THE TRAVELER'S HANDBOOK

Edited by Melissa Shales

in association with
Martin Rosser
Kent Redding
and
Richard Harrington

Chester, Connecticut

Contents

GETTING THERE BY AIR

GETTING THERE BY ROAD

GETTING THERE BY OTHER MEANS

WHAT TYPE OF TRAVEL

EQUIPPING FOR A TRIP

A BASIC GUIDE TO HEALTH

KEEPING TRACK

MAPS

DIRECTORY
General

Rules and Regulations

Training, Help and Advice?

Publishers and Publications

a regular army officer, later becoming an explorer, traveller, writer and
rabist. He has worked in the Arab
world for many years, as personal
assistant to the Mayor of Jeddah,
Director of the Save the Children
Fund in Yemen and most recently as
curator of the Armed Forces Museum
in Muscat, Oman. He has also contributed to many newspapers and magazines, including writing a regular
column on Arab Heritage for the
Oman Daily Observer. He has led
several expeditions, is a Fellow of the
Royal Geographical Society and a
member of the Society of Authors.

Hilary Bradt was once an occupational
therapist but now divides her time
between leading trips in South America for an American adventure travel
company, and writing and publishing
guide books for independent travellers.

Since 1963, **Greg Brookes** (born 1944)
has interspersed three periods of full-time study with teaching in France,
Kenya, England and Northern Ireland. He has travelled widely in
Eastern and Central Africa and in
Western and Southern Europe.

Tania Brown has a degree in Linguistics from Lancaster University. She
speaks fluent German, French and
Spanish and worked for two years as
an administrator before resigning to
join Keith Kimber on a trip round the
world. They left their parents' homes
in Anglesey, North Wales in 1983 and
expected to have covered ¼ million
kilometres in over 60 countries before
returning in 1988.

Tony Bush is Editor of the international trade and finance magazine
Export Times, which he joined in 1984.

He is also author of the *Business Travel
Planner* (pub. Oyez), an undatable
book which aims to help travellers
arrange trips and avoid pitfalls.

Enver Carim, PhD, is managing editor of the Panos Institute in London,
an independent information and policy research unit. He has travelled
widely and is co-author of *AIDS: The
Deadly Epidemic* (published by Victor
Gollancz) and editor-in-chief of *Third
World Development*. He edited the UN
report *The State of the World's Women*
and has published novels and short
stories on the modern human condition.

John Carlton is a keen walker and
rucksack traveller. He has been a
member of the YHA for over 33 years
and has also worked in the travel trade
for the same time. After a long period
of service on voluntary committees of
the Association, he decided to bring
both his interests together and for the
last 15 years has been found behind the
counter of YHA Travel in London. He
has visited most countries in Western
and Eastern Europe, Morocco, Canada and the USA.

Roy Carter writes on corporate security and risk management for the international business and professional
press. He has lectured on related subjects at the Loughborough University
of Technology. He is a former Head of
Consultancy for an international group
of security companies.

Roger Chapman, MBE, BA, FRGS,
was commissioned into the Green
Howards after completing a Geography degree at Oxford and a spell at
Sandhurst. He has been involved in a
great many expeditions – down the
Blue Nile and Zaire Rivers, to Central

Introduction

Tourism is the world's fastest growing
industry. An American Express survey in 1986 put the world's total
expenditure on travel and related areas
at three *trillion* dollars. To many
countries, it represents their sole
source of foreign currency and the
lion's share of the national budget. It
is, in short, Big Business. But it is a
business built on dreams – dreams of
lazy days on a sunny beach, of the
excitement of new places and people,
of adventure, of pushing yourself to
the limits of endurance and coming out
on top.

Yet even dreams require information, planning and preparation if
they are to become a reality without
turning into a nightmare. And when
you are dealing with distances of thousands of miles, alien cultures, new and
often harsh climates, and health hazards, this all becomes infinitely more
difficult. In many places, we are
almost back to childhood, unable to
communicate, ignorant of the simplest
things in life such as how to eat without
giving offence or how to make a telephone call. Even getting into some
countries is a monumental battle,
while deciding how to get there often
provides you with so many options
that you are tempted to give up and
stay at home. However experienced we
are as travellers, whatever type of

travel appeals to us, whether we are
on a whistlestop business trip or the
fabled journey of a lifetime, we still
need help.

This is what *The Traveller's Handbook* is aiming to provide: enough
information on how to go about your
planning about the various different
forms of travel to help you decide what
you want to do and which questions
to ask in more detail; enough contact
names and addresses to ensure you will
always be able to find an answer;
enough hard facts to start your preparations, save you time before you go,
and keep you safe while on the road.
This book is not a guide to the various
places you may want to visit, although
the directory will provide you with
many of the most important details
about individual countries. Once you
have chosen your destination, you will
need other books that will tell you
what to see, and where to stay, so we
have included a hefty list of recommended reading to help you fill in
those final gaps.

This is the fifth edition of The Traveller's Handbook. The first four
expanded dramatically each time they
appeared. This time, we felt that if it
got any larger, it would be too big to
take with you and would lose much of
its usefulness. Instead, therefore, we
have pared down some of the articles

and replaced them with other of greater practical value. Several new listings have been added to the directory section and everything has been thoroughly overhauled and updated, to ensure total accuracy at the time of going to press.

As before, the book is split into two main sections – a series of chapters on every aspect of travel we could think of, from booking your air ticket to surviving after you've been robbed, from travelling by canoe or camel to keeping in touch with home. The second section is a series of listings with the names and addresses of useful suppliers, organisations, embassies etc. and such details as health and visa requirements, driving conditions, climate, banking and shopping hours and even what to tip.

Who is it all aimed at? Everyone who is travelling independently, for whatever reason. Some chapters will be specific to overlanders, expeditioners, or budget travellers while others, such as the sections on health and safety are applicable to anyone crossing an international border. At first glance some sections would not seem to apply to business travellers, but on closer inspection, even they will find an enormous amount aimed specifically at them, such as how to hire a car without risk, or how to obtain discounts on First Class travel.

Inevitably, with the vast amount of information we have included here, some of it will change during the life-time of this book. We ask you to forgive inaccuracies caused by circumstances beyond our control. Inclusion of the name of a firm or association should not be taken to signify the approval of the editor or publishers. Nor are the views expressed or statements made by the text contributors anything but their own. There are over 80 contributors, all of them experts in their particular fields, and all extremely experienced travellers. Inevitably, they have all developed their own ways of doing things and will advise others to do likewise. This may, on occasion, lead to conflicting advice.

Thanks are due to all the many organisations and individuals who responded to our requests for information, particularly the several hundred WEXAS members who found themselves confronted by a twelve page questionnaire and took the time to fill it in. And my special thanks go to Martin Rosser, Kent Redding, Louise Parsons, Sue Stevenson, Rosemary Davis and Ruth Hodgson all of whom have spent endless hours on the telephone, or at the typewriter, researching facts and compiling lists and generally helping me survive and the book get published.
Melissa Shales
Editor

We should like to ask all readers to keep us up to date with any changes or new information that they feel should be included in the next edition.

Notes on Contributors

Major Sir Crispin Agnew of Lochnaw, Bt., Royal Highland Fusiliers, was born in 1944 and began his career in exploration 22 years later as a member of the Royal Navy Expedition to East Greenland. He has since led Services Expeditions to East Greenland and Chile and has been a member of expeditions to Elephant Island, Nuptse – where he reached about 7,925m – and Everest. He has climbed in the UK and the Alps since 1960. He is also Chief of the Clan.

Paulette Agnew was brought up in the Lake District and Scotland, and took a BSc in Biochemistry at Manchester University. For the last five years, she has been working for Wilderness Expedition and Survival Training, based in Ross-shire, as a principal instructor. She has travelled extensively in Europe and the United States and is a keen sportswoman. She especially enjoys mountaineering, skiing and walking.

Sarah Anderson grew up in London. After leaving school, she worked in a bookshop and then spent two years in the United States, travelling and working. After this, she travelled extensively in Asia. On returning to England she took a degree in Chinese which was followed by further spells in bookshops. In 1980, she opened London's first travel bookshop selling

both old and new books – thus combining her two main interests of t and books. She still finds time for elling as well!

Julie Batchelor is a teacher who ti elled extensively during school a university vacations. Her husba John Batchelor is a Fellow of the Roy Geographical Society and currei Vice-President of the Globetrotter Club. He has travelled extensively in Africa including a one-year trans-Africa expedition and a trip through Africa on a motorcycle. The lastest of their many expeditions was across Central Africa from coast to coast in 1986. They have recently published two books – *The Congo* and *The Euphrates* – and run safaris in Zaïre and Tanzania.

Dominic Boland is Editor of *Practical Photography*, the UK's best selling photographic magazine. Apart from the magazine, he also runs a freelance photographic and copyrighting service from his Norfolk home and has broadcast throughout the UK on the subject of photography. Most of his travelling has been within the confines of Europe, the United States and the Indian Ocean. Without doubt, however, his most arduous journey was on British Rail from King's Lynn to Liverpool Street in February 1986.

Peter Boxhall began his working life

and South America, to East Greenland with the British Schools Exploration Society, and Papua New Guinea with Operation Drake amongst them. A novelist, and white water expert, he is currently Director of Plans of Operation Raleigh.

Michael Colbourne, OBE, MB, ChBEd. 1942, FRCPEd. 1970, M. 1962, FFCM 1974, DPh University of London 1951 is an ex-Editor of *The Tropical Doctor* magazine. He is currently a part-time lecturer at the Ross Institute, London and a member of the World Health Organisation's expert panel on Malaria.

Nick Crane rode a bicycle to the top of Kilimanjaro in 1984 and in 1986 cycled over the Himalayas, Tibetan Plateau and Gobi Desert to the place in the world most remote from the open sea. He has five books to his credit, has travelled in Europe, Africa, the USA and Asia and is a Fellow of the Royal Geographical Society.

Ingrid Cranfield edited three previous editions of this book: *Off the Beaten Track* (1977), *The Independent Traveller's Handbook* (1980) and *The Traveller's Handbook* (1982). She is a freelance writer and journalist, a translator, consultant and broadcaster. Her first book was *The Challengers: British and Commonwealth Adventure Since 1945* (1976) and her latest *Skiing Down Everest and Other Crazy Adventures* (Severn House, 1983). She is a Fellow of the Royal Geographical Society and a Member of Council of Endeavour Training Ltd.

Sheila Critchley is a Canadian journalist now based in London. She is currently running an airline in-flight magazine – perfect therapy for her (now cured) fear of flying.

René Dee was born in Switzerland in 1946 and educated in Britain, where he became a regular soldier in the Intelligence Corps, serving in Singapore and Malaysia. In 1967, after leaving the army, he travelled overland to India and Nepal and in 1969 led a series of three weeks adventure holidays to Morocco, from which stemmed his love of desert travel. By 1972, he had formed his own company specialising in treks by camel and mule. This ceased to trade in 1975 owing to economic hardships and he went on to work for Twickenham Travel before working for a time at Young World in Twickenham.

John Douglas, author and photographer, is a former Army officer who has travelled solo and with expeditions throughout southern and south-east Asia, and through much of Africa and the Arctic. His most recent book is *Creative Techniques in Travel Photography*. He is a director of Geoslides Photo library and advises a number of Third World countries on tourist development.

Doris Dow became a single expatriate in Central Africa, married, and spent 24 years there before returning to the UK. She is by profession a secretary and teacher of commercial subjects, and is actively involved with the Women's Corona Society in London on the information and briefing services. She is also Editor-in-Chief of the Society's series of *Notes for Newcomers*.

Peggy Drage is a sociologist, painter and grandmother of seven. She has travelled widely in Europe and India, Sri Lanka and Nepal. On retirement, she and her husband did a six-month journey through the Americas following the Andes-Rockies chain, as well as visiting the Amazon Basin and the Galapagos Islands. She has returned several times since to Mexico, which greatly influenced her painting. She had an exhibition in 1981 at the Anglo-Hispanic Institute in London.

Dr John Frankland is a General Practitioner who has been a caver for over 30 years and Medical Officer to the Cave Rescue Organisation for more than fifteen. He has advised many British caving expeditions and explored caves in Europe and North and South America.

Michael Furnell has been involved with property journalism for more than three decades; he has edited *Homefinder* magazine since 1953 and in 1965 he founded *Homes Overseas*, the monthly specialist periodical devoted to the needs of people wishing to purchase a holiday or retirement home in the sun. He is a broadcaster on overseas property matters and recently had a book published entitled *Living and Retiring Abroad*.

Adrian Furnham is a lecturer in psychology at London University. He holds degrees from the University of London, Strathclyde and Oxford and is particularly interested in applied and medical psychology. He has written a book called *Culture Shock: psychological consequences of geographic movement* with Professor F. Bochner, which was published by Methuen (London) in 1986.

Jon Gardey grew up in California and has lived in Alaska, Switzerland and England. He is the author of a book on Alaska and his writing and photogra-phy have appeared in most of the major magazines in the world. He travels regularly to the remote parts of the globe. He is currently involved in the production of travel-related documentaries and feature films.

Jan Glen, born in Australia, has travelled independently in West Africa, the Sahara, Europe and through Asia. She is joint author, with her husband, of *The Sahara Handbook*.

Simon Glen is an Australian who has lived and worked in Central and West Africa for over twenty years. He is a teacher by profession and has travelled independently in his own vehicle through Africa, Asia and throughout Australia and New Zealand. With years of experience and an intimate knowledge of desert life and travel, he has compiled, with his wife, *The Sahara Handbook*, now in its rewritten and much enlarged second edition.

Rupert and Jan Grey have undertaken many journeys to the remoter parts of the world, both before and after they had children, of which they now have three, aged between six months and six years. On their most recent expedition, they travelled through the interior of Borneo with their two eldest children, an expedition about which a number of stories have been published in UK magazines. Rupert is a solicitor in the City with a litigation practice and his articles and photographs have been widely published. Jan devotes herself to bringing up the children full time. They live in Kensington and Sussex.

Susan Griffith was born in London Ontario and came to England in the late 1970s to do a post-graduate degree at Oxford. She writes and edits books in the *Traveller's Survival Kit* series published by Vacation Work Publications as well as regularly revising *Work Your Way Around the World*. Although she has herself never taught English in Turkey, nursed the sick in Papua New Guinea or even picked raspberries in Scotland, she frequently travels to distant parts to meet the hardy travellers who are doing these things.

Hugo Gurdon is airline correspondent for *Travel News*, the London-based travel-trade weekly newspaper. He has been a journalist since 1980 and has served as a foreign correspondent for the *Financial Times* in Khartoum. An inveterate traveller, his favourite destinations are Rajasthan and St Mortiz.

Robin Hanbury-Tenison, OBE, is a well-known explorer, author and broadcaster who has taken part in well over a dozen major expeditions in South America, Africa and the Far East. He has been a Vice-President and Gold Medallist of the Royal Geographical Society and in 1977/8, led their largest scientific expedition ever to the Gunung Mulu National Park in Borneo. He has written a book about this expedition called *Mulu – The Rain Forest* and has also written several other books, his latest being an autobiography, *Worlds Apart*. He is currently President of Survival International, the organisation that seeks to prevent the extinction of the world's remaining tribal groups.

Geoff Hann was born in 1937 and began travelling extensively in 1969 after a period in industry. He founded Hann Overland in 1972, after travelling overland to Kathmandu, and has operated overland tours and adventure holidays since thenn, leading many of them personally.

Nick Hanna is a freelance travel journalist contributing regularly to a wide variety of publications. He has travelled widely, particularly in Europe, Africa and Asia, and is currently roaming the world researching *The Tropical Beach Handbook* to be published by Virgin.

Bryan Hanson is an executive member of The Globetrotters Club and editor of the *Globetrotter's Handbook* as well as being a guest editor of the Globetrotters' magazine. He has worked as a driver and courier for the Overland Company, has lived in Africa and travelled extensively.

Richard Harrington is a widely travelled freelance travel writer.

Dagmar Hingston is presently employed part-time as an electricity board sales lady. Her experience with disabled travellers began after her husband was diagnosed as suffering from multiple sclerosis. Together they have travelled to many countries and are determined to keep doing so. She is now freelancing as a travel writer and broadcaster on the subject of disabled travel and is currently writing a book for disabled travellers in her local area.

John Hoban used to be Director of Publicity for the BBC External Services.

David Hodgson, AIIP, was senior staff photo-journalist and later picture editor with Features International. He has travelled throughout the world on assignments and his work has appeared in many magazines including *Life*, *Match*, and *Stern*. He is the author of eight books on photography.

Robert Holmes has travelled extensively to remote places throughout the world. He is an experienced mountaineer and has taken part in many expeditions. He is widely known and acknowledged as one of Britain's most accomplished wilderness photographers – his work has appeared in numerous books and magazines. He is presently living in California where, in between his travels, he continues to photograph, write and teach. He is contributing editor to *Darkroom Photography* magazine and teaches wilderness photography at the California Academy of Sciences. He has already been elected to membership of the prestigious American Society of Magazine Photographers.

Malcolm Irvine is presently a registered Insurance broker. He has specialised in insurance for adventure and overland travellers for the last fifteen years.

Jack Jackson is an experienced expedition leader and overland traveller, explorer, mountaineer, author, lecturer and diver. He is co-author with Ellen Crampton of *The Asian Highway* (Angus and Robertson, London 1979) and author of *The Four Wheel Drive Book* (Gentry, London 1982), detailed and authoritative manuals for the overlander. He is a professional photographer specialising in expedition and underwater work.

Keith Kimber has a degree in electronics from Southampton University and worked for four years as an electronics engineer before resigning his job and selling everything to travel at the age of 25. He is expecting to be away for five years, travelling with Tania Brown on a 500cc Honda motorcycle.

Robin Knox-Johnston, C.B.E, R.D., was the first man to sail single-handed non-stop around the world in 1968–69, completing the journey in 313 days. He was world class 2 multi hull champion in 1985 and is currently Chairman of the BOC Challenge Around Alone.

Peter Lane is a Veterinary Surgeon currently working in the pharmaceutical industry in Hertfordshire, England.

Colin McElduff is a Fellow of the Royal Geographical Society, the Royal Anthropological Institute and the Society of Antiquaries (Scotland). He served in the Royal West African Frontier Force in India, Burma and Africa during World War II. On leaving the Army, he joined the Colonial Police Service, serving in Malaysia, Cyprus, Nigeria and Borneo. He gained invaluable experience as a commander of special forces in Malaya and Cyprus and as a Staff Officer Operations during two national emergencies, co-ordinating police and military operations. In 1965 he returned to the UK and worked for the Royal Automobile Club. He is now retired and is living in Barnard Castle, Co. Durham. He is the author of several books on long-distance motoring.

Julian McIntosh lived in Africa for several years and has travelled extensively, doing close to 100,000 miles of rough driving by Land Rover. A keen interest in the performance of equipment and the difficulties faced by travellers has prompted him to make a thorough study of practical water treatment from the traveller's point of view. Julian now runs his own specialist tropical equipment firm, SafariQuip.

Alex McWhirter, born in 1948, has worked in the travel industry since he left school; with a large tour operator in Toronto, Canada in the early days, and later, back in the UK, with all kinds of travel outlets from sleepy suburban offices to the travel departments of multi-national oil and chemical companies. He joined *Business Traveller* magazine as their Travel Adviser in 1979 and is now the editor. He has travelled widely in North America, Australia, Europe, the Middle East and Far East.

Paul Melly has worked as News Editor of *Export Times* and freelance, reporting foreign news, business and travel and specialising in West Africa. He has stayed in everything from five star hotels to fishing boats. He has written for *Export Times*, *The Guardian*, *The Globe & Mail* (Toronto), *Africa Analysis*, *The Scotsman*, *Echo de la Bourse* (Brussels), *World of Business Travel* and other titles.

Wendy Myers was born in Sheffield, England in 1941 and left home at the age of eighteen to see the world, returning seven years later. The story of her hitchhiking, living and working experiences abroad is recounted in her book *Seven League Boots* (Hodder and Stoughton, 1969). She is a SRN, a State Certified Midwife, a Health Visitor and has studied at the Hospital for Tropical Diseases, London. She has done medical work in the Solomon Islands, Nepal, and Burkina Faso and is currently employed by the Save the Children Fund.

Diane Nightingale joined the YHA at fourteen. Her travels have taken her overland to India, on the Trans-Siberian railway to Japan, to Iceland, Morocco, Kenya, Tanzania, Southern Africa, Israel, Thailand and North America. She stays at hostels wherever possible and works as YHA Development Officer for London and the South East.

David Orchard was a station commander for the British Government in Antarctica. He now works as a tour leader for Guerba Expeditions of Westbury, Wiltshire, and consequently spends much of his time in Africa. He writes about his travels from time to time for various magazines.

Chris Parrott was born in 1946 in Aldershot, England, and has lived in France, Singapore, Spain and Brazil, as well as travelling extensively in Europe, the Middle East and the Americas. Until July 1977 he was Head of Geography and Physical Education in the British School, Rio De Janeiro. He has been a director of Journey Latin America since 1981.

E. G. Peacock, MBE, worked overseas as a Customs Officer for 27 years. From 1947 to 1962 he was Serving Officer in the Customs and Excise of Malaya. In 1964, he moved to Malawi, where in 1969, he was promoted to Deputy Controller of Customs and Excise.

Tony Pearson is one of few people in Britain to have made a serious study of outdoor equipment at an academic level. He followed this by working for several years for Field and Trek (Equipment) Ltd and, while there, wrote a regular equipment column, Gear Up, for *The Traveller*. At present he is a freelance consultant to the outdoor equipment trade.

Christopher Portway has been a freelance travel writer for the best part of a decade, is the author of twelve books, and Travel Editor of a women's magazine. He is a member of the Guild of Travel Writers and a Fellow of the Royal Geographical Society.

Paul Pratt has been a ship's radio officer in the British Merchant Navy and an electronics engineer in Britain and Scandinavia. His interest in motorcycles began with cross-country sporting trials and now he claims the longest continuous journey in motorcycle history which, between 1966 and 1979, took him through 48 countries, a distance of nearly 165,000km. He gives illustrated lectures, and his book *World Understanding on Two Wheels* is now in its second edition.

Philip Ray has been a journalist for the whole of his career and has specialized in writing about the airline and travel businesses for the past eighteen years. He was Deputy Editor of *Travel News*, the weekly UK travel trade newspaper from 1969 to 1978, when he switched to freelance writing and market research consultancy. He has travelled widely throughout the world on business but his favourite holiday pursuit is walking in the Alps, the Lake District of the UK or the Scottish Highlands.

Kent Redding is a graduate of Trinity University in San Antonio, Texas who is travelling throughout Europe, the Middle East, and Africa. He has lived in London for the past year, starting his journalism career at *The Traveller*.

Martin Rosser is a freelance writer living in a remote area of Scotland. He is also a self-professed vagabond. He began to develop his writing in London and his vagabond skills in Africa, Australia and Europe. He has

previously worked at WEXAS as Assistant Editor of both *The Traveller* and *The Traveller's Handbook*.

Dave Saunders taught English and Geography in secondary schools for three years – one in England and two in Jamaica. He then worked for two years as a feature writer and technical reporter on *Amateur Photographer* magazine. In 1979 he went freelance and now contributes regular articles to the photographic press in Britain and Australia as well as writing on travel and adventure sports for a wide variety of magazines and newspapers. He has been Travel Editor of *Adventure Sports and Travel* and has edited *Sportscope* magazine. He has written and illustrated four books. His colour/black and white picture library covers the Caribbean, North and South America, Africa, Europe, Australia, New Zealand, India, Nepal and Singapore.

Mary Schantz is a freelance writer who contributes to *Mother Earth News* and writes a regular column on cookery for *Wilderness Camping* magazine. She also teaches 'Trek Out', a *symca* - sponsored camping and wilderness survival programme. She has done most of her camping in Alaska and in the Northern Appalachians.

Douglas Schatz is the Manager of Stanford's International Map Centre, in Covent Garden, London. Stanford's is the world's largest map and travel book shop.

Gilbert Schwartz, a teacher and veteran traveller, spent over a year researching and compiling his book, *The Climate Advisor* (Climate Guide Publications, New York), which has met with considerable success and is now in its second printing.

Melissa Shales was brought up in Zimbabwe, but returned to Britain to take a degree in History and Archaeology at Exeter University. Since graduating, she has been a journalist, taking over as Editor of *The Traveller* in 1982. She left in mid-'87 to work as a freelance travel writer and editor. She has travelled widely in Africa and Europe and is a Fellow of the Royal Geographical Society and a member of the British Guild of Travel Writers. This is the second edition of *The Traveller's Handbook* she has edited.

Anne Sharpley joined the Evening Standard in 1954 and for a number of years covered world events, starting with the Cyprus Emergency and Suez. She has won awards as Woman Journalist of the Year and Descriptive Writer of the Year. She has now 'retired' to travel writing.

James and Sheila Shaw are a husband and wife writing team who enjoy sea travel and writing about their various adventures. Their 18 month honeymoon was composed of no less than four back-to-back freighter trips which took them around the continents of Africa and South America on voyages lasting up to four months. Today, Jim is a freelance journalist for a number of international transportation journals while Sheila is taking an extended absence from teaching high school mathematics to care for sons Ian (3 years) and Nathan (1 year) at their Oregon home.

Ted Simon rode a Triumph 500cc motorcycle round the world, starting in 1973 and returning in 1977. He travelled extensively in Africa, Latin America, Australia and Asia and his articles appeared in the *Sunday Times*. His book on the journey is called *Jupi-*

ter's Travels (Hamish Hamilton, UK and Doubleday, USA). He now lives in California.

Anthony Smith is a Zoologist by training and a writer, broadcaster, and presenter of telvision programmes, including the *Wilderness* series on BBC Television. His first expedition was to Iran with an Oxford University team in 1950. Since then he has ridden a motorcycle the length of Africa, written an account of the Royal Geographical Society/Royal Society Mato Grosso Expedition of 1967, and built and flown hydrogen-filled balloons and airships. He was co-founder of the British Balloon and Airship Club and sits on the RGS Expeditions Committee.

Richard Snailham was born in 1930. He read Modern History at Oxford and was a teacher until, in 1965, he became a Senior Lecturer at the Royal Military Academy, Sandhurst. He has been on expeditions to the Middle East, Ethiopia, Zaire, Jamaica, Ecuador, Honduras and Nepal and recently led parties of tourists to Ethiopia and China. He was co-founder and first Honorary Secretary of the Scientific Exploration Society, is the author of three expedition books and lectures widely on his travel experiences. He is Secretary for the council of the Young Explorer's Trust and President of the Globetrotters Club.

Dr Peter Steele was born in 1935 and qualified as a doctor in 1960. He was climbed in Britain, the Pyrenees, the Alps, North Africa, Mexico, Nepal and the Cordillera Vilcabamba. He has worked at a mission hospital in Kathmandu and with the Grenfell Flying Doctor Service in Northern Labrador, where he travelled the coast by dog team and boat. With his wife,

Sarah, he has driven overland to India, and with his family comprising two children under the age of four, travelled on mule-back across the Himalayan Kingdom of Bhutan. In 1972, he hitchhiked around South America with his ten-year-old-son. He was physician to the International Expedition to Mount Everest in 1971. Author of several books on exploration and exploration medicine, he is now in practice in Whitehorse, Yukon Territory, Canada.

Harry G. Stevens is Austrian by birth but has spent most of his adult life in Britain, where he owns and runs an engineering and electronics automation firm. His business travels frequently take him out of the country, particularly to Europe and the Far East.

Ludmilla Tüting is a freelance journalist and publisher, specialising in tourism, development and environmental issues, women and racism, and the author and editor of several books and films. Widely travelled throughout the world, she now lives alternately in Berlin and Kathmandu. In 1974, she founded the German Globetrotters Club which she ran for ten years.

Steve Usdin is a Washington DC-based consultant and journalist. He has worked and lived in England, Italy, Hong Kong and Japan and has used computer communications networks in most Western European nations as well as China, Panama, Mexico and other developing nations. He is currently involved with the establishment of an international teleconferencing network. He is a regular contributor to *Manufacturing Week* in the United States and *Business Times* of Singapore.

Penny Watts-Russell was born in 1948, obtained a degree in Social Anthropology and Swahili at the London School of Oriental and African Studies and became the first Editor of the WEXAS magazine, then called *Expedition*. Since leaving this post, she has been Sub-Editor on *The Illustrated London News* and Assistant Editor of *Arts and Adventure* and *Executive World*. Currently she is a freelance editor and researcher.

P. J. Whyte is a registered nurse and author who has practised in West Africa, notably Gabon and Angola.

Anne Wilson was born in 1952 in Birmingham. Armed with a BA Hons. in Social Psychology from Sussex University, she came to London where she quickly joined the Consumers' Association. Three years working on *Which* magazine were followed by another four exploring the globe and writing reports for *Holiday Which* a job which embraced anything from Motorway Service Areas in Britain to the Indian pyramids in Mexico. From 1981–1985 she worked freelance and is now a feature writer for a women's weekly.

Shane Winser is Information Officer of the Royal Geographical Society and its Expedition Advisory Centre. She studied Zoology and Information Science at university in London, before helping her husband to organize scientific expeditions to Sarawak, Pakistan, and Kenya. She currently provides the answers for The Traveller Replies column of *The Traveller*.

Nigel Winser is the Expedition Officer of the Royal Geographical Society and their Expedition Advisory Centre. He is currently Director of Operations for the 1988 RGS/Linnean Society Bicentenary Project in Australia following a detailed investigation of the Wahiba Sands in Oman, 1985/87. He has been responsible for the field logistics and support for the last three projects put into the field by the RGS including Mulu (Sarawak), Karakoram (Pakistan) and Kora (Kenya).

David Woolley is a freelance aviation writer. After gaining experience as a pilot and air traffic controller, he wrote for several magazines including *Flight International* (as Air Transport Editor) and *Airports International* (as Editor). From 1983 to 1986, he was Air Transport Editor of *Interavia*. He lives in deepest Sussex.

Carol Wright has been a travel writer fro 20 years. At present she is Travel Editor of *House and Garden* and on the committee of the Guild of Travel Writers. She has written 30 books including *The Travel Survival Guide*.

Where and When

Places in Vogue

by Richard Harrington and Melissa Shales

The sociology of the holiday is a strange affair. It is as easy to tell what a person is like from where they went last summer as by looking at their bookshelves. The holiday brackets one mentally (the nearest art gallery or the knobbly knees competition), physically (lie on a beach or climb a mountain), and financially (fish and chips or Beluga caviare). They also involve a great deal of one-upmanship. The Joneses went to Scotland, so the Smiths must go to Greece, and because the Smiths are going to Greece, Miss Williams down the road sets off with a smirk for Nepal. Soon, not to be outdone, the Smiths and the Joneses will also end up in Nepal. In such a way does mass tourism grow.

Of course, there are people who travel because of a genuine interest in the world around them – a great many – but mass tourism is a product of advertising, financial incentives and peer pressure. The destinations popular with independent travellers today are destined to be the big resorts of ten years hence. Bali, for instance, was big with the *cognoscenti* of the 1930s, but it was not until the 1970s that it started to feature in the glossy tour brochures. And by now there is a travelling clique that has pronounced Bali 'quite ruined' and has gone off in search of a less developed piece of paradise.

The true independent travellers – horrified as they may be to admit it – act as trailblazers, both opening the eyes of the local inhabitants to the financial incentives of tourism, and those of the operators to a new area for development. Greece, in the 1960's, was a hippy hang-out.

The chain starts with airports, or more precisely, runways – runways that can take 707s, DC-8s and 747s. A classic example is the Seychelles, which blossomed in the early 1970s after the opening of an airport built to accommodate the big jets.

With the airports come the hotels, mostly of the same plastic American kind that has become the mark of resorts everywhere. And with the hotels comes a proliferation of other effects – good and bad – radiating out in circles to influence the rest of the country concerned. Tourist facilities, from surf boards to souvenir shops, provide a whole alternative economy, offering a chance of seasonal wealth to the locals. More and more people become involved, abandoning traditional lifestyles in favour of easier, richer pickings, until the whole area is totally dependent upon tourism for economic survival.

Yet tourism is a fickle commodity,

dependent on all manner of external factors from the state of the economy in richer nations – holidays are the first thing to go when the standard of living falls – to fluctuations in the world currency market; from revolutions to the whims of fashion. More easily than any other industry, tourism is threatened by disaster. Even Europe, safest of all destinations lost some 25 per cent of its tourist revenue in the summer of 1986 from the combined effect of the American bombing of Libya and the Chernobyl disaster. Europe can stand the financial blow. Smaller countries could not.

Changing Fashions

The popular resorts of the 1970s are easy to name. In the Caribbean, Jamaica and the Bahamas faded, while Barbados and St. Lucia came into vogue. In black Africa, it was Kenya that won all the prizes for attracting cash-loaded tourists – in the process of which they turned Malindi into a giant German-speaking brothel. Further north, Egypt came, went, and came again, according to the vagaries of the war with Israel. The Tunisians implemented the Italian marketing plan they had commissioned in the 1960s and turned tourism into a massive foreign exchange earner, compensation for being an oilless country flanked by oil-rich Algeria and Libya.

The late 1970s brought into fashion countries that had previously been out of reach of the Western masses. French and German tourists flocked to the Maldives, Nepal, India, Thailand and Sri Lanka. The beautiful state of Ladakh, once the remote home of gentle Tibetan people, is now flooded each summer around the capital of Leh with souvenir-hunting tourists from Europe. Priceless artefacts have been sold for a pittance. Tough, money-hungry Kashmiri traders have moved in to monopolize most commercial activities. And all this because the Indian government opened a new airline to Leh a few years ago.

Not far away, in Nepal, the highland peoples' traditional ways of life are increasingly affected by tourists. There are still beautiful treks to be made in Nepal, but the one to be avoided is one few can resist – to Everest Base Camp,

Thousands now take the traditional route from Lukla airstrip or further afield, and the main hazards of the trip are human pollution and hepatitis.

The Encroaching Masses

The hippy trails of the East have given way to mass tourism; the brothels of Bangkok, the ripoffs of Pataya Beach, the Australian hordes on Bali's Kuta Beach all add up to a pathetic picture of mass tourism at its worst.

For the rich, China was the fashionable destination of the early '80s. Trips were made, not just to Beijing, but further afield to Urumchi, where New York's Linblad Travel beat London's Thomas Cook by two weeks in the race to bring the first Western tour group since before the war. Since then, China has become the 'in' destination and Tibet, more recently opened up, has taken over as the 'real' traveller's goal.

Linblad, which caters for the ultra-rich and exclusive, is now offering luxury cruises to the Antarctic.

The last couple of years have seen some major changes in long-haul travel as the Nile Route has become far less certain politically; and the final nail has been put in the coffin of the tottering route overland to Asia, with Iran dubious, Afghanistan impossible, and the area around the India/Pakistan border unsettled.

The Caribbean has been left almost entirely to the jet set and the package tourists. India and Nepal are getting so crowded they are becoming positively commonplace. Traffic between Europe and the United States is at an all time high with the advent of cut-price Atlantic travel led by Virgin and People Express.

Cheap round-the-world air tickets are opening up a great many gateway cities such as Singapore, Hong Kong and Los Angeles, and bringing even Australia and the South Pacific within more people's budgets. Interest in Australia and New Zealand as holiday destinations is growing, where previously travel was confined to the so-called VFR (Visiting Friends and Relatives) market.

Tropical islands that look like sets for *South Pacific* have already suffered from American and Australasian tourism. But as the European hordes arrive, spearheaded as ever by the Germans (who are, on average, a good ten years ahead of the British), places like Tahiti will get even worse – which is saying a lot, for Polynesia already combines all that is worst in colonial snobbery with all that is worst in the manners of the metropolitan French.

South America stands out as the last part of the world to succumb *en masse*, yet even here, things are now changing. The trail to Machu Picchu is getting crowded, while the mainland Caribbean coast is beginning to attract the traffic which previously went to the islands.

A Tidal Effect

If it all sounds awful, mostly it is. But in the inevitable process, some money is getting through to the people of the countries concerned. It hasn't made the people of Barbados any nicer over the last ten years, but now at least they are better fed and clothed and educated.

During the 1970's, people got used to going abroad, whether to Ibiza or Yugoslavia. The 1980's are seeing them now becoming more adventurous, prepared to fly further, and less inclined just to sit on a beach once they get there.

In the meantime, all over the world, a small number of Westerners are sitting on empty tropical beaches buying genuine artefacts for next to nothing, being invited into the homes of locals, exchanging smiles with people along the road, sharing their food with children who do not ask for money. They are the forerunners by some ten years of the hordes who will follow when Third World governments conspire with big business to put in hotels and airports. These pioneers are of course not all good, and neither, necessarily, is the small impact they make as they go. What is certain, however, is that these visitors are lucky. There will soon be a time when there are no such places left to visit.

Countries at War

Ingrid Cranfield and Kent Redding

People, especially politicians, on both sides of the nuclear divide, like to congratulate themselves that 'we have had forty years of world peace'. Are we really so inured to violence that we don't notice any more wars going on before our eyes? True, modern war is a difficult activity to define. Prior to 1945, wars were usually formally declared. This has not happened since. Istvan Kende, an expert on conflict, has defined war as any armed conflict in which all the following elements exist.

1. Fighting by regular armed forces (including military police forces and other armed services) on at least one side – that is, the presence and engagement of the armed forces of the government in power.

2. A certain degree of organization and organized fighting on both opposing sides, even if this organization extends only to organized defence.

3. A certain continuity between the armed clashes, however sporadic.

4. Centrally organized guerrilla forces are also regarded as making war, insofar as their activities extend over a considerable part of the country concerned.

By this definition, the idea that we have had years of unbroken peace is a ghastly self-delusion.

A *major armed conflict* includes most wars, but excludes most terrorist acts. Since 1720, there have been 654 conflicts recorded and in the 504 cases between 1720 and 1985 in which deaths were recorded, 93 million people have died. There have been three instances of conflict in which over 10 million people have died, the largest being 38 million during World War II. Together, World War I and II account for 55 per cent of the total number of recorded deaths.

Since 1950, the total number of conflicts started has been increasing to an average of 40 per year. This increase has been roughly proportional to the increase in world population. Not only has the number of conflicts increased, but so has the average duration which has been at 5 years since 1950.

Statistics also indicate that more people are now dying due to internal conflicts rather than international ones. About 85 per cent of the wars in the period between 1945 and 1979 were civil wars, aimed at overthrowing the ruling régime or fought for tribal, religious, minority or similar reasons. Between 1962 and 1975 there were 105 military coups in various parts of the world and in 1975 alone, 25 per cent of all member states of the United Nations were ruled by military governments.

The United Kingdom has been fighting a guerrilla war in Northern Ireland since 1969. This is the only war currently being fought in a 'modern', developed country.

Some conflicts are complex as well as lengthy. The Kurds, four million strong in Iran alone, have long been demanding regional autonomy for Kurdistan and the preservation of their language and culture. Kurdish guerrillas are fighting government forces in Iran, Iraq, and Turkey, adopting hit and run tactics and often crossing borders to strike at strategic targets.

Modern wars are not always fought by modern means. The uprising in Vanuatu, then the New Hebrides, in 1980, pitted the British and French governments, condominium rulers of 92 years' standing against an island chief and a handful of men armed with bows and arrows.

The Middle East

The volatile Middle East continues to suffer bloodshed and devastation which stops just short of all out war. The Israeli invasion of Lebanon in 1982 broke – albeit temporarily – the power base of Yasir Arafat, adding still further rival factions to the already divided Palestinian movement. The Palestinian refugees, whom the PLO claims to represent, have never been assimilated by the nations which have harboured them. This latest round of fighting makes their assimilation even more remote especially in such countries as Lebanon.

Syria, which originally entered Lebanon in 1976 as part of the Arab Deterrent Force, remained after other countries withdrew and continues to regard that country as coming under its protection. Despite the additional problems caused by Iranian inspired fundamentalism, Syria has endeavored to remain a stabilizing force in Beirut. Syria, which receives its military equipment from the Soviet Union, is seen by Israel as a possible security threat and its presence in Lebanon is a potential problem between the two countries. Lebanon's populace remains highly fragmented and partition of the country seems the most likely outcome of the disturbances.

From the traveller's point of view, it is advisable to avoid Lebanon (although it is possible to visit the Christian enclave north of East Beirut) and the military zones in western Syria. Although there is widespread military activity in Syria, civilians can move freely as long as not too much time is spent near military installations. The régimes of Syria and Iraq are on the worst possible terms and it may be impossible or inadvisable to travel directly between the two capitals; Amman is the obvious link. By and large, Jordan, Turkey and the whole of the Arabian Peninsula are safe enough for travellers.

Iran-Iraq

Iran and Iraq have been locked in battle since September 1980 and it is possible that it will escalate further, causing the involvement of other countries such as Kuwait. The original engagement stemmed largely from reciprocal accusations of interference in domestic affairs. Both countries have oil-based economies which have been severely disrupted by the conflict.

Iran's oil exports, flowing mainly from the Kharg Island oil terminal in the Gulf, total 2,000,000 barrels of oil a day, bringing in an annual revenue of $25,000 million. Kharg Island has come in for frequent bomb attacks by Iraq, forcing Iran to move its traffic eastward along the Gulf. Iraq is also attempting to weaken the Iranian economy by firing direct at civilian targets. By the same token, Iran has blocked sea traffic from the southern Iraqi town of Basrah and has destroyed two Iraqi oil-loading terminals in the Gulf. Both sides attribute loss of shipping to the other. When, in late 1983, Iran tried to destroy Iraq's oil export pipeline through Turkey, Iraq retaliated with attacks on cities and towns, using long-range artillery and surface-to-surface missiles, causing 200 deaths.

At the time of writing, Iran and Iraq have both received weapons from abroad. Iraq's primary supplier is the

Soviet Union but France has been a significant source for aircraft and missiles. Iran has bought arms in the open market, often at exorbitant prices. Suppliers include Israel, the United States (just ask Ronald Reagan), China and Vietnam. There is significant risk to sea traffic in the Gulf although air flights to Gulf States have not been at risk.

Until 1980, overland journeys through Asia were usually routed through central Iran and Afghanistan. Tour operators were then obliged to seek alternative routes, e.g. from Isfahan, Iran to Quetta, Pakistan via Baluchistan, or to overfly the trouble spots, linking Istanbul, Damascus or Amman with Karachi. Late in 1982, certain overland tour operators reverted tentatively to the practice of traversing Iran, keeping open their option of overflying in case of difficulty.

Afghanistan

In Afghanistan, the government of Babrak Karmal was installed by a Soviet-executed coup on 27 December 1979. Internal and external opposition to the invasion was widespread. The Western powers pressed for Afghanistan to be declared neutral and non-aligned. Inside the country, Muslim rebels, the Mujaheddin, called for a holy war to repel the invaders and joined forces with deserters from the regular Afghan army to mount guerrilla attacks on the Soviet troops. There is now an indication that there may be a Soviet withdrawal from Afghanistan, but the details of the withdrawal still have not been agreed upon. Soviet air power has been built up to the point where bases in Afghan-

istan could provide Soviet naval forces in the Indian Ocean with air cover. Troops are established in considerable strength on the eastern border with Iran. The foothold in Afghanistan offers the Soviets the opportunity to intervene in the internal politics of Iran and Pakistan. It was estimated in late 1983 that there were between 110,000 and 120,000 Soviet troops stationed in Afghanistan, on a six-month tour of duty, with perhaps an additional 20,000 to 40,000 troops during periods of overlap. Afghanistan watchers predict however that there will be no let-up in internal resistance to the occupying forces. The Afghanis are well known for their fierce independence. Travel is not possible here.

Southeast Asia

Khmer Rouge activists continue to make incursions into northern Kampuchea in an attempt to unseat the Vietnamese-installed régime in Phnom Penh. Reasonable law and order have been re-established in Vietnam itself and in Laos, other than in the areas of the Kampuchean border, and in military-ruled Thailand away from the northern border country. Kampuchea is gradually becoming more normal as the central government becomes more stable. Guerrilla incursions do exist throughout the country and should be considered. Local difficulties make travel hard in Portuguese Timor, West Irian and northern Burma (the latter being little problem to tourists who are normally permitted to stay no longer than one week in the country). The activities of the Indonesian security forces can prove a burden to travellers, especially in Sumatra and outlying islands.

In the Philippines, there have been many conflicts between governmental and rebel forces and the post-Marcos government has not been able to quell the troubles with the exception of a short-lived cease-fire in 1987. Support for the rebels is increasing as is the existence of anti-rebel vigilantes. The main area of unrest is Davao province, but outbreaks can occur in most places. Other dangers to visitors are civilian crime and police repression, particularly outside Manila.

South and West Asia

Dhofar in Oman is temporarily quiet, since an understanding has been reached between South Yemen and Oman. Discontent rumbles in Jammu and Kashmir, without flaring up; however Assam and north-eastern parts of India, which have recently seen fierce and massive rioting, are areas to steer clear of. At the time of writing, there is a state of emergency in the Punjab. In Sri Lanka, problems between the government and Tamils in the North have permeated throughout the country and travel could be dangerous. Check with the proper authorities before going.

Northern and Western Africa

Conflicts in this region are fuelled by many factors, not at least of them fuel itself. Although Morocco and Mauritinia vie with one another for control of the uranium deposits which lie under the Sahara, Morocco has established itself in the region and has erected a barrier around the areas nearest its natural resources. Attacks by the Polisario movement which seeks a homeland in Western Sahara, though localised and well away from the population centre, force the maintenance of tight military control in the region. Morocco is in serious debt for various reasons, including a decline in phosphate prices and its involvement in the war in the Western Sahara. Whether or not a referendum resolves the nearly ten-year conflict between Morocco and the Polisario rebels defending their unilaterally declared Saharan Arab Democratic Republic, the area will remain uncomfortable for some time to come.

Libya has achieved a recent rapprochement with Morocco through an arrangement to exchange its oil for Moroccan resources; but Libya's military engagement in Chad is a heavy drain on its oil wealth. Chad has seen a measure of reconciliation between the numerous factions within its borders, but fighting continues between Libyan forces and the Hobre government which receives French support. The area north of the 10° parallel is a military zone.

In other areas, ancient disputes continue to rumble, such as the quarrel between Burkina Faso and Mali over boundaries, the legacy of nineteenth century French rule. Sudan's régime has lately become more repressive with the adoption of ancient harsh and repressive Arab laws for the maintenance of law, order and morality as they interpret it. The separatist movement in the south, which has religious roots, continues to reject government control. Travel in the area is dangerous and is not recommended. The Ethiopian government remains locked in combat with the forces for Eritrean liberation. Somalia and the Horn of Africa harbour one of the world's greatest concentrations of refugees.

Any change of régime in the region gives rise to immediate difficulties and travellers are advised to keep a sharp eye on the short term.

Eastern and Southern Africa

South Africa seems unable to quell the activities of the outlawed African National Congress and other nationalist movements, which infiltrate trained terrorists into South Africa and attack selected key targets. The South African security forces have increased their controls over black communities and violence, though still predominantly black versus black, now sometimes occurs between blacks and whites. There are certain areas where travel is impossible, but there are also unrestricted areas where it is unwise for whites to go. The country is, however, still far from seeing an open revolution. South Africa lost its mandate over Namibia (South West Africa) in 1966 and its administration of the area since is not recognized by the United Nations. Swapo, the nationalist movement, aims to establish a government in Namibia, a prospect viewed by Pretoria as a sell-out of whites and a submission to Soviet Communism. Swapo has been unable to mount a significant campaign or to draw widespread support from its allies, the Ovambo people. Insurgency continues throughout Mozambique and Angola. Uganda remains a problem but Zaire's economic stringencies are forcing the government to adopt a more positive attitude towards tourism.

Central and South America

Central America continues to be the subject of international concern, with some form of conflict occurring in most of its countries. In Nicaragua, President Daniel Ortega has centralized the government and increased his own power. A new constitution was signed in 1986 and then most of its provisions suspended because of the continuing threat from US-backed Contra Rebels. This conflict has had a great effect on the countries bordering Nicaragua due to reprisals for raids originating outside of the country. US aid to the Contras is in jeopardy due to a democratically controlled Congress and the controversy surrounding diverted profits from the 'Iranscam' scandal. Travel can be dangerous, but Nicaragua continues to be a trendy spot for 'lefties'.

In El Salvador, legislative elections were held in 1985 with President José Napoléon Duarte's Christian Democratic Party attracting 54 per cent of the vote. The army, with much aid from the US, has had some success in supressing the FMLN rebels, but not eliminating them. They have reverted to terrorist-type activities while the church tries to mediate. Other Central American countries like Honduras and Costa Rica receive a large amount of US aid and are therefore more receptive to US policies.

In Guatemala, Colombia and Bolivia, right-wing 'death Squads' of the government security forces are accused of torturing and killing many hundreds of suspects and detainees. Bolivia has in the past been very unstable politically, experiencing no fewer than six coups between 1958 and 1963. Chile's government has extended emergency powers in response to continuing demonstrations against the President by the Democratic Alliance. It has also had to deal with severe criticisms on its human rights policies and police and army brutality. The 'Beagle Island' conflict with Argentina has been resolved and no confrontations are forseen.

The Outlook

It should go without saying that travellers, unless they are war correspondents, are well advised to keep out of war zones, even assuming they could gain entry in the first place. The risks are obvious. Any Westerner in Kabul today could easily be taken for a Russian. Tourists react quickly to news of war and internal conflict. Once the troubles are over it may take years for some semblance of normality to return – and the tourists with it. A few travellers, in the right place at the right time, have noticed that the post-conflict period can be an ideal one for travel, with the whole country virtually theirs alone.

Conflict will almost certainly continue to increase in the Third World. Any one of the many present or future wars could escalate to a war involving the Superpowers and thence to a world war, whether nuclear or not. Third World wars are, therefore, of crucial concern to us all.

Note: The authors would like to acknowledge the help given in preparing this article by Major S Robert Elliot, Information Officer at The International Institute for Strategic Studies. Interpretations and judgements are, however, ours alone. The reader will appreciate that the picture of international politics is constantly changing and that events occur at a much faster rate than the revision of published texts.

When to Go

by Richard Harrington

Inexperienced travellers may not think too much about when to go before setting off. They know it's always hot in Indonesia and cold in the Arctic. Seasoned travellers, on the other hand, will plan their trip very carefully around certain times of the year.

Airlines, hotels and tour operators all have off-peak seasons, when they adjust their prices downwards. Prices are governed by demand rather than by climatic seasons – most Mediterranean countries are at their most idyllic in May, when charter flights are at their lowest. However, a great deal of Mediterranean tourism is governed by school holidays, so the demand is comparatively low during the term. And sometimes one-way traffic distorts the fare structure, e.g. westbound fares across the Atlantic are at their lowest when the climate is at its best in many of the destination countries, but are governed by the amount of traffic travelling in the other direction.

Climate – rainfall, humidity, temperature – produces the most obvious type of season. Climates that are no trial to local people may have devastating effects on those ill-adapted souls arriving from more temperate regions.

Hurricanes Hardly Happen

For reasons still little understood, certain tropical regions of the globe are subject to seasonal monsoon rains, cyclones, hurricanes and tornadoes. For most people, these are non-travel seasons. On the other hand, travel deals may be so attractive in these periods that you may decide to make the trip because you know you could never afford it at any other time. A surfer may choose to travel in the stormiest seasons of the year, knowing that these are usually the times for the biggest and best waves.

There are other types of season too. Big game and birdlife may be more spectacular in certain months. Endemic diseases may be caught more easily at certain times of year. In Arctic Canada and Alaska there are two great torments: an icy wind in winter and mosquitoes in summer. The blessing is that you never get both at the same time.

The going may be physically impossible, or almost so, in certain months. Few have dared to move on the Arctic ice cap during the continuous night of freezing winter. Yachtsmen crossing the Atlantic from west to east avoid a winter crossing on the northern route, and those sailing on the Pacific circuit from North America to Hawaii, Tahiti and New Zealand try to complete the last leg of the voyage before the summer cyclones begin. In the jungles of the African West Coast and of 'Africa's armpit', Cameroon, the Congo, Zaïre etc. – the going is very rough and extremely unpleasant during the rainy season from May to August. The best time to start a trans-Africa crossing from London would be September/October when the height of the Saharan summer and the rainy season further south have both passed. Autumn and, better still, spring are the best times for a Sahara crossing.

Trekking in Nepal has become so popular that it's worth knowing the best times for it. The best visibility, lowest precipitation, brightest weather, and most tolerable night time temperatures occur between the end of September and the end of May, and,

within this period the best 'subseason' is autumn, from October to mid-December. January and February are very cold, with snow above 3,000m, but visibility is good and trekking is still possible. Spring arrives around late February or early March. The monsoon, with its poor visibility, mud and leeches, has its onset about the end of March.

A little-known fact is that since hot air is thinner than cold and hot airs rises, the air at altitude will be even thinner than when cold. While the heat itself, in high altitude cities like Mexico City, La Paz, Addis Ababa or Nairobi, is unlikely to be overwhelming, the rarified air may leave you exhausted for several days if you don't take it easy when you get there. If you are susceptible to altitude, then winter is probably the best time to go. The heat is also likely to be less overpowering then.

Man, Maker of all Seasons

Man too creates seasons which can affect the traveller, and the Westerner will sometimes find them hard to predict. The festivals of the Orthodox Church do not often coincide with those of the Western churches. The Islamic religious calendar is based upon the lunar month and is therefore always out of step with our own progression of months and years. The Kandy Perahera festival in Sri Lanka is one of a number of events whose exact dates are settled by astrologers at inconveniently short notice. So if, for instance, you plan to visit a Muslim country during Ramadan, the month of fasting, bear in mind that the local people will do without food from sunup to sundown. Various services will be disrupted or unavailable. Meals will be hard to obtain outside the tourist areas. And you may be woken by whole families noisily eating a meal before dawn puts an end to the revelry. However a meal shared with an Arab family during Ramadan is a treat to be remembered. In the Haj season, when Muslims from West Africa to Indonesia flock to Mecca on pilgrimage, air services along the necessary routes are totally disrupted for ordinary travellers.

Come and Join the Dance

In the West Indies, Guyana and Brazil, Carnival is the time of year when normally poor people are given the chance to forget their worries and feel rich. Cities like Port of Spain in Trinidad and Rio de Janeiro in Brazil have become magnets for tourists, but are to be avoided at that time if you have business to do there and are not interested in the Carnival itself.

Major festivals in Europe and elsewhere always attract culture seekers. The centres concerned become impossibly crowded; hotels fill up; airline passengers get 'bumped' off overbooked aircraft; and visitors pay over the odds for everything because all prices in town have been doubled for the duration. So, for certain countries, especially in Central and South America, a look at the festivals calendar should be part of your planning.

If you decide to beat the crowds and travel to a well-touristed area out of season, there is one more thing to watch out for. The weather could still be glorious, the swimming perfect, but from one day to the next, everything can close down and you could find yourself without transport, entertainment and even food. There is little benefit to be gained from avoiding the crowds if all museums and places of interest are closed, and you have a choice of one place to eat for your entire visit.

Also read a geography book about the place you intend to visit. You may learn things that the tourist brochures and propaganda guidebooks won't tell you for fear of discouraging you.

Checking the seasons will affect your choice of clothes for the trip, the amount of money you take, possibly the choice of film for your camera.

But even knowing all this, the experienced traveller – or the inexperienced traveller with a taste for adventure – will often seek consciously to avoid the 'best' time. Climates and seasons present their own challenge. Who can claim really to know India who has not felt the crashing force of the monsoon rains? Or to be acquainted with Islamic culture without experiencing the tension of the month of Ramadan?

Climate and Its Relevance to Travel

by Gilbert Schwartz

Prospective travellers may prepare for their trip carefully, consulting guidebooks, choosing the most desirable accommodation, designing an appropriate itinerary and making thorough preparations in general. But they frequently fail to investigate the most important ingredient affecting the failure of success of the trip – the weather.

Well, maybe there isn't much you

can do to guarantee good weather but you can do some things to help minimize disappointment.

Be sure to do your homework. Look up reference books on the subject and use them to help select the most favourable times and travel locations. Remember, when interpreting climate information, some statistics are necessary but they could sometimes be misleading. Look for comparisons. Especially compare the prospective location with an area at home or with which you are familiar. For example, San Francisco, California, has a temperature range for July from a maximum average of 18°C to a minimum of 12°C with no precipitation. This becomes more meaningful when it is compared to New York city which has a range of 29°C to 20°C and, on average, eleven days during the month have rain of 0.25cm or more.

So, in spite of the fact that California has a reputation for being warm and sunny, if you're planning a trip to San Francisco in the summer, don't forget to take a sweater! The average temperatures are cold and the winds a brisk 17.5kmph, windier even than Chicago, the 'windy city'.

Sources

Up-to-date weather conditions and forecasts may be obtained from various sources. A current weather map, which is based on information furnished by government as well as private weather services, is the main way of getting a general picture of weather patterns over a large area. These weather maps show conditions around the country at ground level. Elements which are of particular interest to travellers and may be shown on the map include temperature, pressure changes, wind speed and direction, cloud type, current weather, and precipitation.

Of course, the weather information and projected forecasts must be interpreted. You may do well to alter your itinerary and stay clear of areas that project undesirable or threatening weather conditions. Especially keep alert for severe weather conditions such as storms, heavy rains, etc. For example, you should remember when travelling in mountainous regions that flash floods can strike with little or no warning. Distant rain may be channelled into gullies and ravines, turning a quiet streamside campsite into a rampaging torrent within minutes.

Incidentally, there is excellent literature available through the US Government Printing Office prepared by the National Weather Service. For example, information on safety during lightning, flash floods, hurricanes and tornadoes, as well as publications containing summaries and other data pertaining to weather and climate are available. Write to Superintendent of Documents, US Government Printing Office, Washington DC 20420, for a list of publications. In the UK, information on overseas climate and weather is obtainable from the Overseas Enquiry Bureau, Meteorological Office, Bracknell, Berkshire (Tel: (0344) 420242 ext. 2267).

Basic Elements

After you have had an opportunity to review reference materials on climate and sources for weather forecasts you should become acquainted with the meaning of some basic weather

WIND CHILL CHART

Estimated Wind Speed in kmph	Actual Thermometer Reading (C)											
	10	4.5	−1	−6.5	−12	−17.5	−23	−28.5	−34	−39.5	−45	−50.5
	Equivalent Temperature (C)											
calm	10	4.5	−1	−6.5	−12	−17.5	−23	−28.5	−34	−39.5	−45	−50.5
8	9	3	−3	−9	−14.5	−20.5	−26	−32	−38	−44	−49.5	−55.5
16	4.5	−2	−9	−15.5	−23	−29.5	−36	−43.5	−50	−56.5	−64	−70.5
24	2	−5.5	−13	−20.5	−22	−38	−43	−50	−58	−65	−73	−80
32	0	−8	−15.5	−23.5	−31.5	−39.5	−47	−55	−63.5	−71	−79	−86.5
40	−1	−9	−18	−26	−34	−42	−50.5	−59	−66.5	−75.5	−83.5	−91.5
48	−2	−10.5	−19	−22	−36	−44.5	−53	−61.5	−70	−78.5	−87	−95.5
56	−3	−11.5	−20	−28.5	−37	−45	−55	−63.5	−72	−80.5	−89.5	−98.5
64	−3.5	−12	−21	−29.5	−38.5	−47	−56	−65	−73.5	−82	−91	−100

(wind speeds greater than 64 kmph have little additional effect)	LITTLE DANGER for properly clothed persons	INCREASING DANGER	GREAT DANGER
			Danger from freezing of exposed flesh

elements and learn how they may affect your travel preparations.

Perhaps the most crucial weather element is temperature which is a good indicator of body comfort. The ideal air temperature is around 27°C.

Temperatures generally decrease at higher latitudes and at higher elevations, on average by around 1.7°C for every 300m increase in elevation up to 9,000m.

Wind, which is air in motion, is another important weather element. Winds are caused by pressure gradients, the difference in pressure between two locations. Air moves from an area of high pressure toward an area of low pressure. The greater the pressure gradient, the faster the wind. Sea breezes form when cool high pressure air flows from the water onshore to the low pressure area created by warm air over the land. On a clear, hot summer day, the sea breeze will begin mid-morning and can blow inland as far as 16 kms at wind speeds of 16-24kmph. In the evening, the process is reversed. An offshore land breeze blows at a more gentle speed, usually about half the speed of the daytime onshore wind.

A somewhat similar situation occurs in the mountains and valleys. During the daytime, the valley floor and sides and the air above them warm up considerably. This air is less dense than the colder air higher up so it rises along the slopes, creating a 'valley wind'. In the summer, the southern slopes receive more sun and heat up more, which results in valley winds that are stronger than their north slope cousins. At night, the process is reversed and downslope 'mountain winds' result from the cold air above the mountain tops draining down into the valley.

Winds are also affected by such factors as synoptic (large area) pressure differences and by day-night effects. The sun produces maximum wind speeds while at night winds near the ground are usually weak or absent. Wind speed is also influenced by how rough the ground is. Over smooth water surfaces, the wind speed increases very rapidly with increasing altitude and reaches a peak speed at a height of about 180m. Over rough terrain, the wind speed increases more gradually with increasing altitude and does not reach its peak until about 450m.

Comfort

As we well know, wind, temperature and humidity have a bearing on our comfort. To indicate how combinations of these elements affect the weather we experience, two indices should be understood; wind chill factor and temperature/humidity comfort index.

The *wind chill factor* is the cooling effect on the body of any combination of wind and temperature. It accounts for the rate at which our exposed skin loses heat under differing wind-temperature conditions. In a wind of 32kmph, -4°C will feel like -19°C. This effect is called 'wind chill', the measure of cold one feels regardless of the temperature. Chill increases as the temperature drops and winds get stronger, up to about 72kmph, beyond which there is little increase. Thus at 12°C, increasing the wind from 0 to 8kmph reduces temperature by only two degrees, but a change in wind speed from 64-72kmph reduces it only 0.5°C.

The wind may not always be caused naturally. For example, someone skiing into the wind may receive quite a chill. If one is moving into the wind, the speed of travel is added to the wind speed; thus if the wind is blowing at 16kmph and one's speed is 24kmph into the wind, the actual air movement against the body is 40kmph. At -9°C this air speed gives a wind chill equivalent to -30°C. This is easily cold enough for exposed parts of the body to sustain frostbite.

A combination of *warm temperatures and humidity* also has a significant bearing on our comfort, particularly in warmer climates when the higher the relative humidity, the less comfortable we are. This is a result of the corresponding decrease in the rate at which moisture can evaporate from the skin's surface. Since the cooling of the air next to the skin by the evaporation of perspiration is what causes a cooling sensation, a day with 70 per cent relative humidity and 27°C temperature is far less comfortable than one with 25 per cent humidity and 43°C temperature. The THI was developed in order to measure this relative comfort. But remember, where there is low humidity and a high temperature, your comfort can mislead you, for though you feel safe, you may be in danger of burning.

Layman's Forecast

Lacking the sophisticated instruments and sources for weather data, you may still be able to project your own forecasts. Become familiar with basic weather elements such as pressure signs, clouds, wind changes, etc. Learn how these indicators change before the weather does. A layman should beware of the climate statistics he sees in many tourist brochures. The climate will almost always be more severe than is evident from the quoted rainfall, temperature and sunshine figures. All-important humidity figures are usually not given (Bali might be empty of tourist half the year if they were), and temperature figures may be averages over day and night, and well below (or above) actual normal maximum (or minimum) temperatures. Or they may represent averages recorded at 0600 or 1800 hours, because these figures will look most attractive to visitors.

Something else you will not find easily is water temperature. Winter sun holidays are now extremely popular. A lot of people do not realize however that although the daytime air temperatures may be in the low 20°C, water temperatures may only be about 5-15°C and swimming without a wetsuit impossible.

The sea takes longer to warm up than the land each summer. Conversely it takes longer to cool down in the autumn. Reckon on a lag between sea and land temperatures of about one and half months. In Tunisia, the sea is a lot cooler in March than in October. On the other hand, by March air and land temperatures are already rising with the beginning of summer. They will reach their highest point in June/July, but the sea will take until August/September to be fully warmed up.

In winter, comfortably warm water is almost a certainty in the tropics, but more doubtful in the subtropics, for which you should find and study year-round water temperatures. You may just decide to go in summer instead, even though it will probably cost more. In short, warm air and warm water don't always go together.

Familiarity with climate information, whether you rely on primary or secondary sources, will go a long way towards permitting you to get the most of your next trip.

A Guide to Seasonal Travel
by Paul Pratt and Melissa Shales

Africa

North – the climate here varies widely from the warm and pleasant greenery of a Mediterranean climate in the coastal regions to the arid heat of the deep Sahara.

Rains on the coast usually fall between September and May and are heavy, but not prolonged. It can get cool enough for snow to settle in the mountainous areas, but temperatures will not usually fall below freezing, even in winter. In summer, temperatures are high (up to around 40°C) but bearable.

The Sahara, on the other hand, is extreme, with maximum summer temperatures of around 50°C and minimum winter temperatures of around 3°C. The temperature can fall extremely rapidly, with freezing night following blisteringly hot days. What little, if any, rain there is can fall at any time of year. The desert is also prone to strong winds and dust storms.

West – at no time is the climate in West Africa likely to be comfortable, although some areas and times of the year are worse than others. The coastal areas are extremely wet and humid, with up to 2,500mm of rain falling in two rainy seasons – in May and June and then again in October. In the north, there is considerably less rain, with only one wet period between June and September. However, the humidity is still high, only lessened by the arrival of the *harmattan*, a hot, dry, dusty, north-easterly wind blowing from the Sahara. Temperatures remain high and relatively even throughout the year.

East – although much of this area is on or near the equator, little of it has an 'equatorial' climate. The lowlands of Eritrea, Somalia and Djibouti in the extreme east have a very low, uncertain rainfall, creating near desert conditions plagued by severe droughts. Further down the coast, the high lowland temperatures are moderated by constant sea breezes. The temperatures inland are brought down by high altitude plateaux and mountain ranges to about the level found in Britain at the height of summer. They are reasonably stable all year round although the Kenya highlands have a cooler, cloudy 'winter' from June to September. There are two rains in most areas in April and May and for a couple of months between July and November, depending on the latitude.

South – the whole area from Angola, Zambia and Malawi southwards tends to be fairly pleasant and healthy, although there are major variations from the Mediterranean climate of the Cape Province with its mild winters and warm, sunny summers to the semi-desert sprawl of the Kalahari and the relatively wet areas of Swaziland, inland Mozambique and the Zimbabwe highlands in the east. In the more northern areas, there is a definite summer rainy season from December to March when the temperatures are highest. On the south coast, there is some rain all year round. The west coast, with little rain, has cloud and fog due to the cold Benguela current, which also helps keep down the temperature. The best times of the year to visit are April/May and September when the weather is fine, but not too hot or humid.

North America

Almost half of Canada and most of Alaska in the north is beyond the Arctic Circle and suffers from the desperately harsh weather associated with this latitude. The ground is tundra and rarely melts for more than a couple of feet and even though summer temperatures are often surprisingly high, the summers are short-lived. Snow and frost are possible at any time of the year, while the northern areas have permanent snow cover. The coast is ice-bound for most of the year.

The whole centre of the continent is prone to severe and very changeable weather, as the low-lying land of the Great Plains of the Canadian Prairies offers no resistance to sweeping winds that tear across the continent both from the Gulf and the Arctic. The east is fairly wet, but the west has very little rain, resulting in desert and semi-desert country in the south.

Winter temperatures in the north can go as low as -40°C, and can be very low even in the south, with strong winds and blizzards. In the north, winter is long-lived. Summers are sunny and often scorchingly hot.

In general, the coastal areas of North America are far kinder than the centre of the continent. The Pacific coast is blocked by the Rockies from the sweeping winds, and in the Vancouver area, the climate is similar to that of Great Britain. Sea breezes keep it cool further south.

Seasons change fairly gradually on the east coast, but the northerly areas still suffer from the extremes of temperature which give New York its fabled humid heatwaves and winter blizzards. New York, in spite of being far further north, is often much hotter than San Francisco. The Newfoundland area has heavy fog and icebergs for shipping to contend with. Florida and the Gulf States to the south have a tropical climate, with warm weather all year round, winter sun and summer thunderstorms. This is the area most likely to be affected by hurricanes and tornadoes, although cyclones are possible throughout the country.

Mexico and Central America

The best time to visit this area is during the dry season (winter) from November to April. However, the mountains and plains facing the Caribbean have heavy rainfall throughout the year, which is usually worst from September to February. The mountains and plains facing the Pacific have negligible rainfall from December to April.

Central and North Mexico tend to have a longer dry season and the wet season is seldom troublesome to the traveller as it usually rains only between 1600 and 1700 hours. The temperature is affected by the altitude. The unpleasant combination of excessive heat and humidity at the height of the wet season should be avoided, if possible, at the lower altitudes.

South America

The climatic conditions of the South American continent are determined to a great extent by the trade winds which, if they originate in high pressure areas, are not necessarily carriers of moisture. With a few regional exceptions, rain in South America is confined to the summer months, both north and south of the equator. The exceptions are (i) South Brazil and the eastern coast of Argentina and Uruguay; (ii) the southern Chilean coastal winter rainfall region; (iv) the coastal area of north-east Brazil. The highest rainfall in South America is recorded in the Amazon basin, the coastlands of Guyana and Suriname, the coastlands of Colombia, Ecuador and south-west Chile. Altitude determines temperature, especially in the Andean countries near to the equator: hot – up to 1,000m; temperate – 1,000 to 2,000m; cold – above 2,000m.

Ecuador
Dry season: June to October. The coast is very hot and wet, especially during the period December to May. The mountain roads can be very dangerous during the wet season owing to landslides.

Peru
During the colder months, June to November, little rainfall but damp on the coast, high humidity and fog. From December to May, travel through the mountains can be hazardous owing to heavy rain which may result in landslides, causing road blockage and long delays.

Bolivia
Heavy rainfall on the high western plateau from May to November. Rains in all seasons to the eastern part of the country.

Chile
Just over the border from Bolivia, one of the driest deserts in the world faces the Pacific coast.

Argentina
The winter months, June to October,

are the best time for visiting Argentina. Buenos Aires can be oppressively hot and humid from mid-December to the end of February. Climate ranges from the sub-tropical north to sub-antarctic in Tierra del Fuego.

Paraguay

The best time for a visit is from May to October when it is relatively dry. The heaviest rainfall is from December to March, at which time it is most likely to be oppressively hot and humid.

Brazil

The dry season occurs from May to October apart from in the Amazon basin and the Recife area which has a tropical rainy season from April to July.

The Far East and South-East Asia

Japan

Japan lies in the northern temperate zone. Spring and autumn are the best times for a visit. With the exception of Hokkaido, the large cities are extremely hot in summer. Hokkaido is very cold in winter. Seasonal vacational periods, especially school holidays, should be avoided if one is going to enjoy visiting temples, palaces and the like in relative comfort.

Korea

Korea is located in the northern temperate zone, with spring and autumn the best times for touring. The deep blue skies of late September/October and early November, along with the warm sunny days and cool evenings, are among Korea's most beautiful natural assets. Though it tends to be

rather windy, spring is also a very pleasant time for a Korean visit. There is a short but pronounced wet season starting towards the end of June and lasting into early August. At this time, over 50 per cent of the year's rain falls and it is usually very hot and humid.

Hong Kong

Subtropical climate: hot, humid and wet summer with a cool, but generally dry winter. Typhoon season is usually from July to August. The autumn, which lasts from late September to early December, is the best time for visiting, as the temperature and humidity will have fallen and there are many clear, sunny days.

Macao

Macao has a similar climate but the summers are a little more bearable on account of the greater exposure to the breezes and there is also an abundance of trees for shelter during the hot summer.

Thailand

Hot, tropical climate with high humidity. Best time for touring is from November to February. March to May is extremely hot and the wet season arrives with the South-West Monsoon during June and lasts until October.

Malaysia

There are no marked wet or dry seasons in Malaysia. October to January is the wettest period on the east coast, October/November on the west coast. Sabah has an equable tropical climate; October and April/May are usually the best times for a visit. Sarawak is seldom uncomfortably hot but is apt to be extremely wet. Typhoons are almost unknown in East Malaysia.

Singapore

Like Malaysia, Singapore has no pronounced wet or dry season. The even, constant heat is mitigated by sea breezes. The frequent rain showers have a negligible cooling effect.

Philippines

The Philippines have a similar climate to Thailand. The best time to travel in the islands is during the dry season, November to March. March to May is usually dry and extremely hot. The South-West Monsoon brings the rain from May to November. The islands north of Samar through Luzon are prone to be affected by typhoons during the period July to September.

The Visayas Islands, Mindanao and Palawan, are affected to a lesser degree by the South-West Monsoon and it is still possible to travel comfortably during the wet season south of Samar Island, as long sunny periods are usually interspersed with heavy rain showers.

The Indian Subcontinent

Sri Lanka

The South-West Monsoon brings rain from May to August at Colombo and in the south-west generally and the North-East Monsoon determines the rainy season from November to February in the north-east. The most popular time for a visit is during the northern hemisphere's winter.

India

The climate of south India is similar to that of South-East Asia, warm and humid. The South-West Monsoon brings the rainy season to most parts of India, starting in the south-west and spreading north and east from mid-May through June. Assam has an extremely heavy rainfall during monsoon seasons. Generally speaking, the period from November to April is the best time to visit. From April until the start of the South-West Monsoon, the northern Indian plains are extremely hot though the northern hill stations provide a pleasant alternative until the start of the monsoon rains. These places usually have a severe winter.

Nepal

March is pleasant, when all the rhododendrons are in bloom. The monsoon rains begin in April.

Middle East

A large proportion of this area is desert – flat, low-lying land with virtually no rain and some of the hottest temperatures on earth. Humidity is high along the coast and travellers should beware of heat exhaustion and even heat stroke. What little rain there is falls between November and March. To the north, in Iran and Iraq, the desert gives way to the great steppes, prone to extremes of heat and cold, with rain in winter and spring. Melting snow from the surrounding mountains causes spectacular floods from March to May.

The climate is considerably more pleasant in the Mediterranean areas with long, hot, sunny summers and mild, wet winters. The coast is humid, but even this is tempered by steady sea breezes. The only really unpleasant aspect of the climate here is the hot, dry, dusty desert wind which blows at the beginning and end of summer.

Europe

Only in the far north and those areas a long way from the sea does the climate in Europe get to be extreme. In northern Scandinavia and some of the inland eastern bloc countries such as Bulgaria, there are long, bitterly cold winters with heavy snow and, at times, arctic temperatures.

In western Europe, the snow tends to settle only for a few days at a time; in Britain, the Benelux countries and Germany, winter is characterized chiefly by continuous cloud cover, with rain or sleet. In the Alps, heavy snow showers tend to alternate with brilliant sunshine, offering ideal conditions for winter sports. There are four distinct seasons, and while good weather cannot be guaranteed during any of them, all are worth seeing. Summer is generally short, and the temperature varies widely from one year to the next, climbing at times to match that on the Mediterranean.

For sun worshippers, the Mediterranean is probably the ideal location, hot for much of the year, but rarely too hot or humid to be bearable. Rain falls in short, sharp bursts, unlike the continuous drizzle to be found further north. Winter is mild and snow rare.

Australasia

Australia

For such a vast land mass, there are few variations in the weather here. A crescent-shaped rain belt follows the coast to provide a habitable stretch around the enormous semi-desert 'outback'. The Snowy Mountains in the east do, as their name suggests, have significant snowfalls, although even here it does not lie long. The east is the wettest part of the country owing to trade winds which blow off the Pacific. The rainfall pattern varies throughout the country: the north and north-east have definite summer rains between November and April; the south and west have winter rains; while in the east and south-east the rains fall year-round. Tropical cyclones with high winds and torrential rain occur fairly frequently in the north-east and north-west.

Tasmania, further south and more mountainous, has a temperate climate similar to Britain's.

New Zealand

Although at a different latitude, the great expanse of water around New Zealand gives it a maritime climate similar to Britain's. The far north has a sub-tropical climate with mild winters and warm, humid summers. There are year-round snow fields in the south, and snow falls on most areas in winter. Although the weather is changeable, there is a surprising amount of sunshine, making this country ideal for most outdoor activities. The best time to visit is from December to March, at the height of summer.

Papua New Guinea

The climate here is a fairly standard tropical one – hot and wet all year, although the time and amount of the rains are greatly influenced by the high mountains that run the length of the country. The rains are heavy, but not continuous. While the coast tends to be humid, the highlands are pleasant.

Finding Out More

Choosing Maps

by Martin Rosser and Ingrid Cranfield

A few years ago, an explorer, who had better remain nameless, travelled a vast distance through South America, relying for his route-finding on a linear list of place names he could expect to encounter en route and a rudimentary sketch map with his projected route inked in – both items prepared for him by someone else. It was a bit like orienteering on a giant scale – to reach Brazil, turn right at Santiago – except that compass bearings were virtually ignored in the master plan because the use of a compass was also beyond our explorer's ken. To make progress, he had first to find out where he was and then ask the way to the next place on the list. That he got anywhere at all speaks volumes for the power of the spoken word and the generosity of the local people.

Needless to say, our explorer was not much of a hand with maps. And, of course, he is not alone. Thousands of motorists lurch along to their destination by following signposts or asking directions, ignorant perhaps of the fact that a map would be a better source of the necessary information. However, as a wide ranging international traveller you should be aware (whatever American Express may say) that it is maps you cannot afford to leave home without. You may protest that, like the explorer mentioned above, you're inexperienced and a bit nervous about the whole business. No need. Grasp a few basics and the rewards will outweigh the effort.

Elements of a Map

The first thing to think about is scale, which is the measure that relates distances on the map to corresponding distances on the ground. Though there is much confusion on this subject, there is an easy way to remember the difference between small and large scale maps. On a small scale map features appear small, while on a large scale map features appear large.

For most practical purposes, maps at a scale of about 1:1,000,000 or smaller are generally considered small scale, while those, say, between 1:20,000 and 1:1,000,000 are considered large. Scales larger than 1:20,000 are used on town plans, maps of individual properties, or installations and the like.

Map readers may find it useful to make a mental note of one scale and the measure it represents. All other scales can then be compared with it. Thus a scale of 1:100,000 means that a centimetre on the map represents 100,000 centimetres, or one kilometre, on the ground. Metrication in mapping has meant a transition from scales representing round distances in miles (1:63,360 = 1 inch to 1 mile) to scales using multiples of ten (1 to 50,000; 1:250,000 and so on). The official body that produces maps of the UK is the Ordnance Survey (OS), which in the last fifteen years or so has been phasing out its maps based on the mile and replacing them with metric maps.

The choice of scale in a map naturally depends on the purpose for which the map is intended. A motorist planning a route across country will probably find a map at 1:500,000 quite satisfactory. Thus, travelling at 50kmph he will cross 10 cms of map every hour. A rambler, eager to note smallish features in the fields, be they tumuli or pubs, would be well advised to acquire a map, or more frequently, several adjoining map sheets, drawn on 1:50,000 or 1:25,000. Travelling at 4kmph he would thus cross 8cms or 16cms of map in an hour.

Many official mapping authorities base their map series on a national grid, a network of lines which divide the country into small units and represent the edges of individual map sheets. An index for the series (available for consultation at the map retail outlet or in some cases printed on the back of each sheet in the series) shows which sheets are needed to cover the area of the purchaser's interest.

The second major distinction to be made amongst maps is that between topographic and thematic. Topographic maps (which category includes most OS maps) show the general nature of the country: the lie of the land, the location and extent of forests, marshes, farmland, etc., the courses of roads, railways and other lines of communication, the presence of waterways and any other salient features whether natural (mountains, sea-cliffs etc.) or man-made (airports, quarries etc.)

A thematic map focuses instead on one particular aspect of the region, be it relief (configuration of the land), communications, climate, land use, population distribution, industry or agriculture. Thus a road map gives, or should give, detailed information on the road network and such associated features as petrol stations, or motorway exit points, but it may give little or no indication of relief, built-up areas, or features of interest to travellers. Similarly a 'tourist' map will show attractions for the sightseer – castles, museums, lakes, archaeological sites, parks, but will probably skimp on information on the exact road pattern, and other features of, presumably, peripheral interest to the tourist. Think carefully about which type will be of most use to you. For most travellers, it will probably be a combination showing major tourist attractions, a reasonable road network and the main geographical features such as mountains.

All maps employ symbols, and it is a good policy to familiarise oneself with the symbols used before taking a map into the field. Some map-makers use simplified drawings of features, others use abstract or geometric symbols, such as the triangles of different colours used to represent different products at industrial sites. The representation of relief is subject to much variation. Methods include hill shading, which simulates the appearance of the terrain from the air, and contouring, where lines join points on the hillside that are of the same height.

Since maps are two dimensional representations of a three dimensional world, some aspects of the truth are necessarily compromised. The way in which the globe, or a part of it, is transferred onto paper is called a map projection. There are many types of projection and the type used is nearly always specified on the map. You need not worry too much about which map projection you have in front of you. The larger the scale of the map the less the projection matters anyway, since the flat sheet of paper more nearly represents a small area of the ground, which is nearly flat, than it can represent the globe, which is spherical. Be a little wary, however, of using a map in a way for which it was not designed. On an equal area projection, for example, you will go astray if you try to extract accurate bearings from it.

What to Look for in a Map

When you begin to consider which map to buy from the many that stare at you in a good map retailers a part of your final decision will depend on your taste in maps. I, for instance, always prefer to have a map that is good to look at as well as accurate and functional, so I have a tendency to go for strongly coloured maps. Then, months after the trip I can get out my pretty map and remember the places I passed through and dream about those I narrowly missed. There are, however, certain absolutes that bear checking no matter what your personal preferences are.

The first of these is undoubtedly the date the map was published. Everyone who bothers to think about it will realise that maps go out of date, some more quickly than others, yet it is surprising the number of people who don't think to look at the publication date of a map to see whether it is a mere year old or dating from the days of the British Empire.

Having checked out the date, then you need to know how reliable the maps are. Even local Lands and Surveys Offices having varying standards. The Swiss, for instance, are excellent as you might expect. The same goes for New Zealand. North America, surprisingly, is not so hot as you might imagine, but good none the less. At the other end of the scale (no pun intended) are various countries that do not have the native expertise available to make first class surveys, and lack the funds (and perhaps the will) to bring in outside experts to do it for them. The result is non existent or unreliable maps.

Here you run across the need to seek expert advice. You would be well advised to go to a major retailer or to public map rooms (for example in the Royal Geographical Society or the British Museum) if you want a map that is in any way out of the ordinary. After all, if you are spending £2,000 or thereabouts to travel in darkest Peru for a month, it is worth the cost of a train ticket to get some good advice. Especially considering that otherwise you may never learn of the existence of the maps you want, much less be able to obtain them.

You will probably find that the map you are considering is part of a series, like the Landranger series from OS. It is the series, rather than any individual map or publisher that gathers a reputation – good, bad or indifferent.

There is one series covering the Middle East, for instance, that has a high reputation, published by Geoprojects. The Middle East is a boiling pot of local quarrels, perhaps the most furiously bubbling area in the world, and any cartographer is putting his neck on the line trying to please all the parties with one interpretation of current boundaries. Since the vast majority of information on any country has to be authorised by the relevant authorities (or no map reaches the shop) it is a tightrope walk of tact. Geoprojects specialises in this sensitive locality and hence has the best reputation for maps there. Not perhaps the most precise cartography in the world, but clear to read and with nice use of colour.

Nelles Maps have a range that covers South East Asia, India, and the Himalayas with a scale (1:1,500,000) suitable for touring rather than for travelling on foot. The maps are not the result of a re-survey, but are a collation of all the most up-to-date information available. It is probably fair to say that it is the best map series of the area since colonial days. So what makes them good? Well, for a start, all the maps in the range are of a consistent scale, very important if you are crossing from one map to another. It takes time to get used to a scale, and chopping from one to another just gives you unnecessary trouble. There are no contours marked on the maps, but the relief colouring in the more mountainous areas is clear and attractive. There are distances marked off on the roads, and quite a lot of information given on places of interest to the traveller. Also, some of the larger cities that appear on the maps appear again as insets, showing the main highways through.

The sheets are printed both sides, something I call a disadvantage. Too many times I have had to reverse such maps in high winds or enclosed spaces. However, if you are sensible enough to follow the directions given for using the map, instead of immediately opening it wide, you may well find it easy to use. The other pros and cons to such double-sided maps are simple. They give you more map for less weight, but are a nuisance for laying side by side while planning routes.

In the same part of the world, another map series by Freytag-Berndt and Ataria is scaled for travel on foot (at 1:50,000) and shows the popular approaches to Everest. There are seven maps in the series and they are beautiful examples of relief shown clearly and attractively by shading. Contour lines are added at intervals of 40m (with stressed contours at 200m intervals). This means that you can plan route times and will be able to navigate with the aid of an altimeter. Though the series covers nothing west of Kathmandu, simply looking at the maps is enough to make you up and pack.

Covering a far wider range in total is the Bartholomew World Travel series, and one map in particular in the series bears looking at because of its complete covering of one area: South-East Asia. Scaled at 1:5,800,000 it stretches from Hong Kong down to Java and from Burma across to New Guinea. To give an overall view to those travelling or planning to travel through South-East Asia it is a godsend. As Spike Milligan said, everyone has to be somewhere, and I for one prefer to know where I am both on a micro-scale (where is the nearest pub) and the macro-scale (which country borders to the south). As usual, this series cannot be all things to all men. By captioning areas neatly it becomes necessary to vary scales widely from map to map across the series.

Bartholomew maps in general use a distinctive layer colouring to show relief that may well be familiar to you as they do the mapping for the illustrious Times Atlas. You may even come across sheet maps that reappear in the atlas at the same scale and detail.

Detail in depth and fabulous relief colouring are not always the making of a map, however. Take a series very well known to the off-beat, adventurous traveller: the Michelin Africa maps. Three of these are scaled at 1:4,000,000 and one in particular has a longstanding reputation – no. 153 covering the Sahara. The map looks bland, and shows extensive details only when relating to roads and tracks: towns you pass through, where there are petrol stops, and where you can get drinking water for instance. But then how many people want to travel the Sahara on foot or off the tracks? These maps are updated every year and are generally accepted as the best for travelling with. But if your criteria demands that it should look good on your living room wall, perhaps you should think again and choose (maybe) a Bartholomew covering the same area. It probably won't be as detailed or as current for travelling the roads with, but it will look good.

Here endeth the first lesson in maps. Once you narrow down what you want, choosing between the many options becomes so much easier.

So much for what makes a series good and bad. Now a look at some maps that I would label as a last resort for travellers.

Two series spring immediately to mind. The Operational Navigation Charts (ONC) that cover the world at a fixed scale of 1:1,000,000 and the Tactical Pilotage Charts (TPC) at a fixed scale of 1:500,000 that at present covers around half the world. These series were printed primarily for use in navigation from the air, so they are overprinted with navigation beacons and runway approaches. A further disadvantage is that from the air one town looks much like another, so as often as not towns are not named on the map. On top of that, there are areas of the world where the surveyors could not get information, so on the maps you sometimes find in big letters 'RELIEF DATA INCOMPLETE'. All around is bare.

Despite these drawbacks, there will be times when no other maps are available to you. Thus an air navigation chart is better than nothing.

It is interesting to round off a discussion on maps with a look at what maps may look like in the near future. Here rises the spectre of satellite imagery.

For the last twenty years or so, the Earth has gradually been photographed from every available orbit, until now it is unlikely that there is anywhere not covered by satellite imagery. Such images are not of much use as maps in their raw form. Roads and towns may be visible, but nothing is named. The colouring of the image has to be standardised, and any required legends overprinted before the image is of use to travellers. Given that the original cost of the image will be many times the cost of the most expensive regular style map, it is not feasible to produce your own maps this way.

Recently, however, some publishers have made an investment in satellite images and have had printed up a number of maps. There is already available a Chinese published atlas of Tibet, a map of the Himalayan ranges, and Stanfords in London have had printed a map of Kilimanjaro in Tanzania, overprinted with the routes to the summit from the plains below. The cost then comes down to a little above that of a good map or atlas of the regular kind. Stanford's claim, incidentally, to be able to obtain NASA Landsat images of most parts of the world.

An interesting point about satellite imagery takes us back to map projections. Because the imagery is built up from a series of shots taken on orbit, and grouped together in a mosaic, the resulting projection will probably be very irregular. How accurate, then, will be long range bearings taken from such a map?

Background Reading

by Hilary Bradt and Melissa Shales

With all the fuss involved in preparing for a trip, background reading often stays in the background or is neglected altogether. Yet the proper choice of a travel guide can make all the difference between a relaxed, enjoyable trip and one fraught with anxiety and disappointment, and a good travel book can heighten enjoyment by lending familiarity to the places visited.

Of course, your reading requirements depend on the type of trip you are planning. There's little point in buying a book on the archaeology of Tunisia if all you plan to do in North Africa is lie on a beach; or in buying one of those $25 a Day books on how to enjoy cities cheaply if you plan to spend as short a time as possible in them.

Broadly speaking, guidebooks are designed to inform you on necessary preparations for your trip, and to guide you on your travels, while travel books are out to entertain, providing useful information in passing. There has been a vast proliferation in travel publishing over the last few years, both of guides and literature. Not only are more and more travellers writing about their experiences now, but there are numerous imprints such as *Eland Books* which specialise in reprinting the best of past travel literature. For more popular countries, this means that you can not only read what they are like now, but what they have been like for the last hundred years. This can be a fascinating progression, made even more interesting by the way the traveller's viewpoint has changed. With out of the way places, you may find that the only books available were written 50 or more years ago. And don't ignore coffee table books either. Most do not have a vast amount of information in them, so would probably not be worth buying, especially as they can be incredibly expensive, but leafing through the photographs is an excellent way to get the feel of a place.

For most people, background reading involves the use of libraries, both local reference libraries and specialist ones such as those at the Royal Geographical Society, the Natural History Museum, and universities. It is much easier to read up on a specific subject than a general one, and those seeking specialist information will have little trouble (though it is surprising how often, having decided to go to an offbeat country, you will find that there is not a single guidebook, up-to-date or not, in existence). It is the first time travellers, with little knowledge of what is aimed at whom, who find the wealth of information on their chosen country or continent bewildering and are likely to be overwhelmed by choice. They are advised to begin by reading an informative and interesting travel book which gives the general feel of the place. Such a book will probably have an annotated bibliography directing the reader to other recommended books.

The *National Geographic* magazine is an excellent source of background material (although reality is often a little disappointing after those marvellous photos). Large libraries bind the magazine in six-month batches, plus a separate index, which makes it a simple matter to look up your special interest. Articles from other magazines, such as *The Traveller*, and newspapers are particularly useful for busy people with a thirst for knowledge, and have the added advantage that they can be cut out and taken on the trip. Newspapers are frequently the only place where you can get a good picture of what the political situation is like – essential if you know there could be trouble. A list of the contents of past issues can often be had on request, especially if accompanied by a s.a.e. Articles which appeared only mildly interesting when read at home become quite riveting once you're in the country described. The same applies to books. Holiday reading matter should be carefully selected, however, and in no sense should it be heavy, or it will be left at the hotel while you sit on the beach guiltily reading magazines.

Overland travellers with unlimited time will prefer to do much of their reading en route, when they have had the chance to decide which aspects of a country most interest them. The British Council libraries in capital cities are often useful (although the emphasis is on British Culture) and national libraries sometimes have books in English, as do universities. English language bookshops will also have a better selection of titles on that country than can be found at home. And don't neglect to ask other travellers, particularly those heading in the opposite direction, if they have anything to recommend and/or give or swap.

The proper selection of a guidebook is as important to the traveller as the choice of luggage or footwear. It should advise and inform, be evocative yet objective, and help you plan your trip and make maximum use of your travel time. The price of books has risen so sharply in recent years that travellers are often reluctant to buy them. Yet most guidebooks cost only as much as a meal in a restaurant and, in contrast, can be thoroughly sampled before buying. Surely books are still among the best bargains available!

A Guide to Guides

by Douglas Schatz

With an ever-expanding market of international tourism, there has been a corresponding explosion in the publishing of international travel guides. For the traveller of independent means, or the independent traveller of no means, for coverage of the most common, or uncovering the uncommon, the question now is one of choice: 'Which guide?' There are 'Blue' guides, 'Red' guides and 'Green' guides. There are guides that promise you 'Insight' or a 'Companion'. Guides for 'Visitors' and for 'Travellers', that offer a 'Cultural' experience, or a 'Rough' time, or even just 'Survival'. And most arcane of all, there are guides for those whose holiday has some connection with Mobil oil, or who carry American Express cards.

A comparison between the alternatives may be made initially on the general balance of information a guide contains, whether it be cultural description or practical reference on accommodation, for example. One can easily compare the relative detail of the information, which is usually reflected in the price of the book, and note should be taken of the publication date, bearing in mind that the research for a guide usually predates publication by six months to a year. The style of a guide, its prose and presentation, can usually be assessed by its use of maps, indexes or illustrations. The aim, finally, is to match the guide to your individual travel needs and interests.

The survey below briefly highlights the distinguishing features of the main travel guides now available, most of which are series of books covering a variety of places in a consistent format. There may not always be more than one choice of guide for a particular destination, but whether there is or not, this may help indicate which is the most appropriate for your travels.

Newer Series

The expansion of the travel market over the last ten years is best reflected in the development of the *Lonely Planet* series of guide books. What began in 1975 with a single traveller, Tony Wheeler, and his guide to *South-East Asia on a Shoestring*, is now an international company producing an impressive list of 37 guide titles. Lonely Planet are based in Australia and their list is dominated by coverage of Asian locations. As the titles suggest, (there are *Travel Survival Kits* for individual countries while continents are covered *on a Shoestring*), the guides are strong on the hard practical information on visas, transport, inexpensive places to stay and eat, etc. For individual travel in the more adventurous parts of the world, these guides are paramount.

A very different kind of series specialising in the countries of Asia, the regions of America, and more recently the Caribbean and Europe, is the illustrated *Insight Guides*. The publisher, Apa Production, is aptly named, for each book is the collaborative 'production' of several writers and photographers, and credits are given to a producer, a director and designer, and an editor, as with a film. The guides contain detailed descriptive texts, many colour illustrations, and sections of practical information aimed, in contrast to Lonely Planet, at the 'sophisticated traveller'. The guides were originally subtitled with this epithet, and indeed have secured a strong place at the upper end of the market.

Colour Coding

Of the aforementioned guides identified by colour, possibly the most popular are the *Michelin Red Guides*. Published annually, they are an incomparable reference to the hotels and restaurants of Europe, with countless location maps, information on facilities and prices, and of course, their famous symbols of recommendation. They are not descriptive but hugely informative.

While there are basic listings of principal tourist sights in the Red Michelin guides, more substantial touring information is found in the series of *Green Michelin Tourist Guides*. These contain detailed introductions to the history and art of an area, followed by an alphabetical survey of places of interest that is remarkably detailed for the price of the guide, (still under £5.00 for 1987). Their distinctive tall format, the many maps, the star classification of sights, and the clear layout make them easy to use. One of the most impressive features of both the Red and Green Michelin guides is that they are cross-referenced in detail to each other, and to the separate Michelin maps. There are currently 22 Green Tourist Guides available in English, mainly covering European countries, and a similar number in French, mostly for regions of France itself.

The professed aim of a *Blue Guide* is give an account of a country or city 'without omitting anything... which might appeal to the intelligent visitor'. Indeed the long established Blue Guides are justly renowned for their comprehensive treatment of the art, architecture, and history of their subject. In consequence of the incomparable detail of their scholarship they can be rather dry to read, and also contain little practical travel information. They are, however, the last intelligent word on many European locations.

In a similar tradition to the Blue Guides is the series of *Phaidon Cultural Guides*. As their title suggests these guides are designed for a specific purpose, containing detailed alphabetical surveys of the art and architecture of their European subjects. They are handsomely produced hardback books with many colour illustrations, and one cannot but commend works of such detail.

American Giants

One of the giants of guide book publishing, with over 100 titles in the list, is the American produced series of *Fodor's Guides*. These are updated annually, and cover much of the world, though the majority are for countries and cities in the Western world. Often accused of sanitising travel, Fodor's guides are in fact a useful and dependable resource. They maintain a practical balance between their description of sights and the hard information on transport, monies, and accommodation and restaurants, including recommendations of the latter that cover a range of budgets. Travel may be less of an adventure, but is also less likely to go wrong.

Another series, which like Fodor's, originates in America and bears the name of its founder and editorial master, is Arthur *Frommer's Guides*. The 73 titles in the list are updated every second year, and they cover countries and cities worldwide with an emphasis on Europe. As is suggested by their *Dollarwise* and *So Many Dollars a Day* titles, they concentrate on finding value for money. Though not as detailed as some on sights or culture, they contain the most extensive descriptive assessments of hotels, restaurants and nightlife published.

More fluent and subjective cultural

description than any surveyed so far can be found in the series of *Companion Guides*, of which there are nineteen titles for cities and regions of Europe now in print. Of practical information they give no more than brief lists, but if you have a preference for discursive prose over gazeteers of information, these detailed and literary texts will prove worthy companions.

Small But Beautiful

An expanding series from the small travel publisher Michael Haag, which consists of a select list of more distant places (e.g. Turkey, Rajasthan, Zimbabwe...), is distinguished like the Companion Guides by the quality of the writing. The detailed and cultured texts of these guides are accompanied by informal but trustworthy sections of practical information.

A relatively new series to a rather mixed bag of places is the *Cadogan Guides*. They are still seeking to establish an individual character as a series, aiming to be high quality descriptive guides in the model of the *Companion Guides*. On the evidence to date, the quality of the texts is variable; the guides to Scotland and Turkey are superior to those of India or the Caribbean, for example. They each contain sections of general practical information.

For the traveller of less means it would be hard to compete with the *Let's Go* series of budget travel guides covering Europe and America. The guides are researched and written annually by teams of Harvard students, and they contain all of the practical information that the budget traveller requires for life 'on the road'.

I recall on my own budget Grand Tour tearing out sections of the tome-like *Let's Go Europe* country by country and, when used, passing these on to others or simply leaving them behind in order to lighten my travel load.

Another list aimed at the budget traveller is the *Rough Guides* series. Like Let's Go they contain practical travel information, though their recommendations on lower priced accommodation and restaurants are more informal and less comprehensive. While the guides are also culturally informed, the 'rough' of their title refers not only to their style of travel, but to the irreverence of their prose. In addition to European locations, they now also cover places such as China, Kenya, and Peru.

A distinctive and popular series on regions of the United States is the *Mobil Travel Guides*. These are large format paperback books that are updated annually, and are primarily useful for their extensive listings of hotels, motels and restaurants across America. They also give brief tourist information, and have a mini atlas of road maps.

For the more adventurous traveller, Hilary Bradt publishes a series of *Backpacking Guides*, specialising in South America, but also including titles on Africa, Greece and Italy. These are a worthy genre of 'grass roots' guides wherein the wealth of honest personal research is apparent. They contain first hand commentary on walking routes, sketch maps and much advice.

In recent years a successful range of general purpose guides has been the *AA/Baedecker Guides*. There are extensive lists of European 'Country', 'City' and 'Regional' guides, each of which is packaged in a plastic wallet with an accompanying map. The heart of each guide is an illustrated A-Z of principal sights, a gazeteer of adequate cultural substance. The section of practical information is a minimal listing of addresses, without description or recommendation.

Pocket-sized Guides

Competing in the same market is Moorland's new series of *Visitor's Guides* to countries of Europe, joining their useful regional guides to Britain and Europe. In their list they have chosen several locations not heretofore covered by any English language guide, for example, Norway and Corsica. They are pocket-sized books that comprise a clear and dependable mix of touring itineraries, tables of sights, and illustrations. They are not strong on practical travel detail, nor are their texts particularly substantial; they occupy the middle ground.

Hildebrand's Travel Guides do for Asia and Africa what Baedeker's do for Europe. That is, they are pocket-sized, illustrated guides in clear plastic wallets with a separate map, and though their descriptive texts are of necessity brief, I find the discursive prose a more attractive form than the gazeteer of the Baedeker series. The practical information is virtually non-existent, and I would suggest that these pocket guides are intended for package travellers rather than independent ones.

Also pocket-sized, general guides are the *Traveller's Guides* from Jonathan Cape publishers. It is unfortunate that their list is limited to a few titles covering the Mediterranean region, because they achieve a more substantial balance of cultural text and practical instruction than the other general guides just mentioned. The guides to Morocco and Crete are worth singling out.

Another series of pocket guides to be recommended is the *American Express Pocket Guides*, the style of which is especially appropriate for their city subjects. The size is deceptive, for they contain intelligent and relatively detailed cultural surveys, very useful descriptive listings of practical information, good maps, and even walking itineraries.

The most pocket-sized guides of all are the *Berlitz Guides* and *Traveller's Phrase Books*, each measuring less than four by six inches. These series are marvels of packaging. The guides contain basic tourist guidance with colour illustrations, and are sufficient for any short package visit. Similarly, the phrase books are renowned for their packaging of language into practical travel phrases for all occasions, (eliminating the inadvertent 'my uncle is a shoemaker'). The lengthy list of titles is dominated by European locations, though there are several exceptions.

Outstanding Individuals

Space permits no more than brief mention of several important individual publications which are of proven quality and/or enjoy current distinction. (The publisher appears in brackets to facilitate identification.)

The South American Handbook (Trade and Travel) – the bible for South and Central American travel, now (1987) in its 68th annual edition.

The Sahara Handbook (Lascelles) –

likewise, an obligatory guide for survival overland.

Trekking in Nepal (Cordee) – Stephen Bezruchka's detailed guide is still easily the best for high altitude fell walking.

Ladakh – Zanskar Guide and *Hiking in Ladakh – Zanskar* (Cordee/Artou) – an illustrated general guide, and detailed itineraries with maps, respectively, from an experienced Swiss trekking company.

South Pacific Handbook, Indonesia Handbook (Springfield/Moon) – comprehensive, practical handbooks.

A Handbook for India, Pakistan, Bangladesh and Sri Lanka (J. Murray) – encyclopaedic in an avuncular academic tradition, now in its 22nd edition.

The Tropical Traveller (Pan) – John Hatt's wisdom and humour on travel in warm climates.

Turkey's Southern Shore, Aegean Turkey (J. Murray) – George Bean's elegant classics of popular archaeology.

Venice for Pleasure (Cape) – Yes, John Link's incomparable walking tour of Venice is a pleasure indeed.

Trans-Siberian Rail Guide (Bradt) – the only current guide for the 'Big Red Train Ride'.

Work Your Way Around the World (Vacation Work) – invaluable practical directory for the working traveller.

The proliferation of guide book publishing goes on apace, and this survey is therefore inevitably incomplete. When possible, visit a specialist travel bookseller, where you will find the widest range of choice, and possibly even some advice.

Great Journeys Overland

Down and Around Africa

by David Orchard and Melissa Shales

Since Rhodes first dreamed of a railway running from Cape Town to Cairo, travelling the length of Africa has been one of the world's greatest, and most romantic overland routes. Much of it can now be driven on paved roads, but crossing Africa is still no easy undertaking. There is an immense variety of climates, terrain, peoples and history, all of which add together with an extremely 'fluid' political situation to make it a true challenge in all terms.

Across the Sahara

Crossing the Sahara is still quite an expedition, beginning either at Tangiers (through the High Atlas and into Algeria), Alger (via the old Roman city of Constantine), or Tunis (past the huge Roman Amphitheatre at El Djem and across the Chott El Djerid).

From here there are three major trans-Sahara routes: the eastern; the central (the trade route) via Gardaia along the tar-sealed road to Tamanrasset; and the western route along the Libyan border to Djanet, crossing the Fadnoun Plateau, with an optional trek into the Tassil N Ajjer to see the 3,000-year-old rock paintings. From Djanet, travellers are advised to go west past the Hermitage of P. de Foucauld at Assekrem and on to Tamanrasset. From Tam, the route heads due south past Assamarka, the isolated Foreign Legion fortress (no photos permitted) that is the border with Niger, past the salt workings at Tegguiddan Tessoum, where salt caravans, camels laden with tablets of salt, plod their way south and into Agadèz, with its silversmiths still making crosses by a molten wax method as their forefathers did.

As one heads south to Kano or south-west to Niamey, the vegetation thickens, and there are more people and more cattle. This is Fulani country – ornately bejewelled people congregating around wells with goats, camels and cattle. The western route goes from Béchar across the Tanezrouft down to Gao (remember to make an excursion to Tombouctou) and into Niamey.

From Kano or Niamey it is a simple run south on good roads into the thickening forests to Accra, Lomé or Lagos. If the Nigerian border is closed (this seems to happen frequently, usually with no warning) there is a well-used route from Niger skirting round the shore of Lake Chad, into Cameroon.

These routes all remain open to travellers who have made the proper preparations, although the Algerian authorities are becoming extremely reluctant to let anyone through whom they feel they might have to rescue later. So be warned, you will be unlikely to be allowed to undertake the journey in a clapped-out *Deux Chevaux*.

Recent reports coming back to Britain indicate that bribery is on a sharp upward curve and it is proving extremely expensive to satisfy all the outstretched hands in this section of the Sahara.

Trans-Africa (West to East)

From the coastal highway at Accra, Lomé or Lagos, the route follows the tar-sealed road down to Douala (a short, unsealed section near the border), past Mount Cameroon to Yaoundé, the very French capital in the highlands of the Cameroons. Further east past Boali Falls is Bangui, capital of the Central African Republic. The traditional route then took you north-east to Juba in southern Sudan, where you could join the Cairo/Nairobi route south via Lake Turkana. However, since southern Sudan has been closed, due to civil war, for some time, and seems unlikely to reopen in the foreseeable future, the only reasonable route left open is through Zaire, then on to Kigali in Rwanda or Bujumbura in Burundi and across the border into north-west Tanzania. This is a spectacular route scenically, leading through the 'Volcano National Park', where you may be lucky enough to catch a glimpse of the mountain gorillas, past the southern shore of Lake Victoria and through the Serengeti to Nairobi or east via Mount Kilimanjaro to Dar Es Salaam. I wouldn't recommend attempting to enter Uganda as, while several travellers have done this

route and sent back favourable reports, the political situation in the country is still so explosive it is difficult to guage from one day to the next how you are likely to be greeted.

If you are hoping to head south without crossing to East Africa, from Kinshasa it is possible to make for Lubumbashi and cross the Zambian border here.

Whichever route you choose, the roads will be poor for large sections of the journey, supplies are hard to come by, as is fuel. But people are friendly and a ball-point pen can still be bartered for two dozen oranges.

A final warning, however. Zaire has also taken to closing its land borders on occasion with no warning and seemingly for no reason. If this happens again, and Africa's political map does not change there is no safe way through.

Cairo to Nairobi

While southern Sudan remains closed, Uganda is unsafe, and Ethiopia impossible to enter by land, this famous route is, sadly impassable. We have left in a description in the hope that during the life of this edition, it will once more prove possible to make this magnificent journey.

Egypt has been a Mecca for travellers for many years with its pyramids, the ancient temples of Luxor and Karnak and the Valleys of the Kings and Queens. Only recently have foreign registered vehicles been allowed into the country, but a tar-sealed road stretches from Alexandria to Aswan. The ferry on Lake Nasser no longer carries vehicles, and you will have to get special permission to drive south from Aswan, from both the Egyptians and the Sudanese. It is possible, but involves a great deal of complicated paperwork.

From Wadi Halfa, the track leaves the Nile and takes a straight route across the Nubian Desert to Abu Hamed, from where the route follows the Nile all the way to Juba. From Khartoum, where Blue Nile meets White Nile, African meets Arab, one goes south via Sennar, Kosti to Malakal and the beginning of the Sudd, that vast area of marsh and moorland, the size of the UK, where herds of a hundred giraffe are commonplace, where the Dinka stride the plains with nothing but a spear, and life has changed little in a thousand years.

Juba, the capital of the south, is not a hustling, bustling city. At the time of writing, however, it is the centre of the rebel movement and even aid workers need an amnesty to reach it. Excitement can be stirred up by a rogue hippo in the Nile or the arrival of supplies on the steamer from the north.

From Juba, the route takes the traveller through the narrow corridor to Lokichokio and on to Lake Turkana (the Jade Sea of Hillaby fame). South of Lodwar the road separates, west via Kitale for banks, beers and supplies, or east to Lakes Baringo and Beroria for flamingoes by the thousand. The roads join at Nakuru for the tar-sealed road to Nairobi. This route has often been described as 'Africa the old and new': the tomb of Tutankhamun, the temple of Queen Hatshepsut, and the cities of Cairo and Nairobi are the old and new elements linked vaguely by the Nile.

Nairobi to Cape Town

The best route south to Tanzania is through the game reserves of Masai Mara and Serengeti, by the Ngorongoro Crater to Arusha, a climb up Kilimanjaro (5,963m), an extinct, snow-capped volcano and the highest point in Africa, and on to Dar es Salaam. The road west to Lusaka follows the line of the Tazara railway and is an easy section of the journey. It is not on the main route south, but it may be worth considering a small detour to Malawi. This beautiful country is all but neglected by tourists, but is one of the most beautiful spots in southern Africa. Further south, another worthwhile detour is into Swaziland, again rarely visited in the rush to fall off Africa at Cape Point.

From Lusaka, passing through Zambia's copper belt, the traveller has a choice of routes, south-east into Zimbabwe, past Lake Kariba and through the Hwange National Park, or southwest, past the Victoria Falls and the wildlife parks at Chobe and on the Okavango Delta on the edge of the Kalahari desert in Botswana.

Alternatively, you can swing east to Harare, and go south to Mutare on the Mozambique border, through the mountain ranges of the Eastern Highlands, then down past the Great Zimbabwe ruins and cross in South Africa via Beit Bridge.

Once in South Africa, the route goes through the gold city of Johannesburg, through the Orange Free State, across the Karoo (a wonderful sight in spring when the desert is covered by sheets of flowers) to Cape Town and Table Mountain: a dramatic end to a dramatic continent.

A four-wheel-drive vehicle is not

necessary for most of these routes providing one travels in the dry season. The west/east section is probably the most difficult with little available in the way of fuel and supplies. High ground clearance, such as on a VW Campervan, is essential. The problems that will arise will be primarily politically closed borders, visa difficulties, military takeovers or outright wars. But with a clear head and luck, it is still the journey of a lifetime.

Around South America

by Chris Parrott

The Gringo Trail (not to be confused with the Inca trail) is what everyone calls the most frequently travelled route through and around South America. *Gringo* is derived either from 'Green go home' in the days when the US Army used to wear green uniforms, or from *Greigo*, the Spanish word for Greek. Despite assurances in the guide-books that the term is so widely used to refer to anyone with a pale complexion that it has lost its unfriendly connotations, it is definitely not a complimentary form of address. If you need confirmation, watch how a blond Argentine reacts to being called *Gringo*.

The Trail begins in whichever gateway happens to be the cheapest to fly into from Europe or the USA. Let's start in the north, in Colombia. The coast here boasts beautiful golden beaches, clear water and crystal streams cascading down from the 5,800 metre summits of the Sierra Nevada. To the south is the big industrial port of Barranquilla and then Cartagena, an impressively fortified town dating from 1533, through which, for nearly three hundred years, gold and treasures were channelled from throughout the Spanish colonies. Passing through the hot swampland and then inland up the attractive forested slopes of the Cordillera Occidental, the traveller emerges on a high plateau where Bogotá is sited, at 2,620 metres. The Gold Museum has over 10,000 examples of pre-Columbian artefacts. An hour away are the salt mines of Zipaquira, inside which the workers carved an amazing 23 metre high cathedral.

South from Bogotá are the Tequendama Falls, the splendid valley of the Magdalena river and, high up on the Magdalena Gorge, the village of San Agustín. Here hundreds of primitive stone statues, representing gods of a little known ancient Indian culture, guard the entrances to tombs. The road then loops back over high moorland to Popayan, a fine city with monasteries and cloisters in the Spanish style. The tortured landscape near here has been said to resemble 'violently crumpled bedclothes'; tilled fields on the opposite mountain faces 'look nearly vertical'.

So the road crosses into Ecuador. Just north of Quito, the equator, *La Mitad Del Mundo*, cuts the road, a few hundred metres from the grand stone monument built to mark the meridian. Quito itself is at 2,700 metres, ringed by peaks, amongst them the volcanoes of Pinchincha. It has much fine colonial architecture including, according to *The South American Handbook*, eighty-six churches, many of them gleaming with gold.

The Andes

Travellers then cross the Andes, passing from near-Arctic semi-tundra, through temperate forest, equatorial jungle and down to the hot total desert of the Peruvian coast, punctuated by oases of agricultural land where irrigation has distributed the melt-waters from the Andes over the littoral. Here too the ancient empires of the Chavin, Mochica, Nazca and Chimu people flourished. Ruined Chan-Chan, near Trujillo, was the Chimu capital; nearby Sechin has a large square temple, 3,500 years old, incised with carvings of victorious leaders and dismembered foes.

A popular detour here is to turn inland at the fishing port of Chimbote and head for the Callejon de Huaylas. The route passes through the spectacular Can óon del Pato, where the road is literally drilled through the rock wall of the canyon, with 'windows' down to the roaring maelstrom of the Santa river below. The Callejon de Huaylas valley runs along the foot of the Cordillera Blanca; here the 1970 earthquake buried the town of Yungay under an avalanche of mud. The towns of Caraz and Juaraz make good centres for walking and trekking in the Cordillera, and the road south across the mountains has spectacular views of the snowcapped Cordillera Blanca.

The coast near Lima is picturesque and rich in fish and birdlife, owing to the Humboldt Current. Lima itself has both shanty towns (*barrios*) and affluent suburbs, parks and fine beaches. Well worth seeing are the National Museum of Anthropology and Archaeology, the Gold Museum at Monterrico on the outskirts of town, and the Amano private museum.

South from Lima

From Lima, there are two routes south. One branches into the mountains – the pass reaches 4,800 metres – through the zinc smelting town of La Oroya, to Huancayo. The road continues through Ayacucho and Abancay to Cuzco, and though Lima/Cuzco looks a relatively short distance on the map, it actually represents about fifty hours of continuous travel overland. The other route follows the fast coast road through the desert past the wine centre of Ica to Nazca with its vast and little understood lines, on to Arequipa. There are several cut-off routes – from Pisco or Nazca, for example, or you can take the train from Arequipa in a grand circle, to get to Cuzco.

One thing that is certain: any route in Peru that crosses the Andes is tortuous, time-consuming, and stunningly spectacular.

Cuzco sits in a sheltered hollow at 3,500 metres. This was the capital of the Inca Empire. Inca stonework forms the base of many of the Spanish buildings and the ancient city layout survives to this day. Overlooking Cuzco's red roofs is the ruined fortress of Sacsahuaman. Nearby too are the ruins of Pisac and Ollantaitambo and, reached by train only, down the valley of the Urubamba (further up-stream, this is called the Vilcanota), the 'Lost City of the Incas', Machu Picchu. This magnificent ruined city sited nearly 500 metres above the river was overgrown with jungle until its discovery in 1911. There are several legends which add to the mystery of the lost city. One states that after the sacking of Cuzco, the Virgins of the Sun fled to this city, whose existence was unknown to the Spanish. Others say that the Incas themselves had erased all mention of the city from their oral histories, retribution for some now forever-censored local uprising long before Pizarro and his men set foot in Peru.

From Cuzco, the road crosses the watershed of the Andes to the dry and dusty Altiplano, a high treeless plateau stretching from here across much of the Bolivian upland. Here lies Lake Titicaca, at 3,810 metres the world's highest navigable lake, blazing a deep blue because of ultra-violet rays. On the floating reed islands of the lake live the Uru-Aymará Indians. Across the border in Bolivia are the ruins of Tiahuanaco, relic of an ancient race; the main feature is the carved 'Gate of the Sun'.

La Paz lies in a valley just below the rim of the Altiplano, the city centre lying at approximately 3,500 metres.

La Paz and Beyond

From La Paz, there are three possible routes, depending on the size of the circuit that you intend making.

1. Eastwards through the relatively low-lying city of Cochabamba to Santa Cruz, then on by rail to Corumba on the Brazilian border, from where you can head for São Paulo or the Iguaçu Falls. The road from Santa Cruz to Corumba and any of those from Bolivia to Paraguay are suitable for four-wheel-drive only.

2. Southwards via Cochabamba to Sucre and the mining town of Potosi to Villazón on the Argentine border and points south. NB: Since April 1982, British passport holders have required a visa to enter Argentina. At the time of going to press, visas issued in London take several months to pro-

cess; it helps to have a sponsor (friend or relative, etc.) oiling the wheels at the other end. Visas are handled by the Brazilian Embassy (Argentine Interests Section) at 111 Cadogan Gardens, London SW3 1RQ (tel: 01-730 7173). Holders of Irish passports do not need visas.

3. Southwards to Arica in northern Chile. The roads gradually peter out over the salt pans and quicksands that stretch over this region – a region that should only be traversed in the dry season (May to November) and then with very great care. The road passes through the very beautiful Lauca National Park, and then continues (for the most part tar-sealed) through the Atacama desert, the farmlands and vineyards of central Chile to the so-called 'Little Switzerland' of mountainous southern Chile.

There is no road in Chile south of Puerto Montt, and the most usual point of crossing the border south of Santiago is that near Osorno to reach Bariloche, now a fashionable ski resort in Argentina. This route may not be passable in winter (June to October). The road from Santiago to Mendoza via Uspallata is kept open all year round, though in winter the road uses the railway tunnel and does not pass the famous Christ of the Andes statue. Travel south from Bariloche takes you over often unmade roads in the foothills of the Andes through the beautiful Argentine lake district to Viedma and Calafate. Here the lakes are fed by melt-waters from the Patagonian ice-cap, and 'arms' of the lakes are sometimes blocked by tongues of glacial ice. The scenery around Lago Argentino, for example, is some of the most spectacular anywhere in the world. Roads here are passable at most times of year, though from June to October, four-wheel-drive is advisable.

The South

It is possible to reach South America's southernmost tip, Tierra del Fuego, by ferry from near Rio Gallegos, or from Punta Arenas across the border in Chile.

In winter it's impossible to cross the mountains by road to reach the small town of Ushuaia on Tierra del Fuego's south coast, but there are regular flights throughout the year from nearby Gallegos and Rio Grande.

A worthwhile excursion from Punta Arenas (Chile) is to Puerto Natales and the famous Torres del Paine National Park; a must for mountaineers, and an unforgettable experience for anyone who thinks that those etchings by early explorers always made mountains look ridiculously precipitous.

The fast, straight east coast road through temperate scrubland takes you north again via Comodoro Rivadavia, Puerto Madryn with its Welsh-speaking colony, to Bahia Blanca and Buenos Aires. This cosmopolitan city of nearly ten million inhabitants lies on the estuary of the River Plate, a few hours by ferry from Montevideo in Uruguay.

Most travellers tend to bypass the rolling cattle-grazed plains of Uruguay in favour of the roads northwards, either through Santa Fe and Resistencia to Asunción, or direct to Iguaçu via Posadas and the Misiones province. Though there are several ferries, there are only three bridging points across the Paraná River between Buenos Aires and Asunción. The first and newest is at Zarate; the second is the tunnel from Santa Fe to Rosario; and the third is the bridge between Resistencia and Corrientes.

There is a good fast road from Asunción to Foz do Iguaçu where the frontier is crossed by bridge. Car and passenger ferries from Foz do Iguaçu (Pôrto Meira) in Brazil to Puerto Iguaçu (or Iguassu) in Argentina, make it possible to visit these spectacular falls from both sides of the river.

Plantations of Brazil

The dense forest that once spread across Brazil from Iguaçu to Rio and beyond is gradually making way for coffee and soya bean plantations, though there is a particularly special stretch of road between Curitiba and São Paulo, since the new road follows the Serra do Mar coastal range. Carriageways are often separated by several kilometres as east-bound traffic goes around one side of a jungle-clad mountain, while westbound takes the high road.

From São Paulo there are two routes to Rio – one through Santos and Angra dos Reis along a beautiful coast road; the other the fast motorway, along the ridge of the mountains via the steel town of Volta Redonda.

Rio is a focus; from here routes divide once more.

1. The north-east coast road through Salvador, Recife and Fortalaza to Belém at the mouth of the Amazon. Many travellers feel that this route, passing through the regions first settled by Portugal and her slaves four centuries ago, is the real Brazil.

2. North-west via Belo Horizonte and the old mining towns of Minas Gerais province, such as Ouro Preto, Congonhas, Tiradentes and Mariana. This route leads to that oasis of mod-

ernity, that ultimate in planned cities, Brasilia.

There are several routes up to the Amazon basin from Brasilia, the fastest and easiest of which is direct to Belém via Anapolis. On this road there is a cut-off at Estreito, along the Transamazónica Highway to Altamira and Santarém.

Alternatively you can follow the newer road west to Cuiabá, and then take the Transamazónica north to Santarém. At both Belém and Santarém there are river steamers to Manaus though, for anyone with their own vehicle to ship, car ferries are few and far between. A more practical route in this instance is that to the west, to Cuiabá and Pôrta Velho, and then north along the new road via Humairá to Careiro on the south bank of the Amazon opposite Manaus. From here there are three ferries daily across to Manaus.

In the days when Brazil held a monopoly of rubber supplies, Manaus built a splendid (and recently restored) opera house for the best mezzosopranos in the world; and the rubber barons lit their cigars with 1,000 *millreis* notes. Most of that glitter has faded, though edifices built of stone imported from Britain are still to be seen.

From here, riverboats ply the Rio Negro and the Rio Branco, tributaries of the Amazon, and they provide a break from overlanding and a convenient, if primitive, way of visiting remote villages. North from Manaus the authorities have 'subdued' the Indians who, for years threatened white lives on the road to Boa Vista, and the route is now passable in safety.

Angel Falls

The road between Boa Vista and the gold mining town of El Dorado (Venezuela) winds through spectacularly beautiful country passing the sheer-sided 'lost world' of Mount Roraima at the junction of the three countries. Side trips can be taken to the world's highest waterfall, Angel Falls (979 metres), either from El Dorado or from Puerto Ordaz (shortly to become part of the new city of Ciudad Guayana).

After crossing the Orinoco, you'll soon reach Caracas, having completed almost a full circle of the continent. If you've still not seen enough, there's a route eastwards that is definitely not on the Gringo Trail. It is not possible, owing to border disputes, to cross the frontier from Venezuela to Guyana. From Boa Vista (Brazil) however, there is a road of sorts to the frontier and a fordable river into Lethem. In the dry season, it's possible to drive all the way to Georgetown, and from there along the coast to the Corentyne River. Getting across that and into Nieuw Nickerie in Suriname will cause problems for those with their own vehicles, though there is an infrequent ferry. In fact, it's possible to drive all the way to Cayenne in French Guiana, though the road is little more than a sand track in places, and there are a number of rivers that have to be crossed by ferry.

Saint Laurent lies just over the river from Suriname, in French Guiana, and the remnants of both this penal colony and the better-known one of the Isles de Salut are beginning to prove something of a tourist attraction. Devil's Island is part of the Isles de Salut Group, but is hard to reach.

At Cayenne, the road ends, though it is possible to fly either direct to Belém at the mouth of the Amazon or to Saint Georges, just across the river from the Brazilian river port of Oiapoque, from where a road runs all the way to Macapá. There are ferries to Belém from there, and that puts you back on the route southwards to Rio either along the north-east coast, or south to Brasilia. In fact, you could just keep circling and recircling the continent in ever decreasing circles, clockwise and anticlockwise. It's a very dizzying part of the world in every respect!

Overland Through Asia

by Geoff Hann

Several factors have combined to disrupt the traditional overland route to Asia of late, notably internal turmoil and changes of government within Iran and Afghanistan, together with the Russian invasion of Afghanistan, the Iran/Iraq war, which is beginning to spill into the other Gulf states, and even ripples from the civil war in Lebanon. Bureaucracy too has increased in many of the Asian countries. Pre-departure documentation has become all important. Woe betide the traveller who arrives on the border of India without a *carnet de passages* for their vehicle, correct in every detail. Flexibility of attitude and mind is as important now as it was to the early Victorian traveller.

In some circumstances, overflights of extremely troubled areas have to be considered. The route through Iran is still theoretically open, although there may be a difficulty in getting visas, but travellers are being advised in the strongest possible terms not to drive through until the situation both within the country and with Iraq has been resolved. Afghanistan is very definitely closed to tourists and is likely to remain so for the foreseeable future.

The most used overland route begins in London, crosses the Channel by ferry to either Ostend or Zeebrugge and connects with the E5 road for a rapid transit through Belgium, Germany, Austria, Yugoslavia and Bulgaria to Turkey. There are, of course, minor variations, but whether one travels at a leisurely pace or a gallop, the first major halt is Istanbul, introduction to the East, a noisy meltingpot of nationalities and full of historical interest. A place too to gather your breath, rest, repair vehicles, and pick up news of the road ahead from fellow travellers.

Istanbul Connections

From Istanbul there is a choice of route. The shortest one is through the north of Turkey onto the great Anatolian Plateau. The road travels via Ankara, the modern capital of Turkey, and passes through Sivas, Erzurum and Ağri to the border with Iran. Doğubayazit, the last Turkish town, is overlooked by Mount Ararat, the traditional seat of Noah's Ark. This border post, known universally as Bazargan, is now the main crossing for all traffic. Many of the other crossings such as Serou, just south of Lake Van, are subject to local conflicts. Make careful local enquiries before attempting to use them.

Turkey has so much to offer however that most travellers will want to proceed more slowly. The most effective way to do so is to backtrack slightly from Istanbul to the Dardanelles. The Cannakale crossing is the usual way and the road follows the coastline very closely. Troy, Bergama (Pergamon), modern Izmir and ancient Ephesus are just some of the places to visit. From Ephesus, the road loops inland before coming back to the coast at Antalya. Another long scenic drive directly by the sea passes by and through Alanya, Silifke, Mersin and Adana. For those intending to cross into Iran by the Bazargan border, an ideal route is north from Mersin onto the Central Turkish Plateau via the volcanic tufa area around Nevşehir and Kayseri. The small towns of Urgup and the villages such as Göreme are world famous for the early Christian churches and tombs carved out of the rock. The underground city of Derinkuyu also should not be missed.

It is only a few hours from this area to resume the northern route at Sivas. Those intent on seeing something of eastern Turkey should follow the road to Malataya, Elâzığ, Bingol, and Lake Van – beautiful scenery and a Kurdish area. At Van, the border crossing of Serou is close by, as is a road leading north to Bazargan.

The Middle East Route

At the time of writing, this route is closed by the war in Iran/Iraq, but should it reopen, it is well worth considering with a great deal of interest to see on the way.

It begins at Adana, where one turns south and follows the path used by many invaders, through the Syrian Gates to Antakya, ancient Antioch. It is a short distance to the border and

Baba El Hawa, the Syrian entry post. Business takes a while here and travellers should be patient.

Syria is much underrated by travellers, suffering a bad press as it does because of its political stance. But it offers unbounded Arab hospitality and contains a staggering quantity of historical remains. Many of the sites have romantic settings, such as Palmyra, Rosafya, crumpled remains out in the desert and great Crusader castles set on mountain peaks. Halav (Aleppo) is the first introduction to the Arab world, noisy, but full of interesting people, ruined sites and good food. Travelling on southwards through Hamah, with its great eighteenth-century water wheels, and Homs, one reaches Damascus, the capital. Here are the beautiful Ommayad mosque, Saladin's tomb and the biblical 'Street called Straight', together with a huge *souk* or market.

Continuing south, cross the border at Deraa into Jordan, a country with a Western approach, where tourism is a major source of income. But nothing can detract from Petra, Jordan's premier attraction. This fabulous hidden valley lined with rock tombs is approximately 280km south of Amman off the Desert Highway. A natural continuation of this diversion would be a further trip south, to the beaches of Aqaba, before returning to Amman, Jordan's capital.

God-given Relief

From Amman, the overland route turns east, heading straight into the stony desert towards Iraq with Baghdad ('gift of God' in Arabic) as a welcome relief at the end. The city is a large sprawling one. Babylon is nearby, as are the holy cities of An Najaf and Karbala, important centres for the Shi'ite Muslim faith. For the overlander, the usual route is to Al Basran (Basra), another long desert journey. This city is the most southerly in Iraq, famous for its date groves and as the birthplace of Sinbad the Sailor. Normally a ferry crossing and a drive of twelve kilometres into Iran towards Abadan would have sufficed for the next section. However, Basra is currently at the very heart of the fighting, with all the land around bitterly disputed, so the traveller must turn around further north and head back to Turkey.

Back in Turkey, return to Bazargan, refuelling before crossing the Iranian border, since fuel may become very difficult to obtain for some distance. Maku and Tabriz are the main cities with a Turkish flavour. The countryside is delightful – winding valleys lined with poplar trees through low hills – until one comes to the flat plain that stretches to Tehran. Tehran is one of the fastest-growing cities in the world and its hideous traffic and pollution are striking. Travellers will need to guard their language in present circumstances, as people are sensitive. Travellers used then to go through Afghanistan, but this is obviously now no longer possible, and it seems unlikely that the route will open again, so there is no choice but to travel south, bypassing Qom, the theological centre, to Esfahan, known for its mosques and handicrafts. Further south is Persepolis, ancient palace and religious city of the Persians, burnt by Alexander the Great when he conquered the Empire. Close by is the garden city of Shiraz, tree lined and populated by courteous people.

Wild Country

To resume the overland route, return to Esfahan and turn south-east to Yazd, home of the Fire Worshippers and the Towers of Silence. Skirting the Dasht-e-Lut desert, the road travels via Kerman and the oasis of Bam to Zahedan, Motorists should pay particular attention to their vehicles before leaving Esfehan for this stretch of their journey. Conditions can be difficult and spare parts are not readily available.

From Zahedan, the next section is rough and very remote from civilisation as we know it. The province of Baluchistan is quite removed from the rest of Pakistan, a wild country of wild people, with extremes of temperature. Dalbandin is the first major town along this route, some 160km into the country beyond the Customs post. Next comes Quetta, capital of the province, an interesting town in which to relax after the strenuous journey from Esfehan. Thence the road travels from the Bolan Pass – famous from the great days of the British Army – on to Sukkur and Multan and then to Lahore. The North West Frontier and Khyber Pass, which would have formed part of the route from Afghanistan, have recently been closed to travellers in an attempt to try to clear up the drug-trafficking in the area.

Lahore is modern and bustling but with a red fort and many Moghul remains and gardens; many good restaurants and a fine museum too. It is also an excellent place for motor repairs and spare parts.

The Karakoram Highway and the Khunjerab Pass on the Chinese border have recently opened and provide an exciting alternative route through

Tibet, from where you can either cross into Nepal or travel through China to Beijing. It is not yet open to private vehicles however and is only a possibility if travelling by public transport.

India

To cross into India, go from Lahore to the Wagha border. This is only open three times a month, and you are only allowed through in an escorted convoy, which drives straight through to Delhi, bypassing Amritsar which is only a short distance down the road and the first stop within India. In the old part of the town is the Golden Temple, heart of the Sikh religion. The Punjab area is closed due to fighting between the Sikhs and Hindus, and has been officially declared to be in a state of emergency. There is no alternative route.

From Amritsar the Grand Trunk Road carries on through the prosperous Punjab to Delhi – for many travellers, journey's end, and a place to luxuriate in modern hotels, buy handicrafts and sightsee. Others go on to Nepal, either to trek in the Himalayas or to fly to Bangkok and south-east Asia. Other still divert north to Kashmir, a two or three-day journey up a scenic mountain road to Srinagar. Here house-boats on Dal Lake offer every luxury. High in the mountains are Leh and Zanskar.

If you want to explore more of India, leave Delhi slightly south-west on a very good road for Jaipur, city of pink sandstone and centre of the precious-stone trade. Jaipur to Agra is another day's travel. Here one passes Fatepur Sikri, the deserted sixteenth-century city, and Agra, home of the incomparable Tah Mahal, also of the red fort, Little Taj and Great Mosque.

From Agra the road leads south to cross the Chambal river and through Gwalior to Khajuraho, with its amazing temples set in the midst of scrub jungle.

In another day, the traveller can be in Varanasi (Benares), situated on the holy Ganges, a place of pilgrimage for Hindus and of insight into the Hindu faith and therefore India itself for the traveller. A few kilometres from the city is Sarnath, scene of the Buddha's first sermon.

Magical Moment

If you head north, you pass through Gorakhpur and approach the foothills of the Himalayas. It is a magical moment when the great mountain peaks first come into view. The India/Nepal border is a very Asian affair and is best left to the morning if possible.

The route to Pokhara, up through the mountains, is the easier of the two routes into Nepal and also gives the opportunity of seeing more of the country. A complete day is required to reach to Pokhara valley but to arrive at sunset and glimpse the slopes of the Annapurna mountain range turn pink in the evening light is to witness one of the earth's most splendid sights. Pokhara is something of a Shangri-La and is a good trekking centre.

A journey of between seven and ten hours takes one to Kathmandu, once a mysterious city, now a thriving tourist centre. Kathmandu and its valley are worth many days' exploration – nice people, good food, a magnificent backcloth of the world's highest mountains, art treasures in every street. What traveller could ask for more?

From Nepal, it is possible to cross into China, although you are still not able to circle round and drive through Malaysia. The only way to continue on the old route to Australia is to take a boat from Calcutta, but as this means that your vehicle will spend more time afloat than on land for the rest of the journey, it is more sensible to resign yourself to public transport from here onwards. Either fly into Rangoon to have your seven days touring Burma, or straight on to Bangkok or Singapore, from where you can backtrack to explore Thailand and Malaysia before heading south through the Philippines and Indonesia towards Australia.

Great Train Journeys

by Christopher Portway

A famous express can never die. Witness the appeals of the *Direct Orient Express* that ran from Paris to Istanbul which, in substance if not wholly in route, has been resurrected by private enterprise and, in spite of exorbitant fares, is booked solid for months ahead. There are many travellers who obtain their kicks from riding those famed expresses of the world, crossing countries or continents in a manner no other machine can offer, whether it flies, floats or rolls.

For its last decade and more the *Direct Orient* was, alas, the dullest, slowest and most inefficient of trains with all its former glory lost to the caprices of politics and the whims of individual nations along the route. The through express may have passed into history but the line remains inviolate – even if one does have to change at Belgrade. And in case you didn't know – and few do – there's still a real Orient Express which runs between Paris and Bucharest via Strasbourg, Munich, Vienna and Budapest.

Europe

Let's take a look at some famous names – and possibly a few not so famous – in railway express train fame and consider their offerings and delights.

We'll start in Britain – and the names that come immediately to mind are *The Flying Scotsman* and *The Royal Scot*. Neither quite looks as it used to as they streak between London and Edinburgh and Glasgow in five hours or so headed by their unromantic diesel or electric units. But efficient they are, whatever opinions you may hold of British Rail in other realms.

The continent of Europe is a treasure trove of titled expresses. Most bear names that are not only evocative-sounding but also indicate their route either directly – like the *Venezia Express* (between Venice and Athens via Belgrade) – or indirectly, such as the *Chopin* (between Vienna and Moscow via Warsaw) or the *Wiener Walzer* on which I remember trotting happily but not particularly efficiently from Basel, via Graz, Vienna and Budapest to Bucharest some years ago. Even if you're not a wizard with a compass the *Nord-West Express* between London, Hook, Hamburg and Copenhagen, the *Ost-West Express* between London, Brussels, Cologne, Berlin, Warsaw and Moscow (plus a Paris section), the *Nord Express* (same route as the *Nord West*) and the *Sud Express*

(Paris-Lisbon) indicate their direction of travel. Only the *Remus* (Vienna, Venice, Milan, Rome), the *Romulus* (ditto), the *Lusitania* (Madrid-Lisbon) and *Britannia* (London, Cologne, Munich) might not make their intentions clear.

For interest and incident, I suggest either the *Ost-West Express* or the *Hook of Holland-Moscow*, which follow the classic invasion route across central and eastern Europe. What with traversing the territory of two Germanies, two Berlins, Poland and European USSR, not only do you experience some entertaining frontier controls (they used to be particularly vicious at Brest Litovsk) but you pass over the blood-soaked battlegrounds resulting from the crazed ambitions of Napoleon and Hitler.

The above are all international expresses, but there are many named and sometimes very much glossier and faster Trans-Europe, TGV and Intercity services such as the *Cisalpin* (Paris-Milan), *Rembrandt* (Amsterdam-Stuttgart), *Le Capitole* (Paris-Toulouse) and the famous *Train Bleu* (Paris, Marseilles, Ventimiglia) which run between destinations in often no more than one or two countries, particularly France, which knows a thing or two about fast, smooth-running trains. I have not yet sampled the *Citalia* between London, Rimini and Rome which serves only clients of CIT , the Italian Tourist Organisation.

North America

The USA has some notions of train namings very different from those of Europe. First, it must be pointed out that only the trains of the United States East Coast can, on the basis of speed, be looked on as expresses at all. This said, let me recommend with enthusiasm a journey across that great country in the hands of Amtrak, the United States rail passenger handling corporation, who run slow but impressive long-distance trains bearing the most striking names of all. On the East Coast, train services are thin on the ground but what they lose out on in speed and frequency is made up by comfort and sense of occasion. Transcontinental trains offer observation domes, cocktail lounges, restaurants and sleeping cars – including roomettes – and cinema shows interspersed with Bingo. Some of the most well known of these 'expresses' are the *San Francisco Zephyr* (Chicago-Oakland), the *Montrealer* (Montreal-Washington DC, *Silver Meteor* and *Silver Star* (New York-Miami), *Broadway Limited* (New York – Washington DC – Chicago), *Coast Starlight* (Seattle – Los Angeles), *Empire Builder* (Chicago – Portland) and *The Crescent* (New York – New Orleans). A host of exciting names including the famed *Metroliner*, serve the New York - Philadelphia - Washington DC lines, many at high speed.

Canada too has brought its competing private companies to heel and put its passenger-carrying services under a centralized handling authority, this one called VIA. The most famous express – although again more in substance than in speed – is the *Canadian*, making the three-day journey between Montreal, Toronto and Vancouver a delight and offering similar facilities to those supplied by Amtrak. I once made the run in the cab of the locomotive, arriving at Calgary an hour and a half late because the driver kept saying 'I'll go slow round the next bend as there's a good view for you to photograph!

Asia

An even vaster land mass covered by a rail network is the USSR and the one express name that trips off the tongue without much bidding is the *Trans Siberian Express* though the name of the train is actually the *Russia*. I spent nine days on it some years ago grinding – again at no more than 30mph – the 6000 miles from Moscow to Vladivostock, stopping at all 98 stations in between. Soviet trains, with their wide guage track, are spacious and quite comfortable. Endless tea is supplied in half-pint glasses by the lady coach attendant who draws it from the ever-operating samovar. And in the restaurant car, at least a few of the dishes of the dozens listed in the menu are available and, occasionally, it includes caviar – if you're quick enough. Otherwise it's Borsch, Borsch and more Borsch. A Western visitor may only travel Soft Class (First Class in Imperialistic terms) but has to make up his/her own bed, while a strange contradiction to the usual prim and proper Russian attitude is that, as likely as not, you'll be expected to share a 'bedroom' with a member of the opposite sex. Only three cities along the way are open to the likes of you and me – Novosibirsk, Irkutsk, and Khabarovsk. Don't try and alight at Omsk as I did – it doesn't work – and Vladivostock is emphatically out of bounds (though you can reach Nahodka if you are in transit to Japan).

Asia can raise some interesting and quite well-known expresses which are more fun than efficient. From Istanbul to Baghdad runs the *Taurus Express*

which takes three days for the journey and is invariably hours late. Leaving from Istanbul's Haydarpasa Station, it passes through Turkey, Syria and Iraq, so be ready for trouble, but you do meet some priceless characters within its smoke-begrimed coaches.

A return to the balmy Victorian era of elegant train travel can be experienced on some of the long distance but nameless expresses of Chinese railways. On the Hong Kong to Canton, Shanghai, Peking express or that from Peking to Datong, I not only had revolutionary opera interwoven with travel instructions of the TV but lace curtains and silk lampshades à la Brighton belle and a thermos of jasmin tea in my compartment.

India, of course, is the very epitome of railway heritage and it produces some fine and famous expresses to match. Two that will be recognized are the *Frontier Mail* (Amritsar-Delhi-Bombay) and the *Taj Express* (Delhi-Agra). On the former, I spent many uncomfortable hours – that ran into days – squeezed, standing up, in a then Third Class compartment containing 39 bodies. But by travelling air-conditioned or First Class at ludicrously low prices, you can move around India in almost super-luxury. And you'll never go hungry on an Indian train. Actually, the best place to eat on the sub-continent is the railway station where there are often not only different classes of restaurants, but those catering for Indian, vegetarian and European tastes. On similar, but better value lines to the *Venice-Simplon Orient Express* is a tourist train called the *Palace on Wheels* that makes a seven-day circuit of Rajasthan, giving the passenger a taste of train travel as it was understood by the maharajas.

Even its golden coaches were ex-maharajan owned, while Rajasthan itself is full of magic maharajan castles, forts and palaces. More down-to-earth expresses of Indian Railways include the *Rajdhani Express* (Delhi-Calcutta), *Gitanjale Express* (Calcutta-Bombay) and the *Howrah-Kalka Mail* (Calcutta-Delhi-Kalka) which connects with a delightful narrow-guage railcar that zigzags up the hill to Simla.

Still to Sample

There are, as yet, a number of express trains that, alas, I have not yet managed to ride. South Africa – a name synonymous with great trains – has its ultra-famous *Blue Train* upon which I have my sights. It runs between Pretoria and Cape Town via Johannesburg and Kimberley from March until the end of August about three times weekly and is the last word in luxury with even staterooms available for those who can afford them.

In Australia, the old *Ghan Express* is no more, but a less romantic but probably more efficient train runs the long hot desert miles between Adelaide, Port Pirie and Alice Springs. However it is a route, rather than a particular train, that is, perhaps most famous; the Transcontinental Railway from Sydney to Perth – the 'long straight' as it is sometimes called, all 2,230 miles of it. And while at this end of the world one shouldn't overlook New Zealand's *Northerner* running daily between Auckland and Wellington.

Japan, of course, is famous for its bullet trains or super expresses out of Tokyo, but soullessly, they are given no names.

Nor does Thailand go in for fancy titles though the 500 mile route between Bangkok and Chiang Mai is covered by a train sometimes known as the *Northern Express* which makes a delightful ride through the jungle and paddy fields of that steamy country.

I managed to ride the East African Railways before the split-up of the federation, but Kenya Railway's Mombasa-Nairobi-Malabe service is worthy of the term 'famous express' with its superb views of the Great Rift Valley and the wild animals that take the passing trains for granted.

When is an express not an express? With railways, it's not just a matter of speed but of prestige, route and the pure joy of travel they offer.

Getting There by Air

In Control of Aviation

by Philip Ray and Hugo Gurdon

The world of air travel is littered with the initials of the official bodies which appear on the face of it to control virtually every aspect of flying – ICAO, IATA, FAA, CAA etc.

It could well be asked why this particular branch of economic activity should be singled out for special treatment by governments. The international shipping industry, after all, is not subject to nearly the same constraints and a virtually free market exists. But when the governments of the world met in Chicago in 1944 to prepare the way for the post-war pattern of civil aviation, they agreed the fundamental principle, now enshrined in international law, that each nation has sovereignty over its own airspace. This means that any government has the power to grant or refuse permission for the airline of another country to overfly its territory, to make a technical stop – to refuel, for instance – or to pick up and set down fare-paying passengers. By extension of this principle, governments also lay down the conditions under which foreign airlines may pick up traffic – for instance, by agreeing the routes which can be served, imposing restrictions on capacity or approving the fares that can be charged. In practice, all these questions are resolved between governments on a bilateral basis in air service agreements (ASAs) which are subject to termination by either side after giving twelve months' notice. The best-known ASA is the Bermuda Agreement which governs air services between the UK and the USA.

Regulation

But every government in the world also exercises regulatory control over its own domestic airline industry to a greater or lesser extent. Perhaps the strongest argument in favour of this is the uncontroversial need to supervise safety standards. Otherwise, it is argued, airlines might cut corners in order to save costs. The main area of current debate and controversy is the extent to which regulatory bodies should exercise economic control over the airlines in terms of the allocation of routes, the entry of new carriers into the market and fares charged.

Only the USA has gone for complete domestic deregulation, so that airlines are free to open up new routes or move into markets already served by other carriers without having to seek approval. Elsewhere, competition is tightly controlled. In France, for example, the national carriers, Air France and UTA, have traditionally been allocated designated operating areas with no provision for their competing directly with each other. However, there has recently been a slight easing of this policy and both airlines are now allowed to operate from Paris to the US West Coast. Most other European countries have only one major international flag carrier airline to operate scheduled services – Germany with Lufthansa, Italy with Alitalia, and so on. Perhaps the most liberal attitude outside the USA has been adopted by the United Kingdom, whose Civil Aviation Authority has authorized competition between the two major international airlines, British Airways and British Caledonian, on certain routes and has also licensed smaller airlines like Virgin Atlantic to operate trans-Atlantic routes. The Dutch Government has also adopted a liberal policy and has signed what amounts to an 'open skies' agreement with the UK government on air services and fares between the two countries.

Crucial to the argument on deregulation is the balance that has to be drawn between the need to give the traveller the better deal which competition often provides and the desirability of maintaining a financially strong airline industry.

A more detailed look at some of the leading regulatory bodies in world aviation may provide some pointers as to how the present system works in practice.

ICAO (International Civil Aviation Organization)

ICAO is not exactly a household name, and its activities are rarely publicized in the lay press, but it plays an important behind-the-scenes role in laying down standards and controlling the legal framework for international civil aviation.

It is based in Montreal and was set up following the Chicago Convention of 1944 which laid the foundations of the international air transport system as we know it today. It is made up of representatives of some 150 governments and its controlling bodies are the Assembly, which normally meets every three years, and the Council, which controls its day-to-day activities.

The organization also lays down international standards for air navigation, air traffic control, technical requirements and safety and security procedures and was responsible for concluding international agreements on the action needed to deter aircraft hijackings. ICAO works closely with the United Nations and controls assistance development programmes in Third World countries under the UN Development Programme.

ICAO came into the headlines when it investigated the shooting down the Korean Airlines Boeing 747 in September 1983. Its report was inconclusive but it led to the calling of an extraordinary session of the Assembly in 1984 which agreed an amendment to the Chicago Convention embodying in international law for the first time a specific ban on the use of weapons against civil aircraft.

On the economic front, ICAO monitors the finances and traffic patterns of the world's airlines and issues research reports from time to time.

IATA (International Air Transport Association)

IATA is a much more controversial body than ICAO because, as the trade association for over 100 of the world's international scheduled airlines, it is often criticized by consumer interests as being a fare-fixing cartel. This has always been contested by IATA, which points out that a true cartel would not just fix prices but would also share out capacity and market quotas among its members. It could also be argued that if IATA is a cartel, it is a remarkably unsuccessful one, given the appalling financial results of the world's airlines over the past few years.

IATA's fare-fixing role is one which has, effectively, been thrust upon it. The world's governments agreed in the Chicago Convention that they would retain ultimate control of the fares to be charged by airlines picking up or setting down traffic in their countries but in practice they delegated this task to the airlines. To this day, fare agreements by airlines are normally rubber-stamped by governments. But most governments do use their reserve powers to direct their airlines to charge special fares for certain routes or for certain categories of travellers – seamen on duty, for instance. Even here, though, the 'directives' are often inspired by the airlines themselves because they have not been able to secure agreement for a particular fare within IATA. Sometimes, too, the importance of IATA's fare-fixing role can be exaggerated. It frequently happens that the airlines serving a particular region cannot agree on a new fares package, but this rarely spells disaster. Fares between the various countries are simply agreed bilaterally by the respective national airlines and are then approved by governments.

Agreement of tariffs is only one of IATA's functions, albeit the best known. In fact, there is now a move towards a much more liberal approach to fares. Between Europe and the USA, for instance, the IATA airlines agree only a 'zone of reasonableness' for fares and the carriers can then make adjustments up or down within this band without having to go back to the conference table.

Many of IATA's activities are less publicized. While ICAO has been agreeing standards at an international level on technical matters like air safety procedures, meteorological services, engineering and so on, it has had to lean heavily on the advice of the airlines via IATA. From the passenger's point of view, the greatest benefit has come from agreements between IATA members on a standard form of airline ticket which enables the passenger to travel round the world on one ticket with, say, six different airlines, and make only one payment which is then apportioned between the carriers by the IATA Clearing House. It is also IATA which lays down the consumer protection standards for the travel agencies which it appoints to sell international air tickets.

The association has also been active in campaigning against government-imposed increases in user charges – which are ultimately reflected in higher fares – and in fighting for the elimination of airport red tape by encouraging Customs and Immigration authorities to improve the traveller's lot with innovations like the red/green channel system.

DoT (US Department of Transportation)

With the disbanding of the US Civil Aeronautics Board (CAB) in 1985 and the implementation of complete deregulation, the Federal Department of Transportation's powers are limited.

Its most important role is to define and implement policy on international aviation, including the selection of American airlines to operate on specific routes. It also co-operates with the State Department on the negotiation of bilateral air-service agreements with other countries. With the assistance of the Department of Justice, it administers the anti-trust laws, with the aim of ensuring that carriers do not reach any restrictive agreements behind the scenes. It is also responsible for approving or disallowing airline mergers.

FAA (Federal Aviation Administration)
Not affected by the demise of the CAB, the FAA deals mostly with airport management, air traffic control, air safety and technical matters. Despite their complete economic freedom, all US airlines still have to conform with FAA safety standards.

Canadian Ministry of Transport (MoT) and Canadian Transport Commission (CTC)
Transport policy in Canada was going through its biggest period of reform for 20 years at the time of going to press and the future shape of regulation for the airline industry was still not entirely clear. Previously the CTC, a semi-autonomous body reporting to the Minister of Transport, exercised a high degree of control through its air transport committee in selecting airlines for new routes and the approval of tariffs. It also controlled the complete range of Canadian transport activities, including railways, shipping, pipelines and so on.

A new National Transportation Bill, going through the Canadian Parliament during 1987, was expected to weaken the CTC's powers greatly. It

will probably now disappear and be replaced by a new, as yet unnamed, body. The CTC's air transport committee will certainly cease to exist, leading to a much more liberal regime for the airlines in what will amount to a modified form of the deregulated US system. Essentially, new airlines will have to demonstrate only that they conform to safety standards and have adequate financial backing.

The Ministry of Transport will retain responsibility for the international-relations aspects of civil aviation, liaising with the Minister for External Affairs.

Air safety standards and the investigation of air accidents are already the responsibility of an autonomous body, the Canadian Aviation Safety Board, which works at arm's length from the Government.

DTp (UK Department of Transport)
Control of civil aviation in the UK has shuttled between one Ministry and another over the years, but now appears to be fairly securely housed in the Department of Transport, which also controls shipping, railways and road construction.

DTp is responsible for laying down overall policy on the airline industry and airports, usually after consultation with the CAA (see below). The Secretary of State of Transport also considers appeals against CAA decisions on new route licences and at one time overruled the Authority only rarely. Under the Thatcher Government, Transport Secretaries have increasingly tended to intervene and allow appeals where they have felt the CAA was being over-cautious about allowing increased competition.

DTp also handles the international-relations aspects of civil aviation and regulates the activites of foreign airlines in the UK in the same way that the CAA controls British carriers. Legally the Transport Secretary has to approve fares charged by foreign airlines, although in practice this vetting is carried out mainly by the CAA.

The Department has acquired new powers under the Airports Act 1986 to control airport charges and lay down rules for the distribution of traffic between the UK airports, again with advice from the CAA. The Transport Secretary has also taken temporary powers to exercise detailed economic regulation over four major UK airports – Heathrow, Gatwick, Stansted and Manchester – to ensure that there are no monopoly abuses like predatory pricing. These powers will revert to the CAA in due course.

An important role of the Department is the investigation of aircraft accidents. These investigations are carried out by a highly-respected team of inspectors who are independent of political control but work in close liaison with the CAA.

CAA (UK Civil Aviation Authority)
Airline regulatory bodies are usually an integral part of a government ministry, but the CAA is unusual in being only an agency of government which operates at arm's length from whichever government is in power.

It functions under guidelines laid down by Parliament in the Civil Aviation Act and Airports Act, but this is a fairly loose framework which gives it considerable freedom to develop its own policies without Ministers breathing down its neck, although the Thatcher Government has been more interventionist than its predecessors.

At the same time, the Authority is an important source of advice to the government on aviation matters, including airport policy.

Broadly, the CAA's role combines those of the now-defunct CAB and the FAA in the States. It has a particularly important function in the monitoring of safety standards, notably in the licensing of airports and aircrew and in the approval and inspection of airlines' operational procedures. Most of the publicity about the CAA's activities, though, concerns its economic-regulatory functions in approving fares and granting licences for new routes. It monitors the financial integrity of both the UK's airlines and the leading package-tour operators which use air services. The UK airline scene is particularly dynamic, so the Authority often has the difficult task of choosing between two or three applicants for a particular route. The CAA's powers do not extend to foreign airlines, which come under the control of the Department of Transport (see above), but the Authority is usually represented in bilateral negotiations on air routes with foreign governments.

The CAA acquired an important new role under the Airports Act 1986, to regulate charges at the larger airports. Airport operators now have to apply to the CAA for permission to levy charges and the Authority has power to impose conditions so as to ensure that there are no abuses of a monopoly position. Airport charges will also be subject to regular review by the Monopolies and Mergers Commission (MMC).

The Authority has a general advisory role to the Government on matters like noise restrictions or drafting rules on the distribution of traffic between airports. It also has the job of enforcing any such rules once they are agreed by the Government.

OFT (UK Office of Fair Trading)

The OFT, a semi-autonomous agency of the Government, acquired new powers relating to civil aviation in 1985 as a back-up to the licensing role of the CAA (see above). The Director-General of Fair Trading can now investigate and refer to the Monopolies and Mergers Commission any anti-competitive practices on international charter flights. He can also ask the Commission to investigate potential monopolies on domestic flights or on international charters. The Secretary of State for Trade and Industry has the power to make monopoly references to the MMC on air transport generally, including international scheduled services.

DoA (Australian Department of Aviation)

The Department of Aviation administers civil aviation in Australia under powers granted by the Commonwealth Air Navigation Act 1920. As well as imposing safety and operational controls, it determines the general conditions of flights over Australian territory, classifies and licenses air services, approves timetables, negotiates international air transport agreements and approves international fares and freight rates. The Department also licenses aircraft and crews and is responsible for air traffic control.

Both the Federal and State governments may exercise control over intra-state domestic flights. New South Wales, Queensland, Western Australia, Tasmania and the Northern Territory license services within their borders but within Victoria and South Australia only the federal regulations have to be satisfied.

The Federal Government is responsible for the general shape of Australian aviation, which is generally reckoned to be one of the most tightly regulated outside the Eastern bloc. Qantas is the only airline allowed to fly on international routes and is debarred from carrying passengers between domestic points in Australia, while domestic trunk routes are restricted to the privately-owned Ansett and State-owned Australian Airlines (formerly TAA).

This two-airline policy for domestic routes was established way back in 1947 because Ansett and TAA were required to operate flights not only to the main cities but also to the more remote communities which would not have been viable in a deregulated environment. However, it has now been challenged by East West Airlines, which has persuaded the Government to give it permission to import Boeing 737s, enabling it to compete on trunk routes.

The Canberra Government has commissioned an inquiry into the two-airline policy, whose findings were expected early in 1987. But no change can be effected until 1990 because the policy is enshrined in the Airlines Agreement Act 1981. This can be ended only after three years' notice, which may be given no earlier than 1987.

THE TRAVELLER'S PROTECTION / 63

MoT/ASLA (New Zealand Ministry of Transport/Air Services Licensing Authority)

Air transport in New Zealand is controlled by the Ministry of Transport, administering the Civil Aviation Act of 1964. However, the actual licensing of air services is done by the Air Services Licensing Authority, an independent three-person body set up in 1983, whose decisions are subject to appeal in the Administrative Division of the High Court.

International services and fares are government-controlled along lines laid down by the Air Services Licensing Act 1947 and the Civil Aviation Act 1964. In 1985 the New Zealand Government issued a policy statement rejecting wholesale deregulation of civil aviation. Instead, it declared its priority as being the creation of an environment for aviation which would maximise the economic benefits to the country, including a concern for tourism as well as for broader foreign-policy considerations.

This broad view has led to some liberalisation, including permission for the Australian airline Ansett to set up a domestic airline in New Zealand.

The Traveller's Protection

by Philip Ray

More people probably suffer financial loss through dealing with shady second-hand car dealers than through booking a holiday with a company that goes bust. But the buyer of a package holiday undoubtedly enjoys a higher level of financial protection than applies to any other product or service industry.

Some economic pundits might question whether such a high level of protection is really necessary. Surely, they would argue, there is no reason why the rule 'let the buyer beware' should not apply to the purchase of a holiday as much as to anything else. But a holiday is different from most other commodities. If you buy a car or a television set and it doesn't work, you have a claim against the dealer and, in any case, you can inspect the goods before you buy them. With a holiday, you are buying a dream and you are parting with your money months in advance on the strength of that dream. The temptation of this little pot of cash flow has been too much to resist for some dubious entrepreneurs in the past.

The financial failure of a tour company also has implications in terms of diplomatic relations with other countries. It is certainly embarrassing for the Government if hundreds of thousands of holidaymakers are stranded on some foreign shore with their hotel bills unpaid by a bankrupt tour company.

Need For Protection

It was the travel trade itself which saw the need to offer better protection for the public way back in 1964 when a company called Fiesta Tours collapsed. But it took until 1970 for a proper scheme to emerge when members of the Tour Operators' Study Group (TOSG), which accounts for about three-quarters of all package tour sales, agreed that they would each provide a bond to cover consumers against financial failure. Two years later a similar scheme was drawn up for all other tour operators belonging to the Association of British Travel Agents (ABTA).

At the same time, the Civil Aviation Authority was given statutory powers to license tour-operating companies which organized package tours based on charter flights and, again, provision of a bond was made a condition of being granted an Air Travel Organizer's Licence (ATOL for short).

Everyone thought at the time that there would be little danger of a consumer losing money in future through the failure of a tour company. But in August 1974, the Court Line group of companies collapsed at the height of the holiday season when cash flow should theoretically have been at its strongest and it looked as if customers of its tour companies, Clarksons and Halcyon, might collectively lose millions of pounds.

So the government stepped in and set up a new statutory organization, the Air Travel Reserve Fund Agency, which repaid the Court Line holidaymakers out of a Treasury loan which was repaid through a levy on holidays over the next two or three years. The ATRFA was wound up in February 1986 and its accumulated funds of £22 million were transferred to a new organization, the Air Travel Trust. This is administered by the CAA and the trustees are all members or officials of the Authority. The trust's work is overseen by the Air Travel Trust Committee, which is made up of four independent members, five representatives of the travel trade and two of the trustees.

Present Position

Apart from the winding-up of the ATRFA and the transfer of its powers to the Air Travel Trust, this remains the basic structure of consumer protection for the UK holidaymaker. The CAA requires all tour operators selling package tours based on charter flights to provide a bond of at least ten per cent of their anticipated turnover, and the figure is set at fifteen per cent for new applicants.

If an operator fails, the bond is drawn on to recompense disappointed holidaymakers and when the fund is exhausted – and only then – the Air Travel Trust can be called on.

But protection on the so-called 'licensable' holidays is only part of the story, because there is a tremendous variety of holidays (almost one-third of the total) which do not need to be licensed by the CAA – those based on many scheduled flights or on rail, coach or sea travel, for example. The CAA and Air Travel Trust have no involvement in these, and it is left to ABTA, TOSG, the Bus and Coach Council and the Passenger Shipping Association to offer voluntary protection schemes.

ABTA insists on bonds to the tune of ten per cent of anticipated turnover for all its member operators for the whole of their 'non-licensable' turnover and this is backed up by an insurance scheme which provides cover to the tune of £2 million to serve as a second line of defence in the same way that the Air Travel Trust does for licensable holidays.

The eighteen members of TOSG have gone a stage further by bonding non-licensable business at twenty per cent of anticipated turnover and also by providing a £2.5 million back-up insurance cover.

ABTA also protects consumers

against the financial failure of any of its 6,400 High Street travel agents. All new members have to provide a bond of up to £15,000 and there is also an indemnity insurance scheme which protects customers against the failure of any retail agent to the tune of £50,000 per outlet. As a final line of defence, ABTA has a retailers' fund which currently stands at more than £200,000.

ABTA's consumer-protection machinery is underpinned by an agreement known as Stabilizer, under which member travel agents may not sell non-ABTA tours and member operators may not trade through non-member travel agents, although some dispensations from this rule are granted. This Stabilizer system was approved by the Restrictive Practices Court in 1982 as being in the public interest and the judge cited the importance of the protection offered by ABTA on 'non-licensable' holidays.

Loopholes

The holiday purchaser does now appear, on the face of it, to be adequately protected against a tour operator's failure by virtue of the CAA/Air Travel Trust/TOSG/ABTA machinery.

But there is still no formalized system to guard consumers against the failure of scheduled airline – witness the successive collapses of Laker Airways and Braniff International within two months in 1982, when thousands of travellers lost their money. Customers who booked package tours with Laker's holiday companies eventually got their money back, but those who booked seats on the Skytrain scheduled service were not refunded till some four years after the airline's collapse. Even then the payment came only as a result of the settlement in an anti-trust court action brought in the USA against British Airways and other airlines by the Laker liquidator. Better protection against the collapse of an airline still needs to be provided. Failures are not too common, but over the past few years, several other American carriers have followed Laker and Braniff into oblivion.

Another grey area of consumer protection in the UK that has to be tackled involves package holidays based on scheduled flights. In some cases – broadly, those where a tour operator makes an advance financial commitment for a block of seats on a scheduled flight – a CAA licence is required. But frequently a tour-operating firm simply buys aircraft seats as and when it needs them, in which case it is regarded as an agent of the airline and does not require a licence.

The result is that a brochure based on scheduled flights may contain some holidays which are 'licensable' and some which are 'non-licensable'. Confusion then arises because a number of operators still imply that all the holidays shown in their brochures are covered by the Air Travel Trust when, in fact, they may not be.

The ideal solution in the long term would be for all air-based package tours to require a CAA licence, irrespective of whether they are based on scheduled or charter flights.

Credit Card Protection

The position of holidaymakers who pay for a package holiday by using a credit card is still the subject of some legal uncertainty, which was highlighted during the negotiations over refunds to clients of the Laker holiday companies. TOSG, which held the Laker bonds, argued that people who had used their credit cards to buy their holidays had a claim against the card companies under the Consumer Credit Act of 1974. This was contested by the companies who argued that there was no reason why they should be liable when the holidaymakers were already protected by the TOSG/ATRFA machinery.

In the end a compromise agreement was reached and the Laker clients were refunded, but it would have been useful if there had been a ruling in the courts on the true legal position. However, an agreement with Access by the CAA, ABTA and TOSG and a separate scheme drawn up by Barclaycard now ensure that no one need have any qualms about buying a holiday with a credit card.

Under the agreement with Access, clients who use their card to pay for a holiday will be repaid out of the tour operator's bond in the event of its failure. Only when the bond has been exhausted will Access reimburse clients itself, with the Air Travel Trust remaining the final line of defence. Access clients can also assign their claim against a failed tour company to another operator or travel agent so that they can immediately book an alternative holiday. At the time of going to press, a similar scheme was being prepared to cover holders of the Trustee Savings Bank's Trustcard.

Barclaycard has adopted a different approach by insisting that tour operators with which it deals must take out an indemnity insurance, but it then pays out to clients immediately in the event of an operator's failure without having to wait until the bond is exhausted. Holidaymakers receive a straight refund and cannot assign their claims to another operator or agent.

Holders of other Visa cards, apart from Trustcard, appear to be covered under the Consumer Credit Act.
This article is applicable to the UK only.

Understanding Air Fares

by Philip Ray and Alex McWhirter

The world of airline tariffs is an incredibly complex one, but given the help of a well-trained airline reservations clerk or travel agent you can make some substantial savings on your travel by using the various loopholes and legitimate discounts which the system provides.

There are so many permutations of possible fares that, as any travel agent handling complicated itineraries for business executives will tell you, six different airlines will quote six different fares for a particular trip.

To generalize, full-rate First Class and Business Class fares have shown a steady increase over the years but the cost of some promotional discounted fares has been held down, if not actually reduced. And quite apart from the vast range of 'official' fares there are also the special deals offered through the 'bucket-shops'.

On major international routes like London-New York, some 30 different fares are available depending on the airline you fly with, the time of the year and even, in some cases, the day of the week.

On other routes to the US – for

instance, London-Los Angeles – it can sometimes be cheaper to take an indirect flight and change at a US airport like Chicago. Within the US, domestic fares are changing so rapidly that many airlines have given up publishing fare tables and update the information every day on the computer systems used by their travel agents and reservations staff.

Here are the main types of fare available:

First Class
Completely flexible fares; reservations can be changed to alternative departure date or to another airline. No cancellation charges. Valid one year; stopovers permitted; when travelling between two points IATA regulations allow mileage deviation of up to 20 per cent at no extra cost. For example, if paying full-fare from London to Cairo you could travel out via Paris, Zurich and Athens and return via Beirut, Rome and Amsterdam at no extra cost. On a long journey such as London-Sydney, you could fly via Hong Kong at no extra cost or via the USA or Japan at only a small surcharge. You can exceed this 20 per cent mileage allowance by up to 25 per cent by paying a surcharge. This comes in increments of 5 per cent. For example, a journey London-Paris-Frankfurt would incur a 10 per cent surcharge, whereas London-Brussels-Zurich would be included in the mileage allowance. When using this extra mileage allowance, back-tracking is not permitted. Should the 25 per cent allowance be exceeded you must pay the cost of each individual sector: for instance, London-Brussels, Brussels-Paris, Paris-London. Concorde fares are based on

the normal first-class fare plus a supplement of about 30 per cent.

Holders of first-class tickets qualify for the full range of 'perks', including a generous free baggage allowance (usually 30 kilos) and in some cases free ground transport, special lounges, sleeper seats with plenty of leg-room, lavish in-flight cuisine and VIP treatment both on the ground and in the air.

Business Class/Full Economy Class
Completely flexible fare with same concessions for mileage deviations as First Class(see above). Business Class, which is marketed under a variety of brand-names like Super Club, Clipper Class or Ambassador Class, usually offers an enhanced standard of in-flight service and more comfortable seating but sometimes involves a premium of between 5 per cent and 20 per cent on the normal economy fare. Special facilities like executive lounges and dedicated check-in desks are often provided for Business Class passengers.

Point-to-Point Economy
Applies mainly to travel between the UK and US and on some routes to the Far East and southern Africa and, as the name implies, is valid only for travel between the two points shown on the ticket. This means that no mileage deviation is permitted, nor can the ticket be used for connecting flights with another airline. A similar fare within Europe, known as Eurobudget, is available at a discount on the full fare but is subject to a cancellation charge of up to 50 per cent.

Apex/Super Apex

Stands for Advance Purchase Excursion. It has become the airlines' main method of official discounting and is normally available only on a round-trip basis, except to the Far East where one-way Apex fares are available. Must be booked and paid for some time in advance, ranging from two weeks to one month depending on destination, and usually a minimum stay abroad is required. No stopovers are permitted and there are cancellation and amendment fees which vary with the destination. Reductions on some long-haul routes can be as high as 60 per cent off the normal full fare.

Pex/Super Pex

Stands for 'Public Excursion' fare and is similar to Apex, except that there is no restrictive advance-purchase requirement. Applies mainly in Europe and your stay must normally include a Saturday night at the destination. There is a penalty of up to 50 per cent for cancellation.

Excursion Fares

Available on many long-haul routes, with restrictions on minimum and maximum length of stay. Normally for round-trip travel only but fewer restrictions than Apex or Pex – flights can be changed, for example. Typical saving on the full economy fare is between 25 per cent and 30 per cent.

Spouse Fares

Apply on routes throughout Europe. If one partner pays the full Business Class or Club Class fare, the other partner can travel at a 50 per cent discount. Tickets have a maximum validity of five days. No stopovers are permitted and husband and wife must travel together on both the outbound and inbound journeys. Airlines will, however, sometimes make an exception when company regulations or insurance policies stipulate that a couple must always travel separately.

ITX Fares

Now an almost extinct category, ITX fares are used by travel agents to construct tailor-made inclusive packages. Now that new low fares like Apex and Pex are available, the demand for ITX fares has diminished and they are now available only on flights to Germany and the USSR.

Children's and Infants' Fares

An infant under two years of age accompanied by an adult and not occupying a separate seat is carried at 10 per cent of the adult fare. Any additional infants under two years of age occupying a separate seat and accompanying the same adult, and children aged 2-11 inclusive, are carried at half the adult fare. Some fares do not carry these reductions – for example, many Apex fares allow only a one-third discount for children – and certain standby fares allow no reduction at all.

Student Fares

Provided the necessary forms are completed, *bona fide* students are entitled to a reduction of 25 per cent off the full fare. Student fares are not available on the North Atlantic routes and are becoming less widely used elsewhere because so many other fares like Apex offer bigger reductions.

Youth Fares

Available for travel on many routes inside Europe for young people between the ages of 12 and 21. The reduction is 25 per cent off the full fare but, again, a cheaper fare like Apex or Pex is usually available.

Standby Fares

Generally available only on routes to the USA, and even then only in the peak season. Available only on day of departure. Standby tickets are also available on some UK domestic routes. Akin to the standby fare is the late-booking fare offered by British Airways to Athens, Malta and Gibraltar. This can be bought up to three months in advance but seat availability is not confirmed until the day before departure.

Round-the-World (RTW) Fares

An ingenious method of keeping down your travel costs is the Round-the-World (RTW) fare offered by a number of airlines or combinations of airlines – for example, British Airways with Qantas and United Airlines. The first sector of your itinerary usually has to be booked about three weeks in advance, but after that you can book your flights as you go along. You usually have to make a minimum number of stopovers and you are not allowed to 'backtrack'. You can even buy a First Class RTW ticket with some airlines which actually undercuts the normal economy fare.

Advance-Booking Charters

Advance-booking charters (ABCs) still exist across the Atlantic, mainly during the peak summer season, although there are fewer flights nowadays because of the wide variety of attractive fares available on scheduled services. The rules for ABCs are similar to those governing the scheduled airlines' Apex fares. You have to book at least 21 days in advance and you must be away at least seven days. On flights to the US, charters can sometimes provide worthwhile savings on the normal scheduled fares but to Canada charter fares are usually at or about the Super Apex level. Charter services operate from a number of provincial points, which makes them more convenient than scheduled flights for many people.

Charters

Within Europe, there is a well organized network of charter flights which can give savings of up to 70 per cent off the normal IATA fare. These flights operate not only to the Mediterranean sunspots but also to cities like Geneva and Munich and, for legal reasons, are ranked technically as package tours, so the fare will probably include very basic dormitory accommodation. Charters can be booked up to the time of departure but return dates may not be so flexible as on scheduled flights. For instance, you may be able to return only seven days or 14 days after the outward journey.

Scheduled Consolidation Fares

These are charter-priced seats sold for travel on scheduled flights. They are usually intended to be the basis of inclusive packages but often end up as flight-only tickets sold through bucket-shops. These fares are administered by 'consolidators', as they are known in the trade. Their role is to take advantage of special rates for group bookings by making commitments for large blocks of seats which they then make available to travel agents on an individual basis.

Airpasses

Special Airpasses are available in a number of countries which enable you to make big savings on domestic travel.

Some of the best value is to be had in the US, where all the major airlines offer Airpass deals giving virtually unlimited travel on their networks, although you are frequently allowed to make only one stopover per city and there is a ceiling on the number of stopovers you can make. You may be restricted from flying at busy periods. Airpasses usually have to be bought before arrival in the US.

To qualify for some of the best deals you have to travel to the US on a particular airline's trans-Atlantic services. The best plan is to find out which airline has the network which conforms most closely to your preferred itinerary.

A number of other countries with well-developed air services, including Australia, Brazil, India and New Zealand, also offer Airpass schemes.

Discounts and Deals

by Philip Ray

The high level of airfares is always fair game as a topic of conversation when frequent travellers get together. It is an even more popular topic for politicians who appear to believe, probably erroneously, that cheap fares are a good vote-catcher. Some fares are certainly high, but it is still possible to fly to most parts of the world for considerably less than the full standard fare, given the assistance of a switched-on professional travel agent.

The key word when it comes to the difference between high fares and low fares is 'flexibility'. If you are prepared to be flexible as to the day or time of year when you want to travel and let the airline slot you onto a flight which it knows is likely to have empty seats you can nearly always find a cheap fare. But this may well mean you have to buy your ticket either several weeks in advance or at the very last minute on a standby basis. Frequently your stay at the destination must include at least one Saturday night – a frequently-criticized requirement which is imposed by airlines to minimize the risk of business travellers trading down from the normal full fare to the cheap rate (on the theory that few business people want to spend a Saturday night away from home). And with most cheap fares, once you have booked your flight you can usually switch to an alternative service only on payment of a fairly hefty cancellation penalty.

The other side of the flexibility coin is that if you want complete freedom to change or cancel your flight without penalty, you have to pay for the privilege, which means in practice the expensive full fare.

Economics

The economics of the wide gap which exists between the highest fare and the lowest are not quite so crazy as might appear at first sight. If business travellers want the flexibility to change or cancel their reservations at short notice, seats will often be empty because the airline has been unable to resell them, and the cost of flying that seat still has to be paid for.

So there is an implicit bargain

between the airline and the passenger when it comes to a cheap fare. The airline offers a discount in return for a commitment from the passenger, underpinned by a financial penalty, that he or she will actually use that seat.

One airline, British Caledonian, has tried to rationalize its fare structure on European services by ironing out some of the more irksome restrictions, although its efforts have been thwarted by some foreign governments. Under the BCal 'Timeflyer' system, the fare is based purely on the time of departure, so that a passenger who wants to fly at the peak time of day pays the highest fare, while someone who is prepared to travel at a less popular time qualifies for the cheaper rate.

A similar scheme operates domestically in Sweden, where SAS and Linjeflyg offer big reductions on offpeak flights throughout the year, and these cuts are extended to all flights during the peak summer period when few business executives are flying.

Flexibility

Many business travellers can probably be more flexible about their air-travel schedules than they would like to admit and can still save quite a lot of money, provided that they don't mind travelling at the back of the aircraft with the masses.

For example, if you are planning to attend a conference, the date of which is known a long time in advance, you can frequently buy an advance-purchase excursion fare (Apex) at anything up to half the cost of the full fare. But always bear in mind those heavy financial penalties if you suddenly decide to cancel or change your flight.

Business travellers will also find that it is often worth looking around for a package trip, like those offered by specialist tour operators to tie in with a trade fair. Some travel agencies and tour operators also offer attractive packages to long-haul destinations like Tokyo which provide not only the airfare but also hotel accommodation for a total price which is often less than the normal Business Class fare.

Once again, though, this type of package does not offer the flexibility of the full-fare ticket and you will probably not be able to change your flight if your business schedule overruns.

If you are planning an extensive tour within North America it is well worth investigating the many 'Airpasses' issued by US and Canadian domestic airlines which offer unlimited travel over their networks for a given period, although there are usually some restrictions on routing. For travel to the USA, there are also some remarkably good-value deals on fly-drive trips, with car-hire being charged at only nominal rates in many cases.

Some of the best deals for business travellers are to be found in the round-the-world fares offered by a number of airlines which can enable you to plan a complicated itinerary at a knockdown rate.

Frequent Flyer Programmes

Business travellers who have to cross the Atlantic several times a year should certainly have a look at the various 'frequent flyer' programmes offered by most major US airlines and designed to secure passenger loyalty. The essence of the schemes is that passengers taking part accumulate points depending on the mileage flown. At a given threshold they then qualify for one of a range of 'goodies' – typically a free Economy Class ticket or an upgrade to First Class. Some frequent-flyer schemes are also linked to hotel chains so that it is even possible to build up a national air mileage by staying on the ground.

The frequent-flyer schemes do not really seem to have caught on in the UK, probably because of the justifiable fear that the Inland Revenue authorities might take a hard line towards passengers who accrue 'taxable benefits'. Some American airlines insist that passengers taking part in frequent-flyer schemes should have a US mailing address, although others are quite happy to enrol British residents.

British airlines generally seem uninterested in developing their own frequent-flyer schemes, mainly because of the unsporting attitiude of the Inland Revenue. An exception is British Midland Airways which offers an item of lead crystal glassware to passengers who complete a given number of flights on specified routes.

Regular British business travellers should certainly subscribe to one or both of the specialist monthly magazines – Executive Travel or Business Traveller – which list all the latest special offers on airfares, as well as deals on hotel accommodation, car hire and so on.

Bucket Shops

The best-known source of discounted air tickets is the so-called 'bucket shop', a phrase which was first coined at a travel industry conference in the early 1970s to denote an outlet specializing in the sale of air tickets at an 'illegal' discount. Such is the power of the media that the term – which was derived from shady activities in the nineteenth century US stock market – is now universally understood, even by those who have never flown in their lives.

Back in the early 1970s, the world of bucket shops was a pretty sleazy one, based on back rooms in Chinese supermarkets, or in flyblown first-floor offices in Soho. One or two of the early entrepreneurs actually ended up in prison and some of the cheap tickets which found their way into the market place had, in fact, been stolen. One bucket shop which traded as a 'reunion club' ended up owing more than £620,000 to thousands of people who had been saving up to visit relatives abroad, not to mention another £614,000 owed to the airlines.

The owner of this club was eventually jailed for trading with intent to defraud. He knew that the 'club' could not meet its liabilities and yet he continued to trade for almost a year.

Failures still do occur but it is noticeable that the bucket shop is beginning to 'come out'. Outlets are being opened in the High Streets of provincial cities by respected companies with long experience of the travel business, and even some of the household names in retail travel are now able to supply discounted tickets. At one time the Association of British Travel Agents (ABTA) officially banned its members from offering 'illegally' discounted air fares, but dropped this rule when the restrictive-practices legislation began to bite on the travel business. Nowadays many 'bucket shops' are members of ABTA and are covered by the association's consumer-protection machinery.

It is worth taking a closer look at the

discounting phenomenon and at what makes it 'illegal', if indeed it is. It is an ecomonic fact of life that, on average, the world's scheduled airlines fill only two-thirds of their seats, so there is a very powerful inducement to fill the remaining one-third by any means possible. Assuming that overheads have been covered by the two-thirds paying 'normal' fares (although this is not necessarily a valid assumption), anything earned from one extra passenger means a bigger profit or, more likely, a smaller loss – provided that they can earn some valuable hard currency.

The 'illegality' of discounting stems from the internationally agreed convention that governments can approve airines using their airspace, and most countries have provision in their legislation which makes the sale of tickets illegal at other than the officially-approved rates. In the UK the legal position is not quite so clear-cut. British airlines are regulated by the Civil Aviation Authority and there is specific legislation which lays down heavy penalties against discounting. Foreign airlines, however, are separately controlled by the Department of Transport and, depending on whether there is a specific provision on tariffs in their permits, they may or may not be liable to be brought before the courts for discounting. There is a third class of airline – the so-called offline carriers – which do not actually operate services into the UK but which maintain sales offices here. These airlines can, quite legally, do whatever they want in terms of discounting, because there is no law that can catch them.

All this is somewhat academic in the real world because no British government has ever tried to enforce the law, which suggests that perhaps it is time for it to be repealed.

Yield Improvement Programmes

In the UK the airlines themselves have tried out to stamp out unofficial discounting through a series of what are euphemistically called Yield Improvement Programmes. All the major carriers in a particular market sign an undertaking that they will maintain the agreed tariffs and this agreement is then policed by inspectors who make test purchases of tickets. The tickets are bought at the discounted rate and are then presented to the airlines for refund at the officially-approved fare, the difference representing a 'fine' for non-compliance with the agreement.

These Yield Improvement Programmes have generally been backed up by the introduction of legitimate new cheap fares, so that discounting is effectively brought out into the open. Discounting on some routes – from the UK to Australia, for example – often takes a different form these days. Instead of being given a straight discount on the fare, travellers are offered inducements like free travel to the airport or a free stopover in the Far East.

The Passenger's Viewpoint

The consumer's dilemma has always been that an element of risk is still attached to the bucket shop market because it is perceived as operating at the fringe of the law. The passenger, it must be stressed, does not commit any offence in buying a bucket shop ticket and, to confuse matters still further, a high proportion of tickets sold in bucket shops are perfectly legitimate anyway – for example, the many round-the-world scheduled fares or low-cost European charter flights.

The risk element can be exaggerated. Only a tiny proportion of bucket shop clients suffer financial loss in any year, and there are plenty of satisfied customers who have managed to make substantial savings on their trip. Perhaps word-of-mouth recommendation from a friend is a good way to find a reliable outlet for a discount fare deal.

It is a good sign if a bucket shop has been established for some time in good premises with a street-level office. If possible you should make a personal visit to assess the knowledge of the staff rather than just relying on a telephone call. Ask as many questions as possible and find out any likely snags – like a protracted stopover en route in an unattractive part of the world – and make sure which airline you're flying with.

It is a good indication of a bucket shop's reliability if it holds an Access or Visa appointment because the card firms check the financial integrity of their appointed outlets very thoroughly. Use of a credit card also gives you added security because, under the Consumer Credit Act, the card company becomes liable for provision of the service you have bought in the event of the retailer's failure.

It is also a good sign if the office is a member of the Association of British Travel Agents (look for the ABTA sticker on the door) because you are then protected by the association's financial safeguards (*see page 63*).

And readers of this Handbook will not need reminding that WEXAS is a long-established and reliable source of discounted tickets to all parts of the world, backed up by the guarantees which come through membership of IATA.

How to Read an Airline Ticket

by Philip Ray and Alex McWhirter

An airline ticket is really a legal contract which specifies and restricts the services that passengers may expect and when they may expect them. On each ticket, the duties and liabilities of both passenger and airline are clearly stated – whether it is a scheduled or a charter flight – and each passenger must be in possession of a ticket for the journey to be undertaken. An agreement known as the Warsaw Convention limits the liability of most airlines in cases of injury or death involving a passenger and also for baggage loss or damage. This agreement is usually explained on the inside cover of the ticket or on a summary inserted in a loose-leaf form.

The format of tickets issued by IATA-appointed travel agents in the UK and a number of other countries has been changed to conform with the requirements of the so-called Bank Settlement Plan (BSP). Instead of having to keep a stock of tickets for each airline with which they deal, agents now have one common stock of 'neutral' tickets, but a special plate is slotted into the ticket validator at the time of issue to indicate which airline is legally issuing the ticket. The whole BSP operation is essentially aimed at simplifying accounting procedures for both travel agents and airlines. Tickets issued direct by airlines still carry the normal carrier indentification.

Flight coupons contain a fare construction box which, on a multi-sector itinerary, indicates how the fare is to be apportioned among the different carriers. Cities are denoted by their three-letter codes, e.g. LHR is London Heathrow, ROM is Rome, CPH is Copenhagen, LAX is Los Angeles and so on. The fare construction may be shown in FCU's (Fare Construction Units), a universal 'currency' in which fares are frequently expressed. The amount in FCUs is converted into the currency of the country of issue which is shown in the fare box in the left-hand corner. The British pound sterling is shown as UKL so as to distinguish it from other sterling currencies. Where local taxes are to be paid these are also shown and the final amount to be paid is shown in the total box.

At the bottom of the right-hand side is the 'Form of Payment' box. If you pay for the ticket by cash, it will either be left blank or the word 'cash' will be written in. If it is paid by cheque, the word 'cheque' or abbreviation 'chq' will be used. If the ticket is bought with a credit card, the letters 'CC' will be written, followed by the name of the issuing company, the card number and its expiry date. If you have an account with the travel agent the clerk will write 'Non ref', which means that no refund can be obtained except through the issuing office.

In the 'Baggage' section of the ticket, only the 'Allow' column is completed by the agent. This shows the free baggage allowance to which you are entitled. The number of pieces, checked and unchecked weights are completed when the passenger checks in. 'PC' indicates that the piece concept is in operation, as it is on more and more routes. There are validity

boxes immediately above the cities on your itinerary. These 'not valid before' and 'not valid after' entries relate to promotional fares with minimum/maximum stay requirements and the relevant dates will be shown here. If you have a full-fare ticket where there is no mimimum stay requirement and the maximum is one year, these boxes are frequently left blank.

Immediately to the right of the itinerary there is a column headed 'Fare/Class basis'. The letters most commonly inserted are 'F' for First Class, 'C' for Business Class, or 'Y' for Economy Class. The 'Y' will often be followed by other letters to describe the fare, especially if it is a promotional type. For example, 'YH' would mean a high-season fare, 'YZ' a youth fare, 'YLAP' a low-season Apex, 'YE' Excursion etc.

Under the 'Carrier' box is the space for the carrier code, e.g. LH for Lufthansa or BA for British Airways. However, the airline industry has now run out of possible combinations of two-letter codes, and three-letter codes are being introduced during 1987, so that the code for SAS Scandinavian Airlines, for example, will change from SK to SAS. Next follows the flight number and class of travel on that particular flight. Most international flight numbers consist of three figures but for UK domestic flights four figures are frequently used. The date is written as, for example, 04 JUN and not as 4th June, while the time is shown on the basis of the 24 hour clock, e.g. 14.30 hrs is written instead of 2.30pm (The twelve hour clock is still used for domestic travel within the USA). In the 'Status' box the letters 'OK' must be written if you have a confirmed flight, 'RQ' if the flight has been requested but not yet confirmed and 'WL' if the flight has been wait-listed. If you haven't decided when you want to travel, the word 'OPEN' is written, spread out across the flight number, date, time and status boxes. Infants, who travel for a ten per cent fare on international journeys, are not entitled to a seat or baggage allowance so that the reservations entry will be marked 'No seat' and the allowance marked 'nil'. Your ticket is valid for travel only when date-stamped with a travel agency or airline validator which is completed with the clerk's signature or initials.

Listings of airline, airport and city codings, to help you read your ticket, are given in the Directory section of this book.

Choosing an Airline

by Alex McWhirter and Philip Ray

Airlines spend huge amounts on advertising to tell us all about their exotic in-flight cuisine, their glamorous stewardesses and their swish new aircraft. But surveys conducted regularly among frequent travellers – particularly those who have to fly on business – tell us that all these 'service' factors are not terribly important when it comes to choosing an airline.

What does count, though, is a particular airline's punctuality record. When Lufthansa did some market research in 1986, it discovered that punctuality was the most important criterion demanded by business travellers, being mentioned by 98 per cent of the respondents. Close behind were favourable departure times, mentioned by 97 per cent, while separate check-in was demanded by only 78 per cent and a good choice of newspapers by no more than 44 per cent.

Another survey among readers of the Swedish business journal *Svensk Export* produced similar results. Asked to put a priority on the service features which they regarded as most crucial when choosing an airline, 92 per cent cited departure times and 87 per cent regarded punctuality as 'very important'. So a lot of airline advertising probably does no more than reinforce a choice which the consumer has already made.

Going Direct

Most people will want to choose a flight which involves as few changes en route as possible. For departures from London this means, as often as not, that there is a choice between only two or three carriers: British Airways, British Caledonian and the flag-carrier of the destination country. There are a few exceptions like the routes from London to New York (Kennedy) and to Los Angeles, on each of which there are two British and two American airlines, or the London-Hong Kong route, on which there is extremely tough competition between BA, BCal and Cathay Pacific, Hong Kong's own airline.

A close examination of the *ABC World Airways Guide* – which lists every scheduled service worldwide – does reveal a few exceptions, though. Between London and Paris, for example, there are services by no less than twelve airlines, and between London and Frankfurt there are thirteen. Many of these services are 'tail-end' sectors of long haul flights originating in the Far East or North America and are frequently the source of some interesting discount fare deals. But they are usually operated at a low frequency and are of little interest to the traveller in a hurry.

One word of warning: don't always assume that what appears to be a through flight is necessarily so. Some American airlines, in particular, are fond of operating what are called 'change-of-guage' services which are shown as a through service with the same flight number but in fact involve a change of aircraft en route. This is a misleading practice which the regulatory authorities would be well advised to stamp out.

Choice of Carrier

London's two airports, Heathrow and Gatwick, have direct flights to such a tremendous range of destinations that there is generally no need to fly to a continental airport and change flights there. But passengers living away from the South-East often have the choice of flying either to London or the Continent to pick up their connection. Amsterdam's Schiphol Airport and KLM, the national carrier of the Netherlands, have been extremely active in trying to persuade more Britons to fly via Amsterdam, which now has feeder-airline connections from most provincial UK points. It is always worth checking to see if there is a convenient connection via a continental gateway, but in general, there is usually a wider range of destinations and a higher frequency via London.

When choosing an airline for a long-haul flight, the general rule is to choose the carrier with the fewest stops, not only to avoid fatigue, but also to reduce the chance of incurring delays while on the ground.

If you are not in a desperate hurry to reach your destination on a really long-haul route like UK-Australia, a stopover en route is recommended because it will help mitigate some of the worst effects of jetlag (see page 92). The flight from London to New Zealand via Los Angeles is one of the longest in the world, but London-LA is a tiring enough flight as it is and a stopover for a night or two is a good idea.

Third World Standards

Some passengers have doubts about flying with airlines of the Third World countries. In a few cases these fears may be justified – some domestic airlines in South America, for instance, have pretty poor safety records – but in fact they are often represented by progressive and efficient carriers like Singapore Airlines and Air India.

The standards of on-board service offered by carriers from the Far East are probably the highest in the world – service is not a dirty word in Asia – but to generalize, it is probably true to say that the most efficient in terms of punctuality and operational integrity are those of Europe and North America. British Airways, for instance, has had a lot of criticism over the years but it is generally regarded as a world leader in setting high operational and technical standards. Now that its punctuality has been vastly improved, it will be a force to be reckoned with. Other highly regarded airlines include British Caledonian, Swissair, SAS, Lufthansa, KLM and Japan Air Lines.

Many passengers may be worried

about terrorist attacks or hi-jackings after the events of recent years, although the chances of being involved in an accident of this kind are statistically remote. The most sensible advice is to make a mental note of any airlines or airports which appear to be particularly vulnerable and avoid them. Airlines serving the Middle East area are not necessarily bad risks. Israel's national airline, El Al, probably has the most rigorous security standards of any carrier and it was thanks to its own security staff at Heathrow that a catastrophic mid-air bomb explosion was avoided in 1986.

Unless price is your main consideration, avoid flying with Aeroflot, the Soviet Union's national carrier, which dumps seats onto the market at massively discounted prices to raise hard currency. Some of the deals it offers involve a stopover at an airport transit hotel in Moscow, which by all accounts is not a particularly enjoyable experience.

Some Third World airlines which excel in in-flight service may not be so good on the ground. When travelling in Third World countries, never attempt to make your reservation by phone, but visit the airline's office and get them to validate your ticket in front of you. Always check and double-check your reservation, as some airlines in out-of-the-way parts of the world do not have computerized reservation systems and mistakes are frequently made.

Charters

The network of charter flights both inside and outside Europe is wider than many people imagine. On international routes within Europe, char-

ters account for more than half the market in terms of passenger kilometres. Most charter flights within Europe carry passengers going on conventional package tours but more and more flights are taking passengers on a 'seat only' basis, albeit with nominal accommodation provided to conform with government regulations.

Some charter flights still operate across the North Atlantic during the summer despite competition from cheap Super-Apex fares offered by the scheduled airlines. The popularity of charters between Europe and North America tends to go in cycles: when the dollar is strong, charters do well because North Americans realize that they can buy a cheap holiday in Europe. Equally, when the dollar is weak, European passengers can find attractive deals on American-originating charters because blocks of seats are often made available to tour operators at knockdown rates. All these North Atlantic charters operate under the ABC (Advance Booking Charter) rules, which mean you have to book at least 21 days before departure.

In general, though, there are fewer charters across the Atlantic than there used to be, partly because of the increased range of scheduled services which are now available. The Canadian airline Wardair, for instance, now operates a number of scheduled services out of the UK which have replaced its long-standing charter operations.

Extras and Specials

For many scheduled flights it's possible to request certain special meals such as kosher or vegetarian and to put in seat requests – for example, window, aisle, smoking or non-smoking etc. If travelling on a long-haul flight, it's a good idea to advise the airline of your contact phone number, so that you can be informed on the day of your departure if there is a major delay.

VIP treatment can take the form of better handling on the ground. An airline representative will smooth you through all the hassles of check-in and will escort you to the airline's own VIP lounge. The cabin crew will be informed of your presence and will make every effort to ensure that your flight is a comfortable and enjoyable one. Airlines normally grant VIP treatment to senior government officials and commercially important customers. Some airlines will allow you to use their VIP lounges if you have paid the First Class or full Economy Class fare and your travel agent has cleared this facility with the airline's sales department beforehand. Other airlines insist that you must be a member of their executive club or 'frequent traveller' club before they grant you admittance, while some carriers merely charge an annual membership fee which allows you to use their executive lounge whether or not you're actually flying with them. But don't expect VIP treatment if you're travelling at a discount rate.

Human Cargo

In really off-beat parts of the world, cargo aircraft may offer cheap travel, although creature comforts are largely ignored and safety even more so. Remote airstrips are the most likely places to find such services, but cargo aircraft do fly all over the world, even into larger terminals. Approach the captain at the airport office of the cargo company to find out whether there are any flights available and if they will take passengers. You will have to be ready to go at short notice and keep in frequent touch with the office as there may be no timetable to speak of and the pilot will simply take off when he and the load are ready.

It is sometimes possible to get free flights on military aircraft, especially in Latin America. Travellers should investigate this option on the spot and should also take account of any political considerations.

Airports and How to Get the Most Out of Them
by Philip Ray and David Woolley

You just can't generalize about airports. An airport can be a teeming, sprawling terminal like London's Heathrow, or New York's John F. Kennedy, or it might be a concrete strip in the African desert or the Australian outback. Or it could be a grass field with a tin shed on the Orkney island of Westray, where the sheep have to be cleared off the 'runway' before the aeroplane takes off on the world's shortest flight to the neighbouring island of Papa Westray.

All experienced travellers will have their favourite and not-so-favourite airports, but the problem is that we don't always have a choice. If, for example, you want to fly from London to Johannesburg, you will have to go from Heathrow, even if you can't stand the place. But if you are travelling from the centre of London to Manhattan, you do have a choice. You can either fly from Heathrow to JFK

– the world's Blue Riband air route –
or you can use two less congested airports in the shape of Gatwick and
Newark.

It's worth listening to airport horror
stories recounted by friends and
acquaintances because they can provide some pointers in planning your
journey and help you avoid some of the
world's air-travel black-spots.

In the past, airports like New York's
JFK, Los Angeles International and
Miami International acquired a bad
name because of their congested terminals and the long delays in processing jumbo-loads of passengers through
Customs and Immigration. Wise travellers, in particular those making US
domestic connections, have got themselves in via a less congested airport
like Boston's Logan International
rather than JFK. Others have discovered that they can reach Los Angeles
just as quickly by changing flights and
clearing Customs in, say, Dallas/Fort
Worth, which has fewer international
flights and, hence, less congestion at
the processing points. To be fair,
though, the airport authorities in both
New York and Los Angeles have been
making determined efforts to improve
conditions.

Basic Requirements

The basic requirement of an airport
for any traveller is that it should be
easy to reach and that it should have
all the facilities to make the journey
as smooth and hassle-free as possible.
This means, ideally, that it should not
be too congested, it should be well
signposted, and there should be moving walkways or rapid-transit systems
to eliminate those long route marches
which are so notorious at some air-

ports. Bussing should not be necessary
to reach one's flight and, for arriving
passengers, baggage delivery should
be as speedy as possible (although this
is frequently the responsibility of the
airline rather than the airport authority).

Allow plenty of time to get to the
airport. It is always best to assume that
you are going to be delayed by late-
running buses or trains or by traffic
congestion if you are driving. Not so
long ago, airlines started trimming
their minimum check-in times, but
now the trend has gone in the reverse
direction because of the regrettable
need to allow time for security checking. Flights are frequently delayed,
particularly in the holiday peak season, because there are simply not
enough X-ray machines to cope with
the number of passengers.

Of course, these days, the airport
authorities actually want you to check
in early because they reckon you will
have time on your hands and money to
spend in the restaurants and in those
tempting duty-free shops. Shopping is
now big business for the airport authorities, particularly in Europe where
most passengers are travelling on
international services. In 1985-1986,
the British Airports Authority notched
up a trading profit of £111 million from
its commercial activities, which also
included car-parking concessions. It
actually lost money on the fees which
it charged the airlines, so if it had not
been for the commercial income, user
charges would have gone up, pushing
up airfares in turn.

The BAA is currently mounting an
even more aggressive marketing campaign for its duty-free shops and
claims to be making higher profits
from retailing than the giant Tesco

supermarket chain. And the popularity of Amsterdam's Schiphol Airport has been built up largely on the bargain-basement shopping facilities which it provides. The level of prices in the duty-free shops is sometimes criticized on the basis that the profit margins are allegedly excessive, but the fact remains that they are usually well below High Street prices on items like liquor and tobacco which attract a high rate of duty. The criticisms are frequently more valid on items like cameras or electronic goods where the price savings are often insignificant.

Many airports are becoming attractive shopping centres in their own right, quite apart from their popularity as a source of duty-free liquor and perfume. The airports serving Copenhagen and Stockholm, for example, have excellent shops where you can buy local gastronomic specialities. The largest selection of shops is probably to be found at Frankfurt (see below). Another important slice of revenue for airport authorities is derived from restaurants and bars. The trend nowadays is for airports to go in for fastfood or cafeteria-style service rather than waiter-service gourmet restaurants because most people are spending only a relatively short time at the airport while waiting for their flights. Catering standards obviously vary between one airport and another, but on the whole they offer reasonable value for money.

Parking is also big business for most airports and is frequently operated by a concessionaire. It can be worth inquiring if an alternative service is offered by an off-airport company because the rates are likely to be rather cheaper, if only because there is no concession fee to pay to the airport operator. This is certainly the case at major British Airports Authority airports like Heathrow or Gatwick, and not surprisingly the BAA does not go out of its way to supply information about the off-airport operators. Tour operators with flights from UK airports often have special arrangements with off-airport parking companies and will send details with your holiday confirmation.

Another increasingly important 'fringe' operation is the provision of airport hotels. Details of convenient hotels are usually available from the airport information desk, and a courtesy coach service usually operates between the hotel and the airport.

One nasty shock which you may encounter at some airports, particularly outside Europe and North America, is a demand for payment of an airport tax when you check in. In some countries the amount may be purely nominal, but in Hong Kong it is more than £10. Airport taxes exist within Europe but almost invariably they are built into the airfare. It would be a great boon to air travellers if the same practice was adopted worldwide.

Some Major Airports

London Heathrow

It's fashionable to knock Heathrow, but in reality, it is a remarkably efficient operation and it remains the world's busiest international airport, both in terms of the number of passengers handled and the number of destinations served. In fact, you can reach almost any destination in the world from Heathrow with no more than one or two changes in aircraft. The main point to watch is to double-check which of the four terminals your flight departs from. Three of the terminals are in the Heathrow central area but the new Terminal 4, opened in 1986, is located on the south-east periphery of the airport and has separate road access network and parking facilities. There is also a separate Tube station. At the time of writing, Terminal 4 was used mainly by British Airways, for all its intercontinental flights and its Paris and Amsterdam services. It was also used by the Dutch carrier KLM plus its commuter-airline subsidiary NLM and Air Malta.

London Gatwick

Undoubtedly Britain's biggest airport success story, Gatwick has had a history of uninterrupted expansion over the past decade and is now the world's second busiest international airport after Heathrow. It has the best communications of any UK airport with its direct rail and motorway links and it is now quicker to get from central London to Gatwick by the non-stop British Rail Gatwick Express service from Victoria than it is to take the Tube to Heathrow. The last major expansion at Gatwick was the opening in 1983 of its circular satellite pier, which is linked to the main terminal by an automated rapid-transit system running on an overhead guideway. Gatwick reached its theoretical maximum capacity of 16 million passengers a year towards the end of 1986, and the airport is likely to become increasingly congested until the new north terminal opens in 1988, a year behind schedule because of Government restrictions on capital expenditure. The opening of this terminal will enable Gatwick to expand to its ultimate ceiling of 25 million passengers a year.

Amsterdam (Schiphol)

Schiphol remains a convenient and simple airport to use, although it is becoming increasingly busy as a result of its success as a main traffic hub. The railway station, linked to the single passenger terminal by a short underground tunnel, now offers a direct rail service to Amsterdam's Central Station (a twenty-minute journey), as well as to Rotterdam, The Hague and other cities in the Netherlands, plus Antwerp and Brussels.

Sticking to its policy of providing capacity well ahead of demand, the airport authority is building a new pier, 340 metres long and able to handle ten large aircraft at once, due to come into operation late in 1987.

Schiphol's duty-free shopping centre, stocking everything from whisky to video equipment, continues to live up to its reputation for good value. And leave time to buy a bunch of flowers from one of the colourful florist's shops.

Frankfurt

A new runway has been built at Frankfurt, amid warlike confrontations with environmental protesters, and delays have been reduced as a result. The airport's single passenger terminal can be very crowded and is not very well signed. Be prepared for quite long walking distances and leave time for the duty-free shop, which is tucked away up a staircase near the departure gate.

The subterranean labyrinth below the terminal contains a railway station with an excellent service which is part of the city's S-Bahn urban transit network (a ten-minute ride to the city centre). Lufthansa runs special trains, for airline passengers only, to Cologne,

Bonn and Dusseldorf, and a number of inter-city expresses also serve the airport.

Also in the terminal basement is a large supermarket – buy your wine here, not in the duty-free shops – together with the now-famous Dr Muller's sex shop and a disco night-club said to be among the city's more fashionable spots.

An agreeable feature of the Frank-furt terminal is that it has a choice of quite small restaurants, cafés and bars, rather than the usual mass catering.

The airport authority has a US$1.2 billion building programme for the next five years, which includes con-struction of a second passenger ter-minal.

Paris (Charles de Gaulle)

Also known as Roissy, the main Paris airport has two terminals, No.1 mainly for foreign airlines and No.2 for Air France plus the domestic airline Air Inter and Sabena. Terminal 1 is a cir-cular concrete monolith, a showpiece of airport architecture now showing signs of premature old age. Circular buildings are notoriously confusing, so watch the signs to avoid extra walking. The duty-free shops are cramped and not among Europe's cheapest.

Terminal 2 is altogether more mod-ern and convenient, but check which of the two separate buildings you need: 2A is mainly for Air France's long-haul and Mediterranean destinations, 2B for northern Europe.

There is a railway station in the air-port, but you need to use a shuttle bus to reach it. The trains serve the Gare du Nord (journey time 30 minutes) and also the RER suburban network. The Air France bus service from each terminal to the Porte Maillot is more

convenient if you want that part of Paris and takes no longer, except per-haps in the rush hour. If you need to transfer to Orly Airport on the other side of the city, there is a helicopter link as well as a bus service.

Zurich

An impressive new terminal at Swit-zerland's main airport has created ample capacity and has made the air-port even less crowded than before. Swiss security checks are reassuringly thorough – the walk-through weapon detectors seem more sensitive than those anywhere else – and the immi-gration formalities must be among the world's most expeditious. On arrival, your baggage may well be waiting for you when you reach the conveyor.

The new building, Terminal A, serves domestic and European flights and Terminal B is for long-haul ser-vices.

The airport railway station is con-venient to both terminals and has ser-vices to Zurich's main station (journey time eleven minutes) and to most parts of the country, including the federal capital, Berne. You can check in your baggage for the return flight at many railway stations in Switzerland.

New York (John F Kennedy)

As usual at major US airports, there is a terminal at Kennedy for each of the major airlines, plus an international terminal. Unusually for the USA, a foreign carrier – British Airways – also has its own terminal. The drawback with this arrangment is that a change of airline means a change of terminal, and congestion in the terminal area can be a problem. The Port Authority has done something to alleviate conges-tion, but the chief hope for the future lies in an ambitious plan for 'people mover' systems to shuttle passengers via a central 'transportation center'. Another passenger terminal is due to be built in the next six years, but congestion is likely to persist until then.

For downtown links, there are the JFK Express Subway – a shuttle bus takes you to the station first – and several bus services, all of which offer a journey time of about an hour. There are also helicopter services – perhaps the most comprehensive of any airport – to other New York airports and to four heliports in the downtown area.

Atlanta (Hartsfield International)
Atlanta boasts one of the world's busiest airports, but between half and three-quarters of the travellers using it are merely changing flights and not visiting the city at all. The single passenger terminal, designed with this fact in mind, is vast, but easy to get around in. It has its own underground trains to whisk you from one airline's patch to another's or to the main building with its check-in areas, baggage claim, restaurants, bars and shops. The trains are fully automatic, even to the extent that a recorded voice will rebuke you if you obstruct the closing doors.

For such a large airport, the shopping facilities are surprisingly poor, so Atlanta is an excellent place for changing flights but not somewhere in which to linger.

If you are one of the minority wanting to go downtown, a bus service connects with the MARTA rapid transit rail service to the city.

Los Angeles International
Completion of a massive building programme has made life much more bearable for the traveller at Los Angeles International Airport. Road traffic now circulates more freely, thanks to the conversion to two levels of the road which circles the central area and serves the several individual airline terminals.

Another major part of the building programme was the impressive Bradley International Terminal, also in the central area, providing service for the many long-haul airlines that call at Los Angeles. The eternal queueing for Customs and Immigration, so long a feature of the American scene, is now much improved. But efforts to integrate the two services have not been entirely successful and the traveller can be kept waiting.

Rather unusually for the USA, the airport offers a good selection of bus services from the central area to several parts of the vast surrounding urban sprawl, including Anaheim and Disneyland, Orange County and Palm Springs. It can be a problem finding out exactly where each bus company picks up passengers and when, but it's worth persevering.

Hong Kong
The approach by air to the single runway at Hong Kong's Kai Tak Airport is so notorious – head for that mountainside, turn right towards the airfield, look into the windows of the apartment blocks as you pass by – that pilots treat it with kid gloves. As a result, the safety record at Kai Tak is one of the world's best.

Once on the ground, you are pitched into a hectic but on the whole well-ordered Oriental crowd scene. The Far East is where the big growth in air traffic is taking place and Hong Kong is one of the key hubs. Thankfully a large proportion of travellers in the region move in regimented groups and can therefore be circumvented.

The passenger terminal is serviceable but unattractive, run as it is by a Government department, and shopping is more fun downtown. The restaurant and bar services are not good.

Bus services take you to Kowloon and Hong Kong Island. It isn't far but traffic conditions are such that the journey can take 45 minutes or more.

When you leave Hong Kong, be prepared for an early check-in time. The standard is two hours before scheduled departure, although many airlines offer to get their First Class and Business Class passengers through the procedures in less than half that time.

Singapore

The amazing success of Singapore Airlines has taken its tiny home country to tenth place in the world league by size of airline industry and has helped to make Changi one of the key hub airports in the Far East since it was opened about five years ago.

This development has faltered a little in recent economic conditions, but as an expression of confidence in the future the Government is now engaged on a ten-year programme of expansion. A second passenger terminal, due to open in 1989, will double the passenger capacity from ten million to twenty million a year.

The airport was designed by Singaporeans, who first studied the successes and failures of airport designers all over the world. They seem to have avoided the pitfalls and have produced a passenger terminal which is efficiently run and pleasant and easy to use. Not the least of its attractions is

the availability of duty-free shops on arrival as well as departure.

Tokyo

Airlines hate Narita because the landing charges are among the world's highest. This relatively new airport handles an enormous volume of passengers and is already beginning to run out of space. Work on doubling its size has now begun, involving two more runways and a second passenger terminal.

Narita's chief problem is the time taken to get downtown, a distance of some 40 miles. Officially the journey time is put at one hour, but it can take twice that. However, a plan for an express train service (47 minutes) has been announced. Most of the tracks already exist, so it may be running before too long.

Making Claims Against Airlines

by Philip Ray and Alex McWhirter

You have only to read the correspondence columns in the specialist business travel magazines each month to see what a fashionable occupation it is to complain about airline services. Some people seem to enjoy writing letters of complaint so much that they make a profession of it. They complain at the slightest hiccup and write long letters detailing every flaw, claiming huge sums in compensation and threatening legal action if it is not forthcoming by return.

But the fact is that no matter how much their inefficiency costs you in time, trouble, missed meetings, lost deals and overnight hotel bills, the airlines in many cases are not obliged to pay you anything. They are covered for most eventualities by their Conditions of Carriage which are printed on the inside cover of the ticket. However, this is not to say that, in an increasingly competitive environment, the more enlightened airlines do not take their customers' attitudes seriously. Some airline chief executives take a personal interest in passenger complaints and have frequent 'purges' when they insist on seeing every letter of complaint that comes in on a particular day.

If you have a complaint against an airline which you cannot resolve satisfactorily it is worth contacting the Air Transport Users' Committee (129 Kingsway, London WC2B 6NN). The committee is funded and appointed by the Civil Aviation Authority but operates completely independently and, indeed, has frequently been known to criticize some of the authority's decisions. The committee has only a small secretariat and is not really geared up to handle a large volume of complaints, but it has had some success in securing *ex gratia* payments for passengers who have been inconvenienced in some way. All the same, the committee likes to receive passenger complaints because it is a useful way of bringing to light some serious problems which can lead to high-level pressure being brought to bear on the airline or airlines involved. Some of the subjects dealt with by the committee in 1986 included European and domestic airfares, passenger safety measures, communications with airports and noise restrictions.

Procedure

Here are some tips which may make complaining to an airline more effective:

1. The first person to write to is the customer relations manager. You can write to the chairman if it makes you feel better but it makes little difference – unless that happens to be the day that the chairman decides to have his 'purge'. If you've made your booking through a travel agent, send them a copy of the letter and if the agent does a fair amount of business with that carrier (especially if it is a foreign airline) it's a good idea to ask them to take up the complaint for you.
2. Keep your letter brief, simple, calm and to the point. Remember also to give the date, flight number, location and route where the incident took place. All these details seem obvious but it's amazing how many people omit them.
3. Keep all ticket stubs, baggage claims and anything else you may have from the flight involved. You may have to produce them if the airline requires substantiation of your complaint.
4. If you have no success after all this, write to the Air Transport Users' Committee. Send it copies of all the correspondence you've had with the airline and let it take the matter from there.

Lost Luggage

Most frequent travellers will at some time have experienced that sinking feeling when the carousel stops going round and their baggage is not on it. The first thing to do if your luggage does not appear is to check with an airline official in the baggage-claim area. It could be that your baggage is of a non-standard shape – a heavy rucksack, for example – which cannot be handled easily on the conveyor belt and it will then be brought to the claim area by hand. But if your baggage really has not arrived on the same flight as yourself you will have to complete a Property Irregularity Report (PIR), which will give a description of the baggage, a list of its contents and the address to which it should be forwarded.

It is sometimes worth hanging around at the airport for an hour or two because there is always the chance that your baggage may arrive on the next flight. This sometimes happens if you have had to make a tight flight connection and your baggage hasn't quite made it. But if there is only one flight a day there is no point in waiting and the airline will forward the baggage to you at its expense. In this case, ask the airline for an allowance to enable you to buy the basic necessities for an overnight stay – nightwear, toiletries, and underwear for example.

If your baggage never arrives at all, you should make a claim against the airline within 21 days. Airlines' liability for lost luggage is limited by international agreement and the level of compensation is based on the weight of your baggage, which explains why it is filled in on your ticket by the check-in clerk. The maximum rate of compensation at present is US$20 per kilo for checked baggage and US$400 per passenger for unchecked baggage, unless a higher value is declared in advance and additional charges are paid.

The same procedure applies to baggage which you find to be damaged when you claim it. The damage should be reported immediately to an airline official and, again, you will have to fill in a PIR form which you should follow up with a formal claim against the airline.

Overbooking

Losing one's baggage may be the ultimate nightmare in air travel but the phenomenon of 'bumping' must run it a close second. 'Bumping' occurs when you arrive at the airport with a confirmed ticket, only to be told that there is no seat for you because the flight is overbooked.

Most airlines overbook their flights deliberately because they know that there will always be a few passengers who make a booking and then don't turn up ('no shows' in airline jargon). On some busy routes like Brussels-London on a Friday evening, some business travellers book themselves on four or five different flights, so that there is a horrendous 'no-show' problem and the airlines can, perhaps, be forgiven for overbooking.

The use of computers has enabled airlines to work out their overbooking factors quite scientifically, but just occasionally things don't quite work out and a few confirmed passengers have to be 'bumped'.

If you are unlucky enough to be 'bumped' or 'denied boarding', to adopt the airline jargon, you may be entitled to compensation under a scheme drawn up by the major European airlines. You are entitled to a 50% refund of the one-way fare for the sector involved – subject to a ceiling of £150, plus reasonable expenses incurred during the delay, including accommodation if necessary. The Air

Transport Users' Committee is putting pressure on US airlines operating out of the UK, which at present do not feel bound by the European airlines' compensation system, to come into line and offer a similar scheme.

An increasing number of airlines, including British Airways and British Caledonian, are introducing an alternative type of scheme under which passengers are invited to volunteer for offloading from an overbooked flight. In return, they receive compensation on a sliding scale, depending on how long they have to wait for an alternative flight, and in the case of BA more than half the 'bumpees' at Heathrow are now volunteers.

Under the BCal scheme, passengers on a European or domestic flight who are 'bumped', either voluntarily or involuntarily, receive compensation of £30 if their alternative flight leaves within six hours. If they get away within six to twelve hours they receive £40 and for anything in excess of twelve hours the compensation is £50. On long-haul services, there is compensation of £100 if the alternative flight leaves within six hours, £125 for between six and twelve hours, and £150 for more than twelve hours.

Compensation for Delays

Whatever the Conditions of Carriage may say, airlines generally take a sympathetic view if flight delays cause passengers to miss connections, possibly entailing overnight hotel accommodation. Our own experience is that most of the better-known scheduled carriers will pull out all the stops to ensure that passengers are quickly rebooked on alternative flights and they will normally pick up the tab for hotel accommodation and the cost of sending messages to advise friends or contacts of the revised arrival time.

The position is not so clear-cut when it comes to charter airlines because the extent of their generosity usually depends on whatever arrangement they have with the charterer. But a number of British tour operators have devised delay protection plans which are usually included as part of the normal holiday insurance. Thomson Holidays, for instance, will normally provide meals or overnight accommodation in the event of long flight delays, and if a flight is delayed for more than 24 hours passengers have the right to cancel their holiday and receive a full refund. If they decide to continue their holiday they receive compensation up to a maximum of £60, in addition to any meals or accommodation which may have been provided.

Injury or Death

Airlines' liabilities to their passengers were originally laid down by an agreement called by the Warsaw Convention which was signed in 1929. The basic principle was that the infant airline industry could have been crippled if it had been forced by the courts to pay massive amounts of compensation to passengers or their relatives for death or injury in the event of an accident.

The trade-off was that the airlines undertook to pay compensation up to a set ceiling irrespective of whether negligence on their part was proved. The limit of compensation was set at 250,000 French gold francs, an obsolete currency which is nevertheless still used to this day as the official unit of compensation and converted into local currencies. In the UK, for instance, the sterling equivalent is currently laid down by statute as approximately £12,000, which is generally accepted to be a hopelessly inadequate level of compensation.

The parties to the Warsaw Convention met in Montreal in 1975 and signed four protocols which would have substituted for the gold franc the Special Drawing Right (SDR), the international unit of account devised by the International Monetary Fund. But these protocols have not yet been ratified by the necessary 30 states and the gold franc remains the official unit of compensation worldwide.

In a number of countries, the airlines now offer a higher level of compensation than the Warsaw limits, either voluntarily or as a result of government directive. In the UK, for example, it is a condition of all British airlines' licences that they should set their liability limit at 100,000 SDR's (equivalent to about £76,000).

Even if international agreement to ratify the Montreal protocols cannot be reached there seems a strong case for makng it a condition that every airline flying into the UK should adopt the 100,000 SDR limit, and this is a view which appears to be shared by the British Government. In 1986 the Minister of Aviation said the current limits were far too low and warned that the present arrangements could not continue indefinitely. If there was no prospect of other countries ratifying the Montreal protocols, said the Minister, the UK Government would consider 'all the alternatives open to us' including, possibly, a requirement that all airlines using British airports should provide compensation well above the present limits.

It is worth noting that an airline's liability is unlimited if gross negligence or wilful misconduct can be proved.

The Ticket Out

by Ingrid Cranfield

Many countries require travellers to show a ticket out of the country before they are issued with a visa or allowed over the border. This onward ticket is normally expected to be a plane ticket, though sufficient evidence of the traveller's respectability and solvency can ensure that a ticket for some other means of transport will be accepted.

Onward tickets are no problem for travellers who wish to use them, but many people, especially overlanders, want to enter a country, but have no intention of flying out. For them, it will be desirable to try and get a refund.

Some countries require that the onward ticket be shown on application for a visa, but not therafter. The purchaser can get a visa and then cash in his ticket before actually leaving home. If you do this, it is best to buy the ticket on credit, so that no cash need change hands either on purchase or on refund.

However, countries with this precondition for a visa will nearly always want to see the onward ticket at the point of immigration. If the buyer does not intend to use it, he will have to obtain a refund either in the country or after leaving. For many reasons, it is best, therefore, to buy direct from a large carrier with many offices in convenient places and not through a travel agency, and to pay in cash or traveller's cheques.

Buying outside the region for travel to the Third World, you should use a hard currency which will be foreign to your destination. In many countries you will not be allowed to purchase in any but a hard currency. If you buy in one soft currency, you cannot expect to be refunded in another, and this could prove inconvenient. Some Third World authorities are anxious to prevent export of their currency and will prefer refunds to be given in hard currency. Elsewhere, they will be desperate to get their hands on your hard currency and refunds will be given in the local currency, which will generally be a soft one. If your original purchase was in a hard currency, you are, at least, in a stronger position when requesting the same in exchange.

Buying in the region is usually cheaper, especially if the black market rate is favourable, except where ticket taxes are very high. To avoid paying such taxes, buy elsewhere, or get a friend to buy you a ticket in another country and post it to you (suitably disguised).

The rules on refunding tickets vary from one place and one carrier, sometimes even one office, to another. Tickets are sometimes stamped 'non-refundable' (and the ink is sometimes eradicated by unscrupulous travellers), but such tickets are, in any case, usually transferable. Refunds in the form of MCOs (Miscellaneous Charges Orders) should be accepted, as these can be used to buy any airline ticket or service. An MCO can even serve as an

altered ticket and, like a ticket, can be cashed in separately.

Finally, make a note of the ticket number in case of loss; buy yourself a return or onward ticket to avoid being stranded if you're visiting a really remote destination; and do, for the airline's sake, cancel any reservation you don't intend to use.

Flying in Comfort

by Richard Harrington

Flying is physically a lot more stressing than a lot of people realize. And there's more to the problem than time zones. Modern jet aircraft are artificially pressurized at an altitude pressure of around 1,500-2,000m. That means that when you're flying at an altitude of, say, 12,000m in a Boeing 747, the cabin pressure inside is what it would be if you were outside at a height of 1,500-2,000m above sea level. Most people live a lot closer to sea level than this and to be rocketed almost instantly to a height of 2,000m (so far as their body is concerned) takes a considerable amount of adjustment. Fortunately, the human body is a remarkably adaptable organism, and for most individuals the experience is stressful, but not fatal.

Although it might seem more practical to pressurize the cabin to sea level pressure, this is currently impossible. A modern jet with sea level cabin pressure would have to have extremely strong (and therefore heavy) outside walls to prevent the difference between inside and outside pressure from causing the aircraft walls to rupture in mid-flight. At present, there is no economically viable lightweight material available that is strong enough to do the job. Another problem is that if there were a rupture at, say, 14,000m in an aircraft with an interior pressure equal to that at sea level, there would be no chance for the oxygen masks to drop in the huge sucking process that would occur as the air inside emptied through the hole in the aircraft. A 2,000m equivalent pressure at least gives passengers and oxygen masks a chance if this occurs.

Inside the cabin, humidifiers and fragrance disguise all the odours of large numbers of people in a confined space. On a long flight you're breathing polluted air.

Surviving the Onslaught

What can you do to help your body survive the onslaught? First you can loosen your clothing. The body swells in the thinner air of the cabin, so take off your shoes (wear loose shoes anyway, it can be agony putting tight ones back at the end of the flight), undo your belt, tilt your seat right back, put a couple of pillows in the lumbar region of your back and one behind your neck, and whether you're trying to sleep or simply rest, cover your eyes with a pair of air travel blinkers (ask the stewardess for a pair if you haven't brought any with you). Temperatures rise and fall notoriously inside an aircraft, so have a blanket ready over your knees in case you nod off and wake up later to find that you're freezing.

When I look at all the space wasted over passengers' heads in a Boeing 747, and all those half-empty hand baggage lockers, I often wonder why aircraft manufacturers don't arrange things so that comfortable hammocks can be slung over our heads for those who want to sleep – or better still, small *couchettes* in tiers like those found in modern submarines. Personally, I'd prefer such comfort, whatever it might do to the tidiness of the cabin interior.

Circulation, Consumption and Comfort

It's tempting, on a long flight, to feel you're not getting your money's worth if you don't eat and drink everything that's going. Stop and resist the temptation, even if you're in First Class and all that food and drink seems to be what most of the extra cost is all about. Most people find it best to eat lightly before leaving home and little or nothing during the flights. Foods that are too rich or spicy and foods that you're unaccustomed to will do little to make you feel good in flight. Neither will alcohol. Some people claim that they travel better if they drink fizzy drinks in flight, although if inclined to indigestion, the gas can cause discomfort as it is affected by the lower pressure in the cabin. Tea and coffee are diuretics (increase urine output) and so have the undesirable effect of further dehydrating the drinker who is already in the very dry atmosphere of the cabin. Fruit juices and plain water are best.

Smoking raises the level of carbon monoxide in the blood – and incidentally in the atmosphere, so that non-smokers can also suffer the ill effects if seated close to smokers – and reduces the smoker's tolerance to altitude. A smoker is already effectively at 1,500-2,000m before leaving the ground, being more inclined to breathlessness and excessive dryness than the non-smoker.

Walk up and down as frequently as possible during a flight to keep your circulation in shape, and don't resist the urge to go to the toilet (avoid the queues by going before meals). The time will pass more quickly, and you'll feel better for it, if you get well into an unputdownable novel before leaving home and try to finish it during the flight. This trick always works better than half-heartedly flicking through an in-flight magazine.

You may try to find out how full a plane is before you book, or choose to fly in the low season to increase your chance of getting empty seats to stretch out on for a good sleep. If you've got a choice of seats on a stretched DC-8, for example, remember that there's more leg room by the emergency exit over the wings. On the other hand, stewardesses tend to gather at the tail of the plane on most airlines, so they try not to give seats there away unless asked. That means you may have more chance of ending up with empty seats next to you if you go for the back two rows (also statistically the safest place in a crash). Seats in the middle compartment over the forward part of the wing are said to give the smoothest ride; the front area of the plane is however the quietest.

You might try travelling with your own pillow, which will be a useful supplement to the postage-stamp sized pillows supplied by most airlines.

Finally, if you plan to sleep during the flight, put a 'Do Not Disturb' notice by your seat and pass up the chance of another free drink or face towel every time your friendly neighbourhood stewardess comes round.

You probably won't arrive at the other end raring to go, but if you've planned it wisely to arrive just before nightfall, and if you take a brisk walk before going to bed, you might just get lucky and go straight to sleep without waking up on home time two hours later.

Jetlag

by Melissa Shales

Every year, as the holiday season swings into action, millions of people join that bleary-eyed band of professional travellers who stumble their way around the world muttering sourly about jetlag. For holiday-makers, jetlag is an irritating waste of precious time away from the office, but for the many businessmen, politicians, air crew and public figures for whom travelling is unavoidable, it can be an expensive disaster. Scientific research is now proving that jetlag can lower mental and physical efficiency by up to twenty per cent. And that means that many vital decisions are being taken while your mental abilities are considerably below par. Former US Secretary of State John Foster Dulles publicly admitted responsibility for the Suez Crisis, claiming that his hasty and poorly thought decisions were the result of chronic jetlag.

Causes and Symptoms

Initial symptoms include extreme fatigue, which can affect concentration, memory and performance. Other effects can be constipation or diarrhoea, insomnia, loss of appetite, headache, impaired night vision and peripheral vision. On a flight half way round the world, total readjustment can take up to a fortnight.

Since the 1940's, it has been known that the human body functions through a complicated series of cyclical rhythms governing every natural process from ageing and reproduction to breathing and swallowing. This 'circadian' rhythm is governed by the five senses of sight, sound, touch, taste and smell, as well as three less physically obvious senses. The sense of place is similar to the more highly developed instinct that causes birds to migrate within a particular pattern and area, or whales to cross the earth to calve; the sense of time has a natural cycle of around 25 hours, which is adjusted by external factors, such as light and dark, to regulate our daily living – the 'internal clock' that wakes you just before the alarm goes off and tells you when it is time for a meal; and the sense of well being is dependent on the synchronization of the other senses to make our bodies function efficiently – when you live an erratic life you use far more nervous energy just trying to cope with the day to day demands of living. If any of these senses is disrupted, the disorientation is physical as well as mental as the body's chemistry adapts to the new rhythms caused by major displacement in both time and space. This disruption, caused by rapid movement to a totally different time cycle, is what is known as jetlag.

Effects

The effects of jetlag normally only become serious if the time difference is over three hours, so many north-south flights, although they will result in travel fatigue, will not actually cause much jetlag. A rough guideline suggests that 24 hours recovery time is required for every two hours time difference, although this will obviously vary according to each individual. Some organizations, such as the International Civil Aviation Organization (ICAO) are now building a recovery formula into travel schedules and time is allowed for recuperation before any work is done. One firm of management consultants in the USA has ruled that no major financial decision should be taken by its executives during the recovery period.

The effects of jetlag can be altered by personal attributes and habits. Generally, the younger you are, the less it will affect you, to the point where small babies, who almost sleep the clock round, are totally unaffected. A person with rigid habits will suffer more if they are disrupted, while people who are either very early risers or night owls can make their habit work for them, dependent upon the direction in which they are travelling.

Prevention

The effects of jetlag cannot be avoided, but there are ways of lessening their impact. Dr. Charles Ehret of the Argonne National Laboratory in the USA has devised a dietary programme designed to miminize the effects of jetlag by adjusting the body over a four-day period prior to flight. It was originally used by the US Army Rapid Deployment Force, but is now available to the public through a book which Dr. Ehret has written in conjunction with Lynne Waller Scanlon – *Overcoming Jetlag* (Berkeley Books). During the pre-flight period, you alternately 'feast' and 'fast', swopping meals of either high protein value to stimulate activity and high carbohydrate to induce sleep, or fasting, to 'deplete the liver's store of carbohydrates and prepare the body's clock for resetting'. It seems to help, but requires willpower which, when even tea and coffee are severely regulated, few possess.

In a more general book, *The Jetlag Book* (Crown Publishers), writer Don Kowet offers a wide selection of ways to help relieve the misery caused by long-haul flying. As well as the causes and effects of jetlag, he discusses in some depth why the actual flight is so tiring and offers a number of solutions, many of which are pure common sense if we thought them out for ourselves. These will not help combat jetlag, but will mean you do not also have to combat travel fatigue. *(See also the article on Flying in Comfort on page 90).*

I find that a little self-delusion helps. Change your watch the moment you board the plane and try not to convert back to 'home' time. By the time you arrive, your brain, if not your body, will be convinced enough to keep you going on a local schedule. I also force myself to stay awake until the new bedtime – or go to sleep at what my body tells me is lunchtime (easier if you haven't allowed yourself to realise that they really served dinner at eight in the morning) – however hard it may be, and usually find that I will only notice the time difference for a couple of hours the next day.

Jetlag is an inconvenience that is here to stay and has to be faced by an ever-growing population of air travellers, but with some commonsense and willpower, the effects can be minimized to the point where you might no longer need to spend half your stay abroad recovering from the journey.

Fear of Flying

by Sheila Critchley

More people fly today than ever before, yet many – experienced air travellers as well as novices – suffer anguish and apprehension at the mere thought of flying. A survey by the Boeing aircraft company in the USA suggested that as many as one out of seven people experience anxiety when flying and that women outnumber men two to one in these feelings of uneasiness. The crews know them as 'the white-knuckle brigade'.

A certain amount of concern is perhaps inevitable. The sheer size of modern jet aircraft, which appear awkward and unwieldy on the ground, makes one wonder how they will manage to get into the air – and stay there. Most of these fears are irrational and are perhaps based on the certain knowledge that once in the aircraft, we, as passengers, are powerless to control our fate, which depends solely on the skill and training of the crew. There is little comfort for these people in the numerous statistical compilations which show that modern air transport is many times safer than transport by car or rail. According to Lloyds of London, it is 25 times safer to travel by air than by car. A spokesman for Lloyd's Aviation Underwriting said that if you consider all the world's airlines, there are some 600 to 1,000 people killed every year on average. This figure compares to an annual toll on the roads of some 55,000 in the

United States, 12,000 in France and 5,000 in the United Kingdom. One sardonic pilot used to announce on landing, 'You've now completed the safest part of your journey. Drive carefully.'

Anxiety

Most people's fear remains just that – anxiety which gives rise to signs of stress but remains on a manageable scale. For others, however, the anxiety can become an unimagineable fear, known as *aviophobia* or fear of flying. Symptoms include feelings of panic, sweating, palpitations, depression, sleeplessness, weeping spells, and sometimes temporary paralysis. Phobias are deep seated and often require therapy to search out the root cause. Psychologists studying *aviophobia* suggest that in serious cases, there may be an overlap with *claustrophobia* (fear of confined places) and *aerophobia* (fear of heights). Professional help can be obtained from specialists in behavioural psychotherapy. Unlike other phobias, though, which may impair a person's ability to function in society, those suffering from *aviophobia* may simply adopt avoidance of air travel as a means of coping. Only those whose lifestyles necessitate a great deal of foreign travel are forced into finding a solution.

One source of many people's fear of flying is simply a lack of knowledge about how an aircraft works and about which sounds are usual and to be expected. Visiting airports and observing planes taking off and landing can help overcome this problem. Reading about flying can also help (though air disaster fiction can hardly be recommended). Talking to other people who fly regularly can be reassuring. Frequent air travellers are familiar with the sequence of sounds which indicates everything is proceeding normally: the dull 'thonk' when the landing gear retracts on take-off; the seeming deceleration of the engine speed to cruising velocity; the resonance of the engines at certain speeds among other things. Since most people are familiar with the sounds in their cars and listen almost subconsciously to the changed 'tones' that indicate mechanical difficulties, people who are unsure about flying often feel a certain disquiet when they can't identify 'normal' from 'abnormal' sounds in an aircraft.

Air turbulence can also be upsetting. Most modern aircraft fly above areas of severe winds (such as during thunderstorms) and pilots receive constant reports on upcoming weather conditions from monitoring towers. Nonetheless, air currents up to 20,000 feet may buffet aircraft and the 'cobblestoning' effect can be frightening even to experienced air travellers. Flight crews are aware of this problem and usually make an announcement to allay undue worries.

If you are afraid to fly, tell the stewardess when you board so that the crew can keep an eye on you. Hyperventilation is a common sympton of anxiety; the cure is to breathe slowly and deeply into a paper bag. Remember that all aircraft crew are professionals; their training is far more rigorous than, say, that required to obtain a driving licence.

Emergencies

It is probably worth mentioning that the cabin crew's main responsibility is not dispensing food and drink to passengers but rather the safety of everyone on board. There is usually a minimum of one flight attendant for every 50 passengers. The briefings on emergency procedures which are given at the beginning of every flight are not routine matters: they can mean the difference between life and death and should be taken seriously. Each type of aeroplane has different positions for emergency exits, oxygen supplies, and design and positioning of life jackets. The air crews' demonstrations of emergency prodedures are for the benefit of everyone on board and should be watched and listened to attentively. In an emergency situation, action needs to occur in the first fifteen seconds – there is no time to discover that you don't know where the emergency exits are situated. Learning about what to do in an emergency should reduce fear, not increase it.

Relaxation

One way of coping with fear of flying (at least in the short term) is to learn how to relax. In fact, in-flight alcohol, movies, reading material and taped music are all conducive to relaxation.

If these are not sufficient to distract you, some airlines conduct programmes for those they call 'fearful flyers'. These seminars consist of recorded tapes offering advice on relaxation techniques, statistical information on how safe it really is, group discussions where everyone is encouraged to discuss their fears and recorded simulations of the sounds to be expected in flight. Familiarization is the key concept behind all of these behaviourist therapy programmes; instruction in rhythmic deep breathing and sometimes even hypnosis can assist the person in learning to control his or her physical signs of anxiety. A graduate of one of these programmes confirmed its beneficial effects: 'I enjoyed the course, especially sharing my misgivings with other people and discovering I wasn't alone with my fears. At the end of the course, we actually went up on a one-hour flight and I was able to apply all the techniques I had learned. In fact, I actually managed to enjoy the flight – something I would not have ever believed I could do.'

A certain amount of anxiety about flying is to be expected. For most people, a long distance flight is not something one does every day. On the other hand, there is always a first time for everyone, even those who have chosen to make flying their career. The more you fly, the more likely you are to come to terms with your fears. Some anxiety is inevitable, but in the case of flying, the statistics are on your side.

Getting There By Road

Overland by Truck or Van

by Simon Glen and Jack Jackson

Travelling overland in your own vehicle gives you independence, freedom to go where you like and when you like, and a familiar bolthole away from the milling crowds and the alienation one invariably feels in a different culture. The vehicle may seem expensive to start with and can involve you in mountains of bureaucratic red tape, but when one takes into consideration the cost of transport and accommodation, it begins to become more realistic, particularly if you can escape the bed bugs and filth that often seem to accompany the cheapest accommodation.

Which Vehicle?

The choice of a vehicle is often a problem. Everyone has to make a compromise between what they can afford, what can best handle the terrain to be encountered and whether all spares and fuel need to be carried or are available en route. A Land or Range Rover is superb in the sands of the Sahara's Bilma Erg, for example, but it is impossible to sleep full length without the tailgate open and all the stores, fuel and water removed. Moreover, they are very fond of petrol. After a while, one longs for the con-venience and comfort of the Volkswagen Kombi. Renault 4 or Citroen 2CV panel vans are even more cramped than the Rovers, but are far more economical to buy, run and repair.

For a protracted transcontinental or round-the-world journey, you need to consider first what sacrifices have to be made in order to have the advantages of the more cramped vehicles; secondly, the length of time you expect to be on the road; and third, the degree of home comforts you will want along the way.

If you do not plan to encounter soft sand, mud or snow and your payload is mostly people who, when necessary, can get out and push, then you really only need a two-wheel-drive as long as it is of the truck type with enough strength and ground clearance.

Where tracks are narrow, overhung and subject to landslides, such as in outlying mountainous regions like the Karakorams, then the only useable vehicles are the smallest, lightweight four-wheel-drives such as soft-topped Land Rover 88's and Jeep CJ5s. These vehicles also give the best performance when traversing soft sand and steep dunes, but their small payload and fuel carrying capacity restrict them to short journeys.

Avoid big American-style conver-sions. They have lots of space and other home comforts like showers, toilets, microwave ovens and loads of storage, but their fuel consumption, weight, low clearance, poor traction, very small front and rear approach and departure angles and sheer size make them most unsuitable for a journey off the beaten track.

If costs were no problem and all spares were to be carried the ideal vehicle would be a four-wheel-drive with a payload of one ton, evenly distributed between all four wheels, short wheelbase, forward control, high ground clearance, large wheels and tyres, good power to weight ratio and reasonable fuel consumption. The vehicles best fitting this specification are the Mercedes Unimogs, the Fiat PC65 and PC75 models and the Land Rover Military 101″ one tonne. All these are specialist vehicles for best cross-country performance and are soft-topped to keep the centre of gravity low. However, the costs involved in buying, running and shipping these would deter all but the exceptionally wealthy.

Taking into account price, availability of spares and working life, the most commonly used vehicles are the long wheelbased Land Rover, the smaller Mercedes Unimogs and the four ton Bedford M type trucks. For two-wheel-drives, the VW Type 2 Kombi and the Ford Transit (although the latter has problems with a very low front axle and inferior traction) are most popular. These are big enough to live in and carry food, water, spares, stoves, beds, clothes, extra fuel, sand ladders and two people in comfort, yet remain economical to run, small enough to negotiate narrow bush tracks and light enough to make debogging less frequent and easier.

A high-roofed vehicle is good to stand up in and provides extra storage, but is more expensive on ferries and ships. It also offers increased wind resistance, thus pushing up fuel consumption and making the engine work harder and hotter, shortening its life and increasing the risk of mechanical failure.

Unimogs

Where heavier payloads are envisaged, such as in Africa where you will often have to carry large stores of spare fuel, the most popular four-wheel-drive vehicles are the Bedford M type trucks and Mercedes Unimogs. Bedford Trucks are cheap, simple, and in some parts crude. They have good cross-country performance when handled sensibly and slowly, but are too heavy for soft sand. They go wrong often, but repairs can usually be improvised.

Ex-NATO Mercedes Unimogs are near to perfect for heavy overland or expedition work. Their cross-country performance is exceptional, their portal axles give them extra ground clearance, though this also makes them easier to turn over. It is almost impossible to get them stuck in sand, though they will stick in mud. Ex-NATO Unimogs usually have relatively small petrol engines, so you need to use the gearbox well, but fuel consumption is good. The standard six-speed, one-range gearbox can be altered to a four-speed, low-range gearbox, which is useful in sand. Four-wheel-drive can be engaged at any speed without declutching. Diff locks are standard. The chassis is cleverly arranged to give good weight distribution over all four wheels at almost any angle, but gives a bad ride over corrugations.

Mechanically, the Unimog is over-complicated. It doesn't go wrong often, but when it does, it is difficult to work on and needs many special tools. Later models have the clutch set to one side of the transmission, instead of in line with it, making it much easier to change.

Unimogs are best bought from NATO forces in Germany. Spares must be carried with you. Diesel Unimogs are usually ex-agriculture or building contractor and are therefore less well maintained than forces vehicles.

Land Rovers

Despite some weaknesses, Land Rovers are the most durable and reliable four-wheel-drive small vehicles on the market. Their spartan comforts are their main attributes; most of their recent challengers are too softly sprung and have too many car-type comforts to have any real reliability in hard, cross-country terrain. There are also plenty of spare parts available worldwide and they are easy to work on because everything bolts on. The aluminium alloy body does not rust, so the inevitable bent body panel can be hammered back into rough shape and then forgotten. You don't have to be Hercules to change a wheel.

No vehicle will remain in mint condition after cross-country use, but in the UK at least, Land Rovers can currently be resold after a year's hard work for a thoroughly respectable proportion of the original price.

The short wheelbase is usually avoided because of its small load-carrying capacity, but in off-road use, particularly on sand dunes, it has a dis-tinct advantage over the long wheelbase models. Hard-top models are best for protection against thieves and safer when rolled unless you have had roll bars fitted.

When considering long wheelbase models, it is best to avoid the six-cylinder models, including the one ton and the forward control. All of these cost more to buy, give more than the normal amount of trouble, are harder to find spares for and recoup less on resale.

The six-cylinder engine uses more fuel and more engine oil than the four-cylinder engine and the carburettor does not like dust or dirty fuel, which means that it often needs to be stripped and cleaned twice a day in very dusty areas. The electrical fuel pump always gives trouble. The forward control, which is now discontinued, except in Spain, turns over very easily and, as with the six-cylinder, Series I and Series IIA Land Rovers, rear half shafts break very easily if the driver is at all heavy-footed.

It is generally agreed that the four-cylinder models are under-powered, but the increased power of the six-cylinder does not compensate for its dis-advantages.

The V8 Land Rover has continuous four-wheel-drive and differential lock, which on tests in Africa have proved to reduce petrol consumption in sand and save on wear and tear on suspension over corrugations, owing to improved pace. There is only one major drawback: there is no room to fit jerry can brackets in the front, and rear brackets tend to put undue stress on the back panels.

The Land Rover 110's are designed for speed, economy and comfort on the newer, improved roads in Africa and

Asia. Built on a strengthened Range Rover type chassis and suspension with permanent four-wheel-drive and centre differential lock, stronger gearbox, disc brakes on the front and better doors all round, the vehicle is a vast improvement on earlier models. It is ideal for lightweight safari or personnel carrier use, but for heavy expedition work, the difficulty in uprating coil springs could easily prove to be a major drawback.

Military Land Rovers will continue to be of the leaf spring Series 111 type, so spares for these will be most widely available worldwide.

The current Range Rover is not spacious enough nor has it the load carrying capacity for use on major journeys.

Basically, any hard top or station wagon Land Rover will suit you if you do not intend to go off the road much when heavily loaded. If you buy a new Land Rover, run it for a few months before setting off on a trip. This allows the wet weather to get at the hundreds of nuts and bolts which keep the body together. If bolts rust in a bit, it will save you a lot of time later on. If you take a brand new Land Rover into a hot climate, you will regularly have to spend hours tightening nuts and bolts that have come loose, particularly those around the roof and windscreen.

Early Land Rover diesel engines were not renowned for their reliability. The new five-bearing crankshaft diesel engines are better but still under-powered. Land Rover Ltd still refuse to believe that the Third World requires a large, trouble-free diesel engine, and it is sometimes more sensible to fit another engine such as the Isuzu 3.9 litre or the Perkins 4,203 or 4,154.

Kombis

The Volkswagen Kombi, Bus or Type 2 can be seen in use in almost every country outside the Soviet bloc and China. Anyone who has travelled overland through Africa, Asia, the Americas, or around Australia will have to agree the VW Kombi is, without doubt, the most popular independent traveller's overland vehicle. Its ability to survive misuse (up to a point), carry heavy loads over rough terrain economically, and at the same time provide the privacy of a mobile home are some of the factors which make it so popular. Moreover, it is one of the few forward control vans in the world to pass strict US Dept of Transport crash tests in which the driver and front seat passenger can expect to survive a 52 kmph head-on collision if seat-belted.

The Kombi has a one-tonne load and far more living space in it than a long wheelbase Land Rover or Land Cruiser. It lacks the four-wheel-drive capability but partly makes up for it with its robust independent suspension, high ground clearance and engine weight over the driven wheels. With experience and astute driving, a Kombi can be taken to places that will amaze some four-wheel-drive pundits. The notorious 25km 'sea of sand' between In Guezzam and Assamaka in the Sahara has ensnared many a Land Rover for hours while Kombis have stormed through unscathed in minutes.

The Kombi suspension and chassis are very strong and have a reputation equal to that of the Land Rover, Land Cruiser, Peugot 404 and 504, and Citroen 2CV for taking punishment in rough conditions as well as for surviving protracted owner neglect and abuse. The alloy engines are similarly reliable and resistant to neglect. Being air-cooled they have no radiators, hoses and water-pumps to corrode or water passageways to freeze up or clog up with mineral deposits. They are low-stressed engines that are simple to maintain and easy to understand. If in trouble, local knowledge in the ways of VW motors, spare parts, and expert service, can be found in almost every corner of the globe.

A Kombi is considerably cheaper to run than petrol-driven Land Rovers or Land Cruisers and probably the only reasonably sized four-wheel-drive vehicles able to match its fuel consumption are the four-cylinder Land Rovers and Toyota diesels. However, for the price of a basic new four-cylinder long wheelbase Land Rover without any extra equipment or conversion, one could have a new 1600 Kombi fully converted as a pop-top camper with jerrycans, sand ladders, spare parts etc.

Petrol Versus Diesel

Weight for weight, petrol engines have more power than diesel engines, but for hard usage in off-beat areas, they have several disadvantages. In hot countries, there is a considerable risk of fire and the constant problem of vapour lock, which is at its worst on steep climbs, or on long climbs at altitude. Dust, which often contains iron, gets into and shorts out the distributor. High tension leads break down and if much river crossing has to be accomplished, water in the electrics causes you more trouble. A further problem is that high-octane fuel is not usually available and low-octane fuel will soon damage a sophisticated engine. However, petrol engines are more easily repaired by the less experienced mechanic.

Diesel fuel does not have the fire risk of petrol and is usually about one-third of the price of petrol, outside Europe. It also tends to be more available, as it is used by trucks and tractors.

Diesel engines are heavier and more expensive to buy, but are generally more reliable and need less maintenance, though a more knowledgeable mechanic is required if they do go wrong. An advantage is that extra torque is available at low engine revolutions. This allows a higher gear in the rough, which improves fuel consumption, which means less weight of fuel needs to be carried for a section without fuel supplies – and this improves fuel consumption still further. There is also no electrical ignition to malfunction where there is a lot of dust or water. Against this is the fact that diesel engines are considerably louder than petrol ones which can be bad for morale on a long, tiring trip.

A second filter in the fuel line is essential to protect the pump from bad fuel in the Third World. A water sedimentor is useful, but needs to be well protected from stones and knocks.

Tyres

Long-distance travellers usually have to cover several different types of terrain, which makes it difficult to choose just one set of tyres suitable for the whole route. Unless you expect to spend most of your time in mud or snow, you should avoid the aggressive tread, so-called cross-country or all-terrain tyres. These have a large open cleated tread which is excellent in mud or snow, but on sand they tear away the firmer surface crust, putting the vehicle into the softer sand underneath. These open treads also tear up quickly on mixed ground with sharp stones and rocks.

If you expect to spend a lot of time in soft sand, you will need high flotation tyres with little tread pattern which tend to compress the sand, causing least disturbance to the firmer surface crust. Today's standard for such work is the Michelin XS, which has just enough tread pattern to be useable also on dry roads. These, however, are dangerous on wet roads or ice. The XS is a soft flexible radial tyre, ideal for low pressure sand use but easily cut up on sharp stones.

As most travellers cover mixed ground, they need a general truck type tyre. These have a closed tread with enough tyre width and lugs in the outside of the tread to be good mixed country tyres, although obviously not as good in mud or soft sand. Such tyres, when fitted with snow chains, are as good as any all-terrain tyre for snow or mud use and, if of radial construction, can be run soft to improve their flotation on sand. The best tyre in this category is the Michelin XZY series.

Radial or Cross Ply?

Radial tyres are more flexible and have less heat build-up when run soft in sand than cross-ply tyres. They also have less rolling resistance, thus improving fuel consumption. For heavy expedition work, Michelin steel braced radials are preferable. With radial tyres you must have the correct inner tubes, preferably by the same manufacturer. Radial and cross-ply tyres should not be mixed.

Radial tyres 'set' in use, so when changed around to even out tyre wear, they should preferably be kept on the same side of the vehicle. A further advantage of radials is that they are easier to remove from the wheel rim with tyre levers, when you get punctures away from help.

Radial tyres have soft side walls which are easily torn on sharp stones, so if you have to drive over such stones, try to use the centre of the tyre, where the tread is thickest.

For soft sand use, radial tyres can be run at 40 per cent pressure at speeds below ten miles an hour and 75 per cent pressure for mixed terrain below 20 miles per hour. Remember to reflate to full pressure as soon as you return to firm ground.

Tubeless tyres are totally impracticable for this type of work, so always use tubed tyres and carry several spare inner tubes.

A vehicle travelling alone in bad terrain should carry at least one spare tyre beside the one on the spare wheel. Several vehicles travelling together should all have the same types of tyres for full inter-changeability.

Conversions

An elevating roof or fibreglass 'pop-top' campervan conversion has several advantages over a fixed roof van. Not only is it lower, but it can sleep extra people upstairs (eg children) provide extra headroom while camped, and insulate well in tropical heat. Some well-designed fibreglass pop-tops do not collect condensation even when you cook inside them when the roof is laden with snow. Some of the disadvantages are that they can, in extreme cases, be easier to break into; they look more conspicuous and more inviting to thieves than a plain top; and they have to be retracted before a driver, disturbed in the night, can depart in a hurry.

In some vans, the hole cut in the roof will actually weaken the structure of the vehicle. The ordeal of driving through Africa, especially, will cause structural failures and cracks in the body and chassis – failures that would not normally occur if the vehicle spent its life in Europe. Vans such as all VWs, the Toyota Hiace, Ford Transit and Bedford CR should all have room-mounted support plates added along with the pop-top to give torsional support to the chassis. The roof is not an integral part of the structure of the Land Rover and cutting a hole in it does not affect the chassis.

A demountable caravan fitted to four-wheel-drive pick-ups like the Land Rover, Land Cruiser or Toyota Hi-Lux could provide a lot more room and comfort, but demountables are not generally robust enough to stand up to the off-road conditions of an overland journey through Africa. They also add considerably to the height and width of the vehicle and are altogether more expensive than a proper conversion. Moreover you cannot walk through from the cab to the living compartment.

In deserts, if one doesn't have a campervan, sleeping on the roof-rack can be a most pleasant way of keeping cool and avoiding spiders and scorpions. 'Air Camper' folding roof-rack tents offer these advantages but they can also be miserably cold in some climates and make one vulnerable to thieves and other ill-intentioned people.

Furnishings and Fittings

Preferably camper conversions should have furniture made of marine plywood rather than particle board, as it is stronger, more durable, lighter and not prone to disintegration when wet. If your vehicle is finally destined for the US, it must satisfy US Dept of Transport and State regulations for the basic vehicle and the conversion. The same applies to campervans destined permanently for Australia where equally strict Australian Design Rules apply to both the vehicle and the conversion.

Most water filtration systems (eg Katadyn) are portable, though Safari (Water Treatments) Ltd produce a wall-mounted model which can be fitted to a campervan. On many campervans, the water tank and even a gas bottle are mounted beneath the floor where they are most vulnerable away from made-up roads.

Front opening quarter vents in the front doors are sometimes most appreciated in warm climates as are a pair of fans built into the through-flow ventilation system. However, front quarter vents can be attractive to thieves. Fresh air is essential when sleeping inside a vehicle in tropical lands and a roof vent is just not enough to create an adequate draught. Louvred windows provide the answer. Equip them also with mosquito gauze and, because they are louvred, they can be left wide open even in heavy rain allowing a draught of cool air without admitting either mosquitos or thieves.

Having up-to-date information along the route can be a big help, forewarning you of riots, floods, cyclones, earthquakes, revolutions, strikes, currency problems and fuel shortages. A dash-board mounted short-wave radio will enable you to listen to the excellent services of BBC World Service, Voice of America and other international stations.

On a long transcontinental journey, one will normally have to do without a fridge. (It is often preferable to use the space and weight for more fundamental items like jerry cans or spare parts). However, if you are carrying large quantities of film or medicines, one could consider one of the tiny, lightweight, dry-operating, thermoelectric 'Peltier-Effect' fridges (Koolatron Industries), a product of American aerospace technology.

Roof-racks

These need to be strong to be of any use. Many of those in the market are flimsy and will soon break up on badly corrugated piste. Weight for weight, tubular section is always stronger than box section and it should be heavily galvanised.

To extend a roof-rack to put jerry cans of water or petrol over or even beyond the windscreen is absolute lunacy. The long wheelbase Land Rover, for instance, is designed so that most of the weight is carried over the rear wheels. The maximum extra weight allowed for in front is the spare tyre and a winch. It does not take much more than this to break the front springs or even the axle. In any case, forward visibility is impossible when going downhill with such an extended roof-rack. A full-length roof-rack can be fitted safely but it must be carefully loaded. And remember that Land Rover recommend a total roof weight of not more than 90kg and a good full-length rack will weigh almost that on its own.

Expect damage to the bodywork and reinforce likely points of stress. A good design will also have its supports positioned in line with the main body supports. It will also have fittings along the back of the vehicle to prevent it from juddering forward on corrugated roads. Without these fittings, holes will be worn in the roof.

Nylon or terylene rope is best for tying down baggage as hemp rope doesn't last too well in the sun. Hemp is also hard on the hands from all the absorbed dust and grit. Rubber roof-rack straps are useful, but those sold in Europe soon crack up in the sun. You can use circular strips from old inner tubes and add metal hooks to make your own straps. These will stand up to the constant sunlight without breaking.

Other Extras

Stone-guards for lights are very useful, but you need a design which allows you to clean the mud off the lights without removing them (water hoses do not usually exist off the beaten track) and such a design is hard to find. Air horns must be fitted in such a location that the horns do not fill with mud, eg on the roof or within the body. Horns can be operated by a floor-mounted dip-switch. An isolator may be located on the dashboard to prevent accidental operation of the horn.

A good powerful spotlight fitted on the rear of the roof-rack will be invaluable when reversing and will also provide enough light for pitching a tent. Normal reversing lights will be of no use.

Finally, whatever type of vehicle you take and however you equip it, you should aim to be as self-sufficient as possible. You should have food to last for weeks, not days, clothing to suit the changing climatic and social conditions, and the tools, spare parts and personal ability to maintain your vehicle and keep it going. Without these, and in spite of the occasional, genuinely kind person, you will be conned, jilted and exploited to the extent that the journey will be a major ordeal. With adequate care and preparation, your overland journey will be one of the most pleasurable experiences of a lifetime.

Buying and Selling a Car Abroad

by Paul Melly

Who wants to get rid of a car in Jakarta?

Well, if you've just spent seventeen weeks driving all the way from London, there's a fair chance that a plane, at seventeen hours, will seem much the most attractive mode of travel back home. Or, you may plan to fly on to Australia.

Either way, if you do sell a car or camper van, make sure that anybody who could be affected knows what you've done. Whether you think you still own the vehicle is merely the first stage. The important thing is to be certain that the authorities both where you bought it and where you sell it understand the position. What you have to tell them partly depends on

where you bought the vehicle and what its status is.

Buying

Traditionally, the favoured marketplace for those planning long overland trips, especially Australians and New Zealanders, is a car park near Waterloo Station and the Festival Hall on the South Bank of the Thames in London. On Fridays, Saturdays and Sundays, this is busy with travellers haggling over battered camper vans, many of them various conversions of VW Kombis.

Prices can range from several hundred to several thousand pounds, with £1200 as average, but real bargains are becoming fewer as dealers begin to muscle in on the market. Many vehicles are actually registered on the continent, with some of the cheapest coming from the Netherlands. Provided the car is not kept in the UK for more than twelve months at a stretch – unlikely if you are buying it specially for a trip – you do not need to incur the costs of UK registration.

However, many of those sold at Waterloo have already done a huge mileage and, although there may be nothing obviously wrong with them, vital parts can be almost worn out, landing you with hefty repair bills soon afterwards.

A more reliable option can be the normal secondhand market – classified adverts, car auctions and so on. *Complete Car Auction* magazine gives information on sales all over the UK together with guideline prices. Of course, a vehicle bought this way will probably be registered in the UK.

Obviously, tyres, brakes and suspension should be checked wherever you buy. But, if a long trip is planned through countries where spares will be hard to get, it is worthwhile investing in a professional check over the vehicle – the AA charges around £35-40 for this. After all, even if the seller does provide some kind of guarantee, you're going to have difficulty enforcing it in Kurdistan or Mizoram.

Insurance

Before leaving, it is also essential, if you can, to get full details of the vehicle registration rules for any country you could be passing through. These are often available from tourist offices or embassies. Insurance cover providing for at least local vehicle recovery is also a good idea. If you should have an accident or breakdown and decide to abandon the car altogether, there is much less chance of slipping away unnoticed with your battered suitcases than in the days before computers made police and governments across the world more inquisitive, or at least more efficient at being inquisitive.

Insurance can be expensive, but it probably won't be as expensive as the fine or recovery fee you may end up having to pay a foreign government or embassy for leaving them to clear away what was left of your camper van.

The AA and RAC have cooperation deals with their European counterparts, but once you've crossed the Bosphorous, Mediterranean or South Atlantic, you will probably have to turn to someone offering worldwide cover such as Europ Assistance (252 High Street, Croydon CR0 1NF, UK).

When you come to sell at the other end of the journey, immediately contact the insurers to cancel the balance of insurance time remaining, for which you should get a rebate.

Before leaving you should take two photocopies of all your motoring documents – proving insurance registration, ownership, road tax, and if applicable, MOT, together with your passport. You should keep the originals with you, keep one copy in a locked compartment in the vehicle and deposit one copy with the bank or a PO Box number at home where it can be checked out if necessary. This should help you to prove ownership if the police in any country or the insurance authorities require it.

The papers will also be useful when it comes to selling the car – showing that you own it and are therefore entitled to sell.

Selling

When you sell, it is vital to make sure that the transaction is recorded in the presence of a witness who can be easily contacted later if necessary. Motoring journalist Brian Charig recalls the case of an American student who found a garage willing to buy his camper van in India. There it was actually the customer who asked the manager of the hotel where the student had just paid his bill with an American Express card (which is traceable) to witness the deal formally. They wanted to be protected in case something went wrong.

Written proof of sale is a safeguard against someone else committing a motoring offence, or even using the car for a serious crime, after you have sold it. You can demonstrate to the local police that it was nothing to do with you. In fact, it is best to tell the police anyway when you sell the car.

One final point: when you sell your

car you hope to keep, or spend, all the money you are paid for it. So it is vital to make sure the contract of sale stipulates that the local buyer will meet the cost of all taxes, import duties or other official fees involved. When a foreigner sells a vehicle to a local that normally constitutes an import, so be certain the price you agree is net of all Customs dues, sales tax etc. And, before you leave home, check (anonymously) with the embassy of the country where you plan to sell as to how the deal will be viewed by officials. If they record the fact that you bring in a car on your passport or entry document, the people checking you out at the airport Customs or Passport Control may well want to know what you have done with it.

There are one or two legal ways to beat the import duties, which can be as much as 400 per cent of the value of the vehicle. If you have owned the car for at least a year, plan to own it for another two, and it is the first you have imported into that country, you can normally take it in duty free. If the buyer is remaining in the country, they could leave it in your name for the required two years. Only do this however if you know the buyer well enough, either personally or by repute, to ensure that they are trustworthy. Or you can legally sell it in the zone between two borders, although this would mean the buyer would have to have access to free passage of a fairly large sum of money across the borders. Or you can sell it to another traveller, diplomat or foreign resident who is, for whatever reason, not bound by local laws. But you may well find that in many countries, such as Zimbabwe, while foreign currency is in desperately short supply, there is no shortage of local currency, and buyers will be queuing, even with the high price demanded by the duties, for vehicles such as Land Rovers in a good state of repair.

Using the Money

A further factor to bear in mind, which could influence your choice of country to sell in, is currency status and regulations. Many, but by no means all, Third World countries have a currency which is not internationally exchangeable and a large number of these have controls on what you can take out in both local money and foreign exchange.

So ideally choose a country which has an internationally convertible currency, such as the Singapore Dollar, or the CFA (African franc, underwritten by the Bank of France). That way, if you do take the payment for the car out you will be able to change it into money you can spend at home such as sterling or dollars. Or you may even be able to buy western currency in a local bank.

If you cannot plan to land up in a hard currency nation, find out what the local exchange control rules are. Otherwise you may find that you cannot take money out in either cash or traveller's cheques, local or foreign. Many countries are so short of hard currency they must restrict its use to buying essential imports, and these are unlikely to include fifth hand cars from foreign tourists. Even some countries which do have a convertible currency restrict what funds can be taken abroad.

The simplest answer is to check before you leave what you can buy with the local money – clearly food, souvenirs, and often hotel accommodation, sometimes even air tickets – and spend your takings on the spot. The problem is to guess how much you may be paid for the car.

But then, interesting travel is never without its complications.

PS. The career of the amateur currency smuggler is a hazardous one, especially if you aren't much good at telling lies. And Customs officers have a talent for mental arithmetic designed to catch you out as you try to persuade them you lived in their country for a week on £3.

Hiring a Car

by Paul Melly

First hire your car . . .

Yes, there are a lot of countries where it is a big advantage to have your own personal transport, especially if you must keep to a tight work schedule or have bulky luggage.

Yes, it is relatively easy to book in advance anything from a Fiesta to a limousine for a fair number of the world's destinations, including some which are surprisingly off-beat.

Yes, it can be very expensive – and certainly will be if the pre-departure homework is neglected. One journalist acquaintance, who thought he knew what travelling was about, managed to burn up £89 with a day and a half's car hire in Brittany by the time he'd paid all the extras.

The key rule is: don't just read the small print, work out what it actually adds up to. For example, a mileage charge really can rack up the cost, especially if you haven't measured in advance quite how far you will be travelling.

It's no use, after the event, holding a lifelong grievance against the big car hire companies. By and large they do fairly well in providing a comprehensive and reliable service in a wide range of countries, if at a price.

Travelling Cheaply

If you want a better deal, you must expect to work for it and be prepared to tramp the backstreets looking for a local outfit that is halfway trustworthy. It costs Hertz, Avis, Europcar and Budget and the rest a hefty investment to provide that easy-to-book, uniform service across national frontiers and linguistic boundaries. Centralised computer-based reservation networks don't come free.

If you really want to keep the cost down, perhaps public transport is worth a fresh thought. Shared, long-distance taxis or minibuses are surprisingly fast and cheap in many parts of the Third World and, using them, you may have an easier time with police, army or Customs road checks, which have a habit of springing up every few kilometres in some countries. If it's not you who is driving, then it's not you – foreign and unfamiliar with the local situations – who has to judge whether it is correct paperwork or a small bribe that is required. Quite apart from the ethical dilemma, there is the practical one: having to pay back-handers is bad, offering them when they are not expected is worse and can get you into far more trouble.

However, it would be stupid to allow such worries to discourage travellers from doing the adventurous thing, and hiring a car can give you the freedom to go where you want at your own pace, stopping in small villages or at scenic viewpoints when it suits you.

The big car hire firms give thorough coverage of much of the developed world and quite a number of tourist and/or business destinations in other regions. But they certainly do not have outlets everywhere and there are many places where you will have to rely on local advice in finding a reliable rental outfit. Advance reservation before you arrive may well be impossible. In this case, one option, if your time is tight, could be to ask friendly officials in the country's embassy in your home country for suggestions. Most will have a telephone directory for their capital city at least, even if it is a little out of date.

For a few pounds, you can then ring to book in advance – or just to check availability – easier, of course, if the country is on direct dialling. This could well be more effective than asking a small High Street travel agent used to selling Mediterranean package tours to try and arrange something for you. It is also worth contacting agencies which specialise in a particular region of the world – perhaps the people who arranged your half-price, bucket-shop ticket.

For most places, it is still definitely worth considering the big hire companies. In recent years they have developed a good range of lower price services to complement the plusher luxury options for those with fat expense accounts. Thanks both to the recession and the growing interest small firms are taking in foreign markets, there are plenty of businessmen who cannot afford to travel five star all the time.

And, though you may be abroad for work, very often you can, with forethought, make use of the special packages designed for tourists. Not only are these cheaper, but they also have the advantage of simplicity, being tailored to the needs of leisure visitors who are either not used to or do not want to be bothered with organising everything for themselves.

Meanwhile, if you are going on holiday, there is something to be learnt from those who have to travel for work, or from their companies. Clearly, big firms have buying power in the car hire market which a private individual does not, but they also pick up a lot of experience.

Here are some useful tips suggested by the travel manager of one multinational company: read the small print, get your insurance, avoid mileage payments and large cars, and watch out for the chance to save money on the pre-booked deal.

Price, in particular, takes some calculation because of the extras which are hard to evaluate exactly. Car hire is sometimes offered per mile or per kilometre, but it is best to go for an unlimited mileage deal, even if the base price is slightly higher. While you cannot be sure how much petrol you will use or how much you will pay for it, at least it is fixed what actually hiring the car for, say, six days will cost you in local currency.

Legalities

There is room for savings on insurance too if you arrange your own. Car hire forms always include some reference to Collision Damage Waiver (CDW) and Personal Accident (PA). A customer can be held responsible for a share of loss or damage to the hire vehicle, regardless of who is at fault. But if you accept the CDW clause and pay the daily charge for it, the rental company waives this liability for damage caused by collision or roll-over, provided the customer sticks within the conditions of the hire agreement.

Clearly if you rent a car, you must be insured against damaging it, and, more importantly, any other people or vehicles. But accepting the CDW option can prove an expensive form of protection – sometimes up to £5 per day.

So it is essential to explore other possibilities. Your own personal car insurance at home may provide cover or you may be able to get it built into your travel insurance. Those going abroad for work will often find that their company policy provides all the protection necessary, or at least includes Third Party cover.

Another legal aspect it is vital to check is whether the hire agreement allows you to drive where you want. This may seem an irrelevant point to make for anyone restricting themselves to Europe, but it is a key question if you are visiting the developing world, or even, for example, the more rural corners of Canada.

If the conditions insist you stick to metalled roads, that may severely limit your freedom to get, quite literally, off the beaten track. And yet you may only have decided to hire a car in the first place because you wanted to get away from the main routes.

Driving Conditions

Perhaps this is the place to warn that roads in many countries make quite a change from Britain's consistent, if occasionally pot-holed or contra-flowed tarmac. Clearly a good map, if you can buy one, is indispensable. But it is unlikely to give you the up-to-date or seasonal information you really need before setting out.

Many highways are actually made of dirt or gravel and can become almost impassable at rainy times of year. If they are major trading routes this can be made even worse as huge trucks lurch through the mud, cutting deep wheel ruts which fill with water. Maps will not always show the state of the roads, or what they are made of.

Of course, in the dry season, such routes may be dusty, but they become much easier to use.

In some areas, where the vegetation is fairly stunted, lack of tarmac can make it quite hard to follow where the road actually goes.

Nor do these warnings go for tropical countries alone: the famed Alaska Hi-way from Dawson Creek in Canada through to Fairbanks is largely gravel surfaced. And many minor roads in Canada turn into muddy bogs, with cars sinking up to their axles in black gumbo when it rains. The worst time of year can be the spring thaw – just when a European visitor might be expecting conditions to get easier!

Meanwhile, if you are likely to drive through mountains, including the relatively domesticated Alps and Pyrenees, make sure your car is equipped with snow tyres, or has chains, and you know how to put them on. The Alps may be crossed by motorways and tunnels, but that does not stop winter blizzards. Nor does it stop the local police from making spot checks – and spot fines – on roads where chains or snow tires are obligatory (normally indicated by a sign as you enter the relevant stretch). This advice applies particularly to people who go on business in winter to cities near the mountains and decide to hire a car and pop up the hill for a day's skiing – your tyres may feel OK in downtown Turin, but it's not so sure you'll still feel confident in a traffic queue on the nineteenth ice-covered hairpin bend up to the ski resort, with no room to turn round.

You should also check about road construction, especially in the Third World, where massive foreign aid spending can make it happen all of a sudden on a huge scale.

This may sometimes cause a mess, but it can also mean a new hard-top road existed where there was only a mud-track before, opening up fresh areas for relatively easy exploration with a normal hired saloon car. On the other hand, there can be surprising gaps in otherwise fairly good networks.

By mid-1986, the tarmac on the main North-South highway in Côte d'Ivoire had still only reached the outskirts of Ferkessédougou, the last important town before the frontier with Burkina Faso. Once across the border bridge in Burkina the blacktop started again, but to get there meant a rough and muddy six hours' drive from Ferké.

The basic rule is: before you do something unusual, tell the car hire outlet where you picked up the vehicle and signed it out. Avis, for one, says that if the normal road network in a country is poor, it is assumed that anyone hiring a car will still use it. Equally, chains and a roof-rack for skis will be provided if there are mountains nearby. But you must check first with the hire firm if you plan to stray off the tar, because the details of contract conditions can vary. And if you should have an accident or break down, telephone the hire firm before paying for expensive repairs. Otherwise you may not be reimbursed. The firm may want to make its own arrangements.

What Car?

Deciding what size of car to hire is one of the simplest questions. The main firms use fairly standard brands with which you will probably be familiar at home, though it is probably safe to say that you are rather more likely to get a Japanese make in Asia, a French in West Africa, and an American in the US. But when working out costs, don't forget that larger vehicles are also thirstier.

You should remember this especially when booking in advance – sometimes the rental deal will stipulate that if the car of your choice is not available then the agency will provide one in a higher category for no extra charge. In other words, if you reserve a small car and then turn up to find it isn't there, you may end up with one that uses far more petrol – an expensive penalty if you are hiring it for a long trip. So if you hold a firm booking for a Ford Fiesta or Renault 5 size car, that's what you should insist on.

Nor should petrol bills be forgotten when you return the vehicle. Most agreements stipulate that the car is provided with a tankful of fuel and returned topped up. Check that it is full before you take it out and make the final fill-up yourself. You will probably pay less than the hire office would charge for doing it on your behalf.

Reservation in advance is usually worth consideration, not just for peace of mind but because you may get a discount of up to 30 per cent on the hire charge if you book before leaving home. This is especially true if you buy one of the special holiday packages offered by the big groups. Hertz, for example, has a whole range branded as 'Affordable' Asia, Africa, Pacific Islands etc. And these cover a surprisingly wide range of countries, not just the biggest tourist destinations.

There is rarely a penalty if you fail to take up a booking, though of course, you may have needlessly prevented someone else who really would have used the car from reserving.

If you are not sure whether to rent or not, it is possible to buy vouchers in advance, valid for so many days hire of a specified grade of vehicle. Once on the spot and able to check on public transport alternatives you can decide whether to use them or not. This does not give you the security of a reservation, but it can enable you to try for further savings, provided your bank account will stand the cost of the vouchers until you return home and cash them in (they are normally fully refundable). Then when you arrive abroad, ask for tips about reliable hire deals – the hotel porter is often a good source of advice.

Another way of getting the price below that officially quoted by the sales office of a big rental firm back home is to go and see the local outfit without revealing that you have vouchers in your pocket. Their own special offers can be much more attractive than those quoted by the parent franchising company back home and according to which the vouchers for hire time are priced. This way you get the reliable vehicles and maintenance standards of the big names, but at bargain rates.

The big groups claim to offer the same level of service whether through their own offices or franchisees. In some Third World countries, however, new cars are far more valuable than gold dust, the roads are far heavier on wear and tear, and local drivers lack finesse. You will always be given the best possible option available, but it might not always match up.

One option for cutting costs and red tape if you are staying somewhere for a lengthy period, or regularly visit the same destination – perhaps you have a regional office there – can be leasing. This is normally provided for conventional business car fleets, but you may find that if you, or a group of people, regularly need a car in one place, a lease could be cheaper. It is also simple, because the deal can include repairs and service. Avis has recently introduced a budget option – 'Econolease' – under which you can get a much lower price, provided you accept a car which is four months old (having previously been used in the firm's normal rental). Though launched in the UK, there were hopes this deal could soon be extended abroad. However, lease contracts are usually for at least twelve months unless, as an existing regular customer, you can arrange a special short-term deal.

Safety

Of course, the bottom line when you hire a car is safety. Does the vehicle work and can you trust it?

Unless you are a natural, or at least good amateur, mechanic, there isn't much chance of really assessing whether the car is roadworthy. But one can make a few simple checks which are at least a pointer as to how well it's maintained.

Try the steering and test out the brakes by driving a few feet in the hire shop forecourt and of course listen for any faults in the first mile or two. Have a look at the tyre treads to see if they are still fairly deep and test the lights. If you are in a tropical country check the air-conditioning, if any, and in any very cold territory, such as Canada between October and April, be sure that it is winterised. Just because the first snow of autumn hasn't survived in the city centre doesn't mean it has melted in the surrounding countryside and suburbs too.

A rather more subtle approach and probably just as effective is recommended by the travel manager at a big oil company. Have a look in the rear seat ashtrays. If they are still stuffed with cigarette butts and rubbish it suggests the hire firm either hasn't had time or can't be bothered to check over the car thoroughly after the previous customer returned it. Then make sure that any faults such as bumps or scratches are detailed on the hire form before you take the car out. Otherwise you could find yourself held liable when you return it.

It is also a good idea to make sure you are allowed to use the car where you want to. Tell the hire firm if you plan to cross national borders, just to make sure the insurance cover extends across the frontier. And remember that while many discount rental deals allow you to drop the car off where you want in the country where you collected it, there is usually a surcharge for leaving it at one of the firm's offices in a completely different country.

Getting the right paperwork is also vital. Take photocopies of all hire agreements, insurance etc. as well as such basics as an International Driving Permit *(see article on Documentation for the International Motorist on page 246)*. And remember that in many countries travellers are expected to register with the local police on arrival in a town and stop at police posts by the roadside too. Often, as a foreigner, you may get less hassle than the locals. Though when it comes to frontiers, if the border is closed for the night, you will have to wait until morning to cross, even if there is no physical barrier in your way. Otherwise you could have problems when you come to leave and your passport lacks the proper entry stamps. Probably the only reliable way to check whether you're allowed across is to ask the drivers of local bush taxis which may have pulled in to wait for dawn.

In the end, when it comes to officialdom, patience and politeness are probably more important than anything else.

But first hire your car . . .

Off-Road Driving

by Jack Jackson

Off-road driving techniques vary with the ability and weight of the vehicle as well as the skill of the driver. Some vehicles have greater capabilities that many drivers can handle and may offer more than one solution to a problem. Taking a driver training course before you leave will educate you in the vehicle as well as your own strengths and is something I would strongly recommend. As four-wheel-drive is necessary in most off-road situations, I have biased this article towards this type of vehicle.

Before you do any off-road driving, look under your vehicle and note the position of its lowest points – springs, axles, differentials and gearbox. These will often be lower than you think and the differentials are usually off centre. Remember their clearance and position when traversing obstacles which you can't get round.

Alert but restrained driving is essential. A light foot and low gears will usually get one through soft or difficult ground. Sheer speed may sometimes be better, but if you lose control at speed you could suffer severe damage or injury. And don't hook your thumbs round the steering wheel. The sudden twist of the wheel when a front wheel hits a stone or rut can easily break them.

Scouting Ahead

Always travel at a sensible speed, keeping your eyes some twenty yards ahead, watching for difficulties. If you are on a track and another vehicle may come the other way, have a passenger keep a look out further ahead while you concentrate on negotiating the awkward areas. Travel only at speeds which allow you to stop comfortably within the limit of clear vision. Always travel slowly when approaching the brow of a hump or a sharp bend. There may be a large boulder, hole or sheer drop into a river bed behind it.

Most situations where four-wheel-drive is needed also require low range, which gives you better traction, torque and control. They will also normally require you to stop and inspect the route on foot first, so you will be able

to engage low range before starting off again. On soft sand, however, it is useful to be able to engage low range on the move. On some vehicles with non-synchromesh gears this requires double declutching. Practice before you go as being able to achieve this smoothly will usually save you from getting stuck. For most situations, first gear low range is too low, and you might spin the wheels. Use second or third gear, except over bad rocks.

With full-time four-wheel-drive systems, remember to engage lock before entering difficult situations. If you have been in four-wheel-drive on a hard surface, you may find that when you change to two-wheel-drive or unlock the centre differential lock this change and the steering are difficult. This is due to wind up between the axles, which will scrub tyres and damage the drive train. If you are lightly loaded, you can free this by driving backwards for about ten yards, whilst swinging the steering wheel from side to side. If, on the other hand, you are heavily loaded you will have to free it by jacking up one front wheel clear of the ground.

Don't drive on the outside edge of tracks with a steep drop, they may be undermined by water and collapse under the weight. If you have to travel along deep ruts, try to straddle one of the ruts rather than being in both with your transmission dragging the ground in the centre.

Ground Inspection

All difficult sections should be inspected on foot first. This can save you a lot of hard work getting unstuck later. If you are not sure of being able to see the route or obstacles clearly from the driving seat, get a passenger to stand in a safe place where he can see the problem and direct you. Arrange a system of hand signals beforehand, as vocal directions can be drowned by engine noise.

You might be faced with having to build up a route, putting stones or sand ladders across drainage ditches or weak bridges, chipping away high corners or levering aside large boulders. If you have to rebuild a track or fill in a hole completely, do so from above, rolling boulders down instead of wasting energy lifting them from below. Where possible bind them together by mixing with tree branches or bushes.

In Third World countries, always inspect local bridges before using them. If there are signs that local vehicles cross the river instead of the bridge, then that is the safest way to go.

If a rock suddenly appears and you cannot stop in time, hit it square on with a tyre, which is more resilient and more easily repaired than your undercarriage. To traverse large boulders, use first gear low range and crawl over, using the engine for both driving and braking. Avoid slipping the clutch or touching the brakes or you will lose control.

If you get stuck fast in a rut on firm ground, try rocking out by shifting from first to reverse gear. In sand or mud, however, this will only dig you in deeper. If you can't rock out, then jack up the offending wheel and fill up the rut with stones or logs. A high lift jack makes this much easier and can, with care, also be used to shunt a vehicle sideways out of the rut.

Slopes

When going downhill on a loose surface, it is essential to use four-wheel-drive low range with engine braking. Never touch the brakes or change gear or you will lose traction and could lose control. If you lose traction going up such a hill, try swinging the steering wheel from side to side – you may get a fresh bite and make the top. If you fail going up a steep hill, make a fast change into reverse, make sure you are in four-wheel-drive with the centre differential locked and use the engine as a brake to back down the same way you came up. Do not try to turn round or go down on the brakes. Always be prepared to stop quickly on the top of a hill or dune, the way down the other side may be at a completely different angle. Make use of the rhythm of suspension and touch the brakes as you approach the crest of a hump and release them as you pass over it to stop you from flying.

When you come to a sharp dip or rut, cross it at an angle, so that only one wheel dips into it at a time. Steer towards and over the terrain's high point to maintain maximum ground clearance. Also cross narrow river beds at an angle so that you don't get stuck in a dip at 90° with no room left for manoeuvre. *Do not* tackle steep hills diagonally; if you lose traction and slip sideways, you may turn over or roll to the bottom. Only cross slopes if absolutely necessary. If you must do so, take the least possible angle and make any turns quickly.

Crossing Water

Before crossing water, stop and inspect it first, if possible by wading through. Is the bottom solid or moving? Are there any large holes which must be filled in or driven round? Is there a sensible angle into it and out on the other side? Is there a current fast enough to necessitate your aiming upstream to get straight across? How deep is it? Will it come above the exhaust, cooling fan or vehicle floor? Four-wheel-drive vehicles should have poppet valves on the axle breathers, which will keep out water whilst the oils are hot and there is good pressure within, but if you get stuck under water for several hours, the axle oils will need to be changed. Some vehicles have a plug which should be screwed into the clutch housing when much work is done in water, but this should be removed as soon as possible afterwards.

If the water comes above the fan, then the fan belt should be disconnected. If the water comes above the floor, move any articles which could be damaged by it. Petrol engines should have plenty of ignition sealant around the coil, ignition leads and distributor.

Difficult or deep water should be crossed in low range four-wheel-drive, keeping the engine speed high. This keeps enough pressure in the exhaust to stop the back pressure of the water from stalling the engine, whilst the forward speed is not high enough to create a bow wave and spray water over the electrics. Diesel engines are a great advantage here. If you stall in the water, remove the spark plugs or injectors and try driving out in bottom gear on the starter motor. This works over short distances.

On easy crossings, keep the brakes dry by keeping the left foot lightly on the brake pedal. Once out of any water, dry out the brakes by driving a couple of miles this way. Disc brakes are self-cleaning, but drum brakes fill up with water and sediment, so should be cleaned regularly. Don't forget the transmission brakes on some vehicles.

A vehicle stuck in glacier melt water or sea water for more than a couple of hours will need very thorough washing and several oil changes to get rid of salt and silt. With salt water, electrical connections can be permanently damaged.

Sand

Sandy beaches are usually firm enough for a vehicle between high tide mark and four yards from the sea itself, where there is likely to be an undertow. Beware of the incoming tide, which is often faster than you envisaged and can cut you off from your point of exit. Where there are large puddles or streaming water on a sea beach, beware of quicksand.

The key to soft sand is flotation and steady momentum; any abrupt changes in speed or direction can break through the firmer surface crust, putting the wheels into the softer sand below. Use as high a gear as possible, so that you do not induce wheelspin. If you do not have special sand tyres, speed up as you approach a soft section and try to maintain an even speed and a straight line as you cross it. If you find yourself sticking, press down gently on the accelerator. If you have to change down, do it very smoothly to avoid wheelspin. In large soft sand areas, use flotation tyres and/or reduced tyre pressure and drive slowly in four-wheel-drive.

Do not travel in other people's tracks, the crust has already been broken and your vehicle's undercarriage will be that much lower, and therefore nearer to sticking to start with. Keeping your eye on other people's tracks will warn you of soft sections, but do not follow them for navigation, as they may be 50 years old.

In general, flat sand with pebbles or grass on its surface, or obvious wind blown corrugations, will support a vehicle. If in doubt, get out and walk the section first. Stamp your feet. If you get a firm footprint then it should support your vehicle, but if you get a vague oval, then it is too soft. If the soft section is short, you can make a track with sand ladders, but if it is long, then low tyre pressures and low range four-wheel-drive will be needed. Bedford four ton trucks will not handle soft sand without the assistance of sand mats and lots of human pushing power.

Dry river beds can be very soft and difficult to get out of. Drift sand will always be soft. If you wish to stop voluntarily on soft sand, find a place on top of a rise, preferably pointing downhill and roll to a stop instead of using the brakes and breaking the crust.

Many vehicles have too much weight on the rear wheels when loaded and these often break through and dig in, leaving the front wheels spinning uselessly on the surface. A couple of passengers sitting on the bonnet can help for short bad sections, but you must not overload the front continuously or you will damage the front axle.

Sand dunes need proper high flotation sand tyres; you need speed to get up a dune, but must be able to stop on the top, as there may be a sheer drop on the other side. Dunes are best climbed where the angle is least, so known routes in opposing directions are usually many miles apart, to make use of the easiest angles. In the late afternoon, when the sun is low, it is difficult to spot sudden changes in dune strata and many accidents occur with vehicles flying off the end of steep drops, so do not travel at this time of day. Most deserts freeze overnight in the winter months, making the surface crust much firmer. Even if they do not freeze, there is always some dew in the surface crust, making it firmest around dawn, so this is the time to tackle the softest sections. Local drivers often travel at night, but unless you know the route really well this will be too dangerous, so start at dawn and then camp around mid-afternoon before the light gets too difficult and the sand is at its softest.

In large sand dune areas when travelling longitudinally, stay as high up the dunes as possible, then if you feel your vehicle begin to stick, you can gain momentum by aiming downhill and try again. The bottom of the well between dunes usually has the softest sand.

Getting Unstuck in Sand

Once you are stuck in sand, do not spin the wheels or try to rock out as you will only go in deeper and may damage the transmission. First unload the passengers and with them pushing try to reverse out in low range. The torque on the propellor shafts tends to tilt the front and rear axles in opposite directions relative to the chassis. So, if you have not dug in too deep, when you engage reverse, you tend to tilt the axles in the opposite direction, thus getting traction on the wheels that lost it before. If you stopped soon enough in the first place, this technique will get you out. If it does not, then the only answer is to start digging and use sand ladders. It is tempting to do only half of the digging required, but this usually fails and you end up working twice as hard in the end. Self-recovery with a winch does not work well either. Sand deserts do not abound with trees and burying the spare wheel or a stake deep enough to winch you out is as hard as digging the vehicle out in the first place. A second vehicle on firm ground with a winch or tow rope can help, but you will have to dig out the stuck vehicle first, so resign yourself to some hard labour.

Long handled shovels are best – you have to get right under the diffs and small shovels and folding tools are useless. Recce the area and decide whether the vehicle must come out forward or backwards. Dig the sand clear of all points which are touching it, dig the wheels clear and then make a sloping ramp for all wheels to the surface in the intended direction of travel. Lay down sand ladders in the ramps by the back wheels only if things are not too bad, all four wheels if they are very bad. Push the ends of the ladders under the wheels as far as possible so that they do not shoot out. A high lift jack can help here. If you are using sand ladders as opposed to perforated steel plates, then mark their position in the sand with upright shovels as they often disappear in use and can be hard to find later. Then with only the driver in the vehicle and all passengers pushing, the vehicle should come out using low range. If the passengers are very fit, they can dig up the sand ladders quickly and keep placing them under the wheels of the moving vehicle. Sometimes, when a ladder is not properly under a wheel when the vehicle first mounts it, it can pop up and damage a body panel or exhaust pipe, so an agile person has to keep a foot on the free end to keep it down. Remember to move very quickly, once things are safe, though, or you'll get run over!

Bringing the vehicle out backwards is usually the shortest way to reach firm ground, but you still have to get across or around the bad section. Once out, the driver should not stop again until reaching firm ground, so the passengers may have a long, slow walk carrying the sand ladders and shovels. With a large convoy, a ramp of several ladders should be made up on bad sections.

Vehicles of one ton or under need only carry lightweight sand ladders, just long enough to fit comfortably between the wheel base. One vehicle alone needs to carry four, but vehicles in convoy need only carry two each, as they can help each other out. Heavier vehicles need to carry heavy perforated steel plate. It is silly to weigh down lightweight vehicles with this, as one often sees in Africa.

Sand ladders and perforated steel plate bend in use, so when you have finished all the soft sand sections, lay them on hard ground and drive over them to straighten them out.

Salt Flats (Sebkhas, Chotts) are like quick sand, you sink fast and if you cannot be towed out quickly, it can be permanent. In areas known for their salt flats, stick to the track and preferably convoy with another four-wheel-drive vehicle. If you are unlucky enough to hit one, try to drive back to firm ground in a wide arc. Do not stop and try to reverse.

Dirt Roads

On dirt roads, watch out for stones

thrown up by other vehicles (and in some countries, small boys), which break your windscreen. Do not overtake when you cannot see through the dust of the vehicle ahead, there may be something coming the other way. Use the horn to warn vehicles that you are about to overtake. If you cannot overtake, drop back clear of the other vehicle's dust. On dirt roads, culverts do not always extend to the full width of the road, so watch out for these when overtaking. Avoid driving at night. Potholes, culverts, broken down trucks, bullock carts and people are hard to see and many trucks drive at speed without lights and then blind you with full beam on spotting you. In many countries, there are unlit chains and logs across the roads at night as checkpoints.

Corrugations are parallel ridges across ungraded roads caused by the return spring rates of heavy traffic and, in really bad conditions, can be up to ten inches deep. They give an effect similar to sitting on a pneumatic drill to both the vehicle and its occupants. Heavy vehicles have no choice but to travel slowly, but lightweight vehicles often 'iron' out the bumps by finding the right speed to skim over the top of the ruts. This is usually 30-40mph, any faster can be dangerous. Going fast over corrugations increases tyre temperatures, thus causing more punctures. Softly sprung vehicles such as the Range Rover, Toyota Land Cruiser and American four-wheel-drives can go faster more comfortably on corrugations, but often blow tyres and, as a consequence end up turning over, usually with fatal consequences. Short wheelbase (i.e. less than a 100 inches) vehicles are very unstable on corrugations and often spin and turn

over. The only sensible answer is to travel at a reasonable speed, make regular stops to ease your growing frustration and be extra vigilant for punctures. One is often tempted to try travelling beside the corrugations, but remember that thousands of other vehicles have tried that before and given up – hence the corrugations. So take it steady and try to be patient.

Third World ferries should be embarked and disembarked in four-wheel-drive.

Mud

Momentum is also the key to getting through mud, but there are likely to be more unseen problems underneath the mud, than in sand. If it is not too deep, the wheels might find traction on firm ground beneath, so if there are existing tracks and they are not deep enough to ground your transmission in the centre, then such tracks are worth using. Otherwise, slog through in as high a gear as possible, as you would with sand, avoiding any sudden changes of speed or direction.

If the mud is heavy with clay, even aggressive tread tyres will soon clog up, so unless you are using self-cleaning mud tyres such as dumper tyres, or terra tyres, then you will gain a lot by fitting chains.

Muddy areas are likely to be near trees, one of the few areas where a winch is useful.

If you stick badly, digging out can be very heavy work. It is best to jack up the vehicle and fill in the holes under the wheels with stones, logs or bushes. A high lift jack can make things much easier here, but be careful of it slipping. If there is a lot of water, dig a channel to drain it away. Perforated steel plate can be useful in mud, but sand ladders become too slippery.

When you get back on the paved road, clear as much mud as possible off the wheels and propellor shafts, or the extra weight will put them out of balance and cause damage. Drive steadily for several miles to clear the tyre treads or you could skid.

If you are unlucky, you might get the centre of the vehicle's undercarriage stuck on rocks or a tree stump. The answer to this is to jack up one side of the vehicle and build a ramp under the wheels. If you cannot go forwards or backwards, unload the vehicle and use a high lift jack to lever the front and rear ends sideways, one end at a time. This is done by jacking up the vehicle at the centre of the front or rear bumper or chassis and then pushing it sideways off the jack. Beware of injury to yourself and check that the vehicle will not land in an even worse position before you do it.

Snow and Ice

Snow is the most deceptive surface to drive on because it does not always conform with the terrain it covers. If there is a road or track, stay in the middle of it to avoid sliding into ditches or culverts at the side. Drive slowly in four-wheel-drive, in as high a gear as is possible and avoid any sudden changes in speed or direction. Use the engine for braking. If you have to use the brakes, give several short pumps to avoid the wheels locking.

Snow chains are better than studded tyres for off-road use and should be either on all four wheels, or on the rear wheels only. Having chains on the front wheels will only put you into a spin if you touch the brakes going downhill. If the vehicle is empty, put a couple of hundredweight sacks of sand over the rear axle. Chains on all four wheels are the only sensible answer to large areas of ice.

If you drive into a drift, you will have to dig out and it is easiest to come out backwards. Off-road driving in snow will be easier at night, or in the early morning, when the snow is firmest and the mud below is frozen. As with sand, high flotation tyres are an advantage. If they are fitted with chains, they should be at the correct pressures, not at low pressures or the chains will damage them. Carry a good sleeping bag in case you get stuck, and have a long wait for help. Use only the strongest heavyweight chains; having to mend broken chains in freezing conditions is not a pleasant experience. If you start to spin, do not touch the brakes; depress the clutch, then, with all four wheels rolling free, you will regain the steering.

In very cold conditions, if you have a diesel engine, dilute the diesel fuel with one part petrol to fifteen parts diesel to stop it freezing up (use one to ten for arctic temperatures).

Convoy Driving

When travelling in convoy, it is best for the vehicles to be well spread out so that each has room to manoeuvre, does not get into other vehicles' dust, and has room to stop on firm ground should one or more vehicles get stuck.

It is good to use a system where any vehicle which gets stuck, or needs help, switches its headlights onto mainbeam. This is particularly important in desert situations. All drivers should keep an eye out for headlights in their mirrors, as these can usually be seen when the vehicle cannot. If the vehicle ahead of you is stuck, you will see when you catch it up anyway. Thus if someone is stuck, other vehicles stop where possible and return to help; on foot, if necessary, in soft sand. In a convoy situation, the rear vehicle should have a good mechanic and a good spare wheel and tyre, in case of breakdown.

Drivers should keep to the allotted convoy order to avoid confusion and unnecessary searches. In difficult terrain, the convoy leader should make stops at regular intervals to check that all is well with the other vehicles.

Notes

1. Air conditioning causes the radiator water temperature to rise. One way to create the opposite effect if the radiator temperature is getting too high is to turn on the heating – not very pleasant in tropical heat, but it may save your engine from blowing.
2. If you deflate the tyres for off-road driving, remember to reflate them again when you return to the highway. Don't deflate tyres too much off-road if the vehicle is heavy.
3. You should know the maximum weight supportable by each wheel at maximum tyre pressure. You should inflate the tyres below the maximum tyre pressure unless GVW is close to tyre maximum. The tyre manufacturer should supply a chart showing optimum pressure for different loads on different terrains (usually limited to on/off-road).
4. Never drive a deflated tyre over sharp rocks.
5. To get the correct tyre pressure, measure pressure when the tyres are cold before use.

6. Remember that the weight of one imperial gallon of petrol is around 4 kgs and the weight of one imperial gallon of water is around 4.5 kgs. These figures are extremely important on a long trip when it comes to calculating GVW without the help of a truck weighing scale. An imperial gallon is about 25 per cent greater in volume than a US gallon.
7. If your radiator is gathering a lot of insects, you will help cooling by cleaning them off from time to time. You'll also help keep the temperature down by not mounting spare tyres, jerry cans and other pieces of equipment in front of the radiator grille.
8. Don't mix two different types of engine oil if you can help it.
9. When filling up with engine oil, bring the level up to halfway between the high and low marks on the dipstick and no further.
10. Rotate your five tyres every 6,500 kms (8,000 kms for radials, which should only be changed front to rear and vice versa on the same side).
11. Try to get clearly written guarantees with everything you buy for your travel needs and return the warranty cards to the manufacturers for registration.

Motorists' Checklist

by Jack Jackson

If you are an experienced off-road motorist, you are, without doubt, the best person to decide exactly what you need to do and take for your trip. Still, even extensive experience doesn't guarantee perfect recall and everyone might find it useful to jog their memory by consulting other people's lists.

These lists do assume some experience – for without some mechanical expertise, for example, an immaculately stocked toolbox is of limited use. It is also assumed that the motorist in question will spend at least some time driving off-road, most probably in a four-wheel-drive vehicle.

Vehicle Spares and Tools

Petrol Engines

3 fan belts
1 complete set of gaskets
4 oil filters (change every 5,000 kms)
2 tubes of Silicone RTV gasket compound
1 complete set of radiator hoses
2 metres of spare heater hose
2 metres of spare fuel pipe hose
½ metre of spare distributor vacuum pipe hose
2 exhaust valves
1 inlet valve
1 valve spring
Fine and coarse valve grinding paste and valve grinding tool
1 valve spring compressor
1 fuel pump repair kit (if electric type, take a complete spare pump)
1 water pump repair kit
1 carburettor overhaul kit
2 sets of spark plugs
1 timing light or 12 volt bulb and holder with leads
3 sets of contact breaker points (preferably with hard fibre cam follower because plastic types wear fast and close up in the heat)
2 rotor arms
1 condensor
1 spark plug spanner
1 distributor cap

1 set of high tension leads (older wire type)
1 ignition coil
Slip ring and brushes for alternator or complete spare alternator
If you have a dynamo, carry spare brushes
2 cans of spray type ignition sealer for dusty and wet conditions
2 spare air intake filters if you do not have the oil-bath type

Extras for Diesel Engines

Delete spark plugs, contact breaker points, rotor arms, distributor cap, high tension leads, and coil from the above and substitute:

1 spare set of injectors plus cleaning kit
1 complete set of injector pipes
1 set injector seating washers
1 set injector return pipe washers
1 metre plastic fuel pipe plus spare nuts and ferrules
A second in-line fuel filter
4 fuel filter elements
3 spare heater plugs if fitted

Brakes and Clutches

2 wheel cylinder kits (one right and one left)
1 flexible brake hose
1 brake bleeding kit (or fit automatic valves)
1 brake master cylinder seals kit
1 clutch master cylinder seals kit
1 clutch slave cylinder kit
(It is important to keep all these kits away from heat)
1 clutch plate
If you have an automatic gearbox, make sure you have plenty of the special fluid for this and a spare starter motor.
If you have power steering, carry the correct fluid and spare hoses.

General Spares

2 warning triangles (compulsory in most countries)

1 good workshop manual (not the car handbook)

1 good torch, or, better still, fluorescent light with leads to work from vehicle battery, plus spare bulbs or tubes

1 extra tyre in addition to the spare wheel, making two spares in all

One spare wheel only will be necessary if two identical vehicles are travelling together

3 extra inner tubes

1 large inner tube repair kit

1 Schrader spark plug fitting tyre pump if you have a petrol engine or 1 Schrader model 202 12 volt electric tyre pump if you have a diesel engine

Plenty of good quality engine oil plus

2 litres of distilled water or 1 bottle of water deionising crystals

12 volt soldering iron and solder

Hand drill and drills

16 metres of nylon or terylene tow rope strong enough to upright an overturned vehicle

1 set of tyre levers and 1 kg sledge hammer for tyres

5 spare inner tube valve cores and 2 valve core tools

1 good jack and wheel brace (if hydraulic, carry spare fluid)

1 (at least) metal fuel can e.g. jerry can

1 grease gun and a tin of multi-purpose grease

1 gallon (4.5 litres) of correct differential and gearbox oil

1 large fire extinguisher suitable for petrol and electrical fires

4 inner tube valve dust caps (metal type)

1 reel of self-amalgamating rubber tape for leaking hoses

1 pair heavy duty electric jump leads at least 3 metres long

10 push fit electrical connectors (or type to suit vehicle)

2 universal joints for prop shafts

½ litre can of brake and clutch fluid

1 small can of general light oil for hinges, door locks etc.

1 large can WD40

1 starting handle, if available

2 complete sets of spare keys kept in different places

1 small Isopon or fibreglass kit for repairing fuel tank and body holes

2 kits of general adhesive, e.g. Bostik or Araldite Rapid

1 tin of hand cleanser (washing up liquid will do in an emergency)

Spare fuses and bulbs for all lights including those on the dash panel which are often part of the charging circuit

1 radiator cap

Antifreeze if route passes through cold areas

Spare windscreen wipers for use on return journey (keep away from heat)

Inner and outer wheel bearings

A good tool kit containing:

Wire brush to clean dirty threads plus large and small flat and round files

Socket set

Torque wrench

Ring and open ended spanners

Hacksaw and spare blades

Selection of spare nuts, bolts and washers of type and thread to fit vehicle

30 cms Stillson pipe wrench

1 box spanner for large wheel bearing lock nuts

Hammer

Large and small cold chisels for large and stubborn nuts

Self-grip wrench

Broad and thin nosed pliers
Circlip pliers
Insulating tape
3 metres electrical wire (vehicle type not mains)
1 set of feeler guages
Small adjustable wrench
Tube of gasket cement e.g. Red Hermetite
Tube Loctite thread sealer
Large and small slot head and Phillips head screwdrivers
Accurate tyre pressure guage
Hardwood or steel plate to support the jack on soft ground

Extra for off-road use
1 pair of 1½ metre sand ladders
3 wheel bearing hub oil seals
1 rear gearbox oil seal
1 rear differential oil seal
1 rear spring main leaf complete with bushes
1 front spring main leaf complete with bushes
4 spare spring bushes
4 spring centre bolts
1 set (=4) of spring shackle plates
1 set (=4) of spring shackle pins
If you have coil springs, carry one spare, plus 2 spare mountings and 4 bushes
1 set of shock absorber mounting rubbers
2 spare engine mountings
1 spare gearbox mounting
2 door hinge pins
1 screw jack (to use on its side when changing springs and/or bushes)
2 metre length of strong chain and bolts to fix it for splinting broken chassis axle or spring parts
Snow chains for rear wheels if you expect a lot of mud or snow
5 cms paint brush to dust off the engine so that you can work on it

Large groundsheet for lying on when working under the vehicle or repairing tyres, so as to prevent sand from getting between the inner tube and the tyre
1 high lift jack in case of bogging
2 small shovels for digging out
2 steering ball joints
2 rear axle U bolts
1 front axle U bolt
2 spare padlocks
Radiator stop leak compound (porridge will do in an emergency)

Maintenance Check Before Departure

1. Change oil and oil filter
2. Clean air filter and change oil bath
3. Lube driveshafts, winch, speedometer cable
4. Lube all locks with dry graphite; adjust and lube all doors
5. Clean or replace all fuel filters
6. Inspect undercarriage for fluid leaks, loose bolts etc.
7. Rotate all five tyres inspecting for cuts and wear
8. Adjust brakes if needed
9. Check adjustments of carburettor
10. Check fanbelts and accessory belts
11. Check sparkplugs. Clean and regap if needed (replace as necessary)
12. Check ignition timing
13. Check and top up:
    front and rear differentials
    swivel-pin housings
    transmission
    transfer case
    overdrive (if applicable)
    steering box
    battery
    battery and clutch fluid
    cooling system
    crankcase
14. Check that there are no rattles

15. Inspect radiator and heater hoses
16. Check breather vents on both axles
17. Check all lights
18. Check wheel balance and front end alignment and always do so with new tyres and wheels.

Running Repairs

by Jack Jackson

Before you go, use your vehicle for several months to run in any new parts properly, enable you to find any weaknesses and become acquainted with its handling and maintenance. Give it a thorough overhaul before leaving. If you fit any extras, make sure that they are as strong as the original vehicle. For precise navigation, you should know how accurate your odometer is for the tyres fitted. Larger tyres e.g. sand tyres, will have a longer rolling circumference.

Once in the field, check the chassis, springs, spring shackles and bushes, steering, bodywork, exhaust and tyres every evening when you stop for the day. Every morning when it is cool, check engine oil, battery electrolyte, tyre pressures, and cooling water and fill the fuel tank. Check transmission oils and hydraulic fluids at least every third day. In dusty areas, keep breather vents clear on the axle and gearbox. Keep an eye on electrical cables for worn insulation, which could lead to a fire. Make sure that you carry and use the correct oils and fluids in all cases. Deionizing water crystals are easier to carry than distilled water for the battery. Remember to oil door hinges, door locks, padlocks etc., and remember that in many deserts you need antifreeze in the engine for night temperatures. Brush all parts clear of sand or dust before working on them. Have a tarpaulin to lie on and keep things clean when working under the vehicle. Clear goggles will keep the dirt out of your eyes. A small vice fitted to a strong part of the vehicle will aid many repairs. In scrub or insect country you will need to brush down the radiation mesh regularly.

Maintenance

By using several identical vehicles travelling in convoy, you can minimize the weight of spares and tyres to be carried. The idea of using one large vehicle to carry fuel etc., accompanying several smaller, more agile vehicles, does not work out well in practice. The larger vehicles will often be heavily bogged down and the smaller vehicles will have difficulty in towing it out, often damaging their own drive train in the process. Also the vast difference in overall journey speed and the extra spares needed cause many problems, unless you are to have a static base camp.

Overloading is the largest single cause of broken-down vehicles and the easiest to avoid. Calculate your payload against the maker's recommendation for the vehicle. Water is ten pounds per gallon, fuel roughly eight pounds per gallon, plus the container. Concentrate on the essentials and cut back on the luxuries. It could make all the difference between success and failure.

For rough terrain, trailers are not advisable. They get stuck in sand, slip into ditches and overturn on bad tracks. Even powered trailers have been known to overturn the prime vehicle. On corrugated tracks, trailer contents soon become unrecognisable. Trailers are impossible to manhandle in sand or mud and make life difficult if you have to turn around in an awkward situation.

If you must take a trailer, make sure that it has the same wheels and tyres as the towing vehicle, that the hitch is the strong NATO type and that the wiring loom is well fixed along the chassis where it will be protected.

Overturned Vehicles

Short wheelbase vehicles have a habit of breaking away or spinning on bends and corrugations, often turning over in the process, so drive these vehicles with extra care. Given the nature of the terrain they cover, overturned vehicles are not unusual on expeditions. Usually it happens at such a slow speed that no one is injured nor even windows broken. First make sure the engine is stopped and battery disconnected. Check for human injury, then completely unload the vehicle. Once unloaded, vehicles can usually be uprighted easily using manpower, through a second vehicle and/or winch can make things easier in the right conditions. Once the vehicle is righted, check for damage, sort out all oil levels and spilt battery acid and then turn the engine over several times without the plugs or injectors in to clear the bores, before running the engine again.

Punctures

Punctures are the most common problem in off-road travel. Rear wheel punctures often destroy the inner tube, so several spare inner tubes should be carried. Wherever possible,

I prefer to repair punctures with a known good tube and get the punctured one vulcanized properly when I next visit a larger town, but you should always carry a repair kit in case you use up all your inner tubes. Hot patch repair kits do not work well enough on truck inner tubes. Michelin radial tyres have the advantage that their beads almost fall of the wheel rim when flat. If you cannot break a bead, try driving over it or using a jack and the weight of the vehicle. If the wheel has the rim on one side wider than the other, only attempt to remove the tyre over the narrowest side, starting with both beads in the well of the wheel; narrow tyre levers are more efficient than wide ones. Sweep out all sand and grit, file off any sharp burrs on the wheel and put everything back together on a ground sheet to stop any sand or grit getting in to cause further punctures.

When refitting the tyre, use liquid soap and water or bead lubricant and a Schrader valve tool to hold the inner tube valve in place. Pump the tyre up enough to refit the bead on the rim then let it down again to release any twists in the inner tube. Then pump the tyre up again to full rear tyre pressure. If the wheel has to be fitted on the front at a later date, it is easy to let some air out.

Foot pumps have a short life in sand and are hard work. If your vehicle does not already have a compressor, then use a sparkplug fitting pump if you have a petrol engine, or an electric pump if you have a diesel engine. Keep all pumps clear of sand. When using electric pumps, keep the engine running at charging speed.

Damaged steel braced radial tyres often have a sharp end of wire internally, causing further punctures. These should be cut down as short as is possible and the tyre then gaitered, using thicker truck inner tubes. The edges of the gaiter need to be bevelled and the tyre must be at full pressure to stop the gaiter from moving about. On paved road, gaitered tyres behave like a buckled wheel, so they are dangerous. Most truck tyres including Michelin XZY, can be legally recut when worn, and the re-cuts are useful to use on sharp stones where tyres cut up easily.

Wheelbraces get overworked in off-road use, so have a good socket or ring spanner available, to fit the wheel nuts.

In soft sand, use a strong one-foot-square metal or wooden plate under the jack, when jacking up the vehicle. Two jacks, preferably including a high lift jack, are often necessary in off-road conditions.

With a hot wheel after a puncture, you may need an extension tube on the wheel brace to undo the wheel nuts, but do not retighten them this way or you will cause damage.

Fuel Problems

Bad fuel is common; extra fuel filters are useful for everyone and essential for diesel engines. The main problems are water and sediment. When things get bad, it is quicker in the long run to drain the fuel tank, decant the fuel and clean it out. Always keep the wire mesh filter in the fuel filler in place. Do not let the fuel tank level fall too low as this will produce water and sediment in the fuel lines. With a diesel engine, you may then have to bleed the system. If fuelling up from 40 gallon drums,

give them time to settle and leave the bottom inch, which will often be water and grit. If you have petrol in jerry cans in a hot, dry country, always earth them to discharge any static electricity, before opening. Fuel starvation is often caused by dust blocking the breather hole in the fuel tank filler cap. Electric fuel pumps are very unreliable; carry a complete spare. For mechanical fuel pumps, carry a reconditioning kit. In hot countries or in low gear at altitude, mechanical fuel pumps on petrol engines often get hot and cause vapour lock. Wrap the pump in bandages and pour water on it to cool it down. If this is a constant problem, fit a plastic pipe from the windscreen washer system to the bandaged fuel pump and squirt it regularly.

Low pressure fuel pipes can be repaired using epoxy resin glues, bound by self-vulcanizing rubber tape. High-pressure injector pipes need to be braised or completely replaced. Carry spares of these and spare injectors. Diesel engine problems are usually fuel or water, and you should know how to bleed the system correctly. If this fails to correct the problem, check all pipes and joints, fuel pump and filter seals for leaks. Hairline cracks in the high pressure injector pipes are hardest to find. Fuel tank leaks repair best with glass reinforced fibre kits.

Electrical Problems

These are another constant problem. With petrol engines, it is well worth changing the ignition system to an electronic system without contacts. Carry a spare distributor cap, rotor arm, plugs points, condenser and coal

– all tend to break up or short out in hot countries. Replace modern high-tension leads with the older copper wire type and carry a spare set. Keep a constant check on plugs and points. If you are losing power, first check the gap and wear on the points. Spray all ignition parts with sealer to keep out dust and water. Keep battery connections tight, clean and greased. Replace the battery slip-on connections with the older clamp-on type. Keep battery plates covered with electrolyte, top up only with distilled water or deionized water. Batteries are best checked with a battery hydrometer. There are special instruments for checking the modern sealed-for-life batteries.

Alternators and batteries should be disconnected before any arc welding is done on the vehicle. Never run the engine with the alternator or battery disconnected. Alternators are not as reliable as they should be. If the diodes are separate, carry spares, if not, carry a complete spare alternator. Always carry a spare voltage regulator. On some vehicles the red charging warning light on the dash board is part of the the the circuit, so carry spare bulbs for all lights. Make sure you carry spare fuses and fan belts.

Arctic temperatures are a very specialist situation. Vehicles are stored overnight in heated hangars. When in the field, engines are either left running or else have an electric engine heater, which is plugged into a mains power supply. Oils are either specialist or diluted to the makers' recommendations. Petrol is the preferred fuel for lighter vehicles, but for heavier uses, diesel vehicles have heaters built into the fuel tank and

the fuel is diluted with petrol. All fuel is scrupulously inspected for water before being used. Batteries must be in tip-top condition, as they lose efficiency when cold.

General Problems and Improvisations

Steering locks are best removed; if not leave the key in them permanently in dusty areas. A spare set of keys should be hidden safely somewhere under the body or the chassis.

When replacing wheel hub bearing oil seals, it pays to replace the metal mating piece also.

Wire hose clips are best replaced with flat metal Jubilee type clips. Carry spare hoses, although these can be repaired in an emergency with self-vulcanizing rubber tape. Heater hoses can be blocked with a spark-plug.

Bad radiator leaks can be sealed with epoxy resin or glass reinforced fibre. For small leaks, add some Radweld, porridge or raw egg to the radiator water. Always use a torque wrench on aluminium cylinder heads or other aluminium components.

In sand, always work on a ground sheet and don't put parts down in the sand. In sand storm areas, make a protected working area around the vehicle using tarpaulins.

Clean the threads of nuts and bolts with a wire brush before trying to remove them.

If you get wheel shimmy on returning to paved roads, first check for mud, buckled wheels, gaitered tyres and loose wheel bearings. If it is none of these, check the swivel pins, which can usually be dampened by removing shims. Carry any spare parts containing rubber well away from heat.

If you cannot get into gear, first check for stones caught up in the linkage.

If you use jerry cans, carry spare rubber seals. Always carry water in light-proof cans to stop the growth of algae.

Lengths of strong chain with long bolts plus wood, or tyre levers can be used as splints on broken chassis parts, axles or leaf springs. If you do not have a differential lock, and need one in an emergency, you can lock the spinning wheel by tightening up the brake adjuster cam, but only use this system for a few yards at a time.

For emergency fuel tanks, use a jerry can on the roof, with a hose connected to the fuel lift pump. Drive slowly and never let the can get lower than half full.

If one vehicle in a convoy has a defunct charging system, swap that vehicle's battery every 100 kilometres.

For repair work at night, or camp illumination, small fluorescent lights have the least drain on the battery.

If the engine is overheating, it will cool down quickest going downhill in gear using the running engine as a brake. If you stop with a hot engine then, unless it is showing signs of seizure, keep the engine ticking over fast; this will cool it down quicker and more evenly than if you stop it.

With oil bath type air cleaners, make sure that there are not any pin holes in the rubber connecting hose between the air cleaner and the engine inlet manifold.

Roof-mounted air inlets pipes are best avoided as they tend to break on corrugations.

If you have a partially seized six-cylinder engine, remove the piston and connecting rod, disconnect the spark plug and high tension lead (or the injector if diesel). Close the valves by removing the push rods or rocker arms if overhead cam. If diesel, feed the fuel from the disconnected fuel injector pipe to a safe place away from the heat of the engine. Drive slowly. If you have a hole in the block, seal it with any sheet metal plus glass reinforced plastic and self-tapping screws to keep out dust or sand.

In an emergency, you can run a diesel engine on kerosene (paraffin) or domestic heating oil, by adding one part of engine oil to 100 parts of the fuel, to lubricate the injector pump. In hot climates, diesel engine oils are good for use in petrol engines, but petrol engine oils should not be used for diesel engines.

Bent track rods should be hammered back as straight as possible to minimize tyre scrubbing and possibility of a roll.

If you break a rear half shaft, you can continue in two-wheel-drive by removing both rear half shafts and putting the vehicle into four-wheel drive. If the rear differential is broken remove both rear half shafts and the rear propeller shafts and engage four-wheel-drive. If a permanent four-wheel-drive jams in the centre differential lock position, remove the front propeller shaft and drive on slowly.

Temporary drain or filler plugs can be whittled from wood and sealed in with epoxy resin.

Silicone RTV compound can be used for most gaskets, other than cylinder head gaskets. Silicone RTV compound or PTFE tape is useful when putting together leaking fuel line connections.

Paper gaskets can be reused if covered in grease.

If you develop a hydraulic brake fluid leak and do not have a spare, travel on slowly, using the engine as a brake. If the leak is really bad, you can disconnect a metal pipe upstream of the leak, bend it over and hammer the end flat, or fit an old pipe to which this has already been done. Rubber hoses can be clamped, using a round bar to minimize damage. If you have a dual system, then the brakes will still work as normal, but if not, you will have uneven braking on only three wheels. When replacing brake pipes, copper ones are more easy to work with.

If you lose your clutch you can still change gear, by adjusting the engine speed, as with double declutching. It is best to start the engine with it already in second gear.

Four-wheel-drive vehicles are high off the ground and it is often easier to work on the engine if you put the spare wheel on the ground and stand on it. If your bonnet can be hinged right back, tie it back so that the wind does not drop it on your head.

Steering relays which do not have a filler point can be topped up by removing two opposite top cover bolts and filling through one till oil comes out of the other.

If you burst an oil gauge pressure pipe, remove the T-piece, remove the electric pressure sender from it and screw this back into the block. You will then still have the electric low pressure warning light.

Motor Manufacturers' Concessionaires and Agents

by Colin McElduff

Motor manufacturers have concessionaires and agents throughout the world who are responsible for the importation of vehicles, availability of services and spares etc. Once you have decided on the vehicle to use you should approach its manufacturer for a list of their representatives in the countries you are visiting, so that you are able to evaluate its spares potential.

Today, motor manufacturers are constantly reviewing their viability in terms of production and sales. The effect on universal availability of spares is, however, long term, so the transcontinental motorist derives little immediate benefit. Nevertheless, there is the possibility that the spares of one manufacturer's vehicles will be suitable for another and a careful study of the subject is always worthwhile.

Whatever you do, choose a vehicle with a good spares potential, for it is inevitable that you will be faced with a breakdown at some stage of your journey. Be prepared by finding out your vehicle's weak points and use this as a basis for choosing spares to be taken with you, for you must not rely too much on being able to obtain them en route. When it comes to the crunch, the factors concerning spares availability may be divided into three – the assumed, the known, and the unknown.

It is unwise to assume, because you have a list of the vehicle's concessionaires and agents, that the spares you require will be readily available. They never are, for some of the countries you are visiting may have broken off old ties and now no longer enjoy the expertise and use of equipment so provided in the past. This is often the case in Third World countries. Sometimes the cause of shortages may be the country's balance of payments problems, at other times, just downright political instability.

A great deal is known and can be used to get round the problem of no spares, however, such as using parts designed for another vehicle. To reiterate, check out the manufacturer of your vehicle and obtain a family tree of its affiliations, so that you will have some idea where to direct your search should the need arise. For example, vehicles produced by Vauxhall and Opel have parts common to each other, as also do Ford (UK) and Taunus (Germany) together with Saab, whose V4 engine is used in some Ford models. British Leyland and Innocenti (Italy) also have an affiliation and Honda have joined them to produce certain models. Talbot (UK) and Talbot/Simca (France) are similarly affiliated. Polski Fiat and Fiat produce models based on the Fiat design. Because of the intricate spider's web representing connections between manufacturers, it would be confusing to expand on this here, but look into it for your own vehicle.

As always, the unknown is legion, but when in doubt, apply logic. Ask yourself how a local would approach your situation where, for instance, there is little hope of obtaining that urgently needed spare part? The answer? He will cannibalise, and is an expert in doing so. The 'bush' mechanic exists by virtue of his resourcefulness and his ability to adapt under any conditions. He may not know what a concessionaire is, but he does know, as John Steele Gordon puts it in *Over-*

landing, how to make the 'radiator hose of a 1953 Chevrolet serve as an exhaust pipe for a 1973 Volkswagen and vice versa'.

Shipping a Vehicle

by Tania Brown and Keith Kimber

'The duplicate will be delivered to the Gate-Keeper who wlieln doors on the dack of thepuantity as will be passed by him' – English instructions printed on an Indian Shipping Bill.

To find the best shipping for your vehicle you must know who sails to your destination. Most people begin by looking through the Yellow Pages and contacting shipping agents, but this will never give you a complete list of all the ships using the port. The secret is to locate the industry paper that serves the port and get the latest copy. They appear under a variety of obvious names like *Shipping Times, Shipping Schedules,* and some less obvious ones like *The Bulletin* in Panama. Start by asking for them at shipping offices. Most are published weekly and contain a goldmine of information. Listings indicate destinations and arrival/departure dates for all ships in port along with pier and berth numbers that tell you exactly where the ships are located. Also indicated are the shipping line, its local agent and types of cargo carried. The same information is given for ships at sea scheduled to arrive and there's a directory of agents' telephone numbers and addresses. In some countries this information appears as a weekly supplement to a regular newspaper.

Contact the agents that list sailings

to your destination and compare freight costs (always based on volume). The basic freight rate always has three surcharges added to it: a bunker surcharge which follows fluctuating fuel costs; a currency adjustment factor to compensate for exchanging rates; and wharfage charges. Make sure these are included in any quotes you receive. At times the bunker surcharge or currency adjustment factor can be negative values and represent a discount.

Unconventional Channels

But don't only follow conventional channels. The paper will list unscheduled ships using the port – mission boats, training ships, all kinds of 'oddball' one-off vessels that might take you on board. They won't have agents at the ports so you'll have to contact the Captain direct. Where port security is minimal and/or corrupt, enter the docks and speak to the Captain personally. Any *visual* material like photos and maps of your journey are invaluable as an introduction. One good photo can jump the language and cultural barriers and get him interested enough to talk to you. If port security is strict, there is another way. When a ship docks it is immediately connected to a telephone line. Each berth has a different telephone number. In Sydney, for example, the numbers are listed in the telephone directory. Consult your *Shipping Times* for the ship's berth, look up the number and you can speak directly to the ship. If the numbers aren't in the phone book, ask at the Shipping and Port Manager's office.

Write to the Captain with your visual material and a covering letter explaining what you are doing and where you want to go. Follow it up two days later to receive his reply. That way he can see what you are doing and you get a chance to speak to him on the phone. If he's amenable, ask for a working passage or free shipping for your vehicle, but be prepared to follow up with a realistic offer of payment if his interest starts to wane. If you work your passage, as we did in 1985, then your vehicle is taken free. But we've also received offers from regular shipping lines to take our vehicle unaccompanied to various parts of the world. For this you should approach the Operations Manager or General Manager of the shipping line or its agent. Again, write and interest them in what you are doing. If you are on an expedition, you can generate publicity for them – point this out. If not, don't worry. Offer to give a talk and slide show for the staff in return for free shipping, plus any number of large colour photographs they can use for advertising showing the company logo on your vehicle as you tackle the next desert or jungle. The *way* you approach them is really more important than what you offer in return. Don't forget, people in poor countries can't always understand the desire for hard travelling and a frugal lifestyle but some dramatic photos of your journey can work wonders.

Packing Your Vehicle

Your next concern is how the vehicle will travel. Try to avoid crating it if you can. Crating is expensive and involves a lot of backbreaking work. Even in countries where labour is cheap, timber is costly. It's also inconvenient – you can't drive your vehicle to the ship when it's in a crate. If you *must* crate, visit an import agent to try and obtain a ready-made crate the right size. Uncrated, the vehicle can go 'break-bulk', roll-on/roll-off or containerised. Containerised is the best. The vehicle is protected from theft and the elements, can't be damaged during loading or unloading and you can leave all your luggage inside. 'Roll-on/roll-off' services are very convenient. The vehicle is driven onto the ship and stored below deck – just like a regular car ferry. But these only operate on certain routes and your luggage shouldn't be left in the vehicle. 'Break-bulk' means it is carried as it is, either in the ship's hold or on deck surrounded by all the other break-bulk cargo.

Countries with weak economies may insist you pay for your freight in US dollars. It's advisable to carry enough US dollars (rather than pounds) for this purpose.

A forwarding agent can do all the paperwork for you although it's cheaper to do it yourself. The best way is to team up with a 'hustler' who works for a forwarding agent. These young lads spend all day pushing paperwork through the system. They known where to find port trust offices, the wharf storekeeper's office, main Customs building, port Customs building, etc., etc.; buildings and offices that are usually spaced far and wide across the city. They know how to persuade Customs officers to inspect the vehicle and wharf officers to certify documents. Better still, they know what sort of 'tips' are expected down the line. I've always found them friendly, helpful types with great sympathy towards anyone on the same side of the counter as themselves, pitted

against the officials! They've never objected to my tagging along to push my own paperwork through the system. In return, I buy them cold drinks and a good meal each day we're together, and give a few dollars to thank them for their help at the end.

Be well prepared to do your own paperwork. Take a dozen sheets of carbon paper, a handful of paper clips (there will be a lot of copies), a *good* ball point pen, some large envelopes and a pocketful of small denomination notes in the local currency. Commit your passport number, engine and chassis number, vehicle weight and local address to memory so you can double check details as the officials type them out (this is also good practice for any overland traveller when crossing land borders). Remember if a single digit is incorrect in the serial numbers you will *not* be entitled to your own vehicle at your destination. People *have* lost their vehicles this way. I also carry a small 'John Bull' type india rubber kit to make up my own rubber stamps. It saves hours filling out forms – especially if you are doing a number of vehicles. It's normal practice to have to buy the forms you use for a nominal sum – either at the port or a stationer's in town. In Western countries the paperwork is often simplified and it's quite easy to do it yourself.

Clean the vehicle thoroughly before shipping, especially under the mudguards where dirt collects, to avoid the cost of it being quarantined on arrival. For instance, you will be charged $80 Australian for fumigation at Darwin. Smear exposed deck cargo with grease or paint it with diesel oil. Grease the disc brakes as well. Don't worry, they *will* work afterwards. Remove wing mirrors and, on a motorcycle, the screen and indicators.

Cars should be lashed on deck with chains and bottle screws, not rope which will fray and stretch. If only rope is available look for nylon rope which won't stretch when it gets wet. Motorcycles should be off the centre-stand, wheels chocked front and back, and tied to a post using wooden spacers. Look ahead and be prepared to take your own rope. On the *MV Chidambaram* in India we ended up using the guy ropes from our tent and every webbing strap we had to tie our motorcycle securely. Don't leave a vehicle unaccompanied at the dock. Paperwork can usually be done two days before sailing, then the vehicle is inspected, cleared by Customs and loaded on board the day it sails. In Third World countries, insist on being allowed to supervise loading. Use rope slings, don't let them use a net. Sling a motorcycle through the back wheel and under the steering head. A car should be lifted using pairs of boards or poles chained together under the wheels. If the correct tackle is unavailable, drive the car into an empty container so it can be lifted on board. If the vehicle *must* be left on the dockside and loaded in your absence, don't leave any luggage inside, don't leave the key with anyone and lash it to a wooden pallet so they can forklift it to the ship and winch it on board.

Don't leave the country before you've seen the vehicles off in case they don't load it for some reason.

Meet the ship on arrival and confirm your cargo will be unloaded. When we arrived in Malaysia, they told us our bike was destined to continue to Singapore. We had an awful time convincing them they were wrong! The vehicle will then be held in Customs until you complete the paperwork to release it. Insist it goes inside a locked shed. There may be a nominal storage charge but often the first three days are free.

Philosophically, be prepared to accept some minor damage. Put any dents down to adventure!

Air Freight

Motorcyclists can consider airfreight as a viable alternative to shipping. Over short distances, it's often cheaper and sometimes may be the only way of getting somewhere – inland, for example. In a passenger aircraft, the motorcycle lies on its side in the cargo hold, so construct a set of crash bars to support it without damage. It must fly completely dry – no fuel, engine oil, brake fluid, coolant, battery acid or air in the tyres. People worry their battery will be ruined by draining the acid. I've drained mine many times and once left it dry for more than two weeks with no ill-effects. It doesn't even lose any charge. But don't use it before refilling with acid and don't plug the breather hole or the whole thing will explode. A wad of cotton wool over the hole will soak up any acid drops and allow it to breathe. Freight charges are based on weight.

Special notes:
Depending on the political situation in Sri Lanka you can sail to Talaimannar by ferry from Rameshwaram Island, India. Vehicles and passengers cross the Pamban Channel by train from Mandapam, the last stop on the mainland. There is no road bridge. Motorcycles are lifted into the goods carriage, cars go on a low loader which costs extra. The ferry moors ¼ mile

offshore and is loaded by 'lighters' – small wooden boats. Cars go on a flat raft or two lighters tied together – a hair-raising experience. Paperwork takes a full day.

I have met people who have been obliged to spend US$1500 on anti-pollution devices for their cars arriving in California to comply with state laws. This doesn't apply to everyone, but if in doubt, ship to one of the other 49 states.

From personal experience, Columbus Shipping Lines take excellent care of vehicles, keeping them regularly washed down with fresh water to reduce the effects of the salty sea air.

On entering Panama, you have to specify where the vehicle will be shipped from. If undecided, specify 'Colon'. When you've organised your shipping, visit head Customs at Ancon, off Curundu Road to make any changes. International motorcyclists in Panama shipping round the Darien Gap can contact the Road Knights Motorcycle Club at Albrook US Air Force Base for advice, use of workshops, and up to two weeks' free accommodation. It will be cheaper to ship cars to Ecuador than Colombia.

Finally, shipping really isn't all that bad. Things always go smoother and quicker than you think and there are always people who will help you out. If you encounter just a quarter of the problems mentioned here you've had an unusually bad trip!

Translation of the 'Indish' Shipping Bill instructions:

'The duplicate will be delivered to the gatekeeper who will endorse on the back of the shipping bill the quantity passed by him.'

1987 Shipping Costs Using Scheduled Services

A$ = *Australian Dollars* US$ = *United States Dollars*

Route	Line	Cost		
		Motorbike (2cbm)	Land Rover (SWB 12 cbm)	VW Combi (15 cbm)
Australia to Japan	AJCL	A$340	A$950 (packed in container by owner on own premises) A$2040 (packed in container by AJCL)	A$950 (packed in container by owner on own premises) A$2550 (packed in container by AJCL)
	ANL	A$365	A$2196	A$2745
UAE to Pakistan	P&OCL	US$595	US$595	A$595
		(All containerised – no LCL service. Unpacking charges at Karachi are extra.)		
Australia to Singapore	VB Perkins	A$224	A$900	A$1010
		(All vehicles carried uncrated underdeck)		
Singapore to Japan	P&OCL	US$550	US$550	US$550
		(All vehicles containerised)		
W. Coast USA to Australia	Wiltrans	US$3872	US$2322	US$2902
		(Vessel is RO-RO – vehicle stowed underdeck)		
Sri Lanka to Australia	ANZCL	A$385	A$2305	A$2882
	P&OCL	US$237 (crated) US$295 (uncrated)	US$1140	US$1425
Australia to New Zealand	ANZCL	A$320	A$1920	A$2400

England to East Coast USA	P&OCL	US$142 Freight plus £67 UK port charges plus US$190 US port charges	US$400 Freight plus £14/1000kg UK port charges plus US$60 US port charges	US$400 Freight plus £14/1000kg UK port charges plus US$60 US port charges
Australia to Singapore	ANL	A$412	A$2315	A$2265
Australia to East Coast USA	PACE	A$571 (All vehicles containerised)	A$3428	A$4285
Panama to Ecuador	Boyd Steamship Corporation	US$141	US$590	US$725

GLOSSARY

Shipping Line abbreviations:

AJCL = Australia Japan Container Line
ANL = Australia National Line
P&OCL = P&O Container Lines
ANZCL = Australia New Zealand Container Line
PACE = Pacific American Container Express

Commonly used abbreviations:

LCL = Less than a container load
B/L = Bill of Lading
BS/BSC or BAF = Bunker surcharge or bunker adjustment factor.
CAF = Currency adjustment factor
CBM = Cubic metre
USD = US Dollars
RO-RO = Roll on – roll off
B.B. = Break-bulk (i.e. cargo not in a container)

Shipping container dimensions (standard worldwide): full size 40' x 8' x 8'6";
half size: 20' x 8' x 8'6"

Getting There by Other Means

Overland by Public Transport

by Chris Parrott

It's not everyone who has the resources to plan, equip, and insure a full-scale Range Rover expedition across one of the less developed continents, although it's the sort of thing we all dream about. One possible answer is to travel with an overland company, but here the drawback is that you can neither choose your travelling companions nor your itinerary. You can, however, do it all more cheaply on your own, by public transport. Generally speaking, wherever overland companies take their trucks, public transport goes too. And often public transport goes where overland companies cannot – over the snow-bound Andes to Ushuaia in Tierra del Fuego, across Siberia to the Pacific.

Of course, Damascus to Aleppo is not quite the same as getting on a coach to Washington DC at the New York Greyhound Terminal, nor does 'First Class' imply in Bolivia quite what it does on the 18.43 from Paddington to Reading.

A Schedule of Surprises

The Damascus to Aleppo bus is an ancient Mercedes welded together from the remains of past generations of Damascus/Aleppo buses, and pro-

pelled in equal proportions by a fuming diesel engine, the Will of Allah, and the passengers (from behind). It makes unscheduled stops while the driver visits his grandmother in Homs, when the driver's friend visits the Post Office in the middle of nowhere, and when the whole bus answers the call of nature – the women squatting on the left, and the men standing on the right (the French normally display more cool at moments like this).

First Class in Bolivia means hard, upright seats, already full of people and chickens spilling over from Second Class; whimpering children; no heating, even in high passes at night in winter; passageways blocked by shapeless bundles and festering cheeses; impromptu Customs searches at 4am; and toilets negotiable only by those equipped with Wellingtons and a farmyard upbringing. Trains rarely arrive or depart on time, and the author has experienced a delay of 26 hours on a journey (ostensibly) of eight hours. But these trains are nothing if not interesting.

The secret of the cheapness of this means of travelling lies in the fact that it is *public* – and therefore the principal means by which the public of a country moves from place to place. It follows that if the standard of living of the majority of people is low, so will the cost of public transport be low. A 20 hour bus ride from Lima to Arequipa in southern Peru can cost as little as $10; a 20 hour bus ride in Brazil from Rio de Janeiro to the Paraguayan border costs about $20; whilst a 20 hour bus ride through France or Germany would cost $40 or more. It all depends on the ability of the local population to pay.

Of course there are disadvantages to travel by public transport:

1. Photography is difficult at 70mph, and though most drivers will stop occasionally, they have their schedules to keep to.

2. You may find that all transport over a certain route is fully booked for the week ahead, or there is a transport strike.

3. You may find that your seat has been sold twice. In circumstances like this, tempers fray and people begin to speak too quickly for your few words of the local language to be of much use.

Efficiency of reservation arrangements varies from one part of the world to the next. The following may serve as a general guide to travelling in the undeveloped parts of the world.

Booking

Whenever you arrive in a place, try and find out about transport and how far ahead it is booked up. It may be, for example, that you want to stay in Ankara for three days, and that it's usually necessary to book a passage four days in advance to get to Iskenderun. If you book on the day you arrive, you have only one extra day to wait; if you book on the day you intended leaving, you have four days to kill. This is a basic rule and applies to all methods of transport.

Routing

Try to be as flexible as possible about your routing and means of transport. There are at least six ways to get from La Paz in Bolivia to Rio de Janeiro in Brazil. Check all possible routes before making a final decision.

Timing

Don't try and plan your itinerary down to the nearest day – nothing is ever that reliable in the less developed world (or the developed world for that matter). You should allow a ten to twenty per cent delay factor if, for example, you have to be at a certain point at a certain time to catch your plane home.

Possessions

Baggage is often snatched at terminals. Be sure, if you are not travelling within sight of your bags, that they have the correct destination clearly marked, and that they do actually get loaded. Breakfast in New York, dinner in London, baggage in Tokyo happens all too often. Arriving or leaving early in the morning or late at night you are particularly vulnerable to thieves. This is the time when you must be most on your guard. Never leave anything valuable on a bus while you have a quick drink, not even if the driver says the bus door will be locked.

Borders

Prices rise dramatically whenever your route crosses a national frontier. Usually it's cheaper to take a bus as far as the frontier, walk across and then continue your journey by the local transport in the new country. 'International' services are always more expensive, whether airlines, buses, trains or boats. (The author recalls that a donkey ride to the Mexican frontier cost him 20 *pesos* but to have crossed the international bridge as far as far as the Belize Immigration Office, an extra 40 metres, would have increased the cost to 40 *pesos*.)

Fare and Medium

Each particular medium of transport has its own special features.

Trains are generally slower than buses, and the seats may be of wood. There is often no restriction on the number of seats sold, and delays are long and frequent. However, slow trains make photography easier, and the journeys are usually more pleasant than on buses if not too crowded. It's often worth going to the station a couple of days before you're due to leave and watching to see what happens. It will tell you whether you need to turn up two hours early to be sure of a seat.

Buses reflect the sort of terrain they cross. If the roads are paved and well maintained, the buses are usually modern and in fair condition. If the journey involves unmade mountain roads, your bus and journey are not going to be very comfortable.

If you are travelling through bandit country – or a country where political stability conforms to the Third World stereotype – the company may be a consolation when the whole bus is stopped and robbed by bandits or searched by transit police (robbed too, some say). If you're in your own vehicle or hitchhiking, it is somehow far more demoralizing. You probably lose the same things or have your Tampax broken in half by over-zealous soldiers in search of drugs, but it affects you less if you're just part of a coach load.

Urban transport. One of London's biggest failures has been its inability to provide a cheap mass transit system within the city. Other Western industrialized capitals seem to have managed it to a greater or lesser extent, but the Third World has really got the problem licked – for the locals at least. Most urban dwellers in the Third World own no car; they have to travel by public transport – by train, rickshaw, undergound and so on. The networks are labyrinthine in the complexity, the services frequent and the fares cheap. Everyone uses the system; which generates which, I don't know, but it works. The problem is that there is rarely any information on the extent of the network available for the tourist or traveller. He or she is meant to go by taxi or limousine. Buy yourself a city map, jump on a bus and explore. It's a great way of seeing the city cheaply with no censorship, getting your bearings, and spending next to nothing in the process.

Boats. This, if you're lucky, could mean an ocean-going yacht that takes passengers as crew between, say, St Lucia and Barbados, a cement boat from Rhodes to Turkey, or an Amazon river steamer. With a little help from your wallet, most captains can be persuaded to accept passengers. A good rule is to take your own food supply for the duration of the trip and a hammock if there is no official accommodation.

Cargo boats ply the rivers Amazon, the Congo and Ubangi in Zaire, the Niger in Mali, the White Nile in the Sudan, the river Gambia and Ecuador's river Guaya, where an all night crossing costs about thirteen *sucres* (30p).

Planes. In areas where planes are the only means of communication, they are often very cheap or even free. Flying across the Gulf of Aden to Djibouti, for example, costs as little as sailing. A good trick is to enquire about privately owned planes at mission schools (in Africa) or at aeroclubs. Someone who is going 'up country' may be only too pleased to have your company. Similarly, in parts of South America, the Air Forces of several countries have cheap scheduled flights to less accessible areas, though, of course, one must be prepared for canvas seats and grass runways.

The Train Now Standing ...

by Christopher Portway

Trains... A word spelling the daily grind to and from work for many, the gateway to new worlds for some, a vehicle to adventure for a few. Somewhere in between come those people who love trains simply for the railway's sake and just a few eccentrics like me who find in world train travel something of the elixir of life.

Planning a long distance train journey is part of the attraction. The *Thomas Cook International Timetables* are the bibles of the likes of me; their snippets of information unearthed from a morass of footnotes spelling out the shape of wanderings still to come. I donated one such footnote, which I find a source of great pride and I also donated the Ibarra-San Lorenzo train timings as nobody else could prize them out of the Ecuadorian State Railway Headquarters. This notwithstanding, what is still not made quite clear by Mr Cook is that first class travel on this amazing line means riding a converted British Leyland *bus* while lesser breeds in second class have

to make do with the back of a British Leyland *lorry*. Both types of vehicle have a habit or running out of petrol in tunnels, and passengers – first and second class – are expected to dig their way out of the frequent landslides to which the line is prone.

Cook's Turkish Railway section also contains some gems of understatement only appreciated by those who have sweated out the journey between Istanbul and Baghdad.

'Passengers in direct transit by rail should allow at least eight hours for connections between trains' reads a footnote, from which it can be deduced that some Turkish trains do not stick too laboriously to their published timetable. If they did, I can assure you that nobody would catch them. When I was last on such a train it won my accolade for being the slowest in the world and there was a kind of rapport between driver and passengers that allowed for walking beside the train picking flowers and fruit en route. The cooking of meat on charcoal burners on the carriage floor was another original activity and if you weren't asphyxiated by smoke coming in the window while the train was in tunnels then you were by that coming from within your compartment.

For a final word on the Thomas Cook tomes and what they do and do not tell you in their cryptic fashion, take Table 5942 of Pakistan Railways as an example. The Quetta-Kahedan (southern Iran) line is one to be avoided. Even I found it hard going. The intense heat of the Baluchistan Desert frequently buckles the rails; anti-government tribes have a penchant for venting their wrath on the trains; progress across the shifting sands that cover the tracks is dead slow; and, with only two trains in each direction a week, overcrowding is rife. Again passengers are expected to help repair track when necessary.

Standards of Comfort

One thing about travelling such trains in Asia is that you will never want for food. At every stop vendors fall over themselves to serve you titbits of cooked meat and cake. Select what you eat with care or you risk a variety of tummy upsets.

The general comfort of train travel will, of course, vary from country to country and from railway to railway. All over Western Europe, the trains are luxurious, efficient and expensive. In eastern Europe too the trains are generally good. The one exception might be Albanian Rail, but since I'm one of the few Westerners to have risked the wrath of the totalitarian Albanian People's Republic by commuting between Tirana, Durres and Elbasan on crackpot trains that are forbidden to foreigners, this is of little interest to most travellers. Soviet trains are paragons of plain comfort and timekeeping. In Cuba, in spite of a personal application made to Dr Castro, I was allowed nowhere near a train.

In the United States, the railway is very thin on the ground and train travel is looked upon by Americans as no more than once-in-a-lifetime fun way to cross the country.

The railways of South America are less efficient and less comfortable but cheaper to travel and, most importantly, offer their passengers a window onto the countryside.

You are also amongst the local people, which is a major attraction of this type of travel. The cheaper seats are intolerably hard and the carriage windows have a tendency to remain immovably open or closed, but one's fellow travellers are the more colourful. In Peru is the Central Railway from Lima to Oroya on to Huancayo and Hauncavelica which is one of the wonders of Latin America. The line reaches its maximum altitude of 4,782m to make it the highest passenger-carrying railway in the world. White-coated medical staff flit about the corridors equipped with oxygen apparatus for the use of altitude-stricken passengers.

Arrangements

You can, if you prefer, leave all the arranging of a multi-country journey to a travel agent but these gentry usually have little imagination or knowledge where trains are concerned and simply book your seats on the more reliable expresses or deflect you to the airlines. However, always be prepared for the unexpected when you come to put your rail itinerary to the test. Trains may come and trains may go, but not always the way you thought.

With the ever-spiralling cost of petrol, it is cheaper to travel by train – even in the UK where rail transportation is looked upon as expensive – than it is by car, although, of course, this depends on numbers carried in the car. Very many of the railway orientated nations give the intending rail traveller a variety of special offers that, in numerous circumstances, reduce fares dramatically. In the UK it has become almost as complex a business to sort them out as is the selection of best-buy fares across the Atlantic.

British Rail ties in with several rail systems on the continent to arrange inclusive rail holidays or tours while youngsters under 26 can obtain Inter-Rail passes covering a month's unlimited travel in Europe for £139, at the moment. And once there, a maze of rail travel offers are on tap. To find out more about them it is an idea to write in advance to your nearest tourist office or the country concerned. France, in particular, has many fine rail travel bargains in the shop window.

One big advantage of trains over coach travel and flying is that there is space to move around and you will have better opportunities for meeting fellow-passengers. You can eat on a train, sleep on a train, and it is certainly a more restful method of covering distances than any other mechanical means of propulsion. On some railways you can buy tickets in advance, on some you can't, but the train invariably gets there more or less on time. Board in the right frame of mind and it's fun too.

Hitchhiking

by Wendy Myers

For the person who likes conversing with strangers, relishes using newly acquired languages and yet enjoys being (often suddenly) quite alone, far off the beaten track, hitchhiking must be hard to beat as a principal way of getting about. I say 'principal' because, in my opinion, nobody should set off on a journey intending to be completely reliant on other people's goodwill. Those who set out on foot,

hoping for a lift, but feeling happy to walk, will be pleasantly relieved when one comes, whereas the type of attitude that feels it to be the duty of total strangers to transport one from A to B free of charge whenever one wishes could mean a long series of disappointments.

One April morning, I left England to 'walk around the world'. Seven years and over a hundred countries later, I returned home with enough interesting material to fill the equivalent of eight books and enormous experience of hitchhiking, which had been my main method of travelling.

Firstly, even for a long trip, the amount of luggage you take is extremely limited when hitchhiking. Only take as much as can be carried comfortably while walking. My own rucksack, which I carried with reasonable ease, weighed 16 kgs. As a guide to clothing, I suggest strong shirts, shorts and trousers, plus a sweater for cold weather. T-shirts worn next to the skin will both decrease the pressure of the rucksack straps and mop up perspiration. Strong, comfortable shoes are a must, while sandals and 'flip-flops' come in handy for hot climates or if one has blisters. Finally three 'musts' – sunhat, water bottle and diary...

Rules of Thumb

People give lifts for a number of acceptable reasons and, if these can be discovered as soon as possible and complied with, a pleasant journey should ensue. It could be that, facing a long, tedious road ahead, a driver wants to ensure against falling asleep, or maybe he wishes to practise his English, or just 'likes foreigners'. Perhaps help with driving is hoped for ... I had a wonderful tour around New Zealand's North Island with a holidaying resident who had been ill and was on the look-out for a possible co-driver. On another occasion I rode with an illiterate Australian cattle drover for whom I had to read the names on the signposts. Drivers also sometimes find hitchhikers who are foreigners like themselves useful sources of information on places to stay, the local territory and other potential passengers.

In Third World countries, it is not only foreigners who hitchhike but the locals themselves, who are usually either young middle-class students, poor people or military personnel going home on leave. The first group are the most fruitful contacts for a driver as they prove, on the whole, to be well-informed and hospitable.

Conduct will make or mar the future for hitchhikers; those who snore for hours in the back seat or eat whatever food they can find are hardly a good advertisement.

In my experience, it is very rare actually to have to 'thumb down' a vehicle – and waving an outstretched arm in front of moving traffic is downright dangerous. Upon seeing a hiker, drivers will stop – if they want to. Waving a flattened palm is the most appropriate gesture if one is needed. If in doubt, ask other hitchikers what they do.

Lifts are given most readily to mixed couples. Women are safer travelling in pairs. Three or more hitchhikers may prove too many and could do better if they split up for a while. Too little luggage can be taken as the mark of a 'bum'; too much is a hindrance. A girl with no luggage, thumbing a lift, will often stop a car, but if a boyfriend suddenly emerges from hiding with two large rucksacks, the driver of a small vehicle will be understandably infuriated.

The politest way of requesting a lift was one I discovered in Fairbanks, Alaska.

'If you want to get a ride from here, phone the radio people', I was told. 'Your message will be broadcast immediately. This is a remote town so we all try to help each other.' I did just that and somebody phoned to offer me a lift the same day.

In order to get a lift in the more conventional way, it is advisable to look as 'straight' and as clean as possible. Avoid wearing sunglasses (which prevent eye-to-eye contact with the driver) and wear light coloured clothes so that you are more visible. Stand where traffic is slow, where you can be easily seen, and where drivers are able to stop. Petrol stations, border posts and police checkpoints, ferry terminal exits, roadside restaurants, traffic lights and road intersections can all be good places. At night, make sure the spot you choose is lit. If there are two of you, one should wait by the road while the other speaks to drivers who have already stopped to use whatever facility or comply with whatever regulation there is at that place. The unwritten rule in hitchhiking is that more recent arrivals move further down the road.

Hikers bound eastwards for the Middle East stand a good chance of getting their first long distance lift at the German-Austrian border near Salzburg, probably in a lorry. Lorries nearly always have to stop at borders and in places may not pass at all on a Sunday. This is a good opportunity for the hiker to talk to the drivers and find himself an offer. If you are in a town, you could telephone trucking companies to ask if there are any vehicles about to go your way.

Being helpful and courteous to people along the road is always a good policy; it can also get you lifts. Stopping to help the owner of a broken-down vehicle may earn you gratitude in the form of something to help you on your way.

Sign Here

A sign indicating your desired destination is useful. Make the destination fairly local so that neither you nor the driver is committed in advance to a very long journey together. If you find you are congenial, you can always discuss further stages of the journey later. The sign must bear a name written in the local language and script, and even here, courtesy pays. Some people have had success with a sign reading simply 'please'. Deliberately making an obvious bad mistake on the sign can work well too. Write 'East' on the sign and then stand on the side of the road where the traffic flows west and some drivers will stop to point your your mistake. You feign confusion and soon you're away with one of these benevolent drivers – headed westwards, which is where you wanted to go in the first place.

Keep an eye on vehicle registration numbers. They are useful for gaining an idea of where any vehicle has come from or may be heading, and for tracking down the owner in case of theft or trouble.

Before you accept a lift, size up the car's occupants. Don't get into a car with drunks or maniacs. If you do and find out too late, ask to be put down. Saying you have to relieve yourself usually does the trick. When a mixed couple are travelling together, it is customary for the man to sit next to the driver, at least until everyone's confidence is assured. In some countries, unmarked cars are in fact taxis and lorry drivers expect to earn something from their passengers. If in doubt, ask if there will be a charge. Except in an emergency, never let a driver set you down in the middle of nowhere; you may be stuck there for hours, even days. And if you're set down in a town, make it the far side and not the near, so that you're not thrown back on public transport or walking.

Hikers should be prepared to give something in exchange for a ride such as interesting conversation, help with map reading or an English lesson. If they join the vehicle for a longish time, say more than a day, they should offer to pay their share of petrol, and tolls, and of course, pay for their own food and lodging. And they should remember they are guests on someone else's property. That means no requests for adjustments to windows, heating etc. unless prompted by the driver. When wet and muddy, it is considerate to wait and see whether one's host wishes to protect the car seat or floor before one enters. The hiker should be prepared to leave a vehicle when asked to. Drivers may require time to themselves for the last lap of a journey and they should certainly not be made to feel guilty if their destination falls several kilometres short of one's own. On the whole, people who give lifts are kind and unselfish.

Around the World

All over Europe, Australia, and New Zealand, drivers are 'geared' to hitchhikers, but elsewhere it can be a different matter. In many Far Eastern countries, car travel is popular now and hikers will readily be offered lifts through Sri Lanka, Thailand, Malaysia, Singapore and Japan. In rural India, cars are less common, but there drivers go out of their way to aid a traveller – which may not only involve transport but board and lodging as well. In the Philippines, hitchhiking on trucks is relatively easy, but not always advisable for girls. The same applies for South America, along whose roads *camiones* with cheerful drivers (often ex-cowboys) rumble for days and nights on end.

Through most of East, West and South Africa, there is considerable traffic. In Central African countries, where long distances over inhospitable terrain must be covered, trucks are the commonest vehicles to be found, and the same applies to the Sahara. To cross the Desert the two most popular routes northwards run from Gao and Agadez. The latter is the longer, more varied route and that is the one I chose. An Algerian driver smuggling Nigerian sheep took me all the way across the Sahara to his home in El Golea. With this hospitable desert Arab and his companions, I spent bitterly cold nights beneath a canvas spread on the sand, got chased by police between In Salah and Ragane, cheered when we escaped and kept the pre-Ramadan fast.

In jungle-covered lands such as Zaire, and the Gambia, roads are less frequented than rivers. The same applies to the Amazon region of Brazil and parts of Laos. There, one's transport may vary – from the pillion of a motor-bike to enormous trucks with 34 wheels on the ground. When one gets right off the beaten track, it is not uncommon to find people who own little boats or private planes. Two of the occasions on which such free lifts were offered to me involved a boat journey along the Mekong river from Vientiane to Savannakhet in Laos and a flight between St Louis (Senegal) and Nouakchott (Mauritania). At times one may cover vast distances in the same vehicle, such as when a new car is being delivered from one country to another.

Here I should mention one exception to walking on for miles between lifts, and that is through the vast sretches of sparsely populated territory, where it is either very hot or very cold. It has been known for hikers to perish in such conditions, for most are either unequipped with adequate warm gear for the one or enough water for the other. One such place is Australia's Nullabor Plain. The traveller who enters it on foot must beware. The temperature can soar to 45°C in the shade and in many places it has not rained for years. At a place called Karalee stands the only hotel between Coolgardie and Southern Cross. Right on the railway line, it is the only place within 185km that can supply one with a drink. Villages shown on the map become increasingly smaller on the ground as one penetrates the desert, diminishing to one house in the scrub with a sign up saying 'No Petrol Here'.

Rivers too can foil the hitchhiker. In the same country, the road between Wyndham and Darwin may suddenly become impassable from mid-November when the rivers begin to run.

Between Lifts

The traveller off the beaten track will encounter a great variety of types of lodging, from free sleeping places such as railway stations, barns and beaches, to paid accommodation. Invitations to stay with people should never be expected, but it would be a rare hiker who returned home without having enjoyed the thrill of living as 'one of the family' with hosts of other lands.

One soon discovers that there are situations where both hiking and hitchhiking would be unwise or impossible. Then one must investigate the possibility of paid transport, which can range in price from the hundreds of dollars for visiting the Pacific Islands on a liner to a matter of pence to rent a bicycle in Sarawak for 24 hours.

Problems

There are many potential problems to be faced by the hitchhiker, starting with language. Most people who offer lifts speak English or another 'international' tongue such as French, Spanish or German. And if not, a friendly smile and the use of sign language are universally accepted methods of communication. Hitchhiking, on the whole, need be considered dangerous only in Western countries.

There are the obvious hazards faced by a girl travelling alone. As one who knows, I can confidently assure readers that if a girl is mod-estly attired and makes clear her reasons for hitchhiking, problems should be minimal. My only really frightening experiences resulted from travelling with drivers who, unpredictably, were to get themselves intoxicated with drugs (such as from chewing *coca* leaves) or alcohol. A direct 'Will you come to bed with me?' type of approach from a normal male can be invariably rebuffed by laughing it off, discussing his family, expressing great anxiety at such a proposal, or by pleading sudden sickness and leaving the vehicle rapidly...

In the States, in particular, there is a growing trend of violence towards hitchhikers, male and female, that now leads to over 1,000 deaths a year. This does not necessarily mean you should stop altogether, but you should certainly think more carefully about alternative forms of transport, and vet potential lifts more thoroughly before you get into the car.

Finally, it is sad but true that many a journey through otherwise unspoiled lands is hindered by political disputes and sometimes violence. Such was my experience in Ethiopia and Sudan.

My rule here would simply be 'obey the rules' and 'never interfere'. A politely worded, sensible-sounding request to continue one's journey is generally granted, as long as one remains courteous and carries travel documents which are in impeccable order.

Here then are some tips gleaned from my personal experience. Prices and politics alter over the years but people themselves change very little, and those who travel as worthy ambassadors of their own nation will win many hearts overseas.

So, good luck to you on your travels and, should lifts at times be few and far between, remember these words of a Chinese philosopher: 'The journey of a thousand miles begins with one step.'

Backpacking

by Hilary Bradt

The word 'backpacking' was imported from America, along with some of the lightweight equipment which made feasible the whole concept of walking for days carrying the necessary food and shelter. 'Backpacking' is often rather loosely used to cover hitchhiking and rough overland travel, but here we take it in its narrower sense, meaning to explore and enjoy the undeveloped parts of the world in the best way possible as an independent traveller – on foot. If you have only hiked in Britain you'll have little concept of wilderness in the American sense where you can walk for several days without passing human habitation. The Third World offers a different possibility – that of seeing the country, its rural life and natural history by hiking along paths worn smooth by the feet of countless peasants who habitually walk long distances from village to town, or hut to pasture.

Planning and Preparation

Equipment and provisions should be chosen with care, but only after you've researched the climate and terrain of your chosen region. Remember that high altitudes mean cold or freezing nights, and burning sun in the day, that tropical vegetation at low altitudes means humidity and mosquitoes, that equatorial countries have a rainy and dry season, rather than summer and winter, and that you'll be walking along mostly good paths in the Third World but on rougher terrain in the more developed countries where trails may be poorly maintained. Essential equipment includes a tent (this needn't weigh more than 2-3kg), sleeping bag (down-filled if you're hiking in dry areas, artificial fill if heavy rain is expected), stove, and some dried food (which can be supplemented by the ubiquitous package soup). Bear in mind that if your pack weighs more than one quarter of your body weight you're not going to enjoy walking with it. If you are new to backpacking, get expert advice before buying your equipment. A good sports shop should help you, and there are many books on the subject.

Obviously you must be reasonably fit before setting out on a backpacking trip, but don't be overly concerned about it. After all, you can stop for the night more or less when and where you want, so there's no excuse for marathon daily mileage. I always start gently doing about eleven kilometres a day until I'm adjusted to the terrain and properly acclimatized.

Health

Backpacking is an excellent cure for the usual traveller's maladies – by preparing your own water (purifying it if necessary), any stomach problems you started with will soon disappear. But remember that should you become sick or injured, help may be days away. So be prepared and bring such essentials as antibiotics, surgical tape and dressings in your medical kit.

Perhaps the biggest health hazard facing backpackers is altitude sickness, which can be fatal. Acclimatize properly by climbing as slowly as possible, and spending several days at a high altitude before starting your hike. (*See section on Health on page 327*).

Finding Your Way

If you are planning to backpack in the national parks or protected areas of the developed world, you'll have no trouble finding books and maps to guide you along every mile of your chosen route. There are few books describing hikes in the Third World, however, but here it's more exciting to discover your own route. What you do need is some sort of map, even if it's only a good road map, and a compass. Providing the area you've selected is populated by indigenous people, there'll be plenty of paths. Quite good topographical maps are available in most countries (*see article on Choosing Maps on page 25*). Ex-British colonies usually have excellent ones, though they may be a little out of date. Local mountaineering clubs are often good sources of information.

Although you may lose your way from time to time, don't confuse it with being lost. After all, the whole point of backpacking is to see interesting wildlife and people, so who cares if your destination changes during the course of your hike? As long as you keep to inhabited areas, there'll always be people to advise you. It's when you venture into real wilderness that you may find yourself in trouble. Above the treeline, the lack of paths presents no particular problem, providing you have a compass, but lower down it is dangerous and stupid to continue if the path has petered out. And you must remember that that scant high altitude vegetation turns into dense, unfriendly jungle as you lose height. Believe me, once you've tried forcing your way through spiny, stinging shrubs while rotting logs collapse under your feet and vines catch on your pack, you'll never again be too proud to retrace your steps.

Guides

Most people exploring unknown country rely on guides, and if you have a specific goal, such as some ruins hidden in the jungle or a distant mountain peak, it is obviously sensible to take a local person along to show you the way. Mere backpackers, however, will usually enjoy themselves more without the incessant chatter or blackmail which is unfortunately a frequent accompaniment. Guides often get lost, too. As you can see, I'm prejudiced against guides because the few times I've been obliged to use them, they've been inefficient or downright crooked, and spoiled the feeling of adventure. To me, nothing in travel comes close to the exhilaration of approaching a pass and having no idea what you'll see from the top, or what is round the next corner. This is the essence of backpacking.

Minimum Impact

Wherever you hike you have a responsibility to leave the place unchanged by your passing. This consciousness of your impact on the environment can vary from keeping to the path and designated campsites in heavily used areas such as some American National Parks, to respecting the customs and traditions of 'primitive' indigenous people. It goes without saying that you should leave no litter, or evidence of your campsite, but fewer travellers realize the harm they may be done to a fragile culture by the indiscriminate handing out of gifts or money.

Conclusion

There are few truly wild places left in the world for the traveller to explore. Many are accessible only on foot and the adventurous backpacker will see scenery, people and wildlife denied to the car-bound explorer. And if, from time to time, hikers indulge in more conventional forms of travel, they can take comfort in the knowledge that they are carrying food and shelter on their backs to tide them over any emergency.

The Two-Wheeled Traveller

by Nicholas Crane

Ever since John Foster Fraser and his buddies Lunn and Lowe pedalled around the world in the 1890s, the bicycle has been a popular choice of vehicle for the discerning traveller. It is the most efficient of any human-powered land vehicle.

The bicycle is cheap, and because it is a simple machine, is also reliable. Its basic form is similar the world over, with component mechanics as available in downtown Manhattan as they are in Douala. With the exception of remote settlements reachable only on foot, most of the world's population is acquainted with the bike. It can never be as extreme a symbol of wealth as a motor-vehicle and neither can a bike rider be alienated from his/her surroundings. It's a humble vehicle, approachable, friendly and less of a threat than an English August breeze.

Bird-song and scents are as much a constant companion as voices and faces. Cycling is slow enough to keep you in touch with life but still fast enough to bring daily changes. A fit rider ought to be able to manage an average of 80 – 100 kilometres a day, putting you part way between pedestrians and motorcars. A bike can manage a daily distance of four times that of a walker, a third that of a car.

Bikes can be carried in planes, trains, boats and cars, on bus roofs, or in taxi boots, and parked in hotel bedrooms and left luggage stores. They can be carried and taken apart.

'Isn't it hard work?' Sometimes, but for every uphill there's a down that's as much fun as flying.

'What happens when it rains?' You get wet. Or stop in a bar.

'How many punctures do you get?' On my last ride (5,200 kilometres) I got two.

'How do you survive with so little luggage?' It's leaving behind the junk of everyday life that makes bike touring such fun.

That's enough glibness for now. Here are some practicalities.

Ready to Ride

If you are unsure of your stamina, choose for a first trip somewhere mild such as East Anglia in the UK, or northern France. Beware of being tricked by the map. It's not always the places with the highest mountains that are the most tiring to ride through. Scotland, where the roads often follow valley bottoms, is a lot easier than the south-west of England where the roads helter-skelter up and down at ferocious angles. Holland and the Ganges Delta may be as flat as a pancake but it's this flatness that allows the wind to blow unchecked – exhilerating if it's going your way, but if it isn't...

You may already have a clear idea of where you would like to ride. Hilliness, prevailing winds, temperature, rainfall, whether the roads are surfaced or dirt, are all factors worth quantifying before you leave. The actual route you take will fit with the places of interest (and accommodation). There may be duller sections of your route that you would like to skip. If so, you need to find out in advance whether you can have your bike transported on buses or trains.

You do not have to be either an athlete, or able to run up three flights of stairs without collapsing to ride a bicycle. It is a rhythmic, low-stress form of exercise. Riding to work, or school, or regularly during evenings and weekends, will build a healthy foundation of fitness. If you have never toured before, try a day ride from home (50kms maximum), or a weekend ride.

Once you know how many miles you can comfortably ride in a day, you can plan your tour route. *Always* allow for the first couple of days to be 'easy' – set yourself distances that you know you can finish easily, and this will allow you to adjust to the climate (if abroad), and to the extra exercise. It

will also let your bike and luggage 'settle in'.

Main roads must be avoided. This means investing in some good maps. As a general rule, scales of 1:200,000 will show all minor roads. For safe cycling on rough tracks, you'll need maps of 1:50,000.

What type of accommodation you decide upon affects the amount of luggage you carry and the amount of money you spend. Camping provides the greatest flexibility but also the greatest weight of luggage. With (or without) a tent you can stay in all manner of places. Farmers will often consent to the use of a field-corner, and in wilderness areas you camp where you choose (leave nothing; take nothing). With two of you you can share the weight of the tent, cooking gear and so on. If you are using youth-hostels, bed-and-breakfasts or hotels, you can travel very lightly but your route is fixed by available accommodation.

The Bike and Clothing

Unlike the purchase of a motorised expedition vehicle, the bicycle need cost no more than a good camera or backpack. Neither need it be an exotic mix of the latest aluminium alloys and hi-tech tyres. Foster Fraser covered 19,237 miles through seventeen countries on a heavy steel roadster fitted with leather bags. Destinations are reached through the urge to make the journey, rather than the colour of the bike frame.

Given the determination to succeed, virtually any type of bike can be used for making a journey. The author Christa Gausden made her first journey, from the Mediterranean to the English Channel, on a single-speed shopping bike. My own early rides across Europe were made on the heavy ten-speed I had used for riding to school. Spending time and money on your bike however will increase your comfort and the bike's reliability.

For road touring, the most comfortable machine is a lightweight ten or twelve speed. Gear ratios in the UK and USA are measured somewhat quaintly, in inches – the given figure representing the size of wheel which it would have been necessary to fit to a Penny Farthing to achieve the same effect! *Richard's Bicycle Book* (and various others) contain detailed gear ration tables. For normal touring, the lowest gear should be around 30-35 inches; the highest, 80-90 inches. With these ratios a fit rider ought to be able to pedal over the Pyrenees while the top gear is high enough to make the most following winds.

Good quality wheels and tyres are important. If you can afford it, have some wheels built by a professional wheel-builder, asking him to use top quality pre-stretched spokes and the best hubs and rims. For European continental touring, it's handiest if the rims are of the size to take the metric 700C tyres. Some rims (eg Mavic M3CD) will take a variety of tyre widths, allowing your one set of wheels to shod either with fast, light road tyres, or heavier, fatter tyres for rough surfaces. Buy the best tyres you can afford. Quality tyres such as the Specialized and Nutrak series can be expected to run for 8,000 kilometres on a loaded bike over mixed road surfaces.

'Drop' handlebars are more versatile than 'uprights', giving your hands several different positions, distributing your weight fairly between your arms and bottom, and also providing for riding in the 'crouch' position – useful for fast riding, or pedalling into headwinds. Drop handlebars come in different widths; ideally they should match the span of your shoulders. The saddle is very much a question of personal preference; try several before deciding. (Note that you should fit a wide 'mattress' saddle if you have upright handlebars, as most of your weight will be on your bottom.) Solid leather saddles need treatment with leather oils and then 'breaking in' – sometimes a long and painful process, but one which results in a seat moulded exquisitely to your own shape. Also very comfortable are the padded suede saddles, which require no breaking in. Since they never change shape, be sure this sort of saddle is a perfect fit before you buy. Steer clear of plastic-topped saddles.

It is very important that your bike frame is the correct size for you. There are several different methods of computing this, but a rough rule of thumb is to subtract 25 centimetres from your inside leg measurement. You should be able to stand, both feet flat on the ground, with as least three centimetres between the top-tube and your crotch. The frame-angles should be between 71 and 73°. The strongest and lightest bike frames are commonly made from Reynolds tubing, most usually of the '531' specification (look for the label). On lighter models it may be 'double-butted'. An option for those with bigger purses is to have a bike frame built to your own specifications and size.

Generally speaking, the more you spend on your brakes and pedals, the stronger and smoother they will be. Pedals should be as wide as your feet (note that some Italian models are designed for slim continental feet rather than the flat-footed Britisher). Toe-clips and straps increase pedalling efficiency.

Luggage should be carried in panniers attached to a rigid triangulated carrier that cannot sway. Normally, rear panniers should be sufficient. If you need more capacity, use a low-riding set of front pannier carriers (such as the Blackburn model) and/or a small handlebar bag. Lightweight items, such as a sleeping bag, can be carried on the top of the rear carrier if necessary. The guiding rule is to keep weight as low down and as close to the centre of the bike as possible. Never carry anything on your back.

Clothing chosen carefully will keep you warm and dry in temperate climates; cool and comfortable in the heat. Choose items on the 'layer' principle: each piece of clothing should function on its own, or fit when worn with all the others. The top layers should be windproof, and in cold or wet lands, waterproof too. Goretex is ideal. Close fitting clothes are more comfortable, don't flap as you ride, and can't get caught in the wheels and chainset. In bright conditions a peaked hat or beret makes life more comfortable, and cycling gloves (with padded palms) will cushion you from road vibration. Cleated cycling shoes, as worn by racers, are impossible to walk in and not worth taking. Choose shoes with a stiff sole (i.e. not tennis shoes) that will cushion your foot from the pedal, and which are also good for walking. Specially designed touring shoes can be bought at the bigger bike shops.

Mountainbikes

If you're planning to venture off the beaten track, on rough roads and tracks, a mountainbike will provide the greatest strength and reliability. Mountainbikes evolved in California during the early '80s and are now readily available in most Western countries. They are heavier than a road-bike and, on tarmac, a lot slower. But on dirt roads and trails mountainbikes are in their element; easy to control, with good grip and resistant to vibration, knocks and crashes. Mountainbikes generally come with fifteen gears, with a bottom gear of around 25 inches, powerful cantilever brakes and heavy-duty ribbed tyres that are virtually puncture proof. Lighter tyres with smoother tread patterns and higher pressures can be fitted for road-riding. For sheer toughness, a mountainbike is impossible to beat, but you pay for this toughness by pedalling more weight in a less efficient riding position. Oh – I forgot to mention: mountainbikes are great fun!

Buying Secondhand

Buying secondhand can save a lot of money if you know what to look for. Touring bikes and mountainbikes are advertised regularly in the classified columns of the cycling magazines. Before buying, check the frame is straight, first by sight, and then by (carefully) riding no-hands. If the bike seems to veer repreatedly to one side, the frame or forks are bent. Spin the wheels and check they are true. Wobble all the rotating parts; if there is a lot of 'play', the bearings may be worn. Above all, only buy from someone you feel is honest.

On the Road

The greatest hazard is other traffic. Always keep to your side of the road, watching and listening for approaching vehicles. In Asia and Africa, buses and trucks travel at breakneck speeds and expect all to move from their path. Look out too for carts and cows, sheep, people, pot-holes and ruts, all of which can appear without warning and spell disaster for the unwary.

Dogs deserve special mention. Being chased up-hill by a mad dog is the cyclist's ultimate nightmare. I've always found the safest escape to be speed, and (touch wood) have yet to be bitten. If you are going to ride in countries known to have rabies, consider being vaccinated before departure.

Security need not be a problem if you obey certain rules. Unless you are going to live with your bike day and night, you need a strong lock. The best are the hoop-shaped hardened steel models. Always lock your bike to an immovable object, with the lock passing round the frame and rear wheel. For added security, the front wheel can be removed and locked also. Before buying, check that the lock of your choice is big enough for the job. Note that quick-release hubs increase the chance of the wheels being stolen. Always lock your bike in a public place, and if you're in a café or bar, keep it in sight. In most Third World countries, it is quite acceptable to take bicycles into hotel bedrooms. Elsewhere, the management can usually be persuaded to provide a safe lock-up.

Expedition Cycling

Bikes have been ridden, carried and dragged in some ridiculous places: across the Darien Gap, through the Sahara and up Kilimanjaro. They have been pedalled around the world many times, and they have been used as a sympathetic means of transport into remote little-visited corners of the globe. The step up from holiday touring in Europe to prolonged rides to the back-of-beyond requires sensible planning. Choice of bicycle and equipment will have great bearing on the style of the ride. If you want to be as inconspicuous as possible, the best machine will be a local black roadster. Such a bike will probably need constant attention, but will pay off handsomely in its lack of Western pretension. I once pedalled across the African Rift Valley on a bike hired from a street market in Nairobi. The bike fell apart and had to be welded and then rebuilt, but the ride was one of the most enjoyable I've ever had.

For serious journeys defined by a set goal and time-scale, you need a well-prepared, mechanically perfect machine. If much of the riding is on dirt roads, a mountainbike well may be the best bet. If you can keep your weight down, a lightweight road-bike will handle any road surface too. On the 'Journey to the Centre of the Earth' bike ride across Asia with my cousin Richard, our road bikes weighed ten kgs each, and our total luggage came to eight kgs each. We carried one set of clothes each, waterproofs and a sleeping bag, picking up food and water along the way. Objectivity obliges me to note that I've seldom come across other cyclists travelling this light, most voicing the opinion that they'd rather carry their cooking stove, pans, food, tent and extra clothes. The penalty is a bike that's too heavy to lift, with wheels enduring unfair strain.

Spares

Lightness gives you speed. One spare tyre and one spare inner tube, and a few spokes are the basic spares. Rear tyres wear faster than front ones, so switch them round when they are part worn. For rides of over 5,000 kms, in dry or gritty conditions, a replacement chain will also be necessary. The tool-kit should include a puncture repair kit, appropriate Allen keys, chain-link remover, freewheel block remover, small adjustable wrench and cone-spanners for the wheel-hubs. Oil, grease and heavy tools can be obtained from garages and truck-drivers along the route.

Saving weight saves energy. Look critically at your equipment, and have some fun cutting off all unnecessary zips, buckles, straps, labels and discard superfluous clothing and knick-knacks. Make sure there are no unnecessary pieces of metal on the bike (such as wheel-guides on the brakes).

It is useful to know what the absolute maximum is that you can ride in one day, should an emergency arise. On a loaded bike ridden on tarmac when fully fit, this should be 200-300 kms.

With a constant air-flow over the body, and steady exertion, a cyclist loses body moisture rapidly. Particularly in hot climates, it's possible to become seriously dehydrated unless you drink sufficient liquid. You need a minimum of one-litre carrying capacity on the bike; whether you dou-ble or treble this figure depends on how far from habitation you are straying. In monsoon Asia, I've drunk up to thirteen litres a day.

Motorcycling

by Ted Simon

It seems pointless to argue the merits of motorcycles as against other kinds of vehicles. Everyone knows more or less what the motorcycle can do, and attitudes to it generally are quite sharply defined. The majority is against it, and so much the better for those of us who recognize its advantages. Who wants to be part of a herd? Let me just say that I am writing here for people who think of travelling through the broad open spaces of Africa and Latin America, or across the great Asian land mass. Riding in Europe or North America is straightforward, and even the problems posed in Australia are relatively clear cut. As for those fanatics whose notion of travelling is to set the fastest time between Berlin and Singapore, I am all for abandoning them where they fall, under the stones and knives of angry Muslim villages.

Here then are some points in favour of the motorcycle, for the few who care to consider them. In my view, it is the most versatile vehicle there is for moving through strange countries at a reasonable pace, experiencing changing conditions and meeting people in remote places. It can cover immense distances, and will take you where cars can hardly go. It is easily and cheaply freighted across lakes and oceans, and it can usually be trucked out of trouble without much difficulty, where a car might anchor you to the spot for weeks. If you choose a good bike for your purpose, it will be economical and easy to repair, and it can be made to carry quite astonishing amounts of stuff if your systems are right.

Sit Up and Take Notice

In return the bike demands the highest level of awareness from its rider. You need not be an expert, but you must be enthusiastic and keep all your wits about you. It is an unforgiving vehicle which does not suffer fools at all. As well as the more obvious hazards of potholes, maniacal truck drivers and stray animals, there are the less tangible perils like dehydration, hypothermia and plain mental fatigue to recognize and avoid.

The bike, then, poses a real challenge to its rider, and it may seem to verge on masochism to accept it, but my argument is that by choosing to travel in a way that demands top physical and mental performance you equip yourself to benefit a thousand times more from what comes your way, enabling you quite soon to brush aside the discomforts that plague lazier travellers.

You absolutely must sit up and take notice to survive at all. The weather and temperature are critical factors; the moods and customs of the people affect you vitally; you are vulnerable and sensitive to everything around you; and you learn fast. You build up resistances faster too, your instincts are sharper and truer, and you adjust more readily to changes in the climate, both physical and social.

Here endeth the eulogy upon the bike.

After all these generalizations, it is difficult to be particular. There is no one bike for all seasons, nor one for all riders. The BMW is a splendid machine with a splendid reputation for touring, but is *not* infallible, and it *is* expensive. British bikes need a lot of maintenance but they are ruggedly engineered and easily repaired, given the parts or a Punjabi workshop to make them up. Japanese bikes have a shorter useful life, but they work very well, and their dealer networks are incomparable. They are hard to beat as a practical proposition provided you go for models with a tried record of reliability.

On the whole, I would aim for an engine capacity of between 500cc and 750cc. Lightness is a great plus factor. Too much power is an embarrassment, but a small engine will do fine if you don't mean to hump a lot of stuff over the Andes, or carry another person as well.

One's Company

I travelled alone almost all the way around the world, but most people prefer to travel in company. As a machine the motorcycle is obviously at its best used by one person, and it is my opinion that you learn faster and get the maximum feedback on your own, but I know that for many such loneliness would be unthinkable. Even so, you need to be very clear about your reasons for choosing to travel in company. If it is only for security then my advice is to forget it. Groups of nervous travellers chattering to each other in some outlandish tongue spread waves of paranoia much faster than a single weary rider struggling to make contact in the local language. A motorcycle will attract attention in most places. The problem is to turn that interest to good account. In some countries (Brazil, for example) a motorcycle is a symbol of playboy wealth, and an invitation to thieves. In parts of Africa and the Andes, it is still an unfamiliar and disturbing object. Whether the attention it attracts works for the rider or against him depends on his own awareness of others and the positive energy he can generate towards his environment.

It is very important in poor countries not to flaunt wealth and superiority. All machinery has this effect anyway, but it can be much reduced by a suitable layer of dirt and a muted exhaust system. I avoided having too much glittering chrome and electric paintwork, and I regarded most modern leathers and motorcycle gear as a real handicap. I wore an open face helmet for four years and never regretted it, and when I stopped among people, I always took it off to make sure they saw me as a real person. My ideal was always to get as far away as possible from the advertised image of the smart motorcyclist, and talk to people spontaneously in a relaxed manner. If one can teach oneself to drop shyness with strangers, the rewards are dramatic. Silence is usually interpreted as standoffishness, and is almost as much a barrier as a foreign language.

Care and Repair

Obviously you should know your bike and be prepared to look after it. Carry as many tools as you can use, and all the small spares you can afford. Fit a capacitor so that you don't need a battery to start. Weld a disc on the swing stand to hold the bike in soft dirt. Take two chains and use one to draw the other off its sprockets. This makes frequent chain-cleaning less painful, something that should be done in desert conditions. Take a tin of Swarfega or Palmit; it's very useful where water is at a premium and for easing off rims. Buy good patches and take them (I like 'Tip-Top'); you won't get them there. The Schrader pump, which screws into a cylinder in place of the spark plug, is a fine gadget, and one of the best reasons for running on two cylinders. Aerosol repair canisters, unfortunately, do not always work. The quickly detachable wheel arrangement on the Triumph saved me a lot of irritation too.

Change oil every 2,500kms and don't buy it loose if you can avoid it. Make *certain* your air filter is good enough. Some production models will not keep out fine desert grit, and the consequences are not good. Equally important are low compression pistons to take the strain off and to accept lousy fuel.

I ran on Avon tyres and used a rear tread on the front wheel, which worked well. A set of tyres gave me 19,000kms or more. The hardest country for tyres was India, because of the constant braking for oxcarts on tarmac roads. It was the only place where the front tyre wore out before the rear one because, of course, it's the front brakes that do most of the stopping.

Insurance is a problem that worries many people. Get it as you go along. I was uninsured everywhere except when the authorities made it impossible for me to enter without buying it. This was most definitely illegal and I do not recommend it: if you get clobbered you have only yourself to blame. (*See Insurance on page 240 and Driving Requirements on page 631*).

Other things I found essential were: a stove, a good, all-purpose knife, some primitive cooking equipment and a store of staples like rice and beans. Naturally you need to carry water too, up to four or five litres, if possible. I found the ability to feed myself when I felt like it was a great protection against sickness, as well as an incentive to wander even further off the beaten track. In the end I finished with quite a complex kitchen in one of my boxes, but of course that's just a matter of taste.

Don't...

Finally a few things I learned not to do:

Don't ride without arms, knees and eyes covered and watch out for bee swarms, unless you use a screen, which I did not.

Don't carry a gun or any offensive weapon unless you want to invite violence.

Do not allow yourself to be hustled into starting off anywhere until you're ready; something is bound to go wrong or get lost.

Do not let helpful people entice you into following their cars at ridiculous speeds over dirt roads and potholes. They have no idea what bikes can do. Always set your own pace and get used to the pleasures of easy riding.

Resist the habit of thinking that you must get to the next big city before nightfall. You miss everything that's good along the way and, in any case, the cities are the least interesting places.

Don't expect things to go to plan, and don't worry when they don't. Perhaps the hardest truth to appreciate when starting a long journey is that the mishaps and unexpected problems always lead to the best discoveries and the most memorable experiences. And if things insist on going too smoothly, you can always try running out of petrol on purpose.

River Travel

by John and Julie Batchelor

Wherever you want to go in the world, the chances are that you can get there by river. Indeed, the more remote your destination, the more likely it will be that the only way of getting there, without taking to the air, will be by river. This is particularly true of tropical regions where, throughout the history of exploration, rivers have been the key that has opened the door to the interior. It is still the case that for those who really want to penetrate deep into a country, to learn about the place and its peoples through direct contact, the best way to do so is by water.

River travel splits neatly into three categories: public transport, private hire and your own transport.

Public Transport

Wherever there is a large navigable river, whether it be in Africa, South America, Asia or even Europe, you will find some form of river transport. This can range from a luxury floating hotel on the Nile to a dug-out canoe in the forests of Africa and South America. And between these extremes, all over the world there can be found the basic work-a-day ferries which ply between villages and towns carrying every conceivable type of commodity and quite often an unbelievably large number of people.

Let's start by examining travel on an everyday ferry. First you must buy your ticket. The usual method is to turn up at the waterfront, find out which boat is going in your direction and then locate the agent's office. With luck, this will be a simple matter, but on occasion even finding out where to purchase your ticket can be an endless problem. Don't be put off. Just turn up at your boat, go on board and find someone, preferably someone in authority, to take your money. You'll have no difficulty in doing this, so long as you do not embarrass people by asking for receipts.

Board the boat as early as possible. It is probable that it will be extremely crowded, so if you are a deck passenger you will need to stake out your corner of the deck and defend it against all comers. Make sure of your sleeping arrangements immediately. In South America this will mean getting your hammock in place, in Africa and the Far East making sure you have enough space to spread out your sleeping mat. Take care about your positioning. If you are on a trip lasting a number of days do not place yourself near the one and only toilet on board. By the end of the journey the location of this facility will be obvious to anyone with a sense of smell. Keep away from the air outlet from the engine room unless you have a particular liking for being asphyxiated by diesel fumes. If rain is expected, make sure you are under cover. On most boats a tarpaulin shelter is rigged up over the central area.

Try to get a spot near the middle as those at the edges tend to get wet. Even if rain is unlikely it is still a good idea to find shade from the sun. For those unused to it, sitting in the tropical sun all day can be unpleasant and dangerous.

Go equipped. There may be some facilities for food and drink on board, but in practice this will probably only mean warm beer and unidentified local specialities which you might prefer not to have to live on. Assume there will be nothing. Take everything you need for the whole journey, plus a couple of days just in case. On the Zaire river, for instance, it is quite common for boats to get stuck on sand banks for days on end. And don't forget the insects. The lights of the boat are sure to attract an interesting collection of wildlife during the tropical night, so take a mosquito net.

Occasionally, for those with money, there may be cabins available on the larger river boats, but don't expect too much of these. If there is supposed to be water, it will only be intermittent at best, and there certainly won't be a plug. The facilities will be very basic and you are almost certain to have the company of hordes of cockroaches who will take particular delight in sampling your food and exploring your belongings. Occupying a cabin on a multi-class boat also marks you out as 'rich' and thus subject to attention from the less desirable of your fellow passengers. Lock your cabin door and do not leave your window open at night. In order to do this you will also have to go equipped with a length of chain and padlock. On most boats the advantages of a cabin are minimal.

Longer journeys, especially on African rivers, tend to be one long party. Huge quantities of beer are drunk and very loud music plays throughout the night. It is quite likely that you will be looked on as a guest and expected to take an active part in the festivities. It's a good way of making friends, but don't expect a restful time.

Given these few commonsense precautions, you will have a rewarding trip. By the time you reach your destination you will have many new friends, have learnt a few essential words of the local language and have offers of accommodation, all of which make your stay pleasanter and your journey easier.

Private Hire

In order to progress further up the river from the section navigable by larger boats, you will have to look around for transport to hire. This may be a small motor boat, but is more likely to be a dug-out canoe with an outboard motor. When negotiating for this sort of transport, local knowledge is everything: who's reliable and owns a reliable boat or canoe. With luck, your new-found friends from the first stage of your journey will advise you and take care of the negotiations over price. This is by far the best option. Failing that, it is a question of your own judgement. What you are looking for is a well-equipped boat with a well-serviced motor and a teetotal crew. In all probability such an ideal combination doesn't exist – at least we have never found it. So we are back to common sense.

Look at the boat before coming to any agreement. If possible try to have a test run just to make sure the motor works. Try to establish that the boatman knows the area you want to go to. If he already smells of drink at ten in the morning, he may not be the most reliable man around. This last point could be important. If you are returning the same way you will need to arrange for your boatman to pick you up again at a particular time and place. The chances of this happening if he is likely to disappear on an extended drunken binge once he has your money is remote in the extreme. Take your time over the return arrangements. Make sure that everyone knows and understands the place, the day and the time that they are required to meet you. Don't forget that not everyone can read or tell the time. If you have friends in the place, get them to check that the boatman leaves when planned. Agree on the price to be paid before you go and do not pay anything until you arrive at the destination. If the part of the deal is that you provide the fuel, buy it yourself and hand it over only when everyone and everything is ready for departure. Establish clearly what the food and drink arrangements are as you may be expected to feed the crew.

Once you are on your way, it is a question again of common sense. Take ready-prepared food. Protect yourself from the sun and your equipment from rain and spray. If you are travelling by dug-out canoe, it will be a long uncomfortable trip with little opportunity for stretching your legs. Make sure you have something to sit on, preferably something soft, but don't forget that the bottom of the canoe will soon be full of water.

Once you have arrived at your destination, make sure that you are in the right place before letting the boat go If the boatman is coming back for you, go over all the arrangements one more time. Do not pay in advance for the return if you can possibly avoid it. If the boatman has the money, there is little incentive for him to keep his part of the bargain. If absolutely necessary, give just enough to cover the cost of the fuel.

Own Transport

After exhausting the possibilities of public transport and hire, you must make your own way to the remote headwaters of your river. You may have brought your own equipment, which will probably be an inflatable with outboard motor or a canoe. If you have got this far, we can assume that you know all about the requirements of your own equipment. Both inflatables and rigid kayaks are bulky items to transport over thousands of miles so you might consider a collapsible canoe which you assemble once you have reached this part of your trip. We have not used them personally but have heard very good reports on them in use under very rigorous conditions.

Your chances of finding fuel for the outboard motor on the remote headwaters of almost any river in the world are negligible. Take all you need with you. Your chances of finding food and hospitality will depend on the part of the world you are exploring. In South America, you are unlikely to find any villages and the only people you may meet are nomadic Indians who, given present circumstances, could be hostile. You will have to be totally self-sufficient. In Africa the situation is quite different. Virtually anywhere that you can reach with your boat will have a village or fishing encampment of some description. The villagers will show you hospitality and in all probability you will be able to buy fresh vegetables, fruit and fish from the people. Take basic supplies and enough for emergencies but expect to be able to supplement this with local produce.

Another alternative could be to buy a local canoe, although this option is fraught with dangers. Buying a second-hand canoe is as tricky as buying a second-hand car without knowing anything about mechanics. You can easily be fobbed off with a dud. We know of a number of people who have paddled off proudly in their new canoe only to sink steadily below the surface as water seeped in through cracks and patches. This is usually a fairly slow process so that by the time you realize your error you are too far away from the village to do anything about it. A word or two about dug-out canoes: these are simply hollowed-out tree trunks and come in all sizes. The stability of the canoe depends on the expertise of the man who made it. They are usually heavy, difficult to propel in a straight line, prone to capsize, uncomfortable and extremely hard work The larger ones can weigh over a ton which makes it almost impossible for a small group to take one out of the water for repairs. Paddling dug-outs is best left to the experts. Only if you are desperate – and going downstream – should you entertain the idea.

Travel Etiquette

When travelling in remote areas anywhere in the world, it should always be remembered that you are the guest. You are the one who must adjust to local circumstances and take great pains not to offend the customs and traditions of the people you are visiting. To refuse hospitality will almost always cause offence. Remember that you are the odd one out and that it is natural for your hosts to be inquisitive and fascinated by everything you do. However tired or irritable you may be, you have chosen to put yourself in this position and it is your job to accept close examination with good grace. Before travelling do take the trouble to research both the area you intend to visit and its people. Try to have some idea of what is expected of you before you go to a village. If you are offered food and accommodation accept it. Do not be squeamish about eating what is offered. After all, the local people have survived on whatever it is, so it is unlikely to do you very much damage.

No two trips are ever the same, thank goodness! The advice we have tried to give is nothing more than common sense. If you apply this to whatever you are doing, you will not go far wrong. Just remember that what may be impossible today can be achieved tomorrow . . . or perhaps the next day . . . or the next. Don't be in a hurry. There is so much to be enjoyed. Take your time . . . and good luck!

Sailing

by Robin-Knox-Johnston

Sailing beneath a full moon across a calm tropical sea towards some romantic destination is a wonderful dream, but to make it become a reality requires careful preparation, or the dream can turn into a nightmare.

The boat chosen should be a solid, robust cruiser. There is no point in buying a modern racing yacht as it will have been designed to be sailed by a large crew of specialists and will need weekly maintenance. The ideal boat for a good cruise should be simple, with a large carrying capacity, and easy to maintain. Bear in mind that it is not always easy to find good mechanics or materials abroad, and most repairs and maintenance will probably be done by the crew.

It is important to get to know the boat well before sailing so that you will know how she will respond in various sea states and weather conditions. This also enables one to make out a proper checklist for the stores and spares that will need to be carried. For example, there is no point in taking a spare engine, but the right fuel and oil filters, and perhaps a spare alternator, are advisable. Try and standardise things as much as possible. If the same size of rope can be used for a number of purposes, then a spare coil of that rope might well cover nearly all your renewal requirements.

Electronics

There is a huge array of modern electronic equipment available, and these 'goodies' can be tempting. It pays to keep the requirement to a minimum to reduce expense and complexity. Small boat radars are now quite cheap, and these can be used for navigation as well as keeping a lookout in fog. Around the Northern European coastline, a Decca Navigator can be useful, but this system does not exist elsewhere, and if going to North America, the alternative is Loran. There is a world wide system of Radio Direction Beacons and a receiver for these stations is not that expensive although the range is not great. Once out at sea, and out of range of the coastal systems, Satellite Navigation is accurate and not too expensive, and newer versions are in the pipeline. All these 'Black Boxes' are only aids to navigation however, and the knowledge of how to use a sextant and work out a position from the readings is still essential.

Radio communications are now everywhere and are important for the boat's safety. Short range, Very High Frequency (VHF) is in use worldwide for port operations and for communications between ships at sea. It is best to buy a good, multi-channel set and make sure that the aerial is at the top of the mast, as the range is not much greater than the line of sight, so the higher the aerial, the better. For long range communications, there is a worldwide maritime communications network using Single Side Band in the medium and high frequency bands. There are now easy to operate SSB sets at quite reasonable prices and with patience, I have managed to contact the UK from the Caribbean with only 150 watts of output. Before sailing it is advisable to study the Radio Telephone procedure and if possible take the operator's examination which is organised in Britain by the Royal Yachting Assocation. The Admiralty publish lists of frequencies for all Radio Communications and Direction Finding stations worldwide.

Meteorology plays an important part in any voyage and the rudiments of weather systems, and how they are going to affect the weather on the chosen route is essential knowledge for anyone making any voyage. Weather forecasts are broadcast by most nations, but it is possible to buy a weatherfax machine which prints out the weather picture for a selected area, and costs about the same as an SSB radio set.

Crew

The choice of crew will ultimately decide the success or otherwise of the venture. They must be congenial, enthusiastic, and good work sharers. Nothing destroys morale on board a boat more quickly than one person who moans or shirks their share of shipboard duties. Ideally the crew should have previous sailing experience so that they know what to expect, and it is well worth while going for a short shakedown sail with the intended crew to see if they can get on well and can cope. Never take too many people, it cramps the living quarters and usually means there is not enough work to keep everyone busy. A small, but busy crew usually creates a happy purposeful team.

Beware of picking up crew who ask for passage somewhere at the last minute. For a start, you will not know their backgrounds and you will only find out how good or bad they are once you get to sea, which is too late. In many countries, the Skipper of the boat is responsible for the crew, and you can find that when you reach your destination, the Immigration will not allow the marine 'hitch-hiker' ashore unless they have the fare or ticket out of the country to their home. If you do take people on like this, make sure that they have money or a ticket and I recommend that you take the money as security until they are landed. I once got caught like this in Durban with a hitch-hiker who told me I would have to give him the airfare back to the US. However, he 'accidently' fell into the harbour, and when he put his pile of dollars out to dry, we took the amount required for his fare.

Never hesitate to send crew home if they do not fit in with the remainder. The cost will seem small in comparison to a miserable voyage.

Provisions

Always stock up for the longest possible time the voyage might take, plus ten percent extra. The system that I use for calculating the food requirement is to work out a daily menu for a week for one person. Then I multiply this figure by the number of weeks the voyage should take plus the extra, and then multiply that figure by the number of crew on board.

Always take as much fresh food as you can. Root vegetables will last at least a month if kept well aired and dry, greens last about a week. Citrus fruit will last a month. Eggs, if sealed with wax or vaseline, will last a couple of months. Meat and fish should not be trusted beyond a day or two unless smoked, depending on the temperature. Flour, rice and other dry stores will last a long time if kept in a dry sealed container.

The rest of the provisions will have to be canned, which are of good quality in Europe, the US, South Africa, Australia and New Zealand, but not so reliable elsewhere. Code all the cans with paint, then tear off the labels and cover the whole tin with varnish as protection against salt water corrosion, then stow them securely in a dry place onboard.

Freeze dried food is excellent, but you will have to take extra water if you do use them.

When taking water on board, first check that it is fresh and pure. If in doubt, add Chloride of Lime to the water tanks in the recommended proportions. Very good fresh water can be obtained from rain showers. The most effective method is to top up the main boom, so that the sail 'bags' and the water will flow down to the boom and along the gooseneck where it can be caught in a bucket.

Paperwork and Officialdom

Before setting out on a long voyage, make sure that someone at home, such as a member of the family or your solicitor, knows your crew list, their addresses, and your intended programme, and keep them updated from each port. Make sure your bank knows what you are planning, and that there are enough funds in your account for emergencies. It is better to arrange to draw money at banks en route rather than carry large sums on board.

It is always wise to register the boat. Not only is this proof of ownership and nationality, but it also means that your boat comes under the umbrella of certain international maritime agreements.

A Certificate of Competence as a Yachtmaster is advisable. Some countries (eg Germany) are starting to insist on them.

The crew must have their passports with them, plus visas for any countries to be visited that require them, such as the USA, Australia and India. More countries are demanding visas these days and it is advisable to check with the embassies or consulates of the countries you wish to visit on this point. You should also check the health requirements and make sure that the crew have the various up to date inocculation or vaccination certificates. It is always advisable to have Tetanus jabs.

Finally, before setting out, obtain a Clearance Certificate from Customs. You may not need it at your destination, but if you run into difficult officials, it will be helpful.

On arrival at your destination, always fly your national flag and the flag of the country you have reached on the starboard rigging and the quarantine flag (Q). If the Customs and Immigration do not visit the boat on arrival, the Skipper only should go ashore to find them and report, taking the Registration Certificate, Port Clearance, crew passports and any other relevant papers.

Foreign officials, particularly in less developed countries, can be extremely rude and peremptory. Always be polite, even if you have to grit your teeth sometimes. If you get into serious difficulties ask for assistance from the local national Consul.

Smuggling and Piracy

Smuggling is a serious offence and the boat may be confiscated if smuggled items are found on board, even if the Skipper knew nothing about it.

There are certain areas where smuggling and piracy have become common, and, of course, it is largely in the same areas that law enforcement is poor. The worst areas are the Western Caribbean, the North Coast of South America, the Red Sea and the Far East. There have also been a number of attacks on yachts off the Brazilian coast.

The best protection is a crew of fairly tough-looking individuals, but a firearm is a good persuader. Never allow other boats to come alongside at sea unless you know the people on board, and if a suspicious boat approaches, let them see that you have a large crew and a gun. Call on VHF Channel 16, as this might alert other boats, and if the approaching vessel is official, they are probably listening to that channel. When in a strange port, it is a good rule never to allow anyone on board the boat unless you know them or they have an official identity card.

If you do carry a firearm, make sure you obtain a licence for it.

Murphy's Law says that if you carry a rifle, you will never have to use it – it is what the Law says if you don't carry one that causes concern!

Travel By Freighter

by James and Sheila Shaw

Travel by ocean-going freighter has been on the rise again following its near elimination in the early 1980s. Conversion to container ships by many of the world's steamship companies and rising labour costs forced most firms to curtail the carrying of passengers on working cargo vessels through the late 1970's. Fortunately, a number of operators are now making space for passengers again. Behind this movement lie high demand and a willingness by travellers to pay higher fares than before. A few years ago, an around-the-world freighter trip cost the average freighter traveller as little as $35 per day. Today, that same trip costs closer to $125 a day. Nevertheless, many people still consider travel on a working cargo ship to be one of the great adventures of life – and a very good buy for the money.

Such travel, however, is not for everyone; what is adventure for one may be inconvenience for another. Travel agents are quick to point out that cargo dictates the operation of freighters, and few such vessels travel on a set schedule. Consequently a ship's departure may be delayed for days, it may have to wait off-shore instead of going immediately into a berth, and an expected port of call may be eliminated or a new port added after the voyage is underway. For these reasons freighter travellers must have an abundance of time, patience, flexibility and stamina. Most today are retired people in their 60s or 70s with the financial means to afford such travel and the time to pursue it. But this does not rule out freighter travel for everyone else! There are a number of companies that offer either short duration round-trip voyages or that operate their ships on such a tight schedule that they can be successfully incorporated into holiday plans. Where there's a will there's a way.

Finding Out

One of the quickest ways to find out what freighter trips are available, and how much they will cost, is to visit a travel agent or library and browse through a recent issue of the *ABC Passenger Shipping Guide* (ABC International, Dunstable, Beds. LU5 4HB, U.K.). This is a monthly listing of all the companies in the world offering passenger transportation by sea except for very short ferry runs or excursion boats. It lists passenger-carrying freighter services by geographic area and gives a complete breakdown of voyage itineraries, durations, ships, fares and sailing frequencies. Also given are the passenger capacity and tonnage of each vessel and the name of the operating company and their worldwide agents.

Once a decision has been made as to a particular shipping line or the intended area of travel, the next move should be to talk with a reputable travel agent who specializes in freighter travel. These people are likely to have travelled on or visited many of the ships in question and they should be familiar with the companies involved. This is almost essential with freighter travel as cargo lines are not as adept at handling passengers and their many requests as a cruise line or full-time passenger line might be. An agent will be able to ask the right questions and get the right answers. Important points to consider will be the registration of the ship and the nationality of its crew and officers (this will determine what language is spoken), the location of the passenger accommodation on the vessel as compared to its public rooms and dining room (some ships require the use of several staircases and are not equipped with lifts), the availability of laundry facilities and deck chairs on board, and the existence of a bar and 'slop chest' where passengers can purchase alcohol, cigarettes and sundry items during the voyage.

There are very few traditional 'breakbulk' cargo vessels left on the high seas in this modern age. Breakbulk vessels were the ships that loaded all sorts of bales and crates into their holds and spent days in port, giving their passengers more than enough time to get a good look around. Today, more often than not, the freighter traveller's choice of ships will be limited to a containership or a roll-on/roll-off vessel, both designed with the intent of spending as little time in port as possible. A travel agent familiar with freighters will also have a good idea of how long each vessel will usually spend in port. Agents can also arrange sightseeing excursions in ports-of-call, including excursions that leave the ship in one port and rejoin it in another. This is one way interior points can be visited when the stay in port is short.

Accommodation

Cabins aboard most present-day freighters are large, much larger than comparably priced cabins on cruise liners. Unlike cruise liners, however, passengers cannot always choose their cabin in advance. Because of the abnormally long booking schedule of a cargo ship, some passengers may have booked years in advance. The best cabins in any given price range are usually awarded automatically to those who make their reservations first. A travel agent or the shipping company should be able to provide a diagram showing the layout of the cabins on a particular ship. Remember that the forward-looking windows on a container vessel will be blocked from view when the ship is carrying a full load.

Once reservations for a freighter trip have been secured, the waiting process begins. Apart from a few lines which sail on a set schedule, most freighters sail only when all cargo is aboard. This can be held up by a variety of things, including late arriving cargo, indus-trial disputes, weather and mechanical problems. The intending passenger must put up with this and realize that several nights may have to be spent in a motel near the port (at his or her expense) until the go ahead to board the ship is finally received. Even finding the ship can be an adventure in itself as many of the large container terminals are now located far from urban areas. The ship's agent in the port should be contacted for advice and assistance in boarding.

Once aboard, the passenger's welcome may be a waiting officer, completely ambivalent crew, or no one at all. Quite often, and particularly in a ship's home port, the vessel will be virtually empty of crew until just before sailing. This is one reason why passenger boarding times are sometimes delayed until the last hour. If an officer or steward is not present upon boarding, it is best to ask for the Captain. Even if the vessel's crew is non-English speaking, the Captain, Radio Officer and usually the first mate will have some command of English.

Life On Board

If there is some time between boarding and the ship's scheduled departure, a quick inspection of the cabin and galley should be made to determine if anything should be purchased before you set sail. A better grade of toilet paper, face tissues, special laundry soaps, aspirin, cigarettes, alcohol and snack items are the things that most passengers usually wish they had brought aboard. A freighter's scheduled departure time will be noted on a board placed at the gangway, but it is wise to confirm this with the Captain before leaving on any trips back to town.

Life aboard a freighter at sea can be very relaxing, one reason why there is such demand for this type of travel. The hustle and bustle found on cruise ships is completely lacking, and, as there is usually little or no organized entertainment, there are few decisions to make. Some of the newer cargo ships now carry small swimming pools and gyms. These will be shared with the ship's crew and/or officers. Passengers should check to see if there are regulations or set times governing their use. Meal times are set and should be observed. A ship's crew has 'time on' and 'time off' while at sea and a steward may have to work his own 'off time' to serve someone who is late for a meal. On many American ships the dinner time is unusually early, sometimes as early as 4:30 p.m. because of union regulations. Food on freighters is normally good, but this depends entirely on the cook and the provisions that the ship is allowed to take on board.

Safety at sea is an important issue today and passengers will be required to follow set regulations determined by the ship's country of registration and its Master. Cooperation in following the rules is to everyone's advantage. A lifeboat drill is usually given during the first day at sea. If by some chance it is not, a passenger should make certain of lifejacket location, which is usually in the cabin closet, and his or her muster station. As freighters tend to get a bit untidy while loading and discharging cargo it becomes important to watch one's footing and one's head while the ship is in port. Grease and cables may be lying on the deck and cargo rigging may be in a lowered position – and be careful on the docks too. A ship's decks are usually cleared of debris once she returns to sea. As tanks may have been cleaned or plumbing work done in port, it is a good idea to allow water to run from taps and shower heads before using. *Always* test the water temperature on older ships before using as it may come straight from the boilers.

Quite often passengers will be asked to surrender their passports or travel documents to the Captain during the course of the voyage. This is normal and allows for smoother immigration procedures at the vessel's various ports-of-call. A few countries, such as Saudi Arabia, will restrict passengers to the ship in port unless they have visas. In other ports it may not be advisable to go ashore at the time because of local political or health problems. The ship's agent, who will usually be the first person to board the ship once it ties up, should be able to recommend shore-based excursion operators. These people, as well as hawkers of souvenirs and money changers, may swarm aboard the ship in certain ports. It is highly advisable to check with the Captain or agent before doing business with any of these people. In most instances the Captain or steward will be able to furnish or change small amounts of the local currency and advise passengers on transportation from and to the docks. If you leave the ship in a foreign port it's helpful to have the ship's name and location written down in a form understandable to a native taxi driver in case you lose track of time and need to return to the ship hastily.

Entertainment

While the Captain may be a continual source of information during the voyage he should not be over-taxed. In port he will be busy with agents, immigration and customs people, and salesmen as soon as the ship docks. At sea he can be called to the bridge at any time and for long periods. If his office or cabin door is closed respect his privacy and contact another of the ship's crew to ascertain if the Captain is up or not. Often he will be sleeping during the day after a long night on the bridge while you slept undisturbed. Some Captains enjoy joining passengers at meals; others dine in their cabins. One well-known Asian firm stopped carrying passengers on its freighters because the Chinese Captains didn't like making small talk at the dinner table. Socializing is not part of the Captain's job, be sensitive to this.

A Captain who enjoys having passengers aboard his ship is easy to recognize. He will usually extend an invitation to join him on the bridge at one time or another. For some this is a high point of the voyage, a time in which technical questions can be posed. The bridge usually becomes off limits in very rough weather, when navigating confined or congested waters and when a pilot is aboard. Don't abuse your Captain's kind invitation. Similarly, an interested passenger may be invited to the engine room by the Chief engineer or one of the engineering officers. Whether on the bridge or down below it is wise to wear good, rubber soled shoes. New ships, especially those which have steel decks rather than wood, are extremely dangerous when there is the least bit of water or oil about.

Dress aboard freighters is usually very informal. However, some passengers dress up for one or two dinners, particularly if the Captain is hosting a cocktail party or reception. On at least one British line it is now custom to dress formally for dinner. A travel agent or the steamship company's ticketing office will be able to advise in this matter as well as furnish information regarding mail, baggage, tipping and safe-keeping facilities on board. In regard to the latter it is important to keep cabin doors locked while in port and valuables should be entrusted to the Captain's safe. The sudden loss of money, jewellery or travel papers can quickly ruin what would have otherwise been a very enjoyable voyage.

An excellent way to find out other people's reactions to a certain ship or line and day to day life at sea is to subscribe to one of two newsletters printed for freighter travel enthusiasts. The first is *Freighter Travel News* printed each month by the Freighter Travel Club (P.O. Box 12693 Salem, OR, 07309, U.S.A.). The second is *TravLtips*, a monthly publication produced by TravLtips, P.O. Box 1008, Huntington, NY, 11753, USA. Both offer passenger voyage reports each month and current information on upcoming sailings.

Working Your Passage

As for working one's passage, there is little opportunity for this type of travel on freighters in the 1980s. Crews have been drastically reduced on most ships and unions are strictly against the employment of unrenumerated labor. These days, there is a much higher chance of obtaining a working passage on a private yacht than a commercial cargo vessel. Unfortunately, the best places for finding such passages are at mid-voyage points such as Panama and Tahiti, where other crew members may have become disillusioned with yacht travel and returned home by air. As with the freighters of old, it is a case of contacting the Captain and telling one's story. Tenacity is often the ingredient that will spell success.

Travel With a Pack Animal

by Roger Chapman

The donkey is the most desirable beast of burden for the novice and remains the favourite of the more experienced camper – if only because the donkey carries all his equipment, leaving him free to enjoy the countryside unburdened. Although small and gentle, the donkey is strong and dependable; no pack animal excels him for sure-footedness or matches his character. He makes the ideal companion for children old enough to travel into the mountains or hills and for the adult who prefers to travel at a pace slow enough to appreciate the scenery, wildlife and wilderness that no vehicle can reach.

Rock climber, hunter, fisherman, scientist or artist who has too much gear to carry into the mountains may prefer to take the larger and faster mule, but if he is sensible, he will practice first on the smaller and more patient donkey. The principles of pack animal management are the same, but the mule is stronger, more likely to kick or bite if provoked, and requires firmer handling than the donkey. The advantage of a mule is obvious. Whereas a donkey can only carry about 50kgs (100lbs), the mule, if expertly packed, can carry a payload of 100kgs (200lbs). Although both are good for fifteen miles a day on reasonable trails, the donkeys will have to be led on foot, whereas mules, which can travel at a good speed, require everyone to be mounted: unless their handlers are fast hikers.

Planning

To determine the number of animals needed before an expedition or holiday the approximate pack load must be calculated. The stock requirement for a ten-day trip can be calculated by dividing the number of people by two, but taking the higher whole number if the split does not work evenly. Thus, a family of five would take three donkeys. It is difficult to control more than ten donkeys on the trail, so don't use them with a party of twenty or more unless certain individuals are prepared to carry large packs to reduce the number of animals. Mules are usually led by a single hiker or are tied in groups of not more than five animals led by a man on horseback. This is the 'string' of mules often mentioned in Westerns; each lead rope passes through the left-hand breeching ring of preceding animal's harness and is then tied around the animal's neck with a bowline. One or more horses are usually sent out with pack mules because mules respect and stick close to these 'chaperones'.

Whichever method you decide to use, don't prepare a detailed itinerary before your journey; wait and see how you get on during the first few days, when you should attempt no more than 8-10 miles (12-16kms) a day. Later you will be able to average 12-

15miles (20-24kms), but you should not count on doing more than 15 miles (24kms) a day although it is possible, with early starts and a lighter load, if you really have to.

Campers who use pack animals seldom restrict themselves to the equipment list of a backpacker. There is no need to do so, but before preparing elaborate menus and extensive wardrobes, you would do well to consider the price of hiring a pack animal. The more elaborate, heavy equipment, the more donkeys or mules there are to hire, load, unload, groom and find pasture for. In selecting your personal equipment you have more freedom – perhaps a blow up mattress instead of a 'Karrimat', or a larger tent instead of the small 'Basha' – but it should not exceed 12kgs (24lbs) and should be packed into several of those small cylindrical soft bags or a seaman's kitbag. You can take your sleeping bag as a separate bundle and take a small knapsack for those personal items such as spare sweaters, camera, first aid kit and snacks required during the day. But there are some special items you will require if you are not hiring an efficient guide and handler: repair kit for broken pack saddles and extra straps for mending harness. An essential item is a 100lbs spring scale for balancing the sacks or panniers before you load them on the pack animals in the morning. Remember too that each donkey/mule will be hired out with a halter, lead rope, tow 'sacks', a pack cover and a thirty-foot pack rope. In addition, there will be pickets and shackle straps, curry combs, froghooks, canvas buckets, tools and possibly ointment or powders to heal saddle sores.

Animal Handling

The art of handling pack animals is not a difficult one, but, unfortunately you cannot learn it entirely from a book. With surprisingly little experience in this field, the novice soon becomes an expert packer, confident that he can handle any situation which may arise on the trail and, above all, that he has learnt that uncertain science of getting the pack animal to do what he wants it to do. The donkey is more responsive than the mule and is quick to return friendship, especially if he knows he is being well packed, well fed and well rested. The mule tends to be more truculent, angry and resentful until he knows who is in charge. Therefore, an attitude of firmness and consideration towards the animal is paramount.

Perhaps the easiest way to learn the techniques of handling pack animals is to look at a typical day and consider the problems as they arise.

Collecting in the Morning

Pack animals can either be let loose, hobbled or picketed during the night. The latter is preferable as even a mule which has its front legs hobbled can wander for miles during the night searching for suitable grass. If the animal is picketed, unloosen the strap around the fetlock which is attached to the picket rope and lead him back to the campsite by the halter. If the animals are loose, you may have to allow a good half hour or so to catch them. Collect the gentle ones first, returning later for the recalcitrant animals. Approach each cautiously, talking to him and offering a palmful of oats before grabbing the halter.

Tying Up and Grooming

Even the gentlest pack animal will

need to be tied up to a tree or post before packing. The rope should be tied with a clove hitch at about waist height. Keep the rope short, otherwise the animal will walk round and round the tree as you follow with the saddle. It also prevents him stepping on or tripping over the rope. It is advisable to keep the animals well apart, but not too far from your pile of packed sacks or panniers.

Often donkeys, in particular, will have a roll during the night, so they require a good work-over with the brush or curry comb to remove dust or caked mud. Most animals enjoy this, but you mustn't forget that one end can bite and the other end can give a mighty kick. Personally, I always spend some time stroking the animal around the head and ears, talking to him before I attempt to groom him. Ears are a very good indicators of mood. If the ears are upright he is alert and apprehensive, so a few words and strokes will give him confidence; soon the ears will relax and lie back. If the ears turn and stretch right back along his neck, then there is a good chance you are in for trouble. The first time he nips, thump him in the ribs and swear at him. He will soon learn that you do not appreciate this kind of gesture.

Your main reason for grooming is to remove caked dirt which may cause sores once the animal is loaded. Remove this dirt with a brush and clean rag, and if there is an open wound, apply one of the many animal antiseptic ointments or sprinkle on boric acid powder which will help to dry it up. Finally, check each hoof quickly to see that no stone or twig has lodged in the soft pad. Lean against the animal, then warn him by tapping the leg all the way down the flank, past the knee to the fetlock, before lifting the hoof; otherwise you will never succeed. If there is a stone lodged between the shoe and the hoof, prise it out with a frog hook.

Saddling and Loading

Animals are used to being loaded from the left or near side. First you fold the saddle blanket, place it far forward then slide it back into position along the animal's back so that the hair lies smooth. Check that it hangs evenly on both sides, sufficient to protect the flanks from the loaded sacks. Stand behind the mule or donkey – but not too close – and check it before you proceed further. Pick up the pack saddle – two moulded pieces of wood jointed by two cross-trees – and place it on the saddle blanket so it fits in the hollows behind the withers. Tie up the breast strap and rear strap before tying the girth tight. Two people will be required to load the equipment in the soft canvas sacks onto the saddle pack, but it is essential to weigh the sacks before you place them on the cross-trees; they should be within 2kgs of each other. If the saddle is straight, but one sack is lower than the other, correct the length of the ear loops.

On the Trail

Morning is the best time to travel, so you must hit the trail early, preferably before seven am. At a steady 2kms an hour, you will be able to cover the majority of the day's journey by the time the sun is at its hottest. This will allow you to spend a good three hours rest-halt at midday before setting off once more for a final couple of hours before searching for a campsite. Avoid late camps, so start looking by four pm.

During the first few days you may have some trouble getting your donkeys or mules to move close together and at a steady pace. One man should walk behind each animal if they are being led and if there are any hold ups, he can apply a few swipes of a willow switch to the hind-quarters. It is a waste of time to shout at the animals or threaten them constantly as it only makes them distrustful and skittish. The notorious stubbornness of the mule or donkey is usually the result of bad handling in the past. Sometimes, it is a result of fear or fatigue, but occasionally it is sheer cussedness or an attempt to see how much he can get away with. The only occasion when I could not get a mule moving was travelling across some snow patches in the mountains of Kashmir. Eventually, after losing my temper and lashing him with a switch, I persuaded him to move forward slowly across the snow, only for him to fall through the icy surface and disappear into a snow hole. It took my companion and me three hours to unload him, pull him out and calm him down before we could repack. I learned a good lesson from my lack of awareness of the innate intelligence of the mule.

Understanding

There is no problem with unpacking which can be done quickly and efficiently. Just remember to place all the equipment neatly together so it is not mixed up. Keep individual saddles, sacks and harnesses close enough together to cover with the waterproof cover in case of rain. Once unloaded, the donkeys or mules can be groomed, watered and led off to the pasture area where they are to be picketed for the night.

Recently, I took my wife and two young daughters on a 120-mile journey across the Cévennes mountains in south-east France. We followed Robert Louis Stevenson's routes which he described in his charming little book *Travels With a Donkey*. We took three donkeys – two as pack animals and one for the children to take turns in riding – on a trail which had not changed much over the past hundred years. It made an ideal holiday, and we returned tanned, fitter, enchanted by the French countryside and aware that it was the character of our brave little donkeys which had made our enjoyment complete.

The speed with which the children mastered the technique of pack animal management was encouraging because it allowed us to complete our self-imposed task with enough time to explore the wilder parts of the mountains and enjoy the countryside at the leisurely pace of our four-footed companions. We also took a hundred flies from one side of the Cévennes to the other, but that is another story.

Travel by Camel

by René Dee

In this mechanized and industrial epoch, the camel does not seem to be an obvious choice of travelling companion when sophisticated cross-country vehicles exist for the toughest of terrains. Add to this the stockpile of derisory and mocking myths, truths and sayings about the camel and one is forced to ask the question: why use camels at all?

Purely as a means of getting from A

to B when time is the most important factor, the camel should not even be considered. As a means of transport for scientific groups who wish to carry out useful research in the field, the camel is limiting. It can be awkward and risky transporting delicate equipment and specimens. However, for the individual, small group and expedition wishing to see the desert as it should be seen, the camel is an unrivalled means of transport.

Go Safely in the Desert

From my own personal point of view, the primary reason must be that, unlike any motorized vehicle, camels allow you to integrate completely with the desert and the people within it – something it is impossible to do at 80kmph enclosed in a 'tin can'. A vehicle in the desert can be like a prison cell and the constant noise of the engine tends to blur all sense of the solitude, vastness and deafening quiet which are so intrisic to the experience.

Travel by camel allows the entire pace of life to slow down from a racy 80kmph to a steady 6.5kmph, enabling you to unwind, take in and visually appreciate the overall magnificence and individual details of your surroundings.

Secondly, camels do, of course, have the ability to reach certain areas inaccessible to vehicles, especially through rocky and narrow mountain passes, although camels are not always happy on this terrain and extreme care has to be taken to ensure they do not slip or twist a leg. They are as sensitive as they appear insensitive.

Thirdly, in practical terms, they cause far fewer problems where maintenance, breakdown and repairs are concerned. No bulky spares or expensive mechanical equipment are needed to carry out repairs. Camels do not need a great deal of fuel and can exist adequately (given that they are not burdened with excessively heavy loads) for five to ten days without water. Camels go on and on and on and on until they die; and then one has the option of eating them, altogether far better tasting than a Michelin tyre.

Lastly, camels *must* be far more cost effective if you compare them directly with vehicles, although this depends on whether your intended expedition/journey already includes a motorised section. If you fly direct to your departure point, or as near as possible to it, you will incur none of the heavy costs related to transporting a vehicle, not to mention the cost of buying it. If the camel trek is to be an integral portion of a motorized journey, then the cost saving will not apply, as, of course, hire fees for camels and guides will be additional.

In many ways, combining these two forms of travel is ideal and a very good way of highlighting my primary point in favour of transport by camel. If you do decide on this combination, make sure you schedule the camel journey for the very end of your expedition and that the return leg by vehicle is either minimal or purely functional, as I can guarantee that after a period of ten days or more travelling slowly and gently through the desert by camel, your vehicle will take on the characteristics of a rocket ship and all sense of freedom, enquiry and interest will be dulled to the extreme. An overwhelming sense of disillusion and disinterest will prevail. Previously exciting sights, desert towns and Arab civilization, will pall after such intense involvement with the desert, its people and its lifestyle.

First Steps

For the individual or group organizer wanting to get off the beaten track by camel the first real problem is to find them, and to gather every bit of information possible about who owns them, whether or not they are for hire, for how much, what equipment/stores/provisions are included, if any, and lastly, what the guides/owners are capable of and whether they are willing to accompany you. It is not much good arriving at Tamanrasset, Timbouctou or Tindoug without knowing some, if not all, of the answers to these questions. Good predeparture research is vital but the problem is that 90 per cent of the information won't be found from any tourist office, embassy, library or travel agent. Particularly if you're considering a major journey exclusively by camel, you'll probably have to undertake a preliminary fact-finding recce to your proposed departure point to establish contacts among camel owners and guides. It may well be that camels and/or reliable guides do not exist in the area where you wish to carry out your expedition.

I would suggest, therefore, that you start first with a reliable source of information such as the Royal Geographical Society, which has expedition reports and advice which can be used as a primary source of reference including names and addresses to write to for up-do-date information about the area that interests you. Up-to-date information is without doubt the key to it all. Very often this can be gleaned from the commercial overland companies whose drivers are passing

your area of interest regularly and may even have had personal experience of the journey you intend to make. Equally important is the fact that in the course of their travels, they build up an impressive collection of contacts who could well help in the final goal of finding suitable guides, smoothing over formalities and getting introductions to local officials, etc. Most overland travel companies are very approachable so long as you appreciate that their time is restricted and that their business is selling travel and not running an advisory service.

In all the best Red Indian stories, the guide is the all-knowing, all-seeing person in whom all faith is put. However, as various people have discovered to their cost, this is not always so. Many so-called guides know very little of the desert and its ways. How then to find someone who really does know the route/area, has a sense of desert lore and who preferably owns his own camel? I can only reiterate that the best way to do this is through personal recommendation. Having found him, put your faith in him, let him choose your camels and make sure that your relationship remains as amicable as possible. You will be living together for many days in conditions which are familiar to him but alien to you, and you need his support. Arrogance does not fit into desert travel, especially from a *nasrani*. Mutual respect and a good rapport are essential.

Pack Up Your Troubles

Once you've managed to establish all this and you're actually out there, what are the do's and don'ts and logistics of travel by camel? Most individuals and expeditions (scientifically orientated or not) will want, I imagine, to incorporate a camel trek within an existing vehicle-led expedition, so I am really talking only of short-range treks of around ten to fifteen days's duration, up to 400km. If this is so, you will need relatively little equipment/stores and it is essential that this is kept to a minimum. Remember that the more equipment you take, the more camels you will need, which will require more guides, which means more cost, more pasture and water, longer delays in loading, unloading, cooking and setting up camp and a longer wait in the morning while the camels are being rounded up after a night of pasturing.

Be prepared also for a very swift deterioration of equipment. In a vehicle, you can at least keep possessions clean and safe to a degree, but packing kit onto a camel denies any form of protection – especially since it is not unknown for camels to stumble and fall or to roll you over suddenly and ignominiously if something is not to their liking, such as a slipped load or uncomfortable saddle. My advice is to pack all your belongings in a seaman's kitbag which can be roped onto the camel's side easily, is pliable, hardwearing and, because it is soft and not angular, doesn't threaten to rub a hole in the camel's side or backbone. (I have seen a badly placed baggage saddle wear a hole the size of a man's fist into an animal's back.) If rectangular aluminium boxes containing cameras or other delicate equipment are being carried, make sure that they are well roped on the top of the camel and that there is sufficient padding underneath so as not to cause friction. Moreover, you'll always have to take your shoes off while riding because over a period of hours, let alone days, you could wear out the protective hair on the camel's neck and eventually cause open sores.

Water should be carried in goat skin *guerbas* and 20 litre round metal *bidons* which can again be roped up easily and hung either side of the baggage camel under protective covers. Take plenty of rope for tying on equipment, saddles etc, and keep one length of fifteen metres intact for using at wells where there may be no facilities for hauling up water. Don't take any cooking stoves – the open fire is adequate and far less likely to break down. Don't take any sophisticated tents either; they will probably be ruined within days and anyway are just not necessary. I have always used a piece of cotton cloth approximately six metres square, which, with two poles for support front and rear and with sand or boulders at the sides and corner, makes a very good overnight shelter for half a dozen people. Night in the desert can be extremely cold, particularly of course in the winter, but the makeshift 'tent' has a more important role during the day when it provides shelter for the essential two hour lunch stop and rest.

The Day's Schedule

Your daily itinerary and schedule should be geared to the practical implications of travelling by camel. That is to say that each night's stop will, where possible, be in an area where pasture is to be found for the camels to graze. Although one can take along grain and dried dates for camels to eat, normal grazing is also vital. The camels are unloaded and hobbled (two front legs are tied closely together), but you will find they can wander as much as three or four kilometres overnight and there is only one way to fetch them – on foot. Binoculars are extremely useful as spotting camels over such a distance can be a nightmare. They may be hidden behind dunes and not come into view for some time.

Other useful equipment includes goggles for protection in sandstorms, a prescription-suited pair of sunglasses and, of course, sun cream. Above all, take comfortable and hardwearing footwear for it is almost certain that you will walk at least half the way once you have become fully acclimatized. I would suggest that you take Spanish fell boots or something similar, which are cheap, very light, give ankle support over uneven terrain, are durable and very comfortable. The one disadvantage of boots by day is that your feet will get very hot, but it's a far better choice than battered, blistered and lacerated feet when one has to keep up with the camels' steady 6.5kmph. Nomads wear sandals, but if you take a close look at a nomad's foot you will see that is not dissimilar to the sandal itself, i.e. as hard and tough as leather. Yours resembles a baby's bottom by comparison – so it is essential that you get some heavy walking practice in beforehand with the boots/ shoes/sandals you intend to wear. (If your journey is likely to be a long one, then you could possibly try sandals, as there will be time for the inevitable wearing-in process with blisters, as well as stubbed toes and feet spiked by the lethal acacia thorn).

For clothing, I personally wear a local, free-flowing robe like the *gandoura*, local pantaloons and a *chèche* – a three metre length of cotton cloth which can be tied round the head and/or face and neck for protection against the sun. You can also use it as a rope, fly whisk and face protector in sandstorms. In the bitter cold nights and early mornings of winter desert travel, go to bed with it wrapped around your neck, face and head to keep warm. If local clothing embarasses and inhibits you, stick to loose cotton shirts and trousers. Forget your tight jeans and bring loose fitting cotton underwear. Anything nylon and tight fitting next to the skin will result in chafing and sores. Do, however, also take some warm clothing and blankets, including socks and jumpers. As soon as the sun sets in the desert, the temperature drops dramatically. Catching cold in the desert is unbearable. Colds are extremely common and spread like wildfire. Take a good down sleeping bag and a groundsheet. Your sleeping bag and blankets can also serve as padding for certain types of camel saddle. In the Western Sahara you will find the Mauritanian butterfly variety, which envelopes you on four sides. You're liable to slide back and forth uncomfortably and get blisters unless you pad the saddle. The Tuareg saddle is commonly used in the Algerian Sahara. This is a more traditional saddle with a fierce looking forward pommel which threatens man's very manhood should you be thrown forward against it. In Saudi Arabia, female camels are ridden and seating positions are taken up behind the dromedary's single hump rather than on or forward of it.

Culture Shock

Never travel alone in the desert, without even a guide. Ideal group size would be seven group members, one group leader, three guides, eleven riding camels and three baggage camels. The individual traveller should take at least one guide with him and three or four camels.

Be prepared for a mind-blowing sequence of mental experience, especially if you are not accustomed to the alien environment, company and pace, which can lead to introspection, uncertainty and even paranoia. Travel by camel with nomad guides is the complete reversal of our normal lifestyle. Therefore it is as important to be mentally prepared for this culture shock as it is to be physically prepared. Make no mistake, travel by camel is hard, physically uncompromising and mentally torturing at times. But a *Méharée* satisfactorily accomplished will alter your concept of life and its overall values, and the desert's hold over you will never loosen.

Working Your Way

by Susan Griffith

Camels, trains and sailing boats have their peculiar advantages as means of travelling to those corners of the world you wish to visit. But there may be times when you will decide to stop for a while to rest or absorb the atmosphere in one sitting. Working is one way of getting inside a foreign culture, though the kind of job you find will determine the stratum of society which you will experience. The traveller who spends a few weeks picking olives for a Cretan farmer will get a very different insight to the traveller who looks after the children of a wealthy Athenian businessman. Yet both will have the chance to participate temporarily in the life of a culture rather than merely to observe.

Financial considerations are usually the traveller's immediate impetus to look for work. To postpone having to cash the last traveller's cheques, many people begin to look around for ways of prolonging their trip. They may find paid work (though few of the jobs which travellers undertake will make them rich) or they may decide to volunteer their labour in exchange for a bed and food, for example by planting trees in the Australian outback or digging for Biblical remains in Israel. While the sole ambition of some is to extend their travels, others go abroad specifically in search of highly paid jobs. This is easier for people with acknowledged qualifications such as nurses and agronomists, divers and pipe-fitters who often do find better paid opportunities abroad than they can at home. A few might even have their future career prospects on view when they go abroad to teach English as a foreign language or drive a combine harvester. But the majority are trying to put off or escape from career decisions.

Even the unskilled can find jobs which pay high wages. The high minimum wage in Denmark, for example, means that a pot-washer in a hotel or a strawberry picker can earn enough in a short time to fund long periods of travel. In Japan, the demand for university graduates (of any subject) willing to give English lessons is so great that many foreigners can earn $12 an hour and work as many hours as their stamina will allow. Some Japanese language schools even pay the airfares of teachers whom they recruit abroad. Similarly American summer camps pay the airfares of thousands of young people who go to the US each summer to instruct and look after children, though in this case, the advanced airfare is subtracted from the counsellor's end-of-session wages, which are modest even at the outset. Paid fares are a rarity no matter what job you find.

Volunteering

It would be wrong, of course, to assume that the love (or shortage) of money is at the root of all decisions to work abroad. Paid work in developing nations is available only exceptionally to the unskilled and yet many arrange to live for next to nothing by doing something positive. For example, enterprising travellers from Turkey to Thailand have been welcomed into the homes of locals who are eager to share longterm hospitality in exchange for informal lessons in English. More structured voluntary opportunities exist worldwide and there are many charities and organisations which can introduce you to interesting projects such as helping a local Indian settlement to build a community centre in Northern Canada or assisting a study of migration patterns in Pyrenean birds or bringing in the coffee crop in Nicaragua. Many such organisations require more than a traveller's curiosity about a country; they require a strong wish to become involved in a specific project and, in many cases, an ideological commitment. The fact that few of them can offer more than very modest living expenses deters the uncommitted in any case.

Some travellers are fortunate enough to fix up a job in advance. This means that they can be reasonably assured of an immediate income once they have arrived. The traveller who sets off without a pre-arranged job has less security, and should take sufficient reserves in case his or her job search fails. In the course of my researches, I have met many examples of the fearless traveller who is prepared to arrive in Marseilles or Mexico City with virtually nothing. They have remained confident that it will be possible to work their way out of their penury. In most cases they have done just that, though not without experiencing a few moments of panic and desperation. It goes without saying that this situation is best avoided, for it may result in your being forced to take an undesirable job with exploitative conditions, or to go into debt to the folks back home, or, worst of all, to ask your embassy to repatriate you (an expensive and humiliating step).

Seasonal Work

Jobs which are seasonal in nature are those which travellers are most likely to find. Unemployment statistics barely concern themselves with this large and important sector of the economy. In times of recession the number of temporary jobs available may even increase since employers are less eager to expand their regular staff but will need help from outside at busy times.

The two categories of employment which appeal most to travellers (and least to a stable working population) are fruit-picking and tourism. Many farmers from the south of France to the north of Tasmania (with the notable exception of the developing world) cannot bring in their harvests without assistance from outside their vicinity. Similarly the tourist trade in many areas could not survive without a short-term injection of seasonal labour. These economic facts may provide little consolation to the hopeful job-seeker who finds that all the hotels in town are already staffed by local students or that all the fruit is traditionally picked by itinerant Mexicans or Moroccans. Nevertheless, farmers and hotel/restaurant managers remain the best potential sources of employment.

English teaching is more specialised though there are many countries in the world where it is possible to find hourly work with only fluency in the language and a neat appearance as recommendations. You need only learn the words 'English Language School' in the relevant language before you can make use of the Yellow Pages and begin a school-to-school job search. This is unlikely to be productive in countries where English is widely taught and spoken (India, the Netherlands etc) but can be surprisingly effective in many other countries (Spain, Taiwan etc).

It is not easy to look up 'domestic', 'au pair' or 'live-in' positions in the Yellow Pages. But young people (mainly, but not only women) who desire the security of a family placement and who may also wish to learn a foreign language often choose to work with children for little money. Such positions can be found on-the-spot or in advance through a relevant agency or by means of an advertisement.

Paperwork

It has to be admitted that many of these jobs do involve more potential for exploitation than 'proper' jobs. Permanent jobs are usually more carefully regulated by laws and trade unions. A problem which bedevils foreign workers and which inevitably weakens their bargaining position is the problem of work permits. Almost every country of the world has legislation to prohibit foreigners from taking jobs from nationals (although citizens of EEC countries can work freely throughout the Community). Even without any legal prohibitions, few employers would select a foreign applicant over an equally qualified national. The bureaucracy involved in obtaining a work permit is usually discouraging enough to prevent travellers from applying.

Furthermore, it would be impossible to get a work permit for casual jobs such as cherry-picking or hamburger-making. A few countries do have special schemes and visas to cover holiday jobs (eg Canada and Switzerland) but these schemes are usually restricted to a small minority.

There are many organisations, both public and private, charitable and commercial, which can offer advice and practical assistance. Some accept a tiny handful of individuals who satisfy stringent requirements; other accept anyone who is willing to pay the required fee. School and university careers counsellors are often a good source of information, as are newspaper advertisements and the specialist literature. The work schemes and official exchanges which do exist require a large measure of advance planning. It is not unusual for an application deadline to be six to nine months before the starting date of the scheme.

Improving Your Chances

A number of specific steps will improve your chances of being accepted on an organised work scheme and of convincing an employer in person of your superiority to the competition. For example, before leaving home you might take a short course in teaching English as a foreign language, cooking, word-processing or sailing, all skills which are marketable around the world. If you are very serious you might learn (or improve) a foreign language or you might simply undertake to get fit.

Contacts, however remote, can be valuable allies. Everyone has ways of developing links with people abroad, even if he or she is not lucky enough to have friends and family scattered around the world. Penfriends, fellow members of travel clubs and foreign students or visitors met in your home town might be able to help you find your feet in a foreign country. The idea is to publicise your plans as widely as possible since the more people who are aware of your willingness to work, the better the chance of a lead. Once you actually embark you will be grateful for any extra preparation you have done.

Even if you set off without an address book full of contacts, it is not difficult to meet people along the way. Your fellow travellers are undoubtedly the best source of information on job prospects. Youth hostels can be a gold-mine for the job-seeker; there may even be jobs advertised on the notice board. Any local you meet is a potential source of help, whether a driver who gives you a lift while hitchhiking or members of a local club which interests you, such as cycling or jazz. The expatriate community might also be willing to help, and can be met in certain bars, at the English-speaking church etc.

Of course, not all jobs are found by word-of-mouth through intermediary contacts. The local English language newspaper may carry job advertisements appropriate to your situation. The most effective method is to walk-in-and-ask. It may be necessary to exaggerate the amount of relevant experience you have had and to display a little more bravado than comes naturally to you. Persistence and optimism are essential. A resilient personality is essential for such a venture, since there will be a time when it will be necessary to pester 40 hotel managers before one will offer you a job as a chambermaid or to visit the offices of an employment agency on many consecutive days before your eagerness will be rewarded. With such an attitude, it is indeed possible to work your way around the world.

What Type of Travel

The Packaged Traveller

by Hilary Bradt

In 1841 Thomas Cook advertised that he had arranged a special train to take a group of temperance workers from Leicester to Loughborough for a meeting some ten miles away. From this humble beginning has grown a giant tourist industry which has helped the balance of payments in countries all over the world as well as enabling almost anyone to have a taste of 'abroad'. Experienced travellers often scorn package holidays as appealing to the 'If it's Tuesday, this must be Belgium' mentality, without realising how much time and money can be saved, and how many worthwhile places seen, by joining a tour. And now that package tours have expanded into activity holidays a new world, often impenetrable by all but the most determined individual, has opened up for the adventurous person in search of the safely exotic.

The most convenient way of booking any sort of package tour is through a travel agent. Although you can usually deal directly with the company offering the trip, a good travel agent will save you hours of time and hassle. Not everyone realises that travel agents earn their income from commissions on sales and not from any charge levied on the customer, so you pay nothing for their services. If your travel agent is a member of ABTA or has the Air Tour Operator's Licence (*see The Traveller's Protection on page 63*) you are less likely to become the victim of overbooking or other travel malpractice, and if something does go wrong and it's the company's fault, you do have some recourse.

Do your preparatory brochure reading carefully. If you choose a trip to Greece in mid-summer and can't stand the heat, that's not your travel agent's fault. Nor can they be held responsible for the inefficiencies that are inherent in Third World travel. An honest guide book will warn you of the negative aspects of the countries you are interested in, and likewise, a brochure is more likely to be taken seriously if the picture painted is not too rosy. Beware of advertising jargonese that could be fluffing over the fact that your half-built hotel is a couple of miles from the sea, which can just be glimpsed tantalisingly from one room on the top floor.

Short Haul

Under this heading we can include a two-week holiday in Turkey, a 'weekend break' in Majorca, or a day's sightseeing in some foreign city. Prices are generally low, as it is this category which covers the vast bulk of package holidays, and there are also plenty of bargains to be had, especially off season or if booking late, as a glance at any travel agent's window or the holiday section of the newspapers will show you. Just be careful to check the credentials of any company offering unbelievably cheap trips. Even if they are legitimate, prices are being kept down by lowering the standard of accommodation, using flights that leave at two in the morning and switching to more and more self-catering.

Going on a package tour does not necessarily mean travelling in a group. Often the 'package' consists of air tickets and accommodation only, and you are free to explore during the day. And you don't *have* to stay in the allocated hotel; sometimes the savings on the airfare are such that you can afford to use the hotel for a couple of nights then head off on your own and do some travelling. More and more charter companies are now offering flight only sales, with nominal accommodation thrown in purely to satisfy legal requirements, and with no expectation that you would actually use it.

Even brief sightseeing tours are often well worth while for independent travellers. Some of the world's most fascinating places are virtually impossible to get to on your own, and even if easily accessible, sightseeing can be tiring and uninformative without transport or a guide. Tours are easily arranged. Your hotel should be able to recommend a reliable agency, you can look in the yellow pages of the phone book, or simply walk down the main street until you find one. When setting up your tour it helps to have some information on the sight or sights you want to visit. Try to meet your guide the day before to make sure he/she is knowledgeable and speaks good English, and if you enjoy walking, make it clear that a tour on foot would be preferable to spending all day on a bus.

Wherever you are going, these short haul packages come off a mammoth production line, are simple to book and easy to use, leaving you with few more decisions to take than what kind of suntan cream to take. Long haul and 'adventure' packages are more demanding, mentally, physically and on the pocket, and booking can be more complicated as there are fewer departures and a limited number of places. Far more care should be taken to ensure that you find precisely what you are looking for.

Long Haul

Overland journeys lasting several months are the most popular form of 'adventure' package tour for young people, pensioners and others for whom time is no object. And for those with less time to spare, plenty of companies offer two- or three-week tours which still use the converted trucks which are the hallmark of long overland trips. Dodge three-ton trucks, completely stripped and rebuilt to suit the needs of each company, are the vehicles preferred, being rugged enough to cope with the varied terrain and conditions found on a trans-continental journey. Nights are spent in tents or simple rest houses, and most overlanders cook their own meals on a rota system and eat occasionally in local restaurants.

Most long haul trips involve journeys through Africa, Asia, South America and, to a lesser extent, Australia. The most popular routes are London to Kathmandu, which is open again despite problems in the Middle East, and Africa, which offers various possibilities such as the Nile route from Egypt to Kenya, the Sahara from Morocco to French West Africa, Nairobi down to southern Africa, or even North Africa all the way to Cape Town. South America is nearly as popular, with a variety of routes.

These are rugged trips and a great test of psychological fortitude as well as physical endurance. Being with the same group of people for several months in often trying conditions can be a strain on even the most sociable traveller, so if you suspect your patience may snap after a few weeks, don't try it. A long overland trip is a bargain in terms of daily expenditure. Eighteen weeks through Africa costs about £1,700 or £13 per day.

Choose your overland company with care. Some have temptingly low prices but unscrupulous employees like the driver I met in Africa. After dropping his group to do some sightseeing, he drove away and sold the truck. No doubt a rare occurrence, but you are safer if you use a reputable company or go through an organisation like WEXAS (45 Brompton Road, London SW3 1DE) which has long experience of dealing with overland companies.

Special Interest

Many holidaymakers are no longer content just to lie in the sun, but are looking for something more active. Several companies now specialise in activity holidays or adventure travel, which is the fastest-growing area of the travel business, and their brochures show a wide range of trips, from hanggliding in Nepal to weaving in Ecuador, trekking in Africa or taking part in conservation projects or archaeological digs (*see Joining a Project Overseas on page 192*). Activity holidays appeal most to professional people in their 30s and 40s, probably because they are the most expensive form of package tour (three weeks trekking in the Himalayas can cost up to £1,000 or more, excluding the airfare) and the most demanding mentally and physically. Most trips are graded to indicate the degree of fitness required, but the companies point out that even the lowest graded tours are designed for active people and the fitter you are, the more you'll enjoy the trip. Many of the companies involved in organising these tours have age barriers (usually no children and often an upper limit of as little as 45) and others will ask anyone over a certain age to visit them and provide medical certificates to prove their fitness for the trip.

These tours often involve an impressive amount of organisation; providing transport to remote areas, porters or pack animals to carry the luggage, doctors to attend the sick, instructors, interpreters, guides and experts of all sorts. No wonder they are expensive. Carefully planned to give the feeling of adventure without the danger, they enable people to see and experience aspects of a country or culture they could not experience on their own, or take part in an activity or sport impossible in their own country.

Before selecting an activity holiday, you will want to send for as many brochures and catalogues as possible. A good travel agent specialising in this sort of tour will advise you and newspapers and magazines generally carry numerous small ads for these companies. Don't make price the main consideration when comparing brochures. If this is going to be the trip of your life, an extra £100 is not going to make much difference. Check that the price quoted includes the airfare. In Britain it usually does, but American companies usually quote the land costs only. Don't hesitate to contact the company and ask for names and phone numbers of clients who've been on the trip you're interested in. A successful company will have no qualms about putting you in touch with such people.

Once you have signed up and paid your deposit, the company should send you an equipment list, reading list, medical information and so on. If you are dealing with a travel agency rather than the company running the tour, make sure you receive these. It is inconvenient and often impossible to shop for special items once you are there.

Joining a Project Overseas

by Nigel and Shane Winser

There are many operators in Britain and abroad offering adventurous holidays and 'expeditions', which can be ideal for somebody who wants an unusual trip. Naturally you pay to join one of these, but the preparation and responsibilities are correspondingly few. The WEXAS Discoverers brochure lists a number of such trips; others are advertised in the outdoor magazines. There are also two useful books: *Adventure Holidays* published by Vacation Work Publications Ltd which lists holidays by the type of sport or activity, and *Adventure and*

Discovery published by the Central Bureau (for Educational Visits and Exchanges) which gives its listings by country.

There are also many informal groups which set out on adventurous trips which are not expeditions – the main difference being that an expedition aims to prove, alter or discover something and to bring back results, while a holiday does not. Magazines like *Private Eye* or *Time Out* and the travel magazines are useful for finding out about these. However, you should beware that the informal group you team up with is not just trying to pay for a holiday for themselves. However tempting the trip sounds, don't join up if you don't like or trust the people you are going to have to travel with (*see Selecting a Travelling Companion on page 215*).

Joining a genuine expedition demands considerable preparation, commitment and teamwork. Expedition organisers and leaders nowadays demand that a participant has some special skill or expertise, without which he or she will be of little use.

In Britain, the Royal Geographical Society is in the mainstream of serious research expeditions or study projects abroad. Nearly all major expeditions with a geographical content mounted from the UK march by under its gaze, hoping to attract its approval and/or its support. There is, however, no way in which an interested individual can join an RGS-supported expedition through the offices of the Society itself since the Society does not officially oversee the formation of expedition groups. Ready-made parties apply annually (by late January) for the Society's nod of approval or a grant.

Expedition organisers, members or originators still in search of a group or any kind of expedition advice should go direct to the Expedition Advisory Centre, set up by the RGS and the Young Explorers' Trust and housed in the RGS building at 1 Kensington Gore, London SW7 2AR (tel: 01-581 2057). The EAC exists to help those planning overseas expeditions and provides a number of services including a register of forthcoming expeditions. Particularly valuable are its publications, *The Expedition Planner's Handbook and Directory*, and a booklet entitled *Joining an Expedition* which lists most of the organising bodies of 'pure' expeditions, for young people.

Other expeditionary bodies include the Brathay Exploration Group, Brathay Hall, Ambleside, Cumbria LA22 0HP (tel: (09663) 3042) which sends out several expeditions each year for young people aged between 16 and 22, both in the UK and abroad. All provide experience of living in a remote region and many of the overseas projects also have a significant scientific content. The British Schools Exploring Society, 1 Kensington Gore, London SW7 2AR (tel: 01-584 0710) organises one or two major expeditions each summer for 16 to 19 year olds.

For budding archaeologists, Archaeology Abroad, 31-34 Gordon Square, London WC1H 0PY (tel: 01-387 6052) is an organisation which helps directors of overseas excavations to find suitable personnel through its bulletins.

For those with more time available, there are a number of US-based organisations whose functions are to help or staff expeditions. One is Earthwatch, Box 403, Watertown, MA 02172, USA, (tel: (617) 926 8200), a private, non profit-making body which identifies qualified volunteers to staff and finance research expeditions. It was founded in 1971 to serve as a bridge between the public and the scientific community, and has since fielded thousands of people on research expeditions in around 60 countries. Volunteers do not need to have any special skills to join expeditions and anyone aged 16-75 may apply. Funds are raised from the participants and other private sources. For two- and three-week expeditions, costs range from $500 to over $2,000, and cover all field expenses. Work on an expedition may qualify participants for academic credit. Membership, which costs $20 a year or $35 for two years, makes one eligible to join expeditions and secures a magazine, published three times a year, giving updates and advance notices of research projects. Working in conjunction with Earthwatch is the Center for Field Research – at the same address – which arranges financial support for research investigators whose projects can constructively utilise non-specialists in the field. Projects approved by the Center are recommended to Earthwatch for support.

The University of California Research Expeditions Program (UREP), University of California, Desk L, Berkeley, CA 94720, USA, (tel: (415) 642 6586) mounts expeditions to conduct scientific fieldwork in various disciplines and geographical locations, providing opportunities for interested donor-participants to become members of the field team and receive instructional materials and field training. Again, no special academic or field experience is necessary and the age limits are 16-75.

Members contribute equal shares to the cost of the expedition and a limited number of partial scholarships are available to students and teachers. Academic credit may be granted for participation in certain projects.

In Australia, the Association for Research Exploration and Aid Ltd (AREA), GPO Box 4692, Sydney 2001 both mounts its own environmentally-based expeditions and acts as an umbrella organisation in placing volunteers elsewhere.

It is possible to travel in a group and never make contact with the people of the countries you pass through. The Commonwealth Youth Exchange Council promotes contact between groups of young people of the Commonwealth by funding visits by groups from Britain to an overseas Commonwealth country or vice versa. The programme, to attract CYEC funding, must be useful in its own right and involve contact between visitors and hosts, preferably including joint activities. The aim is 'to provide meaningful contact and better understanding between Commonwealth young people' and if possible should lead to a continuing two-way link. Visits must be arranged through an established organisation and led by a responsible person. Two-thirds of each group must consist of people aged between 15 and 25 years. Further information is available from the Executive Secretary, Mr R.F. Grey, CYEC, 18 Fleet Street, London EC4Y 1AA (tel: 01-353 3901).

People wishing to work or study abroad without necessarily joining an expedition should consult the Central Bureau, Seymour Mews House, Seymour Mews (off Wigmore Street), London W1H 9PE (tel: 01-486 5101) whose publications are extremely useful. The Bureau, which also has offices in Edinburgh and Belfast, has details of jobs, study opportunities, youth organisations and holidays in some 60 countries.

A Year Off, published by CRAC Publications, Hobsons Press (Cambridge) Ltd, Bateman Street, Cambridge CB2 1LZ (tel: (0223) 354551) provides information about voluntary service, work camps and summer projects, paid work, *au pair* work, study courses, scholarships and travel, adventure and expeditions. Aimed at people with time to spare between school and higher education, it discusses the pros and cons of using that year in this special way, giving the views of both students and career experts.

Study Abroad, published by UNESCO, 7 Place de Fontenoy, Paris 75007, France and available from HMSO, PO Box 276, London SW8 5DT, describes some 2,600 opportunities for post-secondary study in all academic and professional fields and details of scholarships, assistant-ships, travel grants and other forms of financial assistance available.

Vacation Work Publications of 9 Park End Street, Oxford OX1 1HJ, (tel: (0865) 241978) publish many guides and directories for those seeking permanent jobs or summer jobs abroad, unusual travel opportunities, voluntary work and working travel.

Often travel for its own sake seems insufficient for those who wish to provide practical help for those who live in the country they are to visit. The Brandt report has made those of us who live in industrial Europe (the West) more aware of the acute differences between 'North' and 'South'. If you feel that you have both the time and the specialist skills needed to be a volunteer you should probably start by reading two very helpful directories: *Volunteer Work* from the Central Bureau and/or *The International Directory of Voluntary Work* by David Woodworth, published by Vacation Work. Both books give an outline of the organisations who are willing and able to accept volunteer workers on overseas projects and the skill and commitment required of the volunteer.

At this stage you should be aware that the majority of host countries who welcome volunteers usually require skilled personnel such as nurses, teachers, agronomists and civil engineers. They may be unable to pay even your air fares although many provide board and lodging, and you may be expected to help for at least a year or two. Remember that during that time you probably won't be travelling but will be based in a poor urban community or remote rural village.

If you feel that you are suitably qualified and have the emotional maturity to be a volunteer you may like to discuss your hopes and ambitions to serve with someone who has already been one. You can contact an ex-volunteer through their own organisation: Returned Volunteer Action, 1 Amwell Street, London EC1R 1UL (tel: 01-278 0804) which maintains a register of volunteers who have served on projects in many different areas of the world. They may even be able to direct you personally to an organisation which is appropriate to both your and their needs. Their publication *Thinking About Volunteering* is very frank about some of the problems you

may face before and after you have been a volunteer.

Finding the right organisation for you takes time, so don't expect to leave next week. The four main agencies who send out volunteers from the UK as part of the British Government's Overseas Aid Programme are: The Catholic Institute for International Relations (CIIR), International Voluntary Service (IVS), United Nations Association International Service (UNAIS) and Voluntary Service Overseas (VSO). Over 400 volunteers go abroad each year through these organisations, all are over 21 with professional work experience. The British Volunteer Programme, based in the UNAIS offices at 3 Whitehall Court, London SW1A 2EL (tel: 01-930 0679) has a leaflet which will give you information about these organisations and where to apply to be considered as a volunteer.

If you wish to apply to work for an international aid organisation then the International Recruitment and Index Service of the Overseas Development Administration, Abercrombie House, Eaglesham Road, East Kilbride, Glasgow G75 8EA (tel: (035 52) 41199) will be able to advise you through its booklets *Why Not Serve Overseas?* and *Opportunities Overseas with International Organisations*.

For further names and addresses of useful organisations, see the Directory Associations list on page 768.

The Student Traveller

by Nick Hanna and Greg Brookes

Student travellers can take advantage of a comprehensive range of special discounts both at home and abroad which enable you to go almost anywhere in the world on the cheap.

To qualify for reduced rates to most destinations you need an *International Student Identity Card* (ISIC) which is obtainable from local student travel offices or by post from ISIC, PO Box 90, London WC1. Holders of NUS full-time cards simply need to pay £3.50 to get the ISIC portion validated. All full-time students are eligible; applications should include proof of student status, a passport photo, full name, date of birth, nationality and the £3.50 fee. Postal applicants should also include a SAE.

The ISIC card is issued by the Geneva-based International Student Travel Conference, who, in conjunction with the NUS, publish a booklet called *The International Student Travel Guide* which tells you exactly what discounts students are eligible for. The ISIC card is recognised all over the world and allows holders reduced rates at many art galleries and other places of cultural and educational interest, as well as reductions on local transport.

The ISIC card is not, however, officially recognised in Eastern Europe where they have their own equivalent, the International Union of Students Card. These are difficult to obtain in Britain, although it is worth asking your local student travel office, and you will probably have to apply to the student authorities once you get into Eastern Europe.

The Council of Europe Cultural Identity Card is available free to post-graduate (not undergraduate) students, teachers, and a few other groups. It gives reduced or free admission to places of cultural interest in all member countries of the Council of Europe, and the Vatican; but not in the country of issue and only when produced with a passport. The card may not be used by those travelling for commercial reasons. For information and the application forms, write to the CBEVE (*see page 773*).

Accommodation

A useful booklet published by ISTC is *Low Cost Accommodation: Europe* which is available from student travel offices for £1. It lists over 1,200 places to stay divided into four price categories (budget, inexpensive, moderate or expensive) and a system of symbols indicates whether the hotel is near the station, airport or beach and what percentage discount they give to students.

For cheap accommodation in the USA, students can get a *Where to Stay US* card which costs £3.50 to ISIC holders. It entitles you to a 25 per cent discount on hotels and motels listed in their 48 page directory.

In West Germany students can use university catering facilities (Mensas) which are decent, reasonably priced and open all year round. Student accommodation is available, though usually only during local university vacations.

Travel

Cheap rail travel is now dependent hiefly upon age and is generally open to everyone under the age of 26, but student discounts are available on coaches. It pays to compare prices carefully between coach and rail because although coaches are normally considerably cheaper, sometimes the difference can be as little as £5, and trains are obviously preferable in terms of speed and comfort. Apart from these exceptions, coaches are generally substantially cheaper than trains, and both Euroways Coaches and Supabus offer discounts to ICIS holders on most (but not all) routes.

Ferries also offer student discounts. On Irish Sea Ferries, it is 25 per cent, crossing the North Sea 20 per cent, and on DFDS Ferries to Germany, 50 per cent. Student fares are also available on some cross-channel and Mediterranean ferries.

Within Britain, National Express gives students a 33 per cent reduction on all standard fares (but not Rapide services) on production of a *Student Coach Card* (£3.50).

Air

Valuable discounts are available for air travel. Student charters are operated by the major student travel organisations under the umbrella of the Student Air Travel Association. Most of the flights are in the long summer vacation, and are generally open to ISIC card holders under 30 (some are only open to those under 28) and their spouses and dependent children as long as they are travelling on the same flight.

Students travelling between their home and place of study abroad are also eligible for 25 per cent off standard fares if they arrange beforehand to get a Student Certificate from the airline (apply well in advance). Because these reductions only apply to standard fares, you might be better off with a discount ticket from elsewhere. Local student travel offices often have preferential arrangements with particular airlines and so are able to offer special bargains.

Travel Offices

Student travel offices are a good source of information about every kind of discount: there are nearly 60 of them in Britain, one for every campus or university town. They are coordinated by the National Association of Student Travel Offices (NASTO). Staff are often themselves seasoned travellers and can be a mine of information on budget travel in foreign countries. But check out the High Street travel agent as well and compare prices before making a final decision.

Another source of information on student travel discounts is *The Student Travel Manual* produced annually by STA Travel (to obtain a free copy contact STA Travel, 74 Old Brompton Road, London SW7 (tel: 01-581 1022). Although they started out life as Student Travel Australia, the services offered by STA now cover both hemispheres, making them Britain's biggest and most influential student travel operator. They have three offices in London and others throughout Australia, South East Asia, the Far East and the USA.

Another major operator is Worldwide Student Travel (for a free brochure contact them at 39 Store Street, London WC1E 7BZ (tel: 01-580 7733). Also worth checking out is London Student Travel (Head Office: Victoria Travel Centre, 52 Grosvenor Gardens, London SW1W 0AG (tel: 01-730 8111) who have three offices in London and others in Bristol, Dundee, Glasgow, Liverpool, Manchester and Oxford.

Working and Studying Abroad

There are several very good references

for students who wish to work abroad such as *Working Holidays* published by the Central Bureau for Educational Visits and Exchanges, and a very useful series of books from Vacation work Publications. *(See Joining a Project Overseas, on page 192, and booklist on page 814).*

North America is a favourite destination for students who want a working holiday. The British Universities North America Club (BUNAC) is a non profit-making organisation that exists to give students the chance to get to the States. They've got six programmes in the USA and Canada, offering a wide choice of jobs and locations, and for all of them, BUNAC gets you that vital work permit.

The general work and travel programme, Work America, allows you a visa so that you can take virtually any summer job you find yourself; the airfare has to be paid in advance – they suggest that bank managers will usually oblige with a loan. Places are limited, so it's vital that the lengthy application process is started early. Hundreds of opportunities can be found in BUNAC's *Job Directory*.

If you enjoy the company of children, then they have a BUNACAMP programme which places students in summer camps as counsellors. The round trip ticket is paid for, and you get full board and lodging plus pocket money. Students with specialist skills (music, sports, arts or science) are preferred, but more importantly, you must be able to deal with children.

Another deal that provides you with airfares, full board and lodging and a job is KAMP, the kitchen and maintenance programme. Contact BUNAC at 232 Vauxhall Bridge Road, London SW1V 1AV, (tel: 01-630 0344).

Camp America provides similar facilities with a free flight, free board and work permit all as part of the package. The placement procedure likewise takes a long time, so apply early. They are at Queens Gate, London SW7 5HR (tel: 01-589 3223).

To study abroad, you must first be sure you can cope adequately with the local language. Organisations such as the CBEVE and the British Council should be able to help, as should the Cultural Attaché at the relevant embassy. If possible, ask someone who has just returned for more details about local conditions and lifestyle.

Grants

Ask your university/polytechnic/higher education department/local authority if it has any special trust funds for student travel. If it has, it won't be much, but every little helps. Two handbooks on grants are *The Directory of Grant Making Trusts* and *The Grants Register*. Both are expensive, but should be in your student library. The library noticeboard is also a good place to look for details of bursaries or exchange scholarships which could well lead to a year's studying or travelling upon graduation.

Age-related Discounts

There are also a number of travel discount schemes that are not dependent upon student status, although most of these are nevertheless youth schemes, for which you cease to be eligible once you reach between 24 and 26. *The Federation of International Youth Travel Organisations* is made up of 125 organisations throughout the world which specialise in youth travel. A membership card entitles you to a range of concessions similar, although not identical to those given by ISIC. It is available to everyone under the age of 26, and is issued with a handbook listing all the concession entitlements. Youth Hostels and the YM (or W) CA are now open to everyone, regardless of age, offering a good network of cheap, clean if spartan accommodation around the world (*see Hostelling on page 364*).

There are two alternatives for cheap train travel. The first is an Inter-Rail card, which gives you unlimited free travel for one month in nineteen countries in Europe and North Africa, and costs £139. The card also allows you half price (but not free) travel on British Rail, and there are reductions on many shipping lines. It is available without condition to everyone who is under 26 and national of the UK or Ireland or a country whose railways do not participate in the scheme. If nationals of these countries can prove they live in the UK or Ireland, they are also eligible.

The second option is a BIGE ticket, which like the Inter-Rail card is open to anyone under 26. These give you half price fares to over 2,000 European destinations and are valid for two months. The main specialists are Transalpino and Eurotrain.

Travelling round Britain there are worthwhile savings to be made. An absolute must is a Young Person's Railcard – for those under 26 – which costs £12, is valid for a year, and entitles you to a third off British Rail tickets. It can be used on most journeys except where there are restrictions like minimum fares at peak hours. At the other end of the scale, there are similar rail cards for old age

pensioners, who can also travel extremely cheaply on National Express coaches at certain times, and can travel free by London Transport.

A half price youth rail card is also available in West Germany from GSTS. *The Deutsche Bundesbahn Junior Pass* allows half price rail travel for everyone under the age of 23.

Timeshare and Home Exchange

by Michael Furnell and Melissa Shales

The majority of people believe that timesharing is something new which has only developed over the last fifteen years or so, but in fact it is not really a new concept because as far back as the last century villagers were time-sharing water in Cyprus where there was no piped supply.

Property timeshare is believed to have been initiated in the 1960s when certain French developers of ski apartments experienced difficulties in selling their leisure accommodation outright and decided to offer for sale the ownership of weekly or fortnightly segments at the same time each year for ever.

The idea spread to other parts of Europe including Spain. On the Costa Blanca a British company, which was building apartments in Calpe, offered co-ownership of two-bedroom flats in the main shopping street, near the sea. Prices were as little as £250 per week's usage in the summer in perpetuity. Winter periods were even cheaper at £180 for a month and easy terms were available on the payment of a £50 deposit with the balance payable at £4.50 per month over three years.

The Americans soon recognised this form of holiday home ownership, and in the early stages converted condominiums, motels and hotels which were not viable in their original form into time-share units. Often these had rather basic facilities and it is only in recent years that developers in Florida and elsewhere have realised that top-quality homes with luxury facilities are the key to successful multi-ownership.

It was not until 1976 that timesharing was launched in Britain. The first site was in a beautiful lochside location in the Highlands of Scotland. This was a luxury development with excellent sporting facilities and prices were set from about £5,000 per week.

The aim of timesharing is to provide luxury quality holiday homes for which a once only capital sum is paid at today's prices, so that future holidays are secure whatever happens, for no hotel bills or holiday rents need to be paid in the coming years, just a reasonable annual sum to cover maintenance expenses.

With the initial costs being shared among a number of owners the standard of accommodation and the luxury specifications can be much higher than normal and often the furnishings and equipment are better than in most permanent homes.

Timesharing is sold by several different methods at prices from as little as £500 to nearly £11,000 for a week. When a freehold is purchased, the period of time which you buy is yours to use 'forever', and you may let, sell, assign or leave the property to your heirs in your will. In England and Wales the law only permits ownership for a maximum of 80 years, but in Scotland and many other parts of the world, ownership in perpetuity is possible.

Membership of a club which grants a right to use a specified property for a stated number of years is an alternative scheme. Here the assets of the club, i.e. buildings, lands and facilities are generally held by a trustee which is often a Bank or Insurance company. A transferable membership certificate is normally issued to each purchaser.

The formation of a public limited company with the issue of ordinary shares which vary in price according to the time of year chosen for occupancy has also been used as a vehicle for marketing timeshare. Each share provides one week's occupancy for a set number of years, usually 20 or 25 years. The properties are then sold in the open market and the proceeds divided among the shareholders.

One company uses capital contributed by members to purchase land and build holiday homes in various parts of Europe. Each member is entitled to holiday points which can be used for a vacation of a week or more in a chosen development at any time of year.

Another provides for the funds contributed by participants to be divided between the acquisition of timeshare property and the purchase of gilt-edged certificates. The income from the latter pays for management and maintenance fees. Holiday points are issued to bond holders according to the amount invested and these are used to select the use of one of the properties owned by the club. The properties are valued on a points per week basis depending on the size, location and season chosen. Investors are permitted to encash their bonds at any time after two years.

New Trends

One recent trend has been towards group ownership where each property is sold to a small number of owners, from four to ten.

This involves the purchase of the title for, say, a quarter of each year. Each owner is allotted two weeks use at the height of summer, one month in either spring or autumn plus six weeks during the remainder of the year. Occupation dates revolve annually to give each owner the opportunity of holidays at each season. Capital outlay is of course greater but still enables a family to enjoy part ownership of a superb villa in a very pleasant location for around £13,500.

To ensure adequate maintenance and administration of the properties, a management company is established on each scheme. This may be part of the developer's organisation or a nominee employed by them. After a scheme has been completed, the individual owners may join together to establish their own management organisation. The cost of management is recovered from an annual fee payable by all owners and should cover insurance, staffing, renovation, heat and light, gardening and the care of all communal facilities. Fees vary between about £50 and £150 per annum and are sometimes linked to the cost of living index.

Golden Rules

The Golden Rules to be remembered when buying a timeshare home are:

1. Purchase from a well established developer or selling agent who already has a reputation for fair dealing and offering really successful schemes.

2. The location of the property is vital, so be sure to select a well situated development with adequate facilities and a quality atmosphere. Be sure that it appeals to the family as well as yourself to ensure that you are all able to enjoy regular visits. If you are likely to want to resell in the future, the location could be even more important.

3. Check carefully the annual maintenance costs and be sure you know what they cover. Part of the yearly charges should be accumulated by the management to cover replacements, new furnishings and regular major redecorations.

4. If all the amenities promised by the sales staff are not already in existence, get a written commitment from the vendors that they will be completed.

5. Ascertain the rights of owners if the builder or management company gets into financial difficulties, and ascertain if it is possible for the owners to appoint a new management company if they are not satisfied with the service of the original one.

6. Before signing any documents which commit you to purchasing time, and also management contracts, have the wording checked by a solicitor. It is better to pay a fee for legal advice than to be committed to an unsatisfactory transaction.

7. Talk to an existing owner wherever possible before purchasing.

8. Find out if the vendor owns the property, and if they do not, discover who holds the freehold and if there is any mortgage on the property.

9. The experts believe that any timeshare scheme should have a minimum of ten units to be viable. If it is too small, amenities may be lacking and each owner's share of management costs may be excessive.

10. Are payments held in trust pending the issue of title documents, or a licence to use, and has a trustee been appointed to hold the master title deeds?

Investment

Timesharing is not a conventional money-making investment in property, although some owners who purchased time in the earliest schemes have enjoyed substantial capital appreciation over the past ten years. Essentially, you are investing in leisure and pleasure but you cannot expect inflation-proof holidays. What you are buying is vacation accommodation at today's prices. Expenditure on travel, food and entertainment is still likely to rise in future years according to the rate of inflation.

Exchange Facilities

It was recognised long ago that after a few years, many timeshare owners may want a change of scene for annual holidays, and as a result, organisations were established to arrange exchange facilities for timesharing owners. There are exciting possibilities for owners wanting to swap their seaside apartment in, say, England's West Country, for a contemporary style bungalow in, perhaps, Florida or an Andalucian type *pueblo* in Spain. Today there are three major exchange organisations operating in the UK and between them they offer an immense variety of timeshare accommodation in many holiday destinations. All had their origins in America and now have their offices in England.

RCI, the largest established exchange organisation, has over 350,000 subscribers in 36 countries who are offered 1,000 holiday locations. Interval International now has over 150,000 member families who are offered the choice of 400 resorts in 30 countries, while Exchange Network has over 25,000 listings.

There is normally an annual membership fee payable by each participant and the developer usually pays this for each owner in the first two or three years. In addition, a modest fee ($45-65) is due when an exchange is successfully organised.

Orderly Growth

There are now three professional timeshare associations – the British Property Timeshare Association, Westminster Bank Chambers, Market Hill, Sudbury, Suffolk (tel: (0787) 310749); the European Holiday Timeshare Association, 112 Westbourne Grove, London W2 (tel: 01-221 9400); and The Timeshare Developers Group, 2 Queen Anne's Gate Buildings, Dartmouth Street, London W1 (tel: 01-222 3203). These were formed to try and ensure the orderly growth of the industry, and will offer consumer advice and protection. An insurance bonding scheme for members is being processed and information providing surveys among owners are being conducted.

An encouraging aspect for the future well-being of the timeshare industry is the active participation of well known building firms who all have their own developments in the UK, Spain or Portugal, lending respectability to an area renowned for its appalling press and dodgy operators.

In an attempt to protect the public

from the shady side of the business, the UK Dept. of Trade and Industry has published a leaflet about timeshare entitled *Your Place in the Sun: or is It? – The Timeshare Buyer's Checklist* which is available from them or through Citizens' Advice Bureaux.

Homeswop

Many British home owners fancy the idea of exchanging their home with another family in Europe or elsewhere for a fortnight or a month, in order to enjoy a 'free' holiday – apart from transport costs. Although the idea is attractive, there are many problems to be overcome unless you arrange the swop with friends. A number of relatively small organisations have been established to arrange holiday home exchanges, but few of them have been successful.

Ideally, a swop should be with a like-minded family or group of a similar size, so both will feel at home, and will look after the property well. The various organisations work in two ways. Some simply publish a directory listing the property, with size, location and basic features, and leave it to the individual to make contact and iron out all the details of the arrangement. Others work more like a dating agency, visiting the property, taking down its – and your – details, together with what you are looking for, whether you are prepared to lend your car, feed cats, water plants etc. They will then cross-match you with another suitable scheme member. This obviously costs more but, from the amount of hassle saved, is probably worthwhile.

Whichever method you use, make sure that every eventuality has been covered and agreed in writing, that your insurance cover is full and up to date, and that neighbours or friends are primed before you leave. Put away anything you are worried about and leave detailed notes about how the washing machine works, what the rabbit eats, where the nearest transport is, and all possible numbers needed in case of emergency. At the end of your time in someone else's home, be sure that you leave it sparkling, replace anything damaged or broken, or leave the money for them to do so, and generally behave in the way you hope they are also behaving. Some people have become hooked on homeswopping as a way of travelling, and do so at least once a year, loving the opportunity to live within a real community and meet the 'natives' while away. Others, who have had more sobering experiences, swear never to try again, and normally swear even if you mention the idea. It is a more risky business than a normal holiday in a purpose-built hotel, but the rewards can, if you're lucky, be infinitely greater. You just have to be prepared to take the risk.

The Expatriate Traveller

by Doris Dow

Nowadays governments, large organisations and big companies all compete for expertise and skills they require. More and more people leave their own country to live and work abroad. These expatriates go off with high hopes and expectations but in spite of increased earning power, some are disappointed and frustrated and return home for good. Others adapt well to the challenge of a new life and continue in the expatriate scene for many years, finding it difficult to repatriate. 'Expatriates' should not be confused with 'settlers' – people who originated (years or generations back) from other countries but have a permanent commitment to their adopted country.

Contracts

It is important that the terms of the contract are understood and signed both by the employer and the employee; if it is another language, a reliable translation should be obtained before signing on the dotted line. Contracts should set out the terms and conditions of employment, including minimum length of contract, working hours and overtime, remuneration, allowances for/provision of accommodation, car, education, medical and dental cover, leave and terminal gratuities/bonuses, dismissal clauses and compassionate leave arrangements. Many jobs abroad offer what seem to be on paper very large salaries, but the attitude of employers, their willingness to accept responsibility and to offer support when necessary, are often worth more than money. Expats International, 62 Tritton Road, London SE21 (tel: 01-670 8304) is an association for expats which not only has a large jobs advertisement section in its magazine, but will advise on contracts and finance.

Documentation

Before departure, visas, work permits, driving licences, health regulations and other documentation must be attended to. Getting the necessary visas from embassies can entail many visits and long waits, but the first lessons of an aspiring expatriate are quickly learned – the acquisition of tolerance, patience, perseverance and good humour. For those working for a large company or international organisation, the documentation is usually done for them.

Preparations for the Move

Time spent doing some 'homework' on the country you are going to, its lifestyles, traditions and customs is very worthwhile. Mental preparation is just as important as the practical plans, as working and living in a country is quite a different experience from a holiday there. Search libraries and bookshops for travel books and up-to-date guides. For Commonwealth countries, there are excellent permanent exhibitions at the Commonwealth Institute, Kensington High Street, London, as well as an excellent bookshop. Embassies should also be helpful on specific information on currency, import regulations etc. – also on what *not* to import.

Other valuable sources of information are: The Women's Corona Society, Minster House, 2074 Vauxhall Bridge Road, London SW1V 1BB, (tel: 01-828 1652/3) whose *Notes for Newcomers* series for over 100 countries (£2 per set) give practical details on what to take, what will be found there, education, health, leisure activities, etc.; and Monitor Press, Great Waldingfield, Sudbury, Suffolk, CO10 0TL, (tel: (0787) 78607) who, in conjunction with The Royal Commonwealth Society and The Centre for International Briefing, also produce good detailed notes (£10 per set). *(For other publications, see book list and list of periodicals in the reference section).*

Finance

Arrangements should be made to continue National Health Insurance contributions, as these are an extremely good investment. All financial aspects of the move should be studied and arranged *before* departure – tax clearance, financial regulations and exchange controls in your country of destination, investments etc. There are firms and consultancies specialising in this field e.g. Wilfred T. Fry Ltd, 31 Queen Street, Exeter, Devon EX4 3SR (also London and Worthing) and The Expatriate Consultancy Ltd, 32 Trumpington Street, Cambridge CB2 1QY.

Despatch and Arrival of Effects

There are many international firms who specialise in overseas removals. For those who have to make their own arrangements, it is advisable to approach more than one firm for an estimate.

When travelling by air, include as many basic essentials as possible in the accompanied baggage in order to be self-sufficient for the first few days, including several paperbacks to get through lengthy waits and sleepless nights due to jetlag. Always ensure that personal luggage is locked and insured.

Many people find airfreight the quickest, easiest and safest way of consigning goods. Lists of all contents should be available for Customs clearance, shipping agents, insurance etc., and two copies of these lists should always be retained. Baggage allowances are usually generous and first entry into a country generally permits duty-free import of personal and household effects. In many countries there is a ready sale for secondhand possessions at the end of a contract, often at advantageous prices, so it is worthwhile making full use of the allowance. There are only a few instances where what is imported must be taken away again in its entirety.

Heavier items for sea freight should be crated and listed – translation into the appropriate language can often hasten Customs clearance. Hiring a good local agent who knows the ropes can also be a good investment. Realistic insurance of all effects is essential.

Arrival at Destination

If possible, arrange to be met at the airport, and/or have a contact telephone number. Make sure that hotel accommodation has been booked and keep all receipts for later reimbursement. Salary may be delayed so try to have some traveller's cheques to cover this eventuality.

A long journey and the shock of new climatic conditions can be depressing until acclimatisation is achieved – so use your commonsense and allow yourself time to adjust. Be prepared for long delays at Customs and Immigration – patience and good humour will pay dividends. Don't judge the country by its officialdom. *Do not* exchange money, except through official channels.

Housing

It is unlikely that permanent accommodation will be available immediately, necessitating a few days or even weeks stay in a hotel. Make use of this freedom to get acquainted with local sources of supply etc.

To many expatriates, disappointment can begin with housing and furniture, which often does not match up to expectations. Reserve judgement at the beginning, because what may seem a drawback can turn out to be an advantage. There is a big difference in standards between local and expatriate employers, and there is no firm basis for comparison. In oil-rich states, it may well be that expatriate housing is much humbler than that of the nationals. On the other hand, accommodation may be very luxurious and spacious. The less fortunate expatriate should refrain from envious comparisons and, with careful thought and inexpensive ingenuity, make the best of what comes along. Work camps/compounds and high rise flats are all very real challenges to the good homemaker.

Medical Care

Primary medical care is sometimes much better than one might expect, easily contacted and near at hand. Further care may be available, but if not, serious cases are flown out for emergency or specialist treatment. Large organisations often have their own hospitals, clinics and doctors. Government contracts usually provide free medical facilities. It is always wise to have a good dental check-up before departure from home. Anybody needing medication on a regular basis should take a good supply to last until an alternative source is established.

Education

Very young children are often well catered for by play groups and nursery schools. Later, there are international schools, company schools, and private or state schools. These vary considerably, but given a good school and parents who take advantage of all there is to offer in the locality, a child will have made a good start. There is often a waiting list and information about schools should be obtained, and an early approach made for enrolment, well ahead of departure. For those going to outlying areas, it may be

necessary to consider correspondence courses e.g. World Wide Education Service, Strode House, 44-50 Osnaburgh Street, London NW1 3NN (ages 5-15).

Many contracts provide for boarding school in the UK and regular holiday visits to parents. As the older child might well lack stimulation and local schooling might be inadequate, early consideration should be given to choosing a boarding school. An Educational Trust will assist. It is a hard decision to take, but the partings at the end of the holidays are compensated for by the pleasure with which children look forward to travelling out to their parents at the end of term. In most places, special events are laid on for them, they feel special having a home overseas and travelling experience makes them more responsible, confident and resourceful. The Women's Corona Society also provides an escort service from airport to school trains etc.

Children are often used as an excuse for the wife to return home, but for children at boarding school, it is often more important for them to feel that they have a solid family base than to have Mum on the doorstep.

Marriage

The move should be talked over very carefully as it can have a profound effect on a marriage. For busy working parents and weary commuters, expatriate life can be an opportunity to spend more time together as a family, and if both partners are keen, the novelty of the strange environment can be a rewarding experience. I would advise against married men taking single person's contracts or splitting the partnership for long periods of time, as it places too great a strain on communication. Starting again could help rebuild a shaky marriage, but it could also split it apart completely if an unwilling person is ripped away from everything familiar. So think before you move

Single Men and Women

Single (or unaccompanied) men often live in camps which are isolated. They have frequent short leaves and money to spend. A special interest – sport or hobby – gives them the chance to form stable friendships and does away with propping up the bar for company in their spare time.

A single woman usually has to establish a home as well as tackling the job. However the job, with a real and worthwhile challenge, gives her an advantage over many wives who often find themselves at sea with nothing to do but keep house. A single woman is generally in great demand in a lively social whirl, but this needs to be handled with great care. She is often an object of great interest to the local population who find it difficult to understand that she has no man to tell her what to do, and may receive many offers of marriage because of this

Wives

While women are generally expected to be supportive of their husbands as they come to terms with a new job, it should also be remembered that they too need support and encouragement as they establish a new home, meet new people and adapt to a different lifestyle.

At all times, the rules and regulations and laws of a country must be obeyed. Western women often find the new cultures and traditions difficult to embrace and inhibiting, e.g. in a Muslim country, and it is essential to prepare for this. *Living Overseas* one day courses for men and women are designed by the Women's Corona Society to counsel on adaptation to a new lifestyle and provide an opportunity to meet someone with current knowledge of their country. These courses are held at regular intervals, or at special request, and cost £20 per person.

Many women give up careers or interesting part-time jobs to accompany their husbands overseas, and in a number of places, there is no opportunity for them to get a job. Work permits can often be obtained in the teaching or medical professions but not always where her husband is posted. If your husband is with a big company, it might be worth asking them about jobs, or otherwise considering the possibilities of working on your own or doing voluntary work.

Careful planning and preparation for the use of leisure time, whether it is because of no outside employment or greater freedom from household duties because of servants, is essential to counteract boredom and initial loneliness. There are many hobbies and interests to be resurrected or embarked upon. Join groups with local knowledge e.g. archaeological, historical, wildlife, photographic, amateur dramatics etc. Involvement in the local scene through clubs and organisations helps understanding and leads to more tolerant attitudes towards cultural differences. Learning the language, a correspondence course to gain new qualifications or just for pleasure – the possibilities are many and varied for the wife determined to make the most of her stay in another country. There may be a lack of facilities (she may have to cut the family's hair), she may have to put up with a number of uncongenial conditions, but there are so many other rewards to supply the icing for the cake.

Expatriates are on the whole friendlier and less inhibited than in their home environment. The sun, outdoor pursuits, less clothing, often make people appear more attractive and relaxed. Social life is important for, except in the big cities, self-entertainment is necessary. This often provides scope for great ingenuity and many find latent and surprising talents hitherto undeveloped. In what is often a male-orientated society, it is important for the wife to cultivate her own interests, making sure of an independent identity, rather than identifying too much with her husband's job and position. And with servants, there is more time to experiment, as she is no longer saddled with the day to day chores involved in running the house.

Servants

The availability of domestic help brings an easier lifestyle and is recommended for hot and humid climates where the energy gets sapped. Many people are diffident about employing servants and don't know how to cope with them. With an initial trial period and the advice of someone who speaks the language and has kept a servant for some time, it is possible for a good relationship to be formed. Settle for a few qualities or skills suitable for the family's needs and be tolerant about other shortcomings. Establish what is wanted and agree time off. A servant who is respected becomes part of the extended family.

Lifestyle

Respect the local customs and laws about behaviour and dress, etiquette and the Highway Code, etc., and be aware of local sensitivities so you don't offend them. Be prepared for what might appear odd or rude behaviour. Cultural differences can lead to all sorts of misunderstandings. Reserve judgement, take advice from happily established residents and concentrate first on personal relations. Forget efficiency and don't expect things to happen in a hurry. Polite conversation and courtesy are priorities – sincere interest, tolerance and a joke work wonders. Beware of criticising before you've attempted to understand a situation.

Security

Security can be a problem, but commonsense measures, security guards and alarm systems are used in greater or lesser degree according to local hazards. Wilful violence is rare. It is possible for the expatriate to get caught up in political reprisals, but this is fortunately very rare indeed. It is wise to register with the Consular Section of your Embassy or High Commission so they know where to find you in cases of emergency – don't wait until trouble arises as communications can be difficult.

Summary

The expatriate's life can suffer considerable privation through lack of consumer goods and a low standard of living, or can be extremely rewarding with higher standards of housing and a hectic social life as well as a worthwhile job.

The challenge of helping a country to develop can be very stimulating and addictive – whatever the conditions encountered – which is the reason why so many expatriates return overseas again and again. Friendships made abroad are often more binding and congenial, through shared experiences, than those made at home. Valuable experience in a job often leads to promotion. The tolerance and understanding of other races and cultures learned through the expatriate experience of shorter or longer duration means that life will forever afterwards be enriched.

In the Lap of Luxury

by Carol Wright

A dictionary definition of 'luxury' is 'anything not necessary but used for personal gratification'. This applies particularly to travel since many have a dream goal – a vision of real pampering on the move on Concorde or QE2 or in five-star hotels. Hotel maids in New York have saved all their lives to board the QE2's world cruise. One widow gradually sold her treasures, eventually even her home, to make that voyage each year.

In most luxury travel dreams, there is much looking back in nostalgia to a time of slower pace, innumerable porters and servants; no need to manhandle luggage on wheels, take self-service meals or fight for space round a pool. In those days, social hostesses took banana boats to Jamaica to escape winter and recover from the rigours of the season. Pre-war it was said on transatlantic liners that 'only snobs drank a *second* bottle of champagne before breakfast'.

Cruising

Alas, champagne breakfasts have almost disappeared according to the restaurant manager of QE2's top grill room, and security has ended the magnificent sailing day parties. But cruising is probably still considered the nearest we still have to old-time luxury. It's a pricy indulgence with fuel prices pushing up touring by sea. The cheapest berth on QE2's 1987 ninety-six day round the world cruise including flights from Britain to New York and back by Concorde costs £10,890. QE2's top price was £55,050 per person in the top-grade suite with their own private sundeck over the bridge, split level living room with stereo centre, silver drinks service, special porcelain service for breakfast and afternoon tea, gold plated taps in the two bathrooms and specially designed bed linen.

Concorde

QE2 links one-way Concorde flights on transatlantic trips. Concorde scores with speed, alleviating jet lag, swollen ankles and the boredom of overnight Atlantic flights – it's just three hours to New York – but it is somewhat cramped in seating space. The curved earth scenes looking like sixteenth century maps and purpling upper atmosphere are stunning, but service, because of lack of space, is trimmed to simpler - than - other - First-Class, though the champagne flows and the food, like other British Airways food, is designed by top international chefs like the Roux brothers.

First Class plane travel is certainly a luxury, not a necessity; the back end, and hopefully the luggage, will all arrive at the same time. However, for any journey over five hours, if one can afford the extra, First Class travel is definitely worthwhile. The copious food and champagne are pleasant, but space, toilet access when wanted and the pampered élitist feeling are more satisfying. Sleeperette chairs on most international lines prevent the tray on your knees and prodding in the behind cramps of Economy Class. With foot rest and good recline angle and, on British Airways, adjustable head rest and seat contoured by a Guy's Hospital back expert, one can lie on one's side and sleep. Air Canada have the most capacious wool blankets, not those static-filled, lacy, string-like shawls of most airlines.

Philippine Airlines, as well as good food and good service, has the most luxurious relaxer, called Cloud 9. Here, for a small supplement on the First Class fare, one can book a full-length bed with sheets, blankets and pillows. One has the normal seat downstairs for meals and movie times. Upstairs, the lights are kept dim throughout the trip and, with a seat-belt over the stomach, the traveller can (theoretically) sleep through landings, stopovers and takeoffs. One-upping PAL on sky-high sleep (unless, like Mrs Thatcher on her return from Williamsburg, you buy the upper First Class section of a British Airways jumbo and have a bed installed) is Regent Air's service between Los Angeles and New York. On their 727, there is a maximum of 36 passengers (compared to the normal 130) carried amid art deco surroundings with champagne, caviar and fresh lobster all the way and a choice of four private compartments with queen-sized beds. The fare is about $1000 above the standard First Class fare.

For short flights it is not a costly luxury to hire your own plane if there are four or more passengers. Often the joys of having your own plane where and when you want it are cheaper than the sum of the scheduled return fares. Details can be obtained from the Air Transport Operators Association, Clembro House, Weydown Road, Haselmere, Surrey GU27 2QE, UK (tel: (0428) 4804).

Rail

Trains in India like the Rajasthan Express have become popular with tourists and the revival of the Venice-Simplon Orient Express shows a yearning for older style luxury. Though overrated and overpriced, it is an experience to rattle on these ancient coaches on modern rails, lurching to the dining car over slicing plates of steel linking carriages, that makes one realise the advance British Rail's Inter-City 125 has made in rail comfort.

India's Palace on Wheels is a collection of old maharajah's coaches. Luxurious is an overrated adjective, but it is preferable to touring by air, and each eight-bedded carriage (with two washrooms with showers) has two attendants to cope with snacks, drink bearing and laundry.

And all around the world, other countries have seen these successes, are getting their old trains out of storage, dusting and polishing them, and realising that people are prepared to pay to be pampered and that as we all get used to jet travel, travelling slowly has once again become the chic option.

A Villa in Jamaica

In the lordly days when all hotels seemed to be called Westminster or

Bristol, it was smart to have a private yacht or villa for the season. Both are still available though flotilla sailing and egg-box Costa apartments are not luxurious modern answers. It is however also possible to rent big and beautiful yachts and power cruisers of every size and shape in the Mediterranean and Carribean; basic rental costs per week are anything from $5,000 upwards for five or more passengers.

Hiring villas can be grand as in Jamaica or southern Portugal where servants come in the package and there is usually a pool or garden in the property. Bears House in Barbados is just one example of super-luxury with a staff of butler, cook, laundress, maid and gardener, with four bedrooms with *en suite* bathrooms and huge private pool. You can even hire private islands, with a price tag of up to £15,000 per person per week.

At the end of the day however, any pampered traveller will be looking for a hotel. There are glossy hotels like the Manila, with its crystal glass trees in the Champagne dining room where background music is supplied by a section of the National Philharmonic; the L'Ermitage in Beverly Hills where lengthy white cadillacs are provided to take you shopping; or the Nova Park in Paris, with its open plan bathroom/bedroom/bar which you divide yourself with curtains, its purple erotic decor, 24 hour video film library and restaurant and entertainment in the hotel complete with 20 resident musicians. Or there are those which trade on their heritage, such as Britain's stately homes, where you sleep in four posters, and dine with a duke off game shot on the estate.

But the ultimate for me is a Given-chy suite at Singapore's Hilton Hotel. The spacious rooms with big garden terraces are on a separate floor serviced by Chinese butlers dressed in pin stripe who fix appointments, take breakfast orders, deliver parcels and messages. On arrival, a maid brings a glass of champagne and unpacks for you, taking away soiled or crumpled clothes to be returned the next day fresh and pressed; and each day all laundry is done free. While she works, you can nibble a handmade chocolate from a salver decorated with orchids and, like the massive mound or tropical fruit, kept topped up each day, or sip a drink from the array of cut glass decanters filled with spirits, read papers or magazines, watch TV or write a note at a desk well supplied with personalised notepaper. To unwind from the flight or sightseeing, the bathroom has its own Turkish steam cabinet and bath with gold-plated taps and jacuzzi whirlpool which billows the free Givenchy bath foam into candy floss clouds as you soak it out and decide whether to take Chinese food on the roof top, *nouvelle cuisine* based on what was fresh in the market that morning in the downstairs restaurant, or full afternoon tea in the music room – an area which changes pace all day until it ends as a sophisticated late night disco with music tuned so only the dancers get its full benefit, not the talkers around the floor.

True luxury is something that everyone should experience at least once in their lives, that indescribable feeling that the world has been organised solely for your pleasure. To make a habit of travelling this way however is something few of us can ever try more often without living in penury for the rest of the year.

Your Special Needs

Selecting Travelling Companions

by Nigel Winser

'I would say that this matter of relationships between members... can be more important than the achievement of the stated objective, be it crossing a desert or an ocean, the exploration of a jungle or the ascent of a mountain peak.' – John Hunt

'Bill always takes his boots off inside the tent and Ben has yet to cook a decent meal... yackety yack, moan, moan.' A familiar and typical cry, triggered by lack of privacy and repetitive food. Add to the melting-pot such problems as financial mismanagement, change of itinerary, ill health and a stolen rucksack, and you may realise that you have not given as much thought to the choice of your travelling companions as you should. While the fire remains hot there is little you can do about it, so it is worth thinking about before you depart.

All travelling groups will have storms, so don't kid yourself that they won't happen to you. But perhaps you can weather them without breaking up the party.

I am not concerned here with choosing specialist members of a scientific team for an expedition. That is up to the leader of the group. The more specialised the positions, the more specific the qualifications required. My own experience is with more formal expeditions, but any travellers, from those on a budget package to overlanders will run up against many of the same problems, and should be able to learn from the techniques used by countless expeditions around the world.

Expedition leaders are fortunate to be able to draw on the experiences of many past ventures as well as long-term projects in Antarctica where all nations have studied personnel selection and interview techniques in detail. It is lucky we all don't have to go through such interviews because you and I probably wouldn't make it.

Common Sense

In theory, choosing your companions is common sense. You are looking for good-humoured individuals who, by their understanding and agreement of the objectives, form a close bond and so create a functional and cohesive team. It also helps if you like each other.

People go on journeys to satisfy ambitions, however disparate. The more you understand everyone else's ambitions, the better you will be at assessing the bonds that maintain the group. But it is not that easy. A common problem arises when, for instance, en route you require someone to do a job such as repair a vehicle. Suddenly your good friend has to be moulded into a mechanic, a role for which he or she may or may not be fit. The other solution is to have in your party a mechanic whom you have never met but who has to be moulded into a 'good friend'. There are no black-and-white guidelines here. If any virtues were to be singled out to aid your decision, high tolerance and adaptability would be two.

So, with no fixed guidelines, how can you begin to choose your companions? The single factor most likely to upset the group on a journey will be that an individual does not satisfy his or her own reasons for going. Fellow members of the party will be directly or indirectly blamed for preventing such satisfaction. Travelling itself acts as a catalyst to any dispute and provocations and pressures may build up to intolerable levels. Any bonds that have formed will be stretched to the limit, as individuals continually reassess their expectations.

It is assumed that differing personality traits are to blame here. While there are, of course, exceptions, I do not believe that personality clashes are sufficient to account for groups breaking up. I see them as symptoms of disorder within the group, and a lack of cohesion within the group owing to ill-matched objectives to be the original cause. It is worth mentioning here that the 'organisation' of the trip will come under fire whenever difficulties arise; and while no one wants to lose the freedom of individual travel, the machinery of group travel (shared kitty, agreed itinerary, overall responsibility) should be well oiled.

Practical Tips

From a practical point of view, you may like to consider the following tips, which apply as much to two hitchhikers as to a full-blown expedition:

1. Get to know one another before you go. If necessary, go to the pub together and get slightly pickled, then see if you can get on just as well in the morning.
2. Discuss openly with all members of the group the overall objectives of the trip and see how many members of the group disagree. Are all members of the group going to be satisfied with the plans as they stand?
3. Discuss openly the leader's (or the main organiser's, if there is one) motivation in wanting to undertake this particular journey. Is he or she using the trip to further selfish ambitions? If these are made clear beforehand so much the better, particularly if the others are not connected with the hidden objective.
4. Discuss and plan to solve the problems which will certainly crop up. The regular ones are poor health, stolen goods, accidents, insurance, itinerary. If everyone knows where they stand before the chips are down, the chance of remaining a group improves.
5. If possible, have the team working together before departure, particularly if there has been allocation of duties. To know where you fit in is important.
6. If there is to be any form of hierarchy, it must be established before leaving and not enforced en route. If everyone can be made to feel that he or she is an integral part of the group and the group's interdependence, you will all stay together throughout the

journey and have a rewarding and enjoyable experience.

The Woman Traveller

by Ludmilla Tüting

Strict moral codes make the life of female travellers all over the world more difficult. If you want to avoid trouble you must listen to some unwritten rules.

'You can judge a man by the cut of his suit' – I don't like that saying. For me, it reflects the whole mendacity and dual morality of our society. Whenever I have to pack my rucksack to travel to Asia my trouble with clothes begins. Each time the same thing: shall I take some of my good stuff with me? A nice little skirt would open doors much faster and would afford me more respect. Things can be made much easier in Muslim countries. The more I play up to being a lady or the more determined and authoritarian my appearance becomes, the less I'll be regarded as a plaything. But that whole façade is so repugnant to me that until now I've unpacked my 'good' stuff again.

Western women are, in fact, regarded in most of the underdeveloped countries, and even in Southern Europe, as nothing better than loose women. Even the company of a man doesn't help much in Muslim countries. For instance, Iranians are especially prone to touching our breasts or grasping up between the legs in the bazaars or on the streets. As I was propositioned frequently in non-Muslim countries, although accompanied by a male, I began to think about the

situation. But it took me years to realise my mistake: I just didn't behave in a feminine way.

Stay in Stereotype

Clichés which are used to stereotype the role of women can be expected and found mainly in the orthodox countries. I have never played this role. On the contrary, I always started discussions about the contrast between East and West, or about the fact that daughters and sons go through with arranged marriages not having seen each other before. I talked enthusiastically about how beautiful it is to travel alone, how you are more open to experience and its many other advantages. Apart from that, I liked to look people straight in the face, but I should not have done this with men. My most chaste dress was in vain if I looked deep into their eyes. They usually took it as an invitation. These men are not used to it; their women avoid eye contact. I try to do so too, but it is difficult. I do not feel obliged to live a lie, but the stiff moral concepts applicable to women leave me with no choice. I find I have to accept other countries as they are, otherwise I had better stay at home. So:

– If I travel with a 'constant' partner, we act as a married couple and tell people we have at least two sons, daughters being worthless.

– If I travel alone, I carry with me a photo of 'my husband and our sons' and show it around when necessary. The photo should never show wealthy surroundings; as a background, nature is the best of all.

– On principle I wear a real wedding ring, none of the cheap ones. Wearing the ring on the left hand in these countries means that you are married. Ten years ago, the same stupid trick was even sometimes necessary at home.

– I now avoid eye contact with men. In strong Muslim countries it is a good idea to wear sunglasses with opaque mirror lenses.

– The most successful method of warding off molestation is to learn defensive replies in the native tongue of those countries which are renowned for this problem.

– I only give obvious reasons for why I travel on my own: because of my profession, my studies, or because I want to visit friends or relations.

– I only wear small T-shirts with a bra underneath and a waistcoat on top. I always cover my shoulders, upper arms, and, of course, my legs. Nearly everywhere naked legs are considered disrespectful to the customs of the country, particularly in places like temples. Having bare legs is as bad as wearing nothing at all.

– It is only when I have known people for a long time that I am willing to discuss controversial topics.

– I try to avoid everything which could possibly give the impression that I am 'game'. Whether in Asia or Latin America, it is a matter of prestige for many men to go to bed with a white woman. Accordingly, if they scent a chance, they will use all their charm and tricks to gain their objective. A few times I have been very disappointed and very angry when they tried to use force, although I was a guest of the whole family. Especially in Latin America, as you may know, the macho cult demands that a man has a mistress as well as a wife and this state of affairs is generally accepted. The Koran allows a man to take four

women as long as he can ensure that he will provide each of them with similar material conditions.

– The Western-oriented men in the cities are the most dangerous. Television has a great deal to do with this. In under-developed countries you will notice that many low-cost American trash programmes make up a large part of the station's schedule. And from these, many men get the impression that Western women are only to be regarded as objects of sexual amusement, and frequently the victims of direct violent acts.

– If you find yourself in the position when you are actually about to be raped, there is only one thing to do: keep cool! Panic only angers the perpetrator. As bad as it is, normally the woman will not die and after a few minutes it's all over. It is important that you don't become paranoid about being attacked and even if it should happen to you, don't become a psychological wreck. Therefore here are three tips which you may find useful:

* Try to start a conversation with your attacker. Possibly warn him that you have venereal disease.

* Beat or bite his testicles so that he is forced to let you go because he is in pain.

* Simulate excitement so that he feels secure and the possibility of killing you does not enter his mind.

I have recovered from several attempted rapes. The first time it happened to me was in a little village hospital in Pakistan, when I naïvely went for a medical examination because of acute appendicitis. Three doctors immediately made passes at me. And even though I was in agony because of the pain they merely offered me whisky and howled 'Let's have a party '

Peculiarly, the setting of another attempt was in a heavily guarded building in Brazil: that is, in the German Consulate in Rio, where marksmen stood on guard to protect a visiting ambassador from abduction. However, in the corridor, a messenger, already stripped down to his underpants, was waiting for me.

In India, there is a pocket-book against hippies which created a sensation in 1974 and encouraged the opinion that every tourist who doesn't wear elegant clothes and stay at the Sheraton must be a hippy. This book is a collection of all imaginable prejudices against young Westerners but was sold as an 'analysis'. The author, an officer, came to the conclusion that hippies are only involved in sex and drugs. They come to India, distribute themselves, stink and leave behind a heap of rubbish.

It is also important to know that in most countries, exchange of tenderness in public is scorned. One is only allowed to express tender feelings within one's own four walls. For example, when a couple meet again at an airport in Delhi, the women at best fling themselves into the dust to kiss their husband's feet. An embrace is impossible, but on the contrary it is usual to see men holding hands when going for a stroll and it doesn't automatically mean they are homosexual.

Morals, Traditions and Taboos

The strict moral codes, made by men to protect women, begin on our own doorsteps, with the Italians. In Italy, as late as 1981, a law was abolished which allowed extenuating circumstances to men who murdered their wife, daughter or sister for having immoral sex, just to rescue their honour.

In Muslim society, a similarly peculiar interpretation of honour exists (male honour of course; female honour doesn't exist). If an unmarried female member of the family loses her virginity, the honour of the man is in danger; he loses face. He himself can be the worst lecher but that will not matter. In Berlin, among the migrant workers, Turkish gynaecologists replace young Turkish girls' hymens, otherwise they wouldn't be able to find a husband.

Where false upbringing and the acceptance of foolish role-playing attitudes can lead, we know only too well from our own countries. However, over here I have the right to criticise. Nevertheless, if I mention that women in menstruation are, in many countries, regarded as unclean, I still say it with unbelievable astonishment. A woman should therefore be quiet about her period or she could, for instance, be refused admission to temples, and she may not touch certain foods and men.

The worst violation, in my opinion, is the circumcision of young women in the Northern part of Africa from Egypt to Senegal, where the clitoris is cut out and the vulva are stitched together, leaving only a minute opening. I always shiver when I think how the procedure takes place under primitive, unhygienic conditions. For procreation, the vulva are temporarily separated. The moral: your wife remains clean, the man finds sexual satisfaction elsewhere.

Muslims like to emphasise the advantages the Koran brought to their women, which is also true. They finally acquired material security during the marriage – but that was in the seventh century. They still have few rights, and if not married, none at all.

It is a question of interpretation of the Koran when Muslim men maintain the tradition that their women wear veils. Even in Europe, the orthodox Muslim adheres more to tradition than Mohammed, because Mohammed wrote that face, hands and feet may stay exposed. What is important about that? The hair should be covered, which is why a scarf worn by tourist women in strict regions can only be an advantage. An Arab once said to a friend: 'A woman who shows her hair might as well present herself naked.' The veil in the Middle East is called the *hidscaab* or *tschador* and on the Indian subcontinent, *pardah*. Under the veil, which in Afghanistan completely covers the face, the women wear the latest cosmetics. If a woman walks through the streets with her legs bared and unaccompanied, she should not wonder if she is looked upon as a whore. By walking through a bazaar, she further risks running the gauntlet. More than a few women tourists do this even on purpose, but do so to the detriment of other women. Just as scorned are those on the border separating Colombia and Venezuela who acquire the coveted visas from immigration officers by going to bed with them. So much more is the anger of the women who won't submit and have to travel the 500 kms back.

Something to be aware of when striking up friendships while abroad is that you could only be the means to an end. A marriage contract is often the only way of entering a Western country and a romance with a local man could, in fact, just be his ticket out. However, it would be absurd to avoid all relationships while travelling, on whatever basis they are formed.

For contraception on long journeys, the coil is supposed to be the most suitable method, but it should be tested long before setting out for compatibility. Those who wish to take the pill should take an ample supply, and be careful on long flights with time differences and in cases of diarrhoea. Condoms are highly recommended for use while travelling as they are obtainable everywhere and also give protection against venereal disease.

Sex aside, a few years ago, one noticed that few women travelled alone. Today there are many, often travelling in pairs. Many had bad experiences before the journey started while looking for male partners – only frisky young girls are sought as travelling companions. From whichever angle I look at it, I always seem to arrive back at the same theme. Perhaps it is time more women travellers spoke out in favour of a little respect.

This article has been reprinted from the Globetrotters Handbook, whom we would like to thank for permission to use it.

Travelling with Children

by Rupert and Jan Grey

The difference between travelling with children and travelling without is not unlike crossing the Sahara on foot as opposed to in a Land Rover: you go much slower, it is much harder work, but it is (arguably) much more fun.

Given the choice, we always take ours with us, for they open doors that were previously closed. Parenthood is an international condition, and the barriers erected by race and language fall away in the presence of children. Of equal importance for the travelling parent is the opportunity to experience, with and through their children, the newness of their world, their innocence and their instinctive fear of the unknown. The reactions of children are not yet blunted by the passage of years and the compromises of adulthood, and a journey to the jungles of the equator or the forests of the north can be one of discovery between as well as by parent and child.

Children require explanations, and their passion for knowledge is as infectious as their imagination is vivid. The dark recesses of a cave in the heart of Borneo were, for ours, the home of dragons, and crocodiles long since mourned by conservationists lurked in the darkening shadows over the rivers. The reality of adulthood suddenly became rather boring.

So, of course, is changing nappies. In many parts of the world the locals will regard you with amazement; they will probably have never seen disposable nappies, and for children over six months they regard them as superfluous in any event. Nappies, clothes, children's games and books are items which suddenly become indispensable, and the notion of travelling light becomes a part of your past along with many other aspects of pre-children life.

Preparation

Eric Shipton, so he said, used to plan his expeditions on the back of an envelope. Not with children, he didn't. Detailed organisation and preparation is not an optional extra. It is vital.

What you take will depend on the age and individual requirements of your children. If they have a passion for a pure wool Habitat duck, as our eldest daughter did the first time we took her to Malaysia at the age of 2½, take it. Take a second one just in case the first one gets lost. It will probably be your most crucial item of equipment.

Your choice of clothes will of necessity be dictated by the climate; cotton clothes with long legs and sleeves are best for the tropics, and for fair-skinned children a sun hat (also made of cotton) is essential, particularly if travelling on water.

While children generally adapt to heat better than adults, the younger ones are much more vulnerable to cold. Warm clothing should be in layers and easily washable, and if you put children still in nappies into ski suits you will need the patience of Job.

No less important than choosing the right equipment is packing it in the right way. There will be a rucksack - that - is - only - opened - at - night (all the things necessaryforsleeping); the rucksack - that - you - have - beside - you - at - all - times (which has a few nappies, drinks, a couple of children's books/games, the teddy, guide books etc.); and there will be a rucksack just for nappies and a rucksack just for toys, a rucksack for clothes and one little tiny rucksack for each of the children (containing a couple of nappies apiece: it is bound to get lost) to give them a sense of participation.

As important as sorting out your equipment is preparing the children. This calls for a lot of topical reading and story-telling, spread over several weeks or months before departure. The object of the exercise here is twofold: firstly to instil a sense of adventure and anticipation, and secondly as a sort of advance warning that life is going to be very different. If you are about to expose your children to a radically different culture, an extreme of climate, fly them through eight different time-zones into a world of extraordinary insects, holes in the ground for lavatories and a completely unfamiliar diet, it is an advance warning that they will need. You won't, for you will probably have already been there. The demands on your children will be far greater than on you.

The children should help in the preparations. Erect the mosquito nets for them to play in, let them pack and unpack the rucksacks, read them the story of how the elephant got his trunk (Kipling) or show them pictures of how the Eskimo catch their fish, and tell them all about aeroplanes.

Flights

There are only two classes of air travel: with children and without. The former is a nightmare and the latter (in relative terms) nirvana. There are airlines that go out of their way to cater for children and there are those who merely tolerate them. This is a field all of its own. Bear three rules in mind: do not rely on the airline to supply nappies; the best seats are behind the bulkhead between the aisles, and book them well in advance (with the cradle that hitches to the bulkhead – the children may not like it, but it is useful for stowing toys and books); give them a boiled sweet before each descent and take-off; and if they want to run about the aircraft, let them. They can't fall off, they can't get lost and they might make some friends. If they cause mayhem, it is easy to pretend they're not yours.

In the Field

Tired children are grumpy, and the grump-factor escalates in direct proportion to the number of time-zones you cross. The longer you allow for their sleeping patterns to get back to normal the better, particularly if, like ours, they are not too good at going to bed in the first place. If travelling to South-East Asia, for example, find somewhere peaceful to spend a three or four day adjustment period in one place before engaging in any major adventures.

The usual routine for independent travellers who have a month at their chosen destination is to see as much as possible. This does not work with children. Whatever plans you fancy by way of an itinerary, the most critical ingredient is flexibility. The yardstick of a successful journey is no longer the scaling of a mountain, the descent of a river, or a visit to the Taj Mahal. It is ensuring that laughter predominates over tears, that children get enough sleep, don't get too bored for too long, and eat food *they* find edible with reasonable regularity. The Taj Mahal will leave them completely unmoved, but the goldfish (or whatever lives in those fountains that appear in the foreground of all the photographs of the Taj) will keep them going for hours.

It is no good thinking that your children ought, for the good of their cultural souls, to learn to enjoy chowmien or boiled monkey's testicles. You will have plenty of problems without inviting arguments over food, so keep packets of dried mince and Safeway's noodles in the rucksack-that-you-have-beside-you-at-all-times. A little bit of what they fancy will do them good, and more to the point, what does them good does you better.

This principle, indeed, governs the whole journey, and it is not one that is easy to contend with for fathers who are accustomed to seeing their children in the evenings and at weekends, nor for parents who have developed an efficient pre-children system for surviving and enjoying life on the road. Forget the stories about local babysitters; they might be on hand at Marbella, but they are pretty scarce in Borneo. Even if you found someone you could trust, they already have enough novelties to contend with.

The trick, as with all expeditions, is to select targets that will motivate the expedition members and build your plan around them. A two or three day river journey, for example, is excellent value for children of almost any age; a dug-out canoe, a little bit of slightly exciting white water, a log cabin or longhouse, a couple of fishing rods, the prospect of sighting a crocodile or a bear and a camp-fire under the stars are all good ingredients for success.

Sightseeing should not be on the agenda at all. If the parents must go to a museum, select it with reference to the running around space. Driving long distances will only be a success if done for one day at a time and punctuated regularly with diversions, the excitement of which can be built up as the journey progresses.

Disasters

There will be several of these, even for the most circumspect and cautious of parents.

The first one to avoid is losing your child at the airport, particularly at Terminal 3, Heathrow. We managed this very successfully when Katherine was 2½. She was there, and then all of a sudden, she was not. Thirty minutes later, after public announcements and private panics, she appeared through the legs of the crowd bearing a plate of chocolate cakes. She seemed quite unmoved by the experience. We both vowed that this would be our last international journey with children.

The second disaster, which is less easy to avoid, is illness. This happened to Katherine within about four hours of the first disaster. She developed tonsillitis on the plane, which was then grounded in Abu Dhabi on the grounds that she had a contagious disease, there being no doctor available to suggest otherwise. We were not popular with the other 373 passengers on board.

The best book on being ill abroad is *The Pocket Holiday-Doctor* (Chapman and Lucas, Corgi 1983), which was inspired by Caroline Chapman's ten year old daughter, Katherine, developing diarrhoea, vomitting and a high temperature in a remote corner of Turkey where there were no doctors or telephones for miles. Both Katherines survived their ordeals, but a bad time was had by all.

The acquisition of a little basic knowledge, i.e. when to worry and get moving fast, and when to hold a hand and mutter sweet nothings, is the best that a parent can do. Aside from bellyache, your children are no more likely to be ill in Singapore or the Sahara than in Brighton or Benidorm.

The third disaster is injury. As a general guideline, the louder they scream, the more likely they are to be all right. A bit of sticking plaster and a lot of cuddles usually suffice to mend the wound, and an exhaustive supply of both is recommended. Katherine, then aged 4½, disappeared through the split-bamboo floor of a longhouse in Borneo in front of our very eyes a short while ago. Directly below were the longhouse pigs. Her howls of protest, which were sweet music to us, put the pigs into a panic instead, and the subsequent rescue programme was further hampered by the fact that we were both stark naked, being engaged at the time in having what passes in longhouses for a bath. Equanimity was eventually restored by a combination of Thomas the Tank Engine, an unlimited supply of cuddles and quite a few bits of elastoplast.

The following practical tips may help to avoid or mitigate these disasters:

1. If your child knows his/her name and address you are less likely to lose him/her permanently.

2. Watch out for monsoon drains. In the wet season, your child may be swept away and drowned, and in the dry season there are things in them that it would be better that your child did not eat or roll in.

3. Small children freeze more quickly than large children, so watch them carefully when the temperature drops.

4. Children dehydrate much more quickly than adults. Watch their level of fluid intake, particularly on long flights, in hot climates, and most of all, if they contract a fever or any illness that involves diarrhoea or vomitting. Get him/her to take water mixed with sugar and a little salt. The juice of an orange will make it more palatable.

5. If your child contracts a temperature over 103°F, find a doctor fast. If you are in a foreign capital, the British Embassy will help. Members of the expatriate community are often a good source of information about good doctors.

6. Select your medicine bag carefully before you go, preferably in consultation with your family doctor.

7. Children do not like malaria tablets. They will be more palatable if buried in a piece of fruit and nut chocolate (thus disguising the pill as a nut) with the aid of a penknife. Even then, watch them carefully. Our youngest, aged 1¾ when we took her to Borneo recently, used to tuck them in her cheek and spit them out when we were not looking anything up to an hour later. The other trick was to feed them to the nearest dog. We must have left a trail of malaria-free dogs behind us on our progress around Asia!

8. Sun cream is a vital commodity.

Hotels

Travelling with children is a great deal more strenuous than travelling without them. This is partly because children are an exhausting business anyway, but mainly because the routine of home life, which provides a measure of defence for beleaguered parents, is banished by the unpredictability of life on the road. This is where hotels come in. Expensive ones, the sort that have a laundry service, room service, clean bathrooms for grubby children and a bar for distressed parents. A swimming pool with reclining chairs in the shade for Mum and Dad to take it in turns to sleep is an added bonus.

It may sound extravagant, but this is money well spent. It is only in this kind of circumstance that parents on holiday with their children have a chance to find some peace and even a little time on their own.

Age of Children

There are no rules about this. The best time to start, from the children's point of view, is when they start to enjoy the world about them. There is not much point before they can walk, and better still to wait until they are out of nappies, at least during the day. At the other end of the scale, when they reach their mid-teens they will be thinking in terms of becoming independent travellers themselves, so you have about twelve to fourteen years to show them the world. No time to waste.

The Elderly Traveller

by Peggy Drage

In terms of the traveller, 'elderly' would seem to mean not so much advancing years as diminishing physical endurance. I hope to show that, given a little time and forethought, the elderly can still manage to travel independently and enjoy it.

Of course, there is the attitude of others to take into account. For instance, some freighter companies, car hire firms, and even adventure holiday companies will not accept clients beyond the age of 65 or 70 and it is wise for people of this age to look closely at the small print of any travel insurance they may wish to take out. On the other hand, some countries have 'bonuses' for the retired, such as the *Carte Vermeil* in France which allows retired people of any nationality to travel by rail at reduced fares. We have found, too, that Immigration and Customs officials tend to be less suspicious these days, assuming perhaps that 'oldies' are less likely to be involved in drug rackets or looking for jobs.

Time on Your Side

One of the advantages of being retired is that, paradoxically, time is on your side. You are no longer obliged to rush back to family or job and can travel in a more leisurely manner. So it is possible to break up journeys into smaller, more manageable portions and allow for rest periods when necessary. This is particularly true when driving. We have just completed a long drive through Mexico where, although the roads are fairly good, you have to contend with their narrowness, the dazzling light, other people's often reckless driving and also a great many extra-long vehicles and buses, all of which add up to hard driving conditions. We found that by limiting our daily mileage, starting early in the morning and sometimes staying not one night in a place but two or three, the whole trip was made much easier. There are benefits in this: you arrive reasonably fresh for the hassle of finding accommodation in a strange town and any sightseeing can be done in a leisurely manner. Moreover, an unhurried meal and a chat with a 'local' can be far more rewarding than trying to rush around and see the sights. Another small tip for the driver who may have back trouble (and this is apt to hit people of all ages) is to place a thick guidebook between the seat back and the bottom of your spine – a small thing, but a real help and also an excuse to bring that heavy book!

Similarly, a long haul flight can be broken up for an overnight – or longer – stay without necessarily incurring extra expense. For instance, many US airlines give very cheap vouchers for domestic travel if you buy your ticket before leaving Europe. This means that you can get a cheap and comparatively short transatlantic flight and, after an overnight stop, carry on the next day. This way you can see another city and, after all, one has to sleep somewhere! This can also be a help with jetlag. Off-peak travel is good value if time is not of the essence. Also worth looking into are the round-the-world airfares being offered by several airlines. These are very cheap, last a long time, if you are not in a hurry and allow you a large number of stopovers within the original fare, as long as you keep going in the same direction.

Health

Two of the most unpleasant and disruptive hazards of travel are traveller's diarrhoea and altitude sickness. These can hit both young and old: I have seen a busload of school children completely laid out by *soroche* on the top of Popocatapetl in Mexico, but to older people they can be more dangerous than mere temporary symptoms. Any elderly traveller thinking of going to the Andes, Himalayas or any other high spots of the world should be a little wary. Competent medical advice and a check-up should be sought before deciding on the trip. Some holiday companies sensibly ask for a fitness certificate before selling their more strenuous trips, and if you are travelling independently, there is even more reason to follow the same precautions as there will be no one there to help you should you get ill.

On arrival at high altitude, get plenty of rest, even if you feel quite well and however tempting it is to rush out and 'see'. Above all, the altitude should not be varied more than necessary. Spending a few days at a high altitude, coming down for a 'rest' and then going on somewhere else just as high can be disastrous. I did this, mistakenly, in the Andes and blithely dismissed the consequences, feeling that a stiff upper lip was indicated. The result was that I suffered permanent heart damage which has prevented full enjoyment of subsequent journeys in Nepal and Mexico. Altitude and extremes of heat and cold should be treated with respect.

If you are going to use your retirement to catch up on all the travelling you haven't done before, it is vitally important, particularly if wandering off the beaten track, to know you own physical limitations. If you get ill or break a limb when elderly, it will take a lot longer to heal and it is often doubtful as to whether you will fully recover your strength. Even ordinary exhaustion, something common to most eager travellers, can be far more debilitating than in a younger person. Get as fit as possible before you go, and deprive yourself of as few comforts as possible on your journeys.

Double Your Money

In these days of few or no porters in the more affluent countries and long walks at airports, the old adage about planning your money and your luggage and then doubling the former and halving the latter is more applicable than ever. Try to travel in your heaviest clothes rather than pack them and remember that an anorak is better than a coat anywhere – that is, unless you are going to attend formal gatherings en route, when a good-looking raincoat is lightweight and useful. Instead of taking guidebooks, make notes beforehand. It is surprising what reading matter can be found or swapped with fellow travellers in different parts of the world.

Above all, hand luggage should be limited to a minimum and there should not be too much indulgence in the Duty Free shop.

Provided sufficient care is taken to match partners, home exchange works very well (*see article on page 199*). The exchange does not even need to be simultaneous: some people live in caravans or stay with relatives or have a country hide-away they use while the exchangers are in their home and in this way, the best of all worlds is available – you can go away in winter and allow the exchangers to come in summer and everyone is happy.

Camping and trailer parks are another way of life for people with plenty of time. Thousands of retired people in the USA and Canada spend their winter trailing south as far as Mexico, living largely on the fish and game they catch, and return home in the spring. They are known as 'snowbirds' and almost literally drive south in flocks, not always to the delight of residents or other motorised travellers.

One more bonus of the mature is that they have had time to acquire more experience, knowledge and perhaps a language or two widen and enrich the pleasures of travel. To travel not in order to arrive but to enjoy should perhaps be our motto.

The Disabled Traveller

by Dagmar Hingston

Perhaps the most daunting task facing the disabled traveller is ensuring that the holiday remains free from disaster. With common sense, modern technology, willpower and the help of friends virtually anything is possible, and disability should no longer be a bar to travel. Over the years I have not encountered any problems, simply because I have found that people are only too willing to lend a hand. Provided advance warning is given to everybody concerned, everything will go smoothly. The key, as so often in travel, is meticulous planning.

As a sufferer from multiple sclerosis, diagnosed twelve years ago, my husband has travelled to many countries, with my help and his doctor's blessing. As anyone who suffers from this disease of the central nervous system knows, the symptoms occur in various different ways, so that it is difficult to lay down any hard and fast rules concerning travel abroad. Bearing this in mind, the handicapped traveller and their helper will be able to judge the type of journey they can undertake.

Rail

Being British, most of our rail travel has been on British Rail, who publish a very useful leaflet entitled *British Rail and Disabled Travellers*. It is free of charge and can be obtained at any railway station. It is a self-explanatory leaflet which can be used as a general guideline. However, facilities may differ from area to area and it is advisable to telephone the station manager if there are any specific problems you wish to discuss.

Having given advance warning to railway staff about the time of arrival and the disabled traveller's needs, arrangements will be made for you to be met at the station entrance. In most stations, disabled traveller can be wheeled into the luggage lift and onto the appropriate platform, and, if necessary, British Rail will supply a wheelchair.

Once on board, the wheelchair can be positioned close to the seat while its user is helped into a normal seat. In the latest second class coaches, a table has been omitted from one group of seats nearest the entrance and next to the toilet. Consultation with one's own G.P. will enable them to advise about incontinence aids to be taken on a journey. Toilet facilities are not suitable for wheelchairs and the doors are too narrow. Truly wheelchair-bound passengers will also find it difficult to enter the restaurant car for a meal, but drinks and refreshments may be brought to passengers in their seat. Radiopaging ahead ensures that the disabled passenger and helper will be met by railway staff at connecting stations.

Of course, conditions abroad will vary widely, although most Western countries have facilities as good as, or better than those found in Britain. In the Third World, it is probably more sensible to hire a car rather than rely on the generally erratic and uncomfortable public transport.

At the Airport

It is the responsibility of the traveller and/or any able-bodied people travelling with him or her to make sure that all arrangements will go smoothly on arrival at the airport. Again, advance warning is essential; a week before the holiday commences, a telephone call will confirm that all is well.

From the time you have checked in with an airline, until the end of the journey, the airline should provide any help needed. When a booking is made through a travel agent, ask them to explain to the airline staff the nature of the disability and whether a wheel chair and/or any special diet will be required.

Each airline has its own handling agent who will arrange for someone to help when you arrive at the airport, provided they know in advance how and when you are travelling, and the time of your flight. Direct line telephones to the handling agent are available at the set-down and pick-up points. Seating, reserved for disabled people, has also been provided at these areas. Special facilities are indicated by signs displaying the wheelchair symbol. Unisex toilets, conforming to the latest standards, are also indicated by this sign.

A disabled person is always boarded first on an aircraft and is taken by a member of staff past all the necessary formalities, via ramps and lifts, to the departure lounge. *Who Looks After You?* leaflets can be obtained by writing to the publications department of any main airport.

Each airline makes its own arrangements for assisting handicapped travellers. British Caledonian, British Airways and other major airlines will wheel the disabled passenger from the departure lounge, through the tunnelled entrance to the aircraft. If the disabled person cannot walk to the seat, a small carrying chair will be made available. These seats carry all the latest equipment conforming to safety standards. On most flights, if empty seats are available, airline staff will invite the disabled passenger to make use of two or three seats to stretch out and enjoy a well-earned sleep. A useful booklet, *Care in the Air*, is obtainable from the Airline Users' Committee, Space House, 43-59 Kingsway, London WC2B 6TL. Also available from the same address is *Flight Plan – Hints for Airline Passengers*.

If your journey involves connections with different airlines, be sure to inform each airline individually, and don't rely on the message being passed down the line. And if your final destination is not an international airport, check beforehand on the facilities available for disabled passengers. They may consist of a couple of strong men who will carry you off the plane and leave you in a corner until such time as your own wheelchair is found.

The disabled passenger is usually the last to leave the airport and, once again, carrying seats will be used to carry the handicapped person either to a wheelchair or a motorised vehicle. The larger American airports have a delightful vehicle which transports passengers to the terminal building. The tailgate lift eases the wheelchair passenger into a special compartment whilst other passengers use an upper level.

North America

Travelling throughout the United States and Canada is indeed a most pleasurable experience. There are a number of domestic airlines operating flights between all major centres in the United States, although at some of the smaller airports a disabled passenger will usually be carried bodily into the smaller aircraft.

The wide four-lane freeways leading out of most major cities make for effortless driving and several major hire firms are able to offer cars with hand controls. The Greyhound Bus network, which spans the United States, offers a range of tourist tickets which make touring inexpensive and folding wheelchairs and crutches are not charged as excess baggage. There are many access guides to different regions and towns all over the United States. These are available from the Travel Survey Department, Rehabilitation International USA, 1123 Broadway, New York, NY 10010, USA. Another useful publication is *The Wheelchair Traveller* by Douglas Innand, Ball Hill Road, Milford, New Hampshire 03055, USA.

American hotels and public buildings have long been fully equipped to look after disabled travellers' needs: ramped pavements everywhere; disabled rooms for the handicapped, with large, wide-spaced doorways, call buttons, showers with seats, levered handles instead of awkward taps on wash basins and baths, and raised toilet seats. All the public buildings have unisex toilet facilities, ramped entrances, telephones at waist level and special entrances into banks make life a great deal easier for the disabled traveller.

Coach Travel

There are, as yet, very few coaches in Britain which are, in any way, adapted to take disabled people, although many social services departments and voluntary organisations own adapted vehicles which are always fully utilised. However, some local coach operators, although they do not own specially adapted vehicles, will hire coaches to groups of disabled people and helpers. Although a few seats may sometimes be removed to allow more space for wheelchair users, it remains necessary for disabled people to be lifted up the coach steps. On some of these trips, the helpfulness of staff can more than make up for the lack of carrying chairs and luxury coaches have all the necessary facilities on board including a video recorder and TV screen to enjoy a film show and toilet facilities reached by a few steps. On the older type of coach these are situated at the back and on the level. Air conditioning and fully reclining seats add to the passenger's comfort. On the many stops throughout the journey, the drivers will ensure that restaurant and toilet facilities are within reach of a wheelchair passenger.

Hotels

More and more hotels are offering facilities for the disabled traveller and access guides are available for most countries. In my experience, I have found that many hotels will gladly send details and illustrations of their premises and the surrounding countryside. Public transport drivers in many countries are extremely helpful – we found them particularly so in Yugoslavia. Even if there are, as yet, no specific access guides for the dis-

abled in a particular area and it seems at first glance to be sensible to keep to the hotel area, there are usually many excursions available to surrounding places of interest and the courier will be able to advise on their suitability. Two excellent books are *Directory for the Disabled* compiled by Ann Darnbrough and Derek Kinnade and *Holidays for the Handicapped*, a publication of the Royal Association for Disability and Rehabilitation (now in two parts – one for the UK and one for the rest of the world, mainly mainstream destinations).

Finally, it is most advisable to take out a holiday insurance policy. Disabled people might find that they encounter a problem here since insurance companies might, in their policies, exclude pre-existing conditions. Your tour operator or travel agent can advise on the best type of cover, and it is essential to check the small print to make sure that your disability does not figure as one of the policy exclusions. Two insurance brokers I can recommend are C.R. Toogood and Co Ltd, Duncombe House, Ockham Road North, East Horsley, Leatherhead, Surrey KT24 6NX and The Insurance Programme for the Disabled, Greenway Insurance Brokers (UK) Ltd, First Floor, Peek House, 20 Eastcheap, London EC3M 1DR.

(*For further information, please see the Disabled section of the booklist on page 807, and the Disabled Associations list on page 771*).

Paperwork

Visas

by Jack Jackson

The queue at the Libyan Embassy visa section stretched all the way around the room, out of the door and down the steps. But the traveller wasn't too worried. He'd been warned that the Libyans and the Nigerians were slower than anyone else in issuing visas.

He'd also been tipped off about getting translators to fill out his form in Arabic and this had been done, except – as he discovered about two hours later when he slipped his documents across the counter – for one thing. The year that his passport expired was not in Arabic script.

The error was pointed out. The traveller responded with a friendly nod and a wink. Perhaps the clerk could simply correct it. But no, that couldn't be done.

So, biting his tongue, the traveller collected up his bits and pieces and shot around the corner to his translator, who was fortunately nearby because of the number of Arab embassies in the area.

The correction was made and the traveller joined the queue again. Another hour or so passed and he was back at the counter. But no – he was still not going to get a visa. Why? The explanation was absurdly simple. The form couldn't accepted because it has a crossing out on it where the Arabic script replaced the old figures.

Why hadn't this been pointed out the previous time around? The clerk looked impassive; the question hadn't been asked... Of course, there is no longer a Libyan Embassy in London, but this cautionary tale is as valid for a host of other countries as well.

So, beware! On the face of it, getting a visa doesn't look too difficult. You are told to produce your passport, fill out a form, provide two or three passport-sized photographs and, perhaps, a letter of guarantee from an employer if you are going on company business. That done, it should then just be a case of handing over your money (cash or postal order; cheques aren't accepted) and, in return, receiving a slip of paper or a stamp in your passport.

But if it was that easy visa clerks wouldn't have any fun, human nature would have changed and the world would be a better place to live in.

Tourists Not Wanted

The first thing to remember is that many of the most interesting countries just don't want tourists – or visitors of any kind, come to that, beyond the bare minimum necessary to keep the wheels of commerce and diplomacy turning. Libya is one such. On both religious and ideological grounds, its rulers regard it as desirable to keep out the godless, capitalistic, lascivious Western hordes. Furthermore, the country has vast oil revenues and has no need of the foreign exchange that tourists might bring in. It is therefore a seller's market where visas are concerned. It can afford to pick and choose.

Fanatical Muslim countries are hard on women travellers. Libya will not give visas to unmarried women under 33 years of age or men under 26 years of age. Saudi Arabia will not give visas to unmarried women at all and even married women find it almost impossible to get one. For transit use, girls travelling with men can 'obtain' Muslim marriage licences in Amman (Jordan).

Nigeria and Gabon, though not as rich as Libya, are equally difficult to penetrate. Once again, the presence of oil has meant that neither has felt the need to set up a tourist industry or to make it easy for independent travellers to get in. Those who enter generally do so in spite of the visa section of the relative embassy, not because of it. The Gabonese Embassy in London is a citadel. It is difficult to get through to it on the phone and it is difficult to persuade anyone to answer the front door when you turn up in person. Once inside, you find that all visa applications must be referred to Libreville for 'clearance' (the kiss of death). You are required to send the telex requesting your visa at your own expense and that, generally, is the last you hear of it, since no one in Libreville seems inclined to reply.

The Nigerian system is, if anything, even more frustrating and obscure. Tourist visas are almost impossible and business visas are not issued unless supported by a comprehensive series of testimonials.

Passing the Buck

The same syndrome is particularly prevalent in Africa, but also quite widespread elsewhere. More and more embassies seem to be appreciating the subtle merits of passing the buck by referring all applications 'home' to be vetted. Somali embassies throughout the world have been onto this super dodge for years, creating almost foolproof system whereby only people who have visited the country before and can produce cast-iron local references on demand are able to get in.

Oman, South Yemen and Cuba also come into this category. The oddity of the practice in Somalia's case, however, is that the government would like to see the number of tourist arrivals increase. Individual embassies deliberately frustrate this objective, it would seem, partly to skip all that troublesome paperwork and partly to avoid taking the blame if any tourist should misbehave in Mogadishu.

The general point to be made from all this is that visa officers from most countries that are not well established tourist destinations operate on the simple principle of 'if in doubt, don't'. They have absolute power over your application and neither the time nor the inclination to engage in individual rulings. It therefore pays to be polite and to persevere with dignity. Fill in all forms accurately and without quibbling and don't get irritated if you have to sit around for a long while.

Be Prepared

A tip to remember is that the embassy

at home of the country you wish to visit may behave differently from the embassies of the same country overseas. If you want to visit, say Sierra Leone, don't worry too much if you find it difficult to pick up a visa here. Wait until you are out in West Africa and put in your application at the Sierra Leone High Commission in Banjul (Gambia) or in any other country where there is a Sierra Leone mission. Chances are your visa will be granted without any hassle. It follows that it is good sense on any extended trip over a number of borders, to carry at least twenty technically perfect passport photos of yourself and also some sheets of carbon paper to speed up the business of filling in forms in triplicate.

Whatever precautions you take, however, and wherever in the world you take them, several countries have odd quirks that can temporarily defeat an otherwise perfect application. Carbon copies of forms may not be enough, for instance. The work-to-rule bloodymindedness of some officials can lead them to demand that all forms be filled out painstakingly and individually by hand. Chad will no longer accept visas issued by its own embassy in Algiers, since the embassy is not sympathetic to the President! And it is also worth remembering that a number of countries now refuse to accept visa applications in red or green ink – on the grounds that ink is 'blue'.

Cash on Delivery

There are other, more serious, pitfalls to watch out for than the colour of your pen. Ghanaian embassies and high commissions will not issue your visa until you have purchased minimum daily expenditure vouchers in the local currency to cover the duration of your trip. The visas clerk will require you to pay for these in cash and will not accept a cheque – a nuisance, if you are in a hurry, as the Ghanaian embassy in London, for instance, is some distance from any bank. The ostensible reason for this is that the authorities wish to make certain that you do not go broke on Ghanaian soil. In fact it is done to ensure that at least some of your expenditure as a tourist passes through the official banking system rather than through the roaring black market. Since Ghana is a genuinely nice country presently going through troubled times, it seems only fair to comply with this rule to the letter (the way round it is to take a visa for two days and extend it on arrival). If you do buy *cedi* vouchers to cover your whole trip, however, don't assume they will be anything like sufficient to your needs. A different problem arises in Poland and some other Eastern bloc countries where the same system exists. Here, the independent budget traveller would be extremely hard pressed to spend up to the daily limit without buying everything in sight and eating round the clock – and you can't change your money back into hard currency.

Pariah Visas

Certain visas on your passport may not, in themselves, be difficult to get, but can exclude you from travelling to other countries. Anyone with an Israeli stamp will be refused entry by every country in the Arab League. Similarly, don't try to go to China if you have evidence on your passport of a visit to Taiwan, or to visit much of black

Africa if you have a South African visa. The British authorities will generally issue two passports to anyone needing to travel in these contentious areas. However, there are signs that this loophole may not longer be wide enough. Nigerian diplomats, for instance, are reluctant to put a visa on a new passport until they have vetted the applicant's old one for South African stamps.

Iraq is not currently issuing tourist visas but when it does, it requires a baptismal certificate as proof that the bearer is Christian and not Jewish.

The bureaucratic wrangles described, it is worth adding, are not just something inflicted on hapless Western tourists by 'them out there'. Britain is often an extremely difficult country for anyone from the Third World to visit with stringent entry regulations wielded like so many blunt axes by the churlish, aggressive and sometimes vulgar immigration officers at Heathrow and other airports. And quite a few British citizens tell horror stories of their reception in the United States. Before commenting too disparagingly on the motes in others' eyes, we should try to remove our own particular beam.

Guidelines

Here are some of the bare facts about visas and some points to note when obtaining them:

– Allow plenty of time for obtaining visas. For most Asian countries, you will need three to five days if getting your visas in London, for African countries, it will often be a lot longer. And for those countries who don't have representation in your home country, it will be longer still. For instance, countries such as Mali or Syria don't have embassies in London and you would have to apply to Paris. If applying by post, allow at least three weeks, but check with the individual embassies before posting your passport, and then add on another week. You may also be required to enclose your vaccination certificate and proof of purchase of airline tickets for onward travel. Always use registered post.

It is often far easier (and safer) to use a visa agency. Their charge is money well spent if it means that your passport is returned safely and properly stamped in good time for your departure.

– Some countries, e.g. Nepal, Sudan and Egypt, require proof of available funds, a letter from a known operator if you are travelling on an organised tour, or that you change a certain amount of hard currency into local currency at the official bank rate. This problem can sometimes be avoided when a visa is obtained in a bordering country, but the situation can never be guaranteed and will often change at short notice. In most cases, it is easiest to get a visa in your country of origin, one notable exception being that German nationals cannot obtain a Sudanese visa in Germany, but can do so in the UK. You will occasionally find that you will only be allowed to obtain a visa in your home country, so check very carefully before leaving home.

– Some countries, e.g. Ethiopia, require a letter of introduction from your embassy if you apply for a visa in a country other than your country of origin. Most embassies are used to this and have form letters, but the charge for them is steep.

– Some countries, such as Algeria and many Eastern European countries, require such a large amount of money to be changed into local currrency before entry that no traveller who is not making full use of local hotels would consider it worthwhile.

– During periods of unrest, some countries will only issue business visas. Another growing trend is for people to be issued visas only if they fly in and out of the main airport.

– If you are travelling on, or overland, many countries will not issue a visa unless you already have a visa for the next country en route, so get all your visas in the reverse of the order in which you will use them. This is especially true for travel through Africa. However, many visas are valid for three months from the date of issue, so for lengthy overland journeys, visas must be obtained en route.

– Visas often state specifically the port of entry into the country, so overlanders should make sure they stick to their proposed route.

– Visas obtained in your country of residence will be full tourist visas (different types of visas are issued to people on business or working or studying in a country). Do not rely on obtaining visas on, or just before the border. This was once possible but, with tightening restrictions, visas can usually be obtained in capital cities only, e.g. Nepalese visas are easily obtainable in Delhi and Burmese visas in Kathmandu.

– In London, some consulates, e.g. Sudan and Yemen Arab Republic, will only accept payment in postal orders, even if you attend personally. Others will only take cash. Very few will consider a cheque or plastic. And be warned to add the cost of visas into your travel budget, prices have been doubling and tripling each year. At the time of writing, a single-entry Indian or Egyptian visa costs £20, others are even higher. If you need multiple-entry for several countries, the cost can be enormous.

– If your passport gets filled up and you still have a valid visa in it, a new passport can be tied to the old one with a seal, thus retaining the use of that visa. British nationals who renew their passports abroad should ensure that the new passport has written into it that 'the owner has the right of abode in the United Kingdom' or they can be refused entry on their return home.

– Most countries will extend a full tourist visa two or three times for a fee, but only when the present visa has almost expired and normally only in the capital city. Once you have had a tourist visa extended, you will often also need an exit visa before you can leave and will also have to provide definite proof of onward travel. This takes two or three days to get, so apply early. Some countries require an exit visa anyway, e.g. Yemen Arab Republic. Do not overstay a tourist visa without renewing it: this can involve a heavy fine, an appearance in court (Iran), or, in times of political unrest, a spell in prison.

– Finally watch out for the duration of visas. If you have a long stay in any country, however relaxed its entry regulations may appear to be, get your visa before you go. Thailand is a good example of this. You are allowed to enter for up to fifteen days without any visa at all, provided you have money and a ticket to get out. You simply get a stamp in your passport as you arrive at the airport showing the date by which you must leave the country. The problem is that if you do not leave by then you will end up wasting at least a day in custody explaining yourself to an immigration officer and paying a fine. The alternative is a visa issued in London or elsewhere by a Thai embassy or consulate. The visa is valid for up to 60 days. It can be extended while in Thailand but – and this is an absolutely immoveable constraint – the fifteen day entry permit cannot be extended under any circumstances.

Permits, Registration and Restricted Areas

by Jack Jackson

Fifteen years ago, travel in the Third World was, for a Westerner, relatively easy, with few restrictions and little in the way of police checks, paperwork or permissions to hold the traveller back. Europe, in those days, offered more barriers with frequent Customs and police enquiries. Nowadays the position is reversed. In most Third World countries the hindrances to free travel grow yearly in number and variety.

Ambiguous taxes are demanded at borders and airports. The legality of these may be questionable, but the man behind the desk is all-powerful, so the traveller does not have any choice.

Many countries with unstable monetary systems and flourishing black markets now require the traveller to complete on entry a currency declaration, detailing all monies, jewellery, cameras, tape recorders etc. This is checked on departure against bank receipts for any money changed. Algerian authorities are very thorough in their searches of departing travellers. Countries with the same regulations include India, Nepal, Tanzania, Kenya, Sudan, Zimbabwe and others. With groups, border officials naturally try to cut down massive form filling by completing just one form for the group leader. This can make life very difficult later if one person in a group wishes to change money at a bank and does not have his/her own individual form, and cannot immediately produce either the group form or the leader. Individual forms should be obtained if possible.

Deliberate Delays

Some countries purposely delay the issue of permits. The Nepalese authorities keep travellers waiting in Kathmandu for their trekking permits so that they will spend more money there. As most trekkers are limited for time, a straightforward Tourist Tax would be more acceptable.

In many places, the law requires that you register with the police within 24 hours of arrival. Often a fee is even charged for this. If you are staying at a hotel they will normally take care of your registration and the costs are included in your room charges, but if you are in a very small hotel, camping or staying with friends, you will either have to do it yourself or pay someone to do it for you. As it often entails fighting through a queue of several hundred people at the Immigration Office – with the chance you have picked the wrong queue anyway – *baksheesh* to a hotel employee to do it for you is a good investment. Most of these countries require you to register with the police in each town you stop in, and in some cases you may even have to report to the police in every town or village you pass through. In smaller places, registration is usually much easier.

Permission from central government may be necessary to travel outside the major cities. This is so in the Yemen Arab Republic, the Sudan, Ethiopia, and China among others. Usually you go to the Ministry of the Interior for this permission, but if a Tourist Office exists, it is wise to go there first. Any expedition or trekking party will have to do this anyway; only Nepal has a separate office for trekking permits.

Restricted Areas

Most countries have restricted or forbidden areas somewhere. To visit Sikkim or Bhutan, you must apply to the central government in Delhi. In some other restricted areas, permission remains with the local officials, e.g. Tamanrassett or Djanet for the Algerian Sahara; Agadez for the Niger Sahara; and the District Commissioner in Chitral for Kafiristan. Any country suffering from internal unrest will usually bar tourists from entering troubled areas. As these can fluctuate from day to day, all you can do is wait until you get to the capital before asking.

Asia and Africa both have large areas of desert or semi-desert. Restrictions on travel in these areas are formulated by the government for travellers' safety and take account of such obvious things as ensuring that the travllers have good strong vehicles, are carrying plenty of drinking water and fuel and that they will be spending the nights in safe places. Unfortunately, officials in these out-of-the-way places tend to be the bad boys of their profession. Forced to live in inhospitable places they are usually very bored and often turn to drink and drugs. Hence when a party of Westerners turns up they see this as a chance to show their power, get their own back for the old colonial injustices, hold the travellers up for a day or more, charge them *baksheesh*, turn on a tape recorder and insist on a dance with each of the girls and suggest they go to bed with them. If there is a hotel locally, they may hold them up overnight so as to exact a percentage from the hotel keeper. Unfortunately your permit from the central government means nothing here. These people are a law unto themselves.

Some have been known to insist on a visa from nationals of a country who do not require one, which often involves returning to the nearest capital where incredulous officials may or may not be able to sort things out.

The police in Djanet (Algerian Sahara) really have it tied up. You cannot get fuel to leave without their permission and to get that you have to spend a lot of money with the local tourist organisation and hotel as well as fork out *baksheesh* to the police themselves.

Local officials also have a habit of taking from you your government permit and then 'losing' it. This makes life difficult both there and also with local officials later on in other areas. It is therefore best to carry ten or so photostats of the original government permission (photocopiers are always available in capital cities) and never hand over the original, but always give them a photostat instead.

If you are travelling as a group, all officials will want a group list from you, so carry a dozen or more copies of a list of names, passport numbers, nationalities, dates of issue, numbers of visas and occupations.

Photographic Permits

Some countries, e.g. Sudan, Mali and Cameroon, require that you get a photographic permit. These are usually available in the capital only, so overland travellers will have problems until they can get to the capital and obtain one. As with currency declarations, officials obviously like to save work by giving one permit per group, but it is best to have one per person. I have known several instances where big-headed students have made 'citizens' arrests' of people taking photographs – who then had to spend a couple of hours at the police station waiting for their leader with the photo permit to be located.

Possession of a photo permit does not necessarily mean that you can take photos. Many historic monuments have a total ban, and I have known people to be arrested even when their paperwork is correct in every detail. It is usually best to enquire with the local police first.

In theory, you should be able to find out about documents and permit requirements from the consulate in your country of origin, but in the Third World, this can never be relied on as local officials make their own rules. Information from source books such as this one and recent travellers are your best guide.

Do as much as you can before you leave home, but carry plenty of passport-sized photos and be prepared for

delays, harassment, palms held out and large doses of the unexpected.

Travel Insurance

by Malcolm Irvine

One of the most important aspects of planning a major trip abroad is insurance, but it is frequently overlooked until the last minute or costed inaccurately into the budget.

Personal

The first and most important thing to determine is that you are buying the correct insurance for your particular activities and involvements. It is much better to deal with a professional insurance broker than make the mistake of buying a mundane travel insurance policy from your local High Street travel agent. A policy designed for a few weeks in the sun on the Costa Brava is of no help to you if you end up as a stretcher case in deepest Africa in need of immediate air evacuation. Don't be afraid to ask for an explanation of the insurance policy that you are purchasing or written confirmation that it is suitable for your purposes. A major travel insurance scheme underwritten at Lloyd's of London, and aimed principally at long period travel on a worldwide basis, gathered the following statistics in 1986. Almost exactly 50 per cent of the claims paid related to baggage and personal effects, 25 per cent to medical expenses and 25 per cent to cancellation. The average claim came to £128 and the highest single claim paid under that particular contract during the three years up until 1986 was for £42,000 worth of medical expenses.

It is most common nowadays to purchase an inclusive policy where the sums insured for the various sections of cover have been tailored to suit 99 per cent of travellers. A breakdown of such an inclusive policy would be as follows:

Medical Expenses. This must surely be considered the most important of all forms of insurance – one can replace lost belongings, but one cannot replace one's health or body. Over the last few years, inflation and the more general availability of expert medical attention has resulted in a large increase in the cost of medical care, and the need to have adequate cover is therefore essential. At the time of writing in 1987 we would recommend a minimum sum insured of £100,000 and it is quite common for a higher figure to apply, perhaps £250,000. Make sure your cover is total rather than giving specified maximum amounts for any individual section such as ambulances, hospital beds, surgery etc. A high sum insured is of no help to you if you can only spend a limited part of it on any one aspect of your treatment.

If you are in a remote area, then suitable treatment may not be available locally and in such cases, it might be necessary to incur ambulance charges, airfares or air ambulance charges in order to obtain treatment. In exceptional circumstances, this might even involve repatriation. A personal air ambulance can obviously be very expensive, but even if you are able to use scheduled flights, as a stretcher case you would need to have four seats on a plane, plus another seat for a nurse or companion to accompany

you. Airlines will not accept stretcher cases on their own.

In such a case, you won't have the opportunity to shop around for a cheap ticket. You will have to travel as a scheduled passenger and pay the full fare for all of the seats or spaces that are needed. The charge for an air ambulance can vary according to the severity of the injury or illness and the consequent amount of medical attention that is needed during the flight. As a rule of thumb from, say, North Africa back to the UK, one might be looking at a charge of about £10,000 whereas from the remote parts of Africa, Asia or South America the cost can escalate to as much as £35,000. However, in practical terms, such flights are very seldom arranged due to logistical problems and it is much more likely that a flight would simply be arranged to the nearest country where expert medical attention was available.

Air evacuation from remote areas would be covered by medical insurance if it were necessary because of an accident or illness. 'Search and rescue expenses' would not be covered unless you had specified them and paid an additional premium.

Most policies will include a 24 hour emergency service in respect of medical or accident claims. This will entail your making contact with the UK so can only be put into operation if you are able to request help. In most cases, the emergency service will provide financial guarantees so that treatment or transport arrangements can be made.

Be wary of relying on an everyday private health insurance policy that might already be in existence. Although it may operate outside your normal country of residence, there are bound to be gaps in the cover and almost certainly will be limited as to how much can be spent on any single aspect of treatment. It is unlikely, for instance, to cover the cost of any ambulance charges, repatriation expenses etc., since the basis of private medical cover is that treatment in the UK at least is normally only received after consultation with your GP, for illness or treatment needed where there is no desperate urgency.

Personal Accident Insurance. Most comprehensive policies would automatically include personal accident insurance, normally for an amount of £5,000. This is payable in the event of death, loss of a limb or an eye or total disablement by an accident. While reassuring, it is not generally considered to be important, since any person who is concerned about such matters will probably have a policy operative on a regular basis. It is surprising how many people worry about an accident while in another country yet do not consider the possibility that they could just as easily be involved in an accident in their normal country of residence. Unless the activities that you are going to be involved in are particularly hazardous, there is no more reason to think you will have an accident overseas than at home.

Cancellation or Curtailment. This covers irrecoverable deposits or payments made in advance where a journey has to be cancelled or curtailed for some good reason such as the insured's own ill health or that of a relative or travelling companion. The sum insured obviously has to relate to the type of prepayments that are being made – as a general rule it's about £2,000. If you only have air tickets, the cancellation charges, and consequently the amount that might be lost, are sometimes quite low, but look at it from the worst possible point of view. An airline may make just a ten per cent cancellation charge if you notify them that you cannot use the seat and they consequently resell it, but what would happen if you were to become ill two hours before departure, and, in airline jargon, become a 'no show'? In such circumstances, the value of your ticket might be lost altogether.

Personal Liability. This gives protection for compensation payable for injury, loss or damage to other people or their property. However, it excludes risks which should more properly be covered by a separate insurance such as Third Party motor insurance. A domestic policy may include this cover, but if not, it is included within most travel policies without cost.

Strike and Delay. This section relates to industrial action, breakdown, or adverse weather conditions, which cause a delay on the first outward or first return leg of the journey. As a rule, compensation of £20 per day is payable for a maximum of three days, but only after an initial twelve-hour delay. If, alternatively, on the outward journey only total abandonment is possible, a refund of the cancellation charges imposed by the tour operator or airline would be made. This section of cover tends to be included within most comprehensive policies or is available on payment of a small additional premium.

Travel Trade Indemnity. This covers you in the event of the financial failure of an airline. It was introduced following the collapse of some airlines in the early 1980s and if you are fortunate may be included within some comprehensive policies.

Baggage and Personal Money

There can sometimes be difficulties in obtaining this cover for overland journeys, although most long-distance independent travellers tend to take with them little of great value other than photographic equipment. Such items should already be insured on what is known as an 'all risks' basis, and this cover often operates worldwide for a limited period of time, which it is quite easy to extend.

Most policies will be subject to a non-extendable limit for valuable items. Travel insurance is meant to cover those risks which are not already insured in your home country. If you have valuables which you have been using uninsured in the UK, then you might as well continue to do so while away.

If you are on an expedition and have supplies and scientific equipment with you, there may be difficulty in obtaining insurance cover. Do check that the insurance includes items which you might be sending in advance as freight and for certain areas, check whether you need *Carnet de Passages* documents.

It is a condition of insurance that one acts as if uninsured. For some unknown reason, many travellers tend to adopt a careless attitude when overseas and do things they would not think of doing at home such as leaving valuable photographic equipment on a beach whilst bathing, or suitcases containing all your worldly goods on the luggage rack of a train while going for a cup of tea. All Insurers have adopted the same attitude recently, which is simply that if a client can't act with a reasonable amount of commonsense then insurers will not deal with the claim. In particular this applies to valuable items where it is now a condition that they are kept about one's person at all times. Theft from unattended motor vehicles is also excluded.

One is effectively covered for actual cash, traveller's cheques, documents etc. However, if the loss of traveller's cheques is reported in the correct manner, there is no monetary loss and it is often a condition of the insurance that such action is taken. Most policies will cover the additional expenses involved – perhaps telex charges to notify a bank or additional accommodation expenses whilst waiting for replacement funds to be sent.

Within the money section, most insurances will also include air tickets, and whereas money cover is normally limited to £200, on the more specialised policies for long-haul travellers, air tickets are insured for a much higher amount. Some airlines will provide replacement tickets without any difficulty, but there are a few that will insist on full payment being made for replacements, with a refund unavailable for as long as eighteen months afterwards. It is almost unheard of for a thief to try and use an airline ticket, but these few insist on waiting before accepting the position.

Vehicle Insurance

Once outside the European area, vehicle insurance does present certain difficulties and it is certainly not possible to arrange a single comprehensive insurance policy as we know it in this country. This is due to the varying legislation in different parts of the world on liability or Third Party insurance. Vehicle insurance can be understood by the following equation:

Third Party liability +
Accident Damage, Fire and Theft
= Comprehensive

Within the European 'Green Card' area, a single comprehensive insurance policy can be arranged – either as a one-off policy on a short period basis or as an extension of an existing policy. At the time of writing, the Green Card area includes all of Europe plus Morocco, Tunisia, Turkey and Iran. However, not all insurers are prepared to give cover in the more outlying parts of Europe.

Third Party Liability. This will need to be arranged locally at each border, which can, in itself, present problems. In some parts of the world, such as Algeria, insurance is nationalised and there is a reasonably efficient method of selling it to travellers. The cost is relatively low – about £20 for one month, but the cover given is also low by European standards, often as low as £5,000, whereas in Europe liability limits are generally from £250,000 upwards.

Theoretically, Third Party insurance is a legal requirement in virtually every country in the world, but there are several who are totally indifferent as to whether travellers have it or not. If it is not automatically offered at the border, it is strongly recommended that you seek it out. However limited, it does at least give you some measure of protection and the cost will certainly be low by our standards.

Because of difficulties with liability claims in the USA, the legal requirements there are surprisingly low by UK standards. It is therefore possible if one is hiring a vehicle in the States to purchase additional liability limit before departure from the UK, which tops up the insurance available under the contract of hire to a more realistic level.

Warning

1. Cover is not readily available at some borders and in many areas covers bodily injury claims only, which means you may have to pay the cost of damage to other people's property yourself.

2. Although liability limits are absurdly low by European standards, there is no other means of arranging this cover.

3. It is not uncommon to hear of relatively large amounts being demanded for local certificates (one can only guess whether the premium is passed on to the insurance company).

Accidental Damage, Fire and Theft. As you will see from the equation earlier, this is the other half of a comprehensive insurance policy and simply covers damage to one's own vehicle as the result of an accident, fire or theft. It is in no way connected with liability risks and is available from Lloyds of London on a worldwide basis. Unfortunately, this cover is expensive, since in nearly all claims underwriters have to pay out for repairs with very little chance of recovering their outlay, even if you were not at fault. Whatever the circumstances, it is surprising how many witnesses will suddenly appear to claim that the local driver was blameless and the visitor totally at fault!

This insurance is very strongly recommended on valuable vehicles. In the event of an accident occurring, contact the local Lloyds agent. Repairs would then be completed by the most suitable repairer. In many cases, temporary repairs are carried out at the time and full repairs left until the vehicle returns home. As a general rule, repairs are authorised very quickly, since the insurers are aware of the inconvenience that any delays might cause and because the insurers are responsible for the repairs, irrespective of liability in the accident.

Carnet Indemnity Insurance. This is arranged in conjunction with *Carnet de Passages* documents issued by the Automobile Association. Before issuing the *Carnet* the AA will require a financial guarantee equal to the highest possible duties payable on the vehicle in the countries it is intended to visit. Generally, this figure is about twice its UK value, although for India, and some South American and East African countries the figure can be considerably higher. *Carnet* Indemnity Insurance has not been available for India since 1985, due to the abnormal volume of claims originating from that area. It is hoped that this situation may be remedied, but at the moment the only means of obtaining *Carnet* documents for India is to provide your own bank guarantee or indemnity. If insurance indemnity is to be arranged, the premium is calculated at 3½ per cent of the indemnity figure indicated above, but the premium is on a sliding scale and for very large amounts reduces down as low as one per cent. In addition, the AA will require a service charge of about £30 and a refundable deposit of £250.

Life Assurance

As a general rule, life assurance cover is not taken out specifically for overseas travel, since most people who have family responsibilities will already have a policy in force. Life assurance policies are not normally subject to exclusions but if your journey is of a hazardous nature, it would be as well to give written details to the life office concerned and ask for their written confirmation that they accept the position. They may impose an additional premium just for the period whilst you are away, but the amount involved is generally quite low and it is worth the peace of mind that it gives to know that your cover is fully operative.

Arranging Insurance and Claims

As I've said before, I would recommend the advice of an experienced, professional insurance broker for anything other than the totally standard European holiday. Be sure to outline your proposed activities, and if you are buying a standard policy, ask for written confirmation that it is suitable for your needs.

If you are booking through one of the specialist travel agencies that deals with overland or long-haul travel, they will almost certainly have a tailormade policy available. A normal High Street agency clerk, however, may have little knowledge of the type of insurance you will be looking for.

As far as vehicle insurance is concerned, a proposal form will need to be completed and you must disclose all material facts relating to both your own driving experience and that of any other person who might be using the vehicle. It is much better to spend some time giving all the information about yourself and your requirements to the insurer than finding, after an accident, that there is a gap in the cover. This also relates to personal medical insurance.

As far as claims are concerned, do be patient. Contrary to popular belief, insurers do like paying claims. However, they do require certain information and if it is not available, there are going to be inevitable delays in dealing with paperwork. Any expenditure will need to be supported by a written statement from the local police authorities, airline or government agency.

If possible, claims should be left until you return home. Under no circumstances should you send original documentation by post from overseas, since it can go astray so easily. Unless you have incurred large expenditure for which you require reimbursement while you are still away, it is much better to leave things until you return, when you can collate everything and present your claim in a concise manner. Most claims can be dealt within about two weeks, but if you happen to lose a valuable item, don't be surprised if the insurers insist on seeing a receipt, valuation or some other documentation relating to the original purchase.

Most claims will be subject to an excess – this is normally £25 for personal claims and is imposed by insurers simply because of the cost of dealing with small claims can sometimes be more than the value of the claim itself. Vehicle insurance claims will generally be subject to a much higher excess, which is imposed in order to keep the premiums to a reasonable level and to cut out claims for the inevitable minor scratches or dents that will occur on any long journey.

Documentation for the International Motorist

by Colin McElduff

The following advice is directed principally towards motorists from the UK and should be used as a general guide only, for each and every case produces its own requirements, dependent on the countries concerned and the circumstances and regulations prevailing at the time. As many travellers neglect documentation – some of which should be obtained well in advance of departure – list all that is known to be relevant to your trip and make enquiries as to the remainder. I have included only those documents specifically related to vehicles. Details on personal documentation are to be found elsewhere in the book. In any case, on most overland trips you will need the following:

1. Driving Licence

2. Insurance – Third Party and/or

3. International Motor Insurance Certificate (Green Card)

4. International Registration Distinguishing Sign (GB etc.)

5. Vehicle Registration Certificate

Depending on your country of departure and those through which you will be travelling, you may additionally need your birth certificate, extra passport photographs and:

6. *Acquits à Caution*

7. Bail Bond

8. *Carnet* ATA

9. *Carnet Camping*

10. *Carnet de Passages en Douane*

11. Certificate of Authority for Borrowed or Hired Vehicle

12. International Certificate for Motor Vehicles

13. International Driving Permit (IDP)

14. Motoring Organisation Membership Card

15. Petrol Coupons

1. *Driving Licence.* Most countries will allow you to drive for six months on your national licence. After this you must have an IDP or take a local test. In Italy, a translation of the visitor's National Driving Licence is required. This may be obtained from the motoring organisations. Motorists in possession of an IDP do not require a translation. It is probably also useful to have a translation if travelling in Arab countries.

2. *Third Party Insurance.* This is essential to cover claims relating to bodily injury to or death of third parties as a result of the vehicle's use. When travelling in countries outside the scope of the 'Green Card' – which is generally outside Europe – Third Party insurance should be taken out at the first opportunity on entering the country.

3. *International Motor Insurance Certificate (Green Card).* Whilst a Green Card is technically no longer necessary in EEC countries it is extremely unwise to visit these countries without it, as it remains as readily acceptable evidence of insurance to enable a driver to benefit from international claims-handling facilities. In any case, a Green Card is required in all European countries outside the EEC. It should be obtained from the insurance company that is currently insuring your vehicle.

4. *International Registration Distinguishing Sign.* This sign is mandatory and should be of the country in which your vehicle is registered, thus identifying your registration plates.

5. *Vehicle Registration Certificate.* This is an essential document to take. However, further proof of ownership or authority to use the vehicle may sometimes be required.

6. *Acquits à Caution.* This is a French Customs document, guaranteed by the Automobile Club France and in turn by the motoring organisations issuing it. The document permits entry into France of spare parts for the repair of a temporarily imported vehicle without payment of customs duties or taxes. The spare parts may be imported at the same time as the vehicle or on their own.

7. *Bail Bond.* If you are visiting Spain, it is a wise precaution to obtain a Spanish Bail Bond from a motoring organisation. A driver involved in an accident may be required to lodge a deposit with the local Spanish court both for civil liability and criminal responsibility. Failure to meet this demand may result in imprisonment for the driver and detention of the vehicle until funds are available.

8. *Carnet ATA.* This is a Customs document, valid for twelve months, which facilitates the entry without payment of Customs, duties etc. of professional equipment, goods for internal exhibition and commercial samples, temporarily imported into certain countries, a list of which may be obtained from the London Chamber of Commerce and Industry, 69 Cannon Street, London EC4 (Tel: 01-248 4444) or through one of their many offices throughout the UK.

9. *Carnet Camping.* An international document jointly produced by the three international organisations deal-

ing with camping and caravanning – the *Fédération Internationale de l'Automobile*, the *Fédération Internationale de Camping and Caravanning* and the *Alliance Internationale de Tourisme*. It serves as an identity document and facilitates entry to sites under the wing of these organisations, sometimes at reduced rates. In addition, the document provides personal accident cover up to a specified sum for those names in it. You should approach a motoring organisation for this document.

10. *Carnet de Passages en Douane*. This is an internationally recognised Customs document. If acceptable to a country, it will entitle the holder to import temporarily a vehicle, caravan, trailer, boat etc, without the need to deposit the appropriate Customs duties and taxes.

The issuing authority of the *carnet* is made directly responsible for paying of Customs duties and taxes if the *carnet* is not discharged correctly, i.e. if the owner violates another country's Customs regulations by selling the vehicle illegally. Consequently, any substantial payment will be recovered from the *carnet* holder under the terms of the signed issuing agreement.

Motoring organisations are issuing authorities and will provide and issue documents upon receipt of a bank guarantee, cash deposit or an insurance indemnity from an agreed firm of brokers, to cover any potential liability. The sum required is determined by the motoring organisation, taking into consideration the countries the vehicle will enter, which will naturally have to be declared when application for the *carnet* is made.

Normally the amount of the bond required as security is related to the maximum import duty on motor vehicles required in the countries to be visited, which can be as high as 400 per cent of the UK value of the vehicle.

In the case of a bank guarantee, you need to have collateral with the issuing bank or funds sufficient to cover the amount required to be guaranteed. These funds cannot be withdrawn until the bank's guarantee is surrendered by the motoring organisation. This is done when the *carnet* is returned correctly discharged. The procedure is for the bank manager to provide a letter of indemnity to the motoring organisation.

If you have insufficient funds or security to cover the bond, you may pay an insurance premium (the AA and the RAC have their own nominated insurance companies with which they have *carnet* indemnity agreements) and the company will act as guarantor (*See article on Travel Insurance on page 240*).

There are certain points to watch, however. The car must usually be registered in the country where the *carnet* is issued. In some cases, at the discretion of the issuing club or association, being a citizen of the country where the *carnet* is issued is an alternative, even though the car has been registered elsewhere. In all cases membership of the issuing club is a requirement.

A *carnet* is required for most long transcontinental journeys and should be obtained regardless of the fact that some of the countries on the itinerary do not require it, for example Nigeria. To be without one where it *is* required usually means being turned back if you have insufficient funds to cover the Customs deposit for entry.

A *carnet de passages en douane* is valid

for twelve months from the date of issue and may be extended beyond the expiry date by applying to the motoring organisation in the country in which the holder is at the time. The name of the motoring organisation is shown in the front cover of the *carnet*. An extension should be noted on every page and not just inside the cover in order to avoid difficulties at border checks. When a new *carnet* is required, the application must be made to the original issuing authority. *Carnets* are issued with five, eleven or twenty-five pages, depending on the number of countries to be visited, and a nominal fee is charged accordingly to cover administration.

Each page contains an entry voucher *(volet d'entrée)*, exit voucher *(volet de sortie)* and a counterfoil *(souche)*. When the vehicle, etc. leaves the country, the Customs officer endorses the exit part of the counterfoil and detaches the appropriate exit voucher, thus discharging the *carnet*. If you have not taken care to have this done, the validity of the *carnet* may be suspended until it is rectified.

11. *Certificate of Authority for Borrowed or Hired Vehicle.* This is required when a vehicle is borrowed or hired and should bear the signature of the owner. This must be the same as on the Registration Certificate which must also be taken. A motoring organisation will provide a 'Vehicle on Hire-/Loan' certificate.

12. *International Certification for Motor Vehicles.* In countries where the British Vehicle Registration Certificate is not accepted, this document is required and is issued by a motoring organisation.

13. *International Driving Permit.* An IDP is required by the driver of a vehicle in countries that do not accept the National Driving Licence of the visiting motorist. It is issued on request by motoring organisations for a small fee and is valid for twelve months from the date of issue. An IDP can only be issued in the country of the applicant's National Driving Licence.

14. *Motoring Organisation Membership Card.* Most countries have a motoring organisation which is a member of the *Alliance Internationale de Tourisme* (AIT) or the *Fédération Internationale de l'Automobile* (FIA) and provides certain reciprocal membership privileges to members of other motoring organisations.

15. *Petrol Coupons.* These are issued to visiting motorists in some countries either to promote tourism or where there are restrictions on the residents' use of petrol. Motoring organisations can advise which countries issue petrol coupons.

Passports and Medical Advice

United States

Application for a new passport must be made in person to:
1. A postal employee designated by the postmaster at selected post offices.
2. A passport agent at one of the Passport Agencies listed below.
3. A clerk of any Federal court.
4. A clerk of any State court of record.
5. A judge or clerk of selected probate courts.

6. A US embassy in a foreign country.

The applicant must present:

1. Proof of US citizenship i.e.

(i) a certified copy of his/her birth certificate under the seal of the official registrar; or

(ii) a naturalization certificate; or

(iii) a consular report of birth or certification of birth; or

(iv) his/her previous passport.

2. Two recent identical photographs that are good likenesses. (Note 1).

3. Identification, e.g. a valid driving licence with a signature and containing a photograph or physical description.

The application:

1. is usually processed in ten days or less.

2. costs $42.00 for adults; $27.00 under 18.

The passport:

1. is valid for ten years from the date of issue for adults; five years for persons under 18.

2. comes in two sizes, the standard 24 page size and the 48 page size. (Note 2).

3. can be supplied with extension pages. (Note 3).

Application for passport renewal by a passport holder can be made in person at any of the places listed above, or in certain circumstances by mail, together with a complete form DSP-82 'Application for Passport by Mail', (available from tourist agencies and the places listed above), the previous passport, two new photographs and $35 (Note 4).

Note 1: Photographs need not be taken professionally as long as they are clear and show the applicant full-face and with no hat against a plain white or light coloured background. Photo-graphs must measure 2in x 2in. Machine photographs are not acceptable.

Note 2: Travellers intending to visit Third World and other countries where visas are required and copious entry and exit stamps are entered into passports should ask specifically for the 48 page passport.

Note 3: An accordion sheet of extra pages can also be issued to provide additional space in a valid passport, by any consulate or passport office abroad.

Note 4: When a passport expires, so too do all the visas and permits contained therein. These must be reapplied for after obtaining the new passport. The same is true if a passport is lost or replaced.

Visas and Tourist Cards

A visa is an official permit to enter a country, granted by the government of that country. Visas are usually stamped in the passport and are valid for a particular purpose and stated time. Visa and tourist card requirements change frequently, according to the vagaries of political circumstance. To check the current situation, consult form M-264 *Visa Requirements of Foreign Governments*, available at any passport agency.

For the address of the nearest consulate or consular agent, consult the *Congressional Directory*, available in most libraries.

US Passport Agencies

Boston

Room E123, John F. Kennedy Building,

Government Center, Boston, MA 02203.
Tel: (617) 223-3831.

Chicago
Suite 380, Kluczynski Federal Building,
230 South Dearborn Street,
Chicago, IL 60604.
Tel: (312) 353-7155.

Honolulu
Room C-106, New Federal Building,
300 Ala Maona Boulevard, P.O. Box 50185, Honolulu, HI 96850.
Tel: (808) 546-2130.

Houston
One Allan Center, 500 Dallas St.,
Houston, TX 77002.

Los Angeles
Hawthorne Federal Building, Room 2W16, 1500 Aviation Boulevard,
Lawndale, Los Angeles, CA 90261.
Tel: (213) 536-6503.

Miami
Room 804, Federal Office Building,
51 Southwest First Avenue, Miami,
FL 33130.
Tel: (305) 350-4681.

New Orleans
Room 400, International Trade Mart,
2 Canal Street, New Orleans, LA 70130. Tel: (504) 589-6161.

New York
Room 270, Rockefeller Center,
630 Fifth Avenue, New York,
NY 10020.
Tel: (212) 541-7710.

Philadelphia
Room 4426, Federal Building,
600 Arch Street, Philadelphia,
PA 19106.
Tel: (215) 597-7480.

San Francisco
Room 1405, Federal Building,

450 Golden Gate Avenue, San Francisco, CA 94102.
Tel: (415) 556-2630.

Seattle
Room 906, Federal Building, 915 Second Avenue, Seattle, WA 98174.
Tel: (206) 442-7945.

Stamford
One Landmark Square, Broad and Atlantic Streets, Stamford, CT 06901

Washington
Passport Office, 1425 K Street, NW, Washington DC, 20524.
Tel: (202) 783-8170.

in the UK
US Embassy,
Passport and Citizenship Unit,
24 Grosvenor Square,
London W1A 2LQ
Tel: 01-499-9000 ext 2563/2564
Open: 8.30 – 16.00

Medical Information for US Citizens

The US Public Health Service (USPHS) is the main source of information for the traveller on medical requirements. There are two centres: The USPHS, National Communicable Disease Center, Atlanta, GA 30333, deals with health requirements and animal and plant quarantine regulations for the US and other countries and publishes a small booklet *Health Information for International Travel*, which is available on request. The USPHS, 330 Independence Avenue, SW, Washington DC 20201, provides information on vaccinations and other immunizations required for visitors to foreign countries and in some cases will also administer the necessary shots.

United Kingdom

A UK passport is valid for five to ten years and is obtainable from regional passport offices:

UK Passport Offices

Belfast
Hampton House, 46-53 High Street,
Belfast, BT1 2QS.
Tel: (0232) 232371

Glasgow
1st Floor, Empire House, 131 West
Nile Street, Glasgow G1 2RY.
Tel: 041-332 0271

Liverpool
5th Floor, India Buildings,
Water Street,
Liverpool L2 0QZ
Tel: 051-237 3010

London
Clive House, 70 Petty France,
London SW1H 9HD.
Tel: 01-213 3434

Newport
Olympia House, Upper Dock Street,
Newport, Gwent NPT 1XA.
Tel: (0633) 56292.

Peterborough
55 Westfield Road, Peterborough
PE3 6TG.
Tel: (0733) 895555
Offices open Mondays to Fridays
9.00 to 16.30.

British nationals must apply for a passport on a special form obtainable from passport offices or any main post office. The application must be countersigned by a bank manager, solicitor, barrister, doctor, clergyman or someone of equal standing who knows the applicant personally. The application should be sent to the passport office for the applicant's area of residence. Two full face photographs must accompany the application. The fee is £15 for a 30 page passport or £30 for one of 94 pages. Fees are slightly higher if a spouse is included on the passport. Four weeks should be allowed for the application to be processed except between April and August when it can take longer.

For travel within Western Europe (excluding the German Democratic Republic and East Berlin), you can travel on a British Visitor's Passport. This costs half as much as a full passport, but is valid for twelve months only. British Visitors' Passports and application forms for them are available from any main post office. The British Visitor's Passport is not available from passport offices, other than in Belfast, and is only available to British citizens, British Dependent Territories citizens or British Overseas citizens for holiday purposes of up to three months. It is not renewable.

If you lose your passport, tell the local police first. Then contact the nearest British Embassy or Consulate by telephone or telegram. The telegraphic address of any British Embassy is PRODROME, of a High Commission UK REP and of a British Consulate BRITAIN followed by the name of the town.

Normally the Consul will issue a new passport, valid for up to twelve months, as soon as possible after checking with the issuing office in the UK. For this reason, it is highly advisable to keep a separate note of your passport number and its date and place of issue. The new passport is valid in all the countries in which the original was valid and costs the same. On expiry, it can be extended to a full ten year passport when you return to the

UK, at no extra charge, if your original passport has not been found.

In case of emergency, the Consul can issue instead a Single Journey Emergency Passport, which enables the holder to return to the UK but will be confiscated on his return. Or the consul may issue a passport that is valid for a month – without checking with the issuing officer – and this permits the holder to return to the UK via several other countries.

Medical Information for UK Citizens

The Department of Health and Social Security, Alexander Fleming House, Elephant and Castle, London SE1, publishes a leaflet *Protect Your Health Abroad* (SA 35) which contains up-to-date inoculation requirements for travellers. This may be obtained by telephoning the DHSS on 01-407 5522 ext. 6711. The main offices from which the leaflet may be obtained in Wales, Northern Ireland and Scotland are, respectively:

Welsh Office
Cathays Park
Cardiff CF1 3RT
Tel: (0222) 825 111 (ext. 3336)

DHSS
Dundonald House
Upper Newtownards Road
Belfast BT4 3SF
Tel: (0232) 63939 (ext. 2593)

Scottish Home and Health Department
St. Andrew's House
Edinburgh EH1 3DE
Tel: 031-556 8501 (ext. 2438)

The Health Control Unit, Terminal 3 Arrivals, Heathrow Airport, Hounslow, Middlesex TW6 1NB Tel: 01-759 7208 gives similar information.

Sources of advice on the prevention of tropical diseases are:
The London School of Hygiene and Tropical Medicine
Keppel Street
London WC1E 7HT
Tel: 01-636 8636

The Hospital for Tropical Diseases
4 St Pancras Way
London NW1 OPE
Tel: 01-387 4411

The Liverpool School of Tropical Medicine
Pembroke Place
Liverpool L3 5QA
Tel: 051-708 9393

British Airways Medical Department
75 Regent Street
London W1
Tel: 01-439 9584

The Vaccination Clinic
53 Great Cumberland Place
London W1
Tel: 01-262 6456

Australia

Passport applications should be made in person at an Australian Post Office or Passport Office. The form PC1 should be used and supporting documents (previous passport and 2 45mm x 35mm colour photographs) and general evidence of identity, e.g. drivers licence, credit cards, etc. are required.

Exemptions:

1. Applicants who have permanently resided for no less than one year at an address which is more than 100kms from the nearest Passport Office,

Official Australian Post Office or Diplomatic or Consular Mission overseas.

2. Unmarried applicants under the age of eighteen years.

3. Applicants requiring amendments or endorsements to their current Passports, except where the Passport bears an observation stating personal attendance is required.

Applications can be made in the UK at:

1. Australian High Commission, Strand, London, WC2B 4LA

2. Australian Consulate, Chatsworth House, Lever Street, Manchester, M1 2QL

3. Australian Consulate, 80 Hanover Street, Edinburgh, EH2 2HQ.

The Consular and Passport Section at the High Commission in London is open to the public from 10.00 – 16.00, Monday to Friday. Tel: 01-438 8464 or 01-438 8118.

A Business Passport (which has 48 pages instead of the usual 32) may be issued to business persons who can show substantial filling of their regular passports. Also required is a letter from an employer, preferably signed by the Chief Officer, explaining why a Business Passport is needed.

Current passport fees for adults are $A60 or £26.00 in the UK and A$25 or £10.85 in the UK for unmarried children under the age of 18. All telephone enquiries within Australia can be be made toll free to 008 (026022).

Australian Passport Office Addresses
In all cities: Box 9807
Australian Central Territory
22 West Row, Canberra.

New South Wales
No. 1 Chifley Square, Sydney
Mercantile Mutual Building,
456 Hunter St, Newcastle.

Victoria
3rd Floor, Building B, The World Trade Centre, Corner Spencer and Flinders Streets, Melbourne.

South Australia
Sun Alliance Building, 45 Grenfell Street, Adelaide.

Queensland
Commonwealth Government Centre, 295 Ann Street, Brisbane.

Western Australia
St. Martin's Tower, 44 George's Terrace, Perth.

Tasmania
4th Floor, T&G Building, Corner Collins and Murray Streets, Hobart.

Northern Territory
Arkaba House, Esplanade, Darwin.

Medical Information

Most information about immunization requirements is available from GPs, but further information can be obtained from the offices of the Commonwealth Department of Health:

Central Office
The Secretary, Commonwealth Department of Health (CDH), PO Box 100, Woden ACT 2606.

New South Wales
CDH, Commonwealth Government Centre,
Chifley Square, Corner Phillip and Hunter Streets, Sydney, NSW 2000.
Tel: 239 3000.

Victoria
CDH, Commonwealth Centre,
Corner Spring and LaTrobe Streets, Melbourne, Vic. 3000.
Tel: 662 2999.

Queensland
CDH, Australian Government
Offices, Anzac Square, Adelaide St,
Brisbane, Qld 4000.
Tel: 225 0122.

South Australia
CDH, I.M.F.C. House,
33-39 King William Street, Adelaide,
S.A. 5001,
Tel: 216 3911

Western Australia
CDH, Victoria Centre,
2-6 St George's Terrace, Perth, W.A.
6000.
Tel: 323 5711

Tasmania
CDH, Kirksway House,
6 Kirksway Place,
Hobart, Tas 7000.
Tel: 20 5011

Northern Territory
CDH, M.L.C. Building,
Smith Street, Darwin N.T. 5794.
Tel: 80 2911

**Australian Capital
Territory**
C.T.H.C. Building,
Corner Moore andAlinga Sts,
Canberra City, A.C.T. 2601.
Tel: 45 4111.

Canada

A Canadian passport is valid for 5 years
at a cost of CAN$21. Applicants
should supply a previous Canadian
passport plus proof of citizenship (citizenship card or birth certificate) and 3
passport sized photos.

Applications can be made to passport offices located in most Canadian
cities.

Edmonton
Suite 800, 10 Jasper Avenue,
Edmonton, ALTA TSJ 1WB,
Tel: (403) 420 2622/23.

Montreal
Suite 215, West Tower, Guy Favreau
Complex,
200 Dorchester Blvd West,
Montreal, Quebec H27 1X4.
Tel: (514) 283 2152

Quebec
10th Floor Suite 1000,
2590 Blvd Laurier, Saint-Foy,
Quebec G1V 4M6.
Tel: (418) 648 4990/92

Toronto
Box 171, Suite 1031, Atrium on Bay,
20 Dundas St West, Toronto,
Ontario M5G 2C2.
Tel: 973 3251.

**Medical Information for Canadian
Citizens**
Information about vaccinations and
other medical information questions
can be obtained from the following
Department of National Health and
Welfare Travel Information Offices:

Newfoundland
Health and Welfare Canada (HWC),
Room 410, Sir Humphrey Gilbert
Building, Duckworth Street,
PO Box 5759, St. John's, NFLD
A1C 5X3.
Tel: (709) 772 5571.

Nova Scotia
HWC, 2129 Kempt Road, Halifax
B3K 5N6. Tel: (902) 426 3998.

New Brunswick
HWC, 89 Canterbury Street, Room
513, Saint John, NB E2L 2C7.
Tel: (506) 648 4862.

Quebec

Services Médicaux, Santé et Bien-être Social Canada, Le Complex Guy-Favreau, 200, Dorchester Blvd West, Montreal, Quebec H2Z 1X4.
Tel: (514) 283 4880

Ontario

HWC, 3rd Floor, 55 St. Clair Avenue East, Toronto, Ontario M4T 1M2.
Tel: (416) 966 6245.
or
7Medical Services, HWC, 301 Elgin Street, Ottawa ONT K1A Ol3.
Tel: (613) 990 0641.

Manitoba

HWC, Room 500 303 Main Street, Winnipeg MAN R3C OH4.
Tel: (204) 949 3616.

Saskatchewan

HWC, 1855 Smith Street, Regina SAS S4P 2N5.
Tel: (306) 359 5413

Alberta

HWC, 401 Toronto Dominion Tower, Edmonton Centre, Edmonton ALTA T5J 2Z1.
Tel: (403) 420 2697.

British Columbia

HWC, 5th Floor, 2130 Government Street, Victoria BC V8W 1Y3.
Tel: (604) 566 3387
or
HWC, 7th Floor, 1133 Melville Street, Vancouver, BC V6E 4E5.
Tel: (604) 666 6196.

New Zealand

A New Zealand passport is valid for ten years at a cost of NZ$30. Processing can usually be completed in 21 days. The following must be included with a completed application form:

1. Proof of New Zealand citizenship (by birth, British subject by birth, grant of New Zealand citizenship, or by descent).
2. Previous New Zealand passport.
3. 2 passport sized photographs.
4. An identification certificate signed by a non-related person over 18 years of age who has known the applicant for at least 12 months.

In New Zealand, applications should be sent to the nearest passport office of the:

Department of Internal Affairs

Auckland (P.O. Box 2220)
4th Floor, T. & G. Building
17 Albert Street
Tel: 31 184

Rotorua (P.O. Box 1146)
2nd Floor, Government Building
Haupapa Street,
Tel: 477 680

Wellington (P.O. Box 10476)
2nd Floor, Local Government Building, 114-118 Lambton Quay
Tel: 738 205

Christchurch (P.O. Box 1308)
M.L.C. No. 2 Building
159 Manchester Street
Tel: 790 290

Dunedin (Private Bag)
2nd Floor, Public Trust Building
442 Moray Place,
Tel: 771 274
Offices open 9.00 to 16.00, Monday to Friday.

In the UK, applications cost £18.50 and should be made at:
The Passport Office
New Zealand High Commission
New Zealand House
Haymarket
London SW1Y 4TQ

Medical Information for NZ Citizens
Advice and information are available from GPs and district offices of the Department of Health. A booklet entitled *Health information for travellers*, is available from Government Print Offices or by post from the Department of Health, PO Box 5013, Wellington, New Zealand.

Auckland
Bledisole State Building, Civic Square, Auckland. Tel: 774 494

Christchurch
10 Reserve Bank Building, 158 Hereford Street, Christchurch. Tel: 799 480.

Wellington
Education House, 178-182 Willis Street, Wellington. Tel: 858 769.

Money

Hard and Soft Currencies

by Christopher Portway

The subject of international currency is one of vast proportions but it only needs to be touched on here insofar as its ramifications are felt by the traveller abroad.

We have all heard of hard and soft currencies, yet do we all know exactly what the terms mean? Basically 'hard currency' is another phrase for *strong* currency: in other words, a currency that is in demand (and therefore useful) because everyone has faith in it. 'Soft currency' is the direct opposite. But what makes things somewhat blurred at the edges are the ever-changing degrees of hardness and softness. Classed as hard currencies at present are those of the Western European nations together with the American and Canadian dollars and the Japanese *yen* – though, even here some are harder than others. Soft currency areas include many of the Third World countries and the Communist bloc – though again with fluctuating degrees of 'softness'; the Yugoslav *dinar*, for instance, being more in demand – and therefore stronger – than the Russian *rouble*.

Thus when the traveller goes abroad, he or she will obviously choose hard currency cash or traveller's cheques to take since they will be acceptable – even welcomed – in varying degrees all over the world. A traveller, in fact, will have little choice, since soft currency is virtually unobtainable in most of the hard currency territories, while currencies like the Yugoslav *dinar* and the Egyptian pound – somewhere between hard and soft – are only obtainable in small quantities. Their countries of origin additionally impose severe restrictions on re-exportation.

Financial Advantages

What are the *financial* advantages of taking either one's own currency, foreign currency purchased locally, or traveller's cheques? When making a brief visit to most countries I usually take sterling notes since it avoids the hassles and dilatoriness of some foreign banking systems and their sometimes erratic opening and closing times. But for the traveller seeking economy rather than convenience a better bet would be to make use of the 'retail' facilities for a bank transfer – which is what traveller's cheques are all about. These cheques are normally made in the currency of the country of the issuing bank – though they need not be: dollar traveller's cheques are issued by banks all over the world nowadays. While the British traveller carries, for example, Midland Bank sterling traveller's cheques, he is not yet 'in' foreign currency – he is merely carrying a negotiable claim on his bank which a foreign bank will not normally accept. When the traveller exchanges this sterling claim in, say, France, the French bank pays out francs and will mail the traveller's cheque back to the Midland. When the Midland receives it, it, in turn, will credit the sterling to the London account of the French bank – which the French bank will have to sell at the prevailing sterling-franc rate if it wants to regain its original francs.

Thus a traveller's cheque involves the foreign bank in a degree of foreign exchange risk for the time it takes for the traveller's cheque to clear. Because of this, and also the relatively expensive collection process, rates on traveller's cheques, while normally more favourable for the traveller than those obtainable by buying foreign notes, are still significantly less favourable than the rates a traveller may see quoted in the financial pages of the newspapers.

Local Currency

There are variations on this theme introduced by individual banks to make the purchase of goods, services and local currency that much simpler – but at a not inconsiderable handling charge. Most of the big banks are keen to involve a holidaymaker or traveller in Europe and the Mediterranean countries in their Eurocheque scheme wherein specially supplied cheques, up to a certain limit, are negotiable when supported by a Eurocheque Encashment Card. This way you can pay an account in the local currency without the trouble of having to work out the sterling equivalent prior to settlement by traveller's cheque or cash sterling.

However, the choice of carrying banknotes, traveller's cheques or whatever may also be affected by the possibilities of a change in currency values. Because the traveller gets 'in' to foreign exchange earlier when buying foreign notes at their own bank, this may be to the traveller's advantage should the 'home' currency fall suddenly against the foreign currency. Alternatively, if the traveller fears devaluation by the destination country, he or she will be better off staying in sterling or dollars either in the form of cash or cheques as long as possible, buying foreign currency on arrival in small amounts as the need arises.

This may all sound complicated and worrying, but it has no need to be so. While we happily bet our shirts on horses, dogs, Ernie and even the stock market, and take an active interest in doing so, why not the involuntary act of money exchange? It's all part of the game called 'travel'.

Money Problems – The Legal Side

by Harry Stevens and Melissa Shales

I belong to that generation whose first real experience of foreign travel was courtesy of HMG – when European towns were teeming with black marketeers trying to prove to every young serviceman that 200 British cigarettes were really worth 200, or even 300DM. Traveller's cheques and banks hardly existed and credit cards, like ballpoint pens, had not yet been invented. So my trust in ready cash as the essential ingredient for trouble-free travelling is no doubt due to this early conditioning.

Cash is, of course, intrinsically less safe to carry than traveller's cheques, especially when these are fully refundable when lost – but not all of them are, particularly when a 'finder' has cashed them in before the loss has been reported.

Nowadays, I carry all three: traveller's cheques, credit cards and cash; but only a slim book of traveller's cheques, which I hold in reserve in case I *do* run out of cash – and for use in countries which do not allow one to bring in banknotes of their own currency. If travelling in Europe, it is also worth applying for a Eurocheque book and card which allows you to write cheques on the continent as you would at home. Particularly on short trips, this could mean that you don't have to go to the trouble of getting foreign exchange before departure. However, the cash I carry always includes a few low denomination dollar bills useful for 'emergency' tips, or taxi fares almost anywhere.

Small Change

There are a number of cogent reasons for equipping yourself with the currency of the country you are about to visit before you get there.

1. Even on the plane you may find you can make agreeable savings by paying in some currency other than sterling.
2. Immediately on arrival it may be difficult, or even impossible, to change your money and in any case, you may

be doubtful as to whether you are being offered a good rate of exchange.
3. Yes, the immediate problem of tipping a porter, making a phone call and paying for a taxi or airport bus must be solved long before reaching your hotel. And when you do eventually get there, this does not necessarily solve your problem as not all hotels exchange traveller's cheques for cash (and not necessarily at any time of day or night) and if they do, the vexed question of the rate is exchange arises once more.

Many countries do not allow unrestricted import or export of their currency – and in a number of countries for 'unrestricted' read 'nil'! So one *has* to exchange traveller's cheques or hard cash on arrival (there is usually a small advantage in favour of the cheques). In addition, if several countries are to be visited, it is usually best not to keep bank notes of a currency no longer required on that journey (although I do hold on to small change and some low denomination notes, if there is a likelihood of a next time). Every such exchange results in a loss but the sums involved are usually not large and one can console oneself with the thought that the next taxi ride will help to recoup it. Remember to keep a record of all financial transactions, particularly in sensitive countries, as you may well be asked to account for everything before you are allowed to leave.

Nest Eggs

If you are planning to be away for a long time, and possibly travel through many countries, there is one other way to ensure that you don't have to carry too much with you and risk losing it all in some remote village. Before you leave home, set up a number of accounts along the way through banks affiliated to your own and arrange for money to be wired over to you at regular intervals. Ask the foreign section of your bank to advise you on the best way of doing this.

It is a simple-sounding operation, but as with most aspects of travel, reality is infinitely more complex, each transaction taking weeks longer than claimed and your money being misplaced en route or misfiled on arrival. The bureaucracy alone could make the whole exercise too difficult to be worthwhile, never mind the fact that you are having to place an immense amount of trust in bank staff who may be corrupt. It is probably not worth while unless you are planning to spend some considerable time in the country. Whatever you decide to do, don't rely on having money waiting for you – keep an emergency fund for survival while you try to wring your money out of them.

Even if you haven't set up accounts along the way, ask your bank for a list of affiliated banks in the countries you will be visiting. In an emergency, you can ask for money to be wired out from home to any bank, but if you can choose one that is already in contact, it should make life considerably easier. Always ask for a separate letter, cable or telex confirming that the money has been sent and specify that it should be sent by SWIFT (express).

Be careful not to wire more money than you will need into countries with tight export restrictions. No one will mind the sterling coming in, but they may well object to it leaving again, and if not careful you could find yourself with a nest egg gathering dust in a country you are never likely to visit again.

Money Problems – The Illegal Side

by Jack Jackson

Black markets usually operate best in ports where it is easy to ship money out and goods back in and where, with the help of a little *baksheesh* to Customs officers, nobody in government pay need know or admit knowing. However, a new quasi black market has been growing in recent years, operated by European or American technicians working in oil fields or on international aid or construction programmes. These people are usually paid an allowance in local currency which is more than they need to live on and are often keen to get rid of some of it in exchange for dollars, at a good rate to the buyer. In much of Islamic Africa and the poorer Middle Eastern countries, you will also find Egyptian, Syrian or Palestinian teachers employed in smaller villages who are very keen to convert their salary into US dollars.

Another method of dealing, common in Islamic Africa, Kenya and Uganda, is for a local businessman or hotel owner to 'lend' you funds locally, which you repay in hard currency into his own, or a relative's, bank account in the UK. Those who travel regularly often arrange this in the UK before leaving, but local businessmen will also take a risk on an unfamiliar traveller if they are reasonably dressed and staying in recognized (though smaller) hotels, because their own currency is worthless to them. Even in large, top quality hotels, the cashiers will often take payment in hard currency at black market rates, if the customer pays them outside the manager's normal working hours. Many of the same methods are found in South America, although travellers should particularly avoid street trading there, as they are more likely to be robbed.

On-the-spot black market deals are always for cash and nearly always for US dollars. A few countries with strong links with the UK or Germany will trade in pounds sterling or *deutschmarks*, but no other currencies, even strong ones such as the Swiss franc, will find black market buyers. *Deutschmarks* go down well in Turkey and Iran; pounds sterling in Pakistan, India and Nepal and parts of Southern Africa such as Zambia and Zimbabwe. Elsewhere, the US dollar is the prime requirement.

Normally, larger denomination notes fetch a higher rate as they are easier to smuggle out. However, since a recent spate of forgeries, many dealers no longer like to accept $100 bills. Avoid the older $100 bills which do not have 'In God We Trust' written on them; even though they may not be forgeries, most dealers will not touch them. Also avoid English £50 and £20 notes which may be unknown to smaller dealers. There is no longer any problem attached to taking money out of the UK, so it is best to buy dollars there before you leave.

Declaration Forms

Many countries with black market problems insist on a declaration of all money and valuables on entry and check this against bank receipts on exit. Remember that you may be searched both on entry and exit and any excess funds will be confiscated. If you want to take in some undeclared money for use in the black market, you should understand the risks. Obviously you must change a reasonable amount of money legally at a bank and keep receipts so that you will be able to explain what you have lived on during your stay. You will also need these receipts if you are going to try and change local currency back into hard currency when you leave. It is most inadvisable to try, since most countries make it very difficult for you to do this, despite their literature claiming that you may. The local officials – who probably don't read the literature – like to remove your excess local money and keep it for themselves. The bank clerk who tells you he cannot change your money is in on the act. He informs the Custom officials how much money you have and they, acting on his tip-off, search you as you try to leave.

Currency declaration forms are taken very seriously in Ethiopia and Algeria and you must have an explanation for any discrepancy. If, for instance, any money which is entered on your form is stolen, get a letter about it from the police or you may have trouble when you come to leave the country.

Some countries, e.g. Sudan and Ethiopia get around some of the black market by making you pay for hotels in hard currency at the legal business rate which is often lower than the official tourist rate and much lower than the black market rate.

International airline tickets will always be charged the same way plus a premium ordered by IATA to cover currency fluctuations. Hence, such tickets are much cheaper if bought in Europe. Internal air tickets can usually be bought with black money but you may have to pay a local ticketing agent to do it in his name.

Beware of black market currency quotations by normally acceptable press, such as upmarket Sunday papers, *Newsweek* and the BBC, as they quote local correspondents who have to be careful what they say for fear of deportation. They will usually stick to the lower end of the scale, which means you could get half as much again.

Street Trading

Black market dealers are usually found where budget travellers are most likely to be, e.g. in smaller hotels, bars, shops selling tourist items; in very small towns try the pharmacy. In the main streets of a city or port, street traders will chase you and, assuming you don't know the correct rate of exchange, will start with a very low rate. It is usually worth bargaining to see how high you can go – and then approach safer places such as small hotels to check the real rate. Street trading is very risky. You should never show that you have a lot of money, as there is a high risk that you will be short-changed, have money stolen from the bundle by sleight of hand, see all your money grabbed and run off with, or meet one of those dealers who has a crooked, profit-sharing partnership with the police. In general, show only the amount of money you want to exchange and keep all other money out of sight beneath your clothes.

One part of the world in which to be particularly wary is Eastern Europe, where there is a great demand for hard currency that can be exchanged for exorbitant rates if a person has the right contacts. Here the money-changer and their client are in more danger than anywhere else because of particularly close surveillance by the authorities, who crack down hard on black money transactions. It's also believed that the authorities use their own people as a plant, so the unsuspecting 'client' could find themselves negotiating with a state official. It's advisable not even to ask what the rate is.

Refuse any approaches to buy your passport or traveller's cheques. This kind of trading is becoming so common that embassies delay issuing fresh passports to travellers who may or may not have genuinely lost their own. Getting traveller's cheques replaced in the Third World can take months.

Black market rates fluctuate with both inflation and availability. Rates will increase dramatically in the Islamic world when the time for the annual pilgrimage to Mecca (the Haj) approaches and decreases rapidly when a lot of upmarket travellers are in town, or a cruise ship or fleet ship is in port. Dealing out of season commands a better rate.

Central London banks often carry an excess of Arab currency and one of their branches may be happy to offload a weak currency at a good rate. It is always worth checking whether this is so before you buy.

In very remote areas the local people do not handle money and like instead to be paid in kind: preferred items are T-shirts, jeans and shoes and, in some parts of Eastern Europe, good clothing, records and tapes. In countries such as Zimbabwe, where many people have plenty of local currency, but luxury items are unobtainable, electrical goods, such as hairdryers, calculators or cameras will fetch astronomic prices – sometimes enough to finance your whole trip.

Wherever you are, always check that you have not been shortchanged. Bank cashiers try this regularly in the Third World. Many people end up changing money on the black market just because it can take up to two hours to go through legal channels.

Begging

Begging is one of the world's oldest professions. In the Muslim and Hindu world, giving a percentage of one's income to the poor is considered a legal form of paying tax. However, with the increase of mass upmarket tourism, begging is becoming an increasingly popular way of living, not only amongst the obviously poor people of the Third World, but also amongst Western hippies and confidence tricksters who claim to be refugees.

In some countries, beggars are terribly persistent, knowing full well that wearing you down produces results. Mere persistence may not be too hard for you to repel, but worst of all are the young children, often blind or with deformed limbs, who are guaranteed to arouse your pity. What you may not realise is that the child may have been intentionally deformed or blinded by his or her parents in order to make them a successful beggar. The child is almost certainly encouraged by the family to beg and may be their chief source of income, since the child beggar can perhaps earn more in a day than his or her father, working in the fields or factories. Remember also that a child who is out begging is necessarily missing school, which they should be attending. Adults with no education or experience other than begging tend to be less successful than a child. What are their options? Crime, if they are fit, destitution if crippled. Begging is obviously easier than work, but to give money is to contribute to a vicious circle. By witholding money you may help to eradicate these appalling practices.

Travel Now, Pay Later: Travel Finance Schemes

by Ingrid Cranfield and Kent Redding

To read about exotic destinations and yet be unable to travel because of financial restraints is both tantalizing and frustrating. Perhaps a few hints on where to raise that necessary and apparently elusive cash will inspire you to take the plunge and travel now.

You may wonder what the hurry is. Why travel at all in the short term? The answer is that if you delay, you may well see your objective changed out of sight or its frontiers closed to visitors – an all too frequent occurrence these days. A young man once asked desert traveller Wilfred Thesiger: 'Can I expect to travel as you have done?' The answer was a simple 'No'. Thesiger was not being deliberately discouraging, but merely stating the fact that the world and its people change so rapidly that sometimes it is not possible to recapture things seen and achieved only a few years previously, let alone to retrace routes travelled by explorers 30 or 40 years ago.

The message is: travel now and pay later, if necessary.

Figure It Out

In general terms, it is easier to get finance against a recognized package holiday (where discount is sometimes available on prepayment), be it overland in Africa or Asia or a cultural experience in China. If all you want is to purchase isolated elements of a journey, you may find that you can only get an advance against airfares ex-UK. The ground arrangements will then have to be purchased locally, and for these you will need a cash loan. Some banks and schemes give cash that will cover all travel finance (see below). Borrowing money from other that a recognised source is not to be recommended.

How much will it cost? Figures will vary and should be checked with your bank, but the rate of interest will be the same as for any personal loan, currently fluctuating from about ten percent to fifteen percent. If, as seems likely, you will need to borrow a four figure sum, this could mean you must be prepared to keep paying it off for a couple of years.

Security to cover the loan may be required. You can calculate varying rates of interest as the APR (Annual Percentage Rate) changes.

Credit Sources

Travel Agents and Associations. Some travel agents are familiar with travel credit, but the majority will give you a strange look and nod towards the exit. Most will, however, accept major British credit cards and some American ones, but usually only after reference to airlines – who may accept the credit card when the agent may not.

1. AA Travel Services (Member's Loan Plan)

Sums from £50 to £7,500 are available, with repayments monthly. The current APR is 24.9 per cent. Available for travel services – a leaflet is available from any AA office.

2. RAC Members' Finance

Sums from £50 to £5000 are available, with 12 to 60 monthly repayments. Credit protection is available. The current APR is 25.9 per cent. The loans are arranged through Lombard Finance.

3. Thomas Cook Budget Account

Up to £3,000 can be borrowed (i.e. up to fifteen times the amount you can afford to pay back monthly). £1,005 can be instantly confirmed if you have a bank current account and you agree to pay by standing order. You also need a bank card and proof of your address. Interest is charged at prevailing APR on any outstanding balance.

If you enter the scheme before you travel, interest will also be paid on your savings. Finance is arranged through Forward Trust Ltd and a leaflet is available.

Credit and Charge Cards. Credit and charge cards may be used not only to purchase air tickets etc., but also while travelling, to pay bills and, in some instances, for a cash advance. Check with the issuers of your card before you travel as to whether it is valid for your route.

1. Visa

A card is issued free with a set credit limit. No interest is charged on outstanding amounts if paid within the time limit. Interest on outstanding balance: 26.8 per cent per annum. The card is widely accepted internationally.

2. Access

The card is issued free with a set credit limit. No interest is charged on the outstanding amount if paid within the time limit. Interest on outstanding balance: 26.8 per cent per annum. The card is widely accepted internationally and is interchangeable with the Mastercard in the USA or the Eurocard in Europe.

3. American Express

Green Card: £25.00 annual subscription (with a £12.50 initial enrolment fee). No interest is charged on credit but repayment is expected in full immediately upon receipt of the monthly statement. There is normally no specific pre-set spending limit. The card gives access to over 1,000 American Express offices throughout the world, where English speaking staff not only give travel advice but will cash personal cheques up to £500 (subject to local regulations).

Added to this is the benefit of £75,000 worth of travel accident insurance and *poste restante* facilities. Gold Card: £50 per annum subscription (plus £20 enrolment fee – waived if the applicant is already the holder of a Green Card). Credit and payment arrangements are the same as for the Green Card. Possession of the Gold Card, however, gives the holder £10,000 unsecured overdraft facilities at Lloyds Bank and up to £1,000 in cash or travellers' cheques through a personal cheque cashed at American Express offices worldwide. The deposit for car hire is waived for holders of the Gold Card, which also carries £250,000 of travel accident

insurance and qualifies for access to a 24-hour emergency telephone service.

Both Green and Gold charge cards are well worth having, but to qualify for a Green Card you must be earning around £8,500 per annum and for a Gold Card £20,000 per annum. American Express is not linked to the Eurocheque system. Local rules concerning the use of American Express cards vary considerably, so it is best to get the leaflet and check with reference to specific time, place and circumstances.

4. Diners Club International

The annual subscription is £27.50 (with an initial enrolment fee of £20). No interest is charged on credit but the debit balance has to be paid in full, monthly. There is no spending limit and the card is widely accepted by airlines, car hire firms etc.

5. British Airways – Air Travel Card

(International or North American)

This card is issued on payment of a US$425 cash deposit. This is not a limit to its use. The card is used both by individuals and by businesses to purchase air tickets to and from major cities everywhere in the world. No service charge is made on unlimited credit for air travel.

6. Car Rental Credit Cards

These too can be useful for defraying costs, as settlement is expected monthly. No charge is made for the card, which in some instances – not all – carries a discount and a waiver of deposits.

7. British Telecom International Telephone Credit Card

This card may be used for calls to the UK from abroad and is useful as a way of keeping a supply of cash for other travel expenses and of avoiding the surcharges often imposed by hotels for the use of the telephone.

8. Company Cards

Airlines, hotel groups and other companies provide credit or offer discount cards to regular users. Ask around.

Banks. Major banks operate personal loan schemes. Credit varies from £1,000 to £5,000. Leaflets are available from Midland, Barclays and National Westminster, all of whom promote such schemes. A cashflow account is another option, allowing you to both save in advance and pay back what you have borrowed at your own rate, without make specific arrangements for each trip. Alternatively, approach your bank manager for an individual arrangement.

MCO (Miscellaneous Charges Order). Obtained through a travel agent or airline, this document (which looks like an air ticket) may be used to purchase air tickets or pay for other air travel facilities such as excess baggage charges. Its cost, which varies according to your requirements, may be reclaimed if it is not used, but only at the purchasing source. An MCO is accepted by all IATA airlines. Your travel agent will tell you if it is valid for your area of travel.

Mortgage. If you own a house, you could consider a second mortgage. It all depends on how much importance you attach to travelling.

International Travel Card AE (USA). Of the various types of travel credit available in the USA, note in particular the International Travel Card, which costs $35 for a year or $49.50 for two years. Member benefits include the facility to purchase unlimited American Express foreign traveller's cheques by mail, and free currency exchange by mail or at any Mutual of Omaha counter at US or Canadian airports. The card is available from: International Travel Card, PO Box 5080, Des Plaines, IL 60018, USA. Tel: numbers in mainland USA (credit card orders) toll free: (800) 874-4400 ext. 208 or in Florida (800) 453 8777; enquiries to (904) 299 8300.

Shop around as schemes change and new ones develop. The pointers we have given may at least stimulate your ideas and give you access to money for a journey you have dreamed about but not previously contemplated actually making.

Equipping For a Trip

Luggage

by Hilary Bradt

The original meaning of 'luggage' is 'what has to be lugged about'. Lightweight materials have made lugging obsolete for sensible travellers these days, but there is a bewildering choice of containers for all your portable possessions.

What you buy in the way of luggage and what you put in it obviously depends on how and where you are travelling. If your journey is in one conveyance and you are staying put when you arrive, you can be as eccentric as the Durrell family who travelled to Corfu with 'two trunks of books and a briefcase containing his clothes' (Lawrence) and 'four books on natural history, a butterfly net, and dog and a jam jar full of caterpillars all in imminent danger of turning into chrysalids' (Gerald, author of *My Family and Other Animals*, from which the quotations come).

If, however, you will be constantly on the move and rarely spend more than one night in any place, your luggage must be easy to pack, transport and carry.

What to Bring

There are two important considerations to bear in mind when choosing luggage. First, weight is less of a problem than bulk. Travel light if you can, but if you can't, travel small. Second, bring whatever you need to keep you happy. It's a help to know yourself. If you can travel, like Laurie Lee, with a tent, a change of clothes, a blanket and a violin, or like Rick Berg, author of *The Art and Adventure of Travelling Cheaply* who took only a small rucksack (day pack) for his six-year sojourn, you will indeed be free. Most people however are too dependent on their customary possessions and diversions suddenly to abandon them and must pack accordingly.

Suitcase or Backpack

Your choice of luggage is of the utmost importance and will probably involve making a purchase. Making do with Granny's old suitcase or Uncle John's scouting rucksack may spoil your trip.

Anyone who's had to stand in a crowded Third World bus or the London Underground in rush hour wearing an external frame rucksack will know how unsuitable they can be for travelling. You take up three times more room than normal, and the possessions strapped to the outside of your pack may be out of your sight, but will certainly not be out of the minds of your fellow passengers, or out of their eyes, laps and air space. No wonder back-packers have a bad name. And because they do many Third World countries are prejudiced to the extent of banning them. On arriving at the Paraguay border some years ago I was forced to wrap my pack in a sheet sleeping bag and carry it as luggage in the most literal sense.

That aluminium frame is fragile, as you will soon discover when someone stands on it, and since you carry the backpack behind you, you're particularly vulnerable to thieves. Or have you ever hitch-hiked in a Mini carrying your pack on your lap? Can you honestly say you were comfortable? Leave the frame packs to the genuine backpackers they were designed for. Hitch-hikers and travellers should still carry a backpack, but one with an internal frame. This small variation in design makes all the difference – the pack can be carried comfortably on your lap, it need be no wider than your body, and everything can be fitted inside. It can be checked onto a plane with no trouble, and carried on a porter's head or mule's back.

For the average overland traveller, the ideal solution is the combination bag and backpack. This type of luggage has become justly popular in recent years. Basically it is a sturdy bag with padded shoulder straps that can be hidden in a special zip compartment when approaching a sensitive border or when travelling by plane.

If you are joining an organized group or do not expect to carry your own luggage, you will find a duffel bag the most practical solution. Or two duffel bags since you have two hands. These soft zipped bags are strong and light and can fit into awkward spaces that preclude rigid suitcases. They fit snugly into the bottom of a canoe or the back of a bus and are easily carried by porters or pack animals. In the Third World, small boys with the strength of Hercules throng bus stations in the hope of earning your small tip for carrying luggage.

When selecting a duffel bag, choose one made from a strong material with a stout zip that can be padlocked to the side or otherwise secured against thieves. Avoid those khaki army sausage bags with the opening at one end. The article you need will invariably be at the bottom.

Suppose you're a regular air traveller, what will be the best type of luggage for you? Probably the conventional suitcase, and in that case, you will be well advised – as with most travel purchases – to get the best you can afford, unless you want to replace your 'bargain' luggage after virtually every flight. Cheap materials do not stand up to the airline handling. Now that some airlines have eliminated the weight allowance in favour of a limit of two pieces, neither of which must measure more than 67 inches (that's height by length by width), it's as well to buy luggage that conforms to that size. Suitcases with built-in wheels are a great advantage in the many airports which do not supply trolleys.

If you are using soft-sided luggage, choose items made from a strong material, e.g. nylon. Leather items should be scrutinised for cracking around the expanded areas: the leather should be of a uniform thickness throughout the item. Check the zip, which should not only be strong but also unobtrusive so as not to catch on clothing etc., and the stitching, which should be even and secure with no gaps or loose threads. If you have the choice, get a bag with one handle only:

porters tend to toss luggage around by one handle and this can play havoc with a bag designed to be carried by two. Conveyor belts have a nasty habit of smearing luggage: darker colours stand up to this treatment more happily. Before walking away with your purchase, remember to ask about its care, especially which cleaning materials you should use.

Carry-on luggage should be used for anything you can't do without for a few days, whether it's photos of your children, your own special sleeping tablets or the address of the friend you're going straight from the airport to visit. Not to mention 'uninsurables' such as sums of money or vital papers. To fit under an aeroplane seat, a carry-on bag must measure no more than 450 × 350 × 150 mm (18 × 14 × 6 ins).

As well as a carry-on bag, you are allowed the following free items: a handbag (women only – sorry men; as this is in addition to the carry-on luggage, better take as big a handbag as possible to make the most of your luck), an overcoat, an umbrella or walking stick, a small camera, a pair of binoculars, infant's food for the flight, a carrying basket, an invalid's fully collapsible wheelchair, a pair of crutches, reading material in reasonable quantities, and any duty-free goods you have acquired since checking-in.

Some thought should be given to accessory bags. Everyone ends up with more luggage than they started with because of presents, local crafts, maps etc. collected on the way, and a light foldable bag is very useful. Canvas and straw have their followers. I'm devoted to plastic bags myself and carry a good supply, even though the

bottoms usually fall out or the handles tear.

Security

Choose your luggage with security in mind. Your possessions are at risk in two ways: your bag may be opened and some items removed, or the whole bag may be stolen. Most travellers have been robbed at some time or other, the most frequent occurrence being that small items simply disappeared from their luggage. Make sure that your luggage can be locked. With duffel bags, this is no problem – a small padlock will secure the zip to the ring at the base of the handle. Adapt the bag yourself if necessary. Combination locks are more effective than standard padlocks as they are rarely seen in the Third World and so thieves have not learned how to pick them. They also protect the clients of those manufacturers whose products are all fitted with the same key! It is harder to lock a backpack; use your ingenuity. One effective method is to make a strong pack cover with metal rings round the edges, through which can be passed a cable lock to secure the cover round the pack. Luggage may also be slashed, but this treatment is usually reserved for handbags. Apart from buying reinforced steel cases there is little you can do about it. A strong leather strap around a suitcase may help to keep your luggage safe and will be a lifesaver should the clasps break.

For easy identification, try coloured tape or some other personal markings on the outside. Stick-on labels are safer than the dangling kind, as they cannot be ripped off so easily.

During my travels, I've been robbed of five small bags. I finally learned never to carry something that is easily run off with unless it is firmly secured to my person. If you keep your most valuable possessions in the centre of a locked heavy pack or bag they're pretty safe. If you can barely carry your luggage, a thief will have the same problem.

Allowances for Air Travel

On international flights, the IATA Tourist and Economy Class allowance is normally 20 kgs (44 lbs), that for First Class 30 kgs (66 lbs). For transatlantic flights and some others (e.g. USA to South America), however, you can take far more luggage since the weight system has been cancelled and the only restriction is to two pieces of luggage no larger than 67 inches. Before you fly, always check with the airline on luggage allowances and ask if the same applies to the home journey. For instance, if you fly Ecuatoriana from Miami to Quito, you will fly down on the two piece system, but will be restricted to 20 kgs for your return – a nasty shock for the present-laden tourist.

What to do if you have excess baggage? You could, of course, just pay the charges, but we assume that you'll want to do something more interesting than that. If you know in advance, you could send the excess freight (*see article on Freight on page 299*). You could hang around at the check-in desk until you spot an amiable-looking passenger with space to spare and ask if they will pool. (If you are the amiable passenger, *do not* agree just to take a suitcase for someone else. Make sure they are with you and that they also check in. They could be landing you with drugs or bombs.) If you are not much over the limit, don't worry. The airlines will usually give you some leeway. My record is five bags weighing a total of 70 kgs transported from South America to Miami (weight limit 20 kgs) and on to London (piece limit – two) without paying excess charges.

Packing

Joan Bakewell, in *The Complete Traveller*, suggests thinking of what to take under the following headings: toiletries and overnight, unders, overs, accessories, paperwork and extras. Whilst it is true to say that everything can be classified under these headings, campers and others who must take with them the appurtenances of home will almost certainly find that the 'extras' section expands dramatically over the normal few extras required by, say, airline passengers.

The latter should be warned that aerosols and the ink in fountain pens tend to leak in the pressurised atmosphere of an aeroplane – such items should not should not be packed in your suitcases but may be safe enough in your hand luggage where you can keep an eye on them. Lighter fuel is not permitted on an aircraft. Knives, even pen-knives, may be confiscated from your hand-luggage. You are meant to get them back, but in practice this is rare.

When packing, put irregular-shaped items such as shoes at the bottom, remembering the case will be on its end while being carried (and don't forget to fill up the shoes with soft or small items such as underwear or jewellery), topped by clothes in layers separated by sheets of plastic or tissue paper. Trousers, skirts and dresses, still on their hangers or folded with tissue paper between layers, go towards the top, but the topmost stratum in your case should be occupied by T-shirts, blouses and shirts, small items of clothing, and then some enveloping piece such as a dressing gown or shawl over everything. Some travellers like to keep their toilet items in different groups, which makes sense when you consider that you don't wash your hair with the same frequency as you wash your face or go out in strong sun.

Do not overpack: if you have to force the lid of your suitcase to close, you may bend the frame or break the hinges, with the obvious ensuing risk to the contents. Underpacking, especially in soft-sided luggage is also undesirable since the cases need to be padded out to resist tears to the outer covering.

Travel Clothing

by Jan Glen, Tony Pearson and Melissa Shales

Your method of travel can be a big deciding factor in your choice of suitable clothing. The amount of storage space available is the ultimate restriction for backpackers, a major one for motor-cyclists, less so for motorists who can pack clothes for every climate and other eventuality. On a business trip, you will need suits, ties, and all the other paraphernalia involved on making you look fresh, eager and keen. If you are going off into the bush, you need not see a suit for months. Choosing which clothing to pack initially is often a matter of trial and error. Clothes that prove

unnecessary can, of course, be posted home and additional clothing bought along the way if routes and climates change. However, prices and quality en route may not be to your liking. Good quality shoes and boots are often extremely difficult to find, so take these with you.

Climate has to enter into one's calculations. If several different climatic zones are to be crossed, then the problem is compounded. If, for example, one travels from Britain to the Sahara by road in mid-winter, warm winter clothing has to be packed for the European leg of this journey. However, the Sahara at this time of the year is cold during the night only and some warm clothing could become redundant.

Travelling in deserts really causes few problems, provided all clothing is wrapped in plastic to protect it from the fine, penetrating dust. Cotton clothing is best for both men and women and a wide-brimmed hat is a good idea if you intend walking in the sun. Flip-flops or thonged sandals suffice for footwear in most places, except in Sahel regions where scorpions and large lethal thorns are hazards.

Rain forest, with its tropical heat and clammy humidity, is a very different story. Humidity can be very exhausting and may make the actual temperature seem much higher than it really is. For walking one must keep in mind the hazards of this environment. Muddy and slippery leech-infested tracks make sandals or flip-flops less suitable than closed-in leather or rubber shoes or boots. Cottons are again more comfortable than synthetics, and in both desert and rain forest environments, cotton underwear can minimise discomfort.

Custom and Status

Social custom is also a very important consideration. When in someone else's country, the last thing one wishes to do is offend. Yet this is often done unintentionally and local people are frequently too polite to complain. If you are able to swim where you are travelling, remember that local custom may find bikinis and men's brief trunks offensive. It is always safer to have modest wear: one-piece costumes for women and well-covering trunks or shorts for men. Careful observation of how local people dress when and if they swim can set your standard.

Because a Western woman's status is quite superior to that of her counterparts in other societies, she should be especially cautious in her dress. Some countries, Malawi for example, have been very concerned since the 1960s about the dress of their Western visitors. Dresses above the knee, shorts and trousers for women are actually illegal in that country. In the Saharan oasis town of Tamanrasset a Western girl, wearing only a tight pair of shorts and a bikini top, and with bare feet, was physically thrown out of a bar. In Algeria, Morocco, Tunisia, Libya, Iran and many other Muslim countries, the sort of dress which would arouse least hostility towards a Western woman would include both a headscarf, a long, dark-coloured skirt, and a top that covers your shoulders. Iran, especially since the Revolution, is even stricter than some other Islamic states. In many Islamic countries, women are rarely seen, seldom heard, and when they are seen they are covered up from head to toe. Let the local standard be your guide even if allowances are made for Westerners.

Even Mediterranean countries can be a problem for women if the customs of modesty are not observed. Many are the stories of women being approached and having their bottoms pinched, or worse, in Greece and Italy. Bikinis and shorts in these places should be reserved strictly for resorts where they have become acceptable for foreigners. In Athens, a seemingly cosmopolitan city, I have been harassed when dressed in conservative jeans and accompanies constantly by my husband.

Papua New Guinea has long been a home for expatriates, chiefly Australians, who are renowned for casual dress and an 'anything goes' attitude. However, attitudes have been modified to conform to local custom. Bikinis and shorts are generally out and although a long skirt is not at all necessary in Port Moresby it would be wise to be careful in outlying regions.

When visiting India, dress conservatively out of respect for that country's large Muslim population. Hindu women also wear long saris, are very modest and often have an inferior social status. If visiting a Sikh temple, it is also customary to wear a hat or some form of head covering.

Although anything theoretically goes in Western countries, girls hitchhiking there in very provocative shorts or bikinis are really offering to pay for their ride in a sometimes violent way they may not have anticipated.

Further complications to your luggage occur when you are going to be mixing trips off the beaten track with city stops and the social and cultural occasions these entail. Try and have at least one dress or skirt that rolls up into a ball, comes out looking pristine and will do for a formal evening. You will often find expat communities, in particular, still dress for dinner, trips to the theatre etc.

Men's Wear

A man's position is quite different when travelling in male dominated societies. Because of the significant difference between formal and informal dress for men, they should carry both types. In isolated hot regions where no local people will be encountered, men can comfortably wear shorts and flip-flops and go about shirtless. In towns and at borders, however, the traveller's appearance should be much more formal. Long, straight-legged trousers, a clean, conservative shirt, shoes and tidy hair will give a look of affluence and respectability. Even a tie may be handy at times. The impression this dress creates will promote a more gracious attitude from shopkeepers and businessmen and could well moderate the zealousness of authoritarian border officials.

In Australia, New Zealand, and southern Africa, shorts are the accepted daily dress even for businessmen. However, even in cosmopolitan London they attract curious glances. Therefore, shorts are best reserved for the out of the way places.

Long hair and untidy beards on men are a bone of contention in many countries. Malawi forbids entry to men with long hair and flared trousers. Morocco's entry requirements empower border officials to refuse entry to men with long hair or 'hippy appearance' despite their having valid travel documents. And even where this disapproval is not specified by law,

it often exists in practice. Officials may discriminate against travellers of 'unsuitable' appearance by considerably delaying their entry. Incidentally, men with greying hair are often well respected in less developed countries.

Blend In

Dress is far more important for the independent traveller than for the regular tourist on the more beaten track, who has the protection of tour guides or companies and the safety of numbers. Offending the local people can have unpleasant consequences for the individual alone and away from civilisation. Adopting local dress because of a desire to 'go ethnic' is suitable when actually travelling and living as the locals do. One example of this would be as a member of a camel caravan, where it would not only be justified but sensible to adopt the *tagoulmoust* to protect your face from the dust and dryness. On a camel, you would also be more comfortable wearing a *sarouel* (baggy trousers) and loose shirt. The *jellabah*, the flowing Arab gown found all round the world is an extremely useful garment, and one that I would consider taking anywhere. It can be used as everyday wear in most Muslim countries. It is cool in the sun, protecting you from fierce mid-day heat, and warm at night. You can use it as a cover-up on the beach over a swimming costume, instead of pyjamas for sleeping in, or even, if glamorous enough, as a woman's evening wear. On top of this, it is modest enough not to offend local custom anywhere in the world.

However, in many circumstances, no matter how practical the local dress may be it is wise to wear it with discretion. Imagine how ridiculous a Western tourist would look on the streets of Port Moresby wearing nothing but some 'arsegrass' strung around his waist. You surely don't wish to offend the local people, but neither do you want to become a laughing stock to them. A good idea is to aim to blend in rather than stand out as a foreign visitor. As a foreigner, you are at times already at a disadvantage but you can try to minimise this by, for example, avoiding pretentiousness. Wearing a ten gallon hat, pith helmet or slouch hat tends to attract unwanted attention.

It is strictly illegal for tourists to wear military clothing in the Niger and, however cheap army surplus may be, it is best avoided in many other countries too, where it can have unwanted connotations. This is especially so in 'white mercenary' sensitive Africa. 'Obvious' jewellery is also best avoided by travellers because its style will be unusual and it is regarded as a sign of wealth. Displaying it invites theft. Moreover, worn by men, together with shorts, it has other meanings. An example is the attractive young man, shirtless, with shorts, silver bangles and neck chains, in a Saharan oasis hotel, who was most put out because he had been approached and propositioned by several local men. Homosexuality occurs internationally and advances are made to willing-looking men in the same way as they are made to women in the heterosexual sense. The author's husband, always a conservative dresser, did once forget this in Beirut and wore standard Australian businessmen's shorts and long socks. The resultant cat calls and wolf whistles from the young men sent him fleeing back to his hotel to change into long trousers.

A pair of overalls or very tatty old clothes are most useful for dirty work such as vehicle maintenance en route, allowing you to protect your other clothes from grease and dirt.

If you run out of small change or presents to reward local people who have been very helpful, especially in less developed countries, secondhand Western clothing is often prestigious and it can suit everybody if you give away some clothes as you travel. Jeans are a popular example.

By urging conservative and demure dress in Third World countries, one is not being prudish. Rather, by dressing sensitively, one can travel unharassed in almost any area. In places still relatively untouched by Western influence, the impression one creates can ensure that travellers who follow are welcome visitors.

Cold Weather Clothing

The totally synthetic clothing system for general backpacking or trekking is almost upon us, with the exception of a small cotton content in one or two garments and woollen socks. Consider, for example, this layered clothing system which has become my own personal choice within the last few years.

It starts with polypropelene underwear, Lifa by Helly Hansen in warm weather, and heavier warmer top and long johns by Mountain Equipment in the winter. This layer is topped by an all-nylon fibre-pile jacket, again Helly Hansen, and a pair of either polyester/cotton breeches (Rohan) or polyester/cotton trousers by Mountain Equipment. A polyester/cotton double jacket (Rohan) acts as a windproof and multi-pocketed storage system and the whole assembly is then covered in really foul weather by a Gore-Tex nylon suit from The North Face. Add to this lot a pair of mitts (nylon outer, synthetic pile inner) and a Thermafleece synthetic balaclava and we're almost there. Socks are still basically wool, though with nylon added to increase their durability. Finally, my boots are currently leather, but their water resistance owes a great deal more to the skills of the chemist than to nature.

The advantages of this synthetic personal environment I create are largely connected with drying times, which are conveniently short, and weights, which are kept to a minimum. The disadvantages are the static buildup (which can be spectacular when undressing) and the much quicker rate at which the synthetic underwear becomes unsavoury. No doubt many people will leap to the defence of wool and cotton on reading this, but all tastes are subjective and my choice is based on experience of both natural and synthetic fabric clothing, and for me at least, technology wins hands down.

Look out in the shops for an absolute profusion of garments made from a fabric called fleece (the Americans call it bunting). This is destined to take over from fibre-pile as the number one fabric for what I call intermediate warmwear, that is, the layers between underwear and windproofs. Fleece is all-synthetic and has a rather tighter weave than fibre-pile, making it marginally more wind resistant. But don't be misled by talk of 'windproofing qualities' as this is a gross exaggeration. It certainly has an attractive look and feel to it with its exceptionally soft texture and it wears a little like wool, going 'agreeably shaggy' in the words of Mountain Equipment. As to whether it is warmer than fibre-pile, the laboratories say it certainly is, my experience in the hills says that it isn't and so the argument will go on.

Lightweight Equipment

by Martin Rosser

When I first came to lightweight backpacking I knew very little and didn't bother to ask for advice. I learned from bitter experience and very exciting (interspersed with misery) it was too. The main drawback to that method is expense. Based on trial and error, costs soon mounted to prohibitive proportions before I had what I wanted. The end lesson was – if you're beginning a little advice is worth a lot. When you become more practiced, then is the time for bitter experience to take over.

In this article I intend only to cover the main purchases you will make, missing out on the way food, clothing, and any more technical sporting equipment. This leaves (in descending order of what it will probably cost you) tent or shelter; sleeping gear; rucksack; boots; and cooking and eating gear.

If you are going backpacking, there are a number of objectives you will have in mind. Weight is usually at the top of the list; you want everything as light as possible. Performance; you want it to be good enough for everything you are going to put it through. Expense; you have to be able to afford it. These three criteria form what could be termed the eternal triangle of backpacking.

As we go on you will see the compromises come up, but one aspect of weight can be covered now. Most lightweight gear comes marked with a weight, but manufacturers being manufacturers, these are not always as accurate as they might be. Furthermore, some sleeping bags come marked with the weight of the filling only. It is easy to become confused or misled. The easiest answer is to shop for your kit armed with a spring balance. Something going up to 15 lbs is easily enough, if it can be read to the nearest ounce or two. If you want to know where to get one, ask a fisherman.

Tents and Shelters

At one time, the ridge pole was the only tent you could get, short of a marquee. Then some bright spark designed an A-pole ridge so that the pole didn't come straight down in the doorway. Today you can still get both these designs and the ridge pole (in the form of the Vango Force Ten) is still preferred by many as a heavy duty tent that can take a lot of punishment.

However, with the advent of flexible poles that could be shoved through sleeves, new designs became possible, and new advantages arose. Such models give you plenty of headroom, something as important as groundspace if you intend to live in your tent during bad weather. There are disadvantages of course. The tents are both more expensive and more fragile. To get a structurally strong flexible-pole tent you have to go up-market to the geodesic designs and that costs a lot of money.

After flexible poles, Gore-tex made its mark on the tents scene with single skin tents. Reputably water tight, with built-in breathability, you get a condensation free tent that weighs even less than regular flexible pole types. These tents also tend to employ flexible poles so the space inside is good. However, Gore-tex is a very expensive material, so as the weight goes down, the price goes up.

Single skin tents soon became available in one man versions with only the barest skeleton of a frame. Because the material breathes it doesn't matter if there is no circulation of air around it. With one hoop at the front these tents resemble a tunnel that you have to crawl into feet first. Then the hoop was removed and the Gore-tex 'bivi-bag' was born – a waterproof and fully breathable covering for your sleeping bag. These are probably the ultimate luxury in bivouacing, but the cost is again high. However, weighing in at next to nothing, these bags are well worth considering.

Last but not least comes the humble bivouac sheet or, to use the army parlance, the basha sheet. This six foot by eight foot piece of PU nylon has tags around the outside so that it can be pegged down. It is the most versatile, lightweight, inexpensive, and durable of all the shelters so far discussed. It is limited only by the ingenuity and expertise of the user, and therein lies its fault – you need to know how to use it. But if you don't have any money, or if you can put the occasional soaking down to experience, give it a go.

So which one do you choose? Narrow the field by asking yourself these questions. How many people do you want it to sleep? How high up are you going to camp? (The higher you camp the harsher the conditions, so the sturdier the tent you need.) Is headroom important to you? (Perhaps you want a flexible hoop design.) Do you want it to last a long time? (You will have to go for a heavier duty model.)

It has to be said that even if you designed the tent yourself compromises would have to be made, so be prepared to make them when buying. However, with care and if you scrutinise the maker's specifications you should get something suitable.

Whatever you end up with, try to get a tent with mosquito netting on every entrance, even the vents. Rare indeed are the countries with no flying biters. The tent you end up with will probably have a superthin groundsheet to save weight so you might want to get some 2mm foam to use as an underlay. It will keep you surprisingly warm and will cut down on wear and tear. However, this will add to the weight and bulk of your tent system. Bear this in mind before you reject the heavier tent with the stronger groundsheet.

Sleeping Gear

Without a shadow of a doubt the best you can sleep in is a down bag. It promotes fine dreams, is aesthetically pleasing, is lighter for any given warmth rating than any other fill, and packs away smaller than any other bag, lofting up afterwards to cosset you at night. Nothing else comes close to down, unless, of course, you are allergic to feathers.

Yet down has a terrible Achilles heel. If it gets wet it is next to useless and very unpleasant to be next to. Furthermore, wet it a few times and it starts to feel very sorry for itself, losing efficiency rapidly.

If your bag is likely get wet, steer clear of down. The alternative is a man-made fibre bag.

These come in many guises but the principle is the same in all. A long, man-made fibre is hollow and thus traps air. As with down it is the trapped air that keeps you warm. Call it Holofill, Superloft, Microsoft or whatever, the concensus of opinion is that the difference in performance is marginal. The fibres probably differ slightly to get around patents rather than to improve performance.

The advantages of artificial fibres are clear. The bags are cheaper than down, they are warmer underneath you (because they are harder to compress), they keep you warmer when wet, and they are easier to keep clean. Disadvantages? They are substantially heavier and bulkier than down, and won't last you anywhere near as long.

The compromise is clear. If you can stay out of the wet and can afford to pay more, invest in down which lasts longer, so costing the same in the long run. If you constantly get wet when camping, buy a man-made fibre bag and stick to feeling the down bags in the shops lovingly.

There is one more alternative – Buffalo Bags, made from fibre pile covered in pertex. These are unique and have their own special advantages, though the disadvantages can be stated easily – they are very heavy and bulky. Buffalo Bags are based on the layer system, making it handy to add layers for cold weather and subtract for hot. They are tough and very washable. Thanks to the pertex covering they aren't easily wetted, and if they do get wet, the pile wicks away moisture and the pertex cover dries it out rapidly. The same pertex covering makes the bag very windproof. The bag is very good for those who bivouac and can be used to effect with a good down inner bag. Handle or better still borrow one to try before you buy.

Try the bag on in the shop, however foolish you feel, and leave your clothes on while you do so. This minimises embarassment, and one day you might be cold enough out in the wilds to sleep fully clothed. Pull the hood of the bag tight around your face to cover the head. If you can't do this, the bag can't be used for any kind of cold weather. A large part of the body's heat loss is from the head. Shove your feet into the bottom of the bag and wriggle. If the bag constricts you it is too small. Any point where you press against the bag will turn into a miserable cold spot at night. If you are a restless sleeper make sure the bag is wide enough around the middle to contain all your squirmings. If you feel like a solitary pea rattling around in an empty pod, the bag is too large and you will waste heat warming up empty space.

General good points in a bag include a box or elephant-type foot; a draw-cord at the shoulder *as well as* at the head; and the option of a right or left handed zip so that in an emergency you can share your warmth with an extra special friend. Zips should all be well baffled to prevent loss of heat. If the sack you choose is a man-made fibre one, check to see if it comes with a compression stuff sack. If it doesn't and you want one, this will add a few pounds to the final price.

I have deliberately ignored baffle constructions as the subject is complicated and best covered with examples to hand. Seek advice on site. Similarly with the season rating of the bag. The 'season' system is simple but should only be used as a rough guide. One season (summer) for very casual use in warm weather; two season (summer and spring) is a little better; three seasons covers autumn too; four seasons should be good for winter use; and five seasons for use in severe conditions. However, simple systems like this leave room for manufacturers to fudge their claims. One man's three seasons is another man's four. Query the general reputation of the bag you fancy with as many experts as you can find and average their views. I find that 'lowest temperatures' to use the bags in are next to useless. They are inevitably rated for still air, and who camps in that? As well as ignoring the massive effect of wind chill, they ignore the fact that some people maintain a higher body temperature at night than others.

Last but not least with sleeping gear, you would be well advised to put something under your sleeping bag; namely a 'kip mat'. The most widely used is the closed cell foam type, which is bulky but lightweight and durable. Ignore all advice that tells you they are all made of the same stuff and that for expensive ones you simply pay for the name. It is patently untrue. A simple test is to inflict severe damage on various types – such damage as scoring, tearing, and compressing flat. Choose one that withstands these injuries best and it will probably be the one that feels warmest when pressed between the palms. It will probably cost more too, but in my experience, the cheap ones are simply not worth it.

Rucksacks

With rucksacks two things are important from the outset; size and water-proofness. You have available to you any size of 'sack you want, and (whatever the manufacturer may say to the contrary) none of them are waterproof.

The capacity of a 'sack is measured in litres. A small day pack weighs in at about 25 litres. From there you have various sizes up to a general all round 'sack sized at 75 litres. With one of these you will be able to manage anything up to mountaineering (at a push), but you pay a price for the facility. Having 75 litres to play with you feel a terrible urge to fill up all the space, even for summer camping in the lowlands. To restrict yourself to what you *need* rather than what you have room for takes discipline. Because of this, some people prefer a 65 or even a 50 litre sack. Going upwards from 75 litres, there is almost no end, but the higher you go the more specialised the use; expedition travel overseas perhaps or for humping all you need up to a base camp from which you intend making sorties with smaller loads.

When you look at the vast array of rucksacks available you will find that fashion dictates two things at present. First is the anatomical, internal frame system. External frames are fuddy duddy now, though the internal frame is not the all round answer to carrying loads. The second (and far less valid) fashion is adjustable harnesses. If you can (and it gets harder every season) avoid these. There are more fiddly bits that can go wrong, usually at an awkward moment (mine went halfway up the ascent to a glacier), and as your back shouldn't be due to change shape significantly for another 30 years at least you may as well save yourself some bother. Settle for a 'sack that is fixed at one size and just happens to fit you.

Something that has always been a very important asset to a rucksack is a hip belt. When walking, the hip belt transfers roughly 60 per cent of the pack weight to your legs, leaving only 40 per cent for your more delicate shoulders and back. Therefore any rucksack you buy should have a wide, sturdy, and very well padded hip belt. That thick padding should also appear at the shoulder straps. Thin bands will cut off the circulation, giving you the unusual sensation of having two useless and heavy ropes dangling from your shoulders instead of arms.

After those important criteria the rest more or less comes down to personal preference. If you are organised in the way you pack, a one section rucksack is simpler and more effective. It is an advantage if your pockets can be detached, but having them fixed saves a bit of weight. Some harnesses leave more room for air to circulate between you and the 'sack. If you hate getting hot and sweaty as you walk, try for one of these.

When you buy your pack, enquire about the repair service. Well established manufacturers such as Karrimor and Berghaus give excellent service, often without charging. Some will even go so far as to give a lifetime's guarantee, though I can never work out if this applies to the life of the 'sack or the life of its owner.

Boots

As far as boots are concerned, leather is still the most wonderful material going. Fabric boots have come and gone, and plastic shell boots have managed to retain only a very small part of the market. Meanwhile, leather goes from strength to strength.

To spot a good leather boot is fairly simple. It is as far as possible made from one bit of leather. The stitching is double, sometimes triple. The ankle is well padded to give comfortable support. The inside of the boot is lined with soft leather, and there are no rough seams around the heel. Feet tend to blister in disapproval of poor design.

Check the weight of several different pairs. It costs you energy to clump around with a heavy weight on each foot, and you may well decide that the terrain you usually walk on isn't demanding enough to require such solidness.

If you intend to use your boots with crampons, however, you will need a fairly rigid sole at the least. If you intend to go front pointing you will need a boot with a steel shank in the sole. For the common walker, though, these should be avoided. The boot becomes very heavy and uncomfortable to walk in over any great distance.

Traditionally, two pairs of socks are worn with boots, and some celebrated old timers even wear more, choosing oversize boots to compensate. However, modern thinking says that boots aren't as uncomfortable as they used to be and one pair of socks is quite enough. So unless you suffer terribly from cold feet, prepare to try on your boots with just one pair of thick socks. With the boots on and laced up, rap the heel on the floor and check to see if you can wiggle your toes freely. If you can, the boots are not too tight for you, the blood will still circulate and you should be free from the horrors of gangrene and cold toes.

Cooking and Eating

For this pleasant pastime you will need a stove, something to cook in, something to eat out of, something to eat with and (very importantly) something to carry water in.

A water container should hold about a litre and can be of any shape or design that takes your fancy. The solid plastic army types are robust but heavy. The thin aluminium ones are lighter but more fragile. One rule goes with all water bottles, though. Put anything other than water in them and they will be tainted for life.

The essential part of the 'something to eat with' is a general purpose blade. This will cut up anything you want to eat into manageable portions as well as whittle sticks and slice your tongue open if you lick it once too often. Beyond this, you only need a spoon. Anything more is redundant. Save the weight by cutting down on the number of utensils you take rather than by using flimsy 'camping' ones which bend the first time you use them.

For those who are into time and motion, what you eat out of is also what you cook in. Those who find this idea displeasing will know best what they want. However, when you look for a cooking/eating billy make sure of two things. Firstly, it should have a good handle, preferably one that will not get too hot to hold whilst cooking is in progress. Secondly, it must have a close-fitting lid. This too must have a handle, so it can be lifted on or off, or be used as a frying pan by those terrible people who can suffer fried eggs and bacon for breakfast.

There are many styles of billy available to choose from. I use a two pint 'paint tin' type, because I like the shape and enjoy hanging it over wood fires. Others choose the rectangular army type that hold up to a litre. These fit nicely into the side pocket of a rucksack and can be filled with snack foods and brew kit for the day's use. The choice is yours.

On now to the more complex subject of stoves. The choice here is between solid fuel, liquid or gas.

Solid fuel comes in blocks that resemble white cough candy. A packet fits neatly into the metal tray that you burn them in. The whole affair is little bigger than a pack of playing cards. The system is foolproof since you merely set a match to the blocks and add more for extra heat, take away for less heat. The fuel is resistant to water, though you may have trouble lighting it if it is damp. Its main drawback is that it doesn't produce an intense heat and so is slow to use. It also produces noxious fumes and so should not be used in an enclosed space.

Moving on to liquid stoves your choice increases considerably. Most simple of all is the meths burner. Here you have a container into which you pour meths and then set fire to it. The more sophisticated (and expensive) sets have a windshield built round the container which also neatly holds the billy. Again the design is foolproof. Its advantages include a cleaning burning flame, and quite a range of burners, from inexpensive to high-tech and costly. However, the fuel is relatively expensive and may be difficult to get hold of if you are off the beaten track. Furthermore, the rate of burn cannot be controlled. The choice is simply on or off.

Still in the liquid fuel range, there are the pressurised burners, running on either paraffin or petrol. The burner for paraffin is the well known primus stove. Though it is a relatively complicated device compared to other stoves it can be readily mastered. Once burning, the flame is intense and efficient and can be adjusted to give various rates of heat. As a fuel paraffin is cheap and almost universally available. The disadvantages of pressurised paraffin are that a small amount of a second fuel must be carried to prime the stove, and that the stove itself needs some maintenance such as greasing pump washers and replacing burner washers now and again. However, primus stoves are known in most parts of the world, so spare parts should not be too much of a problem.

An alternative to pressurised paraffin is pressurised petrol. Again this type of stove is quite complicated and needs occasional maintenance. Furthermore it usually demands to be fed unleaded petrol, so buying fuel whilst travelling could present problems. Like paraffin, however, it burns hot and fast, heating quickly and efficiently. Petrol and paraffin also produce noxious fumes and both should be used in a well ventilated space.

Gas stoves are simple to use. They are relatively cheap to buy but are expensive to run. They burn cleanly and the flame can be controlled, but when pressure runs low the flame stays stubbornly and annoyingly feeble. You can usually find somewhere to buy replacement canisters, but in out of the way places the cost will be high. The little Camping Gaz canisters that are ubiquitous around Europe are difficult to find in the Third World, and you are not allowed to take them on planes. Unlike paraffin, gas is not an everyday fuel in most places. Using gas stoves in low temperatures is inadvisable as their performance drops dramatically.

As with most areas of equipment, there is a stove to beat all stoves. It can run on any liquid fuel you care to feed it, including (apparently) vodka, should you be so inclined. It comes with an attachment that screws directly into a regular metal fuel bottle and away you go. Should you be interested in seeing one, enquire after a multi-fuel stove. Should you be interested in buying one, be prepared to spend a lot.

Once again, compromise is the final solution. You will generally find that pressurised paraffin is the tried and trusted stove for most formal expeditions, and is the general favourite of many. Solid fuel I find a useful last resort to have available when you are travelling light, relying on wood fires, and there is no way of lighting one. Gas fuel is simply a consumer convenience stove that is simple to use in all but extreme conditions. You pays your money and you takes your choice.

Afterword

With so much wonderful equipment around it is easy to get carried away and aim for the best in everything. A large rucksack to carry a five season down bag with a Gore-tex bivi-bag, a 'super stove' and a geodesic dome tent. Thankfully most people's pockets refuse to support such notions.

In reality, if you think over the use to which your equipment will be put carefully you will often find that the best is not suitable for you and you are just as well off with something cheaper. Then, when your style of

travelling or camping does demand the best, the expense becomes worthwhile and supportable. So don't end up being par boiled in a five season sleeping bag which you only ever use in summer. The money could be better spent elsewhere.

Space to Spare

by Jack Jackson

If you have a roomy vehicle, aren't worried about weight, and are not constantly on the move, you might as well plan to make yourselves as comfortable as possible. Don't stint on things which might seem frivolous before you leave but can make an enormous difference to your morale. This is particularly true if camping.

If you plan to sleep without a tent, you need a mosquito net in some areas. There are several types on the market, but they are not usually big enough to tuck in properly, so get the ex-army ones which have the extra advantage of needing only one point of suspension. A camera tripod or ice axe will do for this if there is not a vehicle or tent nearby.

Mattresses

In cold places, you should not sleep directly on the ground, so use some form of insulation. Air beds are very comfortable, and are said by some to be a better form of insulation than foam, but they do have disadvantages. They are generally too heavy to carry unless you have a vehicle and inflating them is hard work unless you get one of the more recent, self-inflating varieties. These, however, are considerably more expensive. Thorns and sunlight all work against them and you will certainly spend a lot of time patching them up. If you decide to use one, be sure it is rubber and not plastic, and then only pump it halfway. If you pump it any higher, you will roll around and probably fall off. Even on cold nights you will wake up in a puddle of perspiration unless you have put a blanket or woollen jumper between yourself and the mattress.

Camp beds tend to be narrow, collapse frequently, tear holes in the groundsheet and soon break up altogether. Worst of all, cold air circulates underneath the bed. Since your body weight compresses the bedding, only several layers of blankets will give you the insulation you need.

The best mattress for cold weather camping is made of polythene or rubber foam. Unfortunately the majority of those on the market are cheap and not dense enough to be adequate. Only one brand stands out above all others in density and thickness. This is made by P.T.C Langdon and is called Spatzmola. Spatzmola foams are not easy to find and may have to be ordered. In the UK, you can usually get them at Pindisports or order them from other camping suppliers. Though they cost twice the price of the others, they are by far the most comfortable and are highly recommended.

All foams tend to wear very easily but if you make a washable cotton cover which fully encloses them, they will last for several years. Foams, being bulky, are best wrapped in strong waterproof covers during transport. Personally, I use only half a Spatzmola, enough for hips to shoulders and use a climer's closed-cell foam insulating mat called Karrimat, known in the USA as insulite, for my legs and feet. This cuts down on bulk. One advantage of foam mattresses is that the perspiration that collects in them evaporates very quickly when aired so they are easy to keep fresh and dry. Remember to give the foam an airing every second day. Karrimat make mats of any size to order. They also come in a 3mm thickness suitable for putting under a groundsheet for protection against sharp stones or on ice, where otherwise the tent groundsheet could stick to the ice and be torn while trying to get it free.

Furniture and Utensils

The aluminium chairs on the market today are covered with light cotton. This rots quickly in intense sunlight. Look around for nylon or terylene covered furniture or replace the cotton covers with your own. Full-size ammunition boxes are good for protecting kitchenware and also make good seats.

When buying utensils, go for the dull-grey aluminium ones. Shiny-type aluminium pans tend to crack and split with repeated knocks and vibration. Billies, pots and pans, plates, mugs, cutlery etc. should be firmly packed inside boxes or they will rub against each other and end up as a mass of metal filings. A pressure cooker guarantees sterile food and can double as a large billy, so if you have room it is a good investment.

Kettles with lids are preferable to whistling kettles, which are difficult to fill from cans or streams. For melting snow and ice, it is best to use billies. Big, strong aluminium ones are best bought at Army and Navy auctions or surplus stores.

A wide-range of non-breakable cups and plates is available, but you will find that soft plastic ones leave a bad aftertaste so it is better to pay a little more and get melamine. Stick to large mugs with firm wide bases that will not tip over easily. Insulated mugs soon become smelly and unhygienic because dirt and water get between the two layers and cannot be cleaned out.

Many people like metal mugs but if you like your drinks hot you may find the handle too hot to touch or burn your lips on the metal. Melamine mugs soon get stained with tea or coffee but there are cleaners available, or Steradent is a perfectly adequate and much cheaper substitute. Heavyweight stainless steel cutlery is much more durable than aluminium for a long expedition.

For carrying water, ex-military jerry cans are best, as they are lightproof and therefore algae will not grow inside them as it does with normal plastic watercans.

Stoves and Gas

The 2.7 kgs gas cartridge or the 4.5 kgs gas cylinder are the best sizes to carry. Gas is, without doubt, the easiest and cleanest fuel to use for cooking.

Liquid petroleum gas is usually referred to as Calor Gas or butane gas in the UK and by various oil company names worldwide, such as Shellgas or Essogas. Though available worldwide, there are different fittings on the bottles in different countries and these are not interchangeable. Where you use a pressure reduction valve on a low-pressure appliance, there will always be a rubber tube connection. Make sure that you carry some spares of the correct-size rubber tubing.

Gas bottles are very heavy and refilling can be a major nuisance. Refillable Camping Gaz bottles as supplied in Europe are meant to be factory refilled, but in some countries e.g. Algeria, Morocco, Yemen Arab Republic, they are available with an overfill release, so that you can fill them yourself from a larger domestic butane gas supply. Neither butane nor propane is readily found in Asia. Enterprising campsite managers in Turkey and Iran have discovered ways of filling gas bottles from their own supply. Stand well clear while they do it as the process involves pushing down the ball valve with a nail or stone and then overfilling from a bottled supply of higher pressure. This can cause flare-up problems when the bottle is used with standard cooking equipment so if you use this source of supply, it is advisable to release some of the pressure by opening up the valve for a couple of minutes well away from any open flame before hooking it up.

Lighting stoves is always a problem in cold climates or at altitude. Local matches and Russian matches never work unless you strike three together, so take a good supply. The best answer seems to be a butane cigarette lighter kept in your trouser pocket where it will be warm. Remember to carry plenty of refills.

Space Blankets

Space blankets, very much advertised by their manufacturers, are, on the evidence, not much better than a polythene sheet or bag. Body perspiration tends to condense on the inside of them, making the sleeping bag wet so that the person inside gets cold. In hot or desert areas, however, used in reverse to reflect the sun, they are very good during the heat of the day to keep a tent or vehicle cool. If necessary, a plastic sheet or space blanket can be spread over a ring of boulders to make an effective bath.

Buying

When buying equipment be especially wary of any shop that calls itself an expedition supplier but does not stock the better brands of equipment. All the top-class equipment suppliers will give trade discounts to genuine expeditions or group buyers such as clubs or educational establishments and some, such as Pindisports and Field and Trek, have special contract departments for this service.

Checklist

For a party of four with no worries about travelling light:

Good compass, maps, and guidebooks

Selection of plastic bags for waste disposal, etc.

Clingfilm and aluminium foil for food and cooking

Large bowl for washing up and washing

4 x 20 litre water jerry cans – strong ex-military type

Fire extinguisher

Large supply of paper towels, toilet paper, scouring pads, dish cloths and tea-towels

Large supply of good matches in waterproof box and/or disposable lighters

Washing up liquid for dishes (also good for greasy hands)

Frying pan

Pressure cooker

Selection of strong saucepans or billies

Kettle with lid (not whistling type which is difficult to fill from cans or streams)

Tin opener – good heavyweight or wall type

Stainless steel cutlery

Plastic screw-top jars for sugar, salt, etc.

1 large sharp bread knife

2 small sharp vegetable knives

1 large serving spoon and soup ladle

Good twin burner for your gas supply, otherwise petrol or kerosene twin burner cooker

Good sleeping bag or sleeping bag combination for the climate expected, plus mattress of your choice

Combined mosquito and insect repellent spray

Battery-powered fluorescent light

4 lightweight folding chairs

Plates and/or bowls for eating

Wide-bottomed mugs which do not tip over easily

Large supply of paper plates if you have room

Short-handled hand-axe

Thin nylon line to use as clothesline, plus clothes pegs

6 plastic or wire lightweight clothes hangers

Washing powder for clothes

6 metres of plastic tubing to fill water tank or jerry cans

2 tubes of universal glue/sealant e.g. Bostik

Chamois leather

Sponges

6 heavy rubber 'tie downs'

Water purification filters plus tablets or iodine as backup

Phrase books/dictionaries

2 torches plus spare batteries
Kitchen scissors
Ordinary scissors
Small plastic dustpan and brush
Soap, shampoo, toothpaste, towels
Medical first-aid kit plus multivitamins
Elastic bands
Sewing kit and safety pins
Cassette player and selection of cassettes
Selection of reading material
Hidden strong-box or money belt

Many other things can be taken along, but most of these are personal belongings. They include: dental floss, waterproof watch, tissues and handkerchiefs (good for many other reasons than blowing your nose), clothing and underwear, socks, trousers, shirts, tie (for the formal invitation that may crop up; store the tie rolled up in a jar with a lid), dress (for that same occasion), jackets, coats, raincoats, gloves, bathing suits, shoes, jumpers, belts, parkas with hoods, moisturising cream, toothbrushes, comb, pocket-knife, camera, film, photographic accessories, antimalarial tablets and salt tablets where required, sun barrier cream, sunglasses, medicaments, spare spectacles if worn, passports, visas, traveller's cheques, inoculation certificates, car papers, insurance papers, money, airmail writing paper, envelopes and pens.

Food on the Move

by Ingrid Cranfield, Mary Schantz and Paulette Agnew

'Good food makes up for rain and hard beds. Good fellowship is at its best around good meals.'

Whoever said this did so aptly. Wholesome, mouthwatering food, and plenty of it, can make the most miserable conditions more bearable. But no matter how fantastic the scenery, soft the beds, or fine the weather, enjoyment quickly wanes when the food is lousy. The problem is, how do you ensure you'll have good food when travelling?

Living a regular life, in one place most of the time, people get to know what foods they like and dislike and base a balanced diet on this rather than on text book nutrition. When travelling, however, you are constantly faced with new foods and it can be easy to lose track of how you are eating, simply because your rule of thumb menu planning breaks down. This can lead to tiredness and lack of energy and even poor health.

Essentially there are two ways of coping. You can either pick up local food as you travel, or you can take with you all your needs for the duration. Eating local food may give you the feeling of being closer to a country's way of life – but could also make you severely ill. Taking your own supplies is safe and very necessary if you are going into the wilds – but how do you stop your palate becoming jaded with endless supplies of dried food?

It is sensible to be able to recognise what all foods are made up of and know what is necessary to keep you well fed. A balanced diet breaks down into six main areas. Sugars, carbohydrates, fats, proteins, minerals/vitamins/salts, and water are all needed, some in greater quantities than others, to make it up.

Sugars:

These should really be called simple sugars if you want to be technically correct, but if you don't, it is enough to know that sugars are the simplest form of energy-stored-as-food. Because they are simple, the body finds them easy to absorb into the bloodstream – hence the term blood sugar. From here sugars are either turned directly to energy, or are stored as glycogen. The brain is very partial to using sugars for energy and if it is forced to run on other forms of food energy it complains by making you feel tired, headachy, and generally wobbly-kneed. Though it is important to have some sugars in your diet, try not to depend on them too much. Weight for weight they give you less calories than other food types and if you take on lots of sugars at once, the body will react by over-producing insulin because your blood sugar is too high so that in the end, your blood sugar is taken down to a lower level than before. If you feel a desperate need for instant energy, try to take sugars with other food types to prevent this happening. Whilst travelling it is simple enough to recognise foods with lots of sugars – they're sweet. Simple enough, too, to avoid sugar excesses. The pitfalls are well documented in the West and in less developed areas, sugar is still something of a luxury.

Carbohydrates:

Basically, carbohydrates are complex structures of simple sugars. Plants generally store energy as carbohydrate while animals store food energy as fat or glycogen. Carbohydrates have to be broken down into simple sugars by the body before they can be used as energy, so it takes longer to benefit from them after eating. Weight for weight, however, you will get three or four times more calories from carbohydrates than from sugars.

Recognising carbohydrates is simple. They are stodgy, starchy and very filling. Hence breads for the Western world, mealies in Africa, rice for the East etc. The majority of food energy in the world comes from carbohydrates, so when travelling, find the local equivalent and base a diet round it.

Fats:

Next to carbohydrates, most of our energy comes from fats. Our bodies store energy as fat because it is the most efficient way to do so. Weight for weight, fats give you nearly three times the energy of carbohydrates, so they are an extremely efficient way of carrying food energy. The body takes quite a while to break down fat into a usable form however – from minutes to half an hour.

Fats, of course, are fatty, oily, creamy and sometimes congeal. Hence high fat foods such as butter, dairy foods etc. although there are other high fat foods that are less well known, such as egg yolk or nut kernels. Fats are necessary now and again because one reclusive vitamin is generated from a fat, and more obviously because without these concentrated doses of energy it would take a lot longer to eat all the food you need, as with cows or elephants.

Proteins:

One of the most misunderstood types of food in the West is protein. Traditionally thought of as something essential, and the more the better, the truth is that for adults very little is needed each day and bodies in the West work very hard to convert unnecessary protein into urea so that it can be flushed away.

Protein is used to build and repair bodies, so children need plenty of it, as do adults recovering from injury. Otherwise, the amount of protein needed each day is small – maybe a small egg's worth. Other than that, protein cannot be readily used for energy, and the body doesn't bother converting it unless it is heading for a state of starvation. Those people on a red meat diet are using very little of the protein it contains, relying on the fat content which can be up to 45 per cent.

When you are wondering where protein appears in your food, bear in mind that protein is for growth, so young mammals have protein-packed milk, unhatched chicks have their own supply in the meat of an egg and to help trees off to a good start there is a healthy package of protein in nuts. Even the humble grain of wheat has a little, if it isn't processed away.

Minerals, Vitamins and Salts:
All of these are essential for all round health and fitness. Most of them can't be stored by the body and so they should be taken regularly, preferably daily. Ten days' shortage of vitamin C, for instance, and you feel run down, tired and lethargic – perhaps not knowing why.

In the normal diet, most of your minerals and vitamins come from fresh fruit and vegetables. If you feel that you may not get enough fresh food, take a course of multivitamin tablets

with you for the duration of your travels. They don't weigh very much and can save you lots of trouble. If you are getting your vitamins and minerals from fresh foods, remember that they are usually tucked away just under the skin, if not in the skin itself. Polished and refined foodstuffs have lost a lot, if not all, of their vitamins, minerals and dietary fibre.

As regards salts, there is little cause for concern. It is easier to take too much than too little, and if you do err on the low side your body often tells you by craving salty foods. So don't take salt tablets. You could upset your stomach lining.

How Much

Nutritionists have a term for the amount of food energy needed to keep a body ticking over – the basal metabolic rate. Take a man and put him in a room at ideal temperature, humidity etc. and make sure he does no work at all except stay alive and he will use about 600kCal in a day. This is his basal metabolic rate.

Of course, not many people lie stock still in a room all day, but we still spend that much energy just keeping the metabolism ticking over. Add to that energy needed for working an average day and keeping warm in an average climate and the rough daily energy rate goes up to about 2500kCal. If you are going to be physically active (backpacking say) in a temperate sort of climate, your energy use will go up to around 3500kCal per day. If you do that same hard work in an extreme cold climate, your energy usage could go up to 5000kCal. To need more than this you would need to do immense amounts of work or have an incredibly fast metabolism. Sadly for women, they do not burn up nearly as much.

A little experience will tell you whether you need a little more or a little less than the average. Knowing that you are ready to plan just how much food you need to take for the number of days you are travelling.

When you come to work out amounts of various foodstuffs that make up your calorie intake for the day, books for slimmers or the health conscious are invaluable. They list not only calories, but often protein and other nutritional breakdown. Sometimes, too, the nutritional breakdown of food is given on the packet.

Eating Local Food

Canned, powdered and dried foods are usually safe to eat, provided they are made up with purified water. They are safe because they are often imported, but this does tend to make them more expensive, especially outside the major cities. Staples such as flour and cooking oils are nearly always safe.

Meat, poultry, fish and shellfish should look and smell fresh and be thoroughly cooked, though not overcooked, as soon as possible after purchasing. They should be eaten while still hot or kept continuously refrigerated after preparation. Eggs are safe enough if reasonably fresh. Milk may harbour disease-producing organisms (tuberculosis, brucellosis). The 'pasteurised' label in underdeveloped countries should not be depended upon. For safety, if not ideal taste, boil the milk before drinking. (Canned or powdered milk may generally be used without boiling for drinking or in cooking). Butter and margarine are safe unless obviously rancid. Margari-

ne's keeping qualities are better than those of butter. Cheeses, especially hard and semi-hard varieties, are normally quite safe, though soft cheeses are not so reliable.

Vegetables for cooking are safe if boiled for a short time. Do check, though, that on fruit or vegetables the skin or peel is intact. Wash them thoroughly and peel them yourself if you plan to eat them raw.

Moist or cream pastries should not be eaten unless they have been continuously refrigerated. Dry baked goods, such as bread and cakes, are usually safe even without refrigeration.

Always look for food that is as fresh as possible. If you can watch livestock being killed and cooked or any other food being prepared before you eat it, so much the better. Don't be deceived by plush surroundings and glib assurances. Often the large restaurant with its questionable standard of hygiene and practise of cooking food ahead of time is a less safe bet than the wayside vendor from whom you can take food cooked on an open fire, without giving flies or another person the chance to recontaminate it. Before preparing bought food, always wash your hands in water that has been chlorinated or otherwise purified (*for further information on how to purify water and the equipment available to do so, see page 322*).

In restaurants, the same rules apply for which foods are safe to eat. Restaurants buy their food from shops just as you would. It is wise to avoid steak tartare and other forms of raw meat in the tropics as there is risk of tapeworm. Fruit juice is safe if pressed in front of you. Protect freshly bought meat from flies and insects with a muslin cover. Meat that is just 'on the turn' can sometimes be saved by washing it in strong salty water. If this removes the glistening appearance and sickly sweet smell, the meat is probably safe to eat. Cold foods may have been left standing and are therefore a risk. Ice-cream especially is to be avoided in all underdeveloped countries. Rice and other grains and pulses will probably have preservatives added to them. These will need to be removed by thorough washing as they are indigestible.

Off The Beaten Track

There is no right menu for a camping trip, because we all have slightly different tastes in food. Besides, there is an almost endless number of menu possibilities. So, what should you pack? Here are a few points you'll want to consider when choosing the right foods: weight, bulk, cost per kg.

Obviously, waterweighted, tinned foods are out. So are most perishables, especially if you are going to be lugging your pantry on your back. You'll want only lightweight, long lasting, compact food. Some of the lightest, of course, are the freeze drieds. You can buy complete freeze dried meals that are very easily prepared, just add boiling water and wait five minutes. They have their drawbacks, however. First, they're mighty expensive. Second, even if you do like these pre-packaged offerings, and many people don't, you can get tired of them very quickly. I find that a much more exciting and economical method is to buy dehydrated foods at the supermarket and combine them to create your own imaginative dinners. Dried beans, cereals, instant potato, meat bars,

crackers, dry soup mixes, cocoa, pudding, gingerbread and instant cheesecake mixes are just a few of the possibilities. But don't forget to pack a few spices to make your creations possible.

Quantity and Palatability

Most people tend to work up a big appetite outdoors. About 0.9kg to 1.2kg of food per person per day is average. How much of which foods will make up that weight is up to you. You can guess pretty accurately about how much macaroni or cheese or how many pudding mixes you are likely to need.

Last, but not least, what do you like? If you don't care for instant butterscotch pudding or freeze dried stew, don't take it along. You'll probably like it even less after two days on the trail. And if you've never tried something before, don't take the chance. Do your experimenting first. Don't shock your digestive system with a lot of strange or different new foods. Stick as closely as possible to what you're used to in order to avoid stomach upsets and indigestion. And make sure you pack a wide enough variety of foods to ensure you won't be subjected to five oatmeal breakfasts in a row or be locked into an inflexible menu plan.

Packaging your Food

After purchasing your food, the next step is to repackage it. Except for freeze dried meals or other specially sealed foods it's a good idea to store supplies and spices in small plastic freezer bags. Just pour in your pancake mix, salt or gingerbread mix, drop an identifying label in if you want to take all the guesswork (and fun) out of it, and tie a loose knot. When in doubt use a double bag. Taking plastic into the wilderness may offend one's sensibilities but believe me, it works well. On a month long expedition into the rainy south east of Alaska, I learned just how handy these lightweight, flexible, recyclable, moisture-proof bags really are.

Preparing Great Meals

Although cooking over an open fire is great fun, many areas don't allow and can't support campfires. So don't head off without a stove. When choosing a stove (see page 388) remember that the further off the beaten track you go, the more important become size, weight and reliability. Aside from a stove, you'll also need a collapsible water container, means of water purification and a heavy bag in which to store your soot-bottomed pans. You'll also need individual eating utensils: spoon, cup and bowl will do. Also take a few recipes with you, or learn them before you leave. You can even have such luxuries as fresh baked bread if you are prepared to make the effort.

Some of the things I've learned about camp cooking – the hard way:
– cook on a low heat to avoid scorching
– taste before salting – the bouillon cubes and powdered bases often added to camp casseroles, are very salty. Don't overdo it by adding more!
– add rice, pasta etc. to boiling water to avoid sticky or slimy textures
– add freeze dried or dehydrated foods early on in your recipes to allow time for rehydration
– add powdered milk and eggs, cheese

and thickeners to recipes last when heating
– when melting snow for water, don't let the bottom of the pan go dry or it will scorch – keep packing the snow down to the bottom
– add extra water at high altitudes when boiling – water evaporates more rapidly as you gain altitude.

Cleaning Up

Soap residue can make you sick. Most seasoned campers, after one experience with 'soap sickness of the stomach' recommend using only a scouring pad and water. Boiling water can be used to sterilise and (if you have ignored the above advice) is good for removing the remains of your glued-on pasta or cheese dinners. Soak and then scrub.

Use those recyclable plastic bags to store left overs and to carry out any litter. Leave the wilderness kitchen clean – and ready for your next feat of mealtime magic!

Shopping List

Here's a sample list of lightweight, inexpensive, versatile, easily packable, mostly non-perishable foods to feed four or five people for two weeks off the beaten track.
Food in kilos:
macaroni 1.8
noodles 1.4
rice 1
spaghetti 1
pearl barley 0.5
navy beans 0.5
split peas 0.5
wheatgerm 0.25
cornmeal 1
green beans (freeze dried) 0.5

onion flakes 0.5
corn (freeze dried) 0.5
peas (freeze dried) 0.25
carrots (freeze dried) 0.25
raisins 2.25
prunes 1
apricots (dried) 0.5
apple (dried) 0.5
mixed fruit (dried) 0.5
tomato base powder 1
beef base powder 0.25
soup mixes 1.8
bacon bits (vegetable protein) 0.5
meat bars 2.25
peanut butter 2.25
peanuts 2.25
sunflower seeds 0.5
walnuts 1
coconut 0.25
popcorn 0.25
margarine 4.5
powdered eggs 0.5
powdered milk 2.25
hard cheddar cheese 4.5
crackers (cheese or plain) 2.25
brown sugar 3.6
cocoa 2.25
honey2.25
tea 0.25
instant coffee 0.5
fruit drink crystals 2.25
jelly mix 0.5
pudding mix 0.5
gingerbread mix 0.75
instant cheesecake mix 0.5
chocolate slabs or drops 1

Spices in grams:
salt 450
pepper 60
oregano 30
onion powder 30
garlic powder 30
curry powder 15
chilli powder 15
dry mustard 15

basil 7
cinnamon 100
ginger 7
nutmeg 7
baking powder 100
baking soda 60
vanilla 60
yeast 7

Total Weight (approx) 52kg or between 10.4kg to 13kg per person to last two weeks.

This list is a suggestion. If you choose to use it, be sure to tailor it to your tastes. In other words, if you want powdered scrambled eggs and bacon bits for breakfast every morning, you're going to need more of both. And less oatmeal

Emergency Rations

These are an important part of any expedition, whether you are on a day walk into the hills or driving a Land Rover across the desert. These extra provisions, taken over and above day to day meals, mean that should you be unfortunate enough to be stranded or misplaced for a day or so, you are carrying enough sustenance to keep you alive and alert for long enough to do something about it.

If you are travelling on foot, you won't want to take much, one or two days' supply at the most. Anything more and the extra weight is more likely to get you into trouble than keep you out of it. The food should be balanced nutritionally, but consist mainly of easily transformed energy such as carbohydrates and sugars. The sugars give you a quick boost and the carbohydrates keep you going for a few hours at a time. Some fats should be included, but not much. Package them into units for 24 hours, each weighing around fourteen ounces, containing about 1500kCal, in a watertight, airtight container. That way they can sit in your pack and go unnoticed until needed. As for what you put in your emergency rations, it is as well to remember that the benefits are as much psychological as physical. Because of this, you should always pack food that you like. Your favourite ever chocolate bar, along with a cup of hot tea to warm you will do wonders for your morale. And there lies another good reason for packing such rations into a separate container. They should be so good to eat that they wouldn't last until the emergency unless they were out of sight and out of mind.

One of the commonest problems regarding emergency rations is water. In the desert water is scarce; at sea water is plentiful, but undrinkable. In the Arctic/Antarctic, suprisingly enough, water can be a problem too. The water is either not there at all or is in a frozen form that requires fuel to make the transformation to liquid sustenance. In the latter instance it is not advisable to run out of fuel – it means that you run out of water and food at the same time since the rations you will have for such an environment will undoubtedly be dehydrated.

Lifeboat rations are worth looking at for emergencies. Designed for use at sea they are lightweight and compact and require little water. In fact they can be eaten raw if needs must. They are made up of sugar and carbohydrate, bound together by fats, so the food content is very balanced. Military 'rat packs' are another solution, each containing sufficient sustenance for 24 hours.

Personal Freight and Unaccompanied Baggage

by Paul Melly

Few people bother to think about baggage. Until, that is, they find they are that annoying person at the front of the airport check-in queue, searching for a credit card to pay the extortionate bill for bringing home an extra suitcase on the same plane.

The alternative – shipping separately – is often disregarded, or looked upon as the sort of thing that people did in the days when Britain had an empire, conjuring up images of gigantic Victorian trunks, or battered teachests creaking home from the Far East in the hold of a mail steamer.

But it's actually worth checking up. With just a little planning, you can save a fair sum of money at the cost of relatively little, if any, delay by sending your surplus bags as freight.

The alternative is to pay the full whack for excess baggage, and make your personal contribution to airline profits. This is such a good earner it is given a separate entry in the multimillion dollar revenue graph of one Middle Eastern carrier's annual report.

Costly Limits

The reason excess baggage charges are so high is the strict limit on how much weight an airliner can carry. There is a premium on the limited reserve space.

So, if you significantly exceed your individual quota as a passenger, and want to take that extra bag on the same flight, you must pay dearly for the privilege.

Of course, it then comes up on the luggage carousel with everything else at the end of your journey, which is more convenient, but it is also very much more expensive than sending it unaccompanied by air, sea, road or rail. And with advance planning, you can arrange for items sent separately to be waiting for you on arrival.

For those caught unawares, one UK operator, the London Baggage Company, has actually set up an office near Victoria, the station which houses the central London check-in terminal for many of the airlines using Gatwick. The firm is also present at Gatwick, while Turner's Air Agency, which pioneered the business in the late '60s, is in London's West End, a few minutes' taxi or tube ride from most main airline offices.

Of course, freight services are not only useful for those who have too much travel baggage. If you're going to work abroad, take an extended holiday, embark on a specialist scientific expedition, or even a business trip, you may well have equipment or samples to take. And if you have just finished or are about to start a course of academic or vocational study there could be a hefty pile of books for which your normal baggage allowance is totally inadequate.

The More You Send...

However, although one, two, three or even half a dozen cases may seem a lot to you, for a specialist freight forwarder, airline or shipping company, handling hundreds of tonnes, it is peanuts.

Generally, in the cargo business, the more you send, the cheaper the price by weight – above a basic minimum which, unless you are sending small, expensive items express, can be more than most private individuals want to send. You can of course send less than the minimum, but you still have to pay that standard bottom rate, because most freight companies are in business to cater for the needs of industry, not personal customers.

When industry does not come up with the traffic, however, they can be glad to get what private business is around. The depressed oil market in 1986 led to an economic slowdown in the Gulf and a consequent slump in export cargo to the region, but airline freight bookings out of Bahrain, Abu Dhabi and Dubai were bolstered by expatriate workers sending home their goods and chattels as their contracts expired and were not renewed.

However, there are specialist outfits catering for the private individual using their bulk buying power to get cheap rates which are then passed on to customers. They can also help with technical problems; how to pack, what you cannot send, insurance, and so on.

Sending by Sea

Seafreight is little used these days, except for shipments between Europe and Australia or New Zealand, where the great distances involved make it a lot cheaper than air. It might cost £143 to send a 30 kgs suitcase from London to Sydney by plane, and just £43 by ship. The difference in time is between seven weeks (sea) and perhaps seven to ten days (air). Air takes longer than one might expect because of red tape, the time needed to clear Customs and the wait until the freight company has a bulk shipment going out.

The London Baggage Company reports that nearly all its seafreight bookings are for Australasia, with most of the remainder for New York or California. On these routes, there is enough business for freighting firms to arrange regular shipments of personal cargo, but when it comes to the Third World, traffic is so limited that the price is higher and it is often just as cheap – and more secure – to use air.

Seafreight is charged by volume rather than weight, and is therefore particularly suitable for books or heavy household items. The goods can be held in the UK and then shipped out to coincide with your expected date of arrival in, for example, Melbourne or Auckland.

If you want to send stuff straight-away, you should remember it will wait an average of seven days before actually leaving – freight forwarders book a whole container and only send it when there is enough cargo to fill it.

Shipping on some routes is regarded as high risk so insurance premiums come up too, further reducing any price differential from airfreight.

Road and Rail

Within Europe, rail is a useful option, especially for Italy. There is only limited and relatively expensive airfreight capacity from London to Milan and Rome. A rail shipment to Naples from the UK may take six to eight days and one agent quotes a price of £120-140 for a 30 kgs case, but cheaper rates can probably be found. Rail freight is measured by weight.

It has the added advantage that most stations are in the city centre so you can avoid the tiresome trek out to an airport cargo centre to collect your bags. Of course, it may well be cheaper to travel by train yourself and pay porters at each end to help you carry the cases, than to spend hundreds of pounds having items sent separately while you fly. There is normally no official limit on what baggage you are allowed to take free with you on a train.

Trucking is also an option for continental travellers. There is a huge range of haulage services and some carriers do take baggage. But prices are often comparable to airfreight and journey times are probably a day or two slower. Door-to-door road service from London to Milan in a guaranteed 48 hours (or your money back) costs £90 for a 25 kgs case at one operator.

European airfreight is a highly competitive business and can actually be cheaper than trucking if you measure size and weight carefully. There are direct routes to most destinations and delivery can normally be guaranteed the next day. However, the short distances involved mean that rail and road operators can often compete on timing as, although most flights last only a couple of hours, or less, many hours can be used up waiting for a consolidation (bulk air shipment) or, at the end of the trip, for Customs clearance. Express services, operated by the airlines themselves or specialist companies, are growing rapidly, but they are expensive and only worthwhile for high value items or those of commercial value such as scientific equipment, computer disks, spare parts or industrial samples. Normally these will offer a guaranteed or least guideline transit time.

Whatever your method of shipping there are some practical problems to be warned of. For example, the Spanish and Portuguese Customs can be finicky if items are sent by truck and you may find yourself paying duty on some goods when they arrive although you had been told you would not have to.

Into Remoter Regions

More surprising is the ease of getting stuff to quite remote, long-haul destinations.

The key question is: how far is your final delivery point from the nearest international airport? Normally you, or someone representing you, will need to collect the bags at the place where they clear Customs and it is often impossible to arrange local onward shipment, at least under the umbrella of the baggage service in your home country. Delivery can sometimes be arranged within the city catchment area of the airport, but that rarely extends to more than 20 or 30 kms away. From Europe, it is also often difficult to get detailed information about onward transport services in the Third World, by air, train, truck or even mule.

One option is to go to a specialist freight forwarder who has detailed knowledge of a particular region of the world and is competent to arrange for local distribution. However, as a personal customer providing a relatively small amount of business, you may not be able to get an attractive price and it could prove cheaper in the end to collect the bags from the airport yourself. There do not have to be direct flights from London, as long as your cargo can be routed to arrive in a country at the right city and pass Customs there.

You can take the bags into a country yourself across the land border, but you may face more complication taking five suitcases alone through a small rural frontier post than if they arrive at the main airport under the aegis of an established freight company. Customs regulations are complex and it is vital that the status of research equipment or commercial samples is checked on arrival with Customs by the freight group's local agent.

There is no firm rule as to which places are most difficult to reach but perhaps the complications are greatest when you want to ship to a remote corner of a large Third World country and you may well find the only reliable option is to collect the bags from the capital yourself. Life is not even always easy in places which are regarded as being 'developed' – the US is changing its certificate regulations and when a consignment of carpets arrived in Memphis recently, Customs officers wanted to check whether it had been treated for bugs.

Shipping to small island destinations, such as Fiji, Norfolk Island or the Maldives can be fairly routine, but there are also good services to some places with a particularly tough reputation. London Baggage Comapny specialises in Nigeria using the freight forwarder IML and British Caledonian. If bags are delivered to the firm's Victoria office by early afternoon, it is rare that they will have to wait more than 24 hours for a flight.

Cut-price Gateways

Because of the volume of traffic, prices

are quite low: £23 fixed service charge plus £1.49 per kilo. Accra is also popular and therefore attractively priced and you can save a lot on the direct flight rates to other West African cities if you are prepared to have your freight flown via either there or Lagos. For example, direct to Abidjan in Côte d'Ivoire might cost £3-4 per kilo but you can probably save £1 on that if you take the routing through Ghana or Nigeria.

Similar pricing patterns can be found for other regions of the world. Beirut used to be the hub of Middle East traffic but because of the fighting there, and the on/off closure of the airport that role has now been taken over by Dubai, Bahrain, Athens and Cyprus, so prices to these points are lower than those for other cities which do not have such a good range of flights from Europe. Another factor which helps to bring prices down for the Gulf is its role as a stopover point for flights to the Far East. Dubai is probably the most heavily served centre and it might cost £100 to send a 30 kgs case there, while a shipment to Doha – which is actually half an hour's flying time nearer Europe – would be priced £25-30 higher because it is not an important travel hub or stopover city.

Substantial savings can be achieved if you ship via Cairo to the Middle East or Africa, but the airport is notorious for luggage 'going missing'. On the other hand, if you are insured, the goods are easily replaceable and if you needed to keep costs down you might decide the risk was worthwhile.

Miami is another high risk airport but it does have excellent connections throughout Latin America and can offer competitive prices. Theft is a common problem, or there can be serious delays, sometimes caused by the police searching for drugs. But, as with Cairo, Lagos and Accra, if you don't mind waiting and take the precaution of insurance, there are big savings to be made. Other more important reliable hub centres for South America are Rio de Janeiro, Montevideo (for Argentina while direct flights from the UK remain suspended), Sao Paulo and – in Europe – Paris and Lisbon.

Johannesburg has been the principal hub for southern Africa, including the black 'front line' states, but of course, any ban on direct flights from Europe as part of the campaign to end apartheid would change that situation. There are alternative direct flights to, for example, Lusaka, but prices to ship on these are currently usually higher.

Pricing in general has two elements: a standard service charge, usually in the £15-30 range, which covers documentation, handling and administration by the shipping agent, and a freight charge per kilo which varies according to the airline, destination and the particular bulk shipment deal the agent has been able to negotiate. Storage can be arranged, and also collection within their catchment area. Outside this radius, you will probably have to use a domestic rail or road parcels service, rather than asking the agent to arrange a special collection, although a few larger companies do have regional offices.

Do's and Don't's

There are a number of important practical tips to bear in mind. A highly individual distinguishing mark on the case or carton will make it easier for you to pick out when you go to collect it from a busy warehouse or office. It is also important to mark it with your address and telephone number in the destination country so the receiving agent there can let you know when it's arrived.

If you must send really fragile items, pack them in the middle of a case and tell the freighting office. Many have full packaging facilities and will certainly let you know if they think a bag should be more securely wrapped – for some destinations they cover boxes with adhesive banding tape so that anyone can see if it has been tampered with. You should not overload a case and you should watch out for flimsy wheels or handles that could easily be broken off. The agent's packers can provide proper crates if needed. Proper packing is vital – especially if you plan to ship the luggage by road. In many countries the wet season turns cart-tracks into swamps. Expeditions or development aid teams will often have to ship into remote areas with poor roads.

If you are moving abroad, do try and differentiate between household items and personal effects such as clothing or toiletry. The latter are covered by a quite strict legal definition for regulations. You may find it best to send heavy household items separately by sea.

If you have something awkwardly shaped to send, like a bicycle, the agent is probably much more experienced in packing it safely than you will be. He also knows what the airline rules are: some carriers will not accept goods unless they are 'properly' packed and that can sometimes mean banding with sticky tape, on Iran Air for example.

Insurance is essential. You may find you are covered by your own travel or company policy but the agents can also provide cover specially designed for unaccompanied personal freight. Without insurance, you are only protected against provable failure by the freighting company you booked the shipment with, and only in accordance with the strict limits of their trading terms and conditions.

As with normal airline baggage, there are certain items you cannot put in the hold of a plane. This is an extraordinarily hotch-potch list, but here are some of the main banned items: matches, magnetised material, poison weedkiller, flammable liquids, camping gas cylinders, most aerosols, car batteries, glue or paint-stripper. For shipment by sea or land there are also strict restrictions on dangerous goods, which have to be packed specially.

If you buy things in the UK for immediate shipment abroad, you are entitled to claim back the Value Added Tax (15 per cent) paid on the purchase. Turners have a special scheme which allows you to have the goods sent straight to them certified for export and thus reclaim the tax more quickly. Several other countries operate similar schemes which are worth checking out.

One key point to watch is payment. Special vouchers called Miscellaneous Charges Orders (MCOs), available from airlines, can be used at the traveller's convenience to pay for freight. But these are made out for that particular airline and can only be used on another if specially endorsed by the airline which issued them. They can be used with some freight companies, but they could restrict the agent's ability to get you the best price if, for example, he had a cheap deal arranged on a carrier competing directly with the company which sold you the MCO. Clearly the issuing airline would probably not be prepared to endorse the MCO so that you can ship on this rival.

You should particularly avoid MCOs which specify that they can only be used for 'excess baggage' because you may then be forced to pay the full excess rate that than the lower unaccompanied freight price.

And having bothered to make all the arrangements to ship your personal freight unaccompanied, and more cheaply, that would be a pity.

The prices quoted in this article are all UK-based and current at the time of going to press in 1987.

A Basic Guide to Health

Getting Organised

by Drs Peter Steele and John Frankland

The unprepared and the unwary are those for whom expeditions abroad can end in misery and expense. You are off on the trip of a lifetime. If you are a wise traveller you prepare documents, check equipment and carry spares in case of emergency. It is logical to take as much care of your health, for if this lets you down you may be throwing away a great experience and risking huge costs. At least one member of the party and preferably all would profit from a formal course in first aid as organised by the St John Ambulance or Red Cross. Much of this can be forgotten again but the basic principles are essential, as is the ability to improvise, since accidents never happen in close proximity to your first aid supplies.

Preparations

Besides your travel documents, do not forget:

1. Form E.111 (UK) or your medical insurance policy. If you are taking any medicines or drugs regularly, take an adequate supply with the dosage and *pharmacological* name marked on the bottle since proprietary names vary from country to country. If you have any current or past significant illness, get medical advice on how sensible an undertaking your trip represents. Advice on how any relapses or complications might be handled and whether any particular drugs are available for these should also be sought.

2. Personal medical information which can be imprinted on a bracelet or medallion; blood group, allergies, diabetic or steroid treatment dosage, recurring illnesses and continuous medication. This is safer than a card carried in the pocket and may be life-saving in an emergency.

3. A doctor's letter setting out any special medical problems, with translations into appropriate languages. If you are taking large amounts of medication with you, this should also be mentioned, so that it can be shown at Customs if necessary.

4. Spare spectacles and your lens prescription.

Tooth fillings tend to loosen in the cold, so a dental check-up may save agony later. If you suspect piles, seek an examination. Feet should be in good shape as much may be expected of them.

If you are not in the peak of condition, build up your fitness with regular graded activity over some months before departure and seek medical advice if this brings on any health problems.

Insurance – British Travellers

Falling ill abroad can be very expensive. The European Economic Community will allow eligible citizens of any member country to get *urgent* treatment free, or at a reduced cost, during temporary stays. Continuing treatment for a pre-existing illness, eg asthma, high blood pressure, etc. may not fall within the definition of urgent treatment and may not attract these benefits. Also, these arrangements do not apply if you are working or living in another EEC country. In these circumstances, you should write to the DHSS Overseas Branch at Newcastle-upon-Tyne NE98 1YX, seeking information on your rights to health care in another country.

Not all are eligible for urgent treatment, this being determined by your current or previous National Insurance contribution status. The self-employed and the unemployed may find themselves ineligible. The current position is that somebody who is insured as self-employed, if they *have been employed* at some time, is eligible and will continue to be so after retirement. Any person who has been self-employed for the whole of their working life is ineligible, even though every due National Insurance contribution may have been paid. Discriminatory, but true. Students also beware.

Even in some EEC countries (eg France, Belgium and Luxembourg) you will be covered for approximately 70 percent of treatment only and the remainder may be costly. You may also have to pay the full cost initially and then claim back the 70 percent share. For these reasons, travellers should consider taking out private insurance to cover the part of the cost they may have to meet themselves. See the DHSS leaflet SA.36, *How to Get Treatment in Other EEC Countries.*

Outside the EEC, some countries offer emergency care either free or for a part fee only. This concession may apply only in public hospitals and not in private clinics and it is often necessary to show your National Health Service medical card as well as your UK passport. The following countries offer reduced rate or free medical care (subject to certain provisos) for UK citizens: Austria, Bulgaria, Channel Islands, Czechoslovakia, Finland, East Germany, Hungary, Malta, New Zealand, Norway, Poland, Portugal, Romania, Sweden, USSR and Yugoslavia.

To get full details, obtain leaflet SA.28/30, *Medical Treatment During Visits Abroad* at your local DHSS office. If you are then travelling through EEC countries, complete form CM1 at the back of this leaflet and return it to your local DHSS office as soon as you know the dates of your visit, but not more than six months before you plan to leave. You will be sent form E.111 which you must then carry with your passport to be eligible for benefit in all EEC countries (except Denmark, Gibraltar, and the Irish Republic which do not require form E.111).

Elsewhere, the cost of consultation, medicines, treatment and hospital care must be paid by the patient. As this could be financially crippling, full health insurance is a wise precaution (*see Travel Insurance on page 240*). In America, if you are taken gravely ill or appreciably injured, the final medical account may seem astronomic – American doctors really earn big money.

Discuss with your travel agent the adequacy of your cover should high technology care be needed.

If you incur medical expenses, present your policy to the doctor and ask him to send the bill direct to your insurance company. Many doctors will demand cash and the level of their fees may alarm you. Keep a reserve of traveller's cheques for this purpose, insist on a receipt and the insurance company will reimburse you on return.

Do not expect the medical standards of your home country in your wanderings. Some practitioners include expensive drugs routinely for the simplest of conditions and multi-vitamin therapy, intravenous injections and the inevitable suppositories may be given unnecessarily to run up a bigger bill. Be prepared to barter diplomatically about this, to offer those drugs you are carrying for treatment if appropriate and even to shop around for medical advice.

Insurance – American Travellers

Travel protection plans offered by the travel agencies or insurance companies do not normally include sickness insurance in the States. On the other hand, domestic group or individual health policies usually cover the holder outside the United States.

Blue Cross and Blue Shield plans give some protection to travellers in the form of reimbursement on their return to the USA, although medical expenses must be met initially as they arise. Medicare does not give coverage outside the USA and its possessions, but people who are eligible for it may take advantage of a special extra programme offered by Blue Cross and Blue Shield which *does* cover them outside the country.

Travel health insurance policies do not typically cover previously existing illnesses which arose within a given prior period of time (sometimes as much as a year) nor such conditions as pregnancy, childbirth, miscarriage, abortion, nervous or mental disorders, dental treatment or cosmetic surgery.

Even with adequate health insurance, the traveller is very likely to have to pay for any treatment received abroad at the time and direct to the institution or practitioner involved. Occasionally, a foreign hospital may permit a traveller to pay on his return home. Travellers must keep receipts for presentation to the insurance company which is to reimburse them.

In some countries, American visitors are eligible for free, or reduced rate treatment. In the UK, Denmark and New Zealand, where there are free health or accident programmes, Americans are entitled to the same benefits as citizens of those countries. Elsewhere, eg in Yugoslavia, health care may be free to its citizens but not to American tourists. In the USSR, a doctor's visit is free, but patients must pay for any medication or hospital treatment. In other countries, e.g. the Netherlands, people with insufficient funds may be excused payment.

Immunisation

Immunisation can protect you from certain infectious diseases that are common in countries abroad but rare at home. Your local District Community Physician's Department (UK) or Public Health Service Office (USA) will advise you on the inoculations necessary for a particular country you may wish to visit and how to obtain them, either at a clinic or through your family doctor. Do not leave it to the last moment as a full course can take up to three months.

Immunisation is not obligatory in Europe or North America, but it is wise to be protected as follows:

1. Typhoid, paratyphoid A & B and tetanus (TABT). Two injections are given one month apart. An unpleasant reaction, with a sore arm and headache, is not uncommon, and you must avoid alcohol for 24 hours. After a wound from a dirty object or an animal bite, you should obtain a booster dose of tetanus toxoid. Full protection against tetanus is essential to anyone roughing it in the tropics where this nasty illness is more prevalent.

2. Cholera, yellow fever and smallpox. World Health Organisation certificates of vaccination against these three diseases exist and you may need to show them to gain access to certain countries. No documentary evidence of other immunisations is needed, but this does not mean they should be ignored.

In 1979, the World Health Organisation declared the world free of *smallpox* after two years had elapsed since the last reported case despite meticulous surveillance. Since then, the only need for smallpox vaccinations has been to satisfy frontier bureaucrats in a very few developing countries, who have been subject to pressures to withdraw this requirement. Officially, no one requires this anymore, but some travellers report having been asked for the certificate in the last few years.

Cholera certificates are still definitely needed to cross many frontiers. There are two injections a minimum of ten days apart. This injection can be combined with TAB (TAB Chol). The certificate is valid for six months only, so on a long journey, have the injections just before you go.

Yellow fever immunisation is needed for Central and South America and Central Africa and for travellers in other countries who have journeyed through or come from these areas. In the UK this can be given only in designated centres. Get the address from your GP, who can do all the others him/herself. A single injection is necessary. There are no reactions and the certificate is valid for a period of ten years.

If a smallpox vaccination is also needed, get the yellow fever injection first and the smallpox can be given a week later – if you do it the other way round there has to be a three-week interval between the two. Most people will have had childhood immunisation against *diphtheria, polio* and *tuberculosis* (BCG). However, these last two can be real hazards in developing countries, especially off the tourist track, so check your immunisation status and consider a poliomyelitis booster dose. Most countries do not make immunisation an entry requirement.

The polio vaccine is given by mouth. Even in parts of Europe and around the Mediterranean, polio cases are not infrequent. Protection is very well worth having, as polio can kill or paralyse and is irreversible.

Three months should be allowed for a full course of immunisation, but in an emergency, a 'crash course' of smallpox, TABT, yellow fever (and cholera) can be given in fifteen days.

(*For information on protection against malaria, see article on page 338*).

3. Infectious hepatitis (jaundice) is a

real hazard to travellers through areas without or with primitive sewage systems. Perhaps more return with this ailment than with all the exotic diseases. An injection of 750mgm of human gamma globulin gives reasonably effective passive immunity for up to six months against the commonest strain and is recommended. In the UK, this has been available free on the NHS to all at-risk travellers since 1976. If you decide to have this, leave it to the last possible minute before you leave as the effect tails off during the six month period and could leave you unprotected towards the end of your trip. Never have a gamma globulin injection in a Third World country. It is a blood-based product, and unless the blood has been carefully screened and heat treated as now happens in the UK, there is a danger that you could be infected by the AIDS virus.

Where vaccines are contra-indicated for a particular patient, this should be noted on their International Certificate and you would be wise to secure written permission to enter a country without the relevant vaccination, from its consulate.

On Your Return

On returning from a long trip most travellers will experience some euphoria and elation as family reunions occur and interested friends want to hear all about their adventures. After this, as relaxation and perhaps jet lag set in, a period of apathy, exhaustion and weariness can follow. Recognise this and allow a few quiet days if it is feasible. There are usually many pressures at this stage especially if equipment is to be unpacked and sorted out, photographs processed etc.

Another pressure, for most people, is the none too welcome thought of returning to the mundane chores involved in earning one's daily bread.

If your travels have been challenging, then a couple of recovery days will probably make you work more efficiently thereafter and cope more expeditiously with the thousand tasks which seem to need urgent attention.

After a time of excitement and adventure, some will go through a period of being restless and bored with the simple routine of home and work. They may not be aware of this temporary change in personality but their families certainly will be. Having pointed out this problem, we cannot suggest any way of overcoming it except perhaps to recommend that everyone concerned try to recognise it and be a little more tolerant than normal. This may not be a sensible time to take major decisions affecting career, family and business.

Some people will be relieved to arrive in their hygienic home after wandering in areas containing some of the world's nastiest diseases. Unfortunately, the risk of ill health is not altogether gone, for you may still be incubating an illness acquired abroad – perhaps a few months e.g. hepatitis, or at the extreme, for a few years with rabies.

After your return any medical symptoms or even just a feeling of debility or chronic ill health must not be ignored – medical help should be sought. Tell your physician carefully where you have travelled, including brief aeroplane stopovers. It may be that you are carrying some illness outside the spectrum normally considered. Sadly this has been known to cause mistaken diagnoses so that malaria has been labelled as influenza with occasionally fatal consequences. Tropical worms and other parasites, enteric fevers, typhus, histoplasmosis (a fungus disease breathed in on guano, so cavers are particularly at risk), tuberculosis, tropical virus diseases, amoebic dysentery and hepatitis may all need to be excluded and for this to be done efficiently, many patients will need the special expertise of a Tropical Diseases Unit. Some doctors may not consider this referral but if you feel appreciably ill and a clear diagnosis is not rapidly forthcoming, then it is sensible to request diplomatically that your doctor refer you to a unit with experience in tropical diseases.

Human nature being as it is, some will arrive home with venereal disease, which is much more prevalent in some developing countries than in the UK. If you have been at risk of acquiring this, a visit to the Special Clinic (VD Clinic) at any hospital is sensible. No appointment or referral from a general practitioner is necessary.

After leaving malarial areas, many will feel less motivated to continue their anti-malarial drugs. It is strongly recommended that these be taken for a minimum of 28 days (some now suggest up to eleven weeks) after leaving the endemic area. Failing to do this has caused many, much to their surprise, to develop malaria some weeks after they thought they were totally safe. This is more than a nuisance – it has occasionally caused deaths.

Fortunately the majority of travellers return home with nothing other than pleasant memories of an enjoyable interlude in their lives.

Travel Stress

by Hilary Bradt

The scene is familiar; a crowded bus station in some Third World country; passengers push and shove excitedly. An angry discordant voice rings out: 'But I've got a reserved seat! Look, it says number 18, but there's someone sitting there!' The foreigner may or may not win this battle, but ultimately, he will lose the war between 'what should be' (his expectations) and 'what is' (their culture) and become yet another victim of stress.

It is ironic that this complaint, so fashionable among businessmen, should be such a problem for many travellers who thought they had escaped such pressures when they left their home country. But by travelling rough, they are immediately immersing themselves in a different culture and thus subjecting themselves to a new set of psychological stresses.

The physical deprivations that are inherent in budget travel are not usually a problem. Most travellers adjust well enough to having a shower every two months, eating beans and rice every day and sleeping in dirty, lumpy beds in company with the local wildlife. These are part of the certainties of this mode of travel. It's the uncertainties that wear people down; the buses that double-book their seats, usually leave an hour or so late, but occasionally slip away early; the landslide that blocks the road to the coast on the one day of the month that a boat leaves for Paradise Island; the inevitable *mañana* response; the struggle with a foreign language and foreign attitudes.

Culture Shock

It's this 'foreignness' which often comes as an unexpected shock. The people are different, their customs are different, and so are their basic values and moralities. Irritatingly, these differences are most frequently exhibited by those who amble down the Third World Corridors of Power, controlling the fate of travellers. But ordinary people are different too. Believers in Universal Brotherhood often find this hard to accept, as do women travelling alone. Many travellers escape back to their own culture periodically by mixing with the upper classes of the countries in which they are travelling – people who were educated in Europe or America and are westernised in their outlook. Come to think of it, maybe this is why hitch-hikers show so few signs of travel stress – they meet wealthier car owners and can often lapse into a childlike dependence on their hosts.

Fear and Anxiety

At least hitch-hikers can alternate between blissful relaxation and sheer terror, as can other adventurous travellers. Fear, in small doses, never did anyone harm. It seems a necessary ingredient to everyday life; consciously or unconsciously, most people seek out danger. If they don't go rock climbing or parachute jumping, they drive too fast, refuse to give up smoking or resign from their safe jobs to travel the world. The stab of fear that travellers experience as they traverse a glacier, eye a gun-toting soldier or approach a 'difficult' border is followed by a feeling of exhilaration once the perceived danger has passed. A rush of adrenalin is OK. The hazard is the prolonged state of tension or stress, to which the body reacts in a variety of ways: irritability, headaches, inability to sleep at night and a continuous feeling of anxiety.

The budget traveller is particularly at risk because shortage of money provokes so many additional anxieties to the cultural stresses mentioned earlier. The day-to-day worry of running out of money is an obvious one, but there is also the fear of being robbed (no money to replace stolen items) and of becoming ill. Many travellers worry about their health anyway, but those who can't afford a doctor, let alone a stay in hospital, can become quite obsessional. Yet these are the people who travel in a manner most likely to jeopardise their health. Since their plan is often 'to travel until the money runs out', those diseases with a long incubation period, such as hepatitis, will manifest themselves during the trip. Chronic illnesses like amoebic dysentery undermine the health and well-being of many budget travellers, leaving them far more susceptible to psychological pressures. Even the open-endedness of their journey may cause anxiety.

Tranquillisers

Now I've convinced you that half the world's travellers are heading for a nervous breakdown rather than the nearest beach, let's see what can be done to ease the situation (apart from bringing more money).

There are tranquillisers. This is how most doctors treat the symptoms of stress since they assume that the problems causing the anxiety are an unavoidable part of everyday life.

Travellers should not rule them out (I've met people who consume Valium and marijuana – another effective tranquiliser – until they scarcely know who they are), but since they have chosen to be in their situation, it should be possible to eliminate some of the reasons.

They can begin by asking themselves why they decided to travel in the first place. If it was 'to get away from it all' then journeying for long distances seems a bit pointless; better to hole up in a small village or island and begin the lotus-eating life. If the motive for travel is a keen interest in natural history, archaeology or people, then the problems inherent in getting to their destination are usually overridden in the excitement of arriving. However, those who find the lets and hindrances that stand between them and their goal too nerve-wracking – and the more enthusiastic they are, the more frustrated they'll become – should consider relaxing their budget in favour of spending more money on transportation etc., even if it does mean a shorter trip.

The average overlander, however, considers the journey the object and will probably find that time on the road will gradually eliminate their anxieties. Like a young man I met in Ecuador. He was forever thinking about his money situation, but when I met him again in Bolivia, he was a changed man, relaxed and happy.

'Well,' he said, in answer to my question. 'You remember I was always worrying about running out of money? Now I have, so I have nothing to worry about!'

If a traveller can learn the language and appreciate the differences between the countries he visits and his own, he will come a long way towards understanding and finally accepting them. Then his tensions and frustrations will finally disappear.

But travellers should not expect too much of themselves. You are what you are, and a few months of travel are not going to undo the conditioning of your formative years. Know yourself, your strengths and weaknesses, and plan your trip accordingly. And if you don't know yourself at the start of a long journey, you will by the end.

Culture Shock

by Adrian Furnham

Nearly every traveller must have experienced culture shock at some time or other. Like jet lag it is one of the most negative, but difficult to define, aspects of travel. But what precisely is it? When and why does it occur? And perhaps more importantly, how can we prevent it or at least cope with it?

Although the experience of culture shock has no doubt been around for centuries, it was only 25 years ago that an anthropologist called Oberg coined the term. Others have attempted to improve upon and extend the concept and have come up with bits of jargon like culture fatigue, role shock and pervasive ambiguity but most people still talk of culture shock.

Strain

What is culture shock? From the writings of travellers and interviews with tourists, foreign students, migrants and refugees, psychologists have attempted to specify the exact nature of this unpleasant experience. It seems that the syndrome has six facets. Firstly, there is *strain* caused by the effort of making necessary psychological adaptations like speaking another language, coping with the currency, driving on the other side of the road etc. Secondly, there is often a *sense of loss* and a *feeling of deprivation* with regard to friends, possessions and status. Where nobody knows, loves, respects and confides in you, you may feel anonymous and deprived of your status and role in the society as well as bereft of familiar and useful objects. Thirdly, there is often a feeling of *rejection* – you rejecting them *and* them rejecting you. Travellers stand out by their skin, clothes, and language. Depending on the experience of the natives, they may be seen as unwanted intruders, an easy rip-off, or friends. When Londoners wear T-shirts with 'I'm not a bloody tourist – I live here' on them, a foreigner may well experience some feeling of rejection.

A fourth symptom of culture shock is *confusion*. People feel confused about their roles, their values, their feelings and sometimes about who they are. When people live by quite different moral and social codes to yourself, interacting with them for even a comparatively short period of time can be very confusing. Once one becomes more aware of cultural differences typical reactions of *surprise*, *anxiety*, even *disgust* and *indignation* occur. The way foreigners treat their animals, eat food, worship their god, or perform their toiletries often cause amazement and horror to naive travellers. Finally, culture shock often involves *feelings of impotence* due to not being able to cope with the new environment.

Little England

Observers of sojourners and long-term travellers have noted that there are two extreme reactions when coping with culture shock – there are those individuals who act as if they 'never left home' and those who immediately 'go native'. The former chauvinists create 'little Englands' or 'American ghettoes' in foreign fields, not compromising on their diet or dress and like mad dogs go out in the midday sun. The latter reject all the aspects of their original culture and enthusiastically do in Rome as the Romans do. It is usually easy to identify them as bogus.

Most people, however, experience less dramatic, but equally uncomfortable, reactions to culture shock. These may include excessive concern over drinking water, food, dishes and bedding; fits of anger over delays and other minor frustrations; excessive fear of being cheated or robbed or injured; great concern over minor pains and interruptions; and, of course, a longing to be back at the idealised home where you can get a good cup of tea and talk to sensible people.

But, as any seasoned traveller will know, one begins to get used to, and even to like the new culture. In fact writers have suggested that people go through a number of phases when living in a new culture. Oberg, in his original writings, listed four stages: a *honeymoon* stage which is characterised by enchantment, fascination, enthusiasm and admiration for the new culture and cordial, friendly but superficial relationships. In this stage people are, by and large, intrigued and euphoric. Many tourists never stay long enough to move out of this stage. The second phase heralds *crisis* and *disintegration*. It is now that the traveller feels loss, isolation, loneliness and inadequacy, and tends to become depressed and withdrawn. This happens most often after two to six months of living in the new culture.

The third stage is the most problematic and involves *reintegration*. In this phase people tend to reject the second culture and become opinionated and negative to others, partly showing their self-assertion and growing self-esteem.

The fourth stage of *autonomy* finds the traveller assured, relaxed, warm and empathic because he or she is socially and linguistically capable of negotiating most new and different social situations in the culture.

Finally the *independent* stage is reached and is characterised by trust, humour and the acceptance and enjoyment of social, psychological and cultural differences.

U-curve

For obvious reasons, this is called the U-curve hypothesis. If you plot satisfaction and adaptation (x axis) over time (y axis) you see a high point beginning, followed by a steep decline, a period at the bottom, but then a steady climb back up. More interestingly, some researchers have shown evidence not of a U-curve but a W-curve – that is, once travellers return to their home country, they often undergo a similar re-acculturation, again in the shape of a U. Hence a double U or W.

Other research has shown similar intriguing findings. Imagine, for instance, that you are going to Morocco for the first time. You are asked to describe or rate both the average Briton and the average Moroccan in terms of their humour, wealth, trustworthiness etc. both before you go and after you return. Frequently it has been found that people change their opinions of their *own* countrymen and women *more* than that of the foreigners. In other words, travel makes you look much more critically at yourself and your culture than most people think. And this self-criticism may itself be rather unhelpful.

The trouble with these stage theories is that not everyone goes through the stages. Not everyone feels like Nancy Mitford when she wrote: 'I loathe abroad, nothing would induce me to live there . . . and, as for foreigners, they are all the same and make me sick'. But I suspect Robert Morley is not far from the truth when he remarked: 'The British tourist is always happy abroad so long as the natives are waiters'.

Then there is also the shock of being visited. Anyone who lives in a popular tourist town soon becomes aware that it is not only the tourist but also the native who experiences culture shock. Of course, the amount and type of shock that tourists can impart to local people is an indication of a number of things, such as the relative proportion of tourists to natives, the duration of their stay, the comparative wealth and development of the two groups and the racial and ethnic prejudices of both groups.

Of course not everybody will experience culture shock. Older, better educated, confident and skilful adults, particularly those who speak the language, tend to adapt best. Yet there is considerable evidence that sojourners, like foreign students, voluntary workers, businessmen, diplomats and even military people become so confused and depressed that they have to be sent home at great expense to their organisations. That is why many organisations attempt to lessen culture shock by a number of training techniques. The foreign office, the British Council and many multi-nationals do this for good reason, learning from bitter experience.

Training

Information giving – by lectures, pamphlets etc – is very popular but not very useful for a number of reasons. The 'facts' that are given are often too general to have any clear, specific application in particular circumstances. Facts emphasise the exotic and ignore the mundane (i.e. how to hail a taxi). This technique also gives the impression that the culture can be learnt easily, which is misleading; and even if facts were retained they do not necessarily lead to action. After all, it would be bizarre to teach people how to drive only by giving them information on how to do it.

A second technique is called isomorphic training. The idea is that a major cause of cross-cultural communication problems is that people offer different explanations for each other's behaviour. For instance, a friend might explain their failure to pass their driving test by claiming that the examiner was unfair and there was heavy traffic. You might believe it was simply due to their lack of ability or insufficient training. This technique describes various episodes that terminate in embarrassment, misunderstanding or interpersonal hostility between people from two different cultures. The trainee is then presented with four or five alternative explanations of what went wrong, all of which correspond to different attributions of the observed behaviour. Only one is correct from the perspective of the culture being learned. This is an interesting and useful technique but depends for much of its success on the relevance of the various episodes chosen.

Perhaps the most successful method is skills training. It has been pointed out that socially inadequate or inept individuals have not mastered the social conventions of their own society. Either they are unaware of the rules and processes of everyday behaviour or, if aware of the rules, they are unable or unwilling to abide by them. They are therefore like strangers in their own land. People newly arrived in an alien culture will be in a similar position and may benefit from simple skills training.

This involves analysing everyday encounters such as buying and selling, introductions, refusing requests; observing successful culture models engaging in these acts; practising yourself while being videotaped and watching the tape. This may all sound very clinical, but can be great fun and very informative. Again, it's just like learning to drive a car . . . it does need practice. And it works, as many organisations have found out.

Funny Side

But as all travellers know, culture shock can also have its beneficial side. It can be highly motivating, lead to new learning and the development of many new skills. It can also be funny, though the consequences can be very important. Not long after the war, a journalist called Telberg noted that many clashes at the United Nations arose simply because of cultural misunderstandings.

One of the most deeply rooted, and largely unconscious, features of any culture is what psychologists call the *time perspective*. Within the United Nations, at least three quite different time perspectives operate.

'Gentlemen, it is time for lunch, we must adjourn,' announces the Anglo-Saxon chairman in the unabashed belief that having three meals a day at regular hours is the proper way for mankind to exist.

'But why? We haven't finished what we were doing,' replies an Eastern European delegate, increasingly puzzled and impatient. In his country people eat when the inclination moves them and every family follows its own individual timetable.

'Why, indeed?' enquires the Far Eastern representative who hails from a country where time and life are conceived as a continuous stream, with no man being indispensable, with no life process needing to be interrupted for any human being. Members of the electoral bodies walk in and out of the room quietly, getting a bite to eat when necessary, while meetings, theatre performances, and other arranged affairs last without interruption for hours on end. Individuals come and go, are replaced by others, mediate or participate as the occasion requires, without undue strain, stress, or nervous tension.

As one or the other group persists in its own conception of the time perspective, as the Anglo Saxons demand that the duration of meetings and conferences be fixed in advance and that meals be taken regularly at fixed hours, the Russians sit irritated and the Latins puzzled and the Secretariat frantic. As this condition continues, mutual friction grows, murmurs of 'unreasonableness' are heard around the room; and, when the issue under discussion is an important one, overt accusations are hurled across the room of 'insincerity', 'lack of serious approach to the problem', and even 'sabotage'.

I don't think we can blame all international conflict or xenophobia on cultural misunderstandings or culture shock, but it can make the problems of cross-cultural encounters all the more difficult.

Practical Advice

Many travellers, unless on business with considerable company resources behind them, do not have the time or money to go on courses that prevent or minimise culture shock. They have to leap in at the deep end and hope that they can swim. But there are some simple things that they can do that may well prevent culture shock and improve communications.

Before Departing:

It is important to learn as much about the society one is going to in order to be effective in it. Areas of great importance include:

Language – Not only vocabulary but polite usage; when to use higher and lower forms; and particularly how to say 'yes' and 'no'.

Non-Verbal Cues – Gestures, body contact, and eye gaze patterns differ significantly from one country to another and carry very important meanings. Cues of this sort for greeting, parting, and eating are most important, and are relatively easily learnt.

Social Rules – Every society develops rules that regulate behaviour so that social goals can be attained and needs satisfied. Some of the most important rules concern gifts; buying and selling; eating and drinking; time; 'bribery and nepotism' etc.

Social Relationships – Family relationships, classes and castes, and working relationships often differ from culture to culture. The different social roles of the two sexes is perhaps the most dramatic difference between societies, and travellers should pay special attention to this.

Motivation – Being assertive, extravert and achievement-oriented may be desirable in America and Western Europe but this is not the case elsewhere. How to present oneself, maintain face etc. is well worth knowing.

On Arriving

Once one arrives at one's destination, there are a few simple steps that one can take to reduce perplexity and to understand the natives.

Choose a Host National Friend – Avoid only mixing with compatriots or other foreigners. Get to know the natives who can introduce you to the subtleties and nuances of the culture.

Practical Social Activities – Don't be put off more complex social encounters but ask for information on appropriate etiquette. People are frequently happy to help and teach genuinely interested and courteous foreigners.

Avoid Good/Bad or Us/Them Comparisons – Try to establish how and why people perceive and explain the same act differently, have different expectations etc. Social behaviour has resulted from different historical and economic conditions and may be looked at from various perspectives.

Attempt Mediation – Rather than reject your or their cultural tradition, attempt to select, combine and synthesize the appropriate features of different social systems whether it is in dress, food or behaviour.

On Returning

To be a useful learning experience, the benefits of foreign travel and the prevention of the W curve may be facilitated by:

Becoming More Self-Observant – Returning home makes one realise the comparative and normative nature of one's own behaviour which was previously taken for granted. This in turn may alert one to which behaviours are culturally variant (and perhaps, why) which will be very helpful in future travel.

Helping the Foreigner – There is no better teaching aid than personal experience. That is why many foreign language schools send their teachers abroad not only to improve their language but to experience the difficulties their students have. Remembering this, we should perhaps be in a better position to help the hapless traveller who comes to our country.

Travel does broaden the mind (and frequently the behind), but it does take some effort. Preparation, it is said, prevents a pretty poor performance and travelling in different social environments is no exception. But this preparation may require social, as well as geographic, maps.

Water Purification

Julian McIntosh

Polluted water can at best lead to discomfort and mild illness, at worst to death, so the travelling layman needs to know not only what methods and products are available for water purification, but also in an emergency, how to improvise a treatment system.

Three points about advice on water treatment cause misunderstanding. Firstly, there is no need to kill or remove all the micro-organisms in water. Germs do not necessarily cause disease. Only those responsible for diseases transmitted by drinking water need be treated. And even some water-borne diseases are harmless when drunk. Legionnaires' disease, for example, is caught by breathing in droplets of water containing the bacteria and not by drinking them.

Secondly, in theory, no normal treatment method will produce infinitely safe drinking water. There is always a chance, however small, that a germ might, by virtue of small size or resistance to chemicals or heat, survive and cause disease. But the more exacting your water treatment process, the smaller the risk, until such time as the risk is so tiny as to be discounted. The skill of the experts lies in assessing when water is, in practice, safe to drink. Unfortunately different experts set their standards at different levels.

Thirdly, beware the use of words like 'pure', 'disinfect' and 'protection', common claims in many manufacturers' carefully written prose. Read the descriptions critically and you will find that most are not offering absolutely safe water but only a relative improvement.

Suspended Solids

If you put dirty water in a glass the suspended solids are the tiny particles that do not readily sink to the bottom. The resolution of the human eye is about one-hundredth of a millimetre, a particle half that size (5uM) is totally invisible to the naked eye and yet there can be over ten million such particles in a litre of water without any visible trace. Suspended solids are usually materials such as decaying vegetable matter or mud and clay. Normally mud and clay contamination is harmless, but extremely fine rock particles including mica or asbestos occasionally remain in glacier water or water running through some types of clay.

Chemical Contamination Including Taste and Odour

Most people will have experienced the taste of chlorine, the metallic taste of water from jerricans or the stale taste from water out of plastic containers. These tastes, and many others including those from stagnant water, are caused by minute quantities of chemicals that make the water unpleasant or even undrinkable but can easily be removed by charcoal or carbon filtration.

Microbiological Contamination

1) Eggs, worms, flukes, etc.

Organisms, amongst others, that lead to infections of roundworm

(Ascaris), canine roundworm *(Toxocara canis)*, guinea worm *(Dracunculus)* and bilharzia *(Schistosomiasis)*. They are relatively large, although still microscopic, and can be removed by even crude forms of filtration.

The very tiny black things that you sometimes see wriggling in very still water are insect larvae, not germs, and are not harmful. Practically any form of pre-treatment will remove them.

2) Protozoa

In this group of small, single-celled animals are the organisms that cause Giardiasis *(Giardia lamblia)*, an unpleasant form of chronic diarrhoea, and amoebic dysentery *(Entamoeba histolytica)*. Both of these protozoa have a cyst stage in their life cycle, during which they are inert and resistant to some forms of chemical treatment. However, they quickly become active and develop when they encounter suitable conditions such as the human digestive tract. They are sufficiently large to be separable from the water by the careful use of some types of pre-filter.

3) Bacteria

Very small, single-celled organisms responsible for many illnesses from cholera, salmonella, typhoid and bacillary dysentery, to the many less serious forms of diarrhoea known to travellers as Montezuma's Revenge or Delhi Belly. A typical healthy person would need to drink thousands of a particular bacterium to catch the disease. Luckily, the harmful bacteria transmitted by drinking contaminated water are fairly 'soft' and succumb to chemical treatment as their minute size means only a very few filters can be relied upon to remove them all.

4) Viruses

These exceptionally small organisms live and multiply within host cells. Some viruses such as Hepatitis A and a variety of intestinal infections are transmitted through drinking water. Even the finest filters are too coarse to retain viruses. The polio and hepatitis viruses are about 50 times smaller than the pore size in even the finest ceramic filter.

Selection of a Water Supply

Whatever method of water treatment you use it is essential to start with the best possible supply of water. Learning to assess the potential suitability of a water supply is one of the traveller's most useful skills.

Good points:
– Ground water, eg wells, boreholes, springs
– Water away from or upstream of human habitation
– Quickly running water
– Water above a sand or rock bed
– Clear, colourless and odourless water

Bad points:
– Water close to sources of industrial, human or animal contamination
– Stagnant water
– Water containing decaying vegetation
– Water with odour or a scum on its surface
– Discoloured or muddy water

Wells and boreholes can be contaminated by debris and excreta falling or being washed in from the surface, so the top should be protected. A narrow wall will stop debris. A broad wall is not so effective as people will stand on it and dirt from their feet can fall in. Any wall is better than no wall at all.

Quickly running water is a hostile

environment for the snails that support bilharzia.

Pre-treatment

If you are using water from a river, pool or lake, try to not to draw in extra dirt from the bottom or floating debris from the surface. If the source is surface water such as a lake or river and very poor, some benefit may even be gained by digging a hole adjacent to the source. As the water seeps through, a form of pre-filtration will take place, leaving behind at least the coarsest contamination.

Pouring the water through finely woven fabrics will also remove some of the larger contamination. If you have fine, clean sand available, perhaps taken from a stream or lake bed, an improvised sand filter can be made using a tin can or similar container with a hole in the bottom. Even a sock will do. Pour the water into the top, over the sand. Take care to disturb the surface of the sand as little as possible. Collect the water that has drained through the sand. The longer the filter is used the better the quality of the water will become so re-filter or discard the first water through. Discard the contaminated sand after use.

If you are able to store the water without disturbing it, you could also try sedimentation. Much of the dirt in water will settle out if left over a long enough period. Bilharzia flukes die after about 48 hours. The cleaner water can then be drawn off at the top. Very great care will be needed not to disturb the dirt at the bottom. Siphoning is the best method.

If the water you are using has an unpleasant taste or smell, an improvement can be achieved by using coarsely crushed wood charcoal wrapped in cloth. When the 'bag' of charcoal is placed in the water or the water is run through the charcoal (like a sand filter) the organic chemicals responsible for practically all the unpleasant tastes and smells will be removed. Some colour improvement may also be noticed.

The water will still not be safe to drink without further treatment but you should notice some benefit.

Treatment of a Water Supply

Boiling:

Boiling at 100°C kills all the harmful organisms found in water except a few such as slow viruses and spores which are not dangerous if drunk. As your altitude above sea level increases however, the weight of the atmosphere above you decreases, the air pressure drops, as does the temperature at which water boils. A rule of thumb method for calculating this is that water boils at 1°C less for every 300 metres of altitude. Thus if you are on the summit of Kilimanjaro, at 5,895m, the water will boil at only 80°C.

At temperatures below 100°C most organisms can still be killed but it takes longer. At temperatures below 70°C some of the harmful organisms can survive indefinitely and as the temperature continues to drop, they will even flourish.

There is one more important consideration. When water is boiling vigorously there is a lot of turbulence and all the water is at the same temperature. While water is coming to the boil, even if bubbles are rising, there is not only a marked and important difference between the temperature of the water and the temperature at a full boil but there can also be a substantial difference in temperature between water in different parts of the pan with the result that harmful organisms may still be surviving.

To make water safe for drinking you should bring water to a full boil for at least two minutes. Boil water for one minute extra for every 300 metres above sea level. Do not cool water down with untreated water.

Filtration:

The keys to understanding the usefulness of a filter are:

a) how small are the particles that the filter will reliably separate and

b) what dirt load can the filter take before it clogs up. If the pores in the filter are too large harmful particles can pass through. If small enough to stop harmful particles, the pores can block up quickly, preventing any more water from being filtered.

To reduce this problem, manufacturers employ ingenious means to increase the filter area, and filter in progressively smaller stages. But even in one apparently clean litre of water there can be a hundred thousand million particles the same size or larger than bacteria. And to stop a bacterium the filter has to take out all the other particles as well. If the filter is small, of the drinking straw type for instance, or if the water is at all visibly dirty the filter will block in next to no time.

There are three solutions: water can be filtered first through a coarse filter to remove most of the dirt, and then again through a fine filter to remove the harmful bacteria; a re-cleanable filter can be used; or finally, only apparently clean water could be used with the filter. The use of a coarser filter is called pre-filtration.

Viruses are so small they cannot be filtered out of drinking water by normal means. However because they are normally found with their host infected cells and these are large enough to be filtered, the finest filters are also able to reduce the risk of virus infection from drinking water.

A filter collects quite a lot of miscellaneous debris on its surface and in order to prevent this providing a breeding ground for bacteria the filter needs to be sterilised from time to time. Some are self-sterilising and need no action but others should be boiled for 20-30 minutes at least once every two weeks. Where filters are described as combining a chemical treatment, this is for self-sterilisation. The chemical is in such small concentrations and in contact with water passing through the filter for such a short period that its use to improve the quality of the filtered water is negligible.

1) Pre-filtration

Pre-filters should remove particles larger than 5uM-10uM in size and be very simple to maintain. They will be more resistant to clogging since they take out only the larger particles. They will remove larger microbiological contamination including protozoal cysts, flukes and larger debris that might form a refuge for bacteria and viruses. Pre-filtration is normally adequate for washing. Further treatment is essential for safe drinking supplies.

2) Fine filtration

To remove all harmful bacteria from water a filter must remove all particles larger than 0.5uM (some harmless bacteria are as small as 0.2uM). Filters using a disposable cartridge are generally more compact and have high initial flow rates but are more expensive to operate. Alternatively there are ceramic filters that use porous ceramic 'candles'. These have low flow rates and are fairly heavy. Some need special care in transport to ensure they do not get cracked or chipped enabling untreated water to get through. Ceramic filters can be cleaned easily and are very economic in use.

3) Activated carbon/charcoal filters
Carbon filters remove a very wide range of chemicals from water including chlorine and iodine and can greatly improve the quality and palatability of water. But they do not kill or remove germs and may even provide an ideal breeding ground unless self-sterilising. Some filters combine carbon with other elements to make a filter that improves the taste as well as removing harmful organisms.

Chemical Treatment

There are broadly three germicidal chemicals used for drinking water treatment. For ease of use, efficiency and storage life the active chemical is usually made up as a tablet suitable for a fixed volume of water, although the heavier the contamination, the larger the dose required. Germs can also be embedded in other matter and protected from the effects of a chemical, so where water is visibly dirty you must pre-filter first. Chlorine and iodine have no lasting germicidal effect so on no account should untreated water be added to water already treated.

1) Silver
Completely harmless, taste free and very long lasting effect, protecting stored water for up to six months. The sterilisation process is quite slow and it is necessary to leave water for at least two hours before use. Silver compounds are not effective against cysts

of Amoeba and Giardia and so use pre-filtration first if water is poor quality.

2) Chlorine
Completely harmless, fast acting and 100 per cent effective if used correctly. A minimum of ten minutes is required before water can be used. The cysts of Amoeba and Giardia are about ten times more resistant to chlorine than bacteria but both are killed if treatment time and dose are adequate. If in doubt, we recommend that the period before use be extended to at least 20 and preferably 30 minutes. If heavy contamination is suspected, double the dosage. Alternatively, pre-filter. Some people find the taste of chlorine unpleasant particularly if larger doses are being used. The concentration of chlorine drops quickly over several hours and more so in warm temperatures so there is very little lasting effect. Excess chlorine may be removed by using Sodium Thiosulphate or a carbon filter.

3) Iodine
Fast acting and very effective, normally taking ten minutes before water is safe to use. It has a quicker action against cysts than chlorine. Double dosage and extended treatment times or pre-filtration are still very strongly recommended if heavy contamination is suspected. Iodine is more volatile than chlorine and the lasting effect is negligible. Excess iodine may be removed by Sodium Thiosulphate or a carbon filter.

Note: Iodine can have serious, lasting physiological side effects and should not be used over an extended period. Groups particularly at risk are those with thyroid problems and the unborn foetuses of pregnant women. Thyroid problems may only become apparent when the gland is faced with excess iodine, so in the unlikely event of the use of iodine compounds being unavoidable, ask your doctor to arrange for a thyroid test beforehand or use a good carbon filter to remove excess iodine from the water.

Rules

Order of treatment:
If chemical treatment and filtration are being combined, filter first. Filtration removes organic matter which would absorb the chemical and make it less effective. If of a carbon type, the filter will also absorb the chemical leaving none for residual treatment. In some cases, the filter may also be a source of contamination. If water is being stored prior to treatment then it is worthwhile treating chemically as soon as the water is collected and again after filtration. The first chemical dose prevents algae growing in the stored water.

Storage of water:
Use separate containers for treated and untreated water, mark them accordingly and don't mix them up. If you are unable to use separate containers take particular care to sterilise the area round the filler and cap before treated water is stored or at the time treatment takes place. Containers for untreated water should be sterilised every two to three weeks in any case.

Treated water should never be contaminated with any untreated water.

Treated water should never be stored in an open container.

Treated water left uncovered and not used straight away should be regarded as suspect and re-treated.

Sun and Snow: Illness and the Elements

by Drs Peter Steele and John Frankland

For travellers from temperate countries, one of the greatest problems they have to face while abroad is the dramatic difference in climatic conditions. No matter how often you tell yourself it is going to be hot, nothing can prepare you for the way it will hit you in the Sahara or the equatorial jungle.

Sun

The sun can be a stealthy enemy. Sunlight reflects strongly off snow and light coloured rocks; its rays penetrate hazy cloud and are more powerful the higher you climb. Until you have a good tan, protect yourself with clothing and a hat. An ultraviolet barrier cream screens the skin, but with excessive sun it merely acts as fat in the frying process. Rationing sunlight is cheaper and more effective.

If you are planning to travel in hot weather, train for it by exercising in the heat beforehand and/or spending a few sessions in a sauna bath. This way your body will learn to perspire at lower temperatures and the network of capillaries in the skin will increase so that more blood can travel to the skin. Enzymes in the body will also change, allowing you to make more physical effort while producing less heat. On the trail, stop frequently to rest, drink and eat before you need to so as to replace all the salts necessary to prevent cramps and weakness. Salt tablets, part of the White Raj in a pith helmet, are needed less than most imagine. In the tropics most people will produce almost salt-free perspiration after acclimatisation, especially if conditioning is gone through, and generous salt supplements on food will keep a satisfactory salt level in the blood. In the first week of exertion in the heat it may be reasonable to offer them, but after this it is generally not necessary. However, some will feel better if they take them and it is perhaps unfair to deny them this placebo response.

Sunburn: Calamine soothes shrimp pink, prickly-hot skin. If you turn bright lobster you are severely burnt and should obtain a steroid cream.

Heat exhaustion and heatstroke ('sunstroke'): If you develop a high temperature and feel ill after being in strong sun, cool yourself with a cold water sponging or ice packs, take ample fluid, drink slowly, and take Aspirin to lower your temperature and relieve headache. This, together with salt and rest, is the treatment for heat exhaustion, which is a fairly common condition that can occur in or out of the sun, e.g. after heavy work in shaded, but hot and humid conditions. Heat exhaustion can be due to: a) simple faints precipitated by heat, b) water loss, c) salt deprivation or d) psychological factors.

Rarely, a more serious condition occurs, mainly in elderly or ailing people. On a humid day, an overheated body may attempt to cool by a massive sweating, with little effect, for it is the evaporation of the sweat that cools, not the sweating alone. Excessive water loss will eventually cause the body's heat regulating mechanism to break down and inhibit any further sweating. The patient's temperature may rise to 40.5°C or more. Collapse from heatstroke warrants urgent medical help, as there is danger of damage to internal organs and the brain and a 25-30 per cent death rate. Meanwhile keep the patient cool, by immersion in cold water if possible or in a well-ventilated place. Try to reduce their temperature and keep it from rising again above 38°C.

Snowblindness: is caused by an ultra-violet burn on the cornea, resulting in intense pain and swelling of the eyes. It can be prevented by wearing dark glasses or goggles; horizontal slits cut in a piece of cardboard will do in an emergency. Amethocaine drops will ease the pain enough to reach help. Then put Homatropine drops and Chloromycetin ointment in the eyes and wear dark glasses or cover with eyepads and a bandage if the pain is severe.

Exposure/Exhaustion Syndrome

Hypothermia occurs when the temperature of the central core of the body falls below about 35°C owing to the combined effect of wind, wet and cold. Exhaustion and low morale worsen it. If someone behaves in an uncharacteristic manner – apathetic, stumbling, swearing, uncontrolled shivering – be on your guard. They may suddenly collapse and die.

First priorities are to stop and shelter the victim in a tent, lean-to or polythene bag and to re-warm them by skin-to-skin contact, by dressing them in dry clothing and by putting them in a sleeping bag, in close contact with someone else if possible. Then give them hot drinks, but no alcohol. If this condition does not improve, you may have to call help and evacuate them by stretcher.

Those travelling in areas where exposure is likely should read up the features and treatment of this very real hazard. (*See also Surviving in the Cold on page 428*).

High Altitude Ills

Up to 3,500m you have little to fear – no more than on an ordinary mountain walking holiday. If you are not shaping up too well, reconsider the wisdom of climbing higher, for you are entering the realm of the high, thin, cold, dry air. Slow ascent is the secret of easy acclimatisation to altitude. Breathing and heartbeat speed up; a thumping headache and nausea make you feel miserable. At night, sleep is elusive. You may notice a peculiar irregularity in the pattern of breathing (Cheyne Stokes respiration) when, for a short period, breathing appears to have stopped and then gradually increases in stepwise fashion until it eventually falls off again. The normal output of urine may be diminished and very dilute.

The unpleasant symptoms of acclimatisation usually pass off in a few days, but they may develop into Acute Mountain Sickness. This rarely starts below 4,500m so is unlikely in the Alps, but may occur in Africa, the Andes or the Himalayas.

If you begin to feel more ill than you would expect for your own degree of fitness and acclimatisation, go down quickly and stay down rather than battle on for glory – and end up under a pile of stones on the glacier. Acute Mountain Sickness can quickly develop into High Altitude Pulmonary (lung) Oedema, or Cerebral (brain) Oedema (known in the USA at HAPE – High Altitude Pulmonary Edema, and HACE – High Altitude Cerebral Edema). This is swelling due to abnormal water retention. Women are more susceptible in the days before their periods. This is a potentially lethal disease, the cause of which is not understood, but it can affect all ages, the fit and the unfit, those who have risen quickly and those who have not.

If someone suddenly feels, and looks puffy in the face, goes blue round the lips, has bubbly breathing and even pink sputum, evacuate them urgently to a lower altitude. Oxygen (if available) and a diuretic drug such as Frusemide (*Laxis*) may help to clear water from the lungs, but they are no substitute for rapid descent which has a miraculous effect. Those who have suffered once are likely to do so again and should therefore beware.

Thrombosis: Persistent deep calf tenderness and slight fever and pain – more than muscular ache – may indicate a vein thrombosis. Women on the pill are especially at risk. You should rest, preferably with the legs bandaged and elevated, and start an antibiotic. This is a serious illness, so descend and seek medical advice.

Piles, which commonly trouble people at high altitude, are probably due to raising the pressure inside the abdomen by overbreathing while carrying heavy loads. A haemorrhoidal suppository (*Anusol*) gives temporary relief.

Dry cough is eased by inhaling steam. Codeine Phosphate 15 mgm dampens it. In a bout of violent coughing, you can fracture a rib. The agony may make you think you have had a heart attack but the chances are slim.

Frostbite should not occur if you are clothed properly and take common-sense precautions. If you get very cold, rewarm the part quickly against warm flesh (someone else's if possible). *Do not* rub it or you will damage the skin and cause further wounding which may become infected. Drugs, which dilate the blood vessels (vasodilators) have no specific action against frostbite although they make you feel a warm glow inside. This can be very dangerous as you are losing heat from the rest of your body and you may be tipped into exposure.

If a foot is frozen, it is better to walk on it back to a low camp where you can rewarm it rapidly in water of 42-44°C. Thereafter the victim must be carried.

Dehydration

The sedentary dweller from a moderate climate may well find that tropical temperatures plus the need for a high work rate will cause weakness and suboptimal performance due to dehydration, despite an increased fluid intake. In deserts, in small boats and also at high altitude, dehydration can be a real risk.

Owing to immobility from any cause, particularly if fever or diarrhoea are present, the fluid intake may fall to a level where dehydration can develop. In a temperate climate, around 1500ml (2.6 pints) of fluids daily are adequate but working hard in the tropics may cause this volume of perspiration in just one and a half hours.

Dehydration is best expressed as a percentage loss of body weight, one to five percent causing thirst and vague discomfort, six to ten percent causing headache and inability to walk and ten to twenty percent, delirium leading to

coma and death. Drinking sea water or urine only causes a more rapid deterioration.

To estimate fluid requirements, assume that an average unacclimatised man working out of doors in extreme hot/wet or hot/dry conditions will drink seven to nine litres (twelve to sixteen pints) of fluids per day. 'Voluntary dehydration', symptomless initially, is common if drinking fluids are not within easy reach and palatable.

In temperate climates the average diet contains an excess of salt which is excreted in sweat and urine. Over two to three days in the tropics, adaptation reduces the amount of salt in sweat and urine to negligible levels. During the first two weeks dehydration may be accompanied by salt depletion so that supplements are of value. Generally the treatment is simply rest and an increased fluid intake until the urine volume is adequate (around one or one and a half pints a day) and visibly normal or pale in colour.

In early days of heat exposure a definite self-discipline in achieving a sufficiently high fluid intake is necessary. Those treating ill patients must watch and encourage this aspect of their treatment. The most obvious features of marked dehydration are sunken eyes and a looseness of the pinched skin. If these cannot be corrected by oral fluids a serious situation is developing and medical aid should be sought as intravenous fluids are likely to be needed.

Immersion in Water

Prolonged immersion in all but tropical waters carries a life-threatening hazard of hypothermia which is probably a bigger risk than drowning.

The amount of subcutaneous fat will affect survival time considerably but a naked man of average build will be helpless from hypothermia after 25-30 minutes in water at 5°C and one and a half to two hours in water at 15°C.

If thick clothing is worn these intervals will be increased to 40-60 minutes at 5°C and four to five hours at 15°C. Thus, if a ship is to be abandoned or a small boat is threatened, warm clothing should be donned with a waterproof outer suit if one is available. Cold can cause dilation of blood vessels in the hands and feet and thus increase heat loss so that mitts and footwear are also desirable as is protection for the head and neck.

Some flotation aid such as a lifejacket, wreckage, an upturned bucket or even air trapped in a waterproof coat should be sought. When in the water, float quietly instead of swimming. With the stress of cold water combined with a threatening situation, swimming is a normal reaction but, because of its stirring effect on the surrounding water, and despite the heat it generates, swimming will merely accelerate loss of body heat. Swim only if no flotation aid is available, if threatened by a sinking ship or if rescue by others is not possible and land is within reach. Whilst waiting for rescue, float quietly as all exercise will accelerate cooling.

Nature's Annoyances

by Drs Peter Frankland and John Steele

From flies and mosquitoes, bees, wasps, ants and hornets; from fleas, lice and bed bugs; from sea urchins and jellyfish; and from a host of other creepy-crawlies we pray deliverance. Repellent sprays and creams (usually based on Dimethylphthalate) last only a few hours but are essential for those prone to a severe reaction to insect bites. They will generally already be aware of this. Though everyone will be bitten, fierce reactions and distress will be caused only in a few. Remove any stings. Calamine cream or lotion or *Anthisan* (Mepyramine Maleate) cream will help. If distress remains, antihistamine tablets, e.g. *Piriton* (Chlorpheniramine) 4mgm three times daily, with Aspirin as a pain killing adjunct, should be used. Good hygiene is necessary to prevent large reactions to multiple bites from becoming infected. If this happens, rest, antihistamine tablets, antibiotics and clean dressings will usually effect a cure.

Anthropods: Lice, fleas and bed bugs are kept at bay by ICI Louse and Insect Powder.

Worms: Worms are common in tropical countries. They cause an itchy bottom and can often be seen in stools. Take one Peperazine (*Pripsen*) sachet.

Mosquitoes are usually only a bother at lower altitudes. A net makes sleeping more comfortable but does not guarantee protection from malaria. *(See article on Malaria on page 338).*

Chiggers are larval mites which carry scrub typhus, in eastern and southern Asia and the islands of the southern and western Pacific. Hikers in grassy areas are most likely to contract the disease, which can be cured by the use of a Tetracycline or Chloramphenicol.

Snakes: Clean the area of the bite (not by urinating on it). Try to identify the snake. If possible, kill it and take it to the hospital with you for identification. In the USA, where rattlesnakes and cottonmouth snakes prevail, sucking the wound is favoured in a victim who is well covered in fat. To prepare for this, sterilise a knife in a flame, make a cut into each fang mark about half a centimetre long and half a centimetre deep. Suck the wound, spitting out the venom, for about fifteen minutes. If more than half an hour has passed since the victim was bitten, do not suck or cut the wound, as this may do more harm than good. In South America, Africa and Asia, sucking is, in any case, useless, since cobra venom is the main hazard and this is not easily removed by suction.

Keep the victim quiet, do not move the affected part, e.g. in the case of a bite on the foot, do not allow them to walk even one step. In any case, the victim should be carried to hospital, if possible, instead of walking. Meanwhile apply a cloth of elastic bandage between the wound and the heart to slow the circulation of the venom. Loosen the bandage for a minute or two in every fifteen. Give no stimulants, e.g. alcohol, as this dilates the blood vessels and accelerates circulation of the poison, but give a sedative.

Local hospitals probably carry a serum against the bites of common local snakes. Polyvalent antivenin is available but it is expensive, difficult to get hold of and itself very hazardous because of the risk of inducing shock. If given, it should be injected, but not more than three hours after the bite and *never* unless the features of poisoning develop – despite assurances from some quarters that its use is mandatory. Watch the patient for signs of allergic shock; shivering, rapid heartbeat, and low pulse. If ice is available,

wrap it in a cloth and pack it around the affected part. In case of infection, give antibiotics. Consider also giving painkilling medication and antihistamine. If the patient survives the first 24 hours after being bitten, they will probably recover, though some deaths do occur after this interval. It is worth mentioning, however, that only 30 percent of victims of venomous snakes die.

Dogs: Rabies exists in most countries with a fortunate few exceptions such as Britain and Australia. To help limit the spread of this awful disease, abide strictly by the anti-rabies regulations and never smuggle animals home from abroad. The new human Diploid cell 'Merriaux' anti-rabies vaccine has completely superseded Duck Embryo vaccine but will probably not be available in primitive countries and may not be available in the USA either. Anyone handling bats, small mammals etc. should have this before departure. The British should cease to be dog lovers abroad and should leave well alone any animal displaying abnormal behaviour. A bite from a dog or any other mammal always warrants a doctor's advice on the prevalence of rabies in the district and the advisability of vaccination for a victim not already so protected. At the very least, an anti-tetanus booster is recommended. If at all possible, capture the animal so that it can be tested for rabies.

Wash the wound as soon as possible with soap and water and follow this with a three percent solution of hydrogen peroxide. In the absence of water or hydrogen peroxide, wash with any sterile liquid – beer, cold tea or coffee or any carbonated drink will do.

(For further information, see article on Rabies on page 342).

Scorpions: Only a few species have a severely poisonous sting. As with snakes, prevention is better than cure. Carry a stout stick to test the nature of anything you can't identify. Wear thick boots and watch where you put your feet. Before donning clothes and boots in the morning in scorpion territory, i.e. dry country, shake them out.

If bitten, the treatment is rest, analgesics, antihistamines and probably a course of antibiotics. Tarantula-type spider bites come into this category. Whip scorpions are harmless.

Leeches are most troublesome during and shortly after the monsoon in the tropics. You do not feel them bite and may only notice a bootful of blood at the end of the day. Open sandals let you see them early and insect repellent discourages them – a lighted cigarette or salt makes the leech drop off.

Wasp stings -vinegar. *Bee stings* – antihistamine ointment.

Bilharzia is widespread in many tropical areas, so avoid swimming in slow-flowing rivers and lakes where the flukes breed.

(For further information, see separate article on Bilharzia on page 336).

Poisoning: Try to make the person sick by sticking fingers down his throat. Under ideal conditions, the treatment of choice in children is syrup (not fluid extract) of ipecacuanha where there is a risk of toxicity, provided that treatment is given under medical supervision within four hours of ingestion and that the poison is not corrosive, a petroleum distillate or an antiemetic. For adults, support of vital functions should be the primary concern of those administering first aid, followed by a

stomach washout. Though giving a salt solution is no longer the preferred treatment, it will be the best available under most expedition or trip conditions.

Delhi Belly to Dysentery

by Drs Peter Steele and John Frankland

The following advice aims to help you avoid illnesses commonly met abroad, most of which you can treat yourself in the first instance. If, however, the condition doesn't improve, or even rapidly worsens after the first 24-48 hours, you should seek medical help. In some areas the most highly trained person around will be the local pharmacist who will both dispense medication and perform medical treatment. Your consulate or embassy or the nearest office of the Peace Corps will usually have a doctor. In the remotest places sponsored mission hospitals may offer an excellent and devoted service, probably with English speaking staff. When your trip is over, if you do not wish to ship home drugs and dressings, they will be more than glad to accept them.

Travel Sickness

If you suspect travel sickness could upset you, take antihistamine tablets starting one hour before the journey. All of these can make some people drowsy, so if you need to be alert, e.g. to drive, find one with which you are safe. *Piriton* (Chlorpheniramine) 4mgm three times daily is usually as good as any.

Travel sickness is caused by the conflict of messages received by the brain from the eyes, inner ear and sensors in the muscles and joints. *Stugeron*, long prescribed in maladies involving dizziness or loss of balance, has begun to emerge as a remedy for seasickness. The manufacturers, Jansen Pharmaceutical Ltd., claim that *Stugeron* (Cinnarizine) in 15mg doses, does not cause undue drowsiness.

Traveller's Diarrhoea

Gippy Tummy, Delhi Belly, Kathmandu Quickstep – traveller's diarrhoea has as many names as patent remedies. It strikes most travellers at some stage in their journey, making more trouble than all the other illnesses put together. The causes are usually untraceable but may include gluttony, change in climate and an upset in the bacteria that are normal and necessary in the bowel. Infection by disease-causing organisms carried in water and food is less common.

Much of the pleasure of travelling abroad comes from eating local food and drinking wine; it is hardly worth going all that way for beer, fish and chips. But be moderate to prevent the tummy upset that will spoil your trip. *Prevention:* Food and especially water warrant the utmost care. *(See Food on the Move on page 292 and Water Purification on page 322).*

Hygiene: Lavatories abroad are aften dirty. You may have to squat and keep your balance by holding onto the walls. Wash your hands carefully with soap as soon as possible afterwards. Take your own toilet paper as newsprint is rough and fragile. At campsites, dig a latrine hole well away from the tents and your water supply. If, in cramped surroundings, any member of a group gets diarrhoea, all the others should become more fastidious in personal hygiene, particularly with hand washing after visiting the toilet and before preparing food or eating.

Cholera: 1973 saw a worldwide epidemic, notably in parts of Italy, and cases have been reported from several Mediterranean countries recently, as well as in more obvious places. The cholera organisms come only from the human intestine and are spread by faecally contaminated water, not by direct contact or inhalation.

Raw shellfish collect the bug and so are particularly dangerous. A sudden onset of profuse watery diarrhoea in an epidemic area calls for immediate attention. Unfortunately, the immunizations against this disease are not too effective. Tourists should be particularly careful as the rapidly worsening pollution problem around major resort areas is paving the way for cholera outbreaks of epidemic proportions if precautions are not taken.

Treatment: The illness usually clears up on its own in two to three days. You may also vomit and, because a lot of body water is lost, you may feel groggy. Go to bed and drink unlimited fluids (at least half a litre an hour). Avoid eating – except dried toast and peeled, grated apple gone brown (pectin).

For the vast majority of travellers with diarrhoea, by far the most effective remedy is to take nothing at all by mouth except fluids. This will achieve a cure more rapidly than a normal diet combined with any medication in the world. Certainly an unaccustomed, probably more exotic, diet and any form of therapy are likely to mean a more prolonged period of bowel disturbance and thereby perhaps acute distress. Simply resting your disturbed alimentary tract by not giving it solid food which will be speedily evacuated is the basis of the effective cure.

Many find this advice hard to accept and particularly under expedition circumstances, sufferers may have to go on working and thus may choose to continue eating. In this case, antidiarrhoeal tablets will be of value.

Lomotil (four tabs initially and then two tabs four times daily as required) or Codeine Phosphate tablets 30mg – two tabs four times daily are required – are probably as effective and compact a medication as any.

Antibiotics, though fashionable, should not be used blindly since they kill normal bacteria, which are protective, as well as poison-producing ones. They also contribute to the development of antibiotic-resistant strains of the organisms.

Lomotil, a narcotic analogue, provides symptomatic relief only. It is not recommended for children, pregnant women, or in cases of acute bacillary dysentry or diarrhoea complicated by other symptoms e.g. the existence of gross blood or pus in the stool.

Enterovioform, once a popular remedy, is of doubtful therapeutic or prophylactic value and has even been implicated in neurological disease. At present this drug is not licensed in the USA.

An antimicrobial drug, *Vibramycin,* has shown good results in some cases but is only recommended for people who are especially susceptible or at high risk and then only for short periods, because of the difficulties encountered with antibiotics mentioned above. Incidentally, advancing age is associated with a lower incidence of traveller's diarrhoea.

Recuperation can be hastened when the time is right by appropriate fluid intake – not water or bottled sodas, which lack potassium and other vital ingredients. The WHO has recommended the following solution for rehydration in severe attacks of diarrhoea: Potassium chloride, ¼ tspn; Sodium bicarbonate, ½ tspn; Sodium chloride (table salt) ½ tspn; Glucose 2 tspn; or Sucrose 4 tspn; added to one litre or one quart of water. Or the following two solutions – less accurate, but more readily obtainable – can be made up and drunk alternately:

1. Orange or other fruit juice, 225gm; table salt, one pinch; honey or corn syrup, ½ tspn; or table sugar one tspn; and

2. Pure water, 225gm; and baking soda (sodium bicarbonate), ¼ tspn.

Other liquid should be taken freely, but preferably not milk, coffee, strong tea, cocoa or soft drinks containing caffeine.

Dysentery

If diarrhoea does not stop within 24 hours of this treatment, or if blood appears in the stools, consult a doctor as you may be suffering from dysentery. If you cannot find help, the best drug to start with is Cotrimoxazole (*Septrin, Bactrim*). Bacillary dysentery starts suddenly with acute diarrhoea, fever and malaise. Amoebic dysentery causes slimy mucus and blood and warrants laboratory investigation and treatment. Its severity builds up slowly over several days.

Indigestion

Any antacid will ease gutrot, indigestion, and perhaps a hangover. Tablets are more portable than mixtures and are just as effective. Magnesium trisilicate acts as a laxative and, as some diarrhoea often coexists, aluminium hydroxide *(Aludrox)* tablets may be more suitable. Everyone will need them on most journeys even if only to cure indiscreet eating and drinking. *Maxalon* (Metaclopramide) tablets four times daily will help suppress vomiting.

Constipation

Drink plenty and eat fruit. If this fails, take two laxative tablets.
NB: Beware the person who feels sick, has no appetite, a dirty, coated tongue and pain in the belly. If the abdomen is tender, particularly in the lower right quarter, suspect appendicitis and visit a doctor. If no doctor is available, rest the patient, give fluids only with antibiotics and pain killers. Evacuation must then be considered.

Bilharzia

by P.J. Whyte

Though improved sanitation ˜ and general hygiene measures have gone some way to eradicating bilharzia on a global basis, it still ranks as one of the most important, and least heeded diseases in the tropics and sub-tropical regions. It is particularly prevalent in North African countries, most especially in the Nile Delta, but most other African countries are affected as far south as South Africa, while different strains of a limited nature occur in many parts of the Far East and Brazil.

It is also referred to as *Schistosomiasis*, or 'blood fluke disease' because the schistosoma, which enters the blood, is a trematode worm or 'fluke'.

Infection

These parasites are dependent on aquatic snails, man and water contaminated with the faeces and urine of infected persons. Thus, wherever there are humans, there is a chance of the disease. The larvae of the worms develop in the snail and are then discharged into the fresh water. As the snails prefer a warm stagnant habitat, these are the areas of which to be particularly careful. Confident statements by the locals that their particular river is too high, too cold, or too fast-flowing should, however, be treatedØwith scepticism. Try and avoid *all* natural, untreated water in potentially infected areas. Man is usually affected when bathing, or drinking, but it is easily as common for him to be affected while simply crossing a river where there is no bridge.

The mode of entry is through the skin or, if the water is drunk, the larvae (now called cercariae) burrow through the lining of the mouth and throat. They need man to mature and the cercariae waste no time in entering the bloodstream, and then graduating to a base in the liver. Here a development process occurs, the adult parasites forming, and then migrating to attack either the bowel or the bladder.

Symptoms

While there can often be no signs of

having contracted the disease, some species of cercariae will leave an irritating rash at the point of entry through the skin. This will normally appear about 24 hours after infection and will disappear again after about 48 hours. For the disease to mature (the first eggs to form) and other symptoms to start can take 25 to 28 days with one form and anything from 50 to 80 days with the others. At this point, the sufferer may develop a general body pruritus, accompanied by a severe fever, marked by a very high temperature and annoying agitation. Where the parasitic adults form illustrates the subsequent symptoms that appear. If in the bowel, there is bloody diarrhoea, abdominal pain, anorexia, loss of weight, and a general feeling of mental apathy. The bladder presents signs of cystitis and blood in the urine. This 'haematuria' can last for several months, while in the chronic stage stones may form in the bladder.

Anaemia is common to all with such obvious blood loss, and this in turn leads to further paleness, breathlessness, palpitations and, in particular, fatigue.

Treatment

Anyone who has been in contact with natural water in the tropics would be well advised to have a diagnostic test on their return home, so that if they have contracted the disease, it can be caught and treated in the early stages. There is, as yet, no vaccine and while work continues on trying to develop one, it seems unlikely that the position will change for some time. The disease can, however, be treated with a wide range of drugs, Meridizol being the most common of them.

If the disease is allowed to progress too far before treatment, the patient can be too weak to tolerate the rigours of the drug therapy, in which case bed rest plays a major part.

Prevention

Most emphasis needs to be placed on the prevention methods necessary to combat the disease. Awareness of bilharzia's existence, and the conditions in which one is likely to catch it go a long way towards helping avoid contact. Those who do know have a duty to 'educate' others in its dangers and prevention. One should not urinate or defaecate in the vicinity of water, or bathe in fresh water channels and streams, a remark also applicable to washing clothes. All wells should be protected, and while proper sanitation would go a long way towards preventing the spread of the disease, it will be a long time before this is universal.

The vast progress that has seen massive irrigation schemes to increase crops has also increased the areas that the snails can thrive in. These intermediate hosts favour quiet streams close to living communities, but must also have plant life to survive. If the snails themselves cannot be eradicated, attempts should be made to kill off the plant life. But even private swimming pools are not exempt, particularly if the water comes from a local stream, though isolation methods greatly reduce this hazard.

The traveller may consider personal physical protection as a starting point: always wear shoes in pools and bathing streams, and cover the ankles and feet when wading through water. Try to avoid the inland waters, and to use the bridges however inconvenient they may appear. I would recommend cotton wool ear plugs if you have to submerge your head.

Unless actually filtered, all water for drinking should be boiled or treated with chlorine tablets, and products such as Dettol added to water used for bathing.

An added precaution could be to apply a barrier repellant lotion to the exposed areas of the body, except the eyes. With all these creams, the degree of protection depends on the individual, sweat loss, temperature of the water, and the potency of the creatures. Nevertheless, they can assist. If you are unfortunate enough to suffer an accidental contact, immediately rub the skin dry with clean, unaffected cloths, being extremely careful to make sure you have left no area out.

There are many who consider that the complete eradication of the snail and worms nigh-on impossible, and instead iron supplements are freely given to combat the anaemia, which is the main presenting illness. But the determined traveller must not ignore his own education or his moral duty in preventing any further spread of bilharzia.

Malaria

by Michael Colbourne

Malaria remains one of the most prevalent of tropical diseases, causing sickness and death to those living in malarious countries and posing a threat to the traveller.

Malaria is an infection caused by a parasite that develops in the red blood corpuscles which it eventually destroys, causing fever, headache and anaemia. There are two main types of malaria. The malignant *Plasmodium falciparum* is the more severe as the infected corpuscles 'stick' in the internal organs. If this occurs in the brain it may lead to coma and even death if the infection is not treated. Falciparum malaria is commoner where the temperature is high; untreated it may last for up to two years.

The second type is 'benign' *(vivax)* malaria which causes the same headache, fever and anaemia but rarely the life-threatening complications associated with falciparum malaria. Vivax malaria has a greater tendency to relapse, even after treatment and attacks may occur up to four years after the original infection. It is common in tropical countries, except in West and Central Africa, but its distribution is wider both to the north and the south than that of falciparum malaria. In the summer it is found in many non-tropical areas. Before it was eliminated after the Second World War, it was common in many parts of Europe.

Infection

The way malaria passes from person to person is peculiar. Most of the organisms which cause infection, such as influenza or tuberculosis, pass from person to person through the air. Malaria is transmitted by the bite of a female mosquito. Mosquitoes, when they bite someone suffering from malaria, may suck up blood containing malaria parasites which develop within the mosquito. After about ten days, the mosquito may pass on the parasites to her next victim. The parasite will only develop in certain species of anopheline mosquitoes; in any other species, the parasite will die within the mosquito.

Most people know there is a connection between mosquitoes and malaria. Not so many know that the mosquito merely transfers the disease carrying malaria parasites from one person to another. The anopheline mosquito responsible usually comes unobtrusively in the night; the common 'nuisance' mosquitoes are seldom malaria carriers. Exact knowledge of the habits of these mosquitoes helps us understand and control the disease, but it is the malaria parasite that causes the disease and is our more immediate enemy.

Distribution

It is generally known that malaria is commoner in tropical countries (see map on page 340) but there is less understanding of the widely different risk of getting malaria in different places. The risk can be measured by considering the chance of being bitten by a mosquito carrying malaria parasites. In the lightly stippled areas on the map, the chance is less than 1:2,000 per year of exposure; in the more heavily shaded areas, it varies from this low risk to more than 100 infected bites a year. The very dangerous areas are tropical Africa and coastal New Guinea. This variation means that for many travellers, taking preventive measures is a sensible precaution like wearing a seat belt. For those visiting really dangerous places, neglect of these precautions is like crossing a busy road with your eyes shut. You may 'make it' once or twice, but it will not be long before you succumb – and the malaria found in trop-

ical Africa is usually the more malignant type that is often fatal.

These facts are important, otherwise people who have avoided malaria without taking precaution in areas with little malaria, such as Morocco, will think they will be equally safe if they take their family on a holiday to the Kenya coast and neglect to protect themselves.

Another misconception is that malaria was practically eliminated from the world in the '60s. Some people think that after its virtual elimination, it is back again and even worse than before. There is some truth in these views, but the position is rather more complicated. Many countries that were originally malarious are now free of the disease – usually, but not entirely, the more temperate areas – Europe, North America, Australia, much of North-East Asia; but also most of the Caribbean Islands, Taiwan, Hong Kong and Singapore are free of the disease. Good progress is still being made in South America, in parts of the Middle East and in some countries in Asia.

Protection

In the most malarious areas, especially tropical Africa, in spite of considerable research into methods of controlling the disease, little has been achieved either in reducing the burden of malaria on residents or in making these countries safer for the visitor.

Protecting the traveller from malaria depends on avoiding mosquito bites, especially at night, and the use of anti-malarial drugs to destroy the parasite should infection take place.

The best way to avoid dangerous mosquito bites is to sleep in a mosqui-

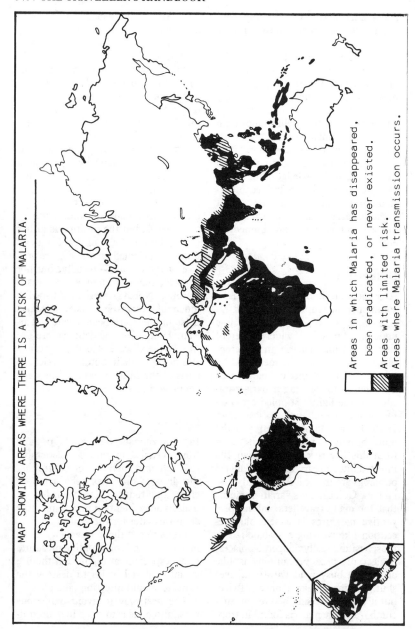

MAP SHOWING AREAS WHERE THERE IS A RISK OF MALARIA.

Areas in which Malaria has disappeared, been eradicated, or never existed.

Areas with limited risk.

Areas where Malaria transmission occurs.

to proof bedroom or, if that is not possible, under a mosquito net. It is important to get rid of any mosquitoes in the room by using a 'knock-down' insecticide before retiring. Between sunset and going to bed, bites can be reduced by wearing clothes that restrict the biteable area of skin – long sleeves and protection for the ankles which are so loved by mosquitoes. Some temporary protection can be obtained by the use of repellants. There are many commercial brands; those containing diethyltoluamide or dimethylphthalate are recommended. Burning mosquito coils will keep a restricted area mosquito free.

Protection against bites is clearly important, but it can seldom be relied on completely. Unfortunately the selection of the most suitable antimalarial drug has now become more complicated and the position changes even from month to month. For many years it has been known that some of the antimalarials were becoming less effective as the parasites become less sensitive to them. Recently the problem has become really serious as the effectiveness of chloroquine – one of the safest and most useful antimalarial drugs – has become ineffective against *Plasmodium falciparum.*

Advice has to be based on first principles – is the area to be visited malarious? What are the species of malaria parasite to be found in that area? Which antimalarial drugs are effective in these circumstances? Is the possible toxicity of the drug greater than the risk of malaria? Are there any special circumstances which may influence the choice of drug – such as pregnancy (or possible pregnancy) or the extreme youth of the traveller?

Some travellers are uncertain exactly which places they are going to visit and may change their itinerary at short notice; these need special advice. It is very difficult to give simple advice. The adviser with no doubts is likely to be incompletely informed or may be unwilling to balance the risk of malaria against possible toxic effects of the drugs. All travellers would be well advised to seek up-to-date information from specialist sources before leaving home. *(See list on page 588).*

There are two , approaches to obtaining the most appropriate advice: first, make a study of the sources of information and make your own decision; the second, ask your adviser what precautions he would take himself if he were making the same trip. It will be clear that with so many variables, sources of advice are likely to disagree on details, but no one will disagree that some form of prophylaxis is to be recommended when visiting the malarious areas and that it is absolutely essential when going to tropical Africa. Another unpleasant fact is that none of the antimalarial drugs is completely effective and that a few unlucky travellers will get malaria, even if they have followed exactly the best advice available.

Symptoms

It is therefore advisable for the traveller to know what sort of symptoms may occur. There are many excellent descriptions of malarial attacks in medical textbooks – the cold, shivering stage, the hot stage and the stage of profuse sweats as the temperature falls. This cycle takes about 24 hours and is repeated every other day. It is a valid description of *Plasmodium vivax* malaria in those who have had several attacks but is not typical of the first attack of malaria in the non-immune traveller. Malaria can mimic many diseases but it usually starts as a 'flu-like' condition with fever and headache; but vomiting and even diarrhoea may be the more obvious symptoms. It is essential to remember that any illness, even one that occurs several months after a visit to an endemic area may possibly be malaria and your doctor should be informed of the details of the trip. This is especially important after visits to tropical Africa, where symptoms may change from mild to serious with unpleasant speed.

Rabies

by Peter Lane

The tragic death from rabies some time ago of an English woman who had visited India and developed symptoms several months after returning home, must have given many a traveller pause to think. Rabies or, as it is sometimes known, hydrophobia, is one of the most terrible of diseases and the victim suffers dreadfully over a prolonged period before finally dying.

What then are the risks to the traveller, especially in the more exotic parts of the world where disease in animals is not controlled as closely as in Europe? Should one worry and take precautions, or disregard it as a risk to be suffered along with all the other hazards of foreign travel?

Rabies is one of the oldest diseases of man, who invariably contracts it from animals. It was certainly known to the people of ancient Egypt, Greece and Rome, who ascribed it to evil spirits when ordinary docile and friendly animals became suddenly aggressive and vicious.

Virus

In fact, rabies is caused by a virus which is excreted in large amounts in the saliva of affected animals. The disease is passed on from one individual to another when a healthy animal or human is bitten by an affected animal. It is not even necessary for a bite to occur as the disease can also be transmitted when an affected animal merely licks a slightly scratched hand or, for instance, the saliva of a spitting cat sprays into the eye.

Once the virus has gained entry by these means, it passes into the nearest small nerves and migrates along them to the bigger nerves. It moves gradually along these until it reaches the brain. At the same time, it multiplies and appears in the saliva. This means that it will take longer to reach the brain if the bite is on the hand or foot than if it is on the face or neck, simply because it has further to travel. Thus it can often happen that many months elapse before the disease manifests itself and the victim may not even remember the occurrence that led to their dreadful plight.

In man, the first symptoms are those of fever, lack of appetite, headache, lethargy, nausea and sore throat. Sometimes there are tingling sensations around the area where the infection first entered the body. After a few days, the victim becomes extremely sensitive to light and sound and excessive salivation develops. As it progresses, spasms of the throat muscles begin and swallowing becomes impossible. These spasms can be brought on by the mere sight of water, hence the alternative name, hydrophobia – fear of water. In addition, there are periods when the victim loses all rational behaviour and throws fits. The patient invariably dies after days of suffering.

Recognising Rabies

There must surely be nothing worse than being bitten or licked by a strange looking animal and then waiting for months to see if rabies symptoms begin to develop. However, there is much that you can do to protect yourself. Remember that, outside Britain, you are, with few exceptions, almost certainly entering a land where the disease is endemic in the wild animal population. This reservoir of infection also ensures that domestic animals will also contract it. The disease is even prevalent within mainland Europe – particularly in France and Germany.

The best precaution of all is to completely disregard all animals when abroad. Resist the urge to stroke or fondle any dogs or cats. Remember that all warm-blooded animals can develop rabies and pass it on to humans.

This will cut the risk but not eliminate it entirely. When animals develop rabies, they frequently change their behaviour, and any animal behaving uncharacteristically should be treated with extreme caution. Normally aggressive animals might first become excessively friendly and vice versa. Dogs will sometimes change the tone of their voice and develop a howling type of bark. At a later stage of the disease, infected animals might show signs of terror, become vicious or run madly around with their jaws paralysed in the open position, drooling saliva. If they develop the furious form of the disease, they will travel over many miles during the course of a few days and will attack any other animal or human they encounter. Wild animals, such as foxes, can lose their natural fear of man and will enter dwellings to attack anyone inside. In Central and South America, there exist vampire bats, which bite their victims to suck blood. Even birds are susceptible.

It is unlikely that anyone would contract rabies from a carcass unless the animal had recently died and they were to examine the mouth region with their hands. Nevertheless all dead animals should be given a wide berth, if only because of other diseases which they might transmit.

Vaccination

The second precaution that you can take is to be vaccinated before you set off on your travels. In the old days, a course of rabies vaccination was a series of very painful infections given into the abdomen over a period of days. Nowadays, the procedure is much pleasanter and is simply the normal type of injection given into the arm and repeated two weeks later.

It is probably only necessary to be vaccinated if you are intending to enter a geographical area of high risk or if your journey will bring you into close contact with animals. If you decide upon being vaccinated, see your doctor at least two months before the start of your journey. The vaccine is not normally kept in stock and it can take some time to obtain it. You will also want to ensure that the vaccine has time to stimulate the development of immunity in the body before you leave. The vaccination must, unfortunately, be paid for.

If you are bitten or licked by an animal of which you are suspicious, immediately wash the wound vigorously with soap and water ensuring, in the process, that all dirt is removed. Rinse all the soap away with copious amounts of water. This procedure will often mechanically remove the virus from the tissues before it has a chance to take hold. Then seek out a local qualified doctor and submit to his treatment. But don't rely solely on this and immediately consult your own doctor on your return. If you have any reason to be dissatisfied with the treatment given by the local doctor, change your travel arrangements and obtain professional medical help in a more reliable area. Even if you were not vaccinated before you left home, it still need not be too late to be treated with serum and vaccine after the event.

Most importantly, do not allow fear of rabies to spoil enjoyment of your travels. It can only be contracted in the manner which I have described and you will be quite safe if you follow the general procedures outlined above.

Sexually Transmitted Diseases and the Traveller

by Enver Carim

'Westerners are exporting AIDS. Don't have sex with tourists.'

Public health officials in Sri Lanka began to warn the local population in November 1986 against being intimate with foreign travellers when a 37-year-old bachelor from London registered a positive response to tests for the presence in his blood of the human immunodeficiency virus (HIV), the causative agent of AIDS. So horrified were the authorities by the prospect of the epidemic getting a foothold in their country that the national airline, Air Lanka, which had brought the infected Londoner, refused to fly him back. He had to be evacuated by stretcher on a scheduled British Airways flight via the Middle East.

It turned out that the patient had been treated for three years at St Thomas's Hospital in London. He had been fully aware of his AIDS condition when he set off for Sri Lanka where there are reportedly 2000 easily accessible and inexpensive male prostitutes, many of them young boys. The purpose of his journey was obviously to have 'a good time'. With the money at his disposal he could fly to pretty much any destination, taking with him his virus, his ego and his couldn't-tracless attitude. As a Western tourist, he was, almost by definition, concerned only about his self-gratification. That his behaviour might have endangered an entire community and led to the eventual deaths of any number of people in his holiday 'playground' was the furthest thing from his mind. He had, after all, foreign currency. He had spending power. He had come to believe that nothing else mattered.

The distressing thing is that he was just one of the increasingly large number of international travellers who have been playing havoc with their own and other people's health. Jetting away to distant countries is becoming more and more common. According to the World Tourism Organisation, there were 270 million tourist arrivals in 1979, generating $75,000 million in receipts. By 1985 the number of tourists had grown to 600 million, and the figure is expected to rise to 780 million over the next ten years. And it says a great deal about confidence in overseas travel that one new hotel is opened somewhere in the world every five minutes.

But despite all the publicity in their countries about how rapidly the AIDS virus has been spreading, and the mechanisms whereby it is spread, many relatively well-off Westerners are still flying to foreign climes and having sex there with highly available strangers. They are still going to bed in large numbers with impoverished men and women whose need for the money is much greater than their medical awareness. Lying in the arms of someone whose body is wracked with hunger is bad enough. Pumping the AIDS virus into their bloodstream, and into their family and culture, in the name of 'having a good time', shows an insensitivity that is both aggressive and arrogant.

It is perhaps not surprising therefore that in Japan, with its rather xenophobic traditions, a generalised resentment towards foreigners has begun to be detected by expatriates. Japan's National Institute of Health has indicated that all the ten male homosexuals who have caught the disease got it through sexual contact with visiting foreigners and that the number of locals now carrying the virus is about 11,000. According to one American living in Tokyo:

'For the average Japanese, it is a tiny step from labelling this a foreigner's disease to saying all foreigners are AIDS carriers.'

And when an American aircraft carrier recently arrived at a Japanese port, it was greeted with a newspaper article asking:

'Is it bringing AIDS or nuclear weapons into port?'

Near the US naval base at Subic Bay in the Philippines, angry Filipino 'hospitality women' have accused American servicemen of infecting them with the AIDS virus. During a blood-screening exercise, US military doctors found seventeen of the women to be carrying the virus. The women are demanding compensation for potential AIDS victims. Their community women's group, known as Gabriella, has been compiling material for a law suit against the American government. Moreover, about 500 of the women have signed a petition demanding that servicemen carry certificates showing they are free of the AIDS virus, just as the women have to carry documents showing they have been tested for venereal diseases at regular intervals and found to be clean.

The implications are clear. Any intelligent traveller will realise that sex abroad now has legal as well as medical implications. Having sex can land you in jail as well as in hospital. If you infect your partner, even unwittingly because you didn't know you were carrying the virus, you could be taken to court and made to pay a heavy penalty. A precedent of sorts was set in October 1986 when a 26-year-old salesman in West Germany was found to have passed the AIDS virus to a large number of partners. He was told that he would be charged with murder if one of them died as a result. Bavaria's Justice Minister, August Lang, said at the time:

'This is a crime because he was deliberately infecting others.'

Clearly, sex has ceased to be simply a pleasurable pastime. There is, moreover, hardly a country in the world where the AIDS virus is not at work. It is spreading steadily in all the countries of Europe, with 1050 cases in France by mid-November 1986, 715 in West Germany, 548 in the UK and 345 in Italy. The number of people carrying the virus, as opposed to those who are already ill, is very much higher, e.g. around 100,000 in France and something like 50,000 in the UK. In the United States 15,000 people have already died from AIDS and the death toll there is expected to reach 180,000 by 1991.

The virus is rampant in Brazil, Mexico, Puerto Rico, Australia and is rapidly spreading in the Far East. Epidemiologists estimate that as many as one person in five has been infected in the capital cities of central Africa. Prevalence of the virus is also being reported in the nations of the Eastern bloc, so much so that Soviet medical authorities have recently expressed their willingness to cooperate with Western experts in the search for ways to control the spread of the deadly disease.

What makes AIDS so frightening is not only the fact that it can strike men, women and children without distinction in a great variety of ways – attacking their lungs, guts, eyes, skin, nervous system and brain in ways that invariably prove fatal, sooner or later – but also that there is no cure available or any preventive vaccine. Nor is there likely to be a cure or vaccine in the foreseeable future.

Tourists should now be absolutely clear about two facts. The first is that any medication now on offer against AIDS is either a palliative or a symptom-specific agent with nasty side-effects such as heavy vomiting, nausea and/or loss of hair. It has in the past year become the concensus of virological opinion that *everyone with the virus in their blood is going to die*, sooner or later, in one way or another, whether or not in the short term they show any symptoms at all.

The second relevant fact is that prostitutes, those people who used to make foreign trips so attractive to international travellers, who used to be so willing to satisfy the most kinky requirements, have become a death trap. Prevalence of the AIDS virus among prostitutes is extremely high, whether the prostitutes are men or women. Travellers who use their services, be it in America or Greece, Thailand or Kenya, are almost certainly asking to be infected.

Other STDs

AIDS is the most prominent and deadly sexually transmissable disease in the world today. There is only one sure way to counteract its dire effects and that is: don't get it in the first place. Which means don't have sex with strangers. Don't even have sex with people you know, unless you know for sure that every single one of their previous sex partners in the past five years had not been exposed to the AIDS virus.

But if you must have sex with more than one partner, then use a condom, i.e. wear a protective rubber sheath on your penis if you are a man. If you are a woman, insist that the man wear a condom. Condoms are certainly not fail-safe, but they are better than no protection at all.

This advice is being disseminated by

the World Health Organisation and by medical authorities across the globe because AIDS is killing hundreds of men, women and children every day. But the advice applies equally with regard to the other STDs which could affect sexually active travellers. The risk of contracting *gonorrhoea* and *syphilis* is high in many parts of the world. And these conditions could cause serious long-term disability if effective treatment is delayed. Given the speed of air travel, it is likely that any STD which the traveller has picked up will be in the incubation phase when he or she returns home. It's a wise move, therefore, to have a medical check-up when you get back, especially if you've been 'active'. And only you know if you have.

Among the other STDs to which travellers are vulnerable are *genital herpes*, *viral hepatitis*, *genital warts*, *pendiculosis pubis*, *candidiasis* and *molluscum contagiosum*. According to Michael Adler, Professor of Genitourinary Medicine at Middlesex Hospital Medical School in London, 'the three commonest presenting symptoms are urethral discharge, genital ulceration, and vaginal discharge with or without vulval irritation'. Some of the diseases may also involve pain in the abdomen and scrotum and retention of urine. And because the diseases may affect any system in the body, their symptoms will not necessarily present in the region of the penis, vulva or anus. For example, headache is the main symptom of meningovascular syphilis; convulsions and insanity are later manifestions.

Genital herpes, whose symptoms are stinging or itching sensations in the genital or anal area, accompanied by headache and high temperature, is considered to be of epidemic proportions in the United States. With mouth herpes, small blisters appear on the lips; they burst and leave small ulcers which then scab over. Hepatitis B virus, on the other hand, is endemic in tropical Africa and South-East Asia; eight to twenty percent of those populations are carriers. The latter illness usually begins with non-specific symptoms such as fever, headache and acute tiredness. Jaundice, a condition characterised by yellowing of the skin and eyes, tends to follow.

The world seems to be under a concerted microbiological attack, with all sorts of unpleasant diseases lying in store for people who indulge in casual sex. Upon reflection, however, it becomes clear that it is we who are our own worst enemies. It is we who are wilfully allowing the germs to do the dirty on us. It is we who, in a cultural stupor, have programmed ourselves to believe that we aren't worthy or admirable unless we are regularly banging away at someone's body.

Other Ailments and Injuries

by Drs Peter Steele and John Frankland

Antibiotics must not be eaten indiscriminately, but if you develop an infection with a high fever and rapid pulse when you are away in the wilds on your own, blind therapy with a broad spectrum bug-killing drug may be justified. Cotrimoxazole ß (*Septrin*, *Bactrim*) Amoxycillin (*Amoxyl*) should be taken for a full five-day course. In malarial areas, treatment must also be considered even if regular prophylaxis has been taken; a three day treatment should abort most attacks. If it does not, then seek medical advice. If there is fever, supportive measures such as rest, shade, frequent sponging with cool water, two Aspirin tablets every four to six hours and an adequate intake of fluids are essential.

Waterworks

Urinary infection is more common in women, and begins as frequent passing of urine with burning pain. Drink a pint of water hourly with a tablespoon of bicarbonate of soda and take an antibiotic if it does not improve in a day.

Women travellers have the extra burden of coping with menstrual problems en route. If on the pill it is totally safe to start the new pack immediately after finishing the current pack without the usual six or seven day interval. This will avoid menstrual loss or certainly minimise it, saving quite a nuisance. If, however, a woman on the pill travelling in a mixed party gets diarrhoea for more than one day, the pill may not be absorbed and she should assume she is not protected for that cycle. An unwanted pregnancy in a remote spot will cause much distress!

To complicate the issue the menstrual cycle of both non-takers and takers of the pill may become irregular or stop temporarily while travelling and adventuring. This is harmless and needs no medical intervention. Women on the pill are more at risk from thrombosis and thrush.

Local Infections

Eyes: if the eyes are pink and feel gritty, wear dark glasses and put in chloromycetin ointment. A few drops of Amethocaine will anaesthetize the cornea so you can dig out a foreign body. Homatropine dilates the pupil and relieves spasm but will temporarily blur the vision.

Ears: keep dry with a light plug of cotton wool but don't poke matches in. If there is discharge and pain, take an antibiotic.

Sinusitis: gives a headache (feels worse on stooping), 'toothache' in the upper jaw, and often a thick, snotty discharge from the nose. Inhale steam in Tinct. Benz. or sniff a tea brew with a towel over your head to help drainage. Decongestant drops may clear the nose if it is mildly bunged up, but true sinusitis needs an antibiotic.

Throat: cold dry air irritates the throat and makes it sore. Gargle with a couple of Aspirins or table salt dissolved in warm water; or suck antiseptic lozenges.

Teeth: when it is difficult to brush your teeth, chew gum. If a filling comes out, a plug of cotton wool soaked in oil of cloves eases the pain; gutta percha, softened in boiling water, is easily plastered into the hole as a temporary filling. Hot salt mouthwashes encourage pus to discharge from a dental abcess but an antibiotic will be needed.

Feet: take a hammering so boots must fit and be comfortable. Climbing boots are rarely necessary on the approach march to a mountain; gym shoes are useful. At the first sign of rubbing put on a plaster.

Blisters: Burst with a sterile blade or needle (boiled for three minutes or hold in a flame until red hot). Remove dead skin, spray with Tinct. Benz. Cover the raw area with zinc oxide plaster and leave in place for several days to allow new skin to form.

Athlete's Foot: can become very florid in the tropics so treat this problem before departure. The newer antifungal creams e.g. Canestin, are very effective and supersede antifungal dusting powders but do not eliminate the need for sensible foot hygiene. In very moist conditions, e.g. in the rain forest, on cave explorations or in small boats, lacerated feet can become a real and incapacitating problem. A silicone-based barrier cream in adequate supply in essential under these conditions.

Skin sepsis: in muddy or wet conditions most travellers will get some skin sepsis on small wounds. Without sensible hygiene these can be disabling, especially in jungle conditions. Cuts and grazes should be washed thoroughly with soap and water or an antiseptic solution; five percent Mercurochrome Aq. dabbed on cuts and grazes is an excellent antiseptic as the skin remains dry (creams will leave it greasy and attract dirt). Other suitable antiseptics are potassium permanganate and gentian violet. Large abrasions should be covered with a vaseline gauze e.g. Jelonet or Sofratulle, then a dry gauze, and kept covered until a dry scab forms, after which they can be treated daily with Mercurochrome solution and left exposed. Anchor dressings are useful for awkward places e.g. fingers or heels. If a cut is clean and gaping, bring the edges together with Sterestrips in place of stitches.

Unconsciousness

The causes range from drowning to head injury, diabetes to epilepsy. Untrained laymen should merely attempt to place the victim in the coma position – lying on their side with the head lower than the chest to allow secretions, blood or vomit to drain away from the lungs. Hold the chin forward to prevent the tongue falling back and obstructing the airway. Don't try any fancy manoeuvres unless you are practised, as you may do more harm than good.

All unconscious patients from any cause, particularly after trauma, should be placed in the coma position until they recover. This takes priority over any other first aid manoeuvre.

Fainting: lay the unconscious person down and raise the legs to return extra blood to the brain.

Injury

Nature is a wonderful healer if given adequate encouragement.

Superficial wounds: see above.

Deep wounds: firm pressure on a wound dressing will stop most bleeding. If blood seeps through, put more dressings on top, secured with absorbent crepe bandages and keep up the pressure. Elevate the part if possible.

On trips to remote spots at least one member of the party should learn to put in simple sutures. This is not difficult – a friendly doctor or casualty sister can teach the essentials in ten minutes. People have practised on a piece of dog meat and on several occasions this has been put to good use. Pulling the wound edges together is all that is necessary; a neat cosmetic result is usually not important.

Burns: superficial burns are simply skin wounds. Leave open to the air to form a dry crust under which healing goes on. If this is not possible, cover with *Melolin* dressings. Burn creams offer no magic. Deep burns must be kept scrupulously clean and treated urgently by a doctor. Give drinks freely to replace lost fluids.

Sprains: a sprained ankle ligament, usually on the outside of the joint, is a common and likely injury. With broad Elastoplast 'stirrup strapping', walking may still be possible. Put two or three long lengths from mid-calf on the non-injured side under the foot and, with tension applied and the ankle twisted towards the injured side, attach along the calf on the injured side. Follow this with circular strapping from toes to mid-calf overlapping by half on each turn. First aid treatment of sprains and bruises is immobilization (I), cold, e.g. cold compresses (C) and elevation (E); remember ICE. If painful movement and swelling persist, suspect a fracture.

Fractures: immobilize the part by splinting to a rigid structure; the arm can be strapped to the chest, both legs can be tied together. Temporary splints can be made from a rolled newspaper, an ice-axe or a branch. Pain may be agonizing and is due to movement of broken bone ends on each other; full doses of strong pain killers are needed.

The aim of splinting fractures is to reduce pain and bleeding at the fracture site and thereby reduce shock. Comfort is the best criterion by which to judge the efficiency of a splint but remember that to immobilise a fracture when the victim is being carried, splints may need to be tighter than seems necessary for comfort when at rest, particularly over rough ground. Wounds at a fracture site or visible bones must be covered immediately with sterile or the cleanest material available and if this happens start antibiotic treatment at once. Pneumatic splints provide excellent support but may be inadequate when a victim with a broken leg has a difficult stretcher ride across rough ground. They are of no value for fractured femurs (high bones). If you decide to take them get the Athletic Long Leg splint which fits over a climbing boot where the Standard Long Leg splint does not.

Pain: Pain killers fall into three strengths for different grades of pain: MILD: Aspirin (lowers the temperature but can irritate the stomach). Dose: up to four 300mg tablets initially, then repeat two tablets at four hourly intervals as necessary. Paracetamol is a useful alternative. Dose: up to four 500mg tablets, then repeat two tablets four hourly as necessary. MODERATE: Pentazocine. *Fortral* is probably the best for parties without a doctor who do not wish to impinge on scheduled drug regulations. Dose: up to four 25mg tablets or two 50mg capsules four hourly as necessary. STRONG: Pethidine. Morphine – available on special prescription only and there is a risk of trouble with the law if you are caught with these drugs in your possession. Further, they are potentially hazardous (e.g. they may depress breathing) and *should be used only by those with previous special instruction in their use.*

A Suggested Medical Kit

by Drs Peter Steele and John Frankland

For British travellers our normally generous National Health Service does not supply medication for trips abroad (other than for a pre-existing medical condition), and all drugs needed for this purpose have to be purchased – usually at a considerably greater expense than anticipated. Friendly doctors, usually General Practitioners, may, if feeling generous, defray this expense by donating drug 'samples'. Travellers should otherwise ask their doctor to sign the entire list as a private prescription.

American travellers should also obtain drugs on prescription; in some cases it is illegal to buy or possess them without doing so. Take with you the drug prescriptions supplied with the drugs or photocopies of their descriptions 'with indications, recommended dosage, etc). In the USA all drugs are listed in The Physician's Desk Reference, published annually. American travellers within easy reach of Mexico may consider buying drugs there: many more drugs are available without prescription than in the USA and they are considerably cheaper.

Store your medical kit in a waterproof and dustproof container that is lockable and kept locked. Transfer liquids and tablets to plastic bottles and attach labels with Sellotape as stuck-on labels can come off in wet heat. Certain items can be stored in plastic pouches with zips. If storing the kit in a vehicle, keep it away from the floor, which is likely to be too hot, and keep it easily accessible at all times. At least one person should be thoroughly familiar with the contents of the kit, knowing instantly the exact location and application of each item. The kit therefore needs to be kept permanently in impeccable order. Where possible one person should issue supplies, as open house will encourage rooting about, the opening of new supplies when part-used ones are available, and general chaos. The same person should oversee stocks of drugs and dressings in case more need to be obtained.

For 4–6 persons for 2 months

Basic Dressings	1 Elastoplast dressing strip 91cms
	50 assorted size Elastoplast dressings
	1 Zinc Oxide strapping plaster 2.5cms × 4m
	1 pack Steristrip 0.6 × 10cms – to hold small wounds together
	1 Bandage Crepe 7.5cms
	1 Bandage Cotton 5cms
	1 Bandage Triangular
	12 Gauze squares plain
	16 Melolin dressings 10 × 10cms – place next to dry wounds
	4 Jelonet or Sofratulle dressings 10 × 10cms – place next to moist

wounds

1 small cotton wool pack (compressed)

1 wound dressing No. 15

1 Netelast dressing (Head size) – to retain dressings

Cleansing

1 bar soap

50ml Dettol or TCP solution – to wash wounds

Instruments

1 pair each scissors sharp/blunt

1 forceps – blunt end

1 scalpel blade (sterile)

4 safety pins

2 thermometres (1 'subnormal' if low temperature likely)

Disposable syringes and needles if injectable drugs included

Paper and ballpoint pen to note drugs given

2 × 3.0 chromic catgut sutures

Medicines

Pain killers (mild)

100 soluble Aspirin 300mgs

50 tabs Paracetamol 500mgs

(moderate)

20 caps Fortal 50mgs (*Pentazocine*)

(strong)

10 tabs Pethidine 50mgs or 4 inj. Pethidine 100 mgs – see warning in text

Antibiotics

40 Cotrimoxazole (Septrin, Bactrim) – 2 tablets night and morning for five days

2 ampoules Triplopen

2 ampoules sterile water – 1 injection i.m. Triplopen and sterile water to patient with an infection who can't swallow

Antihistamine

40 tabs Promethazine (Phenergan) 25mgs – 1 at night

50 tabs Chlorpheniramine (Piriton) 4mgs – 1 3× daily as needed

Sleeping

20 tabs Nitrazepam (Mogadon) 5mgs – 1 or 2 at night

Sedation

20 tabs Diazepam (Valium) 2mgs – 1 3 × daily as needed

Diarrhoea

225g Kaolin powder – 2 tspns in water as necessary

40 tabs Codeine Phosphate 30mgs – 2 4× daily as

needed

100 tabs Lomotil (Diphenoxylate) – 4× daily as needed

Constipation 10 tabs Senokot – 1–4 at night as needed

Indigestion 30 tabs Aludrox or Magnesium Trisilicate – 1 or 2 anytime

10 tabs Maxalon – 1 up to four times daily as necessary for vomiting

Salt 20 tabs Slow Na (Slow sodium) 1–3 daily for 2 days

Anti-worm 4 sachets Pripsen (Piperazine) – 1 sachet, repeat in 10 days

Eye and Ears 5ml Neo-cortef eye/ear drops – apply four times daily as necessary

2 minims Amethocaine – to anaesthetise the eyes

2 minims Homatropine – to rest an inflamed eye

Teeth Oil of cloves – apply to aching tooth

1 gutta percha temporary filling

Skin:
Sun 2 tubes Uvistat
1 Lipsyl
1 tube Calamine

cream – apply when necessary

Insects 3 tubes Flypel or equivalent

3 tubes Anthisan cream – apply 3 × daily

Fungal infections 1 tube Canestin ointment – apply 3 × daily

Barrier cream 1 60g Conotrane ointment – apply when necessary

Bruises and sprains 1 × 14g Lasonil ointment – apply 3 × daily

Antiseptic 1 10ml 5% Mercurochrome Aq. – apply daily

Infestations 1 ICI Louse and Insect Powder – dust with this daily as necessary

Haemorrhoids 10 Anusol suppositories – use twice daily

Diuretic (high altitude only) 20 tabs Lasix (Frusemide) 40mgs – 2 tabs 4 hourly

Anti-malarial ask for advice

Directory IAMAT or INTERMEDIC or either directory of English-speaking doctors.

Individual Kit
Dressings 1 plaster strip 30 × 6cms
1 zinv oxide 2.5cms × 3m
4 Melolin 5 × 5cms
1 crepe bandage

	7.5cms
	1 razor blade
	Paper and ballpoint pen
	10 Fortral
	20 Phenergan (25mgs)
Diarrhoea	60 Lomotil
Sun	1 tube Uvistat
	1 Lipsyl
Throat/Skin/Eyes/Ears	
	12 Aspirin
	1 tube (4gms) Neo-cortef eye/ear drops
	100 water purifying tablets

If travelling in a remote area for a long period, add appropriate quantities of antibiotics and antimalarial prophylactics

Personal drugs sufficient for the whole trip or a list of sources from which they can be obtained in the countries to be visited.

Drugs Referred to – Alternative Names Used in Other Countries

The person in charge of the medical kit should understand the appropriate usage and dosage of all the drugs carried. It also helps if brief notes on this are on the labels of all drug containers.

Pharmaceutical Name	Commonest UK Brand Name	Commonest Brand Names in other countries
Aluminium Hydroxide	Aludrox	Maalox (USA)
		Actal (Various countries)
Chloroquine Phosphate	Avlaclor	Aralen Hydrochloride (USA)
Chlorpheniramine	Piriton	Allertab
		Chlormine, Chlortrone
		Histadur (USA) (Canada)
		Telmin
Chlorimazole 1%	Canestin Cream	Lomotrin (USA)
Codeine Phosphate	Codeine Phosphate	Paveral (Canada)
Cotrimoxazole & Sulpha	Septrin or Bactrim	Septra (USA)
Diazepam	Valium	E-Pam
		Serenach (Canada)
		Vival
Dimethicone & Hydrargaphen	Conotrane Oint.	Versotrane (Canada)
Diphenoxylate & Atropine	Lomotil	Diarsed (France)
Frusemide	Lasix	Lasiix (France)
Heparinoid & Hyaluronidase	Lasonil Oint.	Hyazine (USA)
		Wydase (Canada)
Mepyramine Maleate	Anthisan Cream	Antical Cream (USA)
		Statomin Cream (USA)
Mercurochrome Aq 5%	Mercurochrome Aq 5%	Mercurescein (Canada)
Metoclopramide	Maxolon	Maxeran (Canada)
		Reglan (USA)
Mexenone	Uvistat Oint.	Uvicone (Australia)
Neomycin & Hydrocortisone	Neo-Cortef Eye/Ear Drops	Neobiotic (USA)
		Herisan Antibiotic (Canada)
Nitrazepam	Mogadon	Remmnos (Various countries)
Parcetamol	Paracetamol	Capitol
		Dolanex, Tempra
		Febrigesic (USA) (Canada)
		Nebs
Pencillins (Mixture of 3)	Triplopen Inj.	Benapen (S. Africa)
Pentazocine	Fortral	Talwin (Canada & USA)
		Sosenyl (Various countries)
Pethidine	Pethidine	Demeral (USA & Canada)
		Physadon (Canada)
Piperazine	Pripsen	Antepar (USA)
		Piperzinal (Canada)
Proguanil	Paludrine	Paludrinal (Canada)
Promethazine	Phenergan	Promethopar (USA)
		Zipan (USA)
		Histantil (Canada)
Pyrimethamine	Daraprim or Fansidar	Fansidar
		Maloprim (Various countries)
		Falcidar (Colombia & Venezuela)
Slow release sodium chloride	Slow Na	Neutrasil (Canada)
		Trisomin (USA)
Standardized Senna Extract	Senokot	Colonorm (Germany)
Vaseline Gauze	Jelonet Gauze or Sofratulle Gauze	Petroleum Gauze (USA)

A Place to Stay

Camping

by Anthony Smith, Jack Jackson, Melissa Shales and Martin Rosser

Anthony Smith:

The first real camping I ever did was on a student expedition to Persia. There I learned the principle of inessential necessities. We were travelling by truck and could therefore pile on board everything we might possibly need. The truck could transport it all and we only had the problem of sorting through the excess whenever we needed something. Later we travelled by donkey and, miraculously, the number of necessities diminished as we realised the indisputable truth that donkeys carry less than trucks. Later still, after the donkey drivers had failed to coerce higher rates of pay from very empty student pockets, we continued on foot.

Amazingly, the number of necessities decreased yet again as a bunch of humans realised they could carry far less than donkeys and much, much less than trucks. The important lesson learned was that happiness, welfare and ability to work did not lessen one iota as the wherewithal for camping decreased in quantity. It could even have been argued that these three blessings increased as less time was spent in making and breaking camp.

This lesson had to be learned several times over. Sometime later I was about to travel from Cape Town to England by motorbike. As I wished to sleep out, provide my own meals and experience a road network that was largely corrugated dirt, I found no difficulty in compiling a considerable list of necessities. We must have all made these lists – of corkscrews, tin openers, self-heating soup – and they are great fun, with a momentum that is hard to resist. 'Why not a spare tin opener?' 'And more medicine and another inner tube?' 'Isn't it wise to take more shirts and stave off prickly heat?' Fortunately the garage that sold me the bike put a stop to such idiotic thinking. I had just strapped on a sack containing the real essentials – like passport, documents, maps, money and address book – when a passing mechanic told me that any more weight would break the machine's back. (It was a modest machine.) Thus it was that I proceeded up the length of Africa without a sleeping bag, tent, groundsheet, spare petrol, oil, tools, food or even water, and never had cause for regret concerning this lack of wealth. Indeed I blessed the freedom it gave me. I could arrive anywhere, remove my one essential sack and know that nothing, save the bike itself, could be stolen. To have possessions is to be in danger of losing them. Better by far to save the robbers their trouble and start with nothing.

Kippered Hammock

A sound tip is to do what the locals do. If they sleep out with nothing more than a blanket it is probable that you can do likewise. If they can get by with a handful of dates at sunset it is quite likely that you too can dispense with half a hundredweight of dried egg, cocoa, vitamin tablets, corned beef, chocolate – and self-heating soup. To follow local practice then try to improve on it can, however, be disastrous. Having learned the knack of sleeping in a Brazilian hammock, so that my body was as horizontal as if it were in bed, I decided one thunderous night to bring modern technology to my aid. I covered myself with a space blanket to keep out the inevitable downpour. Unfortunately, while I was asleep, the wretched thing slipped round beneath me and I awoke to find my body afloat in the pool of water it had collected. Being the first man to drown in a hammock is a poor way of achieving immortality. I looked over at my Indian travelling companion. Instead of fooling around with sub-lethal blankets, he had built a fire longitudinally beneath his hammock. Doubtless kippered by the smoke, but certainly dry, he slept the whole night through.

Planning and Adventure

One trouble with our camping notions is that we are confused by a lingering memory of childhood expeditions. I camp with my children every year and half the fun is not quite getting it right. As all adventure is said to be bad planning, so is a memorable camping holiday in which the guys act as trip wires, the air mattress farts into nothingness and even the tent itself falls victim to the first wind above a breeze. Adults are therefore imbued with an expectation that camping is a slightly comic caper, rich with potential mishap. Those who camp a lot, such as wildlife photographers, have got over this teething stage. They expect camping to be (almost) as smooth and straightforward a business as living in a house. They do their best to make cooking, eating, washing and sleeping no more time-consuming than it is back home. The joy of finding grass in the soup or ants in the pants wears off for them on about the second day. It is only the temporary camper, knowing he will be back in a hotel (thank God) within a week, who does not bother to set things up properly.

Surviving Natural Hazards

I like the camping set-up to be as modest as possible. I have noticed though that others disagree, welcoming every kind of extra. A night spent beneath the stars that finishes with the first bright shafts of dawn is hardly punishment – but some seem to think it so, and concentrate on removing as much of the natural environment as possible.

I remember a valley in the Zagros mountains where I had to stay with some colleagues. I had thought a sleeping bag would be sufficient and placed mine in a dried-up stream, which had piled up sand for additional comfort. Certain others of the party erected large tents with yet larger flysheets (however improbable rain was at that time of year). They also started up a considerable generator which bathed the area in sound and light. As electricity was not a predominant feature of those wild regions considerable numbers of moths and other insects, idling their way between the Persian Gulf and the Caspian Sea, were astonished at such a quantity of illumination and flew down to investigate. To counter their invasion, one camper set fire to several of those insect repellent coils and the whole campsite was shrouded in noxious effluent. Over in the dried-up stream I and two fellow spirits were amazed at the camping travesty down the way. We were even more astonished when, after a peaceful night, we awoke to hear complaints that a strong wind had so flapped at the flies that no one inside the tent had achieved a wink of sleep.

The most civilised camping I have ever experienced was in the Himalayas. The season was spring and tents are then most necessary both at the lower altitudes, (where it rains a lot) and at the higher ones (where it freezes quite considerably). Major refreshment is also necessary because walking in those mountains is exhausting work, being always up, as the local saying puts it, except when its down. We slept inside sleeping bags on foam rubber within thick tents. We ate hot meals three times a day. We did very well – but then we did not carry a thing. For the six of us, there were 36 porters at the outset, the number being reduced as we ate into the provisions these men were carrying. I laboured up and down mighty valleys, longing for the next refreshment point and always delighted to see the already-erected tents at each night's stopping place. Personally, I was burdened with one camera, the smallest of notebooks and nothing more. The living conditions, as I have said were excellent, but what would they have become if I had been asked to carry everything I needed myself? It is at that point, when neither donkeys, nor incredibly hardy mountain men are available, that the camper's true necessities are clarified. For myself, I am happy even to dispense with the toothbrush if I have to carry the thing all day long. Just a blanket will do if that is what the locals use. My body may not be like theirs in the early days, but, given encouragement, it can become half as good as the weeks go by.

Jack Jackson:
If you aren't worried about weight, and you are not constantly on the move, you might as well make yourselves as comfortable as possible, which can mean virtually building a tented village. Large groups will find it very useful to have a mess tent where the party can all congregate for meals and during bad weather.

On the hard, sunbaked ground in hot countries, the pegs normally supplied with tents are of little use, so have some good, thick, strong ones made for you from 60mm iron, or else use 15cms nails. As wooden mallets will not drive pegs in, carry a normal claw hammer – you can also use the claw to pull the pegs out again. In loosely compacted snow, standard metal pegs do not have much holding power, so it is useful to make some with a larger surface area from 2.5cms angle alloy. Even this does not solve all the problems because any warmth during the day will make the pegs warm up, melt the snow around them, and pull out – so the tent falls down. The answer is to use very big pegs or ice axes for the two main guys fore and aft and then, for all the other guys, dig a hole about 25 cms deep, put the peg in horizontally with the guy line around its centre and compress fresh snow down hard with your boots on it to fill the hole.

Vango now offer a special 'tent anchor' for snow and soft sand; it is not any better in snow than the method described above, but is good in soft sand. Four of these would normally be all you would carry per tent.

If you sleep without a tent, you need a mosquito net in some areas. There are several types on the market, but they are not usually big enough to tuck in properly, so get the ex-army ones which have the extra advantage of needing only one point of suspension. A camera tripod or ice axe will do for this if there is not a vehicle or tent nearby.

Since tents take heavy wear, carry some strong thread and a sailmaker's needle for repairs plus some spare groundsheet material and adhesive. Tents which are to be carried by porters, on donkeys, or on a vehicle roof rack are best kept in a strong kit bag or they will soon be torn.

If it is not a windy area, a 'space blanket' covering the reflecting side of the tent will help keep the tent cool during the day.

Where to Camp

Melissa Shales:

If a large group of you are travelling together in the more civilised parts of the world, you won't have the option of just choosing a suitable area to camp, particularly if you want to explore the towns. In many countries, or in National Parks, it is actually illegal to camp outside the official sites. These, however, are often a very good option, far cheaper and cleaner than inexpensive hotels. Some motels have camp sites attached which allow you the option of using their restaurant facilities, swimming pools etc. The Caravan Club of Great Britain is a useful source of information about good sites in Europe, for tented camping as well as caravanning, and also runs various small sites around the UK.

If there is an option, aim for a smaller site first. During the height of the tourist season, the larger ones tend to get very crowded, to the point where guy ropes are overlapping and you can hear the conversation in the tent next door. Some have hard stands which, while conveniently clean, are exceptionally hard unless you are travelling with the full paraphernalia of air beds etc. They also become horribly sterile areas that destroy virtually the entire ethos of camping. Avoid them if possible. Many of the better sites will either have barbecues or special sites for fires. You will rarely be allowed to have a fire wherever you choose. The caretaker will often be able to supply wood if you ask in the morning. Check the toilets and washing facilities out before you book in. Unless very small, when all you can expect is a primitive or chemical toilet and a standpipe, there should be showers and laundry facilities and a plentiful supply of hot water. In some countries, such as Zimbabwe, the sites will even have servants attached who will do your washing, sweep out the tent, run errands and build your fires for a small fee.

As with hotels, there are listings, and even star ratings in many places. If you want to go to what is obviously a highly rated site, or visit the only one in the area, or are travelling in high season, book first if possible.

Martin Rosser:

It's not the expense of campsites that I object to, but having to put up with the others that are crammed in around you. I camp to find peace and solitude, to commune with nature. How to do that on a canvas conurbation is beyond me. As for facilities, I can and do bathe in the woods and prefer it to slopping around an overcrowded concrete shower block.

If you make the decision to camp freely, you have to decide whether to ask the landowner for permission or to remain discreetly out of sight. Which you do will depend solely on the circumstances at the time. I am aware that campers on other people's land have an awesomely bad reputation, so I prefer just to get on with it quietly. Nine times out of ten I am not discovered and leave everything as it was except for a piece of flattened grass. I doubt if anyone is the wiser. If you are discovered, your best defence is the clean and tidy way you are camping, so that it can be readily seen that nothing has, is, or will be damaged. Being able to greet the person without guilt I have only once received more than a general caution to take care. That once was well deserved. In the days of my mis-spent youth, I was out camping with friends and we had left a cooking fire unattended. The following dressing down was well deserved and the lesson well learned.

When you come to select a spot, remember to avoid all extremes. If the climate you are in is hot, seek shade; if the land is marshy, look for high, well drained ground. Don't leave sel-ecting your site to the last minute, stopping in late twilight and having to choose within a small area. From late afternoon on you should keep an eye

open and be prepared to stop a little short of your planned destination or backtrack a mile or so if need be. A bad night's sleep or wet and damaged gear is well worth avoiding.

Now the choosing of a resting place that is not to be final involves experi-ence, so here I can do little more than outline general dos and don'ts. After that, bitter experience starts to take over. I rarely camp with a tent, prefer-ring a bivi-bag, which makes my cho-ice of spot very versatile. Generally I select somewhere in a sheltered dip or protected by trees. The patch need not be bigger than eight feet by four for me and my gear. I have even slept on substantial slopes, the record being 45°. I avoid all low lying wetlands and even streams in summer, because fly-ing bloodsuckers enrage me to the point of sleeplessness. In areas I know are going to be extra bad, I try to find ground high enough to have a constant stiff breeze. This is the most sure way I have of deterring the Scottish midge and the Australian mosquito alike.

For those who like to carry tents, the rules are slightly different. The ground you are after has to be as flat as possible and with as few rocks etc. Take a leaf out of the London taxi driver's book and come to know the exact dimensions of your tent, as he knows the exact dimensions of his cab. Then, just as he can slide his cab into the most unlikely looking gaps, you know where, and more importantly where not, to pitch. In a tent you have less to worry about on the insect front, but you should be more wary of falling branches and the like. Tents are far easier to damage than biv-ouac sheets, and more expensive to repair or replace. If you have the oppor-tunity, face the tent doors eastwards. That way you don't have to get up, or even fully wake up, to watch the dawn break. For the rest, just apply common sense. Don't pitch a tent with its only door facing into a gale, and don't camp in a dry river bed when the rains are due. Though it has to be said that dry river beds are very comfortable in the right season – flat floor, and plenty of snapped up firewood to hand.

The reason I prefer bivouacing is that it forces you to keep more of an eye open as to what terrain surrounds you. You become more versatile in your camping and more ready to sleep anywhere. I have slept in derelict buildings and under bridges whilst experiencing the low life; up trees; in caves; and I once found a sea cliff with a horizontal crack running three feet high and over ten feet deep. Sleeping in there was an experience and a half as it was 60 feet above a rocky shore on which the waves crashed all night. A friend went on to greater things and slept behind a waterfall, and once in the downturned shovel of an ancient and abandoned mechanical digger.

So if there is a moral to this tale of where to camp it is to use your common sense; break all the rules in the boy scout manual – but sensibly; and finally to be adventurous and try new ways. Even if you carry a tent you don't *have* to use it. Try a bit more of the wild life.

Hostelling

by John Carlton, Diane Johnson and Kent Redding

Youth Hostels are ideal for the budget traveller, offering an extensive network of accommodation around the world of a reasonable standard and at very affordable prices. They are designed primarily for young people, but there is no age limit (except in Bavaria, Germany) and they are used by the 'young at heart' of all ages.

Youth Hostel facilities are provided by a club run not for profit, but to help young people to travel, to know and love the countryside and appreciate other cultures, thereby promoting international friendship. Each country runs its own hostels independently (usually by committees from within its membership) and the national Youth Hostel Associations of each country are linked through the International Youth Hostel Federation. The Federation (a United Nations style organization) lays down basic standards for its members, but each National Association interprets these in the light of its own local culture.

Theoretically, membership of an Association is necessary for all travellers wishing to use the facilities, but this rule is lax in some countries outside Europe. However, membership is worthwhile, even as a precautionary measure. In England and Wales, the annual subscription is currently £1 for 5-15 year olds, £3.50 for 16-20 year olds, £6 for those 21+, a family membership is £12 and it is possible to get a life membership for £60. A similar small fee is the norm elsewhere. It is possible to obtain YHA membership at an Association office (and sometimes at a hostel) outside one's country of residence, but one then pays a much higher fee.

Facilities

Once a member you can stay in any of about 5,000 hostels in 50 countries throughout the world. Basically, a Youth Hostel will provide a bed in a dormitory of varying size, and will normally have anything from four to 100 beds. There are toilet and washing facilities and a communal room where members can meet, all at a cost of the local equivalent of from £1 to £3 for the night. In most countries, members will find facilities to cook their own food. Cooking utensils and crockery are provided, but not always cutlery. In some countries, cheap meals, cooked by the warden or staff in charge, are on offer.

One familiar feature of Youth Hostel life is the sheet sleeping bag – a sheet sewn into a bag with a space for a pillow. Any traveller intending to use the hostels should have one, although at some hostels there are sheets which may, or indeed, must be hired to protect the mattresses. Most hostels provide blankets and consider that these are adequately protected by the traveller's own sheet sleeping bag. In this respect, as in others, Youth Hostel customs vary from country to country.

A full list of the world's Youth Hostels can be obtained from information centres. Ask for the *International Handbook* – Vol. 1, Europe and the Mediterranean, for £3.77, and Volume 2, The Rest of the World, for £3.50. As well as listing the addresses and facilities of each hostel, the handbook summarizes the local regulations for age limits, facilities for families, etc. However, all the information given is subject to correction as circumstances change during the year and, of course, prices will inevitably rise in time.

Europe

Europe (including many countries in Eastern Europe, but not Russia) is well covered by hostels and the wide variation in their characteristics reflects the local culture of each country. Hostels in the British Isles are perhaps now unique in expecting a small domestic duty from members before departure, but this does help to emphasize to members that they are part of a self-helping club. This idea is less apparent in some countries where the Youth Hostel is often run, with the agreement of the National Association concerned, by the local municipality as a service, and relations between members and staff are strictly commercial. The club atmosphere is stronger also in France, Holland, and Greece. For hostel atmosphere, try Cassis, situated in an isolated position on the hills overlooking the *calanques* of Marseilles, 30km from the city. In West Germany, where the Youth Hostel movement started in 1909, Youth Hostels are plentiful – mostly large, well-appointed buildings, but lacking members' cooking facilities. They are largely devoted to school parties. Scandinavian hostels are also usually well appointed, many having family rooms, and there is therefore more emphasis on family hostelling. Iceland has seven simple hostels.

Africa

In North Africa, there are hostels in Morocco, Tunisia, Libya, Egypt and the Sudan. These too reflect the local culture. Try calling at Asne, a hostel in a Moroccan village 65km south of Marrakesh on the edge of the High Atlas mountains. Here the warden has three wives and will talk to you with great charm in French.

The Kenyan YHA has nine hostels, two of which are on the coast. One is at Malindi and the other at Kanami, about 25km north of Mombasa, in an idyllic setting amongst the coconut palms a few yards from a deserted white sandy beach. The Nairobi hostel is a meeting place for international travellers and at Nanyuki the hostel is close to one of the routes up Mount Kenya. Kitale hostel, near the Ugandan border, is part of a farm with accommodation for eight people and the one room serves as dormitory, dining and common room.

The rest of Africa is devoid of hostels until one reaches the south. Lesotho has one hostel, Mazeru, which is well worth a visit. Local young Basutos use the hostel as a youth centre, so travellers have a chance to meet them. There is a South African YHA but, because of the country's apartheid policy, it cannot be a member the the International Federation. The membership cards of white members of the Associations within the Federation will, however, be accepted in South Africa.

Zimbabwe has two hostels.

Asia

Israel's YHA consists of some 30 hostels, the smallest, in the heart of the old city of Jerusalem, having 70 beds. All provide meals, and many have family rooms, but the members' kitchens are poor. Orphira hostel in southern Sinai is fairly new, with superb snorkelling and diving close at hand. Syrian hostels are small and reasonably equipped. Many hostellers travelling to or from India meet in Damascus. There are fifteen very well-equipped hostels in Saudi Arabia, but only one or two are as yet open to women.

There is a good network in Pakistan, mostly well kept, and there are also a number of Government rest houses open to hostellers, as are some schools in certain areas during school holidays. Indian hostels tend to be mainly in schools and colleges and are therefore only open for short periods of the year, although there is a large new permanent hostel in Delhi. Some hostels do not provide any kind of bedding, even mattresses. Sri Lanka has several hostels including one in Kandy and one in Colombo. Here, too, Govermnment rest houses and bungalows provide alternative accommodation at a reasonable price. There is a hostel at Kathmandu in Nepal.

The Philippines, South Korea, Malaysia and Thailand all have some hostels of which the Malaysian ones are particularly well organized. In Thailand, some hostels listed in the *International Handbook* appear not to exist. The Bangkok hostel, however, certainly does. None of the five Hong Kong hostels is in the city itself.

Three hostels have recently been opened in New Caledonia under the auspices of the French Association.

Japan has the most extensive network of hostels outside Europe, numbering some 600. There are two kinds – Western style with the usual bunk beds and the Japanese style with a mattress rolled out on the floor. Television is a common feature. Several hostels aare on the smaller islands of the country such as Awaji, an island in the Inland Sea. Japanese food is served in most hostels – a bowl of rice, probably served with raw egg, fish and seaweed and eaten with chopsticks.

Australasia and America

Australia has over 100 hostels, mostly in New South Wales, Queensland and Western Australia. Distances between them are great. The smaller, more remote ones, do not have a resident warden and the key has to be collected from neighbour.

New Zealand has hostels throughout the country. They are fairly small and simple, with no meals provided, but have adequate cooking facilities. Many are in beautiful country, such as the hostel near Mount Cook.

The Canadians still give preference to those arriving on foot or by bike over motorists. They also run a number of temporary city hostels in the summer. There are not many hostels in North America, considering the size of the continent. There are a few hostels in some of the biggest cities. (In the USA, a city hostel will often turn out to be a YMCA offering rooms to YHA members at reduced rates.) Most are in isolated areas of scenic interest not always accessible by public transport. There are, however, chains of hostels in New England, Colorado and the Canadian Rockies. A feature of the United States is the 'Home Hostel' where accommodation is offered to members in private houses.

In Central and South America, Youth Hostelling has not yet caught on seriously, although there are a few hostels in Mexico, Argentina, Chile, Uruguay and Colombia.

Although in the poorer countries of the world you can obtain other accommodation as cheaply as in the local Youth Hostel, members have the advantage of being able to look up an address in advance at points all over the world. They can then stay at the local branch of their own 'club' finding (albeit minimal) common standards of accommodation and be sure of meeting and exchanging experiences with fellow travellers.

Information from:

England and Wales
YHA
Trevelyan House
8 St. Stephen's Hill
Herts AL1 2DY
Tel: (0727) 55215
YHA Services Ltd
14 Southampton Street
London WC2E 7HY
Scotland
YHA
7 Glebe Crescent,
Stirling FK8 2JA
Tel: (0786) 72821
Northern Ireland
YHA,
56 Bradbury Place
Belfast BT7 1RU
Tel: (0232) 2224733
United States
American Youth Hostels Inc
National Administration Offices
P.O. Box 37613
Washington DC 20013-7613
Tel: (202) 783 6161
Canada
Canadian Hostelling Association
National Sport and Recreation Centre
333 River Road
Tower A, Vanier City
Ottawa
Ontario K1L 8B9
Tel: (613) 748 5638
Australia
Youth Hostel Association
60 Mary Street

Surry Hill
Sydney
New South Wales 2010
Tel: (02) 212 1151
New Zealand
YHA of New Zealand Inc.
P.O. Box 436
Christchurch C1
Tel: 79 99 70

Non-federated Associations
South Africa
YHA
P.O. Box 4402
Boston House
Strand Street
Cape Town 8001
Tel: 419 1853
Zimbabwe
YHA
P.O. Box 8521
Causeway
Harare
Tel: 796436

YMCA

The Young Men's Christian Association – YMCA – has 2,400 locations in 90 countries worldwide. Centres exist in Africa, Asia, the Caribbean, Europe, Latin America, and North America. Although there is an international network, it is very loose and each YMCA is autonomous. Standards and prices vary, but they can generally be counted on to provide a clean room and often a meal. In Britain, the price for one night's stay averages about £10 and rooms can be rented for longer periods of time at a lower rate.

Cooking facilities are not nearly as common as in YHA hostels and while linen is usually provided but you must supply your own towel. In addition, many centres have sports facilities.

Practically all YMCAs are mixed as are the members of its sister organization, the YWCA, although there isn't any real connection between the two. Religious services and Christian fellowship are both a part of the YMCA experience, but it is not mandatory for people who do not wish to participate in these activities. In fact, YMCAs sometimes adapt to their surroundings, as in one part of Africa where there is a Young Men's Chicken Association. Individuals can get access to the YMCA International Directory, but each office usually has only one copy. It is best to contact the National Council in the country you are visiting for the addresses of individual YMCAs:

United Kingdom
64 Forest Road
London E17 3DZ
Tel: 01-520 5599

United States
101 Wacker Drive
Chicago, IL 60606
Tel: (312) 977 0031

Australia
116 Albert Road
South Melbourne
Victoria, 3205
Tel: 03-699 7655

Canada
2160 Yonge Street
Toronto, Ontario M45 2A9
Tel: (416) 485-9447

New Zealand
Ken Hobson Street
P.O. Box 1780
Wellington 1
Tel: 736 950

On a Limited Budget

Christopher Portway

There is a military saying that 'any bloody fool can be uncomfortable' which has a lot going for it. For the traveller it is equally pertinent. However, while the soldier's degree of comfort is governed by strategic circumstances and the disciplinary attitudes of the higher echelons, that of the traveller is usually governed by cost and security with comfort itself being the best on offer between the two.

This is not to say that even a traveller – as opposed to tourist – has to slum it all the time. I myself don't really go much for luxury hotels, although as a travel writer, I'm not always able to escape the multiple star attention at their hands. The trouble is that most quality establishments have a depressing sameness about them. Not that I don't sometimes appreciate their comforts and gastronomic excesses after weeks in the African bush or Asian jungle.

Oddly enough, it's the reverse of the coin that lingers in my memory. Long after the Bournemouth Carlton or Nairobi's Norfolk's expensive attractions are no more than a hole in the bank balance, the recollection of a night of exquisite horror in an Afghan doss-house takes on the allure of fond evocation.

Thus it can be said that the cheaper you go, the more interesting are the people you're likely to meet and, basically, the more satisfaction the traveller is wont to attain. We usually visit a strange country to see how it ticks and you won't learn anything from an air-conditioned, chromium-plated emporium whether it's in Bangkok or Bali. Yet, having said this, let me revert to my opinion that an occasional encroachment into millionaire's row does wonders for morale as well as the state of one's cleanliness.

Vehicle and/or camping is one method of keeping accommodation costs down, but both have their limitations so far as comfort and security are concerned. Even the most basic hotel, hostel, pension or guest house can usually rise to a shower (if only a cold one) and many will rustle up a meal which can make a nice change from eternal self-catering. Leave your luggage somewhere before arriving at the hotel, so as to avoid giving the impression that you are desperate to accept the first room offered. *Always* ask to see the room before deciding to sleep in it, and check the price – not forgetting the government taxes and other additions. In many Third World countries, a vital consideration is security, so it is important to make sure your bedroom door has a lock that works.

Bed and Breakfast

In some countries of the world there are government-run, or state-owned accommodations that are well worth considering on all counts. The *pousadas* of Portugal are a case in point; good value, but not cheap. And, of course, the internationally known and respected Youth Hostel Association has a reputation to uphold. In Europe, too, there are in France, the *gîtes*, a home from home – or at least, someone else's home – where you can stay for periods long or short. But they are not normally bookable for periods of less than one week, reckoned from Saturday to Saturday.

The British institution of Bed and Breakfast is spreading – you'll frequently see *zimmer* and *chambre* in German and French windows and they are fine so far as the room is concerned, but breakfast is usually extra or not at all and France, in particular, does so short-change one with breakfast. But in the United States, they have the right idea with a Bed and Breakfast where a stack of pancakes covered in syrup is added to a mammoth British-style fry-up. The concept has not yet completely conquered North America, but give it time. They still can't quite get rid of their down-at-heel motel image. However, you can, even now, book ahead with one of the B&B 'chains' prior to arrival in the United States and so have your accommodation fixed all along your proposed route.

Throughout Africa and Asia, good and inexpensive board and lodging is provided by 'resthouses'. Those in India I know particularly well. Each varies in character, amenities offered, comfort and – vital to some – the availability of water for washing. In the Himalayas, those built by the forest administration under former British rule were constructed in high, commanding positions far above villages and roads. Here they are built of stone and timber in what might be described as Victorian railway station style, each with two or three bedrooms, plainly furnished, with a bathroom and store-room at the rear. The wooden verandah at the front is the trademark of all such resthouses, while respectfully at a distance are the staff quarters and kitchen. In the more remote areas, all signs of minor luxuries a traveller could respect during the time of the British Raj have vanished, but nearer towns, I found treats in store: freshly painted bungalows valiantly clinging to the remnants of their former glory. Indian Dak bungalows are also available, extremely cheaply, on a first come, first serve basis.

The Communist Countries

In the Communist countries, one is more constrained. China insists you go into a tourist hotel whether you like it or not, and most are enormous barrack-like places, perfectly adequate for comfort though far from luxurious and lacking the slightest individuality or character. No need for security here as violent crime and theft are rare. It was only in Turfan, in Sinkiang, that I came across a charming lodge – a foreign visitor's guesthouse they called it – with a grapevine-roofed forecourt and old-fashioned waterjug and bowls for washing. In Inner Mongolia they offered me a tourist *yurt* which was clean and comfortable, and not at all like the real thing. In Russia, nothing ever worked in the tourist hotels I stayed in: lifts inoperative, telephones that trilled unasked for early morning calls, baths and basins with no plugs, and taps that produced rusty water or none. The East European states, as well as Russia, sometimes make entry conditional upon the purchase of accommodation in advance because of the anxiety to get their hands on our hard currency. But once you are in, a number of People's Republics – but not the Soviet Union – offer a choice of graded hotels, hostels or private house accommodation at a fixed and inexpensive price. Your private house hosts will almost certainly be selected not only for linguistic ability but also for political reliability but, nevertheless, this is a very worthwhile form of board and lodging. I have stayed thus in Bulgaria and Romania and in both countries I was given meals that formed no part of the transaction though I managed to return the compliment by sending my hosts some English books they were unable to obtain locally.

Desperation

I've never yet had to bribe my way into a hotel though the practice is said to be widespread in Third World countries. I have, however, arrived in towns where hotels could not or would not accept me. This happened in Libya. Just try getting a room, however modest, in its capital Tripoli! Making a reservation won't help either, for they'll deny having received your instructions – even if you've got their booking confirmation to wave in their faces. My solution was to lay out my sleeping bag in the lush gardens of the city's central square and prepare for a perfectly satisfactory night under the stars. Within minutes, along came a jeepload of armed police demanding that I sleep in a hotel. 'Find one for me and I will,' I replied. And, you know, they did.

In some countries a visitor can, in normal circumstances, travel only in a group with prearranged accommodation, so hotel booking problems don't arise. I found this in Cuba a few years back. There, whatever the calibre of the hotel, there was no air-conditioning, which meant that summer nights were one long sweat. In these conditions, it's best to escape to the beach or swimming pool – or even the shower, if it works. Another group-minded country is Albania

where its foreign tourist-only hotels leave much to be desired. Even in Tirana's showpiece, Dajti, I flushed the downstairs toilet and sent a river of water through the foyer. At the Adriatik in the port and resort of Durres, water came on only at night, between two and three am. The more pernickety of us adjusted our lives accordingly though I undertook my ablutions in the sea and used the quite undrinkable ersatz coffee for shaving.

Worse than no air-conditioning is too much air-conditioning and the United States is the chief culprit here. I stayed once in the second-best hotel in Dallas; a whole suite of rooms they gave me, but I spent most of my night unscrewing the bolted-up window.

Desert Lodgings

The desert, of course, produces another kind of lodging that comes under the heading of hospitality. A traveller in the Sahara or the Gobi will never lack for food and shelter, for among the great sand seas and stony plains, all men are equal. A Bedouin tent is filthy, full of vermin and dirty sheep, goats and children, while the sand-gritted food offerings are best not too closely observed. But here is to be found the true brotherhood of man: so never abuse such offerings, for the deserts of this world have a way of dealing with the foolish and the selfish.

If you are travelling in Arabia or Yemen, you will come across the *fondouk*, a kind of dormitory where everyone sleeps happily on mattresses on the floor. Many of these community sleeping rooms are multi-sto-rey houses more like medieval forts, and some will supply a simple but satisfying meal. Conveniences and amenities are of the roughest and with no electric light a torch becomes a prime possession if you have to find a toilet in the middle of the night. A problem here is security of one's belongings and the best solution I can offer is to take what you can to bed with you. In a land where hotel accommodation is viciously expensive, the *fondouk* has its points.

Turkey, Iran, Afghanistan, Pakistan, India – the route to the East – can produce some real nightmares of accommodation that you will remember with delight back at home (I speak now of days gone by and – God, war and revolution willing – days to come). The Majestic – no more than a doss-house – in Jelalabad shines darkest in my personal tableau of sheer horror. We slept in rows along a kind of sleeping gallery. My neighbours were bearded, leering Afghan tribesmen in colourful robes and powerful smells, and they went to bed not only with their baggy trousers on but also their daggers, swords and assorted musketry. Trapped in the middle of this snoring mob I lay feeling the rats scurrying over my blanket and, in the early hours, watched the most bulbous spider in history slowly descending towards me from a bug-infested ceiling.

There are no rules for worldwide hotel sojourning, but one important accoutrement for the traveller is an ability to accept life as it comes and appreciate the culture – or lack of it – of the country concerned. Accommodation can, if you let it, tell you a lot about people, particularly in those

lodgings to be had at the lower end of the scale. They'll cost you little but the experience will be immense.

On an Expense Account

by Philip Ray and Carol Wright

Regular business travellers have often complained – with a good deal of justification sometimes – about the high level of scheduled air fares. But it is an undeniable fact that those same travellers have frequently quite happily paid the full 'rack' rate in a five star hotel when they have reached their destination.

Research has shown, though, that hotel costs – including meals and drinks – can often account for more than 60 percent of the total travel bill on a typical business trip, so it is just as important to control this element of expenditure as it is to find ways of saving money on air fares.

The comparison between air fares and hotel rates is, perhaps, not entirely a fair one because the fares in many parts of the world are the result of cartel-type agreements which do not necessarily reflect true market rates. Hotels, though, normally operate in a competitive environment and would clearly reduce their rates if they were unable to fill their rooms.

In the dynamic capitalist environment of some Far Eastern destinations, hotel rates are notoriously prone to the laws of supply and demand. In recent years there has been a tremendous surge in the construction of new hotels in Singapore, for example, leading to over-capacity and massively reduced room rates. One leading Singapore hotel recently offered half-price deals on all its suites, bringing down the price of a night's stay to less than one would pay in a typical British city-centre hotel for a normal room.

In many parts of the world, though, the rates at hotels used by business travellers are distinctly on the high side. This is partly a function of location and high city-centre rents, because the typical business traveller usually wants to stay in a centrally sited hotel. There is also the question of prestige, particularly in the USA, because you may not be so highly regarded by your business contacts if you decide to stay in an unfashionable hotel on the outskirts of town.

Just like the airlines, hoteliers are particularly anxious to secure the patronage of frequent business travellers, first because of the high rates which they – or, more accurately, their companies – are able to pay and also because they produce year-round business in contrast to the holidaymaker who travels only during a limited period of the year and is highly budget-conscious.

It's worth checking before you book with a leading convention firm or magazine as to whether there is a convention on at your chosen destination. The Non-Aligned Conference has closed all upmarket hotels to individual travellers in both Delhi and Harare in recent years as governments have even cancelled firm bookings to fill the hotels with conference delegates. In any case, there is nothing worse than being the single traveller among hearty name-labelled hordes. I once stayed at the 1,407-bedroomed Grand Hyatt in New York along with 1,300 lady masons. It took a half-hour supervised queue to get to an elevator. Service, whether in room or restaurant, disappears when a convention is on.

Perks

For clients paying the full room rate – or even a premium rate in some cases – many of the world's major hotel groups have come up with ideas like Executive Clubs and Gold Cards which offer a variety of added-value benefits. Some provide entire floors of superior-standard rooms with a full-time manager to look after their special requests and possibly valet and butler service as well. More and more are also providing an executive club room with separate entrance, bar, magazines and games. Pre-registration, speeded up check-in and check-out and late check-out, and free use of health clubs are other typical facilities.

SAS International, a subsidiary of the Scandinavian airline, SAS, has capitalised on its airline links by introducing airline check-in desks in the lobby of most of its hotels so that business travellers can check in for their homeward flight in the morning and then go off on a day's round of appointments without having to carry their luggage around all day.

Most of the major chains also include business facilities for clients with secretaries, telex, interpreters and even sometimes radio pagers. Separate facilities for non-smokers are also often available.

The future in hotels, as predicted by the President of the Holiday Inn chain, is a computer terminal in each room, from which dining table, menu and wines can be selected and ordered by remote control. Bathrooms will all contain whirlpool and steam baths in addition to a shower and tub and hotels rooms will be linked to airline seats and luggage transferred automatically to rooms from the plane (some hope here).

Women travelling alone get less than welcoming reactions from some hotels, particularly in Japan where they refuse to believe you travel alone, and in Britain where you are often thought to be someone 'not quite nice'. American hotels often site women near the elevator; noisy, but it saves long night walks along dim corridors. A survey run by Best Western found that women want good lighting, mirrors and security more than the hairdriers, magazines and flowers which are normally the mark of a 'woman's room'. More hotels are now putting in club floors for women travelling alone. The New Otani in Japan has a separate floor for mothers with small children with special baby foods and a nursery.

Which Hotel?

Best value hotels are found where governments are keen to encourage visitors to spread out and see more of their country. The demise of the maharajahs helped India have a set of uniquely sumptuous palace hotels. Sri Lanka has kept up the old raj rest house system for tourists and in Spain and Portugal old manor houses have been turned into *parados* and *pousadas*, beautiful, characterful stopover places at low prices with local food.

Airport hotels are, on the whole, places to be avoided, drawing to themselves the dreariness and characterless practicality of airports; the most dull of nightly international human filing

cabinets. They can be worthwhile however if you need a room for a day on a stopover, so you can have a wash and a rest, or if you need somewhere for business meetings. They are geared to short stays and odd arrival and check-out times and will be far more likely to accommodate you than the more interesting, city centre hotels.

As a general hotel principle, small is beautiful. In anything under 50 rooms, more attention and character are to be expected.

Incentives and Discounts

Most of the large hotel chains operate schemes to reward customer loyalty, either by specially-reduced rates or extra privileges or a combination of both.

These schemes are constantly being changed or enhanced, but at the time of writing the Marriott Hotels chain was operating an 'Honoured Guest Award' scheme under which points are awarded according to the length of stay and the amount spent. Accumulation of a given number of points entitles participants to membership of the chain's Club Marquis which offers bonuses like guaranteed accommodation, with substantial penalties if the guarantee is not honoured.

The Hilton International chain operates its Vista Club, the only requirement for which is an overnight stay at a Hilton hotel at least six times during a year. The privileges of membership include priority reservations handling, extended check-out time, a welcome gift and an automatic upgrade to superior accommodation if it is available.

The Inter-Continental chain plays hard to get when it comes to rewarding frequent travellers. Applications to join its Six Continents Club are on the basis of a questionnaire and the hotel group then assesses how often the respondent is likely to use its properties. Club membership privileges are similar to those offered by Hilton.

One scheme with a difference is operated by Holiday Inn with its Club Europe. There is no requirement for a given number of room-nights but merely the payment of an annual fee (£15 sterling at the time of writing). Club members qualify for preferential reservations handling, secretarial services and superior accommodation.

Despite the proliferation of 'goodies' offered by the hotel chains, financial directors who have to try and control their executives' travel costs are more likely to be impressed by a reduction in room rates than by offers like a free newspaper in the morning, so when evaluating the various club schemes, it is best to look for the ones which give the most favourable reductions.

Most major hotel groups are prepared to offer discounts or 'corporate rates' to business organisations which give them a reasonable amount of business, typically a minimum of 100 room-nights in a year. With careful planning by your company's business travel manager – if you have one – it is

possible to negotiate discounts of up to 20 percent with many leading chains. Even if you are not a regular customer, it is always worth asking for a discount and seeing what happens.

There is a lot to be said for using one of the specialist travel agencies handling business travel who have tremendous buying power. Even if your own company is unlikely to provide insufficient business to a particular hotel group to qualify for corporate rates, it is often possible to pick up a similar deal through one of these agencies on a one-off basis and sometimes to do even better. Their discounts can be as much as 50 per cent.

If your company decides to organise its own hotel bookings, it is essential to ensure that you take advantage of all the special rates and deals which are available. One frequently hears stories about companies enjoying preferential rates with a particular hotel group which are not activated by travellers or their secretaries when they make their reservation because the word has not been passed down the line.

Within the UK, it is also often worth checking the brochures of the many mini-break operators, because some of them offer packages to important business centres, with or without rail travel, at prices which offer huge reductions over the normal hotel rate.

Communicating

Breaking the Barriers

by Jon Gardey

Barriers to communication off the beaten track exist just because of who you are: a visitor from another civilisation. It is necessary to show the local people that underneath the surface impression of strange clothes and foreign manners is another human being like them.

The first step is to approach local inhabitants as if you are their guest. You are. It is their country, their village, their hut, their lifestyle. You are a welcome, or perhaps unwelcome, intruder into their familiar daily routine. Always be aware that they may see very few faces other than those of their family or the other families in the village. Their initial impression of you is likely to be one of unease and wariness. Be reassuring. Move slowly. If possible, learn a few words of local greeting and repeat them to everyone you meet in the village. It is very important to keep smiling, carry an open and friendly face, even if you feel exactly the opposite. Hold out your hands, open, in a gesture that says to them that you want to be with them, a gesture that includes them in your experience. Hold your body in a relaxed, non-aggressive manner. Try to take out of the first encounter anything that might anger them, or turn to shyness their initial approaches to you. If they offer a hand, take it firmly, even if it is encrusted with what you might consider filth. Don't hold back or be distant, either in attitude or voice. On the other hand, coming on strong in an effort to get something from a local person will only build unnecessary barriers to communication.

Words and Pictures

Begin with words. If you are asking for directions, repeat the name of the place several times, but *do not* point in the direction you think it is, or suggest possible directions by voice. Usually the local person, in an effort to please his visitor, will nod helpfully in the direction in which you are pointing, or agree with you that, yes, Namdrung *is* that way, if you say so. It may be in the opposite direction.

Merely say 'Namdrung' and throw up your hands in a gesture that indicates a total lack of knowledge. Most local people are delighted to help someone genuinely in need, and, after a conference with their friends, will come up with a solution to your problem. When *they* point, repeat the name of the place several times more, varying the pronounciation, to check if it is the same place you want to go. It is also a good idea to repeat this whole procedure with someone else in another part of the village and frequently along the way to check for consistency.

In most areas it is highly likely that none of the local people will speak any language you are familiar with. Communicating with them then becomes a problem in demonstration: you must *show* them what you want, or perform your message.

If you are asking for information more difficult than directions, use your hands to build a picture of what you need in the air. Pictures, in the air, on the sand, on a piece of paper, are the only ways to communicate sometimes, and frequently they are the clearest. Use these symbols when you receive blank stares in answer to your questions. Use sound or objects that you have in your possession that are similar, or of which you would like more.

Giving and Getting

Not all of your contact with local people will be to get something from them. Don't forget that you have a unique opportunity to bring them something from your own culture. Try to make it something that will enrich theirs; try to give them an *experience* of your culture. Again, show them what it looks like: postcards, magazines. Let them experience its tools. If you have a camera let the local people, especially the children, look through the viewfinder. Put on a telephoto so they can get a new look at their own countryside. Take along an instant print camera, photograph them, and give them the print (just be careful, or this can get out of hand). Most important – become involved. Carry Aspirin

to cure headaches, real or imagined, that you find out about. If someone in the village seems to need help, say in lifting a log, offer a hand. Contribute yourself as an expression of your culture.

If you want to take photographs, be patient. Don't bring out your camera until you have established a sufficient rapport, and be as unobtrusive as possible. If anyone objects, stop. A bribe for a photograph or payment for information is justified only if the situation is unusual. A simple request for directions is no reason for a gift. If the local people do something out of the ordinary for you, reward them as you would a friend at home. The best gift you can give them is your friendship and openness. They are not performers doing an act, but ordinary people living out their lives in circumstances that seem strange to us.

I have found myself using gifts as a means of *avoiding* contact with remote people, especially children; as a way of pacifying them. I think it is better to enter and leave their lives with as much warmth as I can give, and now I leave the sweets at home. If you are camped near a village, invite some of the local people over to share your food, and try to have them sit among your party.

On some of the more travelled routes, such as Morocco, or the main trekking trails of Nepal, the local children, being used to being given sweets by passing trekkers, will swarm around for more. I suggest that you smile (always) and refuse them. Show them pictures or your favourite juggling act then give them something creative, such as pencils.

If a local event is in progress, stand back, try to get into a shadow, and watch from a distance. You will be seen and noticed, no matter what you do, but it helps to minimise your presence. If you want to get closer, edge forward slowly, observing the participants, especially the older people, for signs that you are not wanted. If they frown, retire. Respect their attempts to keep their culture and its customs as free as possible from outside influence.

The people in the remote places are still in an age before machines and live their lives close to the earth in comfortable routine. Where you and I come from is sophisticated, hard and alien to them. We must come into their lives as gently as possible, and, when we go, leave no marks.

Officialdom

In less remote areas where the local people have had more experience of travellers, you must still observe the rule of patience, openmindedness and respect for the lifestyle of others. But you will encounter people with more preconceived notions about foreigners – and most of those notions will be unfavourable.

In these circumstances – and indeed anywhere your safety or comfort may depend on your approach – avoid seeming to put any local person, especially a minor official, in the wrong. Appeal to his emotions, enlist his magnanimous aid, save his face at all costs. Your own calmness can calm others. If you are delayed or detained, try 'giving up', reading a book, smiling. Should you be accused of some minor misdemeanour, such as 'jumping' a control point, far better to admit your 'mistake' than to be accused of spying – though even this is fairly standard practice in the Third World and shouldn't flap you unduly.

Wherever you go in the Third World, tones and pitches of voice will vary; 'personal distance' between people conversing may be less than you are used to; attitudes and priorities will differ from your own. Accept people as they are and you can hope that with time and a gentle approach, they will accept you also.

Language

Where you have the opportunity of learning or using a smattering of the local language, try make things easier for yourself by asking questions that limit responses to what you understand; by asking questions the replies to which will add – helpfully and manageably – to your vocabulary. Make it clear to your listeners that your command of the language is limited. Note down what you learn and try constantly to build on what you know.

Always familiarise yourself with the cultural limitations that may restrict topics of conversation or choice of conversation partner.

Keep Your Hands to Yourself

Gestures can be a danger area. The British thumbs-up sign is an obscenity in some countries, such as Sardinia and parts of the Middle East, where it means roughly 'sit on this' or 'up yours'. In such places – and anywhere, if in doubt – the way to hitch a ride is to wave limply with a flattened hand.

The ring sign made with thumb and forefinger is also obscene in Turkey and elsewhere. And in France it can mean 'zero', i.e. 'worthless' – the exact opposite of the meaning 'OK' or 'excellent' for which the British and Americans use it.

By contrast, our own obscene insult gesture, the two-finger sign, is used interchangeably in Italy with the Churchillian V-sign. Which way round you hold your fingers makes no difference – it's still understood as a friendly gesture meaning 'victory' or 'peace'.

In Greece, as Desmond Morris tells us in Robert Morley's *Book of Bricks* (London, Wiedenfeld, 1978), there is another problem to do with the gesture called the *moutza*. In this, the hand is raised flat, 'palm towards the victim and pushed towards him as if about to thrust an invisible custard pie in his face'. To us it means simply to 'go back', but to a Greek it is a hideous insult. It dates from Byzantine times, when chained prisoners were paraded through the streets and abused by having handfuls of filth from the gutter picked up by onlookers and thrust into their faces. Though naturally the brutal practice has long since ceased, the evil meaning of the *moutza* has not been forgotten.

Learning a Language

Adapted from an article in Holiday Which? with the kind permission of the Consumers' Association, and updated by Anne Wilson and Kent Redding.

Can you tell a *tarte* from a *torte*, or even a *tortilla*? Or is your contact with the locals confined to school-room French, gesticulating hands or English pronounced slowly and clearly at the top of your voice?

Adult education classes in holiday languages are booming, and in every newspaper or bookshop you can see claims for 'almost instant packaged language learning' using the 'latest wonder method'. So how do you start?

Learning methods

The main ways of learning are:

Group classes – lots available, run by Local Education Authorities, private language schools or cultural institutes – such as the *Alliance Française*, 6 Cromwell Place, London SW7 2JN, (tel: 01-584 1856 or 01-589 7377), or the *Goethe-Institut.*, 50 Princes Gate (Exhibition Road), London SW7 2PH, (tel: 01-581 3344/7). They vary from one evening a week to intensive courses all day for several weeks. Ask your local education authority, local library, the cultural section of an embassy, or look up 'Schools – Language' in the Yellow Pages. Cost: LEA courses are usually cheapest, from about £8 for a term; private schools charge widely varying prices for their courses, anything from around £30 to well over £1,000 for an intensive couse of several weeks. OAPs, under-18s and those doing more than one evening class pay less; as does anyone registered unemployed.

Private tuition – private language schools and some LEAs have private classes. The Institute of Linguists, 24a Highbury Grove, London N5 2EA (tel: 01-359 7445) or regional branches of teachers' associations such as the Modern Language Association (head office at the same address as the Institute of Linguists (tel: 01-359 7953) can give details of private tutors or where to find out about them; also look under 'Tutoring' in the Yellow Pages or the small ads in, for example, the LEA guides to courses. Cost: from £10 to £15 per hour. Intensive courses can be pretty pricy. Berlitz Language School, Wells House, 79 Wells Street, London W1A 3BZ, (tel: 01-580 6482), offers short crash courses for beginners (about £1,500 for one week) and a Total Immersion Course for people with some previous knowledge which costs £2,800 for a two week course. They also have branches in Birmingham, Leeds, Manchester and Edinburgh. Probably the most expensive programme is offered by Stillitron, 72 New Bond Street, London W1, (tel: 01-493 1177. It runs an intensive ten day non-consecutive language programme which is geared towards business clients. They personalise the course towards each person's interests and use direct as well as audio visual methods. Languages included are French, German, Spanish, Portugese, Italian and Arabic. The cost is £3,300.

Correspondence courses – offered by some colleges, listed by the Council for the Accreditation of Correspondence colleges (CACC), 27 Marylebone Road, London NW1 5JS, (tel: 01-935 5391). Cost: from about £40 to £80 – intensive or advanced courses can cost a lot more.

Teach yourself – using books, or a combination of books, cassette tapes, records, radio and television. Books cost from nothing if you borrow a book to around £400 for a full programme of cassettes and learning books.

Language laboratory courses – offered by LEAs, particularly in larger polytechnics or technical colleges, and by private language schools. They may be flexible 'use the lab when you want' schemes or fixed classes, or supplementary to other, mainly group, courses. They vary from simple tape recordings with headphones to computer-controlled systems, with individual booths connected to a master console. In some laboratories, students can work at their own pace, recording and then listening to their own voices. In others, pace is controlled by the teacher, so a student can't play them back. A lot depends on how much supervision the teacher is able to give, and how good the course material is. Repeated drills can quickly become boring.

Residential short courses – details in a calendar (around £1.05 inc. postage) published by the National Institute of Adult Education, 19B De Montfort Street, Leicester. (tel: (0533) 551451). Cost: from about £30 for a weekend and from £80 for two weeks.

Full information about these methods can be obtained from the Centre for Information on Language Teaching and Research (CILT), Regents College, Inner Circle, Regents Park, London NW1 4NS, (tel: 01-486 8221), in particular from their *Information Guide 8, Part time and intensive language study: a guide for adult learners*. CILT's Publications Catalogue (a free booklet) contains many other guides and books you might find useful. Their library has lots of helpful information, including directories and lists of course materials, and will give advice on the type of course to suit you, and where you can get it. Write to them, giving them as many details of yourself and your needs as you can.

Which Method

Every method has advantages and disadvantages. Which you choose may depend on things like how much time you have, whether you can get to a language centre, whether you can do day or evening classes, what LEA facilities are like, and what you are prepared to spend.

Many people seem to find a combination of several ways of learning a language best and most enjoyable – such as group classes which use audio-visual aids and/or a language laboratory, group classes plus a BBC TV or radio course, or a teach-yourself system with individual tuition, or perhaps a short residential summer course. However, it sometimes takes quite a bit of extra effort.

Even within one method of learning, systems of teaching may vary. For example, many courses use 'direct method' teaching – which means that English is banned, and grammar is not taught formally. While this is a popular method for learning holiday words and phrases, it may have drawbacks in that you can only learn a language superficially without grammar – although it might hold your interest better in the early stages.

There are many Local Education Authority courses, with differing levels, aims and approaches, such as 'conversation', 'refresher', 'intensive', 'audio-visual', 'examination' and even some special short or holiday courses. There are day and evening classes, usually for one or two hours, once or twice a week, running from ten to thirty weeks with breaks during school holidays. You're more likely to find the exact class to suit your needs, particularly past the beginner's stage, if you live in or near a large town. In some areas, you have to join an exam course, such as one for GCE O-level. If the language you want to learn isn't offered, try to make up a group yourself. LEAs will usually try to find a teacher if there are about fifteen people wishing to study a subject.

A large proportion of courses use audio-visual aids such as TV, videotape, radio, slides and cassettes or records. Some classes use only the foreign language, others a lot of English. Some are conversational, others concentrate on grammar. Some students find their classes excellent for learning vocabulary, others are disappointed. Quite a few classes use BBC material.

The level of ability in classes varies greatly, particularly in those other than for beginners, in less-populated districts, or for less popular languages. Too wide a range of ability can make for uneven or slow progress, especially when pace is determined by the slowest members of the class.

The standard of teaching also varies, as does the amount of individual help given. In a two-hour session there is not much time for individual help. Enthusiasm for using native teachers, often proudly proclaimed, is not always matched by ability to select a competent one. 'We were taught by a French woman whose English was difficult to understand' and 'Teachers were Spaniards rather than teachers' are typical complaints.

The fall-out rate in LEA courses is high, a fact that some students find to their advantage, since teaching becomes more personal. However, classes can be closed if they fall below a certain size (usually eight or nine – sometimes as many as fourteen).

Overall, classes are enjoyable and can even become social occasions. How well you do depends on how much work you put in. There is a difficulty in achieving any real competence in the language in only one lesson a week, and it is highly advisable to supplement this method with as many short intensive courses as possible. Two or three days' concentrated practice can bring quite surprising progress.

On Your Own

No one teach-yourself method seems to stand out as better than others for all things. The main problems are:

1. The self-discipline needed. You need to set aside regular study periods and resist the temptation to skip over bits of grammar or those aspects which give you trouble.

2. Pronounciation can be a problem. When there is no one to hear and correct you, mistakes – in pronounciation, grammar, and vocabulary – may go unnoticed and so be learnt and repeated.

3. There is no one to answer your questions or check your work and progress. More simply, there is no one with whom to converse. Taking a correspondence course is one way of learning on your own at home which can avoid some of these problems, since you have the advantage of professional guidance.

The main advantages are:

1. You can work at your own pace.

2. After the course is finished, you can always start again, or just repeat certain parts of it.

3. You can listen to records and cassettes while doing other things.

Teach-yourself Techniques

There are many methods available, including books, cassettes and tapes, radio and television courses. A combination of two or more methods can be the most helpful way of covering different aspects of learning a language, so you pay attention to pronunciation as well reading and writing.

Books and tapes – Living French by T.W. Knight, £2.25 and *Beginners' Italian* by Ottario Negro, about £2, are useful for gaining a practical grounding in the language, especially with the accompanying cassettes, about £10 for two. These books are part of a series available in other languages (also with cassettes) published by Hodder and Stoughton, who also publish the *Teach Yourself* series in many languages. The cassettes are available from Tutor Tape Co. Ltd, 100 Great Russell Street, London WC1B 3LE, (tel: 01-580 7552). Tutor Tape offer many other books and tapes, including the *Talking* series by Sofroniou and Phillips, with conversational phrase books 50p, cassettes about £5.

Hugo's Simplified System, a series in several languages titled *...In Three Months*, costs about £25 for the full course of four cassettes or records and book. They also have a conversational course, *Speak French/German/Spanish/Italian Today*, for £5. The *Made Simple* series costs £15 for books and cassettes and available from Students Recordings Ltd, 89A Queen Street, Newton Abbot, Devon, (tel: (0626) 67026).

Audio systems – Linguaphone Institute, Beavor Lane, London W6 9AR, (tel: 01-741 1655), offers beginners' systems utilising cassettes and books in English, French, German, Italian, Spanish and more. An 8 cassette, 4 book system costs £149.50 and a 4 cassette, 3-5 book system costs £129.90. For intermediate students they offer systems in English, French and German, and an advanced system in English is available. Linguaphone's Minilab (£399) allows you to listen, record and repeat and is small enough to fit into a suitcase. For travellers who do not want to take the time to learn a language properly, but who want to be able to communicate in French, German, Italian or Spanish, they offer a Travel Pack which includes 2 cassettes, a map, a dictionary, and captioned picture cards covering emergency holiday situations.

World of Learning's PILL cassette system in French, German, Spanish, Italian, Russian and Afrikaans costs about £85, as does their French conversation course. They also offer portable language labs at about £140.

BBC courses – Television or radio courses usually start at the beginning of October to coincide with the academic calender. You can find out about these from the September *Radio Times* supplement, *Look, Listen, Learn*, your local library, or Educational Broadcasting Information, Continuing Education, A3155, Ealing, London, W5 2PA, (tel: 01-991 8031). There is a variety of courses including combined radio and television courses and short 'crash' courses. You can get past BBC programmes in the form of cassettes and records, as well as accompanying textbooks from BBC Publications, Woodlands, 80 Wood Lane, London W12 0TT, (tel: 01-576 0202, Telex: 265781) or by mail order from BBC Enterprises, PO Box 234, London SE1 3TH, (tel: 01-407 6961), or from your local bookseller. Costs range from 60p to about £20; not all courses have cassettes. For example, there are six short, intensive courses designed to give travellers a basic grounding in vocabulary and conversation, called *Get by in* French, German, Spanish, Italian, Greek or Portuguese, costing £7.48 for the cassettes plus 1.65 per book. There are many other beginners' and more advanced courses. The BBC also produce a German Kit, based on the *Kontakte* series, which is a complete, self-contained language course for beginners costing about £60 for eight cassettes and two books. A similar French Kit costs about £100.

How Long Does It Take?

Experts reckon that an adult can expect to learn 1,000 to 3,000 words during the first year. One student who went on holiday to Leningrad after two terms of weekly group classes (plus four hours of homework a week) said: 'I obviously didn't know very much, but was able to read the names of shops, goods and so on, exchange common courtesies, ask the way and do shopping; it added an extra dimension to my holiday. It was great to be able to read the Cyrillic script. It meant one could confidently go around Leningrad on one's own; one didn't have to stay with the group for fear of getting lost.'

How long *you* will need before you could cope as well depends on many things: the skill of your teacher, your motivation, how much time you have, your ability to learn, and knowledge of other languages.

A few points which might help you:
1. Have a goal at the end of the course, such as a planned trip to the country where the language is spoken.
2. Group classes can be a stimulation, particularly if you are encouraged to chat to your fellow pupils in the language.

3. Lively teaching makes a lot of difference.

4. Audio-visual aids help, particularly when combined with other methods.

5. You need to study regularly (CILT recommends you do homework for double the time you spend in classes each week). In the end it all depends on your commitment. Nothing compensates for laziness and nothing replaces steady daily practice.

Unusual Languages

You need to approach the learning of an unusual language with rather more care and consideration than the more familiar European ones. Mastering a language like Japanese or Arabic, for example, is quite different to brushing up on rusty school French or picking up a closely related language like Spanish or Italian. It still helps if you have already learnt a foreign language, however, as you will have some idea of the basic principles of grammar. You need to be highly motivated to embark on the daunting task of learning a language which has a different alphabet and difficult pronunciation. I would recommend attending a course initially; you will find it much easier than studying on your own.

The opportunities for learning unusual languages are obviously not as wide as for the 'big four' – French, German, Spanish and Italian. It's worth exploring all possible avenues. The Centre for Information on Language Teaching (CILT) publishes a series of very useful *Language and Culture Guides* (costing about £3.50-£4.50 each) on languages less commonly taught in Britain – from Arabic to Chinese, Japanese, Swedish, Serbo-Croat, Swahili and about 25 others.

The guides include lists of courses available, recommended books, and sources of further information. The choice of methods available to you depends on where you live. Your chances of finding a LEA or language school course are much greater in a major town, especially where there is a high concentration of ethnic minorities. In London, for example, ILEA offer courses covering nearly 50 different languages – including tongues as different and distant as Armenian, Afrikaans, Gaelic, Gujarati, Malayan, Mandarin, Persian, Punjabi and Yoruba. If you could interest enough people in learning a particular language for which there is no course available, the LEA will generally try to arrange classes if there is a suitable teacher.

Not only is it advisable to have some professional guidance, but the standard of teaching is even more crucial than with more familiar languages. It can make a world of difference to how easily you are able to grasp the fundamentals. Individual tuition can be very helpful, especially when you start, or if levels of ability differ widely in a group class. The Institute of Linguists offers advice and information; they also set exams in many unusual languages, which can provide a useful goal to work towards. There are a few correspondence courses available for less popular languages, but the degree of self-discipline required and difficult pronunciation present particular problems that make this method less satisfactory in this instance.

The more 'foreign' a language is, the more difficult it is to get to grips with. So time spent on intensive learning is valuable in becoming familiar with the new letters, sounds and constructions.

If possible, professional tuition should be accompanied by as much study on your own as possible. There is a variety of books and tapes available to help with home study – including some of those mentioned in the teach-yourself section above – information and sources are given in the CILT guides. For example, the Hodder and Stoughton *Teach Yourself* series covers 60 languages, including such unusual ones as Czech, Catalan, Cantonese, Icelandic, Indonesian, Samoan, Sanskrit, and so on. The Linguaphone audio system (costing £118) comes in 28 languages. There are BBC publications and courses in Arabic, Chinese, Gaelic, Russian, Greek and Portuguese.

How to be In with Islam

by Peter Boxhall

Like any nation with an important history, the Arab people are proud of their past. Not only because of an empire which once stretched from the far reaches of China to the gates of France, or their many great philosophers, scientists, seafarers, soldiers, and traders; but because they are one people, sharing a common language and culture, following the same religion which has become an integral part of their lives and behaviour.

Language

Arabic is a difficult language for us to learn, but it is a beautiful, expressive language which, in the early days of Islam, came to incorporate all the permissable culture, literature and poetry

of Arab society. Small West African children, sitting under *cola* trees write their Koranic lessons on wooden boards; infant Yemenis learn and chant in unison *Surahs* of the Holy Book; school competitions are held perenially in the Kingdom of Saudi Arabia and elsewhere, to judge the students' memory and knowledge of their written religion.

So, as in any foreign environment, the traveller would do well to try and learn some Arabic. For without the greetings, the enquiries, the pleasantries of everyday conversation and the ability to purchase one's requirements, many of the benefits and pleasures of travel are foregone. Best, too, to learn classical (Koranic) Arabic which is understood throughout the Arabic speaking world (although the farther one is away from the Arabian Peninsula in, for example, the Magribian countries of Morocco, Tunisia, and Algeria, the more difficult it is to comprehend the dialectical replies one receives).

Not long ago, before the advent of oil, when one travelled in the harsh environment of the Arabian Desert, the warlike, nomadic Bedu tribes would, if they saw you came in peace, greet you with *salaam alaikum* and afford you the hospitality of their tents. If 'bread and salt' were offered to you, you were 'on their face': inviolate, protected, a welcome guest for as long as you wished to stay. *Baiti Baitak* (my house is your house) was the sentiment expressed. This generous, hospitable principle still prevails throughout the Arab world.

Bureaucracy

Although they are subordinate to the

overall sense of Arabness, each of the Arab kingdoms, emirates, sultanates and republics has its own national characteristics. In those far-off medieval days of the Arab Empire, there were no frontiers to cross, no need for passports, there was a common currency, a purer language. Today it is different. There is bureaucracy abroad in the Arab world – mostly, it can be said, a legacy of former colonial administrations. So be patient, tolerant and good-humoured about passports, visas, immunisation, currency controls, Customs. Many of the Arab countries emerged only recently to their present independent status and it has taken us, in the West, some hundreds of years to evolve our systems of public administration and bureaucratic procedure.

One has to remember that generally the Arab does not have the same pressing (obsessional?) sense of urgency that we do. No discourtesy is meant. Does it really matter? Tomorrow is another day and the sun will rise again and set.

Neither in his bureaucratic or even everyday dealings with you does the Arab take much notice of your status, official or induced. When I was Personal Secretary to the Governor of Jeddah, important corporation chiefs and industrialists used to visit him in his *majlis*. They were received courteously and served the traditional *qahwa*. The Arab, however, is a great democrat and even these important people had, often to their annoyance, to wait their turn. Yet on one occasion, a comparatively poor *shaiba* came straight up to His Excellency, kissed him on the shoulder and extracting a scroll from the voluminous folds of his *thobe* (the uniform dress worn by all Saudis),

proceeded to read its fill, eulogistic length length in a high-pitched quavering voice.

To the Arab, it is of little importance to know who or what you represent; he is more interested in who you are. If he likes you, you will soon be aware of it. The sense of touch is to the Arabs a means of communication. Westerners, from colder climates, should not therefore be too reticent, distant or aloof.

Watch and listen, for example, to how the Yemenis greet each other: the long repetitious enquiries as to each other's state of health; the handshake; the finger that will sometimes curl towards the mouth, to indicate they are merely on speaking terms, casual acquaintances; sometimes to the heart, to indicate that they are intimate friends. The embrace, the kiss on both cheeks, which are mainly customary in the Near East and Magribian countries . . . If you allow the Arab to take you as a friend in his way, he may even invite you to his house.

Social Conventions

Baiti Baitak is the greatest courtesy. Do not, though, be critical, admiring or admonitory towards the furniture in the house. If you admire the material things, your hospitable host may feel impelled to give you the object of your admiration. Conversely, remember that if your taste in furnishing does not correspond with that of your host, the Arab is not much in the possession of beautiful material goods.

If it is an old-style house, you must always take your shoes off, and may be expected to sit on the floor supported by cushions. Then all manner of unfamiliar, exotic dishes may be served to you. If it is painful to plunge your fingers into a steaming mound of rice, and difficult to eat what are locally considered to be the choice pieces of meat, forget your inhibitions and thin skin, eat everything you are offered with your right hand and at least appear to enjoy it. Remember, your host is probably offering the best, sometimes the last remaining provisions in his house.

Once, in the Jordan desert, I was entertained by an important tribal *sheikh* in his black, goat-hair tent. An enormous platter, supported by four tribal retainers, was brought in and put in our midst. On the platter, surmounted by a mound of rice, was a whole baby camel, within that camel a sheep, within that sheep, pigeons... Bedu scarcely talk at all at a meal; it is too important, too infrequent an occasion. So we ate quickly, belching often from indigestion, with many an appreciative *Al Hamdulillah*, for it is natural to do so. When replete, rosewater was brought round for us to wash our hands and we men moved out to the cooling evening sands to drink coffee and converse, and listen to stories of tribal life, while the tribal ladies, who had cooked the meal, entered the tent from the rear with the children, to complete the feast.

In some Arab countries, alcoholic drink is permitted. In others, it is definitely not. From my two years' experience in Saudi Arabia and three in Libya, I know it is actually possible to obtain whisky, for example, but it is at a price – perhaps £50 a bottle, which, for me at least – is too expensive an indulgence, even if it were not for the penalties if caught.

Coffee and tea are the habitual refreshments: in Saudi Arabia, as was the custom in my municipal office, the small handleless cups of *qushr* are poured from the straw-filled beak of a brass coffee pot. 'Arabian coffee' is also famous: almost half coffee powder, half sugar. One should only drink half or two-thirds though and if you are served a glass of cold water with it, remember that an Arab will normally drink the water first, to quench his thirst, then the coffee, so the taste of this valued beverage may continue to linger in the mouth.

In North Africa, tea is a more customary drink. Tea *nuss wa nuss* with milk, in Sudan, for example; tea in small glasses with mint, in the Magrib; tea even with nuts, in Libya. Whoever was it said that the English are the world's greatest tea drinkers? Visiting the Sanussi tribe in Libya, in Cyrenaica, I once had to drink 32 glasses of tea in the course of a morning. The tea maker, as with the Arabian coffee maker, is greatly respected for his art.

Dress

In most of the Arab world, normal European-type dress is appropriate, but it should be modest in appearance. Again, if, as we should do, we take notice of Arab custom, which is based in history on sound common sense, we might do well to remember that in hot, dusty conditions, the Bedu put *on* clothes to protect themselves against the elements, not, as we Westerners tend to do, take them *off*.

As to whether one should adopt the local dress in the particularly hot, arid countries of the Arab world is probably a matter of personal preference. The *thobe* is universally worn in Saudi Arabia, the *futah* in the Yemens and

South Arabia. I personally used to wear the *futah*, but in Saudi Arabia, although the Governor suggested I should wear the *thobe* I felt inhibited from doing so, as none of the other expatriates appeared to adopt it.

Religion

The final, and perhaps most important, piece of advice I can offer to the traveller is to repeat the need to respect Islam. Not all Arabs are Muslim, but nearly all are, and Islam represents their religion and their way of life, as well as their guidance for moral and social behaviour.

In the same sense that Muslims are exhorted (in the Koran) to be compassionate towards the non-believer (and to widows, orphans and the sick), so too should we respect the 'Faithful'. Sometimes one may meet religious fanatics, openly hostile, but it is rare to do so and I can only recall, in my many years in Arab countries, one such occasion. Some schoolboys in south Algeria enquired why, if I spoke Arabic, I was not a Muslim, and on hearing my answer responded: *'inta timshi fi'n nar'* ('You will walk in the fires (of Hell?)').

In some countries, you can go into mosques when prayers are not in progress, in others, one cannot. Always ask for permission to photograph mosques, and in the stricter countries, women, old men and children.

Respect, too, the various religious occasions and that all-important month-long fast of Ramadan. My Yemeni doctors and nurses all observed Ramadan, so one year I joined them, to see exactly what an ordeal it was for them. Thereafter, my admiration for them, and for others who keep the fast, was unbounded, and I certainly do not think we should exacerbate the situation in this difficult period by smoking, eating or drinking in public.

Ahlan wa sahlan: welcome! You will hear the expression often in the Arab world, and it will be sincerely meant.

Porter, Sir? Guide?

by Richard Snailham

Porters, guides, interpreters and their ilk can be a great nuisance – it is difficult to feel at ease at the Pyramids surrounded by droves of importunate Arabs, all called Mahmoud or Ahmed, and all claiming to be the only and indispensable authority on Cheops, Thutmose, etc. – but they can just as often be invaluable, as when one is about to venture into wild, badly mapped country. I would not recommend venturing far from the Pan-American Highway into the remoter corners of the Ecuadorian Andes, for instance, without local guides.

Faced with the first situation, I find it best to appear indifferent, to affect disdain, flourish a guidebook and make it clear that I can get myself around without Mahmoud's unwelcome attentions. Generally, some persistent boy will tag along regardless and begin telling me the story whether I like it or not. Not only may he turn out to be a tolerable compromise but might prove, as I often found to be the case in the Ethiopian Highlands, an engaging companion whose *pourboire* is thoroughly deserved. It is not difficult to find a guide in well-visited tourist spots; they seem to emerge out of the stones.

At some famous sites, a guide is obligatory, as we find it is in places closer to home. One would not expect to go round a French *château*, for example, without a practised, often multi-lingual cicerone.

Fixing a Price

If a journey is involved, or any form of transport, or any great length of time, it is as well to discover the fee in advance, as one might on engaging a gondola in Venice – if only to allay the shock of the often inordinate sum asked. Some sort of bargaining may be possible, depending on the circumstances: one could haggle with a Tanzanian hire-car driver for a two-day trip to Ngorongoro, but probably not with a Hong Kong Chinese girl courier operating a hotel-to-hotel, all-in bus trip to Repulse Bay and back.

It is also worth being extremely careful about who you choose, and how much you pay if you are going to be dependent for your safety on your guide or porter. There have been several stories in recent years of guides taking travellers into remote regions then refusing to bring them back without a hefty extra payment. The practice seems to be particularly prevalent in the Himalayas.

Guides quite often get lost. In open country, it is as well to maintain your navigation by dead reckoning and repeatedly ask the names of prominent features. Never pose questions like 'Is it far?' because guides rarely have any concept of distance, nor 'Will we get there tonight?' because they tend to wish to please and will give you the answer they know you want to hear.

Porterage is another unpleasant but necessary part of travel. Between airport and hotel, for instance. The scale of the problem varies vastly, from French railway stations with their *prix fixé* per item of baggage (fixed pretty high, too) to the uncharted problem-ridden business of arranging for porters off the beaten track.

Hiring porters amid the clamour of airport or railway station has few rules: follow your gear carefully, have your mind tuned to the local units of currency and the exchange rate, follow the local rules if there are any and don't overtip. I still shudder when I recall watching some of my quite elderly flock walk with their suitcases into a dense mass of grubby bodies outside Karachi airport, the air loud with suppliant screeches and thin, brown fingers clutching urgently at the Gucci handles.

Porterage in the Wilds

Out in the *ulu* there are other, different considerations to keep in mind. Porterage often involves animal transport. Porters and animals have to be fed and perhaps sheltered. If they are to be away from home for many days, some kind of advance payment may be necessary. If you are moving across their country you have to consider how they will get back to their homes.

In all negotiations of this sort, it is best to involve a local middleman. If you have an indigenous student or scientist or an attached police officer or soldier with your party they will be best at overcoming language barriers and agreeing a fair rate for the job. Otherwise, porters or guides are best hired through a local chief or landowner. This is essential in most wild parts of Africa or South America where tribal or semi-feudal societies prevail.

Sometimes local men will not wish to come forward as porters whatever the inducements. Even though we could offer marvellous goodies like planks of wood, rope, slightly dented jerry cans (to a tribe still using gourds), the proud Shankilla of the lower Blue Nile would not carry for us because it would have shamed them: carrying loads is women's work. Blashford-Snell nearly asked them to send their women along but, since that might have been misunderstood, employed the village boys instead. Other tribesmen, like the Bakongo on the banks of the Zaïre River, where porterage has been a minor industry since the advent of Stanley in 1877, have no such compunction. Some of the best porters we ever had were Angolan FNLA refugees in Bas-Zaïre, who, with their broad smiles and outlandish hats, helped us to relaunch our giant inflatables in 1975.

Bonuses

With large numbers of men it is best to deal with a single head porter and pay him for his pains. But pay each man personally, a portion of his cash at the outset, if you wish, but keep the bulk until arrival at your destination. It is an added kindness and a mark of gratitude if there is something in your stores – plastic bags, wire, spare clothing, cigarettes, even empty tins and other containers – which you can distribute as a bonus.

Porters are generally honest, but it is as well to keep your baggage train in the centre of the column in case the odd load should slip off into the bush.

And with this arrangement, it is easier to see and act promptly when a porter who is fatigued or taken ill needs to be relieved.

I am in favour of taking porters and guides into wild country rather than trying to struggle along without them. They may be difficult, like the Shankilla; they may abandon you precipately, as ours did on the slopes of Mount Sangay, but they do add a colourful extra dimension to the journey and they can be a form of security in hostile, lawless country. And when you pay them, be sure to tell the rest of your party you have done so, so that they don't, as happened once in Ecuador, get paid twice.

Anything to Declare?

by E.G. Peacock

When the expedition leaders of the first Younghusband expeditionary force set off, after months of preparation in India, to subdue Tibet and take the forbidden city of Lhasa, they had barely reached the frontier when they were halted by a British officer of the China Customs Post. The experience was perhaps as irritating for Younghusband as it can be today for the traveller. It was probably quite disturbing too for that officer, after months, perhaps years, of surveying the empty snows for the odd package tour, suddenly one day to see the endless columns of laden men and pack mules toiling up the passes. History does not record if he ever recovered from the shock.

Misunderstandings

If there is one certainty in cross-frontier travel today, it is that Customs posts are a universal phenomenon and will be encountered even in the most unlikely places. The problems that frequently arise are often the result of misunderstanding on one or both side, and not, as many harassed travellers feel, deliberate malice.

The average traveller, even the seasoned one, tends to approach a Customs checkpoint with a degree of apprehension. This commonly manifests itself in suspiciously nervous behaviour or, with another type of person, in a kind of defensive arrogance. The Customs officer, on the other hand, also feels some disquiet, especially if inexperienced in passenger examination. The nature of the transaction between traveller and Customs officer seems to engender a special sort of hostility. The bad feelings on both sides of the counter are, however, quite unhelpful and generally unnecessary – unless, of course, the traveller is knowingly breaking the law, in which case he or she has good reason to regard the Customs officer as an adversary.

The majority of countries place considerable importance upon their tourist trade, and with good reason. And most governments concerned with promoting tourism are also aware that the visitor's first and last contact with the country is almost always with the Customs officials. Generally they try to instil in the latter the need to ensure that the impressions so given are favourable. But also, and somewhat paradoxically, they expect Customs officers to display a conscientious diligence in the enforcement of import and export laws.

Remember, therefore, that nine times out of ten you are dealing with an official torn between two apparently conflicting sets of instructions, who is psychologically poised to behave in one of several quite different ways and who may well take his cue from you. Too great a degree of suspiciously nervous behaviour and he can be forgiven for a more than usually thorough examination – even if it is in the middle of a sandstorm. Too overbearing an attitude and he can likewise be pardoned if he stands on his small authority and unreels the red tape.

Tugs, Barges and Cigarette Lighters

One complaint read only too often is of stupidity on the part of a Customs officer. How often do we read some 'amusing' anecdote in travel books about the almost incredible obtuseness of a remote border official who delays an intelligent and law-abiding traveller for hours while going through an incomprehensible pantomime of official nonsense.

True, it happens, and, incidentally, creates some useful 'copy' for journalists. But it must be understood that the innumerable laws and regulations required to be administered by Customs have grown more complex with the months that pass. The traveller that descends in a Land Rover upon an isolated border post, that has perhaps seen a couple of small camel caravans in the last month, and produces for clearance a bewildering array of vehicle parts, camera equipment and the latest drugs for every known ailment must expect to bump into a mental block of considerable proportions.

Inevitably, too, some quaint examples of tariff classifications will arise, especially if the Customs officer has spent the better part of his life in a rural or village environment without much exposure to modern gadgetry. Certainly, he will have been trained, but it is not easy for such training to cope with every eventuality. How, for example, do you explain the fact that a Ronson cigarette lighter does not come under the heading of 'tugs, barges and lighters', or that logarithm tables are not furniture?

Travellers have a right to expect a high degree of competence when passing the frontier of a sophisticated country. But those with a reasonable amount of human understanding will make allowances in other circumstances and, I guarantee, will almost invariably be met halfway. On the odd occasion when they are not, I would be prepared to wager that they have had the misfortune to arrive at the border ten minutes after an irrascible but intrepid travelling salesman blazing new trails with a sample case of microchips.

Horses for Courses

It should go without saying, although it doesn't, that different places have different regulations. It is generally recognised that such items as dangerous drugs and pornography are undesirable imports (although what constitutes these varies wildly from country to country). Almost every country has, in addition, its own large range of apparently illogical prohibitions and restrictions. Malawi, for instance, bans goods bearing the national emblems as a trade mark; the cockerel and the rising sun are both national emblems. However strange regulations like this may seem to travellers, it makes sense to find out about them in advance. Tourist brochures will not normally give the details, so make a point of asking either at the tourist office or the embassy. And also ask about dress regulations or you could find yourself in the undignified position of being given a compulsory haircut at the border post.

Almost everywhere there are particular items which should never be found in your luggage. In some parts of the world you may wish to carry a gun for protection against marauding bandits. Unless you have all the necessary permits in advance, don't do it. Even then the red tape, the suspicion and the potential for trouble are such that it is probably not worth it. The authorities can often be more dangerous than any bandits you are likely to meet and may view the possession of weapons (particularly if unlicensed) as tantamount to armed insurrection. Other countries verge on paranoia when it comes to currency and have stringent regulations governing its import and export. And remember it isn't the Customs who make the laws or prescribe the penalties, so it will do no good arguing with them.

Commonsense Precautions

What can one do when travelling the remote byways to avoid trouble on the frontiers? It is obviously not possible to guard against everything that can happen, but some general tips are well worth observing.

Arrive at border posts at a reasonable time, and in daylight where possible. Avoid local feastdays and holidays.

Be relaxed in manner and smile often. Do not appear overanxious or impatient. Remain polite and friendly whatever the provocation and never make threats of complaint to higher authority even if you intend to do so.

Do not expect the officer to unload, open, unpack or repack luggage but give the impression that you are more than willing to do so.

Do not carry firearms and ammunition unless these are fully covered by local permits. If you have these, produce the items and the permits before being asked. On no account wait until they are discovered.

Do not carry alcoholic beverages into Islamic countries unless you know they are permitted.

Do not carry or wear items of military-looking clothing such as camouflage jackets.

Carry only normal drugs and remedies and then keep them in properly labelled containers. If they are for your regular use, carry a letter to that effect.

Do not carry literature that could be considered even remotely objectionable on either moral or political grounds.

Declare all currency, traveller's cheques and gold.

Declare any item about which you have doubts. Failing to do so is an offence in itself and declaration is at least an indication of honest intent.

Advance Planning

It is always a good idea, before leaving on a trip, to call at the nearest office of the overseas representative of any country you intend to visit to find out what special regulations you should observe. This is particularly advisable if you are travelling by vehicle as quite complicated rules of temporary importation, payment of duty on deposit, acceptances of triptiques, etc. often apply and these may be beyond the powers of the officers at a small border post. Bear in mind that there is no guarantee that you will receive reliable information from embassies, high commissions or consulates. Diplomats are not always *au fait* with their own Customs formalities. If time permits, it is better to write to the Director or Controller of Customs in the country of destination asking specific questions. You can then take his reply with you for production at the border. It will carry a lot of weight.

When I worked as a Customs officer in both Africa and the Far East, I never failed to be amazed by the number of expeditions which neglected to arrange Customs clearance prior to arrival. Months of preparation were often devoted to getting approval from various ministries (the ones concerned with the particular sphere of interest of the expedition). The story was always the same. The Minister of Health, of Mines, of Forestry, of Wildlife or whatever had given his blessing and then forgotten he had done so. Often, too, an interested local benefactor had arranged accommodation and itineraries, entertainment and hospitality. Everything in fact had been organised to a split-second schedule. Full of confidence, the expedition then flew or trucked in, with specialised equipment ranging from cases of pemmican to litres of the latest experimental fertility drug. At this point the unfeeling and obstructive Customs officer entered from stage left and brought the whole show to a grinding halt. The expedition leader would then rush about, tearing his hair, while sheaves of lists were gone through with an exasperating slowness. The letters on ministry notepaper wishing the project well and promising every cooperation invariably failed to make an impression. At the close of play, abuse was heaped on the Customs for fettering academic endeavour with red tape. And only because it did not occur to anyone to consult them in advance.

The Customs officer everywhere is a normal human being who has a complicated and unpleasant task to perform. He will react favourably to a friendly and cooperative response. The barrier across the road is only symbolic after all.

Over the Airwaves

by John Hoban and Melissa Shales

Most people going abroad, whatever the reason, like to keep in touch with what is going on at home and in the world at large. If travelling in politically unstable countries, it is also advisable to keep track of what is happening around you. Finding news – particularly in an understandable language – is not always easy. English language newspapers may not be available and are usually aimed at entertainment rather than hard news. Local radio services, if not actually unintelligible, may be less than reliable. And you will probably have to contend with censorship. So take a radio.

Two-way Radio

For travellers to very remote or dangerous areas, it may even be worth taking a two-way radio or, at the very least, a search and rescue beacon. Chances are that you would never need anything more than a CB-style set-up, so that if you break down you are able to alert someone, whether the authorities or just a passing driver, and request help. If you are planning a large expedition that will be in the field for some months, consider taking a more powerful field radio. It can be an easy way of arranging re-supply, helping with navigation, or summoning aid in an emergency. You can keep sponsors and the media in close contact with the progress of the expedition and it could prove to be a major boost to the morale of expedition members who are away from home for a very long time.

The selection of which type of radio to take is a complicated business, depending on many factors from the conditions in which it will be used (weather and terrain), the type of transport to be taken and what use the radio will be put to. It is an extremely specialist subject and expert advice and training should be sought before you take any decision. A dead radio, or one in the hands of an incompetent operator, is worse than useless. The Expedition Advisory Centre at the Royal Geographical Society, 1 Kensington Gore, London SW7 2AR (tel: 01-581 2057) publishes a set of notes on *Radio Communications for Expeditions* which offers an introduction to the subject with a good list of suggested further reading.

Finally, before you buy make sure you will be allowed to use radio. Most countries license their airwaves, and many ban private use altogether.

London Calling

For the rest of us, however, our only contact over the airwaves will be through a transistor radio. Make sure you take a set that can pick up BBC World Service or Voice of America. For general convenience, you will want a set which has a tuning scale for Medium Wave, Long Wave and VHF. Don't get one which has only one tuning scale for Short Wave; the stations will be crammed so closely together as to make selection difficult. So look for a set with at least three Short Wave tuning scales, and the more it covers the better. Make sure too that it covers at least 49 to 16 metres (6-17 MegaHertz). It should take widely available batteries (and take plenty of spares). These receivers all have a built-in aerial for Medium Wave and a telescopic one for Short Wave and VHF, but not all sets have provision for an external wire aerial and earth. Look for these as, in difficult listening conditions, an external aerial and an earth can be very helpful.

News is the backbone of the BBC World Service with bulletins of world news on the hour, and more detailed half-hour reports regularly. The time between is filled with anything from pop music to test cricket or drama. There are also numerous programmes concentrating on British or financial news. If you have been away from home for a long time, there is something incredibly reassuring about the cool calm Britishness of the presenters. It'll make you homesick, but it also acts as a sort of 'security blanket' when surrounded by undiluted 'foreignness'.

Wandering Frequencies

Only in a few parts of the world can you listen to World Service on Medium Wave, so it normally has to be Short Wave. Unlike Medium Wave, Short Wave frequencies have to change according to the time of day and the time of year. This is not as complicated as it first seems, and if you are in one place for any length of time you will quickly find out which frequencies are most satisfactory at which times. If you are constantly moving, you will have to battle with a new set of frequencies for each place you stop.

The times of broadcasts and the frequencies for different parts of the world are too extensive to set out here, and anyway they change every few months. Though World Service is on the air 24 hours a day, it is not designed to be heard everywhere all that time. The aim is to provide signal at peak listening times of early morning and evening, although some parts of the world get much more than this. The full times and frequencies can be obtained from the BBC. The World Service publishes its own monthly programme journal – *London Calling* – which is available on subscription if you want a regular copy sent to you personally. It can also be picked up free from most British Embassies, High Commissions and Consulates as well as offices of the British Council.

If you want full details, write to BBC External Services Publicity, Bush House, PO Box 76, Strand, London WC2B 4PH, saying where and when you are going. They will then send you the appropriate programme and frequency information for the area together with some useful guidance on how to tune in.

Post and Telecommunications

by Penny Watts-Russell

A crude form of long-distance communication, smoke signals by day and fires by night, used by ancient Egyptians, Assyrians and Greeks, proved effective in its time, as one home-coming traveller as far back as 1084 BC found out to his cost. Beacon fires established on line of sight locations communicated to the faithless Clytemnestra, at her palace of Argos in ancient Greece, the news of the fall of Troy some 800 kms distant and the imminent return of her husband, Agamemnon – and so enabled her and her lover, forewarned, to plan his murder.

In more recent times – up until about 200 years ago – the quickest way of communicating home took weeks, even months, mail being transported by messenger, mail coach and sailing ship. In 1798, it took two months for news of Nelson's victory on the Nile to reach London.

It was the invention of the electric telegraph in the mid-nineteenth century – enabling messages to be sent at the speed of light – that produced a major revolution in communications and heralded *tele-* (i.e. far off, covering a distance) communications. In our own day, these include the use of telegraphy, telephone, radio, television and satellite to transmit messages. The telegrams, telex and telephone that make use of a worldwide telecommunications network are the most relevant in the context of the traveller contacting home while abroad; in addition, of course, to postal facilities.

Post

It is best to send all letters air mail. Those between Europe and the UK automatically go by air, but further afield, you also have the choice of surface mail which, as in the pre-jet age, can take weeks to arrive.

Telegrams

Telegrams are traditionally the speediest way of sending unwordy messages home, though in recent years in business communications, they are losing ground to telex, fax and electronic mail. Three main classes of international telegram are often available: *urgent* rate for priority; *ordinary*; and *letter* (deferred delivery service) designed for lengthy and less urgent messages. In some Commonwealth countries there is also a special greetings letter telegram at a special reduced rate for non-commercial personal messages. To speed up delivery you can address your telegram to your correspondent's telephone or telex number or Registered Telegraphic Address (a unique word providing their name, address and delivery instructions), the last two usually applying to business connections.

Telegraphic facilities are to be found in post and telegraph offices and in some hotels (as in Moscow). For the majority of leisure travellers, telegraphy is likely to be the most convenient method for despatching messages home quickly.

Telex

Telex – acronym for Teletypewriter Exchange Service – is a telegraphic system using telephone lines through which are sent direct current pulses representing characters typed onto a typewriter keyboard. Telexing has the advantage over telegrams in that your messages are not affected by time differences and can be received and recorded even if your correspondent's office is shut. It will also provide a hard copy of essential information or instructions for future reference. With the expansion of the international telex network, which encompasses almost 200 countries, it is therefore understandable that business travellers whose firms are subscribers should turn to telex. Public telex booths and services are located at main post offices and telegraph offices, and in many international hotels.

Fax, a similar system that will send facsimiles of complete documents, is another extremely useful tool for the business traveller, but unless you are prepared to carry your own portable fax machine, it is unlikely that you will be able to find one to use outside the Western industrialised nations.

Telephone

The telephone can provide the most immediate and personal means of communication, made easier and quicker through the International Direct Dialling (IDD) system that – provided you know the dialling codes – enables you to dial direct to and from many countries round the world.

The IDD network does not yet fully interlock, which means that you cannot automatically phone any country within the grid from any other, and there are still some countries that have not been linked in. In these cases, calls will have to be placed through the operator. Where it is possible, you will have to dial a sequence of four numbers: the international access code; the country code of the country you are

phoning; the area code within that country; and the personal number.

Hints

Just a few other words of advice. Write down the number in full before you dial, so that each digit is dialled carefully and without long pauses and be prepared to wait up to a minute before you are connected. The call has to travel a long distance. Remember too to check before leaving for overseas, the STD numbers (area codes within your home country) you are likely to call: dialling the international access code and country code would be to no avail without them. Lastly, there is likely to be a time difference between the two countries, so remember to check that you won't be phoning at three o'clock in the morning.

If you do have to go through the operator, check beforehand as to how long you are likely to have to wait. Apart from Eastern bloc countries, where they keep to an operator system to keep tracks on who is phoning where, it is usually because phone links are extremely limited, and delays can be up to ten hours. The easiest way around this is to book a call for a specific time well in advance. If the phone lines go down, this will also affect telegrams and telexes.

If communication with the outside world is difficult, forget pay phones, book yourself into the best hotel around and be prepared to pay their exorbitant surcharges. The increased likelihood of your being able to get through at all is worth the extra cost.

Publications

British Telecom International Telecommunications produce a series of leaflets called *Phoning and Writing Home*, which includes most European countries plus Japan; and *International Direct Dialling country codes* covering all countries within the IDD system, which are helpful for area codes of their major towns. These can be obtained free by dialling 100 during normal office hours and asking for Freefone 2013.

Also available from most post offices in the UK is a leaflet *How to contact home when you're abroad*.

(For further information see Getting in Touch With Home on page 401).

Electronic Mail

by Stephen Usdin, Martin Rosser and Melissa Shales

In travel and communications, as in all other aspects of life, the computer revolution is beginning to offer a host of new possibilities. Many business travellers are already using portable computers, and more and more of them are discovering the joys of having their own communications terminal, without the hassles of dealing with public telex machines, and with a great deal more flexibility. Anything you can create on your personal computer can be transmitted.

Like more traditional forms of electronic communication – telex, facsimile, cable and telegram – electronic mail offers instant communication with most parts of the world. It has some advantages over these systems, but also some unique drawbacks.

Electronic mail is computer-to-computer communication sent via telephone lines. It can be a powerful and inexpensive way for international travellers to stay in touch, cutting through barriers of time and space, allowing users to send messages regardless of the time of day or distance the message has to travel.

The core of any electronic mail system is a series of mailboxes within a central computer. As a subscriber you are given a mailbox with an address and password. As long as you have the right address and password, you can send a message to any mailbox where it will be stored until the subscriber accesses the box and retrieves it. As you can also access your own box from abroad, it can be an extremely useful way for others to keep in touch with you if you are moving around and difficult to track down.

The telephone may be more appropriate than electronic mail for some communications. Unlike during telephone calls, the two (or more) parties to an e-mail exchange do not have to access the communications network at the same time, so you can't have a discussion, although with some electronic mail services the recipient of your message can read and reply to your message within minutes. However, it is more expensive, and more difficult to transmit hard information – part numbers or flight information, for instance – by telephone. More importantly, time differences can make an international call very inconvenient. Electronic mail is not time dependent, since whoever you are sending to does not have to receive the message in person.

Electronic mail is less expensive than telex, and can transmit a large amount of data in a reasonable amount of time – no need to wait half an hour for the telex to print it out. More importantly there is no need to re-key documents. When an electronic mail message is received, it is easy to store it. You can then make multiple copies, rewrite, or forward to other people. And the biggest and best electronic mail systems have some type of telex gateway, so it is possible to send and receive telexes. In effect, telex is an outdated subset of electronic mail. Some e-mail services also allow you to send laser-printed documents for rapid delivery.

E-mail is comparable in cost to facsimile transmission, but facsimile requires good timing and co-ordination between sender and receiver. It is often necessary to make a voice phone call to arrange a time to send a document or to confirm receipt. Also, facsimile machines are not as portable as computers, requiring a wall socket. There's only one battery powered fax machine on the market, and it's a group II machine. Furthermore, the equipment required for facsimile is generally more expensive than that required for electronic mail.

Telegrams are barely worth mentioning. They are still in use in some parts of the world, but are far more expensive and less effective than electronic mail. They are increasingly being used only for personal messages to people such as family who may not have access to a telex or computer.

E-mail's big disadvantage is that its viability is highly dependent on the country visited whereas public telex machines are available almost anywhere. It is usually possible to send a telex within half an hour of your arrival in any large city. Not so with electronic mail. You can be left to the mercy of the telephone system in that country, sometimes with infuriating results.

Using the Telephone Lines

Electronic mail uses telephone lines in a fairly specialised manner. This means getting the OK from those who run them.

The key to this, in virtually every country except the USA, is getting a dial up service account with the local ministry for posts, telephone and telegraphs. This body is usually known as PTT – and in most countries this stands for Pretty Terrible Telephones. The PTT is usually a government monopoly.

These accounts with the local PTT are almost universally referred to by PTT officials as 'NUI accounts'. This stands for 'network user ID' and consists of both an address (usually an alphanumeric string about ten digits long) and a password. The NUI account with the PTT allows access to local and overseas electronic mail and database systems.

In most countries there are several types of NUI accounts available. As a traveller, it is important to get a dial-up account – one that allows access to the data service without a dedicated line or leased equipment. It will usually take some digging among the bureaucrats at the PTT in order to uncover the dial up accounts – many PTTs wil try to sell a dedicated line and leased equipment first. Before they will grant an account, most countries will require a deposit of around US$100.

One strategy is to get an account in the country before you arrive. In countries where there is a long lead time in setting up an account this is critical. It's sometimes possible to track down the name and address of a person at the PTT through a country's embassy. Tymnet, an American data transmitting service, keeps a record of PTTs and packet switching services. Some PTTs, like Japan's, maintain overseas offices.

In some places, like the UK, it is possible to get a guest account that is good on a temporary basis. In others like Hong Kong and Japan, accounts can be set up relatively quickly – within two or three working days. In the USA, it is not necessary to get any type of account if the electronic mail service being accessed is US based, or if some gateway to an overseas account is available.

Getting on Line

Once an NUI is obtained, logging on to the local electronic mail system, or the electronic mail system back home is relatively simple. First, place a call to the PTT's local access number. The PTT's computer will ask for your NUI address and password. Then it will ask you for the address you wish to send to, in other words which electronic mail service to access. This is equivalent to the NUI identity number belonging to the person you are contacting, and it will tell the PTT's computer which electronic mail system you want to contact. It is essential that you have this address as without it you will not get through, and there are no listings available to let you look it up. Everyone using electronic mail is ex-directory. Tracking down the address of a German electronic mail system when in Japan, for example, may well involve phone calls and telexes back to Germany.

Mail Services Available

There are several hundred electronic mail services available today, but the field is dominated by a handful. Very few are compatible, so be extremely careful when deciding which to subscribe to. The biggest and best are accessible from nearly anywhere in the world. These include Western Union's *Easylink*, British Telecom's *Dialcom* and *Telecom Gold*, MCI's *MCI Mail*, Telenet's *Telemail*, *Geonet* – an independent mail network in Europe, Lockheed's *Dialog* and its international version *Dialmail*.

It may also be worth changing to or adding another electronic mail service to your normal one before departure, as some services are easier to access overseas than others. For links between the USA and Europe, there are some back doors that are worth considering.

Dialmail, for instance, is best used for UK/USA communications because there is no special need for a PTT account. *Dialog* provides its users with a special NUI and password that allows access to Dialog's *Dialmail* service. In the US, the packet switching services send the telecommunications charges to *Dialog*, who then bill users.

Another kind of back door is provided between *Geonet*, the largest European mail network, and *Econet*, a rather small system that is nevertheless on Tymnets packet switching service. *Econet* is run by the Fallorones Institute in California. Other gateways like these are coming on and going off line all the time – investigation of these avenues before the trip can save hundreds of dollars.

Equipment

The equipment for getting on line can

be relatively simple: a computer and a modem. In both these areas the idea is to go for something that is light and portable and there are a couple of ways to go about this. One is to get a cheap laptop micrcomputer, such as those made by Kyocera for Tandy, NEC and Epson. These machines are perfectly adequate for getting on line and have many advantages over more expensive and sophisticated machines. They are simple to use, are battery operated, so there is no problem with power conversion, and are inconspicuous.

IBM PC compatible portables are another option, and they offer a lot more in terms of power. If you have to be able to do Lotus 1-2-3 spreadsheets, or work with someone else's machine or data, they may be the only viable possibility. You will have to pay for this extra power in terms of weight, however, perhaps as much as 3 kilos difference, as IBM machines usually require more paraphernalia – disks, cables, battery chargers, carrying cases etc.

The other component of the equipment is the modem. Some machines will have modems built in; others will require an external modem. There are several standards in use that govern the way modems send and receive data. Virtually every country in the world, with the notable exception of the USA, uses CCITT standards. In the USA there are the Bell 103 (300 baud) and Bell 212 (1200 baud) standards. For other countries, the CCITT V.15, V.21 and V.23 standards are relevant. Some countries like Hong Kong offer both CCITT and Bell standards. At speeds of 1200 baud, it can be possible to use a US standard modem overseas. Though the local PTT won't like

it if they find out, Bell standard modems have been used in London to access local and overseas databases. For travel to anywhere other than the USA CCITT standard modems are best. For travel to the USA Bell standard modems are best. Note that modems in the US are cheaper than in most other parts of the world. It is possible to get 1200 baud modems for US$100 and 300 baud modems for under US$50. Hong Kong also has cheap modems. In other developed countries they are much more expensive.

Costs

Charges for overseas access are almost universally based on the amount of time spent on-line and the amount of information transmitted. Charges usually range from US$6 to US$15 per hour. The amount of data transmitted is measured in segments which have a maximum length of 64 characters. A rule of thumb is that approximately one half of the charges for an electronic mail session will be hourly and one half transmission charges, so just double the hourly rate to get an idea of what the costs are.

There are several ways of reducing transmission costs. One is to transmit messages at high speeds. Most laptop computers come with 300 baud modems; if traffic volume is relatively high, it may be worth getting a 1200 baud modem. The second alternative is more arcane. Data is sent in segments which can be as short as one byte or as long as 64. The key to reducing costs this way is to ensure that all of the segments sent and received contain 64 bytes. In some countries this can be simple and involves only setting the line length when uploading the file to less than 63 (where there are frequent transmission errors, set the number lower to allow for resends). When receiving messages, work a convention that your correspondents will upload their files with this line length. In other countries, getting the most out of the segments can be more difficult, and involves setting parameters on the PTT account. It is best to ask someone in the engineering department of the local PTT about this, or a local user of the PTT's service.

The best solution however is through a system called packet switching. To use this, you call up a local number (or the nearest available) and transmit the message there, together with the codes for its end destination. The switching system gathers together a number of messages for the same general destination and sends them together at extremely high speed. Once in the destination country, the package is broken up and the message passed on. This cuts down dramatically on the amount of long distance phone time needed, so while you pay a small fee for the service, you are effectively only paying for local calls. There are currently about 40 countries with packet switching facilities. A list is available from British Telecom International.

Paying

Paying for e-mail is certainly not as simple as paying for a phone call, as you are paying for your local PTT account and packet switching services as well as the phone line, and this is where many travellers fall down. PTTs are not keen on travellers because of their itinerant nature and the ever-present danger that they may disappear without paying. There are several new ways of avoiding this problem being set up at the moment, the largest of them being Smartcard. This hopes to get international agreements between all PTTs involved with electronic mail to set up one central credit system. You could then set up a Smartcard account, to which all costs will be billed. And as the danger of nonpayment would be removed, it should also become infinitely easier to get an account in the first place.

When All Else Fails

When all else fails, the medium most similar to E.Mail is telex. It may be possible to revert to a system of sending and receiving telexes at a public booth. But because good e-mail systems interface with the telex network, e-mail can be used on at least one end of the transmission.

Electronic mail certainly has a growing place in the world of global communications. It is still new and while it finds its feet, somewhat fragmented, both in the number of different companies offering the service, and in the number of countries capable of processing it. It is useful to anyone who needs to send large documents at speed, such as business travellers or journalists, but until it is more widespread and there are such basic necessities as directories, it will impinge very little on the lives of other travellers. Yet we could well find that in ten years time, it is as crucial a part of our communications network as the telex has become in recent years.

When Things Go Wrong

Avoidable Hassles

By Tony Bush and Richard Harrington

A traveller's best friend is experience – and it can take dozens of trips to build this up the hard way. But, fortunately, there are some tips that can be passed on to help the unwary before they even step on a plane.

Most people have the good sense to work out their journey time to the airport and then add a 'little extra' for unforeseen delays. But is that little extra enough should something major go wrong – if the car breaks down, for instance, or there are traffic tailbacks due to roadworks or an accident?

Remember, too, to try and avoid travelling at peak periods such as Christmas, Easter and July and August, when families are taking their holidays. This applies particularly to weekends, especially Saturdays.

Taxis and Taxes

Most travellers would agree that the task of dealing with taxi drivers could just about be elevated to a science. In some parts of the world overcharging alone would be a blessing. What is really disconcerting is the driver who cannons through red lights or uses part of the pavement to overtake on the inside.

And what about the fare? Without a meter, the obvious foreigner will almost certainly be overcharged. But even the sight of a rank full of taxis with meters should not raise too much hope. Meters often 'break' just as you are getting in.

Two good tips for dealing with the drivers of unmetered taxis are:

1. Know a little of the local language – at least enough to be able so say 'hello', 'please take me to ...', and 'how much?', and 'thank you'. This throws the driver a little. After all, the driver's aim is only to try and make an extra pound or two. He does not want to get involved in a major row at the risk of being reported to the authorities.

2. Try and have the correct amount to hand over. It prevents the driver pleading that he has not got sufficient change – a ruse that often succeeds – particularly when the fare is in a hurry, and it prevents 'misunderstandings'.

A typical misunderstanding might go like this: the traveller hands over a note worth, say, 100 blanks for a trip that he believed was going to cost him 20 blanks. However, the driver, with the note safely tucked into his pocket, tells him he was wrong; he misheard or was misinformed. In fact, the journey cost 30 blanks and 70 blanks is handed over. This leaves the passenger in an invidious position. He cannot snatch his note back and is faced instead with the indignity of having to argue about an amount that may be just over a pound or so (very rarely would a driver attempt to cheat on too large a scale).

In most cases, the traveller will shrug his shoulders, walk away and put his loss down to experience. And this is what the driver is relying on. That is the reason he is not too greedy. He knows that even the most prosperous looking passenger would baulk at too big a reduction in his change.

The traveller should find out before or during his trip whether he will be required to pay an airport tax on departure, and if so, how much. This is normally only a token sum, but it would be frustrating to have to change a £20 or £50 traveller's cheque in order to pay it. Departure taxes are almost always payable in local currency. Occasionally an equivalent sum in US dollars will be accepted. The ideal arrangement is to work out roughly how much transport to the airport will cost, add on the airport tax, if any, and then throw in a little extra for incidentals.

Tea Oils the Wheels

If you must spread around a little 'dash' to oil the palms that facilitate your progress, do so carefully, after checking how to do it properly with someone who knows the ropes. You may be able, for instance, to avoid a few days in a Mexican jail for a mythical driving offence. On the other hand, you could end up in jail for trying to bribe an officer of the law – and then you might have to hand out a great deal more to get out rather than rot for a few months while waiting for a trial. The $1 or $5 bill tucked in the passport is the safest approach if you do decide on bribery, as you can always claim that you keep your money there for safety. But it may only be an invitation to officials to search you more thoroughly – and since all officials ask for identity papers, you could go through a lot of dollars in this way. When you think a bribe is called for, there's no need for excessive discretion. Ask how much the 'fine' is or whether there is any way of obtaining faster service . . . .

Bribes, by the way, go under an entertaining assortment of different names. *Dash* is the term in West Africa, except in Liberia, where the euphemistic expression is *cool water*. *Mattabiche-* which means 'tip', 'corruption' or 'graft' – oils the wheels in Zaïre. In East Africa, the Swahili word for tea, *chai*, serves the same function. *Baksheesh* is probably the best known name for the phenomenon and is widely used in the Middle East. It is a Persian word, found also in Turkish and Arabic, that originally meant a tip or gratuity, but took on the connotation of bribe when it was used of money paid by a new Sultan to his troops. *El soborno* is 'payoff' in Spanish-speaking countries, except Mexico, where the word for 'bite' – *la mordida* – is used. In India you have the *backhander*, in Japan *wairo* or, when referring more generally to corruption *kuori kiri*, which translates lyrically as 'black mist'. The French refer to the 'jug of wine' or *pot-de-vin*, the Italians to 'little envelope', a *bustarella*, Germans have an honestly distasteful term for a distasteful thing: *Schmiergeld*, which means 'lubricating money'. Even here, however, exporters gloss over the matter by simply using the abbreviation *N.A.* –

Nüzliche Abgabe which means 'useful contribution'.

Smiling Strangers

Beware of the Smiling Stranger when abroad. It is here that experience really counts as it is often extremely difficult to separate the con man from a genuinely friendly person.

A favourite ploy is for him to offer his services as a guide. If he asks for cash, don't say you would like to help, but all your money is tied up in traveller's cheques. The Smiling Stranger has heard that one before and will offer to accompany you to your hotel and wait while a cheque is cashed.

The warning about confidence tricksters also applies to some extent to street traders. Not the man who operates from a well set-up stand, but the fellow who wanders about with his arms full of bracelets or wooden carvings. He may give the souvenir hunter a good deal, but prices on the stands or in the shops should be checked first. Sometimes they will be cheaper in the latter, when, frankly, they should not even compare. After all, the wanderer does not have any overheads.

Local Courtesies

One of the biggest minefields for the unsuspecting traveller is local courtesies and customs and most of us have our pet stories about how we unwittingly infringed them.

It is worth knowing that you should not insult a Brazilian by talking to him in Spanish. The Brazilians are proud of the fact that they are the only nation in South America to speak Portuguese.

It's also important to understand that the Chinese, Japanese and Koreans believe in formalities before friendship and that they all gobble up business cards. Everyone should certainly realise that they must not ask a Muslim for his *Christian* name. And it is of passing interest that Hungarians like to do a lot of handshaking.

It is easy to become neurotic about the importance of local customs, but many Third World people today, at least in the major towns, have some understanding of Western ways and, although they do not want to see their own traditions trampled on or insulted, they don't expect all travellers to look like Lawrence of Arabia or behave like a character from *The Mikado!*

Civility, politeness, warmth and straight dealing transcend any language and cultural barriers.

The Model Visitor

Ideally you should always wear glasses (not dark ones, which are the prerogative of the police and the refuge of terrorists). Men should add, a dark suit, white shirt, a dark tie and carry an umbrella. Women should make sure their skirts are well below the knees, their necklines demure and their arms, if not always their heads, covered. In practice, this is not much fun when the temperature is 45°C in the shade, the humidity is 100 per cent and your luggage weighs 35kg. Nevertheless, try to keep your clothes clean, use a suitcase instead of a rucksack if not backpacking. Shave and get your hair cut as close to a crewcut as possible without looking like an astronaut. A moustache is better than a beard, but avoid both is possible. Long hair, as long as it suitably neat, is usually more acceptable for women, who thereby look suitably feminine .

Do not try smuggling anything through customs, especially drugs. Hash and grass may be common in the countries you visit, but be careful if you buy any. A local dealer may be a police informer. Prosecutions are becoming more common and penalties increasingly severe – from ten years' hard labour to mandatory death for trafficking in 'hard' drugs, and sentences hardly more lenient in some countries for mere possession. There's no excuse for failing to research the countries you intend to visit. Talk to people who have lived in or visited them and find out what problems you are likely to encounter. If you go prepared and adopt a sympathetic, understanding frame of mind you should be able to manage without trouble.

Theft – The Second Oldest Profession

by Bryan Hanson, Christopher Portway and Melissa Shales

Obviously one of the most important things to keep in mind while travelling is the safety of your possessions. Do your best to minimise the chances of theft and you will run far less of a risk of being left destitute in a foreign country. Try and separate your funds, both in your luggage and on your person so as to frustrate thieves and reduce losses. And before you leave home, make arrangements with a reliable person whom you can contact for help in an emergency.

American Express probably issue the most reliable and easily negotiable traveller's cheques, have the most refund points in the world and possibly hold the record for the speediest reimbursements. If you don't have plenty of plastic to keep you going for the two to three weeks it can take to get replacement cheques or new funds via the bank, take these.

Play for Sympathy

If you come face to face with your robbers then use all the skills in communication you have picked up on your travels. Try humour. At least try and get their sympathy, and always ask them to leave items which will be of no immediate value to them, but are inconvenient for you to replace. They are usually after cash and valuables which are easily converted into cash. Try to get the rest back and risk asking for enough money for bus or taxi fare if you feel the situation is not too tense. Acting mad can help, as can asking the thieves for help or advice. One man, when approached in Kenya, claimed to be a priest and put on such a convincing act that the robbers ended by giving him a donation!

Many thefts will be carried out without your noticing, from your hotel room, or by pick-pockets in a crowded street. Never use a handbag that isn't zipped, and keep your hand covering the fastener at all times. They can still slit the fabric or leather, but the odds are lengthened as to their success. Never carry anything valuable in a back pocket of your trousers or the outside pocket of a jacket. Even the top inner pocket can be picked easily in a crowd. A money-belt is the most secure method of carrying valuables although even this isn't foolproof.

Never leave valuables in a hotel room, even out of sight. A good thief will know far more tricks than you and is probably likely to check under the mattress, or behind the drawers of the dressing table before searching more obvious places. As long as the hotel is fairly respectable and isn't likely to be in cahoots with local criminals, put valuables in the hotel safe, and make sure you get a proper receipt.

While on the move, never let your luggage out of your sight. Wrap the straps round your leg while sitting down (a good reason for a longer shoulder strap) so you can feel it if not see it. Lock or padlock everything. This will still not deter the most hardened types, but should lessen the chance of casual pilfering. A slightly tatty case is far less inviting than brand new matching leather Gucci.

Violence

The crime of violence is usually committed with the aim of robbery. My advice in this unhappy eventuality is to offer no resistance. It is virtually certain that those who inflict their hostile attentions upon you know what they are doing and have taken into account any possible acts of self-defence on the part of their intended victim. It may hurt your pride, but you live to tell the tale this way and, after all, if you're insured, the material losses will be made good by your insurance company following the submission of a copy of the police report of the incident.

In many poorer countries, it is advisable not to wear or hold anything that is too obviously expensive, especially at night. You should be especially wary in Africa and South America. The most robbery with violence prone city I know is Bogotá, Colombia, where in certain streets you can be 99 per cent certain of being attacked. Having had most of my worldly goods lifted off me – but not violently – in neighbouring Ecuador, I made sure I lost nothing else by walking Bogotá's treacherous streets with a naked machete in my hand. This, however, is probably a little drastic and not generally advised. You could become a target for the *macho* element – and you could get arrested for carrying an offensive weapon.

The British Exporter robbed three times – once at gunpoint – in as many days in basically friendly Rio spent his remaining week there avoiding *favelas* (shanty towns on the outskirts of the city where many thieves live) and making sure that he was in a taxi after nightfall – when local drivers start to shoot the lights for fear of being mugged if they stop. Sometimes rolled-up newspapers are thrust through quarter-lights and drivers find themselves looking at the end of a revolver or the tip of a sheathknife.

One of the worst cities in Africa for theft is Dar Es Salaam where locals tell of Harlem-style car stripping – a practice that is spreading across the continent anywhere cars or parts are in short supply. Drivers return to where they parked to find that their wheels, and often anything else that can be removed down to the windscreen and doors have been removed. An expert gang can pick a vehicle clean in under ten minutes.

In 1977 I walked right through Peru not knowing that the region was infested with cattle rustlers reputed to kill without mercy if they thought they'd been seen. Occasionally, ignorance can be bliss. Since then, of course, the situation in Peru has worsened, the bandits being joined by guerrillas to make the mountains decidedly unsafe.

Within urban areas, the best advice is to stay in the city centre at night. If it is imperative to move away from the lights, go by taxi and try not to go alone. And don't forget to press down the door locks when you get in. There are some countries – Egypt is a prime example – where other people just jump in if the car has to stop for any reason. Naturally, they're normally just an extra fare, but you can never be certain.

If, by mischance, you do find yourself walking along a remote, unlit road at night, at least walk in the middle of it. This will lessen the chances of being surprised by someone concealed in the shadows. And when you have to move over for a passing car, use its headlights as your 'searchlight' over the next ten or twenty metres.

Another good tip when in more rugged parts of the world is to avoid stray dogs. One businessman visiting Sana'a in the Yemen Arab Republic found packs of wild dogs roaming the streets – and there was no shortage of rabies among them.

Protecting yourself from attack by carrying a firearm is *not* recommended. Even in those countries that do permit it, the necessary papers are difficult to come by and in countries where the law is ticklish over the subject of mercenaries, a gun of any sort could brand you as one. One traveller was arrested in Zambia just for having a bullet on him! But that is not the point. The idea that a pistol under the car seat or one's belt is protection is usually nonsense. In many countries

a gun is a prize in itself to a violent thief who will make every effort to procure one.

What To Do Next

Consider what action you can take if you find yourself penniless in a foreign land. Report thefts to the police and obtain the necessary form for insurance purposes. You may have to insist on this and even sit down and write it out for them to sign. Whatever it takes, you mustn't leave without it. It may be essential to you for onward travel.

Local custom may play a part in your success. In Lima, for instance, the police will only accept statements on paper with a special mark sold only by one lady on the steps of an obscure church found with the help of a guide. They have a way of sharing in your misfortune – or sharing it out!

If there is an embassy or consulate, report to them for help. In a remote spot, you are more likely to get help from the latter. You may have to interrupt a few bridge parties, but insist it is your right to be helped. In cases of proven hardship, they will pay your fare home by (in their opinion) the most expedient route in exchange for your passport and the issue of travel papers. If your appearance suits they may also let you phone your family or bank for funds. If they do, proceed with thought.

Have the money sent either to the embassy via the Foreign Ofice or to the bank's local representative with a covering letter or cable sent to you under separate cover. This will give you proof that the money has been sent when you turn up at the bank. I have met many starving people on the shiny steps of banks being denied money which is sitting there in the care of a lazy or corrupt clerk, or in the wrong file. Other countries do not always use our order of filing and letters could be filed under 'M' or 'J' for Mr John Smith. Have your communications addressed to your family name followed by initials (and titles if you feel the need).

Quite an effective, proven way of moving onto a more sophisticated place or getting home, is to phone your contact at home and ask him to telex air tickets for a flight out. They pay at home and the airline is much more efficient than the bank. This has the additional advantage of circumventing the mickey mouse currency regulations which various countries impose. Algeria is a perfect example. The country insists that air fares are paid in 'hard' currency, but that money transferred into the country is automatically changed into Algerian as it arrives. One then has to apply to the central bank for permission to change it back (at a loss) in order to buy your air ticket. A telexed ticket can have you airborne in a couple of hours (I've done it).

Local Generosity

In desperate situations, help can be obtained from people locally. These fall into two main groups. Expatriates, who live unusually well, are often not too keen on the image that young travellers seriously trying to meet the local scene create, but once you have pierced the inevitable armour they have put up from experience, they are able to help.

They often have telex facilities at their disposal, business connections within or out of the country and friends amongst the local officialdom. Their help and experience is usually well worth having.

Next the missionaries. From experience I would suggest you try the Roman Catholics first as the priests come from the working classes and have a certain empathy with empty pockets. Other denominations tend to live better, but put up more resistance to helping. (I came across an American/Norwegian group in the Cameroons suffering from a crisis because the last plane had left no maple syrup). Swallow your principles or keep quiet and repay the hospitality when you can. They often need their faith in human nature boosted from time to time.

You will receive kindness from other temples, mosques and chapels and can go there if you are starving. Again do not abuse assistance and repay it when you can.

Real desperation may bring you to selling blood, and selling branded clothes in which you have thoughtfully chosen to travel, in exchange for cheap local goods. But local religious communities are the best bet and usually turn up an intelligent person who can give advice.

In Third World countries being poor and going without is no big deal – you may be in the same boat as some 90 per cent of the population. A camaraderie will exist, so you will probably be able to share what little is available. It would be wrong to abuse the customs of hospitality, but on the other hand, be very careful of your hygiene, so as not to give yourself even more problems through illness.! However, I recently heard that vomiting over the check-in clerk may get you three seats together so you can sleep on the plane.

Happy travelling!

Mishaps, Major and Minor:
What to Do

Loss or Theft

General Notes: Travel light and leave all valuables at home if at all possible. Keep all valuables and papers safely, either with you in a secure pouch or money belt, or put them in a hotel safe or bank vault. Handbags, jacket pockets and hotel rooms are all notoriously liable to theft. Keep a complete set of copies of all valuable papers in a separate place to the originals. Use copies, not the originals where possible. Never look too affluent; it makes you a prime target.

	To Avoid:	*Notify:*	*Provide:*	*Expect:*
Passport	Keep a note of the passport number, separate from the passport itself.	Police and nearest consulate or embassy.	Passport number, details of your travel plans and dates, photos of yourself.	To be issued with an exit visa, an emergency travel document or emergency passport (for which there is usually a charge).
Traveller's Cheques	Ask for printed advice from issuing bank or authority; follow advice and keep it with you. Keep a note of the serial numbers of the cheques, separate from the cheques themselves.	Police and issuing bank or company (eg Amex).	Details of issuing authority, and if possible, serial numbers of cheques.	From Amex, during working hours, a rapid refund, *or* at weekends and in an emergency, an immediate loan of up to US$100 for Amex cheques, *or* with some delay, replacement cheques from any other issuing body.
Credit Cards	Keep a note of card numbers and of the issuing company's address, separate from the cards themselves.	Police and bank or issuing company (telephone, telex or cable from post office, large hotel, etc.)		Old card to be cancelled to avoid fraudulent use: eventual replacement issued.
Vehicle	Don't leave vehicle unlocked!	Police and insurance company.	All possible methods of identification such as registration, engine , and chassis numbers.	To be issued with a note of confirmation by the police.
Money	Do not carry all your money in the same place; a small, obvious	Police and nearest embassy or consulate; and telex bank asking		Loan from consulate or embassy in an emergency (a small

	amount will often satisfy thieves.	them to authorise a local bank to issue money to you.		charge is made for this service, payable later) and your passport to be surrendered as security. Money cabled out to a Third World country takes at least two weeks and persistent enquiry at the receiving bank.
Luggage and Hand Valuables	Take a copy of your insurance certificate. Air travel: take out extra insurance, available from travel agents, as the carrier's liability is limited. Watch to ensure luggage goes on conveyor belt. Keep receipts.	Police and manager of hotel, campsite, etc. Airline personnel within four hours of arrival. Ensure that they fill in a 'loss or damage' form.	Copy of your insurance certificate.	Carrier to find luggage within three days; or to pay compensation, which on international flights, is based on weight, not value.
Vehicle papers	Keep a full set of photocopies of driving licence, insurance documentation (green card or equivalent), registration book, bail bond or other documents separately from original. One option: get an International Driving Permit and use this *instead* of your licence.	Police	Details of driving licence; photocopies of relevant documents.	To be issued with a note of confirmation by police; in some countries, a temporary replacement of your driving licence to be issued by the national automobile club on provision of details of your licence.

If:

you have a road accident – notify the police and fill in details on the form supplied with your insurance card or, if you don't have one, take down names and addresses of people involved and of witnesses; a photographic record of the incident will also come in useful.

you are stopped for committing a traffic offence – do not remonstrate, pay any fine demanded, but insist on being issued with an official receipt. (This helps to ensure that you are being charged at the correct rate for the offence.)

you witness a crime or accident – you are required in some countries to stay on the scene and render assistance. This does not apply to a civil disturbance or commotion, when it is best to keep clear in order to avoid a false arrest or charge. (Be careful, however, as in some countries e.g. Nigeria, if you take someone to hospital or find a corpse you could be liable for the cost of treatment/burial).

you get into trouble with the police for a suspected crime – insist on speaking to your consulate or embassy, if the police fail to inform them as a matter of course.

you are the victim of a crime – inform the police and your consulate or embassy.

you need a lawyer – consult your consulate or embassy, who will advise you on legal aid and procedures and be able to refer you to English-speaking lawyers and interpreters.

you need to make a telephone call home from a Third World country – the most effective, if expensive, way may be to forgo using a post office or the services of a cheap hotel and actually book into a Hilton or the nearest equivalent so as to use its telephone system. Even this takes time – one traveller reported a fifteen hour wait for a call from the Hilton in Rabat, Morocco. If you can get access to a telex, this is often faster and easier in an emergency.

you fall ill – you will usually be required to pay for some or all of the treatment, even if you can subsequently reclaim expenses. Make sure your insurance company is informed immediately if much cost is involved. And keep an emergency supply of funds to cover this eventuality.

a member of your party dies – consider having the body cremated locally, which may be less distressing and is usually cheaper than the very expensive and complicated procedures involved in having the body transported back home. The ashes can be flown home for internment. Inform the police and nearest consulate or embassy who provide advice and support. You may have to bully them into helping, but they at least know the formalities involved.

Editor's note:
This article draws on material in a feature entitled 'What You Should Do If . . . ' published in the Sunday Times.

In Trouble With the Law

by Bryan Hanson

Ignorance is no more of an excuse abroad than it is at home for having broken the law. Consideration is usually given to the traveller but this is often in direct proportion to the funds available.

Always keep calm; to show anger is often regarded as loss of face. Be humble and do not rant and rave unless it is the last resort and you are amongst your own kind who understand. Try to insist on seeing the highest official possible. Take the names of all others you come across on the way up – this tends to lead you to someone who is high or intelligent enough to make a decision away from the book of rules. Also, in totalitarian régimes 'having your name took' is positively threatening.

Pay the fine

If you are guilty and the offence is trivial, admit it. Do not get involved with lawyers unless you really have to. The fine will most probably be less painful on your funds than their fees.

On the other hand, do not misinterpret the subtleties of the local system. In Nigeria, I pleaded guilty to a trivial offence without a lawyer and found myself facing the maximum sentence. If I had used one, an 'agreement fee' would have been shared with the magistrate and the case dismissed on a technicality. If we had paid the small bribe initially demanded by the police, we would not have gone to court!

More serious situations bring more difficulties and you should make every effort to contact your local national representative. The cover is thinning out – for instance, 'our man in Dakar' has to cover most of West Africa. A lawyer is next on the list to contact, probably followed by a priest.

It is a good idea to carry lists of government representatives in all the countries through which you intend to travel – especially if you are leaving the beaten track. Remember they work short office hours (I once had a long and very fruitless conversation with a Serbo-Croat cleaner because I expected someone to be there before before ten and after noon!). There should be a duty officer available at weekends.

Keep in Contact

Regular messages home are a good practice. Even if they are only postcards saying 'Clapham Common was never like this', they narrow down the area of search should one go missing. If doubtful of the area you are travelling in, also keep in regular contact with the embassy, and give them your proposed itinerary, so that if you don't

show up by a certain time, they know to start looking.

The tradition of bribery is a fact of life in many countries and often reaches much further down the ladder than it does in the Western world. I find the practice distasteful and have avoided it on many occasions, only to find myself paying eventually in other ways. In retrospect, I am not sure if 'interfering with these local customs' is wise. But how to go about it when all else has failed?

In Detention

Once you've been locked up and all attempts to contact officials have been denied, a more subtle approach is needed. One can only depend on locals leaving the place with messages, or more probably rely on a religious representative who may be prepared to take the risk. Sometimes is is possible to use a local lad and send him C.O.D. to the nearest embassy or consulate, even if it's over a border, with a suitably written plea.

Third World detention premises are usually primitive and provide the minimum of filthy food. You may even have to pay to feed yourself. Time has little significance, so make your means spin out. Even though money talks the world over, try not to declare your resources or you may not get any satisfaction until the last penny has been shared out among the locals.

Humour and a willingness on your part to lose face can often defuse a tense and potentially awkward moment. Travelling gives you lifeskills in judging people and an instinctive knowledge of how to act. Use your experience to your advantage and don't let daunting lists of advice keep you quivering at home.

If you have the gall it is often a good idea to learn the names of a few high-ranking officials and name drop blatantly. How far you carry this is up to you, but when I married off my cousin to the Minister of Justice in Turkey, he didn't mind a bit.

and Christopher Portway

Being something of an inquisitive journalist with a penchant for visiting those countries normal people don't, I have, over the years, developed a new hobby. Some of us collect stamps, cigarette cards, matchboxes. I collect interrogations. And the preliminary to interrogation is, of course, arrest and detention, which makes me, perhaps, a suitable person to dwell for a few moments on some of the activities that can land the innocent traveller in prison as well as the best way of handling matters arising therefrom.

There are no set rules governing what are and are not crimes in some countries . Different régimes have different ways of playing the game and it's not just cut-and-dried crimes like robbing a bank or even dealing on the black market that can put you behind bars. Perhaps a brief résumé of some of my own experiences will give you the general idea and suggest means of extracting oneself from the clutches of warped authority.

Espionage: a Multitude of Sins

It is that nasty word 'espionage' that becomes a stock accusation beloved by perverted authority. Spying covers a multitude of sins and is a most conveniently vague charge for laying against anyone who sees more than is good for him (or her). It is the Communist countries of Europe and elsewhere in which you have to be most careful but some states in black Africa, Central America and the Middle East are picking up the idea fast. Spying, of a sort, can be directed against you too. In my time I have been followed by minions of the secret police in Prague and Vladivostok for hours on end. Personally, I quite enjoyed the experience and led a merry dance through a series of department stores in a vain effort to shake them off. If nothing else, I gave them blisters.

In World War II, to go back a bit, I escaped from my POW camp in Poland through the unwitting courtesy of the German State Railway. The journey came to an abrupt end at Gestapo HQ in Cracow. In post-war years the then Orient Express carried me visaless, into Stalin-controlled Communist Czechoslovakia. That journey put me inside as a compulsory guest of the STB, the Czech secret police. I have met minor inconveniences of a similar nature in countries like Russia, Albania, Yugoslavia and several in the Middle East but it was only in the '70s that I bumped into real trouble again. In Idi Amin's Uganda.

Interrogations James Bond Style

The venues of all my interrogations have been depressingly similar. That in Kampala, for instance, consisted of a bare concrete-walled office containing a cheap desk, a hard-backed chair or two, a filing cabinet, a telephone and an askew photograph of Idi Amin. This consistency fitted Cracow, Prague and Kishinev, except that in Nazi days nobody would dream of an askew Führer. Prague boasted an anglepoise lamp but then Communist methods of extracting information always did border on the James Bond.

Methods of arrest or apprehension obviously vary with the circumstances. For the record, in World War II, I was handed over to the Gestapo in Cracow by a bunch of Bavarian squaddies who could find no excuse for my lobbing a brick through the window of a bakery after curfew. In Czechoslovakia I was caught crossing a railway bridge in a frontier zone and, with five burp-guns aligned to one's navel, heroics are hard to come by. In the Soviet Union it was simply a case of my being caught with my trousers down in a 'soft class' toilet and with an out-of-date visa valid only for a place where I was not. And in Uganda there was no reason at all beyond an edict from Idi that stipulated a policy of 'let's-be-beastly-to-the-British'!

Keep Your Answers Simple

But the latter's line of questioning was different. It wasn't so much why had I come, but why had I come for so brief a period? That and the young Ugandan law student arrested with me. Being in close confinement in a railway carriage for 24 hours we had become travelling companions which, coupled with my suspiciously brief stay, spelt 'dirty work at the cross-roads' to Ugandan authority. And rummaging about in our wallets and pockets, they found bits of paper on which we had scribbled our exchanged addresses. It had been the student's idea and a pretty harmless one but, abruptly, I was made aware how small inconsistencies can be blown up into a balloon of deepest suspicion. All along I maintained I

hardly knew the guy. Which reminds me that the Gestapo too had an irksome habit of looking for a scapegoat amongst the local populace.

Then we came to the next hurdle. 'How is it your passport indicates you are a company director and this card shows you are a journalist? To explain that I was once a company director and had retained the title in my passport in preference to the sometimes provocative 'journalist' would have only complicated matters. So I offered the white lie that I was still a company director and only a journalist in my spare time. It didn't help much.

And, you know, there comes a moment when you actually begin to believe that you are a spy or whatever it is they are trying to suggest you might be. It creeps up on you when they catch you out on some harmless answer to a question. In Kampala I felt the symptoms and resolved to keep my answers simple and remember them the second time round.

For instance: 'What school did you attend?' I gave the one I was at the longest. There was no need to mention the other two.

My regimental association membership card came up for scrutiny.

'What rank were you?' I was asked.

'Corporal' I replied, giving the lowest rank I had held. Pride alone prevented me from saying 'Private'.

'Which army?' came the further enquiry. I had to admit that it was British.

Every now and again I would get in a bleat about having a train to catch more as a cornerstone of normality than pious hope of catching it. And there comes a point in most interrogations when there is a lull in proceedings during which one can mount a counter-attack. The 'Why - the - hell - am - I - here? What - crime - am - I - supposed - to - have - committed?' sort of thing which at least raises the morale if not the roof.

Of course, in Nazi Germany such outbursts helped little for, in declared wartime, one's rights are minimal and the Gestapo had such disgusting methods of upholding theirs. But in the grey world of a cold war the borderline of bloody-mindedness is ill-defined. At Kishinev the KGB had the impertinence to charge me a fiver a day for my incarceration in a filthy room in a frontier unit's barracks. I voiced my indignation loud and clear and eventually won a refund. In Czechoslovakia my outburst had a different effect. The interrogator was so bewildered that he raised his eyes to the ceiling long enough for me to pinch one of his pencils. And in the cell that became my home for months, a pencil was a real treasure. Now let it be said, in general, that the one demand you have the right to make is that you be put in touch with your own embassy or consulate. I once wasn't and it caused an international incident.

In another of Kampala's Police HQ interrogation rooms all my proffered answers had to be repeated at dictation speed. It was partly a ruse, of course, to see if the second set matched the first and I was going to be damn sure it did.

I suppose one lesson I ought to have learnt from all this is to take no incriminating evidence like press cards, association membership cards, other travellers' addresses and the like. But a few red herrings do so add to the entertainment.

The Executive Target

by Roy Carter

All over the world, in such diverse areas as Central America, or the Middle East, the level of politically motivated violence increases almost daily. The victim's nationality – or supposed nationality – is often the sole reason for him or her being attacked. Gone forever are the days when kidnap and murder threatened only the wealthy or influential. Instead, political and religious fanatics often regard ordinary citizens as legitimate targets, and this view will become more prevalent as prominent people take ever more effective steps to protect themselves. The average traveller is much more vulnerable, but still worthy of publicity – which is generally the motive behind all terrorist action.

Measuring the Threat

Measuring the threat is difficult, if only because of conflicting definitions of what constitutes terrorist activity. Incidents involving civil aviation, however, afford a generally uncontentious barometer. In the decade to mid-1983 a fearsome total of 748 people were murdered worldwide in terrorist attacks against aircraft or airports. A similar number suffered serious injury, and the problem is by no means confined to the traditionally volatile areas of the world. Of 144 significant terrorist acts recorded against civil aviation in 1983, no less than 55 took place in Europe. Almost all the victims were innocent travellers. And it is self-evident that this single aspect of the problem represents only the tip of a much larger iceberg.

No one travelling to certain parts of

the world can sensibly afford to ignore the danger. If the risk exists everywhere it naturally increases dramatically in known trouble spots. Nor is it wise to rely on the law of averages for protection. Terrorism and crime thrive on complacency and a fatalistic attitude can actually create danger. Awareness is vital, and it is surprisingly easy for any intelligent person to do the sort of homework that can pay life-saving dividends.

The first step is to understand something of the anatomy of political crime. Terrorist violence is rarely, if ever, carried out quite as randomly as it sometimes appears. Particularly in cases of kidnapping, the victim will first be observed – often for a period of days- for evidence of vulnerability.

Simple Precautions

Translating an awareness of the threat into a few simple precautions means offering a difficult target to people who want an easy one. Invariably they will look elsewhere. It is impossible to say how many innocent lives have been saved in this way, because the threat, by its very nature, is covert, but the number is undoubtedly high. The huge majority of terrorist killings and abductions are facilitated by the victim developing a regular pattern of behaviour, or by being ignorant of the dangers in a strange country. No experienced traveller would forego vital inoculations or fail to enquire about the drinking water. Testing the political climate should be regarded as a natural extension of the same safeguards. After all, the object is the same, and the price of failure at least as high.

Of course, the most straightforward response to ominous events is simply to cancel or postpone the visit. *In extremis* this option should not be disregarded, but there will be occasions, especially for the business traveller, when such a drastic answer is difficult or impossible. An intelligent interest in the press and television news is a fundamental requirement in making the final decision. And sensible analysis of media reports will answer many questions about known trouble spots and help predict others. If nothing else, it will highlight areas for further study. Equally important, but easily overlooked, sound research can help put less serious situations into perspective. Unnecessary worry based on sensationalism or rumour can be a problem in itself.

Official Attitude

It is crucial to get a balanced idea of the official attitude in the country to be visited. The host government's status and its relationship with the visitor's country are always critical factors. A basically hostile or unstable government will always increase the danger to individual travellers, either directly, or be such indirect means as ineffective policing. A recent example of the former risk was seen very clearly in the imprisonment of British businessmen in both Libya and Nigeria, following diplomatic rows. The latter risk is exemplified on a regular basis in the Lebanon, Mozambique and Angola.

Finding the truth will usually involve delving below the headlines. In Britain, an approach to the Foreign Office can produce surprisingly frank answers. Next, and more obviously, an analysis of recent terrorist activity should aim to answer three essential questions: when and where it happens, what form it takes and most important, whom it is directed against? The first two answers will help establish precautionary measures. The third may indicate the degree of risk by revealing common factors. A series of identical abductions from motor vehicles in a particular part of the city, involving the same nationalities or professions, for example, should be augury enough for even the most sceptical observer.

Local Feeling

It is also as well to know as much as possible about feelings among the local populace, which are by no means guaranteed to be the same as those of the government. National identity, and even religion, are often viewed quite differently 'on the streets', although the bias is just as likely to be favourable as not. One need not even step outside the UK to demonstrate the validity of this advice, as an Englishman on the streets of West Belfast could quickly discover. And in a country with a large Western expatriate community, for instance, any caucasian will generally be regarded as belonging to the predominant race. Depending on the local situation, this type of mistaken identity can be dangerous or advantageous. At least one case, the March 1985 abduction of three British visitors to Beirut by anti-American Muslim extremists, resulted from a mistake in the victims' nationality.

These attacks, and others involving French and US citizens, took place outside the victims' homes, highlighting perfectly standard terrorist methods. Known reference points such as home or places of work, are always by far the most dangerous. The much-publicised kidnap and subsequent murder of former Italian premier, Aldo Moro, by the so-called Red Brigade was a notable example of this fact.

Soft Targets

Importantly, but often forgotten, this demonstrates more than a need for extra care at home and in the office. It shows equally the terrorists' need for soft targets and their reluctance to proceed beyond basic research to find them. Terrorist resources and abilities are limited and to regard them as omnipotent is both mistaken and dangerous. Sensible precautions, like varying times of arrival and departure, parking in different places – facing in different directions, watching for and reporting suspicious activity before leaving home, and entering and leaving by different doors, sound almost too simple, but they really work. Only the most specific kind of motivation would justify continued surveillance of a clearly unpredictable and cautious target.

Company Image

In addition to this kind of general precaution, the business traveller will usually need to examine more particular issues. He will need to know how his company is perceived by various local factions. Previous threats or attacks on company premises or employees should be studied with great care, as should incidents involving similar organisations. Where applicable, the local knowledge of expatriate colleagues will be useful, but watch for bias or over-familiarity.

In the absence of any actual events, examine the company's standing in the community, especially where a conflict of interests exists between government and opposition groups. Never forget that a company will often be judged solely on the basis of its clients and associates. Always consider the status of the people you intend to visit. In these days of trade sanctions and mutually antagonistic markets the chances are high that any association will offend someone.

Practical Action

But analysis is only a partial answer. The results must be translated into coherent action. In extreme cases, the business traveller might need special training in such areas as defensive driving, emergency communication, and surveillance recognition. Many of the larger companies will provide special briefings but their failure to do so should never be taken as a sign that no danger exists. It could equally indicate a lack of awareness or a misguided decision not to cause alarm. There is nothing at all wrong with alarm, if it is justified. It may even be a necessity.

Regardless of whether special training is given or not, all travellers to high risk areas should follow certain basic rules as a matter of course. Keep friends and colleagues informed of your whereabouts and stay in company as much as possible. Utilise inconspicuous transport, but avoid public transport in favour of taxis. If in doubt, wait for the second cab in the rank. Never take a taxi if the driver is not alone. Dress down and leave expensive accessories as home. Don't book hotels in the company's name. In all, practice being nondescript in public.

Try not to think of these rules as an inconvenience, but as a natural consequence of your stay in a strange country, like remembering to use a foreign language. Relaxing one rule might be tempting but it could be the mistake that negates all the rest. Better to extend precautions than limit them. For example, travelling regularly by the same route can undo all the good work on the home front. The kidnap and murder of German industrialist, Hans-Martin Schleyer, was carried out because his attackers were able to predict confidently both his route and timing. The murder in India of British diplomat, Percy Norris, by Middle Eastern terrorists likewise occurred along his regular route to work. Mr Norris was shot to death in the back seat of his chauffeur-driven car when it halted at traffic lights.

On the Move

Make a habit of changing places in the car if you have a driver, or use a taxi now and then instead. The chances of being attacked on the move are extremely remote. It follows that road junctions, traffic signals, etc. are always more dangerous than stretches of dual carriageway, for instance. A prospective attacker will study his victim's route carefully and identify vulnerable spots. If he can do so, so can you. Be aware of these danger areas and stay on the alert when negotiating them. If driving yourself, keep the car in gear and ready for a quick getaway at temporary halts. Keep sufficient space between yourself and any leading vehicles to avoid being boxed in.

Routinely lock all doors and keep the windows wound up.

Last of all, remember that you stand more chance of being an accident casualty than a terrorist victim. Far from being dangerous, a little knowledge can stack the odds even higher in your favour. You'll probably never know if it passes the acid test – but you'll be in no doubt at all if it doesn't.

Fill the Bath-It Looks Like Civil War

by Anne Sharpley

Don't take it too personally when the shooting starts. They're almost certainly not shooting at you – and if they are, it's even safer since the level of marksmanship is so low, at least in all street-shooting I've been caught up in, that you're almost invulnerable. Hollywood never comes to your aid at such moments. You'd have thought that the rigorous early training we all get at the movies in both armed and unarmed fighting would have got into our reflexes. But it's all so much more muddled when it happens. Far from knowing when and where to duck I could never make out where the fighting was coming from or which side of the wall or handy car to duck behind.

As for hand-to-hand fighting, far from the balletic, clearly defined movements of cinematic bouts, everyone gets puffed, or sick, or falls over in a shambles of misunderstood intentions. Nor is there that crack on the jaw to let you know who's being hit when. So it's even poor for spectator interest.

As a reporter it is usually my actual work to be there and see what's happening. This means I can't follow my own best advice, which is to get out. Sticking around is the easy bit.

It is the next stage of the events, that sets in during and after the street fighting, that is always the real difficulty. The paraphernalia of street blocks, cordons, summary arrests and general paralysis as order is imposed on a troubled area presents the visitor with new problems.

Communications with the outside world cease, public utilities go wrong and airports close.

It is this sort of scene you can guarantee will take over. So forget the bullet proof vest you wish you'd thought of and get on with the practicalities. The first and best rule is worth observing before you leave home – never pack more than you can run with. Always include a smaller, lighter bag such as an airline overnight bag because if things get really nasty you need something handy with a shoulder strap to pick up and clear out with in a hurry.

Essentials

If you're in a situation in which something is likely to happen, it is worth keeping this bag packed with essentials. Don't run about with suitcases, it can't be done for long.

Always bring in your duty-free allowances if you know things are likely to get tough. Even if you're a non-smoking tee-totaller who hates scent, they're the stuff of which bribes and rewards for favours are made. And as banks close or the money exchange goes berserk they may end up as your only bargaining resource. And remember that drink is a useful stimulant, as well as solace. If I have to stay up all night I do it on regular small nips of whisky.

The next bit of advice will seem absurd at first, but you'll regret having laughed if you ever get into one of those long-standing semi-siege situations that sometimes happen when you're stuck in a hotel that either can't or won't provide for you. Take one of those little aluminium pans with a solid fuel burner – so small it will slip into your pocket. You can boil water at the rate of quarter of a pint to one solid fuel stick, which is about the size of a cigarette. You can get the whole thing from camping shops for only a few pounds.

If you take a few tea bags or a small jar of instant coffee, this will not only help if you're an addict of these things, but again wins friends and allies in an hour of need. Serve up in a tooth mug, but don't forget to put in a spoon before you pour in boiling water or you'll crack the glass.

As the water either goes off completely, or turns a threatening colour, it is just as well to have a means of making water sterile. And at the very least it provides a shave.

If things look ugly it is a good idea to fill the bath. You can keep filling it if supplies continue, but you can't get water at all if they really stop. Not only have you a means of keeping the toilet in a less revolting state, but you can wash yourself and keep away thirst (boil the water first, of course.) I always like to carry a small box of biscuits, although this isn't anything more than a psychological trick to reinforce a feeling of self-sufficiency.

If things get really hectic nobody in a hotel wants to know about you, but they get rather interested in your property. It's a great time for getting everything stolen. I came back from Prague in 1968 with scarcely a thing left. What's yours suddenly becomes theirs. So remember that overnight bag and carry it with you everywhere.

Whether you should try to look less conspicuously foreign is a moot point. War correspondents usually get themselves kitted out in a sort of quasi-military set of clothes and where there are women soldiers, as in Israel, I have too. If nothing else, it meant I could fill my taxi with girl soldiers and let them get me past the road blocks with their papers. But when I found myself in action before I had time to change, I was told later by a captured sniper that it had only been my pretty pink blouse that had saved me. He'd had me in his sights and liked the colour so he couldn't bring himself to shoot me!

However, you're much more likely to be holed up in your hotel. If things are exploding, it's as well to get whatever glass is removable down on the floor, draw curtains and blinds against window glass and drape mirrors you can't take down with blankets and towels. Glass is the biggest danger you face. Locate the fire escape and if it's remote get yourself somewhere else to stay either in the same hotel or elsewhere.

Identity in a Crisis

It's always worth trying to pretend you're from a country they're not having a row with, although local knowledge of nationalities is always limited, so don't try Finnish or Papuan. This is for occasional use when they're running around looking for someone to duff up. Hit the right nationality and you're so popular they won't put you down. Crowds are very emotional and the least thing sends them one way or the other. In Algeria, I found I had a winning ticket by saying I was British, or English to be more precise. I became the object of gallant attention from a group of youths who decided to accompany me as a sort of bodyguard. All very honourable and very sweet.

Women are still quite often chivalrously treated in the Middle East. I found that to get through road blocks in Algeria I could simply say I was an 'English Miss' without having to hand over my passport with the damning word 'journalist' in it. What echoes it evoked, why they were so responsive, I never quite found out but I like to think that I'd modestly linked up with those amazing bossy Englishwomen from Hester Stanhope onwards who'd been in the Middle East.

Certainly I found that Muslim sentries were unable to challenge me. I always walked straight through, looking determined.

Another useful tip for visiting women in tricky situations in Muslim countries is to apply to visit the chief wife of whoever is in power. There's always a go-between who will arrange it for a sum, escort you there, and help generally. As women in harems are bored out of their minds, they're usually delighted to see another woman from the outside world. If they like you – which you must make sure of (that's where the duty-free scent or your best blouse or scarf come in) – they'll do a great deal to help. They always have more power than is generally believed.

Keep Calling

While ordinary communications often stop altogether it is a good idea to tell your family or company to keep on telephoning you from outside. So often, I've found it impossible to get calls out while incoming calls made it.

You can always try the journalists' old trick of getting out to the airport and picking a friendly face about to board whatever aircraft is leaving and get them to take a message.

One belief I've always had, which may not necessarily work, but always has for me, is that befriending a taxi driver can be extremely useful. They're a much maligned lot. What you do is practise your basic physiognomy – a derided skill, but it's all you've got – and pick a driver you think you could trust. Then use him all the time, paying him over the odds, of course. Take an interest in him and his family, and you will find a friend.

A taxi driver not only knows where everything is and what's going on, but can also act as interpreter and spare hand.

Explain what you're trying to do and they soon enter into the spirit of things. There was one taxi driver in Cyprus who virtually did my job for me. He was not only fearless, he was accurate too! And we're still friends.

This article first appeared in Business Traveller magazine, by whose kind permission it is reproduced here. – Ed.

Survival in the Cold

by Sir Crispin Agnew of Lochnaw, Bt.

Some of the most wonderful areas in the world have cold environments and living in them poses a constant challenge. Survival becomes a continual battle against exposure which can lead, if not treated, to hypothermia. This occurs when the body loses its heat faster than its mechanism can replace the heat loss. Humans need a constant body temperature of about 36.9°C. If it falls too much below this level, death will occur. In outline, at 33.9°C, the muscles cease to work and the victims become immobile; at 32.8°C, they become confused; at 31°C (a drop of only six degrees Celsius from normal body temperature) they become unconscious and at 28°C they will die.

People who survive longest in the wild are those who never get into difficulties. Prevention is better than cure, so prepare well. Study the environment and carry appropriate and adequate shelter and clothing with sufficient food for the whole trip including a survival reserve. Amongst more slow-burning sources of energy, an emergency food pack should contain simple sugars which are easy to digest and provide immediate heat generation. If it is possible to carry a cooker and provide cooked food, so much the better (see Food on the Move on page 292). The route must be within your capabilities and you should note possible shelter and escape routes along the way.

Caught Out

Now let us consider what must be done if despite all the preparations you are caught out in a survival situation. Three things cause exposure and are therefore the greatest danger to survival. The colder it is, the greater the danger, but linked to temperature are two other factors – wind and wetness.

Wind carries away body heat by convection and this then has to be replaced by burning more body energy. Scientists have shown a direct correlation between wind and temperature which is called the wind-chill factor. The temperature and wind together combine to produce an apparent temperature considerably lower than the real one (see Climate and its Relevance to Travel on page 13).

The third factor in the equation is the wet. Water is a good conductor which destroys the insulation of clothing, for when it evaporates, it extracts heat from the surrounding area and thus lowers body temperature. Physiologists have defined the insulation factor of clothing in Clo's. For normal winter trekking you wear about 2 Clo's of insulation, but if the clothing becomes wet, then the 'Clo' factor falls from 2 Clo's to 0.75 Clo's. Wet clothing increases the speed at which you lose body heat, a process further increased if it is windy. Stay dry at all costs and avoid the often fatal downward cold-wet spiral.

Clothing

Recent technological advances have brought a multitude of new synthetics onto the market, many of which are expressly designed to cope with the stressful conditions imposed by outdoor activities. Vapour-barrier insulation retains heat by preventing evaporative cooling of the body vapour in circumstances where the user is inactive and producing little liquid perspiration. It is therefore an excellent material for sleeping bag liners and such. Polypropylene encourages evaporation but draws perspiration away from the body. Normally, evaporation on the skin has a cooling effect. When the evaporation takes place in a zone that is not in direct contact with the skin, the body suffers less cooling. Polypropylene is therefore a suitable material for clothing for strenuous activity in cold weather conditions, e.g. ski touring. Other increasingly popular materials are Dunova, viloft/polyester and fibre-pile, which are all used for underwear, and Gore-Tex, an excellent outer layer, which allows perspiration to escape while still being completely waterproof. But even this is only a small sample of what is now available, and it is well worth consulting a specialist about your particular needs before you set off.

Good clothing is vital. Even if you have tents and other camping equipment, if your clothing is not good and fitted to the environment then you will be unable to move. Woollens or nylon pile are much to be preferred to cottons or straight nylons because wools and pile retain their warmth much better, particularly when wet. Several layers of clothing are better than one thick layer because they trap the warm air and also give great flexibility in changing temperatures. A suitable combination of clothing for a cold temperature is: (for the top half) a vest, a woollen shirt, a lightweight woollen pullover, a pile jacket, with a windproof anorak and a waterproof cagoule for the outer covering; (for the lower half) good boots and gaiters, woollen socks, long woollen underwear, woollen breeches or trousers and waterproof trousers on top. The body loses a lot of heat through the head which should be covered by a woollen hat. Ensure that there is no gap at the stomach where the body's temperature is generated and maintained. Down

clothing, sleeping bags etc. should be considered, but their weight must be balanced against probable use. If you do decide to take down, make sure it has a waterproof outer skin as wet feathers can be extremely difficult to dry.

You may think that being physically fit will increase your chances of survival if hypothermia sets in. True, it will help a little, but the amount of fat you are carrying is far more important. Body fat reduces the heat loss and provides fuel to keep the blood temperature raised. Women have a layer of subcutaneous fat and will often survive longer than men as a result.

In a survival situation you must maintain the body's core temperature as near normal as possible. When the air temperature drops, the body shuts off blood from the extremities (such as the fingers and toes) in order to shorten the circuit and maintain the core body temperature, which is essentially in the stomach area. There is also shivering, which burns up sugar in the muscles and generates heat. You must try to prevent frostbite by keeping the extremities warm – in your armpits or your crotch – but it is better to lose fingers than to die. It is essential to seek shelter from the wind. At its most basic this might be the lee of a rock or slope but this should be improved upon wherever possible. Above the snow line it may be possible to dig a snow hole or build an igloo, but if this is not possible, tree or rock shelters can be built. A very simple shelter is provided by a two metre polythene bag, which keeps out the wind and rain.

Body Fuels

You should eat well before setting off

in the morning and continue to eat small snacks at regular intervals during the day to maintain the blood sugar level. If you have done this, you will meet any crisis well-nourished. A regular intake of food during the survival period refuels the body and helps it to generate heat. Liquid intake is also important because without fluid the body finds it difficult to digest food. Outdoor winter activity requires an intake of at least two litres of water a day to prevent exhaustion, kidney strain and dehydration. Dehydration is one of those factors which lowers your body's resistance to the elements. Great care must be taken to keep packs as light as possible. Nothing will exhaust a party more than carrying heavy loads, for they may well then be forced to bivouac before reaching their destination.

In the cold, wind and wet you must anticipate and learn to recognize the symptoms of exposure and once they appear, take immediate action to prevent the situation from getting worse. The symptoms can be summed up as 'acting drunk'. A person suffering from exposure may begin to stagger, appear tired or listless, display unreasonable behaviour or have sudden uncontrollable shivering fits. You will notice that they begin to slow down or stumble and may complain of disturbance or failure of vision.

If your party is getting exhausted and liable to exposure, stop early, because it is easier to take the necessary action while you still have spare energy. Seek shelter from the elements. Once in your shelter, put on all your spare clothing, have something to eat and make every effort to maintain your core temperature. Huddle together for extra warmth and keep your hands and feet warm by placing them in each other's armpits. There is a great temptation when feeling cold to try and generate heat through violent exercise; resist it, because you will merely disperse heat by convection and send warm blood to the cold extremities, which will then return to the core at a lower temperature. Vital reserves of energy will then be used to regenerate the heat. Likewise, do not take alcohol as it creates a false illusion of warmth, sending blood to the cold extremities and lowering the body temperature overall.

The Will to Live

Understanding the problem and taking steps to solve it are half the battle for survival, but however good your equipment, shelter and clothing, you will not survive unless your mental attitude is right. The will to live is vital. We have many examples in the annals of exploration: Shackleton's party surviving for many months on Elephant Island in the Antarctic; Walter Bonatti surviving on Mont Blanc for over five days while some members of his party died on the first day in the same conditions. If you do not have the will to live then you will not begin to take the most elementary necessary precautions. Cultivate determination and it will enhance your survival chances.

Nobody can guarantee you comfort in a really cold environment, but with proper practical and mental preparation, you will probably never be engaged in a real life and death struggle.

Safety and Survival at Sea

by Robin Knox-Johnston

A very sensible list of safety equipment to be carried on board a boat is published by the Offshore Racing Council (O.R.C.). The list is extensive, but because it is comprehensive, it is given below:

2 Fire Extinguishers; accessible and in different places

2 Manually operated bilge pumps

2 Buckets; strong construction, fitted with lanyards

2 Anchors and cables (Chain for Cruising is sensible)

2 Flashlights; water resistant, capable of being used for signalling, with spare bulbs and batteries

1 Foghorn

1 Radar Reflector

1 Set International Code Flags and code book

1 Set Emergency Navigation Lights

1 Storm Trysail

1 Storm Jib

1 Emergency Tiller

1 Tool Kit

1 Marine Radio Transmitter and Receiver

1 Radio; capable of receiving weather forecasts

Lifejackets; sufficient for the whole crew

1 buoyant Heaving Line; at least 50 feet (16m) long

2 Life buoys or rings

1 set distress signals
    12 Red Parachute Flares
    4 Red Hand Flares
    4 White Hand Flares
    2 Orange Smoke day signals

1 Liferaft; of capacity to take the whole crew, which has:
    Valid annual test certificate
    Two separate buoyancy compartments
    Canopy to cover the occupants
    Sea anchor and drogue
    Bellows or pump to maintain pressure
    Signalling light
    3 Hand Flares
    Baler
    Repair Kit
    2 Paddles
    Knife
    Emergency water and rations
    First Aid Kit and manual

In addition, it is worth carrying a portable, waterproof VHF radio and an emergency distress transmitter (E.P.I.R.B.)

Medical

The health of the crew is the Skipper's responsibility and he or she should see that the food is nourishing and sufficient, that the boat is kept clean and that the crew practice basic hygiene.

A good medical kit must be carried. There is an excellent book published by HMSO for the British Merchant Navy, called *The Ship Captain's Medical Guide*. It is written for a ship that does not carry a doctor and includes a recommended list of medical supplies. Most doctors will supply prescriptions for anti-biotics when the purpose has been explained.

Safety on Deck

Prevention is always better than the cure. Everyone on board should know their way about the deck, and know what everything is for. A good way of training is to take the boat out night sailing, so that the crew get to know instinctively where everything is and what to avoid. Train the crew to squat whenever the boat lurches – it lowers the centre of gravity and makes toppling overside less likely. In rough weather, make sure that all the crew wear their lifejackets and safety harness when on deck, and that they clip their harnesses to a strong point. If the crew have to go out from the cockpit, they should clip their harnesses to a wire which runs down the middle, the length of the boat, for this purpose.

Man Overboard

If someone falls overside, immediately summon the whole crew on deck and throw a lifebuoy to the person in the water. The problem is to get back and pick the person up as quickly as possible, so post a lookout to keep an eye on the casualty, and the rest of the crew should assist with turning the boat around. It is worth while putting the boat straight into the wind, as this stops you close to the casualty, then start the engine and motor back. On one occasion in the Southern Ocean, we lost a man overside, and we had run on more than half a mile before we could get the spinnaker down. The only way we could see him when we turned round was by the seabirds that were circling him. We got him back, after about 20 minutes, by which time he was unable to assist himself because of the cold.

In the upper latitudes, there is a real danger from hypothermia and it is vital to warm the person as quickly as possible. Strip off their wet clothing and towel them dry, then put them in a warm sleeping bag. The heat is retained better if the sleeping bag can be put into a plastic bag. If the person is very cold, it may be necessary for someone else to strip and climb into the bag with the casualty and warm them with their own body. If the casualty is conscious, feed them hot soup or tea. Remember that it can be a nerve-shattering experience and that they may need time to get over the shock.

Abandoning the Boat

When, as a last resort, it becomes necessary to leave the boat, inflate the liferaft and pull it alongside. Put one or two of the crew on board, and, if there is time, pass over as much food, water, and clothing as possible, plus the Distress Beacon. If the boat's dinghy is available, tie it to the liferaft, as it will be extra space and also helps to create a larger target. Only leave the boat if there is absolutely no alternative. Liferafts are small and uncomfortable and not particularly robust, and it is always preferable to keep the boat afloat if humanly possible.

The usual reason for abandoning a boat is that it has been holed. One method of improving its survivability is to fit it with watertight bulkheads so that its volume is roughly divided into three. This is now a rule for the BOC Challenge Around Alone Race, and means that if the boat is holed, the chances are that it will lose only one-third of its buoyancy, and there will still be dry, safe, shelter for the crew. From the comparative safety of one of the 'safe' parts of the boat, a plan can probably be made to fix the leak.

When it is necessary to abandon the boat, having got as much food and useful equipment aboard as possible, cut the painter and get clear. Then take stock of what you have, and post a lookout. Activate the Distress Beacon to alert aircraft and ships to the fact that someone is in distress.

Ration supplies from the start. The best way to do this is to avoid food for the first day, as the stomach shrinks, and the body's demand for food falls. Ration water to about half a pint (¼ litre) a day and issue it in sips. On no account should sea water be drunk, but it can be used for washing or cooling in hot weather. Humans can last for amazingly long times without food, but they do need water. Any rain should be trapped and saved. The canopy of the liferaft can be used for this purpose, as could the dinghy if it has been taken along. Unless there is a plentiful water supply do not eat raw fish as they are very rich in protein and ruin the liver unless the surplus can be washed out of the system. As a general rule, 1 volume of protein will require 2 volumes of water. Where water is plentiful, fish should be hunted. Most pelargic fish are edible, and quite often they will swim around a boat or dinghy out of curiosity. It is close to land, or on reefs, that inedible fish are found. Keep movement to a minimum to conserve energy, and in cold weather, hold onto urine as long as possible to retain its heat. In hot, sunny weather, try to keep everyone in the shade. Find some mental stimulus in order to maintain morale, and remember that the crew will be looking to the skipper to set an example, so remain positive. Humans have survived for well over three months on a liferaft, but only because they had a strong will to live and were able to improvise.

Further Reading

Seamanship by Robin Knox-Johnston. Pub. Hodder and Stoughton

Ships Captain's Medical Guide H.M.S.O.

Survival in the Desert

by Jack Jackson

The most important thing about desert survival is to avoid the need for it in the first place.

Know your vehicle's capabilities, do not overload it. Know how to maintain and repair it. Carry adequate spares and tools. Be fit yourselves and get sufficient sleep. Start your journey with 25 per cent more fuel and water than was calculated as necessary, to cover extra problems such as bad terrain, leaking containers and extra time spent over repairs or sitting out a bad sandstorm.

Know accurately where your next supplies of fuel and water are. Carry plastic sheet to make desert stills; carry space blankets. Carry more than one compass and know how to navigate properly. Use magnetic compasses away from vehicles and cameras. Do not leave the piste unless you really do know what you are doing. Travel only in the local winter months. Know how correct your odometer is for the wheels and tyres you are using. Make notes of distances, compass bearings and obvious landmarks as you go along, so you can retrace your route easily if you have to.

Observe correct check in and out procedures with local authorities. Preferably convoy with other vehicles. When lost, do not continue. Stop, think and, if necessary, retrace your route.

Back-up Plans

If you are a large party, you should arrange a search and rescue plan before you start out. This would include the use and recognition of radio beacons and/or flares, for aircraft search. Many countries do not allow you to use radio communication.

For most people, an air search is highly unlikely and high flying commercial passenger aircraft overhead are unlikely to notice you whatever you do. A search, if it does come, will be along the piste or markers. Most often this will just be a case of other vehicles travelling through being asked by the local authorities to look out for you, when you fail to check in. Local drivers will not understand or appreciate coloured flares, so your best signal for outside help is fire. At night, if you hear a vehicle, cardboard boxes or wood are quickly and easily lit, but during the day you need lots of thick black smoke. The best fuel for this is a tyre. Bury most of it in sand to control the speed at which it burns (keep it well away and down wind from the vehicles or fuel) and start the exposed part burning with either petrol or diesel fuel with a rag wick. As the exposed part of the tyre burns away, you can uncover more from the sand to keep it going, or cover all of it with sand if you wish to put the fire out. Avoid inhaling the sulphurous fumes.

Headlights switched on and off at night can be used while the battery still has charge.

A Need to Survive

Once you are in a 'need to survive' situation, the important things are morale and water. Concentrate on getting your vehicles moving again. This will keep you occupied and help to keep up morale. To minimise water loss, do no manual work during the day – work at night or in the early morning. Build shade and stay under it as much as possible, keeping well covered with loose cotton clothing. 'Space blankets' with the reflective side out make the coolest shade. Keep warm and out of the wind at night.

Unless you are well off the piste with no chance of a search you should stay with the vehicle. If someone must walk out, pick one or two of the strongest, most determined persons to go. They must have a compass, torch, salt, anti-diarrhoea medicine, loose all-enveloping clothes, good footwear, good sunglasses and as much water as they can sensibly carry. In soft sand, a jerrycan of water can easily be hauled along on a rope from the waist. On mixed ground, tie the jerry to a sand ladder, one end of which is padded and tied to the waist. The person who walks out should follow the desert nomad pattern of walking in the evening till about 2300 hours, sleep until 0400 hours, walk again till 1000, then dig a shallow well in the sand and lie in it under the space blanket, reflective side out till the sun has lost its heat. If they have a full moon they can walk all night. In this way, fit men would make 60 to 70 kilometres on ten litres of water, less in soft sand.

Water

In a 'sit it out and survive' situation, with all manual labour kept to a minimum, food is relatively unimportant and dehydration staves off hunger, but water is *vital*. The average consumption of water in a hot, dry climate is eight litres a day. This can be lowered to four litres per day in a real emergency. Diarrhoea increases dehydration, so should be controlled by medicines where necessary. Salt intake should be kept up.

Water supply should be improved by making as many desert stills as possible. To make one, dig a hole about one-third of a metre deep and one metre in circumference, place a clean saucepan or billy in the centre of the hole and cover the hole with a two-metre-square plastic sheet weighed down with stones, jerry cans or tools at the edges. Put one stone or similar object in the centre to weigh it down directly over the billy can. Overnight, water vapour from the sand will evaporate and then condense on the underside of the plastic sheet, running down and dripping into the pan. All urine should be conserved and put into shallow containers around the central billy can. The water so collected should be boiled and sterilized before drinking.

If you have antifreeze in your radiator, then don't try to drink this, or use it at all, as it is highly poisonous. Even if you have not put antifreeze in the radiator yourselves, there is still likely to be some left in it from the previous use, or from the factory when the vehicle was first manufactured, so this water should be put into the desert still in the same way as the urine and the resulting condensate should be boiled or sterilized before drinking. Water from wells known to be bad can be made drinkable in the same way. Note, however, that solar stills can take a lot of energy to create and will yield little water in return. Until the situation is really desperate, they are probably not worth considering as a viable means of collecting water.

The minimum daily water requirements to maintain the body's water balance at rest, in the shade, are as follows:

Mean daily temperatures °C	Litres of water per 24 hours
35°	5.3
30°	2.4
25°	1.2
20° and below	1.0

It must be stressed that this is for survival. There will be gradual kidney malfunction and possibly urinary tract infection, with women more at risk than men.

The will to live is essential. Once you give up, you will be finished.

If you find people in such a situation and do not have a doctor to handle them, feed them dilute salt water a teaspoonful at a time every few minutes for a couple of hours, before trying to take them on a long tough drive to hospital. Sachets of salts for rehydration are available for your medical kit.

Survival in the Jungle

by Robin Hanbury-Tenison

The key to survival in the tropics is comfort. If your boots fit, your clothes don't itch, your wounds don't fester, you have enough to eat, and you have the comforting presence of a local who is at home in the environment, then you are not likely to go far wrong.

Of course, jungle warfare is something else. The British, Americans and, for all I know, several other armies have produced detailed manuals on how to survive under the most arduous conditions imaginable and with the minimum of resources. But most of us are extremely unlikely ever to find ourselves in such a situation. Even if you are unlucky enough to be caught in a guerrilla war or survive an air crash in the jungle, I believe that the following advice will be as useful as trying to remember sophisticated techniques which probably require equipment you do not have to hand, anyway.

A positive will to survive is essential. The knowledge that others have travelled long distances and lived for days and even months without help or special knowledge gives confidence, while a calm appraisal of the circumstances can make them seem far less intimidating. The jungle need not be an uncomfortable place, although unfamiliarity may make it seem so. Morale is as important as ever and comfort, both physical and mental, a vital ingredient.

Clothing and Footwear

To start with, it is usually warm, but when you are wet, especially at night, you can become very cold very quickly. It is therefore important to be prepared and always try to keep a sleeping bag and a change of clothes dry. Excellent strong, lightweight plastic bags are now available in which these items should always be packed with the top folded over and tied. These can then be placed inside your rucksack or bag so that if dropped in a river or soaked by a sudden tropical downpour – and the effect is much the same – they, at least, will be dry. I usually have three such bags, one with dry clothes, one with camera equipment, notebooks etc., and one with

food. Wet clothes should be worn. This is unpleasant for the first ten minutes in the morning, but they will soon be soaking wet with sweat and dripping in any case, and wearing them means you need carry only one change for the evening and sleeping in. It is well worth taking the time to rinse them out whenever you are in sunshine by a river so that you can dry them on hot rocks in half an hour or so. They can also be hung over the fire at night which makes them pleasanter to put on in the morning, but also tends to make them stink of wood smoke.

Always wear loose clothes in the tropics. They may not be very becoming but constant wetting and drying will tend to shrink them and rubbing makes itches and scratches far worse. Cotton is excellent but should be of good quality so that the clothes do not rot and tear too easily.

For footwear, baseball boots or plimsolls are usually adequate but for long distances good leather boots will protect your feet much better from bruising and blisters. In leech country, a shapeless cotton stocking worn between sock and shoe and tied with a drawstring below the knee, outside long trousers gives virtually complete protection. As far as I know, no one manufactures these yet, so they have to be made up specially, but they are well worth it.

Upsets and Dangers

Hygiene is important in the tropics. Small cuts can turn nasty very quickly and sometimes will not heal for a long time. The best protection is to make an effort to wash all over at least once a day if possible, at the same time looking out for any sore places, cleaning and treating them at once. On the other hand, where food and drink are concerned, it is usually not practical or polite to attempt to maintain perfectionist standards. Almost no traveller in the tropics can avoid receiving hospitality and few would wish to do so. It is often best therefore to accept that a mild stomach upset is likely – and be prepared (*see section on Health, page 333*).

In real life and death conditions, there are only two essentials for survival, a knife or machete and a compass, provided you are not injured, when the best thing to do is crawl, if possible, to water and wait for help. Other important items I would put in order of priority as follows: a map; a waterproof cover, cape or large bag; means of making fire, lifeboat matches or a lighter with spare flints, gas or petrol; a billy can; tea or coffee, sugar and dried milk. There are few tropical terrains which cannot be crossed with these, given time and determination.

Man can survive a long time without food, so try to keep this simple, basic and light. Water is less of a problem in the jungle, except in limestone mountains, but a metal water container should be carried and filled whenever possible. Rivers, streams and even puddles are unlikely to be dangerously contaminated, while rattans and lianas often contain water as do some other plants whose leaves may form catchments, such as pitcher plants. It is easy to drink from these, though best to filter the liquid through cloth and avoid the 'gunge' at the bottom.

Hunting and trapping are unlikely to be worth the effort to the inexperienced, although it is surprising how much can be found in streams and caught with hands. Prawns, turtles,

frogs and even fish can be captured with patience and almost all are edible – and even tasty if you're hungry enough. Fruits, even if ripe and being eaten by other animals, are less safe, while some edible-looking plants and fungi can be very poisonous and should be avoided. Don't try for the honey of wild bees unless you know what you are doing as stings can be dangerous and those of hornets even fatal.

As regards shelter, there is a clear distinction between South America and the rest of the tropical world. In the South American interior, almost everyone uses a hammock. Excellent waterproof hammocks are supplied to the Brazilian and US armies and may be obtainable commercially. Otherwise, a waterproof sheet may be stretched across a line tied between the same two trees from which the hammock is slung. Elsewhere, however, hammocks are rarely used and will tend to be a nuisance under normal conditions. Lightweight canvas stretchers through which poles may be inserted before being tied apart on a raised platform make excellent beds and once again a waterproof sheet provides shelter. Plenty of nylon cord is always useful.

Fight It or Like It

The jungle can be a frightening place at first. Loud noises, quantities of unfamiliar creep-crawlies, flying biting things and the sometimes oppressive heat can all conspire to get you down. But it can also be a very pleasant place if you decide to like it rather than fight it – and it is very seldom dangerous. Snakebite, for example, is extremely rare. During the fifteen months of the Royal Geographical Society's Mulu Expedition, in Borneo, no one was bitten, although we saw and avoided or caught and photographed many snakes and even ate some! Most things, such as thorns, ants and sandflies are more irritating than painful and taking care to treat rather than scratch will usually prevent trouble.

Above all the jungle is a fascinating place – the richest environment on earth. The best help for morale is to be interested in what is going on around you and the best guide is usually a local resident who is as at home there as most of us are in cities. Fortunately, in most parts of the world where jungles survive there are still such people. By accepting their advice, recognising their expertise, and asking them to travel with you, you may help to reinforce their self-respect in the face of often overwhelming forces which try to make them adopt a so-called 'modern' way of life. At the same time, you will appreciate the jungle far more yourself – and have a far better chance of surviving in it.

Keeping track

Buying Equipment for Photography Off the Beaten Track

by David Hodgson

You may have heard of Murphy's Law. It states that if something can go wrong, it will go wrong – at the worst possible moment. Even if you've never heard of the law, you will have experienced it in action on any trip. And especially if you have been involved in photography or filming on the trip. Cameras jam, films get lost or stolen, lenses mist over at the most inconvenient moment or jam on the body when being changed and you miss that essential shot. Twenty years of magazine photography in some of the least accessible parts of the world have convinced me that Murphy's Law is about as inevitable and universal as the Law of Gravity.

In this article I have Murphy's Law very much in mind. But I am also making two other assumptions. The first is that photography is of some importance to you; that you need, and want, to take first-class pictures for serious use rather than a collection of fuzzy snaps for suitable burial in some album. Secondly I assume that funds are limited and that every penny has to be well spent. Incidentally, all the money in the world will not protect you from the ravages of Murphy's

Law. One of the best financed and most lavishly equipped trips I have ever been on started out with £25,000 worth of cameras and I finished up being thankful that I had a battered, secondhand Leica to take their most important pictures.

Choosing Your Equipment

The motto here is: buy tough for travelling rough. The most sophisticated camera in the world is worse than useless if the electronic shutter fails halfway up a mountain. The more things there are to go wrong, the more things will go wrong. Built-in light meters are very convenient, especially if you nip down to the local dealer's when a CdS battery fails. But if the battery goes in the wilds, you will never replace it and the meter will be useless. So, if you are buying especially for the trip, why spend money on a built-in meter? Better to put the additional money towards a sturdy shutter and wind-on mechanism and use a separate, selenium cell meter. This is the type where a cell converts the light directly to electrical energy. There is no additional power supply to fail. I would suggest a Weston Meter. You can safely buy them secondhand at very reasonable prices. They are tough and extremely accurate. If you do decide to use a camera with a TTL (through the lens) metering system, then take along spare cells and make sure they are protected against excessive damp. But wear braces and a belt. Take a Weston along too.

This brings me to a point about back-up systems. Never put together your equipment on the basis that things will go right, but always in the certain knowledge they will go wrong. Have an answer ready when they do. Two camera bodies are a wise investment, especially when you are going to be a long way from repairman and replacements. You can shoot black and white with one and colour with the other, thus improving your chances of making the widest possible sale when you get home (*see Selling Travel Photographs on page 471*). But which bodies?

Unless you have some specialist purpose which requires large format photography, then 35mm cameras have all the advantages. They are light, easy to use, take 36 pictures on one roll of film and produce negatives of sufficiently high quality to stand considerable enlargement – provided the exposure and processing have been correctly carried out.

The single-lens reflex is probably the most popular camera here. It is a well-proven design which allows you to see exactly what you are shooting. This is very valuable when taking close-up pictures, using either a macro lens or extension tubes, or when using telephoto lenses for capturing distant scenes. If you intend to shoot a lot of extreme close-ups or use lenses longer than 200mm frequently, I would advise a SLR. Nikon, Pentax, Canon, Leicaflex and Minolta are cameras which have all been tested under professional conditions and have come through with flying colours. Nikon,

Pentax, Olympus and Canon are probably the most widely used by magazine and newspaper photographers. One of my Nikons was once struck by a jet fighter coming in to land – and went on taking pictures. All four of these manufacturers make models which combine great toughness with lightness in a small handy format. The weight factor could make a great difference to transportation problems and should be considered by an expedition photographer who is going to have to carry his or her own gear across difficult terrain.

But do not dismiss that much less popular type of 35mm camera, the rangefinder camera focus model. Perhaps the best known name here is Leica. Nikon also used to make an excellent rangefinder camera, as did Canon. These were the standard photojournalist's equipment for decades before the SLR pushed them down into the third division.

Rangefinder cameras have a lot going for them as an expedition camera. They are simpler than the SLRs and less to go wrong can mean fewer problems miles from anywhere. Because they are rather unpopular you can buy them cheaply secondhand. The lack of a mirror makes them quieter to use, which makes for easier candid photography and wildlife studies. The rangefinder focus is very positive and easy to use under low light levels. They are much less satisfactory, however, when being used with long lenses (above 200mm) or for extreme close-ups. The need for either type of photography really makes the SLR the front runner.

If you are switching from SLR to a rangefinder model then be sure to practise before starting on serious photography. There is a tendency to confuse the overall sharpness of the image as seen through the rangefinder screen with total picture sharpness and forget to focus as a result! With an SLR, of course, this mistake cannot happen.

Before moving on to the subject of buying cameras secondhand, I should mention the Nikonos, a very specialist camera that can be worth its weight in usable pictures on really tough trips. The Nikonos is an underwater camera with a lens fully sealed behind a glass plate and the controls similarly protected by O-rings. You can use the Nikonos on land as well, in the wettest mud or the worst sandstorms and simply wash it out when the muck gets too solid! If there is any chance of your equipment ending up soaked or seriously muddied then the Nikonos could be the answer. There are, of course, other ways of protecting standard gear.

Additional Equipment

Some photographers set off on trips hung around with more equipment than the average dealer's display window. It is a waste of time, effort and money to take more than you need. Furthermore, too many gadgets get between you and the picture-making. Keep life as simple as possible. You may need specialist gear for particular tasks, but for general shooting, here is a basic shopping list.

Lens hoods for all lenses: I prefer the screw-on variety to the clip-on type. They are less likely to get knocked off and lost. *Ultraviolet filters* for all lenses – to cut down haze at high altitudes or when photographing at sea, and to protect the lenses. *Wide camera straps* are much more comfortable than the normal, narrow variety. A separate *light meter*, for reasons already given. *Lenses* for general purpose 35mm photography: my favourite combination is a slightly wide angle lens (a 35mm focal length is ideal) together with a slightly long lens. My best buy here would be either a 90mm lens or a 135mm. Both are excellent for candid portraiture, getting details of buildings, statues, etc., and landscape photography. The wide angle lens enables you to work close, frame boldly and operate successfully in a crowd.

What you do not need are as follows: A *tripod* solid enough to provide firm support will be too heavy to carry unless you are fully motorised. Even then it is likely to prove more trouble than it is worth. A much better alternative is a clamp which enables you to fasten the camera to a suitable support. I make my own from a Mole wrench with a camera locking screw attached. Given the flexibility of this type of wrench you can almost always find something steady enough to provide a really stable mount for long exposures. I would certainly not rule out *flash guns* completely, but unless you are intending to shoot a great many flash pictures, you will probably find a bulb gun lighter to carry, cheaper to buy and rather more reliable. If you are going a long way off the beaten track, bear in mind that an electronic gun will get through batteries far faster than a bulb gun – and provide less light. *Camera cases* tend to get in the way when you are working fast. There are better methods of protection.

Specialist Equipment

For close-up work you will need either a close-up lens, extension tubes or bellows. Some modern standard lenses will focus to within a few inches and you may find this sufficient for all but the most precise record of work. Otherwise I advise a close-up lens or extension tubes in preference to bellows because they are so much easier to carry around.

Fast focus with long lenses can prove a problem. The best answer is probably the Novoflex follow-focus system where, instead of a helical screw and twist action focus, the lens is focused by pulling in, or releasing, a pistol-like trigger. For very long lenses (400mm and upwards) you will need the shoulder-pod support which is designed especially for use with this lens. Although bulky and cumbersome, Novoflex lenses are the best for action shots of fast moving subjects, e.g. for bird photography. I paint the barrel of my 400mm Novoflex bright yellow. It makes it look less like a large calibre army pistol and in some areas of the world a mistaken identification could prove most unfortunate for the photographer!

Motorised cameras are increasingly popular. But this is something else which can go wrong so I advise you to purchase with an eye to rugged rather than elegant construction and take one along only if it is going to be really essential. Among their main uses are rapid sequence photography, for high speed action work, and remote control pictures via a trigger line or radio control.

Shopping Summary

My own choice, based on personal experience in the rough, would be as follows:
Nikon with 35mm and 135mm lenses.

Weston Meter. Rox carrying case. Hoods. UV filters. Mole wrench converted to camera clamp. Small screwdriver set (as used by watchmakers) for tightening loose screws. One centimetre wide paint brush. Bulb gun with spare battery. Spare batteries for CdS meter if carried. Two bodies for choice. Best buy secondhand: the Nikon F2.

Alternatively: a secondhand Leica M2 with 35mm and 90mm lens or an Olympus with lenses similar to the Nikon. For a motorised camera: the Olympus on the grounds of lightness.

For very rugged work, take a Nikonos with a 35mm lens, but this needs a special flash gun.

I can't guarantee you'll beat Murphy's Law by taking my advice. But you'll be in there with a chance!

Camera Care and Protection

by Dave Saunders and Robert Holmes

You have spent as much as you can afford on good camera gear for your trip abroad. Naturally, you don't *expect* it to fail, but you are realistic enough to include an extra camera body – just in case. Camera repair shops tend to be in short supply in remote regions of the world and you don't want your pictures to turn into the fish that got away.

Even if the journey is short and conditions far from severe, equipment can easily let you down by getting lost, breaking when dropped or simply expiring after long, devoted service.

Minimising the frustrations of such technical hitches calls for attention to detail. Caring for your camera goes beyond dusting it with a brush from time to time. It begins long before you set out and ends with a final check and brush-up when you return home.

Checklist

It is worthwhile following a routine checklist to avoid on-the-spot panics. First decide exactly what equipment you are going to take. This will, of course, be controlled by what you can afford. It will inevitably be a compromise between the full range of camera bodies, lenses and accessories you might conceivably use and the amount of weight you can allocate for photographic gear.

Choose only those items you will need for the specific type of photographs you plan to take, accounting for any harsh conditions such as sand, salt water or humidity you are likely to meet. Coping with travelling can be taxing enough without the additional burden of unnecessary accessories.

You may find two camera bodies, three lenses and a small flash gun are sufficient. A miniature camera in your pocket at all times and a Polaroid camera can also be very handy.

If you need to buy extra bits and pieces, check everything well before you leave. Run at least one test roll of film through the camera, using various shutter speeds and aperture settings. Change lenses, try out the shutter release cable, the self-timer and the motordrive. Make sure it is all clean and working smoothly. Then study the results for anomalies.

Protection

If your travels are going to take you very near salt water, mud, sand or snow, it may be worth investing in a Nikonos underwater camera or waterproof housing, rather than risk destroying your land camera. A camera is generally pretty sturdy, but water will harm it. If you drop the camera in the sea, you have signed its death warrant and may as well give it to the kids to play with and claim a new one on insurance.

You can defend land cameras against salt spray by wiping with lint cloth lightly soaked in WD40 or a similar light oil. If you need to use a land camera in a sand storm, carefully apply 'O' ring grease to joints, mounts, and hinges, using a cotton bud. Tape over parts not in use, such as sync socket and motordrive terminal.

Take spare plastic bags to help protect gear under adverse conditions. Also include spare 'O' rings for the Nikonos, 'O' ring grease, cotton buds, chamois leather, brush, Dust-Off spray and a small watchmaker's screwdriver for on-the-spot maintenance.

A skylight or ultraviolet filter cuts down haze, but is more important as a lens protector. A filter should remain on each lens all the time to protect the coated front element. Scratched filters are much cheaper to replace than lenses. A lens hood can also shield the lens as well as cut down flare on *contre jour* shots.

Bags

Now, where do you put all of this? I prefer to use a large, soft camera bag for most of my photographic gear. It can be taken as hand luggage on a plane and stowed under the seat. Purpose-made bags and pouches by *Camera Care Systems* and *Lowe Pro* are excellent for adventurous photographers who are likely to find themselves hanging off a cliff face or swinging from the crow's nest.

Expensive looking cases are obvious targets for light-fingered locals. Don't rely on locks to keep out the thieves. If necessary, use a steel cable and padlock. Give the case distinguishing marks such as bright paint or coloured tape. You will then be able to identify it quickly and thieves will tend to avoid anything too conspicuous.

A watertight aluminium case will be useful for photography by the sea or in a desert as it will keep out the damp and dust. The sun is reflected by the silver, so the camera and films don't get too hot and you can use the case to stand or sit on. However, they are more awkward to work from when you are constantly 'dipping in' for something.

If you are carrying the minimum of photographic equipment, you may be able to 'wear' your camera bag in the form of a loose-fitting jacket with plenty of pockets – even in the sleeves. This protects your gear and enables you to be more agile – an important consideration if a camera bag is likely to be a hindrance.

Once you know what you are taking, insure it for its replacement value. Some household insurance policies do not cover photographic gear abroad and should be extended. Alternatively, shop around several insurance companies for the best deal, but watch out for small-print exemptions clauses which may exclude travelling in private aircraft, scuba diving or mountaineering.

Keep a separate record of model and serial numbers, as this will help the police when items are lost or stolen.

Reporting the loss will help when your claim is being processed.

By the time you actually set off, the bulk of the work will be done, though special environments will call for special attention.

Extreme Conditions

Cameras should not be left in direct sunlight when temperatures are high, as the glue holding the lens elements in place may melt and be knocked out of place.

When changing lenses or films, finding a sheltered area. If it is sandy or dusty, keep the whole camera in a plastic bag. Cut a hole for the lens and secure the bag around the mount with a stiff elastic band. This can make composing and framing the picture a little difficult, but may save the camera.

Extremely cold conditions will give as many problems as the heat. Batteries are affected by cold and lose power. Many modern cameras depend on batteries for through-the-lens (TTL) metering, or shutter and aperture adjustments.

On the more exposed ridges and summits, keep your camera inside your anorak (possibly inside a plastic bag) until you are ready to take a picture. Once you have decided what to photograph, act quickly; I have had cameras seize up on me after two or three shots taken on windswept ridges. But ten to fifteen minutes under my anorak and all was well again.

Where possible, try to keep cameras and film at a constant temperature.

When changing films or lenses find a sheltered spot and avoid getting snow inside the camera, or even breathing into it. Using a zoom lens reduces the need for continual lens changes.

If you are likely to experience really severe conditions, with temperatures below minus 32°C (minus 25°F) then you should take extra precautions. Older cameras should be winterised. This involves an oil change, using a lighter oil which is less viscous at low temperatures. But new cameras using modern lubricants should operate as smoothly in arctic as in temperate climates.

Tape over parts not in use, such as the flash sync socket and motordrive terminal. Store everything in hermetically sealed metal cases and take plenty of gaffer tape to seal all hinges, cracks and joints against fine snow. Put cameras in airtight plastic bags with silica gel packets *before* coming indoors. Coming into the warm can be a traumatic time for your camera! Water vapour on cold metal and glass surfaces will condense rapidly and mist up with tiny water droplets. When you go out again, this water will freeze.

At the end of the day, wipe off all the moisture, and don't open the camera back or change the lens until the camera has warmed up because condensation inside the camera can give you even more problems.

Besides looking after your camera, don't forget to look after yourself! Keep warm so that *you* don't freeze up, and avoid touching frozen metal parts of the camera with bare skin – it will stick and can be extremely painful! Tape over exposed metal on the back of the camera and fit a large rubber eyecup to the viewfinder.

Cleaning

Cleaning materials are essential for both the camera body and for lenses. Lenses should be cleaned daily to prevent a build-up of dirt, which will cause soft, muddy photographs through flare and loss of definition. If you are using a UV filter, the same cleaning rules will apply to the filter as to the lens.

First remove the dust and loose dirt with a *pocket 'Dust-Off'* which emits a strong jet of inert gas. Be careful to hold the 'Dust-Off' upright otherwise you will get vapour coming out which will leave a deposit on the lens or filter. Next, carefully remove any stubborn dirt with a small *blower brush* and finally use 'Dust-Off' once more. Don't forget to check the rear element of your lens too. If you get a fingerprint on the lens carefully wipe it off with *lens tissues*. Only buy tissues from a camera store. Lens tissues from opticians often contain silicones which can damage the coating on the lens. Breathing on the lens first can help, but be careful. In sub-zero temperatures, the resulting ice will be far worse than any fingerprints!

It's not just the lens that should be cleaned regularly. So should the camera body – inside and out. Clean the outside with a stiff *typewriter brush* which removes even the most stubborn dirt and gets into all the nooks and crannies. Clean out any dirt that does escape into the camera with a blower brush, carefully avoiding the shutter which can be easily damaged. Using 'Dust-Off' for the interior can do more harm than good by blasting dust into the camera mechanism. Look out for the tiny pieces of film which occasionally break off and get into the film, ruining whole rolls with deep scratches. I learnt my lesson recently in Nepal. A single hair from my brush got stuck in the film path and although I couldn't see it through the viewfinder it appeared, in varying degrees of focus, in ten rolls of film before it finally dislodged itself. That will not happen again!

Film and Film Care

by Dave Saunders

Film emulsion is sensitive material. Mistreat it, and it will complain by fogging or assuming a strange colour cast. All film deteriorates with time, and you will accelerate this process with careless handling.

Different films have different properties and some will complain more vehemently than others when subjected to adverse conditions. In general, 'amateur' film is more tolerant than 'professional' film, which is manufactured to more exacting standards. Amateur film is more stable and will last longer before processing. It is therefore the better choice for long trips, especially in hot climates where the deterioration process is speeded up.

Colour Film

So how do you choose from the bewildering array of film types on the market?

For our purposes, there are three broad categories of colour film:
1. Daylight reversal (transparency) films can be used with electronic flash, blue flashbulbs and, of course, in daylight.
2. Tungsten reversal (transparency) for tungsten/artificial light.

3. Colour negative (for prints) used for all lighting conditions and corrected during printing.

Tungsten films can be corrected for daylight, and vice versa, by using filters.

If you are hoping to sell any of your photographs, be warned that magazines, books and brochures prefer to reproduce from transparencies and many will not even consider colour prints. If necessary you can always have prints made from transparencies.

Kodachrome is usually first choice, and some publications and photo libraries insist on it. Kodachrome 25 is the sharpest and least grainy ordinary slide film available, but because it is slow (ISO 25) you forfeit flexibility. In anything other than bright conditions you may find you have to shoot at full aperture, which gives very little depth of field, and/or a slow shutter speed, with the danger of camera shake. I start to feel nervous when using f/1.8 at 1/30th or 1/15th sec.

Kodachrome 64 has similar sharpness and grain to Kodachrome 25, though it is a little more contrasty. The extra 1½ stops provided by the faster film (ISO 64) allows greater flexibility. To warm up skin tones and increase overall colour saturation, use 81 series filters with Kodachrome film. The density and strength of colour (saturation) will also increase if you slightly underexpose reversal film. Kodak has recently introduced Kodachrome 200 Professional Film with a speed of ISO 200, which allows even more flexibility.

Ektachrome 64 has a more saturated colour than Kodachrome and is sharp with little grain. However, all Ektachrome films should be processed soon after exposure and are therefore not suitable for long journeys in remote areas. Kodachrome is more stable and should survive up to six months between being exposed and processed. Black and white film is even hardier and should last for a year.

Ektachrome 200 High Speed film is good for general use and allows the use of faster shutter speeds and/or smaller apertures. This enables you to use a longer focal length lens without the need for a tripod, have greater depth of field and shoot in dull lighting conditions. This film can be uprated by one or two stops, giving even greater versatility. Similarly, Ektachrome 400 can be pushed two stops, making it in effect ISO 1600, but this gives coarse grained results.

The new Ektachrome P800/1600 Profession Film has speeds of ISO 800 or ISO 1600, depending on the way it is processed. Considering its speed, this film is impressively fine grained with good image sharpness and colour reproduction.

Fuji film has improved markedly in recent years and Fujichrome 50, Fujichrome 100 and Fujichrome 400 are now serious competitors to Kodachrome.

Ilfochrome is Ilford's only colour slide film.

Agfachrome CT 100 and CT 200 are general purpose daylight films which have more grain and are less sharp than Ektachrome or Fujichrome.

3M's ISO 1000 film is grainy, but impressively sharp considering its fast speed.

Slow films are generally impractical for travel photography unless you can guarantee bright conditions and/or long exposure.

When buying film, check if processing is included in the price. Kodach-

rome, for example, is process paid only in certain countries. Also check the expiry date of the film, it should be stamped on the packet. If you have no choice but to buy an old film, you may get away with it. The expiry date has a built-in safety margin and out of date films are usually all right for some months after the date indicated.

It is best to take much more film than you anticipate using. You can always bring home unexposed film and use it later. When you are confronted by magnificent scenery or an interesting incident in the street, you don't want to have to scrimp. The chance may never come again.

Running out of film abroad may, at best, be inconvenient. Prices may be highly inflated or your preferred film type may not be available. Kodachrome, Ektachrome, Fujichrome, Ilfochrome and Agfachrome are fairly universal however, and usually available in places where any film is on sale (it is totally unobtainable in far too many countries).

Black and White

If possible, take black and white film as well as colour. Some colour converts into mono satisfactorily if there is enough contrast, but there is inevitably a loss of quality and to get the best quality can cost more per shot than a whole role of black and white film. Certain magazines stipulate that black and white prints must be derived from black and white originals.

Kodak T-Max 125 and Kodak T-Max 400 have finer grain and better control of contrast than Plus X and Tri X which they have replaced. Ilford's equivalent films – FP4 (ISO 125) and HP5 (ISO 400) are also for general use and dull light conditions respectively. In each case, the faster films are grainier, though Ilford's new XP-1 400 is a finer grain fast film using C41 colour processing chemistry. Ilford's Pan F is a fine grain slow film (ISO 50).

Protection

It is a good idea to include the film on your insurance policy for camera equipment. But this normally only covers you for the price of replacement film. If you want them covered for the potential selling price of the pictures, premiums are exorbitant.

X-rays and fluorescent equipment can be a danger to unprocessed film. Some people are happy to pack spare film in the centre of their suitcase. Others will let the camera bag go through the X-ray machine at the airport. I always insist (pleasantly) on a hand search. I do this even if the machine claims to be safe for films because the bag is likely to pass through several airports and several X-ray machines. This can have a cumulative effect on the emulsion and fog the film. The faster the film (higher ISO rating) the more sensitive it will be to X-rays. A hand search may take a little longer, but I haven't missed a plane yet.

Lead-lined bags are available, but the protection they offer is nullified if the power of the X-ray machine is turned up so that the security people can see what's inside.

Some Eastern bloc countries will not let you take a camera as hand luggage, but they should not complain about film. In some countries you may be asked to pay import duty on unexposed film. It might be worth removing them from their packages so they appear to be exposed (for which no duty is payable).

Heat and humidity cause film to lose speed and contrast and colour film may show a magenta or green cast. If fungus grows on the film, there is very little you can do about it. But there are certain precautions you can take.

Leave film in its plastic container or foil wrapping until you need it as this helps protect it. Colour film, in particular, should be carefully stored away from heat, humidity and extremes of cold or dryness.

Try to keep film at a constant temperature. In hot climates store it at or below 13°C (56°F) if possible. When you want to use the film, return it to room temperature slowly to avoid condensation inside the cassette. If you have access to a fridge, store the film there and take it out two hours before loading it into the camera.

Without a fridge, an airtight ice chest with freezer sachets may provide a possible solution. Packets of silica gel in an airtight container absorb moisture in humid climates. And insulated chamois bags are available to protect film from extremes of temperature. Exceptionally cold film becomes brittle and can crack or snap. Wind the film on gently to avoid tearing it, and take similar care when winding it back into the cassette. A motordrive will increase the risk of breaking the film.

Wind off all exposed film so there is no danger of mistaking it for unexposed film and reusing it.

As a final note, unless you are abroad for several months, it is safer and cheaper to keep exposed film with you and have it developed when you return home. If you do opt to send film by post, mark the package 'Film Only – do not X-ray' and send it first class airmail. Some airmail post is x-rayed as a security measure, and it has been known for films to go missing, only to be sold later as unused film!

A Bag of Junk – Useful Extras in the Camera Bag

by Robert Holmes

A photographer's camera bag is not unlike a woman's handbag. To the owner, an invaluable collection of essential paraphernalia; to everyone else, a miscellaneous hoard of junk.

I am always fascinated by what other photographers carry around with them and you may find it enlightening for me to share the secrets of my 'bag of junk'. The list is long, but has evolved over several years of hard travel and there is nothing that I could comfortably leave out.

Aside from photographic equipment and cleaning materials, I always carry a basic tool kit for simple repairs and equipment maintenance. It includes a set of *jeweller's screwdrivers* including a small *Philips screwdriver* to tighten any screws that come loose. Periodically check the screws in both the camera body and lenses because the continual vibration you get from any method of transport can loosen screws surprisingly quickly. I once had a lens literally fall apart in a very remote part of Turkey because I failed to notice the first two screws fall out. A small pair of *jeweller's pliers* will help straighten out bent metal parts or tighten loose nuts.

Two universal accessories which no photographer should ever be without are a *Swiss army knife* and a roll of *gaffer tape*. The Swiss army knife can be used for all the purposes it was made for plus a multitude of photographic applications which are limited only by your imagination. Gaffer tape is a two-inch wide, tough, cloth-backed tape that can be used for anything from repairing torn trousers to holding a damaged camera together. A whole roll is pretty bulky, so I wind off as much as I think I will need around the *spanner* that I carry to tighten the legs of my tripod.

A *black felt-tip* pen that will write on any surface from film leaders to plastic bags and a *red felt-tip* to write processing instructions on blue and yellow Ektachrome cassettes supplement my ever-present *notebook*. However good you think your memory is, take notes. It's always surprising how people and places are forgotten or confused after a few weeks.

Within the last few years more and more *batteries* have found their way into my baggage. I never feel happy unless I have plenty of spares for cameras, motordrives, exposure meters and flash guns. What a headache modern technology is! I used to carry a couple of spare sets for my flash gun and that was that, but now I almost need a portable generator. When you buy batteries, get them from a store with a fast turnover. They must be fresh. Date them as soon as you buy them and use them in date order. Lithium cells have a long shelf life and work in a wide range of temperatures but they may not have enough power output to cope with some of today's all-singing, all-dancing picture machines. If in doubt, ask your dealer.

Down in the bottom of my bag are a few objects that apparently have no place in a photographer's armoury but are nevertheless irreplaceable when needed.

A *small flash light* has saved my bacon on several occasions particularly when there is not quite enough light left to read by and you still have to set your camera settings. It can also be useful to provide a source of light to focus on when the light is fading.

A tripod light enough to travel is also prone to vibration so I carry a *string bag* that I can fill with rocks and hang under the tripod to steady it. It will also prevent vibration in long telephoto lenses if I loop the handles of the bag over the lens, close to the camera body, to weigh it down on the tripod.

Weather rarely does what you want it to and on a cloudy sunless day, a *compass* will help you find out which direction the sun should shining from. It will also tell you where to expect sunrise and sunset, the most photogenic times of day.

I often shoot architectural subjects with extreme wide-angle lenses and without a small *spirit level* I would not be able to keep my verticals vertical. It also keeps my horizons horizontal.

The *metal mirror* in my bag is not because of any narcissistic tendencies. I occasionally use a camera on a tripod at its maximum height, and, although I can see through the viewfinder, I cannot see to set the shutter and aperture. I can hold the mirror above the camera and check all the setting without leaving the ground. It also comes in handy for directing sunlight on to small objects and flowers in the shade.

I always used to worry about leaving equipment cases in hotel rooms so now I carry a *bicycle lock* with me. The long, thick cable type with a combination lock is the best and you can secure your camera cases to radiators or pipes or even the bed. It may not deter the determined thief but it will prevent any casual thefts.

So there it is. My innermost secrets revealed. Some of these things could help you be a better photographer but all of them will help you be a more reliable one.

By the way, there are two more important additions to the bag. However well you think you know your equipment, when something goes wrong in the field, if you have your *camera manual* with you, at least you can check everything before writing the camera off. If you do have to write it off, keep the *international list of service agents* handy.

Photographing Nature

by Robert Holmes

Few subjects facing the camera produce such dismal failures as wildlife. I never again want to have to search for a bird lost in over-abundant foliage or watch the back end of an elephant disappearing into the bush.

The problem is that wildlife photography needs more than just technical expertise. An intimate knowledge of animal behaviour is equally as important, although fortunately you can improve your photographs without studying for an advanced degree in zoology.

Filling the frame

The most common problem is failing to fill the frame with the subject. This, of course, is easier said than done as most wild animals are so afraid of humans that a close approach is often impossible. The traditional method of setting up a hide and sitting there waiting, for hours on end, is out of the question for most travellers, so we have to resort to other methods. But whatever method we choose, this is not an area of photography that can be hurried.

Most animals and birds are less afraid of vehicles than they are of people and particularly in areas such as East Africa, you can drive right up to the wildlife without scaring it away. The vehicle will serve as a perfect mobile hide, but make sure the engine is switched off before you shoot or your camera will pick up the vibration. To steady long telephoto lenses, support the lens with a bean bag in the window opening. This will be much faster and more flexible than using a tripod.

If you approach the animal on foot, keep a low profile in the literal sense. Crouch down and crawl towards the subject. Wear colours that blend with the surroundings and try to avoid jerky movements.

Half the battle is being in the right place at the right time, and this is where a knowledge of animal behaviour comes in. A basic field guide to the animals and birds of the country you are visiting can go a long way towards helping with this problem. Also remember that most animals are active around waterholes and feeding places at dawn and dusk. It is unlikely that you will see much activity in the middle of the day. Many animals will come out into the open at night and if you have a powerful flash you can get some remarkable results.

Talk to locals and ask where you can see wildlife. Children are usually a mine of information in this respect and they will often be delighted to take you along to the good viewing points. Within the reserves, the rangers are often keen photographers themselves and are very sympathetic and knowledgeable.

Zoos

Many good 'wildlife' photographs are taken in zoos. These are the only places where you will be able to get close enough to many animals. You can get natural looking photographs if you take care with your framing, select a natural-looking background and keep bars and wire netting out of the picture. You can do this by using a telephoto lens (100mm or more focal length) at maximum aperture. This will give you minimum depth of field and throw out of focus everything but the subject you are focused on. This technique will also let you shoot through cages without seeing them, if you are close enough to the cage to throw it out of focus. To shoot through glass, remove reflections by using a polarising filter and angling the camera at 30 degrees to the surface.

Equipment

A good long lens is essential if you want to photograph birds, and it will be useful for most mammals too. I use a 400mm apochromatic lens – that is a lens that has special glass elements to ensure the highest colour fidelity. You can use it on maximum aperture and still get top quality results. Of course, specialist equipment like this comes with a high price tag and there are much more economical ways to solve the problem. I ordered my 400mm lens to take on a long trip to Alaska to photograph the wildlife in both Denali National Park and on the remote Pribilof Islands just off the coast of Siberia. The lens arrived two days after I had set off on this five-week journey. The longest lens that I owned was a 200mm, which, with a maximum aperture of f2.8 was pretty fast. I also had a doubler which was made by the same manufacturer, Minolta, and fixed onto the lens. A doubler, or 2x convertor, is an optical accessory that fits between the camera and the lens and doubles the focal length of the lens. A 135mm becomes a 270mm and my 200mm became a 400mm. The disadvantage is that you lose two stops, an f2.8 becomes an f5.6.

When doublers were first introduced several years ago, their optical quality left much to be desired. The bottom of a milk bottle would have produced better results. Fortunately, technology has improved dramatically and the new generation of doublers that are matched to specific lenses produce excellent results. Not only do they provide great versatility but they also take up very little space. I was forced to use this combination in Alaska and it enabled me to take photographs that have sold to one of the most technically demanding markets in the United States. This doubler has now become part of my standard travelling equipment and, with my newly acquired 400mm, I now have up to 800mm at my disposal without having to carry a huge chunk of glass around.

The other lens I find invaluable for wildlife is a 100mm macro. This will focus all the way from infinity to a few centimetres. Most macro lenses are in the 50mm range, but the 100mm lets you get the same degree of magnifi-

cation at a greater distance – and as I have always had an aversion to creepy crawlies, the 100mm focal length is ideal. It also allows you to take close-ups of subjects in inaccessible locations.

The choice of a camera is always a very personal one and my only advice is to get one that can take interchangeable lenses. The semi-wide angle lenses on compact automatic cameras will rarely produce satisfactory wildlife shots. Although I usually advocate using cameras in their manual mode, wildlife photography is one exception where the automatic camera comes into its own. The Minolta Maxxum even has a fast 300mm autofocus lens which allows total concentration on the subject.

Generally, a camera with a black finish is less likely to distract the wildlife than a bright, shiny, chrome-finished model, but a black finish is more susceptible to excessive heating in hot climates. If you are planning to take a range of shots, and not just wildlife, I would suggest that you err towards the chrome finish.

I wish all manufacturers made autowinders for their cameras as well as motordrives. In operation, the difference is that motordrives have a faster film advance rate – and they often incorporate a motorised film rewind.

Both offer single frame mode (you have to press the release for each exposure) and continuous mode (the shutter fires and the film advances continuously as long as the release is depressed). But how often do you need to shoot at five frames a second? In the last couple of years I have shot over 2000 rolls of film and not once have I ever used a motordrive in the continuous mode. Not only are motordrives more expensive than autowinders but they are also bigger and heavier. I would be lost without a winder because it helps me to concentrate completely on the subject, but its noise can be disturbing to some wildlife.

Plants

Rainforests contain some of the most beautiful plants and flowers imaginable – but what a nightmare for the photographer! Water drips continually from the trees and there is barely enough light to see by, let alone for taking photographs.

In the realm of plant photography, a rainforest is about as difficult a location as you will ever encounter. The light can be extremely contrasty, suggesting the use of a slow colour slide film (ISO 25-100) to handle the extremes of light and shade, but the overall darkness under the canopy of the forest cries out for a fast film (ISO 400 or more) which will be incapable of handling both highlights and shadowed detail. You can use the slow film with a tripod and long exposures, but plants are often moving, if only slightly, and none of the resulting photos will be really sharp.

My solution has been to use a fill flash. I use a small flash gun to illuminate the shadowed areas and thus reduce the overall contrast of the scene. With the new automatic flash-guns, this technique is very simple. Measure the light falling on a highlight – a sun-splashed leaf, for example. If the reading for an ISO 64 film is 1/60 second at f16, all you need to do is set the auto setting on the flash gun for an aperture of F16. Make sure you never set the shutter at a speed too high to synchronise with the flash. With most modern SLR cameras this speed will usually be 1/60 or 1/125 second. If you use a shorter exposure, then the illumination will be uneven. An additional advantage to using a flash fill is that the duration of a burst of light from a flash gun is extremely short and will freeze motion.

Plants and flowers in general present many interesting photographic problems. Lighting in the rainforests can be awkward, but a wild flower in a more open landscape can be equally difficult to shoot well. I always carry a small sheet of baking foil that folds down to nothing and yet becomes an excellent reflector that can push light into dark corners and bring life to a bloom that would otherwise be dull and colourless.

Many interesting flowers are so small that you will need a macro, or close-up lens to get an acceptable photo of them. At the short distances involved, the lens will have to be stopped down to a small aperture, maybe as little as f22, to obtain as much depth of field as possible and ensure that all of the flower is in sharp focus. A small aperture means a long shutter speed and a long shutter speed means an inability to freeze movement. A portable wind break may help, or get a friend to provide shelter. Alternatively, resort again to lighting the flower with flash. Even a small gun will let you use an aperture of f16 or smaller if it is used at close range.

There are certain flowers that are impossible to photograph in their natural colour. These reflect an unusually high percentage of the infrared and ultraviolet portions of the spectrum. Colour film is sensitive to these although our eyes are not and resulting colour on the film appears to be a gross distortion of the truth. Blue flowers are particularly susceptible and frequently produce a pinkish hue. Careful use of filter can sometimes help but the problem is almost impossible to eliminate.

Filters

A photographer doesn't have full control over how the image will turn out but can go a long way towards avoiding problems with light.

If you shoot portraits outdoors, there is no problem if the sky is overcast, but if the sun is shining disaster can strike in the form of ugly black shadows. To avoid these, move the subject into open shade. But now you are faced with another problem if you are using colour film. All colour film is balanced for a specific type of light, or should I say, colour temperature. Most of us use daylight film which will reproduce the true colours of any subject illuminated by light that has a colour temperature of 5500° Kelvin, that of normal sunlight. If the colour temperature of the light source is higher, then the subject will come out looking too blue. If it is lower, then it will be too yellow.

Once your portrait subject has moved from direct sunlight into open shadow, the illumination will be from the blue sky which may have a colour temperature of as much as 10,000° Kelvin – which is why portraits taken in the open shade always look too blue. To overcome this problem you can use a small flash gun and, as all electonic flashes are balanced for 5500° K, the colour will then look correct.

Another way is to use warming filters which warm up the light and bring down the colour temperature. Their technical descriptions are series 81 and 85 filters, each of which comes in a variety of different strengths.

Many professionals use a very expensive instrument called a colour temperature meter which will indicate precisely which filter is needed, but for practical purposes in the field, I would use an 81B as a general purpose warming filter.

Another technique that I have used very successfully in harsh sunlight is photographing the subject in reflected light. Look for a light wall or even use a white sheet or towel to bounce light from the sun into the subject's face. Be careful not to place the subject near surfaces with a strong colour or this will be reflected in the skin tones. People standing too close to foliage can look very sea-sick if you are not careful.

My favourite light for portraits is the Vermeer-like north light which gives an almost three-dimensional quality to the photograph. The important thing is to use your eyes and look to see how the light is playing on the subject matter.

Landscapes

This is equally true for landscapes. A landscape that looks dramatic to our eye may not be equally dramatic on film. Again light is usually the problem. Good weather often provides the worst conditions for dramatic landscapes. I prefer to work on days when there are clouds blowing across the skies creating a modulation of light with interesting shadows and highlights – not to mention the beauty of the clouds themselves. Shafts of sunlight on a stormy day will transform any landscape.

Remember that it is the interplay of light and shade that creates the illusion of depth in photographs and provides graphic interest. The higher the sun is in the sky, the shorter the shadows will be. At home in California, I find that the best light is just before dawn until about two hours after and the last two hours before sunset. At these times the sun is still low in the sky, creating long shadows and emphasising the texture of the land. The closer you get to the Equator, the briefer this period becomes until you have only a few minutes when the light is at its optimum. In Europe, there is a much longer period to play with, particularly in winter, but I still think it is difficult to beat dawn light. And for someone who enjoys a nice warm bed as much as I do, that's saying a lot!

I am frequently accused of using special filters to create dramatic effects although in reality I use few. I rely on the light and my knowledge of how film will react to it. The few filters I do use, however, are certainly worth having.

I have already mentioned the 81B warming filter and along with this I also carry a polarising filter and a graduated grey. Graduated filters are what their name suggests. They fade from a strong colour to clear so when used over the lens, a wash of colour affects only part of the photograph.

The coloured grads, as they are called, which create such dramatic effects as brown or green skies are too artificial for my taste. The grey that I use does not affect the colour of the photograph, but brings the tones within the range of the film. For example, if the sky is very bright, it may not be possible to contain foreground detail and sky detail in the same photograph. If the exposure is correct for the foreground, the sky will be washed out. The graduated grey will tone down the sky and help you make a much more dramatic landscape that still has an air of reality.

Polarisers

Of all the filters used by colour photographers, none can surpass the polariser. Not only is it extremely effective but also very simple to use.

Polarised light is everywhere. It bounces off non-metallic surfaces at an angle of 30°, off water, leaves, even from the sky. Its effect is to de-saturate colours. Most of the shine on a green leaf is polarised light; remove that light and you can see the pure, intense green of the leaf. A polarising filter will do this for you, and you can actually see what is happening through the viewfinder.

All polarising filters are supplied in revolving mounts. You screw them onto the front of the lens in the normal way but are still able to rotate the filter through 360°. Look through the viewfinder while you turn the filter and you will see the reflections disappear from surfaces and the sky deepen to a glorious blue. It will not always work. The maximum amount of polarised light in the sky is from the area of the sky at 90° to the sun. Look directly away from the sun – or into it – and the polarising filter will not have any effect. It is also most dramatic when the sun is low in the sky. If you do a lot of tide pool photography, this filter can completely eliminate surface reflections from the water so that you can see everything below the surface. Again you can see this happening through your viewfinder.

I have seen photographers leaving this filter on their lenses permanently, which I feel is a mistake. The disadvantage is that it cuts down the amount of light reaching the film, thus necessitating longer exposures. If it has no effect, then take it off.

And remember, no amount of equipment will improve your photographs unless you learn to use your eyes.

Beneath the Waves

by Dave Saunders

Anyone who has put on a mask and snorkel and floated over a coral garden or sunken boat will have had a glimpse of the fascinating world beneath the the surface of the ocean. But we are not built to exist for long underwater and nor are most cameras. It is an alien environment with a new set of rules for the photographer.

The nice thing about underwater photography is that you can approach it at any level. It is possible to take satisfactory pictures with an ordinary land camera though the 'window' of a glass bottomed boat, or even in rock pools using a bucket or water-tight box with a glass base. If the sun is shining on the subject, the pictures will be bright and clear.

But be careful when you are near water, especially salt water. Ordinary land cameras are like cats – they just don't want to get involved with water. So if you want to take a camera underwater, you will need either a purpose-built underwater camera or a water-tight housing.

Purpose-built Cameras

The cheapest underwater camera is the Minolta Weathermatic A(110), nicknamed the Yellow Submarine. The camera is light, robust and has a built-in flash unit. The manufacturer claims it is waterproof to a depth of five metres, making it ideal for beginners who want to take holiday snapshots.

The Pocket Marine 110, developed by Sea and Sea Products, can be taken down to 40m. It has a built-in flash as well as a socket for an extension flash. Its great advantage is its automatic wind-on mechanism which saves awkward manoeuvres underwater. This makes the camera a little more expensive than the Yellow Submarine.

Both models are also useful in grubby weather conditions on land – in rain, snow or sandstorms – as they are well insulated.

Higher up the range, Sea and Sea Products also make the Automarine 'Splash' and Motormarine 35SE, both automatic 35mm cameras.

The Nikonos is probably the underwater camera most used by the scuba divers. It is no larger than an ordinary 35mm camera, it is easy to operate and can give good results. Based on the French Calypso design, it is continually being improved. The Nikonos IV-A has a fully automatic exposure system, optional motordrive and automatic flash gun. There is no rangefinder for focusing, so you have to estimate focusing distances. Being a non-reflex camera, with a direct vision viewfinder, you may have problems with parallax when close to the subject. An external sportsfinder frame can be fixed to the top of the camera making viewing easier. The latest model, the Nikonos V, has a choice of auto or manual exposure. A bright LCD display in the viewfinder tells you the shutter speed, warns of over or under exposure and has a flash-ready signal.

The standard lens is the W-Nikkor 35mm f2.5. Also available are 15mm, 28mm and 80mm lenses. For detailed shots of coral and tame fish there are special close-up lenses or extension tubes.

Underwater Housings

Rather than investing in a whole new camera system, an alternative approach is to use an underwater housing around your land camera. In shallow water of less than ten metres, flexible plastic housings provide a relatively cheap method of protecting your camera. Controls are operated through a rubber glove set into the case.

In deeper water the flexible design is inappropriate as pressure increases with depth and the housing would collapse. Ikelite housings are made for 110, 35mm reflex and non-reflex and roll film cameras. These are rigid and some models can safely be taken to a depth of 100m.

The housing has controls which link into the focusing and aperture rings, as well as shutter release and film advance mechanisms. Rubber 'O' ring seals produce a water-tight chamber which keeps the camera dry. To avoid flooding, the rings must be cleaned and lightly greased with silicone each time a film is changed. Metal housings are very strong and durable, but are heavy to carry and need careful attention to prevent corrosion. Plexiglass housings are much lighter and cheaper, and are available for a wider range of cameras. However, the plastic

type ages more quickly and will eventually leak.

How Light Behaves

Light is refracted or bent more in water than in air. Objects underwater appear to be larger and nearer than they really are. Your eye sees the same distortion as the lens, so, with a reflex camera, you simply focus through the lens and the subsequent picture will then be in focus. The subject may be one and a half metres away, but will appear closer to the eye and to the lens. However, if you then look at the focusing ring, it will set at about one metre.

Because of the way light refracts through water, the effective focal length of the lens is increased, making it more telephoto when a flat underwater porthole is used. So, in effect, a 35mm lens underwater is approximately equivalent to a 45mm lens on land. Likewise a 15mm lens is equivalent to a 20mm.

A dome-shaped porthole, on the other hand, enables light from all directions to pass through it at right angles. This eliminates the problem of refraction and the angle of view of the fitted lens is unchanged.

Lenses

Wide angle lenses are generally more useful underwater. Visibility is seldom as good as above water, especially if there are numerous suspended particles. For a clear image it is important to move in close so as to reduce the amount of water between the camera and the subject. To include a whole diver in the frame when using a 35mm lens on a Nikonos, you need to be about two metres away. A wider lens, say 15mm, means you can move in much closer to the subject and thus minimise the amount of obstructing material between the camera and the subject.

Generally camera-to-subject distance should not exceed a quarter of the visibility. If the visibility is only one and a half metres (as it often is in temperate seas or inland lakes), you should restrict yourself to only taking subjects up to 0.3m from the lens.

The Nikonos 15mm lens is very expensive, but cheaper lenses and lens converters are available. The most common are the Sea and Sea 21mm lens and the Subatec Subawinder which is an attachment lens clipping onto the standard Nikonos 28mm or 35mm lenses underwater. The attachment can be removed underwater, enabling you to revert to the normal lens when you no longer need the wide angle.

Flash

With high speed emulsions such as Ektrachrome 400 (slides) and Kodacolour 400 (prints), it is often possible to get away without using flash, especially near the surface where it is brighter. When the sun is shining through the surface layers of water you can obtain good results without flash down to about two metres. However, the deeper you go below the surface layers of water, the more the light is filtered out by the water. At ten metres below the surface, all the red has been filtered out of the ambient light, and flash is needed to restore the absorbed colour.

In tropical waters, the guide number of the flash gun (which indicates its power) is usually reduced to about a third of the 'in air' number. It is much safer to bracket your exposures, as the expense of film is nothing compared to the trouble and expense of getting into the water.

Underwater flashguns are either custom-made, or normal land units in plastic housings. Custom-made guns generally have a good wide angle performance, whereas units in housings generally have a narrow angle.

Instead of using a flash gun mounted close to the camera, place it at arm's length away, or even further, to give a better modelling light to the subject. Having two flash guns is even better and will give much greater control over lighting. With the flashgun further from the camera, fewer particles between the camera and the subject will be illuminated. If the flashgun is near the camera, the particles will be illuminated and detract from the subject.

Aiming the flash can be tricky. Although your eye and the camera lens 'see' the subject to be, say, two metres away, it is actually further. As the flash must strike the subject directly in order to light it up, the unit must be aimed *behind* the apparent position of the subject.

Diving Problems

Test your equipment in the swimming pool before you take it into the sea. Plan the shots beforehand. It is always better to have a good idea of what you want *before* you go into the water so you can have the right lens on the camera to do the job.

Keeping yourself stable while trying to take a picture can be a problem. Underwater you should be neutrally buoyant, such that you can hang suspended in the water without moving up or down. By breathing in you should rise slowly, and by breathing out you should gently sink. Wearing an adjustable buoyancy life jacket (A.B.L.J.) will allow you to increase or decrease your buoyancy by letting air into or out of it.

Sometimes you may need to grab onto a piece of coral to steady yourself. A wetsuit will help protect you against stings and scratches. And as you will be moving around slowly when taking pictures, you will feel the cold earlier than if you were swimming energetically, and you will appreciate the warmth the suit gives you.

Near the sandy sea bed it is easy to churn up the water and disturb the sand, making the water cloudy. The secret is to keep still as possible, and remove your fins. Restricting rapid movements also avoids scaring the more timid fish away. Taking a plastic bag of bread down with you usually guarantees plenty of potential subjects for your photography.

Good Subjects

Even with very simple equipment it is possible to record interesting effects simply by looking at what is naturally around you underwater. Rays of light burst though the water in a spectacular way and are especially photogenic when they surround a silhouette. And you can get impressive effects by catching reflections on the surface when you look up at the sky through the water.

The best pictures are usually simple and clear. Select something to photograph, such as an attracive piece of coral, then position yourself to show it off to best advantage without too many distractions in the picture.

With a little thought and planning beforehand, achieving good results underwater is quite straightforward although you should not be deterred by a high failure rate at first.

The Trouble with Photography

by David Hodgson

I have only been in jail three times in my life and, in each case, the stay was mercifully short! This was just as well since the jails were all in Africa and not amongst the healthiest places to spend a holiday. The cause, I hasten to add, was photographic rather than anything more sinister. A question of pointing a lens in the wrong direction at the wrong time. As a magazine photojournalist with an editor and offices to please, I was probably less discreet with my photography than the average traveller would ever need to be. All the same, great difficulties can be created quite unintentionally and with the most innocent of motives.

First of all find out exactly what the restrictions are and then stick to them. In many areas of the world, frontier security problems can turn an innocent border post picture into an excursion into espionage. At best you are likely to find your camera and film confiscated and the worst can be a whole lot worse. Many places now insist on you having a photographic permit. Make sure you get one. It is no guarantee against trouble, but may help, if you wave it under enough noses. Avoid photographing military installations, troop movements, airfields etc., unless you have a compelling reason for doing so. And I mean one which is worth doing time for! Some countries have a ban on photographing examples of civil engineering, scenes that make the country look primitive – i.e. all the most photogenic places – and industrial plants. In Yugoslavia, some years ago, I was arrested for taking shots inside a chemical plant – and this after being given permission to do so. One traveller in Pakistan – which is full of absurd photographic restrictions – was nearly arrested for taking a picture of a river which just happened to have a bridge in the background. Train and aeroplane spotters beware: certain Iron Curtain and Third World countries regard the photographic or written record keeping involved as an offence. A bribe sometimes secures a bending of the rules.

Watch out for religious or cultural prohibitions. These can result in mob violence against you, especially in the remoter parts of the world. If you want to take pictures in places where the natives are far from friendly, then be careful. Respect their dignity and right of privacy. In some places, such as Kenya, reluctant subjects have been persuaded to pose with hefty payments. If you start shooting without their permission and paying the going rate, the mood can turn ugly remarkably fast. So take plenty of change and be prepared to negotiate. When in doubt, use a telephoto from a healthy distance. I should also add that a quite different problem can arise when you are *too* popular as a camera operator. Everybody in the neighbourhood seems to want to get in on the act. This happens mainly when a camera is a rare sight and you are looked on as a

piece of street theatre. My advice here is to go though the pretence of taking pictures. If necessary – and you have sufficient film stock – waste a few frames or even a whole roll. You never know – some of the pictures may be worthwhile and you will satisfy the crowd's curiosity. When all the fuss has died down you can carry on with picture-taking without arousing much interest. If you are staying in an area for some time and want really candid shots, then let everybody get completely used to seeing you with your camera. Reckon on spending several days simply being seen around. Your novelty value will disappear very quickly.

One good way of persuading reluctant subjects to pose and rewarding them if they do is to carry a Polaroid camera around. Take one shot and let them have it. Then shoot your main pictures. But a word of warning – you can get through a lot of expensive Polaroid film unless you save this tactic for an emergency.

Movies on the Move

by Dominic Boland

Simple movie making is actually very straightforward. New skills need to be practiced for the best results but they are neither complicated nor difficult. Before that, however, it's necessary to look at the equipment itself so that the decision between using cine or video can be made.

Video Equipment

Using a video camera is similar to using a tape recorder and an ordinary single lens reflex camera. Most video cameras come fitted with a zoom lens. Look for as wide a range as possible and check how this applies to 35mm camera lenses. For example, on a VHS video camera an 8mm – 48mm zoom is about equivalent to a 50mm – 300mm zoom in SLR camera terms. The comparisons will vary depending upon the tape format being used.

Choice of format is the biggest decision you'll have to make. At the end of the range is U-matic, capable of broadcast quality, with the benefits of interchangeable lenses and able to handle all the post-production facilities you can imagine. Unfortunately U-matic gear is terribly expensive and anything short of a full-scale travelogue production won't justify the cost. Prices for a camera with a zoom lens and all the necessary bits and pieces start at around £3500 and it's possible to pay well over £8000. Rental works out at about £500 plus per week. And don't forget VAT.

With domestic video formats, life is somewhat easier. You don't need to own a video cassette recorder (VCR) to shoot video films. However, there are both VHS and Betamax cameras to complement home VCR machines. You can also choose from one of the mini-formats, VHS-C (which can be played back through a full-sized VHS recorder via an adaptor), or the new 8mm format. This uses a tape little bigger than an audio cassette, yet produces a picture quality equal to that of most full size VHS or Betamax tapes.

Video cameras used to be operated with a separate recorder slung over the shoulder – inconvenient and heavy. Nowadays the two are usually combined into one easily portable 'camcorder' unit. The size of the camcorder depends on the size of the tape format. Although compact, VHS and Betamax camcorders still seem bulky compared to the amazingly small size of 3mm camcorders. Some are little bigger than the book you are holding.

Another major advantage of the camcorder is that most can be plugged directly into a TV for instant replay. In some countries the TV system may be incompatible with your camera so you'll have to rely on the unit's built-in monitor for reviewing. Also, don't go unplugging hotel television sets to watch the day's shooting without checking with the management. Many hotel systems set off an alarm if interfered with – as I've found to my embarrassment!

New or Old?

The video market is very volatile with new models appearing almost monthly, so many good but discontinued units are available. However, buying discontinued or secondhand cameras can be hazardous so take advice, and only buy from reputable shops.

Buying new equipment means you get the latest technology. Don't underestimate auto-focus, which now is fairly standard and both fast and accurate. Look for a CCD (charge-coupled device) sensor as opposed to the more traditional newvicon or saticon tubes; CCD's are more robust, more powerful and last much longer. A typical auto-focus, auto-exposure camcorder will cost in the region of £1200 regardless of format, although prices are slowly coming down. It's worth noting that many identical cameras carry different brand names and are packaged with different accessories, carrying cases, etc. Shop around for the best 'kit' on offer. Remember too that with video the initial cost is high but the running cost is low.

Hiring is a viable alternative to buying if you don't see yourself using the equipment much. A weekend rental will also help teach you what facilities to look for. Look for a 'hire before you buy' scheme where the rental cost is deducted from the price if you decide to purchase.

Cine is Dead?

With video so good why bother with cine? Three main reasons; superior image quality, higher reliability, and ease of editing.

For top-notch quality and robust specification 16mm cine equipment is the gear used by wildlife and news crews. Compared to 16mm cine, U-matic is cheap. For a 16mm camera with a zoom lens and all the bits and pieces needed to use it you won't find much change out of £10,000. Hiring by the week would be in the region of £250. Buying secondhand is much cheaper as there's a healthy market. You could set up for around £2000, but you need to know your onions. The cameras also chew up film 400 feet at a time, so running costs are high. Definitely not the format for the novice.

Enter Super 8mm cine! Using pre-loaded, drop-in film cartridges, this is an extremely convenient format. New equipment is relatively costly because of the small volume of sales following the video boom, but there's an enormous amount of second-hand and redundant as-new stock lying around waiting to be picked up. Again, seek help if buying second-hand.

Super 8mm cine cameras can match video on size and specification quite easily and prices can be surprisingly low. Avoid the simplest 'point and shoot' cameras and aim for something including auto-focus and a zoom lens. At the top of the range are cameras offering specifications rare on video yet at a price well under half that of the better camcorders; variable film speed for fast and slow motion effects, electronic fading, frame-by-frame exposure, ultra close-up focusing, time lapse facilities, sound-on-sound, and so on.

Projectors too come in simple and advanced forms. Some of the better ones costing around £200 offer sound editing facilities that can in effect improve the performance of a simple camera. In certain circumstances it's possible to shoot a sound-stripped film through a simple, silent camera, edit the film and then, using a suitable projector, add a soundtrack with pre-recorded music and effects, even a voice-over commentary.

It's this flexibility, plus ruggedness, that helps cine to score over video. Actually using the equipment is much the same whichever medium you choose – with one important difference. For the price of a film cartridge (about £8 including processing) you get roughly three minutes of non-reusable film, and you can't check what you shot until it's processed. For the same price you can buy 30 minutes of top quality video tape, which can be reviewed instantly and reused almost indefinitely.

Film and Tape

At the moment Super 8mm film is made in both sound and silent versions. Buy film in bulk for discount and make sure it's balanced for daylight and not tungsten light. There's little choice in film sensitivities, ISO 40 being the most common, with ISO 160 also available.

Just like any 35mm transparency film, cine films exhibit the same variety of characteristics from make to make, the most popular brands being Kodak and Agfa. With the exception of Kodachrome, all other types of film incur processing charges. Processing quality varies too, so when you find a good lab stick with it.

Many video tapes, like audio tapes, are sourced from the same manufacturer. Avoid cheap extra-long play tapes. Simply keep to the best named, highest specification brand you can afford. Even so, tapes do wear out with use, particularly if you use freeze-frame when replaying. Tape wear varies with quality. A cheap tape will stretch, snap or show magnetic drop-out on the screen (white lines, dots, etc.) after ten or so showings. Top quality tape will last over 100 showings.

Video tapes play on one side only and are extremely susceptible to damage. Keep them as you would film; heat, moisture and dust are the main enemies, but add to this magnetic fields created by loudspeakers and electric motors. Also, take care of the cassettes themselves. Believe it or not, they contain very advanced and delicate engineering and should be stored upright in their protective sleeves.

Accessories and Protection

Without doubt, cine equipment is far more robust then video. Safety and precaution instructions come with your equipment. So read them *before* you use the gear. Video cameras in particular don't like extremes of heat (*never* point one at the sun) or cold, whilst direct contact with moisture usually results in complete failure. They can't cope with physical drops either and any sharp bang can ruin the 'tracking' of the camera sufficiently to turn it into a write-off. For this reason adequate insurance cover is a must. The key to using video? Be gentle!

Field repairs aren't going to be easy as both cine and video equipment rely heavily on electronic components. Don't open up a video camera. Some delicate parts can be ruined even by moisture from your fingers. But a first aid kit comprising of a set of jeweller's screwdrivers, a 'puffer brush', proper camera cleaning tissues (not cloths) and a roll of gaffer tape will see you through most emergencies.

As for accessories, the boy scout approach of 'essential, useful and luxurious' comes in here. Essential are spare batteries (at least two spare video battery packs – one to be recharging, one to have in the pocket when shooting), plenty of film or tape, and an intimate knowledge of the instruction book. It's also essential to check carefully well in advance the import controls of the countries you intend to visit. Video equipment particularly is often 'confiscated'. Several copies of receipts, equipment descriptions and serial numbers, to be stamped when entering and leaving countries, will be invaluable.

Useful would be a selection of ordinary photographic filters for special effects, a shoulder stock to help hold the camera steady against the body, and a customised bag to carry everything. As video batteries only last about 30 minutes between charges, another very useful accessory is a special vehicle battery adaptor cable. Many overland vehicles deliver higher than normal voltages, so you might need to have the lead regulated accordingly.

Sheer luxury would be a tripod, supplementary lighting, a separate audio tape recorder – and a sherpa.

Shooting Skills

Whether you're intending eventually to use cine or video your first step should be to borrow or hire a video camera so that you can begin learning the techniques without spending a fortune on film.

Golden rule number one is to read the instructions thoroughly. Also, plug into a television when you can. The larger screen is an enormous help.

Golden rule number two is to practice before you head off into the wilderness. This will teach you what works and what doesn't when it comes to using all those wonderful controls at your fingertips.

A good initial training run is to watch television with the sound turned down. See how the director chops and changes not only the scenes, but the angles and viewpoint. Even a twenty second commercial demonstrates the huge variety of techniques available. Don't try to pack it all in like this yourself or your audience will start suffering eye strain, but do experiment with the following ideas.

Calling the Shots

You don't have a film crew with two or three cameras, so don't attempt the type of shoot they could. You're more like the documentary or news reporter. Remember that most of the time you won't have any control over the events you're capturing, so 'storyboarding', where each shot is visualised as an illustration before the camera ever hits the action, won't be too useful. You'll learn far more from simply going and doing.

Where you do have control is over the type of shoot you use and, especially with video, you want to use 'in camera' editing. This just means thinking ahead and trying to put the shots in some logical sequence and not a random, haphazard series of takes that will need days of later editing.

There are four main types of shot you'll find useful. The 'very long shot' (or vista shot) is used to give a sense of place. It will show the setting but isn't trying to capture action.

Next is the 'long shot' which will move in tighter to show a specific point of interest. It could be a group of people, a row of houses, or a general view of an activity. A 'medium shot' moves in closer still. Whereas the previous shot would include heads and feet, the medium shot would show only the head and shoulders of an individual. It's commonly used during dialogue.

Finally, the 'close-up' excludes most extra detail; a tightly cropped head shot, an isolated detail of architecture. Practice using these shots to relate a story. Start off with straightforward sequences, then be more adventurous. For instance, cutting from a long shot of a dangerous waterfall to a medium shot of a small boat drifting down a river, and then back to the waterfall again, implies that the boat is heading toward an accident. And all without a word being said.

Camera Movements

The zoom action of the cine or video lens is a convenient way to change the focal length for each shot. You can of course zoom from one end of the lens range to the other whilst filming. But use this sparingly and gently. Constant zooming in and out of a scene – 'tromboning' – is very tiring for your audience.

Another very good technique to use is panning. Start off with a couple of seconds of still scene, then slowly rotate your body at the hips keeping the camera perfectly horizontal. End the shot with another couple of seconds still scene shooting. A more interesting variation is to follow action whilst panning, ending on a descriptive shot. For instance, film a cyclist working his way down a busy street, past your position. Then let him ride out of shot (you stop panning) leaving the camera focused on a street sign that describes where you're filming.

Tilting is the same as panning but moving the camera vertically instead. Again the start and stop sequences allow the eye a resting place at either end of the shoot. Amateur films tend to include too much panning and tilting, known as 'hosepiping', so as with all techniques use them only when they're applicable.

The transition from one scene to another can be accomplished in a number of ways, the simplest being the cut. Shoot a scene, stop the film or tape movement until you reach your new location, then shoot the next take. Sounds simple, and so it is. As often, the simplest things can be the most useful. Shooting a market scene with long and medium shots, you can add plenty of close-up cuts of hands, faces and other details to add activity and excitement. You can cut into a scene like this or cut out. Medium shots of camel drivers resting and eating can cut out to atmospheric vista shots of the desert with a shimmering heat haze.

If the cut technique is too short and sharp, another transitional device is the fade. Not all cameras allow this, but the idea is to slowly darken (or indeed lighten) the scene until only a blank screen is left. The tape or film is then paused until the opening sequence of the next shot when the new scene re-emerges from a fade. Why not mix cutting and fading? Try fading out from a tranquil vista shot then cut dramatically into a noisy, bustling close-up.

As you can see, there's enormous control available to you. Add to these basics other techniques such as using filters, creative exposure control, 'tracking' shots where the camera keeps alongside the subject as it moves, mixing still and moving pictures, and the exciting possibilities of video and cine seem endless. Do exercise care and caution though. Good camera technique shouldn't really be noticed – unless you have an audience of cameramen you're trying to impress!

Editing

The final act before you reveal your masterpiece to the world lies in editing, and it's arguably the most important single part of the movie making process.

Although expensive, it's the film itself that's cine's major advantage over video – it can be easily edited with special tapes or cement and an inexpensive tool. You simply snip up the film and rearrange it in the order you want it to finally appear. The best way is to have a copy made, edit that until you're happy with the results, then apply it to your original. This way you can edit much faster and avoid scratching the master copy. Unlike video, which is edited in 'real time' sat in front of a TV, cine can be scanned very quickly, speeding the process up enormously. You can also buy commercial clips to edit into your own films, everything from cartoons to exploding H-bombs. Handle with care!

Editing amateur format video is less easy. You can't cut and paste video tape for two reasons. Firstly, any variation in the smoothness of the tape would ruin the delicate replay heads. Secondly, the signals are 'written' onto the tape in an odd way making accurate splicing impossible. If you're lucky your local arts centre may have professional editing equipment available for a fairly modest fee, starting at around £50 per hour (compared to commercial editing rates which can be in excess of £500 per hour). The alternative is to use two video machines. By careful playing and replaying, you can record the original onto the other machine in any order you wish.

Understand that making a video copy will always affect quality. To ensure the highest possible results use the best tapes you can afford, be as careful as possible in your original shooting technique – particularly when it comes to focusing – and at all stages use the best leads that you can afford. Never underestimate the importance of high quality leads in video. Treat all leads with care, and make sure you keep them clean and well-fitting.

When editing cine and video a notepad and stopwatch are essential tools, used in conjunction with a footage counter on the replay machine. Stick to a plan of action and be methodical in your approach. Don't be too ambitious until you've picked up some experience, just be content with a finished product that follows a logical sequence of events.

The more you edit the more you'll appreciate how good shooting technique will improve the results, how a good edit can sometimes rescue a bad film, and how short sequences can relate a complex storyline. Adding sound is a further technique which, in the early days at least, is best kept very simple. However, even the simplest sound equipment is capable of recording the atmosphere of a place. 'Dubbing' voice-overs and sound effects later on can add a touch of professionalism quite easily.

No matter which medium you decide to use shooting moving pictures is a fascinating, highly enjoyable and ultimately addictive way of recording the world you travel through. Don't be put off by the technical side. The end result will always act as a visual spark for the memory, and your journeys will never be forgotten or lost.

The prices given in this article all refer to the UK market at the time of writing, January 1987.

Selling Travel Photographs

by John Douglas

A two-man canoe expedition up the Amazon...a one-man trek through Afghanistan...a full-scale assault on Everest involving a party of sixty...a student group studying the fauna and flora of a remote Pacific island.

Question: What two features do these travellers have in common?

Answer: They will all be short of money and they'll all be taking at least one camera.

The object of this article is to draw attention to the fact that these two features are not unrelated. Too few expeditions or independent travellers, whether they be on the grand scale or simply a student adventure, are aware that the camera can make a substantial contribution to much-needed funds. When it is pointed out that a single picture may realise, say £100, the hard-pressed traveller begins to see that he may be neglecting a very substantial source of revenue. While it is true that income from photography may not be received until some considerable time after arriving home, it can be used to pay off debts – or perhaps to finance the next excursion.

If photography is to pay, then advance planning is essential. Too often planning is no more than quick decisions regarding types of camera and the amount of film to be taken. Of course, these *are* essential questions and something might first be said about their relevance to potential markets.

Unless sponsorship and technical assistance are received, a movie camera is not worth taking. The production of a worthwhile expedition film or travelogue is such an expensive, specialised and time-consuming matter that it is best forgotten. In order to satisfy television and other markets, a film must approach near professional standards with all that implies in editing, cutting, dubbing, titling and so on, to say nothing of filming techniques. Of course, if a film unit from, for example, a regional TV network can be persuaded to send along a crew, then some of the profit, as well as a fine record of the traveller's achievements may accrue. But for the average trip this is unlikely, to say the least. By all means take along a good 8mm movie camera or video but don't think of it as a source of income.

Format and colour

With still photography, the position is quite different. It *is* worthwhile investing in, or having on loan, a good range of equipment. It will probably be advisable to take perhaps as many as three cameras; two 35mm SLR's and a large format camera with an interchangeable back. If the latter is not available, then contrary to advice sometimes given, 35mm format is quite satisfactory for most markets except some calendar, postcard and advertising outlets.

A common planning argument is the old black and white versus colour controversy. It is *not* true that mono reproduction from colour is unacceptable. Expertly processed a large proportion of colour shots will reproduce satisfactorily in black and white. However, conversion is more expensive and difficult than starting in the right medium and there are far more markets for mono than for colour. Although prices paid for black and white will only be some 50 to 60 per cent of those for colour, it is the larger market that makes it essential to take both sorts of film. A good plan is to take one-third fast black and white film and two-thirds colour reversal film. For formats larger than 35mm, take colour only. The reason for this imbalance is that it is easier to improve a sub-standard black and white during processing. To all intents and purposes, the quality of a colour picture is fixed once the shutter closes.

It is advisable to keep to one type of film with which you are familiar. Different colour films may reproduce with contrasting colour quality and spoil the effect of an article illustrated with a sequence of colour pictures. Colour prints will not sell.

Outlets

Before leaving, the travel photographer should contact possible outlets for his work. Magazines generally pay well for illustrations, especially if accompanied by an article. Such UK markets as *The Traveller, The Geographical* magazine, the colour supplements of the Sunday newspapers or *Amateur Photographer* can be approached and, although they may not be able to give a firm *yes* their advice can be helpful. Specialist journals, assuming they are illustrated, may be approached if the trip is relevant, but it should be remembered that the smaller circulation of such journals yields a lower rate of payment. It can be worth advertising the journey in the hope of obtaining lucrative photographic commissions, but beware of copyright snags if the film is provided free.

Overseas magazines such as the American *National Geographic*, often pay exceptionally high rates but the market is tight. Much nearer home, local and national newspapers may take some pictures while the traveller is still abroad. If the picture editor is approached, he may accept some black and white pictures if they can be sent back through a UK agent. If the expedition is regionally based, local papers will usually be quite enthusiastic, but it is important to agree a reasonable fee beforehand, otherwise a payment of, say, £2 will hardly cover the costs involved. Local papers may also agree to take an illustrated story on the return home, but again, it is important to ensure that adequate payment will be made for the pictures published.

It is not the purpose of this article to discuss techniques of photography but the photographer working with an expedition is well advised to seek guidance, before he leaves home, from others who have worked in the area. There can be problems with climate, customs and the like of which it is as well to be aware before starting out.

Finally, one potentially contentious point *must* be settled before the first picture is taken. This is the matter of copyright ownership and the income received from the sale of photographs. In law, copyright is vested in the owner of the film and *not* in the photographer. This can cause headaches if the traveller has had film given to him by a third party.

Universal Appeal

Once the trip has started, the travel photographer should look for two sorts of photograph. Firstly, of course, there will be those which illustrate their travels, the changing scene, human and physical. But secondly, and so easily neglected, are those pictures which have a universal appeal irrespective of their location. Such shots as sunsets, children at play, brilliant displays of flowers and so on always have a market. It is important, too, not to miss opportunities that are offered en route to the main location in which the travel photographer is to operate. Don't pack away your film while travelling to your destination. Have the camera ready on the journey.

Not unnaturally, the question 'what sells?' will be asked. There is no simple answer except to say that at some time or other almost any technically good photograph may have a market. (Throughout, it is assumed that the photographer is able to produce high quality pictures. There is never a market for the out-of-focus, underexposed disaster) Statements like 'the photograph that sells best is the one that no one else has' may not seem very helpful, yet this is the truth. It is no use building a collection which simply adds to an already saturated market. For example, a traveller passing through Agra will certainly visit the Taj Mahal – and photograph the splendid building. Yet the chances of selling such a photograph on the open market are dismal. It's all been done before, from every angle in every light and mood. Perhaps a picture of the monument illuminated by a thunderstorm might be unusual enough to find a buyer but the best that can reasonably be hoped for is that the photographer will hit on a new angle or perhaps a human interest picture with the Taj as a background. On the other hand, a picture of village craftsmen at work might sell well, as will anything around which a story can be woven.

Landscapes have a limited market but, given exceptional conditions of light, then a good scenic picture might reap high rewards in the calendar or advertising markets. The golden rule is to know the markets well enough to foresee needs. Sometimes the least obvious subjects are suddenly in demand.

Such was the case, for example, in 1976 during the raid on Entebbe Airport by Israeli forces. My own agency, Geoslides, was able to supply television with photographs of the old section of the airport and of the Kampala hospital just when they were needed. Yet who would expect a market for such subjects? Perhaps this is just another reason for carrying plenty of film. My own experience on my travels is that I am constantly looking around for subjects. Certainly it is no use sitting back waiting for something to appear in the viewfinder. It is wise not to ignore the obvious, everyday scenes. As I was preparing this article, Geoslides were asked for a photograph of a hailstorm in our Natal collection. Bad weather photographs sell well, so you should not always wait for brilliant sunshine.

Record Keeping and Processing

One most important but easily overlooked point is the matter of record keeping. In the conditions experienced by many travellers, this will not be easy, yet it cannot be emphasized too strongly that meticulous care must be taken to ensure that every picture is fully documented. It is true that certain photographs may be identified at a later date, for example, macrophotography of plants, but no shot should be taken without some recording of at least its subject and location. It is usually best to number the films in advance and to have an identification tag on the camera which will indicate the film being exposed. A notebook can also be prepared before the traveller leaves.

With the advertising market in mind, it is helpful to make sure that good photographs are taken which include the traveller's equipment. Less obviously, there is a market for photographs of proprietary brands of food, magazines, newspapers, items of clothing and equipment and so on in exotic and unusual settings.

If the traveller is to be away for a long time, it can be important to get some of the exposed film back home. There are dangers in this procedure because of the uncertainty of postal services, but provided some care is taken – perhaps with arrangements made through embassies – then there are advantages. Apart from the obvious problem of keeping exposed film in sub-optimum conditions, some preparatory work can be carried out by the traveller's agent. Of course, if the film is sent home, it is essential that labelling and recording are foolproof.

Serious selling

Once the travel photographer has returned home, the serious business of selling begins. Topicality is a selling point, so there is no excuse for taking even a few days off, no matter how exhausted you may feel. Processing the film is clearly the first task, followed by cataloguing and the production of sample black and white enlargements. No one is going to buy if the goods are badly presented, so it is worth making sure that a portfolio of high quality mono enlargements and colour transparencies is prepared with a really professional appearance. Put together a stocklist of all your photos (what countries and subjects, colour and black and white, and how many you have in each area) and circulate it around all the magazines and papers you can think of. As long as it is kept up to date, you should be able to sell one-offs for some way into the future.

The first market to tackle will be the local newspapers. Following up the advances made before you set out is very important, no matter how lukewarm the original response. It often *looks* more professional if there are both a writer and a photographer to produce a magazine article, but it should be made clear to editors that a separate fee is expected for text and illustrations. This is invariably better than a lump sum or space-payment.

A direct source of income from photography can be slide shows for which the audience is charged. These are relatively easy to organize but must be prepared with slides of maps and accompanying tape or live commentary. Incidentally, do not mix vertical and horizontal frames. It gives an untidy appearance to the show even when the screen actually accommodates the verticals. The bigger the screen the better. If these shows are to have a wide audience, it may be necessary to put the organization in the hands of an agent.

A photographic exhibition can provide helpful publicity but it will probably raise little or no income in itself. Branch librarians are usually helpful in accommodating exhibitions and if these showings precede some other event like a lecture or slide show, they can be indirect money spinners. For an exhibition, great care should be taken in making the display as professional as possible. Again, the bigger the enlargements, the better. As far as photography is concerned 'big is beautiful!' It is worth investing in a few really giant blow-ups.

Depending on the standing of the photographer, it can be a good plan to show some prints to the publicity department of the camera company or franchise agent whose equipment has been used, especially if you have made exclusive use of one company's products. The same may apply to the makers of the film that has been used.

If the traveller has not been too far off the beaten track throughout his travels, then travel firms may take photographs with which to illustrate brochures and posters. However, as with the calendar and postcard market, it must be pointed out that this is a specialist field, requiring not only particular sorts of photographs but pictures of a very high technical quality. This also applies to photographs used for advertising, although the suggestions made earlier regarding pictures of proprietary brands leaves this door slightly wider than usual.

Whenever an original transparency or negative is sent to or left with a publisher or agent, a signature must be obtained for it, a value placed on it should it be lost or damaged (anything up to £300 per original) and a record kept of its location.

Using an Agency

Lastly, when the catalogue is complete, the travel photographer will wish to put the whole of his saleable photograph collection on the market. Now a decision must be reached on the thorny issue of whether or not to use an agency. Of course, direct sales would mean an almost 100 per cent profit, while the agency sales will probably net only 50 per cent of the reproduction rights fee. But, as so often happens, it is the enlargement of the market, the professional expertise and marketing facilities of the agency which are attractive. It is worth making enquiries of a number of agencies (see the *Writers' and Artists' Year-Book*) and finding a company which offers the sort of terms and assistance that satisfy the travel photographer's requirements. It is usually preferable to deal with a company which does not expect to hold the collection but simply calls for pictures when needed. This allows much greater freedom to the copyright owner as well as being a check on what is happening in the market. Some agencies offer additional services to associate photographers in the way of help with the placing of literary as well as photographic material and in the organization of lecture services.

It may even be better to contact an agency before leaving. For a small consultancy fee, a good agency may be able to advise on the sort of pictures which sell well and on the level of reproduction fees which should be charged. There is nothing more annoying than selling rights for £25 and then finding that the market would have stood £50. Many amateurs sell their pictures for too low a fee and others assume that there is a set price irrespective of the use to which the photographic material is put. In fact, the market for photographic reproduction rights is something of a jungle and it may be better to gain professional advice rather than get lost. The same applies to locating markets.

It is almost impossible for the inexperienced amateur to identify likely markets for his work. There are thousands of possible outlets and a small fortune could be lost in trying to locate a buyer for a particular picture, no matter how high in quality.

An ambitious and skilled travel photographer should expect to make a substantial profit from his photography, providing an effort is made along the lines indicated. In the case of a specialised and well-publicised trip it is not unknown for the whole of the cost of mounting the venture to be recouped from the sale of pictures. There are some simple points to remember. Don't treat the camera as a toy. Don't give the job of photographer to a non-specialist. Don't put all those transparencies and negatives in the back of a drawer when you get home. As a money spinner, the camera may be the most important piece of equipment the traveller carries.

Travel Writing

by Carol Wright

One airline public relations officer has termed travel writers 'professional holidaymakers'. Indeed, this is the enviable image the world has of the job. To the uninitiated, it is all lying on a palm-shaded beach with rum punch in one hand, a novel in the other. Most of my friends assume I'm on vacation when I go away and their 'have a good time' wishes enrage me. My own image, tempered by reality, is of lugging cases, heavy with handouts and brochures, not souvenirs, round unlovely airports in inevitable delays.

If I am in a resort area, more time is spent 'counting the screws in the loos' or seeing yet more bedrooms and conference halls in new hotels. Of course, it rains on the one free morning allocated to beach lounging and I have seen press trip itineraries where a free morning was defined as not starting the tour before 8.30am.

One often sees resorts out of season – when the paying public don't go. 'You should have been here last week' will be the title of my autobiography – the words are used so often by tourism officials greeting me in monsoon, gale, snow or hurricane. I have toured the Sahara in snow and spent a Hawaiian beach barbecue wrapped in garbage bags against the lash of the Pacific storm.

In the end, you get back jetlagged and are expected to be bright and breezy and take up office and home work without sympathy from those who stayed at home. To be a travel writer requires a special temperament, itchy feet and a knowledge of how to be ahead of the travelling crowd. Social life is wrecked: travel life is often the loneliness of room-serviced evenings and hours on planes next to non-English-speaking passengers.

Getting Started

Having delivered the bad news, travel writing is one of the most exciting jobs around; hard work, but once having made it into that élite circle, it offers the inestimable advantage of being able to see the world at someone else's expense. Getting in involves more than a talent for writing. It is a chicken-and-egg situation. It is difficult to sell stories until you have travelled somewhere and difficult to get travel facilities until you have had some travel stories published. It is as well to use holiday trips where possible as a springboard and when something has been sold to a magazine, hoard that cutting and show it to travel companies.

Anyone who has ever been on holiday thinks they can become a travel writer. I see so many manuscripts submitted to me as travel editor of a national magazine that prove this wrong. Diary-style and school-like 'what I did on my hoiday' efforts are all too common. A subtle blend of a lively and different approach to a well known place coupled with detail of what it means to a reader in terms of food, accommodation, and sightseeing is needed, as well as a paragraph showing ways of getting to a place and how much it will cost; something editors set great store by. This is the one place where advertisers can be mentioned – and it is advertisers who in the end dictate how much space is allocated to travel features. This space is dismally small in the UK: but in the US, many papers have complete travel supplements every week.

It is unlikely that the aspiring writer will easily get a travel editor's job. The most usual way is by transferring from another in-house job within a paper. And old travel writers die hard, the life style is too attractive to give up lightly. The freelance field is wide, competitive and adaptable to the travelling life. Earnings are low and one must work extremely hard to make a living. The advantages are a freedom to sell to the best available market, avoidance of office politics, and having to get editor's approval of where you go.

Good ideas and constant hard sell are essential. Time spent away travelling must be balanced with keeping one's name and ideas in editors' eyes and thoughts. The market must be studied continually and openings examined. A subscription to a magazine like the UK *Press Gazette* is worth while for news of new magazines, editorial changes etc. When attempting to get work in overseas publications, a file of good cuttings and a short biographical note is a help. English language papers abroad often accept travel pieces about the UK from British-based journalists since they then don't have to send their journalists to Britain.

Few, if any, publications will offer any expenses for travelling, although some will do so occasionally if a lot of research is involved. Editors expect travel writers to get to the places to be covered on their own. The *New York Times* refuses articles where free facilities have been accepted. At this point, the travel writer must establish his integrity and independence of line, not always easy when the travel trade is extremely hospitable – not to say generous – with travelling help.

Free Facilities

Travel companies rarely hound writers for coverage after a trip unless they feel they have literally been taken for a ride by someone not intending to write anything. But travel writers who want to remain such get careful about what trips they select. Some airlines still try and bind travel writers seeking long-haul tickets with a signed contract agreeing to publish articles by a certain date. The British Guild of Travel Writers advises members never to sign these and it is doubtful if these 'contracts' have any legal binding power.

Most hospitality is in the form of travel trips. These are getting so many and overlapping that many have to be filled with also-rans or friends of the travel editor. The true travel freelance, as he or she becomes more established, should ignore all of these except occasional well-run tours or those to places it would be very difficult to get to on one's own. The material one can pick up independently while travelling outweighs the time wasted at endless formal banquets and in bars talking with colleagues on these trips.

In considering outlets, there is the 'grey' area of sponsored magazines and press releases. Airlines, tourist boards, trains and hotel chains back magazines which sell their travel image and are usually lucrative forms of writing, although again one's complete freedom is at risk. Brochure writing for tour companies also pays well but the British Guild of Travel Writers is against such writing where the author's name appears in the copy. Anonymous writing is all right and often gives a fresh approach to a stereotyped copy.

A double-edged problem is the press release or feature travel story sent out by tourist offices and others. To enhance veracity and prestige, 'name' travel writers are often hired to write these and again a bias is inevitable. At the same time, other freelancers' markets are at risk since these features often flood provincial papers, house magazines and other publications which will use them and save the cost of commissioning another writer.

Whereas cookery and other writers often appear in advertisement praising some product, the guild would dismiss any member appearing in a travel ad. On the other hand, it is virtually impossible to stop tour operators selecting quotations from published articles and using them in their brochures – which can again give the appearance of bias.

Specialisation

Apart from these dubious outlets as far as integrity is concerned, the travel writer has a wide choice of outlet types. Specialisation is a good idea and gets one's name established faster. One can concentrate on being the expert on a single country or an aspect of travel such as camping, skiing, cruising, trains, aviation, conventions or incentive travel and get close to publications specialising in these areas. As well as 'straight' travel destination pieces, the good freelance, to get more in fees than time and out of pocket expenses involved in a trip would warrant from one piece, will look for spin-off ideas such as local fashion, food, wine, architecture, economics or politics, particularly in areas where newspapers do not have their own correspondents.

Photojournalism is a growing section of travel writing and broadcasting, with more and more radio stations coming on stream, is another source of income for those who can paint lively word pictures on the air, can cope with phone-in programmes on travel information and are prepared to learn to use and or drag around the world the heavy tape recorders used professionally.

Finance

The running costs of a successful travel writer can be heavy. Insurance, inoculations, visa fees and airport taxes, replacing suitcases frequently, all mount up with the added need of a wardrobe that can go skiing, on safari, trekking, cruising; everything from dining in QE2's top grill room with millionaires to sleeping on the jungle floor. Fees are pathetically low and often need to be prized out of publishers. Writing on spec. is wasteful unless at the very beginning and commissions should always be made in writing if possible. Nagging for fees unpaid is tricky if you want to keep in with that paper. But papers need pressure put on them; the bigger they are, the more reluctant they are to pay quickly compared with smaller and trade publications. A freelance is almost investing for the future when writing an article; payment can be literally years ahead.

Writers' Association

Agents are less use for selling most travel features; editors prefer personal contact and exchange of ideas with their writers. But for books, a good agent is worth their ten to fifteen per cent in fees making sure no rip-offs occur in the contract and for making sure payments come through. Membership of the Society of Authors is useful for those wanting to spend most of their time writing books.

I see a declining future for the traditional type of guide book which is being challenged by video and taped touring cassettes. But currently there is a boom in personal travel accounts where writing that takes the reader along a journey, and angle and personality are as important as the place covered. Reliable, readable clean copy will eventually earn the reward of editors coming to a writer with commissions. Belonging to a travel writers' association will advance the writer little but such an organization is useful for home contacts, having your name circulated widely on a membership list, as a general meeting ground for what's going on and maintaining standards of travel writing. Collective clout is sometimes useful in dealing with problematical publishers. Membership, contrary to what many hopefuls think, is not a passport to eternal free jet-set living. In the USA, the Society of American Travel Writers is a large body with an associate membership of high feepaying Public Relations Officers in the travel industry and others who hold and impressive annual convention. The British Guild of Travel Writers (for information, contact the Secretary, 'Mariners', Dormans Park, Nr E Grinstead, Sussex RH19 3NV, (Tel: (0342) 87512) with around 100 members excludes all but established full-time travel writers with income derived primarily from travel writing. Fees are kept low and used to cover guild expenses.

Maps

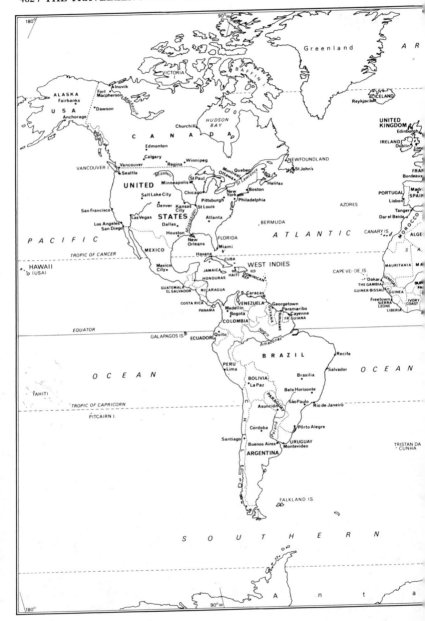

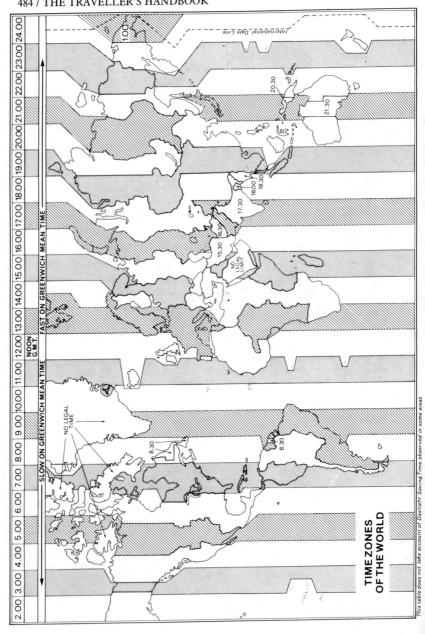

TIME ZONES
OF THE WORLD

This table does not take account of Daylight Saving Time observed in some areas

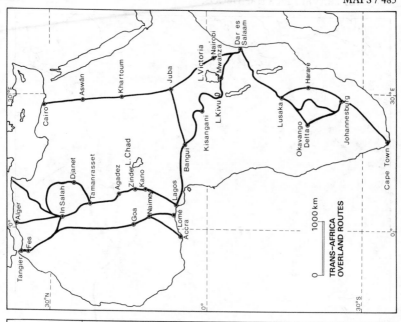

TRANS-AFRICA
OVERLAND ROUTES

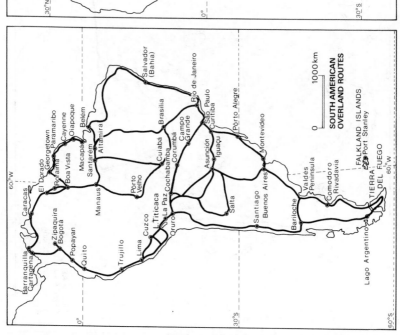

SOUTH AMERICAN
OVERLAND ROUTES

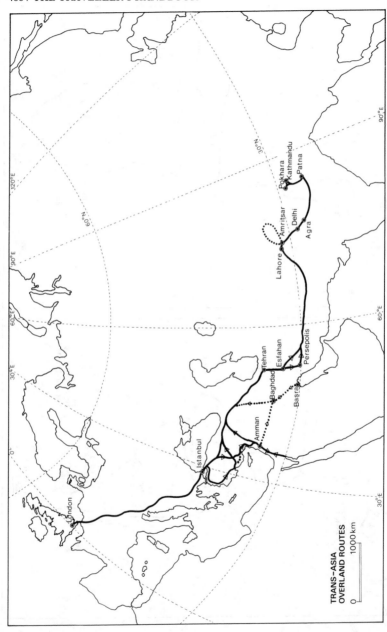

TRANS–ASIA
OVERLAND ROUTES

0   1000 km

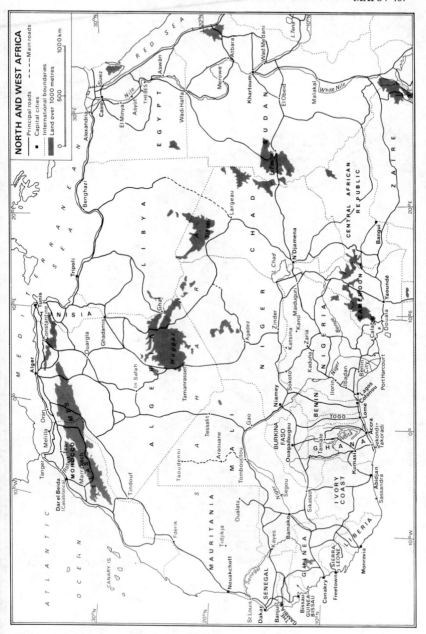

NORTH AND WEST AFRICA

—— Principal roads
----- Main roads
■ Capital cities
International boundaries
Land over 1000 metres

0   500   1000 km

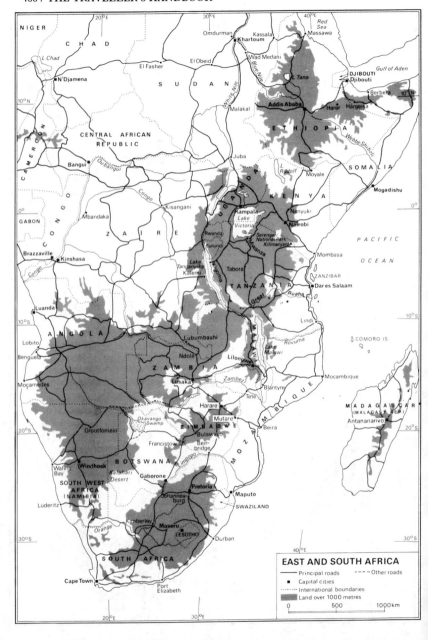

EAST AND SOUTH AFRICA

—— Principal roads ---- Other roads
■ Capital cities
········ International boundaries
▒ Land over 1000 metres

0   500   1000 km

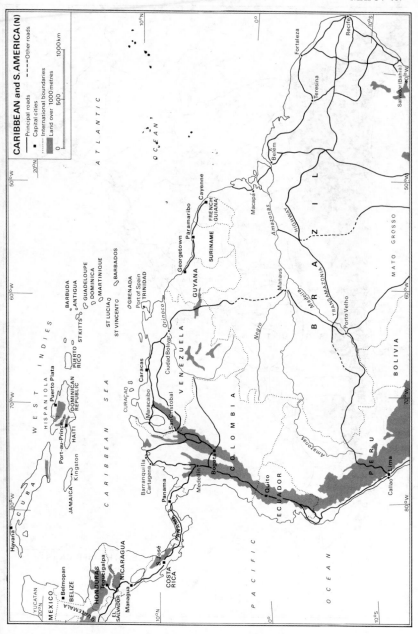

CARIBBEAN and S. AMERICA (N)

■ Principal roads
---- Other roads
■ Capital cities
International boundaries
Land over 1000 metres

0   500   1000 km

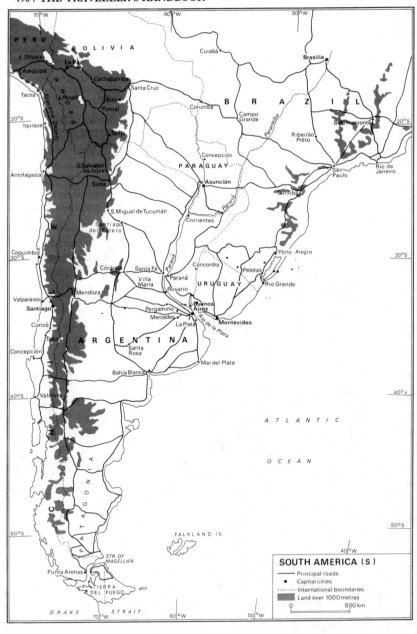

SOUTH AMERICA (S)

— Principal roads
■ Capital cities
········ International boundaries
▓ Land over 1000 metres

0 _____ 500 km

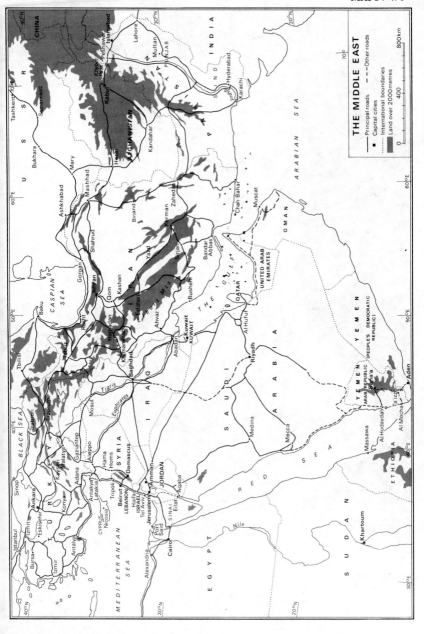

THE MIDDLE EAST

— Principal roads
--- Other roads
■ Capital cities
International boundaries
Land over 2000 metres

0   400   800km

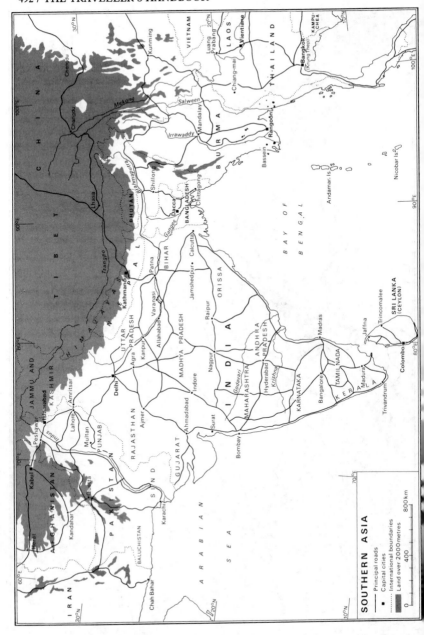

SOUTHERN ASIA

— Principal roads
■ Capital cities
···· International boundaries
▨ Land over 2000 metres

0   400   800 km

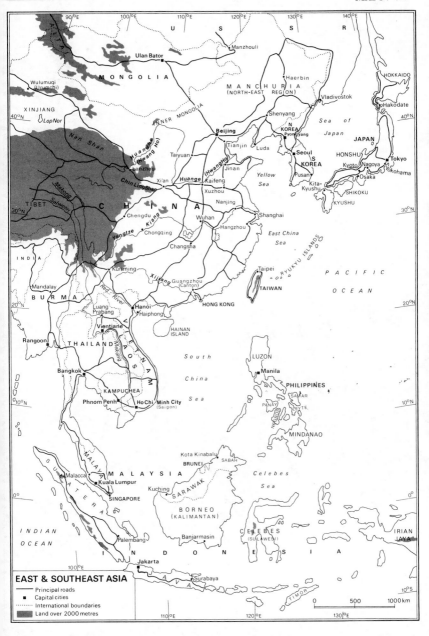

EAST & SOUTHEAST ASIA

—— Principal roads
■ Capital cities
······ International boundaries
▨ Land over 2000 metres

0   500   1000 km

Directory

General

Full List of Countries and Capitals Worldwide

Africa

2,973,000,000km^2
500,000,000 population

Country	Capital	Area (km^2)	Population	Dependency
Algeria	Algiers	2,381,741	23,403,000	
Angola	Luanda	1,246,700	8,298,000	
Benin	Porto Novo	112,622	4,236,000	
Botswana	Gaborone	600,372	978,000	
Burkina Faso	Ouagadougou	274,200	8,119,000	
Burundi	Bujumbura	27,834	4,954,000	
Cameroon	Yaoundé	475,442	9,796,000	
Central African Republic	Bangui	622,984	2,593,000	
Chad	Ndjamena	1,284,000	5,066,000	
Congo	Brazzaville	342,000	1,810,000	
Djibouti	Djibouti	22,000	481,000	
Egypt	Cairo	1,001,449	48,318,000	
Equatorial Guinea	Malabo	28,051	421,000	
Ethiopia	Addis Ababa	1,221,900	36,651,000	
Gabon	Libreville	267,667	600,000	
Gambia	Banjul	11,295	705,000	
Ghana	Accra	238,537	14,216,000	
Guinea	Conakry	245,856	5,897,000	
Guinea-Bissau	Bissau	36,125	460,000	
Ivory Coast	Abidjan	322,463	9,712,000	
Kenya	Nairobi	582,646	21,061,000	
Lesotho	Maseru	30,355	1,559,000	
Liberia	Monrovia	111,369	2,422,000	
Libya	Tripoli	1,759,540	3,748,000	
Malawi	Lilongwe	118,484	7,541,000	
Mali	Bamako	1,240,000	8,233,000	
Madagascar	Antananarivo	587,041	10,322,000	
Mauritania	Sofia	110,912	1,938,000	
Morocco	Rabat	446,550	24,636,000	
Mozambique	Maputo	801,590	12,302,000	
Namibia	Windhoek	824,292	1,206,000	RSA

Niger	Niamey	1,267,000	6,392,000	
Nigeria	Lagos	923,768	94,316,000	
Rwanda	Kigali	26,338	5,821,000	
Sao Tomé e Principe	Sao Tomé	964	106,000	
Senegal	Dakar	190,192	6,654,000	
Sierra Leone	Freetown	71,740	4,112,000	
Somalia	Mogadishu	637,657	6,694,000	
South Africa	Pretoria	1,221,037	34,799,000	
Sudan	Khartoum	2,505,813	21,832,000	
Swaziland	Mbabane	17,363	667,000	
Tanzania	Dar es Salaam	945,087	21,752,000	
Togo	Lomél	56,785	3,158,000	
Tunisia	Tunis	163,610	7,322,000	
Uganda	Kampala	236,036	15,994,000	
Western Sahara	El Aaiun	266,000	80,000	Morocco
Zaîre	Kinshasa	2,345,409	33,601,000	
Zambia	Lusaka	752,614	7,054,000	
Zimbabwe	Harare	390,580	9,119,000	

North America

19,340,000 km^2
270,000,000 population

Country	Capital	Area (km^2)	Population	Dependency
Canada	Ottawa	9,976,139	26,726,000	
St Pierre et Miquelon	St Pierre	241	6,300	France
U.S.A.	Washington DC	9,363,123	236,809,000	

Central America

14,000,000 km^2
142,500,000 population

Country	Capital	Area (km^2)	Population	Dependency
Anguilla	The Valley	150	8,500	UK
Antigua and Barbuda	St John's	442	8,300	
Bahamas	Nassau	13,935	231,000	
Barbados	Bridgetown	431	280,000	
Belize	Belmopan	22,965	161,000	
Cayman Islands	Georgetown	259	20,000	UK
Costa Rica	San José	50,700	2,541,000	
Cuba	Havana	114,524	10,121,000	
Dominica	Roseau	751	88,000	
Dominican Republic	Santo Domongo	48,734	6,874,000	
El Salvador	San Salvador	21,041	5,725,000	
Grenada	St George's	344	120,400	
Guadeloupe	Basse-Terre	1,779	335,000	
Guatemala	Guatemala City	108,889	8,646,000	
Haiti	Port-au-Prince	27,750	6,758,000	
Honduras	Tegucigalpa	112,088	4,514,000	
Jamaica	Kingston	10,991	2,394,000	
Martinique	Fort-de-France	1,102	329,000	France
Mexico	Mexico City	1,972,547	82,734,000	
Montserrat	Plymouth	98	13,000	UK
Netherland Antilles	Willemstad	961	290,000	Netherlands
Nicaragua	Managua	130,000	3,342,000	
Panama	Panama City	77,082	2,162,000	
Puerto Rico	San Juan	8,897	4,448,000	USA
St Kitts and Nevis	Basseterre	258	50,000	
St Lucia	Castries	616	130,000	
St Vincent and the Grenadines	Kingstown	388	138,000	
Turks and Caicos	Cockburn Town	430	8,300	UK
Virgin Islands (UK)	Road Town	153	13,500	UK
Virgin Islands (US)	Charlotte Amalie	344	107,000	USA

South America
17,810,000 km
270,000,000 population

Country	Capital	Area (km^2)	Population	Dependency
Argentina	Buenos Aires	2,766,889	29,013,000	
Bolivia	La Paz	1,098,581	6,547,000	
Brazil	Brasilia	8,511,965	140,344,000	
Chile	Santiago	756,945	12,272,000	
Colombia	Bogotá	1,138,914	29,325,000	
Ecuador	Quito	283,561	9,677,000	
French Guiana	Cayenne	91,000	77,000	France
Guyana	Georgetown	214,970	936,000	
Paraguay	Asunción	406,752	3,789,000	
Peru	Lima	1,285,216	20,855,000	
Suriname	Paramaribo	163,000	460,000	
Uruguay	Montevideo	176,215	3,061,000	
Venezuela	Caracas	912,050	18,959,000	

Asia
50,120,000 km^2
3,000,000,000 population

Country	Capital	Area (km^2)	Population	Dependency
Afghanistan	Kabul	647,497	18,590,000	
Bahrain	Manama	622	369,000	
Bangladesh	Dacca	143,998	104,211,000	
Bhutan	Thimphu	47,000	1,484,000	
Brunei	Bandar Seri	5,765	310,000	
Burma	Rangoon	670,552	41,812,000	
China	Beijing	9,590,961	1,064,000,000	
Hong Kong	Hong Kong	1,045	5,820,000	UK
India	New Delhi	3,287,590	766,515,000	
Indonesia	Jakarta	2,042,012	164,074,000	
Iran	Tehran	1,648,000	45,689,000	
Iraq	Baghdad	434,924	15,988,000	
Israel	Jerusalem	20,770	4,489,000	
Japan	Tokyo	371,313	120,835,000	
Jordan	Amman	97,470	4,032,000	
Kampuchea	Phnom Penh	181,035	7,854,000	
Korea (North)	Pyongyang	120,538	20,543,000	
Korea (South)	Seoul	89,484	42,444,000	
Kuwait	Kuwait	17,818	1,795,000	
Laos	Vientiane	236,800	4,281,000	
Lebanon	Beirut	10,400	3,033,000	
Macau	Macau	16	320,000	Portugal
Malaysia	Kuala Lumpur	329,749	16,295,000	
Mongolia	Ulan Bator	1,565,000	1,962,000	
Nepal	Kathmandu	140,797	16,382,000	
Oman	Muscat	212,457	1,074,000	
Pakistan	Islamabad	803,943	102,689,000	
Philippines	Manila	300,000	57,329,000	
Qatar	Doha	11,000	294,000	
Saudi Arabia	Riyadh	2,149,690	11,220,000	
Singapore	Singapore	581	2,585,000	
Sri Lanka	Colombo	65,610	16,755,000	
Syria	Damascus	185,180	11,337,000	
Taiwan	Taipei	35,961	8,025,000	
Thailand	Bangkok	514,000	53,539,000	
Turkey	Ankara	780,576	52,314,000	
USSR	Moscow	22,402,200	280,693,000	

United Arab Emirates	Abu Dhabi	83,600	913,000	
Vietnam	Hanoi	329,556	61,204,000	
Yemen (North)	Sana'a	195,000	6,702,000	
Yemen (South)	Madinat al Shaab	322,968	2,186,000	

Europe

7,260,000 km²
500,000,000 population

Country	Capital	Area (km²)	Population	Dependency
Albania	Tirana	28,748	3,108,000	
Andorra	Andorra La Vella	453	36,000	France/Spain
Austria	Vienna	32,374	7,448,000	
Belgium	Brussels	30,513	9,873,000	
Bulgaria	Sofia	110,912	7,276,000	
Cyprus	Nicosia	9,251	641,000	
Czechoslovakia	Prague	127,869	15,808,000	
Denmark	Copenhagen	43,069	5,170,000	
Eire	Dublin	70,283	3,536,000	
Faroe Islands	Thorshavn	1,399	47,000	Denmark
Finland	Helsinki	337,032	4,979,000	
France	Paris	547	54,426,000	
Germany (East)	East Berlin	108,178	16,855,000	
Germany (West)	Bonn	248,577	59,992,000	
Gibraltar	Gibraltar	6.5	31,000	UK
Greece	Athens	131,944	9,665,000	
Greenland	Godthaab	2,175,600	52,000	
Hungary	Budapest	93,030	10,890,000	
Iceland	Reykjavik	103,000	245,000	
Italy	Rome	301,225	57,942,000	
Liechtenstein	Vaduz	157	27,000	
Luxembourg	Luxembourg	2,586	356,000	
Malta	Valletta	316	360,000	
Monaco	Monte Carlo	1.5	26,000	
Netherlands	The Hague	40,844	14,458,000	
Norway	Oslo	324,219	4,155,000	
Poland	Warsaw	312,677	37,869,000	
Portugal	Lisbon	92,082	10,266,000	
Romania	Bucharest	237,500	23,322,000	
San Marino	San Marino	61	21,000	
Spain	Madrid	504,782	28,313,000	
Sweden	Stockholm	449,964	8,258,000	
Switzerland	Bern	41,288	6,490,000	
United Kingdom	London	244,046	55,600,000	
Yugoslavia	Belgrade	255,84	23,351,000	

Islands of the Atlantic and Indian Oceans

Country	Capital	Area (km²)	Population	Dependency
Ascension Island	Georgetown	88	2,000	St Helena
Azores	Ponta Delgada	2,335	380,000	Portugal
Canary Islands	Las Palmas	7,273	1,400,000	Spain
Cape Verde	Praia	4,033	356,000	
Cocos (Keeling) Islands		14	600	Australia
Comoros	Moroni	1,862	336,000	
Falkland Islands	Port Stanley	15,800	3,000	UK
Madeira	Funchal	797	285,000	Portugal
Maldives	Male	298	177,000	
Mauritius	Port Louis	2,045	1,057,000	
Mayotte	Dzaoudi	374	72,000	France
Réunion	Saint-Denis	2,510	571,000	France
St Helena	Jamestown	122	5,000	UK
Seychelles	Victoria	280	69,000	
Tristan da Cunha	Edinburgh	202	300	St Helena

Oceania
8,500,000 km^2
25,000,000 population

Country	Capital	Area (km^2)	Population	Dependency
Australia	Canberra	7,686,848	15,512,000	
Christmas Island			4,500	Australia
Cook Islands	Avarua	3,200	21,500	New Zealand
Easter Island	Hanga-Roa	120	1,300	Chile
Fiji	Suva	18,274	694,000	
French Polynesia	Papeete	4,000	167,000	France
Guam	Agana	549	115,000	US Pacific
Kiribati	Tarawa	728	68,000	
Marshall Islands		494	33,000	US Pacific
Micronesia	Kolonia	700	85,000	US Pacific
Nauru	Nauru	21	8,000	
New Caledonia	Noumea	19,058	148,000	France
New Zealand	Wellington	268,676	3,495,000	
Niue	Alofi	259	3,000	New Zealand
Northern Mariana Islands	Saipan	480	19,500	US Pacific
Palau				US Pacific
Papua New Guinea	Port Moresby	461,691	3,708,000	
Pitcairn Islands	Adamstown	27	60	UK
Samoa (American)	Fagatogo	197	35,000	USA
Samoa (Western)	Apia	2,842	180,000	
Solomon Islands	Moniara	28,466	271,000	
Tokelau Islands	Nukunonu	10	1,800	New Zealand
Tonga	Nuku'alofa	699	107,000	
Tuvalu	Funafuti	26	8,400	
Vanuatu	Vila	14,763	138,000	
Wallis Archipelago	Matu-Uta	200	10,000	France

Rules and Regulations

Australian Government Representation Worldwide

Algeria	60 Blvd Colonel Bougara, El-Biar, (BP 43, Alger Gare), Algiers	605601/411/038
Argentina	Avenida Santa Fé 846, Piso Swiss Air Bldg, Buenos Aires	
Austria	Mattiellistrasse 2–4, A-1040, Vienna	
Bahamas	nearest rep. in Jamaica	
Bangladesh	184 Gulshan Avenue, Gulshan	
Belgium	5th, 6th, and 7th Floors, 52 Avenue des Arts, 1040, Brussels	
Brazil	SHIS Q19, Conjunto 16, Casa 1, (Caixa Postal 11-1256), Brasilia DF	
or	Rua Voluntarious Da Patria, 45/5 Andar, 5th Floor, Botfogo-RJ, 22270 Rio De Janeiro, RJ	
Burma	88 Strand Road, Rangoon	
Canada	13th Floor, National Bldg, 130 Slater St, Ottawa, Ontario KIP 5H6	
Chile	420 Gertrudis Echenique, (PO Box 33, Correo 10), Las Condes, Santiago	
China	15 Donzhimenwai St, San Li Tun, Beijing	
Cyprus	2nd Floor, 4 Annis Kominis St, Nicosia	02-473001
Czechoslovakia	nearest representative in Warsaw, Poland	
Denmark	Kristianagrade 21, DK-2100 Copenhagen	
Egypt	1097 Corniche el Nil, Garden City, Cairo	
Ethiopia	Patriots Street, Addis Ababa	
Fiji	7th & 8th Floors, Dominion House, Thomson St, (PO Box 214), Suva	312844
Finland	nearest rep. Sergels Torg, 11157 Stockholm, Sweden	
France	4 Rue Jean Rey, 75724 Paris	
East Germany	1110 Berlin-Niederschoenhausen, Grabbealle 34-40, (Postfach 650149), 1 Berlin 65	
West Germany	Godesburger Allee 107, 5300 Bonn 2	
Ghana	Milne Close, off Dr. Amilcar Cabral Rd, Airport Residential Area, (PO Box 2445), Accra	
Greece	15 Messogeion St, (PO Box 3070), Ambelokipi, Athens 115-26	
Hong Kong	10th Floor, Connaught Centre, Connaught Rd, Hong Kong	
Hungary	1052 Budapest V, Apáczai Csere J., UTCA 12 – 14	188100/346
India	No. 1/50-G Shanti Path, Chanakyapuri, (PO Box 5210), New Delhi	
or	16th Floor, Maker Towers, E Block, Colaba, (PO Box 9937), Bombay	
Indonesia	Jalan MM Thamrin 15, Gambir, Jakarta	323109
or	Jalan Raya, Sanur 146, (PO Box 279), Den Pasar, Bali	
Iran	123 Shalid Khalis Al Islam Buli Avenue, Abassabad, Tehran	

Iraq	Masbah 141/377, Baghdad	
Ireland	Fitzwilton House, Wilton Terrace, Dublin 2	
Israel	185 Hayarkon St, Tel Aviv	
Italy	Via Allessandria 215, Rome 00198	
Jamaica	4th Floor, National Life Bldg, 64 Knutsford Blvd, (PO Box 560), Kingston 5	
Japan	No. 1-14 Mita 2-chome, Minato-Ku, Tokyo 108	453 0251
Jordan	between 4th and 5th Circles, Wadi Sir Road, Jabel Amman, (PO Box 35201), Amman	
Kenya	Development House, Moi Ave, (PO Box 30360), Nairobi	334666
Kiribati	Tarawa, (PO Box 77), Bairiki	
South Korea	5th Floor, Kukong-Shell Building, 58–1 Shinmoonro, 1-Ka, Chongro-Ku, (KPO Box 562 Kang-Uha-Moon), Seoul	
Kuwait	7th Floor, Al-Rashed Building, Fahed Al-Salem St, (PO Box 25057, Safat) Kuwait	241 5880
Laos	Rue J. Nehru, Quartier Phone Xay, (BP 292), Vientiane	
Lebanon	Farra Building, 463 Bliss St, Ras, Beirut	
Luxembourg	51–2 Av. des Arts, B-1040 Brussels, Belgium	02-511 3997.
Malaysia	6 Jalan Yap Kwan Seng, Kuala Lumpur	
Malta	6th Floor, Gaiety Lane, Valletta	
Mexico	Paeso de la Reforma 195, 5°Piso, Mexico City, Mexico 5, DF	
Nauru	Civic Centre, Nauru	
Netherlands	Koninginnegracht 23/24, 2514AB The Hague	
New Caledonia	8th Floor, 18 Rue du Maréchal Foch, (BP 22), Noumea	
New Zealand	72–78 Hobson Street, Thorndon, (PO Box 12145), Wellington	
Nigeria	Plot 738, 16 Adeola Hopewell Rd, Victoria Island, (PO Box 2427), Lagos	
Pakistan	Plot 17, Sector G4/4, Diplomatic Enclave No. 2, (PO Box 1046), Islamabad	
Papua New Guinea	Waigani, Hohola, (PO Box 9129), Port Moresby	
Peru	6th Floor, Edificio Plaza, Natalio Sanchez 220, (Casilla 2977), Lima	
Philippines	China Banking Corporation Bld, Paseo de Roxas (cnr Villar St) Makati, (PO Box 1274), Rizal	
Poland	3/5 Ulica Estonska, Saska Kepa, Warsaw	
Portugal	Avenida de Liberdade 244–40, Lisbon 2	
Saudi Arabia	Off Hamra Road, nr Medina Road, (PO Box 4876), Jeddah	
Singapore	25 Napier Road, (Tanglin PO Box 470), Singapore 10	
Solomon Islands	Hong Kong and Shanghai Bank Bldg, Mendana Ave, (PO Box 589), Honiara	
South Africa *or*	302 Standard Bank Chambers, Church Square, Pretoria. 10th Floor, 1001 Colonial Mutual Building, 106 Adderly St, (PO Box 4749), Cape Town	
Spain	Paseo de la Castellano 143, Madrid 16	
Sri Lanka	3 Cambridge Place, (PO Box 742), Colombo 7	
Sweden	Sergels Torg 12, (Box 7003), S-103 86 Stockholm	
Switzerland	29 Alpenstrasse, Berne	

	or	56–58 Rue de Moillebeau, Petit Saconnex 1211, Geneva 19
Syria		128A Farabi St, Mezzeh, (PO Box 3882), Damascus
Tanzania		7th and 8th Floors, NLC Investment Bldg, Independence Ave, (PO Box 2969), Dar es Salaam
Thailand		37 South Sathorn Road, Bangkok 12
Tonga		Salote Road, Nuku'alofa
Turkey		83 Nenehatun Caddesi, Gazi Osman, Pasa, Ankara
USSR		13 Kropotkinsky Pereulok, Moscow
United Arab Emirates		Sayed Mohammed Glass Tower Building, 14th Floor, Tourist Club Area, nr Tourist Club Gates, (PO Box 559), Abu Dhabi
United Kingdom		Australia House, The Strand, London WC2B 4LA
United States	*or*	1601 Massachusetts Avenue, Washington DC 20036 International Building, 636 Fifth Ave, New York NY 10020 *There are also consulates in Chicago, Honolulu, Los Angeles, and San Francisco*
Vanuatu		Melitco House, (PO Box 111), Vila
Venezuela		Centro Plaza, 18th Floor, Torre A, Avenida Francisco de Miranda, Caracas
Vietnam		66 Ly Thuong Kiet, Hanoi
Western Samoa		Fea Gai Ma Leata Building, Beach Road, Tamaligi, (PO Box 704), Apia
Yugoslavia		13 Cjika Ljibina, 11000 Belgrade 5
Zambia		3rd Floor, Memaco House, Sapele Road (off Southend Road, Cairo Road), (PO Box 35395), Lusaka
Zimbabwe		3rd Floor, Throgmorton House, Cnr Samora Machel Ave and Julius Nyerere Way, (PO Box 4541), Harare

Canadian Government Representatives Worldwide

Algeria		27 bis Rue d'Anjou, Hydra, (PO Box 225, Gare Alger), Algiers	60 66 11
Argentina		Brunetta Bldg, Suipacha and Santa Fé, (Casilla de correo 1598), Buenos Aires	32 90 81/8
Australia		Commonwealth Ave, Canberra, ACT 2600	(062) 733844
	or	17th Floor, Prince's Gate, East Tower, 151 Flinders St, Melbourne, Vic 3000	638431
	or	8th Floor, AMP Centre, 50 Bridge Street, Sydney, NSW 2000	(02) 231 6522
Austria		Dr. Karl-Leuger-Ring 10, A1010 Vienna	43-222-633691
Bahamas		Out Island Traders Bldg, East Bay St, (PO Box 556371), Nassau	(809) 323-2123
Bangladesh		House CWN 16/A, Road 48, Gulshan, (GPO Box 569), Dacca	300181-5
Barbados		Bishop's Court Hill, St Michael	429 3550
Belgium		Rue De Loxum 6, 1000 Brussels	02-513 7940
Bolivia		Alborada Bldg, Office 508, 1420 J. De La Riva St, (Casilla 20408), La Paz	3705224

Brazil	Ave des Nacoes, Number 16, Sector das Embaxadas Sul, (Caixa Postal 07-0961), 7000 Brasilia DF	(61) 2237515
or	Edificio Metropole, Ave Presidente Wilson 165, 6 Andar, Rio De Janeiro	240 9912
or	Edificio Top Center, Ave Paulista 854, 5th Floor, (Caixa Postal 22002), Sao Paulo	287 2122/2234/3240
Burkina Faso	B.P. 548, Ouagadougou	33-20-93
Cameroon	Immeuble Soppo Priso, Rue Conrad Adenauer, (PO Box 572), Yaoundé	222203/222922
Chile	Ahumada 11, 10th Floor, (Casilla 427), Santiago	62256/7/8/9
China	10 San Li Tun Road, Chao Yang, Beijing	521475/571/724/741/684
Colombia	Calle 76, No 11–52, 4th Floor, (Apartado Aero 53531), Bogotá	235 5066
Costa Rica	6th Floor, Cronos Bldg, Calle 3 y Ave Central, San José	23 04 46
Côte d'Ivoire	Immeuble 'Le Général', 4ème etages, Av Botreau-Roussel, (CP 4104), Abidjan 01	32 20 09
Cuba	Calle 300, No 518 Esquina a7a, Mirimar, (PO Box 499), Havana	26421/2/3
Cyprus	Th. Dervis Street, Office 2G, Nicosia	
Czechoslovakia	Mickiewiczova 6, 12533 Prague 6	
Denmark	Kr. Bernikowsgade 1, DK-1105 Copenhagen	
Dominican Rep	Mahatma Ghandi 200, Corner Juan Sanchez, Ramirez, Santo Domingo 1	(809) 689 002
Ecuador	Edificio Belmonte, 6th Floor, Piso Calle Corea 126 y Amazonas, (Casilla 5612-CC1), Quito	
Egypt	6 Sharia Mohamed Fahmi el Sayed, Garden City, (Kasr el Doubara PO), Cairo 23110	
Ethiopia	African Solidarity Insurance Bldg, Unity Square, (PO Box 1130), Addis Ababa	151100
Finland	E. Pohjoisesplanadi 25B, 00100 Helsinki	
Gabon	PO Box 4037, Libreville	71-41-54/56/69
East Germany	Nearest embassy in Warsaw	
Ghana	E 115/3 Independence Ave, (PO Box 1639), Accra	2855/02
Greece	4 L. Gannadiou St, Athens 115–21	
Guatemala	Galerias Espana, 6th Floor, 7 Avenida 11–59, Zone 9, (PO Box 400), Guatemala City	64955/6/7 65839/63049
Guyana	High and Young Streets, (PO Box 660), Georgetown	72081/5
Haiti	Ediface Banque Nova Scotia, Route de Delmas, (CP 826), Port-au-Prince	2-2358, 2-4231 2-4919
Hong Kong	14/15 Flrs, Asian House, 1 Hennessy Road, (PO Box 20264), Hong Kong	5-282222-7
Hungary	1121 Budapest XIV, Budakeszi út 55/d	365738/728
Iceland	Skulagata 20, Reykjavik	25355, 15337
India	7/8 Shanti Path, Chanakyapuri, (PO Box 5207), New Delhi 110021	61 9461
Indonesia	5th Flr, Wisma Metropolitan, Jl Jend Sudirman KAV 29/30, (PO Box 53/JKT), Jakarta	510709
Iran	57 Darya-e-Noor Ave, Takht-e Tavoos, Tehran *Currently no ambassador, Consular Services c/o Royal Danish Embassy Tehran; Immigration Enquiries c/o Canadian Embassy, Kuwait.*	623177/548/549/ 192/629/202 622310/975

Iraq	47/1/7 Al Mansour, (PO Box 323, Central Post Office), Baghdad	5521459/1932/3
Ireland	65/68 St Stephen's Green, Dublin 2	
Israel	220 Hayarkon St, (PO Box 6410), Tel Aviv	222822/3/4/5/6
Jamaica	Royal Bank Bldg, 30–36 Knutsford Blvd, (PO Box 1500), Kingston 5	(809) 926 15006
Japan	3–38 Akasaka 7 – Chome, Minato-ku, Tokyo 107	408 2101
Kenya	Comcraft House, Halié Sélassie Ave, (PO Box 30481), Nairobi	334 033/4/5/6
South Korea	10th Floor, Kolon Bldg, 45 Mugyo-Dong, Jung-Ku, (PO Box 6299), Seoul 1000	776/4062/8
Kuwait	District 1, 28 Quraish St, Nuzha, (PO Box 25281, Safat), Kuwait City	2511451
Lebanon	Immeuble Sabbagh, Rue Hamra, (CP 2300), Beirut	350 660/5
Luxembourg	6 Rue de Loxum, B-1000 Brussels, Belgium	02-513 7940
Malaysia	American International Assurance Bldg, Ampang Road, Kuala Lumpur	89722/3/4
Mexico	Melchor Ocampo 463–7, Mexico 5, DF	533 01 10
or	Hotel el Mirador Plaza, La Quebrada 74, Acapulco	3 72 91
or	Ave Vallarta No 1373, Guadalajara, (PO Box 32–6), Jalisco	(36) 325 9932
Morocco	13 bis Rue Jafaar As-Sadik, (CP 709), Rabat-Agdal	71-373/36/37
New Zealand	ICI Bldg, Molesworth St, (PO Box 12-049), Wellington	739 577
Nigeria	Niger House, Tinubu St, (PO Box 851), Lagos	660130/153/177
Pakistan	Diplomatic Enclave, Sector G-5, (GPO Box 1042), Islamabad	21302/6/18
Paraguay	AZARA 532, (Casilla de corroe 173), Acunción	43506/7
Peru	132 Calle Libertad, Miraflores, (Casilla 1212), Lima	46 38 90
Philippines	4th Floor, PAL Bldg, Ayala Ave, Makati, Rizal	876536/7846
Saudi Arabia	6th Floor, Office Tower, Commercial and Residential Centre, King Abdul Aziz St, (PO Box 5050), Jeddah	6434800/4597/ 4587, 642 9798
Senegal	45 Av de la République, (PO Box 3373), Dakar	210290
Singapore	Faber House, 7th, 8th & 9th Floors, 230 Orchard Road, Singapore 0923 (PO Box 845, Singapore 9016)	737 1322
South Africa	Nedbank Plaza, Cnr Church and Beatrix Streets, (PO Box 26006), Arcadia, Pretoria	28 7062 at night 28-33
Sri Lanka	5 Gregory's Rd, Cinnamon Gardens, (PO Box 1006), Colombo 7	95841-3
Tanzania	Pan Africa Insurance Bldg, Independence Ave, (PO Box 1022), Dar es Salaam	20651
Thailand	Bommitr Bldg, 11th Floor, 138 Silom Road, (PO Box 2090), Bangkok 5	234 1561-8
Tunisia	2 Place Vergile, Notre-Dame de Tunis, (CP 31, Belvédére), Tunis	286 577
Turkey	Nenehatun Caddesi 75, Gaziosmanpasam, Ankara	27 58 03/4/5
USSR	23 Starokonyushenny Pereulok, Moscow	241 9155/ 3067/5070
Venezuela	Ave La Estancia No. 10, 16 Piso Cuidad Commercial Tamanaco, (Apartado del Este No 62302), Caracas	91 32 77
Zaire	Edifice Shell, Coin Av. Wangata et Blvd du 30-Juin, (PO Box 8341), Kinshasa	227 06 243 46
Zambia	Barclays Bank, North End Branch, Cairo Road, (PO Box 1313), Lusaka	75187/8

| Zimbabwe | 45 Baines Avenue, (PO Box 1430), Harare | |

New Zealand Government Offices Worldwide

Australia	Commonwealth Avenue, Canberra, ACT 2600	(062) 73 3611 Telex: 7162019 Cable: KAURI
Austria	Hollandstrasse 2/XII, (PO Box 1471,A-1011), Vienna	264481/2 Tlx:47-136582 Cable: WEKA
Bahrain	1st Floor, Manama Centre Bldg, Government Road, (Box 5881), Manama	259 890 Tlx:490-8748 Cable:TEROTO
Belgium	Blvd du Régent 47, 1000 Brussels	02-512 1040
Canada	Suite 801, Metropolitan House, 99 Bank St, Ottawa, Ont KIP 6G3	(613)238-5991 Tlx:210-534282 Cable: MATAI
Chile	Avenida Isidora Goyenechea 3516, Las Condes, (Casilla 112), Santiago	02-487 071 Tlx:34-40066 Cable:INAKA
China	Ritan Dongerjie No.1, Chao Yang District, Beijing	522 731/2/3/4 Tlx:22124 Cable:RATA CN
Cook Islands	1st Floor, Philatelic Bureau Building, Takuvaine Road, Avarua, (Box 21), Rarotonga	(682) 2065 Ext. 341/2/3 Tlx:722-62009 Cable:KAKAHO-RG
Fiji	10th Flr, Reserve Bank of Fiji Bldg, Pratt St, (PO Box 1378), Suva	311422 Telex: 701-2161 Cable: NIKAU
Finland	E Sergels Torg, 11157 Stockholm, Sweden	
France	7 ter, Rue Leonard da Vinci, Paris 75116	01-500 24 11 Tlx:42-611929 Cable:KOWHAI
West Germany	Bonn-Centre HI 902, Bundeskanzerplatz, 5300 Bonn	(0228)214021/2 Telex:42-886322 Cable:MATANGA
Greece	An. Tsoha 15-17, Ambelokipi, Athens	01-641 0311 Tlx:601-216630 Cable:RAUPO
Hong Kong	3414 Connaught Centre, Connaught Road, (GPO Box 2790), Hong Kong	5-255044 Tlx:802-73932 Cable:KAKA
Indonesia	Jalan P Diponegoro 41, Menteng (PO Box 2439/JKT), Jakarta	(021)330620 Telex:73-46109 Cable: TUI
Iran	Ave Mirzai Shirazi, Afshin St No. 29, (PO Box 128), Tehran	625061/083 Telex:88-212078 Cable:RAHUI
Iraq	2D/19 Zuwiya, Jadriyah (nr Baghdad University), (PO Box 2350, Alwiyah), Baghdad	01-776 8176-8 Tlx: 491-2433

		Cable:MAKOMATA
Italy	Via Zara 28, Rome 00198	06-844 8663/59/ 73/96 Tlx:88-212078 Cable:RANGIORA
Japan	20-40 Kamiyama-cho, Shibuya-Ku, Tokyo 150	03-460 8711 Telex:72-22462 Cable:TITOKI
Korea	Publishers' Association Bldg, No 105-2 Sagandong, Chongr-Ku, (CPO Box 1059), Seoul	02-720 7794/5 725 3707/ 7204255 Cable:TAKAPU
Malaysia	193 Jalan Pekeliling, (PO Box 2003), Kuala Lumpur 16-01	03-486 422 Tlx: 30284 Cable: ARAWA
Mexico	Homero No.229, 8/0 Piso, Mexico CityDF, 11570 Mexico	511 7905 Telex:1763154 Cable:KEA ME
Netherlands	Lange Voorhout 18, 2514EE, The Hague	(070) 46 9324 Telex:44-31557 Cable:TAUPATA
New Caledonia	4 Blvd Vauban, (PO Box 2219), Noumea	27 25 43 Telex: 036NM Cable:KERERU
Niue	Tapeu, (PO Box 78), Alofi	22 Cable:KAHIKA
Papua New Guinea	6th Floor, Australian High Commission Bldg, Waigani, (PO Box 1144, Boroko), Port Moresby	(675) 259444 Telex: 70322191 Cable: MAIRE
Peru	Avenida Salaverry 3006, San Isidro, (Casilla 5587), Lima 27	62-1890/40 Telex:20254PU Cable:KOROMIKO
Philippines	10th Floor, Bankmer Bldg,6756 Ayala Ave, (PO Box 2208 MCC),Makati, Metro Manila	818 0916 Tlx:756-63509/ 754-45284 Cable:MAMAKU-PN
Singapore	13 Nassim Road, Singapore 1025	2359 966 Tlx:87-21244 Cable:TAINUI
Solomon Islands	Soltel House, Mendana Ave, (PO Box 697), Honiara	502-503 Telex:778-66322 Cable:KOKAKO
Switzerland	28 Chemin du Petit-Saconnes, (PO Box 84), CH-1209 Geneva 19	(022)34 95 30 Telex:45-22820 Cable:KONINI
Tahiti	Air New Zealand Ltd, Vaima Centre, (BP 73), Papeete	20170 Telex: none
Thailand	93 Wireless Rd, (PO Box 2719), Bangkok 5	02-251 8165 Cable: MANUKA
Tokelau	Savalalo St, (PO Box 865), Apia, Western Samoa	20822/3 Tlx:86-81165 Cable:TOKALANI
Tonga	Tungi Arcade, Taufa'ahau Road (PO Box 830), Nuku'alofa	21122 Tlx:64-413287

		Cable:KOKUKU
USSR	44 Ulitsa Vorovskovo, Moscow 121069	290 3485/1277 Tlx: 64-413187 Cable:RIMU
United Kingdom	New Zealand House, The Haymarket, London, SW1Y 4TQ	01-930 8422 Telex: 24368 Cable: DEPUTY LONDON SW1
United States	37 Observatory Circle, NW, Washington DC 2008	(202) 320 4800 Telex: 230- 89526/64272 Cable: TOTARA
Western Samoa	Beach Road, (PO Box 208), Apia	21-711/714 Telex: 779222 Cable:TAWA

British Government Representatives Overseas

Afghanistan	Karte Parwan, Kabul	30511/3
Algeria	Résidence Cassiopée, Bâtiment B, Chemin des Glycines, (BP43, Alger Gare), Algiers	605601/411
Angola	Rua Diogo Cao, (CP1244), Luanda	
Australia	Commonwealth Avenue, Canberra ACT 2600	730422
or	Gold Fields House, Sydney Cove, Sydney NSW 2000 *There are also consulates in Melbourne, Brisbane, Perth and Adelaide*	27-7521
Austria	Reisnerstrasse 40, A-1030 Vienna	43-222-31-55-11
Bahamas	3rd Flr, Bitco Bldg, East St, (PO Box N7516), Nassau	(809) 325-7471
Bahrain	PO Box 114, Government Road, North Manama, Bahrain	254002 (7 lines)
Bangladesh	DIT Building Annexe, Dilkhusha,(PO Box 90), Dacca-2	243251-3,244216-8 246867
Barbados	Barclays Bldg, Roebuck St, (PO Box 676-C), Bridgetown	2219
Belgium	Britannia House, 28 Rue Joseph II, 1040 Brussels	32-2-217 9000
Belize	Belmopan, Belize	
Bolivia	Avenida Acre 2732-2754, (Casilla 694), La Paz	51400/29404
Botswana	P. Bag 0023, Gaborone	52841
Brazil	Setor de Empaixadas Sul, Quadra 801 Conjunto K, Brasilia	225 2710/2625 2985/2745
or	Praia do Flamengo 284-2° andar, (Caixa Postal 669-ZC-00), Rio de Janeiro	225-7252
or	Avenida Paulista 1938-17° andar, 01310, (Caixa Postal 846), Sao Paulo	287-7722
Brunei	Room 45, 5th Floor, Hong Kong Bank	26001/2

	Chambers, Djalan Chevalier, Bandar Seri Begawan, Brunei	
Burma	80 Strand Road, (PO Box 638), Rangoon	15700
Cameroon	Le Concorde, Av. Winston Churchill, (BP 547), Yaoundé	220545
Canada	Elgin St, Ottawa, Ontario	(613) 237 1530
Chile	La Concepción Av. 177, 4th Floor, Providencia, (Casilla 72-D), Santiago	239166
China	11 Kuang Hua Lu, Chien Kou Men Wai, Beijing	521961/4
Colombia	Calle 38, 13-35 Pisos 9-11, (Apartado Aero 4508), Bogotá	698100
Costa Rica	Paseo Colon 3203, Apartado 10056, San José	21-55-88
Côte d'Ivoire	5th floor, Immeuble Shell, Av. Lamblin, (BP 2581), Abidjan	22-66-15/32-27-76/ 32-4980
Cuba	Edificio Bolivar, Capdevila 101-103, e Morro y Prado, Havana	61-5681
Cyprus	Alex Pallis St, Nicosia	02-47131
Czechoslovakia	Thunorvska 14, 12550 Prague 1	
Denmark	Kastelvej 40, DK-2100 Copenhagen	
Dominican Rep.	Avenida Independencia No.506, Santo Domingo	
Ecuador	(opp Hotel Quito), Gonzalez Suarez, (Casilla 314), 111 Quito	230070/3
Egypt	Ahmed Raghab Street, Garden City, Cairo	20850/9
El Salvador	17 Calle Poniente No 320, Centro de Gobierno, San Salvador	221014/6989
Ethiopia	Dessie Road, Addis Ababa	182 354
Fiji	Civic Centre, Stinson Parade, (PO Box 1355), Suva	311033
Gabon	Bâtiment Sogame, Blvd de I'Independence, (BP 476), Libreville	72-29-85
Gambia	48 Atlantic Road, Fajara, Banjul	Serrekunda 2133/ 2134/2578/2627
East Germany	Unter den Linden, Berlin 1080	
Ghana	Barclays Bank Bldg, High St, (PO Box 296), Accra	64123/34
Guatemala	Edificio Maya, Via 5, No 4-50, 8°Piso, Zona 4, Guatemala City	61329/64375
Guyana	44 Main Street, (PO Box 625), Georgetown	65881/4
Honduras	Apartado 290, Av. República de Chile, Tegucigalpa	22-31-91
Hong Kong	9th Floor, Gammon House, 12 Harcourt Rd, (PO Box 528), Hong Kong	5-229541
Iceland	Laufasvegur 49, Reykjavik	15883/4
India	Chanakayapuri, New Delhi 21, 110021	690371
or	1 Ho Chi Minh Sarani, (PO Box 9073), Calcutta, 700016	44-5171

or	PO Box 815, Mercantile Bank Bldgs, Mahatma Gandhi Road, Bombay 400023	274874
or	PO Box 3710, 150A Anna Salai, Madras, 2-600002	83136
Indonesia	Djalan Thamrim 75, Jakarta	341091/8
Iran	Avenue Ferdowsi, (PO Box No 1513), Tehran	375011 (10 lines)
Iraq	Sharia Salah, Ud-Din, Karkh, Baghdad	
Israel	192 Hayarkon St, Tel Aviv 63405	03-249171-8
Jamaica	Trafalgar Road, (PO Box 575), Kingston 10	926-9050
Japan	1 Ichibancho, Chiyoda-Ku, Tokyo 102	03-265 5511
or	Hong Kong and Shanghai Bank Bldg, 45 Awajimachi, 4-chome, Higashi-Ku, Osaka 541	06-231 3355/7
Jordan	Third Circle, Jebel Amman, Amman	37374-5
Kenya	13th Floor, Bruce House, Standard St, (PO Box 30133), Nairobi	335944
Korea	4 Chung-Dong, Sudaemoon-Ku, Seoul	75-7341/3
Kuwait	Arabian Gulf St, (PO Box 300), Safat, Kuwait.	439221/2
Laos	Rue Pandit J. Nehru, (PO Box 224), Vientiane	2333/2374
Lebanon	Avenue de Paris, Ras Beirut, Beirut	364108
Lesotho	PO Box 521, Maseru	3961
Liberia	PO Box 120, Mamba Point, Monrovia	221055/107/491
Madagascar	5 Rue Robert Ducrocq, (BP 167), Antananarivo	251-51
Malawi	Longadzi House, (PO Box 30042), Lilongwe 3	31544
Malaysia	13th Floor, Wisma Damansara, Jalan Semantan, (PO Box 1030), Kuala Lumpur	941533
Mauritius	Cerné House, Chaussée, (PO Box 586), Port Louis	20201
Mexico	Lerma 71, Col Cuauhtémoc, (PO Box 96 Bis), Mexico City 5, DF	5114880/5143327
Mongolia	30 Enkh Taivny Gudamzh, (PO Box 703), Ulan Bator	51033
Morocco	17 Blvd. de la Tour, Rabat	20905/6
Mozambique	A. Vladimir I Lenine 319, (Caixa Postal 55), Maputo	26011/2
Nepal	Lainchaur, (PO Box 106), Kathmandu	11081,11588/9
New Zealand	Reserve Bank of New Zealand Bldg, 9th Floor, The Terrace, (PO Box 369), Wellington 1	726-049
or	9th Floor, Norwich Union Bldg, 179 Queen Street, (P.Bag), Auckland 1	32-973
or	PO Box 1762, Christchurch	519-652
Nigeria	11 Eleke Crescent, Victoria Island, (PMB 12136), Lagos	51630/1/2
or	Finance Corporation Building, Lebanon Street, (PMB 5010), Ibadan	21551
or	United Bank for Africa Bldg, Hospital Road, (PMB 2096), Kaduna	22573

Oman	PO Box 300, Muscat	722411
Pakistan	Diplomatic Enclave, Ramma 5, (PO Box 1122), Islamabad	22131/5
or	York Place, Runnymede Lane, Port Trust Estate, Clifton, Karachi-6	53 2041/46
Panama	Via Espana 120, (Apartado 889), Panama City	230451
Papua New Guinea	United Church Bldg, 3rd Floor, Douglas Street, (PO Box 739), Port Moresby	212500
Paraguay	Calle Presidente Franco 706, (PO Box 404), Asunción	49-146/44-472
Peru	Edificio Pacifico-Washington, Plaza Washington, Avenida Arequipe, (PO Box 854), Lima	283830
Philippines	Electra House, 115-117 Esteban St, Legaspi Village, Makati, (PO Box 1970 MCC), Metro Manila	8910-51/8
Qatar	PO Box 3, Doha	321991/4
Rwanda	PO Box 320, Kigali	5905
Saudi Arabia	Jeddah Towers, Citibank Bldg, (PO Box 393), Jeddah	27306/27122
Senegal	20 Rue du Docteur Guillet, (BP 6025), Dakar	27051
Seychelles	Victoria House, 3rd Floor, (PO Box 161), Victoria	23055/6
Sierra Leone	Standard Bank of Sierra Leone Bldg, Lightboot Boston St, Freetown	23961-5
Singapore	Tanglin Circus, (Tanglin PO Box 19), Singapore 10	639333
Solomon Islands	PO Box 676, Honiara	705706
Somalia	Waddada Zasan Geeddii Abtoow 7/8, (PO Box 1036), Mogadishu	22088/9 34072/3
South Africa	6 Hill St, Arcadia, Pretoria 0002	74-3121
	5th Floor, Nedbank Mall, 145/7 Commissioner St, (PO Box 10101), Johannesburg 2000	218161
or	11th Floor, African Eagle Centre, 2 St. Georges St, (PO Box 1346), Cape Town 8000	41-1466/8
or	7th Floor, Barclays Bank Bldg, Field St, Durban 4001	313131(5 lines)
Sri Lanka	Galle Road, Killupitiya, (PO Box 1433), Colombo 3	27611/17
Sudan	New Aboulela Bldg, Barlaman Ave, Khartoum	70760/6-9
Suriname	c/o VSH United Bldg, Vant Hogechuyasstraat, (PO Box 1300), Paramaribo	72870
Swaziland	Allister Miller St, (P.Bag), Mbabane	42581/6
Syria	Quartier Malki, 11 Mohammed Kurd Ali St, Immeuble Kotob, Damascus	712561
Tanzania	Permanent House, Corner Azikiew St/ Independence Ave, (PO Box 9112), Dar es Salaam	29601
Thailand	Wireless Road, Bangkok	2527161/0

Tonga	PO Box 56, Nuku'alofa	21-020
Trinidad & Tobago	Furness House, Independence Square, Port-of-Spain	62-52861
Tunisia	5 Place de la Victoire, Tunis	245100/324/ 649/244805
Turkey	Sehit Ersan Caddesi, 46a Canyaka, Ankara	274310/5
or	Tepebasi, Beyoglu, Istanbul	4475459/498874
Uganda	10/12 Parliament Ave, Kampala	57301/4
USSR	Naberezhnaya Morisa Teresa 14, Moscow 72	2411033 Outside Office hours 231-8511/2 231-2331
United Arab Emirates	PO Box 248, Abu Dhabi	43033/4/5
Uruguay	Calle Marco Bruto 1073, Montevideo	791033
Venezuela	Avenida La Estancia No 10, Ciudad Commercial, Tamanaco, (Apartado 1246), Caracas	91-12-55/91-14-77
Vietnam	16 Pho Ly Thuong Kiet, Hanoi	52349/52510
North Yemen	13 Al Qasr al Jumhuri, (PO Box 1287), Sana'a	5428
South Yemen	28 Ho Chi Minh St, Khorrmaksar, Aden	24801-4
Zaïre	9 Avenue de l'Equateur, 5th Floor, (BP 8049), Kinshasa	23484/6,22666)
Zambia	Independence Ave, (PO Box 50050), Lusaka	216770
Zimbabwe	Stanley House, Stanley Ave, (PO Box 4490), Harare	793781

United States Embassies Worldwide

Telephone numbers are preceded by direct-dial country and city codes where available.

Afghanistan	Wazir Akbar Khan Mina, Kabul	24230/9
Algeria	4 Chemin Cheich Bachir Brahimi, Algiers	601425
Argentina	4300 Columbia, Buenos Aires	54-1-774 7611
Australia	Moonah Place, Canberra	61-62-73 3711
Austria	IX Boltzmanngasse 16, A-1091, Vienna	43-222-31-55-11
Bahamas	Mosmar Building, Queen St, (Box N8197), Nassau	809-322-4753
Bahrain	Shaikh Isa Road, Manama	973-714151
Bangladesh	Adamjee Court, Motijheel, Dacca	244220
Barbados	Canadian Imperial Bldg, Broad St, (PO Box 302), Bridgetown	63574-7
Belgium	27 Blvd du Régent, Brussels	32-2-513-3830
Belize	Gabourel Lane, Belize City	
Benin	Rue Caporal Anani Bernard, Cotonou	31-26-92
Bolivia	Banco Popular Del Peru Bldg, La Paz	591-2-350251

Botswana	Box 90, Gaborone	53982
Brazil	Avenida das Nocoes, Brasilia	55-61-223-0120
Bulgaria	1 Stamboliiski Blvd, Sofia	88-48-01
Burkina Faso	BP 35, Ouagadougou	335442
Burma	581 Merchant St, Rangoon	82055
Burundi	Chaussée Prince Louis Rwagasore, Bujumbura	34-54
Cameroon	Rue Nachtigal, Yaoundé	221633
Canada	100 Wellington Street, Ottawa	613-238-5335
Cape Verde	Rua Hoji Ya Yenna 81, Praia	553
Cayman Islands	nearest representative in Jamaica	
Central African Republic	Avenue President Dacko, Bangui	61-02-00
Chile	1343 Agustinas, Santiago	56-2-710133
China	Guang Hau Lu 17, Beijing	52-2033
Colombia	Calle 37, Bogotá	57-285-1300
Congo	Ave. Amilcar Cabral, Brazzaville	81-20-70
Costa Rica	Avenida 3 & Calle 1, San José	506-33 1155
Côte d'Ivoire	5 Rue Jesse Owens, Abidjan	32-09-79
Cuba	Calzada E/LYM, Vedado, Havana	32-0551
Cyprus	Therissos & Dositheos Sts, Nicosia	02-465151
Czechoslovakia	Trziste 15-12548, Prague,	53-66-41
Denmark	Dag Hammarskjold Alle 21, DK-2100 Copenhagen	45-1-42-31-44
Dijibouti	Villa Plateau du Serpent Blvd, Djibouti	35-38-49
Dominican Rep	Calles Ceasar Nicolas Penson & Leopoldo Navarro, Santo Domingo	682-2172
Ecuador	Avenida 12 de Octobre y Patria, Quito	548-000/548265
Egypt	5 Sharia Latin America, Cairo	28219
El Salvador	25 Avenida Norte, San Salvador	503-26-7100
Ethiopia	Entoto St, Addis Ababa	110666
Fiji	31 Loftus St, Suva	679-23031
Finland	Itainen Puistotie 14A, Helsinki	358-0-171931
France	2 Av. Gabriel, Paris	33-1-296-1202
Gabon	Blvd de la Mer, Libreville	72-20-03
Gambia	16 Buckle Street, Banjul	526-7
East Germany	Neustaedtische Kirchstrasse 4-5, Berlin	37-2-2202741
West Germany	Delchmannsaue, Bonn	49-228-339-3390
Ghana	Liberia and Kinbu Roads, Accra	66811
Greece	91 Vasilissis Sophias Blvd, Athens	30-1-712951
Guatemala	7-01 Avenida de la Reforma, Guatemala	31-15-41
Guinea	Second Blvd and Ninth Avenue, Conakry	41540
Guinea-Bissau	Avenida Domingos Ramos, Bissau	2816
Guyana	31 Main Street, Georgetown	592-02-54900

Haiti	Harry Truman Blvd, Port-au-Prince	509-1-20200
Honduras	Avenida La Paz, Tegucigalpa	504-22-3121
Hungary	V Szabadsag Ter 12, Budapest	329-375
Iceland	Laufasvegur 21, Reykjavik	28100
India	Shanti Path, Chanakyapuri 21, New Delhi	690351
Indonesia	Medan Merdeka Selatan 5, Jakarta	62-21-340001-9
Ireland	42 Elgin St, Ballsbridge, Dublin	353-1-688777
Israel	71 Hayarkon St, Tel Aviv	972-3-654338
Italy	Via Veneto 119/A, Rome	39-6-06-4674
Jamaica	2 Oxford Road, Kingston	809-92-94850
Japan	10-5 Akasaka 1-chome, Minato-Ku, Tokyo	81-3-583-7141
Jordan	King Faisal St, Amman	38930
Kenya	Wabera St, Nairobi	254-2-334141
Korea	Sejong-Ro, Seoul	82-272-2601
Kuwait	Box 77, Kuwait	965-424151
Laos	Rue Bartholomie, Vientiane	3126
Lebanon	Corniche & Rue Ain Mreisseh, Beirut	361-800
Lesotho	Box MS 333, Maseru	22666
Liberia	111 United Nations Drive, Monrovia	231-22991
Libya	Shari Mohammad Thabit, Tripoli	34021
Luxembourg	22 Blvd Emmanuel Servals, Luxembourg	352-40123
Madagascar	14 Rue Rainitovo, Antsohavala, Antananarivo	212-57
Malawi	Box 30016, Lilongwe	730-166
Malaysia	AIA Bldg, Jalan Ampang, Kuala Lumpur	60-3-26321
Mali	Rue Testard & Rue Mohamed V, Bamako	225834
Malta	Saint Anne St, Floriana, Valletta	623653
Mauritania	BP 222, Nouakchott	52660
Mauritius	John Kennedy St, Port Louis	2-3218
Mexico	Paseo de la Reforma 305, Mexico City	905-553-3333
Morocco	2 Av. de Marrakesh, Rabat	30361
Mozambique	35 Rua da Mesquita, Maputo	26051
Nepal	Pani Pokhari, Kathmandu	11199
Netherlands	Lange Vorhout 102, The Hague	31-70-62-49-11
New Zealand	29 Fitzherbert Terrace, Thorndon, Wellington	64-4-722-068
Nicaragua	Km 4½ Carretera Sur, Managua	505-2-23061
Niger	BP 11201, Niamey	72-26-61
Nigeria	2 Eleke Crescent, Lagos	610097
Norway	Drammensvein 18, Oslo	47-2-56-68-80
Oman	Box 966, Muscat	745-231
Pakistan	AID/UN Bldg, Islamabad	24071
Panama	Avenida Balboa & Calle 38, Panama	507-27-1777
Papua New	Armit St, Port Moresby	675-121-211455

Guinea

Paraguay	1776 Mariscal Lopez Ave, Asunción	595-21-201-041
Peru	Avdas Espana & Inca Garcilaso de la Vega, Lima	51-14-286000
Philippines	1201 Roxas Blvd, Manila	63-2-598-011
Poland	Aleje Ujazdowskie 29/31, Warsaw	283041-9
Portugal	Avenida Duque de Loule 39, Lisbon	351-19-570102
Qatar	Fariq Bin Oman, Doha	870701
Romania	Strade Tudor Arghezi 7-9, Bucharest	40-0-12-4-40
Rwanda	Blvd de la Révolution, Kigali	5601
Saudi Arabia	Palestine Road, Ruwais, Jeddah	966-21-6670080
Senegal	Avenue Jean XXIII, Dakar	21-42-96
Seychelles	Box 148, Victoria	23921
Sierra Leone	Walpole & Siaka Stevens Sts, Freetown	26481
Singapore	30 Hill St, Singapore	65-30251
Somalia	Corso Primo Luglio, Mogadishu	28011
South Africa	225 Pretorius St, Pretoria	27-12028-4266
Spain	Serrano 75, Madrid	34-1-276-3400
Sri Lanka	44 Galle Road, Colombo	21271
Sudan	Gamhouria Ave, Khartoum	74611
Suriname	Dr. Sophie Redmondstraat 13, Paramaribo	73024
Swaziland	Warner St, Mbabane	22281
Sweden	Stradvagen 101, Stockholm	46-8-63-05-20
Switzerland	Jubilaeumstrasse 93, Bern	41-31-437011
Syria	Abu Rumaneh, Al Mansur St, Damascus	332315
Tanzania	City Drive, Dar es Salaam	68894
Thailand	95 Wireless Road, Bangkok	66-2-252-5040
Togo	Rue Pelletier Ceventou & Rue Vouban, Lomé	29-91
Trinidad & Tobago	15 Queen's Park West, Port-of-Spain	62-26371
Tunisia	144 Av. de la Liberté, Tunis	282-566
Turkey	110 Ataturk Blvd, Ankara	90-41-26-54-70
USSR	Ulitsa Chaykovskogo 19, Moscow	252-24-51
United Arab Emirates	Corniche Road, Abu Dhabi	971-2-361534
United Kingdom	24 Grosvenor Square, London W1	44-1-499-9000
Uruguay	Calle Lauro Muller 1776, Montevideo	40-90-51
Venezuela	Avdas Francisco de Miranda & Principal de la Floresta, Caracas	58-2-284-7111
North Yemen	Box 1088, Sana'a	72790
Yugoslavia	Kneza Milosa 50, Belgrade	3811-645655
Zaïre	310 Av.des Aviateurs, Kinshasa	25881
Zambia	Box 1617, Lusaka	214911
Zimbabwe	78 Enterprise Rd, Highlands, Harare	791588

Embassies, High Commissions and Consulates in Australia

Argentina	1st Floor, Suite 102, M.L.C. Tower, Woden, Canberra, ACT 2606	824 855/555
Austria	107 Endeavour St, Red Hill, Canberra	591376
Bangladesh	43 Hampton Circuit, Yarralumla, Canberra, ACT 2600	
Belgium	19 Arkana St, Yarralumla, Canberra, ACT 2600	732501/2
Brazil	11th Floor, 'Canberra House', 40 Marcus Clarke St, Canberra City, ACT 2601	
Bulgaria	Double Bay, NSW, 2028	367 581
Burma	85 Mugga Way, Red Hill, Canberra, ACT 2603	
Canada	Commonwealth Avenue, Canberra, ACT 2600	733 844
Chile	93 Endeavour St, Red Hill, Canberra, ACT 2603	
China	14 Federal Highway, Watson, Canberra, ACT 2602	412 4488
Columbia	PO Box 391, Double Bay, NSW, Sydney 2028	
Czechoslovakia	169 Military Rd, Doler Heights, Canberra, ACT	
Denmark	24 Beagle St, Red Hill, Canberra, ACT 2603	
Dominican Rep.	331 King William St, (Box 1017, GPO), Adelaide, S. Australia 5001	518 411
Ecuador	2 Glen St, Hawthorn 3122, Victoria	818 7168
Egypt	125 Monaro Cresent, Red Hill, Canberra ACT 2603	
Fiji	9 Beagle St, Red Hill, (PO Box E159), Canberra, ACT 2600	
Finland	10 Darwin Avenue, Yarralumla, Canberra, ACT 2600	
France	6 Darwin Avenue, Yarralumla, Canberra, ACT 2600	
East Germany	12 Beagle St, Red Hill, Canberra, ACT 2603	
West Germany	119 Empire Circuit, Yarralumla, Canberra ACTACT 2600	(6162) 733 177
Ghana	PO Box 338, Hanuka, Canberra	(6162) 951 152
Greece	1 Stonehaven Crescent, Red Hill, Canberra, ACT 2603	
Hungary	79 Hopetown Circuit, Yarralumla, Canberra, ACT 2600	
Iceland	2 Montalto Avenue, Toorak 3142	
India	3–5 Moonah Place, Yarralumla, Canberra ACT 2600	733 999/774
Indonesia	Piccadilly Court, 3rd Floor, 222 TITT, (PO Box 6), Sydney	
Iran	14 Torres St, Red Hill, Canberra	
Iraq	48 Culgoa Circuit, O'Malley, ACT 2606	861 333/755
Ireland	200 Arkana St, Yarralumla, Canberra, ACT 2606	733 022
Israel	6 Turrana St, Yarralumla, Canberra ACTACT 2600	
Italy	12 Grey St, Deakin, ACT 2600	
Japan	112 Empire Circuit, Yarralumla, Canberra, ACT 2000	
Jordan	29 Roebuck St. Red Hill, Canberra, ACT 2603	
Korea	113 Empire Circuit, Yarralumla, Canberra, ACT 2600	733 044/956
Lebanon	73 Endeavour St, Red Hill, Canberra ACT 2603	957 378
Libya	Jamahiriya, 50 Culgoa Circuit, O'Malley, Canberra	
Malaysia	71 State Circle, Yarralumla, Canberra ACT 2600	731 541/4/5
Malta	261 La Perouse St, Red Hill, Canberra, ACT 2603	
Mauritius	16 National Circuit, Suite 6, Barton, Canberra, ACT 2600	
Mexico	14 Perth Avenue, Yarralumla, Canberra, ACT 2600	
Netherlands	120 Empire Circuit, Yarralumla, Canberra, ACT 2600	733 111

New Zealand	Commonwealth Avenue, Canberra, ACT 2600	
Nigeria	27 State Circle, Deakin, Canberra, ACT 2600	
Norway	3 Zeehan St, Red Hill, Canberra, ACT 2603	
Pakistan	59 Franklin St, Forrest, (PO Box 198), Manuka, Canberra, ACT 2603	(9500) 212 223
Papua New Guinea	Forster Crescent, Yarralumla, Canberra, ACT 2600	733 322
Paraguay	PO Box 481, Mascot 2020, Sydney, NSW	
Peru	94 Captain Cook, Canberra ACT2604	951 016
Philippines	1 Moonah Place, Yarralumla, Canberra, ACT 2600	
Poland	7 Turrana St, Yarralumla, Canberra, ACT 2600	
Portugal	8 Astrolabe St, Red Hill, Canberra, ACT 2603	
Romania	115 Ginahgulla Rd, Belleview, Sydney, NSW	
Seychelles	127 Commercial Rd, South Yarra, Victoria, 3141	
Singapore	81 Mugga Way, Red Hill, Canberra, ACT 2603	
South Africa	Rhodes Place, Yarralumla, Canberra, ACT 2600	732 424/5/6/7
Spain	15 Arkana St, Yarralumla, ACT, (PO Box 256), Woden, Canberra, ACT	
Sri Lanka	35 Empire Circuit, Forrest, Canberra, ACT 2603	
Sweden	9 Turana St, Yarralumla, Canberra ACT 2600	
Switzerland	7 Melbourne Avenue, Forrest, Canberra ACT 2603	733 977
Thailand	111 Empire Circuit, Yarralumla, Canberra, ACT 2600	
Uganda	PO Box 276, Woden, Canberra, ACT 2606	
United States	Yarralumla, Canberra, ACT 2600	733 711
Uruguay	Adelaide House Suite 5, Woden, Canberra, ACT 2606	
USSR	78 Canberra Ave, Griffith, Caberra ACT 2603	959 033
Venezuela	Suite 106, MLC Tower, Woden, Canberra ACT	
Vietnam	31 Endeavour St, Red Hill, Canberra ACT 2603	952 426
Yugoslavia	11 Nuyats St, PO Box 161, Manuka, Canberra, ACT 2603	

Embassies, High Commissions and Consulates in Canada

Antigua	Suite 205, 60 St Clair Ave, East, Toronto, Ontario M4T 1L9	
Argentina	130 Slater St, 6th Floor, Ottawa, Ontario	
Australia	The National Building, 13th Floor, 130 Slater St, Ottawa, Ontario KIP 5H6	
Austria	445 Wilbrod St, Ottawa, Ontario KIN 6M7	
Bangladesh	85 Range Rd, Suite No. 1007, Ottawa, Ontario	
Barbados	Suite 700, 151 Slater St, Ottawa, Ontario KIP 5H4	
Belgium	6th Floor, 85 Range Road, Ottawa, Ontario	
Benin	58 Gleeb Ave, Ottawa, Ontario KIS 2C3	
Bolivia	85 Monterrey Dr, Ottawa, Ontario	(613) 483 4410
Brazil	255 Albert St, Suite 900, Ottawa, Ontario KIP 6A9	
Bulgaria	325 Stewart St, Ottawa, Ontario	232 3215

Burkina Faso	48 Range Rd, Ottawa, Ontario KIN 814	
Burundi	136 Rue Retcal SE, Pièce 210A, Ottawa, Ontario K2P OP8	
Cameroon	170 Clemond Ave, Ottawa, Ontario KIS 2B4	(613) 361 522
Chile	56 Sparks St, Suite 801, Ottawa, Ontario KAP 5A9	
China	415 St. Andrews, Ottawa, Ontario	(613) 234 4721
Colombia	140 Wellington St, Suite No 112, Ottawa, Ontario	
Costa Rica	Suite 2902, 1155 Dorchester Blvd West, Montreal, Quebec	(514) 866 8159/0442
Côte d'Ivoire	9 Av Malborough, Ottawa, Ontario K1N 86E	(613) 236 9919/ 235 9910
Cuba	388 Rue Main, Ottawa, Ontario KIS 1E3	563 0141
Czechoslovakia	1305 Avenue de Pins, West Montreal, Quebec, H3T 1B2	
Denmark	85 Range Rd, Apt, 702, Ottawa, Ontario K1N 8J6	
Dominican Rep.	3435 Drummond St, Suite 5, Montreal, Quebec H3G 1XB	(514) 843 4540
Eastern Caribbean	112 Kent St, Suite 1701, Ottawa, Ontario K1P 5P2	
Ecuador	150 10th St, Suite 407, Ottawa, Ontario, K1P 5W4	(613) 238 5032
Egypt	454 Laurier Ave, East Ottawa, Ontario	(613) 234 4931
El Salvador	'The Driveway Place', 350 Queen Elizabeth Driveway, Suite 101, Ontario, Ontario	
Finland	222 Somerset St West, Suite 401, Ottawa, Ontario K2P 2G3	
France	1 Dundas St West, Suite 2405, (Box 8), Toronto, Ontario M5G 1W3	
Gambia	363 St Francois Xavier St, Suite 230, Montreal, Quebec, H2Y 3P9	
West Germany	1 Waverley St, Ottawa, Ontario KIN 8VA	(613) 534 226
Ghana	85 Range Road, Suite 810, Ottawa, Ontario	(613) 236 0871
Greece	80 Maclaren Ave, Ottawa, Ontario K2P 0K3	
Guinea	Suite 208, Place De Ville, 112 10 St, Ottawa, Ontario	
Guyana	151 Slater St, Suite 309, Ottawa, Ontario, K1P 5H3	
Haiti	Suite 1308 Place DeVille, 112 10th St, Ottawa, Ontario	(613) 238 1133
Honduras	151 Slater St, Suite 300 As Ottawa, Ontario K1P 583	
Hungary	7 Delaware Ave, Ottawa, Ontario K2P OZ2	
Iceland	5005 Jean Talon St West, 3rd Floor, Montreal, Quebec H5P 1W7	
India	325 Howe St, 1st Floor, Vancouver, BC	
Indonesia	225 Albert St, Suite 101, Box 430, Terminal A, Ottawa, Ontario	(613) 236 7403
Iran	Suite 307, 85 Range Rd, Ottawa K1N 8J6	(613) 236 9108
Iraq	215 McLeod St, Ottawa, Ontario K2P O28	(613) 236 9177/8
Ireland	170 Metcalfe St, Ottawa, Ontario K2P 1P3	(613) 233 6281/2
Israel	Laurier Av, West, Ottawa, K1R 5H9	232 2401
Italy	275 Slater St, 11th Floor, Ottawa , Ontario K1P 5H9	(613) 232 2401
Jamaica	Suite 202-204, 85 Range Rd, Ottawa, Ontario	
Japan	225 Sussex Drive, Ottawa, Ontario K1N 9E6	
Jordan	100 Bronson Ave, Suite 701, Ottawa, Ontario KIR 6G8	
Kenya	Suite 600, 141 Laurier Ave West, Ottawa, Ontario KIP 5J3	
South Korea	151 Slater St, Suite 608, Ottawa, Ontario KIP 5H3	(613) 232 1716/7
Lebanon	640 Lion St, Ottawa, Ontario KIS 375	(613) 236 5825

Lesotho	350 Bucks St. Suite 910, Ottawa, Ontario	(613) 236 9449
Madagascar	459 St. Sulpice St, Montreal, Quebec H2Y 2U8	(514) 844 4427
Malawi	112 Kent St, Suite 905, Ottawa, Ontario KIP 5P2	(613) 236 8931/2
Malaysia	60 Boteler St, Ottawa, Ontario KIN 8Y7	(613) 237 518
Mali	50 Avenue Goulburn, Ottawa, Ontario	(613) 232 1501
Mexico	130 Albert St, Suite 206, Ottawa, Ontario KIP 5G4	
Morocco	38 Range Rd, Ottawa, Ontario	
Netherlands	3rd floor, 275 Slater St, Ottawa, Ontario K1P 5H9	(613) 237 5030
New Zealand	Metropolitan House, Suite 801, 99 Bank St, Ottawa, Ontario KIP 6G3	
Nicaragua	Place De Ville, Suite 2224, Tower A, 320 Queen St, Ottawa, Ontario KIR 5A3	
Niger	38 Av. Blackburn, Ottawa, Ontario KIN 8A2	
Nigeria	295 Metcalf St, Ottawa, Ontario K2P 1R9	(613) 236 9521
Norway	Suite 932, Royal Bank Centre, 90 Sparks St, Ottawa, Ontario KIP 5B4	
Pakistan	2100 Drumond St, Apt 505, Montreal, Quebec H3G 1X1	(514) 845 2297
Peru	170 Laurier Ave West, Suite 1007, Ottawa, Ontario KIP 5V5	(613) 238 1777/8
Philippines	130 Albert St, Ste 606-7, Ottawa, Ontario	(613) 233 1121
Poland	773 Daly St, Ottawa, Ontario	
Portugal	645 Island Park Drive, Ottawa, Ontario KIY OB8	
Rwanda	Suite 903, 350 Park St, Ottawa, Ontario KIR 7S9	(613) 238 1603
Saudi Arabia	Suite 901, 99 Bank St, Ottawa, Ontario KIP 5P9	(613) 237 0100
Senegal	57 Marlborough Ave, Ottawa, Ontario	
Somalia	Suite 918, 112 Kent St, Ottawa, Ontario KIP 5P2	(613) 563 4541
South Africa	15 Sussex Drive, Ottawa, Ontario K1N 8R5	(613) 744 0330
Spain	350 Sparks St, Ste 802, Ottawa, Ontario KIR 758	
Sri Lanka	85 Range Rd, Sandringham Suites 102-104, Ottawa, Ontario KIN 8J6	
Sweden	441 Maclaren St, Ottawa, Ontario K2P 2H3	
Switzerland	5 Malborough Avenue, Ottawa, Ontario K1N 8E6	
Tanzania	50 Range Rd, Ottawa, Ontario KIN 8J4	
Thailand	85 Range Rd, Suite 704, Ottawa, Ontario K1N 8J6	(613) 237 1517
Trinidad and Tobago	73 Albert St, Room 508, Ottawa, Ontario K1P 5R4	(613) 232 2418/9
Tunisia	115 O'Conner St, Ottawa, Ontario	
Turkey	197 Laurier Ave, West, Suite 601, Ottawa, Ontario K1P 525	(613) 233 7797
United States	100 Wellington St, Ottawa, Ontario KIP 5T1	(613) 238 5335
Uruguay	1010 Ouest, Rue Ste Catherine, Suite 346, Montreal, Quebec H3B 161	(514) 236 1413
USSR	285 Charlotte St, Ottawa, Ontario K1N 845	(613) 235 4341
Venezuela	Ste 2000, 320 Queen St, Ottawa, Ontario KIR 5A3	(613) 235 5151
Yugoslavia	17 Blackburn Ave, Ottawa, Ontario K1N 8A2	
Zaïre	18 Range Rd, Ottawa, Ontario KIN 8JE	236 7102
Zambia	130 Albert St, Suite 1610, Ottawa, Ontario	

Zimbabwe   112 Kent St, Suite 915, Place De Ville, Tower B, Ottawa,
                    Ontario K1P 5P2

Embassies, High Commissions and Consulates in New Zealand

Argentina	IBM Center, 151-165 The Terrace, 5th Floor, (PO Box 1033), Wellington	
Australia	72-78 Hobson St, Thorndon, Wellington	
Belgium	1 Williston St, (PO Box 3841), Wellington	
Canada	PO Box 12-049 Wellington N, ICI Building, 3rd Floor, Molesworth St, Wellington	739 577
Chile	Robert Jones House, 12th Floor, Jervois Quay, Wellington	
China	No. 226 Glenmore St, Wellington	721 384
Czechoslovakia	12 Anne St, Wadestown, (PO Box 2843), Wellington	
Denmark	18th Floor, Challenge House, 105-109 The Terrace, (PO Box 10035), Wellington 1	
Ecuador	PO Box 2987, Wellington	
Fiji	Robert Jones House, Jervois Quay, Wellington	
France	1 Williston St, (BP 1695), Wellington	
West Germany	90-92 Hobson St, Wellington	
Hong Kong	General Building, G/F, Corner Shortland St & O'Connell St, Auckland	
India	Princes Towers, 10th Floor, 180 Molesworth St, Wellington	736 390/1
Israel	13th Level, Williams City Centre, Plymmet Steps, (PO Box 2171), Wellington	
Italy	38 Grant Rd, (PO Box 468), Wellington	735 339/955
Japan	7th Floor, Norwich Insurance House, 3-11 Hunter St, Wellington 1	
Kiribati	33 Great South Rd, Otahuhu, Auckland	
Korea	12th Floor, Williams Parking Centre Building, Cnr Boulcoutt St & Gilmer Terrace, Wellington	739 073/4
Malaysia	163 Terrace, (PO Box 9422), Wellington	738 185/7
Netherlands	Investment House, 10th Floor, Ballance & Featherstone Sts, Wellington	738 652
Norway	38-42 Waring Taylor St, (PO Box 1392), Wellington	
Papua New Guinea	Princes Towers, 11th Floor, 180 Molesworth St, Thorndon, Wellington	851 2748/9
Peru	3rd Floor, 36/37 Victoria St, Wellington	725 171/2
Philippines	Level 30, Williams City Centre, Boulcott St, Gilmer Terrace, Wellington	729 848
Portugal	47-49 Fort St, Auckland	
Romania	100 Devans Bay Rd, Wellington	
Singapore	17 Kabul St, Khandallah, Wellington	
South Africa	Molesworth House, 101-103 Molesworth St, Wellington	737 413/4
Sweden	PO Box 1800, Wellington 1	
Switzerland	22-24 Panama St, 7th Floor, Wellington 1	721 593
Thailand	2 Burnel Ave, (PO Box 2530), Wellington 1	735 538

United States	29 Fitzherbert Terrace, Wellington	722 068
USSR	57 Messines Rd, Karori, Wellington	721 864
Yugoslavia	24 Hatton St, Wellington 5	

Embassies, High Commissions and Consulates in Britain

Consulates are closed on English Public holidays and on the national holidays observed in their own countries. Visa/consular offices have been listed for preference. Where there is no embassy in the UK, the nearest available has been listed.

Afghanistan	31 Prince's Gate, London SW7 1QQ	01-589 8891/2
Albania	131 Rue de Pompe, Paris 75016, France	553 5132
Algeria	6 Hyde Park Gate, London SW7 1QQ	221 7800/4
Andorra	63 Westover Rd, London SW18	874 4806
Angola	19 Av. Foch, Paris 75116	501 5820
Antigua	Eastern Caribbean High Commission, 10 Kensington Court, London W8	937 9522
Argentina	Brazilian Embassy, Argentine Interest Section, 111 Cadogan Gardens, London SW1 1RQ	730 7173
Australia	Australia House, Strand, London WC2B 4L	438 8000
Austria	18 Belgrave Mews West, London SW1X 8HU	235 3731/4
Bahamas	10 Chesterfield St, London W1X 8AH	408 4488
Bahrain	98 Gloucester Road, London SW7 4AU	370 5132/3
Bangladesh	28 Queen's Gate, London SW7 5JA	584 0081
Barbados	263 Tottenham Court Rd, London W1P 9A	636 9448
Belgium	103 Eaton Square, London SW1W 9AB	235 5422
Belize	15 Thayer Street, London W1M 5DL	486 8381
Benin	125 High St, Edgware, Middx HA8 7HS	951 1234
Bolivia	106 Eaton Square, London SW1W 9AD	235 4255
Botswana	6 Stratford Place, London W1	499 0031
Brazil	6 Deanery Street, London W1Y 5LH	499 7441/4
British Virgin Islands	48 Albemarle St, London W1X 4AR	629 6355
Brunei	Brunei House, 49 Cromwell Rd, LondonSW7 2ED	581 0521
Bulgaria	186-188 Queen's Gate, London SW7 5HL	584 9400
Burkina Faso	150 Buckingham Palace Rd, London SW1W 9SA	730 8141
Burma	19a Charles St, Berkeley Square, London W1X 8ER	499 8841
Burundi	Sq. Marie-Louise 46, 1040 Brussels, Belgium	230 4535/48
Cameroon	84 Holland Park, London W11 3RB	229 7641/4
Canada	38 Grosvenor Street, London W1X 0A	629 9492
Cape Verde Is.	Av. do Rostello 33, 1400 Lisbon,Portugal	613 400/424
Cayman Islands	Hambleton House, 17b Curzon St, Mayfair, London W1Y 7FE	493 5161/7756
Central African Republic	29 Blvd de Montmorency, Paris 75016, France	4224 4256
Chad	65 Rue Belles Feuilles, Paris 75016, France	4553 3675

Chile	12 Devonshire Street, London W1N 1FS	580 6392/4
China	31 Portland Place, London W1N 3AG	636 1835
Colombia	Suite 10, 140 Park Lane, London W1Y 3DF	493 4565
Congo	37bis Rue Paul Valéry, Paris 75016	500 6057
Costa Rica	93 Star St, London W2 1QF	723 1772/9630
Cuba	15 Grape St, London WC2H 8DR	836 7618
Cyprus	93 Park Street, London W1Y 4ET	499 8272
Czechoslovakia	28 Kensington Palace Gardens, London W8 4QY	727 3966
Denmark	55 Sloane Street, London SW1X 9SR	235 1255
Djibouti	26 Rue Emile Menier, Paris 75116	4727 4922
Dominica	1 Collingham Gdns, London SW5 0HW	370 5194/5
Dominican Republic	6 Queens Mansions, Brook Green, London W6	602 1885
Eastern Caribbean Sts	10 Kensington Court, London W8 5DL	937 9522
Ecuador	Flat 3, Hans Crescent, Knightsbridge, London SW1X 0LS	584 2648
Egypt	19 Kensington Palace Gdn Mews, London W8 4QL	229 8818/9
El Salvador	Flat 9, Welbeck House, 62 Welbeck St, London W1M 7HB	486 8182/3
Ethiopia	17 Prince's Gate, London SW7 1PZ	589 7212/5
Fiji	34 Hyde Park Gate, London SW7 5BN	584 3661/2
Finland	38 Chesham Place, London SW1X 8HW	235 9531
France	College House, 29-31 Wright's Lane, London W8	937 1202
Gabon	48 Kensington Court, London W8 5DB	937 5285/9
Gambia	57 Kensington Court, London W8 5DG	937 6316/8
East Germany	34 Belgrave Square, London SW1X 8QZ	235 4465
West Germany	23 Belgrave Square, London SW1X 8PZ	235 5033
Ghana	38 Queen's Gate, London SW7 5HR	584 6311
Greece	1A Holland Park, London W11 3TP	727 8040
Grenada	1 Collingham Gardens, London SW5 0HW	373 7800/8/9
Guatemala	c/o El Salvador Embassy *or* 73 Rue de Courcelles, Paris 75008, France	227 7863
Guinea-Bissau	Rua da Alcolena 17, 1400 Lisbon, Portugal	615371/3
Guinea	24 Rue Emile Meunier, Paris 75116, France	553 7225
Guyana	3 Palace Court, Bayswater Rd, London W2 4LP	229 7684/8
Haiti	Ste 5, 55 Park Lane, London W1	409 3115
Honduras	47 Manchester Street, London W1M 5PB	486 4880
Hong Kong	6 Grafton Street, London W1X 3LB	499 9821
Hungary	35b Eaton Place, London SW1X 8BY	235 2664/4462
Iceland	1 Eaton Terrace, London SW1W 8EY	730 5131/2
India	India House, Aldwych, London WC2B 4NA	836 8484
Indonesia	157 Edgeware Rd, London W2	499 7661
Iran	50 Kensington Court, London W8 5DD	937 5225/8
Iraq	21 Queens Gate, London SW7 5JG	584 7141
Ireland	17 Grosvenor Place, London SW1X 7HR	235 2171
Israel	15 Old Court Place, Kensington, London W8 4QB	937 8050
Italy	38 Eaton Place, London SW1X 8AN	235 9371
Ivory Coast	2 Upper Belgrave Street, London SW1X 8BJ	235 6991

Jamaica	50 St. James's Street, London SW1A 1JT	493 3647
		499 1701/8
Japan	43/46 Grosvenor Street London W1X 0BA	493 6030
Jordan	6 Upper Phillimore Gdns, London W8 7HB	937 3685/7
Kenya	45 Portland Place, London W1N 4AS	636 2371/5
South Korea	4 Palace Gate, London W8 5NF	581 3330
Kuwait	46 Queen's Gate, London SW7	589 4533
Laos	5 Palace Green, Kensington, London W8 4QA	937 9519
Lebanon	15 Palace Gardens Mews, London W8 4RB	727 6696
Lesotho	10 Collingham Road, London SW5 0NR	373 8581/4
Liberia	2 Pembridge Place, London W2 4XB	221 1036
Liechtenstein	c/o Swiss Embassy	
Luxembourg	27 Wilton Crescent, London SW1X 8SD	235 6961
Macau	Airwork House, 35 Piccadilly, London W1V 9PB	734 7282
Madagascar	69-70 Mark Lane, London E3C 7JA	481 3899
Malawi	33 Grosvenor Street, London W1X 0DE	491 4172/7
Malaysia	45 Belgrave Square, London SW1X 8QT	235 8033
Mali	487 Av. Molière, B1060 Brussels, Belgium	345 7589/7432
Malta	Ste 207, College House, Wrights Lane, London W8	938 1140
Mauritania	89 Rue du Cherche Midi, Paris 75006, France	548 2388
Mauritius	32/33 Elvaston Place, Gloucester Road, London SW7 5NW	581 0294/8
Mexico	8 Halkin Street, London SW1X 7DW	235 6393/6
Monaco	4 Audley Square, London W1Y 5DR	629 0734
Mongolia	7 Kensington Court, London W8 5DL	937 0150
Morocco	49 Queen's Gate Gardens, London SW7 5NE	581 5001/3
Mozambique	Av. de Berna 7, 1000 Lisbon, Portugal	771747/773513
Nauru	3 Chesham St, London SW1X 8ND	235 6911
Nepal	12a Kensington Palace Gdns, London W8 4QU	229 6231/1594
Netherlands	38 Hyde Park Gate, London SW7 5DP	584 5040
New Zealand	New Zealand House, Haymarket, London SW1Y 4TQ	930 8422
Nicaragua	8 Gloucester Road, London SW7 4PP	584 4365
Niger	154 Rue de Longchamps, Paris 75116, France	504 8060
Nigeria	56 Fleet Street, London EC4Y 1JU	353 3776/9
Norway	25 Belgrave Square, London SW1X 8QD	235 7151
Oman	44 Montpelier Square, London SW7 1JJ	584 6782
Pakistan	35 Lowndes Square, London SW1X 9JN	235 2044
Panama	24 Tudor Street, London EC4Y 0AY	353 4792/3
Papua New Guinea	14 Waterloo Place, London SW1R 4AR	930 0922/6
Paraguay	Braemar Lodge, Cornwall Gardens, London SW7 4AW	937 1253
Peru	52 Sloane Street, London SW1X 9SP	235 6867
Philippines	1 Cumberland House, Kensington High Street, London W8	937 3646
Poland	73 New Cavendish St, London W1N 7RB	636 4533
Portugal	3rd Flr, Silver City House, 62 Brompton Rd, London SW3 1BJ	581 8722/4
Qatar	115 Queen's Gate, London SW7 5LP	581 8611
Romania	4 Palace Green, London W8 4QD	937 9666/8

Rwanda	Av. Des Fleurs No. 1bis, 1150 Brussels, Belgium	763 0702/05/21
Sao Tomé e Principe	Av. Brugmann 42, 1060 Brussels, Belgium	347 5375
Saudi Arabia	30 Belgrave Square, London SW1X 8QB	235 0303
Senegal	11 Phillimore Gdns, London W8 7QG	937 0925/6
Seychelles	50 Conduit Street, 4th Floor, PO Box 4PE, London W1A 4PE	439 0405
Sierra Leone	33 Portland Place, London W1N 3AG	636 6483
Singapore	5 Chesham Street, London SW1X 8ND	235 9067/9
Somalia	60 Portland Place, London W1N 3DG	580 7148/9
South Africa	South Africa House, Trafalgar Square, London WC2N 5DP	839 2211
Spain	20 Draycott Place, London SW3 2RZ	581 5921/6
Sri Lanka	13 Hyde Park Gardens, London W2 2LU	262 1841
Sudan	3 Cleveland Row, St James, London SW1A 1DD	839 8080
Swaziland	58 Pont Street, London SW1X 0AE	581 4976/7/8
Sweden	11 Montagu Place, London W1H 2AL	724 2101
Switzerland	16/18 Montagu Place, London W1H 2BQ	723 0701
Syria	20 Rue Vaneau, Paris 75007, France	4550 2490
Taiwan	Free Chinese Centre, 4th Floor, Dorland House, 14-16 Regent St, London SW1Y 4PH	930 5767
Tanzania	43 Hertford Street, London W1Y 7TF	499 8951
Thailand	29/30 Queen's Gate, London SW7 5JB	589 0173
Togo	30 Sloane St, London SW1	235 0147/9
Tonga	New Zealand House, 12th Floor, Haymarket, London SW1Y 4TE	839 3287
Trinidad & Tobago	42 Belgrave Square, London SW1X 8NT	245 9351
Tunisia	29 Prince's Gate, London SW7 1QG	584 8117
Turkey	Rutland Lodge, Rutland Gardens, Knightsbridge, London SW7 1BW	589 0360
Turks & Caicos	West India Committee, 48 Albemarle St, London W1X 4AR	629 6355
Uganda	Uganda House, 58/59 Trafalgar Square, London WC2N 5DX	839 5783/9
United Arab Emirates	48 Prince's Gate, London SW7 2QA	589 3434
USSR	5 Kensington Palace Gdns, London W8 4QS	229 3215/6
United States	5 Upper Grosvenor Street, London W1A 2JB	499 3443
Uruguay	48 Lennox Gardens, London SW1X 0DL	589 8835
Venezuela	56 Grafton Way, London W1P 5LB	387 6727
Vietnam	12-14 Victoria Road, London W8 5RD	937 1912/8546
North Yemen	41 South Street, London W1Y 5PD	629 9905/8
South Yemen	57 Cromwell Road, London SW7 2ED	584 6607/8
Yugoslavia	7 Lexham Gardens, London W8 5JU	370 6105
Zaïre	26 Chesham Place, London SW1X 8HH	235 6137/8/9
Zambia	2 Palace Gate, London W8 5NG	589 6655

| **Zimbabwe** | Zimbabwe House, 429 Strand, London WC2R 0SA | 836 7755 |

Embassies, High Commissions and Consulates in the United States

Afghanistan	2100 M St, NW, Washington DC 20037	(202) 234 3770
Algeria	2118 Kalorama Rd, NW, Washington DC 20008	(202) 328 5300
Argentina	1600 New Hampshire Ave, NW, Washington DC 20009	(202) 387 0705
Australia	1601 Massachusetts Ave, NW, Washington DC 20036	(202) 797 3000
Austria	2343 Massachusetts Ave, NW, Washington DC, 20008	(202) 483 4474
Bahamas	600 New Hampshire Ave, NW, Washington DC, 20037	(202) 338 3940
Bahrain	2600 Virginia Ave, NW, Washington DC 20037	(202) 324 0741
Bangladesh	3421 Massachusetts Ave, NW, Washington DC 20007	(202) 327 6644
Barbados	2144 Wyoming Ave, NW, Washington DC 20008	(202) 387 7373
Belgium	3330 Garfield St, NW, Washington DC 20008	(202) 333 6900
Benin	2737 Cathedral Ave, NW, Washington DC 20008	(202) 232 6656
Bolivia	3012 Massachusetts Ave, NW, Washington DC 20008	(202) 483 4410
Botswana	4301 Connecticut Ave, NW, Washington DC 20008	(202) 244 4990
Brazil	3006 Massachusetts Ave, NW Washington DC 20008	(202) 797 0100
Burkina Faso	2340 Massachusetts Ave, NW, Washington DC 20008	(202) 332 5577
Bulgaria	2100 16th St, NW, Washington DC 20009	(202) 387 7970
Burundi	2727 Connecticut Ave, NW, Washington DC 20008	(202) 387 4477
Cameroon	2349 Massachusetts Ave, NW, Washington DC 20008	(202) 265 8790
Canada	1746 Massachusetts Ave, NW, Washington DC 20036	(202) 785 1400
Cape Verde	1120 Connecticut Ave, NW, Washington DC 20036	(202) 659 3148
Central African Republic	1618 22nd St, NW, Washington DC 20008	(202) 483 7800
Chad	1901 Spruce Drive, NW, Washington DC 20012	(202) 882 2999
Chile	1732 Massachusetts Ave, NW, Washington DC 20012	(202) 785 1746
China	2300 Connecticut Ave, NW, Washington DC 20008	(202) 328 2500
Colombia	2118 Leroy Place, NW, Washington DC 20008	(202) 387 5828
Congo	14 E. 65th St, New York, NY 10021	(212) 744 7840
Costa Rica	2112 S St, NW, Washington DC 20008	(202) 234 2945
Cuban Interests	2630 16th St, NW, Washington DC 20009	(202) 797 8518
Cyprus	2211 R St, NW, Washington DC 20008	(202) 462 5772
Czechoslovakia	3900 Linnean Ave, NW, Washington DC 20008	(202) 363 6315
Denmark	3200 Whitehaven St, NW, Washington DC 20008	(202) 234 4300
Dominican Rep.	1715 22nd St, NW, Washington DC 20008	(202) 332 6280
Ecuador	2535 15th St, NW, Washington DC 20009	(202)234 7200
Egypt	2310 Decatur Place, NW, Washington DC 20008	(202) 232 5400
El Salvador	2308 California St, NW, Washington DC 20008	(202) 265 3480
Equatorial Guinea	801 Second Ave, New York, NY 1001	(212) 599 1523
Ethiopia	2134 Kalorama Road, NW, Washington DC 20008	(202) 234 2281
Fiji	1629 K St, NW, Washington DC 20006	(202) 296 3928
Finland	3216 New Mexico Ave, NW, Washington DC 20016	(202) 363 2430

France	2535 Belmont Road, NW, Washington DC 20008	(202) 328 2600
Gabon	2034 20th St, NW, Washington DC 20009	(202) 797 1000
Gambia	1785 Massachusetts Ave, Washington DC 20036	(202) 265 3532
East Germany	1717 Massachusetts Ave, NW, Washington DC 20036	(202) 232 3134
West Germany	4645 Reservoir road, NW, Washington DC 20007	(202) 298 4000
Ghana	2460 16th St, NW, Washington DC 20007	(202) 462 0761
Greece	2221 Massachusetts Ave, NW, Washington DC 20008	(202) 667 3168
Grenada	1424 16th St, NW, Washington DC 20036	(202) 347 3198
Guatemala	2220 R St, NW, Washington DC 20008	(202) 332 2865
Guinea	2112 Leroy Place, NW, Washington DC 20008	(202) 483 9420
Guinea-Bissau	211 E 43rd St, New York, NY 10017	(212) 661 3977
Guyana	2490 Tracy Place, NW, Washington DC 20008	(202) 265 6900
Haiti	2311 Massachusetts Ave, NW, Washington DC 20008	(202) 332 4090
Honduras	4301 Connecticut Ave, NW, Washington DC 20008	(202) 966 7700
Hungary	3910 Shoemaker St, NW, Washington DC 20008	(202) 862 6730
Iceland	2022 Connecticut Ave, NW, Washington DC 20008	(202) 265 6653
India	2107 Massachusetts Ave, NW, Washington DC 20008	(202) 265 6653
Indonesia	2020 Massachusetts Ave, NW, Washington DC 20036	(202) 293 1745
Iraq	1801 P St, NW, Washington DC 20036	(202) 483 7500
Ireland	2234 Massachusetts Ave, NW, Washington DC 20008	(202) 462 3939
Israel	3514 International Drive, NW, Washington DC 20008	(202) 364 5500
Italy	1601 Fuller St, NW, Washington DC 20009	(202) 328 5500
Ivory Coast	2424 Massachusetts Ave, NW, Washington DC 20008	(202) 483 2400
Jamaica	1850 K St, NW, Washington DC 20009	(202) 452 0660
Japan	2520 Massachusetts Ave, NW, Washington DC 20008	(202) 234 2266
Jordan	2319 Wyoming Ave, NW, Washington DC 20008	(202) 265 1606
Kenya	2249 R. St, NW, Washington DC 20008	(202) 287 6101
South Korea	2370 Massachusetts Ave, NW, Washington DC 20008	(202) 483 7383
Kuwait	2940 Tilden St, NW, Washington DC 20008	(202) 966 0702
Laos	2222 S St, NW, Washington DC 20008	(202) 462 8600
Lebanon	2560 28th St, NW, Washington DC 20008	(202) 462 8600
Lesotho	1601 Connecticut Ave, NW, Washington DC 20009	(202) 462 4190
Liberia	5201 16th St, NW, Washington DC 20011	(202) 723 0437
Libya	1118 22nd St, NW, Washington DC 20037	(202) 452 1290
Luxembourg	2200 Massachusetts Ave, NW, Washington DC 20008	(202) 265 4171
Madagascar	2374 Massachusetts Ave, NW, Washington DC 20008	(202) 265 5525
Malawi	1400 20th St, NW, Washington DC 20036	(202) 296 5530
Malaysia	2401 Massachusetts Ave, NW, Washington DC 20008	(202) 328 2700
Mali	2130 R St, NW, Washington DC 20008	(202) 462 3611
Mauritania	2129 Leroy Place, NW, Washington DC 20008	(202) 232 5700
Mauritius	4310 Connecticut Ave, NW, Washington DC 20008	(202) 244 1491
Mexico	2829 16th St, NW, Washington DC 20009	(202) 234 6000
Morocco	1601 21st St, NW, Washington DC 20009	(202) 462 7979
Nepal	2131 Leroy Place, NW, Washington DC 20008	(202) 667 4550
Netherlands	4200 Linnean Ave, NW, Washington DC 20008	(202) 244 5300
New Zealand	37 Observatory Circle, Washington DC 20008	(202) 328 4800

Nicaragua	1627 New Hampshire Ave, Washington DC 20009	(202) 387 4371
Niger	2204 R St, NW, Washington DC 20008	(202) 483 4224
Nigeria	2201 M St, NW, Washington DC 2003	(202) 223 9300
Norway	2720 34th St, NW, Washington DC 20008	(202) 333 6000
Oman	2342 Massachusetts Ave, NW, Washington DC 20008	(202) 287 1980
Pakistan	2315 Massachusetts Ave, NW, Washington DC 20008	(202) 332 8330
Panama	2862 McGill Terrace, NW, Washington DC 20008	(202) 483 1406
Papua New Guinea	1140 19th St, NW, Washington DC 20039	(202) 659 0856
Paraguay	2400 Massachusetts Ave, Washington DC 20008	(202) 483 6960
Peru	1700 Massachusetts Ave, NE, Washington DC 20036	(202) 833 9860
Philippines	1617 Massachusetts Ave, NW, Washington DC 20036	(202) 483 1414
Poland	2640 16th St, NW, Washington DC 20009	(202) 234 3800
Portugal	2125 Kalorama Road, NW, Washington DC 20008	(202) 256 1643
Qatar	600 New Hampshire Ave, NW, Washington DC 20037	(202) 338 0111
Romania	1607 23rd St, NW, Washington DC 20008	(202) 232 4747
Rwanda	1714 New Hampshire Ave, NW, Washington DC 20009	(202) 232 2882
Saint Lucia	41 E 42nd St, New York, NY 10017	(212) 6979360
Western Samoa	211 E 43rd St, New York NY 10017	(212) 682 1482
Saudi Arabia	1520 18th St, NW, Washington DC 20036	(202) 483 2100
Senegal	2112 Wyoming Ave, NW, Washington DC 20008	(202) 234 0540
Seychelles	820 Second Ave, New York, NY 1001	(212) 687 9766
Sierra Leone	1701 19th St, NW, Washington DC 20009	(202) 265 7700
Singapore	1824 R St, NW, Washington DC 20009	(202) 667 7555
Somalia	600 New Hampshire Ave, NW, Washington DC 20037	(202) 234 3261
South Africa	3051 Massachusetts Ave, NW, Washington DC 20008	(202) 232 4400
Spain	27000 15th St, NW, Washington DC 20009	(202) 265 0190
Sri Lanka	2148 Wyoming Ave, NW, Washington DC 20008	(202) 403 4025
Sudan	600 New Hampshire Ave, NW, Washington DC 20037	(202) 338 8565
Swaziland	4301 Connecticut Ave, NW, Washington DC 20008	(202) 362 6683
Sweden	600 New Hampshire Ave, Washington DC 20037	(202) 298 3500
Switzerland	2900 Cathedral Ave, NW, Washington DC 20008	(202) 462 1811
Suriname	2600 Virginia Ave, NW, Washington DC 20037	(202) 338 6980
Syria	2215 Wyoming Ave, NW, Washington DC 20008	(202) 232 6313
Tanzania	2139 R St, NW, Washington DC 20008	(202) 232 0501
Thailand	2300 Kalorama Road, NW, Washington DC 20008	(202) 667 1446
Togo	2208 Massachusetts Ave, NW, Washington DC 20008	(202) 234 4212
Trinidad & Tobago	1708 Massachusetts Ave, NW, Washington DC 20036	(202) 467 6490
Tunisia	2408 Massachusetts Ave, NW, Washington DC 20008	(202) 234 6644
Turkey	1606 23rd St, NW, Washington DC 20008	(202) 667 6400
Uganda	5909 16th St, NW, Washington DC 20011	(202) 726 7100
USSR	1125 16th St, NW, Washington DC 20036	(202) 628 7551
United Arab Emirates	600 New Hampshire Ave, NW, Washington DC 20037	(202) 338 6500
United Kingdom	3100 Massachusetts Ave, NW, Washington DC 20009	(202) 452 1340
Uruguay	1918 F St, NW, Washington DC 20006	(202) 331 1313
Venezuela	2445 Massachusetts Ave, NW, Washington DC 20008	(202) 797 3800

North Yemen	600 New Hampshire Ave, NW, Washington DC 20037	(202) 965 4760
Yugoslavia	2410 California St, NW, Washington DC 20008	(202) 462 6566
Zaïre	1800 New Hampshire Ave, NW, Washington DC 20009	(202) 234 7690
Zambia	2419 Massachusetts Ave, NW, Washington DC 20008	(202) 265 9717

VISA REQUIREMENTS

Country Travelling To	Australia	Canada	New Zealand	UK	USA	Restrictions and Requirements
Afghanistan	Yes	Yes	Yes	Yes	Yes	Only allowed into Kabul. If on business need clearance from Kabul.
Albania	Yes	Yes	Yes	Yes	Yes	* Group visas only.
Algeria	Yes	Yes	Yes	No	Yes	If wish to stay more than 3 mths need a *permit de sejour* obtainable from nearest 'Wilaya'.
American Samoa	No	No	No	No	No	Need visa if over 30 days.
Andorra	No	No	No	No	No	
Angola	Yes	Yes	Yes	Yes	Yes	Letter of invitation from Launda needed.
Anguilla	No	No	No	No	No	
Antigua & Barbuda	No*	No*	No*	No*	No*	* Must have return ticket.
Argentina	Yes	*	Yes	Yes	Yes	* Tourists don't require visas, others do. Must be able to prove solvency.
Australia	—	Yes	No	Yes	Yes	
Austria	No*	No*	No*	No*	No*	* Up to 3 mths; UK to 6 mths.
Bahamas	No	No	No	No	No	
Bahrain	Yes	Yes	Yes	No*	Yes	* Exemption only for those born in or living in UK.
Bangladesh	Yes	No*	No	Yes	Yes	* Yes, if stay exceeds 30 days.
Barbados	Yes	Yes	Yes	No	No	
Belguim	No	No	No	No	No	

Country							Notes
Belize	Yes	Yes	Yes	Yes	No	No	7 days only.
Benin	Yes	Yes	Yes	Yes	Yes	Yes	* Must have a return ticket
Bermuda	No*	No*	No*	No*	No*	No*	
Bhutan	Yes	Yes	Yes	Yes	Yes	Yes	* Tourists don't/others do.
Bolivia	Yes	No	No	No*	No*	No*	
Botswana	No	No	No	No	No	No	
Brazil	Yes	No*	Yes	No*	Yes	Yes	* Need passport endorsed for Brazil (must not expire within 6 mths from date of arrival), a roundtrip ticket and funds to meet expenses.
British Virgin Is	No	No	No	No	No	No	
Brunei	Yes	No (1)	Yes	No (2)	Yes	Yes	1) Up to 14 days. 2) Up to 30 days. British Overseas Citizens require visa. All must have return ticket and sufficient funds.
Bulgaria	Yes	Yes	Yes	Yes	Yes	Yes	Company letter and letter of invitation required for business.
Burkina Faso	Yes	Yes	Yes	Yes	Yes	Yes	Return ticket. Company letter for business visa.
Burma	Yes*	Yes*	Yes*	Yes*	Yes*	Yes*	* Valid for seven days only. No land border crossings. Company letter for business.
Burundi	Yes	Yes	Yes	Yes	Yes	Yes	Return or onward ticket. Sponsorship for business visa.
Cameroon	Yes*	Yes*	Yes*	Yes*	Yes*	Yes*	* Must have return ticket.
Canada	No	—	No	No*	No	No	* British Overseas Citizens need visa.

Country Travelling To	Visa Requirements						Restrictions and Requirements
	Australia	Canada	New Zealand	UK	USA		
Cape Verde	Yes	Yes	Yes	Yes	Yes		Return or onward ticket required.
Cayman Islands	No	No	No	No	No		Return or onward ticket required.
Cent. African Rep	Yes	Yes	Yes	Yes	Yes		
Chad	Yes	Yes	Yes	Yes	Yes		
Chile	No	No	Yes	No	No		
China	Yes	Yes	Yes	Yes	Yes		Formal invit. for business visa.
Colombia	Yes	No	Yes	No*	Yes		* Return or onward ticket required. Business visa needed.
Congo	Yes	Yes	Yes	Yes	Yes		Company letter in French. Apply to Brazzaville.
Cook Islands	No*	No*	No*	No*	No*		* Up to 31 days. Need entry permit. Must have return ticket.
Costa Rica	No (1)	No*	No (1)	No	No (1)		* Need visa after 30 days. 1) Can get Tourist Card if have return ticket. Issued by airlines.
Côte D'Ivoire	Yes	Yes	Yes	No	Yes		
Cuba	Yes	Yes	Yes	Yes	Yes		Company letter for business visa. Personal letter for tourists.
Cyprus	No	No	No	No	No		
Czechoslovakia	Yes	Yes	Yes	Yes	Yes		Letter of invitation for business visas.
Denmark	No*	No*	No*	No*	No*		* Need visa if stay over 3 months.

Djibouti	Yes*	Yes*	Yes*	Yes*	Yes*	* Need return ticket.
Dominica	No	No	No	No	No	
Dominican Republic	Yes	Yes	Yes	No	Yes	UK passport holders of Chinese descent or born in Hong Kong need visa.
Eastern Caribbean	No	No	No	No	No	
Ecuador	No*	No*	No*	No*	No*	* Need visa if staying over 3 mths.
Egypt	Yes*	Yes*	Yes*	Yes*	Yes*	* Visitors must register with the Ministry of the Interior at al-Mugama within 7 days of arrival in Egypt.
El Salvador	Yes*	No	Yes*	No	No	* Valid for 90 days.
Equatorial Guinea	Yes	Yes	Yes	Yes	Yes	
Ethiopia	Yes	Yes	Yes	Yes	Yes	Return or onward ticket. Letter of financial standing.
Fiji	No	No	No	No	No	Return or onward ticket.
Finland	No	No	No	No	No	
France	Yes	Yes	Yes	No	Yes	
French Guiana	No	No	No	No	No	Return ticket required.
French Polynesia	Yes	Yes (1)	Yes	No	Yes (1)	1) 3 mth visa issued on arrival. Return ticket required.
French West Indies	Yes	No (1)	Yes	No (2)	No (1)	1) Up to 21 days. 2) Up to 3 mths.
Gabon	Yes	YEs	Yes	Yes	Yes	Company letter needed for business visa.
Gambia	No*	No*	No*	No*	Yes	* Up to 3 mths. Company letter required for business visa.

Country Travelling To	Visa Requirements						Restrictions and Requirements
	Australia	Canada	New Zealand	UK	USA		
East Germany	Yes	Yes	Yes	Yes	Yes		Must have confirmed accommodation booking. Company letter for business visa.
West Germany	No*	No*	No*	No	No*		* Up to 3 mths.
Ghana	Yes*	Yes*	Yes*	Yes*	Yes*		* Commonwealth citizens need an Entry Permit, company letter and return ticket.
Gibraltar	No	No	No	No	No		
Greece	No	No	No	No	No		Up to 3 mths.
Grenada	No*	No*	No*	No*	No*		* Up to 3 mths. Need a return ticket and proof of funds.
Guatemala	Yes	Yes*	Yes	Yes*	Yes*		* Up to 30 days, and with a return ticket, and visible means of support, a tourist card is OK. Covering letter needed for business visas.
Guinea-Bissau	Yes	Yes	Yes	Yes	Yes		
Guinea	*	*	*	*	*		* No tourist visas.
Guyana	Yes	Yes	Yes	yes	Yes		Company letter for business visas.
Haiti	Yes	No (2)	Yes	No (1)	No (2)		1) Tourist card obtained on arrival. Must have onward ticket. 2) Up to 30 days.
Honduras	Yes*	Yes*	Yes*	No	Yes*		* Tourist cards available for 30 days if only on holiday. Extendable for up to 6 mths.

Hong Kong	No (2)	No (2)	No (2)	Yes	Yes	1) Up to 3 mths. 2) Up to 1 mth.
Hungary	Yes	Yes	Yes	Yes	Yes	
Iceland	No*	No*	No*	No*	No*	* Need return ticket.
India	Yes	Yes	Yes	Yes	Yes	
Indonesia	No*	No*	No*	No*	No*	*Up to 60 days. For tourist purposes only. Must have return or onward ticket.
Iran	Yes*	Yes*	Yes*	Yes*	YEs*	* Cannot stay in Iran. Can get a transit visa which lasts for 2 weeks and allows you to pass through into Pakistan.
Iraq	Yes*	Yes*	Yes*	Yes*	Yes*	* Business visas only. Must get letter of invitation.
Ireland	No	No	No	No	No	
Israel	Yes*	Yes*	Yes*	No (1)	Yes*	* Obtained free on arrival. 1) Onward or return ticket. Max. Stay 3 mths.
Italy	No	No	No	No	No	Up to 90 days.
Jamaica	No (1)	No (2)	No (1)	N0 (1)	No (2)	1) Up to 3 mths. 2) Need proof of citizenship and return ticket for visit not exceeding 6 mths.
Japan	Yes	No (1)	No (1)	No (2)	Yes	1) Up to 3 mths. 2) Up to 6 mths.
Jordan	Yes	Yes	Yes	Yes	Yes	Company letter for business visa.
Kenya	Yes	No	No	No*	Yes	* Visa needed by UK citizens of Asian origin. Visitor's Pass issued on arrival.
Kiribati	Yes	No (1)	Yes	No (2)	Yes	1) Up to 20 days. 2) Up to 21 days.

Country Travelling To	Visa Requirements						Restrictions and Requirements
	Australia	Canada	New Zealand	UK	USA		
North Korea	Yes	Yes	Yes	Yes	Yes		
South Korea	No (1)	No (1)	No (1)	No (2)	No (1)		1) Up to 15 days 2) Up to 60 days.
Kuwait	Yes	Yes	Yes	Yes	Yes		Valid for 28 days.
Laos	Yes	Yes	Yes	Yes	Yes		Permission needed from Ministry of Foreign Affairs, Vientiane.
Lebanon	*	*	*	*	*		* Business only. Need company letter, invitation and approval.
Lesotho	No	No	No	No	No		
Liberia	Yes	Yes	Yes	Yes	Yes		Company letter stating nature of business for business visa.
Libya	Yes	Yes	Yes	Yes	No*		* Only if on business with sponsorship letter from Libyan company. No single women under 35.
Luxembourg	No*	No*	No*	No*	No*		* Up to 3 mths.
Macau	No	No	No	No	No		
Madagascar	Yes	Yes	Yes	Yes	Yes		Letter of recommendation for business visa. Return ticket or evidence of sufficient funds.
Malawi	No*	No*	No*	No*	No*		* Up to 6 mths. Must have return ticket or evidence of sufficient funds.
Malaysia	No (1)	No (1)	No (1)	No (1)	No (2)		1) Up to 6 mths. 2) Up to 3 mths. Must have return ticket or evidence of sufficient funds.

Country						Notes
Maldives	Yes	Yes	Yes	Yes	Yes	Up to 30 days. Issued free on arrival at Male Airport.
Mali	Yes	Yes	Yes	Yes	Yes	1 month only. Must have letter of recommendation for business visa.
Malta	No	No	No	No	No	
Mauritania	Yes	Yes	Yes	Yes	Yes	
Mauritius	No	No	No	No	No	Up to 3 mths.
Mexico	Yes	No*	Yes	No*	No*	* Need to get tourist card which is free of charge, business card isn't. Apply as for visa.
Micronesia	No*	No*	No*	No*	No	* If tourist, for up to 30 days. Authorisation at point of entry.
Mongolia	Yes	Yes	Yes	Yes	Yes	
Morocco	No*	No*	No*	No*	No*	* Up to 3 mths.
Mozambique	Yes	Yes	Yes	Yes	Yes	Need company letter stating business and contacts.
Nauru	Yes	Yes	Yes	Yes	Yes	
Nepal	Yes*	Yes*	Yes*	Yes*	Yes*	* Valid for 3 mths.
Netherlands	No*	No*	No*	No*	No*	* Up to 3 mths.
Netherlands Antilles	No*	No*	No*	No*	No*	Certificate of temp. admission issued on arrival.
New Caledonia	No	No (2)	No	No (1)	No (2)	1) Up to 3 mths. 2) Must have confirmed onward or return tickets and proof of funds.

Country Travelling To	Visa Requirements					Restrictions and Requirements
	Australia	Canada	New Zealand	UK	USA	
New Zealand	No	No (2)	—	No (1)	No (2)	1) Up to 6 mths 2) Up to 3 mths. Need onward ticket and sufficient funds.
	*					
Nicaragua	Yes	No*	Yes	No*	No*	★ Return ticket. Max. stay 90 days.
Niger	yes	Yes	Yes	No	YEs	Max. stay 6 mths. Onward or return ticket needed.
Nigeria	Yes	Yes	Yes	yes	Yes	★ Need return ticket and letter of recommendation.
Niue	Yes	Yes	Yes	Yes	Yes	
Norfolk Island	Yes	Yes	Yes	Yes	Yes	
Norway	No	No	No	No	No	
Oman	*	*	*	*	*	★ Not issuing tourist visas at present. To go to Oman you need a sponsor in Oman to apply for a 'No Objection Certificate' (allows you to travel for 3 mths).
Pakistan	No (1)	No (1)	No (1)	Yes	No (2)	1) Up to 3 mths. 2) Up to 1 mth.
Panama	Yes	No*	Yes	No	No*	★ If possessing a tourist card, for up to 90 days. Onward or return ticket. Company letter for business visa.
Papua New Guinea	No*	No*	No*	No*	No*	★ Up to 30 days, if entering by air to Port Moresby. All need return ticket, evidence of sufficient funds. Company letter for business visa.

						Notes
Paraguay	Yes	No*	Yes	No*	No*	* Up to 90 days. Tourist card issued on arrival.
Peru	Yes	No*	Yes	No*	No*	Tourist card issued by carrier. Company letter for business visa. Onward/return ticket needed.
Philippines	No*	No*	No*	No*	No*	* Up to 21 days. Onward or return ticket.
Poland	Yes*	Yes*	Yes*	Yes*	Yes*	*Valid for 90 days. Letter of invitation for business visa.
Portugal	No (1)	No (2)	Yes	No (3)	No (2)	1) Up to 3 mths. 2) Need visa for Azores. 3) Up to 2 mths.
Qatar	Yes	Yes	Yes	No*	Yes	UK passport holders not born or living in UK need visa.
Réunion	No	No	No	No	No	
Romania	Yes	Yes	Yes	Yes	Yes	Company letter for business visa.
Rwanda	Yes	Yes	Yes	Yes	Yes	Plus certificate of moral conduct.
St Christopher & Nevis	No	No	No	No	No	
St Lucia	No	No	No	No	No	
Western Samoa	No	No	No	No	No	Up to 30 days. Permission needed from New Zealand Dept of Maori & Island Affairs.
Sao Tomé & Principe	Yes	Yes	Yes	Yes	Yes	
Saudi Arabia	Yes	Yes	Yes	Yes	Yes	No tourist visas. Need letter of invitation from Saudi govt. and AIDS free certificate.

Country Travelling To	Visa Requirements					Restrictions and Requirements
	Australia	Canada	New Zealand	UK	USA	
Senegal	Yes	Yes	Yes	Yes	Yes	Plus return ticket. Company letter for business visa.
Seychelles	No	No	No	No	No	6 weeks pass issued free. Renewable up to 3 months.
Sierra Leone	Yes	Yes	Yes	Yes	Yes	Company letter for business visa.
Singapore	No	No	No	No	No	Return ticket or evidence of sufficient funds.
Solomon Islands	No	No	No	No	No	
Somalia	Yes	Yes	Yes	Yes	Yes	
South Africa	Yes	Yes	Yes	No	Yes	Return ticket needed. Employer's letter for business visas.
Soviet Union	Yes	Yes	Yes	Yes	Yes	Letter of invitation for business visa.
Spain	Yes	No*	Yes	No*	No*	* Up to 90 days.
Sri Lanka	No*	No*	No*	No*	No*	* Up to 6 mths. Do need visa plus employer's letter for business visas.
Sudan	Yes	Yes	Yes	Yes	Yes	Letter stating business needed for business visa.
Suriname	Yes	No*	Yes	No*	Yes	* Must have onward or return ticket and tourist card, obtainable on arrival.
Swaziland	No	No	No	No	No	
Sweden	No	No	No	No	No	Up to 3 mths.
Switzerland	No	No	No	No	No	
Syria	Yes	Yes	Yes	*Yes	Yes	* No visas to UK citizens at present.

	No (2)	No (1)	No (2)	No (2)	No (1)	1) Up to 3 mths. 2) Up to 1 mth.
Tahiti	No	Yes	Yes	Yes	Yes	
Taiwan	Yes	Yes	Yes	Yes	Yes	Letter of introduction from Taiwan trade or information service will do if there is no diplomatic representation.
Tanzania	No*	No*	No*	No*	Yes	* Need visitors' pass. Letter of invitation for business.
Thailand	No*	No*	No*	Yes	No*	* Up to 15 days. If leaving by rail need visa. Company letter if on business.
Togo	Yes	Yes	Yes	No*	No*	* Up to 90 days. Company letter if on business.
Tonga	No	No	No	No	Yes	
Trinidad & Tobago	No	No	No	No	No	Onward or return ticket needed.
Tunisia	Yes*	No	Yes*	No	No	* Delivered on arrival.
Turkey	No*	No*	No*	No*	No*	* Up to 90 days.
Turks & Caicos Islands	No	No	No	No	No	
Tuvalu	No	No	No	No	Yes	
Uganda	No	No	No	No	Yes	Company letter for business visa.
United Arab Emirates	Yes	Yes	Yes	No*	Yes	* Up to 30 days, if you have right of abode in UK. Sponsorship letter for business visa.
United Kingdom	No	No	No	—	No	
United States	Yes*	No	Yes*	Yes*	—	* Also evidence to prove you will be leaving the country.

Country Travelling To	Visa Requirements					Restrictions and Requirements
	Australia	Canada	New Zealand	UK	USA	
Uruguay	Yes	No	Yes	No	No	
Vanuatu	No	No	No	No	No	
Venezuela	No*	No*	No*	No*	No*	* Tourist card issued by carrier. Onward or return ticket needed.
Vietnam	Yes*	Yes*	Yes*	Yes*	Yes*	* Group visas only, unless sponsored.
North Yemen	Yes	Yes	Yes	Yes	Yes	Company letter if on business.
South Yemen	Yes*	Yes*	Yes*	Yes*	Yes*	* Need to have booked accommodation before going and a return ticket. Letter of invitation and company letter needed if on business.
Yugoslavia	Yes	Yes	Yes	No*	Yes	* Up to 3 mths.
Zaïre	Yes	Yes	Yes	Yes	Yes	Sponsorship letter certified by govt. if on business.
Zambia	No	No	Yes	No	Yes	
Zimbabwe	No	No	No	No	No	Return ticket required.

Notes:
1) This listing has been put together mainly for the benefit of tourists. Many more countries will require a visa if you are travelling on business.
2) Many countries will demand visas of British Overseas Citizens and UK citizens of Asian origin, so double-check before travelling.

Nationalities Banned Entry

In the interests of space, we have left out the ban on *South Africans* and *Israelis* which are so wide-reaching that nationals of these countries should automatically check whether they are allowed entry. Roughly speaking, Israelis are barred from any Muslim country and South Africans from any predominantly black country, and the bar will also spread to other countries which have close ties.

NB: Travellers should also note that having a stamp in your passport from a barred country can be enough to stop you entering. If you wish, for instance, to go to both Israel and some of the Arab countries, you should get a second passport.

Algeria	Korea, Malawi, Taiwan and Vietnam need special permission.
Australia	Taiwanese must get special permission. Members of racially-segregated sporting groups.
Benin	Morocco, Iran, Iraq.
Bulgaria	South Korea, Taiwan and Northern Cyprus.
Burma	Taiwan, North Korea.
Canada	Bophuthatswana, Ciskei, Transkei, and Venda and passports issued by All Palestine Govt.
Costa Rica	Gypsies, persons of 'unkempt appearance' or without funds ($200 min.).
Côte d'Ivoire	Lebanese living in Liberia.
Egypt	Taiwan, South Yemen, Libya – unless married to an Egyptian national.
France	No admittance via Strasbourg or Tarbes to nationals of Bulgaria, Czechoslovakia, East Germany, Hungary, Poland, Romania and USSR.
Gabon	Angola, Benin, Cape Verde, Cuba, Ghana, Guinea-Bissau, Haiti and Sao Tomé et Principe.
Greece	Nationals of, and people who have visited since 'independence' on November 15, 1983, Turkish Cyprus.
Guinea	Journalists, unless invited by the Government.
Hungary	South Korea.
India	Afghans who have boarded a flight in Pakistan.
Indonesia	Portugal.
Iran	Jordan and Morocco. 'Immodestly dressed' women (Islamic standard).
Japan	Taiwan, North Korea.
Libya	Lebanese with passports issued after 1976.
Malaysia	China, Cuba, North Korea, Taiwan, Vietnam. Anyone not conforming to the dress standard.
Mauritius	Botsphuthatswana, Taiwan, Transkei, Venda.
Morocco	Iran. Anyone scruffy.
Mozambique	Foreigners who were formerly Mozambiquan citizens and didn't renounce it in 1975.
Nepal	Taiwan.
New Zealand	North Korea, Taiwan, Bophuthatswana, Ciskei, Transkei, Venda, Northern Cyprus, and holders of old Rhodesian passports.
Pakistan	Afghanistan.
Papua New Guinea	Taiwan.
Paraguay	Russia, Cuba and all countries with a Communist Government.
Philippines	Passports given by former govts. of Kampuchea or South Vietnam.

Saudi Arabia	South Yemen.
Syria	South Korea, Taiwan.
Taiwan	China.
Tanzania	South Korea, Taiwan.
Thailand	Anyone scruffy. Afghanistan.
Vanuatu	People of doubtful morality. People who might become a public charge.
Zimbabwe	South Korea, Taiwan.

Exit Visas

This list, for the sake of space, includes only those countries which do require some form of exit visa. In other countries it is levied as an airport departure tax (*see list on page 625*). As most countries require some sort of exit visa for nationals and residents, these have not been included.

Afghanistan	Yes, from Immigration Office, unless in transit for less than 72 hours, or if on a tourist visa for 1 mth or less.
Angola	Yes, for all. Apply at the same time as for entry visa.
Benin	Exit visa required. Ask when applying for entry visa.
Burma	Exit visas required by travellers staying more than 30 days. D Form from Immigration and Manpower Dept., Rangoon.
Cameroon	Exit visa plus income tax clearance certificateneeded by all except if on a transit visa.
Central African Rep.	Yes, except for US nationals.
Chad	Yes, if staying longer than 24 hours.
China	Yes, obtain with entry visa.
Comoro Islands	Yes, except if on a service or diplomaticpassport.
Congo	Yes. 48 hours before departure from Emigration Office. Free on proof of having paid your hotel bill.
Cook Islands	Yes, if staying over 30 days. Plus taxclearance.
Cost Rica	Exit visa required if staying over 30 days.
Cuba	Yes, if you have stayed more than 90 days.While you wait from Immigration Office.
El Salvador	Yes, if not on a tourist or transit visa.
Equ. Guinea	Yes, but can usually be arranged at airport.
Ethiopia	Exit visa required if staying over 30 days.
East Germany	Exit visa usually given free to tourists with the entry visa.
Honduras	Yes, if staying over 90 days.
India	No visa required, but you must have your Registration Certificate endorsed before departure. This is done by the Superintendent of Police in all District Headquarters.
Iran	Exit visa should be given at the same time as the entry visa. Must register with the police within 48 hours of arrival.
Laos	Yes, can be obtained from Police, or Immigration, Vientiane.
Liberia	No, but register with Immigration Office within 48 hours if planning to stay over 15 days.
Libya	Exit visa required except if on one-entry visa.

Western Samoa	Yes, if staying over 3 mths.
Thailand	Yes, if staying over 90 days.
Togo	Yes, if staying over 10 days. Apply at least 48 hours in advance to Sûrete Nationale after confirming reservations.
Vietnam	Yes.
North Yemen	Yes, if staying over 7 days. Free from Immigration Dept.Yes, but contained with entry visa.

Restrictions on Working Around the World

Afghanistan	Not granting visas at present, so no work possible.
Algeria	Only possible if with a company that has a govt contract. Need a work permit if staying more than 3 mths and must produce diplomas.
Andorra	There is an annual allocation of work permits that must be applied for personally in Andorra – after the applicant has secured a position.
Antigua & Barbuda	Work permits required. You can only work if locals cannot perform the function. Must arrange the permit in advance.
Argentina	Need a work permit.
Australia	Must have a work permit – they are not easy to get hold of.
Austria	Work permits are required for *all* types of employment, but are never issued for part-time employment.
Bahamas	Need a work permit, but no expatriate may be offered employment in a post for which a suitably qualified Bahamian is available. You may not apply once in the country. Rigidly enforced.
Bahrain	Employer must get permit in Bahrain and send it to the employee to be stamped by the embassy in his own country. Difficult to get renewed.
Barbados	Must have sponsorship from a local employer. Permits only given to people with specialist skills needed by the country.
Bangladesh	Can work for up to three months without a permit.
Barbados	Work permits are issued to employers not employees – you must apply for a job beforehand.
Belgium	The Belgian employer must apply for the permit.
Belize	Work permit required. Must have job offer for which there are no suitable nationals. Apply to Ministry of Labour, Belmopan.
Bhutan	Can work by government invitation only.
Bermuda	Must have a job and work permit before entering.
Benin	Need to have a contract with a company of the Benin Government before applying.
Bolivia	Only residents in Bolivia are allowed employment.
Botswana	Need work permit. No rigid restrictions and there are usually jobs available.
Brazil	Working visas are only issued on the presentation of a work contract, duly certified by the Brazilian Ministry of Labour.
British Virgin Islands	Work permit required.
Brunei	Work permit required in all cases. Must be proposed by a registered Brunei company and have trade qualifications and experience above those available locally.
Bulgaria	It is not possible to get a work permit.
Burma	Government approval required.

Cameroon	You need a work permit, which can be obtained in the Cameroon.
Canada	Work permit required. Must apply from outside the country. Will not be granted if there is a permanent resident or qualified Canadian for the job.
Cayman Islands	You must satisfy the Cayman Protection Board that no local can do the job to get a work permit. Contact the Dept of Immigration. Permits for 1-5 years usually granted to professionals.
Chile	Must have a contract with a company before applying.
China	No work unless either a teacher or technician when one works under contract.
Cocos (Keeling) Is.	All non-locals work for the Australian Govt. No casual work available.
Colombia	Work visa needed. Normally for 2 years at a time. Renewable. Only granted for work no national can do.
Cook Islands	Apply to New Zealand High Commission for temporary residence permit. Not normally given unless you have special skills not available locally.
Costa Rica	Need a signed contract with employer and 'resident' status to be able to work.
Cuba	It is not possible to work here.
Cyprus	Work permit needed – must be obtained by employer. Usually granted for one year but can be renewed. Can be prosecuted and deported for working without one.
Czechoslovakia	Permission to work involves a complicated procedure – enquire at embassy before you go.
Denmark	Nationals of EEC countries do not need permits. Others do, but they are not being issued at present.
Djibouti	Not much work available.
Dominica	Need work permit obtained from country of origin.
Dominican Rep.	Work permit required.
Eastern Caribbean	Work permit offered only if a national cannot do the job.
Ecuador	Work permit required. Available only if being brought in by an Ecuadorean company for professional reasons (ie training, or for your specialist skills). Must register permit on arrival.
El Salvador	Work permit can be obtained for technical or specialized work. Employer must apply.
Ethiopia	Employer must apply on your behalf to Ministry of Labour and Social Affairs. Casual work forbidden.
Falkland Islands	Employer must apply for work permit.
Fiji	Need a work permit before entering Fiji. Rarely given.
Finland	Work permit required.
France	Nationals of EEC countries do not need work permits. Others do.
Gabon	Work permit required.
Gambia	Work permit required.
East Germany	It is not possible to work here.
West Germany	Nationals of EEC countries do not need permits. Others do, but they are only issued once work has been found.
Ghana	Work permit required.
Gibraltar	All foreign nationals except the British need work permits.
Greece	Need a permit issued by the Greek Ministry of Labour. Yearly, renewable. Employer should also apply.
Grenada	Work permit needed.
Guadeloupe	EEC nationals don't need work permits; others do.
Guyana	Work permit needed.
Haiti	First need to get a *Permit de Séjour*, then your employers must apply for a work permit for you.

Hong Kong   You need a work permit if working in the private sector but not if working for the Hong Kong Government or a UK citizen.

Hungary   Work permit needed. Only granted if you are immigrating permanently. Apply to Foreign Nationals Office, Budapest Police HQ.

Iceland   Need a work permit prior to arrival – prospective employer should apply and prove no suitable Icelander is available. Permits renewable yearly.

India   No permit is needed, but you cannot take the money earned out.

Indonesia   Apply for the work permit through Foreign Affairs Dept. and the Dept of Manpower. Getting more difficult and impossible for casual work Must have a skill not available locally.

Ireland   Not required by EEC citizens, but needed by all others.

Iran   Work permit required.

Iraq   Work permit may be arranged by foreign companies working in Iraq. Otherwise it is impossible.

Israel   Apply to the embassy in your home country with letter from your potential employer.

Italy   Nationals of EEC countries may work without permits. All others need them.

Ivory Coast   You are not allowed to work here unless sent by a private company which will arrange your permit for you.

Jamaica   Work permit required.

Japan   Long-term commercial business visa is needed if working for your own company in Japan. Others require work permits. Can do part-time casual work on a study visa.

Jordan   You can only get work through a local company or a foreign company's local offices.

Kenya   Prospective employer in Kenya must obtain a permit for you before you arrive. Heavy fines/deportation for working without a permit.

South Korea   Need a work permit from the Korean embassy in your normal country of residence.

Kuwait   Need a contract from Kuwait before the permit will be issued. No casual work. Can get 2 year contracts for specialist jobs.

Lesotho   Employer must apply and prove no local is suitable. Permits for 2 years but renewable.

Liberia   Work permit required. Must go to Ministry of Labour and Immigration and Labour and pay lots each time. Permits valid for one year but can be renewed.

Liechtenstein   Very rare to be granted a permit.

Luxembourg   EEC Citizens may work without a permit. All other nationals require one.

Macao   Work permit required.

Madagascar   Not required if working for a cultural institution such as the American School. Most expats working for the govt. More difficult for individuals.

Malawi   Work permit required.

Malaysia   Work permit required. You need a sponsor in Malaysia who agrees to assure your maintenance and repatriation.

Malta   Permits only issued for specialized skills not found on the island.

Mauritius   Work permit required. Must provide good reasons and only available if no local can do the job. Permits usually for one or two years, renewable. Fee payable.

Mexico   No work allowed unless you are specifically requested by a Mexican company.

Morocco   Work permit required. Employer must apply. Permit included with residence certificate.

Nepal   Work permits required. Complex process – usually only possible for aid/embassy staff, govt projects and airlines.

Netherlands   EEC citizens do not need work permits. All other nationalities do.

New Zealand	All nationalities except Australians need a work permit.
Nigeria	Work permit compulsory for all foreigners. Employers are given a yearly quota. Two years, renewable. Some expat wives can get part-time 'unofficial' work.
Norway	Work permit required.
Oman	Work permit required. Need a sponsor – either an Omani company or Omani national. Two years renewable permits for specific employment. Casual labour not allowed.
Panama	Permit required. Apply in Panama.
Papua New Guinea	Permit required – usually for 3 year contract – obtained before arrival. Must be sponsored by an employer. Casual work not allowed.
Paraguay	No permit needed.
Peru	Arrange everything in Peru.
Philippines	Permit required. Only given if you already have a job. Employer should apply.
Poland	Foreigners cannot work in Poland.
Portugal	Work permit required.
Qatar	Must have sponsorship and resident's status. Work permit must be obtained by employer.
American Samoa	Severe restrictions. Immigration approval is necessary first, and this is only granted for special needs and skills that cannot be satisfied locally.
Saudi Arabia	Must obtain job and residence permit before arrival. Formalities horribly complicated, so leave it to your employer.
Senegal	Work permits can be obtained in Dakar with great difficulty for working with international or private organisations. Impossible for semi-private or official companies.
Seychelles	Apply for a Gainful Occupation Permit. Permit granted only if the job cannot be filled locally and for the duration of the contract. Difficult and expensive to get without political connections.
Sierra Leone	Required even for casual labour. Apply to Principal Immigration Officer, who is secretary of the Business Immigration Quota Committee. Non-refundable fee of LE500.
Singapore	All non-residents require work permit. Apply to Ministry of Labour and Dept. of Immigration.
South Africa	Not allowed to accept employment without special permission from the Director General, Internal Affairs.
Spain	Permit needed to work legally.
Sri Lanka	Cannot work without Government approval which is rarely given. 1 year permits occasionally granted for specific projects.
St Christopher & Nevis	Permits required but will only be granted when no national is available. Apply to Ministry of Home Affairs.
Sudan	Permits required. Available for aid workers etc. but more difficult for others.
Swaziland	Work permit required.
Sweden	Work permit required.
Switzerland	Work permit required. Employer must apply. Permit renewable annually.
Syria	Work permits required, but whether you'll get one depends on who you'd be working for.
Tahiti	Work permit difficult to obtain. Employer must apply and ensure the employee's return to his country of origin.
Tanzania	Work permit required. Employer must apply on your behalf. If you haven't got a job, write to the ministry concerned with your field to offer your services.
Tibet	Generally no foreigners allowed to work, but a few teachers are being given one year contracts for Lhasa.
Togo	Work permit required.

Tonga	Work permit required. Length of permit depends on individual circumstances.
Trinidad & Tobago	Work permit required. Employer must apply.
Tunisia	Work permit required. Need a job contract before applying to the Ministry of Social Affairs. Only for those skills unobtainable in the country.
Turkey	Working visa required. Minimal restrictions but must apply through prospective employer.
Turks & Caicos	Work and residence permits required.
Uganda	Work permits required – restricted and difficult to obtain. Normally granted for a max. of 3 yrs. for those with skills lacking in Uganda.
United Arab Emirates	Work permit needed. No casual work and permit must be obtained before arrival. Permit normally for 2/3 years dependent on job/nationality. Must be sponsored by a UAE based company or individual.
United Kingdom	Commonwealth nationals aged 17 to 27 can work for two years on a holiday visa. All others need a work permit.
US Virgin Islands	Work permit required.
United States	Work permit (Green Card) required for permanent jobs. Difficult to obtain. Some types of work allowed under exchange or temporary workers' visas.
Uruguay	Work permit needed.
Vanuatu	Work permit required. Given to people in positions which locals can't fill for 1 year. Self-employed prepared to invest US$120,000 receive 3 year permit, renewable annually. Obtained from Labour Dept.
North Yemen	Permit must be obtained by your sponsor before entry. Max. one year.
Yugoslavia	Work permit required.
Zambia	Work permit must be arranged by your employer before you enter. Will only be given for skills not obtainable locally.
Zimbabwe	Apply for a work permit through your prospective employer. Max. stay as an expat is usually 3 years.

Passport Offices
Australia

22 West Row
Canberra City
ACT 2601
Tel: (062) 613810

1 Chifley Square
Sydney
NSW 2000

Mercantile Mutual Building
456 Hunter Street
Newcastle
NSW 2300
Tel: (049) 263655

3rd Floor
Building B,
World Trade Centre
Cnr Spencer and Flinders Sts
Melbourne
Victoria 3000
Tel: (03) 662 1722

Sun Alliance Building
45 Grenfell Street
Adelaide
South Australia 5000
Tel: (08) 212 2466

Commonwealth Government Centre
295 Ann Street
Brisbane
Queensland 4000
Tel: (07) 225 0122

St Martin's Tower
44 George's Terrace
Perth
Western Australia 6000
Tel: (09) 325 4944

4th Floor
T&G Building
Cnr Collins and Murray Sts
Hobart
Tasmania 7000
Tel: (002) 204050

Arkaba House
Esplanade
Darwin
Northern Territories 5790
Tel: (089) 814566

Passport applications can also be submitted to any official Australian Post Office.

Canada

Suite 800
Royal Bank Bldg
10 Jasper Avenue
Edmonton T5J 1WB
Tel: (403) 420 2622/3

Suite 215
West Tower
Guy Favreau Complex
200 Dorchester Blvd West
Montreal H27 1X4
Tel: (514) 283 2152

10th Floor
Suite 1000
2590 Blvd Laurier
Saint-Foy
Quebec G1V 4M6
Tel: (418) 648 4990/2

Box 171
Suite 1031
7 Atrium on Bay
20 Dundas West
Toronto M5G 2C2
Tel: (416) 973 3251

Dept of External Affairs
Ottawa
Ontario K1A 0GJ
Tel: (613) 995 8481

220 4th Ave E
Calgary
Alberta T2G 4X3
Tel: (403) 231 5171

Suite 601
440 King St
Fredericton
New Brunswick
E3B 5H8
Tel: (506) 452 3900

Suite 1210
Barrington Tower
Scotia Square
Halifax
Nova Scotia
B3J 1P3
Tel: (902) 426 2770

Mezzanine Floor
Commerce House
1080 Beaver Hall Hill
Montreal
Quebec H2Z 1SB
Tel: (514) 283 2152

4th Floor
354 Water St.
Box 2185
St. John's
Newfoundland
AIC 6E6
Tel: (709) 772 4616

Suite 605
191 22nd St. E

Saskatoon
Saskatchewan
S7K 0E1
Tel: (306) 665 5106

Suite 228
816 Government Street
Victoria
British Columbia
V8W 1W8
Tel: (604) 338 0213

Suite 308
391 York Ave
Winnipeg
Manitoba
R3C 0P6
Tel: (204) 949 2190

New Zealand

Dept of Internal Affairs
4th Floor
T&G Building
17 Albert Street
Auckland 1
Tel: (9) 31184

Dept of Internal Affairs
The Local Government Building
114/118 Lambton Quay
Wellington
Tel: (4) 738205

Dept of Internal Affairs
MLC No. 2 Bldg
159 Manchester Street
Christchurch 1
Tel: (3) 790290

PO Box 1146
2nd Floor
Government Building
Huapapa Street
Rotorua
Tel: 477 680

2nd Floor
Public Trust Bldg
442 Moray Place
Dunedin

UK

Clive House
70-78 Petty France
London SW1H 9HD
Tel: 01-213 3434/7272/6161

5th Floor
India Buildings
Water Street
Liverpool L2 0QZ
Tel: 051-237 3010

Olympia House
Upper Dock Street

Newport
Gwent NPT 1XA
Tel: (0633) 56292

55 Westfield Road
Peterborough
Cambs PE3 6TG
Tel: (0733) 895555

1st Floor
Empire House
131 West Nile Street
Glasgow G1 2RY
Tel: 041-332 0271

Hampton House
46-53 High Street
Belfast BT1 2QS
Tel: (0232) 232371

United States

Room E123
John F Kennedy Bldg
Government Center
Boston
MA 02203
Tel: (617) 223 3831

Suite 380
Kluczynski Federal Bldg
230 South Dearborn Street
Chicago
IL 60604
Tel: (312) 353 7155

Room C-106,
New Federal Bldg
300 Ala Maona Blvd
PO Box 50185
Honolulu
HI 96850
Tel: (808) 546 2130

One Allan Center
500 Dallas Street
Houston
TX 77002

Hawthorne Federal Bldg
Room 2W16
1500 Aviation Blvd
Lawndale
Los Angeles
CA 90261
Tel: (213) 536 6503

Room 804
Federal Office Bldg
51 Southwest First Avenue
Miami
FL 33130
Tel: (305) 350 4681

Room 400
International Trade Mart
2 Canal Street
New Orleans
LA 70130
Tel: (504) 589 6161

Room 270
Rockefeller Center
630 Fifth Avenue
New York
NY 10020
Tel: (212) 541 7710

Room 4426
Federal Bldg
600 Arch Street
Philadelphia
PA 19106
Tel: (215) 597 7480

Room 1405
Federal Bldg
450 Golden Gate Avenue
San Francisco
CA 94102
Tel: (415) 556 2630

Room 906
Federal Bldg
915 Second Avenue
Seattle
WA 98174
Tel: (206) 442 7945

One Landmark Square
Broad and Atlantic Sts.
Stamford
CT 06901

1425 K Street NW
Washington
DC 20524
Tel: (202) 783 8170

Visa Agencies

Alliance Visa and Consular Services
Room 21, Building 8,
Manchester Airport
Manchester M22 5PJ
Tel: 061-489 3201

Intercontinental Visa Service
Los Angeles World Trade Center
350 South Figueroa Street
Los Angeles
CA 90071
USA
Tel: (213) 625 7175
Specializes in visas, passport photos and travel books.

Port Reps
PO Box 290
Slough SL1 7LF
Tel: (06286) 4714

PVS (UK) Ltd
(Passport and Visa Services)
10b Parlaunt Road
Langley
Slough
Berks SL3 8BB
Tel: (0753) 683160

Ross Consular Services Ltd
6 The Grove
Slough
Berks SL1 1QP
Tel: (0753) 820881
Thames Consular Services
363 Chiswick High Road
London W4 4HS
Tel: 01-995 2492

The Visaservice
2 Northdown Street
Kings Cross
London N1 9BG
Tel: 01-833 2709/2700

Thomas Cook
45 Berkeley Street
London W1A 1EB
Tel: 01-499 4000
Passport Department can obtain visas for almost any destination at £5.00 per person.

Travcour (UK)
270 Vauxhall Bridge Road
London SW1V 1BB
Tel: (01) 834 7356
Specialises in hard-to-obtain visas.

Visas International
3169 Barbara Ct Ste F
Los Angeles
California 90068
USA
Tel: (213) 850 1192
Visa Service and Intourist Representative (USSR Hotels).

Worldwide Visa Shop Ltd
44 Chandos Place
London WC2N 4HS
Tel: 01-379 0419/0376

Customs Regulations
Australia

Each passenger over the age of 18 is entitled to the following duty free admissions:
200 cigarettes
or
250 grams cigars
or
250 grams tobacco
plus
1 litre of alcoholic liquor (including wine and beer).

General Items:

Gifts, souvenirs, household articles unused or less than 12 months old are duty free to a value of A$200.

Goods to the value of a further A$160 are duty-payable at 20 per cent.

You may also take in:
Items of the type normally carried on your person or in your personal baggage including jewellery or toilet requisites, but not electrical items.
Binoculars
Portable typewriters
Exposed film
Photographic cameras
Personal sporting requisites

Bicycles and motorcycles
Clothing (excepting fur apparel, unless it is valued at A$150 or less or you have owned and worn it for 12 months or more).

In order to qualify for duty-free status, goods should be for your personal use, and not have been bought on behalf of someone else, and should have travelled with you.

Prohibited Articles:

Drugs of dependence.
Firearms and weapons.

Wildlife – there is a strict control of all wildlife and wildlife products in and out of Australia. Travellers should be warned that articles of apparel, accessories, ornaments, trophies, etc., made from endangered species of fauna will be seized if imported into Australia. This includes animals such as alligators and crocodiles, elephants, rhinoceros, snakes, lizards, turtles, zebra, and the large cats.

Domestic pets – you cannot bring in cats or dogs, except from the United Kingdom and Ireland, Papua New Guinea, Fiji, New Zealand, Hawaii and Norfolk Island. The animals must have been resident in one of these approved countries for at least six months. A permit is required in all cases.

Other goods – most meat and meat products, dairy produce, plants and plant produce.

Canada

Visitors may bring in duty free all items of personal baggage including clothing, jewellery, etc. Sporting equipment, radios, television sets, musical instruments, typewriters, cameras, are all included in this category.

Alcoholic Beverages:

The age limit is 18 in some provinces, and 19 in others, and should be checked before travelling.
1.1 litres (40 oz) of liquor or wine

or

24 x 336ml (12oz cans or bottles) of beer, or its equivalent of 8.2 litres (28fl oz).

A further 9 litres (two gallons) of alcoholic beverages may be imported (except to Prince Edward Island and the Northwest Territories) on payment of duty.

Tobacco:

Persons over 16 years of age may bring in:
50 cigars
200 cigarettes
0.9kg (2lb) of manufactured tobacco.

Gifts:

Gifts may be imported duty free to a value of $40.

Prohibited and Restricted Goods

Animals – any pet or bird requires a Canadian import permit and a veterinary certificate of health from its country of origin. Domestic dogs and cats may be imported only from rabies-free countries without quarantine or vaccination if: they are shipped directly from the country, and they are accompanied by a vet's certificate, and that the country has been rabies free for the six months prior to the animal's departure.

Endangered species – restrictions on the movement of endangered species stretch also to products made from them. A permit is required for many skins, trophies, etc, as well as live animals.

Foods – meat and meat products are only allowed in if canned and sterile; or commercially cooked and prepared; and the total weight accompanying the traveller does not exceed 10kg per person.

Processed cheese and cooked eggs are the only permissible dairy products.

Food, in general, can be imported duty free provided the amount is only sufficient for two days' personal use by the importer.

Plants: – it is forbidden to import plants or plant produce without permission under the Plant Quarantine Act.

Firearms – handguns are not allowed entry to Canada. Firearms are restricted to those with a legitimate sporting or recreational use. A permit is not required for long guns.

All explosives, ammunitions, pyrotechnic devices, etc, except the following, are forbidden entry to Canada: sporting and competitive ammunition for personal use, distress and life-saving devices such as flares.

New Zealand

Personal effects will be allowed to enter duty free, provided they are your own property, are intended for your own use, and are not imported for commercial purposes. Items such as clothing, footwear, articles of adornment, watches, brushes and toilet requisites can be included here. Jewellery can be included, but not unmounted precious or semi-precious stones, and fur apparel purchased overseas can only be included if you have owned and worn it for more than 12 months.

Tobacco:

Passengers over 17 years of age are allowed the following:
200 cigarettes

or

250 grams of tobacco

or

50 cigars

or

A mixture of all three, weighing not more than 250 grams.

Alcohol:

Passengers over 17 years of age are allowed the following:
4.5 litres of wine (this is the equivalent to six 750ml bottles)

and

One bottle containing not more than 1,125ml of spirits or liqueur.

All passengers are given a general concession on goods up to a combined value of NZ$250. Persons travelling together may not combine their allowances. Children may claim their allowances provided the goods are their own property and of a type a child would reasonably expect to own.

Visitors to New Zealand are also permitted to bring in such items as a camera, a pair of binoculars, a portable radio and camping equipment, on condition that the goods leave the country with them.

Prohibited or Restricted Items

Drugs – the import of drugs is strictly forbidden and incurs heavy penalties. Should they be necessary for your health, carry a letter of authorization and carry the medication in its original, clearly marked bottle.

Firearms – the importation of any weapon is strictly controlled and requires a Police permit. Flick knives, sword sticks, knuckledusters, and other such weapons are prohibited.

Flora and Fauna – the entry of domestic dogs and cats is governed by the Agricultural Quarantine Service to whom you should apply for further details. The following goods must be declared:-
Food of any kind
Plants or parts of plants (dead or alive).
Animals (dead or alive) and animal products.
Equipment used with animals.
Equipment such as camping gear, golf clubs and used bicycles.

United Kingdom

The following chart gives the legal limits of goods which can be brought per adult into Britain duty free. List A is for goods obtained duty free or from outside the EEC. List B is for goods on which duty or tax has been paid within the EEC.

A

Tobacco:
200 cigarettes
or
100 cigarillos
or
50 cigars
or
250 grammes of tobacco.
    These quantities can be doubled if you are resident outside Europe.
Alcholic Drinks:
1 litre of alcoholic drinks over 22% vol (38.8% proof)
or
2 litres of alcoholic drinks not over 22% vol **or** fortified **or** sparkling wine
plus
2 litres of still table wine.
Perfume:
50 grammes (60cc or 2fl oz).
250cc (9fl oz) toilet water.
Other Goods:
Worth £32, but no more than 50 litres of beer and 25 mechanical lighters.

B

Tobacco:
300 cigarettes
or
150 cigarillos
or
75 cigars

or
400 grammes of tobacco.
Alcoholic Drinks:
1½ litres of alcoholic drinks over 22% vol (38.8% proof)
or
3 litres of alcoholic drinks not over 22% vol **or** fortified **or** sparkling wine
plus
3 litres of still table wine.
Perfume:
75 grammes (90cc or 3fl oz).
375cc (13fl oz) toilet water.
Other Goods:
£250 worth but no more than 50 litres of beer and 25 mechanical lighters.

The following goods are restricted or prohibited:

Controlled drugs
Firearms (including fireworks).
Flick knives
Counterfeit coins.
Horror and pornographic literature, films, videos, etc.
Radio transmitters (eg CB) capable of operating on certain frequencies.
Improperly cooked meat and poultry.
Plants, parts thereof and plant produce.
Most animals and birds – alive or dead; certain articles derived from animals including ivory, furskins, reptile leather goods.
Any live mammal – unless a British import licence (rabies) has previously been issued.
Old photographic material valued at £200 or more, portraits over 50 years old and valued at £2,000 or more, antique and collectors' items valued at £8,000 or more, and certain archaeological material are all subject to export controls and formalities should be completed through the Customs and Excise Office before you leave.

Notes:

1. Persons under 17 are not entitled to tobacco and drinks allowances.
2. If you are visiting the UK for less than six months, you are also entitled to bring in all personal effects (except those mentioned above) which you intend to take with you when you leave.

United States

Print:

Everyone entering the United states will be asked to fill in a Customs declaration listing everything except clothes, jewellery, toilet articles, etc, owned by you and intended for your own use. The exceptions are duty free. If jewellery worth $300 or more is sold within three years, duty must then be paid or the article will become subject to seizure.

Alcoholic Drinks:

Adult non-residents can bring in not more than 1 US quart of any form of alcohol for personal use. The amount varies from state to state, and in the more restrictive states, only the legal quantities will be released to you.

If you are only in transit, you are permitted up to 4 litres of alcohol, as long as it accompanies you out of the country.

Liquor-filled candy and absinthe are prohibited goods.

Tobacco

Your personal exemption may include 200 cigarettes (one carton), 100 cigars, and a reasonable quantity of tobacco.

Perfume:

Reasonable quantity.

Gift Exemption:

A non-resident may take in goods valued at up to $100 for use as gifts, provided he/she is to remain in the country for at least 72 hours. This allowance may only be claimed once every 6 months.

Notes:

Antiques are free of duty if produced 100 years prior to the date of entry.

A person emigrating may bring in professional equipment duty free.

If in transit, you may take dutiable goods worth up to $200 through the United States without payment.

Prohibited Items:

Lottery tickets, narcotics and dangerous drugs, obscene publications, seditious and treasonable materials, hazardous articles (e.g. fireworks, dangerous toys, toxic or poisonous substances), products made by convicts or forced labour, switchblade knives, pirate copies of copyright books. Leather items from Haiti.

Firearms and ammunition intended for lawful hunting or sporting purposes are admissible, provided you take the firearms and unfired ammunition with you out of the country.

Cultural objects, such as ethnic artwork, will be allowed in only if accompanied by a valid export certificate from their country of origin.

Bakery items, all cured cheeses, professionally canned foods are permitted. Most plants, or plant products are prohibited or require an import permit. The importation of meat or meat products is dependent on the animal disease condition in the country of origin.

A traveller requiring medicines containing habit-forming drugs or narcotics should always carry a doctor's letter or prescription; make sure that all medicines are properly identified; and do not carry more than might normally be used by one person.

Cats and dogs must be free of diseases communicable to man. Vaccination against rabies is not required for dogs and cats arriving from rabies-free countries. There are controls and prohibitions on all livestock, and anyone wishing to import any should apply to the US Customs for further information.

Vehicles

All countries will let you bring in a vehicle, whether car, camper van or yacht, without paying duty, either on presentation of a *carnet de passages* or on an assurance that you will not sell the vehicle for a certain length of time.

You may have to have the vehicle steam-cleaned to help prevent the spread of diseases in the soil.

Customs Offices:
Australia

The Collector of Customs
Sydney
NSW 2000
Tel: (02) 20521

The Collector of Customs
Melbourne
Victoria 3000
Tel: (03) 630461

The Collector of Customs
Brisbane
Queensland 4000
Tel: (08) 310361

The Collector of Customs
Perth
WA 6000
Tel: (09) 321 9761

The Collector of Customs
Hobart
Tasmania 7000
Tel: (002) 301201

The Collector of Customs
Darwin
NT 5790
Tel: (089) 814444

The Secretary
Department of Business and Consumer Affairs
Canberra
ACT 2600
Tel: (062) 730414

The Australian Customs Representative
Canberra House
Maltravers Street
off Arundel Street
Strand
London WC2R 3EF
Tel: 01-438 8000

The Australian Customs Representative
636 Fifth Avenue
New York
NY 10020
USA
Tel: (212) 245 4078

Officer of the Counsellor (Customs)
Australian Embassy
7th Floor
Sankaido Bldg
9-13 Akasaka
1-Chome
Minato-Ku
Tokyo
Japan

The Australian Customs Representative
c/o Australian Commission
Connaught Centre
Connaught Road
Hong Kong

The Australian Customs Representative
c/o Australian Trade Commissioner
Lorne Towers (9th Floor)
12 Lorne Street
PO Box 3601
Auckland
New Zealand

Canada

Revenue Canada
Customs and Excise
Public Relations Branch
Ottawa
Ontario
Canada K1A 015
Tel: (613) 593 6220

Canada Customs
2 St André Street
Quebec
Quebec G1K 7P6
Tel: (418) 694 4445

400 Carre Youville
Montreal
Quebec H2Y 3N4
Tel: (514) 283 2953

360 Coventry Road
Ottawa
Ontario K1K 2C6
Tel: (613) 993 0534 (8.00am to 4.30pm);
   (613) 998 3326 (after 4.30pm and weekends)

Manulife Centre, 10th Floor
55 Bloor Street West
Toronto
Ontario M5W 1A3
Tel: (416) 966 8022 (8.00am to 4.30pm)
   (416) 676 3643 (evenings and weekends)

Federal Bldg
269 Main Street
Winnipeg
Manitoba R3C 1B3
Tel: (204) 949 6004

204 Towne Square
1919 Rose Street
Regina
Saskatchewan S3P 3P1
Tel: (306) 359 6212

220 4th Avenue SE, Ste 720
PO Box 2970
Calgary
Alberta T2P 2M7
Tel: (403) 231 4610

1001 West Pender Street
Vancouver
British Columbia
V6E 2M8
Tel: (604) 666 1545/6

New Zealand

Box 29
Auckland
Tel: 773 520

Box 2098
Christchurch
Tel: 796 660

Private Bag
Dunedin
Tel: 799 251

Box 940
Hamilton
Tel: 82724

Box 1345
Palmerston North
Tel: 76059

Private Bag
Wellington
Tel: 736 099

United Kingdom

For notices and forms ask at any Customs and Excise office or write to:

HM Customs and Excise
Kent House
Upper Ground
London SE1 9PS

Other customs and Excise offices in major cities in the UK are:

27 King Street
Aberdeen AB9 2SH
Tel: (0224) 648 251

Customs House
Belfast BT1 3EU
Tel: (0232) 234 466

Customs House
Liverpool L3 1DX
Tel: 051-227 4343

19/29 Woburn Place
London WC1H 0JQ
Tel: 01-632 3333

93-107 Shaftesbury Avenue
London W1V 7AE
Tel: 01-437 9800

Customs House
Lower Thames Street
London EC3R 6EE
Tel: 01-626 1515

Customs House
Trafford Road
Salford M5 3DB
Tel: 061-872 4282

39 Quayside
Newcastle-on-Tyne
NE1 3ES
Tel: (0623) 610 981

United States of America

US Customs Service
PO Box 7118
Washington
DC 20044
USA
For detailed information and suggestions write to above address. Customs Hints for Visitors, *and* Importing a Car *are available on request.*

United States Embassy
Grosvenor Square
London W1A 2JB
For complaints and suggestions write to above address. On request Customs Hints for Returning US Residents – Know Before You Go.

Duty Free Allowances Worldwide

Afghanistan	A reasonable quantity of alcohol, tobacco and perfume for personal use.
Albania	A reasonable quantity of alcohol, tobacco and perfume for personal use.
Algeria	200 cigarettes or 50 cigars or 400g tobacco; 1 bottle spirits (opened).
Andorra	No restrictions – duty free country.
Angola	A reasonable quantity of tobacco and perfume (must be opened). Alcohol prohibited.
Anguilla	200 cigarettes or 50 cigars or ½ lb. tobacco. 1 quart of wine or spirits.
Antigua & Barb.	200 cigarettes or 50 cigars or 8oz. tobacco. 1 quart wine or spirits; 6oz. perfume.
Argentina	Goods up to US$1500 in value including 400 cigarettes and 50 cigars and 2 litres alcohol.
Aruba	400 cigarettes or 50 cigars or 250g. tobacco; 2 litres alcohol; ¼ litre perfume; gifts to a value of AWG100. Leather goods and souvenirs from Haiti banned.
Austria	200 cigarettes or 50 cigars or 250g. tobacco; 2 litres wine and 1 litre spirits;

300g. toilet water and 50g. perfume – if arriving from Europe. If arriving from elsewhere, double the quantities.

Bahamas
200 cigarettes or 50 cigars; ½ lb. tobacco; 100 cigarillos; 1 quart spirits; 50g. perfume.

Bahrain
400 cigarettes or 50 cigars or ½ lb. tobacco; 2 bottles of wine or spirits (non-Muslim passengers only); a reasonable amount of perfume. South African and Israeli goods banned.

Bangladesh
200 cigarettes or 50 cigars or ½ lb. tobacco; 2 opened bottles alcohol; reasonable amount of perfume; gifts to the value of BDT500.

Barbados
200 cigarettes or ½ lb. tobacco products; 26 fl. oz. alcohol (1 bottle); 150g. perfume.

Belgium
Duty-paid within the EEC – 300 cigarettes or 50 cigars or 400g. tobacco; 5 litres still wine and 1½ litres spirits and 3 litres liqueur or Luxembourg wine; or 8 litres wine if imported over the Luxembourg frontier; 75g. perfume and ⅜ litre lotion; other goods to the value of BFR2,000. From elsewhere and duty-free within the EEC – 200 cigarettes or 50 cigars or 250g. tobacco; 2 litres still wine and 1 litre spirits or 2 litres liqueur wine; 50g. perfume and ¼ litre lotion; other goods to the value of BFR 2,000.

Belize
200 cigarettes or ½ lb. tobacco products; 20 fl. oz. alcohol; 1 bottle perfume for personal use.

Benin
200 cigarettes or 100 cigarillos or 25 cigars or 250g. tobacco; 1 bottle wine and 1 bottle spirits; ½ litre toilet water and ¼ litre perfume.

Bermuda
200 cigarettes and 50 cigars and 1 lb. tobacco; 1.137 litres spirits and 1.137 litres wine.

Bolivia
200 cigarettes, 1 lb. tobacco or 50 cigars; 1 opened bottle spirits, reasonable amount of perfume.

Botswana
400 cigarettes and 50 cigars and 250g. tobacco; 1 litre wine and 1 litre spirits; up to 300 ml. perfume.

Brazil
400 cigarettes and 250g. tobacco and 25 cigars; 2 bottles alcohol (bought before reaching country). If using duty-free shop on arrival – goods up to US$300 value including a max. of 3 bottles wine, 2 Champagne and 2 spirits per person.

British Virgin Islands
A reasonable quantity of tobacco and alcohol at discretion of Customs officer.

Brunei
200 cigarettes or ½ lb. tobacco products; 1 bottle wine or spirits; reasonable amount of perfume.

Bulgaria
250g. tobacco products; 1 litre spirits and 2 litres wine; 100g. perfume; gifts up to value of LEV50.

Burkina Faso
200 cigarettes or 25 cigars or 100 cigarillos or 250g. tobacco; 1 bottle wine and 1 bottle spirits; ½ litre eau de cologne and a small bottle of perfume.

Burma
200 cigarettes or 50 cigars or 250g. tobacco; 1 quart alcohol; 1 pint perfume or eau de cologne. Must declare jewellery on arrival and get permit to take out Burmese jewellery worth more than K250. Playing cards, gambling equipment banned.

Burundi
1,000 cigarettes or 1 kg. tobacco; 1 litre alcohol; a reasonable amount of perfume. Cameras, radios etc. liable for duty.

Cameroon
400 cigarettes or 125 cigars; a reasonable quantity of tobacco, alcohol, perfume.

Cape Verde
No tobacco or alcohol; reasonable quantity of perfume if bottles are opened.

Cayman Islands
200 cigarettes or 50 cigars or ½ lb. tobacco; 1 quart alcohol.

Central African Republic
1,000 cigarettes or 250 cigars or 2kg. tobacco products (women can only take cigarettes); a reasonable quantity of alcohol and perfume.

Chad
400 cigarettes or 125 cigars or 500g. tobacco (women can only take cigarettes); 3 bottles wine and 1 bottle spirits.

Chile
400 cigarettes or 100 cigars or 500g. tobacco; 2½ litres alcohol; a reasonable quantity of perfume.

China
400 cigarettes (for a stay of up to 6 mths), otherwise 600 cigarettes or equivalent

in tobacco products; 2 litres alcohol; a reasonable quantity of perfume. Exposed but undeveloped film banned.

Colombia 200 cigarettes and 50 cigars and 500g. tobacco; 2 bottles alcohol; a reasonable quantity of perfume and toilet water.

Comoro Islands 400 cigarettes or 100 cigars or 500g. tobacco; 1 litre alcohol; 75 cl. perfume.

Congo 200 cigarettes or 1 box cigars or tobacco (women can only take cigarettes); 1 bottle alcohol; a reasonable quantity of perfume (must be opened).

Cook Islands 200 cigarettes or 50 cigars or ½ lb. tobacco; 2 litres wine or spirits or 4½ litres beer.

Costa Rica 450g. tobacco products; 3 litres alcohol; a reasonable quantity of perfume; one camera and six rolls of film.

Côte d'Ivoire 200 cigarettes or 25 cigars or 250g. tobacco; 1 bottle spirits and 1 bottle wine; a reasonable amount of perfume.

Cuba 200 cigarettes or 25 cigars or 220g. tobacco; 2 bottles alcohol; a reasonable quantity of perfume.

Cyprus 200 cigarettes or 250g. tobacco or cigars; 0.75 litres wine and 1 litre spirits; 0.3 litres perfume and toilet water; other goods to a value of CYL50.

Czechoslovakia 250 cigarettes or equivalent in tobacco products; 1 litre spirits and 2 litres wine; ½ litre of wine. Gifts up to a value of CKR1,000. Half quantities if you are only entering the country for 2 days or less.

Denmark If entering from Europe – 200 cigarettes or 50 cigars or 250g. tobacco; 1 litre spirits or 2 litres fortified wine and 2 litres still wine; 50g. perfume and 0.25 litres toilet water; other goods to the value of DKK 375. Double the tobacco ration if entering from outside Europe.

Dominica 200 cigarettes or 2 packets tobacco or 24 cigars; 52 oz. (2 bottles) alcohol.

Dominican Rep. 200 cigarettes or tobacco products to the value of US$5; 1 opened bottle alcohol (to a value of US$5); a reasonable quantity of perfume (opened).

Ecuador 300 cigarettes or 50 cigars or 200g. tobacco; 1 litre alcohol; a reasonable quantity of perfume; gifts up to the value of US$200.

Egypt 200 cigarettes or 25 cigars or 200g. tobacco; 1 litre alcohol; a reasonable amount of perfume; gifts to the value of EGL40. Cotton as fabric is a banned import.

El Salvador 1 kg. tobacco or 100 cigars or 480 cigarettes; 2 bottles alcohol; a reasonable quantity of perfume; other goods to a value of US$100.

Equatorial Guinea 200 cigarettes or 50 cigars or 250g. tobacco; 1 litre wine and 1 litre spirits; a reasonable quantity of perfume. Spanish newsprint banned.

Ethiopia 100 cigarettes or 50 cigars or ½ lb. tobacco; 1 litre alcohol; ½ litre perfume; gifts to a value of ETB10. May export goods up to value of ETB500 free. Skins and antiques require export certificate.

Fiji 200 cigarettes or ½lb. of cigars or tobacco; 1 quart of spirits or 2 of wine or beer; 4 oz. perfume; other goods to a value of FID50.

Finland 200 cigarettes or 250g. of other tobacco products; 2 litres beer and 2 litres of other mild alcoholic beverages; other goods to the value of FIM1,500. If resident outside Europe you may take in 400 cigarettes or 500g. of other tobacco products.

France From outside the EEC – 200 cigarettes or 50 cigars or 250g. tobacco; 1 litre spirits or 2 litres fortified wine and 2 litres still wine; other goods to the value of FFR300. From within the EEC – 300 cigarettes or 75 cigars or 400g. tobacco; 3 litres of wine and 1½ litres spirits or 3 litres fortified wine; 75g. perfume and 25 cl. toilet water; other goods up to FFR2,000.

French Polynesia 200 cigarettes or 50 cigars or 100 cigarillos or 250g. tobacco; 1 litre spirits and 2 litres wine; 50g. perfume and ¼ litre toilet water; other goods to the value of CFP5,000.

Gabon 200 cigarettes or 50 cigars or a reasonable amount of tobacco (women may only take cigarettes); 2 litres alcohol; 50g. perfume; gifts to value of AFR5,000.

Gambia 200 cigarettes or 250g. tobacco products; 1 quart spirits and 2 quarts wine or beer; ½ pint perfume.

East Germany Tobacco, alcohol, coffee and chocolate allowed completely free of duty as gifts or for personal use. Gifts to value of MRK1,000 (or MRK200 per day of stay up to 5 days). Must have permission to import motor parts, gemstones and jewellery. Can export goods of up to value of MRK100 free.

West Germany From a European country outside the EEC – 200 cigarettes or 50 cigars or 250g. tobacco; 1 litre spirits or 2 litres of fortified wine and 2 litres of still wine; 50g. perfume; other goods to the value of DMK115. From within the EEC – 300 cigarettes or 75 cigars or 400g. tobacco; 3 litres of wine or 1½ litres spirits or 3 litres of fortified wine and 5 litres of other wine; 75g. perfume and 0.375 litres toilet water; other goods to the value of DMK 780. From outside Europe – 400 cigarettes or 100 cigars or 500g. tobacco; alcohol as for countries outside the EEC; other goods to the value of DMK115.

Ghana 400 cigarettes or 100 cigars or 1 lb. tobacco; 1 bottle wine and 1 bottle spirits; 8 oz. perfume.

Gibraltar 200 cigarettes or 100 cigarillos or 250g. tobacco; 1 litre spirits or 2 litres fortified wine or 2 litres table wine; 50g. perfume and ¼ litre toilet water; other goods to the value of £28.

Greece Duty-paid within the EEC – 300 cigarettes or 150 cigarillos or 75 cigars or 400g. tobacco; 1½ litres spirits or 3 litres fortified wine and 5 litres still wine; 75g. perfume and 0.375 litres toilet water; gifts (excluding electronic devices) to the value of DRA32,000. From outside Europe or duty-free in the EEC – 200 cigarettes or 100 cigarillos or 50 cigars or 250g. tobacco; 1 litre spirits or 2 litres wine; 50g. perfume and ¼ litre toilet water; gifts to value of DRA3,500. Windsurfboards banned unless a Greek residing in Greece guarantees they will be re-exported.

Guatemala 80 cigarettes or 3½ oz. tobacco; 2 open bottles alcohol; 2 open bottles perfume.

Guinea-Bissau A reasonable quantity of tobacco and perfume (bottles must be opened). Alcohol banned.

Guinea Republic 1,000 cigarettes or 250 cigars or 1 kg. tobacco; 1 bottle alcohol (opened); a reasonable amount of perfume. All foreign newspapers banned.

Guyana 200 cigarettes or 50 cigars or 225g. tobacco; 0.57 litres spirits and 0.57 litres wine; a reasonable amount of perfume.

Haiti 200 cigarettes or 50 cigars or 250g. tobacco; 1 litre spirits; a small quantity of perfume etc. Coffee, matches, and meths banned.

Honduras 200 cigarettes or 100 cigars or 1 lb. tobacco; 2 bottles alcohol; a reasonable quantity of perfume; gifts to the value of US$50.

Hong Kong 200 cigarettes or 50 cigars or 250g. tobacco; 1 litre alcohol; 60 ml. perfume, 250ml. toilet water. If entering from Macau the quantities are 100 cigarettes or 25 cigars or ¼ lb. tobacco; 1 bottle wine.

Hungary 250 cigarettes or 40 cigars or 200g. tobacco; 2 litres wine and 1 litre spirits; 250g. perfume.

Iceland 200 cigarettes or 250g. tobacco; 1 litre spirits and 1 litre wine or 6 litres beer (8 litres Icelandic beer).

India 200 cigarettes or 50 cigars or 250g. tobacco; 0.95 litres alcohol; ¼ litre toilet water.

Indonesia For a one week stay – 200 cigarettes or 50 cigars or 100g. tobacco. For a two week stay – 400 cigarettes or 100 cigars or 200g. tobacco. For longer stays – 600 cigarettes or 150 cigars or 300g. tobacco. Also 2 litres of alcohol (opened); a reasonable quantity of perfume; gifts to a value of US$100.

Iran 200 cigarettes or equivalent in tobacco products; a reasonable quantity of perfume; gifts with a value on which IRI11,150 would be payable. Alcohol prohibited.

Iraq 200 cigarettes or 50 cigars or 250g. tobacco; 1 litre alcohol; ½ litre perfume. Total value may not exceed IRD100.

Ireland Duty-paid within the EEC – 300 cigarettes or 400g. tobacco or 150 cigarillos or 75 cigars; 1½ litres spirits or 3 litres fortified wine and 5 litres still wine; 75g. perfume and ⅜ litre toilet water; other goods to a value of IR£266. No item may exceed more than IR£58 in value. Duty-free in the EEC or arriving from elsewhere in Europe – 200 cigarettes or 100 cigarillos or 50 cigars or 250g. tobacco; 1 litre spirits or 2 litres fortified wine and 2 litres still wine; 50g. perfume and ¼ litre toilet water; other goods to a value of IR£34. If resident outside Europe, you may increase the tobacco limit to 400 cigarettes or 200 cigarillos or 100 cigars or 500g. tobacco.

Israel   250 cigarettes or 250g. tobacco products; 2 litres wine and 1 litre spirits; ¼ litre eau de cologne or perfume; gifts up to a value of US$125.

Italy   Duty-paid in the EEC – 300 cigarettes or 75 cigars or 150 cigarillos or 400g. tobacco; 1½ litres spirits or 3 litres fortified wine and 3 litres still wine; 75g. perfume and 0.375 litres toilet water; other goods to a value of LIT418,000; 750g. coffee or 300g. coffee extract; 150g. tea or 60g. tea extract. Duty-free in the EEC or from elsewhere in Europe – 200 cigarettes or 50 cigars or 100 cigarillos or 250g. tobacco; 0.75 litres spirits or 2 litres fortified wine; 50g. perfume and ¼ litre toilet water; other goods to a value of LIT15,000; 500g. coffee or 200g. coffee extract; 100g. tea or 40g. tea extract. Passengers from outside Europe may increase their tobacco ration to 400 cigarettes or 100 cigars or 200 cigarillos or 500g. tobacco; and may take in other goods to the value of LIT67,000.

Jamaica   200 cigarettes or 50 cigars or ½ lb. tobacco; 1 litre spirits and 2 litres wine; 12 fl. oz. toilet water and 6 oz. perfume. Coffee is prohibited.

Japan   400 cigarettes or 100 cigars or 500g. tobacco; 3 bottles alcohol; 2 oz. perfume; other goods to the value of 100,000 yen.

Jordan   200 cigarettes or 25 cigars or 200g. tobacco; 2 bottles wine or 1 bottle spirits; a reasonable quantity of perfume.

Kenya   200 cigarettes or ½ lb. tobacco; 1 bottle wine or spirits; 1 pint perfume.

Kiribati   200 cigarettes or 50 cigars or 225g. tobacco; 1 litre wine and 1 litre spirits; a reasonable amount of perfume.

North Korea   A reasonable amount of tobacco and alcohol. Binoculars and wireless sets are banned.

South Korea   400 cigarettes, 50 cigars, 250g. pipe tobacco and 100g. other tobacco (total amount not to exceed 500g.); 2 bottles alcohol (up to total of 1,520 cl.); 2 oz. perfume; gifts to the value of Won100,000.

Kuwait   500 cigarettes or 2 lb. tobacco. Alcohol banned.

Laos   500 cigarettes or 100 cigars or 500g. tobacco; 1 bottle spirits and 2 bottles wine; a reasonable amount of perfume.

Lebanon   200 cigarettes or 200g. cigars or tobacco (goes up to 500 cigarettes and 500g. tobacco for tourists over the summer); 1 litre alcohol; 60g. perfume.

Lesotho   400 cigarettes and 50 cigars and 250g. tobacco; 1 litre alcohol; 300 ml. perfume.

Liberia   200 cigarettes or 25 cigars or 250g. tobacco; 1 litre alcohol; 100g. perfume; other goods to a value of US$125.

Libya   200 cigarettes or 25 cigars; a reasonable amount of perfume. Alcohol, Israeli goods, or goods produced by companies trading with Israel, all food including cans banned.

Luxembourg   Duty-paid within the EEC – 300 cigarettes or 75 cigars or 150 cigarillos or 400g. tobacco; 1½ litres spirits or 3 litres fortified wine and 5 litres still wine; 75g. perfume and ⅜ litre toilet water; other goods to a value of LFR2,000. Duty-free within the EEC, or from outside – 200 cigarettes or 50 cigars or 100 cigarillos or 250g. tobacco; 1 litre spirits or 2 litres sparkling wine and 2 litres still wine; 50g. perfume and ¼ litre toilet water; other goods to the value of LFR2,000.

Macau   A reasonable quantity of tobacco, alcohol and perfume.

Madagascar   500 cigarettes or 25 cigars or 500g. tobacco; 1 bottle alcohol.

Malawi   200 cigarettes or 250g. tobacco; 1 litre spirits and 1 litre beer or wine; ¼ litre toilet water or 50g. perfume.

Malaysia   200 cigarettes or 50 cigars or 225g. tobacco; 2 boxes matches; 1 litre alcohol; opened perfume to a value of RGT200; gifts to a value of RGT200.

Maldives   No restrictions on tobacco or perfume. Alcohol banned.

Mali 1,000 cigarettes or 250 cigars or 2 kg. tobacco; a reasonable quantity of alcohol and perfume in open bottles.

Malta 200 cigarettes or 250g. tobacco; 1 bottle spirits and 1 bottle wine; perfume to a value of MAL2.

Mauritania 200 cigarettes or 25 cigars or 450g. tobacco (women can only take cigarettes); 50g. perfume.

Mauritius 250 cigarettes or 50 cigars or 250g. tobacco; 2 litres wine or beer and ¾ litre spirits; a small quantity of perfume.

Mexico 400 cigarettes or 2 boxes cigars or a reasonable quantity of pipe tobacco; 3 bottles alcohol; a reasonable quantity of perfume; other goods to a value of US$100; one camera and 12 rolls of film.

Micronesia 400 cigarettes or 50 cigars or 250g. pipe tobacco; 3 bottles alcohol; a reasonable quantity of perfume.

Mongolia A reasonable amount of tobacco and alcohol.

Montserrat 200 cigarettes or 50 cigars; 1.14 litres alcohol; 6 oz. (168g.) perfume; gifts to a value of ECD250.

Morocco 200 cigarettes or 50 cigars or 400g. tobacco; 1 litre spirits and 1 litre wine; 50g. perfume.

Mozambique 200 cigarettes or 250g. tobacco; ¼ litre alcohol; a reasonable quantity of perfume (opened).

Nauru 400 cigarettes or 50 cigars or 450g. tobacco; 3 bottles alcohol; a reasonable amount of perfume.

Nepal A reasonable amount of tobacco, perfume and alcohol.

Netherlands Travelling from within the EEC – 300 cigarettes or 150 cigarillos or 400g. tobacco; 1½ litres spirits or 3 litres fortified wine or 5 litres still wine and 8 litres Luxembourg wine; 75g. perfume and 3.8 litres toilet water; other goods to the value of DFL890. Travelling from elsewhere in Europe – 200 cigarettes or 50 cigars or 100 cigarillos or 250g. tobacco; 1 litre spirits or 2 litres fortified wine and 2 litres still wine; 8 litres Luxembourg wine; 50g. perfume; other goods to the value of DFL125. If arriving from outside Europe, you can double this tobacco allowance or 400 cigarettes or 100 cigars or 500g. tobacco.

Netherlands Antilles 400 cigarettes or 50 cigars or 250g. tobacco; 2 litres alcohol; ¼ litre perfume; gifts to a value of AFL100. Leather goods and souvenirs from Haiti banned.

New Caledonia Travelling from Europe, Africa, Americas or Asia - 1,000 cigarettes or 250 cigars or 2 kg. tobacco. From Oceania – 200 cigarettes or 500 cigars or 400g. tobacco. 1 bottle alcohol; a reasonable quantity of perfume.

Nicaragua 500g. tobacco products; 3 litres spirits; 1 bottle perfume.

Niger 200 cigarettes or 25 cigars or 250g. tobacco; 1 litre alcohol.

Nigeria 200 cigarettes or 50 cigars or 200g. tobacco; 1 litre spirits; a small amount of perfume. Sparkling wine prohibited.

Niue 200 cigarettes or 50 cigars or 227g. tobacco or a combination to max. weight of 227g.; 1 bottle wine and 1 bottle spirits.

Norway European residents – 200 cigarettes or 250g. tobacco products; 200 cigarette papers; 1 litre spirits and 1 litre wine or 2 litres wine and 2 litres beer; a small quantity perfume; other goods to a value of K1,200. Others – 400 cigarettes or 500g. tobacco products and 200 cigarette papers; 1 litre spirits and 1 litre wine or 2 litres wine and 2 litres beer; 50g. perfume and ½ litre eau de cologne; other goods to a value of K3,500. Spirits of over 60D (120D) proof banned.

Oman A reasonable quantity of tobacco; 8 oz. perfume; 1 bottle alcohol (non-Muslims only).

Pakistan 200 cigarettes or 50 cigars or ½ kg. tobacco; ¼ litre perfume or toilet water. Alcohol prohibited.

Panama 500 cigarettes or 500g. tobacco; 3 bottles alcohol; a reasonable amount of perfume.

Papua New Guinea 200 cigarettes or 250g. tobacco; 1 litre alcohol; a reasonable quantity of perfume;

other goods to a value of NGK200.

Paraguay   A reasonable quantity of tobacco, perfume and alcohol.

Peru   400 cigarettes or 50 cigars or ½ kg. tobacco; 2 litres alcohol; a reasonable amount of perfume.

Philippines   400 cigarettes or 50 cigars or 250g. tobacco; 2 litres alcohol; a small quantity of perfume.

Poland   250 cigarettes or 50 cigars or 250g. tobacco; 1 litre wine and 1 litre spirits.

Portugal   200 cigarettes or 100 cigarillos or 50 cigars or 250g. tobacco (double these quantities if entering from outside Europe); 1 litre spirits or 2 litres fortified wine and 2 litres still wine; 50g. perfume and ¼ litre toilet water; other goods to a value of ESP3,000.

Qatar   1 lb. tobacco; perfume to the value of QRI20. Must have a licence to import alcohol.

Romania   200 cigarettes or 300g. tobacco; 2 litres spirits and 4 litres wine or beer; gifts to the value of LEI2,000.

Rwanda   200 cigarettes or 50 cigars or 1 lb. tobacco; 2 opened bottles of alcohol; a reasonable amount of perfume.

St Christopher & Nevis   200 cigarettes or 50 cigars or ½ lb. tobacco; 1 quart alcohol; 6 oz. perfume.

St Lucia   200 cigarettes or 250g. tobacco; 1 quart alcohol.

St Vincent & Grenadines   200 cigarettes or ½ lb. tobacco or 50 cigars; 1 quart alcohol.

American Samoa   200 cigarettes or 50 cigars; 2 bottles alcohol; a reasonable quantity of perfume.

Western Samoa   200 cigarettes or 50 cigars or 1½ lb. tobacco; 1 bottle liquor.

Sao Tomé & Principe A reasonable quantity of tobacco, alcohol, and perfume (bottles must be opened).

Saudi Arabia   600 cigarettes or 100 cigars or 500g. tobacco; a reasonable quantity of perfume. Alcohol and contraceptives banned.

Senegal   200 cigarettes or 50 cigars or 250g. tobacco; a reasonable quantity of perfume.

Seychelles   200 cigarettes or 50 cigars or 250g. tobacco; 1 litre spirits and 1 litre wine; 125 cc. perfume and 25 cl. toilet water; other goods to a value of SER200.

Sierra Leone   200 cigarettes or ½ lb. tobacco; 1 quart alcohol; 1 quart perfume.

Singapore   200 cigarettes or 50 cigars or 250g. tobacco; 1 litre wine or beer and 1 litre spirits; a reasonable quantity of perfume. No allowance if arriving from Malaysia.

Solomon Islands   200 cigarettes or 250g. tobacco or ½ lb. tobacco; 2 litres alcohol; other goods to a value of SBD40.

Somalia   400 cigarettes or 400g. tobacco; 1 bottle alcohol; a reasonable amount of perfume.

South Africa   400 cigarettes and 50 cigars and 250g. tobacco; 2 litres wine and 1 litre spirits; 50ml. perfume and 250ml. toilet water; gifts to the value of 200 rand.

Spain   If arriving from Europe or Mediterranean countries - 200 cigarettes or 50 cigars or 100 cigarillos or 250g. tobacco. Others can double the tobacco allowance. Also – 1 litre spirits or 2 litres fortified wine and 2 litres still wine; ¼ litre eau de cologne and 50g. perfume; gifts to the value of PTS5,000.

Sri Lanka   200 cigarettes or 50 cigars or 12oz. tobacco; 2 bottles wine and 1½ litres spirits; ¼ litre toilet water and a small amount of perfume. If a family is travelling together, only 2 may have a duty-free allowance.

Sudan   200 cigarettes or 50 cigars or 500g. tobacco; a reasonable quantity of perfume and gifts. Alcohol, goods from Israel and South Africa, and blank pro-forma invoices banned.

Suriname   400 cigarettes or cigars, or 200 cigarillos or 500g. tobacco; 2 litres spirits and 4 litres wine; 50g. perfume and 1 litre toilet water; 8 rolls film, 60m cine;1-film and 100 metres recording tape (unused).

Sweden   European residents – 200 cigarettes or 100 cigarillos or 50 cigars or 250g. tobacco; 1 litre spirits, 1 litre wine and 2 litres beer; a reasonable amount of perfume; gifts to a value of SEK600. Others may have 400 cigarettes or 200 cigarillos or

100 cigars or 500g. tobacco. Alcohol of more than 60° (120°) proof is banned.

Switzerland	European residents – 200 cigarettes or 50 cigars or 250g. tobacco; 2 litres wine and 1 litre spirits. Others may have 400 cigarettes or 100 cigars or 500g. tobacco.
Syria	200 cigarettes or 50 cigars or 250g. tobacco; 1 litre spirits and 1 bottle wine; a reasonable quantity of perfume.
Taiwan	200 cigarettes or 25 cigars or 1 lb. tobacco; 1 bottle alcohol; 1 used camera.
Tanzania	200 cigarettes or 50 cigars or 250g. tobacco; 1 litre alcohol; ¼ litre perfume.
Thailand	200 cigarettes or 250g. tobacco products; 1 litre alcohol; no limit on perfume for personal use.
Togo	100 cigarettes or 50 cigars or 100g. tobacco; 1 bottle wine and 1 bottle spirits; a reasonable quantity of perfume.
Tonga	200 cigarettes; 1 litre alcohol.
Trinidad and Tobago	200 cigarettes or 50 cigars or ½ lb. tobacco; 1 quart alcohol; gifts to the value of TTD50.
Tunisia	400 cigarettes or 100 cigars or 500g. tobacco; 2 litres wine or beer and 1 litre spirits; ¼ litre perfume and 1 litre toilet water; gifts to the value of TUD200.
Turkey	400 cigarettes or 50 cigars or 200g. tobacco and 50 cigarette papers or 200g. tumbeki; 5 litres spirits; a reasonable amount of perfume and 2 litres eau de cologne; 1 kg. coffee. Only allowed to take in 2 sets of playing cards.
Turks & Caicos	200 cigarettes or 50 cigars or 125g. tobacco; 1 quart alcohol.
Tuvalu	200 cigarettes or 225g. tobacco products; 1 litre wine and 1 litre spirits; other goods to a value of A$25.
Uganda	200 cigarettes or ½ lb. tobacco; 1 bottle alcohol; 1 pint perfume.
USSR	250 cigarettes or 250g. tobacco products; 1 litre spirits and 2 litres wine; a reasonable amount of perfume; gifts to a value of ROU30.
UAE	200 cigarettes or ½ lb. tobacco; a reasonable amount of perfume. Alcohol banned.
Uruguay	400 cigarettes or 25 cigars; 2 litres alcohol; other a value of US$150 to include only two of the following: radio, typewriter, camera, movie camera, projector.
Vanuatu	200 cigarettes or 100 cigarillos or 250g. tobacco or 50 cigars; 1½ litres spirits and 2 litres wine; ¼ litre toilet water and 10cl. perfume; other goods to a value of VUV4,000.
Venezuela	200 cigarettes and 25 cigars; 2 litres alcohol; 4 small bottles perfume. Cuban and Dominican newspapers and magazines banned.
Vietnam	200 cigarettes or 50 cigars or 250g. tobacco; 1 bottle spirits; a reasonable quantity of perfume.
North Yemen	200 cigarettes or 50 cigars or ½ lb. tobacco; 2 pints alcohol; 1 pint perfume.
South Yemen	200 cigarettes or 50 cigars or ½ lb. tobacco; 2 quarts alcohol; 1 pint perfume.
Yugoslavia	200 cigarettes or 50 cigars or 250g. tobacco; 1 litre wine or ¼ litre spirits; ¼ litre eau de cologne and a reasonable quantity of perfume.
Zaïre	100 cigarettes or 50 cigars or equivalent in tobacco; 1 open bottle spirits; a reasonable amount of perfume.
Zambia	200 cigarettes or 250g. tobacco; 1 bottle alcohol (open); 1 oz. perfume.
Zimbabwe	Unlimited cigarettes, but to be included in general allowance of value to ZWD100; 5 litres alcohol including a max. of 2 litres of spirits.

Notes:
1) Alcohol should be taken to mean alcoholic drinks. Fortified wine should also be taken to mean other drinks of between 14° and 22° and most sparkling wines.
2) There is a wide variety in the bottom age limit for those allowed alcohol and tobacco quotas from 10 (Sudan) to 21. People below 21 should check.
3) The gift allowance is normally halved for children.
4) Standard prohibitions such as foodstuffs, plants, animals, pornography, arms, narcotics etc. have not been included in this list due to lack of space. It should be taken as read that you will never be allowed to take these across borders unless you can obtain special permission.

Customs Offices Worldwide

Algeria
Bureau Central des Douanes
12 Blvd Khomisti
Algiers
Tel: 61161/634398

Andorra
Casa de la Vall
Carrer de la Vall,
Andorra La Vella
Tel: 25157

Austria
Bundesministerium fuer Finanzen
Himmelpfortgasse 4
1010 Vienna
Tel: (43) 222 513 1353

Bahamas
HM Customs
PO Box N155
Arawak Cay
Nassau
Tel: (809) 325 6551

Bahrain
Directorate of Customs and Ports
Customs – PO Box 15
Ports – PO Box 453
Bahrain

Barbados
PBX Administration
University Row
Princess Alice Highway
St Michael

Belgium
Douanes et Accises
Rue Picard 1–3
1020 Brussels
Tel: 425 2966

Belize
Customs Department
Belize City
Tel: 02-7091/2/3

Brazil
Secretaria de Receita Federal
Ministério da Fazenda
Esplanada dos Ministe;lrios
Brasilia
Distrito Federal

Brunei
c/o Main Complex
Brunei International Airport

Cayman Islands
The Customs Dept
Box 898
Tower Building
George Town
Grand Cayman
Tel: 92473

Cocos (Keeling) Islands
Dept of Territories
6th Floor
5 Mill Street
Perth
W. Australia

Cook Islands
Customs Dept
Avarua
Rarotonga
Tel: 29490

Cyprus
Dept of Customs and Excise
Ministry of Finance
Ex-Secretariat Compound
Byron Street
Nicosia
Tel: 402321

Ecuador
Dirрección General de Advanas
Pto Maritimo
Guayacil
Tel: 431166

El Salvador
Dirreccio;ln General de la Renta de Advanas
Centro de Gobierno
San Salvador
Tel: 250022

Ethiopia
Customs and Excise Dept
PO Box 1905
Addis Ababa
Tel: 153769

East Germany
Zollverwaltung der DDR
Hauptverwaltung
Grellstrasse 16–23
1050 Berlin

Falkland Islands
Customs Dept
Port Stanley

Fiji
Customs and Excise
Ministry of Finance
Government Buildings
Victoria Parade
Suva
Tel: 22831

France
Centre de Renseignements de Douanes
8 Rue de la Tour des Dames
Paris 75436

Gabon
Direction Générale des Douanes
BP 40
Libreville

Greece
General Directorate of Customs and Excise
Ministry of Commerce

15 Kaniggos Square
Athens
Tel: 361 6241

Grenada
Customs Department
The Pier
St George's
Tel: 2239/40

Guadeloupe
Direction Régionale des Douanes
Cheminot State-Félix E Bové
Basse Terre
Tel: 811822/57

Hong Kong
Customs and Excise Dept;
Hong Kong Trade Centre
14th Floor
161–167 Des Voeux Road
Central
Hong Kong
Tel: 5-8521411

Hungary
Vám-és Pénzu gyo rség
Országos Parancsnokság
Szent Istvàn Tèr 11/B
Budapest 5
Tel: 326943

Israel
32 Agron Street
Jerusalem

Jamaica
Customs Enforcement Division
Scotia Bank Centre
Port Royal Street
Kingston

Kenya
The Commissioner of Customs and Excise
Forodha House
PO Box 40160
Nairobi
Tel: 722095

Lesotho
Customs and Excise Dept
Box MS891
Maseru

Liberia
Ministry of Finance
Customs Dept
PO Box 9013
Broad Street
Monrovia

Luxembourg
Administration des Douanes
4–6 Rue du St Esprit
1476 Luxembourg

Malawi
Customs Authority
Box 257
Lilongwe
Tel: 731694

Malta
The Comptroller of Customs
Vittoriosa
Tel: 821825/7/8

Mauritius
Customs and Excise Dept
Port Louis
Tel: 080251

Morocco
Administration des Douanes et Imports
Place des Nations Unies
Casablanca 01

Nepal
Customs Department
Tripureswar
Tel: 215168/215525

Nigeria
Customs and Excise
Mosaic House
18 Timubu Street
Lagos

Norway
Toll-og Avgiftsdirektorate
Schweigaards gt 15
Postboks 8122 DEP
0032 Oslo 1
Tel: (02) 414960

Papua New Guinea
Bureau of Customs
Stanley Esplanade
PO Box 923
Port Moresby
Tel: 212844

Philippines
Bureau of Customs
Customs Building
Port Area
Metro Manila
Tel: 484 161

Qatar
Customs Dept
Ministry of Finance and Petroleum
PO Box 81
Doha
Tel: 413322

Western Samoa
Customs Authority
Apia Wharf
Matautu-Tai

Senegal
Direction Générale des Douanes
Immeuble SIFA
Place de l'Indépendance
Dakar
Tel: 211328/212879

Seychelles
Customs and Excise Division
Ministry of Finance
Liberty House
Victoria
Tel: 21790

Sierra Leone
Customs and Excise Dept
College Road
Cline Town
Freetown

Singapore
Controller of Customs and Excise
Customs House
Maxwell Road,
Singapore 0106
Tel: 222 3511

Solomon Islands
Customs and Excise
PO Box G16
Honiara
Tel: 22239/23700

Sri Lanka
Customs Dept
3rd Floor
Grindlays Bank Building
York St
Colombo 1
Tel: 21141

St Christopher & Nevis
Comptroller of Customs
Customs Building
Bay Road
Basse Terre
Tel: (809) 465 2128

Sudan
Dept of Customs
Khartoum

Sweden
Generaltullstyrelsen
Skeppsbron 38
Box 2267
S-103 16 Stockholm

Switzerland
Oberzolldirektion
Monbijoustrasse 40
3003 Bern

Tanzania
Idara ya Ushuru wa Forodha
Barabara ya Jiji
SLP 9053 Dar Es Salaam
Tel: 26231

Togo
Ministry of Economics and Finance
Lomé

Tonga
Ministry of Finance
Vuna Road
Nuku'alofa

Trinidad and Tobago
Customs Authority
Abercromby St & Independence Square
Port-of-Spain

Tunisia
Direction Generale des Douanes
Avenue de la République
Tunis

Turkey
Ministry of Customs and Monopolies
Balanliklar
Ankara

Turks and Caicos
Collector of Customs
Grand Turk
Tel: (1-809) 946 2801
and
Provdenciales
Tel: (1-809) 946 4241

Uganda
Customs and Excise Dept
Nile Avenue
Box 444
Kampala
Tel: 257095

UAE
Customs Authority
PO Box 255
Abu Dhabi
Tel: 720700

Vanuatu
Cuswoms Dept
PO Box 431
Port Vila
Tel: 2951

Zambia
Customs House
Kimathi Road
Dedan
Box 30085
Lusaka
Tel: 211932

Zimbabwe
Customs Authority
Cecil House
95 Stanley Ave,
(P. Bag 7715
Causeway)
Harare
Tel: 703153

Currency Restrictions

Many countries impose restrictions on the import or export of local and foreign currency. Often these take the form of ceilings, normally reasonably generous, so that the traveller should rarely be aware of their existence. However, it is worth checking every country you intend to visit.

The following is a list applicable at the time of going to press, of currency regulations which may impinge on the traveller. The list is not comprehensive, as those countries with no restrictions, or restrictions relating only to residents are not included.

KEY TO COLUMNS

(1) Import of local currency prohibited.
(2) Export of local currency prohibited.
(3) Foreign currency may be imported but must be declared.
(4) Foreign currency may be exported by non-residents up to the amoung imported and declared.
(5) Other.
* See notes in Column 5.

Country	(1)	(2)	(3)	(4)	(5)
Afghanistan	yes	yes	yes	yes	
Albania	yes	yes	yes	yes	
Algeria	yes		yes		Non-residents must change a min. of ALD1000 on arrival. Residents ALD700. May re-export amounts above this only.
Angola	no★	yes	yes★	yes★	Sale of imported foreign currency to customs on arrival is obligatory. Can import up to AKZ1000 in local currency. Can re-export foreign currency declared minus AKZ500 for each day's stay.
Anguilla			yes	yes	
Antigua & Barb.			yes	yes	
Aruba	yes	yes			
Australia					The ceiling on local currency leaving the country is A$250 in notes and A$5 in coins. If you wish to transfer more than A$10,000 out of the country, it must be authorized in advance.
Austria					No limit on exporting foreign currency, or Austrian currency, but advance permission is needed to take out more than A$15,000.
Bahamas		no★			No restrictions on foreign currency. Max. of BMD70 per person can be exported without permission.
Bangladesh	no★	no★	yes	yes	Only BDT100 may be imported or exported in local currency.
Barbados			yes	yes	
Belize		no★	yes	yes	Up to BND100 may be exported or imported in local without permission. Foreign currency up to BND400, except for tourists who may take out up to the amount declared on entry.

Benin	no	no★	yes	no★	Residents of the EEC can have unlimited funds. Residents of other areas up to amount declared. Must have authorisation above CFA100,000.
Bermuda		no★	yes	yes	Up to BED250 can be exported in local currency without permission.
British Virgin Islands			yes	yes	
Brunei			yes	yes	Can take in or out up to BRD1,000 in banknotes of local or Singaporean currency. Indonesian and Indian banknotes prohibited.
Bulgaria	yes	yes			Must change at official office and have full set of receipts before being allowed to take any currency out.
Burma	yes	yes	yes	yes	Foreign currency must be surrendered to an authorized dealer within one month of arrival in Burma. Reasonable amounts may be reconverted on departure. Only applicable if on a long stay.
Burundi			yes	yes	
Cameroon		no★			Up to CFA20,000 can be exported.
Cape Verde	yes	yes	yes	yes★	If not declared on arrival, there is a ceiling of CVE6,000 for export of foreign currency.
Cayman Islands		no★			Up to CID50 can be exported in local cash.
Central African Republic	no★	no★	yes	yes	Can import or export up to CFA75,000 in local currency unless in the French monetary area, when it is unlimited.
Chad		no★	yes	yes	Up to CFA10,000 can be exported in local currency.
Chile				no★	Central and South American citizens can take out up to US$200. Others US$800. Sales of US$ are not allowed to non-residents.
China	yes	yes	yes	yes	
Colombia		no★	yes	yes	Can only reconvert up to COP60 on presentation of certificate of exchange. Up to COP500 can be exported in local currency.
Congo		no★	yes	yes	Up to CFA25,000 can be exported in local currency.
Costa Rica					Only US$ accepted for exchange.
Côte d'Ivoire			yes	yes★	Up to CFA10,000 in local currency and equivalent of CFA25,000 in foreign currency. Unlimited amounts in traveller's cheques issued abroad.
Cuba	yes	yes	yes	yes	
Cyprus	no★	no★	no★	no★	Can import and export up to CYL50. Foreign currency of more than US$1000 must be declared.

Czechoslovakia	yes	yes			There is a minimum spending limit of 30DM (approx £8) per day.
Denmark					Must prove that any amount above DKK25,000 was imported to be allowed to export.
Dominica		yes	yes	yes	
Dominican Rep.	yes	yes	yes	yes	No limit on foreign traveller's cheques. Up to US$5,000 in foreign bank notes may be exported. Exchange may take place at authorized dealers only.
Egypt	no★	no★	yes	yes	A max. of EGL20 may be imported or exported in local currency. Must change US$150 on arrival.
Equatorial Guinea	yes	no★			Local currency of up to CFA3,000 may be exported.
Ethiopia	no★		yes	yes	Up to ETB10 may be imported in local currency.
Finland	no★	no★	yes	yes	Local currency of up to FIM500 may also be imported or exported.
France				no★	There is a limit of FF5,00 in foreign or local currency unless you have declared a higher amount on arrival. Traveller's cheques, letters of credit etc. issued abroad are unlimited.
Gabon		no★	yes	yes	Up to CFA200,000 may be taken out in local currency.
Gambia					Will not accept currencies of Algeria, Ghana, Guinea Rep. Mali, Morocco, Nigeria, Sierra Leone and Tunisia.
East Germany	yes	yes	yes	yes	Minimum expenditure requirement of 25 Marks a day to be changed in advance. May re-exchange anything over this amount.
Ghana	no★	no★	yes	yes	Up to GHC20 may be imported or exported in local currency if recorded in passport. Unused currencies may be re-exchanged on presentation of a form to show that they were obtained from an authorized dealer while in Ghana.
Gibraltar			yes	yes	
Greece	no★	no★	no★	no★	Up to DRA3,000 may be imported or exported in local currency. Must declare amounts above US$500 in foreign currency on entry.
Guinea Rep.	yes	yes	yes	yes	
Guinea-Bissau	yes	yes	yes	yes	
Guyana	no★	no★	yes	yes	Up to GYD40 may be imported or exported in local currency.
Honduras			yes★	yes★	US$ only.

Country					Notes
Hungary	yes	yes	yes	yes	Permission for export needed if you've been in the country more than 3 mths.
Iceland	no★	no★	yes	yes	Up to IKR8,000 may be imported or exported in local currency.
India	yes	yes	yes★	yes	Must declare any currency above a value of US$1,000.
Indonesia	no★	no★			Up to RPA50,000 allowed in or out in local currency.
Iran	no★	no★	yes	yes	May bring in or take out up to IRI2,000 in local currency.
Iraq	no★	no★	yes	yes	May bring in or take out up to IRD25,000. Israeli currency banned.
Ireland		no★	yes	yes	Max. of IRL100 in local currency may be taken out. May only export up to IRL500 in foreign currency if not declared on entry.
Israel		no★	yes	yes	A maximum of ILS500 in local currency may be exported. Up to US$3,000 may be reconverted on provision of exchange receipts.
Italy	no★	no★	yes	yes	A maximum of 200,000 lire may be moved in or out, although export requires V2 form, obtained on arrival. Import or export of LIT100,000 notes forbidden.
Jamaica	yes	yes			Unused currency will be exchanged on departure, on presentation of receipts for all exchanges made during the stay.
Japan	no★	no★			A max. of 5 million yen may be imported or exported in local currency.
Jordan		no★	yes	yes	May export up to JOD300 in local currency.
Kenya	yes		yes	yes	Tanzania and Uganda shillings only negotiable as traveller's cheques.
North Korea	yes	yes	yes	yes	
South Korea			yes★	yes	Limited amounts of local currency allowed in or out. Any currency over US$5,000 in value must be declared.
Libya	no★	no★	yes	yes	Up to LBD20 may be taken in or out in local cash.
Madagascar	no★	no★	yes	yes	Can take in or out up to FMG5,000 in local currency.
Malawi	no★	no★	yes	yes	May import or export up to MWK20 in local currency.
Mali			yes	yes	
Malta	no★	no★	yes	yes	Movement of local currency is limited to MAL50 coming in and MAL25 leaving per person.
Mauritania	yes	yes	yes	yes	
Mauritius	no★	no★	yes	yes	Allowed to bring in MAR700 and take out MAR350 in local currency.

Mexico	no*	no*			A max. of 5,000 pesos can be imported or exported in local currency.
Mongolia	yes	yes	yes	yes	
Montserrat			yes	yes	
Morocco	yes	yes	yes*	yes	Foreign currency over the value of MDH15,000 must be declared.
Mozambique	yes	yes	yes	yes	
Nepal	yes	yes	yes	yes	Indian currency also prohibited. This and Nepalese currencies may only be carried by citizens of the countries. May only reconvert 10% of amount converted.
Netherland Antilles	no*	no*			A max. of AFL100 may be imported or exported in local currency.
New Caledonia			yes	yes	
New Zealand		no*			A max. of NZ$100 may be exported in local currency. Must have permission to import any form of finance other than cash, credit cards and traveller's cheques.
Niger		no*			A max. of CFA25,000 may be exported in local currency.
Nigeria	no*	no*	yes	yes	May import or export up to NGN20 in local notes.
Niue		no*	yes	yes	Can export up to NZ$100 in local currency. Must get authorisation from a bank for export of foreign exchange.
Norway			yes	yes	A maximum of K5,000 local cash and up to K10,000 in foreign exchange may be taken out of the country.
Pakistan	no*	no*	yes	yes*	May take up to PAR100 in or out in local currency. Foreign currency above a value of US$500 must be declared on arrival.
Papua New Guinea			yes	yes	
Philippines	no*	no*	yes	yes	May take in or out up to PHP500 of which no more than PHP50 may be coins in local currency.
Poland	yes	yes	yes	yes	A minimum of US$15 must be exchanged for each day of stay.
Portugal		no*		yes*	You can export up to ESP100,000 or equivalent in foreign currency without declaring it on entry.
Romania	yes	yes	yes	yes	Must change a min. of US$10 or equivalent for each day's stay.
Rwanda	no*	no*	yes	yes	Up to FRR5,000 may be imported or exported in local currency.
St Christopher & Nevis			yes	yes	

St Vincent & the Grenadines				yes	Only UK£50 may be brought in in cash. Everything else unlimited.
Sao Tomé & Principe			yes	yes	
Senegal			yes	yes	May export CFA20,000 and other notes to a value of CFA50,000 without declaration on entry.
Sierra Leone	no*	no*	yes*	yes*	May import or export SLE20 in local currency. You may also take in UK£50 and take out UK£25 or equivalent in cash.
Solomon Islands			yes	yes	
Somalia	no*	no*	yes	yes	May take in or out Somali 200 in local currency. Must change foreign currency within 5 days of arrival.
South Africa	no*	no*	yes	yes	Up to R200 may be taken in or out in local banknotes.
Spain		no*			No formal limits on import, but if taking in more than PTS100,000 in local currency and PTS500,000 in foreign currency you should declare it. Can export up to PTS100,000 in local currency.
Sri Lanka	yes	no*	yes	yes	The import of Indian and Pakistani currency is also prohibited. A minimum of US$100 must be changed on arrival. May export up to SLR250 in local currency.
Sudan	yes	yes	yes		
Suriname	no*	no*	yes*	yes	Up to SFL100 may be imported or exported in local currency. Amounts over SLF500 in foreign currency must be declared.
Sweden	no*	no*		yes*	A maximum of 6,000SwKr can be exported or imported in local currency.
Syria			yes	yes	Must change US$100 or equivalent on arrival. Bills at top hotels to be paid in hard currency.
Taiwan	no*	no*	yes	yes	May import or export up to NTD8,000 in local currency. May export up to US$1,000 in cash unless more has been declared on arrival.
Tanzania	yes	yes	yes	yes	
Thailand	no*	no*	no*	no*	You may take in up to BHT2,000 per person or BHT4,000 per family and take out up to BHT500 per person in local currency. You may take in or out up to US$10,000 in foreign currency without declaring it.
Togo	no*	no*	yes	yes	You may take in up to AFR1 million and take out up to CFA25,000 in local currency.
Trinidad and Tobago			yes	yes	

Tunisia	yes	yes	no★		May import up to £500 in foreign currency without declaration. May re-exchange 30% of local into foreign currency up to a max. of TUD100.
Turkey	no★	no★			Can import up to equivalent of US$1,000 in local currency. May re-convert up to US$100 on exit.
Uganda	yes	yes	yes	yes	
USSR	yes	yes	yes	yes	
USA			yes★	yes★	Must declare anything over US$5,00 or equivalent.
Vietnam	yes	yes	yes	yes	
North Yemen					Must change at least US$150 into local currency on arrival.
South Yemen	no★	no★	yes	yes	May import or export up to DYD5,000 in local currency. Must change at least US$150 or equivalent on arrival to cover min. expenditure of US$10 a day.
Yugoslavia	no★	no★			May import or export up to YUD10,000 in local currency. Cannot re-exchange unused local currency on departure.
Zäire	yes	yes	yes	yes★	Export of foreign currency permitted provided it is declared up to the amounts not exchanged into local currency.
Zambia	yes★	yes★	yes	yes	A maximum of ZMK10 can be taken in or out in local currency. Keep a record of all exchanges for reconversion.
Zimbabwe	no★	no★	yes	yes	A maximum of Z$20 can be taken in or out in local currency.

Medical Requirements and Advice

Health Planning and Care

Abbreviations: C = Cholera; YF = Yellow Fever; T = Typhoid; M = Malaria. R = Recommended by DHSS.
1. Vaccinations which are an essential requirement for entry to the country concerned and for which you will require a certificate.
2. Those coming from infected areas, or who have been in infected areas within the past six six days will need a certificate.

| Country | Vaccinations | | | | Quality of Water | Cost & Quality of Health Care |
	C	YF	T	M		
Afghanistan	Yes	Yes[2]	R	R	Unsafe	Few facilities. The vets are good and treat people in the country.
Albania	Yes[2]	Yes[2]	R	No	Unsafe	Hospitals safe. Costs low.
Algeria	R	Yes[2]	R	No	OK in main towns.	Hospitals free but dirty. Doctors good, but nurses poorly trained. Private consultations from 1–200DA each.
Angola	Yes[1]	Yes	R	R	Unsafe	
Argentina	No	No	R	R	Safe in main towns.	
Australia	No	No	No	No	Safe	Standards excellent but costs high.
Austria	No	No	Yes[2]	No	Safe	Excellent.
Azores	No	Yes[2]	No	No		
Bahamas	No	Yes[2]	No	No	Safe but unpleasant	OK, but low overall standard. Fly to Miami for anything more than the simplest treatment. Some good private rooms.
Bahrain	R	Yes[2]	R	R	Normally OK in hotels	Standards good and govt hospitals free. Also private practice at vast expense.
Bangladesh	Yes	No	Yes	R	Unsafe.	
Barbados	No	Yes[2]	No	No	Safe except after floods.	Excellent facilities, private and general.
Belgium	No	No	No	No	Safe.	Excellent facilities and reciprocal agreement with UK.
Belize	No	No	R	R	Safe.	Facilities OK. Up to $20 for a hospital bed a night or $50 for a consultation.

					Water	Notes
Benin	Yes	Yes	R	R	Unsafe.	Poor.
Bermuda	No	No	No	No	Safe.	
Bhutan	R	No	R	R	Unsafe.	
Bolivia	No	Yes	R	R	Unsafe.	
Botswana	No	No	No	R	OK in large towns. Only use bore water in rural areas.	Safe.
Brazil	No	R	R	R	Safe in large towns.	
Brunei	R	Yes[1]	R	R	OK in good restaurants. Boil it elsewhere.	Very good and cheap. Dentists expensive.
Bulgaria	No	No	R	No		
Burkina Faso	R	Yes	R	R	Unsafe.	Dodgy.
Burma	No	No	R	R	Unsafe.	
Burundi	R	R	R	R	Unsafe.	Dodgy.
Cameroon	R	Yes[1]	R	R	Unsafe.	Dodgy.
Canada	No	No	No	No	Safe.	Excellent but expensive.
Cape Verde Islands	Yes[1]	Yes[2]	R	R	Unsafe.	
Cayman Islands	No	No	No	No	Usually safe.	Good, but difficult cases must go to USA.
Central African Rep	R	Yes	R	R	Unsafe.	Poor.
Chad	R	R	R	R	Unsafe.	Poor.
Chile	No	No	No	No	Ok in main towns only.	Good in cities, poor elsewhere and none in Patagonia.
China	No	Yes[2]	R	R	Unsafe in most places.	Good in major centres.
Colombia	Yes[1]	Yes[2]	R	R	Safe in main cities.	Erratic. Surgery etc. very expensive.
Comoro Islands	No	No	R	R	Unsafe.	
Congo	R	Yes[1]	R	R	Unsafe.	

Country	Vaccinations				Quality of Water	Cost & Quality of Health Care
	C	YF	T	M		
Cook Islands	No	No	R	No	Usually OK.	Limited but OK.
Costa Rica	No	No	R	R	Safe only in San José or major hotels.	Good and cheap.
Côte d'Ivoire	Yes	Yes	R	R	Unsafe.	
Cuba	No	No	R	No		
Cyprus	No	No	No	No	Safe.	OK but uncaring.
Czechoslovakia	No	No	No	No	Safe.	Excellent.
Denmark	No	No	No	No	Safe.	Excellent.
Djibouti	Yes	Yes[2]	R	R	Unsafe.	Poor.
Dominica	No	No	R	R	Mains water usually OK.	Safe but limited in scope.
Dominican Rep.	No	No	R	R	Unsafe.	
Ecuador	No	R	R	R	Safish only in Quito.	Private facilities safe, excellent and not too expensive. Govt facilities not as good. Very little in rural areas.
Egypt	No	No	R	R	Mains OK in cities.	
El Salvador	No	No	R	R	Unsafe.	
Ethiopia	Yes	Yes	R	R	Unsafe.	Expensive and not very good.
Falkland Islands	No	No	No	No	Safe.	Excellent, but limited. Will be charged for medication or repatriation.
Fiji	Yes[1]	Yes[1]	No	No	Safe except after cyclones.	Mostly adequate. Some excellent private care.
Finland	No	No	No	No	Safe.	Excellent but expensive.
France	No	No	No	No	Safe	Excellent and reciprocal agreement with UK.
French Guiana	No	Yes[2]	R	R	Unsafe.	
French Polynesia	No	Yes[2]	No	No	Unsafe.	

Country						
Gabon	No	Yes	R	R	Safe in main towns.	High standard but very expensive.
Gambia	Yes[1]	Yes	R	R	Unsafe.	Limited.
East Germany	No	No	No	No	Safe.	Excellent and free to UK citizens.
West Germany	No	Yes	No	No	Safe	Excellent. Reciprocal agreement with UK.
Ghana	Yes	No	R	R	Unsafe.	
Gibraltar	No	No	No	No	Safe.	Good but limited.
Greece	No	No	R	No	Safe.	Good but expensive.
Greenland	No	No	No	No	Safe.	
Grenada	No	No	No	No	Safe.	High standard.
Guam	No	No	No	No		
Guatemala	No	No	R	R	Safish.	
Guinea	No	Yes	R	R	Unsafe.	
Guinea-Bissau	No	Yes	R	R	Unsafe.	
Guyana	No	Yes[2]	R	R	Unsafe.	
Haiti	No	Yes[2]	R	R	Unsafe.	
Honduras	No	Yes[2]	R	R	Unsafe.	
Hong Kong	No	No	No	no	Safe.	Excellent but expensive.
Hungary	No	No	No	No	Safe in towns.	First Aid free. Standards good.
Iceland	No	No	No	No	Safe.	Good and reciprocal agreement with UK.
India	R	Yes[2]	R	R	Unsafe.	Variable. Some excellent private care.
Indonesia	R	Yes[2]	R	R	Unsafe.	OK but expensive in Jakarta, fair to poor in other towns, nothing rural areas.
Iran	Yes[1]	Yes[2]	R	R	Unsafe.	
Iraq	No	Yes[2]	R	R	Unsafe.	
Ireland	No	No	No	No	Safe.	Excellent.

Country	Vaccinations					Quality of Water	Cost & Quality of Health Care
	C	YF	T	M			
Israel	No	No	No	No		Safe.	Excellent.
Italy	No	No	R	No		Safe most places.	Excellent.
Jamaica	No	No	No	No		Safish.	
Japan	R	No	R	No		Safe.	Safe, but expensive.
Jordan	No	No	R	No		Unsafe.	
Kampuchea	R	No	R	R		Unsafe.	
Kenya	R	R	R	R		Safe in major centres.	Good in Nairobi, fair in other urban centres.
Kiribati	No	No	No	No		Safe.	
North Korea	R	R	R	R		Unsafe.	
South Korea	Yes[1]	No	R	R		Unsafe.	
Kuwait	No	No	No	No		Safe.	Good but limited. Free.
Laos	Yes	Yes[2]	R	R		Unsafe.	
Lebanon	R	Yes[2]	R	No		Safe outside Beirut.	US hospital safe but expensive.
Leeward Islands	No	No	No	No		Safe.	
Lesotho	No	No	No	R		Safe in towns.	Safe. Several good private doctors, and South Africa close.
Liberia	Yes[1]	Yes[1]	R	R		Safe in main towns.	Generally poor.
Libya	R	No	R	No		Unsafe.	
Luxembourg	No	No	No	No		Safe.	Excellent but limited.
Macau	No	No	No	No			
Madagascar	R	Yes[2]	R	R		Unsafe.	Doctors and equipment OK in hospitals, but nursing care low and drugs hard to get.
Madeira	No	No	No	No		Safe.	

Country						
Malawi	No	Yes[2]	R	R	OK in cities.	Safe.
Malaysia	No	Yes[2]	R	R	Unsafe.	
Maldives	No	No	R	No	Unsafe.	
Mali	Yes	Yes	R	R	Unsafe.	
Malta	No	No	No	No	Safe.	
Mauritania	No	Yes[2]	Yes	R	Unsafe.	
Mauritius	No	Yes[2]	R	R	Unsafe.	Private clinics OK. Govt. treatment free for those paying UK national insurance, but this is a last resort.
Mexico	No	Yes[2]	R	R	Unsafe.	
Monaco	No	No	No	No	Safe.	
Mongolia	No	No	No	No	Unsafe.	
Montserrat	No	No	No	No	Safe.	
Morocco	No	No	R	R	OK in main cities.	Hospitals OK and treatment free except for drugs. Use private clinics if possible.
Mozambique	R	No	R	R	Unsafe.	Virtually non-existant.
Namibia	No	No	R	R	Safe in towns.	
Nauru	No	No	No	No	Safe in towns.	
Nepal	R	R	R	R	Unsafe.	OK for minor ailments. Leave the country if anything more serious required.
Netherlands	No	No	No	No	Safe.	Excellent.
Neth. Antilles	No	Yes[2]	No	No	Safe.	
New Caledonia	No	No	No	No	Safe.	
New Zealand	No	No	No	No	Safe.	Excellent. Fees below UK levels for illness treatment, free if as a result of an accident.
Nicaragua	No	No	R	R	Unsafe.	
Niger	Yes[1]	Yes[1]	R	R	Unsafe.	Poor.

Country	Vaccinations					Quality of Water	Cost & Quality of Health Care
	C	YF	T	M			
Nigeria	Yes	Yes	R	R		Unsafe.	Private clinics safe, but limited. State hospitals poor and general shortage of drugs.
Norway	No	No	No	No		Safe.	Excellent.
Oman	No	No	No	R		Usually safe.	Treatment of a good standard but very expensive.
Pakistan	R	Yes	R	R		Unsafe.	Poor.
Panama	No	R	R	R		Safe	
Papua New Guinea	No	Yes[2]	R	R		OK in towns.	Just about safe, but insurance essential.
Paraguay	No	Yes[2]	R	R		Unsafe.	
Peru	No	No	R	R		Unsafe.	Public hospitals terrible. Private clinics in Lima good, but terribly expensive.
Philippines	No	Yes[2]	R	R		OK in main centres.	
Poland	No	No	No	No		Safe.	Standard OK and the cost reasonable.
Portugal	No	No	No	No		Safe.	Good.
Puerto Rico	No	No	No	No		Safe.	Good but limited. Anything major goes to USA.
Qatar	Yes	Yes[2]	No	No		Safe from mains supply.	Free care to all. Good for limited ailments and emergencies. Not recommended for serious disorders.
Réunion	Yes	Yes[2]	No	No		Unsafe.	
Romania	No	No	No	No		Should be safe.	
Rwanda	Yes	Yes[1]	R	R		Unsafe.	Poor.
Saint Helena	No	No	No	No		Safe.	
Saint Lucia	No	No	No	No		Safe.	
Saint Vincent and Grenadines	No	No	No	No		Safe.	

Country							
Western Samoa	No	Yes[2]	No	No	No	Unsafe.	
Sao Tomé e Príncipe	R	R	R	R	R	Unsafe.	
Saudi Arabia	No	Yes[2]	No	R	R	Safe in main cities.	Varies tremendously.
Senegal	No	Yes[2]	No	R	R	Unsafe.	Poor.
Seychelles	No	No	No	No	No	Unsafe.	Reasonable free care for minor ailments. Hospital rooms are expensive. Frequent mistakes due to language barrier.
Sierra Leone	R	R	R	R	R	Safe in towns.	Personnel of a high standard but facilities poor, and drugs in short supply.
Singapore	No	Yes[2]	No	No	No	Safe.	Safe to excellent.
Solomon Islands	No	Yes[2]	No	R	R	Best to boil.	Safe, but limited. Must go to Australia for specialist treatment.
Somalia	Yes	Yes	R	R	R	Unsafe.	Poor and limited.
South Africa	No	Yes[2]	No	R	R	Safe.	Excellent.
Spain	No	No	No	No	No	Safe.	Good.
Sri Lanka	R	R	R	R	R	Unsafe.	Private treatment safe and excellent and not vastly expensive.
Sudan	Yes[1]	Yes[2]	R	R	R	Unsafe.	Low cost, but varying standards. Don't get sick in rural areas.
Suriname	No	Yes[2]	R	R	R	Unsafe.	
Swaziland	R	Yes[2]	No	R	R	OK in towns.	
Sweden	No	No	No	No	No	Safe.	Excellent.
Switzerland	No	No	No	No	No	Safe.	Excellent but extremely expensive.
Syria	No	Yes[2]	R	R	R	Safe in Damascus.	Good and not expensive.
Taiwan	Yes[1]	Yes[2]	No	No	No	Safe.	
Tanzania	R	Yes[2]	R	R	R	Unsafe.	Treatment free in govt. hospitals. Usually safe, but limited and shortages of drugs and equipment.
Thailand	No	No	R	R	R	Unsafe.	

| Country | Vaccinations | | | | Quality of Water | Cost & Quality of Health Care |
	C	YF	T	M		
Togo	No	Yes	R	R	Unsafe.	OK but avoid the blood banks.
Tonga	Yes[2]	Yes[2]	No	No	Safe.	Comprehensive service provided by govt.
Trinidad & Tobago	No	No	No	No	Safe.	Safe. Drugs and treatment expensive.
Tunisia	No	Yes[2]	R	R	Public supply safe.	Safe. Private clinics excellent.
Turkey	No	No	R	R	Unsafe.	Excellent in main cities. OK elsewhere.
Turks & Caicos	No	Yes[2]	R	No	Safe.	Fairly good. Anything serious is treated in the USA.
Tuvalu	No	No	No	No	Safe.	
Uganda	R	Yes[1]	R	R	Unsafe.	Mission hospitals OK.
United Arab Emirates	Yes	Yes[2]	No	R	Safe.	Safe but expensive.
USA	No	No	No	No	Safe.	Excellent but astronomically expensive.
USSR	No	No	R	No	Unsafe.	
Uruguay	No	No	R	R	Unsafe.	
Vanuatu	No	No	No	R	Safe.	Reasonable standard. Serious cases flown to Australia.
Venezuela	No	Yes[2]	R	R	Unsafe.	
Vietnam	No	No	R	R	Unsafe.	
Virgin Islands	No	No	R	No	Safe.	
North Yemen	Yes[1]	Yes[2]	R	R	Unsafe.	Private clinics OK; govt. hospitals terrible.
South Yemen	Yes[1]	Yes[2]	R	R	Unsafe.	
Yugoslavia	No	No	No	No	Safe.	Good and free to UK nationals.
Zaire	Yes[1]	Yes[1]	R	R	Unsafe.	Terrible.

Zambia	R	Yes	R	R	Unsafe.	Doctors good but facilities dreadful. Nearest decent treatment in Zimbabwe.
Zimbabwe	No	No	No	R	Mains supply safe.	Private clinics excellent. Generally good but no facilities for complicated surgery.

Notes:

Yellow Fever vaccinations do not apply for children under one year old.

Hepatitis: Travellers to places with primitive sanitation should consider protection again infectious hepatitis (gamma globulin). Seek advice from your doctor.

Tetanus: All travellers should be actively immunized against tetanus.

Polio and meningitis: Anyone travelling on the Indian sub-continent should be protected against these diseases.

We would recommend that although typhoid vaccinations are not strictly necessary in most places, they should be kept up to date at all times.

Vaccination Centres and Information

BELGIUM

In Belgium vaccinations may be given by a GP, in which case the yellow card must be counter-signed by an authorized centre; or by one of the following vaccination centres, when no further endorsement is required:

Ministère de la Santé Publique et de la Famille
Inspection d'Hygiène – Service de Vaccination
Quartier Vesale
B-1010 Brussels
Belgium.

Ministère des Affaires Etrangères et du Commerce Extérieur
Centre Médical
Rue Bréderode 9
1000 Brussels
Belgium

FRANCE

In France vaccinations may be performed by a GP, in which case his signature must be endorsed by one of the following:

Direction de l'Action Sociale, de l'Hygiene et de la Santé
Services des Vaccinations
3bis Rue Mabillon
Paris 75006
France
Tel: 329 21 90

Institut Pasteur
24 Rue du Docteur Roux
Paris 7501515
France
Tel: 306 1919
Other vaccination centres in France:

Aérogare de Roissy
Tel: 862 2263
Hours: 9am-12 noon and 2-6pm

Aérogare d'Orly
Paris
Tel: 853 234
Hours: 9am-12 noon and 2-9pm

Aérogare du Bourget
Tel: 208 9890
Hours: 9-11am and 2.30-5pm

Air France
25 Blvd de Vaugirard
75015 Paris
Tel: (1) 320 1250
Hours: Mon to Fri 9am to 4.30pm
Sun. 9am to 12.00 and 2.00pm to 4.30pm
Smallpox, yellow fever, cholera, typhoid, polio, meningitis, rabies.

Centre Médical d'Air France
1 Square Max Humans
75014 Paris
Tel: (1) 323 94 64

Hours: 9am to 4.30pm Monday to Saturday
Note: on Saturday closed between 12 noon and 2pm.

Centre UTA Vaccinations
50 Rue Arago
92 800 Puteaux
Hours: 9am to 4.30pm. Cholera, smallpox.
Yellow fever by appointment.

Hôpital de l'Institut Pasteur
211 Rue de Vaugirard
75015 Paris
Tel: 567 3509
Hours: 9am to 5pm. All vaccinations including rabies.

Institut Arthur Vernes
36 Rue d'Assas
75006 Paris
Tel: 544 3894.

INDIA

International Inoculation Centre
New Delhi Municipal Committee Office
Town Hall
Parliament Street
New Delhi
Vaccination services in respect of cholera, typhoid and yellow fever are available to international travellers between 10am to 4pm on all working days.

SWITZERLAND

In Switzerland vaccinations are performed by GP's, at clinics or at vaccination centres, with the exception of yellow fever vaccination which can be obtained only at:

L'Institut d'Hygiène
2 Quai du Cheval Blanc
1227 Carouge/Geneva
Tel: (022) 43 80 75
Other vaccination centres in Switzerland are:

Schweizerisches Tropeninstitut Basel
Socinstrasse 75
4051 Basel
Tel: 061-23 38 96
One can also obtain information on vaccinations here.

Ospedale S Giovanni
Pronto Socorso
6500 Bellinzona
Tel: 092-25 03 33
By appointment Thursdays 10-11am

Inselspital Medinzinische Poliklinik
Freiburgstr 3
3010 Bern
Tel: 031-64 25 25
By appointment.

Service du Médecin Cantonal
Départment de la Santé Publique
Route des Cliniques 17
1700 Fribourg
Tel: (037) 21 14 44
By appointment.

Institute d'Hygiène
Service du Médecin Cantonal
Quai Cheval-Blanc 2
1211 Geneva
Tel: 022-43 80 75
Tuesday and Friday 8.30-9.00am without appointment.

Policlinique Médicale Universitaire
Rue César-Roux 19
1005 Lausanne
Tel: 021-20 90 48

Kantonsspital Spitalzentrum
1 Stock
Personalartz
6004 Luzern
Tel: 041-25 11 25
By appointment.

Institut for Med. Mikrobiologie
Frohbergstr 3
9000 St. Gallen
Tel: 071-26 35 55

Swissair
Arzlicher Dienst Schulgebaude A
8058 Zürich Flughafen
Tel: 01-812 68 39

Impfzentrym

Gloriastr 30
8006 Zürich
Tel: 01-257 2006/2626
Hours: Monday 16.30-19.00hrs, Wednesday 13.00-16.00 hrs, Thursday 16.30-19.00 hrs, Friday 9.00-11.00 hrs, without appointment.

UK

In the UK, vaccination against diseases other than yellow fever can be carried out by the traveller's own doctor, or, exceptionally and by arrangement, at a hospital. A list of yellow fever vaccination centres together with details of health precautions for the traveller is given in the booklet *Notice to Travellers: Health Protection* prepared by the Health Departments of England, Wales and Northern Ireland and the Central Office of Information. This is available from the Department of Health and Social Security in London, the Welsh Office in Cardiff, the Department of Health and Social Services in Belfast, the Scottish Home and Health Department in Edinburgh, or from local offices of these departments. Other places where the traveller can be given vaccinations or information about vaccinations are:

British Airways Immunization
75 Regent Street
London W1R 7HG

Tel: 01-439 9584/5
Open Monday to Friday 8.30-16.30 hrs

Central Public Health Laboratories
Colindale Avenue
London NW9
Tel: 01-205 7041
Gamma globulin for immunization against hepatitis, and rabies vaccine are supplied to general practitioner if appropriate. Vaccines for foreign travel are not supplied by the NHS and must be paid for.

Health Control Unit
Terminal 3, Arrivals
Heathrow Airport
Hounslow
Middx TW6 1NB
Tel: 01-759 7209
Can give at any time up-to-date information on compulsory and recommended immunizations for different countries.

Hospital for Tropical Diseases
3 St. Pancras Way
London NW1 0PE
Tel: 01-387 4411

Liverpool School of Tropical Medicine
Pembroke Place
Liverpool L3 5QA
Tel: 051-708 9393

London School of Hygiene and Tropical Medicine
Keppel Street
(Gower Street)
London WC1E 7HT
Tel: 01-636 8636
Provides advice for intending travellers.

Thomas Cook Vaccination Centre
45 Berkeley Street
London W1A 1EB
Tel: 01-499 4000
Vaccinations and certificates given on the spot, also all vaccination information. Saturday mornings appointment necessary.

West London Designated Vaccinating Centre
53 Great Cumberland Place
London W1H 7HL
Tel: 01-262 6456
Hours: 9am to 5pm from Monday to Friday. No appointment necessary.

USA

Convenience Care Centres
World Trade Centre
350 South Figueroa Street
Los Angeles
California 90071
People who need vaccinations prior to their overseas trips can have them taken care of here.

US Department of Health and Human Services
Public Health Service
Center for Prevention Services
Division of Quarantine

Atlanta
Georgia 30333
Publish a booklet annually,'Health Information for International Travel' *($4.25) available from Superintendent of Documents, US Govt. Printing Office, Washington DC 20402.*

The USHPS
330 Independence Avenue SW
Washington
DC 20201

Medical Care Abroad

American Diabetes Association
2 Park Ave
New York
NY 10016
USA
Offers a reprint of travel tips and a list of diabetes organizations throughout the world.

Comité Français pour la Santé
9 Rue Newton
75116 Paris
France
Tel: (1) 723 7207
Publishes a booklet giving practical advice on health for travellers: 'Vous allez partir en voyage ... Mini-guide santé du voyageur.'

Caisse Primaire d'Assurance Maladie de Paris
Direction des Relations Internationales
173/175 Rue de Bercy
75586 Paris Cedex 12
Tel: 346 12 53
The office to which French travellers should apply with any queries or claims about reimbursement of medical expenses incurred abroad.

Elvia Compagnie d'Assurances et d'Assistance
51 Rue de Ponthieu – Entrée D1
75381 Paris Cedex 08
France
Tel: (1) 562 8484
Telex: 290 963 F
One of the two most reliable companies in France offering assistance to the international traveller, instead of reimbursement afterwards.

Europ Assistance
23/23 Rue Chaptal
75445 Paris
France
Tel: 285 8585
Provides a 24-hour service and a worldwide network of representatives, enabling the company to supply immediately a doctor, medic, medically-equipped aircraft or other assistance as needed. One of the two most reliable companies in France offering assistance to the international traveller, instead of reimbursement of expenses afterwrds.

Europ Assistance Ltd
252 High Street
Croydon
Surrey
Tel: 01-680 1234
Provides a worldwide medical emergency service. Specialists in ambulance repatriation. Contracts incorporate medical expenses insurance. The Operational headquarters is fully manned by experienced multi-lingual co-ordinators, 24 hours a day every day.

Exeter Hospital Aid Society
176 Fore Street
Exeter
Devon EX4 3AY
Offers a 'worldwide provident scheme' which can be useful to people whose medical expenses are not covered by their employer.

The Flying Doctor's Society of Africa
London House (AMREF)
68 Upper Richmond Road
London SW15 2PR
Tel: 01-874 0098
Provides financial backing for the East African Flying Doctor Service (part of the African Medical and Research Foundation). Members are guaranteed free air transport if injured or taken seriously ill while on safari in East Africa. Temporary membership is available for tourists or visitors to East Africa and confers the same benefits. (Cost £5.00 for one month, £12.00 for one year.)

Hôpital St. Louis
40 Rue Bichat
75010 Paris
France
Tel: 205 8310
Specializes in tropical and venereal diseases. Tests on returned travellers can be performed here at low costs.

IAMAT
International Association for Medical Assistance to Travellers.
736 Center Street
Lewiston
NY 14092
USA
and
St Vincent's Hospital
Victoria Parade
Melbourne 3065
Australia
and
123 Edward Street
Suite 725
Toronto
Ontario
Canada M5G 1E2
and
188 Nicklin Road
Guelph
Ontario
Canada N1H 7L5
A non-profit organization dedicated to the gathering and dissemination of health and sanitary information worldwide for the benefit of travellers and to help

them find qualified medical care when travelling outside their country of residence. To this end IAMAT publishes a series of charts and a directory of English-speaking doctors who have been trained in Europe or North America, who are on call to IAMAT members 24 hours a day and who have agreed to a set fee schedule.

IAMAT membership is free to any travellers. The association is supported by voluntary contributions.

MASTA
Ross Institute of Tropical Hygiene
Keppel Street
(Gower Street)
London WC1E 7HT
Tel:636 8636
Provides personalised advice for those travelling abroad. Taking into consideration your schedule, where, how and when you are travelling, you will be given a schedule of what jabs to have, a list of what medication to take with you, and a basic guide to health care in the region.

Medic Alert Foundation
Turlock
California 95380
USA
Tel: (209) 668 3333
The Medic Alert Foundation emblem, worn as a bracelet or necklace, is engraved with the wearer's special condition (blood group, a heart condition, an allergy to antibiotics) and a 24 hour emergency telephone number. The phone number (209) 634 4917 USA, which may be called collect from any location in the world, gives access to vital information filed for use in an emergency situation.

Medical Passport Foundation, Inc
PO Box 820
Deland
Florida 32720
USA
Tel: (904) 734 0639
Provides information and advice for those with pre-existing health problems. Provides the Medical Passport, and the emergency Mini-Medical Passport which contain your medical history in portable form for on-the-spot medical identification of your medical record to any physician wherever you are. Contains more than emergency data and has saved lives, warning of allergic reactions or current disorders such as diabetes.

Metpath UK
60 Wimpole Street
London S1E 2UZ
Confidential AIDS testing service. Certification acceptable to Saudi Arabia available on request.

Mondial Assistance
8 Place de la Concorde
75008 Paris
France
Tel: 266 39 42
Medical insurance and emergency service.

The Hospital for Tropical Diseases
3 St. Pancras Way
London NW1 0PE
Tel: 01-387 4411
Returned travellers suspecting disease may be referred here by their general practitioners. (See Vaccination Centres, page 000).

St. John Ambulance Headquarters
1 Grosvenor Crescent
London SW1X 7EF
Tel: 01-235 5231 during office hours.
    01-235 5238 at other times.
Provides doctors and nurses and many members with specialized aeromedical training to escort sick and injured persons by air to or from any part of the world. It runs special ambulances equipped to travel to and from the continent with patients when air travel is not possible. Published definitive First Air Manual in association with The Red Cross.

Trans-care International Ltd
193-195 High Street
Acton
London W3 9DD
Tel: 01-993 6151 (20 lines)
Telex: 934525
Trans-care provides worldwide medical assistance services day and night. Air ambulances, doctors SRNs are always available. Response to all medical emergencies is immediate.

The Traveller's Medical Service
Golden Square
Petworth
West Sussex GU28 0AP
Tel: (0798) 43383
All types of medical advice from 'phone consultation to air ambulance repatriation. Fee paying, not insurance premium.

Note: For Medical Equipment see Equipment: Medical, page 761.

Hospitals or Clinics either run by English speaking doctors or which have interpreters

Algeria   Hôpital Mustapha, Ave Battendier, (nr ler Mai), Algiers. Tel: 663 333.

Argentina	British Hospital, Perdrial 74, 1280 Buenos Aires. Tel: 23-1081
Andorra	Clinica Verge de Meritxell, Escaldes Centre Hospitalari, Andorra la Vella.
Austria	Contact the Osterreichische Arztekammer, Weinburgasse 10-12, 1010 Vienna. Tel: 01043/222/53 69 44 52 679
Bahrain	American Mission Hospital, and International Hospital, Manama.
Belize	Belize City Hospital, Eve Street, Belize City
Bermuda	King Edward V11 Memorial Hospital; St. Brendon's Hospital.
Burma	Kandawgyi Clinic for diplomats and foreigners.
Burundi	Bujumbura
Chile	Santiago and a few major cities offer informal interpreting services but in general the personnel have a basic working knowledge of English.
China	Doctors may speak English in the large cities. Very unlikely elsewhere.
Colombia	Clinica Shio, Bogotá Clinica Marly, Bogotá Clinica Santa Fe, Bogotá Clinica San Juan de Dios, Cali.
Côte d'Ivoire	Chu Cocody Chu Treichville
Czechoslavakia	Fakulini Poliklinika, Karlovo Namesti 42, Prague 2
Dominican Rep	Clinca Gomez Patino, Avenue Independencia, Santo Domingo. Centro Medico Nacional, Ave Maximo Gomez, Santo Domingo Clinica Yunen, Ave Bolivar, Santo Domingo
Dominica	Princess Margaret Hospital, Goodwill, Roseau. Tel: 82231/3 Harlsbro Medical Centre, Hillsborough St, Roseau. Tel: 83332
Ecuador	Hospital Metropolitano, Ave Mariana de Jesus, s/n y Occidental, Quito. Tel: 234936 Hospital Vozandes, Villa Lengua, 267 y Av. 10 de Agosto. Tel: 241540.
El Salvador	Policlinica Salvaforena, SA, 25 Avenida Norte, San Salvador. Tel: 250 588 25 0565 Centro de Emergencias, SA Colonia la Esperanza, 2a Diagonal, San Salvador. Tel: 257 513; 253 583; 254 651; 251 871; 259 303
Ethiopia	Black Lion Hospital, Addis Ababa. Tel: 151211 Yekatit Hospital, Addis Ababa. Tel: 113065 Zawditu Hospital, Addis Ababa. Tel: 448085 Ospidem Hospital, Asmara. Tel: 04-114178
Finland	Helsinki University Central Hospital, Meilahti, Haarrmanink 3. Tampere Central Hospital.
Gabon	Hôpital Chambrier, Hôpital Général de CBV, Hôpital Jeanne Ebarg, Hôpital Josephine Bongo
Guyana	Georgetown Hospital, New Market St, Cummingsburg, Georgetown. St. Joseph's Mercy Hospital, 129-136 Parade Street, Kingston, Georgetown. Medical Arts Centre, 265 Thomas St, Cummingsburg, Georgetown. Woodlands Hospital. 110-111 Carmichael St, Cummingsburg. Davis Memorial Hospital, 121 Durban St, Lodge Prashad's Hospital, 258 Thomas and Middle Streets, Cummingsburg.
Iceland	Borgarspitalinn, Reykjavik Lanndspitalinn, Reykjavik Landakotsspitali, vid Tungotu, Reykjavik Sjukrahusid, Akueryr, Sjukrahusid, Isafirdi Sjukrahusid, Vestmannaeyjum.
Iraq	98% of the Medical Practitioners speak English.
Japan	Kobe Kaisai Hospital, 11-15 Shinohara-Kitamachi 3-chome, Nada-ku. Tel: 871 5201 Osaka University Hospital, 1-50 Fukushima 1-chome, Fukushima-ku. Tel: 06-451 0051 Kyoto – Sakabe Clinic, 435 Yamamoto-cho, Gokomachi, Nijo Sagaru, Nakagyo-ku.

Jordan	Al-Ahli Hospital Italian Hospital Al-Khalidy Hospital Al-Muasher Hospital Shmeisani Maternity Hospital
Kenya	Nairobi Hospital, and Aga Khan Hospital, Nairobi
South Korea	Seoul National University Hospital, 7601-1 Severance Hospital, 322-0161/79 Korea National Medical Centre, 265-91020/5 Songshim Hospital, 267-8111/9 Ewha Woman's Hospital, 762-5061/9 Korea University Hospital 762-5110/30 Korea General Hospital, 725-80021 Songmo Hospital, 771-76 Paik Foundation Hospital, 265-61211/9 Sunchonhyan Hospital, 794-7191/8 Hyonghee University Hospital, 966-1701/5
Lebanon	American University Hospital, Hotel Dieu de France, St Charles Hospital, Hazmieh
Lesotho	Queen Elizabeth Hospital, Maseru Scott Hospital, Morija
Liberia	J.F.Kennedy Medical Centre, Government Hospital, Monrovia St. Joseph's Catholic Hospital (private), PO Box 512, Monrovia. Tel: 261688 Phebbe Hospital, Dr. Kasser's clinic, Cooper's clinic, ELWA Hospital
Madagascar	Hôpital Militaire d'Antananarivo. Tel: 40341 Hôpital Général d'Antananarivo (Befelatanana). Tel: 22384 Clinique de Franciscaines. Tel: 23554 Missionaires de Marie.
Malawi	Adventist Health Centre, Box 51, Blantyre. Tel: 620 006.
Malta	St. Luke's Mangia. Tel: 21251, 607860. Craig Hospital, Gozo. Tel: 556851
Mauritius	Dr A. Sewgobind, Civil Hospital. Tel: 23201
Mexico	American British Cowdray Hospital, Sur 136, Esp Observatorio, Mexico City.
Nepal	Ciwec Clinic, Baluwatar. Tel: 410 983 Patan Hospital. Tel: 522 278/521 034 Teaching Hospital, Maharajganj. Tel: 412 808 Bir Hospital, Manabouda. Tel: 223 807 Himalayan Rescue Association. Tel: 222 014/220 001
Peru	Clinica Anglo Americana, Av. Salazar, (San Isidro). Tel: 403570 Clinica International, Washington 1475 (Lima) Tel: 288060 Clinica San Borja Av, Del Aire 333, (San Borja). Tel: 413141
Portugal	British Hospital, 49 Rue Saraiva de Carvalho, Lisbon
Qatar	Hamad General Hospital. Tel: 446 446 Womens Hospital. Tel: 420 555
Saudi Arabia	Saudi Medical Clinic, Riyadh. Tel: 01-479 0343
Seychelles	Victoria Hospital, Mount Fleurie, Box 52, Mahe. Tel: 24440 Anse Royle Hospital, Anse Royle, Mahe. Tel: 71222 Baieste Ann Hospital, Praslin. Tel: 33333
Sierra Leone	Connaught Nursing Home. Tel: 22001 Netland Nursing Home, 4d College Road, Cohgo Town. Tel: 31476
Sudan	Khartoum Clinic, Street 25, New Extension, Khartoum 2. Tel: 42157
Syria	Medical Care Centre, Damascus. Tel: 718 970/75
Tahiti	Dr. Charles Fichier, Padfai Clinique, BP 545, Boulevard Podare, Papeete. Tel: 30202 Dr. Charles Bronstein, Ardella Clinique, Rue Cardella, Papeete. Tel: 28190
Tibet	Chinese Hospital, just off Jianshe Lu, (east of Potala) Lhasa.
Turkey	American Hospital, Guzelbahce Sokak, Nisantasi. Tel: 148 6030

	French Hospital, Paster, Taskisla Pangalti. Tel: 148 4756
	French Hospital, La Paix, Buyukdere Caddesi, Sisli.Tel: 148 1832
	German Hospital, Siracevizler Caddesi 100. Tel: 143 5500
	Italian Hospital, Defterdar Yokusu, Tophane. Tel: 149 9751
Uganda	Nsambya Hospital, Gaba Road, Kampala. Tel: 268 016/7
Uruguay	British Hospital, Av Italia 2402, Montevideo.
Vanuatu	Vanuatu General Hospital, Port Vila. Tel: 2100
UAE	New Medical Centre, Abu Dhabi. Tel: 332 255
North Yemen	Dar Al Shifa Clinic, Sana'a. Tel: 207 580/1
Zambia	Primary Care Services Ltd, Lusaka. Tel: 215 3858

Travel by: Air, Road, Water and Rail

Travel by

Air

Airlines of the World: Headquarter Addresses

Headquarter addresses and telephone numbers of many scheduled airlines. A list which may be useful for travellers with an unusual itinerary or enquiry or with a complaint about airline service.

Aer Lingus plc
Dublin Airport
Dublin
Ireland
Tel: 370011
Tlx: 25101

Aeroflot
Leningradsky Prospekt 37
Moscow 125167
USSR
Tel: 155 54 94
Tlx: 411969

Aerolineas Argentinas
Paseo Colon 185
Piso 4
Buenos Aires 1063
Argentina
Tel: 308551

Aerolineas Dominicas
Cibao International Airport
PO Box 202
Santiago de los Caballeros
Dominican Republic
Tel: (809 583 3410/1
Tlx: ITT (346) 1023

Aeromexico
Paseo de la Reforma 445 – 1st Floor
Mexico City
Mexico 06500
Tel: 286 4422
Tlx: 1772765

Aeroperu
Av. Jose Pardo
601 Miraflores
Lima
Peru
Tel: 478 900

Aerovias Colombianas
Calle 19
881, Ofic. 303
Bogotá
Colombia
Tel: (57 1) 234 7651

Air Afrique
01 BP 3927
Abidjan 01

Côte d'Ivoire
Tel: 32 09 00
Tlx: AIRAFRIC 785

Air Algérie
Compagnie Nationale de Transports Aériens
1 Place Maurice Audin
Algiers
Algeria
Tel: 639 234/5/6; 642 428

Air Botswana Pty Ltd
Cycle Mart Building
Lobatse Road
PO Box 92
Gaborone
Botswana
Tel: 52812
Tlx: 2413 BD

Air Burkina
BP 1459
Avenue Binger
Ouagadougou
Burkina Faso
Tel: 36155

Air Burundi
PO Box 2460
Bujumbura
Burundi

Air BVI Ltd
Box 85
Roadtown
Tortola
British Virgin Islands
Tel: 52346/7
Tlx: 292 7950

Air Canada
26th Flr, Place Air Canada
500 Dorchester Blvd, West
Montreal
Quebec
Canada H2Z 1X5
Tel: (514) 879 7000
Tlx: 06-217537

Air Djibouti
PO Box 505
Place Rue Marchand
Djibouti
Tel: 3051

Air Europe
Europe House
East Park
Crawley
West Sussex RH10 6AS
Tel: (0293) 519 100
Tlx: 878288

Air France
1 Square May Hymans
75757 Paris
Cedex 15
France
Tel: 4323 8181
Tlx: 200666

Air Gabon
BP 2206
Libreville
Gabon
Tel: 732 197/352/476
Tlx: 5218 GO

Air Guinee
BP 12
Av de la République
Conakry
Guinea
Tel: 3870

Air India
218 Backbay Reclamation
Nariman Point
Bombay 400021
India
Tel: 202 4142
Tlx: 0112 427

Air Inter
1 Avenue du Maréchal Devau
91550 Paray Vieille Poste
France
Tel: 4675 2337
Tlx: 250932F

Air Ivoire
07 BP 10
Abidjan 01
Côte d'Ivoire
Tel: 368 051
Tlx: 43399

Air Jamaica
72-76 Harbour Street
Kingston
Jamaica W1
Tel: 922 3460

Air Lanka
14 Sir Baron Jayatilaka Mawatha
PO Box 670
Colombo-1
Sri Lanka
Tel: 21291
Tlx: 1401

Air Liberia
PO Box 2076
Monrovia
Liberia
Tel: 22144/26464

Air Madagascar
31 Avenue de l'Independence
BP 437
Antananarivo
Madagascar
Tel: 22222

Air Malawi
PO Box 84
Blantyre
Malawi
Tel: Blantyre 620 811
Tlx: 4245

Air Mali
BP 2
Bamako
Mali
Tel: 233 36/235 36

Air Malta
Luqa Airport
Malta
Tel: 824 330
Tlx: MW 1389

Air Mauritanie
BP 41
Nouakchott
Mauritania
Tel: 2211 2681
Tlx: 73

Air Mauritius
PO Box 60
Port Louis
Mauritius
Tel: 08 770
Tlx: 4415

Air Melanesie
PO Box 72
Hong Kong and New Zealand House
Port Vila
Vanuatu
Tel: 2753/2643/2278

Air Micronesia
Box 298
Saipan
Mariana Islands
Tlx: 06-74402

Air Mongol – MIAT
Airport
Ulan Bator
Mongolia
Tel: 1-072 240

Air Moorea
Faaa International Airport

PO Box 6019
Papeete
Tahiti
Tel: 24834/24429
Tlx: 314

Air Nauru
80 Nauru House
Collins St
Melbourne 3000
Australia
Tel: 03-653 5730/5626
Tlx: AA 31158

Air New Zealand Ltd
Private Bag
Air New Zealand House
1 Queen Street
Auckland 1
New Zealand
Tel: 797 515
Tlx: NZ 2541

Air Pacific
Private Mail Bag
Raiwaga
Fiji
Tel: 86444
Tlx: LFJ 2131

Air Panama International
Avenida Justo Arsomena y Calle 34
Panama City
Panama Republic
Tel: 250 213/258 389
Tlx: 665

Air Polynesie
BP 314
Quai Bir Hakiem
Papeete
Tahiti
French Polynesia
Tel: 25850

Air Rwanda
BP 808
Kigali
Rwanda
Tel: 4493/3793
Tlx: AIRWA 554

Air Senegal
BP 8010
Yoff Airport
Dakar
Senegal
Tel: 50764/36913/32790
Tlx: 449 SENELAIR SG

Air Seychelles
Seychelles International Airport
Mahe
Seychelles
Tel: 23603
Tlx: 2314 SZ

Air Tahiti
BP 314
Quay Bir Hakiem
Papeete
Tahiti
French Polynesia
Tel: 25850

Air Tanzania
PO Box 543
Dar Es Salaam
Tanzania
Tel: 42258/111
Tlx: 41253

Air UK
Crosskeys House
Haslett Ave
Crawley
W. Sussex RH10 1HS
Tel: (0293) 517 654
Tlx: 877060

Air Zaire
4 Avenue du Port
BP 8552
Kinshasa
Zaire
Tel: 24986
Tlx: 21313

Air Zimbabwe
PO Box AP1
Harare Airport
Harare
Zimbabwe
Tel: 52601
Tlx: 4548 ZW

Alaska Airlines Inc
19300 Pacific Highway South
PO Box 68900
Seattle
WA 98168
USA
Tel: (206) 244 7000
Tlx: 32303

Alitalia
Palazzo Alitalia
Piazza Giulio Pastore
Rome 00144
Italy
Tel: 5441
Tlx: 61036

ALM – Antillean Airlines
Hato Airport
Curaçao
Neth. Antilles
Tel: 47060

Aloha Airlines, Inc
PO Box 30028
Honolulu
Hawaii 96820

USA
Tel: (808) 936 4125

Alyemda – Democratic Yemen Airlines
PO Box 6006
Khormaksar
Civil Airport
Aden
South Yemen
Tel: 52267/8/9

American Airlines, Inc
PO Box 61616
Dallas/Fort Worth Airport
Texas 75261
USA
Tel: (214) 355 1234
Tlx: 4630158

Andes Airlines
Aeropuerto Simon Bolivar
PO Box 4113
Guayaquil
Ecuador
Tel: 392 0560/070
Tlx: 04-3228

Ansett Airlines of Australia
501 Swanston Street
Melbourne
Victoria 3000
Australia
Tel: 688 1211
Tlx: AA 30085

Ansett New Zealand
PO Box 14
139 Christchurch Airport
Christchurch
New Zealand
Tel: 61415
Tlx: NZ 4811

A/S Norving
PO Box 167
9901 Kirkenes
Norway
Tel: (085) 91694
Tlx: 64304

Australian Airlines
50 Franklin Street
PO Box 2806 AA
Melbourne
Vic 3001
Tel: 665 1333
Tlx: 30109

Austrian Airlines
Fontanastrasse 1
PO Box 50
A-1107 Vienna
Austria
Australia
Tel: 68 35 11
Tlx: 30109

Avensa – Aerovias Venezolanas SA
Av. Universidad -Esq El Clorro
Edf. Torre El Clorro-Piso 13
Caracas
Venezuela
Tel: 562 3022

Aviaco – Aviación y Comercio SA
Maudes 51
Madrid 28003
Spain
Tel: 254 3600
Tlx: 27641

Avianca – Aerovias Nacionales de Colombia SA
Av. Eldorado 93-30
Bogotá
Colombia
Tel: 639 628/511
Tlx: 44427/30

Aviateca – Empresa Guatemalteca de Aviación
Aviateca
Avenida Hincapie
Aeropuerto La Aurora
Guatemala City
Guatemala
Tel: 63227/8
Tlx: 4160

Bahamasair
PO Box N-4881
Nassau
Bahamas
Tel: (809) 327 8451

Balkan Bulgarian Airlines
Sofia Airport
Sofia
Bulgaria
Tel: 751 012
Tlx: 22342

Biman Bangladesh Airlines
Bangladesh Biman Bldg
Motijheel
Dacca
Bangladesh
Tel: 255901
Tlx: 642649

Braathens SAFE Airtransport
Snaroyvn 30
N-1330 Oslo Lufthavn
Oslo
Norway
Tel: (02) 590 090
Tlx: 11066

Braniff Inc.
7701 Lemmon Avenue
PO Box 7035
Dallas
Texas 75209
USA
Tel: (214) 358 6011

British Airways
PO Box 10
Heathrow Airport
Hounslow
Middx TW6 2JA
Tel: 01-759 5511 (Main Switchboard)
 370 5411 (Fares and Reservations)
 370 4255 (Business and Travel Enquiries)
 759 2525 (Flight Enquiries)
 (0293) 3621 (Charters – Concorde and
 Subsonic)
Customer Relations W49
West London Terminal
PO Box 115
Cromwell Road
London SW7 4ED
Tel: 01-370 8881

British Caledonian Airways
Caledonian House
Crawley
Sussex RH10 2XA
Tel: (0293) 27890
Tlx: 87161

British Midland Airways
Donington Hall
Castle Donington
Derby DE7 2SB
Tel: (0332) 810552 (Reservations)
 (0332) 810742 (Administration)
Tlx: 37172

Brymon Airways
Plymouth City Airport
Crownhill
Plymouth
Devon
Tel: (0752) 705151
Tlx: 45462

Burma Airways Corp
104 Strand Road
Rangoon
Burma
Tel: 84566/74874
Tlx: 21204

BWIA International
E & M Hangar Compound
International Airport
Piarco
Trinidad
Tel: 664 4871
Tlx: 29425523

CAAC
PO Box 644
155 Dong-Si Street (West)
Beijing
China
Tel: 558861
Tlx: 22101

Cameroon Airlines
BP 4092

3 Av. du General de Gaulle
Douala
Cameroon
Tel: 422 525
Tlx: 5345 KN

Canadian Airlines Int
2500 Four Rentall Centre
1055 Dunsmuir Street
Box 49370
Vancouver
BC V7X 1R9
Canada
Tel: (604) 270 5211

Cathay Pacific Airways
Swire House
9 Connaught Road C
Hong Kong
Tel: 5-842 5000
Tlx: 73206

Cayman Airways Ltd
PO Box 1101
George Town
Grand Cayman
BWI
Tel: 9-2673

China Airlines Ltd
131 Nanking East Road Sec3
Taipei 104
Taiwan
Tel: 715 2626
Tlx: 11346

Compania de Aviacion Faucett
Aeropuerto Jorge Chavez
PO Box 14239
Lima
Peru
Tel: 513484

Continental Airlines Inc
2929 Allen Parkway
PO Box 4607
Houston
TX 77019
USA
Tel: (713) 630 5000
Tlx: 06 74402

Cook Islands International
50 King Street
Sydney 2000
Australia
Tlx: AA 20143

Cruzeiro do Sul SA Servicios Aereos
Avenida Rio Branca 128
PO Box 190
Rio de Janeiro
Brazil
Tel: 224 0522

Cubana – Empresa Consolidada Cubana de Aviación
Calle 23 No. 64
Havana
Cuba
Tel: 512307 XV/CU

Cyprus Airways Ltd
21 Athanasiou Dhiakou St
Nicosia
Cyprus
Tel: 43054
Tlx: 2225

Danair A/S
Kastruplund Gade 13
DK-2770 Kastrup
Copenhagen
Denmark
Tel: (01) 51 50 55
Tlx: 31205

Delta Air Lines, Inc
Hartsfield Atlanta Airport
Atlanta
GA 30320
USA
Tel: (404) 765 2600
Tlx: 542316

Dominicana de Aviación
Calle Leopoldo Navarro
Edificio San Rafael
PO Box 1415
Santo Domingo
Republic of Dominica
Tel: (809) 687 7111
Tlx: ITT (346) 0394

Douglas Airways Pty Ltd
PO Box 1179
Boroko
Papua New Guinea
Tel: 253 499
Tlx: NE 22145

Dragonair
19F Wheelcock House
20 Pedder Street
Hong Kong
Tel: (5) 810 5015
Tlx: 80253 DRAGH

Eastern Air Lines, Inc
Building 11
Room 1433 (MIALS)
Miami International Airport
Miami
FL 33148 USA
Tel: (305) 873 2211

East-West Airlines Ltd
19th Flr
323 Castlereagh Street
Sydney
NSW 2000

Australia
Tel: 02-219 5111
Tlx: 22610

Ecuatoriana
Torres de la Almagro
Avenida Colon y Reina Victoria
Quito
Ecuador
Tel: 54900

Egyptair
6 Adly Street
Cairo
Egypt
Tel: 922 444/920 999

El Al Israel Airlines
Ben Gurion Airport
PO Box 41
Tel Aviv
Israel
Tel: (03) 976111
Tlx: 31107

Emirates
PO Box 686
Dubai
UAE
Tel: 228151
Tlx: 45728 EM

Ethiopian Airlines
PO Box 1755
Bole Airport
Addis Ababa
Ethiopia
Tel: 182 222
Tlx: 21012

Fiji Air
PO Box 1259
219 Victoria Parade
Suva
Fiji
Tel: 313 666
Tlx: FJ 2258

Finnair
Mannerheimintie 102
00250 Helsinki 25
Finland
Tel: 90/410411
Tlx: 124404

Friendly Islands Airways
Private Bag
Nuku Alofa
Tonga
Tel: 22566
Tlx: 66282 TS

Garuda Indonesian Airways
Jalan Ir H. Djuanda 15
Jakarta
Indonesia
Tel: 370709
Tlx: 49113/4

Ghana Airways
Ghana House
PO Box 1636
Accra
Ghana
Tel: 664 856/7

Gulf Air
PO Box 138
Bahrain
Arabian Gulf
Tel: 322 200
Tlx: GULF HQ BAH BN 8255

Guyana Airways Corporation
32 Main Street
PO Box 102
Georgetown
Guyana
Tel: (02) 59490
Tlx: 2242

Hawaiian Airlines
Honolulu International Airport
PO Box 30008
Honolulu
HI 96820
USA
Tel: (800) 367 5392
Tlx: 7048 3707

Iberia – Lineas Aereas de España
130 Calle Velazquez
28006 Madrid
Spain
Tel: 261 9100/9500/8500
Tlx: 27775

Icelandair
Reykavik Airport
Reykjavik
Iceland
Tel: 690 100
Tlx: 2021

Indian Airlines
Airlines House
113 Gurdwara Rakabganj Road
Parliament Street
New Delhi – 110001
India
Tel: 388 951
Tlx: 031-2131/2576/2810

Iran Air
Mehrabad Airport
PO Box 2600
Tehran
Iran
Tel: 911 2592

Iraqi Airways
Saddam Hussain International Airport
Baghdad
Iraq
Tel: 888 5161/886 3999

Tlx: 28906

Japan Airlines – JAL
2-Chome
Marunouchi
Chiyoda-Ku
Tokyo
Japan
Tel: 213 6211

Jamahiriya Libyan Arab Airlines
PO Box 2555
Tripoli
Socialist People's Libyan Arab Jamahiriya
Tel: 602 083/5, 602092/5

JAT
Sava Center
M. Popovica 9
PO Box JAT
11170 Belgrade
Yugoslavia
Tel: 145 798

Kenya Airways
Jomo Kenyatta
PO Box 19002
Nairobi
Kenya
Tel: 822171
Tlx: 22771

KLM Royal Dutch Airlines
55 Amsterdamseweg
PO Box 7700
1117 ZL Schiphol Airport
Netherlands
Tel: (020) 499123
Tlx: 11252

Korean Air
KAL Building
41-3 Seosomun-Dong
Jung-Gu
(CPO Box 864)
Seoul
Korea
Tel: 751 7114
Tlx: 27526

Kuwait Airways
Kuwait International Airport
PO Box 394
Safat 13004
Kuwait
Tel: 710 167
Tlx: 23036 KT

LACSA – Lineas Aereas Costarricenses SA
La Uruca
San José
Costa Rica
Tel: 323 555

LAN – Chile SA
Huerfanos 757

Piso 8
Santiago
Chile
Tel: 39441
Tlx: (34) 441106

LAP – Lineas Aereas Paraguayas
Olivia 455
Asunción
Paraguay
Tel: 91040/1/2/3/4/5
Tlx: PY LAP 5230

Lao Aviation
BP 119
2 Rue Pan Kham
Vientiane
Laos
Tlx: 310 LAO AVON LS

LIAT (1974) Ltd
Coolidge Airport
Antigua
West Indies
Tel: 30142/3
Tlx: LIAT ANU AK 2124

Lina Congo
Avenue de 28 Aout 1940
PO Box 2203
Brazzaville
Congo
Tel: 3715/6
Tlx: 5243 KG LINCONGO

London European Airways
Luton International Airport
Luton LU2 9LY
Beds
UK
Tel: (0582) 416164
Tlx: 825657

LOT – Polish Airlines
39, 17 Stycznia Street
00 906 Warsaw
Poland
Tel: 460 411
Tlx: 814254

Lufthansa – German Airlines
2/6 Von Gablenzstrasse
D-5000 Cologne 21
West Germany
Tel: (0221) 8261
Tlx: 887 3531

Luxair
L-2987
Luxembourg
Tel: 4798-2311
Tlx: 2372 LGDDAP

Malaysian Airline System – MAS
33rd Floor
Bangunan MAS
Jalan Sultan Ismail

50250 Kuala Lumpur
Malaysia
Tel: 261 0555

Malev – Hungarian Airlines
1051 Roosevelt Square
2 Budapest
Hungary
Tel: 189 005
Tlx: 22-4954

Mexicana – Compania Mexicana de Aviación, SA
Balderas 36
Mexico City 1
DF Mexico
Tel: 585 2422
Tlx: 78870

Monarch Airlines
Luton International Airport
Luton
Beds LU2 9NU
UK
Tel: (0582) 424211

Mount Cook Airlines (NM)
Private Bag
Christchurch
New Zealand
Tel: 488 909

Nigeria Airways Ltd
Airways House
Murtala Muhammed International Airport
Ikeja
Lagos
Nigeria
Tel: 900476
Tlx: 22646

NLM Dutch Airlines
PO Box 7700
Building 70
Schiphol Airport (East)
Amsterdam
Netherlands
Tel: (020) 492 227
Tlx: 1125

Nordair Ltd
1320 Blvd Graham
Ville Mont Royal
Montreal
Quebec
Canada H3P 3C8
Tel: (514) 747 5592
Tlx: 05-826806

Northwest Airlines Inc
Minneapolis/St Paul International Airport
St Paul
Minnesota 55111
USA
Tel: (612) 726 2111

Olympic Airways
96 Syngrou Avenue
11741 Athens
Greece
Tel: (01) 9292-111
Tlx: 215134

Oman Aviation Services Co
Seeb International Airport
PO Box 1058
Muscat
Oman
Tel: 519211
Tlx: 5424 OAS

Orion Airways
East Midlands Airport
Castle Donington
Derby DE7 2SA
UK
Tel: (0332) 812469

Pacific Southwestern Airlines
Lindbergh Field
San Diego
CA 92101
USA
Tel: (714) 574 2361

Pakistan International Airlines – PIA (PK)
PIA Building
Karachi Airport
Karachi
Pakistan
Tel: 412 011
Tlx:2832 PIAC

Pan American World Airways, Inc
Pan Am Building
200 Park Avenue
New York
NY 10166
USA
Tel: (212) 880 1234
Tlx: 620 155/126437

Philippine Airlines
Administrative Offices
Vernida 111 Bldg
Lagaspi Street
Legaspi Village
Makati
Metro Manila
Philippines
Tel: 818 0111

Piedmont Aviation Inc
Smith Reynolds Airport
Winston-Salem
North Carolina 27102
USA
Tel: 767 5100
Tlx: AL WSL 806438

Polynesian Airlines Ltd
NFP Building
Beech Road

Apia
Western Samoa
Tel: Apia 21261
Tlx: 249 PALAPW

Qantas Airways Ltd
Qantas International Centre
International Square
(Box 489 G.P.O.)
Sydney
NSW 2000
Australia
Tel: 236 3636

Quebecair Inc
PO Box 490
Dorval Airport
Dorval
Quebec
Canada H4Y 1B5
Tel: (514) 631 9802
Tlx: 05-822584

Reeve Aleutian Airways, Inc
Passenger Service
4700 West International Airport Road
Anchorage
Alaska 99502
USA
Tel: (907) 243 1112
Tlx: 090-626 357

Royal Air Maroc
Aeroport Anfa
Casablanca
Morocco
Tel: 361620/364 184
Tlx: 21880/21942

Royal Brunei Airlines
PO Box 737
Bandar Seri Begawan
Brunei Darussalem
Tel: 32531
Tlx: BU 2737

Royal Jordanian
Housing Bank Commercial Center
Queen Nour Street
PO Box 302
Amman
Jordan
Tel: 672872
Tlx: 21501

Royal Nepal Airlines Corp
RNAC Building
Kanti Path
Kathmandu
Nepal
Tel: 214 511
Tlx: NP 2212

Ryanair
41 The Quay
Waterford

Ireland
Tel: 0510 78272
Tlx: 80713 BFWT EI

Sabena Belgian World Airlines
35 Rue Cardinal Mercier
B-1000 Brussels
Belgium
Tel: (02) 511 9060
Tlx: 21322

SAHSA – Servicio Aero de Honduras, SA
Ave Colón y 4a Calle
Tegucigalpa
Honduras
Tel: 220131-4
Tlx: 1146

SAS – Scandinavian Airlines
Ulvsundavaegen 193
S-16187 Stockholm-Bromma
Sweden
Tel: 08-780 1000
Tlx: 22263

SATA – Sociedad Acoriana de Transportes Aereos
Av Infante D Henrique 55
9500 Ponta Delgada
Azores
Tel: 27221/9
Tlx: 82276

Saudi Arabian Airlines (SAUDIA)
PO Box 620
Jeddah
Saudi Arabia
Tel: 686 0000

Sierra Leone Airlines
Leone House
PO Box 285
Siaka Stevens St
Freetown
Sierra Leone
Tel: 22075
Tlx: 3242

Singapore Airlines Ltd
Airline House
25 Airline Road
Singapore 1781
Tel: 542 3333
Tlx: RS 21241

Solomon Islands Airways Ltd
PO Box 23
Honiara
Solomon Islands
Tel: 595

Somali Airlines
Via Madina
PO Box 726
Mogadishu
Somalia
Tel: 80487
Tlx: 619

South African Airways
South African Airways Centre
PO Box 7778
Johannesburg
Rep of South Africa
Tel: 713 2206
Tlx: 80651
Sudan Airways
PO Box 253
Khartoum
Sudan
Tel: 41766
Tlx: 257

Suriname Airways Ltd
PO Box 2029
Zorg en Hoop Airfield
Paramaribo
Suriname
Tel: 73939

Swissair
PO Box 8058
Zurich
Switzerland
Tel: 813 1212
Tlx: 825 601

Syrian Arab Airlines
PO Box 417
Damascus
Syria
Tel: 22343/4/6
Tlx: 119192

TAAG – Angola Airlines
PO Box 79
Rua Luis de Camoes
123-6 Andar
Luanda
Angola
Tel: 23523

Taca International Airlines, SA
Edificio Caribe 2 piso
San Salvador
El Salvador
Tel: 232 244

Talair Pty Ltd (GV)
PO Box 108
Goroka
Papua New Guinea
Tel: 721393/233
Tlx: 72519

TAN Airlines – Transportes Aeros Nacionales, SA
Edificio Tan
Tegucigalpa
Honduras
Tel: 28674/5

TAP Air Portugal
Edificio 25

Aeroporto (Apartado 5194)
Lisbon-5
Portugal
Tel: 3511 899121
Tlx: 12331/2

Tarom – Romanian Air Transport
Otopeni Airport
Bucharest
Romania
Tel: 794910/333137
Tlx: 011-181

Thai Airways International
89 Vibhavadi Rangsit Road
Bangkok
Thailand
Tel: 513 0121

THY – Turkish Airlines
Cumhuriyet Caddesi 199-201
Harbiye
Istanbul
Turkey
Tel: 462050/462061
Tlx: 22681

Transbrasil S/A Linhas Aeras
Aeroporto de Congonhas Hangar
Sao Paulo
Brazil
Tel: 240 7411
Tlx: 021471

TWA – Trans World Airlines, Inc
605 Third Avenue
New York
NY 10016
USA
Tel: (212) 692 3000
Tlx: 960124

Tunis Air
113 Ave de la Liberté
Tunis
Tunisia
Tel: 288 100

Uganda Airlines Corp
Kimathi Road
PO Box 5740
Kampala
Uganda
Tel: 32990
Tlx: 61239

United Airlines
PO Box 66100
O'Hare International Airport
Chicago
IL 60666
USA
Tel: (312) 952 4000
Tlx: 287419

UTA – Union de Transports Aériens
50 Rue Arago

92806 Puteaux
France
Tel: 14 776 4133
Tlx: 610692F

Varig – Brazilian Airlines (RG) 042
365 Av. Almirante Sylvio Noronha
Rio de Janeiro G.B. 20 000
Brazil ZC-00
Tel: 292 6600
Tlx: 31373

VASP – Viacao Aerea Sao Paulo
Edificio VASP
04368 Aeroporto de Conganqas
01000 Sao Paulo
SP Brazil
Tel: (011) 240 7011
Tlx: 21493

VIASA – Venezolana Internacional de Aviación SA
Torre Viasa
Av. Sur 25
Plaza Morelos
Los Caobos
Caracas
Venezuela
Tel: 572 9522
Tlx: 21125

Virgin Atlantic
Sussex House
High Street
Crawley
Sussex
Tel: (0293) 38222
Tlx: 877077

Wardair Canada Inc
3111 Convair Drive
Mississauga
Ontario
Canada L5P 1C2
Tel: (416) 671 1331

Windward Island Airways International NV
PO Box 288
Philipsburg
St. Maarten
Netherland Antilles
Tel: 4210

Yemenia Yemen Airways
Airport Road
PO Box 1183
Sana'a
North Yemen
Tel: 232 389
Tlx: 2204

Zambia Airways
Ndeka House
Haile Selassie Avenue
Box 30272
Lusaka
Zambia
Tel: 213 674
Tlx: 43850

Main Airline Offices in the UK

Airline	Address	Telephone	Telex
Air Lingus	52 Poland St, London W1V 4AA	437 8000/734 1212	22179 ALTLON
Aeroflot	69/72 Piccadilly W1V 9HH	493 7436/759 2525	21704 SUSOVA
Aero Virgin Islands	25 Bedford Square, London WC1B 3HG6	637 7961	
Air Afrique	177 Piccadilly, London W1V 0LX	629 6114/493 4881	
Air Algérie	10 Baker Street, London W1M 1DA	487 5709/5903	24606 ALGAIR
Air Botswana	7 Buckingham Gate, London SW1E 6JP	828 4223	267042 CF AIR
Air Burundi	c/o Air France		
Air Canada	140 Regent Street, London W1R 6AT	759 2636/2331	262018 AIRCAN
Air Djibouti	c/o Air France		
Air Ecosse	Aberdeen Airport, Aberdeen, Scotland AB2 0PA	(0224) 724 782/771 177	
Air Europe	Europe House, East Park, Crawley RH10 6AS	(0293) 519 100/ 01-651 3611	878288 AIREUR
Air France	158 New Bond Street, London W1Y 0AY	499 9511/8611	8951888 AF NBS
Air Gabon	c/o Air France		
Air India	17-18 New Bond Street, London W1Y 0AY	491 7979/897 6311	934393 AILHR
Air Inter	c/o Air France		
Air Jamaica	Sabena House, 36-37 Piccadilly, London W1V OJA	437 8732/734 1782	
Air Lanka	1 Little Argyll Street, London W1R 5DB	439 0291/0181	261604 LANKA
Air Madagascar	c/o Air France		
Air Malawi	c/o British Airways		
Air Malta	St James House, 13 Kensington Square, London W8 5HD	937 7181/930 2612	919724 AIRMAL
Air Mauritius	48 Conduit Street, London W1R 9FB	434 4375/79/70	24469 AIR MK

Air New Zealand	New Zealand House, Haymarket, London SW1Y 4TE	930 3434/1088	265206 AIRNZ
Air Seychelles	Kingston House, Stephenson Way, Three Bridges, Crawley, Sussex	(0293) 36313/ 518888/513333	877033 AIRSEY
Air UK	Crosskeys House, Haslett Avenue, Crawley, Sussex RH10 1HSZ	(0293) 517654	877060 AUKK RH
Air Zaïre	29-30 Old Burlington St, London W1X 1LB	734 4210/434 1151	298947 QCZAIR
Air Zimbabwe	Colette House, 52-55 Piccadilly,London W1V	499 8947/491 0009	25251 AIRZIM
Alitalia	205 Holland Park Avenue, London W11 4XB	759 2510/1198/602 7111	27572 ALIT
American Airlines	16th Flr, Portland House, Stag Place, London SW1E 5BJ	629 0195/8817	23939 AMMAIR
Ansett (Australia)	20 Savile Row, London W1X 2AN	434 4071	27365 ANSETT
Australian Airlines	7-9 Swallow Street, London W1R 8DU	434 3864	25325 TAALON
Austrian Airlines	50-51 Conduit St, London W1R 0NP2	439 0741/1851/745 7508	21757 OSLON
Avianca	Ste 246, 162-8 Regent St, London W1	408 1889/437 3664	22896 LONDAV
Bakhtar Afghan	3rd Flr, 169 Piccadilly, London W1V 9DD	629 1611/493 1411	22668 AFGAIR
Balkan Bulgarian	322 Regent St, London W1R 5AB	637 7637	296547 BALKAN
Bangladesh Biman	9 Vigo Street, London W1X 1AL	439 0362/3/4/5	28766 BIMAN
British Airways	Speedbird House, PO Box 10, Heathrow Airport, Hounslow TW6 2JA 75 Regent Street, London W1R 7HG 421 Oxford Street, London W1R 1FJ	759 5511/897 4400	8813983 BAWYSC
British Caledonian	Caledonian House, Crawley,W. Sussex RH10 2XA	(0293) 27890/668 4222	87181 BCAL
	215 Piccadilly, London W1V 0PS	434 1501/2	
British Midland	Donington Hall, Castle Donington, Derby DE7 5SB	(0332) 810 741/552	37172
	1st Flr, Aviation House, Kingsway, London WC2N 6NH	430 2497/581 0864	
BWIA	20 Lower Regent St, London SW1Y 4PH	734 3796/839 7155	918746 BWLON

Canadian Airlines	62 Trafalgar Square, London WC2N 5EW	930 3501/5664	295543 CPAIR
Caribbean Airways	263 Tottenham Court Road, London W1P 9AA	636 2913/2151	23345 BAJAN
Cathay Pacific	7 Apple Tree Yard, Duke of York St, London SW1Y 6LD	930 7878/4444	918120 CATHEX
Cayman Airways	Hambleton House, 17b Curzon St, London W1Y 7FE	491 7756/493 5161	295035 CAYMAN
China Airlines	5th Floor, Nuffield House, 41-46 Piccadilly, London W1V 9AJ2	434 0707	265400 LONCI
Continental	Victoria House, 16 Consort Way, Horley, Surrey RH6 7AF	(0293) 771 681/7764642	877008 CALLGW
CSA-Czechoslovak	17-18 Old Bond St, London W1X 4RB	499 6442-6	21164 CEDOKL
Cubana	c/o Europe Air Promotion, 27 Cockspur St, London SW1Y 5BN	930 1138	893369
Cyprus Airways	Euston Centre, 29-31 Hampstead Rd, London NW1 3AJ	388 5411/5424	23881 CYPAIR
Dan-Air	Bilbao House, 36 New Broad St, London EC2M 1NH	638 1747/680 1011	888973 DANAIR
Delta Airlines	24 Buckingham Gate, London SW1E 6LB	828 5905/668 0935/9135	919210 DELTA
Dominicana de Aviacion	Ste 113, 4th Flr, 27 Cockspur St, London SW1	839 5379	
Eastern Airlines	1st Flr, Princes House, 36-40 Jermyn St, London SW1Y 6DN	734 7637	87450 LGWEA
Egypt Air	296 Regent St, London W1R 6PH	580 5477/734 2395	21832 LONDMMS
El Al	185 Regent St, London W1R 8BS	437 9255/439 2506	22198
Ethiopian Airlines	85-87 Jermyn St, SW1Y 6JD	930 9152/745 4235	917855 ETHAIR
Faucett Peruvian	Ste 163, 4th Flr, 27 Cockspur St, London SW1Y 5BN	930 1136	893369
Fiji Air	2a Thayer St, London W1M 5LG	486 6214	
Finnair	14 Clifford St, London W1X 1RD	629 4349/408 1222	918783
Gambia Airways	c/o British Caledonian		
Garuda	35 Duke Street, London W1M 5DF	935 7055/5036	8954225 GRUDA
Ghana Airways	12 Old Bond St, W1X 4BL	499 0201	21415 GHNAIR

Gulf Air	10 Albemarle St, London W1	409 0191/1951	28591 GFRES
Highland Express	Prestwick Airport, Ayrshire, Scotland KA9 2PL	(0292) 79822	
Iberia	Venture House, 29 Glasshouse St, London W1R 5RG	437 5622/9822	25308
Icelandair	73 Grosvenor St, London W1X 9DD	499 9971/493 6382	23689 ICEAIR
Iran Air	73 Piccadilly, London W1V 0QX	491 3656/409 0971	27285 IRHOMA
Iraqi Airways	4 Lower Regent St, London W1X 9DD	930 1155/7	27128 IRAQI
JAL Japan Airlines	5 Hanover Court, Hanover Square. London W1R 0DR	629 9244/408 1000	23692 JALLON
JAT - Yugoslav	Prince Frederick House, 37 Maddox St, London W1R 0AQ	629 2007/493 9399	261826 JATLON
Kenya Airways	16 Conduit St, London W1R 9TD	409 0277/409 3121	263793 KENAIR
KLM	Time & Life Bldg, New Bond St, London W1Y 0AD	750 9200/9000	934345
Korean Airlines	66-68 Haymarket, London SW1Y 4RF	930 6513/1957	919954 KALLDN
Kuwait Airlines	16-20 Baker St, London W1M 2AD	486 6666/935 8795	262518 KUWAIR
LAN Chile	3rd Flr, 151-153 Great Portland St, London W1N 5FB	636 3005/3006	27706
LAP Paraguayan	c/o Europe Air Promotion, 27 Cockspur St, London SW1Y 5BN	930 1138	893369
LIAT	c/o British Airways		
Libyan Arab Air	88 Piccadilly, London W1V 9HD	499 1016/0381	299519 LIBAIR
Lloyd Aereo Boliviano	Ste 501, 4th Floor, 27 Cockspur St, London SW1Y 5BN	930 1442	893369 FLIGHT
LOT - Polish	313 Regent St, London W1R 7PE	580 5037/8/9	27860 LOTLON
Lufthansa	Lufthansa House, 10 Old Bond St, London W1X 4EN	408 0442/0322	22751
Luxair	Rm 2004, Terminal 2, Heathrow Airport, Hounslow, Middx TW6 1HL	745 4255/4254	935580 LUXAIR
Malaysian Airline System	25/27 St. George St, Hanover Square, London W1R 9RE	499 6286/491 4542	25396 LAYANG
Malev Hungarian	10 Vigo St, London W1X 1AJ	439 0577	24841 MALEVL

Mexicana	35a Byng Road, Barnet, Herts EN5 4NW	440 7830/897 4000	893313 MEXIIC
Middle East Airlines	48 Park Street, London W1Y 4AS	493 5681/6321	24406/265065
Nigeria Airways	11-12 Conduit St, London W1R 0NX	629 3717/493 9726	23474 NIGAIR
Northwest Airlines	49 Albermarle St, London W1X 3FE	491 3270/629 5353	266658 NWAIR
Olympic Airways	Trafalgar House, Hammersmith International Centre, London W6 8SB	846 9966/9080	231135 AIROLY
PIA - Pakistan	1-15 King Street, Hammersmith, London W6 9HR	741 8066/734 5544	262503 PIALON
Pan Am	193 Piccadilly, London W1V 0AD	409 3377/759 2595	261522 PAA COM
Philippine Airlines	19th Flr, Centrepoint, 103 New Oxford Street, London WC1A 1QD	379 6855/409 1177	266479 FILAIR
Piedmont Airlines	36 Seymour St, London W1H 5WD	724 0178	297214 WALLON
Qantas	395-403 King St, London W6 9NJ 169-173 Regent Street, London W1R 8BE	748 3131	935378 QF LON
Royal Air Maroc	174 Regent St, London W1R 6HB	439 4361/8854	263163 RAMLON
Royal Brunei Airlines	Brunei Hall, 35-43 Norfolk Square, London W2 1RX	402 6904/2047	
Royal Jordanian	211 Regent St, London W1R 7DD	437 9465/734 2557	24430 ALIARJ
Royal Nepal	Ste 433, High Holborn House, 52 High Holborn, London WC1V 6RB	242 3131	23770 MSTTGP
Ryanair	240 Kilburn High Road, London NW6 2BS	625 4561	
Sabena	36-37 Piccadilly, London W1V 0BU	437 6950/60	23220 SABLON
SAA	251-259 Regent St, London W1R 7AD	734 9841/437 9621	25215 SAALON
SAS	52 Conduit St, London W1R 0AY	734 6777/4020	8811707 SASLON
Saudia	508-510 Chiswick High Rd, London W4 5RG	995 7755/7777	937957 SAUDIA
Sierra Leone Air	34 St George St, London W1R 9FA	408 0676/491 3291	21445 SLAIR
Singapore	580-586 Chiswick High Rd, London W4 5RB	995 4901/747 0007	935458 SIACHW

Sudan Airways	12 Grosvenor St, London W1X 9FB	629 3385/499 8101	261850 SDLON
Swiss Air	Swiss Centre, 10 Wardour St, London W1X 3FA	734 6737/439 4144	27784 SWRRES
Syrian Arab Airlines	27 Albermarle St, London W1X 3FA	493 2851/499 4707	262943 SYRAIR
TAP Air Portugal	Gillingham House, 38 Gillingham St, London SW1V 1JW	828 2092/0262	261239 TAPLON
Tarom	c/o British Airways		
Thai International	41 Albermarle St, London W1X 3FE	499 9113/491 7953	21491 THAINT
THY Turkish	11-12 Hanover St, London W1R 9HF	499 9240/7/9	262039 LONTHY
TWA	214 Oxford St, London W1N 0HA	636 5411/4090	22343 TWARES
Tunis Air	24 Sackville St, London W1X 1DE	734 7644/437 6236	892605 TUNAIR
Uganda Airlines	2 Mill St, London W1R 9TE	409 2180/1121	299825 UGAIR
United Airlines	7-8 Conduit St, London W1R 9TG	734 9282	22991
UTA	177 Piccadilly, London W1V 0LX	493 4881/629 6114	25965 TELUTA
Varig Brazilian	16-17 Hanover St, London W1R 9HG	759 0722/1179	
VIASA	19-20 Grosvenor St, London W1X 9FD	629 1223/493 5573/7287	28621 VIASAVEN
Virgin Atlantic	7th Flr, Sussex House, High St, Crawley, W. Sussex RH10 1BZ	(0293) 549771/38222	877077 VIRAIR
Wardair	12th Flr, Rothschild House, Whitgift Centre, Croydon CR9 3HN	686 5255	22625 WDLON
Yemenia	5-6 Cork St, London W1X 1PB	434 3926	269292 YEMAIR
Zambia Airlines	163 Piccadilly, London W1V 9DE	491 7521/0658	27127 ZAMAIR

Please note that this is not a complete list of airlines with London offices, but contains the larger ones.

US Offices of Foreign International Airlines

Aeroflot	1101, 16th Street, NW, Washington DC 20036
Aeromexico	8400 NW 52nd St, Miami, FL 33166
Aeroperu	327 SE First St, Miami, FL 33131
Air Canada	25th Floor, 1166 Ave of the Americas, New York, NY 10036

Air Afrique	1350 Ave of the Americas, New York, NY 10022
Air France	666 Fifth Ave, New York, NY 10019
Air India	345 Park Ave, New York, NY 10022
Air Pacific	Suite 108, 32133 West Lindero Canyon Road, Westlake Village, CA 91363
Alitalia	666 Fifth Ave, New York, NY 10019
Ariana Afghan Airlines	535 Fifth Ave, Suite 1609, New York NY, 10017
British Airways	245 Park Ave, New York, NY 10017
BWIA	610 Fifth Ave, New York, NY 10020
China Airlines	1648 K St, NW, Washington DC 20006
Dominicana de Aviación	1270 Ave of the Americas, New York NY, 10020
Egyptair	720 Fifth Ave, New York, NY 10019
El Al	850 Third Ave, New York, NY 10022
Ethiopian Airlines	200 E 42nd St. New York, NY 10017
Finnair	10 E 40th St, New York, NY 10016
Faucett	7720 NW 36th St, Suite 28, Miami, FL 33166
Guyana Airways	6555 NW 36th St, Suite 205-7, Miami, FL
JAL	655 Fifth Ave, New York, NY 10022
Kenya Airways	424 Madison Ave, 6th Floor, New York, NY 10017
KLM	437 Madison Ave, New York, NY 10017
LAB Airlines	310 Madison Ave, Ste 1316, New York, NY 10017
Icelandic Airlines	630 Fifth Ave, New York, NY 10020
LOT Polish Airlines	500 Fifth Ave, New York, NY 10010
Lufthansa	680 Fifth Ave, New York, NY 10019
MAS	Suite 2044, 420 Lexington Ave, New York, NY 10170
Malev	630 Fifth Ave, New York, NY 10020
Middle East Airlines	680 Fifth Ave, New York, NY 10019
Olympic Airways	647 Fifth Ave, New York, NY 10022
PIA – Pakistan Int.	Suite 1027, 17th St, NW, Washington, DC 20036
Philippine Airlines	212 Stockton St, San Francisco, CA 94108
Qantas	360 Post St, San Francisco, CA 94108
Royal Air Maroc	680 Fifth Ave, New York, NY 10019
Royal Jordanian	535 Fifth Ave, New York, NY 10017
SAS	138-02 Queen Blvd, Jamaica, NY 11435
Saudia	747 Third Ave, New York, NY 10017
Singapore Airlines	8370 Wilshire Blvd, Beverly Hills, Los Angeles, CA 90211-2381
South African Airways	605 Fifth Ave, New York, NY 10017
Swissair	608 Fifth Ave, New York, NY 10020
Taca International	PO Box 20047, New Orleans, LA 70141
TAN	PO Box 222, Miami Int. Airport, Miami, FL 33148
Thai Airways	Suite 230, 630 Fifth Ave, New York, NY 10111
UTA	9841 Airport Blvd, Suite 1000, Los Angeles, CA 90045
Zambia Airways	Suite 812, 370 Lexington Ave, New York, NY 10017

Airline Two-Letter Codes

Letters are often used in timetables, brochures and tickets to identify airlines. These are the codes of the main airlines, in alphabetical order.

A

AA	American Airlines
AC	Air Canada
AE	Air Europe
AF	Air France
AG	Aeronaves Del Centro (Passenger)
AH	Air Algérie
AI	Air India
AL	U.S. Air
AM	Aeromexico
AN	Ansett Airlines of Australia
AO	Aviaco
AQ	Aloha Airlines
AR	Aerolineas Argentinas
AS	Alaska Airlines
AT	Royal Air Maroc
AU	Austral
AV	Avianca
AY	Finnair
AZ	Alitalia

B

BA	British Airways
BC	Brymon Airways
BD	British Midland
BG	Biman Bangladesh Airlines
BI	Royal Brunei Airlines
BM	ATI – Aero Trasporti Italiani (Passenger)
BN	Braniff
BO	Bouraq Indonesia Airlines
BP	Air Botswana
BQ	Aliblu
BR	British Caledonian Airways
BT	Ansett N.T.
BU	Braathens S.A.F.E.
BV	Bopair
BW	BWIA International Trinidad & Tobago Airways
BY	Britannia Airways

C

CA	CAAC
CD	Trans Provincial Airlines
CF	Compania de Aviacion Faucett
CG	Ostermans Aero AB (Passenger)
CI	China Airlines
CK	Flinders Island Airlines
CL	Templehof Airways
CM	COPA – Compania Panamena
CO	Continental Airlines, Air Micronesia
CP	Canadian Airlines
CQ	Aerolineas Federal Argentina
CS	Commuter Express
CT	Midcontinent Airlines
CU	Cubana
CW	Airline of the Marshall Islands
CX	Cathay Pacific Airways
CY	Cyprus Airways
CZ	Celtic Air

D

DA	Dan Air Services
DB	Brit Air (Passenger)
DI	Delta Air
DJ	Air Djibouti
DL	Delta Airlines
DM	Maersk Air
DO	Compania Dominicana de Aviacion
DS	Air Senegal
DT	TAAG Angola Airlines
DW	DLT
DX	Danair
DY	Alyemda

E

EA	Eastern Air Lines
EC	Southern Airways
EF	Far Eastern Air Transport
EG	Japan Asia Airways
EH	SAETA
EI	Aer Lingus
EJ	New England Airlines
EL	Air Nippon
EM	Empire Airways
EQ	T.A.M.E.
ET	Ethiopian Airlines

EU	Empresa Ecuatoriana
EW	East-West Airlines
EX	Eagle Airways
EY	Europe Aero Service

F

FA	Finnaviation
FG	Bakhtar Afghan Airlines
FI	Icelandair
FJ	Air Pacific
FO	Western New South Wales Airlines
FR	Ryanair (Dublin)
FX	Express Air
FY	Metroflight Airlines

G

GA	Garuda
GB	Air Furness
GC	Lina Congo
GD	Air South
GE	Guernsey Airlines
GF	Gulf Air
GG	Grenada Airways
GH	Ghana Airways
GJ	Equatorial International Airlines of Sao Tomé
GK	Coast Aero Center
GN	Air Gabon
GQ	Big Sky Airlines
GR	Aurigny Air Services
GS	B.A.S. Airlines
GT	GB Airways
GU	Aviateca
GV	Talair
GY	Guyana Airways Corporation
GZ	Air Rarotonga

H

HA	Hawaiian Airlines
HB	Air Melanesie (Passenger)
HC	Naske Air
HH	Somali Airlines
HK	South Pacific Island Airways
HM	Air Seychelles
HN	NLM – Dutch Airlines
HO	Mid Pacific Airlines
HP	America West Airlines
HQ	Business Express

HR	Friendly Islands Airways
HS	Air North
HT	Air Tchad
HV	Transavia
HX	Holiday Express
HY	Metro Airlines

I

IA	Iraqi Airways
IB	Iberia
IC	Indian Airlines
IE	Solomon Islands Airways
IF	Interflug
IG	Alisarda
IH	Channel Flying
IJ	TAT – Transport Aerien Transregional
IK	Air Caribe International (Passenger)
IL	Bangor International Airline
IN	East Hampton Air
IP	Airlines of Tasmania
IQ	Caribbean Airways
IR	Iranair
IS	Eagle Air
IT	Air Inter
IU	Midstate Airlines
IY	Yemenia Yemen Airways
IZ	Arkia – Israeli Airlines

J

JD	Toa Domestic Airlines
JE	Manx Airlines
JG	Swedair
JH	Nordeste Linhas Aereas Regionais
JJ	Suncity Airlines
JK	Sunworld International Airways
JL	Japan Airlines
JM	Air Jamaica
JN	Japan Air Commuter
JO	Holiday Airlines
JP	Adria Airways
JQ	Trans Jamaica Airlines
JR	Aero California
JU	JAT Jugoslovenski Aerotransport
JV	Bearskin Lake Air Service
JX	Bougair – North Solomons Air Services Pty Ltd
JY	Jersey European Airways

JZ   Golden Air Commuter

K

KA   Dragonair
KC   Cook Islands International
KD   Kendell Airlines
KE   Korean Air
KG   Orion Airways
KI   Time Air
KL   KLM
KM   Air Malta
KN   Temsco Airlines
KQ   Kenya Airways
KS   Peninsula Airways
KU   Kuwait Airways
KV   Transkei Airways
KX   Cayman Airways

L

LA   Lan Chile
LB   Lloyd Aereo Boliviano
LC   Loganair (Passenger)
LF   Linjeflyg
LG   Luxair
LH   Lufthansa
LI   Liat (1974)
LK   Giyani Airlines
LL   Bell Air
LM   ALM – Antillean Airlines
LN   Jamahiriya Libyan Arab Airlines
LO   LOT Polish Airlines
LR   Lacsa
LU   Theron Airways
LV   Aeropostal
LY   El Al Israel Airlines
LZ   Balkan

M

MA   Malev
MB   Midstate Airlines
MC   Transtar Airlines
MD   Air Madagascar
ME   Middle East Airlines
MH   Malaysian Airline System
MJ   LAPA
MK   Air Mauritius
ML   Midway Airlines
MN   Commercial Airways

MO   Calm Air International
MR   Air Mauritanie
MS   Egyptair
MV   Ansett W.A.
MW   Maya Airways
MX   Compania Mexicana
MY   Air Mali
MZ   Merpati Nusantara

N

NB   National Airways
NC   Norskair
ND   Nordair Metro
NE   Air Link
NH   All Nippon Airways
NL   Air Liberia
NN   Air Martinique
NR   Norontair
NV   Northwest Territorial Airways
NW   Northwest Airlines
NZ   Air New Zealand-Domestic

O

OA   Olympic Airways
OG   Air Guadeloupe
OK   CSA (Ceskoslovenske Aerolinie)
OM   Air Mongol – MIAT
ON   Air Nauru
OP   Air Panama Internacional
OQ   Royale Airlines
OR   Air Comores
OS   Austrian Airlines
OY   Sunaire

P

PA   Pan American World Airways
PB   Air Burundi
PC   Fiji Air
PD   Pem-Air
PF   Vayudoot
PH   Polynesian Airlines
PI   Piedmont Aviation
PK   Pakistan International Airline
PL   Aeroperu
PR   Philippine Airlines
PS   Pacific Southwest Airlines
PU   Pluna
PX   Air Niugini

PY	Surinam Airways
PZ	LAP (Lineas Aereas Paraguayas)

Q

QA	Aero Caribe
QB	Quebecair
QC	Air Zaire
QE	Air Moorea
QF	Qantas Airways
QI	Cimber Air
QL	Lesotho Airways
QM	Air Malawi
QN	Air Queensland
QP	Airkenya Aviation
QS	Propheter Aviation
QT	Tampa Airlines
QU	Uganda Airlines
QV	Lao Aviation
QW	Turks & Caicos National Airline
QY	Aero Virgin Islands
QZ	Zambia Airways

R

RA	Royal Nepal Airlines
RB	Syrian Arab Airlines
RD	Avianova
RE	Aer Arann Teo
RG	Varig
RI	P.T. Mandala Airlines (Passenger)
RJ	Royal Jordanian
RK	Air Afrique
RL	Aeronica
RM	Wings West Airlines
RN	Royal Air Inter
RO	Tarom
RP	Precision Airlines
RR	Royal Air Force
RS	Intercontinental de Aviacion
RT	A/S Norving
RW	Air Whitsunday
RY	Air Rwanda

S

SA	South African Airways
SB	Air Caledonie International
SC	Cruzeiro
SD	Sudan Airways
SE	Wings of Alaska

SF	Sunbird Airlines
SH	SAHSA – Servicio Aereo de Honduras
SI	Jet America Airlines
SJ	Southern Air
SK	SAS – Scandinavian Airlines
SL	Rio-Sul
SM	Air Ecosse
SN	Sabena
SO	Austrian Air Services
SP	SATA
SQ	Singapore Airlines
SR	Swissair
ST	Singleton Air Services
SU	Aeroflot
SV	Saudia
SW	Namib Air
SX	Christman Air System
SZ	Pro Air Services

T

TA	Taca International Airlines
TC	Air Tanzania
TD	Transavio
TE	Air New Zealand – International
TG	Thai Airways International
TH	Thai Airways
TK	THY Turkish Airlines
TM	LAM – Linhas Aereas de Moçambique
TN	Australian Airlines
TP	TAP Air Portugal
TR	Transbrasil s/a Linhas Aereas
TS	Transports Aeriens du Benin (T.A.B.)
TT	Tunisavia
TU	Tunis Air
TW	TWA – Trans World Airlines
TX	Tan Airlines
TY	Air Caledonie
TZ	American Trans Air

U

UA	United Airlines
UB	Burma Airways Corporation
UD	Georgian Bay Airways (Passenger)
UI	Norlandair
UK	Air UK
UL	Air Lanka
UM	Air Zimbabwe

UN	Eastern Australian Airlines
UP	Bahamasair
UT	UTA
UU	Reunion Air Service
UW	Perimeter Airlines
UY	Cameroon Airlines

V

VA	Viasa
VD	Sempati Air Transport
VE	Avensa
VH	Air Burkina
VK	Air Tungaru Corporation
VM	Air Vendee
VN	Hang Khong Vietnam
VO	Tyrolean Airways (Passenger)
VP	VASP
VR	Transportes Aereos de Cabo Verde
VS	Virgin Atlantic
VT	Air Tahiti
VW	Skyways of Scandinavia
VY	Highland Express

W

WB	SAN Servicios Aereos Nacionales (Passenger)
WC	Wild Coast Air
WD	Wardair Canada
WF	Wideroe's Flyveselskap
WH	Caribbean Express
WL	Aeroperlas
WM	Windward Island Airways International
WN	Southwest Airlines (U.S.A.)
WP	Princeville Airways
WT	Nigeria Airways

WU	Netherlines B.V.
WW	Maui Airlines
WX	Air NSW
WY	Oman Aviation Services

X

XP	Avior
XT	Island Airlines Inc
XV	Presidential Airways
XY	Ryan Air
XZ	Eastair

Y

YB	Golden Pacific Airlines
YK	Cyprus Turkish Airlines
YP	Ligne Aerienne (Seychelles)
YS	San Juan Airlines
YT	Skywest Airlines
YW	Stateswest Airlines
YX	Midwest Express Airlines
YZ	Transportes Aereos da Guinea-Bissau

Z

ZB	Monarch
ZC	Royal Swazi National Airways Corporation
ZG	Sabair Airlines
ZH	Ecuato Guineana da Aviacion
ZK	Great Lakes Aviation
ZL	Hazelton Airlines
ZO	Florida Express
ZQ	Ansett New Zealand
ZP	Virgin Air
ZT	Satena
ZY	Atlantic Gulf Airlines

Major Airports Worldwide

Country	City	Airport Name	Distance from Town miles	kms	Telephone Number
Argentina	Buenos Aires	Ezeiza	31.5	50	(54) 620 043
Australia	Adelaide	West Beach	5	8	(618) 352 9211
	Canberra	Fairbairn	4	6.5	(61 62) 486 777
	Melbourne	Melbourne	13.5	21	(61 3) 338 2211
	Sydney	Kingsford Smith	6.8	11	(61 2) 667 0544
Bahrain	Manama	International	4	6.5	(973) 321 640
Bangladesh	Dacca	Zia International			310 191
Barbados	Barbados	Grantley Adams	11	18	(1 809) 428 7101
Belgium	Brussels	National	7.5	12	(323) 511 1860
Brazil	Brasilia	International			(55 61) 242 4597
	Rio de Janeiro	International	12.5	20	(55 21) 398 6060
Canada	Montreal	Dorval	7	11	(1 514) 393 3111
	Toronto	Lester B. Pearson Int.	20	32	(1 613) 925 2311
Canary Islands	Las Palmas	Las Palmas			(34 28) 254 140
Cuba	Havana	José Martin			(537) 619 961
Cyprus	Larnaca	International			(357 41) 55533
Czechoslovakia	Prague	Ruzyne	11	17	(42 2) 334
Denmark	Copenhagen	Kastrup	6	10	(45 1) 509 333
East Germany	East Berlin	Schonefeld			(37) 26720
West Germany	West Berlin	Tegal	5	8	(49 30) 41011
	Bonn	Koln/Bonn			(42) 228 401
Egypt	Cairo	International	14	22.5	(202) 968 866
Finland	Helsinki	Vantaa	12	19	(35 80) 82921
France	Paris	Charles de Gaulle	14.5	23	(33 1) 862 1212
		Le Bourget			(33 1) 838 9270
		Orly	9	14	(33 1) 838 9270
Ghana	Accra	Kotoka International	6	10	76171
Gibraltar	Gibraltar	North Front			(350) 76400
Greece	Athens	Hellinikon	6	10	(30) 197 991
Hong Kong	Hong Kong	Kai Tak	4.5	7.5	(852 3) 829 7531
Hungary	Budapest	Ferihegy			(361) 140 400
India	Bombay	Santa Cruz	19	29	(912 22) 535 461
	Calcutta	Dum Dum	8	13	572 611
Indonesia	Bali	Nghurah Raj			Den Pasar 5061/6
	Jakarta	Halim			(62 21) 801 108
Iran	Tehran	Mehrabad			(98 21) 641 171
Ireland	Dublin	Dublin			(353 1) 379 900
Israel	Jerusalem	Atarot	5.6	9	
	Tel Aviv	Ben Gurion	12	19	(972 3) 970 111
Italy	Rome	Leonardo da Vinci	22	35	(39 6) 6012
Jamaica	Kingston	Norman Manley			(1 809) 928 6100

Japan	Osaka	International	10	16	(81 6) 856 6781
	Tokyo	Haneda	12	19	(81 3) 747 0511
		Narita	40	65	(81 476) 322 800
Jordan	Amman	International	20	32	51401
Lebanon	Beirut	International	10	16	(961) 220 500
Libya	Benghazi	Benina Internationale			(218) 613 102
Luxembourg	Luxembourg	Luxembourg			(352) 47981
Mexico	Mexico City	Benito Juarez	8	13	(52 5) 571 3600
Morocco	Casablanca	Nouasseur	19	30	(210) 339 040
Netherlands	Amsterdam	Schiphol	9.3	15	(31 20) 517 9111
New Zealand	Auckland	International	14	22.5	(649) 275 0789
Nigeria	Lagos	Murtala Muhammed			(234 1) 90170
Norway	Oslo	Fornebu	32	51	(47 2) 121 340
Pakistan	Karachi	International	12	19	(92 21) 482 111
Philippines	Manila	International			(63 2) 831 511
Portugal	Lisbon	Da Potela	4.5	7	(351 1) 881 101
Qatar	Doha	International			(974) 321 550
Romania	Bucharest	Oteopeni			(400) 333 137
Saudi Arabia	Jeddah	International	11	17.5	(966 21) 27211
	Riyadh	Riyadh	22	35	(966 1) 64800
Singapore	Singapore	Changi	12.4	20	(65) 542 1122
South Africa	Johannesburg	Jan Smuts	15	24	(27 11) 975 1185
Spain	Madrid	Madrid	10	16	(34 1) 222 1165
Sweden	Stockholm	Arlanda	25	41	(46 8) 244 000
Switzerland	Geneva	Cointrin	2.5	4	(41 22) 983 321
	Zurich	Kloten	7.5	12	(41 1) 816 2211
Sri Lanka	Colombo	Colombo	20	32.2	(941) 302 861
Syria	Damascus	International			430 404/9
Tahiti	Papeete	Faaa			(689) 28081
Tanzania	Dar Es Salaam	International	8	13	(255 51) 42211
Thailand	Bangkok	International	15.5	25	(662) 523 7222
Turkey	Istanbul	Yesilkay	15	24	(90 11) 737 240
USSR	Moscow	Sheremetivo			(7 095) 155 5005
UAE	Abu Dhabi	International	23	37	(971) 237 7277
	Dubai	International	2.5	4	(9714) 224 222
UK	Birmingham	Birmingham			(4421) 743 4272
	London	Heathrow	15	24	(44 1) 759 4321
		Gatwick	27	43	(44 293) 28822
		Stansted	34	55	(44 279) 502 380
		Luton			(44 582) 36061
	Manchester	International			(44 61) 437 5233
USA	Boston	Logan	2.3	3.6	(1 617) 482 2930
	Dallas	Fort Worth	6	10	(1 214) 574 3112
	New York	JF Kennedy	14	22.5	(1 212) 656 4520
		La Guardia	8	13	(1 212) 476 5000
		Newark International	16	26	(1 201) 961 2000

	Los Angeles	International	15	24	(1 213) 646 5252
	San Francisco	International	13	21	(1 415) 761 0800
	Washington DC	Dulles International	27	43	(1 703) 471 7838
Yugoslavia	Belgrade	Surcin	12	20	(3811) 601 555
Zimbabwe	Harare	Harare	7.5	12	50422

Airport/City Codes

For a job well done, you'll surely want to ADD (Addis Ababa) a TIP (Tripoli) to the payment. When things go wrong, such as when someone tries to put the wrong TAB (Tobago) on your luggage, you'll certainly get MAD (Madrid). To ensure that LAX (Los Angeles) luggage handling does not MAR (Maracaibo) your trip, it's a good idea to familiarize yourself with the relevant airport/city code. A selection of these codes are given below, in alphabetical order of city. Have a good flight and may your luggage go with you.

A

AAK	Aranuka, Kiribati
AAU	Asau, Samoa
ABJ	Abidjan, Ivory Coast
ABQ	Albuquerque, NM, USA
ABT	Al-Baha, Saudi Arabia
ABZ	Aberdeen, UK
ACA	Acapulco, Mexico
ACC	Accra, Ghana
ACE	Lanzarote, Canary Islands
ADD	Addis Ababa, Ethiopia
ADE	Aden, South Yemen
AEP	Buenos Aires Aeroparque, Jorge Newbery, Argentina
AGA	Agadir, Morocco
AGP	Malaga, Spain
AIY	Atlantic City, NJ, USA
AJA	Ajaccio, Corsica
AKL	Auckland, New Zealand
AKS	Auki, Solomon Islands
ALC	Alicante, Spain
ALG	Algiers
ALP	Aleppo, Syria
ALY	Alexandria, Egypt
AMM	Amman, Jordan
AMP	Ambon, Indonesia
AMS	Amsterdam, Netherlands

ANC	Anchorage, Alaska, USA
ANK	Ankara, Turkey
ANR	Antwerp, Belgium
ANU	Antigua, Leeward Islands
APW	Apia, Samoa
AQP	Aqaba, Jordan
ARN	Stockholm Arlanda Apt, Sweden
ASP	Alice Springs, NT, Australia
ASU	Asunción, Paraguay
ASV	Amboseli, Kenya
ASW	Aswan, Egypt
ATH	Athens, Greece
ATL	Atlanta Hartsfield Int., GA, USA
AUA	Aruba, Neth. Antilles
AUH	Abu Dhabi, UAE
AXA	Anguilla, Leeward Is
AYT	Antalya,.Turkey

B

BAH	Bahrain
BBQ	Barbuda, Leeward Islands
BBR	Basse-Terre, Guadeloupe
BBU	Bucharest Banfasa Apt, Romania
BCN	Barcelona, Spain
BDA	Bermuda Kindley Field, Bermuda
BEG	Belgrade, Yugoslavia
BEL	Belem, PA Brazil
BEN	Benghazi, Libya
BER	West Berlin, W. Germany

BEY	Beirut, Lebanon
BFS	Belfast, UK
BGF	Bangui, Central African Rep.
BGI	Barbados
BGW	Baghdad, Iraq
BHX	Birmingham, UK
BIM	Bimini, Bahamas
BJL	Banjul, Gambia
BJM	Bujumbura, Burundi
BKK	Bangkok, Thailand
BKO	Bamako, Mali
BLZ	Blantyre, Malawi
BNE	Brisbane, QL Australia
BNJ	Bonn, West Germany
BOG	Bogota;1, Colombia
BOM	Bombay, India
BOS	Boston, MA USA
BRU	Brussels, Belgium
BSB	Brasilia, Brazil
BSL	Basle, Switzerland
BUD	Budapest, Hungary
BUE	Buenos Aires, Argentina
BUH	Bucharest, Romania
BWN	Bandar Seri Begawan, Brunei
BXO	Bissau, Guinea-Bissau
BZE	Belize City
BZV	Brazzaville, Congo

C

CAI	Cairo, Egypt
CAP	Cap Haitien, Haiti
CAS	Casablanca, Morocco
CBR	Canberra, CT, Australia
CCS	Caracas, Venezuela
CCU	Calcutta, India
CDG	Paris Charles de Gaulle, France
CFU	Corfu, Greece
CGH	Sao Paulo Congonhas Apt, SP Brazil
CHC	Christchurch, New Zealand
CHI	Chicago, IL USA
CIA	Rome Ciampino Apt, Italy
CJL	Chitral, Pakistan
CKY	Conakry, Guinea
CMB	Colombo, Sri Lanka
COO	Cotonou, Benin
CPH	Copenhagen, Denmark

CPT	Cape Town, South Africa
CUR	Curacão, Neth. Antilles
CYB	Cayman Brac, Cayman Islands

D

DAC	Dakkar, Bangladesh
DAD	Da Nang, Vietnam
DAM	Damascus Syria
DAR	Dar es Salaam, Tanzania
DEL	Delhi, India
DFW	Dallas/Fort Worth, TX USA
DHA	Dhahran, Saudi Arabia
DKR	Dakar, Senegal
DLA	Douala, Cameroon
DME	Moscow Domodedovo Apt, USSR
DOH	Doha, Qatar
DOM	Dominica
DRW	Darwin, NT, Australia
DUB	Dublin, Ireland
DXB	Dubai, UAE

E

EBB	Entebbe, Kampala, Uganda
EDI	Edinburgh,UK
ETH	Eilat, Israel
EWR	New York Newark Apt, NJ, USA

F

FAE	Faroe Islands, Denmark
FAI	Fairbanks, AK, USA
FAO	Faro, Portugal
FCO	Rome - Leonardo da Vinci, Italy
FNA	Freetown Lungi Int. Apt, Sierra Leone
FNC	Funchal, Madeira
FNJ	Pyongyang, North Korea
FPO	Freeport, Bahamas
FRA	Frankfurt Int Apt, West Germany

G

GBE	Gaborone, Botswana
GCM	Grand Cayman, Cayman Islands
GDT	Grand Turk, Turks and Caicos
GEN	Oslo Gardermoen Apt, Norway
GGT	Georgetown, Bahamas
GIB	Gibraltar
GIG	Rio de Janeiro Int Apt, Brazil
GLA	Glasgow, UK

GND	Grenada, Windward Islands	KTM	Kathmandu, Nepal
GUA	Guatemala City, Guatemala	KUL	Kuala Lumpur, Malaysia
GVA	Geneva, Switzerland	KWI	Kuwait

H

L

HAM	Hamburg, West Germany	LAD	Luanda, Angola
HAN	Hanoi, Vietnam	LAS	Las Vegas, NY, USA
HAV	Havana, Cuba	LAX	Los Angeles, CA USA
HBA	Hobart, TS Australia	LED	Leningrad, USSR
HEl	Helsinki, Finland	LFW	Lomé, Togo
HIR	Honiara, Solomon Islands	LGA	New York La Guardia Apt, NY, USA
HKG	Hong Kong Int Apt, Hong Kong		
HLP	Jakarta Halim Perdana Kusuma Apt, Indonesia	LGW	London, UK - Gatwick Airport
		LHE	Lahore, Pakistan
HND	Tokyo Haneda Apt, Japan	LHR	London, UK - Heathrow Airport
HNL	Honolulu Int Apt, HI USA	LIM	Lima, Peru
HOU	Houston, TX USA	LIS	Lisbon, Portugal
HRE	Harare, Zimbabwe	LOS	Lagos, Nigeria
		LPA	Gran Canaria, Canary Islands

I

		LPB	La Paz, Bolivia
IAD	Washington Dulles Int Apt, DC USA	LTN	London, UK - Luton Int.
		LUN	Lusaka, Zambia
IAH	Houston Int Apt, TX USA	LUX	Luxembourg
IBZ	Ibiza, Spain	LXA	Lhasa, Tibet, China
IHO	Ihosy, Madagascar	LXR	Luxor, Egypt
ISB	Islamabad, Pakistan		
IST	Istanbul, Turkey		

M

IUE	Niue		
IXL	Leh, India	MAA	Madras, India
		MAD	Madrid Barajas Apt, Spain

J

		MAH	Menorca, Spain
		MAN	Manchester, UK
JED	Jeddah, Saudi Arabia	MAO	Manaus, Brazil
JFK	New York John F. Kennedy Apt, NY USA	MAR	Maracaibo, Venezuela
		MBA	Mombasa, Kenya
JIB	Djibouti	MCM	Monte Carlo, Monaco
JKT	Jakarta, Indonesia	MCT	Muscat, Oman
JNB	Johannesburg, South Africa	MDL	Mandalay, Burma
JOG	Yogyakarta, Indonesia	MED	Medina, Saudi Arabia
JRS	Jerusalem, Israel	MEL	Melbourne, Australia
		MEX	Mexico City, Mexico

K

		MGA	Managua, Nicaragua
KAN	Kano, Nigeria	MGQ	Mogadishu, Somalia
KBL	Kabul, Afghanistan	MIA	Miami, FL USA
KEF	Reykjavik Keflavik Apt, Iceland	MIL	Milan, Italy
KHI	Karachi, Pakistan	MLE	Male, Maldives
KIN	Kingston, Jamaica	MLW	Monrovia, Liberia
KMS	Kumasi, Ghana	MNI	Montserrat, Leeward Islands
KRT	Khartoum, Sudan		

MNL	Manila Int Apt, Philippines
MOW	Moscow, USSR
MPM	Maputo, Mozambique
MRS	Marseille, France
MRU	Mauritius
MST	Maastricht, Netherlands
MSU	Maseru, Lesotho

N

NAS	Nassau, Bahamas
NBO	Nairobi, Kenya
NIM	Niamey, Niger
NKC	Nouakchott, Mauritania
NOU	Noumea, New Caledonia
NRT	Tokyo Narita Apt, Japan
NYC	New York, NY USA

O

OKA	Okinawa - Naha Airport, Japan
ORD	Chicago O'Hare Int Apt, IL USA
ORG	Paramaribo Zorg En Hoop Apt, Suriname
ORY	Paris Orly Apt, France
OSA	Osaka Japan
OSL	Oslo, Norway
OUA	Ouagadougou, Burkina Faso

P

PAC	Panama City Paitilla Apt, Panama
PAP	Port au Prince, Haiti
PAR	Paris, France
PBM	Paramaribo, Suriname
PCC	Puerto Rico, Colombia
PEK	Beijing, China
PEN	Penang Int Apt, Malaysia
PER	Perth, Australia
PNH	Phnom-Penh, Kampuchea
POM	Port Moresby, Papua New Guinea
POS	Port of Spain, Trinidad and Tobago
PPG	Pago Pago, American Samoa
PPT	Papeete, Tahiti
PRG	Prague, Czechoslovakia

R

RAK	Marrakech, Morocco
RBA	Rabat, Morocco
REK	Reykjavik, Iceland
RGN	Rangoon, Burma
RIO	Rio de Janeiro, Brazil
ROM	Rome, Italy
RUH	Riyadh, Saudi Arabia
RUN	Réunion

S

SAL	San Salvador, El Salvador
SAO	Sao Paulo, Brazil
SCL	Santiago, Chile
SDA	Baghdad Saddam Int Apt, Iraq
SDQ	Santo Domingo, Dominican Rep.
SDV	Tel Aviv Sde – Dov Int Apt, Israel
SEL	Seoul, Korea
SEZ	Mahé Island, Seychelles
SFO	San Francisco, CA USA
SGN	Ho Chi Minh City, Vietnam
SHA	Shanghai, China
SIN	Singapore
SJO	San José, Costa Rica
SKB	St. Kitts, Leeward Islands
SLU	St Lucia, Windward Islands
SNN	Shannon, Ireland
SOF	Sofia, Bulgaria
STL	St Louis, MO USA
STN	London Standsted Apt, UK
STO	Stockholm, Sweden
SVO	Moscow Sheremetyevo Apt, USSR
SXF	Berlin, East Germany
SXR	Srinagar, India
SYD	Sydney, Australia

T

TAB	Tobago, Trinidad and Tobago
TCI	Tenerife, Canary Islands
THF	Berlin West Tempelhof Apt, W. Germany
THR	Tehran, Iran
TIP	Tripoli, Libya
TLV	Tel Aviv, Israel
TNG	Tangier, Morocco
TNR	Antananarivo, Madagascar
TPE	Taipei, Taiwan
TUN	Tunis, Tunisia
TZA	Belize City Municipal Apt, Belize

V

VIE	Vienna, Austria

VTE	Vientiane, Laos		Canada
	W	YQB	Quebec City, Canada
WAS	Washington, DC USA	YUL	Montreal, Quebec, Canada
WAW	Warsaw, Poland	YVR	Vancouver, BC, Canada
		YYZ	Toronto, Ontario, Canada
	Y		
YAO	Yaoundé, Cameroon		**Z**
YEG	Edmonton, Alberta, Canada	ZAG	Zagreb, Yugoslavia
YOW	Ottawa Uplands Int Apt, Ontario,	ZRH	Zurich, Switzerland

Airport/Departure Taxes

Afghanistan	AFG200	British Virgin Islands	US$5
Albania	None	Brunei	None
Algeria	None	Bulgaria	LEV3.00 for passengers to Libya
American Samoa	None		
Andorra	None	Burkina Faso	None
Angola	National Reconstruction Stamp AKZ20 on Domestic; AKZ200 on International. Embarkation Tax AKZ60 on Domestic; AKZ200 International.	Burma	BUR15.00
		Burundi	FRB1,100
		Cameroons	CFA450
		Canada	None
		Cape Verde	None
		Cayman Islands	CID6
Anguilla	ECD10.00	Cent. African Rep.	Domestic CFA2,500; International CFA4,200
Antigua & Barbuda	Local ECD10.00; International ECD15.00	Chad	Domestic CFA2,500; International CFA4,200
Argentina	Domestic ARA1.00; Uruguay ARA2.50; International ARA8.00	Chile	US$12.50
		China	RMB15
Aruba	US$9.50	Colombia	International US$15; Domestic US$7. Plus Exit Tax of US$20 (if stay over two months).
Australia	A.$20		
Austria	None		
Bahamas	BMD5		
Bahrain	BHD2.00	Comoro Islands	Domestic AFR500; International AFR5,000
Bangladesh	Domestic BDT10; International BDT200	Congo	Domestic CFA500
		Cook Islands	NZ$20; 2-12 yrs NZ$10
Barbados	BB$16	Costa Rica	Residents CRC955; Others CRC313; Stay of less than 48 hrs CRC63
Belgium	From Brussels, BFR300; Antwerp BFR150		
Belize	BND20	Côte d'Ivoire	None
Benin	AFR2,500	Cuba	None
Bermuda	BED10; children under 12 BED5	Cyprus	None
		Czechoslovakia	None
Bolivia	Domestic BOB1.50; International 16.00	Denmark	None
		Djibouti	None
Botswana	None	Dominica	ECD15
Brazil	US$8.83	Dominican Rep.	DOP15.00

Ecuador	US$20	Kenya	US$10
Egypt	None	Kiribati	A$5
El Salvador	SAC45	North Korea	None
Equatorial Guinea	Domestic CFA425; International CFA2,250	Korea	Won 4,000
		Kuwait	None
Ethiopia	None	Lebanon	LEL150: First Class passengers LEL250
Fiji	FID10		
Finland	None	Lesotho	LSL10
France	None	Liberia	LID10
French Guiana	None	Libya	LBD5
French Polynesia	None	Luxembourg	None
French West Indies	None	Madagascar	FMG1,500
Gabon	None	Malawi	MWK10.00
Gambia	UK£7	Malaysia	Domestic RGT3; Brunei and Singapore RGT5; International RGT15
East Germany	None		
West Germany	None		
Ghana	Domestic GHC50; International GHC200	Maldives	MVR50
		Mali	Domestic AFR500; Within Africa AFR1,500; Elsewhere AFR2,500
Gibraltar	£1.00		
Greece	None		
Grenada	ECD25	Malta	None
Guatemala	QUE20	Mauritania	Domestic MOG70; Within Africa MOG70; Elsewhere MOG560.
Guinea-Bissau	Within West Africa US$8; elsewhere US$12		
Guinea	Domestic GNF100; Within Africa GNF150; Elsewhere GNF200	Mauritius	MAR100
		Mexico	MEP Domestic MEP1,500; International MEP US$10
Guyana	GYD275		
Haiti	US$15		
Honduras	US$10 if on a business visa; others US$2.50	Micronesia	Palau $3
		Mongolia	None
Hong Kong	HKD120 per adult; HKD60 per child.	Montserrat	US$6
		Morocco	MDH100
Hungary	None	Mozambique	Domestic MZM100; International MZM350
Iceland	None		
India	Subcontinent INR50; Elsewhere INR100	Nauru	AUD10
		Nepal	Remote areas NER15; Other Domestic NER25; International NER100
Indonesia	Departing Jakarta and Den Pasar - Domestic RPA2,000; International RPA 9,000. Other airports – International RPA2-8,000; Domestic RPA600-1800		
		Netherlands	None
		Netherlands Antilles	Bonaire – Domestic AFL5; Int AFL10; Curaçao – Int AFL10; St Maarten - Int AFL9
Iran	IRI1,500	New Caledonia	None
Iraq	IRD2	New Zealand	NZ$2
Ireland	None	Nicaragua	US$10
Israel	None	Niger	None
Italy	None	Nigeria	Domestic NGN5; 2-12 yrs NGN2.50; International NGN50; 2-12 yrs NGN25
Jamaica	JAD40		
Japan	2,000 Yen; 2-12 yrs 1,000 Yen		
Jordan	JOD7	Niue	NZ$10

Norfolk Island	A$10		SLR51 all other airports SLR2.50
Norway	None		
Oman	RIO3	Sudan	Domestic SUL15; International SUL30
Pakistan	Domestic one-way PAR10; International PAR100	Suriname	None
		Swaziland	None
Panama	BAL15	Sweden	None
Papua New Guinea	Domestic NGK2; International NGK10	Switzerland	None
		Syria	To Arab states SYL5; Elsewhere SYL10
Paraguay	GUA1,200		
Peru	US$10	Taiwan	NTD200
Philippines	Domestic PHP10; International PHP200	Tanzania	TAS200 (US$10)
		Thailand	BHT150
Poland	None	Togo	None
Portugal	None	Tonga	T$5
Qatar	None	Trinidad & Tobago	TT$20
Réunion	None	Tunisia	TUD0.305
Romania	None	Turkey	From Istanbul US$10; other airports US$7
Rwanda	To Burundi, Tanzania, Uganda, Zaire – FRR250; Elsewhere FRR800		
		Turks and Caicos	US$10
		Tuvalu	A$10
St Christopher & Nevis	ECD13.50 (UCD10)	Uganda	UGS10
St Lucia	Caribbean – ECD10; Elsewhere – ECD20	USSR	None
		United Arab Emirates	None
St Vincent and Grenadines	ECD14.00	United Kingdom	None
		US Virgin Island	None
American Samoa	None	United States	None
Western Samoa	SAT20	Uruguay	US$2.50
Sao Tomé et Principe	None	Vanuatu	VUV1,000 (US$10)
Saudi Arabia	None	Venezuela	VBO450
Senegal	Domestic CFA2,000; Within Africa CFA4,000; Elsewhere CFA5,000	Vietnam	None
		North Yemen	International YEM60; Domestic YEM15
Seychelles	None	South Yemen	DYD1,000; Martyr's tax DYD 0,200; Revenue stamps DYD0.250
Sierra Leone	SLE20		
Singapore	To Malaysia and Brunei SID5; Elsewhere SID12		
Solomon Islands	SBD10	Yugoslavia	Domestic YUD700; International YUD2,000
Somalia	SOM100		
South Africa	None	Zaïre	Domestic ZAI200; International US$12
Spain	None		
Sri Lanka	From Colombo, Katunayake – SLR200; From Ratmalana or Kankesanturai –	Zambia	Domestic ZMK20; International US$10
		Zimbabwe	ZWD10

Note: Transit passengers, children and diplomats are often exempted or charged a reduced rate.

International Flight Distances

London (*Heathrow*)	*Direct Flight Distance* (*Most direct aircraft and route*)	
to	(kms)	(miles)
Amsterdam	370	231
Ankara	2,824	1,765
Athens	2,400	1,500
Auckland	18,246	11,404
Beirut	3,459	2,162
Belgrade	1,7042	1,065
Berlin	950	594
Bombay	7,165	4,478
Brussels	347	217
Buenos Aires	11,064	6,915
Cairo	3,501	2,188
Calcutta	7,933	4,958
Copenhagen	978	611
Dublin	446	279
Frankfurt	650	406
Geneva	749	468
Helsinki	1,835	1,147
Hong Kong	9,582	5,989
Johannesburg	9,014	5,634
Kano	4,429	2,768
Karachi	6,296	3,935
Lisbon	1,552	972
Madrid	1,238	774
Malta	2,088	1,305
Milan	974	609
Montreal	5,186	3,241
Moscow	2,491	1,557
Munich	944	590
Nairobi	6,795	4,247
Naples	1,618	1,011
New York	5,504	3,440
Nice	1,035	647
Oslo	1,198	749
Palma	1,333	833
Paris	344	215
Perth	14,413	9,008
Prague	1,040	650
Rangoon	8,930	5,581
Rio de Janeiro	9,194	5,746
Rome	1,451	907
San Francisco	8,562	5,351
Singapore	10,806	6,754
Stockholm	1,437	898
Sydney	16,909	10,568
Tokyo	9,528	5,955
Toronto	5,672	3,545
Vancouver	7,531	4,707
Washington	5,864	3,665
Zurich	784	490

Travel: Consumer Advice and Complaints

Association of British Travel Agents (ABTA)
55 Newman Street
London W1
Tel: 01-637 2444
Professional body of the British travel industry, with a bond to protect travellers against financial collapse.

Air Transport Association of America
1709 New York Avenue NW
Washington
DC 20006
USA
Of all the ATA activities, safety is foremost. Other objectives include the improvement of passenger and cargo traffic procedures, economic and technical research and action on legislation affecting the industry.

Air Transport Users' Committee
129 Kingsway
London WC2B 6NN
Tel: 01-242 3882

Small committee, funded by CAA, but acting independently, to investigate complaints.

American Society of Travel Agents
Consumer Affairs Department
4400 MacArthur Blvd NW
Washington
DC 20007
USA
Can be asked to vouch for, or establish the authenticity of travel agents, or to help with tour problems. Mediates disputes between consumers and travel related suppliers as well as providing 'reliability' checks on the travel industry.

Aviation Consumer Action Project
PO Box 19029
Washington
DC 20036
USA
Was created by Ralph Nader and promotes commercial air safety and passenger rights protection. Those with related concerns may contact the office to dis-

cover how to go about 'Constructive Complaining' to resolve problems.

Civil Aviation Authority
CAA House
45 Kingsway
London WC2
Tel: 01-379 7311
Overall controller of the British airline industry.

Federal Aviation Administration
Community and Consumer Liaison Division
APA-400
800 Independence Avenue SW
Washington
DC 20591
USA
Deals with complaints about air safety.

International Air Transport Association (IATA)
26 Chemin de Joinville
PO Box 160
1216 Cointrin-Geneva
Switzerland
and
West London Terminal
Cromwell Road
London SW7 4ED
Tel: 01-370 8267/4255
Professional body of the world's travel industry offering consumer protection to travellers with member organizations.

Air Taxi/Ambulance Operators

All members of ATOA are certified by the Civil Aviation Authority and subjected to monitoring checks by that body. They comply with the association's code of Practice.

Air Foyle Ltd
Luton Airport
Halcyon House
Luton
Beds LU2 9LU
Tel: (0582) 419 792
Air Foyle is available 24 hours a day, 7 days a week to fly anytime, anywhere.

All Seasons Aviation Ltd
Straverton Airport
Cheltenham
Glos.
Tel: (03843) 77841
Offers a fully approved ambulance service for stretcher cases.

BCA (Aviation) Ltd
Expedier House
Portsmouth road
Hindhead
Surrey GU26 6TJ
Tel: (042873) 7740/4720
Air taxi and air ambulance work.

Cabair Air Taxis Ltd
Elstree Aerodrome
Herts WD6 3AW
Tel: 01-953 4411
24 hour air taxi service.

Continental Flight Services Ltd
Southampton Airport
Hants SO9 1FQ
Tel: (0703) 610 261
Provide a 24-hour, 7 days a week service for executive air taxi and light freight cargo to destinations in UK and Europe.

Crest Aviation
Biggin Hill Airport
Biggin Hill
Westerham
Kent
Tel: (09594) 7500
Specializes in the ad hoc charter of passengers and freight. Suited to long range freight movement.

Fairflight Ltd
Biggin Hill Airport
Biggin Hill
Kent TN16 3BN
Tel: (09594) 7651
Air taxi and air ambulance.

Falcon Jet Centre Ltd
No.2 Maintenance Area
London Heathrow Airport
Hounslow
Middlesex
Tel: 01-897 6021
Air ambulance services.

Gatwick Air Taxis Ltd
Broadwater House
Chawley
Sussex BN8 4JE
Tel: (802) 572 3888
Efficient and economical 24 hour air taxi and air ambulance service.

Glos Air (Charter) Ltd
Bournemouth (Hurn) Airport
Christchurch
Dorset BY23 6DQ
Tel: (0202) 578 601
Provides fast economical travel for up to seven passengers in each of their aircraft throughout Europe, Scandinavia and North Africa.

Jointair Ltd
Executive Jet Centre
London Heathrow Airport
Hounslow

Middlesex TW6 3AE
Tel: 01-759 9933
Executive air taxi ad hoc and contract service for passenger cargo, courier and air ambulance. Economic and efficient over short distances the Lear jets are particularly suited to long range flights to the Middle East, North and West Africa where the high altitude and speed capability shows even greater economy.

Mountleigh Air Services Ltd
Leeds/Bradford Airport
Yeadon
Leeds LS19 7TZ
Tel: Rawdon (0532) 501 242
Specialize in pressurized air taxi and ambulance work throughout Europe and North Africa.

Northern Executive Aviation Ltd
Hangar 522
Manchester International Airport
Wilmslow
Cheshire SL9 4LL
Tel: (061) 436 6666/489 3115
One of Britain's leading air taxi companies. Multipurpose fleet carries out passenger and/or freight flights to and from destinations throughout Europe, the Middle East, Africa, the Far East, Australia, USA, and Canada. Ambulance operations. 24 hours 7 days a week.

Omega Air Travel Ltd
Building 509
Biggin Hill Airport
Westerham
Kent
Tel: (09594) 71901
Fly to Scandinavia, Europe, and North Africa. Air ambulance service.

Shell Aircraft Ltd
Shell Centre
York Road
London SW1 7NA
Tel: 01-934 1234
Operating base: Heathrow and London.

Thurston Aviation Ltd
London Stansted Airport
Stansted
Essex CM24 8QW
Tel: (0279) 815 027
One of the most experienced companies in the air taxi field. A 24 hour service operated from London Stansted airport serving most of Europe, North Africa and the Middle East.

Trans-Care International Ltd
(Associate Member)
193/195 High Street
Acton
London W3 9DD
Tel: 01-933 6151

Aircraft Services

Air Transport Operators Association
Clembro House
Weydown Road
Haslemere
Surrey GU27 2QE
Tel: (0428) 4804
The ATOA, formed in 1967, is a non-profit making business association, and includes most of the major air-taxi companies and a number of third level airlines in its membership. They carry some half-million passengers and several million kilograms of freight each year throughout the UK, Europe, the Middle East and North Africa. Many members operate air ambulance flights.

Air and General Finance Ltd
13 Essex House
George Street
Croydon
Surrey CRO 1PH
Tel: 01-688 9382
Financial services are provided for all aspects of the aviation industry. A leading company in the provision of finance for aircraft aquisition, Air and General Finance specializes in the field of commercial, transport and business aircraft.

Air & General Services Ltd
13 Essex House
George Street
Croydon
Surrey CRO 1PH
Tel: 01-688 9382
Suppliers of aircraft, and will purchase used equipment and act as brokers for the sale and purchase of all aircraft types.

Roebuck Air Services
Roebuck House
Somerset Way
Iver
Bucks
Tel: (02812) 2245
Provide road and air ambulance service to the general public and any business hours with employees abroad 24 hours a day, 7 days a week.

Road

Driving Requirements Worldwide

Countries	Import requirements	Driving Permits	Motor Insurance	Fuel Availability
Afghanistan	Motoring not advised at present.	International licence	No	Scarce. Rationed at times.
Albania	Cannot import.	No private cars. Are not allowed to drive.		Rationed. Not given to tourists.
Algeria	Carnets not valid. Can import free for up to 3 mths.	International licence	Algerian Insurance c. 130DA per month.	Good. Spares are difficult to find.
Andorra	No	International licence	Green Card	Good
Antigua	No	Driving permit obtained at Police Station by showing national licence.	No	Good
Antigua & Barbuda	No	Drivers permit obtained from Police Stations. Cost £2.	No	Good
Argentina	No	International licence	No	Good
Australia	Triptych or carnet will last 12 months.	International licence	Local insurance	Good
Austria	No duty for tourists. Carnet valid.	National licence	Green Gard	Good
Bahamas	Yes, if vehicle in country for 6 months or less.	National licence, up to 3 mths. Bahamian licence costs $10. No test.	Local insurance mandatory.	Good. Spares rare.

Countries	Import requirements	Driving Permits	Motor Insurance	Fuel Availability
Bahrain	Carnet valid. Cars on Arab boycott list barred.	International licence OK after endorsement by Traffic Dept., Ministry of Interior.	Local insurance required. Expensive.	Good
Bangladesh	Carnet valid	International licence	No	OK
Barbados	Need to apply to the Controller of Customs, Bridgetown. Duty payable will be refunded if the vehicle leaves within a year.	Visitors Driving Permit issued by police. Must have valid licence. Fee of BD$30.	Need local insurance	Good
Belgium	No	National licence	Green Card compulsory	Good
Belize	Duty payable up to 75% of car's value.	International licence good for 90 days. Then you must take a local test. Cost $15 pa.	Local insurance mandatory	Good.
Bermuda	Cars older than 6 mths cannot be imported.	Bermuda Driving Licence req. after 30 days residence.	Third Party automobile liability.	Good
Benin		International licence	Local Third Party needed.	OK
Bolivia	Proof that you will be taking the car out again.	International licence issued by a member of Federacion Inter-am de Touring y Automovil Clubs.	No	No
Botswana	Carnet valid. Must buy a Road Fund Licence at the border.	International licence valid if over 18. No test to convert to local. Cost P5.	Local Third Party needed.	Good
Brazil	No	International licence	Local Third Party	No fuel on Sundays or after 8.00 pm every day
British Virgin Islands	No	BVI temporary licence	No	Good
Bulgaria	No	National licence	Green Card	Good

		National licence	Local insurance needed	Good
Brunei	All cars duty-free in the country.	International licence	Local insurance	Good
Burma	No entry overland allowed.	International licence	Local insurance	OK
Cameroon	Carnet valid.	International licence	No	Scarce and difficult to obtain.
Canada	Carnet valid. Must comply with air pollution standards	National licence	Green Card	Good
Cayman Islands	Duty 17.5%. Carnet valid.	International licence. Local can be issued against this without test. Cost CI$5.	Local Third Party	Good
Central African Republic	Carnet valid	International licence	Local insurance needed.	Scarce
Chad	Carnet valid	International licence	Green Gard	Fuel expensive.
Chile	Carnet valid	International licence	No	Petrol fine. Diesel only available on the Pan-American Highway.
China	No foreign vehicles allowed except trade vehicles.			
Colombia	Carnet valid. Duty of 200%	International licence for 6 mths. Local licence officially needs test. Most people pay bribe of £10.	Local insurance needed. All risks essential.	Good
Congo		International licence	Local insurance needed.	Good
Costa Rica	No	National licence	Local Third Party	Good
Côte d'Ivoire	No	The Pine-Leaf Licence & International Licence	Green Card/Third Party	OK
Cuba	No cars allowed in	National	Local insurance	Good
Cyprus	Free for 3 mths. Can be extended up to 1 yr. Carnet valid. Duty 90–150%.	International licence	Local insurance	Good

Countries	Import requirements	Driving Permits	Motor Insurance	Fuel Availability
Czechoslovakia	Must be entered on passport and reexported	International licence	Green Card	Good. Need coupons for diesel. From border and banks.
Denmark	No	National licence	Green Card	Good
Dominica	No carnet. Duty 80%.	Local licence from airport or Police HQ. No test if you have an International Licence. Cost US$30.	Local Third Party necessary but expensive.	Good
Eastern Caribbean	No	Temporary local licence	No	Good
Educador	Carnet valid	National licence OK in theory but better to get a local one.	Local insurance needed.	Good
Egypt	Diesel operated vehicles not allowed in. Carnet valid. No vehicles over 5 yrs old.	International Licence	Compulsory insurance obtained at port on arrival.	Good
El Salvador	Free for 60 days if you have proof of ownership and registration in another country.	National licence	No	Good
Ethiopia	Get given new number plates on entry! Carnet not valid. 190–230% duty on vehicles for private use.	International licence should be exchanged for a local one at the Licencing Office, Asmara Rd, Addis Ababa. No test.	Local insurance advisable	Fuel Shortages. Need coupons from the Ministry of Internal Trade.
Fiji	Yes – refundable on exit.	International licence	Local insurance	Good
Finland	Carnet valid. Duty of 132% otherwise.	National licence & sign attached showing nationality.	Green Card	Good
France	Limited entry free for tourists.	National licence OK for 6 mths. Exchange for Permit	Green Card	Good

		International licence. Local	Local insurance	
Gabon	Limited entry free for tourists.	International licence costs £160.	Full local insurance	Good
Gambia	Free for tourists	International licence	Green Card	Good
East Germany	Free for tourists	National licence	Green Card	Good
West Germany	No	National licence	Not compulsory	Yes – obtainable in small quantities.
Ghana	No. At the moment there's some trouble at the border – overland travel is difficult.	International – must be endorsed by Police Licencing officer	Minimum Third Party Ins	Good
Gibraltar	No	National licence	Green Card	Good
Greece	Free entry for 3 mths	National licence	Green Card	Good
Grenada	35% + 20% VAT + 40% Purchase Tax.	Local licence. No test if you have a valid licence. ECD15 from Licencing Office, St George's.	Not compulsory	Good
Guinea		International licence	Third Party	OK
Guyana	No	Need permission from Chief Licensing officer Licence Revenue Division, Smith & Princes Street, Georgetown.	Third Party	OK
Haiti	Yes – very expensive NB Advised to hire car rather than take one.	International licence	Not compulsory	OK
Hong Kong	No	National licence – after 12 mths must apply for HK driving licence.	Third Party essential.	Good
Honduras		International licence	Local insurance	OK
Hungary	Registration No. must be put on Entry Visa. Carnet valid.	National licence	Green Card	Good. Coupons needed for diesel. Must pay in hard currency at border or IBUSZ offices. Can't change back.

Countries	Import requirements	Driving Permits	Motor Insurance	Fuel Availability
Iceland	Carnet valid. Diesel vehicles must pay a tax for every km driven. Max stay 3 mths with 3 mths extension.	International licence usually OK.	Green Card compulsory	Good, but some types of petrol rationed.
India	AIT Carnet allows 6 mths. Duty is around 300%. Virtually imposs. to get Carnet Indemnity Insurance.	International licence. To get a local one, you must do an oral test. 5 yr licence costs RS20/-.	Local Third Party	Good
Indonesia	Carnet not valid	International licence usually OK. Better to get a local on Bali and in Jakarta. Ask police.	Local insurance not compulsory, but advisable.	Good
Ireland	Limited free entry for tourists.	National licence	UK drivers don't need anything extra. Green Card for others.	Good
Iran	Carnet valid. You usually have to be escorted and pay for it.	International – 2 photos may be required	No – must carry car documents.	OK
Iraq	No bond but vehicles only allowed in for 2 months.	Valid international automobile certificate.	Local Third Party	OK
Israel	Free entry for 1 yr. Duty is 300%.	International licence. Local obtainable from Licensing Office after sight test.	Green Card valid if Israel is listed on it. Third Party compulsory.	Good
Italy	Free entry for 6 mths.	National licence. Must have formal letter or translation (free at border).	Green Card	Good
Jamaica	Import licence needed	National licence	Must be insured	Petrol stations closed on Wednesday and Sunday

Japan	Carnet not valid. Tax has to be paid – customs clearance. And will need modifying to conform to standard. NB Not advised to take car.	International licence for 1 year. Local will be given after sight and coordination tests.	Local insurance	Good
Jordan	Tourist entry free for 3 mths. Diesel cars not allowed. 150–225% duty. Carnet valid.	International licence	Local Third Party available at border.	Good
Kenya	Carnet compulsory	National licence OK for up to 90 days – should have it endorsed at local police station. No test to convert to local. About 20/- for 3 years.	Local Third Party on entry.	Usually OK. Occasional rationing at discretion of garages. Diesel can be difficult in off-beat areas.
Korea	Can only enter through Pusan via Pukwan Ferry. Can drive for 30 days & then extend for another 30 days.	Must be over 25, have valid passport and international licence to drive hired cars.	Local insurance	Good
Kuwait	Carnet needed. Must have Kuwaiti vehicle test.	International Drivers Licence – should be endorsed by traffic authorities. OK for one month.	Preferable to have cars insured with local insurance firm.	Good
Laos	Virtually impossible to take cars in.	International licence	Not compulsory	OK
Lebanon	Carnet valid	International licence	Get insurance from Lebanese border.	OK
Lesotho	No duty if entering from RSA.	International licence	Not compulsory	Good in lowlands. Scarce in mountains.
Liberia	Duty 40%	Local licence costs $20.	Local insurance advisable.	OK, but often rationed from Jan-Apr.

Countries	Import requirements	Driving Permits	Motor Insurance	Fuel Availability
Libya	Carnet valid	International licence good for 3 mths. Local licence costs $35. Test.	Local insurance	Good
Luxembourg	Vehicles imported temp & in brand new condition need Customs Documents. 1 year free if car is 6 mths or older.	National licence. Local costs 80fr from Auto Club.	Green Card	Good
Macao	Not poss. to bring cars in.	No self-drive hire cars.		
Madagascar		International licence	Local insurance	Shortages
Malawi	Carnet valid	International licence OK up to 3 mths.	Local insurance needed.	Good. (Available 0600 hrs – 1800 hrs).
Malaysia	Free import on cond. it leaves within 90 days.	International or Foreign licence endorsed by Min. of Rd. Transport.	Third Party	Good
Mali	Carnet should be OK.	International licence.	Local insurance	Fuel obtainable in big towns.
Malta	No, if imported by tourists for up to 3 mths.	National licence	Third Party	Petrol Stations closed Sundays
Mauritania	Carnet valid	International licence	Local insurance	Shortages
Mauritius	Carnet valid for short period.	International licence endorsed for 1 year at a time.	Local Third Party	Good
Mexico	No. Must produce proof of ownership or rental. Duty 100% and *Valorem*.	International licence. Local obtainable without test for US$6 from AMA or Local Transit Authority Office.	Local insurance	Good
Mongolia	Difficult to get private cars in.	International licence	Local insurance	OK

		International licence	Green Card	Good
Morocco	Carnet not needed. 3 mths free entry. Max of 6 mths a year. Will be entered on passport. Duty is up to 130%.	International licence		Good
Nepal	Carnet required. Lasts a max. of 6 mths in any year.	International licence	Not compulsory	Available in Kathmandu.
Netherlands	No	International licence	Green Card	Good
New Zealand	Carnet will give free entry for 1 year.	International licence	Local Third Party	Good
Nicaragua	No, up to 30 days – extension requires Customs deposit.	No, up to 30 days – after need local licence.	Not compulsory	OK
Niger	Carnet valid	International licence	Insure in case of fire	Usually OK
Nigeria	Carnet or West African 'Brown Card' valid.	International licence lasts 3 mths. Must have a test for a local licence.	Local insurance advisable	Good
Norway	No	National licence	Third Party needed.	Good
Oman	No	National licence lasts 3 mths. Go to police for a local one. Test required.	Green Card	Good
Pakistan	No	International licence	Not compulsory	OK
Panama	Proof of ownership needed. No problem if taking car out again.	International licence	Green Card	Good
Papua New Guinea	80% duty payable	International licence lasts for 1 mth. A local licence costs K20. No test.	Local insurance	Good
Paraguay	No	International licence	Green Card	Good
Peru	No	International licence OK for 90 days.	Local insurance not legally required but advisable.	OK but diesel is difficult in some areas.

Countries	Import requirements	Driving Permits	Motor Insurance	Fuel Availability
Philippines	No	International licence OK for 90 days. Local licence needs a test. Contact the Land Transportation Office.	Not legally required	Good
Poland	No	International licence OK for one month.	Green Card	Have to buy fuel coupons in own country or on border.
Portugal	Carnet valid. 41–44% duty	National licence OK for short period	Greed Card. 3rd Party compulsory	Good
Qatar	Carnet valid	National licence OK for 30 days. Can get a temp. 90 day licence. A full local licence costs 30 Riyals and involves an extremely difficult test. Go to Traffic and Licencing Office.	Local Third Party mandatory.	Good
Romania	No	International licence	Green Card	Good
Rwanda	Carnet valid	International licence	Local Third Party compulsory	OK in patches
Saudi Arabia	Carnets not valid. Fords are banned. Must have an import permit in advance from the embassy.	International licence OK up to 3 months. Women not permitted to drive. Local licence essential for longer stays.	Local Third Party compulsory	Good
Senegal	Carnet valid. Duty 148%.	International licence. National licence can be used to obtain a local one at Service de Mines Routes de Rifirque, Dakar	Local insurance	Good
Seychelles	Duty payable 70–100%	National licence OK for 3 mths, then must convert to a local. Costs SR200 pa.	Green Card	Good

Singapore	Carnet valid. Duty 150%.	International licence	Local insurance	Good
Solomon Islands	Duty payable	International licence	Local insurance	Good
Somalia	NB Tourist visas not issued at moment, so does not apply.			
South Africa	Carnet valid. Duty 115%.	Valid licence printed in English.	Local insurance compulsory.	Good. Petrol Stations open 7–18 hrs Mon.–Fri.
Spain	No	International licence	Green Card. Third Party. Bail Bond advised	Good
Sri Lanka	Carnet valid for 6 mths	Local licence free to tourists from the AA on production of your national licence	Local Third Party	Good
Sudan	Register with the Customs. Free for a limited period. Duty of 100–250%.	International licence OK for 6 mths.	Local insurance needed	Authorities supply Petrol – enough to get you through. Otherwise only available through the black market.
Swaziland	No	International licence	Must be insured.	Good
Sweden	No	International licence	Must be insured.	Good
Switzerland	No	National licence OK for 6 mths.	Green Card mandatory.	Good
Syria	Carnet valid. Duty 200–300% and involves hassle.	International licence	Green Card	Good
Tahiti	No	International licence	Must be insured.	Good
Tanzania	Carnet valid. 100% duty.	International Licence – report to licence issuing authority on arrival.	Local Third Party	Variable. Sometimes rationed. If short, go to the District Office in nearest town.
Thailand	No	International licence	Green Card	Good
Togo	Carnet valid 42% duty.	International licence	Green Card	OK in major towns.

Countries	Import requirements	Driving Permits	Motor Insurance	Fuel Availability
Tonga	No	Local licence required, issued by police dept. Need an international licence and T$3.	Local insurance	Good
Trinidad & Tobago	Duty 45%. Left hand drive cars restricted.	International licence	Comprehensive needed	Good
Tunisia	Free for 3 mths. Renewable.	International licence.	Local insurance.	Good
Turkey	Carnet valid	Local licence from Istanbul Traffik Nudurlugu without test if you have a valid licence.	Green Card valid to Istanbul. Need local insurance in Asia.	Good
Turks & Caicos		National licence OK for 30 days – extendable.	Third Party compulsory. Arrange before arrival.	Good
Uganda	Carnet valid	International licence	Green Card	OK. Some shortages off the beaten track.
USSR	No	Valid Licence in accord with Int. Convention on Rd. Traffic	Green Card	OK
United Arab Emirates	Carnet valid. 2% duty.	International licence OK if driving foreign or rented car.	Green Card as long as it specifies UAE.	Good
US Virgin Islands	No	$2.00 special permit	Local insurance	Good
United States	Free for 1 yr.	National licence OK for 1 yr.	Local insurance	Good
Uruguay	No	International licence OK for 90 days.	No	Good

Vanuatu	Carnet valid. Duty 35%.	No, if British or French (90 days). Others – international. Local licence costs US$10 with licence in lieu of test.	Local insurance	Good
Venezuela	Ownership papers. Declare not going to sell it before entering country.	International licence	Local Third Party	Good
Vietnam	Check with Customs when you enter. Very difficult to get in.	International licence	No	OK
North Yemen	Carnet valid. Duty 125%.	International licence	Local insurance compulsory.	Petrol OK. Diesel sometimes difficult.
South Yemen	NB. Not allowed to take cars or drive (Taxis available).			
Yugoslavia	Carnet valid	International licence	Green Card	Good
Zaire	Carnet valid	International licence	Not required legally.	Shortages
Zambia	Duty free entry for tourists. Duty 150%.	International licence OK for 3 mths. Then get a local. Costs K10 from Police. Need test.	Temp Third Party valid for Zambia obtainable at border.	OK but occasional shortages.
Zimbabwe	Carnet valid.	International licence	Local Third Party needed.	Good

Note:
1) The requirements given here are the minimum accepted by each country. It would always be advisable to use an international licence as opposed to your national one.
2) Many countries will let you take in a car for a brief tourist visit without a carnet and without paying duty, but this should not be relied upon.

International Road Signs

▲ Warning signs   ● Regulative signs   ■ Informative signs

Colours may vary from country to country, but are usually red and black on a white background.

WARNING SIGNS

Right bend

Double bend

Dangerous bend

Danger! Train

Cross roads

Intersection w/minor road

Merging traffic

Road narrows

Uneven road

Slippery road

Other dangers

Round-about

Give way

Dangerous descent

Road work

Tunnel

Opening bridge

Animals

Level crossing with barrier

Level crossing without barrier

Pedestrians

Children

Two-way traffic

Falling rocks

Traffic signals ahead

INFORMATIVE SIGNS

Motorway exit

Priority road

End of priority road

One-way traffic

Hospital

First-aid station

Mechanical help

REGULATIVE SIGNS

Road closed

No entry

No right turn

Direction obligatory

No U-turns

No entry for motorcars

No entry for motor-cycles

No entry for all motor vehicles

No entry for bicycles

No entry for pedestrians

Priority to oncoming vehicles

No overtaking

End of no overtaking

Maximum load

Axle weight limit

Width limit

Height limit

No parking

Maximum speed limit

End of speed limit

End of all restrictions

Halt sign

Customs

No stopping

Use of horns prohibited

International Vehicle Licence Plates

A	Austria		GBJ	Jersey
ADN	South Yemen		GBM	Isle of Man
AL	Albania		GBZ	Gibraltar
AND	Andorra		GH	Ghana
AUS	Australia		GLA	Guatemala
B	Belgium		GR	Greece
BDS	Barbados		GUY	Guyana
BG	Bulgaria		H	Hungary
BH	Belize		HK	Hong Kong
BR	Brazil		HKJ	Jordan
BRN	Bahrain		I	Italy
BRU	Brunei		IL	Israel
BS	Bahamas		IND	India
BUR	Burma		IR	Iran
C	Cuba		IRQ	Iraq
CDN	Canada		IS	Iceland
CH	Switzerland		J	Japan
CI	Côte d'Ivoire		JA	Jamaica
CL	Sri Lanka		K	Kampuchea
CO	Colombia		L	Luxembourg
CR	Costa Rica		LAO	Laos
CS	Czechoslovakia		LAR	Libya
CY	Cyprus		LB	Liberia
D	West Germany		LS	Lesotho
DDR	East Germany		M	Malta
DK	Denmark		MA	Morocco
DOM	Dominican Republic		MAL	Malaysia
DY	Benin		MC	Monaco
DZ	Algeria		MEX	Mexico
E	Spain		MS	Mauritius
EAK	Kenya		MW	Malawi
EAT	Tanzania		N	Norway
EAU	Uganda		NA	Netherlands Antilles
EAZ	Zanzibar		NIC	Nicaragua
EC	Ecuador		NIG	Niger
EIR	Ireland		NL	Netherlands
ET	Egypt		NZ	New Zealand
F	France		P	Portugal
FJI	Fiji		PA	Panama
FL	Liechtenstein		PAK	Pakistan
G	Gabon		PE	Peru
GB	United Kingdom		PI	Philippines
GBA	Alderney		PL	Poland
GBG	Guernsey		PY	Paraguay

R	Romania	SU	USSR
RA	Argentina	SWA	South West Africa (Namibia)
RB	Botswana	SY	Seychelles
RC	Taiwan	SYR	Syria
RCA	Central African Republic	T	Thailand
RCB	Congo	TG	Togo
RCH	Chile	TN	Tunisia
RH	Haiti	TR	Turkey
RI	Indonesia	TT	Trinidad & Tobago
RIM	Mauritania	U	Uruguay
RL	Lebanon	USA	USA
RM	Madagascar	VN	Vietnam
RMM	Mali	WAG	Gambia
RNR	Zambia	WAL	Sierra Leone
ROK	Korea	WAN	Nigeria
RSM	San Marino	WD	Dominica
RSR	Zimbabwe	WG	Grenada
RU	Burundi	WL	St. Lucia
RWA	Rwanda	WS	Western Samoa
S	Sweden	WV	St. Vincent
SD	Swaziland	YU	Yugoslavia
SDV	Vatican City	YV	Venezuela
SF	Finland	Z	Zambia
SGP	Singapore	ZA	South Africa
SME	Suriname	ZR	Zaïre
SN	Senegal		

Metric Tyre Pressure Conversion Chart

Pounds per sq in	Kilograms per sq cm	Atmosphere	Kilo Pascals(kPa)
14	0.98	0.95	96.6
16	1.12	1.08	110.4
18	1.26	1.22	124.2
20	1.40	1.36	138.0
22	1.54	1.49	151.8
24	1.68	1.63	165.6
26	1.83	1.76	179.4
28	1.96	1.90	193.2
30	2.10	2.04	207.0
32	2.24	2.16	220.8
36	2.52	2.44	248.4
40	2.80	2.72	276.0
50	3.50	3.40	345.0
55	3.85	3.74	379.5
60	4.20	4.08	414.0
65	4.55	4.42	448.5

Litre to Gallon Conversion

To convert:	Multiply by
Gallons to Litres	4.546
Litres to Gallons	0.22

Measures of Capacity

2 pints =	1 Quart =	1.136 Litres
4 Quarts =	1 Gallon =	4.546 Litres
	5 Gallons =	22.73 Litres.

Motoring Organizations Worldwide

Andorra
Automobil Club d'Andorre
Babotcamp 4
La Vella
Tel: 20890

Algeria
Fédération Algérienne du Sport Automobile et du Katring-99
Blvd Salah-Bouakouir
Alger

Touring Club d'Algérie
1 Rue Al-Idrissi
B.P. - Alger Gare
Algiers
Tel: 640 837/535 810/633 008

Argentina
Automovil Club Argentino
1850 Avenida del Liberator
Buenos Aires 1461
Tel: 802 6061/7061

Touring Club Argentino
Esmeralda 605
Buenos Aires
Tel: 392 7994/392 8170

Australia
Australian Automobile Association (AAA)
212 Northbourne Ave
Canberra
Act 2601

Automobile Association of the Northern Territory
78–81 Smith Street
Darwin NT 5790
Tel: 813 837

National Roads & Morists Association
NRMA House
151 Clarence Street
Sydney
NSW 2000

RAC of Australia
89 Macquarie Street
Sydney
NSW

RAC of Queensland
CNR Ann & Boundary Streets
Brisbane
QLD

RAC of South Australia
41 Hindmarsh Square
Adelaide
SA

RAC of Tasmania
cnr Patrick & Murray Streets
Hobart
Tasmania

RAC of Victoria
123 Queen Street
Melbourne
Victoria

RAC of Western Australia
228 Adelaide Terrace
Perth
QA

Austria
Osterreichischer Automobil – Motorad – und Touring Club
(OAMTC)
Postfact 252
Vienne 1015
Tel: 0222/72990

Bahamas
Bahamas Automobile Club
West Avenue
Centreville
Nassau
Tel: 325 0514

Bangladesh
Austomobile Association of Bangladesh
3/B Outer Circular Road
Moghbazar
Dacca 17
Tel: 243483/402241

Barbados
Barbados Automobile Association
Room 406
Plantations Building
Broad Street
Bridgetone B.W.

Belgium
Royal Auto-club de Belgique
53 Rue d'Arlon
B-1040
Brussels

Bolivia
Automóvil Club Boliviano
Avenida 6 de Agosto
2993 San Jorge
Casilla 602
La Paz
Tel: 351 667/325 136

Brazil
Touring Club do Brasil
Praca Maua
Rio de Janeiro
Tel: 263 5583/254 2020

Brunei
Persatuan Automobile Brunei
(Automobile association of Brunei – AAB)
Weights and Measures Section
State Secretariat
Brunei
Tel: Bureau du Président 4659

Bulgaria
Union des Automobilistes Bulgares
6 Rue Sueta Sofia
B.P. 257
Sofia
Tel: 878 801/880 002

Burundi
Club Automobile Burundi
B.P. 544
Bujumbura

Canada
Alberta Motor Association
11230-110 Street
Edmonton
Alberta

Canadian Automobile Association
1175 Courtwood Cresent
Ottawa
Ontario
Tel: 237 2150

Canadian Automobile Sports Clubs, Inc
5385 Younge Street
Suite 28
PO Box 97
Willowdale
Ontario M2N 5S7

Hamilton Automobile Club
393 Main Street East
Box 2090
Hamilton
Ontario

Manitoba Motor League
870 Empress Street
Box 1400
Winnipeg
Manitoba

Maritime Automobile Association
Haymarket Square Shopping Centre
Saint John
New Brunswick

Ontario Motor League
2 Carlton Street
Suite 619
Toronto
Ontario

Quebec Automobile Club
2600 Laurier Blvd
Quebec
PQ

Saskatchewan Motor Club Ltd
200 Albert Street North
Regina
Saskatchewan

The British Columbia Automobile Association
PO Box 9900
Vancouver
BC

Touring Club Montreal
1425 Rue de la Montagne
Montreal
PQ

Chile
Automovil Club de Chile
195 Avenida Pedro de Valdivia
Santiago
Casilla 16695 Correo 9
Santiago
Tel: (2) 749 516/258 040

Colombia
Touring y Automovil Club de Colombia
Av. Caracas No 46-64/72
Bogotá
Tel: 232 7580

Costa Rica
Automobile-Touring Club de Costa Rica
Apartado 4646
San José
Tel: 3570

Côte d'Ivoire
Fédération Ivorienne du Sport Automobile et des
Engines Assimilées (FISA)
OI BP 3883
Abidjan

Cuba
Automovil Aero Club de Cuba
Malecon
Bajos
Havana

Cyprus
Cyprus Automobile Association
PO Box 2279
30 Homer Avenue
Nicosia
Tel: 52 521

Czechoslovakia
Ustredni Automotoklub CSSR
Pletalova 29
Prague
CZ 116 31
Tel: 223 592/220 140

Denmark
Foreneda Danske Motorejere
Blegdamscej 124
2100 Copenhagen 0
Tel: 382 112

Ecuador
Automovil Club del Ecuador
Av 10 de Agosto y Callejon Negrete
Quito
Tel: 37779

Automovil Club de Ecuador (Aneta)
Av Eloy Alfaro 218 y Berlin
Casilla 2830
Quito

Egypt
Automobile et Touring Club d'Egypte
10 Rue Kasr-El-Nil
Cairo
Tel: 743 176

El Salvador
Automovil Club de El Salvador
Almeda Roosevelt y 41 Ave Sur 2173
San Salvador
Tel: 238 077

Automovil Club de El Salvador (ACES)
PO Box 1177
San Salvador

Ethiopia
Automobile Club Eritreo
Via Giustino de Jacobis 4-8
BP 1187
Asmara

Finland
Automobile and Touring Club of Finland
10 Kansakoulukatu
Helsinki 00100
Tel: 694 0022

France
Association Francaise des Automobilistes
9 Rue Allatole-de-la-Forge
Paris 75017
Tel: 227 82 00
Touring Club de France
6-8 Rue Firmin-Gillet
Paris Cedex 75737
Tel: 532 2215

Gabon
Fédération Gabonaise de Sport Automobile
Siège B.P. 695
Libreville

Representant en Paris:
M.M. Desert
72 Rue Ampére
75017
Paris

Ghana
The Automobile Association of Ghana
Fanum House
1 Valley View
Labadi Road
Christianborg
Accra
Tel: 75983/74229

West Germany
Allemeiner Deutscher Automobile Club E.V.
8 Am Westpark 8000
Mu nchen 70
Tel: 89/76761

Automobilclub von Deutschland
Lyoner Strasse 16
Postfach 71 0166
D-6000 Frankfurt

Deutscher Touring Automobil Club
Amallienburgstrasse 23
8000 München 60
Tel: 89/811 4048

Greece
Automobile et Touring Club de Grèce
2 Messogion Street
Athens 610
Tel: 779 1615

Touring Club Hellenique
12 Polytechniou Street
Athens 103
Tel: 521 0872

Guatemala
Club de Automovilismo y Tourismo de
Guatemala (Catgua)
Guatemala CA
15 Calle (A) 1251
Case Postale 1337
Zona 1
Tel: 64882/64883

Hong Kong
Hong Kong Automobile Association
Marsh Road
Wanchai Reclamation
PO Box 2045
Hennessy Road
Post Office
Wanchai
Tel: (5) 743394/725832/728504/737474

Hungary
Magyar Autoklub
Remer Floris u 4/a
1277 Budapest PF1
Tel: 152 040

Iceland
Icelandic Automobile Association
Noatun 17
Reykjavik
Tel: (91) 29999

India
Automobile Association of Eastern India
13 Promothesh Barua Sarani
Calcutta 700019
West Bengal
Tel: 479012/5133, 482835

Automobile Association of Southern India
38A Mount Road
PBA 729
Madras 6

Automobile Association of Upper India
14F Connaught Place
New Delhi 110001
Tel: 40409/44312/42063

Federation of Indian Automobile Associations
(FIAA)
76 Vir Nariman Road
1st Floor Churchgate Reclamation
Bombay 400020
Tel: 291085

Western India Automobile Association
76 Vir Nariman Road
Churchgate Reclamation
Bombay 400020

Indonesia
Ikatan Motor Indonesia (IMI)
Gedung KONI
Pusat Senayan
Kotakpos 609
Jakarta
Tel: 581 1102

Iran
Touring and Automobile Club of Islamic Republic of Iran
37 Avenue Marture
dr. Fayaz-Bakhche
Tehran 11146
B.P. 1294 Tehran
Tel: 679 142-7

Iraq
Iraq Automobile and Touring Club
Al Mansour
Baghdad
Tel: 35862

Israel
Automobile and Touring Club of Israel
19 Petah Tikvah Road
PO Box 36144
Tel Aviv 61360
Tel: 622 961/2

Italy
Automobile Club d'Italia
8 Via Marsala
Rome 00815

Tel: 4998
Federazione Italiana del Campeggio e del
Caravania
Uscita 19 'Prato-Calezano'
Autostrada del Sole
Via V Emanuele 11
Florence 50041
Tel: 055-882391/2/3

Touring Club Italiano
10 Corso Italia
Milan
Tel: (2) 809 871

Jamaica
Jamaica Automobile Association (JAA)
14 Ruthven Road
Kingston 10
Tel: (92) 91200/1

Jamaica Touring Club
PO Box 49
Bingston 10

Japan
Japan Automobile Federation
Shiba-Koen
3-5-8 Minato-Ku
Tokyo 105
Tel: 436 2811

Touring Club of Japan
Daini-Maijima Bldg 5F
1-9 Yotsuya
Shinjuku-Ku
Tokyo 160
Tel: (03) 335 1692/1661

Jordan
Royal Automobile Club of Jordan
PO Box 920
Amman
Tel: 22467

Kenya
Automobile Association of Kenya
Nyaku House
Hurlingham
PO Box 40037
Nairobi
Tel: 720 0882

South Korea
Korea Automobile Association
1 PO Box 2008
Seoul

Kuwait
Automobile Association of Kuwait and the Gulf
PO Box 2100
Airport Road
Khalidiyah 72300
Tel: (965) 832 192/408/388
Kuwait Automobile and Touring Club
PO Box 2100
Airport Road
Khalidiyah 72300

Kuwait International Touring and Automobile Club
Khalidiyah 72300
Airport Road
PO Box 2100
Kuwait 72300
Tel: 812 539/815 192/818 406

Lebanon
Automobile et Touring Club du Liban
Avenue Sami Solh Kalot
PO Box 3545
Beirut
Tel: 221 698/9/229 222

Libya
Automobile and Touring Club of Libya
Al Fath Blvd
Maiden-Chazala
PO Box 3566
Tripoli

Liechtenstein
Automobile Club des Furstenturs Liechtenstein
Bannholzstrasse 10
9490 Vaduz

Luxembourg
Automobile Club du Grand Duché de Luxembourg
13 Route de Long W9
Bertrange
Helfenterbruck 8080
Tel: (352) 211 031

Malaysia
Automobile Association of Malaysia
30 Djalan Datuk Sulaiman
Taman Tun Dr. Ismail
Kuala Lumpur
Selangor

Malawi – see Zimbabwe

Malta
Malta Automobile Federation
48 St Publius Street
Saint Paul's Bay

Mexico
Asociacion Mexicana Automovilistica (AMA) AC
Orizaba 7, Colonia Roma
Apartado 24-486
Mexico 7 DF
Tel: 511 1084
Asociacion Mexicana Automovilistica
Av Shapultepec 276
Mexico City
Asociacion Nacional Automovilistica
Miguel E Schultz 140
Mexico 4 DF

Morocco
Royal Automobile Club Marocain
3 Rue Lemercier
BP 94
Casablanca

Tel: (212) 250 030/253 504

Touring Club du Maroc
3 Avenue de l'Armée-royale
Casablanca
Tel: (212) 279 288

Nepal
Automobile Association of Nepal
Traffic Police
Ramshag Path, Opp. Sinadnar
Kathmandu
Tel: 11093/15662

Netherlands
Koninklijke Nederlandse Toeristen Bond
ANWB
Wassenaarseweg 220
BP 93200
The Hague
Tel: (70) 264426

New Zealand
Automobile Association Southland, Inc
PO Box 61
Invercargill
Tel: 89 003

Automobile Association (Otago), Inc
PO Box 174
Dunedin
Tel: 775 945

Automobile Association Nelson, Inc
204 Hardy Street
Nelson
Tel: 88 339

Automobile Association of Marlborough, Inc
PO Box 104
Blenheim
Tel: 83 399

The Automobile Association (Wairarapa), Inc
Chapel Street
Masterton
Tel: 85 006

Automobile Association (South Canterbury), Inc
37 Sophia Street
Timaru
Tel: 84 189

Automobile Association (Taranaki), Inc
46 Brougham Street
New Plymouth
Tel 75 646

Automobile Association (Wanganui), Inc
PO Box 4002
Wanganui
Tel: 54 549

Automobile Association (Central), Inc
AA House
166 Willis Street
Wellington 1

Automobile Association (South Taranaki), Inc
210 Hereford Street
PO Box 994

Christchurch
Tel: 791 280

Automobile Association (Auckland), Inc
PO Box 5
Auckland
Tel: 774 660

Motorsport Association New Zealand (MANZ)
PO Box 3793
9 Tinakori Road
Thorndon
Wellington

The New Zealand Automobile Association, Inc
PO Box 1794
Wellington
Tel: (4) 735 484

Pioneer Amateur Sports Club
Club House
188 Oxford Terrace
Christchurch

Nigeria
Automobile Club of Nigeria
24 Mercy Eneli Surulere Nigeria
Lagos
Tel: 960 514/961 478

Norway
Norge Automobil Forbund
Stopgt 2
Oslo
Tel: (02) 42 94 00

Oman
Oman Automobile Association
PO Box 4503
Ruwi-Muscat

Pakistan
Automobile Association of West Pakistan
14B Shah Jamal
PO Box 76
Lahore
Karachi Automobile Association (KAA)
Standard Insurance House
1 Chundrigar Road
Karachi 0226
Tel: 232 173

Panama
Touring Automovil Club de Panama
Av Tivoli 8
Panama City

Papua New Guinea
Automobile Association of Papua New Guinea
BPO Box 5999
Boroko
Tel: 257 717

Paraguay
Touring Automobil Club Paraguayo
25 de Mayo y Brasil
Casilla de Correo 1204
Asunción
Tel: 26 075

Peru
Touring y Automovil Club de Peru
Cesar Vallejo 6999
Lima 14
Casilla 2219
Lima 100
Tel: 403 270/225 957

Philippines
Philippines Motor Association
689 Aurora Blvd
Quezon City
PO Box 999
Manila
Tel: 780 190

Poland
Polskie Towarzystwo-Turystyczno-Krajoznaw-cze (PTTK)
UL Senatorskall
B.P. 13
Warsaw 00.075
Polski Zwiazek Motorway
UL Kazimierzowska 66
Warsaw 02.518
Tel: (22) 499 361

Portugal
Automovel Club de Portugal
Apartado 2585
Rua Rosa Araujo 24 et 26
Lisbon 1200
Tel: (19) 563 931/775 475

Qatar
Automobile Touring Club of Qatar
Beda Road
PO Box 18
Doha
Tel: 413 265/415 718

Rwanda
Auto Moto Club of Rwanda
PO Box 822
Kigali

Romania
Automobil Clubul Roamn
N. 27 Rue N Beloinais
B.P. 3107
Bucharest 70 166
Tel: 595 270/080

San Marino
Ente di Stato per il Turismo Sport e Spettacolo
Palazzo del Turismo
Republique de Saint-Marin
Tel: (1) 992 102/3/4/5

Senegal
Automobile Club du Senegal
Immeuble Chambre de Commerce
Place di l'Indépendance
B.P 295
Dakar
Tel: 26604/8

Touring Club du Senegal
Bldg. Air Afrique
Place de l'Indépendance
B.P. 4049
Dakar
Tel: 34821

Secretariat d'Etat au Tourisme
3e Étage
Immeuble Kebe Extension
BP 4049
Av. Jean Jaurès x Peytavin
Dakar
Tel: 222 226

Singapore
Automobile Association of Singapore
AA House
336 River Valley Road
PO Box 85
Killiney Road
Singapore 9
Tel: 372 444

South Africa
Automobile Association of South Africa
Corbett Place
66 de Korte Street
PO Box 596
Braamfontein
Johannesburg 2001
Tel: 281 400

The Automobile Association of South Africa
7 Martin Hammerschlag Way
Foreshore
PO Box 70
Cape Town

Spain
Real Automovil Club de Espan;ta
3 José Abascal 10
Madrid
Tel: (1) 447 3200

Sri Lanka
Automobile Association of Sri Lanka
Box 338
Colombo

Ceylon Motor Sports Club
4 Hunupitya Road
PO Box 196
Colombo 2
Tel: 26558

Sweden
Motormñnnens Riksföbund
Box 5855
32 Sturegatan
Stokholm 10248
Tel: (8) 670 580

Svenska Turistöreningen
Box 25
Vasagaten 48
Stockholm 10120
Tel: (8) 227 200

Switzerland
Automobile-Club de Suisse
Wasserwerkgasse 39
3000 Berne 13

Touring Club Suisse
9 Rue Pierre Fatio
Geneva
1211 Geneva 3
Tel: (22) 371 212

Office National Suisse du Toursime
Case Postale 8027
Bellariustrasse 38
Zürich
Psfach 8627
Im Studli 9
Gruningen

Syria
Touring Club of Syria
Rue Baron
Imm Jésuuites
B.P. 28
Alep
Tel: 15210/45847/12230

Touring Club of Syria
Rue Salhie
Place Yousseff al Azme
B.P. 3364
Damascus

Tanzania
The Automobile Association of Tanzania
PO Box 3004
Cargen House
Maktaba Street
Dar es Salaam
Tel: 21965

Thailand
Royal Automobile Association of Thailand
151 Rachadapisek Road
Bang Khen
Bangkok 10900
Tel: (662) 511 2230/1

Trinidad and Tobago
Trinidad and Tobago Automobile Association
14 Woodford Street
Port of Spain
Tel: 622 7194

Trinidad Automobile Association
Room 2
94 Frederick Street
Trinidad

Tunisia
National Automobile Club de Tunisie
29 Avenue Habib Bourguiba
Tunis

Touring Club de Tunisie
15 Rue d'Allemagne
Tunis
Tel: (1) 243 182

Turkey
Turkiye Turing Ve Otomobil Kurumu
364 Sisli Meydani
Istanbul
Tel: 467 090

United Arab Emirates
Automobile and Touring Club for the UAE
PO Bos 1183
Sharjah

United States of America
American Automobile Association
8111 Gatehouse Road
Falls Church
VA 22042

American Automobile Touring Alliance
888 Worcester Street
Wellesley
Massachusetts 02191
Tel: (617) 237 5200

Uruguay
Automovil Club del Uruguay
Av Agraciada 1532
Casilla Correo 387
Montevideo
Tel: 984 710/3 (club)
        911 551/251/2/3 (Rescue Service)

Centro Automobilista del Uruguay
Boulevard Arigas 1773
Montevideo
Tel: 42091/2, 46131, 45016, 412528/9

Touring Club Uruguay
Ave Uruguay 2009–2015
Montevideo
Tel: 44875, 46193/4

USSR
Federacia Automobilnogo Sporta SSSR
(Federation Automobile of the USSR)
BP 395
Moscow D-362
Tel: 491 8661

Intourist
Dept of International Organizations
16 Marx Prospect
Moscow 103009
Tel: 203 6962

UK
The Automobile Association
Fanum House
Basingstoke
Hampshire RG21 2EA
Tel: 20123

The Camping Club of Great Britain and Ireland
Ltd
11 Lower Grosvenor Place
London SW1W OE4
Tel: 01-828 1012/7

Caravan Club
East Grinstead House
East Grinstead
West Sussex RH19 1UA
Tel: 26944

The Royal Automobile Club
PO Box 100
RAC House
Landsdowne Road
Croydon CR9 2JA
Tel: 01-868 2525

The Royal Scottish Automobile Club
11 Blythswood Square
Glasgow G2 4AG
Tel: 221 3850

Vatican City
Commission pour la Pastorale des Migrations et
Tourisme
Palais Saint-Calixte
Tel: (6) 698 7131

Venezuela
Touring y Automovil Club de Venezuela
Centro Integral
Santa Rosa de Lima
Locales 11, 12 13 y 14
Apt. de Correos 68102
Caracas
Tel: 916 373

Vietnam
Automobile Club de Vietnam
17 Duong Ho Zuan Huong
Saigon
Tel: 23273

Yugoslavia
Auto-Moto Savez Jogoslavise
Ruzveltova 18
B.P. 66
Belgrade 11001
Tel: (11) 401 699

Zaire
Office National du Tourisme
Coins Blvd du Bojuin et Avenue de Ritona
B.P. 9502
Kinshasa
Tel: 22417/25828

Zaïre Automobile Federation
Bldg Forescom 118
Avenue du Port
BP 2491
Kinshasa

Zimbabwe
Automobile Association of Zimbabwe
57 Samora Machel Avenue
PO Box 585
Harare C1
Tel: 707 021 (Agent for Malawi)

Main Car Rental Companies

Australia

Avis Rent-a-Car
140 Pacific Highway
N. Sydney
NSW 2060
and
46 Hill St
Perth
WA 6000
Tel: 325 7677

Budget Rent-a-Car
960 Hay St
Perth
WA 6000
Tel: 322 1100

Hertz Rent-a-Car
39 Milligan St
Perth
WA 6000
Tel: 321 7777
All the major car rental companies have offices in the main cities around Australia.

World Travel Headquarters Pty Ltd
Kindersley House
33-35 Bligh Street
Sydney 2000
NSW

Canada

Avis Rent-a-Car
4420 Côte de Liesse Road
Montreal
Quebec
H4N 2V5

Budget Rent-a-Car
680 Michael Jasmin
Dorval
Quebec
Tel: (514) 636 8700

Hertz Rent-a-Car
Tilden
Information phone line
1-800 268 1311

France

Europcar International
65, Avenue Edouard-Vaillant
92100 Boulogne-Billancourt
France
Tel: 46 09 92 20
Telex: 631 421 or 631 425

West Germany

interRent International
Head Office
interRent Autovermietung GmbH
International System Division
Tangstedeter Landstrasse 81
2000 Hamburg 62

UK

Avis Rent-a-Car
Avis House
Station Road
Bracknell
Berks
RG12 1HZ
Tel: (0344) 426644

Budget-Rent-a-Car International Inc
International House
85 Great North Road
Hatfield
Hertfordshire
AL9 5EF
Tel: (07072) 60321
One of the top three car and van rental companies in the world, with 3,000 locations in over 100 countries.

Europcar International
Central Reservations – UK and Worldwide
Bushey House
High Street
Bushey
Herts WD2 1RE
Tel: 950 5050

Hertz Rent-a-Car
Radnor House
1272 London Road
Norbury
London SW16 4XW
Tel: 01-679 1777
Hertz-Rent-a-Car is the world's largest vehicle rental and leasing company, operating a network of 43,000 locations in 119 countries.

InterRent/Swan National Ltd
305/307 Chiswick High Road
London W4 4HH
Tel: 01-995 9242

USA

Avis-Rent-a-Car
World Headquarters
Avis Rent a Car System, Inc
900 Old Country Road
Garden City
New York
NY 11530

Dollar Rent a Car Systems, Inc
World Headquarters
6141 W. Century Blvd
PO Box 45048
Los Angeles
CA 90045
Tel: (213) 776 8100

Hertz-Rent-a-Car
Headquarters
Hertz System Inc
660 Madison Avenue
New York
NY 10021
Tel: (212) 980 2121

Vehicles – Accessories/Spares/ Outfitting

ABC Equipment
The Green
Clayton
Doncaster CN5 7DD
Tel: (0977) 43103
Telex: 547291
Are suppliers of all Land Rover and Range Rover spares, specializing in export. Will ship to all parts of the world at short notice. Special arrangements for expedition requirements.

Auto Accessories
66 Avenue de la Grande Armée
75017 Paris
France
Tel: 4574 7474
All car accessories, sand ladders, jerry cans, air filters.

Brownchurch (Land Rovers) Ltd
Hare Row
off Cambridge Heath Road
London E29 BY
Tel: 01-729 3606
Telex: 299397 BRNCH
Cover all Land Rover needs for trips anywhere, including the fitting of jerry cans and holders, sand ladders, sump and light guards, crash bars, winches, water purifying plants, roofracks (custom-made if necessary), overdrive units. They also supply new vehicles and offer a maintenance and spares service for Land and Range Rovers.

Four Wheel Drives
304 Middlesborough Road
Blackburn South
Vic. 3130
Australia
Tel: (03) 890 509

Manual winches and Land Rover spares.

Michelin Tyre plc
81 Fulham Road
London SW3 6RD
Tel: 01-589 1460
Tyres, maps, guides.

RAC Motoring Services Ltd
PO Box 100
RAC House
Lansdowne Road
Croydon
Surrey CR9 2JA
Sells a range of maps, atlases, guides and touring accessories.

S.E.E.A. Framery
4 Route Nationale
94440 Santeny
France
Tel: (1) 386 0664
Jeep, Dodge, G.M.C. parts and spares.

Société Schneebeli-Chabaud
8 Rue Proudhon
93210 La Plaine Saint-Denis
France
Vehicle heating systems.

Tyre Services (Aust) Pty Ltd
971 Ipswich Road
Moorooka
Brisbane
QLD 4105
Australia
Tel: (07) 392 2766
and
PO Box 4

Moorooka
QLD 4105
Branches at:
Sunshine Coast (071) 435 288
Mackay (079) 513 277
Townsville (077) 794 299
Cairns (070) 519 375
Queensland's largest off-road equipment specialists.

Safariquip
See Equipment: General on page 000.

Vehicles: Purchase, Hire & Conversion

Caravanning and Camping-Cars & Motor-Homes
7 Rue Aude
92210 Saint-Cloud
France
Tel: (1) 771 9171
Have camping vehicles and motor homes for sale and hire and will undertake conversions.

Cross Country Vehicles Ltd
Hailey
Witney
Oxon OX8 5UF
Tel: (0993) 76622
Sell and convert vehicles, prepare them for safari use. Range Rover and Land Rover specialists – new and used vehicles – and any other 4WD vehicle too. They offer service, special preparation, conversion parts (new and reconditioned). Mail order list free application.

Dunsfold Land Rovers Ltd
Alfold Road
Dunsfold
Surrey
Tel: (048 649) 567
Offers free advice to those contemplating overland travel: expedition hardware, air conditioning, left-hand drive conversions, comprehensive stores, rebuilding to owner's specifications; and sales of new and secondhand Land Rovers.

Garage Boursault
11 Rue Boursault
75017 Paris
France
Tel: 293 65 65
Specializes in preparation and fitting out of Land Rovers and Range Rovers.

Harvey Hudson
Woodford
London E18 1AS
Tel: 01-989 6644
Land Rover specialists, suppliers of new and used vehicles to expeditions.

Land Rover Ltd
Direct Sales Department
Lode Lane
Solihull
West Midlands B92 8NW
Tel: 021-743 4242
Manufacturers of Land Rovers and Range Rovers. Purchase must be through authorized dealers.

Manchester Garages Ltd
Oxford Road
Manchester M13 0JD
Tel: 061-224 7301
Service/Sales/Parts.

Mobile Holiday Hire
1a Grosvenor Road
Hanwell
London W7
and
149 Broadway
West Ealing
London W13
Tel: 01-567 6155 and 579 4146
Supply cars, mini-buses, motor caravans and vans for holiday transport.

Scotty's
PO Box 21609
Concorde
CA 94521
USA
Parts, sales and service. Land Rover, Leyland.

Strakit
Bonville
Gellainville
2860 Chartres
France
Tel: (37) 28 54 82

V.A.G. (UK) Ltd
Yeomans Drive
Blakelands
Milton Keynes
MK14 5AN
and
Autorent Manager
V.A.G. (UK) Ltd
95 Baker Street
London W1M 1FB
Have a rental programme called 'Autorent'. Involved with the whole range of Volkswagen and Audi passenger cars. The conversion companies they approve are: Richard Holdsworth Conversions Ltd, Auto-Sleepers Ltd, Auto Homes (UK) Ltd, and Devon Conversions Ltd.

Vehicles: Shipment

P.T. Helu-Trans
Cik's Building, 3rd Floor

84-86 Jalan Cikini Raya
Jakarta Pusat
Indonesia
Tel: 324 679/325 175
Agents for Hermann Ludwig GmbH.
and
100 Albert Road
South Melbourne 3205
Vic
Australia
Tel: (03) 690 21 00
Handle all kinds of transportation worldwide. Deal especially with the shipment of passenger cars by air or sea all over the world. The most frequent shipments are to Canada, the East and West coast of the US, Central America, Australia, New Zealand, West Africa, the Middle East, and to the Far East (Japan, Taiwan, the Philippines).

Hermann Ludwig GmbH & Co
Head Office:
Billstrasse 180
D-2000 Hamburg 28
West Germany
Tel: (040) 781 001
and
PO Box 100240
D-2000 Hamburg 1
West Germany
Eagle House
161-189 City Road
London
EC1V 1LB
Tel: 01-251 0601
and
53 Park Place
Suite 1101
New York
NY 10007
USA
Tel: (212) 608 4140

Kuehne & Nagel, Inc
Suite 7751
One World Trade Center
New York

NY 10048
U.S.A.
One of the largest shipping agents in the U.S. with offices in all major ports.

Malay States Shipping Co. Pte Ltd
Shipbrokers and Shipping Agents
79 Robinson Road
26-00 CPF Bldg
Singapore 0106
Singapore
Tel: 2203266
Telex: RS24057 AB: MMASSCO
Branches at Kuala Lumpur, Port Keland, Penang, Pasir Gudang. Agents for B.P. Shipping Ltd. Yangming Marine Transport Corp. (Yang Ming Line), V.B. Perkins & Co Pty Ltd., Taiwan Navigation Co Ltd.

V.B. Perkins & Co Pty
Box 1019
Darwin
NT 5794
Australlia
Operate a roll-on/roll-off vehicle shipping service between Singapore and Darwin.

Society of Motor Manufacturers and Traders
Forbes House
Halkin St
London SW1
Tel: 01-235 7000
Will advise on shipping vehicles and provide reliable names.

Uni-Ocean Forwarding Co. Ltd
Samheung Bldg
10-4 Bukchang-Dong
Chung-Ku
(CPO Box 7430)
Seoul
Korea
Tel: 77134
Tlx: K26394 UNIFORD
Agents for Hermann Ludwig GmbH; ASG AB of Sweden; PFE Express Ltd (UK).

Water

Passenger Cruise and Passenger/Cargo Freighter Lines

Australia

Canberra Cruises Ltd
P&O Booking Centre
Level 5
Kindersley House
33 Bligh Street
Sydney
N.S.W. 2000
Tel: 237 0333

CTC Lines
6th Floor,
39/43 Clarence Street,
Sydney, NSW,
Tel: 290 3277
Telex: 7174855

Nauru Pacific Line (Aust Pty) Ltd
80 Collins Street
Melbourne
Victoria 3000
Tel: (03) 653 5709
and Prudential Bldgs
39 Martin Place
Sydney
N.S.W. 2000
Tel: 239 9000
Cruises and a Round-the-World Service on the Canberra.

Princess Cruises – P&O Cruises Ltd
P&O Bldg
2 Castlereagh Street
Sydney 2000
NSW
Tel: 231 6655
See USA.

P&O Cruises
Level 5
Kindersley House
33 Bligh Street
Sydney
N.S.W. 2000
Tel: 237 0333
See Canada

Sitmar Cruises
Prudential Buildings
39 Martin Place
Sydney
NSW 2000
Tel: 239 9000
See USA.

Belgium

CMB N.V.
St. Katelijnevest 61
Antwerp

Canada

Canberra Cruises Ltd
3080 Yonge Street
Suite 4000
Toronto
Ontario M4R 3NI
Tel: (416) 488 9984
Cruises and a Round-the World Service on the Canberra.

Freighter Cruise Service
Suite 103
5929 Monkland Ave
Montreal
Quebec
Tel: (514) 481 0447
Agents for all freighter and steamship companies.

Polish Ocean Lines
McLean Kennedy Inc
410 St. Nicolas Street
Passenger Dept
Montreal H2Y 2P5
Modern cargo/passenger vessels. Trips from Europe to Canada, USA, South America, East, West and North Africa, Singapore, Thailand, Hong Kong, Japan, South Africa, New Zealand, Australia, the Middle East and India.

France

Compagnie Générale Maritime
Sotramar Voyages
12 Rue Godot de Mauroy
75009 Paris
Freighter services to the French West Indies, South Atlantic, Madagascar, the Pacific, South America, Canada and the US.
UK Agent – Pitt & Scott.

Paquet Cruises
5 Blvd. Malesherbes
Paris 75008
Tel: 266 5759

West Germany

Columbus Line
Reederei GmbH (Hamburg Sud)
Ost-West Strasse 59
2000 Hamburg 11
Cargo Passenger service from Europe to the South Pacific Islands, Papua New Guinea, Singapore and back to Europe

Containershiffsreederei Elsfleth
Ost-West-Strasse 59
D-2000 Hamburg 11

DEURGO Carl E Press KG
Deichstrasse 11
P.O. Box 11 20 28
D-2000 Hamburg 11
Tel: (040) 3760007-0
*Steamship, Passenger and Cargo Freighter Lines.
Ship all sorts of automobiles and are the head office
for all the various European TASP offices.*

Hamburg South American Lone
Hamburg Sud
Reiseagentur GmbH
Ost-West Strasse 59
Postfach 11 15 40
2000 Hamburg 11

Linea 'C'-Costa Schiffsreisen Gmbh
Schillerstrasse 18-20
D-6000 Frankfurt Main 1
Tel: (069) 20911

Nigerian National Shipping Line
Mattentwiete 1
D-2000 Hamburg 1
Tel: 372 131/363 236
Tlx: 02 173141
See Nigeria

Egon Oldendorff
PO Box 2135
Funfhausën 1
D-2400 Lu beck 1
Tel: (451) 1500-0
*Cargo/passenger services, different routes between
Europe and the USA.*

Reiseorganisation der NAVIS
Billhorner Kanalstrausse 69
D-2000 Hamburg 28
Postfach 10 48 48
D-2000 Hamburg 1
Tel: (040) 789 48-1
*Ships to North and South America, the Baltic, Medi-
terranean, India, Far East, Israel*

Greece

Epirotiki Lines
Head Office: Aktki Miaouli 87
Piraeus
Cruises

Hellenic Lines Ltd
61-65 Filonos Street
Piraeus
Tel: 417 1541, 412 5965
Pacific Cruises.

India

Shipping Corporation of India Ltd
Shipping House
245 Madame Cama Road
Bombay 40041
Tel: 202 6666
Cargo/Passenger services – Bombay/Goa and Indian

*mainland to the Andaman Islands (intending passen-
gers, other than Indian residents, must obtain permission from the Ministry of Home Affairs before
travelling).*

Italy

Lauro Lines
Lauro Bldg
Via Crestoforo Colombo 45
80133 Naples
Italy
Tel: 311 229
*Cargo/Passenger services – Mediterranean to the
Caribbean, Central America and back. Also to
South America.*

Netherlands

Holland America Lijn N.V.
PO Box 7075
3000 HB Rotterdam
Netherlands
Tel: (10) 4388088
Cruises.

Nigeria

Nigerian National Shipping Line Ltd
Development House
PO Box No.326
21 Wharf Road
Apapa
Lagos
Tel: 877 121/262
*Cargo/Passenger service worldwide from West
Africa.*

Norway

Ivaran Lines
PO Box 484
Oslo 1
*Cargo/Passenger service from the US to South Amer-
ica and back.*

Pakistan

Pan-Islamic Steamship Co. Ltd
Writer's Chambers
Dunolly Road
PO Box 4855
Karachi 2
Tel: 228 691
Cargo/Passenger service Pakistan – Arabian Gulf.

Poland

Polish Ocean Lines
10 Lutegoly
Gdynia, 81-364
Passenger Department
Durga 76
80-831 Gdansk
Tel: 31 48 51
Modern cargo/passenger vessels. Trips from Europe to Canada, USA, South America, East, West and North Africa, Singapore, Thailand, Hong Kong, Japan, South Africa, New Zealand, Australia, the Middle East and India.

Singapore

Malay States Shipping Co. Pte. Ltd.
Shipbrokers and Shipping Agents
79 Robinson Road
£27-00, CPF Bldg.
Singapore, 0106
Tel: 220 3266
Telex: RS24057 AB MASSCO
Branches at Kuala Lumpur, Port Kelang, Penang, Pasir Gudang. Agents for B.P. Shipping Ltd. Yangming Marine Transport Corp. (Yang Ming Line), Perkins Shipping Party Ltd., Taiwan Navigation Co. Ltd.

Suriname

Scheepvaart Maatschappij Suriname N.V.
44 Waterkant
PO Box 1824
Paramaribo
Suriname
Tel: 72447
Cargo/Passenger service – Suriname, Brazil, Caribbean, Mexico, US, Suriname. Ship may call, subject to cargo requirements, at one or two Caribbean Islands before Paramaribo. Also Suriname, Europe, Suriname.

United Kingdom

Blue Star Line
34-35 Leadenhall Street
London EC3A 1AR
Cargo/Passenger services from Great Britain to Canada (West Coast) and the USA.

Canberra Cruises Ltd
77 New Oxford Street
London WC1A 1PP
Tel: 01-831 1234, Reservations 01-831 1331
Telex: 885551
Cruises and a Round-the-World Service on the Canberra. Also agents for Princess Line.

Carnival Cruise Lines
Equity Tours (UK) Ltd
77/79 Great Eastern Street
London EC2A 3HU
Tel: 01-235 1656

Costa Line Cruises
2-4 Bywell Place
Wells Street
London W1P 3FB
Tel: 01-637 9961
Telex: 296444

CTC Lines
1 Regent Street
London SW1Y 4NN
Tel: 01-930 5833
Telex: 917193
Pacific Cruises

Curnow Shipping Ltd
The Shipyard
Porthleven
Helston
Cornwall TR1 3JA
Tel: (03265) 63434
Passenger/cargo ships from Great Britain from Great Britain to Tenerife, Ascension Island, St Helena, Tristan da Cunha, Cape Town.

Cunard Line Ltd
South Western House
Canute Road
Southampton SO9 1ZA
Tel: (0703) 229933
30a Pall Mall
London SW1Y 5LS
Tel: 01-491 3930
Cruises

Eileen Houlder
22 Petersham Mews
London
SW7 5NR
Tel: 01-584 9042
Cruises

Epirotiki Lines
127-131 Regent Street
London
W1R 7HA
Tel: 01-734 0805, 734 1487
Cruises

Fred Olsen
111 Buckingham Palace Rd.
London SW1W OSP
Tel: Res. Cruises – 01-630 8844
USA agent – Bergen Line
Cruises and Cargo/Passenger service from Great Britain to Madeira and the Canary Islands.

Gdynia America Shipping Lines (London) Ltd
238 City Road
London EC1V 2QL
Tel: 01-251 3389
Telex: 23256/7
(See Canada)

Geest Line
PO Box 20
Barry

South Glamorgan
Wales CF6 8XE
Cargo/Passenger service from Great Britain to the West Indies. Service is very popular so early application is advised.

Lauro Lines
1st Floor
84-86 Roseberry Avenue
London EC1R 4QS
Tel: 01-837 2157/8
Cargo/Passenger services – Mediterranean to the Caribbean, Central America and back. Also to South America

Nautilus Line
1 Linton Road
Barking
Essex IG11 8HH

Nigerian National Shipping Line Ltd
Ibex House
42-47 Minories
London
EC3N 1DY
Tel: 01-623 7555
Tlx: 897411
and
West Africa House
25 Water Street
Liverpool L2 0TY
Tel: 051-236 5444
Tlx: 629619
See Nigeria.

Norwegian Caribbean Lines
3 Vere Street
London W1M 9HQ
Tel: 01-408 0046
Cruises

Ocean Cruise Lines
6-10 Frederick Close
Stanhope Place
London W2 2HD
Tel: 01-723 5557
Cruises

P&O Cruises
77 New Oxford Street
London
WC1A 1PP
Tel: 831 1131
Cruises and a Round-the-World Service on the Canberra.

Paul Mundy Ltd
11 Quadrant Arcade
Regent Street
London W1R 5PB
Tel: 01-734 4404
Cruises

Royal Caribbean Cruises
Bishops Palace House
2A Riverside Walk
Kingston-upon-Thames
Surrey KT1 1QN
Tel: 01-541 5570
    Reservations 01- 541 5044

Cruises year round from Miami throughout the Caribbean, the Bahamas, Bermuda, and Mexico's Yucatan.

Royal Viking Line (UK)
3 Vere Street
London W1M 9HQ
Tel: 01-491 8813
Cruises around South Africa, in the Mediterranean, to Europe, Canada, the South Pacific, Hong Kong, Alaska.

Schools Abroad
Cruises Dept.
Grosvenor House
Bolnore Road
Haywards Heath
West Sussex RH16 4BX
Tel: (0444) 414 122

Shipping Corporation of India
24 St Mary Axe
London
Ex3A 8DE
Tel: 01-283 4425/7
See India.

Sitmar Cruises
7 Rolls Bldgs
Fetter Lane
London
EC4A 1BA
Tel: 01-405 9266
See entry under USA.

St. Helena Shipping Co. Ltd
Curnow Shipping Ltd
The Shipyard
Porthleven
Helston
Cornwall TR13 9JA
Tel: (03265) 63434
From Great Britain to the Canary Islands, St Helena, Ascension Island, South Africa.

United Baltic Corporation
21 Bury Street
London EC3A 5AU

Wainwright Bros & Co Ltd
200 Moorfields High Walk
London
EC2Y 9DN
Tel: 01-628 2372
Cargo/Passenger service from Europe to South America and back again.

United States

Alaska Marine Highway System
P.O Box R
Juneau
Alaska 98811

American Cruise Lines Inc
Marine Park
Haddam
Conn 06438
USA

Tel: 1-800 243 6755
Cruises

American President Lines
Passenger Department
1800 Harrison Street
Oakland
California 94612
1. Containership service from the US to the Orient and back. Usually keep to set schedule and itinerary.
2. 'Vagabond' Cruises – break-bulk / containership – from the US west coast to a port or ports in the Orient and / or Southeast / west Asia area. Itineraries are indefinite and no specific port-of-call or number of ports can be projected in advance. Voyages vary in length from one to three months. Find yourself in foreign ports rarely visited by other tourists.

Bahamas Cruise Lines, Inc
4600 West Kennedy Blvd
Tampa
Florida 33609
Cruises

Bergen Line
505 Fifth Ave
New York
NY 10017
Tel: (212) 986 2711
US Agents for Fred Olsen. (see United Kingdom)

Bermuda Star Line, Inc.
1086 Teaneck Road
Teaneck, NJ 07666

Black Star Line Ltd
FW Hartmann and Co. Inc
17 Battery Place
5th Floor
New York
NY 10004
Tel: (212) 425 6100
From Canada and US Atlantic and Gulf Ports to West Africa.

Blue Star Line
Three Embarcadero Centre
Suite 2260
San Francisco
CA 94111
Cargo/Passenger services from Great Britain to Canada (West Coast) and the USA.

Canberra Cruises Ltd
555 Fifth Avenue
New York
NY 10017
Tel: (212) 557 4411
Cruises and a Round-the-World service on the Canberra.

Carnival Cruise Lines, Inc
3915 Biscayne Blvd
Miami
Florida 33137
Tel: (305) 576 9260
Cruises

CAST
180 South Lake Avenue

Pasadena
CA 91101

Columbus Line Inc
One World Trade Centre
Suite 3247
New York
NY 10048
Tel: (212) 432 9350

Commodore Cruise Line Ltd
1007 North America Way
Miami
Florida 33132
7-day Caribbean cruises from Miami every Saturday

Cunard Line Ltd
55 Fifth Avenue
New York
NY 10017
Tel: (212) 880 7500
Cruises

Epirotiki Lines Inc
551 Fifth Ave
New York
NY 10017
Tel: (212) 599 1750
Cruises

Freighter World Cruises
180 So. Lake 335
Pasadena
CA 91101
USA
Tel: (818) 449 3106
Offers bi-weekly listings of space available from US to worldwide ports. One year's subscription costs US$47.

Golden Bear Travel
Pier 27
San Francisco
California 94111
Tel: (415) 391 7759
Cruises

Hansen & Tideman Inc
310 Sanlin Bldg
442 Canal Street
New Orleans
LA 70130
Tel: (504) 586 8755
Cargo/Passenger service – Suriname, Brazil, Caribbean, Mexico, US, Suriname. Ship may call, subject to cargo requirements, at one or two Caribbean Islands before Paramaribo. Also Suriname – Europe – Suriname.

Holland America Line
300 Elliot Avenue West
Seattle
WA 98119
Tel: (206) 281 3535
Cruises (see Netherlands)

Home Line Cruises Inc
One World Trade Center
Suite 3969
New York

NY 10048
Tel: (212) 432 1414
Cruises

International Cruise Centre
105 Willis Avenue
Mineola
New York 11501
Tel: (516) 747 8880
Cruises

Jadranska Slobodna Plovidba
180 South Lake Avenue
Pasadena
CA 91101

Lauro Lines
One Biscayne Tower
Miami
Florida 33131
Tel: (305) 374 4120
Cargo/Passenger services – Mediterranean to the Caribbean, Central America and back. Also to South America.

Linblad Travel Inc
One Sylvan Road North
P.O. Box 912
Westport,
Connecticut 06881
USA
Tel: (203) 226 8531
Cruises worldwide – Africa, Canada, Antarctica, Australia/New Zealand, China/Tibet, Danube River, Eastern Europe, Galapagos, Grand Canyon, India, Mississippi River, Orient, Russia, South America, Tahiti.

Lykes Lines
Passenger Dept.
300 Poydras Street
New Orleans
Louisiana 70130
Tel: (504) 523 6611
Box 1139
Houston
Texas 77001
and
320 California Street
San Francisco
CA 94104
Freighter Cruises from the US Gulf to the West Coast of South America, the Far East, Southern and Eastern Africa, the Mediterranean, UK and North Europe. From US Pacific Coast to Japan and Korea.

Mineral Shipping Line
180 South Lake Avenue
Pasadena
CA 91101

Nauru Air and Shipping Agency
China Basin Bldg
185 Berry Street
San Francisco
CA 94107
Tel: (415) 543 1737

Norwegian Caribbean Lines
One Biscayne Tower
Miami
Florida 33131
Tel: (305) 358 6680
Cruises

Norton, Lilley and Co., Inc
Operations Dept
245 Monticello Arcade
Norfolk
VA 23510
Tel: (804) 622 7035
Cargo/Passenger services, different routes between Europe and the USA and worldwide.

Orient Eclipse Cruises, Inc
1080 Fifth Ave
New York
NY 10028
Tel: (212) 831 5059
Cruises

Princess Cruises
2029 Century Park East
Los Angeles
CA 90067
Tel: (213) 553 1770
Fly/cruise to the Mexican Riviera, Panama Canal, Alaska, Caribbean, Europe/Mediterranean, South Pacific and Orient.

Prudential Lines, Inc
Room 3701
One World Trade Centre
New York
NY 10048
USA
Tel: (212) 524 8212/8217
Cargo/Passenger from the US to the Mediterranean and back.

Royal Carribean Cruises
903 South America Way
Miami
FL 33132
Tel: (305) 379 2601, Reservations 379 4731
Cruises year round from Miami throughout the Caribbean, the Bahamas, Bermuda, and Mexico's Yucatan.

Royal Viking Line
750 Battery Street
San Francisco
California 94111
Tel: (415) 398 8000
See UK

Sitmar Cruises
10100 Santa Monica Blvd
Los Angeles
CA 90067
Tel: (213) 553 1666
Cruises to the Mexican Riviera, the Caribbean, through the Panama Canal, Canada, Alaska and the South Pacific.

Society Expedition Cruises
3131 Elliott Ave,
Seattle
Washington

98121
Tel: (206) 285 9400

Special Expeditions Inc
720 Fifth Avenue
New York
NY 10019
Tel: (212) 765 7740
See UK

Sun Line Cruises
1 Rockefeller Plaza
New York 10020
Tel: (212) 397 6400
Fly/cruises to the Caribbean, Panama Canal, Yucatan, the Greek Islands and Turkey. Also US agents for Paquet Cruises.

United States Lines
27 Commerce Drive
Cranford
New Jersey
Tel: (201) 272 9600
Cargo/Passenger service from the US to South and East Africa, the USA to South America and back.

Venezuelan Line
1360 Post Oak Blvd.,
Suite 700,
Houston
TX 70056

Windjammer Barefoot Cruises
PO Box 120
Miama Beach
FL 33119
Tel: (305) 373 2090
Cruises

World Explorer Cruises
3 Embarcadero Centre
San Francisco
CA 94111
Tel: (415) 391 92 62

Cruises

USSR

Black Sea Shipping Co
1 Ul Lastochikina
Odessa 270026
UK and Australian Agent – CTC Lines
Passenger Cruise and Passenger/Cargo Freighter Lines, from Soviet Union to Bulgaria, Turkey, Greece, Cyprus, Syria, Lebanon and Egypt. Subject to alteration. From Soviet Union to Europe

Far Eastern Shipping Co
15, Ul Oktiabria
Vladivostock 690019
UK and Australian Agent – CTC Lines
Cargo/Passenger Service from the Soviet Union to Japan and Hong Kong.

Yugoslavia

Jugolinija
Koblerov trg. bb,
51000 Rijeka

Zaïre

Compagnie Maritime Zaïrosie
BP 9496
UZB Center
Place de la Poste
Kinshasa
Tel: 25183/25830/25029
Telex: 21626
Cargo/Passenger services from Europe to the Canary Islands and West Africa.

Passenger Shipping Agents and Advisory Services

Ask Mr Foster Travel
740 Polhemus Road
San Mateo
CA 94402
USA
Tel: (415) 349 6216
Offers expert advice on freighter travel

Carolyn's Cruises
32 Garner Drive
Novato
CA 94947
USA

Freighter Cruise Service
Suite 103
5925 Monkland Avenue

Montreal
Quebec
Canada H4A 1G7
Tel: (514) 481 0447
Agents for all freighter and all steamship companies. Can also arrange any type of trip by air and land. Reservations should be made well in advance. Handle cruises to South America, the Orient, Yugoslavia and the Mediterranean, South and East Africa, the Middle and Far East, Australia, New Zealand and the South Seas, Hong Kong and Japan.

Freighter Travel Club of America
1745 Scoth Ave, S.E.
PO Box 12693

Salem
OR 97309
USA

Offers members answers to specific questions regarding freighter travel, steamship lines, travel agencies etc. Publish a monthly newsletter Freighter Travel News *which is full of first-hand stories about freighter travel, tips on where to go, what to do while there, where to eat and stay. They do not sell tickets or book passages, nor are they connected in any way with travel agents.*

Freighter World Cruises, Inc
Suite 335
180 S. Lake Avenue
Pasadena
CA 91101
USA
Tel: (818) 449 3106

Offers bi-weekly listings of space available from US to worldwide ports. One year's subscription costs US $28.00.

Halsey Marine Ltd
22 Boston Place
Dorset Square
London
NW1 6HZ
Tel: 01-724 1303

Leading privately owned international yacht charter specialists. Yachts available as far afield as French Polynesia, the Malaysian coast. Also supply yachts and other vessels for commercial purposes.

Ocean Voyages
1709 Bridgeway
Sausalito
California 94965
USA

Tel: (415) 332 4681

A unique organization which provides exotic sailing experiences all over the world. Offers challenging trips for veteran sailors, good learning experiences for novices – and great vacations for all. Can arrange special charters for friends who want to travel together, research expeditions, conferences for business corporations. Island hopping and exploring, long ocean passages, leisurely cruising, deep sea diving, a one-week trip, an eight-week trip or anything in between.

Pitt and Scott
3 Cathedral Place
London EC4M 7DT
Tel: 01-248 6747

Information relating to various shipping lines. Agents for shipping lines (Geest, Polish Ocean Lines, South African Marine corporation (UK) Ltd, Compagnie Général Maritime). Emphasis on freighter travel.

Pearl's Freighter Trips
175 Great Neck Road
Suite 306F
Great Neck
NY 11021
USA

Tel: (516) 487 8351 and (212) 895 7645

Helps plan and book worldwide freighter trips. No charge for the service, but please enclose s.a.e. US money order or other compensations for cost of reply. Preference shown to those taking round trips. Can only control space from the States and no connecting voyages from Europe.

Sea & Cruise Club
32 Berkeley Street
London W1X 5FA
Tel: 01-629 7391

The aims of the club are to provide expert information and booking facilities for worldwide passenger shipping, to act as a voice for members in order to improve and expand passenger shipping facilities, to negotiate, on behalf of its members, beneficial rates on cruises and other travel arrangements, to provide shipowners, ship designers and cruise operators with an understanding of the needs of the sea traveller. Annual Membership: £5.75 (single) £10.00 (Family).

Siemer and Hand Travel
44 Montgomery Street
San Francisco
CA 94104
USA

Stewart Moffat Travel
Zimpel's Centreway
160 St. George's Terrace
Perth 6000
Australia
Tel: 321 2424

General Sales Agents for the Blue Funnel Line vessel Princess Mashuri *which operates South Pacific Cruises out of Sydney and Asian Cruises out of Singapore. Also general sales agents for the Pearl Cruises vessel* Pearl of Scandinavia *which operates exclusively in Asian waters.*

TravLtips
PO Box 1008
Huntington
NY 11743
USA

World Travel Bureau of Anaheim
PO Box 4229
or
839 S. Harbour Blvd.,
Anaheim
CA 92803
USA

Operators of Car Ferries from the UK

B + I Line
PO Box 19
12 North Wall
Dublin 1
Ireland
Tel: 788266
and
155 Regent St
London W1R 7FD
Tel: 01-734 4681/7512
Also offices in Birmingham, Holyhead, Leeds, Liverpool, Manchester and Rosslare.

Belfast Car Ferries
Donegall Quay
Belfast BT1 3ED
Tel: (0232) 226800
Tlx: 74268
and
Langton Dock
Liverpool L20 1BY
Tel: 051-922 6234
Tlx: 627167

Belgian Maritime Transport Authority
22-25a Sackville Street
London W1X 1DE
Tel: 01-437 8405/4495

Brittany Ferries
Milbay Docks
Plymouth PL1 3EW
Tel: (0725) 221321/227104
Tlx: 45380
and
The Brittany Centre
Wharf Road
Portsmouth
Hants PO2 8RU
Tel: (0705) 819416/827701
Tlx: 86878

Channel Island Ferries
Norman House
Albert Johnson Quay
Portsmouth PO2 7AE
Tel: (0705) 864431/819416
Tlx: 869393

DFDS Seaways
Scandinavia House
Parkeston Quay
Harwich
Essex CO12 4QG
Tel: (0255) 554681
Tlx: 987542/53201
and
Tyne Commission Quay
North Shields
Tyne & Wear NE29 6EE
Tel: (091) 257 5655

DFDS Travel Centre
199 Regent Street

London W1R 7WA
Tel: 01-434 1523

Fred Olsen Lines
Victoria Plaza
111 Buckingham Palace Road
London SW1W 0SP
Tel: 01-828 7000

Hoverspeed Ltd
Maybrook House
Queens Gardens
Dover
Kent CT17 9UQ
Tel: (0304) 215205
       01-554 7061 London Reservations.
Tlx: 96323

Irish Continental Line
19-21 Aston Quay
Dublin 2
Ireland
Tel: 774331

Isle of Man Steam Packet Co.
PO Box 5
Imperial Buildings
Douglas
Isle of Man
Tel: (0624) 72468
Tlx: 629414

Isles of Scilly Steamship Co.
Quay St
Penzance
Cornwall TR18 4BD
Tel: (0736) 62009/64013

Jahreline
c/o A/S Winge Travel Bureau of Scandinavia
20 Pall Mall
London SW1Y 5NE
Tel: 01-839 5341

Jersey Ferries
c/o Sea Express
Albert Pier
St Helier
Jersey
Tel: 30773/20361
Tlx: 4192131

Norfolk Line Ltd
Atlas House
Southgates Road
Great Yarmouth
Norfolk NR30 3LN
Tel: (0493) 856133
Tlx: 97449

North Sea Ferries
King George Dock
Hedon Road
Hull HU9 5QA

North Humberside
Tel: (0482) 795141/796145
Tlx: 592349 NSF

Norway Line
Tyne Commission Quay
Albert Edward Dock
North Shields NE29 6EA
Tel: 091-258 5555
Tlx: 537275

Olau-Line (UK) Ltd
Sheerness
Kent ME12 1SN
Tel: (0795) 663 355/666 666
Tlx: 965605

Orkney Island Shipping Co.
4 Ayre Road
Kirkwall
Orkney KW15 1QX
Tel: (0856) 2044
Tlx: 75193 OISCO

P&O European Ferries
PO Box 7
Enterprise House
1 Channel View Road
Dover CT17 9TJ ·
Tel: (0304) 223000
Also numerous other offices throughout the UK.

P&O Ferries
(Orkney & Shetland Services)
PO Box 5

Jamiesons Quay
Aberdeen AB9 8DL
Tel: (0224) 589 111/572 615
Tlx: 73344

Sally Line
Argyle Centre
York Street
Ramsgate
Kent CT1 9DS
Tel: (0843) 595522
Tlx: 96389
and
81 Piccadilly
London W1V 9HF
Tel: 01-409 0536
Tlx: 291860

Sealink British Ferries
163/203 Eversholt Street
London NW1 1BG
Tel: 01-387 1234
Tlx: 291860
Also have numerous other offices and agents around the country. Phone for details of your nearest.

Viking Line
c/o Scantours Ltd
8 Spring Gardens
Trafalgar Square
London SW1A 2BG
Tel: 01-903 9510
Tlx: 919008 SCTOUR

Rail

Representatives of Foreign Railways in the UK:

Australia
c/o Thomas Cook Ltd
Peterborough
Tel: (0733) 502236

Austrian Railways
30 St. George Street
London W1R 0AL
Tel: 01-629 0461
Tlx: 24709

Belgian National Railway
22–25A Sackville Street
London W1X 1DE
Tel: 01-734 1491

Rail Canada Inc
c/o Thomas Cook Ltd
Peterborough
Tel: (0733) 50236

Danish State Railways
c/o DFDS Seaways
Scandinavia House

Parkeston Quay
Harwich
Essex CO12 4QG
Tel: (0255) 554681
Tlx: 987542

Finnish State Railways
Finlandia Travel Agency
130 Jermyn Street
London W1Y 0NP
Tel: 01-493 3873
Tlx: 265653

Luxembourg National Railways – CFL
c/o Luxembourg National Tourist and Trade Office
36/37 Piccadilly
London W1V 9PA
Tel: 01-434 2800

Netherlands Railways
25–28 Buckingham Gate
London SW1E 6LD
Tel: 01-630 1735
Tlx: 269005 HOLLAND

New Zealand Railways Corporation
c/o New Zealand Tourist Office
New Zealand House
Haymarket,
London SW1Y 4TQ
Tel: 01-930 8422

Norwegian State Railways – NSB
21/24 Cockspur Street
London SW1Y 5DA
Tel: 01-930 6666
Tlx: 28380

Polish State Railways
Polorbis Travel Ltd
82 Mortimer Street
London W1N 7DE
Tel: 01-637 4971
Tlx: 8812232

Portuguese Railways
c/o Portuguese National Tourist Office
New Bond Street House
1–5 New Bond Street
London SW1Y 4UJ
Tel: 01-839 4741
Tlx: 918854

French Railways – SNCF
French Railways House
179 Piccadilly
London W1V 0BA
Tel: 01-493 9731/409 1224
Tlx: 24651

German Federal Railway – DB
10 Old Bond Street
London W1X 4EN
Tel: 01-499 5078
Tlx: 25671

Ireland – Coras Iompair Eirann
Ireland House
150/1 New Bond Street
London W1Y 9FE
Tel: 01-629 0564
Tlx: 23513

Italian State Railways
CIT (England) Ltd
Marco Polo House
3/5 Lansdowne Road
Croydon

Surrey CR9 1LL
Tel: 01-686 0677

Japanese National Railways
24–26 Rue de la Pépineière
75008 Paris
France
Tel: 4522 6048

South Africa – Sartravel
48 Leicester Square
London WC2H 7HX
Tel: 01-839 2764
Tlx: 295552

Spanish National Railways
c/o Spanish National Tourist Office
57–8 St James's Street
London SW1A 1LD
Tel: 01-499 0901
Tlx: 888138 TURESP

Swedish State Railways
c/o Norwegian State Railways
21–24 Cockspur Street
London SW1Y 5DA
Tel: 930 6666
Tlx: 28380

Swiss Federal Railways
Swiss Centre
New Coventry Street
London W1V 8EE
Tel: 01-734 1921
Tlx: 21295

USA – Amtrak
c/o Thomas Cook Ltd
Thorpe Wood
Peterborough PE3 6SB
Tel: (0733) 502236

Yugoslav Railways
c/o Yugoslav National Tourist Office
143 Regent Street
London W1R 8AE
Tel: 01-734 5234

Venice Simplon Orient Express
Sea Containers House
20 Upper Ground
London SE1 9PF
Tel: 01-928 6000
Tlx: 8955803

Low Cost Travel Passes

Australia

Aussiepass
Allows unlimited travel on the entire Ansett Pioneer express system for 15 to 60 days.

Austrail Pass
Must be purchases in the UK or Ireland. Allows unlimited First Class travel (or Economy Class if First Class is not available) over all rail systems – interstate, country, suburban (except the metropolitan area of Adelaide) in Australia. Different rates are available for 14 and 21 days, 1, 2, and 3 months.

Eaglepass
Offers unlimited travel on the Greyhound Express Coach network. Contact Greyhound Australia Pty Ltd, Exchange Travel, 66/70 Parker Road, Hastings, East Sussex. Tel: (0424) 443 888.

Europe

Eurail Pass
Available from Britrail Offices and:
Europe by Eurail Inc., Box 20100, Colombus, OH 43220, USA.
Tel: (614) 889 9100.
Unlimited travel for one month in nineteen countries in Europe and North Africa (excluding Great Britain and Northern Ireland, although it is valid in the Republic of Ireland). Only available to those who are not citizens of participating countries.

Interrail
Month-long, travel anywhere in Europe and North Africa ticket for those under 26. Incredible value, but must have been resident in a participating country for 6 months to be eligible. For details, ask British Rail (see below).

India

Indrail Pass
Rail Pass available to visitors and Indians who live outside their country, valid for 7, 21, 30, 60 or 90 days, and permitting unlimited travel in Indian railways.

New Zealand

Kiwi Coach Pass
Unlimited kilometres of First Class coach travel throughout New Zealand on the scheduled services operated by the following motor coach companies; Mount Cook Line, Railways & Road Services, Newmans. Available for 7, 10, 15 or 25 days. Contact New Zealand Tourist Board, or Mount Cook Line Office.

Travel Pass
A railpass, roadpass, seapass – offers unlimited travel on New Zealand railways, coaches, ferries at very reasonable cost. Passes for 15 or 22 consecutive days (can be extended up to 6 additional days). Available from any New Zealand Railway Ticket office, Govt Tourist Bureau, accredited Travel Agent or Trade Commissioners Office.

United Kingdom

Britrail Pass
Unlimited travel throughout England, Wales and Scotland. Are available for either First Class or Economy Class travel for periods of 8, 15, or 22 days or for one month with children from 5 to 15 years travelling half fare. Not available to UK citizens.

Britrail Youth Pass
For 16 to 25-year-olds, unlimited Economy Class travel at two-thirds of the normal price.

Britrail Senior Citizens Pass
Anyone 60 or over can travel first class at a specially reduced rate.

There are also numerous other special deals. For information on all British Rail Services contact any major British Rail Station in the UK, or the following addresses in the USA: Britrail International
800 South Hope Street # 603
Los Angeles
CA 90017

Britrail Travel International
333 North Michigan Ave
Chicago
IL 60601

Inter Rail Point
YMCA Special Programmes
2nd Floor, Crown House
550 Mauldeth Road
Manchester M21 2RX
Tel: 061-881 5321
Offers budget priced accommodation, together with programmed activities such as sight-seeing tours, international evenings and sports events. Run during the summer for young people travelling throughout Europe on the Inter Rail ticket issued by the European network.

Transalpino
71/75 Buckingham Palace Road
London SW1
Tel: 01-834 9656
Transalpino is the world's largest youth rail organization. Offering large discounts off rail/sea/rail services to more than 2000 European destinations.

Tickets valid for 2 months and can be purchased by anyone under 26.

USA

Ameripass
Entitles purchaser to travel over Greyhound's entire route system and routes of other participating bus lines while pass is valid. Stop-overs permitted. (For Greyhound addresses see below.)

Greyhound Lines International Sales
14/16 Cockspur Street
London SW1Y 5BL
Tel: 01-839 5591
For information on Low Cost travel passes in the US and Canada. Also office for Greyhound Australia.

Most countries with a good domestic air network are now running similar air passes. Details should be available from the tourist office or national airline.

Day to Day

Foreign Tourist Offices in Australia

Austria	19th Floor, 1 York St, Sydney, NSW 2000	278 581
Canada	8th Floor, AMP Centre, 50 Bridge St, Sydney NSW 2000	
Denmark	60 Market St, PO Box 5431, Melbourne, Victoria 3001	
West Germany	C/o Lufthansa German Airlines, Lufthansa House, 12th Floor, 143 Macquarie St, Sydney NSW 2000	
Greece	51–57 Pitt St, Sydney NSW 2000	
Hong Kong	Bligh House, 4–6 Bligh St, Sydney NSW 2000	
India	Carlton Centre, Elizabeth St, Sydney NSW 2000	232 1600
Jordan	(Alia GSA) Metralco Services Pty Ltd, 4th Floor, 15 Young St, Sydney NSW 2000	
or	(Alia GSA), 167 St. Georges Terrace, Perth, WA6000	
Macao	Suite 604, 135 Macquarie St, Sydney NSW 2000	
or	GPO Box M973, Perth, WA 6001	
Malaysia	12th Floor, R. & W House, 92 Pitt St, Sydney NSW 2000	23? 3751
Mexico	24 Burton St, Darlinghurst, Sydney NSW 2000	
Singapore	8th Floor, Gold Fields House, 1 Alfred St, Sydney Cove NSW 2000	
South Africa	AMEV-UDC House, 115 Pitt St, Sydney NSW 2001	231 6166
Sri Lanka	FP Leonard Advertising Pty Ltd, 1st Floor, 110 Bathurst St, Sydney 2000	
Switzerland	203–233 New South Head Rd, PO Box 82, Edgecliff, Sydney NSW 2027	
American Samoa	327 Pacific Highway, North Sydney NSW 2060	
Thailand	12th Floor, Royal Exchange Building, corner Bridge and Pitt Streets, Sydney NSW 2000	277 549

Foreign Tourist Boards in Canada

Antigue & Barbuda	Suite 205, 60 St Clair Ave East, Toronto, Ontario M4T 1L9	
Australia	120 Eglinton Ave East, Suite 220, Toronto, Ontario, M4P 1L9	
Austria	2 Bloor St East, Suite 3330, Toronto, Ontario M4W 1A8	
or	Suite 1220–1223, 736 Granville St, Vancouver BC	
or	1010 Ouest Rue Sherbrooke, Montreal, Quebec	
Barbados	615 Dorchester Blvd West, Suite 960, Montreal, Quebec H3B 1P5	
or	Suite 1508, Box 11, 20 Queen St West, Toronto, Ontario M5H 3R3	
Bermuda	Suite 510, 1075 Bay St, Toronto, Ontario M5S 2B1	
British Virgins Islands	Mr W. Draper, 801 York Mills Road, Suite 201, Don Mills, Ontario M3B 1X7	
Cayman Islands	234 Eglington Ave East, Suite 600, Toronto, Ontario	

Denmark	PO Box 115 Station 'N', Toronto, Ontario M8V 3S4
Eastern Caribbean	Suite 205, 60 St. Clair Ave East, Toronto, Ontario M4T 1L9
France	1 Dundas St. West, Suite 2405, Box 8, Toronto, Ontario M5G 1Q3
West Germany	2 Fundy, PO Box 417, Place Bonaventure, Montreal, Quebec H5A 1B8
Greece	1233 Rue de la Montagne, Montreal Quebec, H3G 1Z2
Israel	102 Bloor St West, Toronto, Ontario M5S 1M8
Jamaica	2221 Yonge St, Suite 507, Toronto, Ontario M4S 2B4
Jordan	181 University Ave, Suite 1716, Box 28, Toronto, Ontario M5H 3M7
or	1801 McGill College Ave, Suite 1160, Montreal Quebec H3A 2N4
Kenya	Gillin Building, Suite 600, 141 Laurier Ave, West, Ottawa, Ontario
Macao	Suite 601, 700 Bay St, Toronto, Ontario M5G 1Z6
or	475 Main St, Vancouver, British Columbia V6A 2T7
Mexico	1 Place Ville Marie, Suite 2409, Montreal, Quebec
or	1008 Pacific Centre, Toronto Dominion Bank Tower, Vancouver, British Columbia
Morocco	2 Carlton St, Suite 1803, Toronto, Ontario M5B 1K2
Peru	Mr Raziel Zisman, 344 Bloor St West, Suite 303, Toronto, Ontario
Portugal	Suite 1150, 1801 McGill College Ave, Montreal, Quebec H3A 2N4
South Africa	Suite 1001, 20 Eglington Ave West, Toronto, Ontario M4R 1K8
Spain	60 Bloor St West, Suite 201, Toronto, Ontario M4W 3B8
Switzerland	PO Box 215, Commerce Court, Toronto, Ontario M5L 1E8
Trinidad & Tobago	York Centre, 145 King St West, Toronto, Ontario M5H 1J8
USSR	2020 University St, Suite 434, Montreal, Quebec H3A 2A5
US Virgin Islands	11 Adelaide St. West, Suite 406, Toronto, Ontario M5H 1L9

Foreign Tourist Offices in New Zealand

Australia	15th Floor, Quay Tower, 29 Customs St, (PO Box 1646), Auckland 1
Fiji	47 High St, Auckland
Hong Kong	General Building, G/F corner Shorland St and O'Connell St, (PO Box 1313), Auckland
Ireland	c/o Rodney Walsh Ltd, 87 Queen St, Auckland
Malaysia	Malaysian Airline System, Suite 8, 5th Floor Air New Zealand House, 1 Queen St, Auckland 1
Singapore	c/o Rodney Walsh Ltd, 87 Queen St, Auckland
UK	PO Box 3655, Wellington

Foreign Tourist Boards in the United Kingdom

Albania	C/o Albturist, Regent Holidays, 13 Small St, Bristol	(0272) 211711
Algeria	6 Hyde Park Gate, London SW7	584 5152
Andorra	63 Westover Road, London SW18 2RF	874 4806
Angola	34 Percy Street, London W1P 9FQ	637 1945
Antigue & Barbuda	Antigua House, 15 Thayer St, London W1M 5DL	486 7073/5
Australia	4th Floor, Heathcoat House, 20 Savile Row, London W1X 1AE	434 4371
Austria	30 St. George St, London W1R 0AL	269 0461
Bahamas	23 Old Bond St, London W1X 4PQ	269 5238
Barbados	263 Tottenham Court Rd, London W1P 9AA	636 9448/9
Belgium	38 Dover St, London W1X 3RB	499 5379
Belize	15b Thayer St, London W1M 5LD	486 8381
Bermuda	6 Burnsall St, London SW3 3ST	734 8813/4
Brazil	35 Dover St, London W1	499 0877
British Virgin Islands	48 Albemarle St, London W1X 4AR	629 6355
Bulgaria	18 Prince's St, London W1R 7RE	499 6988
Cameroon	Economic and Commercial Delegation, 48 Holland Park, London W11 3RB	
Canada	Canada House, Trafalgar Square, London SW1Y 5BJ	629 9492
Cayman Islands	Hambleton House, 17b Curzon St, London W1Y 7FE	493 5161
China	4 Glentworth St, London NW1	935 9427
Cook Islands	433 High Holborn House, 52 High Holborn, London WC1V 6RB	242 3131
Cyprus	213 Regent St, London W1R 3DA	734 9822
Czechoslovakia	17–18 Old Bond St, London W1X 4RB	629 6058
Denmark	Sceptre House, 169/173 Regent St, London W1R 8PY	734 2637
Eastern Caribbean	15b Thayer St, London W1M 5LS	486 9119
Egypt	168 Piccadilly, London W1Y 9DE	493 5282
Finland	66 Haymarket, London SW1Y 4RF	839 4048
France	178 Piccadilly, London W1V 0AL	491 7622
Gambia	57 Kensington Court, London W8 5DG	937 9618/9
East Germany	c/o Berolina Travel Ltd, 22 Conduit St, London W1R 9TB	629 1664
West Germany	61 Conduit St, London W1R 0EN	734 2600
Ghana	13 Belgrave Square, London W1	235 4142
Gibraltar	Arundel Great Court, 179 The Strand, London WC2R 1EH	836 0777/8
Greece	195/7 Regent St, London W1R 8DL	734 5997
Grenada	1 Collingham Gardens, Earls Court, London SW5	
Hawaii	15 Albermarle St, London W 1X 4QI	492 1143
Hong Kong	125 Pall Mall, London SW1Y 5EA	930 4775
Hungary	c/o Danube Travel, 6 Conduit St, London W1R 9TG	493 0263
Iceland	73 Grosvenor St, London W1X 9DD	499 9971
India	7 Cork St, London W1X 2AB	437 3677
Indonesia	38 Grosvenor Square, London W1X 9AD	493 2080
Iraq	c/o Iraqui Airways, 4 Lower Regent St, London SW1	930 1155

Ireland	Ireland House, 150 New Bond St, London W1Y 0AQ	493 3201
Israel	18 Great Marlborough St, London W1V 1AF	434 3651
Italy	1 Prince's St, London W1R 8AY	408 1254
Jamaica	Jamaica House, 50 St. James's St, London SW1A 1JT	493 3647
Japan	167 Regent St, London W1R 7FD	734 9638
Jordan	211 Regent St, London W1	437 9465
Kenya	13 New Burlington St, London W1X 1FF	839 4477/8
South Korea	Vogue House, 1 Hanover Square, London W1R 9RD	408 1591
Lebanon	50 Piccadilly, London W1	409 2031
Lesotho	433 High Holborn House, 52 High Holborn, London WC1V 6RB	242 3131
Liberia	c/o Embassy Press Office, 2 Pembridge Place, London W2 4XB	221 1036
Luxembourg	36/37 Piccadilly, London W1V 9PA	434 2800
Macau	c/o Tourism Development Partnership, Airwork House, 35 Piccadilly, London W1V 9PA	734 7282
Malawi	33 Grosvenor Street, London W1X 0DE	491 4172
Malaysia	17 Curzon St, London W1Y 7FE	499 7388
Malta	Ste 207, College House, Wrights Lane, London W8	938 2668
Mauritius	23 Ramillies Place, London W1A 3BF	439 4461
Mexico	7 Cork St, London W1X 1PB	434 1058
Monaco	25 Whitehall, London SW1A 2BS	930 4699
Mongolia	c/o Voyages Jules Verne, 10 Glentworth St, London NW1	486 8080
Morocco	174 Regent St, London W1R 6HB	437 0073
Netherlands	25–28 Buckingham Gate, London SW1E 6LD	630 0451
New Zealand	New Zealand House, 80 Haymarket, London SW1Y 4QT	930 8422
Nigeria	9 Northumberland Ave, London WC2	839 1244
Norway	20 Pall Mall, London SW1Y 5NE	839 2650
Pakistan	c/o M/S Marketing Services, Ste 433, High Holborn House, 52–54 High Holborn, London WC1V 6RL	242 3131
Panama	Eagle House, 2nd Flr, 110 Jermyn St, London SW1	930 1591
Paraguay	Braemar Lodge, Cornwall Gardens, London SW7	937 1253
Peru	10 Grosvenor Gardens, London SW1W 0BD	730 7122
Philippines	199 Piccadilly, London W1V 9LE	439 3481
Poland	c/o Polorbis Travel Ltd, 82 Mortimer St, London W1N 7DE	580 8028
Portugal	New Bond Street House, 1/5 New Bond Street, London W1Y 0NP	493 3873
Qatar	115 Queen's Gate, London SW7 5LP	581 8611
Romania	29 Thurloe Place, London SW7 2HP	584 8090
St Lucia	1 Collingham Gardens, London SW5 0HW	370 0926
St Vincent & Grenadines	1 Collingham Gardens, London SW5 0HW	370 0925
Seychelles	50 Conduit St, London W1A 4PE	439 9699
Singapore	33 Heddon St, London W1R 7LB	437 0033
South Africa	Regency House, 1–4 Warwick St, London W1R 5WB	439 9661
Spain	57/58 St. James's St, London SW1A 1LD	499 0901
Sri Lanka	52 High Holborn, London WC1V 6RL	405 1194

Sudan	308 Regent St, London W1R 5AL	631 1785
Swaziland	58 Pont St, London SW1	
Sweden	3 Cork St, London W1X 1HA	437 5816
Switzerland	Swiss Centre, 1 New Coventry St, London W1V 8EE	734 1921
Tanzania	77 South Audley St, London W1Y 5TA	499 7727
Thailand	9 Stafford St, London W1X 3FE	499 7679
Trinidad & Tobago	20 Lower Regent St, London SW1Y 4PH	839 7155
Tunisia	7a Stafford St, London W1	499 2234
Turkey	1st Floor, 170/173 Piccadilly, London W1V 9DD	734 8681
Turks & Caicos Islands	West India Committee, 48 Albemarle St, London W1X 4AR	629 6355
USSR	292 Regent St, London W1R 6QL	631 1252
USA	22 Sackville St, London W1X 2EA	439 7433
US Virgin Islands	25 Bedford Square, London WC1B 3HG	637 8481
Yugoslavia	143 Regent St, London W1R 8AE	734 5243
Zambia	163 Piccadilly, London W1V 9DE	493 1188
Zimbabwe	Collette House, 52–55 Piccadilly, London W1V 9AA	629 3955

Foreign Fourist Offices in the United States

Australia	1270 Ave of the Americas, New York, NY 10020	489 7550
Austria	545 5th Ave, New York, NY 10017	697 1651
Bermuda	Rockefeller Centre, 630 5th Avenue, New York, NY 10111	397 7700
Brazil	551 5th Ave, New York, NY 10017	682 1055
Britain	680 5th Ave, New York NY 10019	581 4700
British Virgin Islands	370 Lexington Ave, New York, NY 10017	696 0400
Caribbean	20 E 46th St, New York, NY 10017	682 0435
Chile	1 World Trade Center, Suite 5121, New York, NY 10048	
China	159 Lexington Ave, New York, NY	725 4950
Colombia	140 E 57th St, New York, NY 10022	688 0151
Côte d'Ivoire	c/o Air Afrique, 1350 Ave of the Americas, New York, NY 10019	
Dominican Rep	485 Madison Ave, New York, NY 10022	826 0750
Eastern Caribbean	220E 42nd St, New York, NY 10017	986 9370
Ecuador	167 W 72nd St, New York NY, 10023	873 0600
Egypt	630 5th Ave, New York NY 10111	246 6960
El Salvador	PO Box 818, Radio City Station, 200 W 58th St, New York NY 10019	
French Polynesia	200 E 42nd St, New York, NY 10017	
France	610 5th Ave, New York NY 1002 *Also covers the French West Indies*	757 1125

Galapagos Islands	888 7th Ave, New York, NY 10019	
Gambia	19 E 47th St, New York, NY 1003	759 2323
West Germany	747 3rd Ave, New York, NY 10017	308 3300
Ghana	445 Park Ave, Suite 903, New York, NY 10022	688 8350
Haiti	1270 Avenue of the Americas, New York, NY 10020	757 3517
Honduras	501 5th Ave, New York, NY 10017	869 0766
Hong Kong	548 5th Ave, New York, NY 10036	947 5008
Hungary	630 5th Ave, New York	582 7412
Iceland	75 Rockefeller Plaza, New York, NY 10019	582 2802
India	30 Rockefeller Plaza, New York, NY 10020	586 4901
Indonesia	5 E 68th St, New York, NY 10021	
Iraq	14 E 79th St, New York, NY 10021	
Israel	350 5th Ave, New York, NY 10018	560 0650
Jamaica	2 Dag Hammarskjold Plaza, New York, NY	688 7650
Japan	45 Rockefeller Plaza, New York, NY 10020	757 5640
Kenya	15 E 21st St, New York, NY 10022	486 1300
Korea	460 Park Ave, New York, NY 10016	688 7543
Lebanon	405 Park Ave, New York, NY 10022	421 2201
Mexico	630 5th Ave, New York NY 10020	265 4696
Morocco	521 5th Ave, New York NY 10175	557 2520
New Zealand	630 5th Ave, New York MY 10020	586 0060
Panama	630 5th Ave, New York NY 10020	246 5841
Philippines	556 5th Ave, New York NY 10036	575 7915
St. Lucia	41 E 42nd St, New York, NY 10017	867 2950
St Maarten & St. Eustatius	25 W 39th St, New York, NY	840 6655
St. Vincent & Grenadines	220 E 40th St, New York, NY	986 9370
Senegal	200 Park Ave, New York, NY 10003	682 4695
South Africa	610 5th Ave, New York, NY 10020	245 3720
Spain	665 5th Ave, New York, NY 10022	759 8822
Sri Lanka	609 5th Ave, New York, NY	935 0569
Suriname	1 Rockefeller Plaza, Suite 1408, New York, NY 10020	581 3063
Switzerland	608 5th Ave, New York, NY 10020	757 5944
Tanzania	201 E 42nd St, New York NY 10017	986 7124
Thailand	5 World Trade Center, New York NY 10048	432 0433
Tunisia	630 5th Ave, Suite 863, New York, NY 10020	582 3670
Turkey	821 United Nations Plaza, New York, NY 10017	687 2194
Uganda, NY	801 2nd Ave, New York	
USSR	45 E 49th St, New York, NY 10017	371 6953
Uruguay	301 E 47th St, Apt 21–0, New York, NY 10017	
Venezuela	450 Park Ave, New York, NY 10011	355 1101
Zambia	150 E 58th St, New York, NY 10022	758 9450
Zimbabwe	535 5th Ave, New York, NY 10017	

Hostelling Associations

Youth Hostels

American Youth Hostels
National Offices
P.O Box 37613
Washington
DC 20013-7613
USA
Tel: (202) 783 6161
Maintain over 250 hostels in the United States, sponsor inexpensive educational and recreational outdoor travel programmes for all ages, such as bicycling, hiking, canoeing, skiing, and motor trips.

Australian Youth Hostels Association Inc.
60 Mary Street
Surry Hill
NSW 2010
Australia
Tel: (02) 212 1151
Operators of YHA Adventures – Licence B1851.

Canadian Hostelling Association
333 River Road
Tower A, 3rd Floor
Vanier City
Ottawa
Ontario
Canada K1L 8H9
Tel: (613) 748 5638
Telex: 053-3660
Offers inexpensive accommodation, provides facilities for school groups, embraces a wide range of challenging outdoor recreational activities, caters for all ages, backgrounds and tastes. The CHA counts more than 32,000 members and over 70 hostels nationwide.

YHA of New Zealand
PO Box 436
Christchurch C1
New Zealand
Tel: 799 970

Fédération Unied des Auberges de Jeunesse
National Office (admin and enquiries)
6 Rue Mesnil
75116 Paris
France
Tel: (1) 4505 1314

Youth Hostel Association of the UK
Trevelyan House
8 St Stephen's Hill
St Albans
Herts AL1 2DY
Tel: (0727) 55215

YHA Services Ltd
14 Southampton Street
London WC2E 7HY

Polish Association of Youth Hostels
Chocimska 28
Warsaw
Poland

Youth Hostel Association (South America)
Av. Corrientes 1371
1 piso
Buenos Aires
Argentina
For information on Youth Hostels throughout South America.

YMCA

Young Men's Christian Association – YMCA
National Council
64 Forest Road
London E17 3DZ
Tel: 01-520 5599

and

101 Wacker Drive
Chicago
IL 60606
USA
Tel: (312) 977 0031

and

116 Albert Road
South Melbourne
Victoria 3205
Australia
Tel: 03-699 7655

and

2160 Yonge Street
Toronto
Ontario M4S 2A9
Canada
Tel: (416) 485 9447

and

Ken Hobson Street
PO Box 1780
Wellington 1
New Zealand
Tel: 736 950
The YMCA has hostels worldwide. For information and addresses, contact the above.

Young Women's Christian Association – YWCA
9/11 Lockyer Street
Plymouth
Tel: (0752) 660321

and

Alexandra Residential Club
Water Land
Clifton
York
Tel: (0904) 29468
The YWCA has hostels worldwide. For information and addresses contact the above.

Travelmates
496 Newcastle Street

West Perth
Western Australia 6005
Accommodation is structured for young (18-35) back-packers mostly from overseas. There are several large old colonial houses which operate dormitory style on a *do-it-yourself basis. No wardens, curfews, or similar hassles. Kitchen, toilet, showers accessible 24 hrs. No bookings ... simply first come first served. A$6.50 daily, A$44 weekly.*

Accommodation: Home Exchange, Time-sharing

British Property Timeshare Association
Westminster Bank Chambers
Market Hill
Sudbury
Suffolk
Tel: (0787) 310 749

The European Holiday Timeshare Association
112 Westbourne Grove
London W2
Tel: 01-221 9400

The Timeshare Developers Group
2 Queen Anne's Gate Buildings
Dartmouth Street
London W1
Tel: 01-222 3203

Domus Publications Ltd
246/248 Great Portland Street
London W1
Tel: 01-387 7878
Publish a very useful Home Exchange/Timeshare magazine:
Homes Abroad- *covers all aspects of buying and setting up a home abroad. General features cover travel to countries near and far, all types of holidays and hints for travellers.*

Experiment in International Living
Upper Wyche
Malvern
Worcs WR14 4EN
Tel: (05 741) 5280
For those interested in finding out more about the Japanese and their life style, The Experiment in International Living (UK Office) can arrange for you to stay with a Japanese family in many parts of Japan, at a very reasonable cost.

Hapimag
Comser International
Orantecq House
Fairview Road
Timperly
Cheshire
Tel: 061-904 9750

Holiday Service
Ringstr. 26
8608 Memmelsdorf
West Germany
Tel: (0951) 43055
A company in Germany is currently offering a 'Swop Your Home' programme of more than 5,000 home swoppers in 53 countries. The list of potential home *swoppers offered by the company includes about 3,000 offers from the US. Photos of the accommodation offered are available. Full details from above address.*

Homefinders
New Roman House
387 City Road
London EC1V 1NA
Tel: 01-278 9232
Publish the magazine. Homes Overseas, *full of useful information.*

Home Interchange Ltd
8 Hillside
High Street
Farningham
Kent DA4 0DD
Tel: (0322) 864 527

Homesitters
Moat Farm
Buckland
Nr. Aylesbury
Bucks HP22 5HY
Tel: (0296) 631 289
One way to prevent burglary when on holiday is to employ a professional 'Homesitter' to live in your house while you are away. The 'Homesitters' are carefully selected and screened, and they abide by strict rules. They work closely with crime prevention officers.

Intervac – International Home Exchange Service
7000 SW 62nd Ave
Suite 306
S. Miami
FL 33143
USA
Tel: (305) 666 1861

and

6 Siddals Lane
Ailstree
Berks DE3 2DY
Tel: (0332) 558 931
Intervac Home Exchange has been established 35 years, and now has more than 5000 members in 40 countries. A Directory and two Supplements are published each year, and any number of exchanges may be arranged for one annual fee. International hospitality and let/rent arrangements are also possible.

Interval International
World Headquarters

6262 Sunset Drive
Penthouse One
Miami
FL 33143
USA

and

c/o Worldex Europe Inc
Gilmoora House
57-61 Mortimer Street
London W1N 7TD

RCI – Resort Condominiums International
Headquarters
3502 Woodview Terrace
PO Box 80229
Indianapolis 46280-0229
USA
Tel: (441) 821 5588
and

RCI (UK) Ltd
Parnell House
19/28 Wilton Road
London SW1V 1LW
Tel: 01-637 8047
Operates the world's largest exchange programme for time-share owners.

Traveler's Home Exchange Club, Inc.
PO Box 825
Parker
Colorado 80134
USA

Worldwide Home Exchange Club
45 Hans Place
London SW1X 0JX
Tel: 01-589 6055

Main Hotel Chain Reservation Numbers

Ambassador	
UK	01 434 1488
Apart Hotel International	
UK	01 434 1936
Best Western	
Australia	2-212 6444
	Tlx: 26850
New Zealand	9-505418
	Tlx: 60689
Canada & USA	800-528 1234
	Tlx: 165743
UK	01-541 0033
	Tlx: 8814912
Celebrated Country Hotels	
UK	(0628) 372230
Copthorn Hotels	
Australia	008-221 176
UK	(0800) 414741
USA	800-44 UTELL
CP Hotels International	
UK	01 930 8852
Ciga Hotels	
Australia	02-294133
	Tlx: 23430
Canada Toll free Zenith	71060
UK	Freefone 2142
USA	800-221 2340
Crest	
UK	01-236 3242
	Tlx: 83377

USA & Canada	800-548 2323
Hilton International	
Australia	08-217 0711
	008-222 255
Canada	(416) 362 3771
	(514) 861 3301
New Zealand	9-775 874
UK	01-631 1767
	Freefone 2124
USA	(212) 688 2240
	Tlx: 147249
Holiday Inns International	
UK	01-723 1277
Hotel Mercure	
UK	01-724 1000
	Tlx: 24361
USA	800-221 4542
	Tlx: 661831
Hotel Promotion Services	
UK	01-434 4431
	Tlx: 919170
Hotel Representatives, Inc.	
UK	(01) 583 3050
Hotel Sofotel	
UK	01-724 1000
	Tlx: 24361
USA	800-221 4542
Howard Johnston	
Australia	959 3922
	Tlx: 25360
Canada & USA	800-654 2000

New Zealand	774 980
	Tlx: 79163209
UK	01-409 0814
	Tlx: 262354

Hyatt

Australia	008-222 188
	Tlx: 70963
UK	01- 245 6611
	Tlx: 295509
Canada & USA	800-228 9000
	Tlx: 484582

Inter-Continental

Australia	232 1933
Canada	800-268 3785
New Zealand	395 982
UK	01-741 9000
or	(0345) 581 444
USA	800-327 0200

Inter-Europe Hotels

Australia	02-908 3533
	Tlx: AA21281
Canada	800-387 8031
UK	01-450 9388
	Tlx: 893921
USA	800-421 0767
	Tlx: 277541

Ladbroke Hotels

UK	01-734 6000
	Tlx: 897618
USA	800-223 1588

Loews Overseas Reservations

UK	01-487 4005

Lomé (Togo)

UK	01-724 1000
	Tlx: 24361
USA	800-221 4542
	Tlx: 661831

Keytel International

UK	01-402 8182

Mandarin International

UK	01-583 3411

Marriott Hotels and Resorts

Australia	008-221 176
	Tlx: 23430
UK	01-493 1232
USA & Canada	800-228 9290

Maurice Kevan International Ltd

UK	01-367 5175

Mövenpick International

Australia	2-235 1111
New Zealand	9-34526
UK	01-741 1588
USA & Canada	800-228 9822

Meridien Hotels

UK	01-439 1244
USA & Canada	800-543 4300

Novotel

UK	01-741 1555
	Tlx: 934 539
USA	(914) 725 5055
	Tlx: 646887

Omni International

Canada	(416) 424 1765
UK	01-937 7211
	Tlx: 883370
USA	(617) 227 8600
	Tlx:
	7103216707

Penta Hotels

Canada	800-634 3421
UK	01-8997 0551
	Tlx: 939886
USA	800-225 3456
	Tlx: 236608

Ramada Hotels International

Australia/NZ	008-222 431
Canada	(416) 485 2692
	Tlx: 065-22539
UK	01-408 0071
	Tlx: 25991
USA	800-272 6232

Rank Hotels

Australia	02-290 2877
	Tlx: 22152
Canada	(416) 485 7577
UK	01-262 2893
	Tlx: 267270
USA	800-232 5560

Resinter

Australia	235 3965
	Tlx: 176912
UK	01-724 1000
	Tlx: 24361
USA	800-221 4542
	Tlx: 661831

Sheraton

Australia	008-222 229
UK	0800-353 535
USA & Canada	800-325 3535

Southern Sun Hotel Groups

UK	01-636 7087

Steigenberger Reservations Service

Australia	008-221023
Canada	(416) 441 1048
New Zealand	09-396 991
UK	01-486 5754
	Tlx: 226255

USA	800-223 5652		
			Tlx: 6852554
Thistle Hotels		**Utell**	
Australia	02-267 2144	Australia	02-235 1111
	008-222 446	Canada	(416) 967 3442
Canada	(416) 441 1048	New Zealand	09-34526
UK	01-724 1000		Tlx: 63400
	Tlx: 24616	UK	01-741 1588
USA	800-847 4358		Tlx: 27817
	Tlx: 6801035	USA	(212) 397 2449
Tom Eden Associates			Tlx: 424716
UK	01-734 4267	**Western International Hotels**	
Top International Hotels		UK	01-408 0636
Germany (for UK)	(0211) 686 622	**Westin**	
	Tlx: 8581443	Australia	008-222 230
Trust House Forte			Tlx: 24793
Australia	008-222 446	New Zealand	Auckland 794
	Tlx: 121448		861
UK	01-567 3444	UK	01-408 0636
	Tlx: 934946		Tlx: 22144
USA & Canada	800-223 5672	Canada & USA	800-228 3000

Public Holidays

(Dates of some Religious Holidays may change from one year to another according to Lunar Calendar).

Algeria
Jan1; May1; June 19; July 5; Nov 1 (approx. Use lunar months). Europeans observe Christian holidays.

Andorra
Sept 8: National Holiday of Meritxell.

Antigua
Jan 1; Easter; May 31; Whitsun; Nov 1.

Antigua and Barbuda
Dec 25, Jan 1; May 1; Aug 1; Nov 1.

Argentina
Jan 1, Labour Day; May 25, Revolution (1810) Day; June 20, Flag Day; July 9, Independence(1816) Day; Aug 17, Death of General José de San Martin; Oct 12, Discovery of America (Colombus Day); and Dec 25, Christmas. On a number of other days, government offices, banks, insurance companies, and courts are closed, but closing is optional for business and commerce. These include: Jan 1, New Year's Day; Jan 6, Epiphany; and several days with variable dates – Carnival Monday and Tuesday before Ash Wednesday, Holy Thursday and Good Friday before Easter and Corpus Christi: Aug 15, Assumption of the Virgin Mary; Nov 1 All Saints Day and Dec 8, Feast of the Immaculate Conception. In addition, there are local patriotic or religious holidays, which may be observed by part or all of the community in various cities or provinces.

Australia
Jan 1; Australia Day (last Monday in Jan); Good Friday, Easter Sunday, Easter Monday + Bank Holiday; April 25. ANZAC Day; the Queen's Birthday; Dec 25 and 26. Holidays vary from State to State and only ANZAC Day and Australia Day are National Holidays.

Austria
Jan 1; Jan 6; Easter Monday; May 1 Ascension Day; Whit Monday; Corpus Christi; Aug 15; Assumption Day; Oct 26, National Day; Nov 1, All Saints Day; Dec 8, Immaculate Conception; Dec 25; Dec 26.

Bahamas
Jan 1; Good Friday; Easter Monday; Labour Day (early June); Whit Monday; July 10, Independence Day; Emancipation Day (early Aug); Oct 12, Discovery

Day; Dec 25; Dec 26. Those holidays which fall on a Sunday are normally observed on the following day. Offices and stores are generally closed throughout the country on public holidays.

Barbados Jan1; Good Friday; Easter Monday; Whit Monday; First Monday in July, Aug and Sept; Independence Day; Nov 30; Dec 25; Dec 26.

Belgium Jan 1; Easter Monday; May 1; Ascencion Day; Pentecost Monday; July 21, National Holiday; Aug 15. Assumption Day; Nov 11, Armistice Day; Nov 15, King's Birthday (only for administrative and public offices, schools etc); 25 Dec; 26 Dec.

Belize Jan 1; Mar 9; May 1; May 24; Sept 10; Sept 24, National Day; Oct 12; Nov 19; Dec 25, Dec 26, Good Friday. Holy Saturday and Easter Monday. Those holidays which fall on a Sunday are normally observed on the following day.

Bermuda Jan 1; Good Friday, Bermuda Day; Queen's Birthday; Cup Match Somer's Day; Labour Day; Remembrance Day; Dec 25; Dec 26.

Bolivia Jan 1; Feb 3; Carnival Week (preceding Lent); Holy Week (3 days preceding Easter; May 1, Labour Day: May 2, Lake Titicaca (reed and canoe regatta); Corpus Christi: 23 June, St John's Day; 29 June; St Peter & Paul Tizuina; July 15-16 La Paz Day; July 21, Martyrs' Day; Aug 6-7, Independence Festival; Sept 8, Oct 12; Nov 1, All Saints Day, Nov 17-18; Dec 8, Immaculate Conception; Dec 25.

Botswana Jan 1; Jan 2 Easter: May 21, Ascension Day; July 16, President's Day; July 17; Sept 30, Botswana Day; Oct 1; Oct 2; Dec 25; Dec 26.

Brazil Jan 1; Carnival (3 days preceding Lent) Easter; Apr 21, Tiradentes Day; May 1, Labour Day; Sept 7, Independence Day; Nov 2, All Souls' Day; Nov 15, Proclamation of the Republic; Dec 25.

Burkina Faso Jan 1; May; Christian and Muslim holidays.

Burma Jan 4,Independence Day; Feb 12, Union Day; Mar 2, Peasants' Day; Mar 27, Armed Forces Day; mid-Apr Thingyan Water Festival; Worker's Day; early May, Tazaundaing Festival of Lights; Dec 25.

Burundi Jan 1; Ascension; May 1; July 1; Aug 15; Sept 18; Nov 1; Dec. 25.

Canada Jan 1; Easter; May 20; July 1; Sept 2; Oct 14; Nov 11; Dec 25; Dec 26.

Cayman Islands Jan 1, Ash Wednesday; Easter; May 20, Discovery Day; Queen's Birthday; July 1, Constitution Day; Nov 11, Monday after Remembrance Sunday; Dec 25, Dec 26.

Chile May 1; May 21; Sept 18.

China New Year's Day; Spring Festival – Lunar New Year (3 days), May 1; Oct 1+2.

Colombia Jan1; Jan 6; Mar 19; Easter; May 1; Ascension Day; Corpus Christi; June 29; July 20; Aug 7; Oct 12; Nov 1; Nov 11; Dec 8; Dec 25.

Costa Rica Jan 1; St. Joseph's Day; Easter; Apr 11, National Heroes Day; May 1, Labour Day; Corpus Christi; June 29, Sts Peter & Paul; July 25; Aug 2, Our Lady of Angels; Sept 15, Independence Day; Oct 12, Day of the Race; Dec 8, Immacualate Conception; Dec 25; Dec 29-31, Civic Holiday.

Côte d'Ivoire Jan 1; Easter; May 1, Labour Day; Ascension Day; Whit Monday; Aug 15, Assumption of the Virgin Mary; Nov 1, All Saints Day; Dec 7, National Day; Dec 25. Dates for Ramadan and Tabaski (Feast of the Mutton-Muslim) vary from one year to another.

Czechoslovakia Jan 1; Easter Monday; May 1; May 9, Liberation Day; Dec 25; Dec 26.

Denmark Jan 1; Easter; Apr 16, National Day (School Holiday); Queen Margrethe II's Birthday; Great Prayer Day; Ascension Day; Whit Monday; June 5, Constitution Day; Dec 25; Dec 26.

Djibouti June 27.

Dominica Jan 1; Jan 2; Shrove Tuesday and Monday preceding Easter; Whit Monday; May 1; 1st Monday in Aug; Nov 1-3; Dec 25; Dec 26.

Dominican Republic Jan 1; Jan 6; Jan 21; Jan 26, Duarte Day; Feb 27, Independence Day; Easter; May 1, Labour Day; Corpus Christi; Aug 16, Restoration Day; Sept 24, Patron Saint Day; Dec 25.

El Salvador Jan 1; Easter; May 1; Aug 1-6; August Festivities; Sept 15; Nov 2; Dec 25. Banks closed June 29 and 30.

Eastern Caribbean	Jan 1; Easter; 1st Monday in May, Labour Day; Whit Monday; August Monday – National Day of each island.
Finland	Jan 1; Easter, May 1; May 26; June 9, June 23; Nov 3; Dec 6; Dec 25, Dec 26.
France	Jan 1; Easter; May 1; May 8; Ascension Day; Whitsun; July 14, Assumption; Nov 1, All Saints' Day; Nov 11, Remembrance Day; Dec 25.
Gambia	Feb 1, Feb 18; Easter; May 1, Aug 15, Dec 25; Dec 26; Id-El Fizr; Id-El-Kabir; Mawllud-el-Nabi.
East Germany	Jan 1; May 1; Oct 7; Whit Monday.
West Germany	Jan 1; Jan 6, Epiphany; Easter; May 1, Labour Day; Ascension Day, Whit Monday; Corpus Christi; June 17, Day of Unity; Aug 15, Assumption of the Virgin Mary; Day of Prayer and Repentance; Dec 25; Dec 26.
Gibraltar	Jan 1; Mar 12, Commonwealth Day; Easter; May 1; last Monday in May; Queen's Birthday; last Monday in Aug; Dec 25, Dec 26.
Greece	Jan 1; Jan 6, Epiphany; Shrove Monday; Mar 25; Easter; May 1, Labour Day; June 11, Day of the Holy Spirit; Aug 15, Assumption of the Virgin Mary; Oct 28, Ochi Day; Dec 25; Dec 26.
Guyana	Jan 1; Feb 23, Republic Anniversary; Easter; May 1, Labour Day; first Monday in July, Caribbean Day; first Monday in Aug, Freedom Day; Dec 25, Dec 26. You-Man-Nabi; Phagway; Deepavali; Eid-ul-Azha – dates to be decided annually.
Hong Kong	The first weekday in Jan; Lunar New Year's Day; the second and third day of Lunar New Year; Ching Ming Festival; Easter; Tuen Ng (Dragon boat) Festival; the Queen's Birthday, Saturday preceding the Last Monday in July; last Monday in Aug, Liberation Day; day following the Chinese Mid-Autumn Festival; Chung Yeung Festival; Dec 25; Dec 26.
Hungary	Jan 1; Apr 4, Liberation Day; Easter; May 1; Aug 20, Constitution Day; Nov 7, Anniversary of the Great October Socialist Revolution; Dec 25, Dec 26.
Iceland	Jan 1; Easter; Apr 18, first Day of Summer; May 1; Ascension Day; Whit Monday; June 17, National Day; Dec 24,25,26,31.
India	Jan 1; Jan 26, Republic Day;, Aug 15, Independence Day; Oct 2 Mahatma Gandhi's Birthday; Dec 25. Also 32 other religious or special occasions which are observed either with national or regional holidays.
Indonesia	Jan 1; Easter; Mar 13, Hari Maulud Nabi (Muslim Festival); Ascension Day; Waicak Day (celebrating Buddha's birth) June 9; Galunggan in Bali (a New Year Feast lasting 20 days); Sekaten (birth of Mohammed); Aug 17, Independence Day; Sept 25-26, Idul Fitri (Muslim festival); Dec 25. Dates for certain holidays change with the lunar calendar. In addition to the holidays listed, business visitors should note the Islamic month of fasting, Ramadan.
Iraq	Jan 1; Jan 6; Feb 7; Mar 21; May 1; July 14, July 17. In addition there are various religious holidays, including Ramadan.
Israel	All business activity ceases on Saturdays and religious holidays, the dates of which vary from one year to another. Passover, first day; Passover, last day; Israel Independence Day; Shavout (Feast of Weeks); Pentecost; Rosh Hashana (New Year); Yom Kippur (Day of Atonement); First Day of Tabernacles; Last Day of Tabernacles; Hanukkah.
Italy	On Italian National Holidays, offices, shops and schools are closed: Jan 1; Easter; Apr 25, Liberation Day; May 1; Labour Day; Aug 15, Assumption of the Blessed Virgin Mary; Nov 1, All Saints Day; Dec 8, Immaculate Conception of the Blessed Virgin Mary; Dec 25; Dec 26.
Jamaica	Jan 1; Ash Wednesday; Easter; May 23, Labour Day; First Monday in Aug, Independence Day; Third Monday in Oct, National Heroes' Day; Dec 25; Dec 26.
Japan	Jan 1; Jan 2,3,4 Bank Holidays (all commercial firms closed); Jan 15, Adults' Day; Feb 11, National Foundation Day; Vernal Equinox Day (variable date); Apr 29, the Emperor's birthday; May 1; May 3, Constitution Memorial Day; May 5, Children's Day; Sept 15, Respect of the Aged Day; Autumnal Equinox Day (variable date); Oct 10, Physical Culture Day; Nov 3, Culture Day; Nov 23, Labour

Thanksgiving Day; Dec 28, New year's holiday begins (last five to ten days). Also 'Golden Week' in late spring when some firms remain closed. Some manufacturers close for a week during the summer.

Jordan	Jan 1; Mar 22; May 1; May 10; May 25; July 1-14; Aug 11; Sept 6-10; Nov 14; Dec 5; Dec 25.
Kenya	Jan 1; Easter; May 1; June 1; Madraka Day; Oct 20; Kenyatta Day; Dec 12, Independence Day; Dec 25; Dec 26; Idd-ul-Fitr (an Islamic feast at the end of Ramadan).
Korea	Jan 1-3; Mar 1, Independence Day; Apr 5, Arbor Day; May 5, Children's Day; early May, Buddha's birthday; early June, Memorial Day; Korean Thanksgiving Day; Oct 1, Armed Forces Day; Oct 3, National Foundation Day; Oct 9, Hangul Day; Oct 24, United Nations Day; Dec 25.
Kuwait	Religious holidays vary from one year to another. The only fixed holidays in Kuwait are New Year's Day and Kuwait National Day (Feb 25). October to May or June is generally considered the best period for foreign business visitors; business slackens off in the summer.
Liberia	Jan 1; Feb 11, Armed Forces Day; Mar 15, J.J. Robert's birthday; Second Wednesday in March, Decoration Day; April 12, National Redemption Day; Second African Liberation Day; July 26, Independence Day; Aug 24, National Flag Day; 1st Thursday in Nov, Thanksgiving Day; Nov 29, William V.S. Tubman's Birthday; Dec 25.
Luxembourg	Jan 1; Easter; May 1; Ascension Day; Whit Monday; June 23, National Day; Aug 15, Assumption Day; Nov 1, All Saints Day; Dec 25-26. In addition to these Public Holidays there are various Bank Holidays throughout the year.
Macao	Jan 1; Feb, Chinese New Year; Apr, Ching Ming Festival; Easter; Apr 25, Anniversary of Portuguese Revolution; May 1; Jun 10, Camoens Day and Portuguese Communities; June, Corpus Christi, Dragon Boat Festival, Feast of St. John the Baptist; Aug 15, Assumption of Our Lady; Sept Mid-Autumn Festival; Oct 5, Republic Day; Oct 22 Festival of Ancestors; Nov 1-2, All Saints Day – All Souls Day; Dec 1, Restoration of Independence; Dec 8, Feast of Immaculate Conception; Dec 22, Winter Solstice; Dec 24- 25, Christmas.
Malaysia	Jan 1; Feb 1, City Day (for Kuala Lumpur); Feb 2-3, Chinese New Year; May 1, Labour Day; May 15, Wesak Day; June 6, birthday of Dymm Sri Padika Baginda Yand di Pertuan Agong; Hari Raya Puasa (dates vary); Aug 31, National Day; Sept 26, Awal Muharram; Oct 23, Deepavali; Dec 5, Birthday of Prophet Muhammed; Dec 25.
Mali	Jan 1; Jan 20, Festival of the Army; May 1, Labour Day; May 25, Africa Day; Sept 22, National Day; Nov 19.
Malta	Jan 1; Mar 31; Easter; May 1; Aug 15; Dec 13; Dec 25.
Mauritius	Jan 1; Jan 2; Jan 19; Feb 2; Feb 29; Mar 12; Apr 2; May 1; Jun 30; Aug 30; Oct 24; Nov 1; Dec 25.
Mexico	Jan 1; Feb 5; Feb 24; Mar 21; Easter; May 1; May 5; Sept 1; Sept 16; Oct 12; Nov 20; Dec 25.
Morocco	Mar 3; Nov 6; Religious holidays vary from one year to another.
Nepal	Jan 11; Feb 18; Apr 14; Nov 11; Dec 15 & 28; and many other religious, partly public holidays which change every year according to Lunar and other calendars. Biggest festival Dassain (Sept/Oct) when everything closes for a week.
Netherlands	Jan 1; Easter; Ascension Day; Whit Monday; Dec 25; Dec 26; Queen's Day, April 30; and Liberation Day, May 5 are public holidays for the Civil Service, but shops and offices etc need not necessarily be closed.
New Zealand	Jan 1; Feb 6; New Zealand Day; Easter; Apr 25, ANZAC Day; the Queen's Birthday (generally observed in early June); Oct, Labour Day;, Dec 25; Dec 26. Also a holiday for the provinical anniversary in each provincial district i.e Jan 29, Auckland; Dec 16, Canterbury; No 1, Hawkes Bay; Nov 1, Marlborough; Feb 1, Nelson; Feb 6 Northland; Mar 23, Otago; Mar 23, Southland; Mar 31, Taranaki; Jan 22.
Nicaragua	Jan 1; Easter; May 1; July 19; Sept 14; Sept 15; Dec 24; Dec 25.
Niger	Apr 15, National Armed Forces Day; Aug 3, Proclamation of Independence; Dec

	18, Proclamation of the Republic.
Norway	May 17.
Oman	Nov 18 and Nov 19, National Day.
Paraguay	Jan 1; Feb 3, San Blas Patron Saint; Mar 1, Hero's Day; Easter; May 1, Labour Day; May 14 and 15, Independence Day; June 12, Chaco Peace; Corpus Christi; Aug 15, Assumption Day; Aug 25, Constitution Day; Sept 29, Battle of Boqueron (Chaco War); Oct 12, Colombus Day, Nov 1, All Saints Day; Dec 8, Immaculate Conception; Dec 25.
Peru	Jan 1; Easter; May 1, Labour Day; June 24, Countryman's Day/ Day of the Peasant; June 29, St Peter and St. Paul; July 28/29, Independence Days; Aug 30, St. Rose of Lima; Oct 8, Combat of Angamos; Nov 1, All Saints' Day; Dec 8, Immaculate Conception; Dec 25. Banks closed June 30 and Dec 31.
Philippines	Jan 1; Easter; May 1, Labour Day; June 12, Independence Day; July 4, Philippine-American Day; Nov 30, National Heroes' Day; Dec 25; Dec 30, Rizal Day. Additional holidays such as Bataan Day and General Elections Day may be called by the President of the Republic.
Poland	Jan 1; Easter; May 1, Labour Day; Corpus Christi; July 22, National Day; Nov 1, All Saints Day; Dec 25; Dec 26.
Portugal	Jan 1, Shrove Tuesday; Easter; Apr 25; May 1; Corpus Christi; June 10; Aug 15; Oct 5; Nov 1; Dec 1; Dec 8; Dec 25. There are also various local holidays in towns and villages throughout the country. Details from local tourist offices. Carnival is also an important event in the country. Details from local tourist offices. Carnival is also an important event in Portugal and takes place during the four days preceeding Lent.
Qatar	Feb 22, Anniversary of the Accession of HH The Emir, Sheikh Khalifa Bin Hamad Al Thank; Sept 3, Independence Day. Eid Al-Fitr, Eid Al-Adha and Hijri New Year change dates annually as they follow the lunar calendar.
American Samoa	All United States holidays and Apr 17, Flag Day.
Saudi Arabia	During the month of Ramadan (which varies from one year to another according to the lunar calendar), all Muslims refrain from eating, drinking and smoking from sunrise to sunset. Business hours are shortened. Non-Muslims must also observe the fast while in public.
Senegal	All Christian Holidays; All Muslim holidays, which vary yearly; Apr 4; Ascension Day; May Day; Assumption Day.
Seychelles	Jan 1, Jan 2; Easter; May 1, Labour Day; Assumption Day; June 5, Liberation Day; June 29, Independence Day; Corpus Christi; Aug 15, Assumption of Mary; Nov 1, All Saints' Day; Dec 8, Feast of the Immaculate Conception; Dec 25; Sept, La Fete La Digue/Annual Regatta; Nov, Annual Fishing Competition.
Singapore	Jan 1; May 1, Labour Day; May 17, Vesak Day; Aug 9, National Day; Oct 29, Hari Raya Punsa; Dec 25. Holidays with variable dates are Hari Raya Haji, Chinese New Year Good Friday and Deepavali. When a holiday falls on a Sunday, the next day is taken as a public holiday.
South Africa	Jan 1; Apr 6, Founder's Day; Easter; Family Day; Ascension Day; May 31, Republic Day; Oct 10, Kruger Day; Dec 16, Day of the Vow; Dec 25; Dec 26, Day of Goodwill.
Spain	Jan 6; Mar 19; Easter; May 1; June 21; July 25; Aug 15; Oct 12; Nov 18; Dec 8; Dec 25.
Sweden	Jan 1; Jan 6, Epiphany; Easter; May 1, Labour Day; Ascension Day; Whit Monday; Midsummer's Day; All Saint's Day; Dec 25; Dec 26.
Switzerland	Jan 1; Easter; Ascension Day; Whit Monday; Dec 25; Dec 26. Certain Cantons – Jan 2; May 1, Corpus Christi; Aug 1, National Day.
Tahiti	Jan 1; Easter; May 1, Labour Day; May 8, Victory Day; Ascension Day; Whit Monday; July 14, National Day; Aug 15, Assumption; Nov 1, All Saints Day; Nov 11, Armistice Day; Dec 25.
Thailand	Jan 1; Apr 15, the Songkran Festival (Buddhist New Year); May 5, Coronation Day Anniversary; May, Visakhja Pua (Buddhist Festival); June/July, Buddhist

Lent Begins; Aug 12, Queen's Birthday; Oct 23, Chulalongkorn Day; Dec 5, King's Birthday; Dec 31.

Tonga	Jan 1; Easter; Apr 25, ANZAC Day; May 4, Birthday of HRH Crown Prince Tupouto'a; May 13-21, Red Cross Week; early June, Opening of Parliament; June 4, Emancipation Day; July 4 , Heilala Festival; late Aug to early Sept, Royal Agricultural Shows; Nov 4, Constitution Day; early Dec, Music Festival; Dec 4, King Tupou I Day; Dec 25; Dec 26.
Trinidad and Tobago	Jan 1, Easter, Whit Monday; Corpus Christi; Labour Day; first Monday in Aug, Discovery Day; Aug 31, Independence Day; Sept 24, Republic Day; Eid-Ul- Fitr (Muslim Festival), Divali (Hindu Festival); Dec 25; Dec 26.
Tunisia	Jan 1; Jan 18; Mar 20; Easter; May 1; June 1-2; Aug 3; Aug 13; Sept 3; Oct 15.
Turkey	Jan 1; Apr 23, National Independence Children's Day; May 19, Youth and Sports Day; Aug 30, Victory Day (Anniversary of the Declaration of the Turkish Republic).
Turks & Caicos	Jan 1; Easter; June 6, James McCartney Memorial Day; Aug 1, Emancipation Day; Oct 12, International Human Rights Day; Dec 25; Dec 26.
United Arab Emirates	Jan 1; Jan 12 Rabia Al Awal, Prophet's birthday; Jan 27 Rajab Ascension Day; Feb 1, Shawwal; Id Al-Fitr; Aug 6, Accession Day of HH Sheikh Zayed, President of UAE; 10 Aug Dhul Hiffa; Id Al Adha; Sept 1, Muharram; Muslim New Year; Dec 2, National Day.
USSR	Jan 1; Mar 8, International Women's Day; May 1-2, International Labour Day; May 9, Victory Day; Oct 7, Constitution Day; Nov 7-8, October Revolution.
Uruguay	Jan 1; Jan 6; Apr 19, Day of 33 Orientals; May 1; May 18, Battle of Las Piedras; June 19, Birth of Artigas; July 18, Constitution Day; Aug 25, Independence Day; Oct 12, Colombus Day; Nov 2, All Souls' Day; Dec 25; Carnival Week (Feb or Mar) and Tourist Week (Mar or Apr) have variable dates.
Virgin Islands (British)	Jan 1; Feb 23, Commemoration of Visit by HM The Queen; Easter; Commonwealth Day; Queen's Birthday; July 21, Territory Day; First Monday, Tuesday and Wednesday in August; Oct 21, St Ursula's Day; Nov 14, Prince of Wales' Birthday; Dec 25, Dec 26.
Virgin Islands (US)	Jan 1; Jan 6; Jan 15, Martin Luther King's Birthday; Feb 13, Abraham Lincoln's Birthday; Feb 20, George Washington's Birthday; Mar 17, St. Patricks Day; 31 Mar, Transfer Day; Easter; mid-Apr, Rolex Regatta; Apr 23-30, Carnival Calypso Tent on St. Thomas; Apr 30-May 5, Carnival Week, St. Thomas; May 4, Children's Parade; May 5, Adult's Parade; May 31, Memorial Day; June 18, Organic Act Day; July 3, Danish West Indies Emancipation Day; July 4, Independence Day; July 25, Hurricane Supplication Day; Sept 3, Labour Day; Oct 8, Colombus Day and Puerto Rico/Virgin Islands Friendship Day; Oct 19, Hurricane Thanksgiving Day; Nov 1, Liberty Day; Mid-Nov, Virgin Islands Charterboat League Show; Nov 11, Veterans' Day; Nov 22, National Thanksgiving Day; Dec 25; Dec 26, Dec 27, Opening of Crucian Christmas Fiesta.
Yugoslavia	Jan 1; Jan 2; May 1-2; July 4; Nov 29-30.
Zaire	Jan 1; Jan 4; May 1; May 20; June 24; June 30; Aug 1; Oct 14; Oct 27; Nov 17; Nov 24; Dec 25.
Zambia	Jan 1; Mar 17; Apr 20-21; May 1; May 25; July 2-3; Aug 6; Oct 24-26; Dec 25; Dec 26.

Business Hours

Afghanistan	08.00–12.00, 13.00–16.30 Sat–Wed; 08.00–13.00 Thurs.
Albania	07.00–14.00 Mon–Sat, 17.00–20.00 Mon–Tue.
Algeria	7.45–11.50, 14.00–17.00 Mon–Fri. in winter; 7.15–11.00, 15.00–17.30 Mon–-

	Fri in summer.
Andorra	9.00–13.00, 15.00–18.45 Mon–Fri.
Angola	08.00–12.00, 14.00–18.00 Mon–Fri; 08.00–12.00 Sat.
Anguilla	08.00–12.00; 13.00–16.00 Mon–Fri.
Antigua and Barbuda	08.00–13.00, 15.00–17.00 Mon–Fri; 9.00–12.30 Sat.
Argentina	09.00–19.00 Mon–Fri.
Aruba	08.00–12.00, 13.00–17.00 Mon–Fri.
Australia	09.00–17.00 Mon–Fri; 09.00–12.00 Sat.
Austria	08.00–18.00 Mon–Fri.
Bahamas	Nassau and Freeport: 09.00–17.00 Mon–Fri.Opening times vary considerably inthe Family Islands.
Bahrain	07.00–13.00 Sat–Thurs.
Bangladesh	09.00–17.00 Sun–Thurs.
Barbados	08.00–16.00 Mon–Fri; 08.00–13.00 Sat.
Belgium	9.00–17.30 Mon–Fri; 09.00–12.00 Sat.
Belize	08.00–17.00 Mon–Fri; 09.00–12.00 Sat.
Benin	08.00–12.30; 15.00–18.30 Mon–Fri.
Bermuda	09.00–17.00 Mon–Fri.
Bolivia	09.00–18.30 Mon–Fri.
Botswana	08.15–17.00 Mon–Fri.
Brazil	08.30–18.00 Mon–Fri.
British Virgin Is	08.30–17.00 Mon–Fri; 08.30–12.30 Sat.
Brunei	08.00–12.00, 13.30–17.00 Mon–Fri; 08.00– 12.00 Sat.
Bulgaria	08.00–17.00 Mon–Fri.
Burkina Faso	07.00–12.30, 15.00–17.30 Mon–Fri.
Burma	09.30–16.30 Mon–Fri.
Burundi	07.00–12.00, 14,00–17,00 Mon–Fri; 07.00–12.00 Sat.
Cameroon	08.00–12.00, 14.30–17.30 Mon–Fri; 08.00–13.00 Sat.
Canada	08.30–16.30 Mon–Fri
Cape Verde	08.00–13.30, 16.00–18.00 Mon–Fri.
Cayman Islands	09.00–17.00 Mon–Fri.
Central African Rep	07.00–16.00 Mon–Fri.
Chad	07.30–17.00 Mon–Fri
Chile	09.30–18.00 Mon–Fri; 09.00–13.00 Sat.
China	08.00–17.00 Mon–Fri.
Colombia	08.00–18.00 Mon–Fri.
Comoro Islands	07.30–17.30 Mon–Thurs; 07.30–11.00 Fri.
Congo	08.00–17.00 Mon–Fri
Cook Islands	08.00–16.00 Mon–Fri; 08.00–11.30 Sat.
Costa Rica	08.00–17.00 Mon–Fri; 08.00–11.00 Sat.
Côte d'Ivoire	08.00–17.30 Mon–Fri; 08.00–12.00 Sat.
Cuba	08.00–17.00 Mon–Fri.
Cyprus	07.30–13.00, 16.00–18.30 Mon–Fri; 07.30–13.00 Sat.
Czechoslovakia	08.00–16.00 Mon–Fri.
Denmark	09.00–17.30 Mon–Fri; 09.30–13.00 Sat.

Djibouti	07.00–12.30, 15.30–18.00 Mon–Thurs.
Dominica	08.00–13.00, 14.00–16.00 Mon–Fri.
Dominican Rep.	08.30–18.00 Mon–Fri; 08.00–12.00 Sat.
Ecuador	08.00–18.30 Mon–Fri.
Egypt	08.30–19.00 Sat–Thurs.
El Salvador	08.30–12.30, 14.00–18.00 Mon–Fri; 08.00–12.00 Sat.
Equatorial Guinea	08.00–15.00 Mon–Fri; 08.00–12.00 Sat.
Ethiopia	08.00–12.00, 13.00–16.00 Mon–Fri; 08.00–12.00 Sat.
Fiji	08.00–16.30 Mon–Fri.
Finland	08.00–16.00 Mon–Fri.
France	09.00–18.00 Mon–Fri; 09.00–12.00 Sat.
French Guinea	08.00–18.00 Mon–Fri.
French Polynesia	07.30–11.30, 13.30–17.00 Mon–Fri; 07.30–11.30 Sat.
French West Indies	08.00–17.00 Mon–Fri; 08.00–12.00 Sat.
Gabon	08.00–12.00, 15.00–18.00 Mon–Fri.
Gambia	08.00–15.00 Mon–Thurs; 08.00–13.00 Fri, Sat.
East Germany	07.00–16.00 Mon–Fri.
West Germany	08.30–17.00 Mon–Fri
Ghana	08.00–12.30, 13.30–17.00 Mon–Fri.
Gibraltar	09.00–18.00 Mon–Fri.
Greece	08.00–14.00 Mon–Sat in summer; 08.30–13.30, 16.30–19.30 in winter.
Grenada	08.00–12.00, 13.00–16.00 Mon–Fri; 09.00–12.00 Sat.
Guatemala	08.00–18.00 Mon–Sat.
Guinea–Bissau	07.30–13.00 Mon–Fri.
Guinea	07.30–13.00 Mon–Thurs, Sat; 07.30–10.30 Fri.
Guyana	08.00–16.00 Mon–Fri; 08.00–12.00 Sat.
Haiti	08.00–16.00 Mon–Fri.
Honduras	07.30–15.30 Mon–Fri.
Hong Kong	09.00–17.00 Mon–Fri; 09.00–12.30 Sat.
Hungary	08.00–16.30 Mon–Fri.
Iceland	09.00–17.00 Mon–Fri.
India	09.30–17.30 Mon–Fri; 09.00–12.00 Sat.
Indonesia	08.00–16.00 Mon–Fri, 08.00–13.00 Sat.
Iran	08.00–19.00 Sat–Wed.
Iraq	08.00–14.00 Sat–Wed; 08.00–13.00 Thurs.
Ireland	09.00–17.30 Mon–Fri.
Israel	08.00–15.00 Sun–Thurs.
Italy	08.30–19.00 Mon–Fri.
Jamaica	08.30–16.30 Mon–Sat.
Japan	09.00–17.00 Mon–Fri.
Jordan	08.00–13.00, 15.30–18.00 Sat–Thurs
Kampuchea	8.30–15.30 Mon–Fri; 8.20–12.00 Sat
Kenya	08.30–16.30 Mon–Fri; 08.30–12.00 Sat.
Kiribati	08.00–16.15 Mon–Fri.
South Korea	09.00–18.00 Mon–Fri.
Kuwait	08.00–18.00 Sat–Wed.

Laos	07.30–11.30, 14.00–17.00 Mon–Sat.; 08.00–12.00, 13.00–16.30 Mon–Sat. (Mar–Sept).
Lebanon	08.00–13.00 Mon–Sat, summer; 08.30–18.00 Mon–Sat winter.
Lesotho	08.00–16.30 Mon–Fri; 08.30–12.30 Sat.
Liberia	08.00–17.00 Mon–Fri.
Libya	08.00–14.00 Sat–Thurs.
Luxembourg	08.30–17.30 Mon–Fri.
Macao	09.00–17.00 Mon–Fri; 09.00–13.00 Sat.
Madagascar	07.30–17.00 Mon–Fri: 07.30–11.30 Sat.
Malawi	07.30–17.00 Mon–Fri.
Malaysia	08.30–16.30 Mon–Fri; 08.30–12.30 Sat.
Maldives	07.30–13.30 Sat–Thurs.
Mali	07.30–14.30 Mon–Thur, Sat; 07.30–12.00 Fri.
Malta	08.30–17.30 Mon–Fri; 08.30–13.00 Sat.
Mauritania	07.00–15.00 Sun–Thurs.
Mauritius	09.00–16.00 Mon–Fri; 09.30–11.30 Sat.
Mexico	09.00–19.00 Mon–Fri.
Micronesia	07.30–11.30, 12.30–16.30 Mon–Fri.
Mongolia	09.00–18.00 Mon–Fri; 09.00–15.00 Sat.
Montserrat	08.00–13.00 Mon–Thurs; 08.00–12.00, 15.00–17.00 Sat.
Morocco	08.30–18.30 Mon–Fri.
Mozambique	08.00–12.00, 14.00–17.00.
Nepal	10.00–15.00 Sat–Thurs; 10.00–12.00 Fri. Closed Sat.
Netherlands	08.30–17.00 Mon–Fri.
Netherlands Antilles	08.30–12.00, 13.00–17.00 Mon–Fri.
New Caledonia	07.00–11.00, 13.30–17.30 Mon–Fri; 07.30–11.00 Sat.
New Zealand	08.30–17.00 Mon–Fri; 09.00–12.30 Sat.
Nicaragua	08.00–18.00 Mon–Fri; 08.00–12.00 Sat.
Niger	08.00–12.00, 16.00–17.00 Mon–Sat.
Nigeria	08.00–12.30, 14.00–16.30 Mon–Fri; 08.00–12.00 Sat.
Niue	08.00–15.30 Mon–Fri.
Norfolk Island	10.00–16.00 Mon–Fri; Sat morning. Some close Wed afternoon.
Norway	09.00–16.00 Mon–Fri.
Oman	07.30–14.00 Sat–Wed; 07.30–13.00 Thur.
Pakistan	08.30–17.00 Sat–Wed; 08.30–13.00 Thur.
Panama	08.00–12.00, 14.00–18.00 Mon–Fri.
Papua New Guinea	09.00–17.00 Mon–Fri; 09.00–12.00 Sat.
Paraguay	07.30–11.30, 15.00–18.30 Mon–Fri; 07.30–11.30 Sat.
Peru	11.00–20.00 Mon–Sat.
Philippines	08.00–17.00 Mon–Fri.
Poland	07.30–15.30 Mon–Fri.
Portugal	10.00–18.00 Mon–Fri.
Puerto Rico	09.00–17.00 Mon–Fri.
Qatar	08.00–12.30, 16.00–18.30 Sat–Wed; 07.00–14.00 Thurs.
Réunion	08.00–12.00, 14.00–18.00 Mon–Fri.
Romania	07.00–16.00 Mon–Fri; 07.00–12.30 Sat.

Rwanda	Extremely varied.
St Christopher & Nevis	08.00–12.00, 13.00–16.00 Fri–Wed.
St Lucia	08.00–16.00 Mon–Fri.
St Vincent &Grenadines	08.00–12.00, 13.00–16.00 Mon–Fri; 08.00–12.00 Sat.
American Samoa	09.00–14.00 Mon–Thurs; 09.00–17.00 Fri
Western Samoa	08.00–16.30 Mon–Fri; 08.00–12.30 Sat.
Saudi Arabia	09.00–13.00, 16.30–20.00 Sat–Thurs.
Senegal	08.00–18.00 Mon–Fri.
Seychelles	08.00–12.00, 13.00–16.00 Mon–Fri; 08.00–12.00 Sat.
Sierra Leone	08.00–16.30 Mon–Fri; 08.00–12.30 Sat.
Singapore	09.00–17.00 Mon–Fri; 09.00–13.00 Sat.
Solomon Islands	08.00–12.00, 13.00–16.30 Mon–Fri.
Somalia	07.00–14.00 Sat–Thurs.
South Africa	08.30–17.00 Mon–Fri.
Spain	09.00–18.45 Mon–Fri winter; 09.00–14.00, 16.00–19.00 Mon–Fri, summer.
Sri Lanka	09.00–13.00 Mon; 9.00–13.30 Tues–Fri.
Sudan	07.30–14.30 Sat–Thurs.
Suriname	07.00–15.00 Mon–Thurs; 07.00–14.00 Fri.
Swaziland	08.15–17.00 Mon–Fri; 08.15–13.00 Sat.
Sweden	09.00–17.00 Mon–Fri.
Switzerland	80.00–18.00 Mon–Fri.
Syria	08.00–14.30 Sat–Thurs.
Tahiti	7.45–15.30 Mon–Fri.
Taiwan	09.00–17.00 Mon–Sat.
Tanzania	07.30–14.30 Mon–Fri; 07.30–12.30 Sat.
Thailand	08.00–17.00 Mon–Fri; 08.00–12.00 Sat.
Togo	07.30–12.00, 14.30–17.30 Mon–Fri; 07.30–12.00 Sat.
Tonga	08.30–16.30 Mon–Fri.
Trinidad & Tobago	08.00–16.00 Mon–Fri.
Tunisia	08.00–11.00, 14.00–16.15 Mon–Thurs; 08.00–11.00, 13.00–15.15 Fri.
Turkey	08.30–17.30 Mon–Fri. Summer variation.
USSR	09.00–18.00 Mon–Fri.
United Arab Emirates	08.00–13.00, 16.00–19.00 Sat–Thurs, winter; 07.00–13.00, 16.00–18.00 Sat–Thurs, summer.
United Kingdom	09.30–17.30 Mon–Fri.
United States	09.00–17.00 Mon–Fri.
Uruguay	08.30–19.00 Mon–Fri.
Vanuatu	07.30–17.00 Mon–Fri (long lunch); 07.30–11.30 Sat.
Venezuela	08.00–18.00 Mon–Fri (long lunch).
Vietnam	08.00–12.30, 13.00–16.30 Mon–Fri; 08.00–12.30 Sat.
North Yemen	08.00–13.00 Sat, Wed; 08.00–11.00 Thurs.
South Yemen	08.00–14.00 Sat–Thurs.
Yugoslavia	07.00–15.00 Mon–Fri.
Windward Islands	08.00–12.00 Mon–Fri, late opening Fri.
Zaïre	07.00–15.00 Mon–Fri.

Zambia	08.00–17.00 Mon–Fri.
Zimbabwe	08.30–17.00 Mon–Fri; 08.30–12.00 Sat.

Note:
These are only the official hours, and generally apply to the capital. There will be considerable variation according to area and the size of the business. Banking hours are, inevitably, shorter.

Shopping Hours

Afghanistan	08.00–18.00 Sat–Thurs. Closed Thurs. afternoon and all day Fri.
Andorra	08.00–20.00. Varied midday closing.
Antigua & Barbuda	08.30–16.00 Mon–Fri; 09.00–12.00 Sat.
Argentina	Generally 09.00–19.00 Mon–Fri.
Australia	Generally 09.00–17.30 Mon–Fri; 09.00–12.00 Sat. Corner stores open later, but all shops close on Sunday. Late night shopping on Thurs or Fri.
Austria	08.00–18.00 with one or two hour breaks at midday Mon–Fri; Sat. 08.00–12.00 noon.
Bahamas	09.00–17.00 Mon–Sat.
Bahrain	08.00–12.00, 15.30–18.30 Sat.–Thurs. Closed Fri.
Bangladesh	10.00–20.00, Mon–Fri; 09.00–14.00 Sat.
Barbados	08.00–16.00 Mon–Fri; 08.00–12.00 Sat.
Belgium	09.00–18.00 daily.
Belize	08.00–12.00, 13.00–16.00 Mon–Fri; 08.00–12.30 Sat.
Benin	08.00–11.30, 14.30–15.30 Mon–Fri.
Bermuda	Generally 09.00–17.00 Mon–Sat.
Bolivia	08.00–12.00, 13.00–18.30 Mon–Sat.
Botswana	08.00–1300, 14.15–17.30 Mon–Fri; 08.00–13.00 Sat.
Brazil	09.00–19.30 Mon–Fri, 08.00–13.00 Sat.
British Virgin Is.	09.00–17.00 Mon–Fri.
Burma	09.30–16.30 Mon–Fri
Burkina Faso	07.30–12.30, 15.00–17.30 Mon–Fri.
Burundi	07.00–12.00, 14.00–17.00 Mon–Fri.
Canada	Open until 17.30/18.00; Thurs and Fri open till 21.00. Small neighbourhood stores open late.
Cayman Islands	09.00–17.00 Mon–Sat.
Central African Rep	08.00–12.00, 16.00–19.00 Mon–Sat.
Chad	07.00/8.00–18.30/19.00, Tues–Sat with long lunch closing.
Chile	09.00–18.00 every day.
China	08.00–12.00, 14.00–18.00 daily.
Colombia	09.00–16.30 Mon–Sat, 2 hour lunch closing.
Congo	08.00–18.30 Tues–Sun, 2 hour lunch closing.
Costa Rica	09.00–18.00 Mon–Sat.
Côte d'Ivoire	08.00–12.00, 14.30–16.30 Mon–Fri. Close 17.30 Sat.
Cuba	12.30–19.30 Mon–Sat.
Cyprus	Usually 08.00/09.00–12.00, 15.00–18.00/19.00 Mon–Sat.

Czechoslovakia	09.00–12.00, 14.00–18.00 or 09.00–18.00. Some major shops open still 20.00 on Thurs; Sat till noon.
Denmark	09.00–17.30 Mon–Thurs; 09.00–19.00/20.00 Fri; 09.00–12.00/13.00/14.00 Sat.
Djibouti	08.00/09.00–12.00, 15.00–20.00 Mon.–Sat.
Dominica	09.00–12.30, 14.00–15.00 Mon–Fri.
Dominican Rep.	08.30–12.00, 14.00–18.00 Mon–Sat.
Eastern Caribbean	08.30–12.00, 13.00–16.00 Mon–Sat. Half day Thurs.
Ecuador	08.30–18.30 Mon–Fri, 2 hour lunch closing.
Egypt	Usually 09.00–20.00 in summer, and 10.00–19.00 in winter.
El Salvador	09.00–12.00, 14.00–1800 Mon–Fri; 08.00–12.00 Sat.
Ethiopia	08.00–20.00 Mon–Fri, 2 or 3 hour lunch closing.
Fiji	08.00–17.00 Mon–Fri; late night Fri.
Finland	08.00–20.00 Mon-Fri; 08.00–18.00 Sat.
France	Food shops: 07.00–18.30/19.30 Mon–Sat. Others: 09.00–18.30/19.30. Many close for all or half day Monday. Some food shops are open on Sunday morning. In small towns many shops close between 12.00 and 14.00 for lunch.
French West Indies	08.00–12.00, 15.00–18.00 Mon–Sat.
Gabon	08.00–18.30 Tues–Sat. Long lunch closing. Closed Mon.
Gambia	08.00–18.00 Mon–Fri, 2 or 3 hour lunch closing; 08.00–12.00 Sat.
East Germany	09.00–17.00 Mon–Fri; 09.00–13.00 Sat.
West Germany	09.00–18.00 Mon.–Fri; 08.00–13.00 Sat.
Ghana	09.00–15.30 Mon–Thurs; 09.00–15.30, 17.00–18.00 Fri, Closed Sat.
Greece	08.00–14.30 Mon, Wed, Sat; 08.00–13.30, 17.00–20.00 Tues, Thurs, Fri.
Guinea	07.30–16.30, 2 hour lunch closing.
Guyana	08.00–16.00 Mon–Fri. Lunchtime closing. Open Sat morning.
Honduras	08.00–18.00 Mon–Fri. Lunchtime closing. Open Sat morning.
Hong Kong	Central District 10.00–18.00. Elsewhere 10.00–21.00. Most shops remain open on Sunday.
Hungary	10.00–18.00 Mon–Fri; open till 20.00 on Thurs; 09.00–12.00 Sat.
Iceland	09.00–18.00 Mon–Thurs; 09.00–22.00 Fri. Open Sat morning.
India	09.00–18.00 Mon.–Sat.
Indonesia	08.00–18.30 Sat.–Wed.; long lunch.
Iraq	09.00–13.00, 16.00–20.00 Sat–Thurs. Everything closes on Friday.
Israel	08.00–13.00, 16.00–19.00 Sunday–Fri (NB Arab shops are closed on Fri and Christian ones on Sunday.)
Italy	08.30/09.00–12.30/13.00, 15.30/16.00–19.30/20.00 Mon–Sat. In Northern Italy the lunchbreak is shorter and shops close earlier.
Jamaica	08.30–16.30, half day closing Wed in Kingston.
Japan	09.00–17.00 or 10.00–18.00 Mon–Fri; 09.00–12.00 Sat. Closed Sun. Some stores also close one other day in the week.
Jordan	08.00–13.00, 16.00–18.00 Sat–Thurs.
Kenya	08.00–18.00 Mon–Sat. A few shops open Sun. 08.00–13.00
Korea	Dept. Stores: 10.30–19.30. Small shops: 08.00–22.00 Mon–Fri with half day on Sat.
Kuwait	08.30–12.30, 16.30–21.00. Some close Thurs evening. Closed Fri.
Lebanon	Hours vary. Open late in winter.
Leeward Islands	08.00–16.00 Mon–Sat. Closed Thurs afternoon.
Liberia	08.00–18.00 Mon–Sat. Closed for lunch.

Libya	Closed Fri.
Luxembourg	08.00–12.00, 14.00–18.00 Tues–Sat. Closed Mon morning. Only the largest supermarkets remain open at lunchtime.
Macao	09.00–22.00 Mon–Sat (Some stores close earlier depending on the location).
Madagascar	08.00–12.00, 14.00–18.00 Mon–Fri.
Malawi	08.00–16.00 Mon–Fri.
Malaysia	09.30–19.00 Daily. Supermarkets and Dept. Stores. open from 10.00–22.00.
Mali	09.00–12.00, 15.00–18.00 Mon–Fri. Open Sat morning.
Malta	08.30–12.00, 16.00–19.00 Mon–Sat.
Mauritius	08.00–19.00 Mon–Sat.
Mexico	09.00–19.00 generally Mon, Tue, Thurs and Fri.
Morocco	08.30–12.00, 14.00–18.30 Mon–Sat.
Nepal	10.00–20.00 Sun–Fri. Closed Sat.
Netherlands Antilles	08.00–12.00, 14.00–18.00 Mon–Sat.
New Zealand	Normally 09.00–17.00 Mon–Fri. One late night per week usually Fri in each town. Food and ice cream shops known as dairies generally open 09.00–19.00 Sat and Sun sometimes too.
Nicaragua	09.00–12.00, 14.00–16.00 Mon–Sat.
Niger	08.00–12.00, 15.00–18.30 Mon–Fri, 08.00–12.00 Sat.
Nigeria	08.30–12.30, 14.00–17.00 Mon–Fri. Usually closed Sat and Sun.
Norway	09.00–17.00 Mon–Sat.
Oman	08.00–13.00 Sat–Thurs.
Pakistan	09.30–13.00 Mon–Thurs; 9.00–10.30 Sat in rural areas; 9.00–11.30 in main cities.
Panama	08.00–18.00 Mon–Sat, long lunch closing.
Paraguay	07.00–11.30, 15.00–18.30 Mon–Fri; 7.00–11.30 Sat.
Peru	Shops 10.00/10.45–19.00/19.50 Mon.–Fri.
Philippines	09.00–12.00, 14.00–19.30 Mon.–Sat Department stores and supermarkets open Sun.
Poland	07.00–19.00 Food Stores; 11.00–19.00 other shops.
Portugal	09.00–13.00, 15.00–19.00 Mon–Fri; 09.00–13.00 Sat.
Qatar	07.30–12.30, 14.30/15.30–18.00 Sun–Thurs.
Réunion	08.00–12.00, 14.00–18.00.
American Samoa	08.30–16.30 Mon–Fri; 8.30–12.00 Sat.
Saudi Arabia	09.00–13.00, 16.00–20.00 Sat.–Thurs
Senegal	08.00–12.00, 14.30–18.00 Dec–May. Longer lunch and open later June–Nov.
Seychelles	08.00–12.00, 13.00–16.00/17.00 Mon–Fri.
Singapore	Shops in the city: 10.00–18.00; Dept Stores: 10.00–22.00. Most shops are open 7 days a week.
South Africa	08.30–17.00 Mon–Fri. 08.30–12.45/13.00 Sat. Most shops are closed on Sun.
Spain	09.00/10.00–12.00/13.30, 15.00–15.30–19.30/20.00. There are general stores in most towns that are open all day from 10.00–20.00.
Sri Lanka	08.30–04.30 Mon–Fri; 8.30–13.00 Sat.
Sudan	08.00–13.00, 17.00–20.00 Sat–Thurs.
Suriname	07.00–13.00, 16.00–18.00 Mon–Sat.
Swaziland	08.00–17.00 Mon–Fri; 08.30–14.00 Sat.
Sweden	09.30–17.30 Mon–Fri; 09.30–14.00 Sat.
Switzerland	08.00–12.00, 14.00–18.00. Close at 16.00 on Sat. Often close all day Mon.

Syria	08.00–13.30, 16.30–21.00 Sat–Thurs.
Tahiti	07.30–11.30, 13.30–17.30 Mon–Fri; 07.30–11.30 Sat.
Tanzania	08.00–12.00, 14.00–17.00 Mon–Sat.
Thailand	Usually open until 19.00 or 20.00. No standard hours.
Togo	08.00–18.00 Mon–Fri, 2 hour lunch closing. Open Sat morning.
Tonga	08.30–12.30, 13.30–16.40 Mon–Fri; 8.30–12.00 Sat. Closed Sun.
Trinidad & Tobago	08.00–16.00 Mon–Fri and Sat morning. Supermarkets closed Thurs afternoon.
Tunisia	08.30–13.00, 15.00–17.00 Mon–Fri; Sat 09.00–14.00.
Turkey	09.00–13.00, 14.00–19.00 Mon–Sat. Small shops may stay open late and not close for the lunch hour.
US Virgin Islands	09.00–17.00 Mon–Sat.
USSR	Food stores: 11.00–20.00. Some big dept stores: 08.00–21.00. Only food stores open on Sundays – till 19.00.
United Arab Emirates	08.00–12.00, 16.00–19.00. Closed Fri.
United Kingdom	09.30–17.30 Mon–Sat; late night Thurs or Fri; half day on Wed or Thurs in small towns.
Uruguay	09.00–12.00, 14.00–19.00 Mon–Fri. Many stores stay open at lunchtime. 09.00–12.30 Sat.
Venezuela	09.00–13.00, 14.00–16.30 Mon–Fri.
Windward Islands	Usually 08.00–12.00 and 12.00–13.00 or 13.30–16.00. Some closing Wed or Thurs afternoon.
Zimbabwe	08.00–17.00 often with an hour for lunch. Closed Sat afternoon and Sunday. Selected pharmacies have day and night services in all main centres.

Worldwide Currencies

Country	Unit	1 Unit = 100 (unless otherwise stated)
Afghanistan	Afghani (AFG)	Puls
Albania	Lek (LEK)	Qindarkës
Algeria	Dinar (ALD)	Centimes
Andorra	Franc/Peseta	Centimes/Centimos
Angola	Kwanza (AKZ)	Lweis
Anguilla	East Caribbean Dollar (ECD)	Cents
Antigua & Barbuda	ECD	Cents
Argentina	Austral (ARA)	Centavos
Aruba	Guilder/Florin	Cents
Australia	Dollar (A$)	Cents
Austria	Schilling (AUS)	Groschen
Bahamas	Dollar ((BMD)	Cents
Bahrain	Dinar (BHD)	1000 Fils
Bangladesh	Taka (BDT)	Poisha
Barbados	Dollar (BDD)	Cents
Belgium	Franc (BFR)	Centimes

Belize	Dollar (BND)	Cents
Benin	CFA Franc (CFA)	-
Bermuda	Dollar (BED)	Cents
Bhutan	Ngultrum/Rupee (INR)	-
Bolivia	Boliviano (BOB)	Centavos
Botswana	Pula (BTP)	Thebe
Brazil	Cruzado (BRZ)	Centavos
British Virgin Is.	US Dollar	Cents
Brunei	Dollar (BRD)	Cents
Bulgaria	Lev (LEV)	Stotinki
Burkina Faso	CFA	-
Burma	Kyat (BUR)	Pyas
Burundi	Franc (FRB)	Centimes
Cameroon	CFA	-
Canada	Dollar (CAD)	Cents
Cape Verde Islands	Escudo (CVE)	Centavos
Cayman Islands	Dollar (CID)	Cents
Central African Rep	CFA	-
Chad	CFA	-
Chile	Peso (CHP)	Centesimos
China	Ren Min Bi (RMB)	Fen
Colombia	Peso (COP)	Centavos
Comoro Islands	CFA	-
Congo	CFA	-
Cook Islands	New Zealand (NZ$)	Cents
Costa Rica	Colon (CRC)	Centimos
Côte d'Ivoire	CFA	-
Cuba	Peso (CUP)	Centavos
Cyprus	Pound (CYL)	1000 Mils
Czechoslovakia	Koruna (CKR)	Halers
Denmark	Krone (DKK)	Ore
Djibouti	Franc (DFR)	-
Dominica	ECD	Cents
Dominican Republic	Peso (DOP)	Centavos
Ecuador	Sucre (SUC)	Centavos
Egypt	Pound (EGL)	Piastres
El Salvador	Colon (SAC)	Centavos
Equatorial Guinea	CFA	-
Ethiopia	Birr (ETB)	Cents
Falkland Islands	Pound	Pence
Fiji	Dollar (FID)	Cents
Finland	Markka (FIM)	Penni
France	Franc (FFR)	Centimes
French Guiana	French Franc	Centimes
French Polynesia	CFP Franc	Centimes
French West Indies	French Franc	Centimes

Gabon	CFA	-
Gambia	Dalasi (GAD)	Butut
East Germany	DDR Mark (MRK)	Pfennig
West Germany	Deutsche Mark (DMK)	Pfennig
Ghana	Cedi (GHC)	Pesewas
Gibraltar	Pound (UK£)	Pence
Greece	Drachma (DRA)	Lepta
Grenada	ECD	Cents
Guatemala	Quetzal (QUE)	Centavos
Guinea	Franc (GNF)	-
Guinea-Bissau	Peso (GWE)	Centavos
Guyana	Dollar (GYD)	Cents
Haiti	Gourde (GOU)	Centimes
Honduras	Lempira (LEM)	Centavos
Hong Kong	Dollar (HKD)	Cents
Hungary	Forint (FOR)	Fillers
Iceland	Krona (IKR)	Aur
India	Rupee (INR)	Paise
Indonesia	Rupiah (RPA)	Sen
Iran	Rial (IRI)	Dinars
Iraq	Dinar (IRD)	1000 Fils
Ireland	Pound (IRL)	Pence
Israel	Shekel (ILS)	100 Agorot
Italy	Lira (LIT)	-
Jamaica	Dollar (JAD)	Cents
Japan	Yen (JYE)	-
Jordan	Dinar (JOD)	1000 Fils
Kampuchea	Riel	Centimes
Kenya	Shilling (KES)	Cents
Kiribati	Aus. Dollar (A$)	Cents
North Korea	Won (WON)	Jon
South Korea	Won (WON)	Chon
Kuwait	Dinar (KUD)	1000 Fils
Laos	Kip (KIP)	Centimes
Lebanon	Pound (LEL)	Piastres
Lesotho	Maloti (LSL)	Leicente
Liberia	Dollar (LID)	Cents
Libya	Dinar (LBD)	1000 Dirham
Liechtenstein	Swiss Franc	Centimes
Luxembourg	Franc (LFR)	Centimes
Macao	Pataca	Avos
Madagascar	Franc (FMG)	Centimes
Malawi	Kwacha (MWK)	Tambala
Malaysia	Ringit (RGT)	Sen
Maldive Islands	Rufiyaa (MVR)	Laari
Mali	CFA	

Malta	Lira (MAL)	1000 Mils
Mauritania	Ouguiya (MOG)	5 Khoums
Mauritius	Rupee (MAR)	Cents
Mexico	Peso (MEP)	Centavos
Micronesia	US Dollar	Cents
Mongolia	Tugrik	Mungs
Montserrat	ECD	Cents
Morocco	Dirham (MDH)	Centimes
Mozambique	Metical (MZM)	Centavos
Nauru	Aus. Dollar (A$)	Cents
Nepal	Rupee (NER)	Pice
Netherlands	Guilder/Florin (DFL)	Cents
Netherlands Antilles	Guilder/Florin (AFL)	Cents
New Caledonia	Pacific Franc (CFP)	Centimes
New Zealand	Dollar (NZD)	Cents
Nicaragua	Cordoba (COR)	Centavos
Niger	CFA	-
Nigeria	Naira (NGN)	Kobos
Niue	NZ Dollar (NZD)	Cents
Norfolk Island	Aus. Dollar (A$)	Cents
Norway	Krone (NOK)	Ore
Oman	Rials (RIO)	1000 Baizas
Pakistan	Rupee (PAR)	Paisa
Panama	Balboa (BAL)	Cents
Papua New Guinea	Kina (NGK)	Toea
Paraguay	Guarani (GUA)	Centimos
Peru	Inti (PEI)	Centavos
Philippines	Peso (PHP)	Centavos
Poland	Zloty (ZLO)	Groszy
Portugal	Escudo (ESP)	Centavos
Puerto Rico & US Virgin Islands	US Dollar (US$)	Cents
Qatar	Ryal (QRI)	Dirhams
Réunion	French Franc	Centimes
Romania	Lei (LEI)	Bani
Rwanda	Franc (FRR)	Centimes
St.Kitts & Nevis	ECD	Cents
St.Lucia	ECD	Cents
St Vincent & the Grenadines	ECD	Cents
American Samoa	US Dollar (US$)	Cents
Western Samoa	Tala (SAT)	Sene
Sao Tomé & Principe	Dobra (STD)	Centavos
Saudi Arabia	Ryal (ARI)	Hallalah
Senegal	CFA	-
Seychelles	Rupee (SER)	Cents
Sierra Leone	Leone (SLE)	Cents
Singapore	Dollar (SID)	Cents

Solomon Islands	Dollar (SBD)	Cents
Somalia	Shilling (SOM)	Cents
South Africa	Rand (SAR)	Cents
Spain	Peseta (PTS)	Centimos
Sri Lanka	Rupee (SLR)	Cents
Sudan	Pound (SUL)	Piastres
Suriname	Guilder/Florin (SFL)	Cents
Swaziland	Lilangeni (SZL)	Cents
Sweden	Krona (SEK)	Ore
Switzerland	Franc (SFR)	Centimes
Syria	Pound (SYL)	Piastres
Taiwan	Dollar (NTD)	Cents
Tanzania	Shilling (TAS)	Cents
Thailand	Baht (BHT)	Satang
Togo	CFA	-
Tonga	Pa'anga (T$)	Seniti
Trinidad & Tobago	Dollar (TTD)	Cents
Tunisia	Dinar (TUD)	1000 Millimes
Turkey	Lira (TUL)	Kurus
Turks & Caicos	US Dollar (US$)	Cents
Tuvalu	Aus. Dollar (A$)	Cents
Uganda	Shilling (UGS)	Cents
USSR	Rouble (ROU)	Kopeks
United Arab Emirates	Dirham (ADH)	Fils
United Kingdom	Pound (UK£)	Pence
USA	Dollar (US$)	Cents
Uruguay	(Peso NUP)	Centimos
Vanuatu	Vatu (VUV)	-
Venezuela	Bolivar (VBO)	Centimos
Vietnam	Dông	-
North Yemen	Riyal (YEM)	Fils
South Yemen	Dinar (DYD)	1000 Fils
Yugoslavia	Dinar (YUD)	-
Zaïre	Zaïre (ZAI)	Makutas
Zambia	Kwacha (ZMK)	Ngwee
Zimbabwe	Dollar (ZWD)	Cents

CFA = Communauté Financière Africaine.

Clothing Sizes

LADIES

Dresses, Coats, Skirts/JR Sizes — *Misses Sizes*

American	7	9	11	13	15	8	10	12	14	16	18
British	9	11	13	15	17	10	12	14	16	18	20
Continental	34	36	38	40	42	38	40	42	44	46	48

Blouses, Sweaters

American	10	12	14	16	18	20
British	32	34	36	38	40	42
Continental	38	40	42	44	46	48

Shoes

American	4½	5	5½	6	6½	7	7½	8	8½	9	9½
British	3	3½	4	4½	5	5½	6	6½	7	7½	8
Continental	35½	36	36½	37	37½	38	38½	39	39½	40	40½

CHILDREN

Clothes

American	3	4	5	6	6X
British	18	20	22	24	26
Continental	98	104	110	116	122

(For older children, sizes usually correspond with their ages.)

Shoes

American	8	9	10	11	12	13	1	2	3
British	7	8	9	10	11	12	13	1	2
Continental	24	25	27	28	29	30	32	33	34

MEN

Suits

American	34	35	36	37	38	39	40	41	42
British	34	35	36	37	38	39	40	41	42
Continental	44	46	48	49½	51	52½	54	55½	57

Shirts

American	14½	15	15½	16	16½	17	17½	18
British	14½	15	15½	16	16½	17	17½	18
Continental	37	38	39	41	42	43	44	45

Worldwide Voltage Guide

In general, all references to 110V apply to the range from 100V to 160V. References to 220V apply to the range from 200V to 260V. Where 110/220V is indicated, voltage varies within country, depending on location.

An adaptor kit may be necessary to provide prongs of various types that will fit into outlets which do not accept plugs from the traveller's own country. A converter is also necessary where the voltage differs from that of the traveller's electrical appliances. Plugging an electrical appliance manufactured to 110V into a 220V outlet without using a converter may destroy the appliance and blow fuses elsewhere in the building.

A special adaptor will probably be necessary for electronic items such as computers. Check with the manufacturer. Plugging straight in could wipe the memory.

Afghanistan	220V	Finland	220V
Algeria	110/220V	France	110/220V
Angola	220V	French Guiana	110/220V
Anguilla	220V	Gabon	220V
Antigua	110/220V	Gambia	220V
Argentina	220V	Germany	110/220V
Aruba	110V	Ghana	220V
Australia	220V	Gibraltar	220V
Austria	220V	Greece	110/220V
Azores	110/220V	Greenland	220V
Bahamas	110/220V	Grenada	220V
Bahrain	220V	Grenadines	220V
Bangladesh	220V	Guadeloupe	110/220V
Barbados	110/220V	Guatemala	110/220V
Belgium	110/220V	Guinea	220V
Belize	110/220V	Guyana	110/220V
Benin	220V	Haiti	110/220V
Bermuda	110/220V	Honduras	110/220V
Bhutan	220V	Hong Kong	220V*
Bolivia	110/220V	Hungary	220V
Bonaire	110/220V	Iceland	220V
Botswana	220V	India	220V¥
Brazil	110/220V¥	Indonesia	110/220V
British Virgin Is	110/220V	Iran	220V
Bulgaria	110/220V	Iraq	220V
Burma	220V	Ireland	220V
Burkina Faso	220V	Isle of Man	220V
Burundi	220V	Israel	220V
Cameroon	110/220V	Italy	110/220V
Canada	110/220V	Jamaica	110/220V
Canary Islands	110/220V	Japan	110V
Cayman Islands	110V	Jordan	220V
Central African Rep	220V	Kampuchea	110/220V
Chad	220V	Kenya	220V
Channel Islands	220V*	South Korea	220V
Chile	220V¥	Kuwait	220V
China	220V	Laos	110/220V
Colombia	110V	Lebanon	110/220V
Costa Rica	110/220V	Lesotho	220V
Côte d'Ivoire	220V	Liberia	110/220V
Cuba	110V	Libya	110/220V
Curaçao	110V	Liechtenstein	220V
Cyprus	220V¥	Luxembourg	110/220V
Czechoslovakia	110/220V	Macao	110/220V
Denmark	220V	Madagascar	220V
Dominica	220V	Madeira	220V¥
Dominican Rep	110/220V	Majorca	110V
Ecuador	110/220V	Malawi	220V
Egypt	110/220V	Malaysia	110/220V
El Salvador	110V	Mali	110/220V
Ethiopia	110/220V	Malta	220V
Fiji	220V	Martinique	110/220V

Mauritania	220V	Singapore	110/220V★
Mexico	110/220V	Somalia	110/220V
Monaco	110/220V	South Africa	220V
Montserrat	220V	Spain	110/220V
Morocco	110/220V	Sri Lanka	220V
Mozambique	220V	Sudan	220V
Nepal	220V	Suriname	110/220V
Netherlands	110/220V	Swaziland	220V
Neth. Antilles	110/220V	Sweden	110/220V¥
Nevis	220V	Switzerland	110/220V
New Caledonia	220V	Syria	110/220V
New Zealand	220V	Tahiti	110/220V
Nicaragua	110/220V	Taiwan	110/220V
Niger	220V	Tanzania	220V
Nigeria	220V★	Togo	110/220V
Norway	220V	Tonga	220V
Oman	220V	Trinidad and Tobago	110/220V
Pakistan	220V	Tunisia	110/220V
Panama	110V	Turkey	110/220V
Papua New Guinea	220V	Turks & Caicos	110V
Paraguay	220V¥	Uganda	220V
Peru	220	Uruguay	220V
Philippines	110/220V	UAE	220V
Portugal	110/220V	United Kingdom	220V★
Portugal	110V	USA	110V
Qatar	220V	USSR	110/220V
Romania	110/220V	US Virgin Islands	110V
Rwanda	220V	Vanuatu	220V
St. Barthélemy	220V	Venezuela	110/220V
St. Eustatius	110/220V	Vietnam	110/220V
St. Kitts	220V	North Yemen	220V
St. Maarten	110/220V	South Yemen	220V
St. Vincent	220V	Yugoslavia	220V
Saudi Arabia	110/220V	Zaïre	220V
Senegal	110V	Zambia	220V
Seychelles	220V	Zimbabwe	220V★
Sierra Leone	220V		

★ Denotes countries in which plugs with 3 square pins are used (in whole or part).
¥ Countries using DC in certain areas.

English language newspapers/magazines published abroad.

(Those countries where English is spoken widely have not, in the main, been included, as information is easy to obtain.)

Argentina
Buenos Aires Herald – weekly
The Review of the River Plate (on financial matter)

Antigua
Nation's Voice – twice a month
Worker's Voice – once a week
Standard – once a week
Outlet – once a week

Bahamas
Nassau Guardian – daily
Nassau Tribune – – daily
Freeport News- daily

Bangladesh
Bangladesh Observer -daily
Bangladesh Times – daily
News Nation – daily
Holiday – weekly
Bangladesh Today – weekly
Tide – weekly

Barbados
The Advocate – News – daily
The Nation – Mon-Fri
Junior Nation – Mon-Fri
The Sunday Sun
The Bajan – monthly

Belize
Sunday Times – 40¢ weekly
Reporter – 40¢ weekly
Amandala – 40¢ weekly
The Voice-40¢ weekly
The Beacon – 40¢ weekly
Disweek – 40¢ weekly
The Tribune – 40¢ weekly

Bermuda
Royal Gazette – 30¢ daily
Mid Ocean News – 40¢ Fri
Bermuda Sun – 45¢ Fri
Numerous magazines.

Botswana
Botswana Daily News – Free
Botswana Guardian -10 *thebe*, Fri

Burma
The Working People's Daily
The Guardian Daily

Cayman Islands
Cayman Compass – $0.25
Horizon magazine – *Free, bi-monthly*
Nor'Wester – $3.00, bi-monthly
Tourist Weekly – Free
Looking – Free, monthly

China
China Daily
China Reconstructs – monthly
China Pictorial – monthly
Peking Review – weekly

Costa Rica
Tico Times – US $40.00 (annual fee), weekly

Czechoslovakia
Czechoslovakia Life – 5 Czech crowns, monthly
Welcome to Czechoslovakia – US$1.20, quarterly

Commonwealth of Dominica
Dominica Chronical – weekly

Fiji
Fiji Times – daily
Fiji Sun – daily

Gambia
Gambia News Bulletin – twice a week
The Senegambia Sun – daily

Guyana
Guyana Chronical – 25¢, daily
Guyana Chronical – 50¢, Sunday issue.

Hong Kong
South China Morning Post – daily inc. Sunday, HK $1.50
Hong Kong Standard – daily incl. Sunday HK $1.50

Hungary
Daily News – 10p
Hungarian Week – 10p

Iceland
News from Iceland – monthly

Iraq
Baghdad Times – daily, 100 fils (20 pence)

Israel
Jerusalem Post – daily

Jamaica
The Daily Gleaner – daily, J$0.60
The Star – daily, J$0.40

Jordan
Jordan Times 100 *fils* daily
Jerusalem Star – 150*fils*, weekly

Kenya
The Standard – Ksh 2, daily
Nation – Ksh 2, daily
Kenya Times – Ksh 2, daily
The Weekly Review – Ksh 7.50

Korea
Korea Herald – 11 pence, daily excl. Mon
Korea Times – 11 pence, daily excl Mon
Korea News Review – weekly

Liberia
The Observer
The New Liberian
The Scope
The Express
The Mirror
The Bong Crier
Afro Media Magazine

Malaysia
New Straits Times
New Sunday Times
Malay Mail
Sunday Mail
The Star
The National Echo
Sarawak Tribune
Sarawak Vanguard
Malaysia Focus
Sabah Times
Daily Express
Sarawak Herald

Malta
The Times – 5¢ daily
Weekend Chronicle – 5¢ weekly

Mexico
The News – daily
(American newspapers from Sanborns)

Nepal
The Rising Nepal – daily
Media Nepal – monthly

Oman
Oman Daily Observer – daily
Times of Oman – weekly
Akhbar Oman – weekly

Paraguay
Guarani News – Gs 250, monthly

Peru
Lima Times

Qatar
Daily Gulf Times – 1 Qatari Riyal
Weekly Gulf Times – 2 Qatari Riyals

Samoa
Samoa News – 40¢ Fridays
News Bulletin – Free, Mon-Fri
Samoa Journal – 40¢, Thursdays

Seychelles
The Nation – R1 (1 Seychelles rupee)

Singapore
Straits Times – 7 days

Sri Lanka
National dailies pubished in English, Sinhala and Tamil languages.

Swaziland
Times of Swaziland – 17 cents, daily
Swazi Observer – 17 cents, daily

Tahiti
Tahiti Sun Press

Tanzania
Daily News

Trinidad and Tobago
Trinidad Guardian – 50¢ TT, daily

Turkey
Daily News – 50TL
Middle East Review – 200 TL, monthly
Outlook – weekly

Turks and Caicos Islands
Turks and Caicos Current – magazine – bi-monthly

United Arab Emirates
Gulf News – daily
Khaleej Times – daily
Emirate News – daily
Gulf Mirror – daily
Gulf Commercial Magazine – weekly
Recorder – weekly

Main American Express Travel Service Offices Worldwide

American Express Services can be used by cardholders as a post restante address (letters and telegrams only – no parcels) and for emergency cheque encashment. American Express Traveller's Cheques can be bought, exchanged or refunded and a Foreign Exchange Service is also available. Lack of space means that this is necessarily a very shortened list, only covering major centres. For a full list, contact your nearest American Express office.

American Samoa
Pago Pago
Samoan Holiday & Travel Centre
Lumana'l Building
Tel: (684) 688 5336/4692/1144

Andorra
Benguela
Agencias E Biagens Expresso Lda
Rua Joao Belo No. 10
Tel: 2755/3061

Lobito
Agencias E Viagens Expresso Lda
Ave. Marechal Carmona 125/27
Tel: 2412

Antigua
St.John's
Antours
BWIA Sunjet House – Long & Thames
Tel: (809) 462 4788/89

Argentina
Buenos Aires
City Service Travel Agency
Florida 890, 4th floor
Tel: 312 8416/9

Cordoba
Simonelli Viages, S.A.
Av Figueroa Alcorta 50
Tel: (051) 26186/46575/20627

Rosario, Santa Fe
Grupo 3 de Turismo, S.R.L.
Cordoba 1147, Local 01-10
Galeria la Favorite
Tel: 245698/46389

Aruba
Oranjestad
S.E.L. Maduro & Sons (Aruba) Inc.
Rockefellerstraat 1
Netherland Antilles
Tel: 23888/26039

Australia
Adelaide
American Express International, Inc
13 Grenfell Street
Tel: (08) 212 7099

Brisbane
American Express International Inc
68 Queen Street
Tel: (07) 229 2022

Cairns
Northern Australian Travel Agency
91 Grafton Street
Tel: (070) 516472

Canberra
American Express International Inc
Centrepoint
City Walk & Petrie Plaza
Tel: (062) 472333

American Express Travel Service
Australian National University
Melville Line
Tel: (062) 493012/2151

Darwin
Travellers World Pty Ltd
18 Knuckley street
Tel: (089) 814699

Hobart
Webster Travel
60 Liverpool Street
Tel: (002) 380 200

Melbourne
American Express International Inc
105 Elizabeth Street
Tel: (03) 602 4666
Wandana Travel
505 St. Kilda Road
Tel: (03) 267 3711

Perth
American Express Travel Service
51 William Street
Tel: (09) 233 1177

Sydney
American Express Travel Service
American Express Tower
388 George Street
Tel: (02) 239 0666
American Express International Inc
60-62 Castlereagh Street
Tel: (02) 233 3571
*There are many other offices in Australia. For a full
list ask at your nearest AMEX office.*

Austria
Innsbruck
American Express Europe Limited
Brixnerstrasse 3
Tyrol
Tel: (5222) 22491/27386

Salzburg
American Express Europe Limited
5 Mozartplatz
Tel: (0662) 842501

Vienna
American Express Europe Limited
Kaerntnerstrasse 21/23
Tel: (222) 51540

Bahamas
Freeport
Mundytours
Kipling Building B
Ground Floor
Tel: (809) 352444/3526641

Nassau
Playtours
Shirley Street
Tel: (809) 3222931/7

Bahrain
Manama
Kanoo Travel Agency
Al Khalifa Road
Tel: 254081

Bangladesh
Dacca
Vantage International Ltd
Hotel Sonargaon
Karwan Bazar
Tel: 326920/315001-9

Barbados
Bridgetown
Barbados International Travel Services
Independence Square
Tel: (809) 4366543

Belgium
Antwerp
American Express International Inc
Frankrijklei 21
Tel: (03) 232 5920

Brussels
American Express International
2 Place Louise
Tel: (02) 512 1740
American Express International Inc
100 Boulevard du Souverain
Tel (02) 660 2990

Belize
Belize City
Belize Global Travel Services Ltd
Albert Street 41
Tel: 7185/7363-4

Bermuda
Hamilton
L.P. Gutteridge Ltd (R)
Harold Hayes Frith Building
Bermudiana Road
Tel: (809) 2955/4545

Bolivia
La Paz
Magri Tourismo Lda
Av 16 de Julio 1490
5th Floor
Tel: 341201/340762/323954

Borneo
Bandar Seri Begawan
Travel Centre (Borneo) Limited
G6 Tek Guan Place
56-60 Jalan Sultan
Tel: 29601/2

Botswana
Gaborone
Manica Freight Services (Botswana) Pty Ltd
Botsaland House
The Mall
Tel: (31) 52021

Brazil
Brasilia, D.F
Kontik-Franstur S.A.
S.C.S. Ed Central S1001/1008
Tel: (061) 244 9636

Recife Pernambuco
Kontik-Franstur S.A.
Rua da Concordia 278
Tel: (081) 224 9636

Rio De Janeiro
Kontik-Franstur S.A.
Avenida Atlantica 2316-A
Copacabana
Tel: (021) 235-1396

Salvador, Bahia
Kontik-Franstur S.A.
Praca da Inglaterra
Tel: (071) 242-0433

Sao Paulo
Kontik-Franstur S.A.
Rua Marconi, 71
2nd Floor
Tel: (011) 259-4211

British Virgin Islands
Roadtown
Travel Plan Ltd/Romney Associates Consultants
Waterfront Plaza
Tel: 4942872

Bulgaria
Sofia
Interbalkan
Grand Hotel Balkan
Lenin Square 1
Tel: 831135

Burma
Rangoon
American Express Liason Office
51 Golden Valley Road
Tel: 31937/75361

Cameroon
Douala
Camvoyages
15 Blvd de la Liberté
Tel: 422544/423188

Canada
Calgary, Alberta
American Express Canada, Inc
510-5th Street S.W.
Tel: (403) 261 5982

Edmonton, Alberta
American Express Canada, Inc
10303 Jasper Avenue
Principal Plaza Mezzanine
Tel: (403) 421 0608

Halifax Nova Scotia
American Express Canada, Inc
7067 Chebucto Road
Tel: (902) 455 9676
Burgess Travel
1505 Barrington St
Tel: (902) 425 6110

Montreal, Quebec
American Express Canada, Inc
17 Edison Street
C.P. 1345, Place Bonaventure
Tel: (514) 866 3852

American Express Canada, Inc
7525 Rue Sherbrooke Est
Tel: (514) 866 3853

Niagara Falls, Ontario
Matthews Travel International Inc
4685 Queen Street
Tel: (416) 354 5649

Ottawa, Ontario
American Express Canada, Inc
Manulife Tower
220 Laurier Ave, West
Tel: (613) 563 0231

Prince George, BC
Seven Seas Travel Ltd
1553 Third Ave
Tel: (604) 564 7000

Saint John, New Brunswick
Waddell-Leore Travel Agency Ltd
86 Germain Street
Tel: (506) 652 3620

St. John's, Newfoundland
Cook's Travel World
327 Freshwater Road
Tel: (709) 753 8111

Toronto, Ontario
American Express Canada, Inc
2 Bloor Street East
4th Floor
Tel: (416) 964 5650

American Express Canada, Inc
44 Bloor Street East
5th Floor
Tel: (416) 963 6060

Vancouver, BC
American Express Canada, Inc
674 Granville Street
Tel: (604) 687 7686

American Express Canada, Inc
10270 Pacific Centre
Tel: (604) 669 2613

Victoria, BC
American Express Canada, Inc
1701 Douglas Street
Tel: (604) 385 8731

Winnipeg, Manitoba
American Express Canada, Inc
Portage Avenue & Memorial
Tel: (204) 786 5671
*There are many other offices in Canada. For a full
list ask at your nearest AMEX office.*

Cape Verde
Mindelo
Anav
Av. Republica
Tel: 2418/2420/2311

Praia
Anav
Tel: 2418/2420/2307

Chile
Santiago
Turismo Cocha
Agustinas 1173
Tel: 698 2164/698 3341

China
Beijing
American Express Company
East Chang An Avenue
Hotel Beijing
Room 1527
Tel: 553849

American Express International Inc
Shop D
Beijing-Toronto Hotel
Jianguo-Menwai St
Tel: 502266 ext. 2244

Barranquilla
Tierra Mar Aires Lda
Carrera 45
Calle 34 Esquinal
Ocal 2
Tel: 317183/410541

Bogotá
Tierra Mar Aires Lda
Calle 92 #15–63
Tel: 573642/682
Tierra Mar Aire Lda
Local 126
Carrera 10 £27-91
Apartado Aereo 5371
Tel: 283 2955

Costa Rica
San José
Tam Travel Agency
Avenidas Central-Primera, 2Fl
Tel: 33 00 44

Curaçao
Willemstad
S.E.L. Maduro & Sons Inc
Hanchi di Snoa
Tel: 599 9 12301/13853/4/5
S.E.L. Maduro & Sons Curaçao
Rijkseenheid Boulevard
Maduro Plaza
Tel: 76988/76164

Cyprus
Larnaca
A.L. Mantovani & Sons Ltd
King Paul Square, 1
Tel: 52024/5

Limassol
A.L. Mantovani & Sons Ltd
130 Spyro Araouza Str
Tel: (51) 62045/6

Nicosia
A.L. Mantovani & Sons Ltd
35-37 Evagoras Avenue
Tel: (21) 43777/9

Czechoslovakia
Prague
Cedok, Foreign Travel Division
NA Prilope 18
Tel: 22 42 51/9

Denmark
Copenhagen
American Express International Inc
Amagertorv 18 (Stroget)
Tel: (01) 122301

Dominican Republic
Santo Domingo
Vimenca Travel Agency
Abraham Lincoln 306
Tel: 532 2219/533 1306

Ecuador
Guayaquil
Ecuadorian Tours CIA Lda
9 de Octobre 1500 y Antepara
Tel: 397111/394984

Quito
Ecuadorian Tours S.A.
Amazonas 330
Tel: 543722/239777

Egypt
Cairo
American Express of Egypt Limited
15 Sharia Kasr 11 Nil
Tel: 750444
Also 6 other offices.

Luxor
American Express of Egypt Limited
Old Winter Palace Hotel
Tel: 82862

El Salvador
San Salvador
El Salvador Travel Service
Centro Comercial La Mascota
Tel: 230177

Fiji Islands
Nadi
The Travel Company Ltd
Nadi International Airport
Tel: 72325

Suva
The Travel Company Ltd
189 Victoria Parade
Tel: 22345

Finland
Helsinki
Travek Travelbureau Ltd
Katajanokan Pohjoisranta 9-13
Tel: (90) 666 1631

Turko
Travek Travelbureau, Ltd
Humalistonkatu 3
Tel: (921) 337111

France

Bordeaux
American Express V F
14 Course Intendance
Tel: (56) 81 70 02

Cannes
American Express Voyages France S.A.
8 Rue des Belges
Tel: (93) 38 15 87

Nice
American Express Voyages France S.A.
11 Promenade des Anglais
Tel: (93) 87 29 82

Orleans
American Express V.F.
12 Place de Martroi
Tel: (1) 45-44-26-00

Paris
Daro – American Express
101 Rue du Bac
Tel: (1) 4544 2600
Also many more other offices.

Gabon

Libreville
Sata Voyages
Im Les Franipaniers
Blvd Bord De La Mer
Tel: 724117/32/64

Port Gentil
Sata Voyages
Carrefour Seed BP 532
Tel: 753550/753660

East Germany

Berlin
Reisebuero Der D.D.R.
'Berlin-Tourist'
5 Alexanderplatz
Tel: 2150

Dresden
Reisebuero Der D.D.R.
'Elbe-Tourist'
3-4 Kreuzstrasse
Tel: 44001

Leipzig
Reisebuero Der D.D.R.
'Messe-Tourist'
Katherinenstrasse
Tel: 79210

West Germany

Berlin (West)
American Express International Inc
Kurfuerstendam 11
Tel: (030) 882 7575

Bonn – Bad Godesberg
American Express
Dsichmannsaue 29
Tel: (0228) 33-20-66

Dusseldorf
American Express International, Inc
Heinrich Heine Alee 14
Tel: (211) 8022

Frankfurt/Main
American Express International Inc
5 Steinweg
Tel: (69) 21051

Hamburg
American Express International Inc
Rathausmarkt 5
Tel: (040) 221141

Hanover
American Express
Georgstrasse 54
Tel: (511) 12027
Munich
American Express International Inc.
Promenadeplatz 6
Im Bayerischen Hof Bavaria
Tel: (89) 21990

Stuttgart
American Express International Inc
Lautenschlagerstrasse 3
Tel: (0711) 20890

Ghana

Accra
Scantravel (Ghana) Limited
High Street
Tel: 63134/64204

Takoradi
Scantravel (Ghana) Ltd
Atlantic Hotel
Tel: 2201/3300/3301/3302

Tema
Scantravel (Ghana) Limited
Meridian Hotel
Tel: 2878/80 ext. 241

Gibraltar

Sterling Travel Ltd
18/20 John Mackintosh Square
Tel: 71787/71788

Greece

Athens
American Express International
2 Hermou Street
Constitution Square
Tel: (01) 324 4975

American Express International
Vassilissis Sophias Avenue
Athens Hilton Hotel
Tel: 722 0201

Corfu
Corfu Tourist Center Ltd
42 Kapodistriou Street
Tel: (0661) 33975/24055-6

Heraklion, Crete
Creta Travel Bureau S.A.
20-22 Epimendiou Str.
Tel: (081) 2438111/1

Mykonos
Delia Shipping-Travel-Tourism
Quay
Tel: (0289) 22222

Rhodes
Georgiadis Tourism & Shipping
Vass Sophias Street No. 41
Tel: (0241) 27300/27493

Santorini
Pelikan Travel
Fira
Tel: (0286) 22940/22220

Grenada West Indies
St Georges
Grenada International Travel Services
Church Street
Tel: (809) 442945

Guadeloupe, French West Indies
Pointe-a-Pitre
Petrelluzzi Travel Agency
2 Rue Henry IV
Tel: 830399/828230

Guam
Agana
The Travel Store
108 Hernan Cortez St
Tel: (472) 1133-4/(477) 3393

Guatemala
Guatemala City
Clark Tours
7 A Ave 6-53 Zona 4
Edif El Triangulo 2nd Fri
Tel: (5022) 310213/16

Guyana
Georgetown
Guyana Stores Limited
19 Water Street
Tel: 68171/66181/688401

Haiti
Port-au-Prince
Agence Citadelle
35 Place Du Marron Inconnu
Tel: 25900

Honduras
La Ceiba
Agencia de Viajes Trans Mundo, S. De R.
San Isidor
8a Calle Entre Ave and Ave Republica
Tel: 422820/422840

Tegucigalpa
Trans Mundo Tours
Edif Palmira- Nivel 1
Front of Htl Honduras Maya
Tel: 320072

Hong Kong
American Express International, Inc
Golden Crown Court
66-70 Nathan Road, Kowloon
Tel: (3) 7210179

American Express International Inc
New World Tower Building
16-18 Queen's Road Central
Tel: (5) 210211

Hungary
Budapest
Ibusz Travel Bureau
Felszabadulas Ter 5
Tel: 184084/185707/184865

Siofok
Ibusz Travel
Petofi Setany 38
Tel: (3684) 11106

Iceland
Reykjavik
Utsyn Travel Agency
17 Austrustraeti
Tel: (1) 26611

India
Bombay
American Express International
Banking Corporation
276 Dr Dadabhai Naoroji Road
Majithia Chambers
Tel: 265615

Calcutta
American Express International Banking Corporation
21 Old Court House Street
Tel: 236281/232133/230225/230551

Madras
Binny Limited
65 Armenian Street
Tel: 29361/26978/21985

New Delhi
American Express International Banking Corporation
Wenger House
Connaught Place
Tel: 344119/322868

American Express International Banking Corporation
World Health Organization
Indraprastha Estate
Ring Road
Tel: 270181/272230

Srinagar, Kashmir
Kai Travels Private Ltd
Tara Bhavan Place-Blvd 2
Tel: 74366/75373/774180

Indonesia
Denpasar, Bali
P.T. Pacto Ltd
Jalan Sanur Beach
Tel: (0361) 8427 8349

Jakarta, Pusat
P.T. Golden Pacto Jaya
Jalan Sukarjo Wiryopranoto 9
Lippo House
Tel: 652706

Yogyakarta
P.T. Pacto Ltd
JL Mangkubumi 5
Tel: (0274) 2740

Ireland
Cork
Casey Travel Ltd
60 South Mall
Tel: (021) 270123/505859

Dublin
American Express Travel Service
116 Grafton Street
Tel: (01) 772874

Limerick
Riordans Travel Ltd
2 Sarsfield Street
Tel: (061) 44666/49441/44226/44234

Waterford
Harvey Travel Ltd
4 Gladstone Street
Tel: (051) 72048-9/73580

Israel
Haifa
Meditrad Ltd
2 Khayat Square
Tel: (04) 642266

Jerusalem
Meditrad Ltd
27 King George Street
Tel: (02) 222211

Tel Aviv
Meditrad Ltd
16 Ben Yehuda Street
Tel: (03) 294654

Italy
Cagliari, Sardinia
Sartourist Travel Office, S.R.L.
Piazza Deffenu 14
Tel: (070) 652971-3/664374

Catania, Sicily
La Duca Viaggi
Via Etna 65
Tel: (095) 316155/316711

Florence
American Express Travel
Via Guicciardini 49/R
Tel: (055) 212219

Genoa
Aviomar S.N.C.
Via Ettore Vernazza 48
Tel: (010) 587753

Milan
American Express Company S.P.A.
Via Brera 3
Tel: (02) 85571

Naples
Ashiba Professional Travel
Piazza Municipio 1
Tel: (081) 322786/322236

Rome
American Express Company S.P.A.
Piazza Di Spagna 38
Tel: (06) 676411

Venice
American Express Company, S.P.A.
1471 San Marco
Tel: (041) 700844
Also Offices in Ancona, Bari, Bolzano, Padua, Palermo, San Remo and Trieste.

Ivory Coast
Abidjan
Socopao Voyages
Avenue Chardy
Immeuble Alpha 2000,01
Tel: 323554

Jamaica
Kingston
Global Travel Service Ltd
40 Union Square,
Cross Roads
Tel: 929 4329

Montego Bay
Global Travel Service Ltd
Corner of 2 Church Street
Sunshine Plaza
Tel: 952 0124

Japan
Okinawa City
Okinawa Tourist Service
241 Aza-Yamazato
Tel: (0989) 331152

Tokyo
American Express International. Inc
Umeda Mitsui Bldg Kita-Ku
5-10 Sonezaki 2-Chrome
Tel: (06) 315-0781
Also 2 other offices.

Jordan
Amman
International Traders
King Hussein Street
Tel: 6661014/5

Aqaba
International Traders
Municipality Square
Tel: 313757

Kenya
Mombasa
Express Mombasa
Nkrumah Road
Tel: (011) 312461

Nairobi
Silver Spear Tours
Consolidated House
Standard Street
Tel: 334722/28

Kuwait
Safat
Al-Kazami Travel Agencies
Fahed Al Salem Street
Tel: 2450655
Al Kazemi Travel Agency Co
Salhiya Commercial Complex
Tel: 2425421/2425440

La Réunion
St. Denis
Bourbon Voyages
14 Rue Rontaunay
Tel: 216818

Lesotho
Maseru
Manica Freight Services Travel
Kingsway
Tel: (0501) 22554

Liberia
Monrovia
Donkor Travel Agency
Chase Manhattan Plaza
Randall Street
Tel: (22) 1104/4209

Liechtenstein
Vaduz
Reisa Travel Agency
Heiligkreuz 19
Tel: (075) 23734

Malagasy Republic
Antananarivo
Madagascar Airtours
Madagascar Hilton Hotel
Tel: 241192

Malawi
Blantyre
Manica Freight Services Travel
Victoria Avenue
Tel: 634533/634575

Lilongwe
Manica Freight Services Travel
Centre House
Capital City
Tel: 733133
Manica Freight Services Travel
Kamuzu Procession Road
Tel: 721895/617

Malaysia
Kuala Lumpur
Mayflower Acme Tours
18 Jalan Segambut Pusat
Tel: (03) 4866739/486023/667011

Kuching
Sarawak Travel Agencies
1st Floor
70 Padaungan Road
Tel: 23708/222289

Penang
Mayflower Acme Tours
Unit 2, 3rd Floor
Green Hall Bldg
8 Green Hall
Tel: (04) 23724/368121

Maldives
Male
Treasure Island Enterprises Ltd
Furana Resort
8 Marine Drive
Tel: 485 532

Malta
Valletta
A & V Von Brockdorff Ltd
14 Zachary Street
Tel: 624312/621167/623825

Martinique
Fort De France
Roger Albert Voyages
7 Rue Victor Hugo
Tel: 71 55 55

Mauritius
Port Louis
M.T.T.B. Ltd
Corner Sir William Newton and Royal Roads
Tel: (08) 2041-4/4841-22

Mexico
Acapulco
American Express
Costera Miguel Aleman 709-1
Tel: 41095/41520/41601

Mexico City D.F.
American Express
Paseo de la Reforma 234
Tel: (905) 533 0830

American Express
Ave Patriotismo 635
Col Ciudad de los Deportes
Tel: 598 7966

Mexico City
American Express
Centro Commercial Perisur
Periferico Sur 4090
Tel: (905) 652 2788/652 2799
There are many other offices in Mexico. For a full list ask at your nearest AMEX office.

Monaco
Monte Carlo
American Express
35 Blvd Princesse Charlotte
Tel: (93) 25 74 45

Morocco
Agadir
Voyages Schwartz S.A.
87 Place du Marche
Municipal
Tel: 90682

Voyages Schwartz S.A.
Immeuble Tigourramine
Avenue Hassan 11
Tel: 24948/24962

Casablanca
Voyages Schwartz S.A.
112 Avenue du Prince
Moulay Abdullah
Tel: 2731-33/2780-54

Marrakesh
Voyages Schwartz S.A.
Immeuble Moutaouskil 1
Rue Mauritania
Tel: 33321

Tangier
Voyages Schwartz S.A.
54 Boulevard Pasteur
Tel: 33459/33471

Namibia
Swakopmund
Woker Freight Services Travel
Standard Bank Building
Moltke Street
Tel: (0641) 4950 5211

Windhoek
Woker Freight Services Travel
145 Kaiser Street
Tel: (061) 37946

Nepal
Kathmandu
Yeti Travels Pvt Ltd
Hotel Mayalu Jamal Tole
Tel: 13596

Netherlands
Amsterdam
American Express International Inc
Damrak 66
Tel: (020) 262042

American Express
Van Baerlestraat 38
Tel (020) 738550

Rotterdam
American Express International
92 Meent
Tel: (010) 330300

The Hague
American Express International, Inc
Venestraat 20
Tel: (070) 469515

New Caledonia
Noumea
Centre Voyages
27bis Ave du Maréchal Foch
Tel: 284040/285737

New Zealand
Auckland
American Express International Inc
95 Queen Street
Tel: (09) 798243

Christchurch
Guthreys Travel Centre
126 Cashel Street
Tel: (03) 793560

Rotorua
ATA Travel
Cnr Tutanekai & Eruera Streets
Tel: (071) 89 062

Wellington
Century 21 Travel
276 Lambton Quay
Tel: (04) 731 221

Nigeria
Lagos
Mandilas Travel Ltd
96/102 Broad Street
Tel: (01) 666339/663159/663291

Norway
Bergen
Winge Travel Bureau of Scandinavia Ltd
Chr Michelsengt 1-3
Tel: (05) 321080

Oslo
Winge Travel Bureau of Scandinavia
Karl Johans Gate 33
Oslo 1
Tel: (02) 429150

Stavanger
Winge Travel Bureau of Scandinavia Ltd
Ostervay 20
Tel: (04) 530065

Tromso
Winge Travel Bureau of Scandinavia Ltd
Frederick Langes GT 19/21
Tel: (083) 85035

Trondheim
Winge Travel Bureau of Scandinavia
Olav Tryggvassons GT30
Tel: (07) 533000

Oman
Mina-Al-Fahal
Zubair Travel & Service Bureau
BBME Building
Tel: 677739

Muscat
Zubair Travel & Service Bureau
Muscat Intercontinental Hotel
Airport Highway, Qurum
Tel: 601224

Muscat-Ruwi
Zubair Travel & Service Bureau
Bank of Oman, Bahrain & Kuwait Bldg
Mazin Bin Ghadooba St
Tel: 701287/8

Salalah
Zubair Travel & Service Bureaau
Salalah Dhofar
Tel: 461145/462855

Pakistan
Islamabad
American Express International Banking Corporation
Elahi Chambers, I&T Centre
Tel: 29422/528865

Karachi
American Express
International Banking Corporation
Shaheen Commercial Complex
Dr Ziahddin Ahmed Rd
Tel: 520261/265

American Express International Banking
Corporation
1121 RAFE Mansion
Sharhrah-E-Quaid-E-Azam
Tel: 312435/68378-79

Rawalpindi
American Express International Banking Corporation

Ground Floor, Rahim Plaza
Muree Road
Tel: 65766-65/65128

Panama
Panama
Ave. Samuel Lewis
Banco Union Bldg – 12 Floor
Tel: 636005

Papua New Guinea
Port Moresby
Coral Sea Travel Services
P.N.G.B.C. Building
Musgrave & Douglas Streets
Tel: (21) 4422

Paraguay
Asuncion
Inter-Express S.R.L.
Yegros 690
Inter-Express Building
Tel: (90) 111115

Peru
Cuzco
Lima Tours S.A.
Av. Sol Nte 567
Tel: (51084) 228431
Lima
Lima Tours S.A.
Belen 1040
Tel: (95114) 2667/6624

Philippines
Angeles City
American Express International Inc
710 Friendship Highway
Riverside Subdivision
Tel: (055) 5391/4053

Manila
American Express International Inc
Ground Floor, Philamlife Bldg
Ave Ermita
Tel: (05) 509601/599386

Subic Bay
American Express International Inc
Philgam Cultural Centre
U.S. Naval Base
Tel: (460) 8848-448/8848-957

Poland
Gdansk
Orbis
22 Heweliusza Street
Tel: 322081

Krakow
Orbis
Al. Puszkina 1
Tel: (094) 224746/224632

Warsaw
Orbis Travel
Marszalkowska 142
Tel: (022) 267501

Portugal
Estoril
Star Travel Service

Avenida de Nice 4
Tel: (01) 2680839/2692906/2681945

Faro
Star Travel Service
Rua Conselheiro Bivar 36
Tel: (89) 251 125/6

Funchal, Madeira
Star Travel Service
Avenida Arriaga 23
Tel: 32001

Lisbon
Star Travel Service
Avenida Sidonjo Pais 4-A
Tel: (01) 539872/539841-50

Star Travel Service
Praca dos Restauradores 14
Tel: (01) 362501/323336

Praia Da Vitoria, Azores
Star Travel Service
Rua Serpa Pinto 74
Tercira
Tel: 52623/52166

Puerto Rico
Mayaguez
Agencias Soler Inc
8 W. Mendez Vigo Street
Tel: (809) 834 3300

San Juan
Agencias Soler Inc
1035 Ashford Ave
Condado Area
Tel: (809) 725 0950

Qatar
Doha
Darwish Travel Bureau
Clock Tower Square
Tel: 418666

Qatar Tours
Volkswagon Building
Tel: 423465/423453

Rumania
Bucharest
National Tourist Office
Carpati
Boulevard Maghero Nr 7
Tel: 1455 160

Saudi Arabia
Al Khobar
Kanoo Travel Agency
King Khalid Street
Tel: 864 0039/1647/1992

Dammam
Kanoo Travel Agency
King Faisal Street
Tel: (83) 22499/23789/23084/39793

Dhahran
International Travel Agency
Dharan International Hotel
Tel: 891 8555 ext. 420/422/434

Jeddah
Ace Travel
Palestine Street
Alhambra Area N17 W8
Tel: 6605120

Riyadh
Ace Travel
Green Glove Building
Olaya Main Road
Central Prov
Tel: 4648810

Senegal
Dakar
Socopao Voyages
51 Avenue Albert Sarraut
Tel: 22416/222576/212023/222279

Seychelles
Victoria
Travel Services (Seychelles) Ltd
Victoria House
State House Ave
Tel: 22414

Sierra Leone
Freetown
A. Yazbeck & Sons Agencies
22 Siaka Stevens Street
Tel: 22374/24423/220263/26368

Singapore
American Express Travel Service
UOL Building
96 Somerset Road
Tel: 235 8133

American Express International Inc
01-06 Lucky Plaza
Orchard Road 304
Tel: 235 8133

South Africa
Cape Town
American Express/Nedtravel
Union Castle Bldg
1st Floor
55 St. Georges Street
Tel: (021) 215586

Durban
American Express/Nedtravel
1st Floor
Westgard House
Cnr West/Garner Streets
Tel: (031) 301 5541

Johannesburg
American Express/Nedtravel
Merbrook House
123 Commissioner St
Tel: (011) 285100

Pretoria
American Express/Nedtravel
Shops 22/23 Kodoe Arcade
Pretorius Street
Tel: (012) 269182

Spain
Barcelona
American Express Company of Spain
Paseo de Gracia 101
Chaflan Rosello
Tel: (93) 217 0070

Grenada
Viajes Bonal S.A.
Avda de la Constitucion 10
Tel: (958) 267312/6

Ibiza
Viajes Iberia S.A.
Calle Aragon 70
Tel: (971) 302014/300650

Lanzarote
Viajes C.Y.R.A.S.A.
Centro Atlantico
Local NR 60A
Carretera de las Playas
Puerto
Tel: (928) 825851/2

Las Palmas, Gran Canaria
Viajes C.Y.R.A.S.A.
Triana 114
Tel: (928) 364100/300

Madrid
American Express Company of Spain
2 Plaza de Las Cortes
Tel: (01) 429 5775

Mahon, Menorca
Viajes Iberia S.A.
Carrer Nou 35
Tel: (971) 363900

Malaga
Viages Alhambra
Especerias 10
Tel: (952) 222299/219090

Palma De Mallorca
Viajes Iberia S.A.
Paseo Borne 14
Tel: (971) 726743

Puerto de la Cruz, Tenerife
Viajes Iberia S.A.
Avenida Generalismo Franco S/N
Tel: (922) 381350/54

Seville
Viajes Alhambra
Tenient Coronel Sugui 6
Seville 1
Andalucia
Tel: (954) 224435/212923/228331
There are many other offices in Spain. For further details, contact your nearest Amex office.

Sri Lanka
Colombo
Mackinnan Travels Ltd
Mackinnon Bldg
York Street
4 Leyden Bastian Rd
Tel: 22641/29563/29881

St. Lucia
Castries
Carib Travel Agency
5 Jeremie Street
Tel: (809) 452 1529

St. Maarten
Philipsburg
S.E.L. Maduro & Sons, (W.I)Inc
Emmaplein Building One
Tel: 340 7810

St. Vincent
Kingstown
Caribbean International Travel Service
Granby Street
Tel: (809) 4571841

Sudan
Khartoum
Contomichalos Travel & Tourism
Al Barlman Street
Tel: 70929/70601

Suriname
Paramaribo
Travelbureau C Kersten & Co N.V.
Hotel Krasnapolsky
Domineestraat 39
Tel: 74448/77148

Swaziland
Manzini
Manica Freight Services Travel
1V Emocozini Bldg
Ngwant St
Tel: 52237/52872

Mbabane
Manica Freight Services Travel
Allister Miller St
Tel: 42298/42101

Sweden
Goteborg
Fallenius/American Express
Kyrkogatan 56
Tel: (031) 178230

Stockholm
Fallenius/American Express
Birger Jarlsgatan 1
Tel: (8) 235330

Fallenius/American Express
Birger Jarlsgatan 1
Tel: (8) 235330

Fallenius/American Express
Karlavagen 66
Tel: (8) 234545

Switzerland
Basle
Reisbuero Kuendig AG
Aeschengraben 10
Tel: (061) 236690

Berne
American Express International, Inc
Cubenbergplatz 11
Tel: (031) 229401

Geneva
American Express International Inc
13 Chemin Louis-Dunant
Tel: (022) 332550

American Express International Inc
7 Rue Du Mont Blanc
Tel: (022) 317600

Zurich
American Express International Inc,
Bahnhofstrasse 2
Tel: (01) 211 8370

American Express International Inc
Kreuzstrasse 26
Tel: (01) 251 7051

Syria
Damascus
Chami Travel
Rue Fardous
Mouradi Building
Tel: 111652/119553

Tahiti
Papeete
Tahiti Tours
Rue Jeanne D'Arc
Tel: 27870

Thailand
Bangkok
Sea Tours Company Ltd
965 Rama 1 Road
Siam Center
Room 414
Tel: 251 4862/9

Togo
Lomé
Société Togolaise Maritime et Portuaire (STMP)
2 Rue de Commerce
Tel: 6190

Trinidad and Tobago
Port-of-Spain
Hub Travel Ltd
24/28 Richmond Street
Tel: (809) 625 1636/4266

Tunisia
Tunis
Cathage Tours
59 Avenue Bourguiba
Tel: 254 304/325/605/908/391

Turkey
Ankara
Turk Expres
Sehit Adem Yavuz Sokak 14/4
Kizilay
Tel: 90410/252182/180288

Antalya
Pamfilya Travel Agency
30 Augustos Caddesi
No. 57B & C
Tel: (311) 11698/12745/21988

Istanbul
Turk Ikspres Travel
Cumhuriyet Caddesi 91, Kat 6
Elmadag
Tel: (011) 141 0274/5

Turk Ekspres
Istanbul Hilton Hotel
Beyofly
Tel: (011) 140 5640/148 3721

Izmir
Egetur Travel Agency
Nato Arkasi
Talapasa Bulvari 2B
Tel: (051) 217925-7/217921

United Arab Emirates (U.A.E.)
Abu Dhabi
Al Masaood Travel & Services
Al Nasr Street
Tel: 212100

Dubai
Kanoo Travel Agency
Khalid Bin Walid Street
Tel: (4) 434614/421100

Sharjah
Kanoo Travel Agency
Ai Ourooba Street
Tel: (960) 356058

United Kingdom
Aberdeen
American Express Travel Service
4/5 Union Terrace
Tel: (0224) 641050

Belfast
Hamilton Travel
23/31 Waring Street
Tel: (0232) 230321

Birmingham
American Express Travel Service
17/19 Martineau Square
Tel: (021) 233 2141

Douglas, Isle of Man
Palace Travel
Palace Buildings
Central Promenade
Tel: (0624) 73721

Edinburgh
American Express Europe Ltd
139 Princes Street
Tel: (031) 225-7881

Glasgow
American Express Travel Service
115 Hope Street
Tel: (041) 221 4366

Liverpool
American Express Travel Service
54 Lord Street
Tel: (051) 708 9202

London
American Express Travel Service
6 Haymarket
Tel: 01-930 4411

American Express British Travel Centre
4-12 Regent Street
Tel: 01-839 2682

American Express Travel Service
78 Brompton Road

Knightsbridge, SW7
Tel: 01-584 6182

Manchester
American Express Travel Service
1 Cross Street
Tel: 061-833 0121

Newcastle-upon-Tyne
Travelwise
117 Newgate Street
Tel: (0632) 323898

Oxford
Keith Bailey Travel
99 St. Aldgates
Tel: (0865) 790099

St. Brelade, Jersey
Marshalls Travel
1 Quennavais Precinct
Tel: (0534) 41278/45955

Swansea, West Glamorgan
American Express Travel Service
1-5 Belle Vue Way
Tel: (0792) 50321/41631
*There are many other offices in the UK. For a full
list contact your nearest Amex office.*

United States of America
Birmingham, Alabama
Brownell Tours/Brownell Travel
1001 South 22nd Street
Brownell Building
Tel: (205) 323 8981

Anchorage, Alaska
Travel Centre Inc
333 West 4th Street
Tel: (907) 266 6300

Fairbanks, Alaska
Travel Centre Inc
400 Cushman Street
Tel: (907) 542 3611

Phoenix, Arizona
American Express Travel Agency
3003 North Central Avenue
Tel: (602) 264 0673

Tuscon, Arizona
Century Travel
4505 E Broadway
Tel: (602) 795 8400

Los Angeles, California
American Express Travel Agency
The Westin Bonaventure Hotel
404 South Figueroa
Tel: (213) 627 4800

American Express Travel Agency
Beverly Centre
131 N La Cienega Blvd #706
Tel: (213) 659 1682

San Francisco, California
American Express Travel Agency
295 California Street
Tel: (415) 788 4367

American Express Travel Agency
237 Post Street
Tel: (415) 981 5533

Denver, Colorado
American Express Travel Agency
Anaconda Towers
555 17th Street
Tel: (303) 298 7100

American Express/Lakewood Travel Agency
274 Union Blvd, Suite 100
Tel: (303) 986 2221

Stamford, Connecticut
American Express Travel Agency
Landmark Tower Building
101 Broad Street
1 Landmark Sq
Tel: (203) 359 4244

Washington DC
American Express Travel Agency
1919 F Street NT
Tel (202) 289 8800

American Express Travel Agency
1150 Connecticut Avenue NW
Tel: (202) 457 1300

Miami, Florida
American Express Travel Agency
12231 South Dixie Highway
Tel (305) 251 7454

American Express Travel Agency
1351 Biscayne Boulevard
Tel: (305) 358 7350

Tampa, Florida
American Express Travel Agency
One Tampa City Centre
Tel: (813) 273 0310

Atlanta, Georgia
American Express Travel Agency
Colony Square
1175 Peachtree Street N.E.
Tel: (404) 892 8175

Honolulu, Hawaii
American Express Travel Agency
Discovery Bay Shopping Centre
1778A La Moana Blvd
Tel: (808) 946 7741

Maui, Hawaii
American Express Travel Related Services, Inc
Hyatt Regency Maui
200 Nohea Kai Drive
Lahaina
Tel: (808) 667 7451

Chicago, Illinois
American Express Travel Agency
625 North Michigan Avenue
Tel: (312) 435 2570

American Express Travel Agency
Marshall Field & Co
111 North State Street
Tel: (312) 781 4477

New Orleans, Louisiana
American Express Travel Agency
150 Baronne Street
Tel: (504) 586 8201

American Express Travel Agency
The Plaza in Lake Forest
5700 Read Boulevard
Tel: (504) 241 8912

Detroit, Michigan
American Express Travel Agency
200 Renaissance Centre
Suite 127
Renaissance Fashion Circle
Tel: (313) 259 5030

Las Vegas, Nevada
Cole Travel Service Inc
Caeser's Palace
3570 Las Vegas Boulevard S
Tel: (702) 733 9700

New York City
American Express Travel Agency

American Express Plaza Lobby
Tel: (212) 797 3900
American Express Travel Agency
B Altman & Company
361 Fifth Avenue at 34th St
Tel: (212) 683 5367

Philadelphia
American Express Travel Agency
615 Chestnut Street
Independence Mall Area
Tel: (215) 592 9211

American Express Travel Agency
Two Penn Centre Plaza
S.E. Cor, 16th & JFK Boulevard
Tel: (215) 587 2300

Memphis, Tennessee
A&I Travel Service, Inc
606 South Menderhall
Suite 201
Tel: (901) 682 1595

Nashville, Tennessee
American Express Travel Agency
St. Cloud Corner
500 Church Street
Tel:(615) 256 0745

Dallas, Texas
American Express Travel Agency
Bloomingdales
Valley View Mall
13320 Montfort Drive
Tel: (214) 960 1999

Houston, Texas
American Express Travel Agency
30 Greenpoint Mall
Tel: (713) 658 1114

Salt Lake City, Utah
American Express Travel Agency
175 South West Temple
Tel: (801) 328 9733

Seattle, Washington
American Express Travel Agency
Plaza 600 Building
600 Stewart Street
Tel: (206) 682 8622
There are many other AMEX offices across the U.S.A. For a full list, contact your nearest office.

Uruguay
Montevideo
Turisport Limitada
Mercedes 942
Tel: 914823/906300/900474

USSR
Moscow
American Express Company
21-A Sadovo-Kudringskaya Street
Tel: (95) 254 4495/4305/4505/2111

Venezuela
Caracas
Turismo Consolidado Turisol C.A.
CCCT Nivel C2
Local 53F-07 Chuaoh
Tel: 927922

Maracaibo
Turismo Consolidade Turisol CA
Au 4 Res La Guajira
Locales 2 & 3
Tel: 79501/70611

Virgin Islands (U.S.)
Christiansted, St. Croix
Southerland Tours
Kings Alley
Tel: (809) 773 0340

St. Thomas
Tropic Tours
International Plaza
Tel: (809) 774 1855/(800) 524 4334

Western Samoa
Apia
Retzlaffs Tours & Travel
Beach Road
Tel: 21724/5

Yemen Arab Republic
Sana'a
Marib Travel and Tourism
Ali Abdul-Mughni Street
Tel: (9627) 71741/74213/78082

Yugoslavia
Belgrade
Atlas Yugoslav Travel Agency
Mose Pijade 11
Tel: (011) 341471/332522

Sarajevo
Atlas Yugoslav Travel Agency
Ulica HNA 81
Tel: (071) 532 521

Zagreb
Atlas Yugoslav Travel Agency
Zrinjevac 17
Tel: (041) 441003/440654

Zambia
Lusaka
Eagle Travel Limited
Findeco House
Cairo Road
Tel: 214916/214735

Ndola
Eagle Travel
Tel: 216857/217540

Zimbabwe
Bulawayo
Manica Freight Services Travel
Federal Centre
10th Avenue
Tel: (19) 62521

Harare
Manica Freight Services Travel
Wetherby House
Baker Avenue
Tel: 703421/708441

Insurance

Automobile Association
Fanum House
Leicester Square
London W1
Tel: 01-954 7373/7511
Has a reasonably priced scheme to cover overland travel abroad. Will also provide carnets and Green Cards.

Assist-Card
745 Fifth Avenue
New York
NY 10022
Tel: (212) 752 2788
Outside New York 1-800-221-4564

An organization to help with travel crises such as loss of passport, illness, theft. legal trouble. Cardholders may telephone the office (collect) from 28 European countries and both North and South American countries. A multilingual staff is on call 24 hours a day. 5 days – $30.00, 10 days – $50.00, 16 days – $60.00, 22 days – $70.00, 30 days – $80.00, 45 days – $100.00, 60 days $120.00, 90 days – $180.00.

Baggot Evans & Co Ltd
99 Church Road
London SE19 2PR
Tel: 01-771 9691/761 1335
Can arrange insurance on motor vehicles of most types in the UK throughout the whole of Europe including

the USSR. Other countries in Near Middle and Far East as well as Africa are available by special arrangement for which a full itinerary should be sent. They can obtain cover for sea transits of vehicles to countries other than those mentioned and for goods and equipment to all ports of the world. They also offer personal accident, sickness and baggage insurance.

Campbell Irvine Ltd
48 Earls Court Road
Kensington
London W8 6EJ
Tel: 01-937 6981
Specialize in unusual insurance and can offer travellers insurance against medical expenses, repatriation, personal accident, cancellation and curtailment and personal liability, also baggage and money cover subject to certain restrictions. Vehicle insurance can be arranged and usually takes the form of Third Party insurance (for countries where British insurers have adequate representation), accidental damage, fire and theft insurance (worldwide, including sea transit risks) Carnet Indemnity insurance is available in order that travellers can obtain carnet de passages documents from the Automobile Association. Will also do quotations for expeditions.

Centre de Documentation et d'Information de l'Assurance
2 Rue de la Chassée d'Antin
75009 Paris
France
Tel: 4247 9000
Will give advice to travellers on insurance problems.

R.L.Davison & Co Ltd
Lloyd's Insurance Brokers
5 Stone House
London EC3A 7AX
Tel: 01-377 9876
Offer Carnet Indemnity insurance for travellers in Asia and elsewhere.

Kemper Group
Long Grove
IL 60049
USA
Offer a 12 month travel accident policy which gives the same cover and at the same premium as the insurance offered at airport terminals for only 21 days cover. The policy, which must be ordered a week in advance, covers approved charter flights.

Medisure
Frizzell Insurance and Financial Services Ltd.

Frizzell House
County Gates
Poole BH13 6BH
Tel: (0202) 292 333
Medisure is a medical insurance scheme which pays for National Health Service emergency hospital treatment for overseas visitors not covered by reciprocal agreements. Premium payment can be made at any Post Office in the United Kingdom and application forms are available from Post Offices at Heathrow, Birmingham, Wolverhampton and Leicester and from Frizzell's in Poole. Medisure provides medical insurance for up to £50,000 per person with cover available for a maximum period of six months. No age restrictions and the cost is £9.00 for 31 days plus £7.00 for each additional month. Advice is obtainable 24 hours a day on an emergency telephone line.

Midland Bank Insurance Services
Midland Bank PLC
Head Office
Poultry
London EC2P 2BX
Tel: (01) 606 9911 Ext 3215
Telex: 8811822
Offered – up to £1,000 cancellation, unlimited medical expenses, up to £500 hospital benefit, personal accident (death £5,000, other capital benefit £15,000), up to £1,000 on baggage, £300 on money, personal liability up to £500,000, a 24 hour advisory service for emergencies and free cover for children under 2 years of age. Also certain optional extensions.

Pinon Assureur
8 Rue de Liège
75009 Paris
France
Tel: 4878 0298/9530
Is one of the rare insurance companies that will insure cameras and photographic equipment. Premiums amount to about 3 per cent of the value of the items insured and the firm will insure for a minimum premium of 650 Francs.

WEXAS International
45 Brompton Road
London SW3 1DE
Tel: 01-589 3315/0500
Tlx: 297155 WEXAS G
Offers members a comprehensive range of travel insurance packages at extremely competitive prices. Year round insurance as well as the short-term.

Getting in Touch With Home

A Country by Country Guide

Afghanistan
Air mail post to UK: About 7 days.
Telegrams: May be sent from Central Post Office,

Kabul (closes 21.00 hours.)
Telex: Public terminal at PTT Office, Jad Ibn Sina (next to Kabul Hotel).

Telephoning the UK: International operator service, reasonably efficient; shortage of lines may cause delay.

Algeria

Air mail post to UK: 3-4 days.
Telegrams: May be sent from any post office (8.00-19.00). Main post office in Algiers at 5 Blvd Mohamed Khemisti offers 24 hour service.
Telex: At main post office, Algiers; also public facilities at Aurassi and Aletti Hotels.
Telephoning the UK: At main post office, Algiers; also public facilities at Aurassi and Aletti Hotels.
Telephoning the UK: IDD to UK, also international operator service 24 hours, but subject to delays.

Andorra

Air mail post to UK: 4-5 days.
Telegrams: Services available throughout.
Telex: Services available throughout.
Telephoning the UK: Normal code dial system.

Antigua

Air mail post to UK: 3-4 days.
Telegrams: May be sent from Cable & Wireless, High Street, St.Johns or from your hotel.
Telex: From Cable & Wireless, St. Johns.
Telephoning the UK: IDD or through hotel operator, or via Cable & Wireless.

Argentina

Air mail post to UK: About 7 days.
Telegrams: May be sent from General Post Office (Correo Central), corner of Samrieto and L N Alem.
Telex: ENTEL (state-owned telephone and telegraph company) has two booths in Buenos Aires; also from General Post Office.
Telephoning the UK: IDD; also 24 hour international operator service.

Australia

Air mail post to UK: About 7 days.
Telegrams: May be sent from local Post Offices and by telephone.
Telex: Telecom operates Public Telex Bureaux at all capital city Chief Telegraph Offices and at the following Telecom country offices: Canberra, Newcastle, Dubbo, Wollongong, Ballarat, Townsville, Rickhampton, Mt Gambier, Darwin, Alice Springs, Launceston.
Telephoning the UK: IDD; also operator-connected calls.

Austria

Air mail post to UK: 3-5 days
Telegrams: From Post Offices Mon-Fri 0800-1200, 1400-1800. Sat 0800-1000 in selected offices.) Main and station post offices in larger cities open round the clock including Saturdays, Sundays and public holidays).
Telex: From Post Offices.
Telephoning the UK: IDD, from Post Offices or international call boxes.

Bahamas

Air mail post to UK: 3-5 days.
Telegrams: May be sent through BATELCO offices in Nassau and Freeport.
Telex: through BATELCO
Telephoning the UK: IDD and International operator service.

Bahrain

Air mail post to UK: 3-4 days.
Telegrams: Ordinary, letter telegrams may be sent 24 hours a day from Cable & Wireless, Mercury House, Al-Khalifa Road, Manama.
Telex: Public call offices at Cable & Wireless open 24 hours.
Telephoning the UK: IDD

Bangladesh

Airmail Post to UK: 3-4 days.
Telegrams: From telegraph and post offices; major hotels.
Telex Links with almost every country in the world. Hotel Intercontinental in Dacca has a public telex service. Telex facilities also available from Chittagong, Khulna.
Telephoning the UK: IDD

Barbados

Air mail post to UK: 4-7 days.
Telegrams: via Cable & Wireless (WI) Ltd, Wildey, St. Michael.
Telex: via Cable & Wireless
Telephoning the UK: IDD

Belgium

Air mail post to UK: 3-4 days.
Telegrams: In main towns, telegraph offices (usually found in the stations or close at hand) are open day and night.
Telex: Extensive facilities available throughout.
Telephoning the UK: IDD

Belize

Air mail post to the UK: 4-8 days.
Telegrams: Via Cable and Wireless, Belize City, BTA National Telephone System.
Telex: International Telex services available via Cable & Wireless and BTA National Telephone System.
Telephoning the UK: IDD and international operator service.

Bermuda

Air mail post to the UK: 5-7 days.
Telegrams: From all post offices.
Telex: Via Cable & Wireless.
Telephoning the UK: IDD.

Bolivia

Air mail post to the UK: About 4 days.
Telegrams: From West Coast of America Telegraph Co Ltd, main office at Edificio Electra, Calle Mercado 1150, La Paz and Sheraton Libertador, Crillon, El Dorado, Gloria. Ordinary, urgent and letter telegrams.
Telex: Public telex facilities also available at West Coast of America Telegraph offices.
Telephoning the UK: IDD and international operator service.

Botswana

Air mail post to the UK: 7 days.
Telegrams: May be sent via post office.
Telex: Via post offices.
Telephoning the UK: IDD and international operator service.

Brazil

Air mail post to the UK: 4-6 days.
Telegrams: From EMBRATEL (Empresa Brasileira de Telecomunicacoes SA) offices in Rio de Janeiro and Sao Paulo.
Telex: International Telex facilities available at EMBRATEL offices.
Telephoning the UK: IDD.

Burkina Faso

Air mail post to UK: 5-6 days.
Telegrams: Address them to La Poste Centrale.
Telephoning the UK: IDD or international operator service.

Burma

Air mail post to UK: Slow, 7-10 days; air letter forms quicker and more reliable than normal air letters.
Telegrams: From Posts and Telecommunications Corporation, 125 Phayres Street, Rangoon.
Telex: Telex facilities in Tourist Burma office and hotels in Rangoon.
Telephoning the UK: IDD and international operator service.

Burundi

Air mail post to UK: 3-4 days.
Telegrams: From any post office.
Telex: Available from post offices.
Telephoning the UK: Operator only. Often difficult with delays.

Cameroon

Air mail post to UK: 7 days.
Telegrams: Telegraph office does not operate at night, and messages are apt to be delayed.
Telex: Facilities are available from the main telegraph office in Yaoundé and also larger hotels in Youndé and Douala.
Telephoning the UK: IDD and international operator service.

Canada

Air mail post to UK: 4-8 days.
Telegrams: Cannot be sent through the post offices in Canada. Telegrams or 'Telepost' messages should be phoned or deliverd to CN/CP Telecommunications – address and telephone number can be found in the local telephone directory. In Newfoundland and Labrador telegrams are sent through Terra Nova Tel.
Telex: Telex facilities easily located in all major Canadian cities.
Telephoning the UK: IDD

Cayman Islands

Air mail post to UK: About 5 days.
Telegrams: Public Telegraph operates daily from 07.30-18.00 hours Cayman time. Telecommunications are provided by Cable and Wireless (West Indies) Ltd.

Telex: Available at Cable & Wireless office; many hotels and apartments have their own telex.
Telephoning the UK: IDD.

Chile

Air mail post to UK: 3-4 days.
Telegrams: From Transradio Chilena at Bandera 168, Santiago, and at Esmerelda 932, Valparaiso; ordinary and letter telegrams.
Telex: Facilities at Transradio Chilena, Bandera 168, and at ITT Communicaciones Mundiales SA, Agustinas 1054, Santiago.
Telephoning the UK: IDD and international operator service.

China

Air mail post to UK: 4-6 days.
Telegrams: From Administration of Telecommunications at 11 Sichanganjian Street, Beijing, and at Nanking Road East 30, Shanghai, or any telegraph office. Ordinary, urgent or letter telegrams.
Telex: Telex facilities available at Administration of Telecommunications offices.
Telephoning the UK: IDD and international operator service.

Colombia

Air mail post to UK: 5 days.
Telegrams: From any chief telegraph office in main towns. Ordinary and urgent telegrams.
Telex: International telex facilities available at hotels Tequendama and Hilton, Bogotá, at Telecom (Empresa Nacional de Telecomunicaciones) offices and chief telegraph offices in main towns.
Telephoning the UK: IDD and operator service.

Costa Rica

Air mail post to UK: 6-8 days.
Telegrams: Facilities available at all main post offices.
Telex: Telex for tourists not available.
Telephoning the UK: IDD.

Côte d'Ivoire

Air mail post to UK: About 10 days.
Telegrams: May be sent from the post offices.
Telex: Facilities in the post offices.
Telephoning the UK: IDD and international operator service.

Cyprus

Air mail post to UK: 3 days.
Telegrams: From any telegraphic office, including Electra House, Museum Street, Nicosia. 24 hour service. Ordinary and urgent telegrams.
Telex: No public telex offices, but larger hotels have telex facilities.
Telephoning the UK: IDD.

Czechoslovakia

Air mail post to UK: About 7 days.
Telegrams: Facilities available at all main post offices.
Telex: Telex for tourists not available.
Telephoning the UK: IDD.

Denmark

Air mail post to UK: About 3 days.

Telegrams: May be sent from main post offices.
Telex: Facilities available from your hotel or main post offices in major towns.
Telephoning the UK: IDD.

Djibouti

Air mail post to UK: About 7 days.
Telegrams: May be sent from main post offices.
Telex: Available from any post office.
Telephoning the UK: IDD. International telephone calls (by satellite) are possible 24 hrs a day.

Dominica

Air mail post to UK: About 7 days.
Telegrams: Available from All America Cables and Radio ITT, Julio Verne 21, Santo Domingo; RCA Global Communications, El Conde 203, Santo Domingo.
Telex: Facilities available from All America Cables and Radio ITT and RCA Global Communications.
Telephoning the UK: IDD and international operator service.

Eastern Caribbean States

Air mail post to UK: About 7 days.
Telegrams: Services available from General Post Office in capital.
Telex: General post office.
Telephoning the UK: IDD and international operator service.

Ecuador

Air mail post to UK: 6-7 days.
Telegrams: From chief telegraphic office in main towns. In Quito, 24 hour service. Also from Hotel Quito and Hotel Colón up to 20.00 hours. Ordinary and urgent telegrams.
Telex: Public booths at Hotels Quito, Colón and Humboldt, Quito; Hotel Humboldt, Continental, Grand Hotel, Palace, Guayaquil; also at IETEL (Instituto Ecuatoriano de Telecomunicaciones) offices.
Telephoning the UK: IDD and international operator service; sometimes long delays in securing connection.

Egypt

Air mail post to UK: Minimum 2 days.
Telegrams: From telegraph offices. Ordinary telegrams.
Telex: Public telex facilities at major hotels for guests only; other telex services in Cairo at: 19 El Alfi Street (24 hours); 26 July Street, Zamalek; 85 Abdel Khalek Sarwat Street, Attaba; El Tazaran Street, Nasr City; Transit Hall, Cairo Airport.
Telephoning the UK: IDD. International operator calls should be booked in advance.

El Salvador

Air mail post to UK: 7-10 days.
Telephoning the UK: IDD.

Ethiopia

Air mail post to UK: 4 days.
Telegrams: From Telecommunications Authority, Adoua Square, Addis Ababa, and telegraphic offices. Ordinary, urgent and letter telegrams.

Telex: Facilities available at Telecommunications Board, Churchill Road, Addis Ababa, and at Heroes Square, Asmara.
Telephoning the UK: IDD. Link available from Addis 15.00–20.00 East African Time.

Fiji

Air mail post to UK: 5 days.
Telegrams: Overseas telegrams accepted at all telegraph offices. Ordinary and deferred (LT) telegrams.
Telex: International telex facilities available at Fiji International Telecommunications Ltd (FINTEL), Victoria Parade, Suva, or at major hotels.
Telephoning the UK: IDD and international operator service.

Finland

Air mail post to UK: About 7 days.
Telegrams: Can be left with the nearest post office or hotel desk.
Telex: Facilities available at Post Offices.
Telephoning the UK: IDD.

France

Air mail post to UK: 2 days.
Telegrams: Facilities available throughout.
Telex: Extensive facilities available.
Telephoning the UK: IDD.

Gambia

Air mail post to UK: 3 days.
Telegrams: From Cable & Wireless, Mercury House, Telegraph Road, Banjul. Ordinary telegrams.
Telex: Public telex booth at the GPO, Russell Street, Banjul, and at Cable & Wireless, Banjul.
Telephoning the UK: IDD and 24 hour international operator service.

East Germany

Air mail post to UK: About 3 days.
Telegrams: May be sent from post offices.
Telex: From post offices in main centres.
Telephoning the UK: IDD.

West Germany

Air mail post to UK: 5 days.
Telegrams: May be sent from post offices.
Telex: From main post offices and hotels.
Telephoning the UK: IDD.

Ghana

Air mail post to UK: 5 days.
Telegrams: From External Telecommunications Service of Posts and Telecommunications Corporation, Extelcom House, High St, Accra, and Stewart Avenue, Kumasi. Ordinary, urgent and letter telegrams.
Telex: Public call facilities at External Telecommunication Service offices.
Telephoning the UK: IDD. Operator connected calls may be made 08.15-18.15 hours, weekdays only. Often difficult and delays sometimes of 2-3 days.

Gibraltar

Air mail post to UK: 2-6 days.
Telegrams: Via Cable & Wireless in Gibraltar.
Telex: Via Cable & Wireless.

Telephoning the UK: Automatic almost every-where in the world.

Greece
Air mail post to UK: 4-5 days.
Telegrams: May be sent from OYE (Telecom-munications Centre).
Telex: Facilities available from OTE.
Telephoning the UK: IDD.

Guyana
Air mail post to UK: 7-10 days.
Telegrams: Can be sent 24 hours a day from Bank of Guyana Bldg, Avenue of the Republic and Church Street, Georgetown. Ordinary and night letter telegrams.
Telex: Public call offices at the Bank of Guyana Building.
Telephoning the UK: IDD and international oper-ator service at all times.

Hong Kong
Air mail post to UK: 3-5 days.
Telegrams: From telegraphic offices. Ordinary, letter and social telegrams.
Telex: Public telex facilities available at Mercury House, 3 Connaught Road, Central, Hong Kong Island, and at Ocean Terminal, Kowloon and from Kai Tak Airport.
Telephoning the UK: IDD and 24 hour inter-national operator service.

Hungary
Air mail post to UK: About 4 days.
Telegrams: May be sent from hotel desks.
Telephoning the UK: IDD.

Iceland
Air mail post to UK: All items automatically sent by air – 7-10 days.
Telegrams: From Chief Telegraphic Office, Reyk-javik.
Telex: There are no public telex facilities.
Telephoning the UK: IDD and international oper-ator services 24 hours a day.

India
Air mail post to UK: 6-7 days.
Telegrams: From any telegraphic office. Express, letter and urgent.
Telex: International telex facilities available 24 hours a day at large hotels, and at telegraph/telex offices in major cities.
Telephoning the UK: IDD and international oper-ator service.

Indonesia
Air mail post to UK: 7-10 days.
Telegrams: From any telegraphic office. In Jak-arta, facilities available 24 hrs a day.
Telex: Public telex facilities operated from Direc-torate General for Posts and Communications, Medan Merdeka Selatan 12 (24 hours); also in some major hotels; and at the chief telegraphic offices in Semarang; Jogjakarta, Surabaya and Denpasar.
Telephoning the UK: IDD and international oper-ator service 24 hours, seven days a week.

Iran
Air mail post to UK: 4-5 days.
Telegrams: Must be despatched from Chief Tele-graph Ofice, Meidane Sepah, Tehran, which is open all night. Ordinary, letter and urgent tele-grams.
Telex: Public facilities at Chief Telegraph Office and some some hotels.
Telephoning the UK: IDD and international oper-ator service.

Iraq
Air mail post to UK: 5-10 days.
Telegrams: Telegraph office attatched to central post office in Rashid Street, Baghdad, also at Bas-rah, Kerkuk and Musul.
Telex: Facilities available at the PTT in Rashid Street, Baghdad, and at a number of hotels.
Telephoning the UK: IDD

Israel
Air mail post to UK: 4-7 days.
Telegrams: From telegraphic offices. Ordinary.
Telex: Facilities available to guests in most de luxe hotels in Jerusalem and Tel Aviv. Public telex booths at 23 Rehov Yafo, Jerusalem; 7 Rehov Mikve Yisrael, Tel Aviv.
Telephoning the UK: IDD 19.00-07.00 weekdays; 15.00-07.00 Sunday at cheaper rate.

Jamaica
Air mail post to UK: About 10-14 days.
Telegrams: Telegram service available from any post office (inland).
Telex: Telex service available from Jamaica Inter-national Telecommunication Ltd, Jamintel Cen-tre, 15 North Street, Kingston.
Telephoning the UK: IDD

Japan
Air mail post to UK: 4-6 days.
Telegrams: May be sent from the main hotels, from offices of Kokusai Denshin Denwa Co Ltd and from Nippon Denshin Denwa Kosha and from larger post offices in major cities. Ordinary, letter and express telegrams.
Telex: Telex booths are available at main post offices and main offices of Kokusai Denshin Denwa Co Ltd and Nippon Denshin Denwa Kosha.
Telephoning the UK: IDD

Jordan
Air mail post to UK: About 5 days.
Telegrams: Overseas service reasonably good. May be sent from the Central Telegraph Office; Post Office, 1st Circle, Jebel Amman; or any post office.
Telex: Public telex facilities are available at the Central Telegraph Office and in a number of hotels.
Telephoning the UK: IDD.

Kenya
Air mail post to UK: 3-4 days.
Telegrams: Overseas telegrams can be sent from all post and telegraphic offices. Nairobi GPO open 24 hrs. Ordinary, letter and urgent tele-grams.
Telex: Facilities available at Nairobi GPO. New

Stanley and Hilton Hotels have facilities for their guests, otherwise no public call booths.
Telephoning: IDD and operator service.

Korea
Air mail post to UK: 7–10 days.
Telegrams: May be sent by dialling 115 and velivering message in English or by visiting a telegraph office of the Korea International Telecommunications Office (KIT) near Capitol Building and delivering message in written English.
Telex: Telex facilities available in main hotels; also from the Post Office in Seoul and office of Korea International Telecommunications Services.
Telephoning the UK: IDD.

Kuwait
Air mail post to UK: 5 days.
Telegrams: Telegrams sent from Chief Telegraph Office 6 hours after being handed in at the Post Office.
Telex: Facilities available at main hotels or from main Post Office (24 hours).
Telephoning the UK: IDD.

Liberia
Air mail to UK: 3–7 days.
Telegrams: Facilities provided by the Liberian Telecommunications Corporation and French Cables, Monrovia.
Telex: Services provided by the Liberian Telecommunications Corporation.
Telephoning the UK: IDD

Luxembourg
Air mail to UK: About 3 days.
Telegrams: Telegram facilities available at the Main Post Office in Luxembourg City; Bureau de Postes, 8a Avenue Monterey (open 0700–20.45 Mon–Sat); Luxembourg Railways Station Main Post Office, 9 Place de la Gare (open 24 hours, 7 days a week).
Telex: Facilities available from post offices named above. Also Luxembourg Airports Post Office, inside main airport terminal, 1st floor.
Telephoning the UK: IDD

Macao
Air mail post to UK: About 3 days.
Telegrams: May be sent from hotels and from General Post Office in Leal Senado Square.
Telex: Facilities from the General Post Office.
Telephoning the UK: Most hotels have direct dial telephones but otherwise through operators or from the General Post Office.

Malaysia
Air mail post to UK: 4–7 days.
Telegrams: May be sent by phone 24 hours a day by dialling 104, or at any Telegraph office and most post offices. Ordinary, urgent letter and greetings telegrams.
Telex: Public facilities available 24 hours at Telegraph Office, Djalan Raja Chulan, Kuala Lumpur, and most hotels.
Telephoning the UK: IDD

Malta
Air mail post to UK: 3 days.
Telegrams: From TELEMALTA offices and most hotels.
Telex: Facilities from TELEMALTA and most hotels.
Telephoning the UK: IDD.

Mexico
Air mail post to UK: About 7 days.
Telegrams: Telegraphic system maintained by Telegrafos Nacionales, and telegrams to be handed in to their offices. In Mexico City the main office for international telegrams is at Balderas y Colón, Mexico 1 DF.
Telex: International telex facilities available at a numner of locations in Mexico City; hotels reluctant to despatch messages for guests but willing to receive them.
Telephoning the UK: IDD or through operator.

Morocco
Air mail post to UK: At least 5 days.
Telegrams: From all telegraph offices. Ordinary and urgent telegrams.
Telex: International telex facilities available at Hotels Hilton and Tour Hassan, Rabat; Hotels El Manour and Marhaba, Casablanca.
Telephoning the UK: IDD. Calls may be made at any time, but delays might be experienced.

Nepal
Air mail post to UK: 4–10 days.
Telegrams: Telecommunication Office, Tripureshwor, Kathmandu.
Telex: International telex facilities available at large hotels and Telecommunication Office, Kathmandu.
Telephoning the UK: IDD from Kathmandu. International operator service 24 hrs a day.

New Zealand
Air mail post to UK: About 7 days.
Telegrams: From all post offices 09.00–17.00 hours, and telephoned through at any time. Ordinary, letter and urgent telegrams.
Telex: All major hotels, banks, Government offices and some commercial practices have telex facilities.
Telephoning the UK: IDD.

Niger
Air mail post to UK: Varies.
Telegrams: From Chief Telegraph Office, Niamey, and at all other telegraph offices. Ordinary, urgent, and letter telegrams.
Telex: Public facilities available at Chief Telegraph Office, Niamey.
Telephoning the UK: IDD. Good quality, direct telephone line to Paris from Niamey, which links with UK. Service available 08.30, 12.30, 15.30

and 18.00 hours daily in Niamey. Calls should be made by asking exchange for L'Inter Radio.

Oman

Air mail post to UK: 4 days.
Telegrams: May be sent from post offices.
Telex: Facilities available from post offices.
Telephoning the UK: IDD.

Pakistan

Air mail post to UK: 4 days.
Telegrams: Post offices, telegraph offices and hotels. The Central Telegraph Office, 1.1 Chundrigar Road, Karachi, provides 24 hours service.
Telex: The Central Telegraph Office provides telex facilities 24 hrs.
Telephoning the UK: IDD. International operator service.

Paraguay

Air mail post to UK: 7–10 days.
Telegrams: May be sent from post offices, banks, and hotels.
Telex: Facilities available from post offices, banks and hotels.
Telephoning the UK: IDD or via operator.

Peru

Air mail post to UK: About 10 days.
Telegrams: From ENTEL PERU telegraph offices. Ordinary and night telegrams.
Telex: Telex machines with international connections installed at Hotels Bolivar, Crillon and Sheraton in Lima.
Telephoning the UK: IDD or international operator service at all times.

Philippines

Air mail post to UK: 10 days, often more.
Telegrams: From Eastern Telecommunications Philippines Inc. offices. Ordinary and urgent telegrams.
Telex: Public telex booths operated by Eastern Telecommunications Philippines Inc, Globe Mackay Cable and Radio Corporation, and RCA Communications Inc.
Telephoning the UK: IDD or international operator service 24 hrs a day.

Portugal

Air mail post to UK: About 3 days.
Telegrams: Facilities available from all post offices.
Telex: From post offices.
Telephoning the UK: IDD.

Qatar

Air mail post to UK: About 4 days.
Telegrams: For telegraph service dial 130.
Telex: Facilities available from Qatar National Telephone Service (QNTS).
Telephoning the UK: IDD.

Samoa

Air mail post to UK: About 10 days (US mail system).
Telegrams: Available from post office.
Telex: Facilities at post office.
Telephoning the UK: IDD.

Senegal

Air mail post to UK: About 7 days.
Telegrams: Available at most major post offices.
Telex: Via Cable & Wireless.
Telephoning the UK: IDD.

Sierra Leone

Air mail post to UK: 5 days.
Telegrams: From Mercury House, 7 Wallace Johnson Street, Freetown. Ordinary, urgent and letter telegrams.
Telex: Facilities available at Mercury House.
Telephoning the UK: IDD or international operator calls between 11.00 and midnight local time any day of the week.

Singapore

Air mail post to UK: Usually 5 days, but can take 10–14.
Telegrams: From telegraph offices. Ordinary, urgent, letter and social telegrams.
Telex: Public telex facilities available at Central Telegraph Office, 35 Robinson Road.
Telephoning the UK: IDD; operator service 24 hours.

South Africa

Air mail post to UK: 3–7 days.
Telegrams: Telegraph service available in every town, however small.
Telex: Public call facilities available in Cape Town, Durban, Johannesburg and Pretoria post offices. Most hotels and offices have telex.
Telephoning the UK: IDD available from all centres.

Spain

Air mail post to UK: 4–5 days.
Telegrams: May be sent from main post offices.
Telex: Facilities from main post offices.
Telephoning the UK: IDD.

Sri Lanka

Air mail post to UK: 4–7 days.
Telegrams: From all post offices. Ordinary, letter and urgent telegrams.
Telex: Public telex booth at OTS Building, Duke Street, Colombo.
Telephoning the UK: IDD and international operator service 24 hours.

Swaziland

Air mail post to UK: About 6 days.
Telegrams: May be sent from most post offices.
Telex: Facilities from most post offices.
Telephoning the UK: IDD or through exchange no. 90.

Sweden
Air mail post to UK: About 6 days.
Telegrams: Telephone the telegrams in by dialling 0021 or send by post.
Telex: Public Telexes not available.
Telephoning the UK: IDD.

Switzerland
Air mail post to UK: 2–4 days.
Telegrams: May be sent from post offices and hotels.
Telex: Some hotels have telex facilities.
Telephoning the UK: IDD.

Tahiti
Telegrams: Facilities can be found at the Office des Postes et Telecommunications, Boulevard Pomare, Papeete.
Telex: Services from the Office des Postes et Telecommunications.
Telephoning the UK: IDD or dial 19 for international operator service.

Tanzania
Air mail post to UK: About 7 days.
Telegrams: From post office, Ordinary, urgent, letter and greetings telegrams.
Telex: Public telex at post office in Mkwepu Street, Dar Es Salaam, and in some hotels.
Telephoning the UK: IDD or international operator service 24 hrs.

Thailand
Air mail post to UK: 5 days.
Telegrams: From GPO Building, New Road, Bangkok, or any telegraph office. Ordinary, urgent, letter telegrams.
Telex: Public call office facilities at the GPO, New Road, Bangkok.
Telephoning the UK: IDD or international operator service, by contacting Long Distance Telephone Office behind GPO in New Road (tel: 32054 or 37056).

Tonga
Telegrams: Via Cable & Wireless, Salote Rd. Tel: 21–499.
Telex: Via Cable & Wireless. Private booths available.
Telephoning the UK: IDD or dial 913 for International Operator.

Trinidad and Tobago
Air mail post to UK: About 6 days.
Telegrams: Via Trinidad and Tobago External Telecommunications Company Ltd (TEXTEL) located at 1 Edward Street, Port of Spain, Trinidad.
Telex: TEXTEL provide a telex agency service for the receipt of telex messages on behalf of customers who do not have their own installations.
Telephoning the UK: IDD.

Tunisia
Air mail post to UK: About 5 days.
Telegrams: From Central Post Office in Rue Charles de Gaulle, Tunis (24 hrs), and other telegraph offices.
Telephoning: IDD and international operator service 24 hrs a day.

Turkey
Air mail post to UK: 3 days.
Telegrams: From telegraph and post offices. Ordinary and urgent telegrams.
Telex: Public call office at main post office, Ulus, Ankara and at main post office, Telegraf Gisesi, Sirkeci, Istanbul (24 hrs).
Telephoning the UK: IDD or international operator service.

Turks and Caicos Islands
Air mail to UK: 5–10 days.
Telegrams: Via Cable & Wireless.
Telex: Via Cable & Wireless.
Telephoning the UK: IDD or through operator.

United Arab Emirates
Air mail post to UK: 5 days.
Telegrams: Phone and send telegrams from Emirtel offices in each town. Emirtel is the Federal telephone company.
Telephoning the UK: IDD.

USSR
Air mail post to UK: Over 10 days.
Telegrams: Usually reach UK within a few hours. May be sent from hotels. Ordinary, urgent and letter telegrams.
Telex: Telex installed in offices of Commercial Dept of British Embassy, (Kutozovsky Prospekt 7/4).
Telephoning the UK: IDD or international calls booked through the hotel service bureau or by visiting Central Post Office, 7 Gorky Street. Operator service. Be prepared to give STD code number.

USA
Air mail post to UK: 5–6 days but varies. More from West Coast.
Telegrams: From all post and telegraph offices. Full and night letter telegrams.
Telex: Western Union international telex facilities throughout the USA.
Telephoning the UK: IDD.

Uruguay
Air mail post to UK: About 7 days.
Telegrams: Public booths in main banking and commercial offices.
Telex: Facilities in main banking and commercial offices.
Telephoning the UK: IDD or via the operator.

Venezuela
Air mail post to UK: 3–7 days.
Telegrams: Usual telegram services from public telegraph offices, ordinary, and night letter telegrams.

Telex: Public telex facilities provided by CANTV.
Telephoning the UK: IDD.

British Virgin Islands
Air mail post to UK: 5–10 days.
Telegrams: Via Cable & Wireless.
Tele: Via Cable & Wireless.
Telephoning the UK: IDD or through operator.

Virgin Islands
Air mail post to UK: About 6 days.
Telegrams: Extensive facilities available.
Telex: Full facilities available.
Telephoning the UK: IDD or through operator.

North Yemen
Air mail post to UK: 3-4 days.
Telegrams: From any telegraph office. Ordinary, urgent and letter telegrams.
Telex: Telex booths at Cable & Wireless offices in Sana'a, Hodeida and Taiz.
Telephoning the UK: IDD or operator service.
Telephone link available 08.00–20.30 local time.

Yugoslavia
Air mail post to UK: 4–5 days.
Telegrams: Facilities at post offices.
Telex: Via post offices.
Telephoning the UK: IDD.

Zaïre
Air mail post to UK: 4–10 days.
Telegrams: From Chief Telegraph Offices. Ordinary and urgent telegrams.
Telex: Facilities only available at Kinshasa and Lubumbashi Chief Telegraph Offices; also at Intercontinental Hotel.
Telephoning the UK: IDD or international operator service.

Zambia
Air mail post to UK: 5–7 days.
Telegrams: From telegraph offices. Urgent will be accepted at Lusaka Central Telegraph Offices up to 21.00 hrs Mon–Sat.
Telex: Public telex facilities at Lusaka GPO; also main hotels.
Telephoning the UK: IDD or international operator service.

Zimbabwe
Air mail post to UK: About 5 days.
Telegrams: Facilities found in all major cities and tourist centres.
Telex: From all major cities and tourist centres.
Telephoning the UK: IDD or operator service.

Note
Although most countries now have some form of IDD connection, this is often only operative in major centres and even this can involve lengthy delays in some cases. Be warned.

International Direct Dialling

(Reproduced by courtesy of British Telecom)

Countries in alphabetical order to which international direct dialling is available. Country codes are the same from anywhere in the world.

Country	Country Code	Time Difference (based on GMT)
Algeria	213	(+1)
Andorra	33 628	(+1)
Angola	244	(+1)
Anguilla	1 809 497	(−4)
Antigua	1 809 46	(−4)
Argentina	54	(−3)
Aruba	297 8	(−4)
Ascension	247	GMT
Australia	61	(+8–10)
Austria	43	(+1)
Azores	351	(−1)
Bahamas	1 809	(−5)
Bahrain	973	(+3)
Bangladesh	880	(+6)
Barbados	1 809	(−4)
Belgium	32	(+1)
Belize	501	(−6)
Benin	229	(+1)
Bermuda	1 809 29	(−4)
Bolivia	591	(−4)
Botswana	267	(+2)
Brazil	55	(−2–5)
British Virgin Islands	1 809 49	(−4)
Brunei	673	(+8)

Bulgaria	359	(+2)	Hungary	36	(+1)
Burkina Faso	226	(GMT)	Iceland	354	GMT
Burma	95	(+6½)	India	91	(+5½)
Cameroon	237	(+1)	Indonesia	62	(+7–9)
Canada	1	(–3½–9)	Iran	98	(+3½)
Cayman Islands	1 809 94	(–5)	Iraq	964	(+3)
Chile	56	(–4)	Ireland	353	GMT
China	86	(+8)	Israel	972	(+2)
Colombia	57	(–5)	Italy	39	(+1)
Congo	242	(+1)	Jamaica	1 809	(–5)
Cook Islands	682	(–10)	Japan	81	(+9)
Costa Rica	506	(–6)	Jordan	962	(+2)
Côte d'Ivoire	225	GMT	Kenya	254	(+3)
Cuba	53	(–5)	South Korea	82	(+9)
Cyprus	357	(+2)	Kuwait	965	(+3)
Czechoslovakia	42	(+1)	Lebanon	961	(+2)
Denmark	45	(+1)	Lesotho	266	(+2)
Djibouti	253	(+3)	Liberia	231	GMT
Dominica	1 809 449	(–4)	Libya	218	(+1)
Dominican Rep	1 809	(–5)	Liechtenstein	41 75	(+1)
Ecuador	593	(–5)	Luxembourg	352	(+1)
Egypt	20	(+2)	Macao	853	(+8)
El Salvador	503	(–6)	Madagascar	261	(+3)
Ethiopia	251	(+3)	Madeira	351 91	GMT
Faroe Islands	298	GMT	Malawi	265	(+2)
Fiji	679	(+12)	Malaysia	60	(+8)
Finland	358	(+2)	Maldives	960	(+5)
France	33	(+1)	Malta	356	(+1)
French Guiana	594	(–4)	Martinique	596	(–4)
French Polynesia	689	(–10)	Mauritius	230	(+4)
Gabon	241	(+1)	Mexico	52	(–6–8)
Gambia	220	GMT	Monaco	33 93	(+1)
East Germany	37	(+1)	Montserrat	1 809 491	(–4)
West Germany	49	(+1)	Morocco	212	GMT
Ghana	233	GMT	Mozambique	258	(+2)
Gibraltar	350	(+1)	Namibia	264	(+2)
Greece	30	(+2)	Nauru	674	(+13)
Greenland	299	(–3)	Nepal	977	(+5½)
Grenada	1 809 440	(–4)	Netherlands	31	(+1)
Guadeloupe	590	(–4)	Neth. Antilles	599	(–4)
Guam	671	(+10)	New Caledonia	687	(+11)
Guatemala	502	(–6)	New Zealand	64	(+12)
Guyana	592	(–3)	Nicaragua	505	(–6)
Haiti	509	(–5)	Niger	227	(+1)
Honduras	504	(–6)	Nigeria	234	(+1)
Hong Kong	852	(+8)	Norfolk Island	672 3	(+11½)

Norway	47	(+1)	Spain	34	(+1)	
Oman	968	(+4)	Sri Lanka	94	(+5½)	
Pakistan	92	(+5)	Sudan	249	(+2)	
Panama	507	(−5)	Suriname	597	(−3)	
Papua New Guinea	675	(+10)	Swaziland	268	(+2)	
Paraguay	595	(−3)	Sweden	46	(+1)	
Peru	595	(−3)	Switzerland	41	(+1)	
Philippines	63	(+8)	Syria	963	(+2)	
Poland	48	(+1)	Taiwan	886	(+8)	
Portugal	351	GMT	Tanzania	255	(+3)	
Puerto Rico	1 809	(−4)	Thailand	66	(+7)	
Qatar	974	(+3)	Togo	228	GMT	
Réunion	262	(+4)	Tonga	676	(+13)	
Romania	40	(+2)	Trinidad & Tobago	1 809	(−4)	
St Kitts & Nevis	1 809 465	(−4)	Tunisia	216	(+1)	
St Lucia	1 809 45	(−4)	Turkey	90	(+2)	
St Pierre & Miquelon	508	(−3)	Turks and Caicos	1 809 946	(−5)	
St Vincent & Grenadines	1 809 45	(−4)	Uganda	256	(+3)	
			UAE	971	(+4)	
Saipan	684	(−11)	Uruguay	598	(−3)	
American Samoa	684	(−11)	USA	1	(−5–11)	
Western Samoa	685	(−11)	USSR	7	(+3–12)	
San Marino	39 541	(+1)	Vanuatu	678	(+11)	
Saudi Arabia	966	(+3)	Vatican City	39 66982	(+1)	
Senegal	221	GMT	Venezuela	58	(−5)	
Seychelles	248	(+4)	US Virgin Islands	1 809	(−4)	
Sierra Leone	232	GMT	North Yemen	967	(+3)	
Singapore	65	(+8)	Yugoslavia	38	(+1)	
Solomon Islands	677	(−11)	Zaïre	243	(+½)	
Somalia	252	(+3)	Zambia	260	(+2)	
South Africa	27	(+2)	Zimbabwe	263	(+2)	

International Access Code
The International Access Code, to be dialled before the country code varies from country to country. Contact the local operator for the relevant number. UK International Access Code – 010.
Charge Bands, Standard and Cheap Rates
These vary worldwide due to time differences. For further information on charge bands dialling from UK contact British Telecom for their booklet *International Telephone Guide*. IDD cheap rate, available to most countries from the UK, is from 8pm to 8am Monday to Friday, all day Saturday and Sunday. For charge bands and standard rates elsewhere contact the local operator.
Note: New countries are constantly being added to the international network. If you would prefer to dial direct and the number is not listed here, ask the operator for an update.

Climate

Climate

Worldwide Weather Guide

The information given below details temperature and humidity at important cities throughout the world.

Temperature – Average daily maximum and minimum temperatures are shade temperatures. Maximum temperatures usually occur in early afternoon, and minimum temperatures just before sunrise.
Humidity – Measured as a daily figure at one or more fixed hours daily. It is normally lowest in the early afternoon and highest just before sunrise. High humidity combined with high temperatures increases discomfort.
Precipitation – Includes all forms of moisture falling on the earth, mainly rain and snow. Average monthly.

		J	F	M	A	M	J	J	A	S	O	N	D
Accra													
Temperature F	Max	87	88	88	88	87	84	81	80	81	85	87	88
	Min	73	75	76	76	75	74	73	71	73	74	75	75
Temperature C	Max	31	31	31	31	31	29	38	38	38	29	31	31
	Min	23	24	24	24	24	23	23	22	23	23	24	24
Humidity %	am	95	96	95	96	96	97	97	97	96	97	97	97
	pm	61	61	63	65	68	74	76	77	72	71	66	64
Precipitation	mm	15	33	56	81	142	178	46	15	36	64	36	23
Amsterdam – De Bilt													
Temperature F	Max	40	42	49	56	64	70	72	71	67	57	48	42
	Min	31	31	34	40	46	51	55	55	50	44	38	33
Temperature C	Max	4	5	10	13	18	21	22	22	19	14	9	5
	Min	−1	−1	1	4	8	11	13	13	10	7	3	1
Humidity %	am	90	90	86	79	75	75	79	82	86	90	92	91
	pm	82	76	65	61	59	59	64	65	67	72	81	85
Precipitation	mm	68	53	44	49	52	58	77	87	72	72	70	64
Athens													
Temperature F	Max	55	57	60	68	77	86	92	92	84	75	66	58
	Min	44	44	46	52	61	68	73	73	67	60	53	47
Temperature C	Max	13	14	16	20	25	30	33	33	29	24	19	15
	Min	6	7	8	11	16	20	23	23	19	15	12	8
Humidity %	am	77	74	71	65	60	50	47	48	58	70	78	78
	pm	62	57	54	48	47	39	34	34	42	52	61	63
Precipitation	mm	62	37	37	23	23	14	6	7	15	51	56	71
Auckland													
Temperature F	Max	73	73	71	67	62	58	56	58	60	63	66	70
	Min	60	60	59	56	51	48	46	46	49	52	54	57
Temperature C	Max	23	23	22	19	17	14	13	14	16	17	19	21
	Min	16	16	15	13	11	9	8	8	9	11	12	14
Humidity %	am	71	72	74	78	80	83	84	80	76	74	71	70
	pm	62	61	65	69	70	73	74	70	68	66	64	64
Precipitation	mm	79	84	81	97	127	137	145	117	102	102	89	79

		J	F	M	A	M	J	J	A	S	O	N	D
Bahrain													
Temperature F	Max	68	70	75	84	92	96	99	100	96	90	82	71
	Min	57	59	63	70	78	82	85	85	81	75	69	60
Temperature C	Max	20	21	24	29	33	36	37	38	36	32	28	22
	Min	14	15	17	21	26	28	29	29	27	24	21	16
Humidity %	am	85	83	80	75	71	69	69	74	75	80	80	85
	pm	71	70	70	66	63	64	67	65	64	66	70	77
Precipitation	mm	8	18	13	8	0	0	0	0	0	0	18	18
Bangkok													
Temperature F	Max	89	91	93	95	93	91	90	90	89	88	87	87
	Min	68	72	75	77	77	76	76	76	76	75	72	68
Temperature C	Max	32	33	34	35	34	33	32	32	32	31	31	31
	Min	20	22	24	25	24	24	24	24	24	24	22	20
Humidity %	am	91	92	92	90	91	90	91	92	94	93	92	91
	pm	53	55	56	58	64	67	66	66	70	70	65	56
Precipitation	mm	8	20	36	58	198	160	160	175	305	206	66	5
Beirut													
Temperature F	Max	62	63	66	72	78	83	87	89	86	81	73	65
	Min	51	51	54	58	64	69	73	74	73	69	61	55
Temperature C	Max	17	17	19	22	26	28	31	32	30	27	23	18
	Min	11	11	12	14	18	21	23	23	23	21	16	12
Humidity %	am	72	72	72	72	69	67	66	65	64	65	67	70
	pm	70	70	69	67	64	61	58	57	57	62	61	69
Precipitation	mm	191	157	94	56	18	3	0	0	5	51	132	185
Berlin													
Temperature F	Max	35	37	46	56	66	72	75	74	68	56	45	38
	Min	26	26	31	39	47	53	57	56	50	42	36	29
Temperature C	Max	2	3	8	13	19	22	24	23	20	13	7	3
	Min	−3	−3	0	4	8	12	14	13	10	6	2	−1
Humidity %	am	89	89	88	84	80	80	84	88	92	93	92	91
	pm	82	78	67	60	57	58	61	61	65	73	83	86
Precipitation	mm	46	40	33	42	49	65	73	69	48	49	46	43
Bombay													
Temperature F	Max	83	83	86	89	91	89	85	85	85	89	89	97
	Min	67	67	72	76	80	79	77	76	76	76	73	79
Temperature C	Max	28	28	30	32	33	32	29	29	29	32	32	31
	Min	12	12	17	20	23	21	22	22	22	21	18	13
Humidity %	am	70	71	73	75	74	79	83	83	85	81	73	70
	pm	61	62	65	67	68	77	83	81	78	71	64	62
Precipitation	mm	2.5	2.5	2.5	0	18	485	617	340	264	64	13	2.5
Brussels													
Temperature F	Max	40	44	51	58	65	72	73	72	69	60	48	42
	Min	30	32	36	41	46	52	54	54	51	45	38	32
Temperature C	Max	4	7	10	14	18	22	23	22	21	15	9	6
	Min	−1	0	2	5	8	11	12	12	11	7	3	0
Humidity %	am	92	92	91	91	90	87	91	93	94	93	93	92
	pm	86	81	74	71	65	65	68	69	69	77	85	86
Precipitation	mm	66	61	53	60	55	76	95	80	63	83	75	88
Buenos Aires													
Temperature F	Max	85	83	79	72	64	57	57	60	64	69	76	82
	Min	63	63	60	53	47	41	42	43	46	50	56	61
Temperature C	Max	29	28	26	22	18	14	14	16	18	21	24	28
	Min	17	17	16	12	8	5	6	6	8	10	13	16

		J	F	M	A	M	J	J	A	S	O	N	D
Buenos Aires cont'd													
Humidity %	am	81	83	87	88	90	91	92	90	86	83	79	79
	pm	61	63	69	71	74	78	79	74	68	65	60	62
Precipitation	mm	79	71	109	89	76	61	56	61	79	86	84	99
Cairo													
Temperature F	Max	65	69	75	83	91	95	96	95	90	86	78	68
	Min	47	48	52	57	63	68	70	71	68	65	58	50
Temperature C	Max	18	21	24	28	33	35	36	35	32	30	26	20
	Min	8	9	11	14	17	20	20	22	20	18	14	10
Humidity %	am	69	64	63	55	50	55	65	69	68	67	68	70
	pm	40	33	27	21	18	20	24	28	31	31	38	41
Precipitation	mm	5	5	5	3	3	0	0	0	0	0	3	5
Calcutta													
Temperature F	Max	80	84	93	97	96	92	89	89	90	89	84	79
	Min	55	59	69	75	77	79	79	78	78	74	64	55
Temperature C	Max	27	29	34	36	36	33	32	32	32	32	29	26
	Min	13	15	21	24	25	26	26	26	26	24	18	13
Humidity %	am	85	82	79	76	77	82	86	88	86	85	79	80
	pm	52	45	46	56	62	75	80	82	81	72	63	55
Precipitation	mm	10	31	36	43	140	297	325	328	252	114	20	5
Christchurch													
Temperature F	Max	70	69	66	62	56	51	50	52	57	62	66	69
	Min	53	53	50	45	40	36	35	36	40	44	47	51
Temperature C	Max	21	21	19	17	13	11	10	11	14	17	19	21
	Min	12	12	10	7	4	2	2	2	4	7	8	11
Humidity %	am	65	71	75	82	85	87	87	81	72	63	64	67
	pm	59	60	69	71	69	72	76	66	69	60	64	60
Precipitation	mm	56	43	48	48	66	66	69	48	46	60	64	60
Colombo													
Temperature F	Max	86	87	88	88	87	85	85	85	85	85	85	85
	Min	72	72	74	76	78	77	77	77	77	75	73	72
Temperature C	Max	30	31	31	31	31	29	29	29	29	29	29	29
	Min	22	22	23	24	25	26	25	25	25	24	23	22
Humidity %	am	73	71	71	74	78	80	79	78	76	77	77	74
	pm	75	69	67	66	66	70	76	78	77	76	75	76
Precipitation	mm	89	69	147	231	371	224	135	109	160	348	315	147
Copenhagen													
Temperature F	Max	36	36	41	51	61	67	71	70	64	54	45	40
	Min	28	28	31	38	46	52	57	56	51	44	38	34
Temperature C	Max	2	2	5	10	16	19	22	21	18	12	7	4
	Min	−2	−3	−1	3	8	11	14	14	11	7	3	1
Humidity %	am	88	86	85	79	70	70	74	78	83	86	88	89
	pm	85	83	78	68	59	60	62	64	69	76	83	87
Precipitation	mm	49	39	32	38	43	47	71	66	62	59	48	49
Delhi													
Temperature F	Max	70	75	87	97	105	102	96	93	93	93	84	73
	Min	44	49	58	68	79	83	81	79	75	65	52	46
Temperature C	Max	21	24	31	36	41	39	36	34	34	34	29	23
	Min	7	9	14	20	26	28	27	26	24	18	11	8
Humidity %	am	72	67	49	35	35	53	75	80	72	56	51	69
	pm	41	35	23	19	20	36	59	64	51	32	31	42
Precipitation	mm	23	18	13	8	13	74	180	173	117	10	3	10

		J	F	M	A	M	J	J	A	S	O	N	D
Djakarta													
Temperature F	Max	84	84	86	87	87	87	87	87	88	87	86	85
	Min	74	74	74	75	75	74	73	73	74	74	74	74
Temperature C	Max	29	29	30	31	31	31	31	31	31	31	30	29
	Min	23	23	23	24	24	23	23	23	23	23	23	23
Humidity %	am	95	95	94	94	94	93	92	90	90	90	92	92
	pm	75	75	73	71	69	67	64	61	62	64	68	71
Precipitation	mm	300	300	211	147	114	97	64	43	66	112	142	203
Frankfurt													
Temperature F	Max	38	41	51	60	69	74	77	76	69	58	47	39
	Min	29	30	35	42	49	55	58	57	52	44	38	32
Temperature C	Max	3	5	11	16	20	23	25	24	21	14	8	4
	Min	−1	−2	2	6	9	13	15	14	11	7	3	0
Humidity %	am	86	86	84	79	78	78	81	85	89	91	89	88
	pm	77	70	57	51	50	52	53	54	60	68	77	81
Precipitation	mm	58	44	38	44	55	73	70	76	57	52	55	54
Haifa													
Temperature F	Max	65	67	71	77	83	85	88	90	88	85	78	68
	Min	49	50	53	58	65	71	75	76	74	68	60	53
Temperature C	Max	18	19	22	25	28	29	31	32	31	29	26	20
	Min	9	10	12	14	18	22	24	24	23	20	16	12
Humidity %	am	66	65	62	60	62	67	70	70	67	66	61	66
	pm	56	56	56	57	59	66	68	69	66	66	56	56
Precipitation	mm	175	109	41	25	5	0	0	0	3	25	94	185
Hamilton, Bermuda													
Temperature F	Max	68	68	68	71	76	81	85	86	84	79	74	70
	Min	58	57	57	59	64	69	73	74	72	69	63	60
Temperature C	Max	20	20	20	22	24	27	29	30	29	26	23	21
	Min	14	14	14	15	18	21	23	23	22	21	17	16
Humidity %	am	78	76	77	77	78	81	82	81	79	81	79	77
	pm	70	69	69	70	75	74	73	69	73	72	70	70
Precipitation	mm	112	119	122	104	117	112	114	137	132	147	127	119
Harare													
Temperature F	Max	78	78	78	78	74	70	70	74	79	83	81	79
	Min	60	60	58	55	49	44	44	47	53	58	60	60
Temperature C	Max	26	26	26	26	23	21	21	23	26	28	27	26
	Min	16	16	14	13	9	7	7	8	12	14	16	16
Humidity %	am	74	77	75	68	60	58	56	50	43	43	56	67
	pm	57	53	52	44	37	36	33	28	26	26	43	57
Precipitation	mm	196	178	117	28	13	3	0	3	5	28	97	163
Hong Kong													
Temperature F	Max	64	63	67	75	82	85	87	87	85	81	74	68
	Min	56	55	60	67	74	78	78	78	77	73	65	59
Temperature C	Max	18	17	19	24	28	29	31	31	29	27	23	20
	Min	13	13	16	19	23	26	26	26	25	23	18	15
Humidity %	am	77	82	84	87	87	86	87	87	83	75	73	74
	pm	66	73	74	77	78	77	77	77	72	63	60	63
Precipitation	mm	33	46	74	137	292	394	381	367	257	114	43	31
Istanbul													
Temperature F	Max	46	47	51	60	69	77	82	82	76	68	59	51
	Min	37	36	38	45	53	60	65	66	61	55	48	41
Temperature C	Max	8	9	11	16	21	25	28	28	24	20	15	11
	Min	3	2	3	7	12	16	18	19	16	13	9	5

		J	F	M	A	M	J	J	A	S	O	N	D
Istanbul cont'd													
Humidity %	am	82	82	81	81	82	79	79	79	81	83	82	82
	pm	75	72	67	62	61	58	56	55	59	64	71	74
Precipitation	mm	109	92	72	46	38	34	34	30	58	81	103	119
Jeddah													
Temperature F	Max	84	84	85	91	95	97	99	99	96	95	91	86
	Min	66	65	67	70	74	75	79	80	77	73	71	67
Temperature C	Max	29	29	29	33	35	36	37	37	36	35	33	30
	Min	19	18	19	21	23	24	26	27	25	23	22	19
Humidity %	am	58	52	52	52	51	56	55	59	65	60	55	55
	pm	54	52	52	56	55	55	50	51	61	61	59	54
Precipitation	mm	5	0	0	0	0	0	0	0	0	0	25	31
Johannesburg													
Temperature F	Max	78	77	75	72	66	62	63	68	73	77	77	78
	Min	58	58	55	50	43	39	39	43	48	53	55	57
Temperature C	Max	26	25	24	22	19	17	17	20	23	25	25	26
	Min	14	14	13	10	6	4	4	6	9	12	13	14
Humidity %	am	75	78	79	74	70	70	69	64	59	64	67	70
	pm	50	53	50	44	36	33	32	29	30	37	45	47
Precipitation	mm	114	109	89	38	25	8	8	8	23	56	107	125
Kathmandu													
Temperature F	Max	65	67	77	83	86	85	84	83	83	80	74	67
	Min	35	39	45	53	61	67	68	68	66	56	45	37
Temperature C	Max	18	19	25	28	30	29	29	28	28	27	23	19
	Min	2	4	7	12	16	19	20	20	19	13	7	3
Humidity %	am	89	90	73	68	72	79	86	87	86	88	90	89
	pm	70	68	53	54	61	72	82	84	83	81	78	73
Precipitation	mm	15	41	23	58	122	246	373	345	155	38	8	3
Kuala Lumpur													
Temperature F	Max	90	92	92	91	91	91	90	90	90	89	89	89
	Min	72	72	73	74	73	72	73	73	73	73	73	72
Temperature C	Max	32	33	33	33	33	33	32	32	32	32	32	32
	Min	22	22	23	23	23	22	23	23	23	23	23	22
Humidity %	am	97	97	97	97	97	96	95	96	96	96	97	97
	pm	60	60	58	63	66	63	63	62	64	65	66	61
Precipitation	mm	158	201	259	292	224	130	99	163	218	249	259	191
Lagos													
Temperature F	Max	88	89	89	89	87	85	83	82	83	85	88	88
	Min	74	77	78	77	76	74	74	73	74	74	75	75
Temperature C	Max	31	32	32	32	31	29	28	28	28	29	31	31
	Min	23	25	26	25	24	23	23	23	23	23	24	24
Humidity %	am	84	83	82	81	83	87	87	85	86	86	85	86
	pm	65	69	72	72	76	80	80	76	77	76	72	68
Precipitation	mm	28	46	102	150	269	460	279	64	140	206	69	25
Lima													
Temperature F	Max	82	83	83	80	74	68	67	66	68	71	74	78
	Min	66	67	66	63	60	58	57	57	58	60	62	62
Temperature C	Max	28	28	28	27	23	20	19	19	20	22	23	26
	Min	19	19	19	17	16	14	14	13	14	14	16	17
Humidity %	am	93	92	92	93	95	95	94	95	94	94	93	93
	pm	69	66	64	66	76	80	77	78	76	72	71	70
Precipitation	mm	3	0	0	0	5	5	8	8	8	3	3	0

		J	F	M	A	M	J	J	A	S	O	N	D
Lisbon													
Temperature F	Max	57	59	63	67	71	77	81	82	79	72	63	58
	Min	46	47	50	53	55	60	63	63	62	58	52	47
Temperature C	Max	14	15	17	20	21	25	27	28	26	22	17	15
	Min	8	8	10	12	13	15	17	17	17	14	11	9
Humidity %	am	85	80	78	69	68	65	62	64	70	75	81	84
	pm	71	64	64	56	57	54	48	49	54	59	68	72
Precipitation	mm	111	76	109	54	44	16	3	4	33	62	93	103
London (UK)													
Temperature F	Max	43	44	50	56	62	69	71	71	65	58	50	45
	Min	36	36	38	42	47	53	56	56	52	46	42	38
Temperature C	Max	6	7	10	13	17	20	22	21	19	14	10	7
	Min	2	2	3	6	8	12	14	13	11	8	5	4
Humidity %	am	86	85	81	71	70	70	71	76	80	85	85	87
	pm	77	72	64	56	57	58	59	62	65	70	78	81
Precipitation	mm	54	40	37	37	46	45	57	59	49	57	64	48
Madrid													
Temperature F	Max	47	52	59	65	70	80	87	85	77	65	55	48
	Min	35	36	41	45	50	58	63	63	57	48	42	36
Temperature C	Max	9	11	15	18	21	27	31	30	25	19	13	9
	Min	2	2	5	7	10	15	17	17	14	10	5	2
Humidity %	am	86	83	80	74	72	66	58	62	72	81	84	86
	pm	71	62	56	49	49	41	33	35	46	58	65	70
Precipitation	mm	39	34	43	48	47	27	11	15	32	53	47	48
Manila													
Temperature F	Max	86	88	91	93	93	91	88	87	88	88	87	86
	Min	69	69	71	73	75	75	75	75	75	74	72	70
Temperature C	Max	30	31	33	34	34	33	31	31	31	31	30	30
	Min	21	21	22	23	24	24	24	24	24	23	22	21
Humidity %	am	89	88	85	85	88	91	91	92	93	92	91	90
	pm	63	59	55	55	61	68	74	73	73	71	69	67
Precipitation	mm	23	13	18	33	130	254	432	422	356	193	145	66
Melbourne													
Temperature F	Max	78	78	75	68	62	57	56	59	63	67	71	75
	Min	57	57	55	51	47	44	42	43	46	48	51	54
Temperature C	Max	26	26	24	20	17	14	13	15	17	19	22	24
	Min	14	14	13	11	8	7	6	6	8	9	11	12
Humidity %	am	58	62	64	72	79	83	82	76	68	61	60	59
	pm	48	50	51	56	62	67	65	60	55	52	52	51
Precipitation	mm	48	46	56	58	53	53	48	48	58	66	58	58
Mexico City													
Temperature F	Max	66	69	75	77	78	76	73	73	74	70	68	66
	Min	42	43	47	51	54	55	53	54	53	50	46	43
Temperature C	Max	19	21	24	25	26	24	23	23	23	21	20	19
	Min	6	6	8	11	12	13	12	12	12	10	8	6
Humidity %	am	79	72	68	66	69	82	84	85	86	83	82	81
	pm	34	28	26	29	29	48	50	50	54	47	41	37
Precipitation	mm	13	5	10	20	53	119	170	152	130	51	18	8
Miami													
Temperature F	Max	74	75	78	80	84	86	88	88	87	83	78	76
	Min	61	61	64	67	71	74	76	76	75	72	66	62
Temperature C	Max	23	24	26	27	29	30	31	31	31	28	26	24
	Min	16	16	18	19	22	23	24	24	24	22	19	17

		J	F	M	A	M	J	J	A	S	O	N	D
Miami cont'd													
Humidity %	am	81	82	77	73	75	75	75	76	79	80	77	82
	pm	66	63	62	64	67	69	68	68	70	69	64	65
Precipitation	mm	71	53	64	81	173	178	155	160	203	234	71	51
Moscow													
Temperature F	Max	15	22	32	50	66	70	73	72	61	48	35	24
	Min	3	8	18	34	46	51	55	53	45	37	26	15
Temperature C	Max	−9	−6	0	10	19	21	23	22	16	9	2	−5
	Min	−16	−14	−8	1	8	11	13	12	7	3	−3	−10
Humidity %	am	82	82	82	73	58	62	68	74	78	81	87	85
	pm	77	66	64	54	43	47	54	55	59	67	79	83
Precipitation	mm	39	38	36	37	53	58	88	71	58	45	47	54
Nairobi													
Temperature F	Max	77	79	77	75	72	70	69	70	75	76	74	74
	Min	54	55	57	58	56	53	51	52	55	56	56	55
Temperature C	Max	25	26	25	24	22	21	21	21	24	24	23	23
	Min	12	13	14	14	13	12	11	11	11	13	13	13
Humidity %	am	74	74	81	88	88	89	86	86	82	82	86	81
	pm	44	40	45	56	62	60	58	56	45	43	53	53
Precipitation	mm	38	64	125	211	158	46	15	23	31	53	109	86
Nassau													
Temperature F	Max	77	77	79	81	84	87	88	89	88	85	81	79
	Min	65	64	66	69	71	74	75	76	75	73	70	67
Temperature C	Max	25	25	26	27	29	31	31	32	31	29	27	26
	Min	18	18	19	21	22	23	24	24	24	23	21	19
Humidity %	am	84	82	81	79	79	81	80	82	84	83	83	84
	pm	64	62	64	65	65	68	69	70	73	71	68	66
Precipitation	mm	36	38	36	64	117	163	147	135	175	165	71	33
New York													
Temperature F	Max	37	38	45	57	68	77	82	80	79	69	51	41
	Min	24	24	30	42	53	60	66	66	60	49	37	29
Temperature C	Max	3	3	7	14	20	25	28	27	26	21	11	5
	Min	−4	−4	−1	6	12	16	19	19	16	9	3	−2
Humidity %	am	72	70	70	68	70	74	77	79	79	76	75	73
	pm	60	58	55	53	54	58	58	60	61	57	60	61
Precipitation	mm	94	97	91	81	81	84	107	109	86	89	76	91
Oslo													
Temperature F	Max	28	30	39	50	61	68	72	70	60	48	38	32
	Min	19	19	25	34	43	50	55	53	46	38	31	25
Temperature C	Max	−2	−1	4	10	16	20	22	21	16	9	3	0
	Min	−7	−7	−4	1	6	10	13	12	8	3	−1	−4
Humidity %	am	86	84	80	75	68	69	74	79	85	88	88	87
	pm	82	74	64	57	52	55	59	61	66	72	83	85
Precipitation	mm	49	35	26	43	44	70	82	95	81	74	68	63
Ottawa													
Temperature F	Max	21	22	33	51	66	76	81	77	68	54	39	24
	Min	3	3	16	31	44	54	58	55	48	37	26	9
Temperature C	Max	−6	−6	1	11	19	24	27	25	20	12	4	−4
	Min	−16	−16	−9	−1	7	12	14	13	9	3	−3	−13
Humidity %	am	83	88	84	76	77	80	80	84	90	86	84	83
	pm	76	73	66	58	55	56	53	54	59	63	68	75
Precipitation	mm	74	56	71	69	64	89	86	66	81	74	76	66

		J	F	M	A	M	J	J	A	S	O	N	D
Papeete													
Temperature F	Max	89	89	89	89	87	86	86	86	86	87	88	88
	Min	72	72	72	72	70	69	68	68	69	70	71	72
Temperature C	Max	32	32	32	32	31	30	30	30	30	31	31	31
	Min	22	22	22	22	21	21	20	20	21	21	22	22
Humidity %	am	82	82	84	85	84	85	83	83	81	79	80	81
	pm	77	77	78	78	78	79	77	78	76	76	77	78
Precipitation	mm	252	244	429	142	102	76	53	43	53	89	150	249
Paris													
Temperature F	Max	42	45	55	61	69	75	80	79	73	61	50	43
	Min	30	31	37	42	49	55	59	58	53	45	38	33
Temperature C	Max	5	7	13	16	20	24	27	26	23	16	10	6
	Min	−1	0	3	6	9	13	15	14	12	7	4	0
Humidity %	am	89	87	87	84	83	82	79	85	89	92	91	90
	pm	80	72	60	56	56	55	50	54	60	69	78	80
Precipitation	mm	52	46	53	56	69	85	56	89	93	77	80	57
Port-of-Spain													
Temperature F	Max	87	88	89	90	90	89	88	88	89	89	89	88
	Min	69	68	68	69	71	71	71	71	71	71	71	69
Temperature C	Max	31	31	32	32	32	32	31	31	32	32	32	31
	Min	21	20	20	21	22	22	22	22	22	22	22	21
Humidity %	am	89	87	85	83	84	87	88	87	87	87	89	89
	pm	68	65	63	61	63	69	71	73	73	74	76	71
Precipitation	mm	69	41	46	53	94	193	218	246	193	170	183	125
Prague													
Temperature F	Max	49	53	64	73	82	88	91	89	84	71	57	50
	Min	7	10	18	29	36	44	49	47	38	29	24	14
Temperature C	Max	10	11	18	23	28	31	33	32	29	22	14	10
	Min	−13	−12	−8	−2	2	7	9	8	4	−2	−5	−10
Humidity %	am	84	83	82	77	75	74	77	81	84	87	87	87
	pm	73	67	55	47	45	46	49	48	51	60	73	78
Precipitation	mm	18	18	18	27	48	54	68	55	31	33	20	21
Rangoon													
Temperature F	Max	89	92	96	97	92	86	85	86	86	88	88	88
	Min	65	67	71	76	77	76	76	76	76	76	73	67
Temperature C	Max	32	33	36	36	33	30	29	29	30	31	31	31
	Min	18	19	22	24	25	24	24	24	24	24	23	19
Humidity %	am	71	72	74	71	80	87	89	89	87	83	79	75
	pm	52	52	54	64	76	75	88	88	86	77	72	61
Precipitation	mm	3	5	8	51	307	480	582	528	394	180	69	10
Rio de Janeiro													
Temperature F	Max	84	85	83	80	77	76	75	76	75	77	79	82
	Min	73	73	72	69	66	64	63	64	65	66	68	71
Temperature C	Max	29	29	28	27	25	24	24	24	24	25	26	28
	Min	23	23	22	21	19	18	17	18	18	19	20	22
Humidity %	am	82	84	87	87	87	87	86	84	84	83	82	82
	pm	70	71	74	73	70	69	68	66	72	72	72	72
Precipitation	mm	125	122	130	107	79	53	41	43	66	79	104	137
Rome													
Temperature F	Max	52	55	59	66	74	82	87	86	79	71	61	55
	Min	40	42	45	50	56	63	67	67	62	55	49	44
Temperature C	Max	11	13	15	19	23	28	30	30	26	22	16	13
	Min	5	5	7	10	13	17	20	20	17	13	9	6

		J	F	M	A	M	J	J	A	S	O	N	D
Rome cont'd													
Humidity %	am	85	86	83	83	77	74	70	73	83	86	87	85
	pm	68	64	56	54	54	48	42	43	50	59	66	70
Precipitation	mm	71	62	57	51	46	37	15	21	63	99	129	93
San Francisco													
Temperature F	Max	55	59	61	62	63	66	65	65	69	68	63	57
	Min	45	47	48	49	51	52	53	53	55	54	51	47
Temperature C	Max	13	15	16	17	17	19	18	18	21	20	17	14
	Min	7	8	9	9	11	11	12	12	13	12	11	8
Humidity %	am	85	84	83	83	85	88	91	92	88	85	83	83
	pm	69	66	61	61	62	64	69	70	60	58	60	68
Precipitation	mm	119	97	79	38	18	3	0	0	8	25	64	112
Singapore													
Temperature F	Max	86	88	88	88	89	88	88	87	87	87	87	87
	Min	73	73	75	75	75	75	75	75	75	74	74	74
Temperature C	Max	30	31	31	31	34	31	31	31	31	31	31	31
	Min	23	23	24	24	24	24	24	24	24	23	23	23
Humidity %	am	82	77	76	77	79	79	79	78	79	78	79	82
	pm	78	71	70	74	73	73	72	72	72	72	75	78
Precipitation	mm	252	173	193	188	173	173	170	196	178	208	254	257
Stockholm													
Temperature F	Max	30	30	37	47	58	67	71	68	60	49	40	35
	Min	23	22	26	34	43	51	57	56	49	41	34	29
Temperature C	Max	−1	−1	3	8	14	19	22	20	15	9	5	2
	Min	15	15	14	1	6	11	14	13	9	5	1	−2
Humidity %	am	85	83	82	76	66	68	74	81	87	88	89	88
	pm	83	77	68	60	53	55	59	64	69	76	85	86
Precipitation	mm	43	30	25	31	34	45	61	76	60	48	53	48
Sydney													
Temperature F	Max	78	78	76	71	66	61	60	63	67	71	74	77
	Min	65	65	63	58	52	48	46	48	51	56	60	63
Temperature C	Max	26	26	24	22	19	16	16	17	19	22	23	25
	Min	18	18	17	14	11	9	8	9	11	13	16	17
Humidity %	am	68	71	73	76	77	77	76	72	67	65	65	66
	pm	64	65	65	64	63	62	60	56	55	57	60	62
Precipitation	mm	89	102	127	135	127	117	117	76	74	71	74	74
Tehran													
Temperature F	Max	45	50	59	71	82	93	99	97	90	76	63	51
	Min	27	32	39	49	58	66	72	71	64	53	43	33
Temperature C	Max	7	10	15	22	28	34	37	36	32	24	17	11
	Min	−3	0	4	9	14	19	22	22	18	12	6	1
Humidity %	am	77	73	61	54	55	50	51	47	49	53	63	76
	pm	75	59	39	40	47	49	41	46	49	54	66	75
Precipitation	mm	46	38	46	36	13	3	3	3	3	8	20	31
Tokyo													
Temperature F	Max	47	48	54	63	71	76	83	86	79	69	60	52
	Min	29	31	36	46	54	63	70	72	66	55	43	33
Temperature C	Max	8	9	12	17	22	24	28	30	26	21	16	11
	Min	−2	−1	2	8	12	17	21	22	19	13	6	1
Humidity %	am	73	71	75	81	85	89	91	92	91	88	83	77
	pm	48	48	53	59	62	68	69	66	68	64	58	51
Precipitation	mm	48	74	107	135	147	165	142	152	234	208	97	56

		J	F	M	A	M	J	J	A	S	O	N	D
Vancouver													
Temperature F	Max	41	44	50	58	64	69	74	73	65	57	48	43
	Min	32	34	37	40	46	52	54	54	49	44	39	35
Temperature C	Max	5	7	10	14	18	21	23	23	18	14	9	6
	Min	0	1	3	4	8	11	12	12	9	7	4	2
Humidity %	am	93	91	91	89	88	87	89	90	92	92	91	91
	pm	85	78	70	67	63	65	62	62	72	80	84	88
Precipitation	mm	218	147	127	84	71	64	31	43	91	147	211	224
Vienna													
Temperature F	Max	34	38	47	58	67	73	76	75	68	56	45	37
	Min	25	28	30	42	50	56	60	59	53	44	37	30
Temperature C	Max	1	3	8	15	19	23	25	24	20	14	7	3
	Min	−4	−3	−1	6	10	14	15	15	11	7	3	−1
Humidity %	am	81	80	78	72	74	74	74	78	83	86	84	84
	pm	72	66	57	49	52	55	54	54	56	64	74	76
Precipitation	mm	39	44	44	45	70	67	84	72	42	56	52	45
Warsaw													
Temperature F	Max	32	32	42	53	67	73	75	73	66	55	42	35
	Min	22	21	28	37	48	54	58	56	49	41	33	28
Temperature C	Max	0	1	6	13	19	23	24	23	19	14	6	−2
	Min	−7	−6	−2	3	8	12	14	13	9	5	1	86
Humidity %	am	83	82	83	83	79	82	84	88	90	89	90	78
	pm	74	71	64	59	55	60	63	63	63	67	78	43
Precipitation	mm	27	24	25	43	57	88	105	93	58	50	43	
Zurich													
Temperature F	Max	36	41	51	59	67	73	76	75	69	57	45	37
	Min	26	28	34	40	47	53	56	56	51	43	35	29
Temperature C	Max	2	5	10	15	19	23	25	24	20	14	7	3
	Min	−3	−2	1	4	8	12	14	13	11	6	2	−2
Humidity %	am	88	88	86	81	80	80	81	85	90	92	90	89
	pm	74	65	55	51	52	52	52	53	57	64	73	76
Precipitation	mm	74	69	64	76	101	129	136	124	102	77	73	64

Guide to Rainy Seasons

Within each region, the places mentioned in the table are arranged in order of decreasing latitude north of the equator, increasing latitude south of the equator. This is a reminder that at any given time of the year opposite seasons are to be found north and south of the equator. December to February, for example, bring winter to the northern hemisphere, summer to the southern hemisphere. In the belt stretching about up to 10° north and south of the equator, the equatorial climate tends to prevail: the seasons are almost indistinguishable from each other and rain, broadly speaking, is more evenly spread throughout the year than elsewhere. But a lot depends on altitude and other features of geographical location; proximity to the sea or to mountains, and the nature of prevailing winds and currents.

The places listed are not necessarily typical of other places within the same region or country. And they represent only a minute sample globally. Total annual rainfall should always be taken into account, since the rainy season in one place may be less wet than the dry season in another. At best, this table is a rough guide only.

+   represents a month having more than 1/12 of the annual total rainfall.
−   represents a month having less than 1/12 of the annual total rainfall.
●   indicates the month(s) with the highest average rainfall of the year.

	Total annual rainfall, cm	J	F	M	A	M	J	J	A	S	O	N	D	Latitude
Asia														
Istanbul, Turkey	80.5	+	+	+	−	−	−	−	−	−	+	+	●	41°0'N
Beijing, China	134.1	−	−	−	−	−	+	●	●	+	−	−	−	39°50'N
Seoul, Korea	125.0	−	−	−	−	−	+	●	●	+	−	−	−	37°31'N
Tokyo, Japan	156.5	−	−	−	+	+	+	+	+	●	+	−	−	35°45'N
Tehran, Iran	24.6	●	+	●	+	−	−	−	−	−	−	−	+	35°44'N
Osaka, Japan	133.6	−	−	−	+	+	●	+	+	+	+	−	−	34°40'N
Kabul, Afghanistan	34.0	−	+	●	●	−	−	−	−	−	−	−	−	34°28'N
Beirut, Lebanon	89.7	●	+	+	−	−	−	−	−	−	−	−	●	33°53'N
Damascus, Syria	22.4	●	●	−	−	−	−	−	−	−	−	+	+	33°30'N
Baghdad, Iraq	15.0	+	+	●	+	−	−	−	−	−	−	+	+	33°20'N
Nagasaki, Japan	191.8	−	−	−	+	+	●	+	+	+	−	−	−	32°47'N
Amman, Jordan	27.9	●	●	+	−	−	−	−	−	−	−	+	●	32°0'N
Jerusalem, Israel	53.3	●	●	+	−	−	−	−	−	−	−	+	+	31°47'N
Shanghai, China	113.5	−	−	−	−	−	●	+	+	+	−	−	−	31°15'N
Hankow (Wuhan), China	125.7	−	−	−	+	+	●	+	−	−	−	−	−	30°32'N
Kuwait City, Kuwait	12.7	+	+	●	−	−	−	−	−	−	−	−	+	29°30'N
Delhi, India	64.0	−	−	−	−	−	+	●	●	+	−	−	−	28°38'N
Kathmandu, Nepal	142.7	−	−	−	−	+	+	●	●	+	−	−	−	27°45'N
Agra, India	68.1	−	−	−	−	−	+	●	●	+	−	−	−	27°17'N
Cherrapunji, India	1,079.8	−	−	−	−	+	●	●	+	+	−	−	−	25°17'N
Taipei, Taiwan	212.9	−	−	+	−	+	+	+	●	+	−	−	−	25°2'N
Karachi, Pakistan	18.3	−	−	−	−	−	−	●	+	−	−	−	−	24°53'N
Riyadh, Saudi Arabia	9.1	−	+	+	●	+	−	−	−	−	−	−	−	24°41'N
Guangzhou, China	164.3	−	−	−	+	+	●	+	+	−	−	−	−	23°10'N
Calcutta, India	160.0	−	−	−	+	+	●	+	+	−	−	−	−	23°10'N
Hong Kong	216.1	−	−	−	−	+	+	●	●	+	−	−	−	22°36'N
Mandalay, Burma	82.8	−	−	−	−	●	●	+	+	+	+	−	−	22°11'N
Jeddah, Saudi Arabia	8.1	−	−	−	−	−	−	−	−	−	−	●	●	22°0'N

	Total annual rainfall, cm	J	F	M	A	M	J	J	A	S	O	N	D	Latitude
Hanoi, Vietnam	168.1	−	−	−	−	+	+	+	●	+	−	−	−	21°5′N
Bombay, India	181.4	−	−	−	−	−	●	●	+	+	−	−	−	18°55′N
Hyderabad, India	75.2	−	−	−	−	−	+	+	●	+	+	−	−	17°10′N
Rangoon, Burma	261.6	−	−	−	−	+	+	●	+	+	−	−	−	16°45′N
Manila, Philippines	208.5	−	−	−	−	−	+	●	●	+	+	−	−	14°40′N
Bangkok, Thailand	139.7	−	−	−	−	+	+	+	+	●	+	−	−	13°45′N
Madras, India	127.0	−	−	−	−	−	−	−	+	+	●	●	+	13°8′N
Mangalore, India	329.2	−	−	−	−	−	●	●	+	−	−	−	−	12°55′N
Aden (Perim Is.), Yemen People's Dem Rep (South)	4.8	+	−	+	−	−	−	−	+	●	−	−	−	12°50′N
Colombo, Sri Lanka	236.5	−	−	+	●	+	−	−	−	−	●	●	−	6°56′N
Sandakan, Malaysia	314.2	●	+	−	−	−	−	−	−	−	−	+	+	5°53′N
Kuala Lumpur, Malaysia	244.1	−	−	+	●	+	−	−	−	+	+	+	−	3°9′N
Singapore	241.3	●	−	−	−	−	−	−	−	−	+	●	●	1°17′N
Djakarta, Indonesia	179.8	●	●	+	−	−	−	−	−	−	−	−	+	6°9′S
Africa														
Algiers, Algeria	76.5	+	+	+	−	−	−	−	−	−	+	●	●	36°42′N
Tangier, Morocco	90.2	+	+	+	+	−	−	−	−	−	−	+	+	35°50′N
Tripoli, Libya	38.9	+	+	−	−	−	−	−	−	−	+	+	●	32°49′N
Marrakech, Morocco	23.9	+	+	●	+	−	−	−	−	−	−	+	+	31°40′N
Cairo, Egypt	3.6	+	+	+	−	−	−	−	−	−	−	−	+	30°1′N
Tombouctou, Mali	24.4	−	−	−	−	−	−	+	●	●	+	−	−	16°50′N
Khartoum, Sudan	17.0	−	−	−	−	−	−	+	●	+	−	−	−	15°31′N
Dakar, Sénégal	55.4	−	−	−	−	−	−	+	●	+	−	−	−	14°34′N
Zungeru, Nigeria	115.3	−	−	−	−	+	+	+	+	●	−	−	−	9°45′N
Harar, Ethiopia	89.7	−	−	+	+	+	+	+	●	+	−	−	−	9°20′N
Addis Ababa, Ethiopia	123.7	−	−	−	−	−	+	●	●	+	−	−	−	9°2′N
Freetown, Sierra Leone	343.4	−	−	−	−	−	+	●	●	+	+	−	−	8°30′N
Lagos, Nigeria	183.6	−	−	−	−	+	●	+	−	−	+	−	−	6°25′N
Cotonou, Benin	132.6	−	−	+	+	●	●	−	−	−	+	−	−	6°20′N
Monrovia, Liberia	513.8	−	−	−	−	+	●	●	−	+	+	−	−	6°18′N
Accra, Ghana	72.4	−	−	+	+	+	●	−	−	−	+	−	−	5°35′N
Mongalla, Sudan	94.5	−	−	−	+	+	+	●	+	+	+	−	−	5°8′N
Libreville, Gabon	251.0	+	+	+	+	+	−	−	−	−	+	●	+	0°25′N
Entebbe, Uganda	150.6	−	−	+	●	+	−	−	−	−	−	+	−	0°3′N
Nairobi, Kenya	95.8	−	−	+	●	+	−	−	−	−	−	+	+	1°20′S
Mombasa, Kenya	120.1	−	−	−	+	●	+	−	−	−	−	−	−	4°0′S
Kinshasa, Zaïre	135.4	+	+	+	+	+	−	−	−	−	+	●	●	4°20′S
Kananga, Zaïre	158.2	+	+	+	+	−	−	−	−	−	+	●	●	5°55′S
Lilongwe, Malawi	78.7	●	●	+	−	−	−	−	−	−	−	+	+	14°0′S
Lusaka, Zambia	83.3	●	+	+	−	−	−	−	−	−	−	+	+	15°25′S
Harare, Zimbabwe	82.8	●	+	+	−	−	−	−	−	−	−	+	+	17°50′S

	Total annual rainfall, cm	J	F	M	A	M	J	J	A	S	O	N	D	Latitude
Tamatave, Madagascar	325.6	+	+	●	+	−	+	+	≃	−	−	−	−	18° 2′S
Beira, Mozambique	152.2	●	+	+	−	−	−	−	−	−	+	+	+	19° 50′S
Johannesburg, South Africa	70.9	+	+	+	−	−	−	−	−	−	−	+	●	26° 10′S
Maputo, Mozambique	75.9	●	+	+	−	−	−	−	−	−	−	+	+	26° 35′S
Cape Town, South Africa	50.8	−	−	−	+	+	+	●	+	+	−	−	−	33° 55′S
Sub-Arctic														
Reykjavik, Iceland	77.2	+	−	−	−	−	−	−	−	+	●	+	+	64° 10′N
Australasia and Pacific														
Honolulu, HI, USA	64.3	●	+	+	−	−	−	−	−	−	−	+	●	21° 25′N
Tulagi, Solomon Is.	313.4	+	●	+	−	−	−	−	−	−	−	−	+	8° 0′S
Port Moresby, Papua New Guinea	101.1	+	●	+	+	−	−	−	−	−	−	−	+	9° 24′S
Manihiki, Cook Is.	248.2	●	+	−	−	−	−	−	−	−	+	+	+	10° 24′S
Thursday Is., Australia	171.5	●	+	+	+	−	−	−	−	−	−	−	+	10° 30′S
Darwin, Australia	149.1	●	+	+	−	−	−	−	−	−	−	+	+	12° 20′S
Apia, Western Samoa	285.2	●	+	+	+	−	−	−	−	−	−	+	+	13° 50′S
Cairns, Australia	225.3	+	+	●	+	−	−	−	−	−	−	−	+	16° 55′S
Tahiti, French Polynesia	162.8	●	●	+	+	−	−	−	−	−	−	+	●	17° 45′S
Suva, Fiji	297.4	+	+	●	−	−	−	−	−	−	−	−	+	18° 0′S
Perth, Australia	90.7	−	−	−	−	+	●	●	+	+	+	−	−	31° 57′S
Sydney, Australia	118.1	−	+	+	●	+	+	+	−	−	−	−	−	33° 53′S
Auckland, New Zealand	124.7	−	−	−	−	+	+	●	+	−	−	−	−	36° 52′S
Melbourne, Australia	65.3	−	−	+	+	−	−	−	−	+	●	●	+	37° 40′S
Wellington, New Zealand	120.4	−	−	−	−	+	+	●	+	−	+	−	−	41° 19′S
Christchurch, New Zealand	63.8	+	−	−	−	+	+	●	−	−	−	−	+	43° 33′S
Central America and Caribbean														
Monterey, Mexico	58.2	−	−	−	−	−	+	+	+	●	+	−	−	25° 40′N
Mazatlán, Mexico	84.8	−	−	−	−	−	−	+	+	●	−	−	−	23° 10′N
Havana, Cuba	122.4	−	−	−	−	+	+	+	+	+	●	−	−	23° 8′N
Mérida, Mexico	92.7	−	−	−	−	+	●	+	+	+	+	−	−	20° 50′N
Mexico City, Mexico	74.9	−	−	−	−	−	+	●	+	+	−	−	−	19° 20′N
Port-au-Prince, Haiti	135.4	−	−	−	+	●	−	−	+	+	+	−	−	18° 40′N
Santo Domingo, Dominican Rep	141.7	−	−	−	−	+	+	+	+	●	+	+	−	18° 30′N
Kingston, Jamaica	80.0	−	−	−	−	+	+	−	+	+	●	+	−	18° 0′N
Acapulco, Mexico	154.2	−	−	−	−	−	●	+	+	+	+	−	−	16° 51′N
Salina Cruz, Mexico	102.6	−	−	−	−	−	−	+	+	●	−	−	−	16° 10′N
Dominica, Leeward Is.	197.9	−	−	−	−	+	●	+	+	+	+	−	−	15° 20′N
Guatemala City, Guatemala	131.6	−	−	−	−	+	●	+	+	+	+	−	−	14° 40′N
Tegucigalpa, Honduras	162.1	−	−	−	−	●	+	−	+	+	−	−	−	14° 10′N
San José, Costa Rica	179.8	−	−	−	−	+	+	+	+	●	●	−	−	10° 0′N
Balboa Heights, Panama	177.0	−	−	−	−	+	+	+	+	+	●	●	−	9° 0′N

	Total annual rainfall, cm	J	F	M	A	M	J	J	A	S	O	N	D	Latitude
South America														
Caracas, Venezuela	83.3	−	−	−	−	+	●	●	●	●	●	+	−	10° 30′N
Ciudad Bolivar, Venezuela	101.6	−	−	−	−	+	+	●	+	+	−	+	−	8° 5′N
Georgetown, Guyana	225.3	+	−	−	−	+	●	+	−	−	−	−	+	6° 50′N
Bogotá, Colombia	105.9	−	−	+	+	+	−	−	−	−	●	+	−	4° 34′N
Quito, Ecuador	112.3	+	+	+	●	+	−	−	−	−	−	−	−	0° 15′S
Belém, Brazil	243.8	+	●	●	+	+	−	−	−	−	−	−	−	1° 20′S
Guayaquil, Ecuador	97.3	●	●	●	+	−	−	−	−	−	−	+	+	2° 15′S
Manaus, Brazil	181.1	+	+	●	−	−	−	−	−	−	−	−	−	3° 0′S
Recife, Brazil	161.0	−	−	+	+	+	●	+	+	−	−	−	−	8° 0′S
Lima, Peru	4.8	−	−	−	−	+	+	+	●	●	−	−	−	12° 0′S
Salvador (Bahía), Brazil	190.0	−	−	−	●	●	+	+	−	−	−	−	−	13° 0′S
Cuiabá, Brazil	139.5	+	+	●	−	−	−	−	−	−	+	+	+	15° 30′S
Concepción, Bolivia	114.3	●	+	+	−	−	−	−	−	−	−	●	+	15° 50′S
La Paz, Bolivia	57.4	●	+	+	−	−	−	−	−	−	−	+	+	16° 20′S
Rio de Janeiro, Brazil	108.2	+	+	+	+	−	−	−	−	−	−	+	●	23° 0′S
São Paulo, Brazil	142.8	+	+	+	+	−	−	−	−	−	−	+	●	23° 40′S
Asunción, Paraguay	131.6	+	+	−	+	+	−	−	−	−	+	+	●	25° 21′S
Tucumán, Argentina	97.0	●	+	+	−	−	−	−	−	−	−	+	●	26° 50′S
Santiago, Chile	36.1	−	−	−	−	+	●	+	+	−	−	−	−	33° 24′S
Buenos, Aires, Argentina	95.0	−	−	+	+	−	−	−	−	−	+	+	●	34° 30′S
Montevideo, Uruguay	95.0	−	−	●	●	+	+	−	−	−	−	−	−	34° 50′S
Valdivia, Chile	260.1	−	−	−	+	+	●	+	+	−	−	−	−	39° 50′S

Sea Temperatures at 40 Resorts and Cities (in degrees Centigrade)

	J	F	M	A	M	J	J	A	S	O	N	D
Acapulco Mexico	24	24	24	25	26	27	28	28	28	27	26	25
Agadir Morocco	17	17	18	18	19	19	22	22	22	22	21	18
Algiers Algeria	15	14	15	15	17	20	23	24	23	21	18	16
Athens Greece	14	14	14	15	18	22	24	24	23	21	19	16
Bangkok Thailand	26	27	27	28	28	28	28	28	28	27	27	27
Barcelona Spain	13	12	13	14	16	19	22	24	22	21	16	14
Cairo Egypt	15	15	18	21	24	26	27	27	26	24	21	17

	J	F	M	A	M	J	J	A	S	O	N	D
Copenhagen Denmark	3	2	3	5	9	14	16	16	14	12	8	5
Corfu Greece	14	14	14	16	18	21	23	24	23	21	18	16
Dubrovnik Yugoslavia	13	13	13	15	17	22	23	24	22	19	16	14
Faro Portugal	15	15	15	16	17	18	19	20	20	19	17	16
Hong Kong	18	18	21	24	25	27	28	28	27	26	24	21
Honolulu Hawaii, USA	24	24	24	25	26	26	27	27	27	27	26	25
Istanbul Turkey	8	8	8	11	15	20	22	23	21	19	15	11
Kingston Jamaica	26	26	26	27	27	28	29	29	28	28	27	27
Las Palmas Canary Islands	19	18	18	18	19	20	21	22	23	23	21	20
Lisbon Portugal	14	14	14	15	16	17	18	19	19	18	16	15
Los Angeles USA	14	14	15	15	16	18	19	20	19	18	17	15
Malaga Spain	15	14	14	15	17	18	21	22	21	19	17	16
Malta	15	14	15	15	18	21	24	25	24	22	19	17
Miami USA	22	23	24	25	28	30	31	32	30	28	25	23
Mombasa Kenya	27	28	28	28	28	27	25	25	27	27	27	27
Naples Italy	14	13	14	15	18	21	24	25	23	21	18	16
Nassau Bahamas	23	23	23	24	25	27	28	28	28	27	26	24
New Orleans USA	13	14	17	21	26	28	30	30	28	23	18	14
New York USA	3	2	4	8	13	18	22	23	21	17	11	6
Nice France	13	12	13	14	16	20	22	23	21	19	16	14
Palma Majorca	14	13	14	15	17	21	24	25	24	21	18	15
Rio de Janeiro Brazil	25	25	26	25	24	23	22	22	22	22	23	24
Rome Italy	14	13	13	14	17	21	23	24	23	20	18	15
San Francisco USA	11	11	12	12	13	14	15	15	16	15	13	11
Stockholm Sweden	3	1	1	2	5	10	15	15	13	10	7	4
Sydney Australia	23	24	23	20	18	18	16	17	18	19	19	21
Tahiti Fr. Polynesia	27	27	27	28	28	27	26	26	26	26	27	27

	J	F	M	A	M	J	J	A	S	O	N	D
Tel Aviv Israel	16	16	17	18	21	24	25	27	27	24	21	18
Tenerife Canary Islands	19	18	18	18	19	20	21	22	23	23	21	20
Tunis Tunisia	15	14	14	15	17	20	23	25	24	22	19	16
Vancouver Canada	8	7	8	9	11	13	14	14	13	12	11	10
Venice Italy	9	8	10	13	17	21	23	24	21	18	14	11
Wellington New Zealand	17	18	18	17	14	14	13	13	12	14	14	17

Altitudes of Selected Cities (in metres)

Amsterdam, Netherlands	5
Asunción, Paraguay	77
Athens, Greece	0
Auckland, New Zealand	0
Bangkok, Thailand	12
Beirut, Lebanon	8
Bogotá, Colombia	2,590
Bridgetown, Barbados	0
Brussels, Belgium	58
Buenos Aires, Argentina	14
Calcutta, India	26
Cape Town, South Africa	8
Caracas, Venezuela	964
Casablanca, Morocco	49
Cayenne, French Guiana	8
Copenhagen, Denmark	8
Curaçao, Netherlands Antilles	0
Damascus, Syria	213
Dublin, Ireland	9
Frankfurt, West Germany	91
Geneva, Switzerland	377
Glasgow, Scotland	59
Guatemala City, Guatemala	1,478
Havana, Cuba	9
Helsinki, Finland	8
Hong Kong	8
Istanbul, Turkey	9
Jerusalem, Israel	762
Juneau, Alaska	0
Kabul, Afghanistan	2,219
Karachi, Pakistan	15
Kingston, Jamaica	8
La Paz, Bolivia	3,720
Lima, Peru	153
Lisbon, Portugal	87
Madrid, Spain	655
Manila, Philippines	8
Mexico City, Mexico	2,240
Montevideo, Uruguay	9
Moscow, USSR	191
Oslo, Norway	12
Panama City, Panama	12
Port-au-Prince, Haiti	8
Port-of-Spain, Trinidad	8
Quito, Ecuador	2,819
Rabat, Morocco	0
Rangoon, Burma	17
Rio de Janeiro, Brazil	9
Rome, Italy	14
St. George's, Grenada	0
St. John's, Antigua	0
Santiago, Chile	550
Singapore	8
Stockholm, Sweden	11
Suva, Fiji	0
Sydney, Australia	8
Tegucigalpa, Honduras	975
Tehran, Iran	1,220
Tokyo, Japan	9
Vienna, Austria	168

Weather Information

London Weather Centre
284–286 High Holborn
London
WC1V 7HX
Tel: 01-836 4311 Public Enquiries
430 5709 Climatological Enquiries
430 5511 General Enquiries.

Can answer all regional weather enquiries.

Meterological Office
(Overseas Enquiry Bureau)
Bracknell
Berkshire
Tel: (0344) 420242 Ext. 2267

National Meterological Center
5200 Auth Road
Camp Springs
MD 20233
USA

Is the head office. Regional and local offices can also give weather information.

International Time Comparison

Hours ahead (+) or behind (−) Greenwich Mean Time (GMT)

Afghanistan	+ 4½
Algeria	GMT
summer until late Oct.	+ 1
Angola	+ 1
Argentina	− 3
Australia	
New South Wales	+11
Queensland	+10
South Australia	+10½
Tasmania	+11
Victoria	+11
Western Australia	+ 8
summer until late Oct:	
NSW, Qld, Tas, Vic	+10
SA	+ 9½
WA	+ 8
Bahrain	+ 3
Bangladesh	+ 6
Belize	− 6
Benin	+ 1
Bhutan	+ 6
Bolivia	− 4
Botswana	+ 2
Brazil	
Fernando de Noronha	− 2
East, all coast and	
Brasilia	− 3
West	− 4
Territory of Acre	− 5
Brunei	+ 8
Bulgaria	+ 2

Burma	+ 6½
Burundi	+ 2
Cameroon	+ 1
Canada	
Atlantic Time	− 4
Central Time	− 6
Eastern Time	− 5
Mountain Time	− 7
Newfoundland	− 3½
Pacific Time	− 8
Yukon Territory	− 8
summer until late Oct:	
Atlantic Time	− 3
Central Time	− 5
Eastern Time	− 4
Mountain Time	− 6
Newfoundland	− 2½
Pacific Time	− 7
Yukon Territory	− 7
Cape Verde Is	− 1
Cayman Is	− 5
Central African Rep	+ 1
Chad	+ 1
Chile	− 3
mid-March until mid-Oct	− 4
China	+ 8
Colombia	− 5
Comoro Arch.	+ 3
Congo	+ 1
Cook Is	− 9½
summer until late Oct	−10

Costa Rica	− 6
Cuba	− 5
summer until mid-Oct	− 4
Djibouti	+ 3
Dominican Rep	− 4
Ecuador	− 5
Egypt	+ 2
El Salvador	− 6
Equatorial Guinea	+ 1
Ethiopia	+ 3
Falkland Is	− 4
Port Stanley	− 3
Fiji	+12
French Guiana	− 3
French Polynesia	−10
Gabon	+ 1
Gambia	GMT
Ghana	GMT
Guatemala	− 6
Guinea	GMT
Guinea-Bissau	GMT
Guyana	− 3
Haiti	− 5
Honduras	− 6
Hong Kong	+ 8
Iceland	GMT
India	+ 5½
Indonesia	
Central Zone (Kalimantan, Sulawesi, Timor)	+ 8
East Zone (Molucca Is, Irian Jaya)	+ 9
West Zone (Java, Sumatra, Bali)	+ 7
Iran	+ 3½
Iraq	+ 3
Israel	+ 2
Ivory Coast	GMT
Jamaica	− 5
summer until late Oct	− 4
Japan	+ 9
Jordan	+ 2
Kampuchea	+ 7
Kenya	+ 3
Kiribati Rep	+12
Korea, North	+ 9
Korea, South	+ 9
Kuwait	+ 3
Lao People's Dem Rep (Laos)	+ 7

Lebanon	+ 2
Lesotho	+ 2
Liberia	GMT
Libya	+ 2
Macao	+ 8
Madagascar	+ 3
Malawi	+ 2
Malaysia	
Peninsular Malaysia	+ 7½
Sabah, Sarawak	+ 8
Maldive Is	+ 5
Mali	GMT
Mauritania	GMT
Mauritius	+ 4
Mexico	
General Mexico Time	− 6
Lower California & N. Pacific Coast	− 7
Baja California Norte	− 8
summer until late Oct: Baja California Norte	− 7
Micronesia	
Caroline Is except Kusaie, Pingelap & Truk	+10
Guam and Mariana Is	+10
Kusaie, Pingelap	+12
Marshall Is (Kwajelein −12)	+12
Truk	+11
Morocco	GMT
Mozambique	+ 2
Nauru	+12
Nepal	+ 5
New Caledonia	+11
New Zealand	+13
summer until late Oct	+12
Nicaragua	− 6
Niger	+ 1
Nigeria	+ 1
Oman	+ 4
Pakistan	+ 5
Panama	− 5
Papua New Guinea	+10
Paraguay	− 3
Peru	− 5
Philippines	+ 8
Qatar	+ 3
Réunion	+ 4
Rwanda	+ 2
Samoa, American & Western	−11
São Tomé & Principe	GMT
Saudi Arabia	+ 3

Sénégal	GMT	**USA**	
Seychelles	+ 4	Central Time	− 6
Sierra Leone	GMT	Eastern Time	− 5
		Hawaiian Is	−10
Singapore	+ 7½	Mountain Time	− 7
Solomon Is	+11	Pacific Time	− 8
Somalia	+ 3	Alaska, Ketchikan to 58°N	− 8
		58°N–141°W	− 9
South Africa	+ 2	141°W–162°W	−10
Sri Lanka	+ 5½	162°W–Western Tip	−11
Sudan	+ 2	summer until late Oct:	
		Central Time	− 5
Suriname	− 3½	Eastern Time	− 4
Swaziland	+ 2	Hawaiian Is	−10
		Mountain Time	− 6
Syria	+ 2	Pacific Time	− 7
Taiwan	+ 8	Alaska, Ketchikan to 58°N	− 7
		58°N–141°W	− 8
Tanzania	+ 3	141°W–162°W	− 9
Thailand	+ 7	162°W–Western Tip	−10
Togo	GMT	**USSR (Moscow)**	+ 3
Tonga	+13	**Upper Volta (Burkina Faso)**	GMT
Trinidad & Tobago	− 4	**Uruguay**	− 3
Tunisia	+ 1	**Vanuatu Rep**	+11
		Venezuela	− 4
Turkey	+ 3	**Vietnam**	+ 7
Turks & Caicos Is	− 5	**Yemen Arab Rep (North)**	+ 3
summer until late Oct	− 4	**Yemen People's Dem Rep (South)**	+ 3
Tuvalu Is	+12	**Zaïre**	
Uganda	+ 3	Kasai, Katanga, Kivu, Orientale	+ 2
United Arab Emirates	+ 4	Kinshasa, Mbandaka	+ 1
UK	GMT	**Zambia**	+ 2
mid-March until late Oct	+ 1	**Zimbabwe**	+ 2

Equipment

Equipment: General

Austria:

Hof and Turecek GmbH
Expeditions Service
Markgraf Rüdigerstrasse 1
1150 Vienna
Tel: (0222) 92 23 61/95 21 74
Sells emergency and survival equipment, water purifiers, cooking appliances, camping gear, inc. tents, expedition food, lamps, navigational devices, books, maps, clothing, motoring equipment and spares, backpacking equipment, tools and bows and arrows. This shop is closely connected with the Expedition Club Austria. Dispatch of goods all over the world. Please order equipment catalogue free of charge.

Canada:

Austin House, Inc
PO Box 1051
2388 Speers Road
Oakville
Ont L6J 5E9
Tel: (416) 825-2650
(See Austin House, USA.)

Blacks Camping International
2121 Carling Ave
Ottawa Ont K2A 1H2

and

16 Carlton Street
Toronto
Ontario

and

3535 Queen Mary Road
Montreal Que
Make excellent down gear. Catalogue.

Koolatron Corporation
27 Catharine Avenue
Brantford
Ontario N3T 1X5
Manufacture a line of 12-volt portable and build-in electronic coolers which hold up to 20kg of food, 110 or 220 volt adaptors. ABS Case Ltd. Distributorships available. Export pricing from $88 to $181.

Eire:

Cascade Designs Ltd
Dwyer Road
Midleton
Co. Cork
Tel: (021) 632399
Telex: 75490
Supplier of the Therm-a-rest camping mattress.

Lowe Alpine Systems
Sragh Industrial Estate
Tullamore
Co. Offaly
Tel: (0353) 506 41124
Telex: 60818 LASI EL
Manufacturer of specialist outdoor clothing and equipment.

France:

Ets Becker (Igloo)
94 Route Nationale 10
Coignieres
78310 Maurepas
Tel: (1) 30 51 57 81
Katadyn-France SA
24 Blvd du Château
F-94500 Champigny s/Marne
Tel: (1) 48 80 37 70
Make portable water filters which clear and decontaminate water

E. Lacroix
18 Rue Malher
75004 Paris
Tel: 48 87 53 20
Telex: 220672F LACART
Signalling and rescue devices, flares, preventive devices against avalanches, dryness, hail, and miscellaneous safety devices such as luminous alarm signals and the ballasted petard intended to frighten sharks and other tropical fish to protect fishermen.

Manuel
16 Rue la Boétie
75008 Paris
Tel: 42 65 47 27

and

30 Avenue de la Grande Armée
75017 Paris
Tel: 43 80 09 30

and

Sport et Climat
223 Blvd St Germain
75007 Paris
Tel: 45 84 80 99
These three stores specialize in garments for tropical countries from head to foot.

West Germany:

Alles Für Tramper
Bundesallee 88
D-1000 Berlin 41
Tel: (030) 8518069

Därr's Travel Shop
Theresienstr. 66
D-8000 Munich 2
Tel: (089) 28 20 32

Globetrotter Ausrüstungen
Wiesendamm 1
D-2000 Hamburg 60
Tel: (040) 29 12 23
Equipment for travellers; books, maps. Catalogue available.

Katadyn Deutschland GmbH
Schaufeleinstr, 20
D-8000 Munich 21
Tel: (089) 57 20 53
(See Katadyn France)

Transglobe
Weyerstr, 33
D-5000 Koln 1
Tel: (0221) 239 398

Versandhaus Süd-West
Magirstrasse 35
D-7900 Ulm
Tel: (0731) 1701
Telex: 712 640 VSW
Mail order house for mountaineers, backpackers, camping, trekking, survival, etc.

India:

Choomti Trekkers PVT Ltd
Houseboat King's Marina No 67
The Bund
Srinagar 190001
Trekking equipment for sale or hire.

Netherlands:

Tatteljee Products
Nieuwendammerdijk 304
1023 BT
Amsterdam
Hand-made specialist outdoor products, and 'button-beds'. Available in UK through Field and Trek.

Switzerland:

Katadyn Products Inc
Industriestr. 27
8304 Wallisellen
Switzerland
Tel: 01-830 36 77

UK:

ABC Equipment
The Green
Clayton
Doncaster DN5 7DD
Tel: (0977) 43103
Telex: 547291

Are suppliers of all Land Rovers and Range Rover spares, specialising in export. Will ship to all parts of the world at short notice. Special arrangements for expedition requirements.

Allcord Ltd
Ilford Road
Newcastle upon Tyne
NE2 3NX
Tel: 091-284 8444

Alpine Sports
456/8 The Strand
London WC2R 0RG
Tel: 01-839 5161
and
215 Kensington High Street
London W8 6BD
Tel: 01-938 1911
Travel and mountaineering equipment.

Airborne Industries Ltd
Airborne Industrial Estate
Arterial Road
Leigh-on-Sea
Essex SS9 4EF
Tel: (0702) 52565
Telex: 99412
Manufacture portable solar still and water collector based on military survival kit design.

Backpacker Systems
44 Winchcombe Street
Cheltenham
Glos
Tel: (0242) 42200
Travel bags, tents, camping and trekking equipment and clothing for sale or hire.

Baker-Nicol Logistics Ltd
4 Sundew Close
Eaton Socon
St Neots
Cambs PE19 4AN
Tel: (0480) 216825
Supply specialist survival equipment and clothing and advice for remote areas, specialising in polar regions and hot deserts.

Berghaus
34 Dean Street
Newcastle upon Tyne
NE1 1PG
Tel: 091-232 3561
One of Britain's leading suppliers of specialist packs and clothing for hiking and climbing. Suppliers to many expeditions.

Blacks Camping and Leisure Ltd
Gailey
Stafford ST19 5PP
Tel: (0902) 790 721
Head office of the firm formerly known as variously as Blacks of Greenock and Blacks Outdoor Centres. Blacks have tents and camping equipment for hire. Supply lightweight, patrol, frame, mountain, and touring tents; camp furniture, kitchen kits, stoves and lamps; clothing and accessories and convertible specialist and summer-weight sleeping bags. There

are five retail outlets in London and others in Birmingham, Bristol, Cardiff, Dundee, Edinburgh, Exeter, Glasgow, Hull, Leeds, Leicester, Liverpool, Manchester, Newcastle, Norwich, Nottingham, Plymouth, Reading, Sheffield, and Stoke.

Camping Gaz International
Camping Gaz (GB) Ltd
126-130 St Leonards Road
Windsor
Berkshire
Tel: (0753) 855011
The best source of information on the availability of Camping Gaz throughout the world. Camping Gaz cartridges and stoves, heaters, lanterns, portable refrigerators, cookboxes, stainless steel vacuum flasks and the Globetrotter stove, which is very small and light, are available throughout the UK. Worldwide availability list for cartridges and cylinder refills available on request

Caravan Backpacking
1 Newfield Drive
Menston
Ilkley
W. Yorks LS29 6JQ
Tel: (0943) 74870
Manufacture sleeping bags, lightweight tents, and rucksacks.

Colne Valley Sports
Linyards Terrace
Marsden
Huddersfield
W. Yorks
Tel: (0484) 844580

Dales Outdoor Centre
Coach Street
Skipton
N. Yorks BD23 1LH
Tel: (0756) 4305
Mountaineering and trekking equipment and clothing.

Dantex Services Ltd
La Motte Chambers
St Helier
Jersey
Channel Islands
Tel: (534) 767 77
Telex: 4192231
Personal-size water purifier – small enough to fit in pocket or briefcase. Filters and purifies water from all sources except sea water. Safe and effective.

Derby Mountain Centre Ltd
85/89 King Street
Derby DE1 3EE
Tel: (0332) 365650
Specialist lightweight outdoor equipment and clothing.

Direct Adventure Supplies
17 Pages Walk
London SE1
Tel: 01-231 3391
Offer a mail order service with a discount off a comprehensive range of outdoor equipment.

Europa Sport
Ann Street
Kendal LA9 6AB
Tel: (0539) 24740

Field and Trek (Equipment) Ltd
Mail Order:
3 Wates Way
Brentwood
Essex CM15 9TB
Tel: (0277) 221529

Retail Shops:
23-25 Kings Road
Brentwood
Essex CM14 4ER
Tel: (0277) 222230
and
3 Palace Street
Canterbury
Kent CT1 2DY
Tel: (0227) 470023
Field and Trek's illustrated catalogue offers products which are reduced in price by appproximately 14 per cent off normal retail on most leading makes of expedition equipment, including tents, rucksacks, boots, waterproof clothing, sleeping bags and mountaineering gear. They allow a further five per cent discount on orders over £300. Large mail order department. Expeditions entitled to special bulk purchase prices. Please ask for a quotation on expedition letter-head. Contract price list is free of charge. Illustrated retail catalogue and price list is available for £1.50.

Fjallraven Sports Equipment (UK) Ltd
International House
Priestley Way
Staples Corner
London NW2 7AZ
Tel: 01-450 6681
Manufacturer of outdoor equipment and clothing.

Glacier Sport
40-41 Lune Street
Preston
Lancs PR1 2NN
Tel: (0772) 21903
Outdoor and mountain sports equipment and clothing.

Hamish Hamilton
Unit 20
Meemsbrook Works
Valley Road
Sheffield S8 9FT
Tel: (0742) 580611
Manufacturer of Buffalo sleeping bags.

Hazel Constance
Gear for Outdoors
13 The Chase
Coulsdon
Surrey CR3 2EJ
Tel: 01-660 7294
New bags for old! Damaged or worn sleeping bags may be worth saving. The filling from good quality bags can be used in a new shell. Top quality work. Some specialist clothing made to order. Send s.a.e.

or phone for details. *These sleeping bags have been used in places as far apart as Corsica, Yosemite and Everest Base Camp. This can help keep down the cost of equipment.*

Helly Hansen
College Street
Kempston
Bedford MK42 8NA
Tel: (0234) 41431
Manufacturers of good rough weather and outdoor clothing.

Johnson-Progress Ltd
Carpenters Road
Stratford
London E15 2DS
Tel: 01-534 7431
Telex: 896156
Make Millbank Bags for filtering water in two sizes: individual and party/group.

Karrimor International Ltd
Avenue Parade
Accrington
Lancashire BB5 6PR
Tel: (0254) 385911
Karrimor International is particularly known for the excellent quality of its range of rucksacks, cycle luggage, adventure luggage and camera bags; all of which they manufacture themselves. They also act as UK distributors for Asolo/Karrimor Footwear, Trangia stoves, Ajungilak sleeping bags, Salewa winter hardware. Trak, Kneissl and Rolletto skis and a range of small travel accessories.

LD Mountain Centre
34 Dean St
Newcastle-upon-Tyne NE1 1PG
Tel: 091-232 3561
Outdoor and sporting equipment and clothing.

M.L. Industries
c/o 117 Inglesham Way
Hamworthy
Poole
Dorset BH15 4PP
Bivvy bag manufacturers.

Mountaineering Designs
PO Box 5
Bramhall
Stockport
Cheshire SK7 3AX
Tel: 061-439 6009
Will re-cover down sleeping bags.

Mountain Equipment
Leech Street
Stalybridge SK15 1SD
Tel: 061-338 8793
Manufacturers of outdoor and travel clothing and equipment.

Mrs S. Norman-Luthy
37 Town End
Wilsford
nr Grantham
Lincs NG32 3NX
Tel: (0400) 30285
Water purifiers.

Northern Feather Leisure (UK) Ltd
1 Newfield Drive
Menston
Ilkley
W. Yorks LS29 6JQ
Sleeping bag manufacturers.

The North Face
PO Box 16
Industrial Estate
Port Glasgow
PA14 5XL
Scotland
Tel: (0475) 41344
Telex: 777394
Outdoor clothing and equipment manufacturer.

A.B. Optimus Ltd
Sanders Lodge Estate
Rushden
Northants
NN10 9BQ
Tel: (0933) 57412
Are manufacturers of the well known Optimus pressure stoves, lanterns and cookers as well as PLG cooking and heating appliances.

Outdoor Specials
19 Nookston Close
Hartlepool
Cleveland TS26 0PG
Tents and rucksacks.

Overland Vehicle and Supplies Ltd
5 Bridge Industries
Fareham
Hampshire PO16 8SX
Tel: (0329) 239123
Will supply, convert and kit out Land Rovers for overland travel.

Phoenix Mountaineering Ltd
Coquetdale Trading Estate
Amble
Morpeth
Northumberland
NE65 0PE
Tel: (0665) 710 934
Manufacturers of lightweight tents, specialists in high performance ski wear, outdoor clothing, sleeping bags, and Alpine Climbing Helmets.

Pindisports
14-18 Holborn
London EC1
Tel: 01-242 3278
Provided some equipment for the 1972 Everest South West Face Expedition and the 1970 Annapurna South Face Expedition and are suppliers to the John Ridgway School of Adventure at Ardmore, Sutherland. They supply equipment for hill-walking, rock-climbing, big-wall climbing, alpinism, expeditions, shelter and survival; also guidebooks and magazines.

Polywarm Products Ltd
Cambuslang Road
Rutherglen
Glasgow G73 1RS
Telex: 779968

Manufacture a selection of lightweight and compact specialist sleeping bags suitable for the mountaineer and hiker, including conventional and mummy-shaped bags, made of washable man-made fibres and stiched by a special process that prevents the filling from moving. The sleeping bags are all guaranteed for 12 months.

Ranger
PO Box 138
Barnet
Herts EN5 5DL
Clothing and equipment.

Raven Leisure Products
Unit 9-10
Long Furrow Trading Estate
East Goscote
Leicester LE7 8ZS
Tel: (050 981) 6611

Rohan
30 Maryland Rd
Tonywell
Milton Keynes
Bucks
Tel: (0908) 618888
Make specialist clothing for hot and cold climates. Send s.a.e. for clothing system. Catalogue.

SafariQuip
20 Mill Brow
Marple Bridge
Stockport SK6 5LL
Tel: 061-449 8148
Specialists in all kinds of equipment. Give customers special assistance and offer objective and unbiased advice. Catalogue carries an expanded section on useful and often hard-to-come by equipment. Have special 84 inch wide seamfree terylene mosquito netting for sale off the roll so that customers can make their own nets. Offer a wide range of lamps and stoves, and vehicle accessories, offer a design and build service for vehicle equipment. Compasses. Also help people wishing to buy or sell second-hand expedition equipment.

Sanctum
Land of Green Ginger
Front Street
Tyne-mouth
Tel: 091-296 0804
Clothing and equipment supplier.

Robert Saunders (Chigwell) Ltd
Five Oaks Lane
Chigwell
Essex IG7 4QP
Tel: Chigwell 500 2447
Manufacturer of high quality tents.

Shark Sports Ltd
Nordstrom House
North Bromhill
Morpeth
Northumberland
NE65 9UJ
Tel: (0670) 760365
Watersports and survival products.

Slioch Outdoor Equipment
Unit 1
Poolewe
Ross-shire IV22 2JU
Made-to-measure and individually tailored thermal and waterproof clothing.

Snow and Rock
47 Stephenson Street
(New St Shopping Centre)
Birmingham B2
Tel: 021-643 6040
and
188 Kensington High Street
London W8
Tel: 01-937 0872
Camping, trekking, climbing, skiing equipment and clothing.

Peter Storm Ltd
14 High Pavement
Nottingham NG1 1HP
Tel: (0602) 506911
Manufacturer of rough weather clothing.

Surf and Ski Sports Ltd
1-2 Regent Street
Brighton BN1 1UL
Tel: (0273) 673192
and

41 Bells Street
Reigate RH2 7AQ
Tel: (07372) 22218
Clothing and outdoor equipment.

Survival Aids Ltd
Morland
Penrith
Cumbria
CA10 3AZ
Tel: (09314) 444
Telex 64484 Fax (09314)450
Produces a comprehensive Survival Equipment Catalogue and quarterlySurvival News. Firm supplies all sorts of equipment including survival kits, flares, emergency rations, compasses, knives, medical kits and clothing.

Survival Equipment Ltd
Chandos House
42 St Owen Street
Hereford
Tel: (0432) 277739
Mail order outdoor clothing and equipment. Catalogue £1 and SAE.

The Survival Shop
11-13 West Colonnade
Euston Station
London NW1
Tel: 01-388 8353
Over 750 expedition/outdoor equipment and clothing items. A comprehensive selection for the traveller.

Tent Craft Ltd
25 Rusthall Ave
Chiswick

London W4 1BW
Tel: 01-841 2418
Made-to-order tents of all types. Tent repairs.

Tent and Tarpaulin Manufacturing Co.
101/3 Brixton Hill
London SW2 1AA
Tel: 01-674 0121
Suppliers to commercial and private expeditions of all kinds of tent from the marquee to the two-man, of camp beds, air beds, stoves, mosquito nets, sand ladders, jerry cans (water and petrol), wire ropes and slings, towing chains, all typed of ropes and tarpaulins. They also repair tents.

Touringsport
Unit 13
Quay Lane
Gosport
Hants
Tel: (0705) 528711
Discount mail order equipment for wide range of touring sports. Free catalogue.

Traveller International Products Ltd
51 Hays Mews
London WIX 5DB
Tel: 01-499 2774
Manufacturers of electrical products for the traveller, including the Traveller 'Travel Plug' Adaptor. Available from leading retail outlets.

Travelling Light
Freepost
Morland
Penrith
Cumbria
Tel: (09314) 488
Tropical clothing and lightweight accessories. Mail order.

Ultimate Equipment
Ryburne Mills
Hanson Lane
Halifax
W. Yorks HX1 4SE
Tel: (0422) 42011
Manufacturer of high quality camping equipment and outdoor clothing.

Vango (Scotland) Ltd
70 East Hamilton Street
Ladyburn
Greenock PA15 2UB
Tel: (0475) 44122
Supply a lot of specialist climbing, camping and skiing clothing. Do not sell direct to public but will refer public to nearest stockist. Contact above address. Most camping and outdoor shops sell their products and they are well established and respected.

Venturgear
30 Cricklade Road
Swindon
Wilts
Tel: (0793) 692680
Discount mail order clothing and equipment.

Weatherstop
185 Chanterlands Ave

Hull HU5 3TP
Tel: (0482) 445633
Cold weather clothing.

YHA Adventure Shops
14 Southampton Street,
Covent Garden,
London WC2E 7HY
Tel: 01-836 8541
Also 11 other shops throughout the UK. Phone to find the address of the nearest to you. They supply a wide range of good camping and outdoor equipment as well as books and maps.

USA:

Advanced Filtration Technology
2424 Bates Avenue
Concord
CA 94520
Portable water filter and Super Straw

Austin House, Inc
P.O. Box 117, Sta 'B'
Buffalo
NY 14207
Tel: 1 800-268-5157
Specialize in travel accessories such as money belts, miniature packs, locks, hangers, converters, adaptor plugs, transformers, etc.

Banana Republic
Box 7737
San Francisco
CA 94120
Tel: (800) 527 5200
Mail order travel clothing and books.

Basic Designs, Inc
5815 Bennett Valley Rd
Santa Rosa
CA 95404
Tel: (707) 575 1220
Telex: 9103806641
Make the H20 Sun Shower, a solar-heater portable shower consisting of a heavy duty vinyl bag which holds 11½ litres of water and heats the water to between 32 and 49°C depending on exposure and the heat of the day. The pack measures 10×33 cms and weighs only 340g.

L.L. Bean Inc
Freeport
ME 04033
Tel: (207) 865 3111
Operates a mail order service and has a salesroom which is open 24 hours a day, 365 days a year. Firm sells outdoor garments and accessories, boots and other footwear, canoes, compasses, axes, knives, binoculars, thermometers, stoves, tents, sleeping bags, packs and frames, skis and snowshoes, campware, travel bags, lamps, blankets.

The Complete Traveller
199 Madison Avenue
New York
NY 10016

Tel: (212) 679 4339
Annual catalogue US$1.

Early Winters Ltd
110 Prefontaine Pl.
Seattle
WA 98104
Makers of backpacking and outdoor gear, including the Thousand Mile socks which are guaranteed not to wear out before 1 year or 1,000 miles/1,600 km of walking (whichever comes last) and manufacturers of a full line of gore-tex tents and raingear. Free colour catalogue.

Franzus Company, Inc
352 Park Avenue South
New York
NY 10010
Tel: (212) 889 5850
Makes travel irons, blow dryers, garment steamers, beverage makers, converters, converter sets and adapter plug kits. Travel care appliances for worldwide use.

Katadyn USA, Inc
Warehouse + Service-Center
3020 North Scottsdale Road
Scottsdale
AZ 85251
Tel: (602) 990 3131
Telex: 6835045 MAXCH
(See Katadyn France)

North by Northeast
181 Conant Street
Pawtucket
RI 02862

Parks Products
3611 Cahuenga
Hollywood
CA 90068
Tel: (212) 876 5454
Make voltage converters and adaptor plugs to fit electronic/portable appliances anywhere in the world.

Sierra West
6 East Yanonali Street
Santa Barbara
CA 93101
Tel: (805) 963 87 27
Sierra West is a manufacturer of high quality rainwear, outerwear, tents and backpacking accessories. For further information, please write and request a free colour catalogue.

Traveler's Checklist
Cornwall Bridge Road
Sharon
CT 06069
Tel: (203) 364 0144
International mail order company sells hard-to-find travel accessories, including electrical devices, security, health and grooming aids, money convertors and other travel items.

Wilderness Way International
PO Box 334
Northridge
CA 91324

Make the collapsible two gallon/nine litre Water Sack which weighs 3½ oz/100 gm and consists of two bags, the inner being the larger so that it can never expand to its full size and is therefore less subject to stress.

Equipment: Medical

BCB Ltd
Moorland Road
Cardiff CF2 2YL
Tel: (0222) 464464
First Aid and medical kits to any specification. Catalogues available.

John Bell and Croyden
50 Wigmore Street
London W1
Tel: 01-935 5555
Chemists in London who specialize in making up travel and expedition supplies.

MASTA
c/o London School of Hygiene and Tropical Medicine
Keppel Street
(Gower Street)
London WC1E 7HT
Tel: 01-636 8636
Medical advisory service. Will also provide sterile kits of syringes, needles etc. for those going into areas with a high incidence of AIDS or Hepatitis B.

May & Baker Ltd
Dagenham
Essex
RM10 7XS
Tel: 01-592 3060
May & Baker are one of the largest pharmaceutical manufacturers in the UK. They have several remedies for the minor everyday accidents that occur at home or abroad.

Survival Aids Ltd
Morland
Penrith
Cumbria CA10 3AZ
Tel: (09314) 444
Telex: 64484
Fax: (09314) 450
The firm supplies medical kits for general or special requirements and a large range of packed, lightweight expedition rations.

Tender Corp After Bite
Box 42
Littleton
NH 03561
USA
America's leading treatment for the relief of pain and irritation due to insect bites or stings.

Wyeth Laboratories
PO Box 8299
Philadelphia

PA 19101
USA
and
Hunterscombe Lane South
Taplow
Maidenhead
Berks
Tel: (062) 86 4377
Manufacturer of antivenoms against poisonous snakes of the United States. The serum is sold in a freeze dried condition, making it ideally suited for expeditions (no need for refrigeration), and in small quantities.

Equipment: Optical

Heron Optical Co
23-25 Kings Road
Brentwood
Essex CM14 4ER
Tel: (0277) 222 230
and
3 Palace Street
Canterbury
Kent CT1 2DY
Tel: (0227) 470023
Mail Order:
3 Wates Way
Brentwood
Essex CM15 9TB
Tel: (0277) 233 122
Stock all leading makes of binoculars, telescopes. Associate company of Field and Trek (Equipment) Ltd.

Newbold & Bulford
Carlton Park
Saxmundham
Suffolk IP17 2NL
Tel: (0728) 2933
Supplies Sunto compasses and binoculars.

Olympus Optical Co (UK) Ltd
2-8 Honduras Street
London EC1Y 0TX
Tel: 01-253 2772

Equipment: Photographic

Agfa-Gevaert Ltd
27 Great West Road
Brentford
Middlesex
TW8 9AX
Tel: 01-560 2131

Camera Care Systems
Vale Lane

Bedminster
Bristol BS3 5RU
Tel: (0272) 635263/7
Manufacture protective casings for and distribute fine photographic equipment.

Canon UK Ltd
Brent Trading Centre
North Circular Road
Neasden
London NW10 0JF
Tel: 01-459 1266

Ilford UK Ltd
14 Tottenham Street
London W1
Tel: 01-636 7890

Keith Johnson Photographics
11 Great Marlborough St
London W1
Tel: 01-439 8811
Major suppliers for all photographic equipment and accessories.

Kodak Ltd
Kodak House
PO Box 66
Station Road
Hemel Hempstead
Herts HP1 1JU
Tel: (0442) 611 22
Enquiries to: Ext 44228
Supplies a limited number of films on trade terms to expeditions having the support of the Royal Geographical Society, Mount Everest Foundation or a similar authority, provided that purchases are made in bulk on a one order basis at a minimum value of £250. Delivery must be to a UK address (excluding docks and airports).

Minolta UK Ltd
1-3 Tanners Drive
Blakelands
Milton Keynes
MK14 5BU
Tel: (0908) 615 141

Nikon House
380 Richmond Road
Kingston Upon Thames
Surrey KT2 SPR
Tel: 01-541 4440

Olympus Optical Co (UK) Ltd
2-8 Honduras St
London EC1
Tel: 01-864 4422

Pentax UK Ltd
Pentax House
South Hill Avenue
South Harrow
Middlesex HA2 OLT
Tel: 01-864 4422

Photo Paste (Odeon Photo)
110 Blvd St Germain
75006 Paris
France

Tel: 329 4050

Is a photographic developing and printing service that will process photos of films sent from anywhere in the world, and send the results on anywhere. They will undertake a variety of processes; will give advice on film handling and photographic technique; will retain negatives safely until your journey is over; and charge reasonable prices for these services.

Anthony Scott Ltd
14 Britton Street
London EC1M 5NQ
Tel: 01-253 9060
Photographic developing and printing to a high standard.

TAMRAC
6709 Independence Ave
Canoga Park,
CA 91303
USA
Make the TeleZoom Pak (Model 517), Photo Backpack (Model 757) and a full line of instant access foam padded weatherproof cases for 35mm systems.

Freight Forwarders

Air Freight Shipping
West Tech Shipping Dept
3 Woodstock House
London W1
Tel: 01-408 1088
Telex: 895 5642 WTECH G

APL Shipping and Forwarding Ltd
6 Stratford Office Village
4 Romford Road
London E15
Tel: 01-519 0333/0335

CMF Baggage
Debmore House

193 London Road
Staines
Middx TW18 4HR
Tel: Staines 56431

Excess Baggage Co.
Block 6
Avon Trading Estate
Avonmore Road
London W14 8BR
Tel: 01-603 7173/6
(out of hours) 01-944 9742

Freight Agencies International Ltd
38 Mount Pleasant
London WC1X 0AP
Tel: 01-833 3735

London Baggage Co.
262 Vauxhall Bridge Road
Victoria
London SW1V 1BB
Tel: 01-828 6789

Overseas Containers Ltd
Beagle House
Braham Street
London E1 8EP
Tel: 01-488 1313

Personal Shipping Services
35 Craven Street
London WC2
Tel: 01-839 5095/7

SBS Freight Agencies Ltd
Cambrian House
509/11 Cranbrook Road
Ilford
Essex IG2 6EY
Tel: 0-554 8479/8333

Send It Anywhere Directory
Kogan Page Ltd
120 Pentonville Road
London N1 9JN

Listing of freight forwarders

Kodak Processing Laboratories Worldwide

Australia:
PO Box 4742
Melbourne
Victoria 3001

Austria
Albert Schweitzer-Gasse 4
A-1148 Vienna

Belgium:
Steenstraat 20
1800 Koningslo-Vilvoorde

Canada:
9977 McLaughlin Road
Brampton

Ontario L6X 2M4

Denmark:
Roskildevej 16
2620 Albertslund

Finland:
Postilokero 758
00101 Helsinki 10

France:
Rond-Point George Eastman
93270 Sevran

West Germany:
Postfach 369

7000 Stuttgart 60

Greece:
PO Box 1235
GR 100 10 Athens

Italy:
Casella Postale 11057
20 100 Milan

Japan:
Far East Laboratories ltd
Maniki Bldg
No.2-10 Ginza 3-chome
Chuo-Ku
Tokyo

Mexico:
Administration de Correos 68
Mexico 22 D.F.
Mexico 04870

Netherlands:
Treubstraat 11
2288EG Rijswijk Z.H.

New Zealand:
PO Box 3003
Wellington

Norway:

Trollasveien
1410 Kolbotn

Spain:
Apartado de Correos 130
Colmenar Viejo
Madrid

Sweden:
S-162 85 Vallingby

Switzerland:
Case Postale
CH-1001 Lausanne

United Kingdom:
Box 14
Hemel Hempstead
Hertfordshire
HP2 7EH

USA:
1065 Kapiolani Blvd
Honolulu
Hawaii 96814
and
Kodak Park
Rochester
NY 14650

Training, Help and Advice

Associations: Expeditions

The Adirondack Mountain Club
174 Glen Street
Glens Falls
NY 12801
USA

Tel: (518) 793 7737
Founded in 1922, the ADK is a non-profit membership organization. Works to retain the wilderness and magic of New York's Adirondack and Catskill parks. Assists in construction and maintenance of trails and campsites, shelters and permanent facilities on private land acquired for that purpose. Hiking, skiing, snowshoeing, canoeing and mountaineering. Winter mountaineering schools, canoe and wilderness skills workshops, rock climbing schools and other programmes. Publish a series of guidebooks for Adirondack and Catskill Mountains of New York and other books on the Adirondacks. Several types of membership available. For details write to above address.

Amicale des Sahariens
4 Rue de Coetlogon
75066 Paris
France

Association for Research Exploration and Aid (AREA)
GPO 4692
Sydney 2001
Australia
Non-profit organisation set up to help in ecological preservation and encourage sustainable development through research and expeditions. Operate their own and help placement of volunteers on other projects. Send SAE to above address for details.

Brathay Exploration Group
Brathay Hall
Ambleside
Cumbria LA22 OHP
Tel: (0966) 33942 (24 hrs)
Provides expedition and training opportunities for young people – 40 years of experience. Write to the Expeditions Coordinator for details.

British Schools Exploring Society
at The Royal Geographical Society
1 Kensington Gore
London SW7 2AR
Tel: 01-584 0710
Organises major expeditions each year for 16½-20 year olds.

Earthwatch
The Center for Field Research
Box 403
Watertown
MA 02172
USA
Tel: (617) 926 8200
Telex: 5106006452 EARTHWATCH
Research organisation, funding scientific field research. Will take unskilled volunteers who must pay for participation.

Expedition Club-Austria
PO Box 1457
A-1011 Vienna
Austria
Was established in 1978 to hold meetings, publish a newsletter, organize camps, film evenings and other events, and to act as a centre for the exchange of information for anyone interested in long distance travel but particularly between experienced expeditioners and would-be travellers. The club also produces information sheets on relevant countries.

The Explorers Club
46 East 70th street
New York
NY 10021
USA
Tel: (212) 628 83 83
Was founded in 1904 as an institution of serious purpose designed for and dedicated to the search for new knowledge of the earth and outer space. It serves as a focal point and catalyst in the identification and stimulation of institutional exploration, independent investigators and students. The Club has over 3000 members who continue to contribute actively to the constructive role of the explorer. The classes of membership are: Member, Fellow, Student, Corporate, each class being divided into Resident (living within 50 miles of the Headquarters) and Non-Resident. The Club has financed over 140 expeditions and awarded its flag to over 300 expeditions.

The James B Ford Memorial Library contains over 25,000 items, including maps, charts, archives and photographs, and is probably the largest private collection in North America wholly devoted to exploration. The club publishes the quarterly Explorers Journal (see Periodicals, page 784). Lectures, seminars and special events and an annual dinner are held. There is an annual presentation of honours and awards.

There are many formally constituted branches of the club in other areas of the United States and abroad.

The National Geographic Society
17th and M Streets, NW
Washington
DC 20036
USA
The Society's aim is to pursue and promulgate geographical knowledge and to promote research and exploration. The Society often sponsors significant expeditions. (See Periodicals, page 784).

The 153 Club
Hon. Sec. – Marion Herrod
84 Westfield Avenue
London SW13 0AZ
Tel: 01-761 0696
Is a club for 'friends of the Sahara' who have travelled within the confines of the Michelin Map 153. The club publishes a quarterly newsletter. The annual subscription is currently £3.00, but there is presently a waiting list.

Polar Exploration Group
45 Dale Bank Crescent
New Whittington
Chesterfield
Derbyshire S43 2DN
Tel: (0246) 452230
Formed in 1986 to use and build on experience gained on 7 expeditions to polar regions and plan a new series of expeditions to the Arctic. Members must be able to contribute significantly to plans and be prepared to contribute to finances.

Royal Geographical Society
1 Kensington Gore
London SW7 2AR
Tel: 01-589 5466
A focal point for geographers and explorers. It directly organizes and finances its own scientific expeditions and gives financial support, the loan of instruments, approval and advice to some 50+ expeditions each year. The Society honours outstanding geographers and explorers with a series of annual medals and awards.

The RGS maintains the largest private map collection in Europe, with over half a million sheets. It has a library with over 1,000,000 books and periodicals on geography, travel and exploration. There is also an archive of historical records and expedition reports.

There are regular lectures, children's lectures, discussions, symposia and academic meetings in the society's 760-seat lecture hall. Most of the leading names in exploration, mountaineering and geography have addressed the Society. The RGS publishes the Geographical Journal three times a year and a newsletter entitled 1 Kensington Gore, four times a year. There is a Young Member's committee. Anyone with a geographical interest can apply for a Fellowship of the RGS. An applicant must be proposed and seconded by existing Fellows.

Royal Scottish Geographical Society
10 Randolph Crescent
Off Queensbury Street
Edinburgh EG3 7TU
Tel: 031-225 3330
Also has centres in Aberdeen, Dundee, Dunfermline and Glasgow. It offers the following classes of Membership: Ordinary, Life, Student Associate, Junior, School Corporate, Country Areas, and Overseas. The society houses a library, a map collection and over 200 periodicals. It arranges tours, excursions and lecturers, and sells map reproductions and publications.

Scientific Exploration Society
Home Farm
Mildenhall
Nr. Marlborough
Wiltshire
Was formed in 1969 by a group of explorers, many of whom had been together on expeditions, with the aim of making their association more permanent so that personnel and useful equipment would not be dispersed but instead kept together for future undertakings. The society exists to organize expeditions and to help others – universities, schools, services and individuals – to organize their own. It maintains close links with commerce, industry, educational establishments, the services and other kindred scientific and exploration organizations. The society has 500 members, many of them expert explorers. All are eligible to take part in expeditions. Fully sponsored expeditions generally appoint their Leader, Secretary and Treasurer and many of their personnel from among the Society's membership. Other expeditions can be given the approval and support of the SES by the council and may then borrow equipment, receive advice and use the SES name in their publicity. Though the Society 'approves and supports' expeditions it rarely gives cash to any project.

Members have to be proposed and seconded by existing members, and then elected by the Council. Expeditions organized by the Society include Za ire River Expedition, 1974-5, Operation Drake 1978-80, and Operation Raleigh 1984-88.

South American Explorers' Club
Casilla 3714
Lima 100
Peru
Tel: 314480
and
1510 York Street 214
Denver
CO 80206
USA
Tel: (303) 320 0388
Exists to promote travel and sporting aspects of exploration; and to record, co-ordinate and publicise academic research on a wide variety of natural and social sciences. Membership is open to all. It publishes a magazine, The South American Explorer, (see Periodicals on page 000). The Club House, with reading rooms, maps and guidebooks is open most days and people are welcome to visit. The address is: Avenida Portugal 146, Brena District, Lima, Peru, near the US Embassy.

University of California Research Expeditions Program (UREP)
University of California
Desk L
Berkeley
California 94720
USA
Tel: (415) 642 6586
Will take inexperienced volunteers on UREP expeditions worldwide. Wide variety of areas and subjects.

Young Explorers Trust
(The Association of British Youth Exploration Societies)
The Royal Geographical Society
1 Kensington Gore
London SW7 2AR
Tel: 01-589 9724
Exists to promote youth exploration and to provide a forum within which societies and individuals can exchange information and act together for their mutual benefit. It does not organize its own expeditions or make travel bookings. The Trust is a registered charity. Membership is open to groups or

societies wishing to take part in the Trust's activities and to contribute to the Trust's aims. Present members include all major national and regional bodies active in the field of youth expeditions as well as school and university groups.

Information is available on a wide range of topics and on a variety of foreign locations. The Trust has recently taken on a team of volunteer regional co-ordinators to assist with the flow of information and to provide a local focus for members as well as being the 'first link' for the 'unattached' youngster, enabling them to join in adventurous activities. YETMAG, a quarterly magazine which goes out free to all members, carries news, papers and speeches, preliminary expedition reports and other information.

Associations: Travel

Airport Concierge (Heathrow Services)
Room 115, Bldg 223
Norwood Crescent
Heathrow Airport
Middx
Tel: 01-759 3022
Membership organisation to help with messages, meeting, courier and freight and documentation.

Arbeit Tourismus und Entwicklung
Missionsstrasse 21
CH-4003 Basel
Switzerland
Critical non-profit organization

International Airline Passengers Association
PO Box 113
London SW1V 1ER
Tel: 01-828 5841
A consumer watchdog association assisting and bene-fitting the frequent traveller. Representing over 120,000 members worldwide. Membership costs £24.50 per year.

Deutsche Zentrale für Globetrotter
Postfach 60
D-5429 Katzenelnbogen
West Germany
A small informal association of globetrotters mainly from German-speaking Europe, linked by an interest in low cost travel and the desire to study the cultures of other countries at first hand. Founded in 1974, it has some 1,500 members. Publishes a quarterly newsletter, Trotter. Membership is open to those who can prove that they have travelled on their own in countries outside Europe for at least three months. The club operates from a private address. Members meet regularly at different places in Germany. Non-members are also offered information and contacts, but must enclose a s.a.e. with enquiry.

The Experiment in International Living
Upper Wyche
Malvern
Worcestershire
WR14 4EN

Tel: (06845) 62577

Non-profit making organisation aiming to promote international understanding through a homestay pro-gramme for groups and individuals around the world. Also offers training and orientation programme for people wishing to experience another culture.

Fédération Française de la Randonée Pedestre
Comité National des Sentiers de Grande Ran-donée
8 Avenue Marceau
75008 Paris
France
Tel: 47 23 52 32

Foyer International d'Accueil de Paris
30 Rue Cabanis
75014 Paris
France
Tel: 589 8915
Telex: FIAP 205666F
Holds all-discussion 'forums' for the exchange of information between travellers.

Globetrotters Club
BCM/Roving
London WC1N 3XX
An informal association of travellers from all over the world, linked by an interest in low cost travel and the desire to study the cultures of other lands at first hand. Members share their personal experiences and detailed knowledge of local conditions. The club con-centrates on attracting as new members only those 'non-tourists' with a genuine empathy for the people in other lands. Members may advertise in the club's newsletter Globe. Films and talks are held in London, California, Ontario and New York.

Globetrotter Club and Travel Services
Walter Kamm
Rennweg 35
CH-8001
Zurich
Switzerland
Tel: 01-211 7780
Runs a club magazine, Globetrotter, and talks on travel as well as selling travel books and cheap flights.

Gruppe Neues Reisen
Höarthstr. 4
D-8000 München
West Germany
Tel: (089) 368 298
A non-profit club with critical views about tourism. Newsletter – Reisebriefe.

Guilde du Raide
11 Rue du Vaugirard
75006 Paris
France
Tel: 326 9752
Promotes adventure in remote parts of the world. It organizes meetings, conferences, lectures, film even-ings and permanent exhibitions, and a small number of organized tour/treks. Since 1971, it has made annual grants under the heading of National de l'Av-enture to responsible but adventurous expeditions having definite goals, usually those mounted by

individual or small groups. Other grants and donations in money or kind are available through the Guilde, as are also the advice of experts, access to documents, discounts and benefits from associated bodies, and help with the safe-keeping and sale of expedition reports and photos.

International Federation of Women's Travel Organisations (IFWTO)

c/o Montpearl Travel
26 York Street
London W1H 1FE
Tel: 01-935 8823
Tlx: 8952022 (attn: MONTPEARL)
Federation of 60 associations worldwide of women working in the travel industry.

International Globetrotters Club

ERC, Avenue Louise 89
B-1050 Brussels
Tel: 322 511 84 61
International travel club for overlanders and other travellers off the beaten track. Organizes overland expeditions in Africa, Asia and Northern Scandinavia, yacht cruises and exploratory projects, as well as specialty resort holidays. Established in 1973 in Denmark, now a franchisor of specialty travel, and planning to offer franchised offices and operations in several countries over the next few years. Travel and franchise opportunities available.r

JOLT

Journey of a Lifetime
32 Maxwell Road
Northwood
Middlesex HA6 2YF
Tel: (09274) 25453
The Jolt Trust provides journeys, expeditions and holidays abroad in order to advance the education of young persons between the ages of 15 and 19 years who are resident in city areas and who would benefit by reason of their disability, poverty or other social or economic circumstances.

Project Trust

Breacachadh Castle
Isle of Coll
Argyll PA78 6TB
Tel: (08783) 444
Organisation which aids UK young people to spend a year between school and university working overseas: in schools, as field instructors; on sheep and cattle stations; and in child-care and social work.

Travelmates

496 Newcastle Street
West Perth
Western Australia 6005
Hostels and share-houses and share-a-car service.

WEXAS International

45 Brompton Road
Knightsbridge
London SW3 1DE
Tel: 01-589 3315/0500
WEXAS (for World Expeditionary Association) was founded in 1970 to provide an information and travel service for expeditions. Membership has since become open to anyone, and WEXAS currently has

thousands of members spread over 91 countries. *WEXAS's appeal derives from its worldwide programme of discount flights, 'adventure' holidays, hotels, car hire and insurance at special low rates. The Expeditions Committee of the Royal Geographical Society each year selects promising UK based expeditions to receive WEXAS grants. Members of WEXAS receive* The Traveller *magazine (see Periodicals, page 784), and are also eligible to receive other WEXAS publications.*

Women's Corona Society

Minster House
274 Vauxhall Bridge Road
London SW1V 1BB
Tel: 01-828 1652/3
Primarily a support and advice group for expatriate women, offering courses and advice to those about to move abroad and services in the UK such as shepherding children from plane to school and back.

Women Outdoors, Inc.

Curtis Hall
474 Boston Avenue
Medford
MA 02155
USA
Incorporated in 1980 to provide a clearing-house for women with a strong interest in the outdoors. Members receive the quarterly Women's Outdoor *magazine. Aims are to build a network in which women can get in touch with other women who share similar interests, and a clearing-house for information and women who want partners for trips.*

Women Help Women

c/o Frances Alexander
'Granta'
8a Chestnut Ave
High Wycombe
Bucks HP11 1DJ
Tel: (0494) 39481
Organisation to promote international friendship by helping female travellers to stay with other members and their families.

Associations: Specialist Travel

Archaeology Abroad

31-34 Gordon Square
London WC1H 0PY
Tel: 01-387 6052
Archaeology Abroad provides information about opportunities for archaeological field work and excavations outside Britain. Archaeologists, students of archaeology and specialists who wish to be considered for archaeological work abroad are enrolled and information is provided on request to organizers of excavations who wish to recruit personnel.

Others interested in archaeology, and preferably with some experience of excavation, are also eligible for membership. The organization is not an employment agency.

A comprehensive insurance scheme, appropriate for excavation work, has been compiled with Sun Alliance Insurance group and is available to members and others travelling abroad on excavations. Messrs W.F & R.K. Swan (Hellenic) Ltd have for a number of years generously made several free places available on their Hellenic cruises to student members of Archaeology Abroad.

An annual Bulletin (March) and two Newssheets (Spring and Autumn) are available to members by subscription, and these list all projects overseas on which information is received. The organization is small and is entirely dependent on subscriptions from individual members and corporate bodies. For further details write to The Secretary at the above address enclosing an s.a.e.

Christians Abroad
11 Carteret St
London SW1H 9DL
Tel: 01-222 2165
Arranges introductions for people going overseas to the local church in the host country and to people who know that country. Produces a series of information sheets about work abroad, mainly in the 'South' through volunteer, mission and government agencies.

Expats International
62 Tritton Street
London SE21 8DE
Tel: 01-670 4411
and
PO Box 302
Williamsburg
VA 23185
USA
Offers working expatriates job information, tax & legal advice, gift service, club magazine, Home and Away, *and much more.*

International Opportunities
Box 19107
Washington
DC 20036
USA
Information about overseas jobs. Directory: International Opportunities $3.00 (add $1.00 for overseas mail).

Associations: Hitchhiking

France

Allostop
The collective name for the associations Allauto, Provoya and Stop-Voyages. Allostop puts you in contact with drivers with a view to sharing petrol costs. Enrol sufficiently in advance. The sum of 130F (which constitutes an annual subscription

fee and which cannot be refunded) allows you to an unlimited number of journeys in a year starting from the date of enrolment. If you wish to make only one journey, the subscription is 35F.
The main offices are:

Alsace
Allostop-Provoya
5 Rue de Général Zimmer
6700 Strasbourg
Tel: (88) 37 13 13
Open from 15.00 hrs to 18.30 hrs from Monday to Friday and from 10.00 hrs to 12.00 hrs on Saturday.

Bretagne
Allostop-Provoya
Au C.I.J. Bretagne
Maison du Champs de Mars
35043 Rennes
Tel: (99) 30 98 87
Open from 15.00 hrs to 18.00 hrs on Monday to Friday and from 9.00 hrs to 12.00hrs on Saturday.

Languedoc
Allostop-Provoya
9 Rue du Plan de l'Olivia
3400 Montpellier
Tel: (67) 66 02 29
Open from 15.00 hrs to 18.00 hrs on Monday to Friday and 10.00hrs to 12.30 hrs on Saturday.

Midi-Pyrénées
Allostop-Provoya
au C.R.I.J.
2 Rue Malbec
31000 Toulouse
Tel: (61) 22 68 13
Open from 15.30 hrs to 18.30 hrs from Tuesday to Friday and 10.30 hrs to 12.30 hrs on Saturday.

Nord-Pas-de-Calais
Allostop-Provoya
à l'Office du Tourism
Palais Rihour
59800 Lille
Tel: (20) 57 96 69
Open from 15.00 hrs to 18.00 hrs on Monday to Friday and 10.30 hrs to 12.30 hrs on Saturday.

Pays de la Loire
Allostop-Provoya
au C.R.I.J.
10 Rue Lafayette
44000 Nantes
Tel: (40) 89 04 85
Open from 15.30 hrs to 18.30 hrs from Tuesday to Friday and from 10.00 hrs to 12.00 hrs on Saturday.

Provence – Alpes de Sud-Côte d'Azur
Allostop-Provoya
3 Rue du Petit St-Jean
13100 Aix-en-Provence
Tel: (42) 38 37 51
Open from 15.00 hrs to 18.30 hrs on Monday, Tuesday, Thursday and Friday. From 9.30 hrs to 11.00 hrs and 17.00 hrs to 19.00 hrs on Wednesday annd 10.00 hrs to 13.00 hrs on Saturday.

Allostop-Provoya
M.J.X. Picaud

23 Avenue Raymond Picaud
06400 Cannes
Tel: (93) 38 60 88
Open from 14.00 hrs to 18.00 hrs on Tuesday to Friday and 10.00 hrs to 12.00 hrs on Saturday.
Paris
Allostop-Provoya
84 Passage Brady
75010 Paris
Tel: (1) 246 00 66
Open from 9.00 hrs to 19.30 hrs on Monday to Friday and from 9.00 hrs to 13.00 hrs and 14.00 hrs to 18.00 hrs on Saturday.

Rhône-Alpes
Allostop-Provoya
8 Rue de la Bombarde
(quartier Saint-Jean)
69005 Lyon
Tel: 78 42 38 29
Open from 14.00 hrs to 18.00 hrs on Monday to Friday and from 10.00 hrs to 12.00 hrs on Saturday
Voyage au Fil (au Crit)
28 Rue du Calvaire
Nantes
Tel: 40 89 04 85
Agent for Allostop (the hitchhiking service), Billets BIGE (discount on ferry services) and the YHA.

Belgium

The Allostop card can be used for Taxi-stop in Belgium. Taxi-stop offices are:

Infor-Jeunes
27 Rue du Marche-aux-Herbes
100 Brussels
Tel: (02) 511 69 30

Taxi-stop
24 Rue de France
Charleroi
Tel: (071) 31 63 42

Taxi-stop
34 Rue des Dominicains
Liège
Tel: (041) 32 38 70

Taxi-stop
31 Rue de Bruxelles
1300 Wavre
Tel: (010) 22 75 75

Australia

Travelmates
496 Newcastle Street
West Perth
Western Australia 6005
Tel: (09) 328 66 85
Share a Car Service – A unique service operated from their office arranges for people to share cars on Interstate Trips departing Perth. They introduce the owner/drivers to intending passengers who are about
to embark to the Northern Territory or to the Eastern States. Usual arrangement is to share part of the petrol cost and assist with driving. No bookings … simply standby operation; it is only suited to backpackers.
Average part share cost for passengers:
Adel $45, Melb $55, Syd $65, Bris $75, Darwin $75. Office fee $10.

Poland

There is an official hitchhiking scheme run by the National Tourist Office. Drivers get points for helping you. Ask before going.

Associations: Disabled

The Across Trust
Crown House
Morden
Surrey
Tel: 01-540 3897
Operates large luxury fully-equipped ambulances called 'Jumbulances' which take severely disabled people on organized group pilgrimages and holidays across Europe.

Disabled Living Foundation
380/4 Harrow Road
London W9 2HU
Tel: 01-289 6111

The Les Evans Holiday Fund for Sick and Handicapped Children
The Secretary
12a High Street
Brentwood
Essex
or
General Manager
Administration Office
183a St. Mary's Lane
Upminster
Essex RM14 1BR
Tel: Upminster 22920
Holidays arranged for children who are sick or severely disabled. Caters for children aged 8-15 who are accompanied by fully qualified medical staff. Destinations – Florida's Disneyworld & California's Disneyland.

National Handicapped Sports and Recreation Association
Farraqut Station
PO Box 33141
Washington DC 20033
and
Capitol Hill Station
PO Box 18664
Denver
CO 80218 USA

Formed in 1967 and now has a national network of branches across the United States offering recreational and competitive sports for the handicapped, including the 'travelling sports' such as river rafting, diving, riding and skiing.

Mobility International
62 Union Street
London SE1 1TD
Tel: 01-403 5688
Exists to encourage the integration of handicapped people with the non-handicapped, by arranging international projects with a wide appeal, varying from youth festivals to more professional conferences and seminars. Handicap is not the common denominator; rather people attend because of their interest in the topic or emphasis of the particular project. Mobility International News *is published three times a year at £4 p.a.*

Project Phoenix Trust
68 Rochfords
Coffee Hall
Milton Keynes MK6 5DJ
A non-profit organization the Trustees of which organize and run visits overseas. Mixed ability groups of adults include those who (a) would like a holiday which has a focal point, such as art, history, etc, (b) would need some physical help in order to make such a visit possible, (c) would be prepared to provide physical help to others to make the visit viable and may need some financial assistance in order to take part. These tours involve a lot of activity and are probably best suited to energetic and strong disabled people.

RADAR
Royal Association for Disability and Rehabilitation
25 Mortimer Street
London W1N 8AB
Tel: 01-637 5400
A registered charity to help disabled people, by identifying the problems they encounter and then taking the necessary action to reduce or eliminate these problems. RADAR finds suitable accommodation and facilities for holidays for the disabled. Publishes two guides entitled Holidays for Disabled People *and* Holidays *and* Travel Abroad *which are updated each year and a monthly* Bulletin *and a quarterly journal called* Contact. *They also publish excellent comprehensive lists of publications and useful addresses for the disabled holidaymaker. Holidays Officer – Kathy Ellis.*

Rehabilitation Inter USA
1123 Broadway
New York
NY 10010
USA
Disability Society with information on disabled travel in North America

Society for the Advancement of Travel for the Handicapped (SATH)
International Head Office
Penthouse Suite
26 Court Street
Brooklyn
NY 11242
USA
Tel: (718) 858 5483
Is a 'non-profit educational forum for the exchange of knowledge and the gaining of new skills in how to facilitate travel for the handicapped, the elderly and the retired'. Information is available on tour operators, hotels and other travel related services; (s.a.e. requested with written enquiries). Affiliated member of the World Tourism Organisation (UN) and represented on the US Congress Tourism Advisory Board. Membership is open to all who share SATH's concerns.

Youth Exchange Centre
Seymour Mews House
Seymour Mews
London W1H 9PE
Tel: 01-486 5101
The centre is responsible for the development of British policy on youth exchanges. It administers central government grant aid for youth exchanges and promotes training initiatives. There is a special fund for international educational exchange visits undertaken by groups of young disabled people.

Associations – Sporting

The Adirondack Mountain Club
172 Ridge Street
Glenfalls
NY 12801
USA
Tel: (518) 793 7737
(See Associations: Expeditions, page 766.)

Alpine Club
74 South Audley Street
London W1Y 5FF
Tel: 01-499 1542
The Alpine Club is an association of experienced mountaineers, interested in the alps and the Greater Ranges (Himalayas, Andes, etc.). New recruits are welcome but are expected to have a reasonable amount of experience on joining. The Alpine Club Library is open to the public, and is used mainly by people planning treks and expeditions.

British Sub-Aqua Club Expedition Scheme
Gordon Ridley
94 Brownside Road
Cambuslang
Glasgow G72 8AG
Tel: 041-641 4200
Runs a series of expeditions off chartered diving vessels, usually off the West coast of Scotland.

Cyclists Touring Club
69 Meadrow
Goldalming
Surrey GU7 3HS

Tel: (048 63) 7217
Britain's national cyclists' association, working to promote recreational and utility cycling. Range of UK and overseas facets and cycling holidays, and information on all aspects of cycling.

The Eagle Ski Club
Mrs Sue Baldock
10 Orchard Drive
Chorleywood
Rickmansworth
Herts WD3 5QL
Tel: (09278) 2950
Aims to encourage ski-mountaineering and touring through a programme of expeditions, mainly within Europe.

The International Long River Canoeist Club
c/o Peter Salisbury
238 Birmingham Road
Redditch
Worcs B97 6EL
The International Long River Canoeist Club is the only United Kingdom association that can offer details of thousands of rivers around the World, from the As in France to the Zambezi in Zambia, from the Alesk in Canada/Alaska to the Zaïre in Zaïre. Members in 26 countries ready to offer help and advice.

National Handicapped Sports and Recreation Association
Farraqut Station
PO Box 33141
Washington DC 20033
USA
(See also Associations: Disabled on page 771.)

Ski Club of Great Britain
118 Eaton Square
London SW1W 9AF
Tel: 01-245 1033
Telex: 291608 SKIDOM G
Offers members: unbiased advice on resorts, travel and equipment; snow reports; club flights and special discounts; reps in the Alps and UK; British Ski Tests; unique skiing parties for all standards and ages; artificial slope courses for intermediate and advanced skiers; insurance; Ski Survey magazine and a busy programme of lectures, filmshows and parties at the Club House in central London.

Transcyclist International
CPO Box 2064
Tokyo 100-91
Japan

Trancyslist UK
Stuart Lucas
12 Kincaidston Drive
Ayr
Scotland

Transcyslist USA
(West Coast)
Al Jesse
RT 1 Box 130
Carmel Highlands
CA 93923

(East Coast)
Deke Krewson
PO Box 8053
N-Village
N. Charleston
SC 29418-3799
The organization aims to establish a global frame of cross-national and cross-continental channels to allow for and encourage co-ordination and co-operation in motorcycle touring and sporting ventures. Runs travel projects of an unspecified nature for the ambitious individual tourer, at home or overseas, with own machine or use of the TC 'Machine Loan Program'. Also two types of touring rallies – Blitz Rally (two day; weekend), One week Rally. Membership.

Educational Exchange

The Central Bureau
Seymour Mews House
Seymour Mews (off Wigmore Street)
London W1
Tel: 01-486 5101
and
3 Bruntsfield Crescent
Edinburgh EH10 4HD
Tel: 031-447 8024
and
16 Malone Road
Belfast BT9 5BN
Tel: (0232) 664418/9
Established in 1984 by British Government to act as the national information office and coordinating unit for every type of educational visit and exchange. Helps with on-site training in education, placement of students and teachers abroad, a wide variety of exchanges. Will not offer grants, but produces several excellent books about educational placements, working abroad and volunteer schemes.

The Commonwealth Youth Exchange Council
18 Fleet Street
London EC4Y 1AA
Tel: 01-353 3901
Promotes contact between groups of young people in Commonwealth countries through educational visits and exchanges. Grant aids projects which allow for homestays or shared accommodation and lead to joint ventures.

Pressure Groups

Amnesty International
1 Easton Street
London WC1
Tel: 01-833 1771/837 3805

International pressure group working for the betterment of human rights and the release of political prisoners.

Friends of the Earth
377 City Road
London EC1V 1NA
Tel: 01-837 0731
A campaigning organization, promoting policies which protect the natural environment. Their campaigns are pursued worldwide.

Greenpeace
36 Graham Street
London N1 8LL
Tel: 01-608 1461
International ecology pressure group, particularly concerned with saving the whale, rainforests and preventing nuclear disaster.

International Union for the Conservation of Natural Resources (IUCN)
World Conservation Centre
Avenue de Mont-Blanc
CH-1196 Gland
Switzerland
Umbrella organisation coordinating the work of the various charities working in the field of conservation.

Survival International
310 Edgeware Road
London W2 1DY
Tel: 01-723 5535
Telex: 933524 GEONET G
Survival International is an international charity established in 1969. It now has National and Local Groups in many other countries. S.I. has the following objectives:

  *To help tribal peoples to exercise their right to survival and self-determination.

  *To ensure that the interests of tribal peoples are properly represented in all decisions affecting their future.

  *To secure to tribal peoples the ownership and use of adequate land and other resources and seek recognition of their rights over their traditional lands.

  Survival International publishes a quarterly newsletter, an annual review and special documents; organizes public meetings and exhibitions; lobbies governments, companies and international human rights organizations; issues Urgent Action Bulletins etc. Write for details.

World Wildlife Fund – United Kingdom
Panda House
11-13 Ockford Road
Godalming
Surrey GU7 1QU
Tel: (04868) 20551
Telex: 859602
Telefax: 04868-27366

Headquarters:
WWF – International
Avenue du Mont Blanc
CH-1196
Gland
Switzerland
Tel: (022) 64 71 81

Telex: 28183
Telefax: (022) 64 42 38
An international organisation which raises money for the conservation of wildlife, natural habitats and natural resources throughout the world. Founded in 1961 with headquarters in Switzerland, since when it has opened national organisations in 24 countries. Between them these have spent over £60 million on more than 4000 projects worldwide. WWF makes sure that its projects have a sound scientific base by working closely with the International Union for the Conservation of Nature and Natural Resources (IUCN).

Third World Aid and Volunteer Programmes

ActionAid
Hamlyn House
Archway
London
N19 5PG
Tel: 01-281 4101
A charity working in development in some of the poorest communities of the Third World. It aims to help people tackle their own poverty and improve the quality of life for their families.

Action d'Urgence International
10 Rue Félix-Aiem
75018 Paris
France
Tel: 264 74 19
AUD runs training courses for people interested in helping rescue operations in times of natural disasters. Branches in France, Great Britain, Morocco, India, Dominican Republic and Guadeloupe.

British Council
10 Spring Gardens
London SW1A 2BN
Tel: 01-930 8466
Permanent appointments and contracts for teachers, especially of English as a foreign language and some educational advisory options. Arranges for English students to study abroad.

British Red Cross Society
9 Grosvenor Crescent
London SW1X 7EJ
Tel: 01-235 5454
Part of the International Red Cross, the world's largest voluntary organisation for the relief of suffering. It trains people in community care, nursing and first aid. Its voluntary, unpaid members work to help injured, sick, disabled, elderly and housebound people. It is non-political and non-religious and is not supported by government grant, relying entirely on donations to maintain its services. The society operates through local branches across the U.K. and Britain's remaining colonies and dependencies. Almost every country has either a national Red Cross

or Red Crescent Society affiliated to the International body.

Catholic Institute for International Relations (CIIR)
22 Coleman Fields
London
Tel: 01-354 0883
Has a Health Programme in Yemen which takes medically qualified volunteers. Other volunteers are sent to Central America, Peru, Honduras, Zimbabwe, Ecuador and various other countries depending on their needs at the time. Volunteers are usually skilled e.g. teachers.

Christians Abroad
11 Carteret St
London SW1H 9DL
Tel: 01-222 2165
Have three main objectives:
(1) To provide information and advice to volunteers about the countries where their skills could be used to the greatest advantage.
(2) To recruit teachers, health workers, agriculturalists and others for overseas employers.
(3)To provide people going abroad with country advisers in Britain and Christian contacts overseas.

Christian Aid
PO Box No 1
London SW9 8BH
Tel: 01-733 5500
Aims to combat hunger and poverty throughout the world. Funds development projects in poor countries and developmental education in the U.K.

Christian Outreach
34 St Mary's Crescent
Leamington Spa
Warwickshire CV31 1JL
Small Christian charity needing volunteers to work with children in refugee camps.

Crown Agents for Overseas Governments and Administrations
St. Nicholas House
Sutton
Surrey SM1 1EL
Tel: 01-643 3311
Mostly appointments for overseas governments and public authorities in professional and sub-professional posts.

Intermediate Technology
Myson House
Railway Terrace
Rugby CV21 3HT
Tel: (0788) 60631
Charity working for Third World development through the creation of small-scale projects which can be built, operated and repaired by local inhabitants without the continuing presence of Western experts.

International Voluntary Service (IVS)
Ceresole House
53 Regents Rd
Leicester LE1 6YL
Tel: (0533) 541862
Has three programmes for Volunteers:

(1) Long-Term Service
A minimum of 2 years. Must be over 21. The work is in Southern Africa excluding South Africa and the volunteers must be skilled or qualified and have had previous work experience e.g. engineer, agriculturalist, horticulturalist.
(2) Work Camp Programme
This is a short-term programme of 2-3 weeks. A particular project is undertaken, e.g. manual work; social work. The idea being to do a job that wouldn't otherwise get done. The work is in Europe, UK, Turkey, USA and Canada.
(3) Development Education and Exchange Programme
A programme of Development Education which may involve 2 to 3 months as a volunteer in the Third World. Places are very limited on the exchange part of the programme so volunteers must have had a year's involvement with IVS and previous work camp experience. The work involves manual projects which teach the volunteer what life is like in the Third World. Volunteers are sent from the Third World to the UK to gain a similar experience.

Overseas Development Administration
Abercrombie House
Eaglesham Rd
East Kilbride G75 8EA
Tel: (03552) 41199
Mainly government appointments overseas, covering a wide variety of posts including accountancy, engineering, economics, forestry, statistics as well as medical posts.

Oxfam
274 Banbury Rd
Oxford OX2 7DZ
Tel: (0865) 56777
Primary object is to relieve poverty, distress and suffering in any part of the world. Volunteers are occasionally sent overseas at times of disaster, but they must be people with specialist skills and qualifications. The main requirement is that the person recruited should have professional qualifications adaptable to the cultural context overseas, as well as the personal skills needed for a specific assignment.
There is not a demand for unqualified or unskilled staff.

Returned Volunteer Action
1 Amwell Street
London EC1R 1UL
Tel: 01-278 0804
Organisation for returned volunteers. Will offer advice to those thinking of volunteering or about to set off.

Save the Children Fund
17 Grove Lane
Camberwell
London SE5 8RD
Tel: 01-703 5400
Britain's largest international children's charity. Take on paid staff and only those who are fully qualified. Mainly send doctors, nurses and child-care workers overseas.

The TEAR Fund
100 Church Road
Teddington
Middx TW11 8QE
Tel: 01-977 9144
Christian organisation with strong development programmes, needing qualified volunteers prepared to serve two to four years.

United Nations Association International Service (UNAIS)
Whitehall Court
London
Tel: 01-930 0679
Project workers are sent overseas to help development and must be skilled and prepared to work for a minimum of 2 years. The fare to the country is paid by UNAIS and the volunteer also receives a basic wage plus insurances.

US Peace Corps
Washington
DC 20526
USA
Places volunteers in 62 developing countries. Volunteers with all kinds of backgrounds are accepted, though naturally those with specific skills, being more in demand, are easier to place.

Voluntary Missionary Movement
Shenley Lane
London Colney
Herts AL2 8AR
Tel: (0727) 248853
Volunteers must be skilled or qualified and over 21. Work is available for professions such as doctors, midwives, teachers, mechanics, civil engineers and physiotherapists. Volunteers are required to work a minimum of two years and during this time live every close to the native people.

Voluntary Services Overseas (VSO)
9 Belgrave Square
London
Tel: 01-235 5191
Volunteers are selected from people with skills and qualifications e.g. teaching, nursing, agriculturalists, social workers, carpenters to work in the Third World. Volunteers must be aged between 20 and 65 and prepared to work for 2 years minimum. VSO pay the volunteer's airfare and a small wage and living accommodation are provided by the host country.

Travel and Expedition Advice

Baker-Nicol Logistics Ltd
4 Sundew Close

Eaton Socon
St Neots
Cambridgeshire
PE19 4AN
Tel: (0480) 216825
Advice and logistic organisation for expeditions, mainly in the world's harsh climate zones. Small fee payable if advice complex. Can also provide equipment.

Bolivian Adventure Tours SRL
PO Box 8412
La Paz
Bolivia
Tel: 375764/795355
A company offering two kinds of service for those interested in exploring the country, equipment for the extremely varied terrain, including camping gear, specially adapted vehicles, cartographic and photographic data; and information, advice, guides and transport for the various kinds of expedition to which Bolivia lends itself, from alpine climbing to jungle trekking.

Expatriate Consultancy Ltd
32 St Mary at Hill
London EC2P 3AS
Tel: 01-623 3356

Exploration Logistics
Maggs House
78 Queens Road
Clifton
Bristol BS8 1QX
Tel: (0272) 266531
Tailor-made support service for expeditions with consultancy, design and purchase of equipment, survival courses and field support.

Direction des Français a l'étranger et des Etrangers en France
21 bis Rue La Perouse
75016 Paris
France
Tel: 502 14 24
A government office responsible to the Ministry of Foreign Affairs which handles aid to French citizens abroad and so on.

Expedition Advisory Centre
1 Kensington Gore
London SW7 2AR
Tel: 01-581 2057
The Expedition Advisory Centre provides an information and training service for those planning an expedition. It was founded by the Royal Geographical Society and the Young Explorer's Trust and is a Shell International Petroleum Company funded project.

In addition to organizing a variety of seminars and publications including The Expedition Planners Handbook and Directory, *the Advisory Centre maintains a database for expedition planners. This includes a register of planned expeditions, lists of expedition consultants and suppliers, information for leaders on individual countries and a register of personnel who have offered their services to expeditions. Write with s.a.e to the Information Officer for further details.*

Geo Travel
4 Christian Fields
London SW16 3JZ
Tel: 01-764 6292
In addition to acting as consultants to state tourist boards, providing advice on the development of tourism in the Third World, expert advice is available on a consultancy basis for single travellers, groups and expeditions to polar areas, Asia (exl. USSR), Africa and Scandinavia. Lapland specialists.

Odyssey Consultants Ltd
Suite 55
Chesham House
150 Regent Street
London W1R 5FA
Tel: 01-853 3732/439 6288
Commercial, independent source of advice and information both on how to travel and on individual countries for all travellers from expeditions to overlanders.

Dick Philips
Whitehall House
Nenthead
Alston
Cumbria CA9 3PS
Long-established specialist in travel in those parts of Iceland beyond the interests of the mainstream travel trade.

Rainbow Ridge Consultants
Box 190
Kapaau
HI, 96755
USA
Specialists in the Far East and can provide contacts for travellers

SafariQuip
13a Waterloo Park
Upper Brook Street
Stockport SK1 3BP
Tel: 061-429 8700
Advice and equipment supply, specialising in tropical regions.

K. &. J Slavin (Quest 80's) Ltd
Abbey Farm,
Halton-cum-Beckering,
Lincoln LN3 5NG
Tel: (0673) 858274
Telex: 56277 QUEST G
Directors: Kenneth and Julie Slavin
Are expedition and aid consultants offering complete logistical support services to individual and commercial clients on projects throughout the world. They are advisers to Land Rover Ltd in the expeditionary field

and have a special franchise for the direct export of expedition-equipped Land Rovers and Range Rovers.

Trekking Agents Association of Nepal
PO Box 3612
Kantipath
Kathmandu
Nepal
Tel: 211 875
Will provide information on trekking and trekking companies in Nepal. Also publishes a quarterly newsletter with updates on conditions. Cost: US$40 p.a.

Women's Corona Society
Minster House
274 Vauxhall Bridge Road
London SW1V 1BB
(See Associations: Travel on page 768.)

Awards and Grants

Bourses ELF Aquitaine
Direction des Relations Publiques et de la Communication
7 Rue Nelaton
75739 Paris Cedex 15
France
Tel: 571 72 73
Grants to young people working in the field of international relations between France and the country visited.

Guilde du Raid
11 Rue du Vaugirard
75006 Paris
France
Tel: 326 97 52
(See Associations: Expeditions on page 766.)

Mount Everest Foundation
Hon. Secetary: W.H. (Bill) Ruthven
Gowrie
Cardwell Close
Warton
Preston PR4 1SH
Tel: (0772) 635346
Sponsors British and New Zealand expeditions only, proposing new routes or research in high mountain regions. For grant application forms write to above address. Closing dates August 31 and December 31 for the following year. Give 40-50 grants a year from £300 to £1,000.

The Rolex Awards for Enterprise
The Secretariat
PO Box 178
1211 Geneva 26
Switzerland
The Rolex Awards provide financial assistance for persons who have manifested the spirit of enterprise in order to bring to fruition projects which are off the beaten track and come within three broad fields of human endeavour: Applied Sciences and Invention, Exploration and Discovery, the Environment. The

Rolex Awards enjoy world renown. To enter: send for official application form from the 'Rolex Awards for Enterprise Secretariat' at the above address. Project description must be in English.

The Royal Geographical Society
1 Kensington Gore
London SW7 2AR
Tel: 01-589 5466
Administer not only their own awards and grants, but those of many other sponsors through their General Award Scheme. Details and applications forms from the Administrative Secretary at the above address. Applications to be submitted by January 31st each year. (See also Associations: Expeditions, page 766).

Touring Club Royal de Belgique
Rue de la Loi 44
B 1040 Brussels
Belgium
Tel: (02) 233 22 11
Makes grants known as Les Bourses de Voyage Jeunesse to Belgians aged between 16 and 25, for extensive travel. As well as the sizeable grant, successful applicants also receive vehicle accessories, travel tickets and various coupons.

Traveller of the Year Awards
VSO
9 Belgrave Square
London SW1X 8PW
Tel: 01-235 5191
Six annual awards to travellers who have made outstanding journeys during that year. Categories: Traveller of the Year, Adventurous Traveller, Committed Traveller, Family Travellers, Business Traveller and Young Traveller. Nominations early the following year. Awards announced in May. Details from above address.

WEXAS International
45 Brompton Road
Knightsbridge
London SW3 1DE
Tel: 01-589 3315/0500
(See Associations: Travel, page 768.)

Winston Churchill Memorial Trust
15 Queens Gate Terrace
London SW7 5PR
Tel: 01-584 9315
The Winston Churchill Memorial Trust awards about 100 travelling Fellowship grants annually to enable UK citizens, irrespective of their age or educational achievements, to carry out study projects overseas in approximately 10 categories of interest or occupation which are varied annually. Grants are not normally given for formal or academic studies.

Young Explorers Trust
Royal Geographical Society
1 Kensington Gore
London SW7 2AR
Tel: 01-589 9724
Gives grants to school and pre-University expeditions. (See Associations: Expeditions, page 000.)
c/o Elizabeth Nellist, Membership Secretary
National Maritime Museum
Greenwich
London SW 10

Courses: General

The Centre for International Briefing
The Castle
Farnham
Surrey GU9 0AG
Tel: (0252) 721194
Runs short residential courses for people about to go overseas, offering them the chance to meet a variety of specialist speakers, others going to the same country and the use of the excellent library and resource centre.

The Experiment in International Living
(See Associations: Travel on page 768.)

Field Studies Council Expeditions Overseas
Flatford Mill Field Centre
East Bergholt
Colchester
Essex CO7 6UL
Tel: (0206) 298283
Expeditionary courses abroad to study birds, botany, art and archaeology. Open to anyone; only qualification necessary is an enthusiasm for the subject and an interest in exploring new areas.

School for Field Studies
196 Broadway
Cambridge
Massachusetts 021139
USA
Tel: (617) 497 9000
Non-profit organisation that designs and operates month and term long courses around the world for high school and university students who want first hand experience in the environmental sciences. Scholarships and interest-free loans available and academic credits offered.

Women's Corona Society
Minster House
274 Vauxhall Bridge Road
London SW1V 1BB
Tel: 01-828 1652/3
Runs one day initiation courses for those about to move abroad.

Courses: Language

Accreditation of Correspondence Colleges (CACC)
27 Marylebone Road,
London NW1 5JS
Tel: 01-935 5391
Supply lists of correspondence courses

Alliance Français
6 Cromwell Place
London SW7 2JN
Tel: 01-584 1856 or 589 7377

Audio-Forum
31 Kensington Church Street
London W8 4LL
Tel: 01-937 1647
Teach yourself language courses.

BBC Books
Woodlands
80 Wood Lane
London W12 0TT
Tel: 01-576 0202
Telex: 265781
Language courses for beginners to advanced (include French, Greek, German, Russian, Arabic, Italian, Spanish, etc.). Courses suitable for holidaymakers and business travellers alike. Most courses comprise book, audio cassette packs and teacher's notes.

The Berlitz Schools of Languages Ltd
Wells House
79 Wells Street
London W1A 3Bz
Tel: 01-580 6482
Schools in many provincial UK towns. Have native tutors to teach almost any language under the sun. Courses range from leisurely group tuition (up to eight students in a group) to the Total Immersion courses. Private tuition can be arranged at time and schedules to suit the student, or given in the form of a crash course of six hours a day, five days a week. In-company tuition can be given to groups of up to 12 people in the same company, or executive crash courses can be arranged for groups of 3 to 4 people. For all courses held worldwide, multi-media equipment can be bought to enable the student to extend his studies to the home.

Centre for Information on Language Teaching and Research. (CILT)
Regents College
Inner Circle
Regents Park
NW1 4NS
London NW1 4NS
Tel: 01-486-8221
Publishes the Information Guide 8, Part time and intensive language study: a guide for adult learners *(£1.20 plus 45p postage or look at it for free in their library.) The library also contains directories and lists of courses, biographies of course materials and they will give advice on an appropriate course.*

Goethe-Institut
50 Princes Gate (Exhibition Road)
London SW7 2PH
Tel: 01-581 3344/7

The Institute of Linguists
24a Highbury Grove
London N5 2EA
Tel: 01-359 7445
Can give details of private tutors or where to find out about them.

Linguaphone
209 Regent Street
London W1
Tel: 01-734 7572
Offers systems utilising cassettes and books in French, German, Spanish, Italian, and English. Also offers a Minilab and Travel Pack.

National Institute of Adult Continuing Education
19b De Montfort Street
Leicester LE1 7GE
Tel: (0533) 551451
Publishes, twice a year, a booklet Residential Short Courses, *which gives details of languages courses of all kinds for all levels of ability, study tours abroad and short weekend breaks in the UK. Booklet price £1.05p (inc p&p)*

Paradigm Publishing
Brookhampton Lane
Kirkton
Warwick CV35 0BR
Language cassette courses.

Stillitron
72 New Bond Street
London W1
Tel: 01-493 1177
Offers intensive ten day language programme geared towards business clientel. Very expensive.

Students Recordings Ltd.
89a Queen Street,
Newton Abott,
Devon
Tel: (0626) 67026

Tutor Tape Co. Ltd.
100 Great Russell Street
London WC1B 3LE
Tel: 01-580 7552

Courses: Outdoor and Survival Training

Adirondack Mountain Club Inc.
(See Associations: Expeditions, page 766.)

Bremex
London Borough of Brent
Youth & Community Service
65 Forty Avenue
Wembley
Middx HA9 8JR
Tel: 01-904 5811
'Bremex' – The Brent Mountain Expedition Training Scheme – enables young people, including teachers, leaders and their aides to gain the specialized 'know-how' required to plan and enjoy adventurous expeditions. The Mountain Skills Courses cover a wide range of varied interests, and operate on five levels, from basic to post-advanced.

British Mountaineering Council
Crawford House
Precinct Centre
Booth St East
Manchester M13 9RZ
Tel: 061-273 5839
The BMC offers a variety of courses in rock climbing, snow and ice climbing, mountaincraft, and Alpine climbing for most age groups. Cost from £45.00. Apply to C.Dodd at the above address.

The Drake Fellowship
10 Trinity Square
London EC3P 3AX
Tel: 01-481 7050/1
The Drake Fellowship aims to motivate young unemployed people, between the ages of 15 and 25, by the use of challenging outdoor pursuits, in order that they eventually seek, gain and retain full-time employment and make a positive contribution to their community. The Fellowship is a registered charity with centres of activity in London, Bristol, Merseyside, Cardiff, Shatham, Manchester, Newcastle, Glasgow, and Edinburgh..

Endeavour Training (The John Hunt Exploration Group)
17 Glumangate
Chesterfield
Derbyshire
S40 1TX
Tel: (0246) 37201/2
Voluntary organisation providing leadership training through expeditions for young people.

The National Centre for Mountain Activities
Plas y Brenin
Capel Curig
Nr Betws y Coed
North Wales LL24 0ET
Tel: (06904) 280
A very wide programme of training courses including rock climbing, skiing, canoeing, and orienteering for all levels of ability, introductory courses, advanced training and leadership courses, and assessment courses at the highest levels.

Orion
St Just
Nr Penzance
Cornwall
Tel: (0736) 787682
Survival training with a strong adventure sports aspect.

Outward Bound U.K.
Chestnut Field,
Regent Place,
Rugby,
CV21 2PJ
Tel: (0788) 60423
Adventure and expedition courses at five locations in the U.K. Sound basic training in a wide range of outdoor activities such as sailing, canoeing, climbing, hill walking, water and mountain safety. Emphasis on group problem solving, teamwork and leadership.

Outward Bound International
Chestnut Field,
Regent Place
Rugby,
CV21 2PJ
Tel: (0788) 60423
Co-ordination point for twenty-three Outward Bound centres in fourteen countries. High adventure and expedition courses available in Europe, USA, Canada, Africa, New Zealand, Australia, Barbados, Malaya, Hong Kong and Singapore.

School of Survival
22 Langland Drive
Whitecross
Hereford HR4 0QG
Tel: (0432) 55153

W.E.S.T.
Arrina
Shieldaig
Strathcarron
Ross-shire IV54 8XU
Tel: (05205) 213
Weekend and weekly courses in all aspects of survival from navigation and first aid to using the land. One overseas expedition each year. Also E.A.S.T., a survival training programme for business executives.

Courses: Sail Training

Mariners International Club
c/o Elizabeth Nellist, Membership Secretary
National Maritime Museum
Greenwich
London SW 10 9NF
Tel: 01-858 4422
M.I.C., an association for the promotion of traditional sail and related skills, serves as an international forum for tall ship and windjammer activities. It publishes a quarterly magazine which lists current sailing opportunities on tall ships in many different parts of the world and gives news of tall ships and related activities.

Ocean Voyages Inc
1709 Bridgeway
Sausalito
California 94965
USA
Tel: (415) 332 4681
Telex: 470-56L SAIL UI
Organization offering worldwide adventure sailing programmes. (Publish a 48-page brochure detailing these offerings). In addition to scheduled programmes, which offer active sail training for groups of four, six or larger, they can custom design yacht charters, arrange vessels for filming purposes, or for scientific research expeditions.

Ocean Youth Club
Central Office: The Bus Station
South Street
Gosport
Hants PO12 1EP
Tel: (0705) 528421/2

and
Barnett Dock
Belfast Harbour
Belfast BT3 9AF
Tel: (0232) 740008
Adventure training, cruises on 72 foot yachts for young people aged 12-24.

Sail Training Association
2a The Hard
Portsmouth PO1 3PT
Tel: (0705) 832055
Operate two schooners giving adventure voyages for young people between 16 and 25.

Courses: Photographic

New York Institute of Photography
16-20 High Road
Wood Green
London N22 6BX
Tel: 01-888 1242
Photographic studies

The Royal Photographic Society
The Octagon
Milsom Street
Bath
Tel: (0225) 62841
Offers a series of weekend workshops for both amateurs and professionals, aiming to provide background knowledge as well as specialist information. Of special interest to travellers may be the occasional courses on Nature and Travel Photography.

Publishers and Publications

Periodicals

Although most of the titles on this list are aimed at the consumer, I have included a few travel industry publications where I felt them to be of special use. Numbers at right indicate number of issues per year.

ABC TRAVEL GUIDES
ABC International
World Timetable Centre
Church Street
Dunstable
Beds LU5 4HB
Tel: (0582) 600111
Telex: 82168 AIRABC

ADVENTURE TRAVEL 2
1515 Broadway
New York
NY 10036
Tel: (212) 719 6000
Twice yearly travel magazine. $3.95 + p&p per copy.

ATLANTIS
Atlantis Travellers Club
PB 5908
Hegdehaugen
0308 Oslo 3
Norway
Tel: 02-6005 20
Norwegian-language magazine dealing in off-beat travel. Club magazine of Atlantis Travellers Club.

BUSINESS TRAVELLER 10
Perry Publications
49 Old Bond Street
London W1X 3AF
Tel: 01-629 4688
Features, air-fare cost-cutting information that will show quickly and clearly how to save dramatically on your air-travel costs.

CONDE NAST TRAVELER
641 Lexington Ave
New York
NY 10022
USA
Tel: (212) 303 6900

CONSUMER REPORTS TRAVEL LETTER
301 Junipero Serra Blvd
Suite 200
San Francisco
CA 94127
USA
Comprehensive examination of major travel questions, with company-by-company, dollars and cents comparisons of competitive travel services based on 'own original, independent, professional' research. Feature length articles on places, issues.

DEPARTURES
20/21 Suffolk Street
London SW1 4HG
Tel: 01-930 4411
Free, highly glossy magazine for American Express gold card holders. Difficult to get hold of otherwise, but some of the best travel journalism around.

EXECUTIVE TRAVEL 12
Business Magazines International Ltd
Travelpoint House
21 Fleet street
London EC4Y 1Ap
Tel: 01-353 1042
Telex: 24438 TVLPNT
For frequent travellers looking for the best deals and facilities available for their business and leisure transporation and accommodation requirements. News and features about who offers what plus temperature guides and contact numbers. Available on subscription at £11 per year or £5.50 introductory rate to WEXAS members.

EXPATRIATE, THE 12
Expatriate Publications Limited
25 Brighton Road
South Croydon
Surrey CR2 6EA
Tel: 01-681-5545
Investment, pensions information, selection of job advertisements, health, keeping in touch, tax, useful reading, reports on particularly countries. Free sample on request.

EXPEDITION CLUB AUSTRIA CLUB-NACHRICHTEN
Postfach 1457
1010 Vienna
Austria
Newsletter with readers' reports on travels, news of events past and forthcoming, and classified advertisements. (See Associations – Expeditions, page 768.)

EXPLORERS JOURNAL, THE 4
The Explorers' Club
46 East 70th Street
New York
NY 10021
USA
Official quarterly of The Explorers Club. Established 1904. Articles on scientific discoveries, expeditions, personalities and many other branches of exploration. Reviews. Subscriptions: one year $15.00, two years $27.00: three years $40; outside US add $5.00 per year; single copies $3.75. (See Associations – Exploration, page 000.)

FORD'S TRAVEL GUIDES
19448 Londelius Street
Northridge
CA 91324
USA

FREIGHTER TRAVEL NEWS 12
Freighter Travel Club of America
1745 Scotch Ave, SE
PO Box 12693
Salem
OR 79309

USA
News, letters, reports on freighter cruises. Subscription rates $16 per year/$18 foreign.

GEO
Gruner & Jahr AG &Co
Editorial Office:
Warburgstrasse 45
D-2000 Hamburg 36
West Germany
Tel: (040) 41181
Telex: 21952-16
Subscriptions:
Postfach 111629
D-2000 Hamburg 11
West Germany
Travel and places in the style of the National Geographic magazine.

THE GEOGRAPHICAL MAGAZINE   12
1 Kensington Gore
London SW7 2AR
Articles, notes, news, reviews, classfied advertisements.

GLOBE   6
The Globetrotters Club
BCM/Roving
London WC1N 3XX
Newsletter for the Globetrotters Club. Travel information. Articles on individual experiences, news of 'members on the move', tips, mutual-aid column for members.

GOING PLACES   4
Pericles Press Ltd
38 Buckingham Palace Road
London SW1W 0RE
Tel: 01-486 5353
Quarterly glossy magazine dealing in mainstream travel, with lots of destination reports.

GREAT EXPEDITIONS   6
PO Box 64699
Station G
Vancouver, BC V6R 4GT
Canada
Tel: (604) 734 3938
For people who want to travel and explore, offers trips, a free classified ads service, discounts on books, an information exchange, articles and travel notes. Magazine is US$18 annually (6 copies) in North America, US$24 elsewhere. Write for free brochure.

HOME & AWAY   12
62 Tritton Road
London SE21 8DE
Magazine with advertisements, overseas jobs information, offers of services, features on areas and topics of interest to expatriates. Club magazine of Expats International.

ISLANDS   12
3886 State Street
Santa Barbara
CA 93105
USA
Tel: (805) 682 7177

Beautiful looking magazine on – islands. World-wide.

INTERNATIONAL TRAVEL NEWS   12
Martin Publications, Inc
2120 28th Street
Sacramento
CA 95818
USA
News source for the business and/or pleasure traveller who often goes abroad. Contributions mostly from readers. Free sample copy on request. Subscription price; US$12 (year); US$15 (year) outside USA.

LONELY PLANET NEWSLETTER   4
Lonely Planet Publications Pty Ltd
PO Box 88
South Yarra
Victoria 3141
Australia
Quarterly newsletter giving updates on all the LP guidebooks and lots of useful tips from other travellers. Cost A$10 (inc. airmail postage) anywhere in the world.

MILITARY TRAVEL NEWS   6
TRAVEL NEWS   6
PO Box 9
Oakton
VA 22124
USA
Newsletters providing current low-cost travel information on the USA, Caribbean, Europe, Far East and elsewhere. Military Travel News is aimed at the US military member on active duty or retired, and dependants. Price: $6.95 per year. Travel News features travel bargains for all. Price: $7.95 per year.

NATIONAL GEOGRAPHIC MAGAZINE 12
NATIONAL GEOGRAPHIC TRAVELER   4
National Geographic Society
Washington DC
USA
The National Geographic Magazine is a long-established magazine familiar to many. Noted for the quality of its photography, articles cover travel and expeditions and many other fields. The National Geographic Traveler concentrates on travel in the US, Canada and Mexico.

NOMAD
BCM-Nomad
London WC1V 6XX
Newsletter aimed at people on the move and written by peripatetic publisher, with many readers' reports. Current issues are sent to any address on receipt of £1 or US$2.00.

OFFBEAT   4
Marie Mattson Reports
1250 Vallejo Street
San Franciso
CA 94109
USA
Newsletter offering practical advice on visiting. We suggest that reader include international reply coupons when contacting overseas organizations.

OFFICIAL AIRLINE GUIDES   12
Bridge House

4 Lyons Crescent
Tonbridge
Kent TN9 1EX
Tel: 01-930 2915
Telex: 95478
Monthly airline timetable in pocket format, aimed at the consumer.

OUTSIDE MAGAZINE 12
1165 N Clark Street
Chicago
IL 60610
USA
Tel: (312) 951-0990
Outside *magazine is edited for the active adult. It is a contemporary lifestyle magazine that features sports, fitness, photography, adventure travel and portraits of men and women adventurers. Also regularly reviewed: wildlife, outdoor clothing, product news, destinations/travel options, environmental and political issues.*

PASSPORT 12
20 North Wacker Drive
Chicago
IL 60606
USA
Newsletter for discriminating and culturally minded international travellers. Forthcoming cultural events worldwide, plus hotel and restaurant suggestions.

RESIDENT ABROAD 12
F. T. Business Publishing Ltd
Greystoke Place
Fetter Lane
London EC4A 1ND
Telex: 883694 IC LDN G
Magazine for expatriates. Price: £30 pa within UK. Sliding scale up to £60 pa for airmail longhaul.

SAFARIPOSTEN – DENMARK
Topas Globetrotterklub
Safari House
Lounsvej 29
DK-9640 Farsoe
Denmark
Tel: (08) 63 84 00
Tele: 60965 GLOBE DK
Annual expedition publication in Danish. There is also a bi-monthly newsletter of the name 'Globetrotterklub Nyhedsbrev' and a bi-monthly newsletter in English called 'The Globtrotter's Newsletter'.

THE SOUTH AMERICAN EXPLORER 4
South American Explorers Club
Casilla 3714
Lima 100
Peru
Subscriptions:
1510 York Street #214
Denver
CO 80206
USA
Official journal of the South American Explorers Club. Subscription: $15. Accounts of scientific studies, adventure, and sports activities in South America. Also, sections on news, Club activities, book reviews, letters, tips and notes.

BUSINESS MAGAZINES INTERNATIONAL LTD
Travelpoint House
21 Fleet Street
London EC4Y 1AP
Tel: 01-353 1402

TRAVEL AFRICA 4
Europe's only specialist quarterly focusing on news and features about travel to and within the African Continent. Travel Africa knows no political boundaries covering all territories of interest to tourists and business travellers from Cairo to The Cape. Package-tour programmes, hotel facilities, safaris, air and surface transportation are all given prominence. The Indian Ocean islands of the Seychelles and Mauritius are also occasionally included in this colour quarterly. Available on subscription at £4.00 per annum in the UK and $16 elsewhere from the publishers at the above address.

TRAVEL ASIA PACIFIC 6
A specialist magazine, focusing on the latest developments within the Far East and Pacific regions for tourists and business travellers alike. Reviews all the latest package tour programmes, new hotels, air routes, rail, bus and car rental services to and within the region. Subscription £4.00 per annum (including postage) UK: and $16 elsewhere from the publishers above.

THE TRAVELLER 3
WEXAS International
45 Brompton Road
Knightsbridge
London SW3 1DE
Established in 1970 as Expedition. *Photofeatures on travels and expeditions. Letters, latest news on travel, expeditions and overland, book reviews, photography and medical advice. Articles on anything from the philosophy of travel to travel writing. A lifely, informative, entertaining magazine, with excellent photographic standards.*

TRAVEL SMART 12
TRAVEL SMART FOR BUSINESS 12
Communications House
40 Beechdale Road
Dobbs Ferry
NY 10522
USA
Travel Smart
Newsletter for sophisticated travellers who expect honest value for their money. Also discount-cruises, supercharters, hotel, car rentals, etc., for members, $29.00 year year.
Travel Smart for Business
High-level inside information for business travel. Designed to save money by maintaining efficiency. $96.00 per year. Introductory discount rate.

TRAVEL TIPS 6
163–07 Depot Road
Flushing
NY 11358
USA
First person accounts of freighter and passenger ship

travel to all parts of the world. *Cruise guide, budget travel news, tips on trips.*

THE TRAVELWRITER MARKETLETTER 12
c/o Robert Scott Milne
Room 1723
The Plaza Hotel
New York NY 10019
US newsletter for travel writers with excellent news on new publications, freebies on offer and who is looking for what. Monthly. Cost within the USA – $40 pa; $50 overseas.

TROPICAL FRONTIERS
PO Box 1316
Eagle Pass
TX 78853
USA
Newsletter with news, events and travel data on 'the world's most exotic islands'.

TROPICAL ISLAND LIVING
PO Box 7263
Arlington
VA 22207
USA

Information, news on tropical islands.

TROTTER 5–6
Deutsche Zentrale für Globetrotter e.v.
c/o Peter Meyer
Postfach 60
D-5429 Katzenelnbogen
West Germany
German language. News and articles mainly from outside Europe. Tips, readers' reports, reports on the behaviour and misbehaviour of travellers, background information on 'developing countries', classified ads. For club members only, though non-members may advertise or obtain information on payment of 3 International Reply Coupons and SAE.

WORLD 12
Hyde Park Publications
Suite 6
27 Kensington Court
London W8
Tel: 01-938 1103
Glossy magazine about travel and related subjects such as ecology, wildlife etc. Annual UK subscription £18.

Book List

compiled by Melissa Shales

This list, as before, is necessarily selective. Where possble, we have given prices which are correct at the time of going to press, and virtually all books on the list are currently available. We have only included out-of-print books we feel to be classics.

The list is in two sections – a continent and country list of guide books and travel writing, and a list of 'how-to' books on the more general aspects of travel. Books are in alphabetical order by title.

Although some travel 'literature' has been listed, the many reprints of older classics currently on the market have not been included due to pressure of space, but are also well worth reading.

Continent and Country Guides

AFRICA

Africa-the Nile Route
Kim Naylor
Pub. Lascelles £3.95
One of the few guides available which includes the Sudan.

Africa – An Overlander's Guide
P. Cleggett
Pub. Bradt £1.95

Africa on a Shoestring
Geoff Crowther
Pub. Lonely Planet £6.95
Revised and updated edition of this, by now, classic guide to Africa.

Africa South of the Sahara
Pub. Fieldings Guides £11.95

Alexandria. A History and Guide Paros and Pharillon
E.M. Forster
Pub. Michael Haag £5.95/£3.95
A series of short essays which capture the feeling of Alexandria.

Algeria and the Sahara. A Handbook for Desert Travellers
Valerie and Jon Stevens
Pub. Constable £4.95
Guidebook including a detailed survey of the principal motor routes, a review of attitudes to be found towards tourists among Algerians and many travel tips.

Atlas Mountains: Morocco
R.Collomb
Pub. West Col £6.75
Practical trekking and touring guide.

Backpacker's Africa
Hilary Bradt
Pub. Bradt £5.50

Baedeker:
Egypt
Pub. AA £9.95

Berlitz Guides
Egypt
Kenya
Morocco
South Africa
Tunisia
£2.45 each

Beyond the Last Oasis: A Solo Walk in the Western Sahara
Ted Edwards
Pub. John Murray £11.50

Blue Guide Egypt
Pub. E. Benn £10.95
A comprehensive cultural guide.

The Blue Nile
The White Nile
Alan Moorhead
Pub. Penguin £5.95
Starting with Burton and Speke, the author travels to the sources of both the White and Blue Nile.

Children of the Country
Joseph Hone
Pub. Hamish Hamilton £12.95
Amusing account of the white population of Zaire and East Africa.

Cruising the Sahara
Gerald Morgan-Grenville
Pub. David and Charles £2.25
Although published in 1974, this book is still relevant, offering detailed references on all aspects of desert planning and travel.

A Desert Dies
Michael Asher
Pub. Viking £12.95
Account of time spent travelling with the nomads of the Sahara.

Dollarwise Guide to Egypt
Nancy McGrath
Pub. Arthur Frommer £9.95
A guide to hotels, restaurants, nightspots and tours with an emphasis on the medium priced.

East Africa with Zambia and Malawi
Joe Yogerst
Pub. Lascelles £3.95

Egypt – Guide Poche Univers
Pub. Editions Marcus, Paris £8.90
Compact, comprehensive guidebook.

Egypt Travel Guide
Hans Strelocke
Pub. Polygott-Verlag £1.95

Field Guide to the Birds of East Africa
Field Guide to the Birds of West Africa
J.G. Williams/Sersale
Pub. Collins £7.95 each

Field Guide to the National Parks of East Africa
J.G. Williams
Pub. Collins £7.95 **Fodor**
Egypt
Kenya
North Africa
From Hodder and Stoughton £10.50 – 12.95.

The Gambia – A Holiday Guide
Michael Tomkinson
From Luzac £3.95

Guide to Cairo – including the Pyramids and Saqqara
Michael Haag
Pub. Michael Haag £5.95

Guide to Egypt
Michael Haag
Pub. Michael Haag £9.95

Guide to East Africa
Nina Casimati
Pub. Michael Haag £4.95
Kenya, Tanzania and the Seychelles.

Guide to Lesotho
David Ambrose
From Lascelles £3.75
Comprehensive guide with a good map.

Guide to West Africa
Kim Naylor

Pub. Michael Haag £6.95
Based on a journey up the Niger River in the footsteps of Mungo Park.

Guide to Zimbabwe
Melissa Shales
Pub. Michael Haag £6.95

Hildebrand's Travel Guides:
Kenya
Mauritius
Seychelles
South Africa
From Harrap/Columbus £4.95/£5.95

The Innocent Anthropologist: Notes from a Mud Hut.
and
A Plague of Caterpillars
Nigel Barley
Pub. Penguin
Funny, thoughtful accounts of life as an anthropologist in the Cameroons.

In Search of the Forty Days Road
Michael Asher
Longman £8.95
Travel along the old Saharan slave route.

In Search of the Sahara
Quentin Crewe
Pub. Michael Joseph £12.95
Quentin Crewe and pals roaming the Sahara.

Insight Guides:
Egypt
Kenya
Pub. Harrap £9.95 each

Journey to the Jade Sea
John Hillaby
Pub. Paladin £1.95
An account of a 1,100-mile walk through Africa.

Kenya – A Visitor's Guide
Arnold Curtis
Pub. Evans Brothers Ltd

Madagascar Today
Morocco Today
Tunisia Today
Zaire Today
Pub. Editions Jeune Afrique. Each £7.50.
Awkward format, but informative guides.

Morocco. Pocket Travel Guide
From Lascelles £2.50
Chapters on each major city.

Morocco That Was
Walter Harris
Pub. Eland Books £4.95

Muddling Through in Madagascar
Dervla Murphy
Pub. Century £5.95

Nagel Guides:
Algeria
Egypt
Morocco
From G. Cave £8.50-£17

Encyclopedic guides, sometimes out of date, but full of information.

North of South
Shiva Naipaul
Pub. Penguin £2.95
Travels through Kenya, Tanzania and Zambia. Written in a scathing yet revealing way.

The Other Nile – Journeys in Egypt, The Sudan and Ethiopia
Charlie Pye-Smith
Pub. Penguin £3.95
Account and comparison of two journeys, made in 1974 and 1984, along the same route.

Penguin Guide to Ancient Egypt
W.J. Murname
Pub. Penguin £6.95
A wonderful guide.

Rough Guides:
Kenya
Morocco
Tunisia
Pub. Routledge Kegan Paul

The Sahara Handbook
Simon and Jan Glen
Pub. Lascelles £18.95
New edition of this classic guide to the Sahara and all desert travel. Essential reading.

South Africa – A Background to the Crisis
Michael Attwell
Pub. Sidgwick and Jackson £14.95/£9.95
Analysis of events in South Africa by the Weekend World team.

Times/Bartholomew Guide to Egypt
Pub. Bartholomew £4.95

Travellers Guide to:
Egypt
Kenya and N. Tanzania
Southern Africa
Pub. Thornton Cox £3.50 each
Game parks, sights to see, places to stay and eat. Background on history, culture, society.

Travellers Guide:
Central and Southern Africa
East Africa
North Africa
Guide West Africa
Pub. IC Communications £6.95 each
Rather dry, but have places not included in other guides.

The Traveller's Guide – Egypt
Derek and Julie Parker
Pub. Jonathan Cape £6.95

The Traveller's Guide – Morocco
Christopher Kininmonth
Pub. Jonathan Cape £8.95

Voices of Marrakesh
E. Canetti
Pub. M Boyars £3.95
Nobel prize winner's impressions.

The Wildlife Parks of Africa
Nicholas Luard
Pub. Michael Joseph £14.95

AMERICA, CENTRAL AND SOUTH

American Express Mexico
Pub. Mitchell Beazley £4.95

Antigua and Barbuda – The Heart of the Caribbean
Brian S. Dyde
Pub. Macmillan Caribbean £4.50

Back to Cape Horn
Rosie Swale
Pubs. Collins £10.95
Lone woman and her horse travel the length of South America.

Backpacking in:
Chile and Argentina plus the Falkland Islands
Mexico and Central America
Peru and Bolivia
Venezuela, Colombia and Ecuador
G. and H. Bradt
Pub. Bradt. £4.50-£6.95
Firsthand information about regulations, food, accommodation, transport, wildlife, parks, security, culture: with drawings, photos, entertaining asides and anecdotes.

Baedeker:
Caribbean
Mexico
Pub. AA £9.95 each

Berlitz Guides:
Bahamas
Bermuda
French West Indies
Jamaica
Mexico City
Puerto Rico
Rio de Janeiro
Southern Caribbean
Virgin Islands
£2.45 each

Bermuda Today and Yesterday 1503-1980s
Terry Tucker
Pub. Hale £7.95

The Budget Traveller's Latin America
Pub. CIEE, USA £2.95/$4.95
Comprehensive guide with information on low-cost transport to and within nineteen countries. Entry requirements, money, health, history, places of interest, etc.

Caribbean Island Hopping
Frank Bellamy
Pub. Cadogan Books £5.95
Itineraries, prices, ways of getting there.

Caribbean Today
L. Doucet
Pub. Editions Jeune Afrique £7.50

Climbing and Hiking in Ecuador
Rob Rachowiecki
Pub. Bradt £6.50
Up 30 peaks, and hikes through highlands, jungles and along the coast with background advice and information of value to all travellers.

Coups and Cocaine: Two Journeys in South America
Anthony Daniels
Pub. John Murray £10.95

Cut Stones and Crossroads – A Journey in Peru
Ronald Wright
Pub. Penguin £3.95

Eight Feet in the Andes
Dervla Murphy
Pub. John Murray £9.95
Woman, child and donkey walk 1,300 miles from Cahamarca to Cuzco.

The Enchanted Islands: The Galapagos Rediscovered.
John Hickman
Pub. Anthony Nelson £10.95
A history of the islands' discovery and their human inhabitants.

Exploring Cuzco
Pub. Bradt £5.50

Far Away and Long Ago. A Childhood in Argentina
W.H. Hudson
Pub. Eland £3.95
Very evocative.

Fisher's Annotated Travel Guides:
Bahamas
Bermuda
Caribbean
Mexico
Pub. Fisher, NY £3.95-£4.95
Clearly laid out guides with notes in the margin in red.

Fodor:
Bahamas
Bermuda
Brazil
Budget Travel Caribbean
Budget Travel Mexico
Caribbean
Central America
Mexico
Mexico City and Acapulco
South America
Pub. Fodor £5.95-£12.95

Frommer:
$-A-Day:
Mexico and Guatemala
South America £8.50 – £8.95
Dollarwise:
Bermuda and the Bahamas
The Caribbean £8.95/£9.95
City Guides:
Cancun, Cozumel and the Yucatan
Mexico City and Acapulcon £4.50 each
Pub. Frommer

Galapagos: A Natural History Guide
Plants of the Galapagos Islands
From Bradt £14.95/£5.95
About the only guides to these islands.

Grand Bahama
P.J.H. Barratt
Pub. Macmillan £4.50
Strange mix of fact and legend: climate and geology, piracy and bootlegging, the growth of industry and tourism. Good reading.

The Great Explorers – The European Discovery of American
Samuel Eliot Morison
Pub. OUP £8.95

Guide to Jamaica
Guide to Puerto Rico and the Virgin Islands
Pub. Moon £6.95/£7.95

Hildebrand's Travel Guides:
Cuba
Hispaniola
Jamaica
Mexico
From Harrap/Columbus £4.95/£6.95

In Patagonia
Bruce Chatwin
Pub. Picador £2.50
Already a classic – an account of the author's journey through Patagonia.

Insight Guides:
Bahamas
Barbados
Cruising the Caribbean
Jamaica
Mexico
Puerto Rico
Trinidad
Pub. Harrap £9.95 each

Into Cuba
Barry Lewis and Peter Marshall
Zena £18.95
Coffee-table format, but fascinating look at Cuba and its inhabitants.

Latin American Travel Guide including the Pan-American Highway Guide
Ed. Ernst Jahn
Pub. Comsco Publishing, NY
Prepared in cooperation with the Pan-American Union and the American Automobile Association. Facts and figures, not a guide to the tourist attractions.

Let's Go: Mexico
ed. Wade L. Stokes
Pub. Harrap/Columbus £9.95

Mad White Giant
Benedict Allen
Pub. Macmillan/Futura £9.95/£2.95
Travels by canoe along the Amazon.

Masquerade – The Visitor's Guide to Trinidad and Tobago
Jeremy Taylor
Pub. Macmillan Caribbean £4.50

Mexico: a Travel Survival Kit
D. Richmond
Pub. Lonely Planet £3.95

Monuments of the Incas
John Hemming and Edward Ranney
Pub. Hutchinson £30
Stunning black and white photographic portrait and fascinating text. Beautiful, interesting and useful.

Nagel Guides:
Bolivia
Brazil
Central America
Mexico
Peru
From G Cave £14-£17
Comprehensive encyclopedic guides.

Old Patagonian Express
Paul Theroux
Pub. Penguin £2.25
The author's account of a journey to the very tip of South America – all the way by train.

One Man's Mexico
J. Lincoln
Pub. Century £4.95
A reprint from 1967

Penguin Travel Guides:
Caribbean
Mexico
South America
Pub. Penguin £6.95-£7.95

Road to Elizabeth
John Ridgway
Pub. Gollancz £10.95
Account of a journey that the author and his wife made through Peru, which ended in them finding and adopting the daughter of a friend recently massacred.

Rough Guides:
Mexico
Peru
Pub. Routledge Kegan Paul

Saint Lucia – Helen of the West Indies
G. Ellis
Pub. Macmillan Caribbean £3.50

So Far From God
Patrick Marnham
Pub. Penguin £3.95
Subtitled So Close to the United States, *this is an award-winning portrait of life and travel in Central America today.*

South America on a Shoestring
Geoff Crowther
Pub. Lonely Planet £6.95
Greatly expanded version of this budget guide to South America.

South America Overland
I. Finlay
Pub. Deutsch £9.95

The South American Handbook
Pub. Trade and Travel £13.50
Annually revised. Winner of prizes and called 'the best guidebook to anywhere by anyone'.

South American River Trips
G.N. Bradt
Pub. Bradt £5.50

South American Survival
Maurice Taylor
Pub. Wilton House Gentry £6.95
Full details on routes (including Amazonas), regional differences, statistics, sketch maps of countries, regions and towns.

Student Guide to Latin America
Marjorie A Cohen
Pub. E.P. Dutton NY $2.95
Written for the Council on International Educational Exchange.

The Survival of Jan Little
John Man
Pub. Viking £10.95
Incredible story of a blind woman abandoned in the Amazon jungles of Brazil.

Trails of Cordilleras Blanca and Huayhuash of Peru
J. Bartle
Pub. Bradt £6.50

Travels with My Father:
A South American Journey
Daniel and Feliks Topolski
Pub. Elm Tree Books £9.95
Father and son set out on a six-month overland trip through South America.

Trespassers on the Roof of the Amazon
John Ure
Pub. Constable £10.95
History of travel and exploration in South America.

Yuraq Janka, Cordilleras Blanca and Rosko
J.F. Ricker
Pub. Bradt £13.95
Guide and map.

AMERICA, NORTH

Access Guides:
Hawaii
Las Vegas
Los Angeles
New Orleans
New York
San Francisco
Washington DC
Pub. Simon and Schuster £2.50 – £10.95

The Alaska Handbook
R.K. Woerner
Pub. McFarland £19.95

The Alaska-Yukon Handbook
Pub. Moon £7.95

America on Five Valium a Day
Linda Blandford

Pub. Methuen £7.95
Compilation of witty articles written home to The Guardian.

America's Favorite National Parks
National Park Guide
National Parks Recreation Directory (2 vols)
Pub. Rand McNally £5.95 – £11.95

Backpacking in North America
The Complete Guide to Backpacking in Canada
The Canadian Rockies Trail Guide
Rocky Mountain National Park Hiking Trails
Pub. Bradt £4.50 – £7.50

Baedeker:
New York
San Francisco
Pub. AA £4.95 each

Berlitz Guides:
California
Florida
Hawaii
Montreal
New York
From Cassell £2.45 each

Blue Guides:
Boston
New York
Pub. E. Benn £7.95 each

Blue Highways
William Least Heat Moon
Pub. Secker and Warburg £8.95
Marvellous account of travels around backwoods America. Potential classic.

Companion Guide to New York
Michael Leapman
Pub. Collins £6.95
A true companion to this exciting city.

Fodor:
Canada
USA £12.95 each
City Guides:
Atlantic City
Boston
Chicago
Dallas, Fort Worth
Houston and Galveston
Los Angeles
Great Miami and the Gold Coast
New Orleans
New York City
Philadelphia
San Diego
San Francisco
Toronto
Washington DC
Williamsburg, Jamestown and Yorktown £5.95
– £8.95
Budget Guides:
American Cities on a Budget
Budget America
Budget Travel Canada
Budget Travel Hawaii

Area Guides:
Alaska
Arizona
California
Canada's Maritime Provinces
Cape Cod
Chesapeake
Colorado
Far West
Florida
Hawaii
New England
New Mexico
Pacific North Coast
Quebec
South
Texas
Virginia
From Hodder and Stoughton £8.95-£10.95

Dollarwise Guides:
Canada
California and Las Vegas
Florida
New England
The Northwest
SE and New Orleans
The Southwest
Texas £8.95 – £9.95
$-A-Day Guides:
Hawaii
New York
Washington DC £8.50-£8.95
City Guides:
Atlantic City and Cane May
Boston
Hawaii
Las Vegas
Los Angeles
Montreal and Quebec City
New Orleans
New York
Orlando, Disney World and Epcot
Philadelphia
San Francisco
Washington DC
Pub. Frommer £4.50 each

The Hawaiian Islands
Carole Chester
Pub. Batsford £9.95

Hidden Hawaii
Hidden San Francisco and Northern California
Pub. Moorland £8.95 each

The Hip Pocket Guide to New York
T. Page
Pub. Harper and Row £2.95

Honkytonk Gelato
(about Texas)
New York Days, New York Nights
Stephen Brooks
Pub. Hamish Hamilton
Hilarious tales of travel in the USA.

Indian Country
Peter Mathiessen
Pub. Collins £12.95
Portrait of North American Indian culture.
Insight Guides:
Alaska
American Southwest
California: Grand Tour
California: Northern
California: Southern
Canada: Grand Tour
Crossing America
Florida
Hawaii
New England
New York State
Pacific North West
Rockies
Texas
Pub. APA/Harrap £9.95 each

Let's Go:
California and the Pacific Northwest
USA
Pub. Harrap/Columbus £9.95 & £10.95

Lonely Planet:
Alaska Travel Survival Kit
Canada: A Travel Survival Kit
Companion Guide to New York
USA West. A Travel Guide to Hawaii, the Pacific States and SW
Pub. Lonely Planet

Michelin Green Guides:
Canada
New England
New York City
Pub. Michelin £3.60 each

Mobil Regional Travel Guides:
California and the West
Great Lakes Area
Major Cities
Mid-Atlantic States
Northeastern States
Northwest and Great Plains States
Southeastern States
Southwest and South Central Area
Pub. Simon and Schuster £8.95 each

Moneywise Guide to California
Vicki Leon
Pub. Travelaid £5.95
Fun to read and full of practical advice.

Nagel Guides:
Canada
New York
USA
From G. Cave £7-£18.50

Old Glory
Jonathan Raban
Pub. Flamingo £2.95
A journey down the Mississippi.

Passport Guides:
Hawaii at Its Best
Pub. £7.95

Penguin Guides:
Canada
Hawaii
USA
USA for Business Travellers
Pub. Penguin £6.50-£7.50

Rough Guides:
New York
Pub. Routledge Kegan Paul

Scot Free
Alastair Scot
Pub. John Murray £10.95
Hitchhiking from the Arctic to New Mexico.

Travel Brief USA
Nigel Buxton
Pub. Sunday Telegraph £2.95

Travelling and Camping in the National Park Areas:
Eastern States
Mid-America
Western States
Pub. Bradt £4.95 each

Turn Right at Death Valley
John Merrill
Pub. JNM Publications £6.95
Account of and guide to a walk across the USA – coast to coast.

Vagabonding in the USA
Ed Buryn
From Lascelles £6.50

Washington DC – The American Express Pocket Guide
Pub. Mitchell Beazley £4.95

Welcome to:
East Canada
New York
Carole Chester
Pub. Collins £2.95 each

West Coast USA
I. Van Dam
Pub. John Murray £5.95

ARCTIC AND ANTARCTIC

Antarctica: The Last Horizon
John Béchervaise
Pub. Cassell £8.95
An account of Antarctica's unique wildlife, explorations past and present and ecological future by winner of the Queen's Polar Medal.

Antarctica. Wilderness at Risk
B. Brewster
Pub. Reed £5.95

Antarctic Year:
Brabant Island Expedition
Chris Furse
Pub. Croom Helm £14.95

Account of the year long Joint Services Expedition to Brabant Island.

An African in Greenland
Tété-Michel Kpomassie
Pub. Secker and Warburg £8.95
Run-away boy from Togo goes to live with the Eskimoes.

Arctic Dreams
Barry Lopez
Pub. Macmillan £14.95

The Arctic Highway
John Douglas
From Geoslides or Stackpole Books, USA
A full description of north Norway's famous road to the Arctic.

The Fourth World
Sam Hall
Pub. Bodley Head £12.95
Description of lifestyle of Arctic peoples and discussion of the area's future.

The Last Kings of Thule
Jean Malaurie
Pub. Cape £17.50
Wonderfully sensitive portrait of traditional Eskimo life.

South
Ernest Shackleton
Pub. Century £4.95
First published in 1919, this is the story of Shackleton's last expedition 1914-17.

Portrait of Antarctica
Pub. George Philips £9.95
Composite view of life over the last 40 years on the frozen continent by five enthusiasts.

South Pole Odyssey
E. Wilson
Pub. Blandford £3.95
Selection from Edward Wilson's diary.

ASIA – GENERAL

All Asia Guide
Pub. Far Eastern Economic Review £6.50
Classic middle depth guide. 682pp of travel advice for businessmen and travellers from Afghanistan to Japan.

Insight Guides:
Asia: Grand Tour
Pub. Harrap £9.95

Santhana: One Man's Road to the East
Borna Babek
Pub. Bodley Head £6.50
Adventure and mysticism. A fine example of travelling against the odds.

Student Guide to Asia/Budget Traveler's Asia
Ed. David Jenkins for the Australian Union of Students.
Pub. E.P. Dutton, NY $4.95/£3.50
Useful guide to 26 countries for students or other low-budget travellers.

The Traveller's and Business Guide to Asia and Australia
Devine and Braganti
Pub. Sidgwick & Jackson £12.95

Traveller's Survival Kit to the East
Susan Griffith
Pub. Vacation Work £2.95

ASIA – WEST

Among the Believers
V.S. Naipaul
Pub. Penguin £2.95

Arabia Through the Looking Glass
Jonathan Raban
Pub. Fontana £2.95

Arabian Sands
Marsh Arabs
Wilfred Thesiger
Pub. Penguin £2.25 and £2.95

Arabian Travellers – The European Discovery of Arabia
Richard Trench
Pub. Macmillan £12.95
Story of the early European travellers in Arabia.

Baedeker:
Israel £9.95
City Guides:
Istanbul
Jerusalem £4.95 each
Regional Guides:
Turkish Coast £5.95
Pub. AA

Blue Guide to Istanbul
John Freely
Pub. E. Benn £9.95
By the same author as the famous but elusive Strolling Through Istanbul.

Business Guide to:
Egypt
Kuwait
Oman
Saudi Arabia
Pub. World of Information/Longmans £2.95

The Companion Guide to Turkey
John Freely
Pub. Collins £8.50
Reliable, comprehensive guide from Istanbul to the border.

The Economist Business Traveller's Guide:
Arabian Peninsula
Pub. The Economist/Collins £12.95

Fodor:
Israel
Jordan
Turkey
From Hodder and Stoughton £10.50-£10.95

Frommer:
Israel on $25 and $30 a Day.
Pub. Frommer £8.95

Insight Guides:
Israel
Pub. Harrap £9.95

An Insight and Guide to Jordan
Christine Osborne
Pub. Longmans £8.75

Iraq – Land of Two Rivers
Gavin Young
Pub. Collins £15
Starting in Baghdad and central Iraq, this book moves south to Basra and the obscure lagoons and reed-beds of the Marsh Arabs and north to Kurdistan.

Israel Travellers Guide
Pub. Thornton Cox £3.50

Istanbul – A Traveller's Companion
Laurence Kelly
Pub. Constable £12.95/£6.95
Anthology of writings on Istanbul from all periods.

Jerusalem
Colin Thubron
Pub. Century Hutchinson £5.95

Journey to Kars
Philip Glazebrook
Pub. Viking £8.95

Let's Go: Israel and Egypt
Pub. Harrap/Columbus £9.95

Lonely Planet:
Israel and the Occupied Territories
Turkey: A Travel Survival Kit
West Asia on a Shoestring

Mecca and Medinah Today
Kaidi, Bamente and Tidjani
Pub. Editions Jeune Afrique £7.50

MEED Guides:
Bahrain
Jordan
Oman
Qatar
Saudi Arabia
UAE
From Noonan Hurst £7.95-£9.95

Nagel:
Gulf Emirates
Iran
Israel
Turkey
From G. Cave £9-£25

Phaidon Cultural Guide to Jerusalem and the Holy Land
Pub. Phaidon £9.95

Traveller's Guide to the Middle East
Pub. International Communications £4.95
Guide for the businessman or tourist including country-by-country information on how to get there, accommodation, local customs, transport, etc.

The Traveller's Key to Ancient Egypt
Pub. Columbus £8.95
Historical and cultural guide.

Treks and Climbs in the Mountains of Rum and Petra, Jordan
Tony Howard
Pub. Cicerone £9.95

ASIA-INDIAN SUBCONTINENT

Bangladesh. A Traveller's Guide
Don Yeo
Pub. Lascelles £3.50
Only guide to the republic.

Berlitz:
Sri Lanka £2.45

The Best of India: from budget to luxury
Paige Palmer
Pub. Bradt £7.95

Calcutta
Geoffrey Moorhouse
Pub. Penguin £4.95
Riveting account of the city.

Everest: The Unclimbed Ridge.
Chris Bonington and Charles Larke
Pub. Hodder and Stoughton £12.95
Account of the tragic 1982 expedition in which Peter Boardman and Joe Tasker lost their lives.

First Across the Roof of the World
Graeme Dingle and Peter Hillary
Pub. Hodder and Stoughton £9.95
3,000-mile-walk from Darjeeling to K2 – the first traverse of the Himalayas.

Fodor:
India, Nepal and Sri Lanka
From Hodder and Stoughton £12.95

A Guide to Trekking in Nepal
S. Berzuchka
Pub. Cordee £5.95
Detailed descriptions of many routes and advice on organizing a trek.

A Handbook for Travellers in India, Pakistan, Nepal, Sri Lanka and Bangladesh
ed Prof L.F. Rushbrook Williams
Pub. John Murray £25
Periodically revised. First published in 1859.

Handguide to the Birds of the Indian Subcontinent
M. Woodcock
Pub. Collins £3.50

Hildebrand's Travel Guides:
India and Nepal
Sri Lanka
From Harrap £5.95 each

The Himalayan Kingdoms: Nepal, Bhutan and Sikkim
Bob Gibbons and Bob Ashford
Pub. Batsford £9.95

Heart of the Jungle
K.K. Gurung
Pub. Andre Deutsch £9.95
Naturalist and manager of Tiger Tops discusses the Chitwan Valley.

India. A Practical Guide
John Leak
Pub. Lascelles £3.95
If you can't find the Travel Survival Kit – grab this.

India on $25 a Day
Pub. Frommer £8.50

India File
Trevor Fishlock
Pub. John Murray £6.95

India in Luxury – A Practical Guide for the Discerning Traveller
Louise Nicholson
Pub. Century £6.95

India, Sri Lanka and Nepal
Peter Meyer and Barbara Rausch
Pub. Springfield £8.95

An Indian Attachment
Sarah Lloyd
Pub. Futura £2.50
English woman marries a Sikh and goes to live in a Punjab village.

An Indian Summer – A Personal Experience of India
James Cameron
Pub. Penguin £3.95

India's Wildlife and Wildlife Reserves
B. Seshadri
Pub. Oriental University Press £12

Insight Guides:
India
Nepal
Rajasthan

Sri Lanka
Wildlife of India
Pub. Harrap £9.95 each

An Insight and Guide to Pakistan
Christine Osborne
Pub. Longmans £12.95

Into India
John Keay
Pub. John Murray £4.95
An area-by-area coverage of modern India and Indian life.

A Journey in Ladakh
Andrew Harvey
Pub. Chatto £8.50

Lonely Planet:
India: A Travel Survival Kit.
Kashmir, Ladakh and Zanskar
Kathmandu and the Kingdom of Nepal
Pakistan: A Travel Survival Kit
Sri Lanka: A Travel Survival Kit
Trekking in the Himalayas

The Maldives Mystery
Thor Heyerdahl
Pub. Unwin-Hyman £12.95
Heyerdahl turns his attention to the fascinating past of these islands.

Maldives – Via Sri Lanka
Pub. Lascelles £2.95
The only English guide to these increasingly popular islands.

Nagel:
Ceylon
India
From G. Cave £9-£25

Out of India
Tim Piggott-Smith
Pub. Constable £8.95
Anthology of writings on India and diary kept while filming The Jewel in the Crown.

Pakistan. A Travellers Guide
Adamson and Shaw
From Lascelles £6.95
An excellent comprehensive guide.

Plant Hunting in Nepal
R. Lancaster
Pub. Croom Helm£6.95
Useful self-explanatory book.

Post Guide:
Sri Lanka
Pub. Columbus £5.95

Riding the Mountains Down
Bettina Selby
Pub. Gollancz £9.95
On a bicycle through the Himalayas.

A Short Walk in the Hindu Kush
Slowly Down the Ganges
Eric Newby
Pub. Picador £2.50 each
Two highly entertaining journeys.

To the Frontier
Geoffrey Moorhouse
Hodder and Stoughton £9.95
Prize-winning account of travels on the North-West Frontier.

The Traveller's Key to Northern India
Pub. Columbus £8.95
Cultural and historical guide.

Trekkers Guide to the Himalaya and Karakoram
Hugh Swift
Pub. Hodder and Stoughton £6.95
Excellent comprehensive guide.

Trekking in the Himalayas
Pub. Springfield £14.95

A Walk Along the Ganges
Dennison Berwick
Pub. Century Hutchinson £12.95

Where Men and Mountains Meet
John Keay
Pub. Century £4.95

ASIA – SOUTH EAST

A Dragon Apparent
Norman Lewis
Pub. Eland £3.95
Travels in Cambodia, Laos and Vietnam. Written in 1951, it makes poignant reading.

Baedeker:
Bangkok
Singapore
Pub AA £5.95

Berlitz:
Singapore
Thailand
£2.45 each

Crossing the Shadow Line
Andrew Eames
Pub. Hodder and Stoughton £12.95
Young man's journey in Thailand.

Fodor:
Korea
Singapore
South East Asia
From Hodder and Stoughton £7.95/£12.95

Golden Earth
Norman Lewis
Pub. Eland £4.95
About Burma.

Great Railway Bazaar
Paul Theroux
Pub. Penguin £1.95
*A train journey through South East Asia: a modern
classic.*

Hildebrand's Travel Guides:
Indonesia
South Korea
Thailand and Burma
From Harrap £5.95/£6.95

Indonesia Handbook
Bill Dalton
Pub. Moon £14.95
*First-ever comprehensive guide (with detailed maps)
to the islands of Micronesia, Polynesia and Melane-
sia with Papua New Guinea also. Indispensable.*

Insight Guides:
Burma
Indonesia
Java
Korea
Malaysia
Philippines
Singapore
Thailand
Pub. APA/Harrap £9.95 each

Into the Heart of Borneo
Redmond O'Hanlon
Pub. Salamander Press £10.95

**Island Hopping through the Indonesian Archi-
pelago**
Maurice Taylor
Pub. Wilton House Gentry £5.40
*A guide to cheap, leisurely travel through Thailand,
Malaysia, Indonesia. Good town plans and detailed
advice.*

The Land of the Great Sophy
Roger Stevens
Pub. Methuen £8.50

Lonely Planet:
Bali and Lombok: A Travel Survival Kit
Burma. A Travel Survival Kit
Malaysia, Singapore and Brunei. A Travel Sur-
vival Kit
Indonesia: A Travel Survival Kit
Philippines: a Travel Survival Kit
South East Asia on a Shoestring
Thailand: A Travel Survival Kit

The Malaysia Handbook
Pub. Springfield £6.95

Nagel:
Philippines
Thailand
From G. Cave £9-£25

Peoples of the Golden Triangle
Paul and Elaine Lewis
Pub. Thames & Hudson £18

*Coffee-table format, but fascinating guide to the
tribes of northern Thailand.*

Post Guides:
Indonesia
Malaysia
Philippines
Singapore
Thailand
Pub. Columbus £5.95 each

South East Asia Handbook
Stefan Loose and Renate Ramb
From Springfield £8.95
*Detailed guide to travel in Thailand, Singapore,
Indonesia, Brunei, Malaysia and Burma.*

Thailand
Gladys Nicol
Pub. Batsford £7.50
*A description of Thai history and art from Bangkok
to the rain forests.*

ASIA – FAR EAST

Access Guide to Tokyo
Pub. Simon and Schuster £10.95

Alone Through China and Tibet
Helena Drysdale
Pub. Constable £9.95

Baedeker:
Japan £9.95
City Guides:
Hong Kong
Tokyo £4.95 each
Pub. AA

Behind the Forbidden Door – Travels in China
Tiziano Terzani
Pub. Unwin-Hyman £11.95/£3.95

Berlitz:
Hong Kong
£2.45

China
Sarah Allan and Cherry Barnett
Pub. Cassell £6.95
*Gives a historical background to the major cities of
China and general practical advice to the traveller.*

China Companion
Evelyn Garside
Pub. Deutsch £4.95
*A guide to 100 cities, resorts, and places of interest
in the people's republic. The author lived for some
years in Beijing.*

China Off the Beaten Track
Brian Schwartz
Pub. Collins £5.95
*Excellent, if a bit outdated, guide to independent
travel in China.*

China Guidebook
A.J. Keijzer and I.M. Kaplan
Dist. A. and C. Black £4.95
Authoritative guide to over 30 cities and 250 tourist sites.

China's Sorrows
Lynn Pan
Pub. Century £11.95

China Today
Japan Today
Pub. Editions Jeune Afrique £7.50 each

The Chinese. A Portrait
David Bonavia
Pub. Penguin £1.95

Chinese Characters – A Journey through China
Sarah Lloyd
Pub. Collins £12.95

Dollarwise Guide to Japan and Hong Kong
Pub. Frommer £9.95

The Economist Business Traveller's Guide – Japan
ed. Rick Morris
Pub. The Economist/Collins £12.95

Fodor:
Beijing, Guangzhou and Shanghai
Budget Travel Japan
China
Hong Kong and Macau
Japan
Tokyo
From Hodder and Stoughton £7.50 – £12.95

From Heaven Lake
Vikram Seth
Pub. Chatto £8.95
Seth hitchhiked through Tibet to Nepal, an extraordinary journey. Winner of the 1983 Thomas Cook Travel Book Award.

Hildebrand's Travel Guides:
China
Japan
Taiwan
From Harrap £5.95/£6.95

Hong Kong, Macau and Taiwan
Nina Nelson
Pub. Batsford £9.95

The Inland Sea
Donald Richie
Pub. Century £4.95
Travelling in Japan.

Into Japan
John Lowe
Pub. John Murray £6.95

The Insider's Guide to Japan
Peter Popham
Pub. CFW Publications

Insight Guides:
Hong Kong
Taiwan
Pub. APA/Harrap £9.95

The Japan Handbook
Pub. Moon £12.95

Japan Post Guide
ed. Simon Holledge
Pub. South China Morning Post £5.95

Japan. A Travellers Companion
Lesley Namioka
Pub. Vanguard Press, NY r8.95
Explains Japan for the visitor – including explanation of both customs!

Land of the Snow Lion – An Adventure in Tibet
Elaine Brook
Pub. Jonathan Cape £10.95

Lonely Planet:
Hong Kong, Macau and Canton
Japan: A Travel Survival Kit
Korea and Taiwan: A Travel Survival Kit
North East Asia: A Travel Survival Kit.

Low City, High City
Edward Seidensticker
Pub. Allen Lane £16.95
Tokyo from Edo to Earthquake. A fascinating portrait of the city.

Nagel:
China
From G. Cave

On Your Own in China
G. Earnshaw
Pub. Century £4.95
A guide for the adventurous traveller.

A Pedaller to Peking
Christopher Hough
Pub. Methuen £9.95
A cycle ride to China.

Pictures from the Water Trade
John David Morley
Pub. Andre Deutsch £9.95
Experiences of an Englishman living in Japan.

Post Guides:
Hong Kong
Japan
Pub. Columbus £5.95 each

Return to China
Lian Heng and Judith Shapiro
Pub. Chatto and Windus £12.95
A survivor of the Cultural Revolution reports on China today.

Rough Guide to China
Pub. Routledge Kegan Paul

The Silk Road – A History
Irene M. French and David M. Brownstone
Pub. Facts on File £16.95

Slow Boats to China
Gavin Young
Pub. Penguin £2.95
The author travelled from Greece to China by a variety of different boats.

A Traveller in China
Christina Dodwell
Pub. Hodder and Stoughton £10.95

Travels in Japan
David Price
Pub. Olive Press £10.95

Traveller's Guide to the People's Republic of China
Ruth L. Malloy
Pub. Wm Morrow, NY £6.50
Comprehensive English-Chinese phrasebook. Descriptions of 90 cities and special sections for business people.

A Visitor's Guide to China
Elizabeth Morrell
Pub. Michael Joseph £8.95.

AUSTRALIA AND PACIFIC

Across the South Pacific
Finlay and Sheppard
Pub. Angus and Robertson £9.95

Across the Top
Malcolm Douglas and David Oldmeadow
From Lascelles £2.95

Australia
Vicki Peterson
Pub. Cassell £5.95
The author travelled 25,000km to research this book; an excellent overall guide.

The Australians
Ross Terrill
Pub. Bantam £12.95
Portrait of Australia today written to coincide with the Bicentennial celebrations.

Borneo
John Mackinnon
Pub. Time-Life £7.50

Fiji – In Search of an Island
Linda Gill
Pub. Hodder and Stoughton £7.95
Linda Gill, her family, Sir Edmund Hillary and his family all travel together in Fiji.

Finding Fiji
Pub. Moon £6.95

Fodor:
Australia, New Zealand and South Pacific
New Zealand

South Pacific
Sydney
From Hodder and Stoughton £7.95 – £12.95

Frommer:
$-A-Day:
Australia
New Zealand
Pub. Frommer £8.95 each

Guide to the Outdoors
Jeff Carter
From Lascelles £7.50
Practical, simple authoritative book by a man who has spent most of the last 25 years travelling and living outdoors in every corner of Australia.

Hildebrand's Travel Guides:
Australia
New Zealand
From Harrap/Columbus £5.95 each

How to Get Lost and Found In:
Australia
Cook Islands
Fiji
New Zealand
Tahiti
From Lascelles £4.95 each

In Papua New Guinea
Christina Dodwell
Pub. Oxford Illustrated Press £7.95
One of the few up-to-date books on Papua New Guinea

Insight Guides:
Australia
New Zealand
Pub. APA/Harrap £9.95 each

Lonely Planet:
Australia: A Travel Survival Kit
Bushwalking in Papua New Guinea
New Zealand: A Travel Survival Kit
Papua New Guinea: A Travel Survival Kit
Tramping in New Zealand

Long Stays in Australia
Maggie Driver
David & Charles £9.95
Guide to living and working on the continent.

The Micronesia Handbook
Pub. Moon £7.95

On Fiji Island
Ronald Wright
Pub. Viking £10.95
History and lifestyle of the island, published before the coup.

Outback
Thomas Keneally
Pub. Hodder and Stoughton £12.95
Fabulous evocation by Booker Prize-winning author. Magnificent photographs.

Pacific Island Yearbook
Stuart Inder

Papua New Guinea Handbook
Judy Taylor

Pub. Pacific Publications, Sydney £8.50
Description of the country area by area.

Pacific Odyssey
Gwenda Cornell
Pub. Adlard Coles £4.95
The author and her family spent three years sailing round the South Sea islands.

Post Guide: Australia
Pub. Columbus £5.95

The Ribbon and the Ragged Square
Linda Christmas
Pub. Viking £14.95
Nine months spent exploring Australia.

South Pacific Handbook
Bill Dalton
Pub. Moon £13.95
Vocabs, diagrams, maps, town plans, archaeological sites, etc.

The South Seas Dream
John Dyson
Pub. Heinemann £10
Beautifully written account of time spent searching for paradise in the modern South Seas.

Tahiti
John Bounds
From Lascelles £3.95

Tracks
Robyn Davidson
Pub. Granada £1.95
Amazing account of a journey across the Australian desert on camels.

EUROPE

Access Guides:
London
Paris
Rome
Pub. Simon and Schuster £9.95 each

The Aegean
H.M. Denham
Pub. John Murrary £25
A sea-guide with information on cruising, the coast and islands.

Albania. A Travel Guide
Phillip Ward
Pub. Oleander £5.95
Interesting, but sledgehammer politics.

Alpine Pass Route
J. Hurdle
Pub. West Col £3.95

Alta Via – High Level Walks in the Dolomites
Martin Collins
Corsica High Level
Alan Castle
The Kalkapen Traverse
Alan Proctor
Mountain Walking in Austria
Cecil Davies

The Mountains of Greece – A Walker's Guide
Tim Salmon
The Tour of Mont Blanc
Andrew Harper
Tour of the Oisans:
Andrew Harper
Via Ferrata – Scrambles in the Dolomites
Walks and Climbs in the Pyrenees
Kev Reynolds
Walking in Mallorca
June Parker
Walking the French Alps:
Martin Collins
Cicerone Press £2.95 – £7.95
Good practical guides to walking in Europe. Also wide selection of UK titles.

American Express Guides:
Florence and Tuscany
Greece
Paris
Rome
South of France
Spain
Venice
Pub. Mitchell Beazley £4.95 each
Handy, informative pocket guides.

Among the Russians
Colin Thubron
Pub. Heinemann £8.95
View of everyday life behind the Iron Curtain based on conversations with the local populace.

Backpacker's Greece
Marc S. Dublin
Pub. Bradt £5.50

Backpacking in Italy
Stefano Ardito
Pub. Bradt £6.95

Baedeker Guides:
Austria
Denmark
France
Germany
Greece
Holland/Belgium/Luxembourg
Italy
Mediterranean Islands
Portugal
Scandinavia
Spain
Switzerland
Yugoslavia £9.95 each
Regional Guides:
Greek Islands
Loire
Provence/Côte D'Azur
Rhine
Tuscany £5.95 each
City Guides:
Amsterdam
Athens
Berlin
Brussels

Budapest
Cologne
Copenhagen
Florence
Frankfurt
Hamburg
Madrid
Moscow
Munich
Paris
Prague
Rome
Stuttgart
Venice
Vienna
Pub. AA £4.95 each

Berlitz:
45 guides covering countries, areas and cities.
From Cassell £2.45 each

Between the Woods and Water
Patrick Leigh Fermor
Pub. John Murray £13.95
Teenage travels in Europe in the 1930s.

The Big Red Train Ride
Eric Newby
Pub. Penguin £2.25
A journey on the Trans-Siberian railway.

Black Lamb and Grey Falcon
Rebecca West
Pub. Macmillan £6.95
*A masterful mixture of travel, politics, anecdote, etc.
on Yugoslavia.*

Blue Guides:
Athens and Environs
Belgium and Luxembourg
Crete
Cyprus
Florence
Greece
Holland
North Italy
South Italy
Loire Valley
Malta
Moscow and Leningrad
Paris and Environs
Portugal
Rome and Environs
Sicily
Spain
Venice
Pub. E. Benn £3.95-£7.95

Companion Guides:
Florence
Greek Islands
Mainland Greece
Rome
South of France
Venice
Yugoslavia
Pub. Collins £5.95-£6.95

Complete Guide to the Soviet Union
V. and J. Louis
Pub. Michael Joseph £6.95
The authors live in Moscow.

Corsica Mountains
R.G. Collomb
Pub. West Col £5.25

Fat Man on a Bicycle
Tom Vernon
Pub. Fontana £1.95
A trip through France.

Fieldings Guides:
Discover Europe: Off the Beaten Track
Pub. Columbus £9.95

Fight the Wild Island
Ted Edwards
Pub. John Murray £11.95
Solo walk across Iceland.

France for the Independent Traveller
John P. Harris
Pub. Papermac £4.95
Lifestyle guide to France and the French.

Fodor Guides:
Austria
Belgium and Luxembourg
France
Germany
Great Britain
Greece
Holland
Hungary
Ireland
Italy
Portugal
Scotland
Spain
Sweden
Switzerland
Yugoslavia £7.95 – £10.95
Area Guides:
Eastern Europe
Europe
Scandinavia
Soviet Union £12.95 each
City Guides:
Amsterdam
Florence and Venice
Lisbon
Loire Valley
London
Madrid
Munich
Paris
Rome
Stockholm
Copenhagen
Oslo
Helsinki
Reykjavik
Vienna £5.95–£7.95
Budget Guides:
Budget Travel Britain
Budget Europe
Budget Travel France

Budget Travel Germany
Budget Travel Italy
Budget Travel London
Budget Travel Spain £7.50 – £10.95
From Hodder and Stoughton

The French Channel Ports – A Visitor's Guide
David Wickers & Charlotte Atkins
Pub. Papermac £4.95

French Leave
Richard Binns
Pub. Chiltern House £5.95
Third edition of this extremely popular guide.

Frommer Guides:
$-A-Day:
Eastern Europe
England
Europe
Greece
Ireland
Scandinavia
Scotland and Wales
Spain, Morocco, and Canaries £8.95-£9.95
Dollarwise Guides:
Austria and Hungary
England and Scotland
France
Germany
Italy
Portugal, Madeira and the Azores
Switzerland and Liechtenstein £9.95 each
City Guides:
Amsterdam
Athens
Dublin and Ireland
Lisbon, Madrid and Costa del Sol
Paris
Rome
Pub. Frommer £4.50 each

Frontiers
Adam Nicolson
Pub. Weidenfeld & Nicolson £10.95
A journey along the Iron Curtain.

The Greek Islands
Brian Dicks
Pub. Robert Hale £12.95

Guide to Aegean and Mediterranean Turkey
Diana Darke
Pub. Michael Haag £7.95

A Guide to Central Europe
Richard Bassett
Pub. Viking £10.95
Chiefly Vienna, Budapest, and Prague.

Guide to Czechoslovakia
Simon Hayman
Pub. Bradt £6.95

A Guide to Tuscany
James Bentley
Pub. Viking £10.95

High Level: the Alps from End to End
David Brett
Pub. Gollancz £10.95

Vivid account of 600-miles through the Alps with a wealth of information for anyone going there.

A History of Sicily
Finley, Smith and Duggan
Pub. Chatto and Windus £14.95

Hitch-Hiker's Guide to Europe
Ken Walsh
Pub. Pan £2.95

100 Hikes in the Alps
I. Spring and H. Edwards
Pub. Cordee £5.50

The Holiday Which? Guide to France inc. Corsica
Adam Ruck
Pub. Hodder and Stoughton £8.95

Iceland Saga
Magnus Magnusson
Pub. Bodley Head £12.95
Takes a new look at the Icelandic sagas and ties them into the modern landscape.

Iceland: the Visitor's Guide
David Williams
Pub. Stacey Int. £12.95

Insight Guides:
Continental Europe: Grand Tour
France
Great Britain
Greece
Ireland
Italy
Romantic Germany
Spain
Pub. APA/Harrap £9.95 each

Italy
Edmund Swinglehurst
Pub. Batsford £12.95

Journey into Cyprus
Colin Thubron
Pub. Penguin £3.95

Just Across the Channel
Charles Owen
Pub. Cadogan £3.95
Day trips and weekends on the Channel coast.

Le Weekend
Arthur Eperon
Pan £2.95
Day trips and weekends on the Channel coast.

Let's Go:
Britain and Ireland
Europe
France
Greece
Italy
Spain, Portugal and Morocco
Pub. Harvard Student Agencies £9.95-£10.95

Life in Russia
Michael Binyon
Pub. Panther £2.95

Long Stays in Belgium and Luxembourg
Carole Hazlewood
Pub. David and Charles £10.95
Living and working in the two countries.

Michelin Green Guides
10 European countries
19 French Regions
Pub. Michelin £3.60 each

Nagel Guides:
24 European titles
From G. Cave £2-£21

Moscow – A Traveller's Companion
Ed. Laurence Kelly
Pub. Constable £9.95/£5.95
Selection of writings on the city from all nationalities and periods of history.

The Natural History of the USSR
Algirdas Knystautas
Pub. Century £14.95

Next Time You Go to Russia
C.A. Ward
Pub. John Murray £5.75
A guide to historic landmarks and art museums.

On Foot Through Europe:
Austria, Switzerland and Liechtenstein
The British Isles
Europe's Long Distance Footpaths
France and the Benelux Nations
West Germany
Spain and Portugal
Scandinavia
Craig Evans
Pub. Quill Books £7.95 each
Series of seven books covering Western Europe for the walker, ski tourer and climber.

Passport Guides:
Britain at Its Best
France at Its Best
Germany at Its Best
Italy at Its Best
Spain at Its Best
Switzerland at Its Best £7.95 each
City Guides:
London at Its Best
Paris at Its Best £5.95 each
Pub. Columbus

Pauper's Paris
M. Turner
Pub. Pan £2.50
Superb budget guide, packed full of useful tips.

Penguin Travel Guide Europe
Pub. Penguin £8.95

Phaidon Cultural Guides:
Holland
Paris and the Ile de France
Rome and Latium
Pub. Phaidon £9.95 each

Picos de Europa. Northern Spain
R.G. Collomb
Pub. West Col £7.50

Pyrenees, Andorra, Cerdagne. A guide to the mountains for walkers and climbers
A. Battagel
Pub. West Col £6.00

Pyrenees. High Level Route
G. Vernon
Pub. West Col £7.50

Romanian Journey
A. Mackenzie
Pub. Hale £8.50

Rough Guides:
Amsterdam and Holland
Eastern Europe
France
Greece
Paris
Portugal
Spain
Yugoslavia
Pub. Routledge Kegan Paul
Excellent series, a combination of practical information and scholarly fact. Many other titles in the pipeline.

Roumel:
Patrick Leigh Fermor
Pub. Penguin £2.95
Beautifully written book of travels in Northern Greece.

Shell Guide to France
Pub. Michael Joseph £7.95

South From Granada
Gerald Brenan
Pub. CUP £4.95
A classic book on Spain.

Spain
Jan Morris
Pub. Penguin £1.75

Stranger in Spain

Traveller in Italy

Traveller in Rome

Traveller in South Italy
H.V. Morton
Pub. Methuen £5.95-£6.95

A Time of Gifts
Patrick Leigh Fermor
Pub. Penguin £1.95
A journey on foot from England to Hungary.

Times/Bartholomew Guides:
Florence
Paris
Venice
Pub. Bartholomew £4.95 – £5.95

Trans-Siberia by Rail and a Month in Japan
Barbara Lamplugh
Pub. Lascelles £1.95

Trans-Siberian Rail Guide
Robert Strauss
Pub. Bradt £6.95

The Traveler's Guide to the Ocean Ferryliners of Europe
Hippocrene $12.95 each
Two volumes – one on The Northern Seas (N. Europe) and one on The Southern Seas (the Mediterranean).

The Travellers' Guides:
Balearics
Corfu
Crete
Elba
Malta and Gozo
Rhodes
Sardinia
Sicily
Pub. Jonathan Cape £3.50-£7.95

Travellers Guides:
Majorca
Portugal
South of France
Pub. Thornton Cox £1.95-£3.50

The Traveller's Key to Medieval France
Pub. Columbus £8.95
Cultural and historical guide.

Travellers Survival Kit Europe:
K. Brown
Pub. Vacation Work £3.95
Too short to be terribly useful.

Venice
James Morris
Pub. Faber £3.95
Superbly written, revealing account of Venice.

Venice for Pleasure
J.G. Links
Pub. Bodley head £5.95
A guide, based on walks.

The Visitors Guide to:
Corsica
Finland
Holland
Iceland
Norway
Sweden
Turkey £10.95/£7.95
Regional Guides
Brittany
The Dordogne
The French Coast
The Loire
Normandy
The South of France
Austria: the Tyrol
West Germany: the Black Forest
The Rhine, Mosel and Eifel
Italy: Florence and Tuscany £8.50/£5.95
Yugoslavia: the Adriatic Coast £10.95/£7.95
Touring Guides:
Chalkidiki
The Pousadas of Portugal
The Paradores of Spain
The Road to Compostela
Touring Guide to Europe £7.95 – £8.95

Walking Guides:
Walking in the Alps
Walking in Austria
Walking in Northern France
Walking in Central France
Walking in Southern France
Walking in Switzerland £7.95/£5.95
Pub. Moorland

Welcome to Venice
Edmund and Jan Swinglehurst
Pub. Collins £2.95

General

AIR TRAVEL

A Book of Air Journeys
Ludovic Kennedy
Pub. Fontana £3.95
Anthology of writings on air travel from balloon flights to space missions.

Access Travel: Airports
From Consumer Information Centre, Dept 619-F, Pueblo, CO 81009, USA

Airport Information
Pub. British Airport Publications. Free
How to get there, what to expect on arrival, how to get help and information, and where to stay – for all seven airports managed by the British Airports Authority.

Airport International
Brian Moynahan
Pub. Pan £1.75
The inside story on airports and commercial aircraft operations. Revealing.

Charter Flight Directory
Jens Jurgen
Pub. Travel Information Bureau, NY
Revised annually. Tips on air fares, ways of obtaining stopovers, getting airlines to pay for accommodation, etc. Also good address list.

A Consumer's Guide to Air Travel
Frank Barratt
Pub. Daily Telegraph £3.95
Information and advice on air fares to passengers' rights.

The Flier's Handbook – The Traveller's Complete Guide to Airports, Aircraft and Air Travel.
ed. Helen Varley
Pub. Pan £5.95
Covers planning, economics, security airport vehicles, runways; guide to airports and air travel.

Freedom from Fear of Flying
Cummings and White
Pub. Pocket Books (Simon & Schuster), US $3.95

Hickman's International Air Traveller
eds. R.H. and M.E. Hickman
Pub. Mitchell Beazley £6.95
Information on hundreds of countries, airlines, and airports as well as other aspects of travel, such as booking, visas and baggage.

The Jet Lag Book
Don Kowet
Pub. Crown, USA $4.95
Good general book on how to avoid the miseries of long-haul flying from cramp upwards.

Jet Stress
Judith Goeltz
Pub. International Institute of Natural Health Sciences, USA $14,95
One of the most comprehensive books available on jet lag, written by former stewardess.

Overcoming Jet Lag
Dr. Charles Ehret and Lynne Waller Scanlon
Pub. Berkeley Books £4.95
Dietry programme devised for the US Army rapid deployment force to counteract the most vicious effects of jet lag. Seems to work, but requires iron willpower.

Planetalk: The Consumer's Air Travel Guide
Richard C Levi and Sheryl Levi
Pub. Ace, USA $2.95
Covers complaints, how to book and understand ticketing, how to get the best fares, how to stay well while travelling, how to handle baggage, etc.

The Round the World Air Guide
Katie Wood and George McDonald
Pub. Fontana £9.95
How-to guide to air fares and gazeteer of 50 cities worldwide.

ATLASES

Bartholomew Junior Atlas of the World
Pub. Bartholomew £14.95
Classic atlas used as standard in many schools. Contains sections on cartography and map projections.

Bartholomew World Atlas
Pub. Bartholomew £16.95
Now in its 13th edition. Also a concise version at £4.95 and two mini editions.

Philip's World Atlas
Pub. G. Philips £5.50
Smaller size atlas with good coverage and a higher than usual proportion of maps in the total number of pages.

Rand McNally Cosmopolitan World Atlas
Pub. Rand McNally £17.50

State of the World Atlas
Kidron and Segal
Pub. Heinemann/Pan £9.50

The Times Atlas of the World
Pub. Times Books £55
Widely acknowledged to be the best modern atlas.

The Times Concise Atlas of the World
Pub. Times Books £25
Maps reduced in size from those in the comprehensive edition, but still superbly drawn and put together.

The Times Atlas of the Oceans
Pub. Times Books £19.95
272pp and over 317 maps covering history, trade, resources and environment, as well as geography of the oceans. Excellent.

The Times Atlas of World History
Pub. Times Books £25.00
Also a concise version.

TRAVELLING WITH CHILDREN

Baby Travel
Pub. St John's Wood Press £5.95
Sub-titled Choosing, Planning and Enjoying Holidays at Home and Abroad with Your Children.

Children Abroad – A Guide for Families Travelling Overseas
Losos, Clayton, Gerein & Wilson
Pub. Deneau $9.95

Have Kids, Will Travel – The Complete Holiday Handbook for Parents
Susan Grossman
Pub. Christopher Helm £4.95

CYCLING

Bike Touring
Raymond Bridge
Pub. Sierra Club Books £5.95
Comprehensive guide, information from what to buy to where to go.

Bikepacking for Beginners
Robin Adshead
Pub. Oxford Illustrated Press £3.75

The CTC Book of Cycling
John Whatmore
Pub. David and Charles £9.95
The first half is devoted to practical information and the second to actual routes around Britain.

Cycle Touring in Britain and the Rest of Europe
Peter Knottley
Pub. Constable £4.95

Cycling in Europe
Nick Crane
Pub. Pan £3.95
Touring guide to 16 countries.

Fat Man on a Bicycle
Tom Vernon
Pub. Fontana £1.95
Hilariously funny account of a journey from Muswell Hill to La Grande-Motte.

Full Tilt
Wheels within Wheels
Dervla Murphy
Pub. Century/Penguin £4.95/£1.95

Into the Remote Places
Ian Hibbell
Pub. Robson Books £8.95

Journey to the Centre of the Earth
Richard and Nicholas Crane
Pub. Bantam £12.95

Journey to the Source of the Nile
Nick Sanders
Pub. Nick Sanders Ltd £8.50
Cycle ride through the desert by the holder of the fastest time round the world on a bicycle.

The New Cyclist
Tony Osman
Pub. Collins £4.95
A beginner's guide.

The Penguin Bicycle Handbook
Rob Van Der Plas
Pub. Penguin £4.95

Richard's Bicycle Book
Richard Ballantine
Pub. Pan £3.95
A manual of bicycle maintenance and enjoyment.

Round the World on a Wheel
John Foster Fraser
Pub. Chatto £7.95
Record of a 19,000-mile bicycle journey around the world in 1896.

Two Wheel Trek
Neil Clough
Pub. Arrow Books £1.75
Manchester to the Cape of Good Hope by bicycle.
The CTC Route Guide to Cycling in Britain and Ireland
Christa Gansden and Nicholas Crane.
Cycling routes around UK and Ireland.

TRAVEL FOR THE DISABLED

Access at the Channel Ports – A Guide for Disabled People
Couch and Barrett
Pub. RADAR £2.50

Access to the World
Louise Weiss
Pub. Facts on File
Shortlisted for the Thomas Cook guidebook award.

Access Guides
From RADAR, 25 Mortimer Street, London W1N 8AB
Access to British towns and areas and cities abroad. Full publications list available.

Air Travel for the Handicapped
Consumer information free from TWA

Directory of Directories
From Rehabilitation International, NY
Lists 275 handbooks for the handicapped person covering hotels, restaurants, theatres, churches, transport and travel facilities in all countries. Claimed to be the most complete listing available.

Disabled Traveller's International Phrasebook
Ian McNeil
From Disability Press, 60 Greenhayes Ave, Banstead, Surrey

Holidays and Travel Abroad – A Guide for Disabled People
Pub. RADAR £1

A List of Guidebooks for Handicapped Travellers
Pub. The President's Committee on Employment of the Handicapped, 111 20th Street, NY Washington DC 20036, USA
Free pamphlet.

Motoring and Mobility for Disabled People
Ann Darnbrough and Derek Kincade
Pub. RADAR £1

Travel for the Disabled – A Handbook of Travel Resources and 500 Worldwide Access Guides
Helen Hecker
Pub. Twin Peaks Press $9.95

Travel Tips for the Handicapped
From US Travel Service, Dept of Commerce, Washington, DC 20230, USA

The Wheelchair Traveller
Douglas R. Annand
From the author, Ball, Hill Road, Milford, NH 03055, USA $7.95.

EXPEDITIONS

Caving Expeditions
Dick Willis
Pub. EAC/BCRA £3
Desert Expeditions
Tom Sheppard
Pub. Expedition Advisory Centre £5
Expedition Catering
Nigel Gifford

Pub. Expedition Advisory Centre £3

Expedition Equipment Manual
Tony Lack
Pub. Expedition Advisory Centre £4

Expedition Planners' Handbook and Directory
ed. Nigel and Shane Winser
Pub. Royal Geographical Society £9.95

Joining an Expedition
Nigel Winser £1

Notes for Overland Expeditions
Shane Winser £1

Polar Notes
Geoff Renner
Pub. Expedition Advisory Centre £6

The Expedition Handbook
ed. Tony Land
Pub. Butterworth
From: Expedition Advisory Centre £7.50
Initial considerations, planning details, expedition field studies, appendices, including addresses. Tips on fund-raising activities, getting reduced air fares, etc.

Expeditions and Exploration
Nigel Gifford
Pub. Macmillan £14.65
An essential source book for both novice and professional expedition planners.

Expedition Medicine
Robin Illingworth
Pub. Blackwell £1.25

Expedition Medicine
Bent Juel-Jenson
Pub. Expedition Advisory Centre £3

The Expedition Organizer's Guide
John Blashford-Snell and Richard Snailham
Pub. Daily Telegraph
Includes sections on planning, information, research and organization, personnel, finance, stores and vehicles, leadership and winding up an expedition.

Explorers Source Book
ed. Al Perrin
Pub. Harpers and Row, NY
Advice, addresses, etc, on training, equipment, books and maps, governing bodies: by type of activity. Comprehensive and extremely useful.

Tropical Rain Forest Expeditions
Roger Chapman
Pub. Expedition Advisory Centre £5

MEDICINE

A.M.A. First Air Manual
Pub. American Medical Association, 535 N Dearborn Street, Chicago, IL, USA

American Red Cross First Aid Text Book
Pub. The Country Life Press, Garden City, NY

British Airways Travel Health Guide
ed. Dr A.S.R. Peffers
Pub. Johnston and Bacon/Cassell
Useful short paperback.

The Care of Babies and Young Children in the Tropics
From National Association for Maternal and Child Welfare, Tavistock House North, Tavistock Square, London WC1
Free booklet. Mostly about medical problems, their prevention and treatment.

The Cruising Sailor's Medical Guide
Nicholas C Leone MD and Elizabeth C Phillips, RN
Pub. David McKay Co Inc, NY $12.50
Essential lifesaving information in a clear, well organized fashion – injuries, illness, dangerous marine life, emergency procedures at sea, water accidents.

Emergency Dentistry
Dr David Watt
Pub. Clausen Publications
Intended for those who must treat the occasional dental patient. Useful.

Foreign Language Guide to Health Care
Pub. The Blue Cross Association, Blue Cross/Blue Shield, 622 Third Avenue, New York, NY 10017, USA
Free booklet giving translations of phrases and concerning health and medicine into French, German, Italian and Spanish.

Foreign Travel Immunisation Guide
Hans H Neumann, MD
Pub. Medical Economics Co, USA $2.95
Published annually. Guide to the immunizations necessary for each area and a discussion of some common traveller's ills.

Health Guide for International Travellers
Sakmar, Gardner and Peterson
Pub. Passport Books $7.95

Health Hints for the Tropics
ed. Harry Most, MD
Pub. National Institute of Health, USA 75c
Excellent source for travellers, said to be the best small booklet available on the subject.

Health Information for International Travel
Pub. US Dept of Health, Education and Welfare
Published annually. General information on the prevalence of disease and the inoculation requirements of foreign countries. Free. Publication number (CDC) 79-8280.

The Healthy Traveller – An Indispensable Guide to Staying Healthy Away from Home
Beth Weinhouse
Pub. Pocket Books (Simon and Schuster), US

How To Stay Healthy While Travelling
Bob Young
Pub. Ross Erikson $4.95
Preparations, immunizations, diet and nutrition, obtaining medical care abroad, travel for the elderly, health problems associated with foreign travel.

How to Survive Your Holiday
Dr. D. Allan Birch
Pub. Wigmore House £3.95
Reliable guide to many of the potential health hazards encountered abroad.

Medical Care for Mountain Climbers
Peter Steel
Pub. Heinemann £4.75

New Advanced First Aid
A.W. Gardner and P.J. Roylance
Pub. John Wright £4.95

Pocket Holiday Doctor
Caroline Chapman and Caroline Lucas
Pub. Corgi £1.25
A sensible person's guide on how to cope with illness abroad.

Preservation of Personal Health in Warm Climates
Pub. Ross Institute of Tropical Hygiene

Pye's Surgical Handicraft
ed. J Kyle
Pub. John Wright £15.00

Safety and Health Abroad – How to Pack Peace of Mind into Your Next Trip
Giordana and Shea
Pub. Datafax Corp. $4.95

The Ship Captain's Medical Guide
Pub. HMSO £25.00
Excellent handbook for anyone responsible for the health of others and reliant on their own resources.

Stay Healthy in Asia
Pub. Volunteers in Asia, Stanford, CA, USA
Guide for young American volunteers working in Asian communities over extended periods with suggestions on preventing, identifying and treating problems and locating doctors and hospitals.

Traveler's Guide to US Certified Doctors Abroad
Pub. Marquie Who's Who, Inc., USA $9.95
List of over 3,500 English-speaking doctors in 120 countries.

Travel Healthy – The Traveler's Complete Medical Kit
Dr Harold Silverman
Pub. Avon

Traveling Healthy
Sheilah M Hillman and Robert S Hillman, MD
Pub. Penguin NY $7.95
Medical facilities and services in most of Europe plus emergency language, first-aid, self-help and Pharmocopia and Drug Index.

Travellers' Health
ed. Richard Dawood
Pub. OUP £6.95
Superb, detailed guide to travel ills and diseases written by renowned experts. Highly recommended.

The Traveller's Health Guide
Dr Anthony C. Turner
Pub. Lascelles £1.95
Paperback by the Senior Overseas Medical Officer of British Airways Medical Services and Hon. Associate Physician and Lecturer at the Hospital for Tropical Diseases, London. Invaluable for visitors to Africa, Asia or Latin America. Special sections on overlanding and cold climate comfort.

The Traveler's Medical Manual
Scott and Moore
Pub. Berkeley Books
Includes a listing of recommended doctors abroad.

A Word or Two Before You Go
Broughton Waddy, MD and Ralph Townley
Pub. W.W. Norton and Co, NY $3.95
Excellent guide to the medical aspects of travel: all the diseases, likely and unlikely emergencies, etc.

OVERLANDING

Africa Overland – A Trek from Cape Town to Cairo
Iain Finlay and Trish Sheppard
Pub. Angus and Robertson £5.95
Account of a family of four travelling on foot, by bus, train and hitchhiking on their way south. With summaries of historic places visited, prices and places to stay.

The Asian Highway
The Complete Overland Guide from Europe to Australia
Jack Jackson and Ellen Crampton
Pub. Angus and Robertson
Still useful, if now outdated manual for any overlander, giving the benefit of Jack's experience of camping, customs, driving, preparations and bureaucracy.

Jupiter's Travels
Ted Simon
Pub. Penguin £1.95
A 63,000 mile motorbike journey around the world.

Overland
Peter Fraenkel
Pub. David and Charles £4.95
Indispensable money-saving guide to planning, preparation, equipment, vehicle modification, etc. (but not routes), by author with 160,000km of overland experience in Africa, Asia and Europe.

Overland and Beyond – Advice for Overland Travellers
Theresa and Jonathan Hewat
Pub. Lascelles £2.50
Planning equipment and the other essentials of overland travel, based on author's three-year trip around the world in a VW Camper.

Trans-Africa Motoring
Trans-Asia Motoring
Trans-Australia Motoring
Colin McElduff
Pub. RAC, London
Again rather out of date, but useful books with a wealth of information for the overland traveller – from routes to regulations.

Wanderlust – Overland through Asia and Africa
Dan Spitzer
Pub. Richard Marek Publishers, NY

World Understanding on Two Wheels
Paul R. Pratt
From Lascelles £2.50
Based on the author's journey by motorcycle through more than 60 countries.

PHOTOGRAPHY

Creative Techniques in Travel Photography.
John Douglas
Pub. Batsford £9.95
Covers all aspects of travel photography from planning to selling the finished product.

How to Take Better Travel Photos
Lisl Dennis
Pub. Fisher, USA $7.95
What to do before you leave, equipment and how to carry it, lenses, faces/adventure/lanscape/special events, problems, showing photos, turning professional. Readable and copiously illustrated.

The Photographer's Handbook
John Hedgcoe
Pub. Ebury Press £10.95
Use of equipment, procedures, glossary, special projects.

Practical Wildlife Photography
Ken Preston-Mafham
Pub. Focal Press £11.95
Not for the beginner, but very good for the experienced photographer with a serious interest in wildlife and plant photography.

Travel Photography
Pub. Time-Life
From Heinemann £10.25

The Underwater Photographer's Handbook
Peter Rowlands
Pub. Macdonald £9.95
Clearly presented informative book on technical aspects and guide to worldwide diving sites.

RAILWAYS

Eurail Guide – How to Travel Europe and All the World by Train
Martin L. Salzman and Kathryn S. Muilman
From Trade and Travel £5.95

Europe by Rail
Pub. Michael Muller £7.95

The Great Railway Adventure
Christopher Portway
Pub. Oxford Illustrated Press £7.95
Documentation of one man's experiences, travelling the world by train.

Fodor's Railways of the World
ed. Robert Fisher
Pub. David McKay
Timetables to menus – details of trains throughout the world.

Rail Guide to Europe
Pub. AA £9.95

Guide to 18 countries and over 40 destinations plus all connecting rail details.

Train Trips – Exploring America by Rail
Pub. Bradt £7.50

SURVIVAL

Desert Travel and Research
J.L. Cloudsley-Thompson
Pub. Institute of Biology, London

Don't Die in the Bundu
Col. D.H. Grainger
Pub. Howard Timmins, RSA

Desert Survival
Jungle Survival
Sea Survival
Snow Survival
Survival Against the Elements
From Survival Aids Ltd, Morland, Penrith, Cumbria.
All have useful information on first-aid, possible sources of injury, illness or danger.

How to Survive on Land and Sea
Frank C. Craighead Jnr and John J. Craighead
Pub. Airlife £10.95
Comprehensive guide to survival first published by the US Navy.

Outdoor Survival Handbook
David Platten
Pub. David and Charles £4.50
For trekkers and campers.

Stay Alive in the Desert
K.E.M. Melville
Pub. Lascelles £2.50
Deals with the hazards of desert driving, including advice on equipping the vehicle, procedure if stuck or stranded, precautions when driving, against ill health and hygiene.

Survival
Pub. Department of the Air Force, USA
Air Force manual.

Survival Cards
Pub. Survival Cards, Box 805, Bloomington, IN 47401, USA $2.50
Ten small plastic cards giving 300 techniques – solar still, snares, signals, snakebite, hypothermia, amputation, etc, – for temperate, desert, arctic and tropical conditions.

Survival in Cold Water
W. R. Keating
Pub. Blackwell Scientific Publications
Subtitled The Physiology and Treatment of Immersion, Hypothermia and Drowning.

Bikepacking for Beginners
Robin Adshsiology and Treatment of Immersion, Hupothermia and Drowning.

TRAVEL TIPS

Area Handbooks
Compiled by US State Department
From Superintendent of Documents, US Government Printing Office $5-$10
Detailed information on history, politics, economics, population, health of many countries. Request by country.

The Art and Adventure of Travelling Cheaply
Rick Berg
Pub. And/Or Press, USA $4.95
Very useful readable guide to attitude, philosophy and method in travel by all means, especially for the person who travels for Travel's sake.

Background Notes on Countries of the World
Compiled by US State Department
From Superintendent of Documents, US Government Printing Office 35p -75p
Synopsis of countries' history, geography, climate, economy, current exchange rate, etc. approximately 75 countries updated each year.

Cheap/Smart Travel – Dependable Alternatives to Travelling Full Fare
Theodore Fischer
Pub. M. Evans and Co $6.95

The Complete Handbook for Travellers
Hal Gieseking
Pub. Pocket Books, NY r8.95
Useful guide to airlines, hotels, rental cars and other aspects of travel, written by the editor of The Travel Advisor newsletter. Much of the information concerns travel within the USA.

Consumer's Guide to Federal Publications
From Superintendent of Documents, US Government Printing Office
Free catalogue listing government travel publications.

Dos and Taboos Around the World – A Guide to International Behaviour
ed. Roger E. Axtell
Pub. John Wiley & Son $9.95

Expatriate Briefings
Pub. Monitor Press
Detailed guides including information on cost of living, health and educational facilities, housing availability and rent and other useful information for potential residents to a wide range of countries.

Fools Paradise
Brian Moynahan
Pub. Pan £1.75
Horrifically informative account of the tourist industry and the rip-offs inherent therein.

A Guide to Solo Travel Abroad
Eleanor Adams Baxal
Pub. Berkshire Travel Press, USA $5.50
Pros and cons, some personal experiences of solo travel, projecting expenses, dealing with the opposite sex, etc.

Holiday Insurance
Pub. British Insurance Association, Aldermary House, Queen Street London EC4P 4JD
Free leaflet (enclose sae).

Holiday Money – The Best Money Deals for Travellers
Wendy Elkington
Pub. Rosters £1.70
Useful, but only deals with major destinations.

International Youth Hostel Federation Handbook
Pub. IYHF
Guide to youth hostelling principles and regulations with lists of all hostels with notes on their amenities, location, costs, etc.

The New York Times Practical Traveller
Paul Grimes
Pub. Times Books, US

Notice to Travellers
Pub. Bank of England
Free leaflet giving countries with special currency restrictions, sources of best rates of exchange, etc.

1,001 Sources for Free Travel Information
Jens Jurgen
Pub. Travel Information Bureau, PO Box 105, King's Park, NY 11754, USA
Information on around 200 countries.

Penguin International Travel Handbook
Peter and Magda Hall
Pub. Penguin £2.95
Advice and country-by-country guide.

Super Travel
The Complete Handbook of Essential Facts, Regulations, Rights and Remedies for Trouble-free International Travel.
Saul Miller
Pub. Holt, Rinehart and Winston $6.95
For the American travelling abroad.

Survival Kit
Pub. CIEE, USA
Details of many intra-European charter flights and cheap accommodation in 33 countries.

Thomas Cook A-Z of Travel
Edmund Swinglehurst and Janice Anderson
Pub. Constable £6.50

Time Off – A Psychological Guide to Vacations.
Stephen Shapiro PhD and Alan Tuckman, MD
Pub. Anchor Press/Doubleday, USA
Mental preparation to help avoid pre-holiday frenzy and post-holiday blues.

Traveler's Picture Dictionary
Pub. AJS International, USA
Pocket-sized, indexed, picture dictionary with sections on personal needs, drinks, foods, clothes, medical aid, services.

The Travel Survival Guide
Carol Wright
Pub. David and Charles £6.95
Easy to read, practical advice.

Travel Tips
Edythe Syversten
Pub. Tempo/Grosset and Dunlop $1.95
By the editor of the New York Post. Brief paperback

on travelling by all means and in different environments.

Travelling in Tropical Countries
Jacques Herbert
Pub. Hurtig $14.95 (Can)

The Tropical Traveller
Hints, Ideas, Advice for Enterprising Travellers to Hot Countries.
John Hatt
Pub. Pan £2.50

Trouble-Free Travel – What to Know Before You Go
Marty Leshner
Pub. Franklin Watts, NY, $7.95
Choosing means, luggage, staying healthy and sane, etc.

Trouble-Free Travel
Richard Harrington
Pub. WEXAS £2.25

Whole World Handbook – A Student Guide to Work, Study and Travel Abroad
Marjorie Cohen and Margaret Sherman
Pub. CIEE/Frommer, USA
An excellent compendium on student travel, including background reading, reports from students on travel and study abroad.

World Traveller – For First Class Independent Travellers
Pub. Waterhouse and Waterhouse £9.95

YMCA and YWCA directories
Pub. YMCA
List own addresses in over 70 countries, plus other useful addresses of doctors, lawyers, consultates, priests, etc.

VEHICLES

Buying a Car Overseas
Pub. US Environmental Protection Agency
From US Customs Service Offices
Free brochure, revised periodically.

The Four-Wheel Drive Book
Jack Jackson
Pub. Gentry Books £10.95
Comprehensive view of four-wheel-drive vehicles and their uses with excellent sections on overlanding and expeditions.

A Guide to Land Rover Expeditions
Pub. Land Rover Ltd
Free booklet with information on the vehicle, hints on cross-country driving and some general information on travel.

Importing a Car
Pub. US Customs Service
Free brochure, revised periodically.

Petersen's Complete Book of Fourwheel Drive
ed. Spence Murray
Pub. Petersen Publishing Co, USA
Combines history of the military Jeep with practical

tips for modern four-wheel-drives. Includes reports on sixteen vehicles submitted to comparison tests.

WEATHER

The Climate Advisor
Gilbert Schwartz
Pub. Climate Guide Pubs., USA
Non-technical reference guide to climate and weather in North America, with climate charts for over 350 locations.

The World Weather Guide
E.A Pearce and C.G. Smith
Pub. Hutchinson £7.95
Excellent reference with climate charts around the entire world and short sections on altitude and geography of each country.

WOMEN TRAVELLERS

Everywoman's Guide to Travel
Donna Goldfein
Pub. Les Femmes $3.95

Half the Earth – Woman's Experience of Travel Worldwide
ed. Miranda Davies et al
Pub. Pandora – RKP £8.95
Fascinating country-by-country listing of personal experiences of women travellers.

Handbook for Women Travellers
Maggie and Gemma Moss
Pub. Piatkus £4.95

MsAdventures – Worldwide Travelguide for Independent Women
Gail Rubin Sereny
Pub. Chronical Books, USA $5.95
Light reading, hard facts, a good guide for the lone woman traveller.

Travel Sense – A Guide for Business and Professional Women
Barbara A. Pletcher
Pub. Ace Books $5.95

The Traveling Woman
Dena Kaye
Pub. Doubleday, NY $11.95
Practical information on food, clothing, accessories, packing and the pitfalls, pleasures and precautions involved in travel, alone or in company.

WORKING AND LIVING ABROAD

Accepting a Job Abroad – A Practical Guide
M Tideswell
Pub. British Institute of Management Foundation
Useful guide for potential expatriates with good list of sources of information.

Berlitz Business Travel Guide
From Cassell £2.45
Covers 31 countries in West and East Europe.

Brits Abroad
Harry Brown and Rosemary Thomas
Pub. Express Books £3.95

Frommer's Swap and Go – Home Exchanging Made Easy
Albert and Verna Beerbower
Pub. Simon & Schuster $10.95

Guide to the Business Capitals of the World
ed. Graham Boynton
Pub. Perry Books
Compilation of destination features originally published in Business Traveller magazine.

Home Exchanging – A Complete Sourcebook for Travelers at Home and Abroad
James Dearing
Pub. The East Woods Press $9.95

International Herald Tribune Guide to Business Travel and Entertainment Europe
Pub. Thames and Hudson £7.95

International Directory of Voluntary Work.
Pub. Vacation Work £4.50

Living Costs Overseas – A Guide for Businessmen
Pub. Financial Times
Good but very expensive information on living costs in 66 of the world's major business centres.

Living Overseas
Ted Ward
Pub. The Free Press $12.95

Moving and Living Abroad – A Complete Handbook for Families
Albright, Chu and Austin
Pub. Hippocrene, NY $11.95

Summer Jobs Abroad
Pub. Vacation Work £4.95
Covers both short and long-term employment. Invaluable.

Sun, Sand and Cement – A Guide to Buying Overseas Property
Cheryl Taylor
Pub. Rosters £5.99

Travel and Retirement – Edens Abroad
Peter A. Dickinson
Pub. E.P. Dutton $12.95

Work Your Way Around the World
Susan Griffith
Pub. Vacation Work £6.95
Covers both short and long term employment. Invaluable.

Working Abroad
Daily Telegraph Guide to Working and Living Overseas.
Godfrey Golzen and Margaret Steward
Pub. Kogan Page c.£7
Factual profiles of living and working conditions in 39 countries and much other advice and information.

Working Abroad – The Expatriate's Guide
David Young
Pub. Financial Times £9.95
Comprehensive guide to all aspects of expatriate employment.

Expedition Reports

The Royal Geographical Society
1 Kensington Gore
London SW7 2AR
Tel: 01-581 2057
Reports may be consulted in the Map Room, Monday to Friday 10am-5pm. The collection includes reports approved by the RGS, YET and MEF.

Scientific Exploration Society
Home Farm
Mildenhall
nr Marlborough
Wilts.

FURTHER READING

Selected Guide to Travel Books
Susan Nareckel
Pub. Fleet Press, N7
Published in 1974, so dated, but worth looking into for references to background and historical reading.

The Travel Book – Guide to the Travel Guides
Jon O. Heise
Pub. R. R. Bowker Co., NY
A well researched guide to hundreds of travel guides and travel books current and historic. Includes a very well organized index. Published 1981.

Travel Guidebooks in Review
ed. John O. Heise
Pub. Gaylord Professional Pub., Syracuse, NY
Published 1978. Even if you don't agree with the reviews, this is still a worthwhile guide to available literature.

Travel in Asia – Guide to Information Sources
Neal L. Edgar
Pub. Gale Research Co., Detroit
A pot pourri of useful information sources, published in 1983, as well as a good list of recommended reading. Other volumes available on other areas.

Book and Map Publishers and Distributors

AA Publications
Automobile Association
Fanum House
Basingstoke
Hants RG21 2EA
Tel: (0256) 492929
Guide and map publishers and distributors including the Baedeker guides.

John Bartholomew & Son Ltd
12 Duncan Street
Edinburgh EH9 1TA
Tel: 031-667 9341
Publish tourist, road, topographic/general maps and atlases and guides. Free catalogue from Marketing Dept.

BAS Overseas Publications
BAS House
48-50 Sheen Lane
London SW14 8LP
Tel: 01-876 2131/878 7257-8
General sales agent for a wide range of British, American and European timetables, hotel directories, etc.

Bookpeople
2929 Fifth Street
Berkeley
CA 94710
USA

Bradt Enterprises
41 Nortoft Road
Chalfont St Peter
Bucks SL9 0LA
Tel: (02407) 3478
and
95 Harvey Street
Cambridge
MA 02140
USA
Backpacking and trekking guides and books for and about independent travellers.

Cicerone Press
2 Police Square
Milnthorpe
Cumbria LA7 7PY
Tel: (04482) 2069
Publishers of books on outdoor activities including climbing and walking.

Collins
8 Grafton Street
London W1
Tel: 01-493 7070

Columbus Books
19-23 Ludgate Hill
London EC4M 7PD
Tel: 01-248 6444
Telex: 28673 CONSOL G
Guide book publishers including the Harrap series.

Cordee/Diadem Books
3a DeMontfort Street
Leicester
Tel: (0533) 708212
Publish and distribute books on climbing, mountain travel, walking, caving, skiing and other outdoor adventure sports.

David and Charles Ltd
North Pomfret
VT
USA
Distributors for David and Charles and several other British publishers of overland and travel books in the USA.

Department of Defense and Mapping Agency
Hydrographic/Topographic Centre
Washington
DC 20315
USA
Publish charts of oceans and coasts of all areas of the world and pilot charts. Supply maps or photocopies of maps on request provided that the exact area is specified.

Editions Berlitz
1 Avenue des Jordils
1000 Lausanne 6
Switzerland

Freytag Berndt
Kartographische Anstalt
Schottenfeldgasse 62
Vienna VII
Austria
Major high quality map publishers.

Michael Haag
London NW3 4ER
Tel: 01-794 2647
Guide book publisher.

Harian Publications
1 Vernon Avenue
Floral Park
NY 11001
USA
Publishers of retirement, shipping and other travel guides. Books are sent surface rate. Air mail according to weight. All orders prepaid plus postage.

Hippocrene Books
171 Madison Avenue
New York
NY 10016
USA

Hydrographic Department
MOD (Navy)
Taunton
Somerset TA1 2DN
Tel: (0823) 87900
Telex: 46724
Publishes world series of Admiralty Charts and hydrographic publications. Available from appointed Admiralty Chart Agencies.

Institut Géographique National
Direction Générale
136bis Rue Grenelle
75700 Paris
France
Tel: 550 34 95
Mail Order Sales for Individuals:
107 Rue la Boetie
75008 Paris France
Tel: 225 87 90

Publish and sell maps of France and very many of the former French possessions.

Kummerly und Frey Ltd
Hallerstrasse 6-10
CH-3001 Bern
Switzerland
Publish charts and political, topographic, road and other maps.

Roger Lascelles
47 York Road
Brentford
Middlesex TW8 0QP
Tel: 01-847 0935
Guide and map publisher and distributor. Catalogue published twice a year, extensive selection.

Lonely Planet Publications
PO Box 88
South Yarra
Victoria 3141
Australia
Tel: (03) 429 5100
Rapidly turning into one of the world's largest guide books publishers. Extensive selection of off-beat destinations.

Rand McNally & Co
PO Box 3600
Chicago
IL 60680
USA
Large publisher of maps, atlases, guides and globes.

Michelin Guides
46 Rue de Breteuil
75341 Paris
France
Tel: 539 25 00
Publish excellent maps and the famous Red and Green Guides.

Moon Publications
PO Box 1696
Chico
CA 95927
USA
Tel: (916) 345 5473/5413

Moorland Publishing
Moor Farm Road
Airfield Estate
Ashbourne
Derbyshire DE6 1HD
Tel: (0335) 44486
Tlx: 377106 CHACOM GMPC
Guide book publisher.

National Geographic Society
17th and M Streets
Washington
DC 20036
USA
Publish mainly topographical maps to accompany National Geographic magazine. Also sell wall, relief and archaeological maps, atlases and globes. Also magazines and books.

NOAA Distribution Branch, N/CG33, National Ocean Service
Riverdale
Maryland 20737
USA
The National Ocean Service (NOS) publishes and distributes aeronautical charts of the US. Charts of foreign areas are published by the Defense Mapping Agency Aerospace Center (DMAAC) and are sold by the NOS.

Ordnance Survey
Romsey Road
Maybush
Southampton SO9 4DH
Tel: (0703) 775555
The official mapping agency for the UK. The Overseas Surveys Directorate at the same address publishes maps of former and current British possessions.

Passport Publications
20 N Wacker Drive
Chicago
IL 60606
USA
Tel: (312) 332 3571

George Philip & Son Ltd
12 Long Acre
London WC2E 9LP
Tel: 01-836 1915
Publish a wide range of topographical and thematic maps, globes, atlases and charts, and some guides.

Regenbogen-Verlag
Schmidgasse 3
CH-8001
Postfach 240
CH-8025 Zurich
Switzerland
and
c/o Los Amigos del Libro
Casilla Postal 450
Cochabamba
Bolivia
Publish books for the independent traveller.

Routledge and Kegan Paul
39 Store Street
London WC1
Tel: 01-753 9435
Publishers of the Rough Guides.

Royal Geographical Society
Publications Dept.
1 Kensington Gore
London SW7 2AR
Tel: 01-589 5466
Sells maps originally published in the Geographical Journal and maps published separately by the Society. Also expedition pamphlets, G.J. reprints, and other papers on geography, expeditions, and related subjects. Lists available on request.

Simon and Schuster
1230 Ave of the Americas
New York 10022
USA
Tel: (212) 698 7000

and
West Garden Place
Kendal Street
London W2 2AQ
Tel: 01-724 7577

Springfield Books Ltd
Norman Road
Denby Dale
Huddersfield
W. Yorks HD8 8TH
Tel: (0484) 864955
Publishers and distributors of maps and guides, including the Freytag & Berndt maps.

Trade and Travel Publications
5 Prince's Buildings
George Street
Bath BA21 2ED
Tel: (0225) 69141
Telex: 265871
Publishers of the South American Handbook and distributors.

US Department of the Interior Geological Survey
National Cartographic Information Center
(NCIC)
507 National Center
Reston
VA 22092
USA
Information about maps and related data for US areas.

Vacation Work Publications
9 Park End Street
Oxford
Oxon OX1 1HJ
Tel: (0865) 241 978
Publishes books on employment and budget travel abroad.

Wilderness Press
2440 Bancroft Way
Berkeley
CA 94704
USA
Tel: (415) 843 8080
Natural history, adventure travel guides and maps of North America. All mail order, including from abroad, to be paid in US dollars.

Book and Map Retailers

United Kingdom:

The main travel book and map retailers in Greater London are:

Chapter Travel Ltd
102 St.John's Wood Terrace
London NW8 6PL
Tel: 01-586 9451
Telex: 263820 CHAPTR G
Stocks a very wide range of travel books and maps including the complete Ordnance Survey, Michelin and TCI series. Please send s.a.e. for book lists on individual countries. All credit cards are accepted.

Compendium Bookshop
234 Camden High Street
London NW1
Tel: 01-485 9844/267 1525
A useful source of travel books that are difficult to obtain elsewhere.

W.&G.Foyle Ltd
Travel Department
Ground Floor
113-119 Charing Cross Road
London WC2H OEB
Geographia
63 Fleet Street
London EC4
Tel: 01-353 2701

The Good Book Guide Book Shop
91 Great Russell Street
London WC1
Tel: 01-580 8466
Also have worldwide mail order service for books in English through their monthly magazine The Good Book Guide.

The London Map Centre
22-24 Caxton Street
London SW1
Tel: 01-222 2466
Is the main agent for Ordance Survey maps and retailers for all major publishers. At the same address is the retail outlet for the cartographic printing side of the firm, known as Cook, Hammond & Kell Ltd.

London Tourist Board
26 Grosvenor Garden
Victoria
London SW1
Tel: 01-730 0791 (Automatic queuing system)

Map Marketing
92-104 Carnwath Road
London SW6 3HW
Tel: 01-736 0297
Have a range of over 400 maps which have been laminated and can be supplied framed or unframed. The range includes a selection of world maps, more than 50 individual country maps, over 300 section maps of the UK and over 100 specialized UK maps – postal codes, marketing, counties.

McCarta Ltd
122 King's Road
London WC1X 9DS
Tel: 01-278 8276
Are Book and Map Publishers, Distributors and Retailers. They are agents for Kummerly and Frey, IGN (French Official Survey), Touring Club Italiano, Gabelli, and Toubis. As retailers, they have an extensive list of guide books and maps, especially of

Europe. Also have a large range of scientific publications related to geography and geology. Stockists of Columbus globes and pop-up city maps.

Edward Stanford Ltd
12–14 Long Acre
London WC2 9LP
Tel: 01-836 1321
Is the largest mapseller in Europe, carrying a wide range of maps, globes, charts and atlases, including Ordnance Survey and Directorate of Overseas Surveys maps. For anyone within reach of London planning to buy specific maps, Stanford's should be the first port of call.

Trailfinders Travel Centre
42-48 Earls Court Road
London W8 6EJ
Tel: 01-603 1515
Stocks a comprehensive range of travel guides and maps.

The Travel Bookshop
13 Blenheim Crescent
London W11
Tel: 01-229 5260
Is London's first bookshop specializing in travel literature, opened in 1980 to provide a 'complete package for the traveller' including books on particular areas, current and old guide books, histories, cookery books and relevant fiction. Shop also stocks old and new maps and topographical prints.

YHA Bookshops
14 Southampton Street
London WC2E 7AHY
Tel: 01-836 8541
Sell books, maps and guides for backpackers, hostellers, adventure sportsmen and budget travellers.

Travel Bookshops Elsewhere in the UK:

Austicks Polytechnic Bookshop
25 Cookridge Street
Leeds LS1 3AN
Tel: (0532) 445335
Best travel bookshop in Yorkshire. A large map selection including large-scale ordnance survey mapping.

B. H. Blackwell Ltd
50 Broad St
Oxford
Tel: (0865) 249 111

W.Hartley Seed
152-160 West Street
Sheffield
Yorks S1 3ST
Good selection of books and maps.

Heffer
20 Trinity Street
Cambridge CB2 3BG
Tel: (0223) 358 351
Very good selection of travel books.

Heffers Map Shop
3rd Floor
19 Sidney Street
Cambridge CB2 3HL
Are leading mapsellers in the region.

The Map Shop
(A.T. Atkinson & Partner)
15 High Street
Upton-upon-Severn
Worcestershire WR8 0HJ
Tel: (06846) 3146
Agents for Ordnance Survey, large -scale maps and guides for Europe and other areas worldwide in stock or obtained to order. Send for free catalogue stating area of interest.

Parker & Son Ltd
27 Broad Street
Oxford
Tel: (0865) 54156
Telex: 838965 PARKER G
Leading mapsellers with large travel-guide department. Ask for Stuart Kemp.

Dick Phillips
Whitehall House
Nenthead
Alston
Cumbria CA9 3PS
Tel: (0498) 81440
Specializes in books and maps of Iceland and Faroe. He stocks maps at scales of between 1:750,000 and 1:25,000 (general maps) and thematic or specialized maps held in stock or usually obtainable by special order.

Nigel Press Associates Ltd
Edenbridge
Kent TN 8 6HS
Tel: (07332)865 023
Offers a free service to bona fide expeditions for the supply of map-like satellite images, of which they have a large archive covering most parts of the world. These Landsat satellite images can be produced at scales between 1:1,000,000 and 1:200,000 and are useful for navigation or research.

RAC Motoring Services Ltd
Publications Manager
PO Box 100
RAC House
Landsdowne Road
Croydon
Surrey CR9 2JA
Sell guides, handbooks, and maps for motorists and other travellers in the UK and on the Continent, also touring accessories.

Rallymaps of West Wellow
PO Box 11
Romsey
Hampshire SO51 8XX
Tel: (0794) 515 444 (24hr)
Mail order specialists for Ordnance Survey, geological and Michelin maps. Walking, climbing, books, map cases and sundries. Catalogue 25p.

Sherratt & Hughes Bookshop
17 St.Anne's Square
Manchester M2 7DP
Are leading map and guide retailers.

John Smith & Son (Glasgow)Ltd
57-61 St. Vincent Street
Glasgow G2 5TB
Tel: 041-221 7472
Ordnance Survey agents for West of Scotland. Foreign maps, Michelin maps.

Whitemans Bookshop
7 Orange Grove
Bath BA1 1LP
Tel: (0225) 64029
Have a whole room of books and maps devoted to travel including a large range of Ordnance Survey maps and all other major UK maps to street plans; a range of foreign maps covering countries all over the world; atlases; walking guides; natural history guides; 'where to stay' guides and a wide range of books of interest to travellers, mostly of a practical nature, some of which cover unusual countries. Also undertake to order any obtainable map or book (at no extra charge) and operate a worldwide mail order service.

Travel book and map retailers elsewhere:

Australia:

All Maps
431 Pacific Highway
Artarmon
Sydney
NSW

Gregory's Publishing Co
64 Talavera Road
North Ryde
Sydney
NSW
Tel: 02-888 1877
Sells road maps, guides, street directories and auto service manuals.

Universal Press Pty Ltd
64 Talavera Road
North Ryde
NSW 2113
Tel: 02-887 1887
Telex: AA 170274

Austria:

Okista
Türkenstr. 4
A-1090 Vienna
Mainly student travel books.

Belgium:

La Route de Jade
Librairie du Voyageur
Rue de Stassart 116 (Place Stephanie)
B-1050 Brussels
Tel: 512 96 54
Is a travel bookshop selling books, maps and guides on all aspects of travel in five continents. The exclusive distributor of ONC maps in Belgium.

Canada:

Gulliver's Travel Bookshop
609 Bloor St. W
Toronto
Ontario M6G 1K5
Tel: (416) 537 7700

Oxbow Books
Box 244 Clarkson
Mississauga
Ontario L5J 3Y1
Sell out-of-print books on travel, exploration, geography, mountaineering, caving.

France:

L'Asiathèque
6 Rue Christine
75006 Paris
Tel: 4325 3457
Offers books on the Far East and South-East Asia.

L'Astrolabe
La Librairie
46 Rue de Provence
75009 Paris
Tel: 285 42 95
Is the most important map seller in France, carrying Ordnance Survey maps of the UK, national Surveys of Ireland, Norway, Denmark, Czechoslovakia, Guatemala, Peru, Bolivia, Pakistan, India, etc. Topographic maps, nautical charts, geological astronomical and aeronautical charts and maps. Also stocks about 15,000 travel books and guides old and new, in French and English and some in Spanish and German. Some scientific manuals, other personal accounts of travels. One of the few bookshops in Europe that can be of real help to somebody planning a serious expedition, by placing all the relevant literature and large-scale maps at the organizers' disposal. A new Natural History department, for travellers with an interest in ornithology, heretology and geology. Founder member of European Mapsellers Association.

Blondel La Rougery
7 Rue St. Lazare
75009 Paris
Tel: (1) 4878 9554
Maps.

Editions du Buot
30 Rue du Rendez-vous
75012 Paris
Tel: (1) 4343 5903
Maps.

La Grande Porte
4 Rue Dalpozzo
0600 Nice
Tel: 9387 7124
Specializes in books on short- and long-distance travel with works also on seafaring and mountaineering, antiquarian books and postcards. Items also bought.

Librairie E.P.A.
Automobile -moto -train -aviation -marine
83 Rue De Rennes
75006 Paris
Tel: 4548 1514
and
92 Rue St. Lazare
75009 Paris
Tel: 4281 3762

Librairie Gibert Jeune
Second Floor
5 Place St. Michel
75005 Paris
Has a wide choice of route maps and tourist guides.

Librairie Ulysse
Pays et Voyages
35 Rue St. Louis en I'Ile
75004 Paris
Tel: 43 25 17 35
Sells geographical, travel and guide books and maps.

Le Tour du Monde
9 Rue de la Pompe
75116 Paris
Tel: 4288 7359/5806
Sells travel books and guides on all aspects of foreign countries. Also has unique search service for out of print French books. Same address. Tel: 4520 8712.

West Germany:

Darr's Travel Shop
Theresienstr. 66
D-80000 Munich 2
Tel: (089) 28 20 32
Telex: 5215384 DARR D
This establishment has an exceptionally extensive range of maps, guides and other travel handbooks, covering the world but with a concentration of material about Africa, Asia, South America, and other expedition destinations, including Antarctica Catalogue free. Mail order delivery overseas.

Geografische Buchhandlung(Geo Buch)
Rosental 6
D-8000 Munich 2
Has a comprehensive range of travel books and maps.

Globetrott Shop
Karlsgraben 69
D-5100 Aachen
Tel: (0241) 33636
Publishes and sells handbooks for globetrotters and overlanders. Specialists in Africa, world motorcycling, survival training.

Dr Götze & Co GmbH
Hermannstr. 5-7
2000 Hamburg 1
Tel: (040) 322 477
Specializes in maps, guide books and tourist books

Buchhandlung Kiepert KG
Hardenbergstr. 4-5
D-1000 Berlin 12
Has a good selection of travel books, old and new and maps.

Schropp
Potsdamer Strasse 100
1000 Berlin 30
Tel: 261 34 56
Maps, guidebooks, atlases.

Italy:

Liberia Alpina
Via Coronedi-Berti 4
1-40137 Bologna
Tel: (051) 34 57 15
Specializes in books on mountains and mountaineering worldwide, in all languages. Catalogue.

Netherlands:

Pied à Terre
Singel 393
1012 WN Amsterdam
Maps and guide books for walking, cycling and mountaineering. Travel books for globetrotters: Himalayas, Africa, Asia and South America; literature on mountaineering expeditions.

van Wijngaarden
Overtoon 136
Amsterdam 1054HN
Tel: (020) 121 901
Is an established bookshop in the centre of Amsterdam, selling exclusively travel guides and maps – for hikers, cyclists, motorists, tourists, cityplans, maps of the surrounding regions and of the countries of Africa, South America, etc. Also Michelin, Baedeker, Frommer Guides, compasses. Agent of ONC and TPC maps.

Switzerland:

Atlas Reisbuchladen
Schauplatzgrasse 31
CH-3011 Bern
Tel: (031) 22 90 44
Sells travel books, guides, maps. Is the distributor for many map agencies from all parts of the world.

Buchhandlung Bider
Hochhaus Heuwaage

4010 Basel
Tel: (061) 23 00 69
Travel books and maps.

Librairie du Voyageur – Artou
9 Rue de Rive
CH-1204 Geneva
Tel: (022) 21 45 44
Large selection of travel books and maps; also old travel books, trekking and climbing guides.

Travel Book Shop
Gisela Treichler
Rindermarkt 20
CH-8001
Postfach 216
CH-8025 Zurich
Tel: (01) 252 38 83
Is a highly thought of shop selling travel literature – maps, books, guides, timetables, vehicle manuals – of all kinds, and run by a well-travelled lady who is on hand to give advice and travel tips to customers.

USA:

The Complete Traveller
199 Madison Avenue
Corner 35th Street
New York
NY 10016
Tel: (212) 685 9007/679 4339
Books, maps, guides.

Families on the Go
1259 El Camino Road
Menlo Park
CA 94025
Tel: (415) 322 4203
Mail order catalogue of travel and activity books for parents and kids.

Forsyth Travel Library Inc
9154 West 57th Street
PO Box 2975
Shawnee Mission
KS 66201-1357
Tel: (913) 384 3440
Sells maps and travel books, including maps of the USA and Canada, Thomas Cook publications, and many other guides, maps and travel books relating to all destination. Free catalogue on request. Overseas inquiries should enclose four international reply coupons.

Gourmet Guides
1767 Stockton Street
San Francisco
CA 94133
Tel: (415) 391 5903
Is a retail bookshop specializing in travel books and maps (and cookbooks – hence the name), including Fodor, Frommer, Fielding and others; many maps of Asia, the USA, Africa, and Latin America that are extremely difficult to find elsewhere. Owner imports some of these and is the only US source, stocking 'everything I can get hold of in the travel

field'. Mail order. Lists of stock covering particular areas made up and available from time to time.

Hammond Map and Travel Center
57 West 43rd Street
New York
NY 10036
Sells world, road and travel maps, political maps and weather charts.

Hippocrene Books, Inc
171 Madison Avenue
New York
NY 10016
Are specialists in travel literature with Hildebrand and Michael Haag guides, Eland Travel Classics and Orafa guides. Hildebrand, Rectafoldex, Carta, Cartographia maps and Bollmann picture maps.

The Map Center
2440 Bancroft Way
Berkeley
CA 94704
Tel: (415) 841-MAPS

Map Centre, Inc
2611 University Ave
San Diego
California 92104-2894
Tel: (619) 291 3830
Stocks over 5,000 maps and charts, is an agent for defence mapping and National Ocean Survey, nautical and aeronautical maps, plus publications of interest to boat owners, including tide tables, coastal pilots and navigational guides and globes. Motto is: if you can't find it on our maps . . . it's lost.

Pacific Travellers Supply
529 State Street
Santa Barbara
CA 93101
Tel: (805) 963 44 38
Sells a complete selection of guidebooks, specializing in obscure and hard-to-find titles. Have 50,000 maps representing the entire world.

Rand McNally & Co.
10 East 53rd Street
New York
NY 10022
Also in Chicago and San Francisco

Trans-World Visions
PO Box 1028
Cambridge
MA 02238
Tel: (617) 524 0411
Mail order books.

Wide World Bookshop
401 NE 45th
Seattle
WA 98105
Tel: (206) 634 3453
Sells a selection of unusual travel books, many of them imported maps and globes, language tapes and 'other trivia'. Catalogue.